AN ETHNOHISTORICAL DICTIONARY OF THE RUSSIAN AND SOVIET EMPIRES

AN ETHNOHISTORICAL DICTIONARY OF THE RUSSIAN AND SOVIET EMPIRES

EDITED BY
James S. Olson

Lee Brigance Pappas and Nicholas C. J. Pappas
ASSOCIATE EDITORS

GREENWOOD PRESS
Westport, Connecticut • London

Library of Congress Cataloging-in-Publication Data

An Ethnohistorical dictionary of the Russian and Soviet empires /
   edited by James S. Olson ; Lee Pappas and Nicholas C. J. Pappas, associate
   editors.
        p.   cm.
   Includes bibliographical references and index.
   ISBN 0–313–27497–5 (alk. paper)
      1. Ethnology—Russia—Dictionaries.   2. Ethnology—Soviet Union—
Dictionaries.   3. Russia—Ethnic relations—Dictionaries.
4. Soviet Union—Ethnic relations—Dictionaries.   I. Olson, James
Stuart.   II. Pappas, Lee.   III. Pappas, Nicholas Charles.
DK33.E837   1994
305.8′00947—dc20   93–18149

British Library Cataloguing in Publication Data is available.

Library of Congress Catalog Card Number: 93–18149
ISBN: 0–313–27497–5

First published in 1994

Greenwood Press, 88 Post Road West, Westport, CT 06881
An imprint of Greenwood Publishing Group, Inc.

Printed in the United States of America

The paper used in this book complies with the
Permanent Paper Standard issued by the National
Information Standards Organization (Z39.48–1984).

10 9 8 7 6 5 4 3 2 1

Contents

Preface

The photograph said it all. On November 6, 1992, the international wire services distributed a photograph of civil unrest in the Transcaucasian region of Russia. The photograph displayed a squad of armed Ossetian militiamen advancing carefully into an Ingush village where armed Ingush militiamen had been harassing them. The Ossetian homeland is located in the North Ossetian Autonomous Republic of Russia, as well as across the border in the Georgian Republic; the Ingush live in the western part of the Chechen-Ingush Autonomous Republic in Russia, which borders Ossetia. Their argument is an old one. The Ingush are Sunni Muslims while most Ossetians are Eastern Orthodox. During World War II, Josef Stalin accused the Ingush of cooperating with the German invaders, and, in 1944, he relocated almost all of them to Central Asia and Siberia. The Ingush were later rehabilitated, but when they returned from their internal exile in the 1960s, they found that Ossetians had occupied former Ingush land. Today, the Ingush are laying claim to half of the North Ossetian capital of Vladikavkaz. They also argue that the Prigorodny region of North Ossetia is their historic homeland. Ossetians do not accept that claim, and, throughout 1992, there was sporadic fighting in the region between Ossetian and Ingush militiamen. Several hundred people were killed in the fighting during 1992.

The vast majority of Americans and Europeans who saw the photograph in their newspapers and read the caption did not have the vaguest idea of who the Ossetians and Ingush were and why they were fighting. Ossetia and Ingushetia were by no means the only places in the former Soviet Union where mystifying ethnic squabbles surfaced as the country disintegrated. Uzbeks and Kazakhs battled in Uzbekistan, while Armenians and Azerbaijanis killed each other over the Nagorno-Karabakh. Ossetians fought with Georgians, while Jews and Gypsies worried that old ethnic hatreds would soon lead to the holocausts of the past. Uzbeks went after the Meskhetians, and all over the former Soviet Union local ethnic groups reacted against the presence of ethnic Russians. Crimean Tatars, after nearly fifty years of exile, are returning to the Crimean Peninsula, but ethnic Ukrainians and ethnic Russians are resisting the relocation. Ethnic

Russians are re-forming Cossack groups in the Baltics, Moldova, and Siberia to protect their interests. The centrifugal forces of ethnic nationalism destroyed the Soviet Union in 1991, and the possibility that Russia itself may disintegrate for the same reasons is very real. During the 1990s, religious and ethnic issues will be the defining principles of political life in Eastern Europe, Transcaucasia, and Central Asia.

An Ethnohistorical Dictionary of the Russian and Soviet Empires is designed to serve as a ready reference work for students, researchers, and librarians trying to sort out the political and social struggles in that part of the world. The volume includes entries on over 450 ethnic groups. Most of the essays conclude with the disintegration of the Soviet Union at the end of 1991, although some of the essays extend into 1992 for the sake of continuity. Entries conclude with sources of additional information; cross-references are indicated by asterisks after groups that are discussed in separate entries. In developing the topic list and describing most of the subgroups, I have relied heavily on the following works: Ronald Wixman, *The Peoples of the USSR: An Ethnographic Handbook* (Armonk, N.Y.: M. E. Sharpe, 1984); Shirin Akiner, *Islamic Peoples of the Soviet Union* (London: Kegan Paul International, 1983); Alexandre Bennigsen and S. Enders Wimbush, *Muslims of the Soviet Empire: A Guide* (Bloomington: Indiana University Press, 1986); Walter Kolarz, *The Peoples of the Soviet Far East* (New York: Archon Books, 1969); Lawrence Krader, *Peoples of Central Asia* (Bloomington: Indiana University Press, 1966); Bernhard Geiger, *People and Languages of the Caucasus* (The Hague: Mouton, 1959); and Geoffrey Wheeler, *The Peoples of Soviet Central Asia* (London: Bodley Head, 1966). I have defined ethnicity in somewhat narrow terms, focusing on ethnolinguistic groups rather than on peoples defined by purely religious orientations. I am grateful to the reference librarians in the Newton Gresham Library at Sam Houston State University, as well as to the other scholars who contributed essays to the dictionary. My associate editors—Professors Lee and Nick Pappas—have been particularly generous with their time and their intellects. I am the author of all unsigned entries. My editors at the Greenwood Publishing Group have been universally supportive in seeing this project to fruition.

James S. Olson
Huntsville, Texas

A

ABA. See SHOR, SAGAI, and KHAKASS.

ABA KHIZI. See SHOR.

ABA KIJI. See SHOR.

ABADZEG. The Abadzeg, who call themselves the Abadzegh and are known to ethnic Russians* as the Abadzekh, are one of the subgroups of the Adyghes*. They live in the western end of the North Caucasus along the upper Psekups, Laba, and Belaya rivers. See ADYGHE.
REFERENCE: Ronald Wixman, *The Peoples of the USSR: An Ethnographic Handbook*, 1984.

ABADZEGH. See ADYGHE and CHERKESS.

ABADZEKH. See ADYGHE and CHERKESS.

ABAKAN. See KHAKASS.

ABAKAN TATAR. The Abakan (Abaqan) Tatars are part of the larger collection of Siberian Tatars* who originated with the Mongol* invasion of Russia in the thirteenth century. The term ''Abakan Tatar'' is more a reflection of their location in the town of Abakan along the Abakan River in southern Siberia than of any distinct identity as a special group of Tatars*. They were converted to the Sunni Muslim faith, Hanafi rite, by Islamic merchants in the fourteenth and fifteenth centuries. That conversion process among the Abakan Tatars continued for the next five centuries. Most of them were Turkic-speaking Kypchak* tribes known for their geographic mobility and volatility. During the fifteenth century, the region came under Ibak Khan and his Siberian Khanate, which reached north from present-day Kazakhstan to the Arctic Ocean. Russians finally conquered the region in 1581 and established forts at Tjumen in 1586, Tobolsk in 1587, Tara in 1594, and Tomsk in 1604. Contact with Russians brought about the conversion of the Abakan Tatars to Eastern Orthodox Christianity, although the conversion was superficial at best. Strong elements of shamanistic animism survived among them. Until the nineteenth century, most of the Abakan Tatars were hunters and trappers, going after sable, fox, marten, ermine, bear, and wolf. When industrialization began to reach Siberia, some Abakan Tatars went to work in factories, tanneries, and sawmills. After the 1930s, most of the Abakan Tatars found themselves living and laboring on collective farms. Since World War II, Russian ethnographers have classified them with the Khakass*. See KHAKASS and TATAR.

REFERENCES: Shirin Akiner, *Islamic Peoples of the Soviet Union*, 1983; Alexandre Bennigsen and S. Enders Wimbush, *Muslims of the Soviet Empire: A Guide*, 1986.

ABAKANTSY TATAR. See ABAKAN TATAR and KHAKASS.

ABALAK. See KACHA and KHAKASS.

ABAN. See SHOR.

ABANTSY. See SHOR.

ABAQAN. See ABAKAN TATAR and KHAKASS.

ABAQAN TATAR. See ABAKAN TATAR and KHAKASS.

ABAZA. During the twentieth century, Soviet ethnologists and demographers have had a difficult and intellectually controversial time classifying the Abaza people as an ethnic community. They are closely related to the Circassian* ethnic group, and, until the 1920s, most Soviet scholars classified them as the branch of the Abkhaz* people who lived in the region of Kuban. The Abaza call themselves the "Apswa," which is the same term used by the Abkhaz people who are considered a branch of the Circassians. The Abaza and the Abkhaz view themselves as the same people, ethnically and linguistically. The Abaza are also known as Abazin, Abazian, Abazinian, Beskesek Abaza, and Kuban Abkhaz. Russians* call them the Abazin. Their language is part of the northwest branch of the Caucasic linguistic family. In the 1989 Soviet census, the Abaza population was 33,801 people. They live in the Karachai-Cherkess Autonomous Oblast on the northern coast of the Black Sea. The Abaza are divided into distinct groups based on differences in dialect. They are the Tapanta and the Ashkharawa* (Ashkaraua) or Shkharawa. Tapanta-speakers form the largest group of the Abaza people.

The Abaza are an indigenous people of the Caucasus. They originally lived along the Black Sea coast, just north of the contemporary Abkhazian Republic. Between the sixth and twelfth centuries, Christian missionaries from the Byzantine churches brought their religious faith to the northern Caucasus region; during the next several centuries, there was a blending of Eastern Orthodox beliefs with traditional animist rituals and values. The Abaza migrated from the Black Sea coast to their present location between the fourteenth and sixteenth centuries. That migration brought them into contact with Islamic peoples, and Mongol* invaders reinforced the Sunni Muslim faith in the sixteenth century, though some ethnologists argue that it was the Nogais* who first passed that faith on to the Abazas. It was not until the eighteenth century that Muslim missionaries and traders from the Ottomon Empire converted large numbers of the Tapanta Abaza to the new religion. But although Sunni Muslims had considerable religious success among the Abaza, their conversion was not universal, and a significant number of Abaza—primarily the Ashkharawa—remained loyal to Christianity. Not until the middle of the nineteenth century did the Ashkharawa convert to Islam, largely because of the missionary efforts of Mehmet Emin. By the early twentieth century, and today as well, virtually all of the Abaza are loyal to Islam, particularly to the Hanafi rite of the Sunni faith.

During the mid-nineteenth century, the Abaza underwent a severe population decline. Beginning late in the 1500s, Russian* and Ukrainian* Cossacks*, attracted by the rich agricultural lands of the North Caucasus, settled among and eventually outnumbered the Abaza. Catherine the Great then exacerbated the problem in the eighteenth century by relocating even larger numbers of Ukrainian Cossacks to the area. The cultural sources for conflict between the Christian, Slavic-speaking Cossacks and the Sunni Muslim, Caucasic-speaking Abaza were well-established, and competition for land only made the situation worse. When the Russian-Turkish wars erupted, the Abaza were devastated. The Cossacks joined Russia in its attack on the Muslim Turks*, while the Abaza, along with large numbers of other Circassians, joined other Muslim Caucasians and fought against Russia and its expansionist urges. The Russians conducted a war of extermination against the Muslims, and groups like the Abaza, who lived on the open steppes, were especially vulnerable to attack. During the Shamil uprising between 1834 and 1858, the Tapanta sided with the Russians while the Ashkharawa supported Shamil. Thousands of Abaza—especially the Ashkharawa—were slaughtered, and tens of thousands more emigrated to Turkey between 1861 and 1864.

By the end of the nineteenth century, the Abaza had been drastically reduced in numbers. Their economy revolved around animal husbandry, and they were especially successful at raising cattle, sheep, and horses. After the Russian Revolution and the beginning of the Soviet period, government policy collectivized the Abaza herds and pasture lands, much to the opposition of Abaza leaders. Today, the Abaza economy revolves around raising cattle, sheep, and horses and growing feed grains, corn, wheat, and fruits. There has been very little industrialization in the Karachai-Cherkess Autonomous Oblast where most Abaza live, and more than 80 percent of the people still function in a rural lifestyle.

That collectivization process occurred at the same time that Soviet policy became committed to the russification of Abaza culture. Beginning in 1922, the

government closed all Muslim schools, and, in the early 1930s, the state created an Abaza written language based on the Latin alphabet. The alphabet was changed from Latin to Cyrillic in 1938, and all Persian*, Arabic, and Turkic words were outlawed in the language; that is, those words were forbidden to be used or published. The study of Russian in the public schools became mandatory, and the use of Abaza as a language of instruction was prohibited after the fifth grade. In the early 1960s, all use of Abaza in public schools was prohibited. Nonetheless, government attempts to assimilate the Abaza have not been successful. The Abaza people are committed Sunni Muslims, continue to function in traditional economic ways, speak their native language, and remain loyal to their patriarchal, extended family traditions. More than 95 percent of them still use one of the Abaza dialects as their native tongue, and endogamous marriage is the rule.
REFERENCES: Richard Abaza, "The Abazinians," Caucasian Review (1959), 34–40; Thomas Abkhazian, "Literature on Abkhazia and the Abkhazian-Abazinian," Caucasian Review (1958), 125–43; Alexandre Bennigsen, "The Problem of Bilingualism and Assimilation in the North Caucusus," Central Asian Review, 15 (1967), 205–11; Alexandre Bennigsen and Chantal Lemercier-Qualuejay, Islam in the Soviet Union, 1967; Alexandre Bennigsen and S. Enders Wimbush, Muslims of the Soviet Empire: A Guide, 1986; Maxim Kim, The Soviet Peoples: A New Historical Community, 1974; Louis J. Luzbetak, Marriage and the Family in Caucasia, 1966; Ronald Wixman, "Circassians," in Richard V. Weekes, ed., Muslim Peoples, 1984, 203–9; Ronald Wixman, The Peoples of the Soviet Union, 1984.

ABAZGHI. See ABAZA and ABKHAZ.

ABAZGHIAN. See ABAZA and ABKHAZ.

ABAZGI. See ABAZA and ABKHAZ.

ABAZGIN. See ABAZA and ABKHAZ.

ABAZGINIAN. See ABAZA and ABKHAZ.

ABAZGO-CIRCASSIAN. The term "Abazgo-Circassian," or "Abazgo-Kerketian," is an older, generic reference to the languages and peoples of the northwest branch of the Caucasian linguistic family. Included in this group are the Abazas*, Abkhazes*, Ubyks, Adyghes*, Cherkesses*, and Kabards*. See CIRCASSIAN.
REFERENCE: Ronald Wixman, The Peoples of the USSR: An Ethnographic Handbook, 1984.

ABAZGO-KERKETIAN. See ABAZGO-CIRASSIAN.

ABAZIAN. See ABAZA.

ABAZIN. See ABAZA.

ABAZINIAN. See ABAZA.

ABAZINTSY. See ABAZA.

ABAZINY. See ABAZA.

ABHAZ. See ABKHAZ.

ABIN. See SHOR.

ABINTSY. See SHOR.

ABJUI. See ABAZA and ABKHAZ.

ABJUY. See ABAZA and ABKHAZ.

ABKHAZ. The term ''Abkhazians'' (Apsua, or Apswa, in Abkhazian) refers to a northern Caucasian people whose homeland is found between the southern reaches of the Caucasus and the Black Sea coast in the northwest corner of the Republic of Georgia. The Abkhazians in the Commonwealth of Independent States (CIS) number 102,933, according to the Soviet census of 1989. The overwhelming majority (well over 90 percent) of Abkhazians reside in the former Abkhazian Autonomous Republic within the Republic of Georgia, where they make up about 18 to 20 percent of their republic's population. Individuals and small groups of Abkhazians are also found in other regions of the Georgian Republic, as well as in other republics of the CIS. A significant number of Abkhazians also emigrated to the Ottoman Empire in the late nineteenth century, and their descendants today reside in the Turkish Republic and elsewhere in the Middle East. The Abkhazian people constitute a minority in their own republic. In 1979, Abkhazians made up 17 percent of the total population of 486,082 in the republic. Of the other ethnic groups of the republic, 43.9 percent were Georgians*, 16.4 percent were Russians*, 15.1 percent were Armenians*, 2.8 percent were Greeks*, and 2.1 percent were Ukrainians*.

The Abkhazian Autonomous Republic is a triangular region of 8,600 square kilometers in the northwest corner of the Republic of Georgia, encompassing a territory that is bordered by the Caucasus Mountains in the north, Svanetia in the east, the Black Sea in the south, and Mingrelia in the southeast. The climate and vegetation include alpine meadows above an altitude of 2,000 meters, upper foothills with mixed coniferous and deciduous forests, lower foothills forested with a mixture of oak, chestnut, and other deciduous trees, and subtropical coastal lowlands, with palms, citrus, figs, and other ''Mediterranean'' flora.

The language of the Abkhazians is not closely related to the southern Caucasian languages of Georgia (Georgian, Migrelo-Laz, Svanetian*), but rather is a northern Caucasian language, belonging to the Abazgo-Cherkess language group with more affinities to the languages of the northwestern Caucasian peoples such as the Abazas*, Cherkesses*, and Kabards*. The Abkhazian language, like the Cherkess language, is known as polysynthetic, due to its unusual feature of having only two vowels and sixty-five consonants in the northern dialect, which became the literary language, and sixty-seven consonants in the southern dialect. It is interesting to compare these features with those of the neighboring Svanetians, whose language has eighteen vowel sounds. Prior to the Russian annexation, there was no written Abkhazian language; Georgian was widely used by the Christians and some of the Muslims, while Arabic, Turkish, and Persian* were used by others among the Muslims. Abkhazian was developed into a literary language, first using the Cyrillic alphabet, in the mid-nineteenth century by a team consisting of a Russian general who was a specialist on Caucasian languages, two Abkhazian officers in the Russian service, and an Abkhazian Orthodox priest. The first works of Abkhaziar. literature were published by Christian Abkhazians like Dimitri Gulia, G. D. Gulia, and others. Between 1918 and 1938, Cyrillic was replaced by a Latin script, which was in turn supplanted by a Georgian alphabet between 1938 and 1954; the Georgian script was abandoned for a new Cyrillic alphabet after the death of Josef Stalin in 1954. The Cyrillic written language continues to this day. Literary Abkhazian, however, is mostly used only up through the secondary schools, while Georgian and Russian are used more widely in upper-level education. Russian and Georgian language publications have a much wider circulation. In addition, more radio and television broadcasts are presented in the latter two languages.

The Abkhazians have a history that goes back to ancient times. It is perhaps from the Abkhazian folk hero Abrskil that the ancient Greeks received the myth of Prometheus, who brought fire to humanity and was punished by the gods by being tied to the Caucasus Mountains and perennially gnawed at by eagles. The Greeks who founded the Black Sea colonies of Dioskourias (later Sebastopolis and Sukhumi) and Pitiuntas (later Bichvinta) came into contact with a warlike, piratical people they knew as the Heniochi. Some scholars have asserted that the Heniochi were the progenitors of the Abkhazians, who also practiced piracy in early modern times. A number of ancient authors in the Roman era—notably Arrian, Pliny, and Strabo—mentioned a people inhabiting the coastal region of the northeastern Black Sea who were known as the Abasgoi in Greek and the Abasgi in Latin. According to the sixth-century Byzantine historian Procopius, the Abasgoi in his time were under the suzerainty of the Kingdom of Lazica. In his *History of the Wars*, Procopius also described the Abasgoi as warlike and as worshipers of tree dieties. He also claimed that the Abasgoi (Abkhazians) provided eunuchs for the Byzantine court in Constantinople. The Abkhazians, along with Lazic Kingdom, became clients of the Byzantine Empire in the sixth century under the emperor Justinian. With this came the further Christianization of the Abkhazians. The Christian Church already had outposts in the former

Greek colonies of Pitiuntas and Sebastopolis on the Abkhazian coast, with a bishop of metropolitan rank at Pitiuntas.

With the rise of Islam in the seventh century, the subsequent destruction of Sassanid Persia, and the weakening of Byzantium, Abkhazia became independent of Byzantine suzerainty and formed a principality known as Abazgia or Abkhazia. It affiliated with the Khazar khanate about 800 A.D. through the marriage of its prince, Leon II, to a Khazarian princess. Leon II then promoted himself with the title of king and established his capital at Kutaisi in western Georgia. His kingdom controlled the principalities of Svanetia, Mingrelia, and Guria, as well as parts of Imeretia and Lazica. The kingdom was soon threatened by Muslims, who had reached eastern Georgia by the early ninth century. Supposedly, for a brief time in the 830s and 840s, the kings of Abkhazia had to pay tribute to the Caliphate of Baghdad. By the second half of the ninth century, however, Muslim power had receded, and the Abkhazian kings extended their authority into Kartlia and as far as Armenia until the middle of the tenth century. During this period, Georgian influence in Abkhazian statecraft and culture began to be pronounced. The power of the Abkhazian king rested upon a complex feudal pyramid that had as its hallmarks military prowess and kinship. As this feudal authority spread to more vassals, it became much more difficult to maintain.

A Georgian dynasty known as the Bagrations or Bagratids began to extend its influence westward. Amid the anarchy among vassal princes and nobility, the Abkhazian throne passed to Bagrat III, a Bagratid who was the son of an Abkhazian princess. Bagrat and his successors eventually controlled not only Abkhazia, but also all of the Georgian principalities and parts of Armenia. Although the Bagratids were recognized as kings of all Georgia, their title of king of Abkhazia continued to be important, since Muslims continued to call the Bagratid Georgian kingdom Abkhazia or Abkhazistan into the thirteenth century.

In the fourteenth and fifteenth centuries, direct Bagratid rule in Abkhazia was replaced by an *eristavate*, a feudal principality under the Shavashidze family that subsequently ruled Abkhazia under Ottoman suzerainty. In the sixteenth and seventeenth centuries, Abkhazia was plagued with feudal strife among Georgian and Abkhazian nobility, as well as by the increasing incursions and raids by the Ottoman Turks who had occupied the Lazic coastal region to the southeast. By 1578, Abkhazia had become a vassal principality under the Ottomans, and the Abkhazians came increasingly into contact with the Islamic world.

The Islamization of a significant portion of the population began in the seventeenth century and culminated in the conversion of the princely family of Shavashidze in the late eighteenth century. By this time, Turkish rule had become nominal, and Abkhazia was ruled by two branches of the Shavashidzes in the western and eastern coastal regions. The interior highland regions had no central government but rather a clan system similar to that of Free Svanetia to the east.

The Russian annexation of eastern Georgia (Kartlia and Kakhetia) and parts of Mingrelia in 1801 brought Abkhazia increasingly under Russian influence. The Muslim prince, Kelesh-Bey Shavashidze, attempted to develop a modus vivendi with the Russians in 1803, but to no avail. In the midst of the Russo-Turkish War of 1806–1812, Kelesh-Bey was assassinated by his son, Arslan-Bey, who was supported by the Ottomans. His other son, Sefer-Bey, made common cause with the Russians and sought an alliance with them against his brother. Sefer-Bey converted to Christianity, taking the name of George, and was recognized as Prince of Abkhazia under Russian protection in 1809. The Russians captured Sukhumi from the Turks and placed a garrison there, but the rest of the country remained mostly under the Muslim feudatories. The Russian forces remained in order to maintain the feudal authority of the re-Christianized Shavashidzes.

The two sons of George Shavashidze, Dimitri and Michael, had to be maintained in power by the presence of the Russian garrison at Sukhumi. The Russian position in Abkhazia was enhanced during the Russo-Turkish War of 1827–1828, when the Russian annexation of the Black Sea coast from Anapa to Poti allowed the garrison at Sukhumi to be more easily supplied and reinforced. Nevertheless, Russian dominion in Abkhazia was very tenuous. While Michael Shavashidze was Prince of Abkhazia, he directly controlled only the northwest corner of the principality; the rest was under the control of the Muslim branches of the Shavashidze clan, who owed only nominal feudal allegiance to Michael. With Russian help, Michael was able to extend his authority somewhat in later years; yet he still depended on Muslim notables and advisers in his court. The Muslim feudatories and population became increasingly restive in the 1830s and 1840s, as Abkhazia became a base of operations for the Russian campaigns against the Cherkess, with whom the Muslim Abkhazians had religious and ethno-linguistic affinities. British agents were able to persuade one of the Muslim members of the Shavashidze clan, Iskander, to aid them in operations against the Russians in exchange for authority over the Samurzakan district of Mingrelia. Omar Pasha Latas's expeditionary force later landed at Sukhumi and advanced southeast along the coast until the end of hostilities. In the wake of the Crimean War, when the Russians succeeded in subduing and annihilating most of the Cherkess and other Muslim tribesmen of the Western Caucasus, they also decided to eliminate the autonomous principality of Abkhazia. Michael Shavashidze was deposed in 1864, and the Russians then occupied the country.

The Russians quickly annexed Abkhazia as a special province of Sukhumi with three districts—Pitsunda, Ochemchiri, and Dzhebelda. Two years later, in 1866, the Abkhazians staged an armed uprising against Russian rule in response to an attempt by the government to initiate land reform and to assess property for the purpose of initiating a recompensation (taxation) system. This policy was too much for the Abkhazians, whose revolt caught Russian forces by such surprise that the rebels were able to capture Sukhumi for a time. Eight thousand Russian reinforcements had to be called in and the revolt was crushed only with much bloodshed. The Russians confiscated all weapons in the province and declared the Abkhazians to be unfaithful subjects of the tsar. Between 1858 and 1864, and especially following the subjugation of the revolt in 1866, many Muslim Abkhazians followed the lead of over 600,000 Cherkess and other tribesmen and emigrated to the Ottoman Empire, rather than remain under Russian rule. A second uprising occurred during the Eastern Crisis in 1877 and led to further Abkhazian out-migration after it was quelled. According to one source, the Abkhazian population in the 1830s was 90,000, but it declined to 65,000 in 1866 and to 20,000 in 1877. The Russian Imperial Census of 1897, however, gave the population of Abkhazians at a higher figure of 59,481.

The departure from Abkhazia by a large percentage of its natives opened the door to immigration by Georgians, Russians, Ukrainians, Greeks, Armenians, and other nationalities in the late nineteenth and early twentieth centuries. It also created a confessional equilibrium among the remaining Abkhazians. At the time of the Russian annexation, a large majority of Abkhazians were probably at least nominally Muslim, with a minority of Orthodox Christians. The exodus of a significant proportion of the Muslim Abkhazians left the percentage of Christians somewhere between 50 and 70 percent, with corresponding percentages of Muslims. These figures are difficult to verify because, according to most scholars, the Abkhazians are not deeply imbued with either faith, and syncretic elements of both Islam and Christianity have been mixed with traditional Abkhazian folklore and social customs.

Abkhazia, like other areas of Georgia and the Russian Empire, was racked by disturbances during the 1905 revolution in the wake of the Russo-Japanese War. In the revolutionary year of 1917, class and ethnic conflict in the region flared up again. While some of this activity was spurred on by the non-Abkhazian urban classes, the native Abkhazians, led by the native Bolshevik Nestor Lakoba, also broke the remnants of the feudal power of the Abkhazian nobles and their clans. For a brief time, Abkhazia, particularly Sukhumi, came under Bolshevik control in 1918. Between 1918 and 1921, Abkhazia became part of an independent Georgian Republic dominated by Mensheviks and protected by German* and later British forces. This fledgling republic lost control of Abkhazia first to White Russian forces and finally to Bolshevik forces in late 1920 and 1921. Following the demise of the Georgian Republic, Abkhazia became part of the Transcaucasian Federated Soviet Socialist Republic in 1922, which in turn became part of the new Union of Soviet Socialist Republics.

Abkhazia did not participate in the anti-Soviet uprising that broke out in Svanetia, Mingrelia, and elsewhere in Western Georgia in 1924. Nonetheless, a good deal of resistance emerged among Abkhazians over collectivization in 1930 and 1931. The Abkhazian resistance to collectivization was met with arrests and armed intervention by Soviet troops. In order to hasten the drive to collectivization, native and Russian Communist cadres were allowed to form an Abkhazian Autonomous Soviet Socialist Republic, which increasingly submitted to the authority of the Georgian Soviet Socialist Republic. The Georgian Communist Party simultaneously came under the control of Lavrenty Beria, a native of Sukhumi of Mingrelian* origin and head of the Soviet secret police in Transcaucasia. From 1932 through 1938, Beria became Stalin's right-hand man in Georgia and wielded dictatorial powers in the implementation of the Second

Five-Year Plan (1933–1938) and the purges of the Georgian Communist Party. It was during his tenure that Abkhazia was further inundated by Georgians and other immigrants involved in carrying out the goals of the Second Five-Year Plan. This policy of increasing the influx of Georgians led to some resentment and dissent from native Abkhazian communists, led by Lakoba. Beria responded with a purge of Abkhazian Communist leadership. Following the death of Lakoba by a heart attack in late 1936, he and many other members of the native Abkhazian cadre were accused of Trotskyism and national deviationism. Beria implicated forty-seven of Lakoba's comrades and relatives in a plot to assassinate Stalin. Ten of Lakoba's associates were executed, including Samson Chanba, Abkhazia's best-known playwright.

Through much of the Stalin era, Soviet power and Georgian nationalism made inroads through attempts to relegate the native Abkhazian population to the status of an anthropological oddity with claims regarding the longevity of the Abkhazians' lifespan. They have a reputation for having the highest percentage of centenarians in the Caucasus, the former Soviet Union, and indeed the world. At the same time that this element of Abkhazian society and culture was proclaimed as a positive aspect of the new Soviet order, attempts were made to eliminate many of the negative aspects of Abkhazian customary law, such as the blood feud. Still, other more positive aspects of Abkhazian social life and customs were vitiated without allowing for the development of a modern Abkhazian identity. Among educated Abkhazians, the tendency has been either to identify themselves increasingly with the Georgian plurality, with whom many share common customs, religion, and historical development, or to resist assimilation and develop a separate Abkhazian identity with the aid of the Soviet government.

The trends toward geogianization were eased somewhat by the death of Stalin and the liquidation of Beria in 1953. De-Stalinization manifested itself in Abkhazia in the changeover from Georgian to Cyrillic script for the Abkhazian language, the reorganization of the Abkhazian school system to allow further instruction in Abkhazian for native Abkhazians, and the founding of an Abkhazian language and literature section at the Sukhumi Pedagogical Institute. In addition, the party and government issued new Abkhazian newspapers and magazines; it also increased general publishing in the Abkhazian language. Perhaps reaction against the domination of Beria accounted for this flowering of Abkhaz language and culture. Moreover, the increased international attention to the Abkhazians and their supposed longevity, together with the development of Sukhumi as a spa and resort center, no doubt played a role in the liberalization of national policy toward the Abkhazians.

Nevertheless, the demographic trends that militated against the native Abkhazians continued to be fostered by the Soviet regime. By 1926, the native Abkhazians made up less than one-third of the population of the Abkhazian Soviet Socialist Republic (55,918 out of 186,004). Under Russian imperial rule, the coastal lowland regions of Abkhazia had been developed for the cultivation of tobacco, tea, and citrus fruits, which brought in large numbers of Georgians,

Mingrelians*, Armenians, and Greeks as workers, as well as Russians and Ukrainians. In addition, mountaineers from the Georgian highland area of Svanetia settled in the mountain regions of Abkhazia that had been abandoned by Muslim Abkhazians in 1866 and 1877.

The policy of diluting the native presence in Abkhazia was prosecuted with vigor by the Soviets and Georgian Communists. During the aforementioned Second Five-Year Plan, the Soviets began an expansion of tobacco production and processing, as well as projects such as hydroelectric power stations, which promoted further in-migration by Georgians, Russians, Armenians, and Greeks. Even though a large portion of the Greek population of Abkhazia was deported after World War II, nevertheless the proportion of Abkhazians relative to the total population of the republic dropped to an all-time low of 15.1 percent by 1959. The development of the Abkhazian coast as a resort center further encouraged an increased influx of non-Abkhazians.

The 1970 and 1979 Soviet censuses indicated that the Abkhazian population had begun to recoup part of their proportional strength with a growth rate that outstripped all other nationalities except the Georgians. Between 1959 and 1970, the Abkhazian portion of the population grew from 15.1 to 17.1 percent. While the Georgian plurality in the Abkhazian Autonomous Republic also grew (from 39.1 to 43.9 percent), the Russian component declined precipitiously (21.4 to 16.4 percent). In light of these demographic trends, the nationality problems in the Abkhazian Republic increasingly engaged native Abkhazians with the Georgian plurality in Abkhazia, as well as with the government of the Republic of Georgia. Ethnic disturbances and anti-Soviet riots occurred in Abkhazia in 1957, 1967, and 1979, which went unreported until the late 1980s. It is unknown to what extent these incidents involved the expression of Abkhazian nationalism.

The national disputes between Abkhazians and Georgians manifested themselves in 1973, when the communist leadership in the Georgian Republic claimed that elements among the Abkhazian communist leadership in Abkhazian Autonomous Republic were demanding that preference be given to native Abkhazians in the doling out of party and government positions. At the same time, there is evidence that some Georgian party officials in the 1970s and 1980s considered national minorities like the Abkhazians, Ossetians*, Adjars*, and others as subject to eventual assimilation by the Georgians. The national issue became much more pronounced with the advent of *glasnost* under Mikhail Gorbachev in 1985. Soon Abkhazians were demanding more cultural and political autonomy; some sought secession from the Georgian Republic and incorporation into the Russian Republic. These activities were partly a long-term development, but they were also a response to the recrudescence of Georgian nationalism under Zviad Gamsakhurdia and other leaders. As Georgians asserted their nationalism within the republic by the formation of political movements and paramilitary organizations, the Abkhazians and others responded in kind.

The Abkhazian-Georgian rivalry in the autonomous republic came to a head with the outbreak of armed clashes between Abkhazians and Georgians in 1989.

Ostensibly, the confrontation occurred over the organization of a branch campus of the University of Tbilisi in Sukhumi; the fighting had much broader causes, however, as seen in later events. With the move toward Georgian independence in the summer of 1991, Abkhazian demands for secession from Georgia increased. At first, the secessionists called for affiliation with the Russian Federated Republic, but, following the examples of the Chechen*-Ingush* and other north Caucasian autonomous areas, more Abkhazians soon called for independence.

Intermittent battles between Abkhazian irregular forces and the Georgian military continued through 1992. No doubt the combat has had the effect of increasing the exodus of Russians and other ethnic minorities from the republic. The withdrawal of a Soviet or Commonwealth of Independent States military presence in the area has made it a battleground between Abkhazian and Georgian militias. The prospects for a peaceful solution to the Abkhazian issue within the new Georgian Republic become dimmer as fighting drags on. Still, the threat of "ethnic cleansing" and either an Abkhazian or Georgian refugee problem seem more terrifyingly real.

REFERENCES: On Abkhazia and Abkhazians within the history of Georgia, see W.E.D. Allen, *A History of the Georgian People from the Beginning Down to the Russian Conquest in the Nineteenth Century*, 1936; D. M. Lang, *The Georgians*, 1966; D. M. Lang, *Modern History of Soviet Georgia*, 1962; R. G. Suny, *The Making of the Georgian Nation*, 1988; Cyril Toumanoff, "Christian Caucasia between Byzantium and Iran: New Light from Old Sources," *Traditio*, 10 (1954); and "Introduction to Christian Caucasian History," *Traditio*, 15 (1959) and 17 (1961). On the Abkhazians, see I. A. Adshindzhal, *Iz etnografiia Abkhazii: Materialy i Issledovanie*, 1969; W. Barthold and V. Minorsky, "Abkhaz," *The Encyclopedia of Islam*, Vol. 1, 1960; S. Benet. *Abkhazians*, 1956; N. S. Dzanashiia, *Stat 'ei po etnograffii Abkhazii*, 1960; G. A. Dzindzaria, et al., *Ocherk istorii Abkhazskoi A.S.S.R.*, 1960; B. Geiger, *Peoples and Languages of the Caucasus*, 1959; Sh. D. Inal-Apa, *Abkhazy*, 1960; A. E. Kuprava, "Kratki obzor izucheniia istorii Abkhazii za sorok let," *Trudy Abkhazskogo instituta iazyka, literatury i istorii*, 32 (1962); V. Minorsky, *Studies in Caucasian History*, 1953; and Cyril Toumanoff, "Chronology of the Kings of Abasgia and other Problems," *Le Museon*, 69 (1956).

Nicholas C. J. Pappas

ABKHAZIAN. See ABKHAZ.

ABOLTAI. See KACHA and KHAKASS.

ABOLTAY. See KACHA and KHAKASS.

ABUGACH. See KHAKASS.

ABUGACHAEV. See KHAKASS.

ABUGACHAIEV. See KHAKASS.

ABUGACHYEV. See KHAKASS.

ABZHUI. The Abzhui are one of the subgroups of the Abkhaz* people. They are concentrated demographically in the Kodor River valley of the Abkhaz Autonomous Republic. See ABKHAZ.
REFERENCE: Ronald Wixman, *The Peoples of the USSR: An Ethnographic Handbook*, 1984.

ABZHUY. See ABZHUI and ABKHAZ.

ACHA. See KYZYL and KHAKASS.

ACHAN. See NANAI.

ACHAR. See ADJAR and GEORGIAN.

ACH'ARELI. See ADJAR.

ACHIKULAK NOGAI. Most Achikulak live in the Achikulak Rayon in Stavropol Krai. They constitute one of the three geographical subdivisions of the Nogai* people. See NOGAI.
REFERENCE: Ronald Wixman, *The Peoples of the USSR: An Ethnographic Handbook*, 1984.

ACHIKULAK NOGAY. See NOGAI.

ACHIKULAKTSY. See NOGAI.

ACHUKULAK NOGHAI. See NOGAI.

ACHUKULAK NOGHAY. See NOGAI.

ACHIN. See KHAKASS.

ACHINTSY. See KHAKASS.

ACHIQULAQ NOGAI. See NOGAI.

ACHIQULAQ NOGAY. See NOGAI.

ACHIQULAQ NOGHAI. See NOGAI.

ACHIQULAQ NOGHAY. See NOGAI.

ADIGE. See ADYGHE.

ADIGEI. See ADYGHE.

ADIGEY. See ADYGHE.

ADIGHI. See ADYGHE.

ADIGI. See ADYGHE.

ADJAR. Ever since 1926, the Adjar (Adzhar, Achar) people have been classified as Georgians* by Soviet and Russian* ethnologists. They use the term Ach'areli (Adzhareli) as a self-designation, while Russians* refer to them as the Adzhartsy. They live on the southeast coast of the Black Sea, bordering Turkey. Christianity first reached the region in the fourth century, and the Adjars were incorporated into the Georgian kingdom in the tenth century. Their ethnic origins are the same as those of other Georgians; they speak a Gurian dialect that is laced with Turkish words and their literary language is Georgian. The region has historically been overrun by foreign invaders: Seljuks in the eleventh century, Mongols* in the thirteenth century, Timurids in the fourteenth century, and Ottomans in the fifteenth century. The Adjars were under Turkish rule until the Russo-Turkish War of 1877–1878, when the Congress of Berlin awarded the region to Russia. In the late nineteenth and early twentieth centuries, the Adjar capital of Batumi was linked by railroad lines and oil pipelines to Baku and Tbilisi.

Adjar differences with other Georgians are primarily religious. In the late sixteenth and seventeenth centuries, they were converted to the Hanafi rite of the Sunni Muslim religion by the Ottoman Turks (government officials and businessmen) who occupied the region. The Adjars number approximately 150,000 people today, and they remain devoted to their Muslim faith. In July 1922, the Soviet Union established the Adjar Autonomous Soviet Socialist Republic for them, consisting of 1,100 square miles and located southwest of Georgia, bordering on the Black Sea and the Turkish border. Late in the 1920s, the Adjars rose up in rebellion, because of Soviet anti-Muslim religious campaigns and the drive to collectivize farms throughout the country. After crushing the rebellion, Josef Stalin deported large numbers of Adjars to Central Asia. They were also declassified as a nationality and considered a Georgian subgroup from that time on. Today, Batumi is occupied primarily by non-Muslim Russians, Armenians*, and Ukrainians*. Adjar intellectuals have traditionally been oriented more toward Turkey, and most Adjars are bilingual in Turkish and Georgian. See GEORGIAN.

REFERENCES: Shirin Akiner, *Islamic Peoples of the USSR*, 1983; Alexandre Bennigsen and S. Enders Wimbush, *Muslims of the Soviet Empire: A Guide*, 1986; Ronald Wixman, *The Peoples of the USSR: An Ethnographic Handbook*, 1984.

ADURKHAY. See KARACHAI.

ADYGE. See ADYGHE.

ADYGEI. See ADYGHE.

ADYGEY. See ADYGHE.

ADYGHE. The Adyghes, also known as the Lower Circassians and the Kiakhs, are an ethnic group of approximately 127,000 people, living primarily in the Adyghe Autonomous Oblast of the Krasnodar Krai in Russia. They are considered to be the western branch of the Circassian* people. Adyghes also live in the Lazarevskii and Tuapse rayons (administrative districts). The Adyghes first emerged as a self-conscious ethnic group in the thirteenth century, when they may have occupied the entire area between the Don River and the Caucasus mountains and between the Black Sea and the Stavropol plateau. They found themselves overrun in turn by the Sarmatians, Mongols*, Turks*, and Russians*, and they are now much reduced in number and are a minority population everywhere. A large but indeterminate number of Adyghes live abroad, mostly in the Middle East. These are the descendants of Adyghes expelled from Russia in 1864.

The Adyghe homeland is a warm and fertile part of the Russia, with open grassland, rich soil, and numerous rivers carrying Caucasus snow-melt to the Black Sea. It is eminently suitable for agriculture and thus has attracted many Russian and Ukrainian* settlers. The area contains coal, oil, and natural gas. Because of this geographic base, the traditional Adygheian economy has revolved around animal husbandry. Adyghes have a well-earned reputation throughout Central Asia and the Middle East for their skills in breeding horses, cattle, and sheep. They are also well-known for unrivaled horsemanship and marksmanship. Another important feature of the Adygheian economy involves textiles, and their sheepskins and leathers are highly prized throughout Central Asia and the Middle East.

The Adyghe language is part of the larger Abkhazo-Adyg group of Caucasian* languages. All of the Circassian peoples spoke dialects of a single language, but because of their turbulent history, different tribes adopted various loan-words from Russian, Turkish, Georgian*, Persian*, and Arabic. Today there are four mutually intelligible Adyghe dialects: Abadzeg* (Abadzekh), Bzhedug* (Bzhedukh), Temirgoi* (Temirgoj), and Shapsug*. Ethnographers identify ten Adyghe subgroups. The Abadzeg live along the Psekups, Laba, and Belaya rivers on the western side of the North Caucasus. The Beslenei* (Beslenej) are located between the upper Urup and Khozdya rivers, and along the Middle Laba River, in the western reaches of the North Caucasus. Living in a concentrated area near Krasnodar are the Bzhedug. The Temirgoi, Makhosh*, and Egerukai* are between the Laba and Belaya rivers. Between the Pshish and Belaya rivers are the Khatukai*. The Natukhai* dwell along the coast of the Black Sea between the Kuban and Pshad rivers. The Shapsug live on the coast as well, between the Pshad and Shakhe rivers. There are also clusters of Shapsug on the foothills of the Caucasus mountains.

What chiefly distinguishes Adyghes from other Caucasian nations is the simple geographic fact that their rivers drain to the Black Sea, not to the Caspian. Thus they were, from earliest times, peripherally in touch with the Mediterranean ecumene, in contrast to their inward-looking, xenophobic eastern neighbors— the Ossetians*, Karachais*, and Chechens*. Greek and Roman authors described tribes in the northwest Caucasus as particularly noted for their fine horsebreeding and horsemanship. Adyghe women were considered especially beautiful; many were sold into Turkish and Arabian harems. Adyghe men often hired out as mercenaries, and one particularly successful group ruled Egypt for centuries as the Mameluke dynasty. The Adyghes traded with Byzantium in horses, honey, furs, and filigreed jewelry. Some converted to Christianity, which, however, blended with rather than displaced their pagan beliefs. Contact with Byzantium was interrupted in the thirteenth century by the Mongol* conquest. In the fifteenth century, the Adyghes resumed trade with the west through Genoese merchants. Islam gradually penetrated Adygheia in the sixteenth and seventeenth centuries, although this religion, too, only marginally affected their traditional beliefs and customs. The Adyghes seem never to have imitated the fanatical excesses of eastern Caucasians such as the Chechens and Daghestanis*. Their social structures were very loosely organized. Many of their customs are pan-Caucasian, including the vendetta, mandatory hospitality, and bride purchase.

The Adyghes found themselves in a perennial state of war with the Tatar* Khanate of Crimea, and with Turkic groups such as the Karachais, Kumyks*, and Nogais* that had been driven into the Caucasus by the wars of Genghis Khan. Since the western part of Caucasus range is relatively low and gentle, the Adyghes could not retreat into the mountains as did the Chechens and Ossetians. Like other Circassians, the Adyghes alternately sought alliances with Turkey and Russia for protection. A total of three diplomatic missions to Muscovy in the 1550s resulted in what the Circassians called an ''alliance'' and the Russians called a ''voluntary union'' with Russia. Ivan the Terrible then took a Kabard* princess as one of his wives. As Russian settlers followed the Cossacks* into the region between the lower Don and the Kuban, friction with the native Circassians developed.

The Circassians' fate was sealed by the Russo-Turkish wars. The Russians could not tolerate an independent Muslim Kabardia to the rear of their lines, and they forced Turkey to cede that territory (which it had never owned) in 1774. The Kabards rebelled in 1778 but were defeated. More battles took place between 1787 and 1791. Russian troops defeated the Ottoman forces of Batal Pasha on the upper Kuban River in 1790, and founded the *stanitza* (fortress) of Batalpashinsk (now the city of Cherkessk) in 1804; from there, the Georgian Military Road now winds through the mountains down to Sukhumi. General Aleksei Yermolov carried out vicious reprisals against Circassians and other Caucasians who resisted Russia. In 1829, the Turks* gave up any claim to Circassia by the Treaty of Adrianople, but this was hardly the end of warfare between Russians and Circassians. Rebellions and reprisals continued in the 1840s and 1850s. The Circassians, although not di-

rect participants in the Murid Wars, did take advantage of the Russians' preoccupation with suppressing the Imam Shamil and his followers to raid and harass the
west Caucasus forts constantly. Shamil capitulated in 1859, and the Russians completed their conquest of the Circassians in 1864.

Those Circassians who survived the war were then given a choice between
settling on the plains amidst Russians, under Russian control, or emigrating to
Turkey. The number who went to Turkey is variously estimated between 200,000
and 500,000. Conditions were horrible, and many died. Of those who survived,
some were assimilated and some went on to Syria, Jordan, Palestine, and Lebanon. Russians, Ukrainians*, and Armenians* now poured into the depopulated
Circassian lands. Economic development of the Caucasus accelerated in the last
decade of the nineteenth century and the first decade of the twentieth, but it was
strictly a Russian affair. The Circassians remained overwhelmingly rural.

Russian workers established a Kuban-Black Sea Soviet Republic in 1918, but
the area was soon taken by White Guards. When the civil war ended with a
Bolshevik victory, the Circassians in general and Adyghes in particular were
subjected to a seemingly endless round of administrative manipulations designed
to keep them separate and always outnumbered by other groups. The Karachai-
Cherkess Autonomous Oblast, for example, artificially joined the Turkic Karachais with the Caucasian Cherkess. The Kabardino-Balkar Autonomous Republic did the same, for the Balkars* are another Turkic group. It would have
made more sense to create one region for the Balkars and Karachais, and another
for the Cherkesses* and Kabards, but this did not suit Lenin, Stalin, or their
successors. The Adyghe Autonomous Oblast was established in 1922.

Soviet policy in the 1920s and 1930s affected the Adyghes in three ways:
First, the region's economy became heavily industrialized, and thus its value to
the Soviet Union increased. Second, Soviet scholars devised a separate written
language (first using Latin, then Cyrillic script) for the Adyghes. Few publications
ever appeared in Adyghe, and Adyghe children were encouraged to learn Russian
instead (most did so, but strictly as a second language). Third, the Bolsheviks
tried to erase Islam, closing religious schools in 1922. In World War II, the
Germans* occupied the Adyghe Autonomous Oblast and its capital, Maikop, as
well as the Karachai-Cherkess Autonomous Oblast and its capital, Nalchik. In
1944, Josef Stalin decided that the Turkic people had been disloyal, so all Balkars
and Karachais were deported to Central Asia. The Adyghes, who had been more
active in resisting the German occupation, escaped some of Stalin's wrath.

For years, ethnic separatism and local nationalism, so strong in the Eastern
Caucasus and the Transcaucasian republics, was far less threatening in the Adyghe regions. Russians outnumbered Adyghes three to one in the Adyghe Autonomous Oblast, and Cherkesses constitute a mere 10 percent of the population
of the Karachai-Cherkess Autonomous Oblast. Still, in spite of Russian occupation, more than 95 percent of the Adyghes still speak Adyghe as their native
language. Although Adyghe political nationalism and religious devotion never
assumed the dimensions that they did in many other Transcaucasian groups, the

glasnost policies of Mikhail Gorbachev and the subsequent outbursts of nationalist sentiments throughout the Soviet Union eventually affected many Adyghe leaders. The Adyghe-Khase Movement in 1990 began to discuss the questions of nationalism and independence, and, after the dissolution of the Soviet Union in 1991, they talked of secession from Russia and the merger of all North Caucasian peoples into a unified Mountain Republic. Aslan Dzharimov, president of the Adyghe Republic, demanded autonomy for the republic in 1992, with continued association with Russia.

REFERENCES: W.E.D. Allen and Paul Muratoff, *Caucasian Battlefields*, 1953; Alexandre Bennigsen and S. Enders Wimbush, *Muslims of the Soviet Empire: A Guide*, 1986; *Current Digest*, 44 (March 25, 1992), 5–7; Maxim Kim, *The Soviet Peoples: A New Historical Community*, 1974; Louis J. Luzbetak, *Marriage and Family in Caucasia*, 1966; Hugh Seton-Watson, *The Russian Empire, 1801–1917*, 1967; R. T. Trakho, "Literature on Circassia and the Circassians," *Caucasian Review*, 1 (1955), 145–62; Ronald Wixman, "Circassians," in Richard V. Weeks, ed., *Muslim Peoples*, 1984, pp. 203–09.

Ross Marlay

ADYGHEI. See ADYGHE.

ADYGHEY. See ADYGHE.

ADYGHI. See ADYGHE.

ADYGI. See ADYGHE.

ADZHAR. See ADJAR.

ADZHARELI. See ADJAR.

ADZHARTSY. See ADJAR.

AFGAN. See AFGHAN.

AFGANTSY. See AFGHAN.

AFGHAN. The Afghans are a tiny minority in the former Soviet Union. They call themselves the Pashtani, Pukhtu, or Pushtu. Russians* call them the Afgantsy. Ethnologists speculate that the Afghan people originated in southern India and that they are also Tajik* and Turkish in their ethnic heritage. Historical sources first identify the Afghans as a distinct group in the sixth century when they lived in the Sulaiman Mountains. They later expanded to the north and west, and, by the fourteenth and fifteenth centuries, they had reached the Peshawar Valley. By that time, Persian* traders had also introduced the Sunni Muslim religion, which eventually became the dominant faith of the Afghan people. Because of their powerful tribal mentalities, the Afghans only slowly developed any sense of nationalism. Individual Afghan states began to emerge in the eighteenth century; among the most prominent was the Durrani state of Ahmad Shah Durrani.

During the nineteenth century, the Afghan people were caught between the conflicting geo-strategic demands of the British* and the Russians. By 1830, Afghanistan had been divided into three competing principalities. Kabul was ruled by Dost Muhammad, while Kohendil Khan controlled Qandahar; Sadozai Kamran reigned over Herat. Russian and British politicians forged conflicting alliances with these rulers in order to promote their own interests. The Russians were interested in expanding south toward the Persian Gulf and the Indian Ocean, while the British feared that such expansion would permit Russia to control the Hindu Kush—the frontier corridor to the Indian subcontinent. During the second half of the nineteenth century, the British imposed a near-colonial status on Afghanistan, and it became the buffer zone that the British wanted between Russia and India. An 1895 agreement between Great Britain and Russia defined most of the Russian-Afghanistan border, and, in 1907, Moscow declared Afghanistan to be outside the Russian sphere of influence. Great Britain promised not to annex or occupy any part of Afghanistan. Afghanistan became fully independent through the Treaty of Rawalpindi in 1919.

Today there are approximately 9,000 Afghan people living in what used to be the Soviet Union. Most of them live in Tajikistan, Turkmenistan, and Uzbekistan. They are descendants of Afghan immigrants from Pushtun who arrived in the late nineteenth century. Although some of the Afghans are semi-nomadic and support themselves economically by raising sheep, cattle, horses, and camels, most are farmers who raise wheat, barley, millet, rice, and fruit. Others work in the construction industry. The Afghans maintain powerful patriarchal clan loyalties, and they have a traditional resentment toward the Soviet state and Russia, which they feel have historically been intent on culturally eliminating them. The Soviet invasion of Afghanistan in 1979 and its subsequent slaughter of a million Afghans only intensified the Afghan resentment of Russians. Most of the Afghans in the Commonwealth of Independent States are Sunni Muslims of the Hanafi school.

REFERENCES: Shirin Akiner, *Islamic Peoples of the Soviet Union*, 1983; W. K. Fraser-Tyler, *Afghanistan: A Study of Political Development in Central and Southern Asia*, 1967.

AGRJAN. See ASTRAKHAN TATAR and TATAR.

AGRZHAN. See ASTRAKHAN TATAR and TATAR.

AGRZHANTSY. See ASTRAKHAN TATAR and TATAR.

AGUL. Until the time of the Russian Revolution, the Agul people were generally classified as the Lezgin*, itself a generic term used to describe all of the ethnic groups of the highlands southwest of the Caspian Sea in what is today the Daghestan Autonomous Republic. Since then, ethnologists have been more careful in making group identifications, and the once generic Lezgins have become the Lezgins proper, as well as the Aguls, Rutuls*, and Tabasarans*. The Agul language, which has no written equivalent, is part of the Samurian group of the Caucasic languages and closely related to Lezgin. Between the 1920s and the 1950s, Lezgin served as the literary language for the Agul. That practice was terminated by state policy in the 1950s, after Russian* became the written language of the Agul. There are two basic Agul dialects: Agul and Koshan.

The Agul are still among the most isolated of the Daghestani* peoples, and their villages were all but inaccessible even to people of nearby villages. Their closest neighbors geographically have been the Kaitaks*, and they have long engaged in commercial transactions with the Lezgins, who purchased Agul wool, fleece, and cheese. The Agul were historically governed, though only nominally, by the Laks* and then the Tabasarans. When Daghestan fell to Russia in the early nineteenth century, the Agul came under Russian sovereignty as well.

Like other ethnic groups in southern Daghestan, the Agul are Sunni Moslems loyal to the Shafi theological school. Until the fifteenth century, the Agul people were primarily animists with their own folk religions, although Zoroastrianism, Judaism, and Christianity were making inroads. Persian* traders introduced Islam into southern Daghestan in the fifteenth century, while the Golden Horde brought Islam into the northern region in the sixteenth and seventeenth centuries. By the nineteenth century, the Agul had all been converted to Sunni Islam. The Agul are extremely devout in their religious devotions, and, like other Muslim people in the Near East and Middle East in the 1970s and 1980s, they have been influenced by an increasingly strident religious fundamentalism that has dominated the cultural landscape. In spite of more than seventy years of anti-religious state policy, fundamental religious institutions and traditions—such as endogamous marriages, family mosques, religious marriages and burials, observance of Ramadan, and faithful devotion to the teachings of the Koran—still flourish.

A profound anti-Russian* sentiment permeates Agul culture. Just after the Russian Revolution, the government in Moscow created the Mountain Autonomous Republic, with Arabic as the official language of the government and the schools. The Agul, along with many other highland ethnic groups, opposed the policy and rebelled against it. The government then created the Daghestan Autonomous Soviet Socialist Republic in 1921 and, in 1925, launched an anti-Islamic campaign that included closing all Islamic schools, eliminating the use of Arabic, and executing many local imams. At that point, state policy shifted in favor of the Turkic* peoples, and Azeri became the official language of the region. That ended in 1928, when the government declared that Dargin*, Avar*, Lezgin, and Azeri were all official languages. The government also decided at that time, however, to include the Aguls with the Lezgins and the Rutuls*, and to merge the Tsakhurs with the Azerbaijanis*. The government also began to create a Latin alphabet for the Agul language in 1928, but that program was changed back to the Cyrillic alphabet in 1938. Gradually, over the next twenty years, the Russian language was imposed on all schools and government offices in Daghestan.

The constant policies of cultural manipulation by the Soviet government only increased Agul resentment of Russian culture, and they had no intention of merging with the Lezgins. The Agul resisted the russification of their culture and also refused to participate in government programs to relocate them out of the highlands and into lowland towns and collective farms. As a result, all but a handful of the Agul people retain a traditional rural life-style. Economic life still revolves around animal husbandry (sheep and goats in the highlands, cattle in the lowlands), gold and silver smithing, weaving, pottery, and rug manufacturing. Because of their geographic isolation and their resentment of state education policies, Agul education levels are among the lowest in the former Soviet Union.

Although Russians generally refer to them as the Aguly, the Agul have little sense of general group ethnicity. But because of the geographic setting in which they live, the nature of their economy, and their social structure, the Agul are much more familiar with their identity as Agul subgroups based on the canyon where they live near the upper Kurakh and Gyulgeri rivers or the clan to which they belong. The four primary Agul subgroups, based on where they live, are the Aguldere, Kurkhdere, Khushandere, and Khpuikdere. Most of the Agul are among the Aguldere. Within those geographic subgroups, the Agul are further subdivided by their rigid endogamous patriarchal clan systems in which young people are encouraged to marry first or second cousins. The sense of clan cohesion is strengthened by the fact that all land is owned communally by the extended family unit. Although the Agul population underwent a decline between the 1920s and 1950s because of assimilation by the neighboring Lezgins, that trend has stalled in recent decades. Between 1959 and 1970, the Agul population grew from approximately 6,700 people to 12,000 people, and 1991 estimates place them at approximately 14,000 people.

REFERENCES: Alexandre Bennigsen, "Muslim Conservative Opposition to the Soviet Regime: The Sufi Brotherhoods in the North Caucasus," in Jeremy R. Azrael, ed., Soviet Nationality Policies and Practices, 1971; Alexandre Bennigsen and S. Enders Wimbush, Muslims of the Soviet Empire: A Guide, 1986; Bruce Geiger, et al., Peoples and Languages of the Caucasus, 1959; T. S. Halasi-Kun, "The Caucasus: An Ethno-Historical Survey," Studia Caucasic, 2 (1956), 7–16; Brian Silver, "Language Policy and Linguistic Russification of Soviet Nationalities," in Jeremy R. Azrael, ed., Soviet Nationality Policies and Practices, 1971; Ronald Wixman, Language Aspects of Ethnic Patterns and Processes in the North Caucusas, 1980; Ronald Wixman, "Daghestanis," in Richard V. Weekes, Muslim Peoples, 1984, 211–19; Ronald Wixman, The Peoples of the USSR: An Ethnographic Handbook, 1984.

AGULDERE. See AGUL.

AGULSHUJ. See AGUL.

AGULTSY. See AGUL.

AGULY. See AGUL.

AHTA. See LEZGIN.

AHTIN. See LEZGIN.

AHVA. See AVAR.

AHWAH. See AVAR.

AINO. See AINU.

AINU. The Ainu, who are also known as the Kuril and Kurilians, are a dying race, a remnant people whose origin and characteristics have puzzled anthropologists because they seem out of place in Asia. Their light skin, round eyes, wavy hair, and abundance of facial and body hair distinguish them from their Mongoloid neighbors in the Russian Far East and northern Japan. Ainu today are found in only a small part of their former territories, which included Honshu (the main Japanese island); Hokkaido (the northernmost Japanese island); and the following parts of the former Soviet Union: Sakhalin Island, the entire Kurile chain, the Kamchatka Peninsula, and the lower Amur River basin on the Siberian mainland.

Some ethnologists have described the Ainu as a ''proto-Caucausoid'' people, meaning that this racial group was thought to have split off from the white race at an early period. Recent Soviet and American scholarship, however, suggests a racial link to the people of Polynesia and Micronesia, while a minority of anthropologists maintain that the Ainu are related to Australian aborigines. The Ainu language sheds little light on their origin, for although it contains some cognates from the Ural-Altaic family, it is not linguistically related to any other language. Today Ainu is spoken by only a few people who use it when reciting epics and ballads. The language has no written form and will soon be extinct. In fact, one of its three mutually unintelligible dialects, Kurile Ainu, is no longer spoken. The other two, Hokkaido Ainu and Sakhalin Ainu, are rapidly being extinguished by Japanese* and Russian*.

Census counts of the Ainu are plagued by political and definitional problems. The Japanese government maintains that there are no national minorities, so the Ainu are not counted separately. Most sources estimate that 15,000 to 20,000 self-defined Ainu live on Hokkaido, although fewer than 200 are full-bloods. The Ainu were indigenous to the entire Okhotsk Sea Basin but over the centuries were absorbed by other, more numerous tribes, including the Nivkhis*, Itelmen*, Kamchadals*, Nanais*, and Oroks*. Members of these groups have been observed to have some Ainu racial characteristics. A Soviet census of 1926 counted only 32 Ainu. Subsequent censuses apparently have not counted the Ainu as a distinct group.

The Ainu habitat was northerly and maritime, almost constantly cold and wet, but rich in game and fish. Migrating salmon were plentiful and could be harvested with spears, basket traps, mesh nets, and weirs. The Ainu believed that the salmon were spirits who deliberately sacrificed themselves so that the Ainu might live. Herring, sea trout, and sea-urchins were also caught. The Ainu hollowed out logs for dugout canoes usable on lakes and rivers, but these were too unstable for ocean voyages. Bows and arrows were used to bring down bears, and great numbers of deer could be killed by herding them between woven deer fences into a compact mass. Some Ainu practiced a rudimentary agriculture, but the economy was otherwise based on hunting and gathering, supplemented over the past millenium by increasing trade with more advanced cultures. Ainu houses were one-room dwellings, built with a wooden frame and covered with grass or bark. They usually had a sacred window facing east (the west being associated with death). Family life centered around the open fire pit, where dwelt the Goddess of Fire, who had to be appeased with a few crumbs from every meal. Women were responsible for seeing to it that the embers never went out.

Ainu religious beliefs and practices have been recorded in detail. They were pantheists who worshipped the ocean, wind, plants, mountains, stars, rivers, trees and, above all else, the sacred bear. Bear cults were widespread in Siberia—the Ainu practice of carefully raising a cub for ritual slaughter was not unique. The bear's spirit was sent back to its ancestors to show appreciation, for it was believed that the gods provided bears to save people from famine. Shamanism was more highly developed among the Ainu of Sakhalin and the Kuriles than among the Hokkaido Ainu. Shamans (good and bad witches) diagnosed illnesses and brought messages from deceased relatives.

Ainu villages, even households, were self-sufficient. Settlements averaged only twenty to thirty people and were usually located near salmon spawning grounds upriver from the sea. The main cause of Ainu collapse in the face of the Manchus*, Russians, and Japanese was their complete lack of any unifying social or political structure.

Japanese-Ainu wars commenced as soon as the Nara state was formed in the eighth century. Shoguns were dispatched to fight Ainu "barbarism," but the prestigious samurai class may actually have sprung from Japanese-Ainu unions. Japanese power was extended progressively northward in the eighteenth and nineteenth centuries to encompass Hokkaido and Sakhalin. Ainu material culture had already been enriched by a three-way trade with Japan and Manchuria that brought tobacco, knives, brocades, lacquerware, and rice wine in exchange for furs and salmon. Traders were followed by settlers, and in 1868 Hokkaido was formally placed under the administrative control of the Japanese government, which viewed all Russian expansion along the North Pacific rim with suspicion. The Japanese imposed a policy of radical assimilation on the Ainu, ending the bear ceremony, forbidding them to fish for salmon or to hunt deer, outlawing the tradition of unmarried women tattooing their lips, and even banning the Ainu language. An 1899 law regrouped the Ainu into compact settlements, allotted them parcels of land, and established schools where the Ainu were taught to speak Japanese.

Such assimilationist policies must be seen in the light of Russo-Japanese rivalry. The Russians had encountered the Ainu as early as the 1600s, immediately converting them to Orthodoxy and transmitting European diseases. Russification was most extensive among the Ainu of southern Kamchatka and the northern Kuriles who, according to one report, even learned to swear like Russians. Russian exploration of Sakhalin and the Kuriles was intended to provide the basis for legal claims to the land, but Russian settlers were few. The Tokugawa Shogunate, in response, pushed Japanese claims as far north as possible. The Treaty of Shimoda (1855) recognized Japanese sovereignty over the southern Kuriles, where the Ainu lived, and the Treaty of St. Petersburg (1875) gave all the Kuriles to Japan while recognizing Russian claims to Sakhalin. After Japan humiliated Russia in war (1904–1905), the Treaty of Portsmouth divided Sakhalin at the fiftieth parallel, placing all the Ainu of southern Sakhalin under Japanese rule. After the Bolshevik Revolution, Japan for a time occupied northern Sakhalin as well but later withdrew. In the closing days of World War II, the Soviet Union declared war on Japan and took back all of Sakhalin and all the Kuriles as well. The Ainu who had fought with the Japanese Army were interned in Siberia and then repatriated to Japan.

The Japanese government has never recognized Soviet control over the four southernmost islands in the Kurile chain, and Japanese Ainu strongly support their government's position. With the collapse of the Soviet Union in 1991, Japan began to escalate its demand for the return of the islands. On the Kuriles, ethnic Russians responded by organizing Cossack* militia groups to resist any return of Japanese authority. A rapprochement between Japan and Russia hinges on some resolution of this issue, but for the few Ainu who may still live on Kunashir and Iturup, the question is beside the point: Their culture has vanished. Demographers believe that the Ainu have been largely assimilated by the Itelmen, Kamchadals, and Nivkhis.

REFERENCES: John Batchelor, *Ainu Life and Lore*, 1971; E. A. Hammel, "A Glimpse Into the Demography of the Ainu," *American Anthropologist* (1988), 25–41; Neil G. Munro, *Ainu Cult and Creed*, 1963; Emiko Ohnuki-Tierney, *The Ainu of the Northwest Coast of Southern Sakhalin*, 1984; Fred C. C. Peng and Peter Grier, *The Ainu: The Past in the Present*, 1977; Hitoshi Watanabe, *The Ainu Ecosystem: Environment and Group Structure*, 1972.

Ross Marlay

AIRUM. The Airum—also known as the Airym, Airumy, and Airymlary—are one of the subgroups of the Azerbaijanis*. They are a semi-nomadic people engaged in animal husbandry and farming who live in the western reaches of the Azerbaijan Republic. They originally lived in the far northwest region of Azerbaijan, especially in the Kazakh* region, but they then migrated to the

southwest. They are concentrated in the Dostafur Region, the Kedabek Region, and the mountains of the Tauz Region. See AZERBAIJAN.
REFERENCES: Shirin Akiner, *Islamic Peoples of the Soviet Union*, 1983; Ronald Wixman, *The Peoples of the USSR: An Ethnographic Handbook*, 1984.

AISOR. See ASSYRIAN.

AISORY. See ASSYRIAN.

AJAR. See ADJAR and GEORGIAN.

AK. See NOGAI.

AK NOGAI. The Ak Nogais, whom the Russians* call the Ak, Belyy Nogai, or the Kuban Nogai, are Nogais* who live in the northern reaches of the Karachai-Cherkess Autonomous Oblast in Russia. They constitute one of the three geographical divisions of the Nogai. See NOGAI.
REFERENCE: Ronald Wixman, *The Peoples of the USSR: An Ethnographic Handbook*, 1984.

AK NOGAY. See AK NOGAI.

AK NOGHAI. See AK NOGAI.

AK NOGHAY. See AK NOGAI.

AKIITA. See LEZGIN.

AKHTIN. See LEZGIN.

AKHTINTSY. See LEZGIN.

AKHVAKH. See AKHWAKH.

AKHVAKHTSY. See AKHWAKH.

AKHWAKH. Although once considered a separate ethnic group in the former Soviet Union, the Akhwakh (Akhvakh) have been classified as Avars* by Russian* ethnologists since the 1930s. They are, to be sure, in a rapid state of assimilation with the larger Avar community, but there are still several hundred people living between the Avar and Andi rivers in southern Daghestan who are aware of their Akhwakh roots. They are concentrated in the Akhawakh Region and the Sovietsky Region. The Akhwakh language is divided into two dialects with a geographical orientation, one northern and the other southern, and they are mutually incomprehensible. Avar is the literary language for both groups. They call themselves the Atluatii or Ashvado. They are also known as Akh-vakhtsy and G'akhevalal. The Akhwakh are Sunni Moslems. Although it is difficult to estimate the current Akhwakh population because of their census listing with the Avars, demographers estimate that there are as many as 8,000 people who are either consciously Akhwakh or are aware of their Akhwakh origins. See AVAR.

REFERENCES: Shirin Akiner, *Islamic Peoples of the Soviet Union*, 1983; Ronald Wixman, *The Peoples of the USSR: An Ethnographic Handbook*, 1984.

AKNOGAI. See NOGAI.

AKNOGAY. See NOGAI.

AKNOGHAI. See NOGAI.

AKNOGHAY. See NOGAI.

AKSULAK. See UIGUR.

AKSULUK. See UIGUR.

AKWAKH. See AVAR.

ALAR. See BURYAT.

ALATAU KIRGHIZ. See KYRGYZ.

ALATAU KIRGIZ. See KYRGYZ.

ALATAU QIRGHIZ. See KYRGYZ.

ALATAU QIRGIZ. See KYRGYZ.

ALATAU QYRGHYZ. See KYRGYZ.

ALATAU QYRGYZ. See KYRGYZ.

ALATAULAK. See KYRGYZ.

ALATAULUK. See KYRGYZ.

ALATOOLUK QYRGYZ. See KYRGYZ.

ALBANIAN. The term "Albanians" can refer to two peoples who have made an imprint upon Russian* and Soviet history. Certain inhabitants of the eastern Caucasus region in the ancient and medieval periods were called Albanians, while an Albanian kingdom existed in that region between the first century B.C. and the eighth century A.D. "Albanians" also refers to a small group of non-indigenous inhabitants of Russia and the Soviet Union who settled mostly in the Azov region from the southwestern Balkan peninsula in the late eighteenth century.

The Caucasian or Caspian Albanians (known as Aluank in Armenian*, Albanoi in Greek*, and Albani in Latin) inhabited an area of the eastern Transcaucasus between the Kura River and the Caucasus range, mostly within the present Azerbaijan Republic and the southern parts of the Daghestan Autonomous Republic of the Russian Federated Republic. According to the ancient geographer Strabo, Caucasian Albania was divided into twenty-six different tribes and languages, similar to those of today's Daghestan. It is interesting to note that both the Turkish Daghestan and the Latin Albania denote "mountainous land." The Caucasian Albanians seemed to have been under Persian* and Seleucid suzerainty until the second century B.C., when their tribes merged into a kingdom. The kingdom of Albania, together with the kingdoms of Armenia and Iberia (Georgia), attempted to maintain a precarious independence in spite of its unenviable position as a border state between the empires of Rome and Parthia.

In the third century A.D., Albania became a vassal state of the new Sassanid Persian Empire. During the fourth century, Christianity spread among the Caucasian Albanians, as it had among the Armenians and Georgians*. The rise of the Christian Roman Empire, with its new capital in the East at Constantinople (Byzantium), further complicated the relations between the Christian Albanian Kingdom and the Sassanid dynasty. By the fifth century, the Christianized kingdom of Albania, in conjunction with the Armenian and Georgian kingdoms, revolted against Sassanid rule. The Sassanids were able to restore their suzerainty over Albania. The weakening of the Sassanid Empire by its wars with the Byzantines and later the Muslim Arabs in the seventh century gave the Albanian kingdom the opportunity to reassert its full independence.

The Albanian kingdom was again caught between two powers in the seventh century, however. The Khazar khanate in the north and the Muslim Arab caliphate in the south began to make inroads and to weaken its independence. By the early eighth century, most of Albania had come under the rule of the caliphate, and a process of Islamization of the population began, which continued under the regional dynasties of the Sheddadids and Maziadids. A number of potentates in the Transcaucasus—Armenian, Georgian, and Muslim—all continued to lay claim to the kingship of Albania until the twelfth century, although for all intents and purposes, Caucasian Albania had passed into history by the ninth century. Some historians assert that the Armenian region of Nagorno-Karabakh (Nagorno-Karabagh) in Azerbaijan is the successor to Caucasian Albania. While this claim may be somewhat tenuous, it cannot be denied that the Caucasian Albanians of ancient and medieval times played a role in the ethnogenesis of the Armenians

of Nagorno-Karabagh, the Azerbaijanis*, the Georgians of Kakhetia, and some
of the Daghestanis*, notably the Laks*, the Lezgins*, and the Tsakhurs*.

The Albanians who still exist in the Commonwealth of Independent States
(CIS) constitute one of the smallest recognized ethnic groups in the former Soviet
Union, numbering only 4,085 in the 1989 census. They are a part of the Balkan
people who today make up the Republic of Albania and who constitute the
majority population in the Kosovo-Metohija region of former Yugoslavia. They
are also found in sizable numbers in Greece, Italy, Romania, Turkey, Egypt,
and the United States. The Balkan Albanians speak a language that is descended
from the ancient Thraco-Illyrian languages and is considered a separate subgroup
of the Indo-Europeans languages; it is divided into two dialects, Tosk and Geg.
In the Balkans, a majority of Albanians are Muslims (70 percent in Albania;
higher percentages in Kosovo and Turkey), while significant numbers are Orthodox Christians (20 percent in Albania, much higher percentages in Greece,
Romania, and the United States) and Roman Catholics (10 percent in Albania,
higher percentages in Italy).

Those Albanians in the CIS are mostly the descendants of Orthodox immigrants
who came to the Russian Empire in the wake of the Russo-Turkish Wars of the
eighteenth and early nineteenth century. During the Russo-Turkish War of 1769–
1774, Orthodox Albanians and Greeks participated in Russian-inspired uprisings
in Epirus and the Peloponnesus in expectation of Russian naval operations in
the Aegean. While these rebellions failed, many of the insurgents entered service
with the Russian fleet as irregular marines and were organized into *Albanskie
irreguliarnye bataliony* or Albanian irregular battalions. These troops became
known as Albantsi and served alongside regular Russian marines and irregular
South Slav Slaviani in amphibious operations in the Aegean and the Eastern
Mediterranean in the years 1770–1774. It was from these units that the first
Albanians immigrated to Russia.

Following the end of hostilities and the signing of the Treaty of Kucuk Kainarci
in 1774, Russian naval forces were obliged to withdraw from the eastern Mediterranean and to evacuate the Aegean islands under their occupation. Large
numbers of Greek and Albanian volunteers, together with Aegean islanders, left
the area with the Russians to emigrate to newly conquered Russian lands along
the Black Sea. Among these refugees were 1,057 officers and men of the *Albanskie irreguliarnye bataliony* and 656 family members. These immigrants
were organized in 1775 into a unit of military colonists known as the *Albanskoe
Voisko* and were settled around the forts of Kerch and Yenikale in the Russian
area in and bordering the Crimea along the Sea of Azov. The unit grew until,
in 1779, the *Albanskoe Voisko* was reformed into a 1,762-man regular unit known
as the *Grecheskii Pekhotnyi Polk* (Greek Infantry Regiment), renamed the better
to describe the composition of the force. Following the Russian annexation of
the Crimea in 1784, the regiment was transferred from Kerch and Yenikale to
the southern coastal region of the Crimea with its headquarters at Balaklava.
There the unit functioned at regimental or battalion size until 1859. Subsequent
arrivals of Albanians, together with Greeks, were settled in the Odessa region

initially into another military colony known as the *Odesskii Grecheskii Divizion* (the Odessan Greek Detachment) and later as the *Odesskii Grecheskii Batalion* (the Odessan Greek Battalion). Because most of the Albanian immigrants were Orthodox and shared many of the same Greek Orthodox rites and folk customs as the Greeks, many assimilated into the larger Greek communities in southern Russia. No doubt many Orthodox Albanians, like many of their Greek coreligionists, assimilated into the general Russian and Ukrainian* population over the years.

The only significant concentration of Albanians in Russia in the twentieth century is located in three villages in the Azov district of Melitopol province. In the late 1940s, they were organized into village soviets and numbered over 3,000 inhabitants. It seems that these settlements may have a connection with the initial *Albanskoe Voisko* military colony of the eighteenth century. It may be that, when the *Albanskoe Voisko* was reorganized into the *Grecheskii Pekhotnyi Batalion* and transferred to the southern Crimea, most of the Greek-speaking personnel of the unit and their dependents moved to Balaklava and its environs, while most of the Albanian personnel and their families remained in the Azov region. The Albanian-speaking settlers of the area were perhaps supplemented by later arrivals and consolidated into the existing three village communities. Between 1959 and 1989, the Albanian population in the Soviet Union ranged from 5,258 in 1959 to 4,085 in 1989. No doubt a portion of that population was made up of more recent arrivals from the People's Republic of Albania, the fluctuation downward was perhaps caused by the break in Soviet-Albanian relations in the early 1960s.

REFERENCES: On the Albanians of Transcaucasia, see: Movses Dashkuranci, *A History of the Caucasian Albanians*, trans. by C.J.F. Dowsett, 1962; C.J.F. Dowsett, "A Neglected Passage in the History of the Caucasian Albanians," *Bulletin of the School of Oriental and African Studies*, 19 (1957); Vladimir Minorsky, "Transcaucasia," *Journal Asiatique*, 217 (1930) and in *Studies in Caucasian History*, 1953; Cyril Toumanoff, "Christian Caucasia between Byzantium and Iran: New Light from Old Sources," *Traditio*, 10 (1954) and "Introduction to Christian Caucasian History," *Traditio*, 15 (1959), and 17 (1961). On the Balkan Albanians in Russia, see R. P. Bartlett, *Human Capital: The Settlement of Foreigners in Russia, 1762–1804*, 1979; S. K. Batalden, *Eugenios Voulgares in Russia, 1771–1806*, 1982; N. S. Derzhavin, "Albantsy-Arnauty na priazovie Ukrainskoi SSR," *Sovetskaia Etnografiia*, 2 (1948); Walter Kolarz, *Russia and Her Colonies*, 1952; N. Pappas, *Greeks in Russian Military Service in the Late Eighteenth and Early Nineteenth Centuries*, 1991; T. Stoianovich, "The Conquering Balkan Orthodox Merchant," *Journal of Economic History*, 20 (1960), 234–313.

Nicholas C. J. Pappas

ALBANTSY. See ALBANIAN.

ALEUT. The Aleuts are one of the smallest surviving ethnic groups in what used to be the Soviet Union. They are part of the much larger group of Aleutian people of the Arctic region, but most Aleuts live in the United States. The Aleuts in Russia today live on Bering Island and Medny Island, both of which are part of the larger Komandorskiy Island group. The Aleuts call themselves the Unangan

(Unangun), although the Aleuts on Medny Island also refer to themselves as "Aleuts" or Sasignan. Russians* have traditionally called them Unangun. The Aleut language is Paleo-Asiatic in its origins and closely related to Eskimo*. They historically practiced an animistic, shamanist religion, in which they believed that their entire environment was alive with deities demanding appeasement. Traditionally, the Aleuts made their living hunting sea animals, especially sea lions, seals, walruses, and whales. They made their tools out of stones and bones. They were semi-nomadic, living in large, communal dugouts during the winter and in single family huts in the summer.

It was not until the eighteenth century, after the exploratory voyages of Vitus Bering, that Russian hunters reached the Aleutian Islands. The Russian state quickly imposed sovereignty, as well as fur and fur seal taxes, on the Aleut people. At the time of the Russian arrival in 1741, there were more than 15,000 Aleuts living on the Aleutian Islands and the Kodiak region. Many of them were massacred by Russian hunters, and thousands more died of smallpox and other diseases. Starvation also became a problem, because the Russians insisted that the Aleuts hunt for furs rather than for food. By 1840, the Aleut population had fallen to fewer than 1,500 people.

A variety of trading companies assumed actual political control of the Aleutian Islands, and, in 1825–1826, the Russian-American Company transferred about fifty Aleuts from Atka and Attu islands to the Komandorskiy Islands. During the next several decades, Aleuts from the Andreanof, Pribilof, and Fox islands also settled there, increasing the Aleut population to several hundred people. Eskimos, Russians, Komis*, and Gypsies* also settled there, and a great deal of intermarriage began to take place. Their economy also began to change. The Aleuts began to hunt the sea-beaver and the polar fox to sell for cash; they also began to breed cattle, pigs, and goats.

After the sale of Alaska to the United States in 1867, the Russian government leased out the Komandorskiy Islands to a series of trading companies, and the Aleut population suffered under their corporate control. The Aleuts became poorer than ever working for the companies, but they also began the process of russification, since the company bosses they worked for insisted on it. The Russian Orthodox Church established two schools for the Aleuts in the early 1900s, and the language of instruction was Russian. Children soon became bilingual in Russian and Aleut, and the Russian Orthodox faith began to compete with their traditional indigenous religion.

Since the Russian Revolution in 1917, Aleut life has changed even more. The Komandorskiy Islands became designated the Aleutskiy Rayon, which was part of the Kamchatskaya Oblast. Government officials eliminated the influence of the trading companies, organized the Aleuts into village soviets, and put them to work on state fur farms and on state-owned fishing boats. State schools replaced the parochial schools, and, by the late 1930s, there was universal literacy among the Aleuts. Because of the earlier intermarriage with non-Aleut peoples, education, and the influence of the state, the Aleuts have rapidly acculturated to the larger society and are among the most russified of the Siberian peoples. Less than 18 percent of Aleuts still speak the Aleut language, and the 300 Aleuts on Commander Island are, for all intents and purposes, completely russified. The Aleut population is estimated at approximately 600 people.

REFERENCES: James Forsyth, A History of the Peoples of Siberia, 1992; Bryan Hodgson, "Hard Harvest on the Bering Sea," National Geographic, 182 (October, 1992), 72–104; M. G. Levin and L. P. Potapov, The Peoples of Siberia, 1964.

ALI ILI. The Ali Ilis are a distinct subgroup of the Turkmen*. The vast majority of them live in the lower altitude areas of the eastern Kopet Dag mountains in the Turkmen Republic. See TURKMEN.

REFERENCE: Ronald Wixman, The Peoples of the USSR: An Ethnographic Handbook, 1984.

ALILI. See ALI ILI and TURKMEN.

ALIUTOR. See ALYUTOR and KORYAK.

ALLAIKHA. See EVEN.

ALTAI. The 1989 census of the Soviet Union listed the Altai population at 71,317 people. That figure is deceptive, however, because the Altais remain highly divided in terms of subgroup loyalties. A process of ethnogenesis has been at work among them for the past two centuries, but tribal loyalties remain very strong, as do linguistic differences between the various Altai subgroups. Their language belongs to the North Turkic group of languages. The Altais are divided into two well-identified groupings. The Northern Altai—also known as Chernevyje Tatar* or Back Country Tatar—emerged from an ongoing fusion of three tribal groups: the Tubalars, Chelkans*, and Kumandins*. Ethnologists surmise that the Northern Altai tribes first emerged out of a mix of ancient Samoyedic, Kettish, Ugrian, and Turkic peoples. They speak a language belonging to the Old Uigur* group of the eastern division of the Turkic branch of the Uralo-Altaic linguistic family. The Tubalars are actually a group of Tofalars* who broke away and mingled with Chelkans and Kumandins. The Tubalars live primarily along the left bank of the Bya River and in the northwestern coast of Lake Teletskoe. The Chelkans (Lebedin) live in the Lebed' River Basin but retain only the slightest sense of separate identity, as do the Kumandins, who live along the Bya River.

The Southern Altai first emerged between the sixth and eighth centuries as descendants of the ancient Turkic tribes of Saiano-Altais. From the thirteenth through the eighteenth centuries, various Mongolian tribes also joined the mix. The southern Altai speak a language that is part of the Kypchak* division of the Turkic branch of the Uralic-Altaic linguistic family. The language closely resembles Kyrgyz.* Four subgroups went into the making of the Southern Altai:

the Altai Kizhi, Telengit*, Telesy*, and Teleut*. The Southern Altai have also been known historically as the Belyy, Altai, Gornyy, Porubezhny, and Biy Kalmyk. Of the Southern Altai subgroups, the Altai Kizhi and the Teleut retain a strong sense of group identity. Most Altais, both Southern and Northern, live in the Gorno-Altai Autonomous Oblast of the Altai Krai in Siberia. The Altai Krai borders the Mongolian People's Republic and the People's Republic of China on the southeast.

The traditional Altai economy revolved around breeding cattle and hunting. They also bred deer and harvested the animals for their antlers, which were exported to China for use in the manufacture of folk medicines. The money the Altais received from those exports provided them with the cash to purchase trade goods, particularly metal tools and varieties of cloth. They lived in feudal, patriarchal societies. Those centrifugal ethnic forces were strong enough that, as late as the early 1920s, the Altais identified themselves as Tubalars, Chelkans, Kumandins, Altai Kizhis, Teleuts, Telesy, and Telengits rather than as Altais.

Although the Russians* first established contact with the Altais in the seventeenth century, the region remained under the control of the Dzungarian state until the eighteenth century. Dzungaria, also known as Sungaria, encompassed what is today northwestern China. From the eleventh to the fourteenth centuries, the region was under Mongol* control, but the forces of Tamerlane overran the area in 1389. Until 1758, it was under a Kalmyck* confederation, when China incorporated Dzungaria into Sinkiang. The Altai tribes had traditionally been a very proud people, known throughout Central Asia for their ferocity and tenacity. During the first half of the eighteenth century, many of them left Dzungaria and invaded Kazakh* territory, capturing Tashkent and eventually almost reaching the Ural Mountains in the west. After taking control of the region in 1758, however, the Chinese* launched a war of extermination against the Altais. When it was over, only a few thousand of them were alive, most of them isolated in the Altai Mountains. Russia began asserting control over the area several years later, and Russian sovereignty was finalized with the annexation of the region in 1866. The surviving Altais came under the control of ethnic Russians. During the nineteenth century, Russia began the agricultural colonization of the Altai, and the number of ethnic Russians settling there increased dramatically. Russian Orthodox missionaries began working among the Altai and made a significant number of converts, even though strong elements of the traditional Altai animistic religion and folk culture survived.

The extension of tsarist control, however, did not wipe out Altai identity. In fact, it only intensified it. The Altais found Russian culture heavy-handed and assimilationist, and, by the early 1900s, they were openly resisting it. A new religion, termed Burkhanism or White Faith, swept through the Altai tribes. This was a distinctly anti-Russian, messianic faith at whose center was the mythical Oirot Khan, supposedly a descendant of Genghis Khan, who promised to liberate the Altais from Russian domination and restore them to a pre-Russian, pre-Chinese reality. Burkhanism had its formal beginnings in 1904 when Chot Chelpanov, an Altai shepherd, reported being visited by Oirot Khan, who was riding a white horse. The Oirot Khan told Chelpanov to spread the message that the Altai peoples were to adhere to a rigid code of behavior and avoid all contact with Russians and other foreigners; they were not to eat from the same utensils as Christians. The religion spread through the Altai communities, forcing tsarist authorities to arrest Chot Chelpanov and crush the movement. When Japan defeated Russia in the Russo-Japanese War, Burkhanism even acquired a decidedly pro-Japanese* flavor as well.

After the Bolshevik Revolution, Altai nationalism assumed a secular dimension under the leadership of B. I. Anuchin. He convened the Constituent Congress of the High Altai in February 1918 and demanded the creation of an Oirot Republic, which would also include Khakassians* and Tuvinians.* He expected Russia, Mongolia, and China all to surrender territory for the new republic. With Russia in the middle of a civil war, the creation of such a republic appeared to be the only way of stopping a continuing process of russification among the Altai. Many of the Altai leaders sided with the Mensheviks against the Bolsheviks during the conflict. By 1920, the area was under strict Soviet control.

During the early 1920s, Sary-Sen Kanzychakov emerged as a new Altai nationalist leader, and he too demanded creation of a Greater Oirotia state. The People's Commissariat for Nationalities initially responded positively to the idea of an "Autonomous Oirot-Khakassian Province," but the plan was stillborn. Instead, the Oirot Autonomous Oblast was created in the Altai Krai of Russia. The Soviet Union tolerated talk of "Greater Oirotia" and Burkhanism until 1933, when it began denouncing the nationalist movement as a conspiracy by "Chinese merchant capitalists" and the "Mongol-Lamaist bureaucracy." By the late 1930s and during World War II, the government accused Altai nationalists of being pro-Japanese. As a result, much of the Communist Party membership in the Oirot Autonomous Oblast was purged. In 1948, the Soviet Union banned the use of the word "Oirot," which it described as counter-revolutionary. The Oirot Autonomous Oblast was renamed the Mountainous-Altai Autonomous Oblast (Gorno-Altai Autonomous Oblast). The capital city, Oirot-Tura, was renamed Gornoaltaisk. All Soviet reference books and textbooks dropped the use of the word Oirots and called them Altais.

After the Bolshevik Revolution of 1917, the homeland of the Altais underwent rapid industrial development. In the 1920s and 1930s, the first of the Five-Year Plans emphasized the development of the manganese, iron, silver, lead, wolfram, and timber resources of the region. Large numbers of ethnic Russians poured into the area, reducing the Altais from 42 to only 36 percent of the population by 1925 and only 30 percent by 1930. During World War II, when the Stalin regime relocated large portions of Soviet heavy industry east of the Urals to escape Nazi destruction, the Altai Krai was one of the major recipients. The government had already begun to exploit the region's rich timber resources, as well as the extraction of stone, lime, salt, gold, mercury, sandstone, and nonferrous metals, but the war industries and the extremely ambitious development projects after World War II also spawned large-scale chemical, metalworking, and machine tool enterprises, as well as factories assembling tractors, automobiles, radios, televisions, engines, boilers, and electrical appliances. Along with industrial development came hundreds of thousands of Russian and Ukrainian* workers, who reduced the Altais to an even smaller minority in the Gorno-Altai Autonomous Oblast (AO).

The Soviet government made a concerted effort to assimilate and russify the Altais. Altai hunting and breeding operations were collectivized in the 1920s and 1930s, even though this policy inspired a good deal of resistance from Altai farmers and livestock breeders. The government also established what became known as "Houses of the Altai Woman" all over the region. Altai women on the collective farms were required to attend meetings where Russian habits were praised and where they received instruction in cooking, knitting, sewing, child welfare, Russian literacy, poultry breeding, and political indoctrination. Children in the public schools received the same instruction and attempts at russification.

Suppression of Altai nationalism continued throughout the Nikita Khrushchev and Leonid Brezhnev years, but, under Mikhail Gorbachev's policies of *perestroika* and *glasnost*, much of the heavy-handedness of earlier decades disappeared. Altai nationalism resurfaced, again under the name of the Oirot, but it did not have quite the same power as in the pre-World War II years. Decades of indoctrination had reduced Burkhanism to little more than historical mythology, and the continuing influx of ethnic Russians and Ukrainians had made the Altais only a small minority in the Gorno-Altai Autonomous Oblast. But in the Mountain Altai Autonomous Province in the late 1980s, the proposed construction of a hydroelectric dam became a nationalistic rallying cry. The dam would have flooded the Katun Valley, destroying the last region of the Soviet Union in which the Altais retained even a semblance of a traditional life-style. Altai protests eventually caused Mikhail Gorbachev to terminate the project. The Altais began demanding autonomy within Russia after the dissolution of the Soviet Union.

REFERENCES: James Forsyth, *A History of the Peoples of Siberia*, 1992; *The Great Soviet Encyclopedia*, 1973, vol. 1, 301–04; Walter Kolarz, *The Peoples of the Soviet Far East*, 1969; Ronald Wixman, *The Peoples of the USSR: An Ethnographic Handbook*, 1984.

ALTAI KIJHI. See ALTAI.

ALTAI KIJI. See ALTAI.

ALTAI KIZHI. See ALTAI.

ALTAIAN. See ALTAI.

ALTAY. See ALTAI.

ALTAY KIJI. See ALTAI.

ALTAY KIZHI. See ALTAI.

ALTAYAN. See ALTAI.

ALTYM. See KHANT.

ALTYNA KUMANDY. See KUMANDIN and ALTAI.

ALYUTOR. The Alyutors (Aliutor) are one of the major Koryak* groups in Siberia. They dwell in the Kamchatka Peninsula in the Koryak Autonomous Oblast. See KORYAK.
REFERENCE: Ronald Wixman, *The Peoples of the USSR: An Ethnographic Handbook*, 1984.

AMERICAN. Until its 1989 census, the Soviet Union did not track, or at least did not publish, the number of foreign residents by nationality group. The 1989 census did provide those figures, and it indicated that in that year there were 746 American citizens living in the Soviet Union. Ever since the Bolshevik Revolution, there had been Americans like John Reed, the prominent American Communist, living in the Soviet Union. Over the years, other expatriates infatuated with Marxism and the Communist experiment took up residence there. Still, there was never any significant movement of Americans to change citizenship and live their lives in the Soviet Union. There had also been other Americans who, for economic reasons, were very interested in improving the business relationship between the United States and the Soviet Union. Among the most prominent of these individuals was Armand Hammer of Occidental Petroleum. Disillusionment with the Communist Party mounted, in both the Soviet Union and the United States, during the Brezhnev era in the 1970s. The numbers of expatriates declined, but, as Mikhail Gorbachev welcomed American capital and technological expertise, the number of Americans permanently residing in the Soviet Union increased. In 1992, President Boris Yeltsin of Russia revealed that there were still a handful of American citizens who had been captured or trapped in the Soviet Union during World War II living in Russia. Of the 746 Americans living in the Soviet Union in 1989, most were business people hoping to establish an economic foothold there.
REFERENCE: Raymond E. Zickel, ed., *Soviet Union: A Country Study*, 1991.

AMGUEM. See CHUKCHI.

AMUR. See MANCHU.

AMUR-USSURI COSSACK. Early in the nineteenth century, the Amur-Ussuri Cossacks emerged from the Transbaikal Cossacks*, especially after the addition of many Tungusic* and Manchu* peoples into their ranks. The Amur-Ussuri Cossacks claimed the Amur and Ussuri river valleys of southeastern Siberia as their homeland. See COSSACK.

REFERENCES: Philip Longworth, *The Cossacks*, 1969; Ronald Wixman, *The Peoples of the USSR: An Ethnographic Handbook*, 1984.

AN' KALYN. See CHUKCHI.

ANATRI. The Anatris are one of the two main Chuvash* groups. Most of them reside in the southeastern Chuvash Autonomous Republic. See CHUVASH.
REFERENCE: Ronald Wixman, *The Peoples of the USSR: An Ethnographic Handbook*, 1984.

ANDI. See AVAR.

ANDI. In addition to serving as a reference to the Avar*, the term ''Andi'' is a generic one, referring collectively to the Andi*, Botlig*, Godoberi*, Karata*, Bagulal*, Tindi*, Chamalal*, and Akhwakh* people in southwestern Daghestan. They are Sunni Muslims.
REFERENCE: Ronald Wixman, *The Peoples of the USSR: An Ethnographic Handbook*, 1984.

ANDI. The term ''Andi'' (Andii) refers to a contemporary subtribe of the Avars* who call themselves the Qwannal (Kwannal) and are known as the Andi. Russians* call them Andijtsy and they are also known as Handisew. The Andi live in nine villages of the Botlig Region of Daghestan: Andi, Gunkha, Gagatl, Rikvani, Ashali, Chankho, Zilo, Munib, and Kvankhidatl. They use Avar as a literary language; their own spoken language is divided into two dialects: Andi and Munib-Kvankhidatl. They are Sunni Muslims. Although it is difficult to estimate the current Andi population because of their census listing with the Avars, demographers estimate that there are as many as 15,000 people who are either consciously Andi or are aware of their Andi origins. See AVAR.
REFERENCES: Shirin Akiner, *Islamic Peoples of the Soviet Union*, 1983; Ronald Wixman, *The Peoples of the USSR: An Ethnographic Handbook*, 1984.

ANDI-DIDO. The term ''Andi-Dido'' is a generic ethnographic description referring to two groups of people living in southwestern Daghestan. The Andi peoples include the Andis*, Botligs*, Godoberis*, Karatas*, Bagulals,*, Tindis*, Chamalals*, and Akhwakhs*, while the Dido includes the Bezhetas, Didos*, Ginugs*, Khunzals*, Khwarshis*, and Archis*. They are all Sunni Muslims.
REFERENCE: Ronald Wixman, *The Peoples of the USSR: An Ethnographic Handbook*, 1984.

ANDIJTSY. See ANDI and AVAR.

ANDO-DIDO. See ANDI-DIDO.

ANDO-TSEZ. See ANDI-DIDO.

ANKUSH. See DARGIN.

ANTSUKH. See AVAR.

APSUA. See ABAZA and ABKHAZ.

APSWA. See ABAZA and ABKHAZ.

APUKA. The Apuka (Apukin) are one of the main subgroups of the Koryaks*. They are concentrated along the Bering Sea, in the Koryak Autonomous Oblast, and at the outlet of the Apuka River. See KORYAK.
REFERENCE: Ronald Wixman, *The Peoples of the USSR: An Ethnographic Handbook*, 1984.

APUKIN. See APUKA and KORYAK.

APUKINTSY. See APUKA and KORYAK.

AQ NOGAI. See AK NOGAI and NOGAI.

AQ NOGAY. See AK NOGAI and NOGAI.

AQ NOGHAI. See AK NOGAI and NOGAI.

AQ NOGHAY. Scc AK NOGAI and NOGAI.

AQNOGAI. See AK NOGAI and NOGAI.

AQNOGHAI. See AK NOGAI and NOGAI.

AQNOGHAY. See AK NOGAI and NOGAI.

AQSULAQ. See UIGUR.

AQSULUQ. See UIGUR.

ARA. See KHAKASS.

ARAB. In the 1989 census of the Soviet Union, demographers placed the Arabic-speaking population of the country at 11,599 people, most of whom lived in Uzbekistan, Tajikistan, and Turkmenistan. Ethnologists in the Commonwealth of Independent States (CIS) have a number of theories concerning the origins of the Arabic-speaking community, but it is most likely that these Arabs, who call themselves Araby and have also been known as the Arabs of Central Asia, migrated into what used to be the Soviet Union in a number of stages over the course of several centuries. The ancient Semitic tribes from which the Arabs descended were already in the Arabian Peninsula by the second millenium B.C., and, over the next thousand years, the Arab people began to emerge. By the fifth and sixth centuries A.D., the Arabs occupied the entire peninsula. With the rise of Islam, early in the seventh century, they expanded into surrounding areas. Eventually, those Arab conquests resulted in the establishment of the Arab Caliphate, which stretched from India in the east to the Atlantic Ocean in the west, and from Central Asia in the north to Central Africa in the south. The Arab Caliphate survived for three centuries and began to disintegrate only when its subject peoples started to rebel against its domination.

Those Arabs who ended up in Central Asia came from several sources. Some scholars argue that they are descended from Arab invaders who entered the region in the seventh and eighth centuries. Some popular culture theories explain their origins in terms of the invader Timur (Tamerlane), who may very well have brought some Arabs to Samarkand in the fifteenth century. Another theory holds that the present-day Arabs derive from nomadic Arabs who came to Central Asia from northern Afghanistan in the mid-sixteenth century and settled in Bukhara and Samarkand and along the Amur-Darya River. The most widely accepted theory of their origins is that they came to Central Asia in three waves. Some of them are descended from the Arab invaders of Central Asia in the eighth century; others were resettled in Central Asia by Ubaydullah Khan, the Shaibanid ruler of Bukhara, in the sixteenth century. The majority of the Arabs derive from nomadic Arab herders who came out of northern Afghanistan in the eighteenth and nineteenth centuries.

By the mid-nineteenth century, there were more than 30,000 nomadic Arabs living in Bukhara. They were widely known for their skills in raising sheep. After the Bolshevik Revolution, Soviet authorities forced the Arabs to stop their nomadic ways and settle down; as a result, most of them fled back to northern Afghanistan where they could continue their traditional patterns of animal husbandry. By the 1920s, the remaining Arabs who had settled down tended to live separately from the non-Arab population and maintained their clan loyalties. Over the years, those clan loyalties gradually declined and the Arabs mixed with the surrounding Uzbeks*, Turkmen*, and Tajiks*. They remained loyal to the Sunni Muslim religion.

The Arabs living in the CIS speak two mutually unintelligible dialects: Bukharan and Kashka-Daryan. The Bukhara dialect has elements of Tajik, while Kashka-Daryan has been strongly influenced over the years by Uzbek. Today less than one-third of the Arabic population speaks their Arab dialect as a native language, and virtually all of the Arabs are bilingual in Uzbek, Tajik, or Russian. Most of them live in the Zerafshan Valley between Samarkand and Lake Karakul. Smaller groups are located in the lower Kashka-Darya River valley and the Surkhan Darya River valley in Uzbekistan, the Vakhsh Valley in Tajikistan, in the eastern Fergana Valley, and in the cities of Bukhara, Karshi, Katta-Kurgan, Leninabad, and Kuliab. They still tend to marry endogamously, but that is changing, especially among those who speak Uzbek or Tajik as their native languages.

REFERENCES: Shirin Akiner, *Islamic Peoples of the Soviet Union*, 1983; Alexandre Bennigsen and S. Enders Wimbush, *Muslims of the Soviet Empire: A Guide*, 1986; *Great Soviet Encyclopedia*, 1973, vol. 2, 224–25.

Gary R. Hobin

ARABS OF CENTRAL ASIA. See ARAB.

ARABY. See ARAB.

ARCHI. The Archis (Archin), who call themselves the Arishishuw or Arishishttib, are today considered one of the Avar* subgroups. They are Sunni Muslim in their religious loyalties and occupy one village in the Charodin Region of central Daghestan. Most Archis are trilingual in Archi, Lak*, and Avar. Although it is difficult to estimate the current Archi population because of their census listing with the Avars, demographers estimate that there are as many as 2,000 people who are either consciously Archi or are aware of their Archi origins. See AVAR.

REFERENCES: Shirin Akiner, *Islamic Peoples of the Soviet Union*, 1983; Ronald Wixman, *The Peoples of the USSR: An Ethnographic Handbook*, 1984.

ARCHIN. See ARCHI and AVAR.

ARCHINTSY. See ARCHI and AVAR.

ARGUN. See KYZYL and KHAKASS.

ARIANE. See UDMURT.

ARIMINI. See ARMENIAN.

ARIN. See KHAKASS.

ARINTSY. See KHAKASS.

ARISHISHUW. See ARCHI and AVAR.

ARMENIAN. Their 3,000 years of uninterrupted historical presence make the Armenians the oldest ethnic group in the former Soviet Union (Commonwealth of Independent States) and, in many ways, a unique one. They comprised the first Christian state in the world, and became, like the Jews*, a cosmopolitan, educated, and dispersed nationality. Unlike many of their neighbors, they made contacts with the Russians* early on in their history and have, until recently, maintained a pro-Russian orientation. Although they call themselves Hai, their language Hayeren, and their land Hayastan, the Armenians are better known by their Greco-Iranian names as Armenoi, Arimini, or Armenians.

Armenia is a landlocked mountainous plateau with an average altitude of 5,000 feet above sea level. These Armenian highlands, often referred to as "historic Armenia" to distinguish it from the present-day Armenian Republic, stretch roughly between 38 degrees and 48 degrees east longitude and 37.5 degrees and 41.5 degrees north latitude. They cover an area of over 100,000 square miles. In present-day terms, historic Armenia comprised a large part of eastern Turkey, the northeastern corner of Iran, parts of the Azerbaijan and Georgian republics, as well as the entire territory of the Armenian Republic. It was defined by a number of natural boundaries: the Kura River, separating the Armenian highlands from the Caspian and Georgian lowlands in the east and northeast; the Pontic Range, separating Armenia from the Black Sea in the north and northwest; the Taurus-Zagros chains, connecting to the Iranian Plateau and separating Armenia from Kurdistan and Iran in the south and southwest; and the Euphrates River, marking and western boundary of historic Armenia. The Armenian plateau was formed some 50,000,000 years ago during the Tertiary period and is covered with volcanic peaks, the most famous of which is Mount Ararat (16,945 feet), the traditional resting place of Noah's ark. The mountains of Armenia give rise to numerous rivers, all unnavigable, which create deep gorges, ravines, and waterfalls. The longest of these is the Araxes (Arax) River, which flows through the plain of Ararat and the Araxes Valley. A number of lakes are situated in the Armenian highlands, the most important and deepest of which is Lake Van, known for its high borax content, in present-day Turkey; Lake Sevan, the highest (over 6,300 feet above sea level), in the Armenian Republic; and Lake Urmiya, the northern part of which sets the southernmost boundary of historic Armenia.

Armenia lies in the temperate zone and has a variety of climates. In general, winters are long and severe, lasting up to seven months in certain areas, while summers are usually short and very hot. Some plains, because of their lower elevation, are suited for agriculture and have fostered population centers throughout the centuries. The variety of temperatures has enabled the land to support a great diversity of flora and fauna common to western Asia and Transcaucasia. The mountains also supply abundant deposits of mineral ores, including copper, iron, zinc, lead, silver, and gold. There are also large salt mines, as well as borax, obsidian, and volcanic tufa stone. The generally dry Armenian climate has necessitated artificial irrigation throughout history. In fact, the volcanic soil is quite fertile and with sufficient water is suitable to intensive farming, especially at the lower altitudes, while the highlands favor nomadism. Historically, the Armenians took up agriculture and the Kurds* became nomads. The Turks*, later arrivals, at first engaged mainly in nomadism but later divided into settled, semi-settled, and nomadic groups. In addition to cereals, Armenia produced cotton and silk. Armenian fruit has been famous from ancient times, with the pomegranate and apricot (which the Romans called "the Armenian plum") being the most renowned. Lying on the Anatolian fault, the Armenian plateau is subject to earthquakes. Major seismic activities have been recorded since the ninth century, some of which destroyed entire cities. The most recent earthquake, that of December 7, 1988, killed over 25,000 people and leveled numerous settlements.

According to legend, the Armenian people are the descendants of Japeth, a son of Noah, who, after the landing of the ark on Mount Ararat, settled in its valley. This legend was only written down sometime between the fifth and eighth centuries A.D. It not only blends historical facts with legend but places the Armenians in a prominent position within the Biblical tradition. The Armenians, as the descendants of Noah, the "second Adam," who repopulated the earth, were, like the Jews, chosen and blessed by God.

Ancient Greek* historians, writing centuries after the appearance of the Armenians in their homeland but well before the Armenian chroniclers, left other explanations as to the origins of the Armenian people. According to Herodotus, the Armenians originally lived in Thrace, from where they crossed into Phrygia in Asia Minor, and gradually moved across the Euphrates River to what became Armenia. Strabo claimed that Armenians came from two directions, Phrygia and Assyria. By 400 B.C., Xenophon, who passed through Armenia, recorded that the Armenians had absorbed most of the local people, with the exception of a group of mountain dwellers whom we assume were the ancestors of the present-day Kurds. According to the Greeks, therefore, the Armenians were not the original inhabitants of the region.

Modern archaeological finds have presented a more detailed, although not complete, version of the possible origins of the Armenians. Until recently, scholars maintained that the Armenians were an Indo-European group who came into the area from the Balkans with the Phrygians or from the northern Caucasus with the Mitanni and other Indo-Iranian or Aryan groups. They either formed part of the Urartuan federation or were centered around the Euphrates until invasions by the Scythians and Cimmerians weakened the Urartuan kingdom. The Armenians then managed to consolidate their power over Urartu and in time assimilated most of the indigenous groups to form the Armenian nation. More recent scholarship offers another society. It claims that the Armenians were one of the several indigenous Caucasian groups who formed their language from those of later Indo-European arrivals. This may explain why Armenian is a unique branch of the Indo-European language tree that is not related to any other. Pressure from the Hittites and the Assyrians* forced these Caucasian and Indo-European groups to create various federations and, eventually, the Urartuan kingdom. In 782 B.C., the Urartuan king Argishti I built the fortress-city of Erebuni (present-day Erevan, capital of the Armenian Republic). The decline and fall of Urartu allowed the Armenian component of the state to achieve predominance and, by the sixth century B.C., to establish a separate identity.

Located between east and west, Armenia and its people from the very beginning were frequently subject to invasions and conquest. Like the Georgians*, the Armenians adopted features of other civilizations but managed to maintain their own unique culture. Following the demise of Urartu and the emergence of Armenian power, the Medes controlled the region, which soon after became part of the Achaemenid empire of Iran. Armenian governors, most notably the Ervandian family, governed the region as an Iranian satrapy. Alexander the Great's invasion of Iran allowed the Ervandians to declare their independence, and, for the next century, they resisted all attempts by the Seleucids to gain control of Armenia. Around 200 B.C., the Seleucid ruler, Antiochus III, convinced two Armenian generals to rebel against the Ervandians. Antiochus' defeat by Rome in 190 B.C., however, left them independent. One of them, Artaxid, established the Artaxiad dynasty and the first Armenian Kingdom in 189 B.C.

This first Armenian dynasty faced Rome to the west and Parthia to the east. During the first century B.C., when both powers were otherwise engaged, Armenia, with the help of its ally Pontus, managed to extend its territory and influence beyond its borders to include parts of the Middle East, including most of present-day Iran and what used to be Soviet Azerbaijan. The Armenian ruler, Tigranes the Great, was acknowledged by the Parthians as "King of kings," and Armenia became an empire. This period of greatness was very brief, however, for Rome soon sent Sulla, Lucullus, and eventually Pompey to restore its prestige in Asia Minor and Mesopotamia. Parthia also sought to regain its power in the region. Armenia was soon reduced to its former boundaries and stature and continued to balance its policy between Rome and Parthia.

The struggle between Rome and Parthia to install their own government in Armenia was finally settled by the peace of Rhandeia in 64 A.D. The brother of the Parthian ruler became the king of Armenia but was to be crowned by Nero at Rome. Thus, in 66 A.D., Armenia received its second dynasty, the Arsacid. Originally Parthian, the Arsacids became a distinctly Armenian dynasty. During their four-century rule, Armenia became the first state to adopt Christianity and developed its unique alphabet. At the same time, however, Armenia fell under a strong Hellenic influence—religiously, linguistically, and culturally. Parthian feudalism was adapted as well, weakening Armenia's central ruling authority.

The accession of the Sassanids in Iran posed new problems for Armenia. The Sassanids sought a revival of the old Iranian Achaemenid empire, establishing Zoroastrianism as the state religion and destroying all vestiges of Hellenism in Iran. They invaded Armenia, put to death some of its leaders, and forced others to flee to Rome. Rome intervened in 298, forcing the peace of Nisibis on Iran. The forty years of the enforcement of this peace allowed the Armenians to restore their economy and build a new capital at Dvin. Realizing the threat of Zoroastrian Iran, the Arsacids adopted Christianity as the official state religion in the second decade of the fourth century, becoming the first nation to do so. This action promoted Shapur II of Iran to invade Armenia, starting fifty more years of Irano-Roman conflict, with Armenia as the prize. By 387, the two had powers partitioned Armenia, which became a vassal state of Rome, as represented by Byzantium, and of Iran.

Byzantine policy, led by Zeno and Justinian, was aimed at the destruction of Armenian feudalism and the extension of Byzantine administration into Armenia. Iran allowed Armenia to retain its feudal system but periodically tried to Iranianize Armenia by forcing Zoroastrianism upon it. It is very possible that the leaders of Armenia looked for an alphabet for the first time because of fears of partition and the potential loss of an Armenian identity. An alphabet was created in 400 A.D., and a large number of religious translations, most notably the New and Old Testaments, were made within a very short time. The Armenian Church under its supreme patriarch, or *Catholicos*, soon assumed a prominent leadership position and, for both doctrinal and political reasons, split from the churches of Rome and Constantinople to form a national church with its own traditions.

In 451, the Armenians rose up and fought the Iranians* at Avarair. Although the Armenians and their leader Vartan Mamikonian were defeated, their martyrdom fostered a spirit of rebellion, further inspired by the rebellion of the Georgian* king Vakhtang Gorgaslan. By 484, Armenian resistance had resulted in maintaining religious and administrative autonomy within its borders. But, in 555, the Persians* were again appointing governors in Armenia, and, in 591, Armenia was once again divided, with the Byzantines receiving a larger share than before.

The advent of Islam and the arrival of the Arabs* changed the picture drastically. During the Arab occupation, the local Armenian nobles were permitted to rule, provided they paid taxes. The Arabs even accepted a new Armenian dynasty, the Bagratid, which united Armenia in 885 and ruled parts of it until 1045. Cities and trade revived during Bagratid rule. One branch of the dynasty established the Georgian Bagration house, which ruled parts of Georgia until the nineteenth century.

Attacks by the Byzantines and local Arab garrisons stationed near the cities, as well as the rivalries among feudal factions in Armenia, eventually weakened the Bagratid kingdom. Armenia was split into four different kingdoms and several ecclesiastical factions, eventually succumbing to Byzantine attacks. The dynasty and the last Armenian kingdom in historic Armenia ended when Ani, the capital, fell to Byzantine attacks in 1045. The Byzantines, who were experiencing a revival under the Macedonian dynasty, now incorporated Armenia into their empire. The victory was short-lived, however. By destroying their Armenian buffer zone, the Byzantines had to face the Seljuk Turkish onslaught that arrived soon after. In 1071, the Seljuks Turks*, who had already taken most of Iran, defeated the Byzantines in the battle of Manzikert, and the Seljuks Turks entered Armenia.

The Seljuk Turkish invasion differed in one significant respect from all other previous invasions of Armenia: The Turkish nomads remained in Armenia, settling on the land and in the mountains. During the four centuries before the Ottoman Turks conquered Constantinople and entered Europe, the turkification of present-day Turkey took place. The Armenians and Greeks slowly lost their dominance there and became a minority. Emigration, war, and forced conversions depleted the Anatolian Christian population significantly. Many nobles left the region and joined the Byzantine administration or army. Many other emigrated to the Byzantine-controlled Balkans. Those Armenians who remained were leaderless and defenseless. Mountainous Karabagh (Karabakh) and Zangezour were the only regions in historical Armenia where an Armenian nobility, military, church leadership, and education continued to exist.

A number of the Armenian military leaders who had left Armenia for Byzantium settled in Cilicia on the Mediterranean. The Byzantines hoped to set up military posts at the Cilician mountain passes as a buffer against Arab attacks on Byzantium. After fortifying the region, two Armenian families, the Rubenids and Hetoumids, encouraged Armenian immigration there and, by the late eleventh century, had established themselves as the lords of Cilicia. They defied Byzantine commands as well as pressures from the Greek Orthodox Church. The arrival of the Crusaders helped the Armenians to find an ally in Catholic Europe. Together they formed a number of states along the Mediterranean coast. In 1198, European powers recognized Prince Leo of the Rubenid family as King of Cilicia, and a new Armenian Kingdom was born. The kingdom became a center for east-west trade. Armenian rulers made agreements with the Mongols*, and, thanks to that alliance, Armenia became one of the major traders in Asia. The *Pax Mongolica* made it possible for Italian*, Armenian, Arab, Persian, and Indian* merchants to travel to China, and they became the conduits for technological, scientific, and artistic information to the West. Unfortunately, the Cilician kingdom faced Byzantine and Arab incursions, as well as internal feuding among crusader states. In addition, Roman Catholicism, which had made some inroads among the Armenian nobility, was not welcomed by the Armenian masses. The acceptance of Islam by the Mongols around 1300, the resurgence of the Turks under the Ottomans, and the European abandonment of the Levant sounded the death knell of the last Armenian kingdom, which fell to the Mamluks (or Mamelukes) in 1375. Only pockets such as Karabagh (Karabakh) and Zangezour in eastern Armenia and Sasun and Zeitun in western Armenia remained autonomous.

For the next four centuries, Armenians, who had begun their dispersion after the fall of Ani and the Seljuk Turkish invasions in the eleventh century, continued to emigrate. In the meantime, Persia (Iran) experienced a revival under the Shi'i Safavids, who became the adversaries of the Sunni Ottomans. From 1501 until 1639, the two fought each other periodically in Armenia. Armenians were uprooted during these wars, and, in 1604, some 250,000 Armenians were forcibly transferred by Shah 'Abbas to Iran. By the seventeenth century, the Armenians had become a minority in parts of their historic lands. The merchants of Julfa in Nakhichevan were among those who were brought to Iran by Shah 'Abbas; he moved them to a suburb of Isfahan where they built the New Julfa community. The support of 'Abbas and subsequent shahs enabled the Armenians to expand Iran's trade with India, China, Russia, and Western Europe. These merchants helped to make the Persian Gulf an important trade center.

In 1639, the Iranians and Ottomans ended their long period of hostility and partitioned Armenia. Two-thirds of historic Armenia became known as western or Turkish Armenia, while the remaining one-third became eastern or Persian

Armenia. The division lasted for over two centuries, until Russia conquered eastern Armenia and made it Russian Armenia. The hostility between the Iranians and the Turks, and later the Russians and the Turks, kept the two Armenias separate from each other and created two very different Armenian communities. Armenians in Iran and, later, Russia lived under different economic and political conditions than those in the Ottoman Empire.

Sociologically, three groups of Armenians emerged: Armenian peasants; Armenians who lived in the mountains of Karabagh (Karabakh) and who enjoyed a degree of autonomy; and Armenian artisans, bankers, and especially merchants who lived in the great cities of Europe, Russia, India, Iran, and the Ottoman Empire. With the decline of the Ottoman Empire, the peasants bore the burden of taxes and, by the nineteenth century, lived in deplorable conditions. Removed from central authority, the Armenian villages on the fringes of the empire were relegated to local officials who generally did as they pleased. The Armenian merchants had economic power but were far away from historical Armenia and generally out of touch with it. Armenian magnates in India, Russia, and the Ottoman Empire not only opened trading and banking houses but were soon involved in acquiring Western political ideas. They patronized the translation and printing of books and periodicals, through which ideas of British* humanism and the Englightenment were carried to the Armenian population.

The Armenian intellectual revival was thus sparked by Armenians in the diaspora. First among these were the Armenian Mkhitarist priests in Venice and Vienna. These Armenian Catholics were the first scholars to research Armenian history and the literature of its past. At the same time, the children of the Armenian bourgeoisie in the Ottoman and Russian empires traveled abroad, where they were introduced to French* and American* revolutionary ideas of self-determination, freedom, equality, and liberty. Some also became aware of their historical past when European scholars began to examine the ancient history of the Middle East and placed the Armenian language within the Indo-European family tree.

The Armenian cultural and political revival, however, was very different from those of other groups in the Ottoman and Russian empires. The Armenians were scattered around the globe, they possessed different dialects and customs, and their intellectual leaders lived outside the homeland. The Armenians were thus among the last people to demand political changes or autonomy in the Ottoman Empire.

The situation of the Armenians in Russia was far better. The Russian conquest of eastern Armenia following the Russo-Persian Wars of 1804–1813 and 1826–1828 allowed the Armenians a chance to advance. Unlike their kinsmen in the Ottoman Empire, the Armenians in Russia adopted Western ideas and began their national and political revival early. Armenians had achieved economic superiority in most urban centers of Transcaucasia. Tiflis (or Tbilisi, the main city of Georgia) had an Armenian majority. The Russians and Armenians controlled the administration and commerce. The same was true of Baku, where the Armenians, although not a majority, wielded great economic power. Armenian commercial and linguistic connections made it possible for them to join the Russian administration.

The great reforms of Alexander II, combined with some reforms in the Ottoman Empire and Persia, enabled the Armenians to open schools and to print books and newspapers in both Russia and the Ottoman empire. By 1860, the Armenian leadership had begun to break with the past and established the foundations for educating the peasants and artisans who lived in the small towns and villages of historic Armenia. The task was completed in just one generation. The political awakening came next.

Russia had defeated the Ottomans in the Balkans and Asia throughout the eighteenth and nineteenth centuries, and they favored expansion into the Balkans. After all, much of the Ottoman lands in eastern Europe was populated by Orthodox Christians, of whom Russia considered itself the natural protector. With the Armenians' growing political awareness and economic power in Russia, an Armenian lobby emerged, asking for an improvement of conditions in Turkish Armenia. By 1878, the Armenians were strong and prominent enough to have a minister and generals in Russia. They now petitioned Russia to take a more active role in the fate of the Armenians in the Ottoman Empire. Russia did just that when, after defeating the Turks in 1878, it forced them to sign the Treaty of San Stefano, whose article sixteen guaranteed reforms for Armenians in Turkey under Russian supervision. England, which had frustrated Russian attempts before, once again objected and forced the Berlin Conference. The Armenians were abandoned in Berlin for higher stakes—the new European interest in Africa. The Armenians realized that they had waited in vain. They were now ready and more united than before. Communications, books, and journals had awakened enough for them to act.

Armenian political parties emerged in the last two decades of the nineteenth century. Beginning with reformist groups, the Armenian parties began to copy the programs of the Russian Social Democratic Labor Party and the Russian Populists (*Narodniki*). By the twentieth century, the following parties had emerged: *Hnchakian* or Social Democrats (Marxists), *Ramgavars* or Democratic Reformers, Social Revolutionaries, and the *Dashnaktsutiun*, which started as a union of all Armenian political parties and ended up with a socialist-nationalist platform. The parties all agreed that Armenians should be granted self-rule and insisted that major reforms be carried out in the Armenian provinces of the Ottoman Empire.

Armenian political activities angered both the Russians and the Turks. The Russians issued a decree in 1903 that confiscated the property of the Armenian church. They arrested and exiled some leaders and began a general russification program. Armenian surnames were changed, and speaking Armenian was forbidden. The Armenian armed response and the 1905 revolution abrogated the decree. The Russians then proceeded to instigate the Armeno-Azerbaijani* conflict, which lasted for two years (1905–1907). Armenian energies were thus focused on the Azeris and not on Russia. Meanwhile, the Turkish sultan Abdul-Hamid II ordered Armenian massacres in 1894 through 1896. Armenian hopes were raised when, in 1908, the Young Turks overthrew the "bloody sultan" and promised a state where all citizens would be equal. Unfortunately, the Young Turks became increasingly nationalistic. Pan-Turkism and Pan-Islamism, combined with chauvinism and Social Darwinism, broke up the Armeno-Turkish cooperation. Demands for reforms and autonomy in the Armenian provinces angered the Turks. The defeat of the Turkish army in the winter campaign of 1914–1915 gave the Young Turks the excuse to rid Turkish Armenia of its Armenian population. In April 1915, believing the Armenians to be pro-Russia, the Turkish government began the first genocide of the twentieth century by exploiting the war and Armenian-Kurdish tensions. Much of the population of Turkish Armenia was killed outright or died during deportation; 1.5 million people perished. The small number of survivors, mostly women and children, reached Syria or Russia.

The Russian revolution and civil war initially established a Transcaucasian Federated Republic in 1918. On May 26 of that year, however, Georgia, under German protection, pulled out of the federation. Azerbaijan, under Turkish protection, followed the next day. On May 28, 1918, Armenia was forced to declare its independence on the small, backward, and mountainous territory of the former tsarist district of the Erevan Guberniia. Erevan, with a population of 30,000, was one-tenth the size of Tiflis or Baku. It had no administrative, economic, or political structure. The affluent Armenians all lived outside the borders of the republic. A government composed of a majority of Dashnak party members began the new independent state. Armenia was immediately attacked by Turkey but resisted long enough for the war to end. The republic also had border disputes over historical Armenian enclaves that had ended up as parts of the Georgian and Azerbaijani republics. Despite a blockade, terrible economic and public health problems, and starvation, the Armenians hoped that the allied promises for the restoration of historical Armenia would be carried out. The allies, however, had their own agenda (the Sykes-Picot Agreement). Armenia was sacrificed in the peace conferences that divided parts of the Middle East between the French and the British. Although the United States, represented by President Woodrow Wilson, tried its best to help Armenia, the American mandate did not materialize. Armenia was invaded by both Republican Turkey, under the leadership of Mustafa Kemal (Ataturk), and by the Bolsheviks. In December 1920, it became a Soviet state.

Bolshevik rule began harshly for Armenia. Armenian political leaders were either arrested or fled to Iran. Not only did Karabagh (Karabakh) and Ganja remain in Azerbaijan, but Nakhichevan (Nakhchivan), which had always been part of Persian Armenia, together with the adjoining district of Sharur, was handed over to Azerbaijan as well. The Armenian region of Akhalkalaki remained part of Georgia. Armenian regions of Kars and Ardahan, captured by the Russians in 1878, were returned to Turkey. As a final slap, Mt. Ararat, which had never been part of Turkey or Turkish Armenia, was given to Turkey. Thus, Armenia became the junior member of the Transcaucasian Federation.

From 1920 until 1991, Armenia, unlike Georgia and Azerbaijan, and very much like Ukraine, had two groups of intellectual and national leaders. The Armenian Communist Party and its leadership tried to work within the framework of the multi-national Soviet state. Outside the Soviet Union, the rather large Armenian diaspora was itself divided among those who viewed Soviet Armenia as the Armenian government (the Ramgavars and Hnchaks) and those who considered it an illegal usurper (the Dashnaks). The Armenian church split along these lines with the Holy See at Etchmiadzin in Soviet Armenia representing the former view and the Holy See at Antilias, Lebanon, the latter.

The history of Armenia under Communist rule paralleled that of the Soviet Union. Armenia experienced the harshness of "War Communism" and breathed a sigh of relief during the years of the New Economic Policy (NEP). Mountainous Karabakh, with its predominantly Armenian population, was given an autonomous status of an oblast or district. Nakhichevan, separated from Azerbaijan by the Zangezour strip, remained part of the constituent republic of Azerbaijan, but as an autonomous republic. Armenian Communists gradually began to convince the Armenians of the benefits of Communism. Prior to World War I, Armenian capital and intellectual leadership had been concentrated in Tiflis, Baku, Constantinople, Moscow, and other cosmopolitan centers; most had remained outside Armenia. The task of the Armenian Communist leaders was to build a new Armenia to attract immigrants and to compete with the diaspora. Up to 1933, modernization and renationalization were the main object. Modernization meant urbanization. Erevan, a small dusty town of 30,000, was transformed by urban planners into a large city which, by 1990, had a population of over 1.2 million people. Armenia, which had had primarily an agricultural economy, was transformed into an industrial region. By 1929, food production and land cultivation had reached pre-war levels. The five-year plan and the forced collectivization and industrialization, however, changed Armenia forever. Unemployment disappeared, and Armenian workers began slowly to increase at the expense of the farmers. The church was persecuted, and anti-religious propaganda was strong. Women were encouraged to break the domination of men, and youth were told to ignore ancient traditions and join the new world order. Literacy and education were high on the agenda, and this policy enabled the Armenians to achieve full literacy in a short time. Armenian immigrants from the Middle East, Europe, and even parts of Soviet Union came to live in the national homeland. The idea of *korenizatsiia* (nativization and renationalization of the local Communist cells) was encouraged until 1934, when new Armenian leaders—communist but defending Armenian language, literature, and history—emerged. Their national leaders, like their counterparts in Georgia and other republics, were purged by Josef Stalin during the 1936–1938 period. Russians from the central bureaucracy were then brought in to replace the Armenians. In 1937, Lavrenty Beria, head of the Soviet Secret Police, installed his protégé, Grigor Arutiunov, who, in effect, ruled Armenia until 1953.

The Axis* invasion during World War II revived Russian and other minority nationalism as a unifying force in battling the Nazis. The Russian and Armenian churches were permitted to gather funds and to encourage the people to defend the motherland. Armenia was not occupied by the Germans during World War II, but many Armenians served in the Red Army and died or were decorated during the war. After the war, the Soviets revived the issue of Armenian lands in Turkey, but the Cold War soon ended that prospect. Despite economic hardship, Armenians living abroad were invited to "repatriate." Thousands arrived. Some were immediately exiled to Siberia and Central Asia as spies, while the rest were given homes and jobs, which was resented by the locals. The immigrants were never truly happy in Armenia and left the Soviet Union at the first opportunity.

By the end of Stalin's life, any form of Armenian national expression was once again suspect. Stalin's death began the Nikita Khrushchev era and a break with the repressive regime of the past. A period known as the "thaw" emerged in the Soviet Union and Armenia. Arutiunov was replaced by Toumasían, and all the members of the Central Committee of the Armenian Communist Party were also replaced. Khrushchev's friend, Anastas Mikoyan, personally came to Armenia to rehabilitate a number of Armenian authors and to signal the end of the Stalin era. After 1956, therefore, Armenia began to build a new cadre of national leaders. Armenians were once more empowered to run their local ministries. The period of indirect rule had begun. The new Armenian elite penetrated all aspects of society and gained power by making economic and political concessions. They managed to combine the acceptance of Soviet rule with loyalty toward Armenia. The power of this elite was bound up with their popularity; hence, a small group ruled Armenia for thirty-five years with only four heads of state. Unlike Georgia, Armenia did not experience any post–1972 purges, but corruption and bribery did become commonplace.

Armenian industrial and agricultural output rose considerably in this period. By 1975, only 20 percent of Armenians were engaged in any form of agriculture. Their per capita income was higher than that of the Soviet Union as a whole; 38 percent of Armenians were engaged in industry, much higher than in Azerbaijan or Georgia, while 42 percent were employed in services. Similarly, 70 percent lived in cities and over 80 percent had secondary or higher education; over half spoke Russian as a second language. Half of the work force was composed of women, and over 99 percent of Armenians listed Armenian as their primary language. The population of Soviet Armenia, which at the time of the Russian conquest of the Khanate of Erevan consisted of barely 20 percent Armenians, had risen to 90 percent in 1983 and, as a result of Azerbaijani emigration, to over 98 percent today. A large percentage of the Russians, Kurds, and Azerbaijanis living in Armenia have learned Armenian. Out of the 50,000 Kurds in Armenia, half speak Armenian fluently. Armenians also have the lowest percentage of any major ethnic group living within its republic's borders. Of the 4.2 million Armenians in 1980, only 2.8 million lived in Armenia. After the Jews, Armenians were the most widely dispersed people in the Soviet Union. A million lived in Georgia and Azerbaijan, with the rest scattered throughout the various republics of the Soviet Union, primarily in the Russian republic.

Although recent immigration from Azerbaijan and Georgia has changed these numbers significantly, the fact remains that Armenians are still heavily dispersed throughout the former territory of the Soviet Union.

From the mid–1960s to the mid–1980s, Armenia experienced the Brezhnev era—sometimes known as the period of benign neglect of the nationalities. Both Khrushchev and Leonid Brezhnev mistakenly thought that socioeconomic forces would eventually create a sort of melting pot. During these two decades, the Armenian elite became more independent and nationalistic in character. More important, however, was the rise of a new dissident nationalism that was totally independent of the Armenian governing elite. The dissidents opposed the system and demanded major changes. Unlike other regions of the Soviet Union (e.g., Baltic States and Ukraine), the new nationalists did not direct their vocal opposition against Russia or things Russian but against the Turks and the Azerbaijanis. In fact, Russia was viewed as the traditional friend of the Armenians and the one power that could redress the wrongs of the past. Since Armenian nationalism did not threaten the Soviet Union, these differences were treated as an internal matter.

From April 24, 1965, when the Armenians in Erevan openly commemorated the fiftieth anniversary of the Genocide, to 1975, when the issue of Karabagh (Karabakh) was openly discussed by the dissidents, the Armenian elite had to negotiate a delicate road in maintaining the status quo vis-à-vis Moscow. A secret underground Armenian national party (National Unity Party) emerged and demanded the restoration of a united and independent Armenia. A few acts of terror were attributed to this group; some members were arrested, and others were executed. In addition, an Armenian human rights group attached to the Helsinki group had been organized by 1977.

In 1978, during discussions on the new Soviet constitution, Moscow proposed that Armenian, like Georgian and Azerbaijani in their respective republics, be eliminated as an official language. Protests erupted in Tbilisi first; Erevan followed suit, and the proposal was dropped. The question of Karabagh (Karabakh), however, continued to fester. Armenians feared that Karabagh (Karabakh) would suffer the same fate as Nakhichevan (Nakhchivan), whose Armenian population had vanished and whose Armenian historical monuments were being systematically destroyed. Karabagh (Karabakh), with an Armenian population of over 80 percent, had no ties with Armenia, did not receive Armenian television programs, had no Armenian institution of higher learning, and was kept economically backward.

Mikhail Gorbachev's rise marked the culmination of the power of the new Russian elite. His program of *glasnost* and *perestroika* anticipated some difficulties with the Baltic and Ukrainian* minorities, but no one anticipated the great eruption of Armenian nationalism, primarily over the Karabagh (Karabakh) issue. In 1987, petitions were collected and, on February 28, 1988, the Karabagh Soviet of People's Deputies passed a resolution for the transferring of Karabagh (Karabakh) to Armenia. Within the space of a few days, a million sympathetic

Armenians marched in peaceful demonstrations in Erevan. Finally, Gorbachev spoke with a number of Armenian intellectuals and promised that the Karabagh (Karabakh) situation would be investigated at the highest level.

Two days later, the Azerbaijanis carried out a pogrom against the Armenians in the city of Sumgait. From then on, the situation escalated into open conflict. The Armenians expected Moscow to react strongly to the events in Sumgait. When it did not, the Armenians slowly lost faith in Russia. In the meantime, the dissident leaders, known as the Karabagh Committee, had gained credibility with the public, while the Armenian Communist elite lost its popularity. Karabagh (Karabakh) began to receive Armenian television programs, and an economic initiative was promised by Moscow as well. Unfortunately, neither the Armenians nor the Azerbaijanis were willing to compromise.

In May 1988, Karen S. Demirjian was replaced by Suren G. Harutiunian, who promised to take the issue of Karabagh (Karabakh) to the Supreme Soviet. On July 18, 1988, Moscow rejected the transfer. Armeno-Azerbaijani emigrations, accusations, and armed conflict escalated and resulted in the arrest of some Karabagh (Karabakh) Committee members. A crackdown began in Erevan. The result was that, for the first time, Russia, the Armenian government, and even the *Catholicos* were attacked by the dissidents who demanded full independence. A compromise was reached when the dissident leaders were released from jail and put under house arrest. May 28 was declared a national holiday, and Moscow appointed a special commission, headed by Arkadiy Volskii, to administer Karabagh (Karabakh) in place of the Azerbaijanis. Before anything could be enforced, the terrible earthquake of December 7, 1988, took place. Moscow's inept handling of that crisis and its buckling to pressures from Baku to relinquish Karabagh (Karabakh) to Azerbaijan resulted in something extraordinary. Armenians, the most pro-Russian of all ethnic groups, became extremely anti-Russian, and a majority began to demand a change of government. Harutiunian resigned, and, after declaring its intent to separate from the union and a public referendum, the Armenian National Movement, under the leadership of Levon Ter Petrossian, a Karabagh (Karabakh) Committee member, assumed power in Armenia. Following the fall of the Soviet Union on December 26, 1991, Armenia became an independent state, part of the commonwealth of former Soviet republics, and on March 2, 1992, a member of the United Nations. The issue of Karabagh (Karabakh) has not been resolved but has resulted in a full-scale war between the Azerbaijanis and the Armenians that threatens to embroil Turkey and Iran. Armenia is blockaded, and the post-World War I scenario is slowly playing itself out.

REFERENCES: G. A. Bournoutian, *Eastern Armenia in the Last Decades of Persian Rule*, 1982, and *The Khanate of Erevan under Qajar Rule, 1795–1828*, 1992; S. Der Nersessian, *The Armenians*, 1970; R. G. Hovannisian, *Armenia on the Road to Independence, 1918*, 1967, *The Republic of Armenia*, Vols. I & II, 1982, *The Armenian Image in History and Literature*, 1982, and *The Armenian Genocide*, 1992; G. Libaridian, *Armenia at the Crossroads*, 1991; M. Matossian, *The Impact of Soviet Policies in Ar-*

menia, 1962; L. Nalbandian, *The Armenian Revolutionary Movement*, 1963; Y. Rost, *Armenian Tragedy*, 1990; R. G. Suny, *Transcaucasia, Nationalism and Social Change*, 1983, and *Armenia in the Twentieth Century*, 1983; S. Shahmuratian, *The Sumgait Tragedy*, 1990; C. Walker, *Armenia: Survival of a Nation*, 1990, and *Armenia and Karabagh*, 1991.

George Bournoutian

ARMENIAN MUSLIM. See KHEMSIL.

ARMIAN. See ARMENIAN.

ARMYAN. See ARMENIAN.

ARNAUT. See ALBANIAN.

ARSHISHTTIB. See ARCHI and AVAR.

ARSHISHUW. See ARCHI and AVAR.

ARYA. See UDMURT.

AS. See OSSETIAN.

ASAN. See EVENK.

ASHKARAWA. See ASHKHARAWA and ABAZA.

ASHKENAZIC JEW. See JEW.

ASHKENAZIM. See JEW.

ASHKHARAWA. The Ashkharawa are one of the two subgroups of the Abaza* people. Their dialect is closely related to the Abkhaz* language. See ABAZA. *REFERENCE:* Ronald Wixman, *The Peoples of the USSR: An Ethnographic Handbook*, 1984.

ASHQARAWA. See ASHKHARAWA and ABAZA.

ASHTIKULI. See LAK.

ASHVADO. See AKHWAKH.

ASI. See OSSETIAN.

ASSIRIAN. See ASSYRIAN.

ASSIRIY. See ASSYRIAN.

ASSIRIYTSY. See ASSYRIAN.

ASSYRIAN. The Assyrians are a Christian Middle Eastern people who speak a neo-Aramaic dialect of the Semitic language family. They believe themselves to be direct descendants of the ancient Assyrians, whose empire reached its greatest extent in the seventh century B.C., encompassing all of Mesopotamia, the Holy Land, and Egypt. Inasmuch as that state was destroyed in 612 B.C., the exact lineage of those who today call themselves Assyrians is hard to trace. The Assyrians call themselves the Sura'i or Aturai, and they have also been known as the Aisor and Assiriy.

There may be as many as one million Assyrians in the world today; the number is uncertain because of intermarriage and assimilation in all the countries of their diaspora, including the United States and the former Soviet Union. The greatest number of Assyrians (approximately 200,000) can be found in Iraq, followed by Iran, Turkey, Syria, and Lebanon. The 1979 Soviet census recorded exactly 25,170 Assyrians, up from 24,294 in 1970 and 21,083 in 1959. The 1989 Soviet census claimed that there were 26,289 Assyrians in the country. These numbers are thought to be misleading, because many Assyrians were probably pressured by republican authorities to declare themselves to be members of other, more numerous Soviet nationalities. Soviet Assyrians are all immigrants, having sought refuge among Christian Russians* and Armenians* from hostile Muslim Turks*, Persians*, and Kurds*. Assyrians live in the Transcaucasian republics of Armenia, Azerbaijan, and Georgia; in southern Russia, especially around Armavir; and in big cities such as Moscow, Leningrad, and Kiev.

There is little, if any, pan-Assyrian nationalism. Ethnic loyalties have traditionally been quite decentralized, revolving around tribal and religious identities. The Turkish Assyrians are Jacobites, followers of a sixth-century Christian leader named Jacob Baradzi. Like the Armenians* and Copts, they were also known as Monophysites, and their religious beliefs were distinguished by the conviction that Jesus had only one personality and that that personality was divine. Some Iraqi Assyrians are Chaldean, a Uniate Catholic tradition loyal to Rome but retaining local liturgies. Most Assyrians are Nestorian Christians, adherents of a sect that was declared heretical in 431 A.D. Nestorius, the fifth-century patriarch of Constantinople, believed that Jesus had essentially a split personality, one human and the other divine, and that humanity and divinity did not fuse in his personality into a single entity; in other words, Jesus had two distinct personalities. That belief put Nestorians at odds with most other Christian sects, particularly the Monophysites, and clearly established their religious identity. They have clung fiercely to their religion and ancient customs, the more so, it seems, because of constant challenges from their militant Muslim neighbors.

Assyrians came to Russia and the Soviet Union in three main waves. The first group entered the tsarist empire from their homeland around the Lake Urmia region after the Treaty of Turkmanchai (1828) delineated a boundary between Russia and Persia. As a result of the treaty, many Assyrians suddenly found themselves living under Russian sovereignty, and thousands of relatives and friends crossed the border and joined them there. Later, during World War I, the solidly pro-Russian orientation of Nestorian Assyrians led to disaster at the hands of the Ottomans, who correctly suspected the Assyrians of collaboration with Russia. The Assyrian patriarch Mar Shimun led thousands to safety in Russia, but of those who remained in Turkey, many were slaughtered. Kurdish bands, intent on expanding into Assyrian territory in order to establish their own territorial claims at the Paris Peace Conference of 1919 and set up their own independent state, plundered the evacuated Assyrian villages. The violence drove still more Assyrians across the border into Russia. The third wave of Assyrian migration occurred after World War II, when several thousand Assyrians settled in Tbilisi, Moscow, and Leningrad. Following World War II, Moscow tried unsuccessfully to establish a satellite state in Iranian Kurdistan. That attempt met stiff resistance from Iran, and the Soviet Union eventually abandoned the policy. But the withdrawal of Soviet troops from Iran in 1946 left Assyrians exposed to precisely the same sort of retaliation that they had suffered from the Ottomans thirty years earlier. Persians and Kurds turned on the Assyrians, viewing them as a pro-Russian fifth column, and anti-Assyrian violence reached a fever pitch. Persecuted Assyrians fled to the Soviet Union, and most of them ended up in the cities.

Soviet policy toward the Assyrians was contradictory: The Urmian dialect of their language was officially declared to be "literary," but the ancient Nestorian alphabet was replaced by modified Latin and Cyrillic characters. The basis of Russian-Assyrian friendship—shared Christianity—was proscribed by atheist Bolsheviks, who persecuted Assyrian religious leaders and allowed most Assyrian churches to fall into disrepair. Other Stalinist excesses left the Soviet Assyrians leaderless after 1939. The state-sponsored terror resulted in the death or deportation of hundreds of prominent Assyrian tribal and religious leaders.

The Soviet Assyrians are too small a group to wield any political power. They have neither the numbers nor the political consciousness for it. Moscow has made sporadic attempts to exploit them in dealings with Iran, Iraq, and other Middle Eastern states, but, by and large, Soviet Assyrians have been forgotten by the state and have tended to assimilate with the more numerous Armenians* in recent years. Their tendency to gather in major Russian cities has also had the effect of accelerating the assimilation process. There is not much likelihood, however, of the Assyrians disappearing into the larger Soviet population soon. Centuries of persecution at the hands of Muslims, other Christian sects, and Communists have helped them to forge a strong identity. That identity found new expression during the years of *glasnost* under Mikhail Gorbachev. Although they have lived for more than 2,500 years without a nation-state of their own, the Assyrians in general have retained a strong sense of cultural and linguistic identity. During the late 1980s, cultural societies emerged among the Assyrians in the Soviet Union, including the Semiramida Assyrian Club in Leningrad and the Khayadta Assyrian Association in Moscow. Assyrians in Leningrad also began publishing a monthly magazine that they titled *Atra*, or Homeland. Under the leadership of Viktor Kolomanov, Assyrians established the Assyrian Congress of the Soviet Union in 1990; they convened in Moscow, where they discussed questions revolving around ethnic relations in Transcaucasia and Central Asia, as well as the issue of pan-Assyrian identity. Conferees decided to establish a nationwide Assyrian newspaper, implement an annual Assyrian cultural festival, and associate themselves with the All-Union Congress of Assyrians.

REFERENCES: W.E.D. Allen and Paul Muratoff, *Caucasian Battlefields*, 1953; *Current Digest*, March 20, 1991, p. 28; R. S. Stafford, *The Tragedy of the Assyrians*, 1935; William O. McCagg and Brian D. Silver, *Soviet Asian Ethnic Frontiers*, 1979.

Ross Marlay

ASTRAHAN TATAR. See ASTRAKHAN TATAR and TATAR.

ASTRAKAH TATAR. See ASTRAKHAN TATAR and TATAR.

ASTRAKHAN TATAR. The Astrakhan (Astrahan) Tatars are the descendants of the Golden Horde who reached the Volga River region in the thirteenth century. They settled between the Volga and Ural rivers, near Astrakhan, and evolved into two groups: the Kundrov Tatars* and the Karagash (Karashi) Tatars*. The ancestors of the Astrakhan Tatars established the Khanate of Astrakhan in the fifteenth and sixteenth centuries, and they then proceeded to mix culturally with the surrounding Nogais*. The Astrakhan Tatars share a written and spoken language with the Kazan*, or Volga Tatars*, and today those peoples are virtually indistinguishable. Like most other Tatars, they are Sunni Muslim in their religious loyalties. See TATAR.

REFERENCES: Shirin Akiner, *Islamic Peoples of the Soviet Union*, 1983; Alexandre Bennigsen and S. Enders Wimbush, *Muslims of the Soviet Empire: A Guide*, 1986; Ronald Wixman, *The Peoples of the USSR: An Ethnographic Handbook*, 1984.

ASY. See OSSETIAN.

ATAGAN. See BURYAT.

ATLUATII. See AKHWAKH and AVAR.

ATURAI. See ASSYRIAN.

AUGSZEMNIEK. See LATVIAN.

AUKSHTAI. See LITHUANIAN.

AUKSHTAITI. See LITHUANIAN.

AUKSHTAY. See LITHUANIAN.

AUKSHTAYTY. See LITHUANIAN.

AUKSKTAI. See LITHUANIAN.

AUKSTAICIAI. The term "Aukstaiciai," once a tribal division of Lithuanians*, today is used as a territorial reference to those Lithuanians living in eastern and southern Lithuania. See LITHUANIAN.
REFERENCE: Ronald Wixman, *Peoples of the USSR: An Ethnographic Handbook*, 1984.

AUKSTAITI. See LITHUANIAN.

AUKSTAITIS. See LITHUANIAN.

AUSTRIAN. The 1989 Soviet census listed the Austrian population of the country at 731 people. During the first few years after World War II, when Soviet troops occupied Austria, a number of Austrian nationals, including the noted Marxist leader Karl Kurtsky, moved to the Soviet Union for political and educational purposes. During the 1980s, others went there representing corporate interests that hoped to open up the vast Soviet supply of raw materials.
REFERENCE: Raymond E. Zickel, ed., *Soviet Union: A Country Study*, 1991.

AVAGAT. See ICHKILIK.

AVAM. See NGANASAN.

AVAR. One of the major Daghestani* ethnic groups in the Soviet Union is the Avar people, who actually are comprised of a complex mix of related, although quite distinct, ethnic communities. They call themselves the Maarlulal* or Magarulal, and those in the southern reaches of Avar land are known as the Bagulal*. The vast majority of the Avar live in the mountainous highlands of the Daghestan Autonomous Republic. They are concentrated in west central Daghestan and extend across the border in northern Azerbaijan and southeastern Chechenia. The Avar live in the major river valleys and have traditionally dominated commercial relationships in the region. They are Sunni Muslim in their religious faith and speak a language that is part of the northeast branch of the Caucasic linguistic family. Four Avar dialects are still spoken, and they are mutually unintelligible to one another. Those dialects are: Khunzakh, Antsukh, Charoda, and Gidatl-Andalalay-Karkh. Each of these dialects is also divided into a series of sub-dialects. Because the town of Khunzakh has historically been the political and cultural center of the Avar community, as well as of the region in general, the Khunsakh dialect is the dominant one among Avars and the foundation for the Avar written language.

In addition to the Avar proper, there are a number of other small ethnic groups that today are classified as Avar by Soviet demographers and ethnologists. The Andi* ethnic group dwells in southwestern Daghestan in the westernmost reaches of Avar territory, especially along the Upper Andi River. They employ the Khunzakh dialect as their literary and commercial language. The Andi are further divided into eight ethnic subgroups: the Botligs* (Botlikh), Bagulals, Chamalals*, Akhwakhs*, Godoberis* (Gogoberi), Karatas*, Tindis*, and Andis proper. In addition of the Andi groups, there is also the Dido* (Tsez) ethnic group, which is itself divided into the Didos proper and the Bezhetas, Ginugs* (Ginukh), Khwarshis*, and Khunzals*. The Dido groups live in the most isolated regions of the mountains near the border of the Georgian Republic. The final ethnic group classified with the Avars today is the Archis*, who dwell in the southeastern portion of Avar territory. Like the Andis, the Didos and the Archis use the Khunzakh dialect as their literary and commercial language. Collectively, the Avar, Andi, Dido, and Archi peoples numbered more than 604,000 people in the 1989 census of the Soviet Union.

Avar groups were described by Pliny the Elder in the first century, and Ptolemy may have been referring to the Avars when he discussed the "Savirs." In the first half of the eighth century, Arabs*, led by Abu Muslim according to Avar tradition, invaded the region and brought Islam with them. The Mongols* overran the region in the thirteenth century, but, by the fourteenth century, independent principalities, particularly the Avar Khanate, began to break away from the control of the Golden Horde. The Avar Khanate rose to the height of its power in the seventeenth and eighteenth centuries, but even then it was divided by the centrifugal forces of internal tribal loyalties. In 1803, Russia established a protectorate over the Avar Khanate. Avars rebelled against Russian* influence in 1821. In response, Russia abolished the protectorate and began to exercise more direct control.

Like most of the other inhabitants of the region, the Avar are Sunni Muslim in their religious loyalties. Within that Sunni Muslim faith, most Avar are devoted to the Shafi theological school. The Muslim religion came to the Avar from three directions. Arab traders first began introducing the religion in the eighth century; Persian* traders then brought it into the area beginning in the fifteenth century; finally, Mongol invaders carried it in from the north in the sixteenth and seventeenth centuries. By the mid-nineteenth century, the Avar had been thoroughly converted, religiously and culturally, to Sunni Muslim values and beliefs. Today the Avar remain devoted to the faith, attending mosque regularly, praying daily, circumcising male children, and conducting regular Muslim ceremonies for marriages and funerals.

During the nineteenth and twentieth centuries, the policies of the tsars and then of the Communist governments alienated the Avar and intensified their sense of ethnic solidarity. As large numbers of ethnic Russian settlers poured into Transcaucasia in the nineteenth and early twentieth centuries, the Avar found themselves confronted by an alien people who enjoyed the backing of the state. The Russian settlers brought commercialized forms of agriculture and animal husbandry and managed to seize large areas of Avar land. The arrival of large numbers of ethnic Russians in the Daghestani region led to the Shamil Rebellion between 1834 and 1858. The Daghestanis in general, as well as the Laks,* resented the Russians, and, in 1834, Imam Shamil, an Avar Muslim leader, declared independence for Daghestan and imposed the Koran as the law of the land. Older animistic beliefs were crushed, and the government fought the Russian Orthodox church. The Shamil Revolt collapsed in 1858, but, by that time, the Avar hatred for everything Russian was complete. In 1864, Russia changed the Avar Khanate into the Avar District.

Governmental pressures to russianize and then sovietize the Avar people continued during the twentieth century. Just after the Russian Revolution, the Soviet government tried to placate those who wanted to create a single Islamic state out of the entire Muslim population of the North Caucasus region. They established the Mountain Autonomous Republic in 1920, with Arabic as the official language. Most Avars, as well as other ethnic Daghestanis, had no love for Arabic and therefore opposed the decision. They resisted the government, and, in 1921, the state created the Daghestan Autonomous Soviet Socialist Republic as an ethnic subdivision of the larger republic. Policy changed again a few years later when Arabic ceased to be the official language. In the late 1920s, the Soviet government conducted an intense anti-Islamic campaign that included widespread imprisonment and execution of local religious leaders. The government tried to Latinize the Avar language in the early 1930s and then switched to the Cyrillic alphabet in 1938. At the same time, Russian became the only language of instruction in public schools. Early in the 1960s, state policy prohibited the teaching of Avar, as well as of the other Daghestani languages, in the public schools.

In addition to trying to russify Avar culture, the government worked diligently at sovietizing the Avar economy. Traditionally, the Avars owned land and livestock herds communally, so the Soviet government converted those ethnic communal arrangements into economic collectives, with the government owning the land and the herds. The Avars had to sell their produce to government collectives at state-mandated prices. In the end, the Avar community found itself in a poorer economic situation. Because of the state-controlled economy and the heavy-handed attempts to change Avar culture, the Avar sense of ethnicity has only intensified over the years. It is distinctly anti-Communist, anti-Russian, and anti-Christian. More than 95 percent of ethnic Avar speak the native language and are intensely loyal to their Muslim faith. Today they are among Transcaucasia's most nationalistic people clamoring for independence from Moscow.

REFERENCES: Alexandre Bennigsen, "Muslim Conservative Opposition to the Soviet Regime: The Sufi Brotherhoods in the North Caucasus," in Jeremy R. Azrael, ed., *Soviet Nationality Policies and Practices*, 1978; Alexandre Bennigsen and S. Enders Wimbush, *Muslims of the Soviet Empire: A Guide*, 1986; Vladimir Rogov, *Languages and Peoples of the USSR*, 1966; Ronald Wixman, *Language Aspects of Ethnic Patterns and Processes in the North Caucasus*, 1980; George Feizuillin, "The Persecution of National-Religious Traditions of the Moslems of the USSR," *Caucasian Review*, 3 (1956), 69–76; Ronald Wixman, "Daghestanis," in Richard V. Weekes, ed., *Muslim Peoples*, 1984, 211–19; Ronald Wixman, *The Peoples of the USSR: An Ethnographic Handbook*, 1984.

AVARO-ANDI-DIDO PEOPLES. The term "Avaro-Andi-Dido peoples" is a generic reference to all those who are today considered part of the Avar* peoples. Included in this classification are the Andis*, Akhwakhs*, Botligs*, Godoberis*, Bagulals,*, Karatas*, Tindis*, and Chamalals*, who are Avars; the Didos*, Khwarshis*, Bezhetas, Khunzals*, and Ginugs*, who are Didos; and the Archis*. See AVAR.
REFERENCE: Ronald Wixman, *The Peoples of the USSR: An Ethnographic Handbook*, 1984.

AVARO-ANDI-TSEZ PEOPLES. See AVARO-ANDI-DIDO PEOPLES and AVAR.

AVARO-ANDO-DIDO PEOPLES. See AVARO-ANDI-DIDO PEOPLES and AVAR.

AVARO-ANDO-TSEZ PEOPLES. See AVARO-ANDI-DIDO PEOPLES and AVAR.

AVARTSY. See AVAR.

AVGAT. See ICHKILIK and KYRGYZ.

AWAR. See AVAR.

AWARO-ANDI-DIDO PEOPLES. See AVAR.

AWARO-ANDI-TSEZ PEOPLES. See AVAR.

AWARO-ANDO-DIDO PEOPLES. See AVAR.

AWARO-ANDO-TSEZ PEOPLES. See AVAR.

AYRAMOINEN. See AYRAMOISET, FINN, and KARELIAN.

AYRAMOISET. The Ayramoiset, who are known to Russians* as the Evrimeiset, are a Finnish-speaking people who live in the St. Petersburg oblast. They are Lutherans. See FINN or KARELIAN.

REFERENCE: Ronald Wixman, *Peoples of the USSR: An Ethnographic Handbook*, 1984.

AYRUM. See AZERBAIJANI.

AYSOR. See ASSYRIAN.

AZERBAIDJAN. See AZERBAIJANI.

AZERBAIDJANIAN. See AZERBAIJANI.

AZERBAIJANI. The people of Azerbaijan, who call themselves Azerbaijanis, have also been referred to as Turks*, Azeris, Azeri Turks, Tyurks, Azeri Tatars, Tatars of Transcaucasia, and, finally, Caucasian Tatars. The Azerbaijanis are currently one of the most rapidly growing ethnic groups in the Commonwealth of Independent States (CIS): in 1926, their population was 1,706,605, but by 1989 that number had increased to 6,791,106. Three Azerbaijani subgroups maintain a strong sense of individual identity. The Airum*, Padar*, and Shahseven* are all semi-nomadic people. The Airum live in western Azerbaijan, while the Shahseven are located in southern Azerbaijan along the Iranian border. The Padar live in eastern Azerbaijan. The Azeri language is part of the southwestern group of the Turkic* branch of the Ural-Altaic* family of languages. It is divided into four basic groups of dialects, and each of those is further divided into subdialects. The eastern group of dialects included Kuba, Baku, and Shemakha. The western cluster of dialects consists of Kazakh, Gandzha, Karabagh, and Airum. The northern group includes Nukha and Zakatalo-Kazak. Finally, the southern cluster of dialects consists of Nakhichevan and Erevan, as well as those dialects spoken across the border in Iran. The Baku dialect serves as the literary dialect for all Azerbaijanis. At the present time, because of their demographic superiority in the Azerbaijan Republic, the Azerbaijanis are assimilating the Moslem Tats*, Talyshes*, Kurds*, Shah Daghs*, Udis*, Lezgins*, Avars*, and Tsakhurs* living among them.

In the early 1990s, headlines around the world chronicled the growing violence between the Azerbaijanis and the Armenians*. The conflict is rooted in centuries of history and ethnic rivalry. The Azerbaijani homeland lies at the junction of three different historical empires: the Persian (Iranian), the Ottoman, and the Russian. Today, roughly 18,000,000 Azerbaijanis are divided between the former Soviet Republic of Azerbaijan (over 6,000,000 in "northern" Azerbaijan) and the Azerbaijan Province of Iran (12,000,000 in "southern" Azerbaijan). The former Azerbaijan Soviet Socialist Republic is located on the Transcaucasian isthmus, which is nestled between the Black Sea on the west and the Caspian Sea on the east, in what was formerly the southwestern part of the Soviet Union. Transcaucasia includes "Soviet" Azerbaijan and the former Soviet Republics of Georgia on the northwest and Armenia on the southwest. Azerbaijan is also bordered by Daghestan on the north and Iran on the south. It is bounded on the east by the Caspian Sea, and its capital city, Baku, is the best harbor on that sea.

The Azerbaijani people evolved from the intermingling of Persians and Turks, and their culture is a synthesis of both these groups. Despite the expanse of territory that they inhabit and their sizable population, the Azerbaijanis have never really known independence, having been ruled alternately by the Persians, Turks, and Russians*, with brief interludes of independence and British* occupation. The Greeks* and Mongols* also tried to conquer the area, though without meaningful success.

Despite never having enjoyed actual independence, modern Azerbaijan has more than enough natural resources for a viable economy sufficient to sustain an independent nation. Since the late nineteenth century, Azerbaijan's economy has been balanced between industry and agriculture. Azerbaijan was responsible for approximately 10 percent of Soviet agricultural production before the dissolution of the Union, even though it had only 7 percent of the country's arable land. Even that level of productivity was substantially below Azerbaijan's potential. A variety of food crops are grown, and cotton is the leading cash crop. Industry includes equipment manufacture, especially for the oil industry, power generation, and chemical production. Natural resources include lead, zinc, iron, and copper ores. But the major resource and the driving force of the economy has been oil and, to a lesser extent, natural gas.

The Baku oil fields contributed almost half of total world oil production in the early twentieth century. Unfortunately, the profits went primarily to foreign investors, a sore point that prompted Azerbaijani support for the October Revolution of 1918, given the Bolshevik argument that natural resources should not be exploited to enrich foreign investors and the imperialist economies of Western Europe. While Baku's oil production increased steadily until World War II, worldwide production grew much faster, thus reducing the importance of Baku oil. Indeed, the discovery of other oil fields in the Soviet Union reduced Baku's importance within the Union. Baku's proportion of total Soviet production fell from over 90 percent to 75 percent by the 1950s and eventually leveling off at about 5 to 7 percent by 1975. Efforts to revitalize Baku's oil production have been unsuccessful for a variety of reasons: diminishing reserves, the costliness of the technology needed for secondary and tertiary recovery, the lack of pipeline capacity, and a shortage of technological expertise. Rather than commit its resources to expanding production, the Soviet Union chose to diversify the economy by, among other things, increasing mining, steel production, and natural gas exploration and production.

Baku's importance as an international oil center made it very different from the rest of Azerbaijan. It became a cosmopolitan city of genuinely international character. It was an urban mecca in a profoundly agrarian and rural region. While Soviet Azerbaijan was ethnically diverse, Baku was even more so. The better-paying jobs went to Armenians, Russians, and foreign nationals, while the Azerbaijani natives were left with entry-level and unskilled jobs. This has been a continuing source of conflict both within Baku and between Baku and the countryside, especially during the disintegration of the Russian Empire and of the Soviet Union.

Persian culture dominated Azerbaijan from the sixth century B.C. until the ninth century A.D. when Turkish culture became dominant. The one exception was in the area of religion. By the sixteenth century, most Azerbaijanis were Shiite Muslims, in contrast to most other Turks who were Sunni Muslims. The Azerbaijani language is sufficiently similar to Anatolian Turkish that the Turks and Azerbaijanis can understand each other if everyone speaks carefully. Similarly, Turks experience only minor difficulties in reading Azerbaijani. The primary problem is differences between the alphabets. Soviet Azerbaijan used the Arabic alphabet until 1922 when Soviet authorities replaced it with the Latin alphabet. In 1937, the alphabet was changed once again to the currently used Cyrillic alphabet.

By the eleventh century, Persia had regained control over Azerbaijan and governed the region until 1723, although it never fully integrated the Azerbaijanis into Persia. In 1724, Peter the Great annexed the Baku and Derbent regions to Russia, but Persia regained the area in 1736. In the last half of the eighteenth century, Azerbaijan experienced a degree of independence, but the region was fragmented into local power centers and not unified. This, of course, left it attractive and vulnerable to its more powerful neighbors.

While Soviet historians have claimed that Russian influence can be traced back to the twelfth century, actual Russian conquest came much later and was difficult, protracted, and costly. Azerbaijan fell first to anti-tsarist Cossack* rebels under the leadership of Stanka Razin in the seventeenth century, but Cossack control was short-lived. In 1701, Russia began a campaign of conquest that would be completed in 1806. The conquest and control of Baku and northern Azerbaijan were central to Russian ambitions in the Caspian Sea, in part because Azerbaijanis dominated Caspian Sea shipping and also because they were the middlemen in trade between Russia and Persia. The division of Azerbaijan between Russia and Persia was formulated by the treaties of Gulestan in 1813 and Turkmanchai in 1828. Nonetheless, the "northern" Azerbaijanis were not fully united under Russian rule until 1841 and not integrated into Russia proper until the 1860s.

Initially, Russian rule was relatively benign, and many Azerbaijanis were more concerned about Turkish designs than Russian ones. A positive orientation toward Russian rule was greatly encouraged by tsarist authorities who appointed Azerbaijanis to important posts in St. Petersburg and Moscow. Relations became so positive that some Azerbaijani leaders advocated siding with Russia against the Ottoman Empire during the Crimean War of 1854.

Good relations with Russia notwithstanding, the Azerbaijanis did not benefit economically from incorporation into the imperial fold. The purpose of Russian investment was to extract wealth rather than to build the economic infrastructure of the country. Agricultural production declined because Russian military governors did not maintain the irrigation systems. Even oil production fell and did not really recover until tsarist reforms opened Russia to foreign investors. When Russia began to lease crown lands to the highest-bidding oil developers in 1872, the Baku oil boom began in earnest. In 1879, the Swedish Nobel brothers founded what would become the world's largest oil company up to that time.

Benign rule gradually changed, however, as tsarist leaders began a program of national integration. Azerbaijanis resisted this policy through a variety of means, including but not limited to their enduring tactic of passive resistance. In particular, the first decade of the twentieth century was marked by turbulence in Azerbaijan. Following the "Bloody Sunday" St. Petersburg massacre on January 9, 1905, protests and riots erupted in Baku and spread throughout Transcaucasia.

In an attempt to give voice to Azerbaijani discontent, Hummet, a Muslim Marxist organization, was founded in 1904. In 1907, it was destroyed by tsarist agents, who played on the ethnic diversity of the region using tactics of divide and rule to achieve the empire's objectives. This activity heightened ethnic animosities and helped to produce ethnic riots in 1905 and 1906. These riots together became known as the "Tatar-Armenian War" and left resentments and hostilities that have endured to the present day. In 1911, Mehmed Emin Rasulzade organized the Musavat Party, which proved to be more resilient than the Hummet. Though originally socialist, the party quickly became a non-ideological Islamic modernist party.

With the collapse of the Russian war effort in late 1917 and early 1918, Azerbaijan became embroiled in ethnic, ideological, and imperial conflicts. Persia made a brief bid to reunify all of Azerbaijan. Both Britain and the Ottoman Empire at times occupied significant portions of Azerbaijan, and the Azerbaijani people made a courageous, if brief, effort at independence. Ultimately, Russian Azerbaijan was incorporated into the Soviet state.

World War I exacerbated the traditional split between urban Baku and the rural countryside. Baku had become a multinational urban center with no dominant ethnic group. Ethnic Azerbaijanis were a minority in Baku and generally held low-paying, unskilled jobs. This created resentment throughout the Azerbaijani population and ultimately separated Baku from the Azerbaijani-dominated countryside, producing, among other things, significant differences among responses to the Bolshevik revolution. The urban proletariat favored revolutionary ideology while the rural peasants remained loyal to the Musavat agenda.

In the October 1917 elections, the Musavat party won a plurality of the vote but then withdrew, allowing the Bolshevik leader Stepah Shaumyan to become chairman of the Baku soviet. Over the next five months, the Musavat moved sharply to the right and began to portray the Bolsheviks as being anti-Azerbaijanian. By the end of March 1918, Azerbaijan was embroiled in ethnic riots. The rise of Soviet power, so evident in other parts of the former Russian empire, was mirrored in Baku, with the Bolsheviks gaining authority in late 1917 and early 1918. Their hold was broken, however, by ethnic strife and the encroachment of Ottoman forces in the spring of 1918. Later, the "Baku Commune," as the Bolshevik local government was called, succumbed to British intervention.

While the Baku Commune is portrayed in Soviet historiography as a glorious period of the Russian civil war, very few Azerbaijanis supported or participated in it. For example, prior to 1917, not one prominent Azerbaijani was listed among the Baku Bolshevik Party leadership, with the exception of Meshadi Azizbek, who was the Assistant Commissar of the Interior. Shaumyan, the Commune's leader, was an Armenian and a genuine Bolshevik revolutionary. Shaumyan's top assistants were either Georgian (People's Commissar of the Interior Alyosha Dzhaparidze) or Russian (People's Commissar of the Army and Navy Grigory Kurganov, and Chair of the Baku Economic Council Ivan Fioletov). Azizbek, Shaumyan, and approximately twenty-four other Bolsheviks who were executed by the British in September 1918 became celebrated martyrs of the revolution.

During this time, the Musavat nationalist party, which had withdrawn from Baku in late 1917, was headquartered at Gandzha when the Bolsheviks were driven from Baku in March 1918. A small British force was actually the first to occupy the city, but it was driven out by units of the Ottoman army. British occupation forces returned with the collapse of the Ottoman Empire in November 1918, and they remained there until August 1919. During the period of British occupation, those who had cooperated with the Ottomans were removed from power and socialist politicians were reinstated. The British made no attempt to resolve the economic hardships and political disintegration of a region cut off from both its traditional suppliers of bread in the northern Caucasus and its oil markets. In this environment, the Bolshevik underground continued to build substantial strength among Baku workers.

While Russia was distracted with its own civil war, Azerbaijani leaders attempted to take advantage of the situation to gain their country's independence. Because of fears that either victor in the civil war would attempt to reestablish Russian authority over them, Azerbaijani interests lay in not supporting either the Reds or the Whites. Furthermore, Azerbaijani sentiment was divided between the two warring factions: The Bolsheviks had built a relatively strong organization in Baku, but the countryside was hostile to them.

In the period following the Treaty of Brest-Litovsk in January 1918, both the Ottoman Empire and Persia had expansionist designs on Azerbaijan, but neither power was able to enforce its claims. Azerbaijanis attempted to form an independent Transcaucasian federation composed of Azerbaijan, Georgia, and Armenia; this organization declared its independence on April 22, 1918. By May 1918, however, this non-Bolshevik federation had failed because of ethnic and religious conflicts among the three states and because neither Bolshevik Russia, the Ottoman Empire, nor Persia was willing to accept an independent Transcaucasia, in spite of their own disarray.

Although Azerbaijan won *de facto* recognition from the Allies on January 15, 1920, their case for independence fell on deaf ears at the Versailles peace conference. The republic was invaded by Bolshevik forces in April 1920. Without international support, the Azerbaijanis could not stand against Red Army pressures, and thus Baku fell to the Bolsheviks without a fight on April 28. Azerbaijan then became the theoretically independent Azerbaijan Soviet Socialist Republic.

While Azerbaijan was geographically and culturally viable as an independent state, the Bolsheviks would not permit this for three reasons. First, the Bolsheviks understood that Baku was the most important source of oil in Bolshevik Russia at the end of World War I. Second, the Bolsheviks believed that new agricultural policies would transform Azerbaijani agriculture into the nation's most important source of cotton. Third, plans for increasing Bolshevik influence in the Middle East and the Muslim world hinged on the development of Azerbaijan and its integration into the new Soviet state.

Initially, there was a loose constitutional relationship among the Russian, Ukrainian, Belorussian, and Transcaucasian republics, with the latter actually governed by the Caucasian Bureau of the Bolshevik Party (Kavburo). This relationship evaporated in December 1922, when Lenin and the Bolsheviks moved to form the more centralized Soviet Union, largely as a consequence of their mistrust of local Communist leaders and their understanding of republican nationalism. V. I. Lenin envisioned a benign, native nationalism as the cornerstone on which to build a multinational, multiethnic nation. By contrast, Josef Stalin, who was an ethnic Georgian, saw nationalism as a device for manipulation and managed Transcaucasian nationalism because he understood its totalitarian potential. Early Kremlin leaders approved the expression of Georgian, Armenian, and Azerbaijani nationalist aspirations and took a leading role in advancing Transcaucasian nationalism. Later, in Stalin's hands, this policy was used to undermine locally inspired nationalism. Thus, Stalin proposed a Transcaucasian Soviet Federation but not as a vehicle for *rapprochement* between Azerbaijan, Armenia, and Georgia; rather it was used to limit the nationalist tendencies of each. At that time, Moscow was not sufficiently strong to limit the three republics' sovereignty, but the Transcaucasian Federation established an intermediate agency that could. Once the federation's usefulness had passed, Stalin ordered that it be dissolved in favor of individual Soviet republics. Ironically, Stalin's cynical manipulation of nationalism eventually culminated in the disintegration of the Soviet Union.

Despite revolutionary rhetoric supporting ethnic identity and respect for ethnic boundaries, Soviet leaders were not particularly sensitive to ethnic geography in drawing the boundaries of the Transcaucasian Soviet republics. Part of this problem can be attributed to the limits of empire. Each empire in the Caucasus region, as well as those of the Western interlopers, attempted to control as much territory as possible before being effectively checked by another imperialist nation. In many instances, those gains were halted *within* the territory of an ethnic group rather than at the boundaries *between* ethnic groups.

Lenin was sensitive to nationalism and resisted attempts to impose Russian as a national language on non-Russian inhabitants of the Soviet Union. He also advocated drawing political lines consistent with ethnic distributions, arguing that it was reasonable to grant autonomy to ethnic populations consisting of as few as 50,000 individuals. The process of "national statehood" was viewed by Lenin, but not Stalin, as an important means of gaining support among the disparate nationalities and ethnic groups that made up the Soviet Union, especially those such as the Armenians who had endured persecution. Rather than attempting to assimilate these nationalities into a homogeneous russianized culture, the intent was to encourage the development of each nationality's culture within its nation-state and then to integrate that nation-state into the larger mosaic of the Soviet Union. The very name, "Soviet Union," was itself an attempt to avoid the appearance that any nationality was superior in the multinational federation.

Unfortunately, internal and external opposition to Lenin's ideas precluded Azerbaijan's and Armenia's boundaries from being drawn in such a manner. Stalin, for one, did not want boundaries based on clean ethnic lines so that he could use ethnicity as a divide-and-rule strategy. Therefore, in 1923, 2,100 square miles of predominantly Azerbaijani-speaking territory on the Iranian border, the Nakhchivan (Nakhichevan) Region (which was completely surrounded by Armenia), was made into the Nakhichevan Autonomous Republic. Relatedly, the mountain region of Nagorno-Karabakh (Nagorno-Karabagh), which was 80 percent Armenian, was made an autonomous oblast, or province, within Azerbaijan in 1924, *reputedly* because it belonged to Azerbaijan economically. It had also been a center of Armenian resistance to Bolshevik rule. The Nagorno-Karabakh region is separated geographically from Armenia by a thin, sparsely populated mountainous strip of Azerbaijani territory. Eventually, in 1936, the Transcaucasian Soviet Federated Socialist Republic was dissolved and Armenia, Azerbaijan, and Georgia became separate union republics within the Soviet Union. These divisions formed the basis of the violent conflicts that have raged between Azerbaijanis and Armenians since the late 1980s.

Once order and stability had been established and control of the Soviet Union had been consolidated in Bolshevik hands, the somewhat contradictory programs of colonization and state-building were begun. Azerbaijan was the only part of Transcaucasia that was subjected to large-scale Russian colonization. Indeed, Christian Georgia and Armenia enjoyed a special status in the Soviet Union, compared with the other Soviet republics, no doubt partly as a consequence of Stalin's Transcaucasian roots. By contrast, the Azerbaijanis were Muslims, there were extensive oil and natural gas resources around Baku, and the region was populated relatively sparsely. Azerbaijan was therefore treated somewhat differently.

The absence of an independent national identity proved crucial to Soviet calculations for the russification of Azerbaijan, calculations that went beyond agricultural and industrial development as well as state-building. Soviet state-building extended to giving the Azerbaijanis their very name, since they had previously been referred to variously as Caucasian Turks, Muslims, or Tatars*. The Soviets tried to capitalize on Azerbaijan's lack of an independent historical identity to erase all lingering recognition of the region's cultural and historical ties with Persia and to weaken its Turkish heritage as well. To the extent that Turkish and Persian cultural ties were encouraged at all, this was done with a Soviet twist.

With regard to state-building, the Soviets quickly turned to programs for the economic and cultural transformation of Azerbaijan; these were similar to programs imposed on other republics. This process entailed educating and training a native Azerbaijani leadership. This policy served to legitimize the Soviet establishment in Azeri eyes because the Azerbaijanis had always been administered by some other national or ethnic group, particularly Russians and Armenians. There were two problems, however, that the Soviets never solved. Despite the cultivation of Azerbaijani leaders, most political and economic leadership positions remained in predominantly non-Azerbaijani hands.

While Azerbaijanis were willing to accept a degree of westernization, such as the latinization and later cyrillization of the alphabet and the use of Western technology, this acceptance did not mean a lack of nationalist sentiment. The imposition of Soviet state-building met strong resistance as even Azerbaijani Communists rejected subordination to centralized Soviet authority. Between 1921 and 1930, repeated efforts were made to suppress "nationalist deviation" within the Azerbaijan Communist Party. The purge of "Narimanovism" by S. M. Kirov (an ethnic Russian and the party secretary) in 1921 was the first purge in all of Transcaucasia.

On August 27, 1924, an uprising against Soviet rule was instigated by an alliance of all non-Communist groups in Azerbaijan and Georgia. The initial Soviet response was relatively mild. Ultimately, however, Soviet courts imposed death penalties not only on the uprising's leaders but also on participants and even those suspected of plotting against the regime. Such executions of nationalist leaders represented a departure from the leniency shown to nationalists in other regions that had been brought under Bolshevik control. Another purge followed in 1930, this one of reputed Trotskyite-Bukharinist and "bourgeois-nationalist" elements within the party.

The Soviet collectivization of agriculture and the increased production especially of cotton also proved to be a continuing source of conflict between Azerbaijanis and Soviet planners. An extensive and highly successful literacy program was started. As literacy increased, Islamic influence in the rural areas decreased. A primary tactic used to reduce Islamic influence was to co-opt modernist Islamic leaders. Islamic influence was gradually weakened through such indirect means until 1928, when a more direct attack was launched through the League of Militant Atheists. The decline in Islamic influence also resulted in a decline in Azerbaijani nationalism. A series of purges culminating in 1937 wiped out virtually all Islamic-nationalist leadership as well as many top officials of the Soviet Republic, including G. M. Musabekov, former chair of the Council of Commissars of Transcaucasia, and Husein Rakhmanov, secretary of the Central Committee and chair of the Council of Ministers of Azerbaijan.

In addition to its effects on the Communist hierarchy, militant atheism attacked public manifestations of religion as well. Four of the "five pillars" of Islamic faith were suppressed. The *zakat* (or almsgiving) was forbidden, and public prayers became rare. Only two mosques remained open in Baku by 1970, with only fourteen others in the rest of the republic. The month of fasting (*Ramadan*) became impracticable because of work schedules and official discouragement. Only a small number of token pilgrims were permitted to visit Mecca. Since the profession of belief in Allah, the *Shahada*, can be made in the heart, only the fifth pillar escaped direct control by Soviet authorities. Still, the persistence of Islam-approved dress for women in rural areas, religiously oriented names for children, early marriage for women, and the expression of religious proverbs indicated that the strength of Islam was not so much broken as hidden underground. As the Soviet Union collapsed, there was a strong revival of Islam in Azerbaijan, as there was of Christianity in the traditionally Christian regions of the Soviet Union.

The Soviets worked hard to increase Azerbaijani assimilation into Russian culture for several reasons: the Azerbaijanis' Turko-Persian heritage, their Muslim religion, their strong nationalist sentiments, and their importance to the Soviet Union with respect to oil, agriculture, natural resources, and strategic location. While a foundation for greater assimilation existed, the Soviet approach was too coercive and punitive. The emphasis on Azerbaijani acknowledgment of inferiority to Russians and the purges of proponents of the various "deviations" not only stirred Azerbaijani resistance, it also frustrated Soviet objectives in Persia and, to lesser extent, Turkey. While the primary explanation for oppressive Soviet tactics was the attempt to unify the nation and to build allegiance to the national government, much of it can also be attributed to Stalin's own Georgian heritage and the historical animosity of Georgians toward their "hereditary enemy."

Relatedly, Baku's lack of integration into Azerbaijan posed problems in terms of the Soviets' Middle Eastern ambitions. Since Azerbaijan was to be the means for spreading Sovietism to the neighboring Muslim states, it was very important both that enterprises in the republic be successful and that Baku be presented as an integrated part of the republic and accepted as such by the rural Muslim population. That never really happened, although the Soviets asserted that it had.

The Soviets faced other problems in addition to integrating Baku into the Azerbaijan Republic. Soviet planners wanted to increase cotton acreage substantially to give the republic a more profitable cash crop, but this necessitated reducing acreage for grains and foodstuffs because of a lack of arable land with suitable climate. Opposition to this agricultural policy was pervasive, extending even to the collective farms and to the rural and village-based units of the Azerbaijan Communist Party. Despite persistent attempts to sabotage efforts to expand acreage and the problem of insufficient farm mechanization, cotton became the republic's leading cash crop, accounting for almost half of its agricultural income.

By the beginning of World War II, Baku was the fifth-largest city in the Soviet Union and still the largest oil producer, although its proportion of total Soviet oil production was declining and would continue to do so. While Baku's growth leveled off and its relative importance declined, the russification of Azerbaijan continued. Kirovabad, Gandzha, and new towns created under successive five-year plans were developed to exploit the republic's natural resources and create an industrial infrastructure. In almost all instances, the heads of government and economic operations were non-Azerbaijanis. This situation resulted in the development of multiethnic cities as islands in an ethnically homogeneous countryside, which remained a continuing source of conflict between urban and rural Azerbaijanis.

During the time of the German-Soviet Non-Aggression Pact, the Soviets supplied Baku oil to Germany. The Allies initiated plans to bomb Baku, but these were not executed because of Germany's invasion of Norway. Stalin also apparently realized or learned that Baku had become a potential target. Not wanting war with the Allies, Stalin significantly reduced oil shipments and other trade to Germany. When Germany declared war on the Soviet Union, Baku again became a target, as now the Germans, strapped for oil, sought to capture the fields there.

By November 1941, all of southern Russia and much of Ukraine had fallen to the Germans. In the summer offensive of 1942, German units moved out of the Crimea, across the Don River to the Volga River, capturing Rostov, Sevastopol, and the Maikop oil fields and laying siege to Stalingrad. Becoming preoccupied with capturing Stalingrad, Adolf Hitler diverted troops from the Baku oil fields, which otherwise could have been captured. Ultimately, he captured neither, and the German advance in the southwestern Soviet Union had been halted.

The war presented opportunities for Soviet expansion not only in Eastern Europe, but also to the Soviet Union's southwest, specifically Iran. After entering the war, Soviet armies occupied northern Iran, including "southern" Azerbaijan, from 1941 through 1946. The Soviets intended to stoke nationalism among Iranian Azerbaijanis by cultivating and exploiting the common ethnic and linguistic heritage of Soviet and Iranian Azeris. A concerted effort was made to present the Azerbaijan Republic to Iranian Azerbaijanis in the most positive terms and to represent Iranian and Soviet Azerbaijanis as one people, wrongfully divided against the will of both groups.

The Soviets hoped eventually to integrate "southern" (Iranian) Azerbaijan into "northern" (Soviet) Azerbaijan, once Azerbaijani nationalism broke out into open revolt against Iranian rule. While the Soviets worked diligently during this time to foster nationalism and emphasize the common heritage of the two groups of Azerbaijanis, they discovered that even a weak Iran was able to reassert Iranian authority quickly after the withdrawal of Soviet forces. The Soviet dream of unifying all Azerbaijanis under Soviet control would remain, but there would be no more real opportunities for such expansion. Nonetheless, the possibility of such expansion continued to be a real concern in the United States and it was used to legitimize an American military presence in the region.

As throughout the Soviet Union, education in Azerbaijan was emphasized. While the Russian language was certainly favored and essentially mandatory for those aspiring to be upwardly mobile, children could go to school that taught in Azerbaijani, Armenian, or Russian. Azerbaijani was taught as the second language in all Russian-language schools in the republic. Changes in the internal political climate, of course, determined the extent to which non-Russian language schools were tolerated. As the educational level of the general population increased, educational requirements were gradually raised. In 1959, the law required education through the eighth grade; after 1966, emphasis was shifted to universal secondary education. As a consequence, Azerbaijani literacy rates increased substantially, from 31.9 percent in 1927 to 97 percent in 1959.

The arts, like the Azerbaijani language, were encouraged in one sense and discouraged in another, because, like everything else, they were subjected to the Soviet political litmus tests. Standards for such tests were not always clear and occasionally changed capriciously. Nevertheless, traditional arts and those arts reflecting the culture and heritage of the Azerbaijani people were discouraged unless they meshed in some way with the Soviet political agenda. While Azerbaijani musical compositions perhaps have not demonstrated a quality comparable to Armenian and Georgian composers, Azerbaijanis can boast of an impressive literary tradition, even under Soviet rule.

A number of trends developed in Azerbaijan from the late 1950s through the 1970s. The population increased significantly, about 2.5 times more rapidly than in the Soviet Union as a whole. This phenomenon was not confined to the Azerbaijanis. The Muslim population in general was becoming a larger proportion of the total Soviet population. Such growth posed potentially serious political problems with respect to the continued Russian domination of the government, as well as for the military and future labor resources.

The relative youth of the Azerbaijani/Muslim populations meant that this population growth would be a long-term problem. Furthermore (and as in most Western nations), most of the population increase has appeared among Azerbaijanis who were less well educated and less affluent than the Armenian and Russian "elites." In particular, population increases in rural Azerbaijan caused tensions because there was insufficient land for all. While this was a period of relative economic growth, jobs in the cities were not being created fast enough to absorb the surplus rural population. Many were unwilling to move to the cities anyway, and they were surely unwilling to migrate to farmland in Kazakhstan or Siberia. Relatedly, the gap between the more affluent and better educated Armenians and Russians remained a source of ethnic animosity and conflict.

While the Azerbaijanis generally benefited from three decades of Soviet economic growth and the rising standards of living, during the Nikita Khrushchev and Leonid Brezhnev years, they clearly benefited less than did the Russians and Armenians in Azerbaijan. The Azerbaijan Republic as a whole prospered less than many, if not most, other Soviet republics. Despite progress in many areas, the Azerbaijani economy generally did not function well. In the 1970s, Geidar Aliyev, First Secretary of the Communist Party of Azerbaijan, detailed the systemic shortcomings of the Azerbaijan economy. These shortcomings were evident in the relatively low standard of living vis-à-vis other Soviet republics, the uneven levels of productivity, the consistent failure to meet production goals, and a poor distribution of doctors and medical facilities throughout the republic. Despite Aliyev's efforts to stimulate the Azerbaijani economy, the republic continued to fall behind.

Aliyev is the only Azerbaijani to have achieved political prominence in the post-World War II Soviet Union. Prior to being named First Secretary of the Azerbaijan Communist Party, Aliyev spent twenty-eight years in the KGB and headed the Azerbaijan political police from 1962 to 1969. His career prospered rapidly thereafter. He was appointed first secretary to resolve problems of corruption and a faltering economy.

Corruption has been a continuing problem in Azerbaijan and is probably linked to the passive resistance that Azerbaijanis have used in response to centralized Soviet rule. Aliyev apparently produced some results in this area. A number of people were sentenced to prison terms; and, in 1975, five factory and collective farm managers were sentenced to death for "gross corruption." Economic revitalization proved more difficult. Nevertheless, Yuri Andropov appointed Aliyev to the Soviet Politburo as first deputy premier of the council of ministers. His duties included working to revive the Soviet railroad industry and diplomatic missions to Syria. In November 1982, he had the distinction of becoming the first Azerbaijani to be named a full member of the Politburo. Although his nationality would prevent him from being a serious candidate for secretary general, Aliyev was a rising star who quite possibly could have become premier had Andropov lived. Aliyev's ties to Andropov, however, meant that he did not fit in with Mikhail Gorbachev's plans.

As the Soviet economy declined, nationalist sentiments grew in many republics. Ironically, Soviet policies fueled the nationalist resurgence. The prominent role of Russians in the Soviet Union's achievements and their near monopoly of top socio-economic and political positions directly conflicted with ethnic interests. Conflicts over increased independence from Moscow's central direction and over achieving higher status, greater access to the instruments of authority, and greater religious freedom were exacerbated by the Soviet emphasis on science, education, and the rights of workers and peasants, all of which increased awareness and raised expectations. But the most incendiary factor was continued economic decline.

The republics of Transcaucasia were not immune to renewed nationalist sentiments. As early as 1974, the National Unity Party of Armenia was demanding the unification of all Armenia, including not only Turkish Armenia, but also the Armenian enclaves in Azerbaijan, specifically Nagorno-Karabakh (Nagorno-Karabagh). While such demands were guaranteed to cause concern in Azerbaijan, nationalist activities there were more muted. This is ironic, given Armenia's initial acceptance of the Bolshevik Revolution and Azerbaijan's opposition. The tradition of passive resistance by Azerbaijanis was not conducive to the development of a strong national identity, but this fact does not imply that no nationalist sentiment or activity existed. There is speculation that the 1978 murders of a KGB general and the prime minister of Kyrgyzia were related to Azerbaijani nationalist activity. In any event, by 1980, Aliyev was warning the KGB about a potential resurgence of Islam and the need for vigilance in the republics bordering Islamic countries.

The 1980s were marked by economic stagnation and decline through Azerbaijan. For the first few years of Gorbachev's regime, *glasnost* and *perestroika* hardly penetrated Azerbaijan. The First Secretary of the Communist Party of Azerbaijan, Kamran Baghirov, was indifferent, if not opposed, to Gorbachev's reforms. In May 1988, Baghirov was replaced as first secretary by Abdulrahman Vazirov in an attempt to end the Nagorno-Karabakh (Nagorno-Karabagh) Autonomous Oblast (NKAO) insurgency and reinvigorate the Azerbaijani economy.

Vazirov's approach was relatively conservative, emphasizing the building of a stronger party apparatus through improved recruitment and training, the introduction of cadre exchanges, and the rotation of duties. Vazirov also undertook a number of economic programs in an attempt to increase investment and development and to improve housing. His programs addressed economic problems in the poorer rural and mountainous areas as well as in the cities, but his efforts were unsuccessful for two primary reasons. First, both the political and the economic problems facing Azerbaijan were structural. No facelifts achieved by personnel changes, party renewal, or new economic programs within the existing economic structure would erase such problems. Second, the Azerbaijanis were more interested in subordinating the upstart Armenians in the NKAO than in addressing the systemic problems of the republic.

Rather than Gorbachev's top-down process of reform, which began at the center and extended to the periphery, change in Azerbaijan began on the periphery, specifically in the Armenian NKAO. The impetus was a long-held desire by the Armenian majority of the oblast to unify with Armenia. Conflict with Armenia raised the Azerbaijanis' sense of identity and nationalism to heights not seen since the 1920 civil war.

As Soviet-style government disintegrated in other republics, it survived in Azerbaijan largely because independent forces were unable to unify and organize sufficiently to challenge the regime. This was so primarily because the NKAO-Armenian problem consistently prevented independence activists from focusing on the organization and program development needed to challenge the entrenched Communist Party. An additional distraction was the desire among some activists to reestablish ties and improve relations with ''southern'' (Iranian) Azerbaijan. While this might have been an appropriate ultimate objective for an Azerbaijan that had reformed and reestablished its government, it was dysfunctional for Azerbaijanis struggling with a collapsing political and economic system and beset with intractable and violent ethnic conflict.

While long-standing religious and cultural ties with Armenia no doubt constituted part of the NKAO drive for union with Armenia, it would be a mistake to conclude that this development was a consequence of incitement by the Armenian Republic. On the contrary, the impetus seems to have been more directly a consequence of the Azerbaijanis' having ignored the cultural and economic interests of the Armenian minority, including making adequate provision for Armenian education.

Historically, Azerbaijani ministries had ignored specifically Armenian interests, underinvested in the NKAO economy, subordinated local enterprises to the interests and control of the economies of Baku and other cities outside the oblast, and done little to establish cultural ties between the oblast and the rest of the Azerbaijan Republic. NKAO Armenians had been raising these objections without meaningful results for three decades. In the face of such non-responsiveness NKAO Armenians established economic ties with the Armenian Republic—an action that put the oblast in conflict with Azerbaijan's state economic plan. In effect, economic unification with Armenia had taken place even if a political union could not.

Despite the indigenous roots of the NKAO uprising, Azerbaijanis saw the Republic of Armenia as an instigator. As tensions between the two republics mounted, fear spread that Azerbaijanis in Armenia would be persecuted. Azerbaijanis in Azerbaijan took the offensive against the Armenian minority, firing Armenian workers, expelling them from their homes, and conducting armed attacks against them. Anti-Armenian violence spread throughout Azerbaijan. In January 1989, Moscow established a "separate government administration" for the NKAO headed by Arkadiy Volskii. Although too little and too late, the Volskii Commission temporarily eased tensions. While the brief breathing period was not used constructively to come up with a negotiated settlement, many of the Azerbaijani government officials and Communist Party officials who had contributed to the disruptions and violence of 1988 were fired, demoted, or transferred.

In March 1989, approximately two dozen intellectuals met to form the Azerbaijani Popular Front (APF), an organization of individuals rather than a coalition of organizations. Despite differing objectives and strategies, all agreed on rejecting Armenian claims and supporting the maintenance of Azerbaijan's territorial integrity. With respect to the Soviet Union, they recommended greater political and economic independence within the context of a federal structure or commonwealth rather than complete independence. Within this structure, the APF called for sovereignty over the entire republic, including the NKAO and the Nakhchivan (Nakhichevan) Autonomous Soviet Socialist Republic (ASSR), as well as complete control over the republic's natural resources, politics, economics, and culture.

For months, the APF remained a group of intellectuals with neither official status nor a mass following. Its singular appeal centered on anti-Armenianism, a problem that became more acute after the fall of 1989 when some 200,000 Azerbaijani refugees arrived from Armenia and the NKAO. Since Azerbaijanis were not particularly interested in political reform and since these refugees tended to be very activist and vocal, emphasizing anti-Armenianism became the quickest way to build some semblance of mass appeal. The Azerbaijani government's unwillingness to adopt the APF's anti-Armenian agenda resulted in a series of strikes, including a transportation strike aimed at blocking the shipment of supplies to both Armenia and the NKAO. These strikes were sufficiently successful that the government granted several concessions to the APF, including abolishing the Volskii Commission and drafting laws for the political and economic sovereignty of Azerbaijan.

With strikes continuing and a crisis atmosphere developing, negotiations between the APF leadership and the Communist Party finally resulted in legal recognition for the APF. By September 1989, Azerbaijan had drafted a law on sovereignty that included many APF demands. The law proclaimed Azerbaijan an independent nation belonging to a federation of Soviet nations. As such, Soviet law was invalid if it conflicted with Azerbaijani law; the Soviet federation had no role in addressing problems internal to Azerbaijan, which was sovereign over all of the republic's territories, including the NKAO and the Nakhchivan (Nakhichevan) ASSR. Azerbaijan's borders could not be changed without the consent of the Azerbaijani people, and the republic had authority to declare martial law to deal with an internal problem.

For Azerbaijanis, the conflict over the NKAO could now be settled by force of arms, if necessary. With key APF demands enacted into law, the strikes and railway blockade should have ended, but the APF's leadership was too weak to control the forces it had unleashed. Armenians redoubled their determination to take control of the NKAO. By November, the central Soviet government was attempting in effect to wash its hands of the whole problem. The Volskii Commission was dissolved, and administrative control of the NKAO was turned over to a republic-level committee consisting mainly of ethnic Azerbaijani's and appointed by the presidium of the Azerbaijan Supreme Soviet. Security responsibilities for the NKAO were also turned over to Azerbaijani authorities. Azerbaijanis saw this as a restoration of Azerbaijani sovereignty.

Armenia, in conjunction with Armenian representatives from the NKAO, responded by proclaiming the unification of the NKAO with Armenia. Armenia and Azerbaijan were effectively at war, as evidenced by the ensuing violence. In Baku, there were violent attacks on and forced expulsions of Armenians despite their having played no role in the NKAO conflict; Baku's Armenians were simply convenient targets. As the Azerbaijan government's paralysis became obvious (the so-called sovereignty law notwithstanding), Moscow declared martial law and dispatched Soviet military units on January 19, 1990, to impose order. For whatever reason, the martial law was not imposed until all Baku's Armenians had either fled, been deported, or were killed.

Although having faded from the media's eye, the Armenian-Azerbaijani situation has not improved since the final collapse of the Soviet Union and of Soviet-style government in both Armenia and Azerbaijan. A number of truces have been negotiated, only to break down; the toll of deaths mounts daily. In September 1992, Armenia requested a United Nations peace-keeping mission. Tragically, this conflict quite probably could have been avoided if Lenin's objective of having the boundaries of Soviet republics drawn more in accordance with ethnic distributions had succeeded; that is, if Nakhchivan (Nakhichevan) and Nagorno-Karabakh (Nagorno-Karabagh) had been included in the Republic of Armenia in 1923.

The widespread violence resulting from Azerbaijani opposition to Armenian demands had two contradictory effects. First, Azerbaijan became one of the first republics to mobilize independent political forces and the first to cause the collapse, even if a temporary one, of a Stalinist Communist party system. To restore Soviet authority, Gorbachev ordered a massive intervention by Soviet troops in Baku. The ensuing oppression within the context of an intensifying Armenian-Azerbaijani conflict resulted in Azerbaijan's being one of the last republics finally to abandon the Soviet system of governance.

Predicting the future in such volatile situations is always dangerous. Neither republic can afford to continue this conflict. Both Azerbaijan and Armenia are small, impoverished, and living in the shadows of three former giants with past histories of empire-building. Armenia can no longer count on Russian protection against Turkish intervention, and the Turks are unlikely to sit idly by as Armenia attempts to unify the Armenian people. Azerbaijan's position is somewhat better, in that its traditional enemies, Armenia and Georgia, are relatively small and, in the case of Georgia, torn by violent internal strife. The current situation in all three republics almost certainly precludes the resurrection of a Transcaucasian Federation.

In the face of the historic repression of Azerbaijanis and other national minorities in Iran, renewed political instability in Iran could result in nationalistic movements in ''northern'' and ''southern'' Azerbaijan to unify both regions into one independent nation. While this possibility may have been enhanced somewhat by the Soviet occupation of Iranian Azerbaijan during World War II, the facts that greater Azerbaijan never was a unified political entity and that there has been relatively complete separation of the two regions since 1928 would tend to diminish the probability of unification.

Another question is whether a unified Azerbaijan would be viable as a nation. It would be a nation of perhaps 20,000,000 people with a variety of natural resources, an industrial base, arable land, and established institutions of higher education. Key impediments, however, include the facts that the area would still be landlocked (in the sense that the Caspian Sea does not empty into an ocean) and that neither Iran nor Russia is likely to have much interest in seeing a unified, independent Azerbaijan. Armenia's opposition to such a state would be absolute unless their territorial disputes had been settled. Finally, it should not be assumed that Russia, Turkey, and Iran have at last yielded their historical dreams of empire.

REFERENCE: Zev Katz, ed., *Handbook of Major Soviet Nationalities*, 1975; Walter Kolarz, *Russia and Her Colonies*, 1967; William Mandel, *Soviet but not Russian: The "Other" Peoples of the Soviet Union*, 1985; David B. Nissman, *The Soviet Union and Iranian Azerbaijan*, 1987; Mark Saroyan, "The 'Karabakh Syndrome' and Azerbaijani Politics," *Problems of Communism*, 34 (September–October 1990), 14–29; Tadeusz Swietochowski, *Russian Azerbaijan, 1905–1920*, 1985.

Samuel Freeman

AZERBAYDJAN. See AZERBAIJANI.

AZERBAYDJANIAN. See AZERBAIJANI.

AZERBAYDZHAN. See AZERBAIJANI.

AZERBAIDZHANIAN. See AZERBAIJANI.

AZERBAYJAN. See AZERBAIJANI.

AZERBAYJANIAN. See AZERBAIJANI.

AZERI. See AZERBAIJANI.

AZERI TATAR. See AZERBAIJANI.

AZERI TURK. See AZERBAIJANI.

AZERI TYURK. See AZERBAIJANI.

B

BACK COUNTRY TATAR. See ALTAI.

BADJUI. See BAJUI and TAJIK.

BADJUY. See BAJUI and TAJIK.

BADZHUI. See BAJUI and TAJIK.

BADZHUJTSY. See BAJUI, TAJIK, and PAMIR PEOPLES.

BADZHUVEDZH. See BAJUI, TAJIK, and PAMIR PEOPLES.

BADZHUY. See BAJUI and TAJIK.

BADZUWEDZH. See BAJUI, TAJIK, and PAMIR PEOPLES.

BAGAOLAL. See AVAR.

BAGAULAL. See AVAR.

BAGOLAL. See AVAR.

BAGULAL. The Bagulals, who call themselves the Kwantl Hekwa and who are also known as the Kwanadi, are one of the Andi-Didi* peoples who are now considered part of the larger Avar* community. Russians* sometimes refer to them as the Kvanadin or as the Bagulaly and Bagvalaly. Avars call them the Bagvalal. They are Sunni Muslim in religion. The Bagulal live along the Andi River in southwestern Daghestan, primarily in the Tsumandin Region and the Akhwakh Region. Bagulal identity is still highly divided among their own subgroups, with village loyalties and identities transcending generic group loy-

alties. Each village actually has its own recognizable dialect, although the two most prominent dialects are Bagulal and Tlisi. Although it is difficult to come up with current population estimates for the Bagulal, primarily because of their census designation with the Avars, demographers estimate that there are approximately 9,000 people who either consciously identify themselves as Bagulals or who are aware of their Bagulal ancestry. See AVAR.
REFERENCES: Shirin Akiner, *Islamic Peoples of the Soviet Union*, 1983; Ronald Wixman, *The Peoples of the USSR: An Ethnographic Handbook*, 1984.

BAGULALY. See BAGULAL.

BAGVALAL. See BAGULAL.

BAGVALALY. See BAGULAL.

BAIHA OSTIAK. See TURUKHAN SELKUP and SELKUP.

BAIHA OSTYAK. See TURUKHAN SELKUP and SELKUP.

BAIKAL BURIAT. See BAIKAL BURYAT and BURYAT.

BAIKAL BURYAT. The Baikal Buryats are a subgroup of the Buryat* people. They live west of Lake Baikal and are sometimes known as the Cis-Baikal people. See BURYAT.
REFERENCE: Ronald Wixman, *The Peoples of the USSR: An Ethnographic Handbook*, 1984.

BAIKAT. See KHAKASS.

BAIKHA OSTIAK. See TURUKHAN SELKUP and SELKUP.

BAIKHA OSTYAK. See TURUKHAN SELKUP and SELKUP.

BAIKOT. See KHAKASS.

BAIQAT. See KHAKASS.

BAIQOT. See KHAKASS.

BAISHA OSTIAK. See TURUKHAN SELKUP and SELKUP.

BAISHA OSTYAK. See TURUKHAN SELKUP and SELKUP.

BAJUI. The Bajui call themselves the Badjuvedj (Badzhuvedzh, Badzhuwedzh) and are an Ismaili Muslim group who today are considered part of the larger Tajik* ethnic community. More specifically, they are a subgroup of the Shugnan*, a Pamirian* people. See PAMIR PEOPLES or TAJIK.

REFERENCES: Shirin Akiner, *Islamic Peoples of the Soviet Union*, 1983; Ronald Wixman, *The Peoples of the USSR: An Ethnographic Handbook*, 1984.

BAJUY. See BAJUI and TAJIK.

BAKHSAN. See BALKAR and BAKSAN.

BAKHSANCHI. See BALKAR and BAKSAN.

BAKHSANCHILI. See BALKAR and BAKSAN.

BAKHSANCHY. See BALKAR and BAKSAN.

BAKHSANCHYLY. See BALKAR and BAKSAN.

BAKHSANLI. See BALKAR and BAKSAN.

BAKHSANLY. See BALKAR and BAKSAN.

BAKSAN. The Baksan, who call themselves the Bakhsanchi, are one of the subgroups of the Balkars*. They live along the Baksan River in the Kabardino-Balkar Autonomous Republic. See BALKAR.
REFERENCE: Ronald Wixman, *The Peoples of the USSR: An Ethnographic Handbook*, 1984.

BAKSANCHI. See BALKAR and BAKSAN.

BAKSANCHILI. See BALKAR and BAKSAN.

BAKSANCHY. See BALKAR and BAKSAN.

BAKSANCHYLY. See BALKAR and BAKSAN.

BAKSANLI. See BALKAR and BAKSAN.

BAKSANLY. See BALKAR and BAKSAN.

BAKU. See AZERBAIJANI.

BALKALAR. See BALKAR.

BALKAR. The Balkar are a relatively small ethnic group living in what used to be the Kabardino-Balkar Autonomous Soviet Socialist Republic in the former Soviet Union. More specifically, they reside along the northern slopes of the Caucasus Mountains. They call themselves the Malkari, and they have been referred to historically as the Taulu, Mallqarli, Malkarla, Balkalar, Balqar, Malkarlar, the Five Mountain Tatars, and the Five Mountain Societies of Kabarda. Russians* refer to them as the Balkary or Balkartsy. Historical ethnologists searching for Balkar origins suspect that they are descendants of a complex fusion of Hunni, Karachai*, Kypchak*, Khazar, Bulgarian, Alan, and Caucasic peoples. Specific theories have variously considered them Khazars who fled their homelands after the disintegration of the Khazar Khanate in the tenth and eleventh centuries, Volga Bulgarians driven into the North Caucasus by the Mongol* invasion of the fourteenth century, and indigenous Caucasus peoples who assimilated after contact with Turkic-speaking peoples. Their linguistic roots are both Persian* and Turkic. The Balkar language is closely related to Karachai, and they are both part of the Kypchak group of languages, which are in turn part of the Turkic division of the Uralic-Altaic linguistic family. The Balkar use Cyrillic-alphabet Karachai as their literary language. Ethnologists also divide the Balkar into five subgroups, each division of which is based on a geographical location. Those five groups are the Balkar (Malkar*) proper, Bizingi* (Byzungy), Chegem*, Kholam* (Khulam), and Baksan* (Urusbiev). In the 1989 census, Soviet demographers placed the Balkar population at 88,771 people.

Until the mid-eighteenth century, the Balkars were pastoral nomads who followed an animist religion in the Caucasus region. Crimean Tatars* and then Nogais* from the Kuban Basin introduced Islam among them in the eighteenth century. Few places in the world have been the scene of as much ethnic conflict as the northern Caucasus and, to escape marauding tribes, the Balkars gradually migrated to higher altitudes in the mountains, where they adopted less nomadic forms of farming and stock raising. During the years of the Shamil Revolt in Daghestan, between 1834 and 1858, the Balkar conversion to Islam accelerated dramatically. By the early twentieth century, most Balkars had become adherents of the Sunni faith. That conversion, however, was marginal at best. The Balkars retain strong elements of their indigenous animist traditions and are only sporadic in their mosque attendance.

Russian expansion into the Caucasus increased during the early nineteenth century, and, by 1827, they had come to control Balkaria, which at the time was under the domination of the Kabards*. At the time Russians referred to the Balkars as "Mountain Tatars" in order to distinguish them from the Kabards. During the last half of the nineteenth century, there was a large-scale immigration of ethnic Russians into Balkar territory. Large areas of Balkar pastoral land were converted to agriculture by the Russians. In the process, the Balkars were integrated even more deeply into a commercial farming economy. In 1921, after the Soviets had consolidated their power in the North Caucasus, they established the Balkar District as part of the Gorskaja Autonomous Soviet Socialist Republic, and, in 1922, this became part of the Kabardino-Balkar Autonomous Province. That became an autonomous republic in 1936.

The Balkar people underwent a severe population decline during World War II. As part of Josef Stalin's paranoia during the war, the Balkars were uprooted in 1943 and scattered throughout Central Asia and Kazakhstan. The forced relocation was disastrous, and large numbers of Balkar did not survive the move. The Soviet Union also dissolved the Balkar administrative district in the Kabardino-Balkar Autonomous Soviet Socialist Republic and refused any longer to identify the Balkar as a separate people. When the era of de-Stalinization began in 1956, the Soviet Union allowed the Balkar to return to the Caucasus, and their republic was re-established. Today there are still Balkar people scattered throughout Central Asia, although the majority are back in what has been called the Kabardino-Balkar Autonomous Republic since the fall of the Soviet Union in 1991. Most Balkars are farm workers on the large collectives in the region.

The disintegration of the Soviet Union and the heavy-handed ethnic policies of Soviet leaders over the years have produced an increasingly intense sense of ethnic identity among the Balkars. It is difficult for those feelings to find political expression, however, because Balkars constitute only 9 percent of the population of the Kabardino-Balkar Autonomous Republic. They are vastly outnumbered by Kabards and Russians. Because of that demographic reality, many Balkar leaders are opting for pan-Turkic nationalism. In 1991, Balkars joined the Assembly of Turkic Peoples, which consisted of Azerbaijanis*, Kumyks*, Nogais*, and Balkars. They work for cultural, economic, and political solidarity among Turkic peoples and for self-determination.

REFERENCES: William Allen and Paul Muratoff, *Caucasian Battlefields*, 1953; Alexandre Bennigsen, *The Evolution of the Muslim Nationalities of the USSR and Their Linguistic Problems*, 1961; Alexandre Bennigsen and S. Enders Wimbush, *Muslims of the Soviet Empire: A Guide*, 1986; *Current Digest*, 44 (March 11, 1992), 25; Alexsandr M. Nekrich, *The Punished Peoples*, 1978; N. A. Smirnov, *Islam and Russia*, 1956; Ronald Wixman, *The Peoples of the USSR: An Ethnographic Handbook*, 1984; Serge A. Zenkovsky, *Pan-Turkism and Islam in Russia*, 1960.

BALKARTSY. See BALKAR.

BALKHAR. See LAK.

BALKHAR. See BALKAR.

BALOCH. See BELUCHI.

BALQAR. See BALKAR.

BALTDEUTSCHE. See BALTIC GERMAN and GERMAN.

BALTIC GERMAN. The Baltic Germans, who call themselves the Baltdeutsche and are known to Russians* as the Baltiskie Nemtsy, first arrived along the coast of what are today Latvia and Estonia in the thirteenth century. They were Cru-

saders. During World War II, most of the Baltic Germans died in the fighting, were deported to Siberia, or returned with the German army to Germany in 1944 and 1945. Very few of them still live in their Baltic homeland. See GERMAN.
REFERENCE: Ronald Wixman, *Peoples of the USSR: An Ethnographic Handbook*, 1984.

BALTIC PEOPLE. The term "Baltics," or "Baltic peoples," is a generic linguistic term referring to people who speak Baltic languages, such as Latvians* and Lithuanians*. Estonians* are not included in this category because they speak a Finnic language. When the term is used in a geographic sense, however, it includes the Estonians.
REFERENCE: Ronald Wixman, *The Peoples of the USSR: An Ethnographic Handbook*, 1984.

BALTISKIE NEMTSY. See BALTIC GERMAN and GERMAN.

BALTO-FINN. The term "Balto-Finns" is a generic term referring collectively to the Finns*, Izhorans*, Karelians*, and Veps*.
REFERENCE: Ronald Wixman, *The Peoples of the USSR: An Ethnographic Handbook*, 1984.

BALTORUS. See BELARUSIAN.

BALTORUSIN. See BELARUSIAN.

BALTORUSSIAN. See BELARUSIAN.

BALTORUTHENIAN. See BELARUSIAN.

BALUCH. See BELUCHI.

BALUCHI. See BELUCHI.

BALUDJ. See BELUCHI.

BALUDJI. See BELUCHI.

BALUDZH. See BELUCHI.

BALUDZHI. See BELUCHI.

BALUJ. See BELUCHI.

BALUJI. See BELUCHI.

BAQSAN. See BAKSAN and BALKAR.

BAQSANCHI. See BAKSAN and BALKAR.

BAQSANCHILI. See BAKSAN and BALKAR.

BAQSANCHY. See BAKSAN and BALKAR.

BAQSANCHYLY. See BAKSAN and BALKAR.

BAQSANLI. See BAKSAN and BALKAR.

BAQSANLY. See BAKSAN and BALKAR.

BARABA TATAR. The Baraba Tatars, who are also known as the Barabinsk Tatars (Barabintsy or Barabinskije tatary to Russians*), are part of the larger collection of Siberian Tatars*. They call themselves the Paraba. Their traditional homeland was on the Baraba steppes. Islamic merchants converted them to the Sunni faith in the fourteenth and fifteenth centuries. Russians conquered the region in the late sixteenth century, and incoming Russian settlers drove the Baraba Tatars off the best lands. They resettled between the Om' and Tara rivers in the Novosibirsk Oblast of Russia. Until the nineteenth century, most of the Baraba Tatars were hunters and trappers, going after sable, fox, marten, ermine, bear, and wolf. When industrialization began to reach Siberia, some Baraba Tatars went to work in factories, tanneries, and sawmills. After the 1930s, most of the Baraba Tatars found themselves living and laboring on collective farms. They numbered approximately 8,000 people in the 1970s and were divided into several kinship clusters, including the Barama, Tara, Terena, Keleke, Longa, Lovei, and Kargan. Today the Baraba Tatars live in the Om' River valley and along its tributaries in the Baraba steppes, in the Barabinsk, Kuybyshev, Chanov, Kargatsk, and Khyshtov districts and in Severnyi Oblast of Novisibirsk. See TATAR.
REFERENCES: Shirin Akiner, *Islamic Peoples of the Soviet Union*, 1983; Alexandre Bennigsen and S. Enders Wimbush, *Muslims of the Soviet Empire: A Guide*, 1986.

BARABIN TATAR. See BARABA TATAR and TATAR.

BARABINSK TATAR. See BARABA TATAR and TATAR.

BARABINSKIJE TATARY. See BARABA TATAR and TATAR.

BARABINTSY. See BARABA TATAR and TATAR.

BARAMA. See BARABA TATAR.

BARBARI. See KHAZARA.

BARGU BURIAT. See BURYAT.

BARGU BURYAT. See BURYAT.

BARGUT. See BURYAT.

BARGUT BURYAT. See BURYAT.

BARTANG. The Bartang (Bartangi), who call themselves the Bartangidzh, are one of the Pamir* groups who today are classified with the Tajiks*. They are Ismaili Muslims and live along the Bartang River in the Gorno-Badakhshan Autonomous Oblast. See PAMIR PEOPLES and TAJIK.
REFERENCES: Shirin Akiner, Islamic Peoples of the Soviet Union, 1983; Ronald Wixman, Peoples of the USSR: An Ethnographic Handbook, 1984.

BARTANGIDZH. See TAJIK.

BASAGAR. See KYZYL and KHAKASS.

BASHGIRD. See BASHKIR.

BASHGURD. See BASHKIR.

BASHKIR. The Bashkir (Bashkord, Bashkurd, Bashgird, or Bashgurd), who call themselves the Bashkort (Bashkurt), are a Sunni Muslim ethnic group numbering more than 1,500,000 people. They are known to Russians* as the Bashkiry. The 1989 Soviet census placed their numbers at 1,449,462 people. Approximately 900,000 of them live in the Bashkir Autonomous Republic of what used to be the Soviet Union, and a growing number of Bashkirs have settled in the Tatar Autonomous Republic in recent years. Those Bashkir are overwhelmingly rural pastoralists who raise cattle, sheep, and horses. They are active in the production of various grains, sugar beets, feed corn, and potatoes as well. Approximately 500,000 more Bashkir live in the surrounding Chelyabinsk, Perm', Orenburg, Sverdlovsk, Kurgan, and Kuybyshev oblasts. Finally, there are perhaps 100,000 Bashkirs scattered widely throughout Kazakhstan, Uzbekistan, Tajikistan, Kyrgyzia, and Ukraine. Those Bashkirs living outside the Bashkir Autonomous Republic are more likely to be urban workers than the main body of Bashkirs. The region of Bashkiria has long been known for its oil resources, and although ethnic Russians and Tatars* dominate the work in the petroleum fields, small numbers of Bashkirs are employed there as well. The Bashkirs are also known as the best beekeepers in the former Soviet Union.
Soviet demographers and ethnologists long argued about the origins of the

Bashkirs, since they are so closely related linguistically to the Tatars; Bashkir and Tatar are mutually intelligible languages. Bashkir is a Kypchak* language, the northwest Turkic branch of the Altaic family. There are two distinct Bashkir dialects. The Kuvakan dialect is spoken in the northern, forested regions of Bashkiria, while the Yurmatin (Yurmatyn) dialect is spoken in the southern steppes. Because of those linguistic characteristics, as well as their physical similarity to Mongoloid peoples, ethnologists suspect that the Bashkirs first emerged as a self-conscious ethnic group in the sixteenth century when the process of ethnogenesis created them out of a mix of Tatar, Mongol*, Volga Bulgarian*, Oguz, Pechenegs, and Kypchak peoples. They were once considered extremely devout Sunni Muslims, loyal to the Hanafi theological school. The Bashkir capital city of Ufa today remains one of Russia's four Muslim *muftiyats*, or spiritual synods.

When Ivan the Terrible conquered the Tatar states around the Volga in the mid-sixteenth century, the Bashkirs were also affected, coming under Russian sovereignty in the process. Russians established a fort at Ufa in 1574, and similar military installations were soon placed in what is today Kuybyshev and Orenburg. Bashkir lands were seized, heavy taxes were imposed, and the Bashkirs descended into a state of abject poverty. They ended up working as virtual slaves in Russian-owned mines and estates. There were a number of rebellions against Russian authority, of which the largest was led by Salavat Yulai in 1773, but all of them were ruthlessly suppressed. Forced conversions to Christianity also occurred, although they were superficial at best.

Today the Bashkirs are in a state of increasing assimilation. Within the Bashkir Autonomous Republic, the Bashkirs are a small minority, vastly outnumbered by the ethnic Russians who began arriving in the region in large numbers during the late nineteenth century. During the 1920s, when Josef Stalin launched his collectivization schemes, there was intense resistance from the Bashkirs, and, during the civil wars and relocations that followed, the Bashkirs suffered a severe population loss. In self-defense, they aligned themselves more closely with the Tatars during the 1930s and began to assimilate into Tatar life. That process slowed during World War II and the postwar years, but today the Bashkir are also outnumbered by ethnic Tatars.

State policy has also helped to assimilate the Bashkirs. Most Bashkirs lived on 600 collectives and 150 state farms in 1990. The government has collectivized Bashkir farms, pastures, herds, and apiaries (beehives). Although traditional Bashkir patriarchal, extended families dominate local government on the collectives, the clan lifestyle is nevertheless slowly eroding. Bashkir children attend public schools where Russian is the only language of instruction. Only two out of three Bashkir even speak Bashkir as their native language; the others speak Tatar. In addition, more than 70 percent of the Bashkirs are fluent in Russian. Although the Bashkirs remain loyal to the Sunni Muslim faith, they are not as intense in their devotions as many other Muslim ethnic groups. State policy has outlawed polygamy and child marriage. Traditional religious ceremonies for marriage, birth, and death are still observed, but the Bashkirs are increasingly likely to eat pork and drink alcohol and less likely to attend mosque regularly, say their daily prayers, or embark on pilgrimages to special religious sites in Central Asia. Those Bashkirs living outside the Bashkir Autonomous Republic are even more likely to be affected by cultural and economic change. By no means have the Bashkirs become thoroughly, or even superficially, russified, but the forces of acculturation and assimilation are nevertheless at work on their identity.

Two other smaller Soviet groups have recently been classified as Bashkir peoples. The Teptyar* (Tepter or Teptiar) people first came to Bashkiria in the 1600s as descendants of mixed Tatar and Meshchera* groups. They were a highly influential group economically, dominating commercial traffic in Bashkiria and controlling an inordinate amount of land and wealth. By the 1700s, the Teptyar were widely perceived throughout the area as a privileged group. Over the years, they too adopted the Sunni Muslim faith and accepted the Bashkir language as their native tongue. But in spite of their religious and linguistic conversion, the Teptyar remained ethnically distinct because of their unique economic position. During the collectivization campaigns of the 1920s, the approximately 30,000 Teptyar lost much of their property, and, beginning in the 1940s, Soviet ethnologists no longer viewed them as a separate ethnic group. Nevertheless, there are still thousands of Bashkir-speaking people in Bashkiria who are aware of their Teptyar heritage.

The other Soviet ethnic group now classified with the Bashkirs is the Nagaibak*, who call themselves the Noghaibaq (Nogaibak). When large numbers of ethnic Russians began settling in Bashkiria, certain Bashkir groups became highly influenced by them economically and linguistically. Several thousand Sunni Muslim Bashkirs converted to the Russian Orthodox church. Although their language and culture was still overwhelmingly Bashkir, their religion was not, and they came to constitute a distinct ethnic community. Although Russian ethnologists still classify the Nagaibak as a Bashkir subgroup, the classification is a weak one because of the religious cleavage between the two peoples.

In 1917, when the Bolshevik Revolution erupted, the Bashkirs established their own national government at Orenburg in Russia, but it was short-lived. With the Bolshevik victory in 1919, they merged their government with that of the Bolsheviks. Eventually, the Soviets recognized the existence of Bashkir ethnicity with the creation of the Bashkir Autonomous Soviet Socialist Republic (ASSR), but overt expressions of Bashkir nationalism were ruthlessly suppressed. All of that changed with the *glasnost* policies of Mikhail Gorbachev in the 1980s. With so many other ethnic groups in the Soviet Union exerting themselves, the Bashkirs decided to do the same. In June 1990, the supreme soviet of the Bashkir ASSR adopted a draft constitution for what they called the Bashkorostan Republic. The constitution asserted Bashkir control over tax revenues, foreign currency exchange, and natural resources, and it claimed the right for Bashkiria to secede from the Soviet Union. But since ethnic Bashkirs constituted only 22 percent of the republic's population, the constitution encountered bitter opposition from ethnic Tatars and Russians who constituted the majority. The battle over ethnic sovereignty in the republic between Bashkirs, Tatars, and Russians continued after the demise of the Soviet Union in 1991.

REFERENCES: Edward Allworth, ed., *The Nationality Question in Soviet Central Asia*, 1973; Alexandre Bennigsen and S. Enders Wimbush, *Muslims of the Soviet Empire: A Guide*, 1986; *Current Digest*, 44 (March 25, 1992), 5–7, and (July 29, 1992), 29–30; Petr Dostal and Hans Knippenberg, "The Russification of Ethnic Minorities in the U.S.S.R.," *Soviet Geography*, 20 (1979), 197–218; A. A. Rorlich, "Islam Under Communism: Volga-Ural Muslims," *Central Asian Survey*, 1 (1982), 5–42; Ronald Wixman, "Territorial Russification and Linguistic Russianization in Some Soviet Republics," *Soviet Geography*, 22 (1981), 667–75; Ronald Wixman, *The Peoples of the USSR: An Ethnographic Handbook*, 1984.

BASHKIRY. See BASHKIR.

BASHKORD. See BASHKIR.

BASHKORT. See BASHKIR.

BASHKURD. See BASHKIR.

BASHKURT. See BASHKIR.

BATS. See BATSBI and GEORGIAN.

BATSAW. See BATSBI and GEORGIAN.

BATSBI. The Batsbi (Bats), who call themselves the Batsaw and have sometimes been known as the Tsova Tushin, are closely related linguistically to the Ingushes* and Chechens* but today are being almost completely assimilated by Georgians*. See GEORGIAN.

REFERENCE: Ronald Wixman, *Peoples of the USSR: An Ethnographic Handbook*, 1984.

BAYHA OSTIAK. See SELKUP.

BAYHA OSTYAK. See SELKUP.

BAYKAL BURIAT. See BURYAT.

BAYKAL BURYAT. See BURYAT.

BAYKAT. See KHAKASS.

BAYKHA OSTIAK. See SELKUP.

BAYKHA OSTYAK. See SELKUP.

BAYKOT. See KHAKASS.

BAYQAT. See KHAKASS.

BAYQOT. See KHAKASS.

BEJETA. See AVAR.

BEJETIN. See AVAR.

BELARUSIAN. The Belarusians—also known as White Russians, Baltorusins, Baltorussians, Belorussians, Baltoruthenians, Belorus, Belorusins, Beloruthenians, Byelorussians, White Ruthenians, and Krivichis—are a large ethnic nationality group in the former Soviet Union. The term "Krivichi" is an older designation for the Belarusians. Soviet ethnographers identify the Krivichi as a very old group of Eastern Slavs who, as late as the early 1900s, still maintained a rudimentary identity; today they have been assimilated into the larger Belarusian community. Other ancient eastern Slavic groups that evolved into the Belarusians included the Radzimichi, Dregovichi, and Viatichi. Today most of the more than ten million Belarusians live in the Belarus Republic, although there are substantial numbers of them in Lithuania, Ukraine, and Russia. In terms of topography, Belarus is marshy and swampy in its southern lowlands, drier and more elevated (because of the glacial moraines) in the north. The Western Dvina River in Belarusia drains into the Baltic Sea, and that transportation link has long given Belarus close ties with Lithuania and Latvia. Today, the Belarusian economy still maintains its traditional commitment to lumbering and growing potatoes. Since World War II, however, Belarus has also been one of the most rapidly industrializing sections of the Eastern Europe.

The Belarusian language is one of the Eastern Slavic languages, although distinct cleavages between Belarusians and Great Russian Slavs appeared somewhat later than did other Slavic divisions. There are four basic Belarusian dialects, three of which are mutually intelligible but have regional distinctions. These are known as southwestern Belarusian, northwestern Belarusian, and central Belarusian. The differences among the three regional dialects are quite small; literary Belarusian is based on the central dialect, which is spoken in the capital city of Minsk. The fourth Belarusian dialect is more distinct than the others and is spoken by a people known as the Poleshchuk*. They live in the Polesie swamps of southwestern Belarus and northwestern Ukraine. Because of the historically limited economic value of the swampy lowlands, the Poleshchuk have been relatively isolated, and their language is loaded with Ukrainian* words and elements. Within the Poleshchuk, there are identity differences between those who live in and around Pinsk, who call themselves the Pinchuki, and those who live in and around Brest, the Breshyki. Generally, the Belarusian language was a vernacular language confined largely to common people; the elites of the country spoke Russian*, Polish*, or Lithuanian*.

The Slavs are a diverse group of people who originated in Eurasia and slowly pushed into Eastern Europe during the Middle Ages. Around 400 A.D., they reached a frontier running from the Adriatic Sea to the Elbe River, at which point the Germans stalled further expansion west. Two-hundred years later, the Slavic fringe penetrated the Balkans. During the migration, the Slavic communities developed into many political, religious, and linguistic groups. The first groups of Slavs—such tribes as the Krivichi, Radzimichi, Dregovichi, and Viatichi—probably arrived in Belarus in the seventh century. By the ninth century, they had settled over a wide enough area that they had pushed ethnic Lithuanians toward the Baltic Sea. The region became part of the state of Kievan Rus' in the ninth century. What is today Belarus occupied the central western region of Kievan Russia. Like the other inhabitants of Kievan Russia, the Belarusians, then known as the Belaia Rus', accepted Christianity under Vladimir I in 988. At that time, the term "White Russians" came into use; the phrase indicated that the Belarusians paid no tribute at all, neither to the Tatars* in the east nor to the Lithuanians in the west. When the Mongol* invaders swept through Kiev in the fourteenth century, Kievan Russia was divided into three distinct areas: west Russia, south Russia, and northeast Russia. West Russia became known as Belarus, south Russia as Ukraine, and northeast Russia as Russia.

The Mongol invasion dramatically changed Belarusian life. In cultural self-defense against the Mongols, the Belarusians turned west and sought the protection of Lithuania, placing themselves in vassalage to their more powerful but, in the Belarusian mind at least, culturally inferior western neighbors. The Lithuanians accepted the cultural superiority of the Belarusians. Old Slavonic, which eventually evolved into Belarusian, became the official language of the Lithuano-Belarusian state, which was known as the Grand Duchy of Lithuania. Belarusia was part of Lithuania, and Belarusian evolved into the official language of the combined society.

In 1386, Jagiello, the Grand Duke of Lithuania, married Jadwiga, the queen of Poland, creating the Kingdom of Poland and Lithuania. Both countries were interested in a dynastic union as a means of improving their military position vis-à-vis the Teutonic Knights, who were expanding eastward out of German-speaking Europe. Jagiello became known as King Ladislaus II of the Kingdom of Poland and continued as Grand Duke of Lithuania. Gradually, over the years, Belarusians lost their special status. Land and wealth became increasingly concentrated in the hands of a Polish-Lithuanian elite, while Belarusians became confined largely to the lower classes. Polish replaced Belarusian as the official language. Polish culture, which was intensely Roman Catholic, permeated the western portions of Belarus, and the official pressure to convert was intense. Many Belarusians did convert to Roman Catholicism, but the cultural imperialism of the Poles also gave birth to a small but nevertheless intense Belarusian national movement. Those who refused to convert became more politically aware of their Belarusian identity. Finally, in the 1790s, when Poland was partitioned among Prussia, Russia, and Austria-Hungary, Belarusia formally became part of the Russian empire.

The Russian domination of other Slavic groups had always been a central feature of Slavic politics and culture. The Slavs never united because the values they shared—common origins, hatred of the Germans, fear of the Turks—never overcame the political, geographic, religious, and linguistic forces dividing them. By 1840, pan-Slavic nationalism had emerged in central and eastern Europe, but it foundered on multiple Slavic nationalisms. Eastern Slavs consisted of perhaps 25,000,000 Ukrainians, 3,000,000 Belarusians, and nearly 40,000,000 Great Russian Slavs. About 11,000,000 Poles and 7,000,000 Czechs and Slovaks* constituted the Western Slavs, while 3,000,000 Bulgarians*, 6,000,000 Serbs* and Croatians*, and more than 1,000,000 Slovenes made up the Southern Slavs. Each Slavic group possessed its own history and cultural identity, and the Czechs, Slovaks, Poles, Carpatho-Rusyns*, Ukrainians, Slovenes, and Croatians were all preoccupied with the Russians. They envisioned pan-Slavism as a loose confederation of independent subcultures, but what the Russians had in mind was an empire with the throne in Moscow. Other Slavs shuddered at the thought. Because of their relatively small numbers and geographical proximity to Russia, the Belarusians were unable to extract themselves from the shadow of the Great Russian Slavs. In 1840, Tsar Nicholas I forbade the use of the term "Belarusia" and renamed the region the North Western Territory. He also prohibited the use of Belarusian as a language of instruction in the public schools, campaigned to eliminate all Belarusian publications, and insisted that all individuals who, themselves or whose ancestors, had switched from Eastern Orthodoxy to Roman Catholicism under Polish influence return to the Orthodox faith.

The inability to establish a separate national identity and the domination by Russian Slavs were sources of deep resentment among the Belarusians. They felt economically exploited, since more than 54 percent of Belarusians were peasants in 1860. The economic and cultural pressure exploded into revolt in 1863, when Kostus' Kalinouski led more than 75,000 peasants against their Russian, Polish, and Belarusian lords. Kalinouski was captured and executed in 1864. In the process, he became a martyr to Belarusian nationalism and a cultural hero. Belarusian nationalism continued to develop, and, in 1902, students in St. Petersburg established the Belarusian Socialist Hramada, a group dedicated to the establishment of an independent Belarusian state as well as the creation of a socialist economy. With the advent of the Revolution of 1905, Belarusian nationalism surfaced immediately, in the form of Belarusian publications and student movements in Minsk. Belarusian poets like Ianka Kupala and Iakub Kolas wrote of the pain and suffering of the Belarusian past with great poignancy and of the Belarusian future with great hope.

Because of their geographical location and historical experience, the Belarusians have been divided among three religious traditions. Most Belarusians, like their Russian counterparts to the east, are Eastern Orthodox. Their proximity to Poles on the west has converted many Belarusians to Roman Catholicism. Finally, because of the presence of Ukrainians to the south, a good number of Belarusians are Uniate Catholics. The dominant religious tradition in Belarus is Eastern Orthodoxy.

Because of the dominance of the Great Russian Slavs over the Belarusians, Russian Orthodoxy became their religion as well, especially in the eastern reaches of Belarus. The Belarusian Orthodox Church had been organized in 1291 under Greek* jurisdiction, but, over the centuries, it had fallen under the control of the Russian patriarch in Moscow. That change had a weakening effect on Belarusian nationalism. In Western Europe, where Roman Catholicism predominated, religion and nationality were often distinct entities, but, in the East, the church was part of nationhood and the nation was an expression of the church. The Western dualism between church and state gave rise to the idea that all power did not rest in the state and that other segments of the society could criticize and even transcend the political establishment. In the East, a more authoritarian tradition developed. Since the patriarch was an agent of the state, the church could play no role in criticizing national politics. In terms of their religious loyalties, most Belarusians therefore looked to Moscow for leadership.

But there were Belarusians who fell under Polish, and therefore Roman Catholic, influence. Historically, Poles have been among the most devoutly Roman Catholic people in Eastern Europe. When Belarus became part of the larger Polish state in the sixteenth century, Roman Catholicism became an important, although still a minority, religion in Belarus.

During the nineteenth and twentieth centuries, Russia and then the Soviet Union sharpened the Polish sense of identity by relentlessly attacking the Roman Catholic church and the Polish language. During the seventeenth and eighteenth centuries, Russia looked upon Roman Catholicism in Poland as both a political threat and a cultural intrusion. After taking control of Poland in the 1790s, Russia tried in vain to restrict the church and suppress the Polish language. In 1864 and 1865, the tsar ordered that all teaching of religion in public schools be conducted in Russian; shortly thereafter, he ordered that Russian be used as the language of instruction in all public and parochial schools. Russian authorities injected their language into Roman Catholic liturgies. They outlawed crosses on Catholic churches, devotional processions, and parish temperance associations. They demanded prior approval of all clerical appointments, eliminated clerical visitation with parishioners, forbade the construction of new chapels or the repair of old ones, and censored all sermons. But instead of wiping out Roman Catholicism, Russian oppression succeeded only in making the church the premier symbol of Polish ethnicity.

Uniate Catholicism constituted the third element of Belarusian religious identity. In southern Belarusia, the people are still more likely to be Eastern Rite or Uniate Catholics than either Eastern Orthodox or Roman Catholic, primarily because of the influence of the Ukrainians there. Christianity first came to the Ukraine from Constantinople and the Byzantine Empire; it was adopted as a state religion by Vladimir the Great in 988. In the great schism between Roman and Eastern Christianity, the Ukrainians recognized the patriarch of Constantinople, not the pope, as their spiritual leader. They remained Eastern Orthodox until the fourteenth century, when Poland acquired control of Galicia in the western Ukraine and began to catholicize the population. More than two centuries later, in 1595, the Brest-Litovsk Union brought many Carpatho-Rusyns, Belarusians, and Ukrainians back into the Roman Catholic fold. Ukrainians and Belarusians living in what was then the Kingdom of Poland and Lithuania became the nucleus of today's Ukrainian Catholic Church. The pope left the Orthodox rite, complete with its Old Slavonic liturgy and ceremonies, in place, allowed communicants to receive both the bread and wine during the celebration of the Eucharist, and permitted priests to marry before their ordination. Many people in southern Belarus adopted the Eastern Rite (or Uniate) traditions of their Ukrainian neighbors.

In spite of the religious diversity in Belarus, Russian authorities barely tolerated any tendencies toward independence among Belarusians. Culturally, most Russians could not understand ethnic nationalism among Belarusians. As far as they were concerned, any Slav who adopted the Russian language and converted to Eastern Orthodoxy became a Russian, whether or not he was originally Belarusian, Ukrainian, or any other Slavic nationality. To them, a Belarusian is simply a Russian whose language has been vulgarized because of centuries of isolation from mainstream Russian culture. The idea of a distinct Ukrainian or Belarusian identity is silly to most Russians.

Not surprisingly, Russian policy over the centuries has aimed at incorporating the Belarusians into the body politic and cultural life of Russia. Under the tsars and the Bolsheviks, the government was extremely suspicious of distinct Belarusian religious identities. For centuries, Moscow opposed the building of Roman Catholic churches because most Latin, or Roman, Rite Catholics were foreigners. After Russia's acquisition of much of Poland in the 1790s, most Roman Catholics in Russia were Poles and Lithuanians. Moscow at first refused to receive a permanent representative of the Roman Catholic church in Russia, but eventually, the government decided at least to tolerate Catholics; most major cities around the country ended up having at least one Catholic church. The tsars were much less willing to tolerate Eastern Rite (Uniate) Catholics, since they perceived the Eastern Rite of the Ukrainians and Belarusians as a form of incipient, anti-Russian nationalism. During the reign of Nicholas I, whose motto was "Orthodoxy, Russianism, and Absolutism," the government severed the Belarusian Uniate connection with Rome. In 1839, the government voided the Brest-Litovsk Union and forcibly brought most Eastern Rite Catholics back into the fold of Russian Orthodoxy. Privately, of course, they retained their original loyalties. This pattern of pressure and persecution of Eastern Rite Catholics became the norm in nineteenth- and twentieth-century Belarus.

Moreover, the state would not tolerate any sense of independence among Belarusians who were loyal to the Eastern Orthodox tradition. In 1922, under the leadership of Metropolitan Melchizedek, the Minsk Council of Clergy and

Laity established the Belarusian Orthodox Church and declared their religious independence from the Russian Orthodox Church in Moscow. Neither the Russian Orthodox patriarch in Moscow nor Bolshevik officials tolerated the move for independence. Government secret police moved into Minsk, arrested most members of the Minsk Council of Clergy and Laity, and sentenced them to Siberian prisons, from which very few returned. When the German armies invaded Belarus in 1941, a number of Belarusian clerics tried again to create an independent Belarusian Orthodox Church. Russian troops reconquered Belarus in 1944, and another purge of those priests and ministers took place.

There was, of course, a similar reaction to Belarusian demands for political independence. During World War I, when Austro-Hungarian and German troops occupied Belarus and when the Bolshevik Revolution and subsequent civil war sent Russia into disarray, Belarusian nationalism emerged from the political shadows. Belarus proclaimed its independence on March 25, 1918. Its freedom was short-lived. In December 1918, Polish armies moved into western Belarus, while Russian troops occupied eastern Belarus. The Bolsheviks proved to be no more open-minded about Belarusian nationalism than the tsars had been. They treated Belarus as a Russian province. On January 1, 1919, the Soviet government announced the creation of the first Belorussian (Belarusian) Soviet Socialist Republic (BSSR). The borders of the BSSR included practically all ethnic Belarusians; so Belarusian nationalists felt that they had finally achieved their goals.

But their hopes were naive at best. Although the BSSR proclaimed its independence and sovereignty, Moscow ordered the First All-Belarusian Congress to unite the BSSR with Lithuania in a new state, to be known as Litbel. Four Belarusian provinces were absorbed by Moscow, and the last province (Minsk) became part of Litbel. The Belarusian Republic had been all but liquidated. Belarusian ethnic leaders protested loudly, but their complaints were to no avail; the Bolsheviks had dreams of expanding westward and incorporating Poland into the new Soviet state.

The Russian and Polish armies jockeyed for position for the next two years, hoping to secure control of Belarusian territory, and a similar diplomatic jockeying occurred as well. In 1921, with the Treaty of Riga, they formally divided Belarus between them. The treaty constituted a grave injustice to the Belarusian people. More than 40,000 square miles of western Belarusia became Polish territory, while the eastern territory was incorporated into the Russian Soviet Federated Socialist Republic. The center of Belarus, which included only the six districts of the Minsk region, now constituted the BSSR. No Belarusian representatives had been permitted at the treaty negotiations. The Soviet Union then proclaimed a second BSSR, and, at the end of 1922, the BSSR entered a formal union with the Russian, Ukrainian, and Transcaucasian Soviet Socialist republics.

For the next eighteen years, except for some minor territorial acquisitions from the Soviet Union, the BSSR retained this basic profile. Soviet troops occupied Belarusian soil, and a small minority of Russian Communists controlled the government of the BSSR. Russians organized the Belorussian Communist Party, appointed an ethnic Russian to head it, and then ruthlessly subjected the party to the control of the Russian Communist Party. Moscow had decided that, without constant Russian guidance and control, Belarusian nationalism would surface again and threaten the central control of Moscow. Belarusian nationalists deeply resented the stifling of their aspirations, but there was little they could do about it.

Between 1921 and 1928, Lenin's New Economic Policy (NEP) did serve to mollify many Belarusian ethnic leaders. The "Leninist Decree on Land" resulted in the distribution of more than two million acres of land to peasants in 1921. Moscow also responded to Belarusian requests for an expansion of the territory of the BSSR so that more ethnic Belarusians could be included in the republic. In 1924, the territory of the BSSR was expanded by the inclusion of the Gomel, Smolensk, and Vitebsk regions, which increased BSSR territory from 20,310 square miles to more than 43,000 square miles and increased the number of BSSR inhabitants from 1,500,000 to 4,172,000 people. In 1926, two more districts were added, bringing the BSSR population to more than five million people, of whom more than 80 percent were ethnic Belarusians. During the years of the New Economic Policy, Moscow also permitted a flowering of Belarusian ethnic culture. Belarusian leaders established the Institute of Belarusian Culture in 1921 to study Belarusian culture and history. Schools in which Belarusian was the language of instruction also began to appear. The Belarusian State University was likewise founded in 1921. The Belorussian Communist Party even made plans for "Belorussification," in which Belarusian became the official language of all public institutions in the BSSR. A Belarusian infantry division was established in 1927.

But with Lenin's death, NEP was doomed. Josef Stalin supported it as long as he was trying to consolidate his power, but, as soon as he had eliminated his political rivals, he ruthlessly implemented his schemes of industrialization and collectivization. Collectivization of the farms in the BSSR dramatically accelerated in 1930, even though there was considerable resistance from Belarusian peasants. Collectivization was not complete in Belarus until 1937. By that time, Belarusian peasants had suffered more than any other peasants except those of the Ukraine and southern Russia. Stalin deported approximately 15 percent of all Belarusian peasants to concentration camps east of the Ural Mountains where most of them died. Another 5 percent of the Belarusian population starved to death because all of their produce was taken by the state.

Stalin also turned his attention on Belarusian ethnic leaders, accusing them of trying to dismantle the Soviet state and ruthlessly liquidating them in purges. Stalin went after prominent Belarusian political figures and intellectuals. The victims included people like Vatslav Lastouski, Iazep Liosik, Stsiapan Nekrashevich, and Vladimir Picheta. By 1934, Belarusian nationalism had been all but destroyed. Stalin had become the sole ruler of Russia and Belarusia, as well as much of the rest of the Soviet Union. One Belarusian leader later commented that "Not a single man who had labored for the establishment of the Belarusian home under the Soviets in the 1920s was alive or free in 1939."

The Belarusians in eastern Poland did not fare too much better. Poland had secured the region with the Treaty of Riga of 1921. Although the treaty had guaranteed the rights to cultural self-determination of all ethnic groups, of whom Belarusians constituted nearly 80 percent of the population, the results were quite different. Belarusian politicians were harassed, and Poland made sure that Polish officials exercised the only real political power in the Belarusian region. Much Belarusian land was confiscated and redistributed to Polish, not Belarusian, peasants. Poland then promoted an active program of ethnic Polish colonization of western Belarusia. Within a few years 37 percent of all arable land and 90 percent of all forested land in western Belarusia fell into Polish hands, even though Poles constituted only 6 percent of the population. After 1923, the Polish government began to suppress Belarusian schools and insisted that Belarusian children either go to Polish schools or remain illiterate. Belarusian newspapers were suspended, Belarusian libraries and clubs were suppressed, and Belarusian Orthodox churches were closed.

In 1939, the Soviet Union and Germany signed the Non-Aggression Pact (Molotov-Ribbentrop Agreement), and one of its provisions allowed the Soviet Union to occupy western Belarus and eastern Poland. Western Belarus was then incorporated into the BSSR. During World War II, when the Nazi armies overran Belarus, the region came under German* control. That ended in 1944 with the return of the Soviet army. The Curzon Line was then established as the frontier between Belarus and Poland. World War II had been an unmitigated catastrophe for Belarus. Stalin immediately collectivized peasant farms in the Belarusian region that had been Polish territory before 1939, with the same disastrous results that had occurred earlier in the rest of Belarus. He then urged a vicious purge of all Belarusian nationalists, political leaders, and intellectuals in the area. When Germany invaded in June 1941, Stalin began to liquidate "Belarusian enemies of the state." Altogether, more than 300,000 Belarusians in what had been Poland were either killed or deported between September 1939 and July 1941.

Because the BSSR was on a direct route between Berlin and Moscow, it suffered from the German invasion in 1941. During the course of the war, three out of every four Belarusian towns and cities were completely destroyed. More than a million Belarusians died at the hands of the Germans, who were intent on slaughtering large numbers of Slavs and deported tens of thousands more for forced labor in western factories. Some Belarusians retreated to the forests and launched guerrilla warfare against the Germans. Stalin had another 1.5 million Belarusians evacuated east of the Volga River. More than three million people were left homeless as a result of the war. Belarus also lost more than half of its economic assets to the Germans during the war. When the Red Army reoccupied Belarus in 1944, Stalin simply began where he had left off in 1941. Once again, he turned on politicians and intellectuals—anyone who had, in his opinion or in the opinion of anyone else, cooperated with the Nazis. Purges, deportations, enslavement, and murder were the order of the day during the late 1940s and early 1950s. From top to bottom, officials in the Belorussian Communist Party were purged, and all were replaced by ethnic Russians.

Even after the horrors of the Stalin years, Soviet officials continued their campaign against Belarusian identity. The pressure eased somewhat during the Khrushchev years but then intensified during the Kosygin-Brezhnev era of the 1970s. Part of the notion of the "Soviet man," which became a popular idea in the 1970s, was that, as Soviet society moved steadily toward Communism, the people of the Soviet Union would have to abandon parochial national and ethnic identities in favor of a "Soviet identity." In the 1970s, the chief exponent of the "Soviet man" idea was Mikhail Suslov, the hard-line Communist Party ideologue. Suslov wanted to bring about what he called the "merger of nations" in the Soviet Union, and he was especially concerned with Belarus and Ukraine. Russification was most important there, Suslov believed, because the cultural merger of Russia, Belarus, and Ukraine would assure domination of the rest of the empire. Russification would strengthen the economy and reduce ethnic tensions in the Red Army. Russian continued to be the language of Belarusian public schools; it was also the language of Communist Party meetings and of the party bureaucracy in Belarus. Life became economically and politically difficult for Belarusian language publications. Suslov also insisted that, in all non-Russian republics, the first secretary of the Communist Party had to be a russified leader, while the second secretary had to be an ethnic Russian.

The process of russification seemed to go hand-in-hand with urbanization and industrialization for Belarusians. They had been exposed to Russian media for so long that the vast majority became bilingual in Russian and Belarusian. While Belarusians who lived in rural areas and worked on farms retained Belarusian as their primary tongue, increasing numbers of Belarusians living in cities and working in factories came to view Russian as their first language. As Belarus continued to urbanize in the 1970s and 1980s, these linguistic trends continued.

Attempts at russification seemed to have been the most successful in Belarus. For many years, Soviet ethnologists and Communist Party officials did not have to worry much about incipient political nationalism emerging in Belarus. Over the centuries, the Belarusian elites and intelligentsia had been russified, and the violent purges of the Stalin era had destroyed most dissident voices. The BSSR became the most russified of the non-Russian republics in the Soviet Union, even though Belarusians were surrounded by intense dissident nationalisms in Ukraine and the Baltics. By the 1980s, only 70 percent of Belarusians claimed Belarusian as their native language, while approximately 30 percent spoke Russian as their mother tongue. Belarusian was not taught in the public schools, and not a single teacher of Belarusian language and literature had graduated from college since World War II. Soviet officials therefore did not worry about Belarus, at least in terms of the problems of nationalism and dissidence. There had frequently been, of course, some signs of discontent, but these were usually not taken seriously. In 1980, for example, several Minsk university students organized a group known as the Belarusian Workshop to explore Belarusian folklore and literature. They had been inspired by Lech Wałesa's success with the Solidarity Movement in Poland. But suspicious Belarusian officials, led by Communist Party boss Efrem Sakalau, forced the group to disband in 1984.

The rise to power of Mikhail Gorbachev in the Soviet Union and his policies of *glasnost* and *perestroika* exposed the reality of Belarusian nationalism. The Belarusian Workshop of the Minsk students was not a political aberration. Resentment of Moscow was intense in Belarus. Economic life was steadily deteriorating, and a sense of helplessness about it permeated Belarus. The Chernobyl nuclear accident in 1986 only exacerbated matters. Because of incompetent management of the huge nuclear power plant, a catastrophic accident occurred in August 1986, scattering deadly radiation contamination across a wide area. Although the reactor was located in northern Ukraine, the contamination spread across the border into the BSSR. More than 2,000,000 people were exposed to the radiation, more than 800,000 of them children. By 1991, epidemiologists were already detecting unusually high rates of cancer and neurological disorders in the Belarusian population. Since management of the nuclear plants was a responsibility of the central government in Moscow, many Belarusians blamed high Soviet officials for the disaster and demanded autonomy. They also began to insist on the removal of all nuclear weapons from Belarusian soil.

In 1986, the Minsk students also organized the Talaka Historical-Cultural Association, with assistance from Lithuanian nationalists in Vilnius, Lithuania. Their purpose was to bring about a Belarusian national revival. In November 1987, more than 200 Belorussian students gathered in Yanka Kupala Square in Minsk to demand that Gorbachev and Communist Party officials reveal the truth about Stalin's genocidal campaign against the Belarusian people. The demonstration soon assumed all the trappings of a patriotic rally. One month later, representatives of thirty individual Belarusian groups held a conference in Minsk, where they pledged to campaign for constitutional protection of the Belarusian language.

The Belarusian movement gained momentum in 1988. Fueled by the boldness and growing success of the national movements in Lithuania, Latvia, and Estonia, Belarusian nationalists became more radical and outspoken. They held meetings and classes to teach Belarusian history and revived the red-on-white flag and the *Pahonya* coat of arms of pre-Soviet Belarus. They made much of the historic Belarusian ties to Poland and Lithuania while de-emphasizing the connections with the Russian Republic. In the summer of 1988, the Confederation of Belarusian Youth Associations, an umbrella organization, was established in Minsk. In June, Zyanon Paznyak, an archaeologist and historian, published an article describing a mass grave at Kuropaty on the outskirts of Minsk that contained more than 250,000 graves—victims of just one of Stalin's purges. The purges had annihilated university graduates, the intelligentsia, people with even marginally suspect political credentials, and individuals with any connection to Belarusian political activity. Stalin's henchmen had murdered priests—Roman Catholics and Russian Orthodox—and even ordinary people when it was necessary to fill their killing quotas. The article had a dramatic impact on the Belarusian national movement. The Belarusian Council of Ministers issued the "Resolution on Immortalizing the Memory of the Victims of the Mass Repressions of 1937–1941 at the Kuropaty Woods." Older Belarusians, led by the writer Vasil Bykau, joined with the youth groups and, in October 1988, established the anti-Stalinist group Martyrology of Belarusia and the *Adradzhenne* (Renewal) Belarusian Popular Front for *Perestroika*. They openly called for the development of Belarusian sovereignty, a commitment to human rights, and a Belarusian cultural revival. When Minsk officials violently broke up a public rally on October 30, 1988, public sympathy for the demonstrators intensified. Arkady Ruderman, a Belarusian filmmaker, had cameras at the demonstration, and he then produced a documentary about the entire incident, known as *Counter-Suit*. It won first prize at the Leningrad Film Festival of 1989.

In 1989, when Minsk officials refused to allow the Belarusian Youth Association to hold its second annual convention there, Lithuanian officials came to their assistance, providing a convention hall in Vilnius as well as access to printing presses and newspapers to advertise their meetings and point of view. At the convention, Belarusian historians condemned Pan-Slavism as a thinly veiled pretext to justify Russian domination and cultural russification. Belarusian political scientists justified their demand for sovereignty by pointing to Belarusian history and to its current status as an independent voting member of the United Nations. The group *Adradzhenne* promoted its own program, which included an expansion of democracy throughout the republic, the implementation of civil liberties, the protection of ethnic minorities in Belarus, freedom of religion and legalization of the banned Belarusian Catholic Church, the granting of state recognition to the Belarusian language, the legal creation of citizenship status in the republic, and a revival of Belarusian cultural and educational institutions.

Although *Adradzhenne* debated the question of declaring Belarusian independence at the 1989 meetings in Vilnius, it stopped short of doing so. Such a declaration of independence would wait another two years. Paznyak, who had come to be regarded as the voice of free Belarus ever since his 1988 article on the mass grave at Kurapaty, was elected president of *Adradzhenne*. *Adradzhenne* quickly evolved into a political party, and, in the winter elections of 1990, it almost captured control of the government in Minsk, even while doing poorly in rural areas of Belarus. The Communist Party in the urban areas of the BSSR was in trouble. In May 1990, *Adradzhenne* sent representatives to Kiev, where they met with ethnic nationalists from Ukraine, Latvia, Azerbaijan, Lithuania, and Uzbekistan. They formed an umbrella organization—the Union of Democratic Forces—to deal with the issues of sovereignty, nationalism, and independence.

In August 1991, during the events of the unsuccessful coup d'état against Gorbachev, the movement for Belarusian independence gained momentum. The Belarusian legislature formally protested the coup as an illegal "putsch." Nikolai Dementei, chairman of the BSSR Supreme Soviet, organized public protests at Lenin Square in Minsk and decided to continue the protests until the coup aborted. They also declared the independence of Belarus. The coup itself, along with the horrendous economic problems that had beset the Soviet Union, undermined centralized rule from Moscow. The Communist Party was dissolved several weeks after the coup, removing another dimension of centralized authority.

Gorbachev survived the coup, but his power was never the same. Five months after the failed coup d'état, the three republics of Russia, Ukraine, and Belarus signed an agreement creating a Commonwealth of Independent States, with the capital in Belarus at Minsk. Stanislav Shushkevich, the leader of Belarus, first carried the news to Gorbachev. At first, Gorbachev resisted the idea of the commonwealth, but centralized power in the Soviet Union ceased to exist and the Commonwealth of Independent States took its place, with Belarus as an independent nation within the commonwealth.

REFERENCES: Anthony Adamovich, *Opposition to Sovietization in Belorussian Literature, 1917–1957*, 1958; James Billington, *The Icon and the Axe: An Interpretive History of Russian Culture*, 1970; Robert Conquest, *The Great Terror: Stalin's Purges of the Thirties*, 1968; *Current Digest*, 41 (May 3, 1989), 27–28, and 43 (September 18, 1991), 24; Nadia Diuk and Adrian Karatnycky, *The Hidden Nations: The People Challenge the Soviet Union*, 1990; Jan T. Gross, *Revolution from Abroad: The Soviet Conquest of Poland's Western Ukraine and Western Belorussia*, 1988; Steven L. Guthier, "The Belorussians: National Identification and Assimilation, 1897–1970. Part I, 1897–1939," *Soviet Studies*, 29 (January 1977), 37–61; and "The Belorussians: National Identification and Assimilation, 1897–1970," *Soviet Studies*, 29 (April 1977), 270–83; Mikolaj Iwanow, "The Politics of Perestroika in the USSR and Byelorussian Nationalism," *Ukrainian Quarterly*, 48 (Summer 1992), 185–98; Ivan S. Lubachko, *Belorussia under Soviet Rule: 1917–1957*, 1972; David R. Marples, *Chernobyl and Nuclear Power*, 1986; Kathleen Mihalisko, "The Popular Movements in Belorussia and Baltic Influences," in Jan Arveds Trapan, ed., *Toward Independence: The Baltic Popular Movements*, 1990, pp. 123–34; Iurii Shcherbak, *Chernobyl: A Documentary Story*, 1989; Nicholas P. Vakar, *Belorussia: The Making of a Nation*, 1956; Roman Szporluk, "West Ukraine and West Belorussia: Historical Tradition, Social Communication, and Linguistic Assimilation," *Soviet Studies*, 31 (January 1979), 76–98.

BELARUSIAN TATAR. The Belarusian Tatars descended from the Golden Horde invaders who arrived in what was then the Grand Duchy of Lithuania between the fourteenth and the mid-sixteenth century. By the end of the 1500s, there were more than 200,000 Tatars* living there. They soon integrated into the surrounding Belarusian* communities, losing their native tongue but retaining their Muslim religion. The primary Tatar settlements in Belarusia were Hrodno, Minsk, Trakai, and Vilna. It was relatively easy for them to maintain their Islamic culture because of the close commercial relations between these Belarusian settlements and Muslim communities in the Near East. After the union between Poland and Lithuania in 1569, however, those contacts were severed. They came under considerable persecution from Polish* Catholics, who viewed Islam as an alien, anti-Christian religion. Tatar emigration from the region began, and after the end of the eighteenth century, when those parts of what had been the Grand Duchy of Lithuania switched from Polish to Russian hands, the numbers of Tatars steadily declined.

After World War I and the Russian Revolution, Western Belarusia came under Polish authority, while Eastern Belarusia became part of the Soviet Union. During World War II, Germans* and Russians* went after Tatar intellectuals; by 1945, virtually all of them had either been killed or deported. Most of Western Belarusia was re-incorporated into the Soviet Union, which meant that the surviving Tatars were either Lithuanian Tatars or Belarusian Tatars. Josef Stalin's anti-religious terrorism, however, had badly weakened the Tatar attachment to Islam in the Soviet Union. Since they had long since lost their native language, they gradually disappeared as an identifiable ethnic group. Still, there are people in Belarusia who know of their Tatar roots.

REFERENCE: Shirin Akiner, *Islamic Peoples of the Soviet Union*, 1983.

BELIY KALMUK. See ALTAI.

BELIY KALMYK. See ALTAI.

BELIY NOGAI. See NOGAI.

BELIY NOGAY. See NOGAI.

BELIY NOGHAI. See NOGAI.

BELIY NOGHAY. See NOGAI.

BELIY QALMUQ. See ALTAI.

BELIY QALMYQ. See ALTAI.

BELORUS. See BELARUSIAN.

BELORUSIN. See BELARUSIAN.

BELORUSSIAN. See BELARUSIAN.

BELORUTHENIAN. See BELARUSIAN.

BELTIR. The Beltir are of Tuvinian* extraction and today are classified as a Khakass* subgroup. They are concentrated on the middle and upper reaches of the Abakan River. See KHAKASS.

REFERENCE: Ronald Wixman, *The Peoples of the USSR: An Ethnographic Handbook*, 1984.

BELUCH. See BELUCHI.

BELUCHI. The Beluchis (Baluchi, Baloch, Baluch) are a Muslim people of Iranian origin who live in southeast Iran, southwest Pakistan, and the southwest corner of Afghanistan. Russians* call them the Beludzhi. Approximately 18,500 Beluchis (1979 census) live in the Turkmen Soviet Socialist Republic (SSR) and about 500 live in the Tajik SSR. The total world population of Beluchis is uncertain. Published figures differ wildly, due to the difficulty of enumerating nomads, the ambiguity in defining who is Beluchi, and politically motivated undercounts and overcounts. A median figure for Beluchis of all countries would be in the four to five million range. Soviet censuses put the Soviet Union's Beluchi population at 9,974 in 1926; 7,842 in 1959; 12,582 in 1970; 18,997 in 1979; and 29,091 in 1989.

The Beluchis' origins are equally elusive. They firmly believe that their ancestors came from Aleppo, in what is now Syria. Some Beluchi nationalists claim they are descended from the Chaldeans, while others claim Beluchi descent from an uncle of the Prophet Mohammed. Most scholars dismiss these theories. It is certain that Beluchis lived along the southern shore of the Caspian Sea in the early centuries of the Christian era and moved southeastward into their present wilderness homeland in the twelfth to the fourteenth centuries.

Most Beluchis are Sunni Muslims of the Hanafi rite, but a few in Pakistan follow the heretical Zikri sect, and a small number of Shi'ites are found among the Beluchis in the former Soviet Union. Like many other Muslim tribal peoples, the Beluchis practice an unorthodox Islam, incorporating many pre-Islamic elements. For example, the Beluchis pay particular attention to *pirs*, Sufi mystics who claim to be faith healers and clairvoyants. The Beluchis are a mixture of many races, for, in their travels, they came into contact with Persians*, Turks*, Kurds*, Pathans, Punjabis, Sindhis, and even African slaves. At various times, the Beluchis were at war with the empires of the Persians, Greeks*, Scythians, Arabs*, Afghans*, Sikhs and British*. None but the Soviets have ever been able to control them or even make them stay in one place. Despite their turbulent history, the Beluchis have clung to their distinctive culture and language.

Beluchi society is the product of the extremely harsh environment of mountainous southwest Asia. The land is barren and bleak (it has been compared to Mars and the moon); it pitches and rolls in jagged mountains and high plateaus, then descends into arid salt pans. Temperatures reach 120°F in the summer, but winter brings bitter, freezing weather. Few plants grow, except in scattered oases. This forbidding country can support only a meager population, thus accounting for the failure of the Beluchis to evolve any supra-tribal political or social organization. Without that, despite their ferocity, they have been at the mercy of better organized governments in Teheran, Karachi, Kabul, and Moscow.

Tribes inhabiting the most barren parts of Baluchistan are fully nomadic, but most Beluchis are semi-nomadic. They herd sheep and goats, as well as tending small, irrigated plots of drought-resistant barley and wheat. Those who cluster around reliable oases in Pakistan are more settled and have formulated a more complex, feudal social structure. Altogether, there are seventeen Beluchi tribes and hundreds of sub-tribes. They are heterogeneous and diverse, having adapted to varying geographic conditions and having been subject to different imperial powers. They are alike, though, in their strong allegiance to a hereditary tribal *sardar* (chief), whose authority is unquestioned.

The Beluchi language is classified as a western Indo-Iranian tongue and is related to Persian, Kurdish and Tajik*. There are many dialects of Beluchi. The Beluchis of the former Soviet Union speak the dialect of Khorasan. To complicate matters, the Beluchis have partly assimilated the Brahui* people, whose Dravidian language is not even in the Indo-European family, and various loan-words have found their way into Beluchi. In Soviet censuses, Brahuis are classified as Beluchis. There is no widely accepted Beluchi script. Previously, Persian was used as a literary language. Modern Beluchi nationalists have tried with little success to propagate an Arabic script for Beluchi. Soviet scholars have also tried to devise an alphabet for Beluchi, but again with disappointing results. Beluchi culture is preserved and transmitted by minstrels, who draw on a vast repertoire of folk songs, ballads, and historical epics recalling the great fifteenth-century invasions of India. Holidays, religious festivals, and marriage feasts are occasions for the Beluchis to remind themselves of past glories.

Only once, under the hero Nasir Khan (reigned 1750–1793), did the Beluchis unite to create a single, large, independent political unit, but they soon reverted to tribal warfare and could not, despite bitter resistance, ward off British penetration of the Sind and Punjab. By a series of treaties (1854, 1876, and 1879), eastern Baluchistan passed to British control, and an Anglo-Russian convention (1907) even recognized British suzerainty over what is now Iranian Baluchistan. The British allowed the Beluchis a great deal of internal autonomy, but, in the squeeze that characterized the "Great Game," some Beluchis left Sistan (Seistan), a region straddling the Iranian-Afghan border, and headed north to what was then called Russian Turkistan (now the Turkmen Republic). Most of them came from the town of Zaranj (also spelled Chahansur, Chakhansur), while others came from the southern Makran Hills.

By 1917, there were fewer than a thousand Beluchis in Turkistan, most of them in the oasis town of Mary (Merv) and Bayram Ali (Bairam Ali). More Beluchis joined them over the next few years, especially between 1923 and 1928. Reza Khan's (later Shah Reza Pahlavi) vicious Persian pacification campaigns against the Beluchis in the 1920s employed heavy artillery. By contrast, the Soviet Union enjoyed a reputation as a progressive state standing firmly against imperialism. Thus, all Soviet Beluchis are of recent standing; few, if any, have lived in what was the Soviet Union for more than a century.

The last wave of Beluchi nomads arrived in the Soviet Union just as Josef Stalin eliminated his rivals and celebrated his triumph at the fifteenth Party Congress. The Communist Party soon undertook a campaign to abolish Islam and to settle all nomadic people on collective farms. Beluchis, who once had raided freely into Iran and Afghanistan, now were told to become sedentary farmers, and were assigned to *kolkhozes* and *sovkhozes* in the districts of Iolatan', Turkmen-Kala, and Bayram Ali. Only 10 percent of Soviet Beluchis are classified as urban. Some Beluchi leaders disappeared in the early stages of collectivization; others fled to Afghanistan. Soviet Beluchis, constituting a mere one-half of one percent of all Beluchis in the world, were completely cut off from their relatives south of the border. They have strongly resisted cultural assimilation, however. Half have learned Turkmen* as a second language, since the state provides them education with instruction in Turkmen, but only 4 percent know Russian. It is different with the approximately 500 Beluchis who live to the east in the Tajik Republic, for they have married Tajiks and no longer speak Beluchi at all.

The small Beluchi population of the former Soviet Union so far has played no role in the nationalist ferment currently sweeping Soviet Central Asia, which is perhaps fortunate in view of the fact that nuclear-tipped SS–23 missiles are located in Bayram Ali. Nor have Beluchis been used as a Soviet or Russian cat's-paw to meddle in Afghan, Pakistani or Iranian politics. That possibility remains open for the future. Beluchi aspirations for a homeland, if fulfilled, would re-draw the map of southwest Asia. A pro-Russian Baluchistan, with ports on the Arabian Sea, might be an attractive prospect for Moscow some day.

REFERENCES: Alexandre Bennigsen and S. Enders Wimbush, *Muslims of the Soviet Empire: A Guide*, 1986; Selig S. Harrison, *In Afghanistan's Shadow: Baluch Nationalism and Soviet Temptations*, 1981; Sylvia A. Matheson, *The Tigers of Baluchistan*, 1967; William D. McCagg and Brian D. Silver, *Soviet Asian Ethnic Frontiers*, 1979; Robert G. Wirsing, *The Baluchis and the Pathans*, 1987.

Ross Marlay

BELUDJ. See BELUCHI.

BELUDJI. See BELUCHI.

BELUDZH. See BELUCHI.

BELUDZHI. See BELUCHI.

BELUJ. See BELUCHI.

BELUJI. See BELUCHI.

BELY. See ALTAI.

BELY KALMUK. See ALTAI.

BELY KALMYK. See ALTAI.

BELY NOGAI. See NOGAI.

BELY NOGAY. See NOGAI.

BELY NOGHAI. See NOGAI.

BELY NOGHAY. See NOGAI.

BELY QALMUK. See ALTAI.

BELY QALMYK. See ALTAI.

BELYY. See ALTAI.

BELYY NOGAI. See NOGAI.

BELYY NOGAY. See NOGAI.

BELYY NOGHAI. See NOGAI.

BELYY NOGHAY. See NOGAI.

BELYY QALMUK. See ALTAI.

BELYY QALMYK. See ALTAI.

BERBER. See KHAZARA and TAJIK.

BEREZOV. See KHANT.

BEREZOVTSY. See KHANT.

BERING ALEUTS. See ALEUT.

BESERAB. See MOLDOVAN.

BESERABIAN. See BESSARABIAN and MOLDOVAN.

BESERABIAN GERMAN. See GERMAN.

BESERJMANE. See BESERMEN.

BESERMEN. The Besermen are a small group of Sunni Muslims who live in the Glazovskiy and Balezinskiy rayons of the Udmurt Autonomous Republic. Most Russian* ethnologists assume that in ancient times they were a group of Tatars* who assimilated with the Udmurts*. Their primary language today is Udmurt, but it still contains a variety of Tatar words. Russians have classified

them as an Udmurt subgroup for the past sixty years. Russians refer to them as the Besermjane. See UDMURT.
REFERENCES: Shirin Akiner, *Islamic Peoples of the Soviet Union*, 1983; Ronald Wixman, *The Peoples of the USSR: An Ethnographic Handbook*, 1984.

BESERMIAN. See UDMURT and BESERMEN.

BESERMYAN. See UDMURT and BESERMEN.

BESHITL. See AVAR.

BESKESEK ABAZA. See ABAZA.

BESKESEK ABAZIN. See ABAZA.

BESKESEK ABAZINTSY. See ABAZA.

BESLENEI. The Beslenei today are considered to be an Adyghe* subgroup. Their identity as Beslenei is still very strong, almost tribal in its intensity, and much stronger than any sense of loyalty they have to the Adyghe. See ADYGHE.
REFERENCES: Alexandre Bennigsen and S. Enders Wimbush, *Muslims of the Soviet Empire: A Guide*, 1986; Ronald Wixman, *The Peoples of the USSR: An Ethnographic Handbook*, 1984.

BESLENEJ. See ADYGHE and CIRCASSIAN.

BESLENEY. See ADYGHE and CIRCASSIAN.

BESSARAB. See MOLDOVAN.

BESSARABIAN. The term Bessarabian is generally used by Romanians* to refer to Moldovans* living in what used to be the Soviet Union. The name is taken from Bessarabia, the geographical reference to that region. See MOLDOVAN.
REFERENCE: Ronald Wixman, *The Peoples of the USSR: An Ethnographic Handbook*, 1984.

BESSARABIAN GERMAN. Today there are only a handful of ethnic Germans* living in Moldova. They first arrived in the region in the 1700s when Catherine the Great was in power. World War II was their undoing in the Soviet Union. The vast majority of them were either killed in the fighting, slaughtered by Soviet soldiers and partisans who considered them pro-Hitler, or deported to Kazakhstan and Siberia. Most of those who survived joined the retreating German army in 1944 and headed for Germany. See GERMAN.

REFERENCE: Ronald Wixman, *The Peoples of the USSR: An Ethnographic Handbook*, 1984.

BESSERABIAN. See MOLDOVAN.

BESSERABIAN GERMAN. See BESSARABIAN GERMAN and GERMAN.

BESSARABIN. See MOLDOVAN.

BESSARABINTSY. See MOLDOVAN.

BEYENIN. See EVENK.

BEZENGI. See BALKAR.

BEZENGICHI. See BALKAR.

BEZENGICHILI. See BALKAR.

BEZENGILI. See BALKAR.

BEZHETA. See KAPUCHIN and AVAR.

BEZHETIN. See KAPUCHIN and AVAR.

BEZHETINTSY. See KAPUCHIN and AVAR.

BEZHTA. See KAPUCHIN and AVAR.

BEZHTIN. See KAPUCHIN and AVAR.

BEZHTLAS SUKOS. See KAPUCHIN and AVAR.

BIELIY KALMUK. See ALTAI.

BIELIY KALMYK. See ALTAI.

BIELIY NOGAI. See NOGAI.

BIELIY NOGAY. See NOGAI.

BIELIY NOGHAI. See NOGAI.

BIELIY NOGHAY. See NOGAI.

BIELIY QALMUQ. See ALTAI.

BIELIY QALMYQ. See ALTAI.

BIELORUS. See BELARUSIAN.

BIELORUSIN. See BELARUSIAN.

BIELORUSSIAN. See BELARUSIAN.

BIELORUTHENIAN. See BELARUSIAN.

BIELY KALMUK. See ALTAI.

BIELY KALMYK. See ALTAI.

BIELY NOGAI. See NOGAI.

BIELY NOGAY. See NOGAI.

BIELY NOGHAI. See NOGAI.

BIELY NOGHAY. See NOGAI.

BIELY QALMUQ. See ALTAI.

BIELY QALMYK. See ALTAI.

BIELYY KALMUK. See ALTAI.

BIELYY KALMYK. See ALTAI.

BIELYY NOGAI. See NOGAI.

BIELYY NOGAY. See NOGAI.

BIELYY NOGHAI. See NOGAI.

BIELYY NOGHAY. See NOGAI.

BIELYY QALMUQ. See ALTAI.

BIELYY QALMYK. See ALTAI.

BII KALMUK. See ALTAI.

BII KALMYK. See ALTAI.

BII QALMUQ. See ALTAI.

BII QALMYQ. See ALTAI.

BIRAR. See EVENK.

BIRARI. See EVENK.

BIRARY. See EVENK.

BIY KALMUK. See ALTAI.

BIY KALMYK. See ALTAI.

BIY QALMUQ. See ALTAI.

BIY QALMYQ. See ALTAI.

BIZINGI. The Bizingis, who call themselves the Bezengili or Byzyngyly, are a Balkar* subgroup. Today they are concentrated in the Cherek River Valley. See BALKAR.
REFERENCE: Ronald Wixman, *The Peoples of the USSR: An Ethnographic Handbook*, 1984.

BIZINGICHI. See BALKAR and BIZINGI.

BIZINGICHILI. See BALKAR and BIZINGI.

BIZINGILI. See BALKAR and BIZINGI.

BJEDUG. See ADYGHE and CIRCASSIAN.

BJEDUGH. See ADYGHE and CIRCASSIAN.

BJEDUKH. See ADYGHE and CIRCASSIAN.

BLACK KIRGIZ. See KYRGYZ.

BLACK KYRGHYZ. See KYRGYZ.

BLACK KYRGYZ. See KYRGYZ.

BLACK NOGAI. See NOGAI.

BLACK NOGAY. See NOGAI.

BLACK NOGHAI. See NOGAI.

BLACK NOGHAY. See NOGAI.

BLACK QIRGHIZ. See KYRGYZ.

BLACK QIRGIZ. See KYRGYZ.

BLACK QYRGYZ. See KYRGYZ.

BLACK SEA COSSACK. In 1775, the Russian* government officially dissolved the Zaporozhe Cossacks*. Many of them fled across the Danube River into Turkish-controlled territory; those who remained behind evolved into the Black Sea Cossacks. At the conclusion of the Russo-Turkish War of 1787–1791, when the tsar grew extremely suspicious of Black Sea Cossack connections with the Zaporozhe Cossacks across the Danube, they were relocated to the Kuban area, where they evolved into the Kuban Cossacks*. See COSSACK.
REFERENCES: Philip Longworth, *The Cossacks*, 1969; Ronald Wixman, *The Peoples of the USSR: An Ethnographic Handbook*, 1984.

BOHARAN. See BUKHARAN and UZBEK.

BOHARAN JEW. See CENTRAL ASIAN JEW and JEW.

BOHARLIK. See BUKHARAN and UZBEK.

BOHARLUK. See BUKHARAN and UZBEK.

BOHARLYK. See BUKHARAN and UZBEK.

BOIKI. The Boikis (Boiko, Boiky) today constitute a subgroup of the Carpatho-Rusyn* people. Historically, they have been closely related, culturally and religiously, with the Poles* and Slovaks*, and their religious loyalties have been as Uniates—Catholics loyal to the pope in Rome but who retain their own Byzantine/Slavic liturgies and have a married clergy. When the Lvov Oblast and the Ivano-Frankovsk Oblast were brought into the Soviet Union in 1945, the Boikis suffered the public loss of their religion when the church was abolished.

They became nominally Eastern Orthodox, but privately the Uniate faith survived among hundreds of thousands of Boikis. See CARPATHO-RUSYN.
REFERENCES: Alexander Bonkalo, *The Rusyns*, 1990; Paul Robert Magocsi, *The Rusyn-Ukrainians of Czechoslovakia*, 1983; Paul Robert Magocsi, *The Shaping of a National Identity: Subcarpathian Rus', 1848–1948*, 1979; Ronald Wixman, *The Peoples of the USSR: An Ethnographic Handbook*, 1984.

BOIKO. See BOIKI and CARPATHO-RUSYN.

BOIKY. See BOIKI and CARPATHO-RUSYN.

BOKHARAN. See BUKHARAN.

BOKHARAN JEW. See CENTRAL ASIAN JEW and JEW.

BOKHARLIK. See BUKHARAN and UZBEK.

BOKHARLUK. See BUKHARAN and UZBEK.

BOKHARLYK. See BUKHARAN and UZBEK.

BOLGAR. See CHUVASH, TATAR, and BULGARIAN.

BOLGARIAN. See BULGARIAN.

BOLGHAR. See CHUVASH, TATAR, and BULGARIAN.

BORDERLAND KALMUK. See ALTAI.

BORDERLAND KALMYK. See ALTAI.

BORDERLAND QALMUQ. See ALTAI.

BORDERLAND QALMYQ. See ALTAI.

BOSHA. The term ''Bosha'' (Boshin) has been used for years to refer to Gypsies* who abandoned the Romany language and began the long assimilation process with Armenians*. See GYPSY.
REFERENCE: Ronald Wixman, *The Peoples of the USSR: An Ethnographic Handbook*, 1984.

BOSHIN. See GYPSY.

BOSHINTSY. See BOSHA and GYPSY.

BOSTON. See ICHKILIK and KYRGYZ.

BOTLIG. The Botlig call themselves the Buikhatli. They are also known as the Botligh and the Botlikh. They are Sunni Muslims and are today classified as an Avar* subgroup. The Botlig live along the Andi River in southwestern Daghestan, primarily in Botlikh village and Miarsu village in the Botlikh Region. In fact, their identity is based more on a loyalty to their respective villages than on any larger Botlig consciousness. Although it is difficult to come up with current population estimates for the Botlig, primarily because of their census designation with the Avars, demographers estimate that there are approximately 4,000 people who either consciously identify themselves as Botligs or who are aware of their Botlig ancestry. See AVAR.
REFERENCES: Shirin Akiner, *Islamic Peoples of the Soviet Union*, 1983; Ronald Wixman, *The Peoples of the USSR: An Ethnographic Handbook*, 1984.

BOTLIGH. See BOTLIG and AVAR.

BOTLIKH. See BOTLIG and AVAR.

BOTLIKHTSY. See BOTLIG and AVAR.

BOYKI. See BOIKI.

BOYKO. See BOIKI.

BOYKU. See BOIKI.

BRAGUI. See BRAHUI.

BRAGUY. See BRAHUI.

BRAHUI. The Brahuis are a Sunni Muslim ethnic group of Dravidian extraction whose homeland is in South Asia, especially in Pakistan. During the early twentieth century, a small group of Brahuis came to the Soviet Union when the Beluchis* also migrated there. Since then, the Brahuis have all but disappeared into the larger Beluchi community. There are still a handful of Brahuis who speak the native language, and they live in the Mariy Oblast of the Turkmen Republic. Actually, most of the surviving Brahuis consider themselves to be members of the Brahui tribe of the Beluchi people.

REFERENCES: Shirin Akiner, *Islamic Peoples of the Soviet Union*, 1983; Ronald Wixman, *The Peoples of the USSR: An Ethnographic Handbook*, 1984.

BRESHYKI. See BELARUSIAN.

BRITISH. The 1989 census indicated that there were 636 British citizens living in the Soviet Union. Ever since the Bolshevik Revolution, some British expatriates wanted to be part of the Communist experiment and took up residence there. Others were business people interested in tapping into the Soviet market. Of the 636 British living in the Soviet Union in 1989, most were business people hoping to establish an economic foothold there.
REFERENCE: Raymond E. Zickel, ed., *Soviet Union: A Country Study*, 1991.

BUDIAN. See KARACHAI.

BUDUG. The Budugs are a Shiite Muslim group who live in Budukh village in the Konakhkend Rayon in the Azerbaijan Republic. They have been classified for the past several decades as a Shah Dagh* group, but they are distinguished from the Shah Daghs in that most of the Shah Dagh groups are Sunni Muslims. The Budugs' literary language is Azerbaijani*. Although it is difficult to come up with current population estimates for the Budugs, primarily because of their census designation with the Shah Daghs, demographers estimate that there are approximately 2,000 people who either consciously identify themselves as Budugs or who are aware of their Budug ancestry. See SHAH DAGH.
REFERENCES: Shirin Akiner, *Islamic Peoples of the Soviet Union*, 1983; Ronald Wixman, *The Peoples of the USSR: An Ethnographic Handbook*, 1984.

BUDUGH. See BUDUG and SHAH DAGH.

BUDUGTSY. See BUDUG and SHAH DAGH.

BUDUKH. See BUDUG and SHAH DAGH.

BUDUKHTSY. See BUDUG and SHAH DAGH.

BUGIAN. See BELARUSIAN and UKRAINIAN.

BUHTARMAN. See BUKHTARMAN and RUSSIAN.

BUINAKSK. See KUMYKS.

BUJAK. See NOGAI.

BUJAN. See BELARUSIAN and UKRAINIAN.

BUKHARAN. The Bukharans, who call themselves the Bukharlyks (Pukharlyks) and have also been known as Sarts, are a small group of several thousand people in the former Soviet Union. Russians* refer to them as the Bukhartsy. They are primarily located in Tobol'sk, Tara, Tyumen, and Astrakhan today. Their ancestors were Uzbek* merchants from Bukhara who established trading colonies in south central Russia and Siberia in the seventeenth century. They are Sunni Muslims in religion. The region known as Bukhara fell to the Turks* in the sixth century, to the Arabs* in the eighth century, and to the Iranians* in the tenth century, at which time it became a center of Persian culture. Its capital was the city of Bukhara, located today in the southern part of Uzbekistan. At the end of the tenth century, Bukhara came under foreign domination once again, this time that of the Karakhanids, but their rule was soon succeeded by that of Turks, Uzbeks, and others. The Khanate of Bukhara was founded in the sixteenth century. The nomadic Uzbek conquerers took control of the pastures and irrigated plains and pushed the indigenous peoples, mostly Tajiks*, into the mountains. Those Uzbeks established control over the economy and politics of Bukhara, becoming an extremely powerful elite, and those who expanded out into Russia in search of trade became the Bukharans. Early in the 1860s, Russia began its military expansion into Bukhara. The conquest was complete in 1868, when Amir Muzaffar Al-Din signed a peace treaty with the Russian governor-general of Turkistan. The amir retained his throne but only as a puppet. On October 6, 1920, the new Soviet Union abolished the Khanate of Bukhara and established the Bukharan People's Soviet Socialist Republic in its place. Over time, the Bukharans mingled and intermarried with local Siberian Tatar* groups, lost their native language, and became indistinguishable from the surrounding Tatar* groups. Nevertheless, there are still people in the region who are aware of their Bukharan ancestry.

REFERENCES: Stephen Becker, *Russia's Protectorates in Central Asia: Bukhara and Khiva, 1865–1924*, 1968; Alexandre Bennigsen and S. Enders Wimbush, *Muslims of the Soviet Empire: A Guide*, 1986; M. T. Holdsworth, *Turkestan in the Nineteenth Century: A Brief History of the Khanates of Bukhara, Kokand and Khiva*, 1959; Ronald Wixman, *The Peoples of the USSR: An Ethnographic Handbook*, 1984.

BUKHARAN JEW. See CENTRAL ASIAN JEW and JEW.

BUKHARLIK. See BUKHARAN.

BUKHARLUK. See BUKHARAN.

BUKHARLYK. See BUKHARAN.

BUKHARTSY. See BUKHARAN.

BUKHTARMAN. The Bukhtarman, who have also been known as the Kamenshchiks, are part of the larger Starozhily* group of ethnic Russians* who settled Siberia. They are Eastern Orthodox Old Believers who made their living as stonemasons. Today they live along the Bukhtarman River in southern Siberia. See RUSSIAN.
REFERENCE: Ronald Wixman, *The Peoples of the USSR: An Ethnographic Handbook,* 1984.

BULAGAT. The Bulagats are a Buryat* subgroup. They live primarily along the Angara River in southern Siberia. See BURYAT.
REFERENCE: Ronald Wixman, *The Peoples of the USSR: An Ethnographic Handbook,* 1984.

BULGAR. See BULGARIAN.

BULGAR. See CHUVASH.

BULGAR. See VOLGA TATAR.

BULGARIAN. The term ''Bulgarian'' refers to three peoples who have left their impression upon Russian and Soviet history. Two of these peoples known as Bulgarians no longer exist; nonetheless, the term ''Bulgarian'' can still refer to both a Turkic-speaking people of the Kuban-Azov region in early medieval times and to the Turkic-speaking people of the Volga region during the Middle Ages who established the first Muslim state in what is now the Commonwealth of Independent States (CIS) and who played a role in the ethnogenesis of the Chuvash*, Bashkirs*, and Volga Tatars*. ''Bulgarian'' also refers to a Slavic-speaking Orthodox Christian people from the southeastern Balkan peninsula who were important to the present territories of the CIS (chiefly in Moldova and Ukraine) in the eighteenth and nineteenth centuries. While these three historic peoples are very different in their languages, religions, and histories, their common name has revealed a common origin to most scholars.

The Great Bulgarians

References to a people known as Bulgars or Bulgarians began in the fifth century in Byzantine sources. These sources indicate that the Bulgarians were a Turkic* people, also known as Onogurs, who inhabited the steppe region between the Kuban River and the Sea of Azov, an area often referred to as Great Bulgaria. They were organized into a typical steppe polity and ruled by a khan, who broke off ties with the Hunnic empire and maintained relations with the Byzantines. In the mid-seventh century, following the death of their last powerful khan and threatened by the expansion of the Khazar khanate, the Bulgarians broke up into smaller tribal groups.

The Kuban Bulgarians

One group of these Bulgarians remained in the Kuban/Azov region and existed as a separate group known as the "Black Bulgars" in Byzantine and early Slavic sources. These remaining Bulgarians did not establish a strong political entity and were probably assimilated by succeeding groups of steppe peoples (Magyars*, Pechenegs, Polovtsy, etc.) by the eleventh century. They constitute the least-known branch of the proto-Bulgarians, and their connections with modern nationalities of the CIS is most tenuous. Some scholars assert that the remnants of the Black or Kuban Bulgarians may have retreated into the Caucasus, which explains in part the origins of the modern Turkic nationalities in the Caucasus known as the Karachais* and Balkars*. These now make up a population of 156,140 Karachais and 88,771 Balkars, residing mostly in the Karachai-Cherkess Autonomous District and the Kabardino-Balkar Autonomous Republic, respectively.

The Volga Bulgarians

Another group of Bulgarians migrated from the Kuban River north along the Volga and settled in the area south of the confluence of the Kama and Volga rivers, perhaps giving their name to the latter river. There they brought certain Finnic* tribes under their control and established a new state. The Volga Bulgarians (known as Bulghar in Arabic, Boulgaroi in Greek, and Bolgari or B'lgari in Slavic), while having a tributary relationship with the Khazar khan, nonetheless established a separate steppe polity under a *yiltuwar* or *alteber*, their own vassal ruler. Unlike the Khazars (whose leadership adopted Judaism and whose general population was of various confessions), the Volga Bulgarians adopted Islam and established their state along Islamic, as well as traditional Turkic, precepts. Islamization seems to have developed through the active trade in furs and other commodities that the Volga Bulgarians conducted with the Islamic world. By the early tenth century, the ruler of the Volga Bulgarians had adopted Islam. Muslim sources from that period indicate that the Volga Bulgarian state was the northernmost outpost of Islam. Within the area under their control, the Volga Bulgarians established a tribal state under the overall suzerainty of the *yiltuwar*. By the tenth century, the title of the Bulgar ruler had been changed to the Arab term "amir" in conjunction with the establishment of an alliance between the Volga Bulgarians and the Caliphate of Baghdad. With the fall of the Khazar Khanate in the tenth century, the amir of the Volga Bulgarians became an independent ruler.

Ethnically, the Volga Bulgarian state was diverse. Besides the Turkic Bulgarians, there were the Finnic Wisu (Veps*) and Burdas (Mordvinians*), Turkic Savash (Chuvash), Basdjirt (Bashkirs), and Polovtsy. A delicate set of power relationships existed between the Bulgarians and these peoples, due to the fact that the Bulgar amirate had features of both a nomadic steppe polity and a sedentary state, comprising urban, agrarian, and nomadic populations. The center of the Volga Bulgarian state, according to most sources, was a large trading center near the confluence of the Kama and Volga Rivers known as the Great Bulghar or Bolgary, reputedly located some sixty miles south of present-day Kazan. Great Bulghar became a trading crossroads between the tenth and fifteenth century, as reported by such travelers as Ibn Fadlan, Marco Polo, Piano di Carpini, and Ibn Battuta. Beyond Great Bulghar, little is known of other large settlements. Within their state, it seems that the Bulgarians were successful in spreading Islam among the Bashkirs, Chuvash, and Polovtsy, even though they did not have full political control over them. Between the late tenth century and the middle of the thirteenth century, the Volga Bulgarians vied with the Christianized east Slavic principalities for the allegiance of the Finnic tribes and the territories west of the Volga.

The dynamics of this rivalry were drastically altered by the Mongol* invasion of the 1240s. In the wake of the Mongol invasion, the power balance between the Volga Bulgarians and the Eastern Slavs was shattered. The Mongols invaded the Volga Bulgar state and destroyed the capital of Great Bulghar. The Rus' principalities that survived the onslaught or were rebuilt came under the suzerainty of the khanate of Kypchak or the Golden Horde. The khanate established its seat of power at the fortified town of Sarai on the lower Volga near the old Khazar center of Itil and the later town of Astrakhan. Only a minority of members of the Golden Horde were Mongols; the rank and file were mostly Turkic-speaking peoples, including Tatars, Polovtsy, *and* Bulgars. The town of Bulghar was rebuilt and flourished as part of the khanate of the Golden Horde until the end of the fourteenth century. At that time, it was destroyed either in the conquests of Tamerlane or in a raid by Russians*. The rise of the new Muslim center of Kazan and its khanate prevented the resettlement and reconstruction of Great Bulghar. During the period from the Mongol invasion in the 1240s to the destruction of the Kazan khanate by Ivan the Terrible in the 1550s, a process of ethnic assimilation and amalgamation brought an end to the Volga Bulgarians and the creation of the Kazan Tatars*, the Bashkirs, and the Chuvash peoples. The Volga Bulgarian population nonetheless played a role in the ethnogenesis of the Tatars, Bashkirs, and Chuvash. Although the Volga Bulgarians no longer exist today, Tatar intellectuals in the nineteenth century and Chuvash national leaders in the twentieth century have attempted to revive the name Bulgar as a national appellation. Both imperial Russian and Soviet authorities, however, suppressed any attempts to adopt this ancient name because it could be claimed by at least three different peoples of the Volga region. Its use was also discouraged because of the existence of yet another ethnic group known as Bulgarians in the nineteenth and twentieth century.

The Balkan or Slavic Bulgarians

This third group of Bulgarians was related to the Kuban and Volga Bulgarians in that they too lived in the Great Bulgaria of the Black Sea region of the early Middle Ages. This group separated from them around the seventh century, however, and had a very different development. With the breakup of Great Bulgaria, one group, under Khan Asparuch, moved west and south, later carving out a powerful state in the former Roman/Byzantine provinces of Moesia and

Thrace. There these Bulgarians brought recent Slavic settlers of that region under their sway and seriously challenged the Byzantine Empire for control of the Balkan Peninsula for over 300 years. The Turkic element of the Bulgarians began to assimilate with and be absorbed by the Slavic element of their khanate, so that, by the mid-ninth century, pagan Bulgarian khans were bearing the Slavic names of Malamir, Presijan, and Boris. By the tenth century, the old Turkic Bulgarian language had been supplanted by the new Slavonic Bulgarian to such an extent that the only remnants were some elements of vocabulary and grammar.

Under Khan Boris (852–889), the official Christianization of the Bulgarians was initiated. After some vacillation between Latin and Byzantine Christianity, Khan Boris opted for the latter. Missionaries from the exiled Byzantine Moravian mission of Cyril and Methodius brought the Slavonic liturgy and literary language to the Bulgarians, in the form of an alphabet based in part upon Cyrillic characters, named thus by the Greeks after the honored founder of the mission. In succeeding decades, cultural centers of Slavic Christianity such as Ohrid and Preslav arose in Bulgaria and provided translations of most major early Christian and Byzantine works from the Greek, for not only the Bulgarians but also the Kievan Rus' a century later.

The Christianized first Bulgarian Empire flourished and continued to challenge Byzantium for control of southeastern Europe until the eleventh century, when it was absorbed into the Byzantine Empire after a series of debilitating wars. Bulgaria reemerged as an empire in the thirteenth century and vied with Byzantium, the Latin principalities, and Serbia for predominance in the Balkans until the Turkish conquest in the late fourteenth century.

Due to the fact that they had developed a common religion and literary language, the Balkan Bulgarians and Kievan Rus' established significant ties in the medieval period, from the tenth through the fourteenth centuries. Initially, relations between Bulgarians and Russians were belligerent, as seen in the Rus' invasion of Bulgaria under the pagan Prince Sviatoslav in between 967 and 971, which weakened Bulgaria and left it open to Byzantine conquest. In the wake of that conquest, Bulgarian churchmen and leaders emigrated to the newly Christianized Kievan Rus' principalities. Bulgarian churchmen participated in the building of the Russian church and the development of Old Church Slavonic, which was initially based on the Slavic language as spoken in Bulgaria in the ninth and tenth century. The work of translation from Greek to Old Church Slavonic continued in Kiev and other centers in Rus' lands, with Bulgarians, as well as Greeks* and Rus', as translators. Some Bulgarian nobles, unable to reconcile themselves to Byzantine rule or fleeing internal civil wars, sometimes went into exile in Russian lands. For example, Ivan Asen spent his youth in exile in Russia, only to become the most brilliant tsar of the revived second Bulgarian empire with Russian aid.

Cultural ties flowered again in the late fourteenth century, as the second Bulgarian empire succumbed to the Ottoman conquest. Significant numbers of Bulgarians emigrated to Russia and participated in a monastic and literary revival there. Some of these Bulgarians were followers of Euthymius of Trnovo, the last Bulgarian patriarch and a leading exponent of the mystical quietistic movement known as hesychasm. Two Bulgarian émigrés became hierarchs in the Orthodox churches in Lithuania, Ukraine, and Muscovy. Cyprian Tsamblak, a Bulgarian monk who had spent his early years in monasteries at Kilifarevo, Constantinople, and Mount Athos, served as metropolitan of Kiev from 1375 to 1390, later becoming metropolitan of Moscow and all Russia between 1390 to 1406. His nephew, Gregory Tsamblak, served as a priest in Moldavia, Lithuania, and later as metropolitan of Kiev and Lithuania from 1415 to 1420.

These and other Bulgarian and South Slav exiles were instrumental in introducing new literary forms and styles to Russian Old Church Slavonic, a trend known as "the second South Slav influence" to distinguish it from the initial introduction of Old Church Slavonic in the tenth century. This "second South Slav influence" saw the revival of early south Slavic forms in Russian Old Church Slavonic and the development of ornamental formalism, a literary style developed by Byzantine, Bulgarian, and Serbian* writers who had been influenced by hesychasm. It was spread to Russia by South Slavic émigrés in the fifteenth century and remained the dominant literary style in Muscovy up to the seventeenth century.

During the period of Ottoman rule, from the fourteenth through the nineteenth centuries, significant numbers of Bulgarians emigrated to Russia, especially in the eighteenth and nineteenth centuries. Three factors played a role in this emigration. The first was the common religious and linguistic ties between Bulgarians and Russians, which promoted the sporadic emigration of Bulgarian clergy and others in search of aid and asylum in Russia. The second factor was the growth of a Balkan merchant class in the eighteenth century, which, although dominated by Greeks, included Bulgarians and other Balkan peoples; a number of Bulgarians therefore emigrated to the Russian Empire in search of commercial opportunities. The third and most significant factor was the Russo-Turkish wars of the eighteenth and nineteenth centuries, in which Bulgarian lands often became areas of military operations. The vagaries of war, revolt, and reprisal caused large-scale emigrations of Bulgarians. In particular, the Russo-Turkish Wars of 1769–1774, 1787–1791, 1806–1812, 1828, and the Crimean War (1853–1857) brought about the emigration of thousands of Bulgarians to the Danubian principalities of Moldavia and Wallachia (present-day Romania), Bessarabia (present-day Moldova), and the territories of New Russia (present-day Ukraine).

During those wars, Bulgarians participated in uprisings and volunteer military units in support of the Russian war efforts. In the Russo-Turkish War of 1769–1774, when Russian forces advanced into Bulgarian lands, hundreds of Bulgarians served in irregular volunteer units. Likewise, a number of Bulgarians served as irregular marines in *Slaviani* and *Albantsy* battalions attached to the Russian fleet operating in the Aegean. An abortive revolt in Vidin was crushed by the Turks in 1774, and hostilities ended with the signing of the treaty of Kutchuk Kainadji in the same year. In the wake of that war, many Bulgarians, fearing

Ottoman reprisals, emigrated to Wallachia, Moldavia, and Bessarabia. In the following Russo-Turkish wars of 1787–1791 and 1806–1812, Bulgarian volunteer units were again organized and served with Russian forces; in the latter war, a Bulgarian legion was organized under the command of the Greek officer Demetrios Vatikiotes. The Russo-Turkish war of 1828–1829 saw the organization of two volunteer units in Russian service. Other Bulgarian patriots, such as Andrei Deshev, Petur Ivanovich, Nikola Filipovsky, and Vasil Hadzi Vulkov, organized and led later insurrections between the Russo-Turkish wars in Bulgaria in 1841, 1842, 1843, 1847, 1849, and 1850. During the Crimean War, new volunteer units and uprisings were organized by Georgyi Rakovskii, a nephew of Mamarchev (who had led insurgent movements in Bulgaria in 1842) and by Filipovsky. After all these conflicts, as well as the sporadic uprisings in between the wars, many Bulgarian volunteers and rebels and their families moved to Russian-controlled territory or to the autonomous principalities of Moldavia and Wallachia.

During the Balkan crisis of 1875–1878, new Bulgarian formations were organized under Russian command, in particular the Bulgarian militia. The Russo-Turkish War of 1876–1878 brought autonomy to most of the territory of present-day Bulgaria, which eventually achieved its full independence in 1908. Because of the strong ties between Russia and Bulgaria over the centuries, the presence of a Bulgarian émigré community in Russia, and the Russian role in Bulgaria's independence, close relations between the two countries continued, in spite of diplomatic strains, in the years 1878–1914. Indeed, Russophilism among Bulgarians was probably the strongest among all the Slavic and Eastern European peoples outside of Russia, due especially to the important role played by Russia and by Bulgarian communities in Russia in the national revival of Bulgaria.

As mentioned above, some Bulgarians emigrated to Russia for economic opportunities, and the Bulgarian communities in Russia included not only agricultural colonies but significant merchant and crafts communities in such towns as Odessa and Kishinev. The Bulgarian national awakening in the nineteenth century was in part fostered by Bulgarians in Russia and by Russian Slavophiles. Among the Bulgarians in Russia who contributed to the Bulgarian national awakening were Vasil Aprilov and Nikolai Palauzov, wealthy émigrés in Odessa who founded the first Bulgarian school in Gabrovo in 1835. Other schools were later founded elsewhere in Bulgaria. As an example of the Russian contribution to the Bulgarian national renaissance, one of the first modern histories of Bulgaria was written by Iurii Venelin, the Russian scholar of Carpatho-Rusyn* origin, and published in Moscow in 1829. Venelin also compiled the first scholarly attempt at a modern Bulgarian grammar. Other Russian intellectuals like Nikolai Pogodin and Ivan Akaskov supported the development of Bulgarian historical and linguistic studies.

In trying to break away from Greek ecclesiastical and cultural domination in their homeland, the Bulgarians looked to Russia for ecclesiastical and educational support. Aprilov and other Bulgarians in Russia were able to convince the Russian imperial government to sponsor Bulgarian students for study in Russia. In 1840, the Russian Orthodox Theological Seminary in Odessa initiated a program of scholarships for such students. In time, the Russian government and organizations such as the Slavic Benevolent Society expanded scholarship opportunities for Bulgarians at other schools to such an extent that, between 1856 and 1876, nearly 500 Bulgarian students attended schools in Russia. Many more attended after the liberation of Bulgaria, making up the largest foreign student component in many Russian universities. Among the Russian-trained Bulgarians who contributed to the modern Bulgarian enlightenment were Anastasia Tosheva, who became headmistress of one of the first schools in Bulgaria, and Naiden Gerov, who organized new secondary schools in Bulgaria along Russian lines.

In many cases, however, these Bulgarian students did not adapt to the official ideologies of tsarism and pan-Slavism in Russia, but were drawn instead to the views of the Russian radical intellgentsia, especially populism and Marxism. It is significant that the Social Democratic Party of Bulgaria followed the same course of development as did its Russian counterpart. In the early 1900s, it too split into two factions, the broads and the narrows, that mirrored the Bolsheviks and Mensheviks of Russia.

Relations between Bulgaria and Russia were hostile in World War I, as a result of Bulgaria's joining the Central Powers. The Bulgarian defeat in the war and the paradigm of the Russian Revolution stimulated the rise of revolutionary movements, including a Bulgarian Communist Party that attempted a revolution in 1923. The failure of the Bulgarian Communist Party uprising led to the exile of several thousand Bulgarian Communists in the interwar period. In the 1920s the Bulgarians in Ukraine were organized into Bulgarian National Districts, the most important of which was the Vasil Kolarov District in Dniepropetrovsk Province, named after a Bulgarian Communist leader who had emigrated to the Soviet Union after a failed Communist putsch in Bulgaria. During the Axis occupation of Ukraine in 1941–1944, a significant number of Bulgarians were repatriated to Bulgaria. With the Soviet counter-offensive and advance, however, many of these Bulgarians resettled in Soviet Ukraine.

The Bulgarians who still inhabit the CIS and are officially recognized as Bulgarians are mostly the descendants of immigrants who came to the Russian Empire in the wake of the Russo-Turkish wars of the eighteenth and nineteenth centuries. By the end of the nineteenth century, the census recorded that there were 172,700 inhabitants who used Bulgarian as their mother tongue. Actually, Bulgarians in Russia were probably more numerous, as seen in later Soviet censuses. According to these, the number of Bulgarians was 111,200 in 1926, 113,000 in 1939, 324,200 in 1959, 351,200 in 1970, 361,100 in 1979, and 378,790 in 1989.

The sudden drop in numbers between 1926 and 1939, especially in light of later figures, is not hard to explain. The province of Bessarabia, which had a significant Bulgarian population, was part of the Russian Empire from 1878 until 1917, but was not part of the Soviet Union in the years between the Revolution and World

War II. It was annexed by the Soviet Union after World War II and became the Moldavian Soviet Republic and the Bilhorod Dnistrovsky area of the Ukrainian Soviet Socialist Republic. Of the 324,200 Bulgarians in the Soviet Union in 1959, 219,000 lived in Ukraine, over 70 percent in the Odessa district and the Trans-dniester area adjoining Moldova, while 61,652 lived in Moldova proper.

Today the Bulgarian settlements in the CIS continue to be found in the new successor states of Ukraine and Moldova. They are concentrated in the southern areas of Moldova and in the Transdniester, Odessa, Azov, Zaporozhie, and Dniepropetrovsk regions of Ukraine. The Bulgarians constitute one of the larger non-indigenous ethnic groups in the former Soviet Union. According to the 1989 Soviet census, 378,790 Bulgarians reside in the CIS. The overwhelming majority of Bulgarians outside of the CIS live in the Republic of Bulgaria, while the related Slavic Macedonians make up the majority population in the newly formed Macedonian Republic of Skopje. They are also found in sizable numbers in Australia, Canada, and the United States. As mentioned above, the Bulgarians speak a South Slavic language that has a literary form with many affinities to Russian. In the Balkans as well as in the CIS and elsewhere, the overwhelming majority of Bulgarians are Eastern Orthodox Christians with Muslim (Pomak) and Catholic minorities in Bulgaria proper, Turkey, and Greece. No doubt, many Bulgarians in the CIS, like other Balkan immigrants to Russia, have assimilated into the general Russian and Ukrainian population over the years. During the post-war era, the sovietized People's Republic of Bulgaria maintained probably the closest and most subservient relations with the Soviet Union, and, as such, was able to establish and maintain ties with the Bulgarians in the Soviet Union. With the fall of Communism in both Bulgaria and the Soviet Union and the rise of democratizing regimes, it will be interesting to follow the status of Bulgarian communities in the new Ukrainian and Moldovan republics and their relations with the new Bulgarian republic.

REFERENCES: On the Great Bulgarians, see I. Kafesoglu, *Origins of Bulgars*, 1986; David M. Lang, *The Bulgarians*, 1976; Gyula Moravcik, *Byzantinoturcica*, 1958; and Stephen Runciman, *A History of the First Bulgarian Empire*, 1930. For the Kuban or Black Bulgarians, see the works cited above, as well as John R. Dunlop, *The History of the Jewish Khazars*, 1954; *Istoriia Kabardino-Balkarskoi ASSR s drevneishikh istorii balkarskogo narodna*, 1961; K. O. Laipanov, *K istorii karachaevtsev i Balkartsev*, 1957; C. A. Maccartney, "On the Black Bulgars," *Byzantinische-neugriechische Jahrbucher*, 8 (1931). On the Bulgarians of the Volga, see the works above, as well as W. Barthold, "Bulghar," *The Encyclopedia of Islam*, 1913, vol. 1; M. Canard, "Ibn Fadlan chez les Bulgars de la Volga," *Annales de l'Institut d'Études Orientales de l'Université d'Alger*, 1958; R. G. Fakhrutdinov, *Ocherki poistorii Volzhskoi Bulgarii*, 1948; B. Grekov, "Vol-zhskie Bolgary v IX-X vekakh," *Istoricheskie Zapiski*, 14 (1954); I. Hrbek, "Bulghár," *The Encyclopedia of Islam*, 1960, vol. 1; C. G. Sergheraert, *Les Bulgares de la Volga et les Slaves du Danube*, 1939; A. P. Smirnov, *Volzhskie bulgary*, 1951; Zeki Validi Togan, "Ibn Fadlans Reisebericht," in *Abhandlungen für die Kunde des Morgenlandes*, 24 (1939). On the Balkan Bulgarians in Russia, consult A. Alekseev and I. Savenko, "Bulgarian-Soviet Fraternity," *International Affairs*, 7 (1967); R. P. Bartlett, *Human*

Capital: The Settlement of Foreigners in Russia, 1762–1804, 1979; James F. Clarke, "Russia and Bulgaria," *Journal of Central European Affairs*, 5 (1946); N. S. Derzhavin, "Bolgarskie kolonii v Rossii," *Sbornik za narodni umotvoreniia, naukai knizhnina*, 29 (1914), 1–259; *Iz istorii russko-bolgarskikh otnoshenii*, 1958; Walter Kolarz, *Russia and Her Colonies*, 1952; I. Snegarov, *Kulturni i politicheski vruzhki mezhdu Bulgariia i Russiia*, 1953; T. Stoianovich, "The Conquering Balkan Orthodox Merchant," *Journal of Economic History*, 20 (1960), 234–313, and "Russian Domination of the Balkans," in Taras Hunczak, ed., *Russian Imperialism from Ivan the Great to the Revolution*, 1974, 198–238, 352–62; B. H. Sumner, *Russia and the Balkans, 1870–1800*, 1937.

                                                                         Nicholas C. J. Pappas

BULGHAR. See BULGARIAN.

BULGHAR. See CHUVASH.

BULGHAR. See VOLGA TATAR.

BURGUT. See BURYAT.

BURIAT. See BURYAT.

BURYAT. The Buryats (Buriats), who have also been called Buryat Mongols, are a Mongol* people of Siberia. Many belong to the Lamaist branch of Buddhism. Their strategic importance far transcended their estimated population of 425,000, for they were considered potentially subversive by the former Soviet government. At the same time, they were also believed to be conduits for the spread of Russian* influence throughout Inner Asia, particularly to Mongolia and possibly even to Tibet. All past and present Imperial, Soviet, Russian, and post-Soviet policies toward the Buryats must be understood in this light. Buryatia itself has not been the prize. Cultivating and manipulating the Buryats has been a way to influence the huge but sparsely populated Mongolian People's Republic (MPR). Until recently, the MPR was kept on a very short leash, allowed less independence than any of the former Eastern European satellites, and was considered by some to be virtually a sixteenth republic of the former Soviet Union.

  Three administrative subdivisions of the Russian Federation are dedicated to the Buryats: the Buryat Autonomous Soviet Socialist Republic (BASSR, or Buryatia) and two lesser entities, the Ust'Orda Buryat National Okrug of Irkutsk Oblast and the Aga Buryat National Okrug of Chita Oblast. Buryatia, located east of Lake Baikal, occupies an area one-and-a-half times the size of Great Britain. Its low mountains are forested, but its valleys are open steppe. The climate is sharply continental, hot in summer but very cold in winter. Buryatia's location has strategic importance, for the Trans-Siberian Railroad runs around the southern end of Lake Baikal, less than a hundred miles from the Mongolian border.

  The Buryat language is a dialect of Mongolian but different enough from the standard Khalkha* Mongolian of the MPR so that speakers of the two dialects cannot really understand one another. There were formerly twelve sub-dialects of Buryat, corresponding to separate tribes, but these distinctions have now eroded; still, knowledge of five of those subdivisions—Bugalat, Khora*, Ekhirit*, Khongodor*, and Tabunut*—survives among the Buryats. Soviet census figures for Buryats are puzzling and contradictory. If accurate and not an artifact of incomplete counts or deliberate distortion, the census shows that Buryat population declined for sixty years but then turned around, moving from 285,000 in 1897 to 237,000 in 1926, 252,000 in 1959, 314,000 in 1970, 352,000 in 1979, and 421,682 in 1989. Since the Buryats are not known to have suffered deportation or mass killing during the Stalin years, the above figures may be due to nomadic movements, high infant mortality, drunkenness, or disease.

The population includes Buryatized sub-groups of 1) Tuvans (a Turkic tribe); 2) Tungus* (also called Evenks*, native Siberians); and 3) Karymy (half-Russian, half-Buryat). The Buryats have also assimilated the Sartol, Atagan, and Daur*— Mongol peoples who migrated from Mongolia. The only important distinction, though, is between Buryats living west of Lake Baikal (known as Irkutsk Buryats) and those living east of the great lake (the Transbaikal Buryats). The former are somewhat russified, while their eastern cousins remain culturally closer to other Mongols. For example, the western Buryats are mostly farmers, while the eastern Buryats are pastoralists. The western Buryats are more likely to have taken Russian* names, to be literate in Russian, to write Buryat with Cyrillic script, to live in Russian-style houses, and to speak Russian as a second language. The eastern (Transbaikal) Buryats are Buddhists, may write in the Mongolian script, keep camels, and live in yurts (round, portable Mongol tents made from felt).

Buryat society is based on the family, the clan, and the tribe. They were a peripheral "forest tribe" to Genghis Khan, whose military reorganization of Mongol society touched them only lightly. Nevertheless, Buryat culture has much in common with Mongol culture. Their favorite sports include wrestling, horse racing, and archery. Their historical epics consist of enormously long *uligers*, or poems. Marriages are exogamous and arranged.

The Buryat pastoral economy was based on sheep, horses, and cattle. Hence, their diet featured domesticated meat and milk products, supplemented by hunting and trapping. Whole tribes hunted together, sending beaters into the woods to flush game and reaping Siberian stags, reindeer, foxes, and wolves. Lake Baikal, a wonder of nature containing more fresh water than all the North American Great Lakes combined, also offered whitefish and seals.

The original Buryat religion was animistic shamanism, the belief that the world is permeated by good and bad spirits who can be propitiated through chants and rituals performed by shamans (witches). Lamaism (Tibetan Buddhism) spread north from Tibet to Mongolia, reaching the Buryats in the seventeenth century, at the very same time that Russians were bringing Eastern Orthodox Christianity from the west. The result is that among the western Buryats, about half are shamanist and half are Orthodox Christian, while the Buddhism of the Transbaikal Buryats is syncretically mixed with shamanism. Buryats are the most northerly people to accept the authority of the Dalai Lama. By the time of the first Russian contacts, Buryatia had evolved, like Tibet, into a theocracy, in which every family gave sons to the monkhood. The *datsans* (Buddhist monasteries) controlled much of the best land.

Russian explorers, trappers, and later settlers reached Lake Baikal in the 1600s. The territory and its people were taken into the Russian state by the Treaties of Nerchinsk (1689) and Kyakhta (1728), which delineated spheres of influence between tsarist Russia and Manchu* China. Typically, Soviet historians describe the russification of Buryats as "progressive" and the anti-Russian uprisings of 1695 and 1696 as "anti-feudal." Historically, Russian imperialism had a religious tone, and Buryats were sometimes forcibly baptized. Soon the Irkutsk Buryats took Russian names, began wearing Russian-style clothes, and abandoned nomadism for agriculture. They planted wheat, buckwheat, rye, and barley. Soon, too, Buryats were victimized by Russian land policies, including serfdom. Russians settled along Siberian riverbanks and around the shores of Lake Baikal, eventually outnumbering Buryats in the region. They even organized a special army, the Transbaikal Buryat Cossacks*, to guard the Mongolian border.

Buryat leaders were co-opted. Some intellectuals joined Russian political movements; while others promoted Buryat nationalism to preserve their unique culture. These conflicting tendencies brought about much foment and strife among Buryats in the twentieth century. When the Trans-Siberian Railroad reached Irkutsk in 1898, it seemed that Buryat culture might vanish entirely, especially since government officials gave Buryat land to Slavic immigrants. Buryat unrest between 1900 and 1905 greatly concerned the Russian government, but Buryats were not deterred, even by threats from General Aleksei Kuropatkin to destroy their society. Buryat "congresses" were held in Chita in 1905 to demand Buryat-language schools and genuine self-government.

Following these congresses, a prominent Buryat nationalist, Jamtsarano, drew attention to the Mongolian roots of Buryat culture. The Russian government, however, viewed Buryat nationalism with extreme suspicion, because, during the Russo-Japanese War (1904–1905), Japanese* agents spread a "pan-Mongol" ideology in an effort to lure Buryats away from allegiance to Russia. Russia lost the war and ceded certain Far Eastern territories to Japan, but a secret agreement in 1907, followed by a formal treaty in 1912, recognized Outer Mongolia as a Russian sphere of influence. Therefore, pan-Mongolism might now be used as a positive weapon to keep all Mongols in the Russian empire.

Buryats did not play an important role in the Russian civil war of 1918–1922, but Japanese military forays deep into Siberia revived Russian fears of Buryat disloyalty. To many Russians, all Orientals looked alike and were untrustworthy. To keep the Japanese at bay, the Bolsheviks used Buryats to make Mongolia the first Soviet satellite. Buryat radicals and Soviet agents promoted a Mongolian "revolution" in 1921, and a clique of Soviet Buryats actually ran Mongolia until 1928, dominating the indigenous Khalkhas. At times, the government of the MPR pursued pan-Mongol, not exclusively pro-Russian, policies.

In Soviet Buryatia, V. I. Lenin and Josef Stalin created the Buryat-Mongol Autonomous Soviet Socialist Republic (BMASSR) in 1923. Of course, it was a sub-unit of the Russian Federation of the Soviet Union, autonomous in name only. The first six years of Soviet power in Buryatia were relatively peaceful. Then, on May 27, 1929, the Party Central Committee decreed the "socialist re-organization" of Buryat agriculture. The subsequent collectivization and Buryat resistance was an unmitigated disaster for all parties. Buryats slaughtered their livestock rather than see them confiscated. Nomads were forcibly settled on collective cattle and sheep farms. Buryat hunters were made to live in what the Communist Party called "well-equipped hunting stations," and trappers were made to rear sable in captivity. Many Buryats fled to Mongolia, but things were no better there, for the Mongolian Communist Party's politburo was no less faithful in carrying out Stalin's wishes. Outright rebellion in the MPR in 1931 and 1932 forced Stalin to relent, but only because fresh Japanese aggression in Manchuria had raised the value of Mongolian loyalty.

Japanese encroachments fueled Stalin's suspicion of all Asians, especially since Japan in its propaganda often posed as a defender of Buddhists worldwide. The Communists accused Buryat lamas of sabotage and used that as a pretext to destroy monasteries and defrock monks in Buryatia and Mongolia. Buryats had already been removed from power in the MPR; now treason was found in the BMASSR as well. Mikhail Yerbanov, the Buryat party boss, was suddenly discovered to be a bourgeois nationalist and shot, along with fifty-three other leaders, on October 12, 1937. In two years, more than 10,000 Buryats were slaughtered—a time that Bur-yats still refer to as the era of "Red Barbarism." Then Stalin's government re-structured and diminished the territories of the BMASSR, transferring the eastern steppe to Chita Oblast and four western counties to Irkutsk Oblast. The Mongolian script was abolished and replaced by a Cyrillic alphabet. To further dilute the Bur-yat population, special privileges were decreed for Russian and Ukrainian* set-tlers. In 1943, the Stalin government dissolved the autonomous republic of a different Mongol people, the Kalmyks*, and scattered them around the Soviet Union, ostensibly for their collaboration with the axis powers. In 1944, the Soviet government incorporated the formerly Mongolian Tannu Tuva region of Buryat Mongolia as the Tuva Autonomous Oblast.

These bizarre and capricious territorial manipulations continued after Stalin's death. In 1958, when Mao Zedong's overtures to the MPR aroused old Russian fears, the name "Mongol" was taken away from Buryatia: The Buryat Mongol ASSR became the Buryat ASSR. The status of two other Buryat regions (Ust'Orda and Aga) has fluctuated. Sometimes they are elevated to the status of autonomous oblasts (provinces), while, at other times, one or both are down-graded to the lowest possible status, that of autonomous okrug (district).

Buryat cultural and religious expression has been strictly circumscribed and controlled. In 1948, Stalin decided that a Buryat epic, featuring a mythical hero named Geser, actually celebrated Genghis Khan. References to Geser were banned. Buryat youths studying art were enjoined from using their traditional

Buddhist symbolism and told that it would stifle their creativity. Instead they should learn realistic art from the "rich legacy of Russian painting." Buryat music and songs were to tell of the struggle to build a socialistic society. Authority over Buryat education was brought under the supervision of a predominantly Russian university in Irkutsk.

Soviet persecution of the clergy and institutions of Lamaist Buddhism continued. There were only 300 Buryat lamas in 1976, down from 16,000 before the Bolshevik Revolution. But, during the Leonid Brezhnev years, the Communist party and Soviet government tried to use Lamaist Buddhism as part of a worldwide propagnda peace offensive. Buddhism was declared to be a "peace religion," "struggling for peace and tranquility on the planet." One new lamasery, the Ivolginsky Datsan, was opened as a showcase to which tourists and delegations from Buddhist countries could be taken. A small number of Buryat seminarians were sent to Mongolia for study.

Buryatia developed some heavy industry, including a locomotive factory, an airplane factory, a textile mill, sawmills, fish canneries, and tungsten and asbestos mines. Lead is mined in the Aga district. Indeed, Soviet and Mongolian planners have constructed an entire industrial corridor along the road and railroad running south from Ulan Ude (formerly Verkhne-Udinsk, the capital of the BASSR), through Kyakhta and Darhan, to Ulan Bator, the capital of Mongolia proper. Also, 525 kilometers of the new Baikal-Amur Mainline, a second Trans-Siberian Railroad hundreds of miles north of the original (and thus further away from a hypothetical Chinese armored thrust), now runs through northern Buryatia. The industrial towns of the BASSR are populated mostly by Russians, since the Buryats still remain strongly averse to living in cities.

Buryat nationalism has found new expression in the era of *glasnost*. Buryats are pushing for expanded Buryat-language education, and, in the fall of 1990, the BASSR actually declared its local laws supreme over those of the Soviet Union. Even though the Soviet Union was dissolved in 1991, Russian geopolitical interests may dictate continued suppression of Buryat separatism. One of the leading Buryat cultural and political figures today is Dashi-Nima Dondupov, a patriarchal figure who still conducts religious services in villages near Lake Baikal. During the years of the "Red Barbarism," he hid the sacred Buryatian religious texts from the Red Army. Today he vigorously condemns the ruin brought by Communism. Buryat monasteries have reopened in the Buryat capital of Ulan Ude, and talk continues about political sovereignty. Dondupov, along with other Buryat leaders, also speaks constantly of making Buryat the official language of their region and restoring it as a language of instruction in the schools.

REFERENCES: Don Belt, "The World's Great Lake," *National Geographic*, 181 (June 1992), 2–40; *Current Digest*, 41 (March 22, 1989), 22–23; Walter Kolarz, *The Peoples of the Soviet Far East*, 1954; William O. McCagg and Brian D. Silver, eds., *Soviet Asian Ethnic Frontiers*, 1979; Robert Rupen, *How Mongolia is Really Ruled*, 1979; and

Mongols of the Twentieth Century, 1964; K. V. Vyatkina, "The Buryats," in M. G. Levin and L. P. Potapov, eds., *The Peoples of Siberia*, 1964, 203–42; Pyotr Zubkhov, "Buryatia: A Republic on Lake Baikal," *Soviet Life*, 378 (1988), 41–46.

Ross Marlay

BURYAT MONGOL. See BURYAT.

BUZAVA. See KALMYK.

BUZAVIN. See KALMYK.

BUZAWA. See KALMYK.

BUZHAN. See UKRAINIAN.

BYELIY KALMUK. See ALTAI.

BYELIY KALMYK. See ALTAI.

BYELIY NOGAI. See NOGAI.

BYELIY NOGAY. See NOGAI.

BYELIY NOGHAI. See NOGAI.

BYELIY NOGHAY. See NOGAI.

BYELIY QALMUQ. See ALTAI.

BYELIY QALMYQ. See ALTAI.

BYELORUS. See BELARUSIAN.

BYELORUSIN. See BELARUSIAN.

BYELORUSSIAN. See BELARUSIAN.

BYELORUTHENIAN. See BELARUSIAN.

BYELY KALMUK. See ALTAI.

BYELY KALMYK. See ALTAI.

BYELY NOGAI. See NOGAI.

BYELY NOGAY. See NOGAI.

BYELY NOGHAI. See NOGAI.

BYELY NOGHAY. See NOGAI.

BYELY QALMUQ. See ALTAI.

BYELY QALMYQ. See ALTAI.

BYELYY KALMUK. See ALTAI.

BYELYY KALMYK. See ALTAI.

BYELYY NOGAI. See NOGAI.

BYELYY NOGAY. See NOGAI.

BYELYY NOGHAI. See NOGAI.

BYELYY NOGHAY. See NOGAI.

BYELYY QALMUQ. See ALTAI.

BYELYY QALMYQ. See ALTAI.

BYZYNGY. See BIZINGI and BALKAR.

BYZYNGYLY. See BIZINGI and BALKAR.

BYZYNYCHY. See BIZINGI and BALKAR.

BYZYNYCHYLY. See BIZINGI and BALKAR.

BZHEDUG. The Bzhedug, who call themselves the Bzhedugh, are an Adyghe*
subgroup. They are concentrated on the Kuban River near Krasnodar in the North
Caucasus. See ADYGHE or CIRCASSIAN.
REFERENCE: Ronald Wixman, *The Peoples of the USSR: An Ethnographic Handbook*,
1984.

BZHEDUGH. See BZHEDUG, ADYGHE, CHERKESS, and CIRCASSIAN.

BZHEDUKH. See BZHEDUG, ADYGHE, CHERKESS, and CIRCASSIAN.

BZIB. See BZYB and ABKHAZ.

BZIB GUDAUT. See BZYB and ABKHAZ.

BZYB. The Bzyb are an Abkhaz* subgroup. They live in the Bzyb Valley of northwestern Georgia. See ABKHAZ.
REFERENCE: Ronald Wixman, *The Peoples of the USSR: An Ethnographic Handbook*, 1984.

BZYB GUDAUT. See BZYB and ABKHAZ.

C

CABARD. See KABARD.

CABARDIN. See KABARD.

CABARDINIAN. See KABARD.

CABARTAY. See KABARD.

CABARTI. See KABARD.

CACHA. See KACHA and KHAKASS.

CACHIN. See KACHA and KHAKASS.

CADJAR. See KAJAR.

CADZHAR. See KAJAR.

CAHELI. See KAKHETIAN and GEORGIAN.

CAHETIAN. See KAKHETIAN and GEORGIAN.

CAHUR. See TSAKHUR.

CAIBAL. See KOIBAL and KHAKASS.

CAIDAK. See KAITAK and DARGIN.

CAITAK. See KAITAK and DARGIN.

CAIVAN. See VEP.

CAJAR. See KAJAR.

CAKHELI. See KAKHETIAN and GEORGIAN.

CAKHETIAN. See KAKHETIAN and GEORGIAN.

CAKHUR. See TSAKHUR.

CALCHA. See KALCHA and KYRGYZ.

CALCHIN. See KALCHA and KYRGYZ.

CALMAK. See KALMYK.

CALMUK. See KALMYK.

CALMYK. See KALMYK.

CAMASIN. See KAMASA SAMOYED and KHAKASS.

CAMASIN SAMODI. See KAMASA SAMOYED and KHAKASS.

CAMASIN SAMOED. See KAMASA SAMOYED and KHAKASS.

CAMASIN SAMOIED. See KAMASA SAMOYED and KHAKASS.

CAMASIN SAMOYED. See KAMASA SAMOYED and KHAKASS.

CAMASSIAN SAMODI. See KAMASA SAMOYED and KHAKASS.

CAMASSIAN SAMOED. See KAMASA SAMOYED and KHAKASS.

CAMASSIAN SAMOIED. See KAMASA SAMOYED and KHAKASS.

CAMASSIAN SAMOYED. See KAMASA SAMOYED and KHAKASS.

CAMCHADAL. See KAMACHADAL and RUSSIAN.

CAMEN. See KAMEN and KORYAK.

CAMENSHCHIK. See BUKHTARMAN and RUSSIAN.

CAMENTSY. See KAMEN and KORYAK.

CAPSAI. See SUVALKIECIAI and LITHUANIAN.

CAPSAY. See SUVALKIECIAI and LITHUANIAN.

CAPUCHA. See ANDI-DIDO and AVAR.

CARA CYRGHYZ. See KYRGYZ.

CARA NOGAI. See KARA NOGAI and NOGAI.

CARA NOGAY. See KARA NOGAI and NOGAI.

CARA NOGHAI. See KARA NOGAI and NOGAI.

CARA NOGHAY. See KARA NOGAI and NOGAI.

CARA TATAR. See KARA TATAR and TATAR.

CARACAIDAK. See KAITAK and DARGIN.

CARACAITAK. See KAITAK and DARGIN.

CARACALPAK. See KARAKALPAK.

CARACAYDAK. See KAITAK and DARGIN.

CARACAYTAK. See KAITAK and DARGIN.

CARACHAEV. See KARACHAI.

CARACHAI. See KARACHAI.

CARACHAIEV. See KARACHAI.

CARACHAILI. See KARACHAI.

CARACHAY. See KARACHAI.

CARACHAYEV. See KARACHAI.

CARACHAYLY. See KARACHAI.

CARADASH. See KARADASH and TURKMEN.

CARADASHLI. See KARADASH and TURKMEN.

CARADASHLY. See KARADASH and TURKMEN.

CARAGA. See KARAGA and KORYAK.

CARAGASH. See KARAGASH TATAR, ASTRAKHAN TATAR, and TATAR.

CARAGASS. See TOFALAR.

CARAGIN. See KARAGA and KORYAK.

CARAGINTSY. See KARAGA and KORYAK.

CARAIM. See KARAIM and JEW.

CARAIT. See KARAIM and JEW.

CARAITE. See KARAIM and JEW.

CARALPAK. See KARAKALPAK.

CARANOGAI. See KARA NOGAI and NOGAI.

CARANOGAY. See KARA NOGAI and NOGAI.

CARANOGHAI. See KARA NOGAI and NOGAI.

CARANOGHAY. See KARA NOGAI and NOGAI.

CARAPAPAH. See KARAPAPAKH and MESKHETIAN.

CARAPAPAK. See KARAPAPAKH and MESKHETIAN.

CARAPAPAKH. See KARAPAPAKH and MESKHETIAN.

CARASA SAMODI. See KARASA SAMOYED and ENT.

CARASA SAMOED. See KARASA SAMOYED and ENT.

CARASA SAMOIED. See KARASA SAMOYED and ENT.

CARASA SAMOYED. See KARASA SAMOYED and ENT.

CARASHI. See KARAGASH TATAR, ASTRAKHAN TATAR, and TATAR.

CARASIN SAMODI. See KARASA SAMOYED and ENT.

CARASIN SAMOED. See KARASA SAMOYED and ENT.

CARASIN SAMOIED. See KARASA SAMOYED and ENT.

CARASIN SAMOYED. See KARASA SAMOYED and ENT.

CARATA. See KARATA, ANDI-DIDO, and AVAR.

CARATAI. See KARATAI and MORDVINIAN.

CARATAY. See KARATAI and MORDVINIAN.

CARELIAN. See KARELIAN.

CARIM. See BURYAT and RUSSIAN.

CARIN TATAR. See KARA TATAR and TATAR.

CARINSKIY TATAR. See KARA TATAR and TATAR.

CARPATHO-RUS. See CARPATHO-RUSYN.

CARPATHO-RUSSIAN. See CARPATHO-RUSYN.

CARPATHO-RUSYN. The term ''Carpatho-Rusyn'' refers to a small group of people who live in Subcarpathian Rus', a region in Eastern Europe on the southern side of the central portion of the Carpathian mountains. Its boundaries extend to cover the whole Transcarpathian (Zakarpats'ka) Oblast, located in present-day Ukraine, and a section of Slovakia, including the northeastern part of the former Hungarian counties of Szepes, Zemplen, and Saros. The term ''Carpatho-Rusyn'' is often used as the basis for defining an ethnic group that has been known by several names: Carpathorussians, Rusnaks, Rusins, Subcarpathian Rus', and Carpatho-Rusins. Based on census results, there are an estimated 1,000,000 Carpatho-Rusyns living in the borderlands between Ukraine and Slovakia. Because of their small numbers and their cultural proximity to neighboring ethnic groups, the Carpatho-Rusyns have not actually been accepted as a distinct ethnic group. Many neighboring groups have claimed that some or all of the Rusyns are actually Slovaks*, Ukrainians*, Russians*, or Poles*, and many Rusyns, for their part, have assimilated into these groups. In the recent past, a controversy has revolved around the question of whether the Carpatho-Rusyns constitute a separate ethnic group or are simply a branch of the Ukrainian nation.

The Carpatho-Rusyns living in Ukraine and Slovakia speak four separate dialects that linguists have classified as belonging to the Ukrainian language. The Rusyn dialect includes the Lemko, Hutsul*, Boiko, and Transcarpathian dialects. Three out of four dialects (Lemko, Boiko, and Hutsul) cross over the mountains and are spoken in neighboring states. Lemko, for example, is spoken by Eastern Slavs living in northern Romania and in several oblasts in Ukraine. Lemko, Boiko, and Hutsul are also used as terms to designate a local or tribal identity; at various times in the past, the tendency for Carpatho-Rusyns to identify themselves as Lemkos, Boikos, or Hutsuls, rather than as a Rusin or Ukrainian, has prevailed. With the exception of the Hutsuls, however, Rusyns living in Subcarpathian Rus' do not use these local terms as ethnic designations and simply call themselves Rusyns or Rusnaks. In addition to the local divisions, Rusyns are divided geographically between the *dolyshniany* (lowlanders, or those who live in the valleys and on the plains) and *verkhovyntsi* (highlanders).

Traditionally, Rusyns have belonged either to the Orthodox faith or to the Greek Catholic (Uniate) faith. The date of their conversion to Christianity has been the object of a certain amount of controversy. Some scholars have argued that the Rusyns were converted in the ninth century, in conjunction with the mission of Saints Cyril and Methodius to the Slavs. Others have argued that the conversion took place in 988 as part of the Christianization of Kievan Rus'. In any case, a strong pre-Christian element has remained in the practice of Christianity in Subcarpathian Rus'.

The earliest Rusyn settlements in the Carpathian mountains date back many centuries. Some theories suggest that the Rusyns lived in Subcarpathian Rus' and the Carpathian Mountains for several centuries prior to the migration of the Magyars*, but convincing evidence to support these theories has been difficult to ascertain. By the end of the twelfth century, thriving Rusyn settlements had sprung up on both sides of the Carpathian Mountains. During the thirteenth century, the Rusyn population in the region grew noticeably. In response to the incursion of the Mongols* into Central Europe in the mid-thirteenth century, King Bela IV of Hungary invited settlers from Rus' (Rusyns) to populate and defend Hungary's northern frontier. Waves of settlers from neighboring Rus' principalities such as Galicia (Halych) poured into Subcarpathia, fleeing the Golden Horde. For the next three centuries, the Hungarian crown offered favorable terms to both nobles and peasants from Rus' to settle its borderlands.

During the sixteenth and seventeenth centuries, when Hungary was divided between a Transylvanian party and a Hapsburg party, Subcarpathian Rus' became a battleground for the two camps. Both sides vied for control over Subcarpathia, and incursions by foreign powers such as Poland were frequent. Because of their political and religious allegiances, the Orthodox believers of Subcarpathian Rus' were targeted by the Counter Reformation. After several decades of Catholicization among the Rusyn nobility and clergy, an agreement was reached, under which a group of Orthodox bishops accepted the primacy of the pope in exchange for being allowed to maintain their Byzantine Rite. In 1646, the agreement, called the Union of Uzhorod, created the Greek Catholic (Uniate) Church in Subcarpathia (the Greek Catholic Church already existed in Polish-controlled Ukraine). Throughout this period, the Rusyn peasants played an active role in shaping the outcome of events in the region. In 1703, they joined the Transylvanian prince Ferenc Rakoczi in a rebellion against Hapsburg control. From 1500 to 1800, well-armed groups of peasant bandits, known as the *opryshky*, shuttled between the mountainous areas of Poland and Hungary. They robbed landowners, merchants, and townspeople in both countries. Despite their statelessness, Rusyn peasants affected the social and political development of Eastern Europe.

During the first half of the nineteenth century, a national awakening swept Eastern Europe, penetrating even the most remote regions. Like other Eastern European ethnic groups, the Rusyns searched for a historical identity and a national past that would be comparable to those of surrounding peoples. Leading the Rusyns in this quest was the poet and scholar Alexander Dukhnovych (1803–1865). Dukhnovych not only authored a Rusyn grammar and a primer in the local language, but he also published several newspapers. Because of his many contributions, Dukhnovych has been deemed "the awakener of the Carpatho-Rusyn nation."

In the course on the nineteenth century, many members of the Rusyn intelligentsia, including Dukhnovych, turned to Russia for inspiration. The powerful Great Russian state to the east embodied many of the longings of small, stateless Subcarpathian Rus'. The similarity between the name that the Great Russians used for themselves—*russkie*—and the Rusyn's own name—*rusyny*—contributed to Russophile sentiment. In the last decades of the nineteenth century, a "Return to Orthodoxy" movement was launched to persuade Greek Catholic Rusyns to abandon their religious union with Rome and accept Russian Orthodoxy.

The movement for a separate Rusyn consciousness found itself competing not only with Russophilism but also with a Ukrainian movement based in Galicia. The Ukrainians viewed the Rusyns as part of a Ukrainian people that was distinct from the Great Russians. The Hungarian rulers of Subcarpathian Rus' tried to woo the Rusyns as well. By the end of the nineteenth century and the beginning of the twentieth, a sizable number of Rusyns had migrated to the United States, transplanting the question of Rusyn identity onto North American soil. On the eve of World War I, the Rusyns had not universally accepted any national orientation.

In 1918, coinciding with the collapse of the Austro-Hungarian Empire, Subcarpathian Rus' was caught in the middle of a struggle. While some Rusyns favored outright independence, others advocated uniting Subcarpathia with Russia, Ukraine, or Hungary. After lengthy negotiations and debate, a group of Rusyn representatives and the Allied powers agreed that Subcarpathian Rus' would be incorporated into Czechoslovakia as an autonomous region. Though this agreement was formalized by the Peace of Paris, Subcarpathian Rusyn autonomy was never fully acknowledged by the Czechoslovak government. Even without autonomy, the Rusyns living in Czechoslovakia fared comparatively well, in contrast with the minorities living in other Eastern European states. During the inter-war war period (1919–1938), the Czechoslovak government instituted a series of agrarian reforms and, although it generally supported the local Rusyn consciousness over the pro-Hungarian and pro-Ukrainian identities, the Czech government did nothing to suppress Ukrainian cultural activities.

In 1938, the Czechoslovak state, under pressure from Germany, began to collapse. Rusyn activists of all national orientations seized this opportunity and began to press for full autonomy. After the Munich pact in September 1938, Subcarpathian Rus' emerged as the third party in a three-way federal state. Autonomy brought little stability to Subcarpathian Rus' however. Roughly one month after the Munich pact, Hungary demanded and received Hungarian-populated lands in southern Slovakia and Subcarpthia, including the cities of Uzhhorod and Mukachevo. The population and governing apparatus of Subcarpathian Rus', which had been united in their desire for autonomy, split into pro-Hungarian, pro-Ukrainian, pro-Rusyn, and pro-Russian factions. All sides vied for the support of the Czechoslovak government. In the course of the ensuing struggle, the Ukrainian nationalist faction, under the leadership of Reverend Avhutsyn Voloshyn, emerged as the victor and began re-organizing public life in Subcarpathian Rus' around the Ukrainian culture. The pro-Ukrainian Voloshyn government renamed the republic Carpatho-Ukraine and endorsed policies that consistently favored Ukrainian-oriented groups within the region.

The radical Ukrainian nationalist sentiment present in the republic's apparatus brought Carpatho-Ukraine into conflict with Prague. In March 1939, a series of skirmishes took place between Czech detachments and Ukrainian Sich troops when an effort to re-organize Carpatho-Ukraine's governing body was instituted by Prague. When Jozef Tiso announced independence for Slovakia on March 14, 1939, signaling the disintegration of Czechoslovakia, Hungarian troops responded by marching on Carpatho-Ukraine. Faced with the invasion, the government of Carpatho-Ukraine held an emergency session and declared its independence, expecting support from Prague or Berlin. Such support failed to materialize. Carpatho-Ukraine fell the next day.

Under Hungarian occupation, instruction in the local language was allowed, and Rusyns were not pressured to identify themselves as Magyars. Despite this culturally tolerant atmosphere, Hungary was less tolerant of political dissent. Many Ukrainian nationalists were rounded up and imprisoned. In the fall of 1944, Soviet troops crossed the border into Subcarpathian Rus' for the first time. Shortly thereafter, a council of Communists from Subcarpathian Rus' announced their desire to be incorporated into the Ukrainian Soviet Socialist Republic. With Czechoslovak leaders in no position to resist, "Transcarpathian Ukraine" (Subcarpathian Rus') was "united" with Ukraine by a treaty that was ratified in

November 1945. Those Rusyns who lived in eastern Slovakia were given the option of moving to Soviet-controlled territories, but most chose to remain in Slovakia.

Resistance to Soviet occupation and the Czechoslovak Communist government came mainly in the form of low-intensity warfare directed by Ukrainian nationalist guerrillas toward the new regime and its supporters. The resistance, however, was not sufficient to prevent the two states from carrying out their policies in Subcarpathian Rus'. In 1944, the Soviet government initiated a series of campaigns against the Greek Catholic Church. In 1946, the Uniate Church in Western Ukraine was forcibly incorporated into the Russian Orthodox Church by a rump synod; several years later, the Greek Catholic Church was dissolved in Transcarpathia and Slovakia. For the next four decades, the church and its believers were suppressed. Uniates were allowed to resume their activities in Slovakia in 1968 and in Ukraine in 1989.

In the cultural sphere, the Soviet government launched a massive drive to "ukrainianize" Transcarpathia, based on the notion that the Rusyns of Subcarpathian Rus' were simply part of the Ukrainian nation. The local dialects were replaced, in the schools and in print, by standard literary Ukrainian. Rusyn consciousness was portrayed as provincial and old-fashioned. Similar policies were enacted in neighboring Czechoslovakia. The two states' attempts to ukrainianize the Rusyns yielded mixed results. While a majority of people in Transcarpathia identified themselves as Ukrainians in the postwar censuses, evidence suggests that many Rusyns, especially in Slovakia, chose to identify themselves as Slovaks instead of as Ukrainians. When faced with the likelihood of no longer being able to identify themselves as Rusyns, a segment of the population in both countries assimilated and became Slovaks in Slovakia and Russians in the Soviet Union.

Since the onset of *glasnost* and *perestroika*, the "Rusyn Question" has re-emerged as a topic for public debate in Eastern Europe. The Rusyn identity, once thought dead among the younger generation, had made a comeback. In 1989, Rusyn cultural clubs sprang up in the Soviet Union, Poland, and Czechoslovakia. Although the initial purpose of these clubs was ostensibly to preserve local culture, as liberalization progressed, many of these groups jumped into the politics surrounding the question of Rusyn identity. In Transcarpathia, for example, Rusyn groups divided and re-aligned themselves in terms of ethnic identity (pro-Russian, pro-Ukrainian, and pro-Rusyn) and in terms of political orientation (pro-Soviet, pro-Ukrainian nationalist, and pro-Czechoslovak). The recent polls and referendums have sent mixed signals. In March 1991, Mikhail Gorbachev's referendum to preserve the Soviet Union passed by a majority in Transcarpathia, but so did a measure on the ballot for more Ukrainian sovereignty. This was interpreted as both a sign of conservatism and a rejection of Ukrainian nationalism in the region. In the December 1991 referendum on Ukrainian independence, voters in Transcarpathia faced two questions: one on Ukrainian independence and the other concerning autonomy within Ukraine for Transcarpathia. While approving Ukrainian independence by a wide majority, voters supported autonomy for Transcarpathia by the even wider margin of 78 percent.

The politics of the Rusyn question and the debate over ethnic orientation has led to a series of polemics in the Polish, Czechoslovak, and Soviet media. Those who advocate a Ukrainian identity often accuse Rusynism of being a mask for Czechoslovak and Hungarian expansionism or an anti-Ukrainian movement being manipulated by former Communists and Russophiles. Their opponents counter with charges that "Dnieper Ukrainian culture" and "Bolshevism" have been forced upon the Rusyns at the expense of the local culture and local political autonomy. The volatile issue of ethnic identity has split a number of newspapers and organizations. The situation has been complicated by demands for autonomy from Transcarpathia's Hungarian population and by the break-up of Czechoslovakia on January 1, 1993. The new nation of Slovakia included Slovaks, Magyars, and Rusyns. Some Rusyn activists demanded an official Rusyn-Slovak state, but that did not happen when Slovakia split from the Czech Republic. A few Rusyn radicals even proposed creation of a Transcarpathian Rusyn republic independent of both Slovakia and Ukraine.

REFERENCES: Alexander Bonkalo, *The Rusyns*, 1990; Paul Robert Magocsi, *The Rusyn-Ukrainians of Czechoslovakia*, 1983 and *The Shaping of a National Identity: Subcarpathian Rus', 1848–1948*, 1979; Walter C. Warzeski, *Byzantine Rite Rusins in Carpatho-Ruthenia and America*, 1971; Michael Winch, *Republic for a Day*, 1939.

Anthony J. Amato

CARPATHO-RUTHENIAN. See CARPATHO-RUSYN.

CARPATHO-UKRAINIAN. See CARPATHO-RUSYN.

CARPATO-RUSSIAN. See CARPATHO-RUSYN.

CARPATO-RUSYN. See CARPATHO-RUSYN.

CARPATO-RUTHENIAN. See CARPATHO-RUSYN.

CARPATO-UKRAINIAN. See CARPATHO-RUSYN.

CARPATSKO-RUSSIAN. See CARPATHO-RUSYN.

CARPATSKO-RUSYN. See CARPATHO-RUSYN.

CARPATSKO-RUTHENIAN. See CARPATHO-RUSYN.

CARPATSKO-UKRAINIAN. See CARPATHO-RUSYN.

CARTLI. See KARTLI and GEORGIAN.

CARTLIAN. See KARTLI and GEORGIAN.

CARTLIN. See KARTLI and GEORGIAN.

CARTVELI. See KARTVELIAN and GEORGIAN.

CARTVELIAN. See KARTVELIAN and GEORGIAN.

CARTVELIN. See KARTVELIAN and GEORGIAN.

CARYM. See BURYAT and RUSSIAN.

CASHGAR. See KASHGAR and UIGUR.

CASHGARLIK. See KASHGAR and UIGUR.

CASHGARLUK. See KASHGAR and UIGUR.

CASHGARLYK. See KASHGAR and UIGUR.

CASIMOV TATAR. See KASIMOV TATAR and TATAR.

CASOG. See AZERBAIJANI.

CAUCASIAN. The term ''Caucasian'' is a generic reference for all of the various ethnic groups who are indigenous to Transcaucasia and the North Caucasus.
REFERENCE: Ronald Wixman, *The Peoples of the USSR: An Ethnographic Handbook*, 1984.

CAUCASIAN MOUNTAINEER. The term ''Caucasian Mountaineer'' has been used for years in Russia and the Soviet Union to refer to the indigenous peoples of the North Caucasus region. The designation includes the Karachais*, Balkars*, Ossetians*, Ingushes*, Chechens*, and Circassians*.
REFERENCE: Ronald Wixman, *The Peoples of the USSR: An Ethnographic Handbook*, 1984.

CAUCASIAN TATAR. See AZERBAIJANI.

CAYBAL. See KOIBAL and KHAKASS.

CAYDAK. See KAITAK and DARGIN.

CAYTAK. See KAITAK and DARGIN.

CAZAH. See KAZAKH.

CAZAK. See AZERBAIJANI.

CAZAK. See KAZAKH.

CAZAN TATAR. See KAZAN TATAR and VOLGA TATAR.

CAZANLIK. See KAZAN TATAR, VOLGA TATAR, and TATAR.

CAZANLYK. See KAZAN TATAR, VOLGA TATAR, and TATAR.

CAZICUMUH. See LAK.

CAZICUMUK. See LAK.

CAZICUMUKH. See LAK.

CENTRAL ASIAN. The term Central Asian is a generic reference to the Uzbeks*, Tajiks, Turkmen*, Kyrgyz*, Kazakhs*, and Karakalpaks*.
REFERENCE: Ronald Wixman, *The Peoples of the USSR: An Ethnographic Handbook*, 1984.

CENTRAL ASIAN ARAB. See ARAB.

CENTRAL ASIAN GYPSY. The Gypsies* of Central Asia call themselves Mugi or Mughat. That term is often qualified by a regional location, such as Mughat Samarkandi or Mughat Bukhori. They are known as Dzhugi or Mazang to the Tajiks*, Luli to the Uzbeks*, and Sredneaziatskije tsygany to Russians*. Ethnologists suspect that the Gypsies originated in India, but, unlike Gypsy groups located farther to the west, the Central Asian Gypsies have lost their language—Romany. They speak either Tajik or Uzbek. Most of them are Sunni Muslims. The Central Asian Gypsies continued their migratory ways, making their living by peddling, fortune-telling, begging, singing, and dancing, until the 1930s when Soviet policies insisted on settling them. Most settled into Gypsy quarters in major cities. As a result, increasingly large numbers of Central Asian Gypsies have been incorporated into the larger industrial economy. They number today approximately 12,000 people. See GYPSY.
REFERENCES: Rena C. Gropper, *Gypsies in the City: Cultural Patterns and Survival*, 1975; Denis Harvey, *The Gypsies: Wagon Time and After*, 1980; Charles G. Leland, *The English Gypsies and Their Language*, 1980; Judith Okely, *The Traveller-Gypsies*, 1983; Jan Yoors, *The Gypsies*, 1983; Ronald Wixman, *The Peoples of the USSR: An Ethnographic Handbook*, 1984.

CENTRAL ASIAN JEW. The Central Asian Jews—who call themselves Ya-hudi, Isroel, Bane Isroel, and Yahudikhoi Makhalli—and who have also been known as the Bukharan Jews, live primarily in Samarkand, Tashkent, Khokand, and Bukhara. Most of them speak a Tajik* dialect laced with Hebrew words. Many Central Asian Jews also speak Uzbek*. One group of Central Asian Jews are known as the Chala*. They are distinguished by their formal conversion to Islam but their private commitment to Judaism, a phenomenon that over the centuries produced a hybrid religion—part Judaism and part Islam. See JEW.
REFERENCES: Benjamin Pinkus, *The Jews of the Soviet Union: The History of a National Minority*, 1988; and Solomon N. Schwarz, *The Jews in the Soviet Union*, 1951; Ronald Wixman, *The Peoples of the USSR: An Ethnographic Handbook*, 1984.

CENTRAL ASIAN TURK. The term "Central Asian Turk" has had two distinct meanings in Russia and the Soviet Union. On the one hand, it has been used to refer to the Turkmen*, Kazakh*, Kyrgyz*, Karakalpak*, Uzbek*, and Uigur* groups. On the other hand, the term has also sometimes been a reference to the Turks* of Samarkand and the Fergana Valley.
REFERENCE: Ronald Wixman, *The Peoples of the USSR: An Ethnographic Handbook*, 1984.

CHAGATAI. The Chagatai (Chagathai) are today a subgroup of the Tajiks*, although their origins may very well be Mongol.* They live in the Surkhan Darya Oblast of Uzbekistan. A smaller cluster of Chagatais live in southern Tajikistan. See TAJIK.
REFERENCE: Ronald Wixman, *The Peoples of the USSR: An Ethnographic Handbook*, 1984.

CHAGATAY. See CHAGATAI and TAJIK.

CHAGHATAI. See CHAGATAI and TAJIK.

CHAGHATAY. See CHAGATAI and TAJIK.

CHAGATHAI. See CHAGATAI and TAJIK.

CHAIDAQ. See KAITAK and DARGIN.

CHALA. The term "Chala" refers to a relatively small group of Bukharan Jews* who converted to Islam under pressure from surrounding Muslims. Their true spiritual allegiances, however, remained quite Jewish, and they continued to practice Judaism in private. Those who did not practice it privately assimilated into the Muslim community. Over the years, their religion became a syncretic mix of Judaism and Islam. The term "Chala" translates as "imperfect." The word has also been used in Russia and the Soviet Union to refer to an individual

of mixed parentage. For example, a full-blooded Tajik* might refer to an individual of half-Tajik and half-Russian* ancestry as a Chala-Tajik. See JEW.
REFERENCE: Shirin Akiner, *Islamic Peoples of the Soviet Union.* 1983.

CHALA CAZACH. See CHALA KAZAK and KYRGYZ.

CHALA CAZAH. See CHALA KAZAK and KYRGYZ.

CHALA CAZAK. See CHALA KAZAK and KYRGYZ.

CHALA KAZAH. See CHALA KAZAK.

CHALA KAZAK. The Chala Kazak are today considered to be a sub-tribe of the Kyrgyz*. Actually, they are ethnic Kazakhs* living in the Talass Valley of the Kyrgyz Republic who have been largely assimilated by the Kazakhs. See KYRGYZ.
REFERENCE: Ronald Wixman, *The Peoples of the USSR: An Ethnographic Handbook,* 1984.

CHALA KAZAKH. See CHALA KAZAK and KYRGYZ.

CHALCHA. See KHALKHA and MONGOL.

CHALCHA MONGOL. See KHALKHA and MONGOL.

CHALCHIN. See KHALKHA and MONGOL.

CHALCHIN MONGOL. See KHALKHA and MONGOL.

CHAMAL. See CHAMALAL.

CHAMALAL. The Chamalals (Chamal), who call themselves the Chamalali and are known to Russians* as the Chamalintsy, are today considered an Avar* subgroup by Russian ethnologists, even though their sense of identity is highly decentralized, with village loyalties more important than any Chamalal identity. Their language reflects that divided loyalty. Its two major dialects are Gidatl and Gakwari-Gaidari, with Gakwari having five subdialects and Gaidari two. All of the Chamalal are Sunni Muslims who live along the Andi River in the southwestern Daghestan highlands, especially in Tsumadin Rayon. See AVAR.
REFERENCES: Shirin Akiner, *Islamic Peoples of the Soviet Union,* 1983; Ronald Wixman, *The Peoples of the USSR: An Ethnographic Handbook,* 1984.

CHAMALALI. See CHAMALAL and AVAR.

CHAMALINTSY. See CHAMALAL and AVAR.

CHAN. See LAZ and GEORGIAN.

CHANDEIAR. See KHANDEYAR and NENET.

CHANDEYAR. See KHANDEYAR and NENET.

CHANT. See KHANT.

CHANTAIKA. See ENT.

CHANTAIKA SAMODI. See ENT.

CHANTAIKA SAMOED. See ENT.

CHANTAIKA SAMOIED. See ENT.

CHANTAIKA SAMOYED. See ENT.

CHANTAYKA SAMODI. See ENT.

CHANTAYKA SAMOED. See ENT.

CHANTAYKA SAMOIED. See ENT.

CHANTAYKA SAMOYED. See ENT.

CHAPUT. See GAPUT, DZHEK, and SHAH DAGH.

CHAQASS. See KHAKASS.

CHATUCAI. See KHATUKAI, ADYGHE, and CIRCASSIAN.

CHATUCAY. See KHATUKAI, ADYGHE, and CIRCASSIAN.

CHATUKAI. See KHATUKAI, ADYGHE, and CIRCASSIAN.

CHATUKAY. See KHATUKAI, ADYGHE, and CIRCASSIAN.

CHATUQAI. See KHATUKAI, ADYGHE, and CIRCASSIAN.

CHATUQAY. See KHATUKAI, ADYGHE, and CIRCASSIAN.

CHAVCHU. See CHAVCHUVEN, CHUKCHI, and KORYAK.

CHAVCHUVEN. The term "Chavchuven" has been used to refer to those Koryaks* who still pursue a traditional reindeer-herding life-style. It is also the name of one of the nine subgroups of the Koryaks.
REFERENCE: Ronald Wixman, *The Peoples of the USSR: An Ethnographic Handbook,* 1984.

CHAYDAK. See KAITAK and DARGIN.

CHAYTAK. See KAITAK and DARGIN.

CHAYTAQ. See KAITAK and DARGIN.

CHAZARA. See KHAZARA.

CHECHEN. The Chechens are a fiercely anti-Russian, Muslim mountain people of the North Caucasus. There were 755,000 Chechens counted in the 1979 Soviet census, more than double the 319,000 counted in 1939 before their calamitous deportation and scattering across Central Asia. The 1989 Soviet census placed the Chechen population at 958,309 people. Most of them live in the Chechen-Ingush Autonomous Republic in Russia, which is also called Chechenia. On its eastern border is the Daghestan Autonomous Republic, and to the west lies the North Ossetian Autonomous Republic. The southern border of Chechenia is the crest of the central Caucasus range; on the other side lies the Georgian Republic. The Chechen-Ingush Autonomous Republic encompasses a wide variety of terrain. Scanning from north to south, one finds the lowland along the Terek River and the oil fields of Grozny; the Chechen Plain, with mixed fields, pastures, and forests; and the high mountains and glaciers that form the virtually impassable southern wall of Chechen territory.

The names "Chechen" and "Ingush*" were given by the Russians* and were derived from particular villages. The people call themselves "Nakh*" or "Nakh-chuo." The Chechen and Ingush languages are mutually intelligible and may actually be considered different dialects of a single language of the Nakh or Veinakh group of the Caucasian language family. The preferred literary language and script were formerly Arabic, but Chechen is now written with Cyrillic script. The Chechens have clung fiercely to their language, perhaps as an expression of their contempt for Russian culture.

The historical record of the Chechens before the nineteenth century is scanty indeed, but it is thought that they are autochthonous to the north slope of the Caucasus. From there, they could resist mounted steppe nomads such as the Scythians, Sarmatians, and Mongols* by retreating into fortified watchtowers until the marauders departed. The remains of medieval stone churches indicated that some Chechens were once Christians, but, during the sixteenth to nineteenth centuries, they were all converted to Islam by Sunni missionaries from neighboring Daghestan. Xenophobic Chechen nationalism is very much grounded in

Islam. In the terrible wars against tsarist Russia, Chechens found inspiration in fanatical, secretive, and mystical Sufi brotherhoods, specifically the Naqshbandiya and Qadiriya. These organizations are eminently suited to clan-based underground warfare against an occupying power, and they still exist today.

In the eighteenth century, Russia fought the Ottoman and Persian* empires for control of the strategic Caucasus range. The Christian Ossetians*, who live immediately west of Chechenia, welcomed the Russians, but the Muslim Chechens resisted bitterly, starting with the movement of Sheik Mansur in 1785 and continuing to the present day. The brutal Caucasian War (1817–1864) indelibly impressed on both Chechens and Russians the most terrible beliefs about each other. To Russians, the Chechens were dishonest and merciless brigands. They built a 500-mile line of forts from the Black Sea all the way to the Caspian to pacify the unruly tribesmen. From one fort in that line named Grozny, the relentless Russian General Aleksei Yermolov sent punitive expeditions to destroy Chechen villages, burn crops, and kill everyone in sight, sparing neither women nor children. The Chechen hero, Imam Shamil, led the resistance to the Russians until 1858. Victory ultimately went to the Russians, but at a cost. It imbued the Chechens with a permanent enmity that Leo Tolstoy described as ''stronger than hatred, a refusal to recognize these Russian dogs as people.'' Since the north Caucasus was covered in beech and oak forests, and since the Chechens were particularly skilled at forest warfare, the Russians completely deforested the foothills. In 1865, 39,000 Chechens were sent into exile in Turkey, but revolts periodically flared up in Chechenia over the remaining decades of the nineteenth century.

Russian settlers occupied the lowlands from which the Chechens had been driven, especially after 1893, when oil wells were drilled near Grozny and the railroad to Baku was laid through Chechenia. Few Chechens worked in the oil fields or in Grozny. Thus, the cities of Chechenia are predominantly Russian, while the countryside remains heavily Chechen. The two groups rarely intermarry.

Chechens tried again during the years of turmoil from 1917 to 1920 to expel the Russians and reclaim what they regarded as their own land. Sheik Uzun Haji's followers launched a violent jihad (holy war) against White Guard forces, but the Bolsheviks reasserted Russian power after Denikin was expelled from Grozny in 1920. Sporadic banditry and murders of Russians occurred in the early 1920s.

A Chechen Autonomous Oblast was formed in 1922. They were joined with the Ingushes in a Chechen-Ingush Autonomous Republic in 1936. These administrative tricks could not hide the fact that Chechen resistance to russification continued under Josef Stalin, just as it had under V. I. Lenin and the tsars. As always, Chechen resistance was based on folk Islam. Somehow, while organized religion was being extinguished in the rest of the Soviet Union, more and more mosques were being built in Chechenia. A millenarian cult arose in the 1930s, based on the belief that Kunta Haji, a long-dead Chechen leader, would return to earth to usher in an era of righteousness and Sharia law. As late as the spring of 1940, by which time Stalin had utterly crushed resistance to his will elsewhere in the Soviet Union, a new revolt broke in Chechenia, led by a former Chechen Komsomol member.

Chechen resistance to collectivization was predictably violent. The Soviet press characterized the situation as a struggle against "kulaks and mullahs," and authorities in Moscow published a fulsome "Chechen Song of Stalin," in which the dictator was identified as the father and brother of the Chechens. The song contained some unlikely Christian themes: "Holy is the womb that bore thee. Most happy is she above all women whose child is our unfailing sun."

When Nazi Germany invaded Soviet Russia and German* troops neared the Caucasian oilfields, Chechens were found on both sides in the war. Their less-than-perfect record of loyalty to the Soviet homeland resulted in the mass deportation of Chechens from their homeland in February 1944. The 1939 census had counted 318,000 Chechens and 74,000 Ingushes. They were all taken by train to locations scattered across the steppes of northern Kazakhstan, where their culture and language were supposed to die out. Their autonomous region was abolished. Not a word appeared in the press until two years later, when the Supreme Soviet announced that many Chechens had joined volunteer units organized by the Germans while the "main population took no counter-action against the betrayers of the Fatherland."

The Chechens' internal exile lasted thirteen years, until, along with seven other deported nationalities, they were rehabilitated in 1957. Chechen was once again declared to be a literary language, and Chechen-language newspapers reappeared. Resettlement to their homeland proceeded gradually, but naturally there were problems, because Daghestani* families (Avars* and Dargins*) had in the meantime been moved into Chechen villages; now those people in turn had to be expelled. Moscow again arbitrarily redrew the borders of Chechen-Ingushetia; its land area would henceforth be 19,300 square kilometers. The Chechens had clung tenaciously to Islam during their exile. Official Soviet sources estimated in 1975 that fully half the Chechen population belonged to Sufi brotherhoods. Mosques were reopened in 1978. Many Chechens openly defied Soviet authorities by making pilgrimages to the tombs of past religious or military heroes.

Glasnost encouraged Chechens to demand increased autonomy. In the turmoil that followed the failed military coup in Moscow in August 1991, they declared independence. This represented a direct threat to the territorial integrity not only of the Soviet Union but of the Russian Federation itself, of which the Chechen-Ingush Autonomous Republic was a constituent part. Demonstrators knocked down a statue of Lenin in Grozny, blockaded KGB headquarters, and seized radio and television stations. A retired Chechen bomber pilot named General Dzhokhar Dudayev arose as a political strongman. He seized control of Chechenia on September 6, 1991, and he was elected president on October 27. Dudayev claimed the support of 5,000 soldiers and 62,000 volunteers. The only enmity between Chechens and Russians reappeared as a high-stakes showdown between Dudayev and Russian President Boris Yeltsin, who declared emergency rule and sent 1,000 Interior Ministry troops to Grozny, only to have them withdrawn a few days later. In November 1991, Dudayev threatened to sever the Moscow-Baku Highway and to launch terrorist attacks on Russian nuclear power stations, unless Chechen independence were recognized. Dudayev's words would have sounded familiar to Kunta Haji or Sheik Mansur: "Why should our mothers cry, our old people cry, why should our children cry and live in so much fear? Why shouldn't Russia, which is where this evil is coming from, feel fear?" Dudayev also raised the prospect of a Caucasian Federation to unite all the North Caucasus mountaineers, from the Black Sea to the Caspian, and appealed to Iran and Turkey for support.

After the disintegration of the Soviet Union at the end of 1991, the drive for Chechen independence continued. The Chechens were no more happy with Russian domination than they had been with Soviet variety. In announcing their independence, Chechenia also formally separated from the Ingush, dissolving the Chechen-Ingush Autonomous Republic. Tensions escalated throughout 1992, especially when the Ossetians, who are Christians, began attacking the Ingush, who are Muslims. Russia sent troops to quell the civil war in the region, and, when those troops crossed the boundary between Chechenia and Ingushetia in November 1992, President Dudayev called for a holy war against Russia.

REFERENCES: Robert Conquest, ed., *Soviet Nationalities Policy in Practice*, 1967; Oleg Glebov and John Crowfoot, eds., *The Soviet Empire: Its Nations Speak Out*, 1989; Hugh Seton-Watson, *The Russian Empire, 1801–1917*, 1957; Bohdan Nahaylo and Victor Swoboda, *Soviet Disunion: A History of the Nationalities Problem in the USSR*, 1989; *New York Times*, November 18, 1992.

                                                                                Ross Marlay

CHEGEM. The Chegem call themselves the Chegemli. They are a subgroup of the Balkars* and live along the Chegem River in the Kabardino-Balkar Autonomous Republic. See BALKAR.

REFERENCE: Ronald Wixman, *The Peoples of the USSR: An Ethnographic Handbook*, 1984.

CHEGEMCHI. See CHEGEM and BALKAR.

CHEGEMCHILI. See CHEGEM and BALKAR.

CHEGEMLI. See CHEGEM and BALKAR.

CHELKAN. The Chelkan, formerly called the Chernevyje Tatars*, are an Altai* subgroup. See ALTAI.

REFERENCE: Ronald Wixman, *The Peoples of the USSR: An Ethnographic Handbook*, 1984.

CHEMGUI. See TEMIRGOI, ADYGHE, and CIRCASSIAN.

CHEMGUY. See TEMIRGOI, ADYGHE, and CIRCASSIAN.

CHEMSHIL. See KHEMSHIL, ARMENIAN, MESKHETIAN, and AZERBAIJANI.

CHERKESS. The Cherkess are one of the primary subgroups of the Circassian* peoples, which today also includes the Adyghes* and the Kabards.* There has been considerable debate among Soviet politicians and ethnologists over just how to classify the Circassians, and today the term Cherkess generally refers to those Circassians living in the northern portions of the Karachai-Cherkess Autonomous Oblast. The Cherkess language is extremely close to Kabardian and similar to Adyghe. The Cherkess slowly adopted Christianity in the eleventh and twelfth centuries and became widely known for their commercial trading skills. With the thirteenth-century invasion by the Golden Horde, some of the Adyghes moved east toward the Terek River, mixed with the local Alan peoples, and eventually became known as Kabards. Those Adyghes who stayed in the west became known as the Cherkess. Early in the sixteenth century, the Ottomans and their subject state, the Crimean Khanate, brought Islam to the Adyghes, and the conversion process began. That process was a slow one, but, by the early 1800s, most Cherkess had become Sunni Muslims of the Hanafi school. In the 1860s, after Russia had established control over the region, there was a mass exodus of Cherkess to Turkey, reducing their total in Russia at the beginning of the twentieth century to perhaps only 20,000 people.

The Cherkess call themselves Adyge, indicating their close relationship with the Adyghes and other Circassians. But their identity as a people is extremely restricted by the centrifugal forces of tribal loyalties, because the Cherkess also identify themselves by subgroups or tribes. The most prominent of the Cherkess subgroups are the Abadzeg* (Abadzekh), Beslenei* (Beslenej), Bzhedug* (Bzhedukh), Gatjukai (Gatjukaj), Jererukoi (Jereukoj), Kemgoi (Kemgoj), Kheak, Nadkhokuadzh, Shapsug,* and Temirgoi* (Temirgoj).

What chiefly distinguishes the Cherkess from other Caucasian nations is the simple geographic fact that their rivers drain to the Black Sea, not the Caspian. Thus, from earliest times they were peripherally in touch with the Mediterranean ecumene, by contrast with their inward-looking, xenophobic, eastern neighbors—Ossetians*, Karachais*, and Chechens*. Greek* and Roman authors described tribes in the northwest Caucasus as particularly noted for their fine horsebreeding and horsemanship. Cherkess women were considered especially beautiful; many were sold into Turkish* and Arabian harems. Cherkess men often hired out as mercenaries, and one particularly successful group ruled Egypt for centuries as the Mameluke dynasty. The Cherkess traded with Byzantium in horses, honey, furs, and filigreed jewelry. Some converted to Christianity, which, however, blended with rather than displaced their pagan beliefs. Contact with Byzantium was interrupted in the thirteenth century by the Mongol* conquest. In the fifteenth century, they resumed trade with the West through Genoese merchants. Islam gradually penetrated the region in the sixteenth and seventeenth centuries, although this religion, too, only marginally affected their traditional beliefs and customs. The Cherkess seem never to have imitated the fanatical excesses of eastern Caucasians such as the Chechens and Daghestanis*. Their social structure was very loosely organized. Many of their customs, including the vendetta, mandatory hospitality, and bride purchase, are pan-Caucasian.

The Cherkess found themselves in a state of perennial war with the Tatar Khanate of Crimea and with Turkic groups such as the Karachais, Kumyks*, and Nogais* who had been driven into the Caucasus by the wars of Genghis Khan. Since the western part of the Caucasus range is relatively low and gentle, the Cherkess could not retreat into the mountains as did the Chechens and Ossetians. For protection, the Cherkess, like other Circassians, alternately sought alliances with Turkey and Russia. A total of three diplomatic missions to Muscovy in the 1550s resulted in what the Circassians called an "alliance" and the Russians called a "voluntary union" with Russia. Ivan the Terrible then took a Kabard princess as one of his wives. As Russian* settlers followed the Cossacks* into the region between the lower Don and the Kuban rivers, friction with the native Cherkess developed.

The Cherkess' fate was sealed by the Russo-Turkish wars. The Russians could not tolerate an independent Muslim Kabarda to the rear of their lines, and they forced Turkey to cede that territory (which it had never owned) in 1774. The Kabards rebelled in 1778 but were defeated. There were more battles between 1787 and 1791. Russian troops defeated the Ottoman forces of Batal Pasha on the upper Kuban River in 1790, and founded the *stanitza* (fortress) of Batalpashinsk (now the city of Cherkessk) in 1804. From there, the Georgian Military Road still winds through the mountains down to Sukhumi. General Aleksei Yermolov carried out vicious reprisals against the Cherkess and other Caucasians who resisted Russia. In 1829, the Turks gave up any claim to Circassia by the Treaty of Adrianople, but this was hardly the end of warfare between Russians and Circassians. Rebellions and reprisals continued in the 1840s and 1850s. The Cherkess, although not direct participants in the Murid Wars, did take advantage of the Russians' preoccupation with suppressing the Imam Shamil and his followers to raid and harass the west Caucasus forts repeatedly. Shamil capitulated in 1859, and the Russians completed their conquest of the Circassians in 1864.

Those Cherkess who survived the war were then given a choice of settling on the plains amidst Russians under Russian control or emigrating to Turkey. The number who went to Turkey is variously estimated at between 200,000 and 500,000. Conditions were horrible, and many died. Of those who survived, some were assimilated, and some went on to Syria, Jordan, Palestine, and Lebanon.

Russians, Ukrainians*, and Armenians* now poured into the depopulated Cherkess lands. Economic development of the Caucasus accelerated in the last decade of the nineteenth century and the first decade of the twentieth, but it was strictly a Russian affair. The Cherkess remained overwhelmingly rural.

Russian workers established a Kuban-Black Sea Soviet Republic in 1918, but the area was soon taken by White Guards. When the civil war ended with a Bolshevik victory, the Cherkess were subjected to a seemingly endless round of administrative manipulations designed to keep them separate and always outnumbered by other groups. The Karachai-Cherkess Autonomous Oblast, for example, artificially joined the Turkic Karachai with the Caucasian Cherkess. The Kabardino-Balkar Autonomous Soviet Socialist Republic did the same, for the Balkars* are another Turkic group. It would have made more sense to create one region for the Balkars and Karachai, and another for the Cherkess and Kabards, but this did not suit V. I. Lenin, Josef Stalin, or their successors. The Adyghe Autonomous Oblast was established in 1922.

Soviet policy in the 1920s and 1930s affected the Cherkess in three ways: First, the region's economy became heavily industrialized, and thus its value to the Soviet Union increased. Second, Soviet scholars devised three separate written languages (first using Latin and then Cyrillic script) for the Adyghes, Cherkess, and Kabards, where one common written language might have sufficed. Few publications ever appeared in those languages, and Cherkess children were encouraged to learn Russian instead (most did so, but strictly as a second language). Third, the Bolsheviks tried to erase Islam, closing religious schools in 1922. In the 1920s, the Soviet Union officially consolidated all Circassian peoples into two groups. The western group was designated as the Cherkess and the eastern group was designated as the Kabard. Late in the 1930s, the ethnic lines were officially redrawn, with Circassians being subdivided into three groups: the Adyghes as western Circassians, the Cherkess as central Circassians, and the Kabards as eastern Circassians. In January 1922, the government established the Cherkess Autonomous Oblast, and, in July 1922, the Adyghe-Cherkess Autonomous Oblast. The name Cherkess was dropped from the title of the Adyghe-Cherkess Autonomous Oblast in August 1936. The Cherkess Autonomous Oblast was re-established in 1928, which was later combined with the Karachai Autonomous Oblast to form the Karachai-Cherkess Autonomous Oblast.

In World War II, the Germans* occupied the Adyghe Autonomous Oblast and its capital, Maikop, as well as the Karachai-Cherkess Autonomous Oblast and its capital, Nalchik. In 1944, Stalin decided that the Turkic* people had been disloyal, so all Balkars, Karachais, and some Adyghes were deported to Central Asia. From then until 1957, when the punished nations were rehabilitated, the Karachai-Cherkess Autonomous Oblast was simply the Cherkess Autonomous Oblast. Today, ethnic separatism and local nationalism, so strong in the eastern Caucasus and the Transcaucasian republics, is far less threatening in the Circassian regions. The Cherkess population stands at approximately 53,000 people, virtually all of whom are Sunni Muslims. See CIRCASSIAN.

REFERENCES: Shirin Akiner, *Islamic Peoples of the Soviet Union*, 1983; Ronald Wixman, "Circassians," in Richard V. Weekes, ed., *Muslim Peoples*, 1984, 203–9; *The Peoples of the USSR: An Ethnographic Handbook*, 1984.
Ross Marlay and James S. Olson

CHERKESY. See CHERKESS.

CHERNEVIY TATAR. See CHERNEVYJE TATAR or TATAR.

CHERNEVJE TATAR. See ALTAI and CHERNEVYJE TATAR.

CHERNEVYJE TATAR. The Chernevyje Tatars are today known as the Altais.* They are part of the larger collection of Siberian Tatars* who originated with the Mongol* invasion of Russia in the thirteenth century. These Tatars were converted to the Sunni Muslim faith, Hanafi school, by Islamic merchants in the fourteenth and fifteenth centuries. During the fifteenth century, the region came under Ibak Khan and his Siberian Khanate, which reached north from present-day Kazakhstan to the Arctic Ocean. Russians* finally conquered the region late in the sixteenth century. Contact with Russians led to the conversion of some Tatars to Eastern Orthodox Christianity, although the conversion was superficial at best. Strong elements of Islam and their traditional shamanistic animism survived among them. Until the nineteenth century, most of the Tatars were hunters and trappers, going after sable, fox, marten, ermine, bear, and wolf. When industrialization began to reach Siberia, some of the Tatars went to work in factories, tanneries, and sawmills. After the 1930s, most of these Tatars found themselves living and laboring on collective farms. Since World War II, Russian ethnographers have classified the Chernevyje Tatars with the Altais. See ALTAI and TATAR.

REFERENCES: Shirin Akiner, *Islamic Peoples of the Soviet Union*, 1983; Alexandre Bennigsen and S. Enders Wimbush, *Muslims of the Soviet Empire: A Guide*, 1986.

CHERNEVYY TATAR. See ALTAI and CHERNEVYJE TATAR.

CHERNOMORSKIY. See BLACK SEA COSSACK and COSSACK.

CHERNYE KIRGIZI. See KYRGYZ.

CHERNYE KLOBUKI. See KARAKALPAK.

CHERNYE NOGAI. See KARA NOGAI and NOGAI.

CHERNYE NOGAITSY. See KARA NOGAI and NOGAI.

CHERNYE NOGAY. See KARA NOGAI and NOGAI.

CHERNYE NOGHAI. See KARA NOGAI and NOGAI.

CHERNYE NOGHAY. See KARA NOGAI and NOGAI.

CHERNYY KIRGIZ. See KYRGYZ.

CHERNYY KLOBUK. See KARAKALPAK.

CHERNYY NOGAI. See KARA NOGAI and NOGAI.

CHERNYY NOGAY. See KARA NOGAI and NOGAI.

CHERNYY NOGHAI. See KARA NOGAI and NOGAI.

CHERNYY NOGHAY. See KARA NOGAI and NOGAI.

CHETTI PURI. See SAGAI and KHAKASS.

CHETTIBER. See SAGAI and KHAKASS.

CHEVSUR. See KHEVSUR and GEORGIAN.

CHEVSURIAN. See KHEVSUR and GEORGIAN.

CHINALUG. See KHINALUG, SHAH DAGH, and AZERBAIJANI.

CHINALUGH. See KHINALUG, SHAH DAGH, and AZERBAIJANI.

CHINALUKH. See KHINALUG, SHAH DAGH, and AZERBAIJANI.

CHINESE. The 1989 census of the Soviet Union listed a total of 11,418 ethnic Chinese living in the Soviet Union. There were other groups in the Soviet Union that also had counterparts in China—such as the Manchus*, Dungans*, and Koreans*—but ethnic Chinese in this context means primarily Mandarin- and Cantonese-speaking Chinese of Han descent. Ethnic Chinese first arrived in the Russian Far East in the seventeenth century, when the area was used as a place of exile by political authorities in Northern China. When China ceded the Ussuri Province to Russia in the Treaty of Peking of 1860, a small number of Chinese were already living there, most of whom fished and hunted for their livelihoods. In the southern reaches of the area, Chinese farmers raised beans, maize, oats, wheat, melons, red pepper, tobacco, cabbage, garlic, and onions. Each of the major towns of the Russian Far East—Nikolsk Ussuriisky, Khabarovsk, and Vladivostok—had energetic Chinese communities. Each of these cities also had a Chinese Society, which promoted community cultural values, much to the consternation of the tsarist government. Other Chinese immigrated to the Russian Far East in the late nineteenth and early twentieth centuries when the government brought in Chinese contract laborers to work on public works construction projects.

By 1926, there were more than 23,000 Chinese living in Vladivostok and as many as 92,000 Chinese altogether in the Russian Far East. Some observers believed that Vladivostok seemed more like Shanghai than a Soviet community. Government policies worked at assimilating the ethnic Chinese. Between 1929 and 1937 Soviet linguists labored at creating a Latin alphabet for the Chinese language and introduced it to Chinese students in the public schools of the Far East. But the cultural and political winds changed in the late 1930s, and, in 1937, the government ordered the use of the alphabet terminated. There were also years of open hostility between ethnic Russians* and ethnic Chinese. Local Russians blamed the local Chinese for the anti-Russian policies of the Chinese warlords in Manchuria. Mob attacks on ethnic Chinese were not uncommon. A purge of the Far East occurred at the end of the 1930s when Chinese theaters, newspapers, and societies were suppressed. Between 1926 and 1939, the Chinese population of the Soviet Far East declined from 92,000 to 29,000 people. Those numbers continued to decline in subsequent years.

During the 1950s, after the Chinese Revolution that brought Mao Zedong and the Communists to power in China, large numbers of Chinese students and political officials lived in the Soviet Union to receive political training and higher education. Those numbers also began to decline by the early 1960s, however, when the Sino-Soviet split widened. During the 1970s and 1980s, the Soviet Union was not a very attractive place, politically or economically, for very many Chinese. The bulk of the 11,418 ethnic Chinese living there in 1989 were permanent residents of the Soviet Far East.

REFERENCES: John De Francis, *Nationalism and Language Reform in China*, 1950; Walter Kolarz, *The Peoples of the Soviet Far East*, 1969.

CHINESE MOSLEM. See DUNGAN.

CHINESE MUSLIM. See DUNGAN.

CHITRI. See CHUVASH and KHITRI.

CHIURKILI. See DARGIN.

CHOKNGAN. See KRJASHEN, TATAR, and VOLGA TATAR.

CHOLA. See JEW.

CHOLAM. See KHOLAM and BALKAR.

CHOLAMCHY. See KHOLAM and BALKAR.

CHOLAMCHYLY. See KHOLAM and BALKAR.

CHOLAMLY. See KHOLAM and BALKAR.

CHONGODOR. See KHONGODOR and BURYAT.

CHORA. See KHORA and BURYAT.

CHORNIE KIRGIZI. See KYRGYZ.

CHORNIE KLOBUKI. See KARAKALPAK.

CHORNIE NOGAI. See KARA NOGAI and NOGAI.

CHORNIY KIRGIZ. See KYRGYZ.

CHORNIY KLOBUK. See KARAKALPAK.

CHORNYE NOGAI. See KARA NOGAI and NOGAI.

CHORNYE NOGAITSY. See KARA NOGAI and NOGAI.

CHORNYE NOGAY. See KARA NOGAI and NOGAI.

CHORNYE NOGHAI. See KARA NOGAI and NOGAI.

CHORNYE NOGHAY. See KARA NOGAI and NOGAI.

CHORNYY NOGAI. See KARA NOGAI and NOGAI.

CHORNYY NOGAY. See KARA NOGAI and NOGAI.

CHORNYY NOGHAI. See KARA NOGAI and NOGAI.

CHORNYY NOGHAY. See KARA NOGAI and NOGAI.

CHORVAT. See UKRAINIAN.

CHOSHEUT. See KHOSHEUT and KALMYK.

CHOUDOR. The Choudor—also known as Choudur, Chovdor, and Chovdur—are one of the subgroups of the Turkmen*. Those subdivisions are based more on territorial distinctiveness than ethnic differences. The Choudor live in the Khorezm Oasis in the Turkmen Republic. See TURKMEN.
REFERENCE: Ronald Wixman, *The Peoples of the USSR: An Ethnographic Handbook*, 1984.

CHOUDUR. See CHOUDOR and TURKMEN.

CHOVDOR. See CHOUDOR and TURKMEN.

CHOVDUR. See CHOUDOR and TURKMEN.

CHRISTIAN TATAR. See KRJASHEN.

CHUD. See VEP.

CHUDIN. See VEP.

CHUF. See KHUF, RUSHAN, and TAJIK.

CHUFIDJ. See KHUF, RUSHAN, and TAJIK.

CHUFIDZH. See KHUF, RUSHAN, and TAJIK.

CHUFIJ. See KHUF, RUSHAN, and TAJIK.

CHUHAR. See VEP.

CHUHON. See VEP.

CHUI. See TELENGIT.

CHUI-KIZHI. See TELENGIT.

CHUKCHA. See CHUKCHI.

CHUKCHI. The Chukchi—who call themselves the Lyg Oravetlyan and are also known as the Luoravetlan, Chukcha, and Chukot—are an indigenous people of Siberia in Russia. Closely related ethnically and linguistically to the Koryaks* and ethnically to the Itelmen*, the Chukchi speak a Chukotic language, which is part of the larger Paleo-Asiatic family. They live in scattered villages throughout the Chukchi Autonomous Oblast, the Koryak Autonomous Oblast, and the Yakut Autonomous Republic. As late as the early twentieth century, the Chukchi were subdivided into a number of identifiable tribal groups, each with its own ethnic identity. Those subgroups included the western tundra Chukchi, who lived in the Nizhne-Kolymskiy Rayon of the Yakut Autonomous Republic; the Little Anyuy Chukchi, who followed nomadic trails between the Arctic Ocean and Anyuy; the Omolon Chukchi, who pursued a nomadic life-style along the Omolon River; the Chaun Chukchi, who also traveled nomadic trails between Chaun Bay and Cape Schmidt; the Amguema Chukchi, who lived along the Amguema River; the Chukchi of the Chukchi Peninsula; the Onmylen Chukchi of the left tributaries of the Anadyr' River; and the Tuman Chukchi of the Velikaya River and coastal areas south of the Anadyr' River. During the twentieth century, those regional identities have become steadily less significant as the Chukchi have acquired a more generic identity. With a population of more than 15,000 people in 1990, the Chukchi are the largest of the indigenous groups of Siberia.

Traditionally, the Chukchis were divided into two distinct economic groups, and those economic divisions have had strong cultural implications. One group of Chukchi, who call themselves the Chavchu or Chavchuven, were nomadic and semi-nomadic herders whose economy revolved around the reindeer herds. The other group of Chukchis, who call themselves the An' Kalyn, are settled coastal dwellers who live primarily on small peninsulas jutting off the coast so they can hunt sea mammals. The differences in the two ways of life were distinct enough for anthropologists to claim that the coastal Chukchi had more in common culturally with the coastal Koryaks than they did with the nomadic Chukchi. Coastal Chukchis and Koryaks primarily ate the meat and fat of walruses, common seals, and bearded seals. They also hunted the white whales and other whales. The nomadic Chukchi and Koryak ate reindeer. The reindeer provided the nomadic Chukchi with meat, lard, and blood, which they consumed as food as well as skins for clothes, shoes, tents, rope, harnesses, and strings. The Chukchi also used the tendons and horns. For transportation, they harnessed reindeer and attached them to sleds. The coastal Chukchi and Koryak traveled by dog sleds, while the nomadic Chukchi and Koryak traveled by reindeer.

Chukchi religious life resembles that of other aboriginal people around the world. An animistic, polytheistic people, the Chukchis believed that all aspects of creation—animals, plants, insects, lakes, mountains, rivers, oceans, stars, the sun, the moon, and the wind—had souls of their own consisting of some spiritual essence imparted from the source of all life. Human beings were not unique and transcendent but part of a larger, eternal whole. Not only did all things have spirits that gave them life, but all spirit was fundamentally of the same essence, different only in degree and not in kind. Through discipline, observation, and personal tranquility, individuals could learn from the world and make contact with the soul of the universe or any of its creations. Among the Chukchi, the souls of the animals they hunted and herded were particularly significant. In terms of religious rituals and festivals, however, the coastal Chukchi were different from the nomadic Chukchi. Coastal Chukchi ritual life was heavily laced with rituals devoted to whales, walruses, and seals. They sacrificed dogs annually to guarantee good hunts, while the nomadic Chukchi offered bits of entrails, meat, blood, and bone marrow to the gods to protect the reindeer herds.

Ethnic Russians* first encountered the Chukchi in 1642, when the Cossack* Ivan Yerastov met them on the Alazeya River. The Russians built Fort Nizhne-kolymsk in 1644 and Fort Anadir' in 1649. Using those forts as their bases, commercial traders, fur trappers, and hunters then established permanent contact with the Chukchi. Systematic Russian contact with the Chukchis brought a wave of epidemic diseases—influenza, mumps, smallpox, chicken pox, and so on— and the Chukchi underwent a population decline. Moscow authorized the granting of citizenship to any native who converted to Christianity, a process that led to forced baptisms and enserfment by local rulers, who then used these native serfs to increase fur trapping. As the numbers of fur-bearing animals decreased, Moscow lost interest in the area and in the well-being of its natives. The Chukchis were part of this entire administrative process. By the mid-eighteenth century, the Russians and Chukchis were drawn together in an increasingly commercialized economy. They began holding annual fairs, in which the Chukchi would trade reindeer hides and furs for alcohol, iron tools, firearms, ammunition, and tobacco. In the nineteenth century, as greater numbers of ethnic Russians settled in the region, the economic contacts strengthened. Completion of the Trans-Siberian Railroad in 1905 expanded those economic contacts even more.

The Bolshevik Revolution of 1917 had a dramatic impact on the Chukchis. The new Soviet government issued the ''Declaration of the Rights of the Peoples of Russia'' in 1917. This document guaranteed the ''equality and sovereignty of the peoples of Russia; the right of self-determination, including separation and the formation of independent states; abolition of all national and national-religious privileges or restrictions; and free development of national minorities and ethnic groups inhabiting the territory of Russia.'' Under Josef Stalin, who served at the time as Commissar for Nationalities, the program was implemented. When the position of Commissar for Nationalities was abolished in 1924, a new Committee of Assistance to the Peoples of the North (or Committee of the North) assumed responsibility for indigenous affairs.

There was an intense debate among Soviet officials during the 1920s over native policy. The Committee of the North proposed creating large reservations for the indigenous peoples of Siberia, including the Chukchi, where they could be left alone to pursue traditional life-styles. But V. I. Lenin and other Bolsheviks opposed this, ''arguing it would prevent Native People from catching up educationally, politically, and economically with other Soviet nationalities.'' Instead, the Soviet government made the decision to incorporate the native peoples into the larger social, political, and economic body of the country. Between 1929 and 1932, the government created ''national districts,'' or oblasts, which were small territorial administrative units named after each of the native peoples; among these was the Chukchi Oblast. Late in the 1920s and throughout the 1930s, the government also collectivized the indigenous economic activities. For the Chukchi, this meant collectivization of their traditional reindeer-herding economy. Collectivization had a dual purpose: It would implement the communist economic ideology, and it would help to acculturate Chukchi children to Russian values and eliminate the traditionally nomadic, subsistence economy of the Chukchi people. This policy inspired a futile resistance from Chukchi leaders. The government also established "cultural bases" for the indigenous people—settlements complete with boarding schools, hospitals, day-care centers, veterinary dispensaries, and clubs. The government worked to minimize the nomadic nature of Chuckhi life. It was easier for the government to create such bases for the coastal-dwelling Chukchi than for the nomadic Chukchi, but the government encouraged the nomads to settle down as well. The Soviet government also created a Cyrillic alphabet for the Chukchi language in 1931, but, in 1938, Russian became the language of instruction for all Chukchi schoolchildren. Finally, the government launched an assault on Chukchi religion. Russian Orthodox Christianity had been superimposed on the native religion under the tsars, creating a syncretic, mixed faith. Beginning in the late 1930s, the Soviet government prohibited both native and Russian Orthodox religious services among the Chukchi.

Dramatic changes in Chukchi life have occurred since World War II. During the war, when the Soviet government relocated so much of its industry east of the Ural Mountains to keep it out of German* hands or protected from German artillery bombardment, large numbers of ethnic Russian workers suddenly moved into Siberia. State development plans accelerated that process in the 1950s and 1960s, and as a result the Chukchi found themselves herding reindeer on ever smaller amounts of land. More and more Chukchi moved into the settled coastal villages, while fewer and fewer herded reindeer. The collapse of the Soviet economy in the 1970s and 1980s actually slowed that process somewhat, but, even then, the long-term changes in Chukchi life were irreversible. Many Chukchis still followed the reindeer and lived in their *yaranga* tents, but growing numbers abandoned the herds for jobs at construction sites, oil and natural gas wells, and mass-production factories. Moreover, the coastal Chukchis are increasingly assimilating with the Eskimos.*

After 1985, the *perestroika* and *glasnost* policies of Mikhail Gorbachev gave the Chukchi more political freedom and ended the heavy-handed cultural repression they had experienced for fifty years. In 1988, along with other indigenous peoples, the Chukchi contacted Gorbachev shortly after the Communist Party of the Soviet Union (CPSU) established a special nationality commission to strengthen the collective farms and other state businesses, including fur-trading operations. The Chukchi also participated in the creation of the Association of People of the North (APN) on March 31, 1990, during a meeting in the Kremlin. This organization was established to defend the interests of twenty-six northern peoples by slowing the pace of economic development, the influx of ethnic Russian settlers, and the deterioration of the natural environment. The Chuckchi also want the government to ratify both the 1957 International Convention on

Protection and Integration of Indigenous and Other Tribal and Semi-Tribal Populations in Independent Countries and the 1989 Convention on Indigenous and Tribal Peoples in Independent Countries in order to affirm that they have a right to the ownership and possession of lands that they have traditionally occupied.

Ironically, the collapse of the Communist Party and the disintegration of the Soviet Union in 1991 actually made the achievement of Chukchi objectives less likely to occur. More than anything else, the implosion of the economy explained the destruction of the Soviet Union, and one of the major goals of people like Boris Yeltsin was the acceleration of economic development. Since huge volumes of natural resources exist in Siberia, the exploitation and exportation of those resources—especially coal, iron ore, natural gas, timber, and petroleum—represented a relatively quick way of earning hard currency to develop the rest of the economy. Russians began importing Western technology to develop Siberia. In the process, the traditional Chukchi economy became even more threatened. If, during the rest of the 1990s, the development of the Siberian economy continues to accelerate, the pressure on traditional Chukchi ways will become even more intense.

One of the leading advocates of Chukchi rights in the late 1980s and early 1990s is Yuri Rytkheu, a widely published Chukchi poet. He has been openly critical of Josef Stalin's brutal and shamelessly manipulative ethnic policies, which forcibly ended the nomadic Chukchi ways; he has been equally critical of the impact that economic development was having on the tundra environment in which the Chukchis had traditionally lived. Rytkheu has been active in the Congress of Minorities in the North, Siberia, and the Soviet Far East, which lobbied for the protection of their habitat. Economists estimate that, in 1992, the Chukchis were responsible for raising more than 500,000 reindeer on state-controlled breeding regions. A principal demand among Chukchi activists has been for the privatization of the herds, so that Chukchi life could return to its pre-collectivized status. As centrifugal ethnic forces swept through the Soviet Union in 1990 and 1991, they affected the Chukchis as well. Tired of coming under the domination of ethnic Russians, the Chukchis began to demand political autonomy. In February 1991, the Chukchi legislature of the Chukchi Autonomous Region seceded from the Magadan Krai of Russia, renaming themselves the Chukchi Soviet Autonomous Republic. When the Soviet Union disintegrated at the end of 1991, the Chukchi legislature dropped the word Soviet from their name and became the Chukchi Autonomous Republic.

REFERENCES: "A Chukchi Writer's View of Then and Now," *Soviet Life*, (December 1990), 24, 35; Alice Bartels and Dennis Bartels, "Soviet Policy Toward Siberian Native People," *Canadian Dimension*, 19 (1985), 36–44; *Current Digest*, 43 (March 20, 1991), 27; Mike Edwards, "Siberia: In From the Cold," *National Geographic*, 177 (March 1990), 2–49; Constantine Krypton, "Soviet Policy in the Northern National Regions After World War II," *Slavic Review*, 13 (October 1954), 339–53; Piers Vitebsky, "Perestroika Among the Reindeer Herders," *Geographical Magazine*, 61 (June 1989), 23–34; Ronald Wixman, *The Peoples of the USSR: An Ethnographic Handbook*, 1984.

CHUKHAR. See VEP.

CHUKHON. See VEP.

CHUKOT. See CHUKCHI.

CHUKOTIAN. See CHUKCHI.

CHULAM. See KHOLAM and BALKAR.

CHULAMCHI. See KHOLAM and BALKAR.

CHULAMCHILI. See KHOLAM and BALKAR.

CHULAMLI. See KHOLAM and BALKAR.

CHULIM TATAR. See CHULYM TATAR and TATAR.

CHULYM TATAR. The Chulym Tatars, who call themselves the Kjuerik (Kiueriks), are part of the larger collection of Siberian Tatars*. Russians* refer to them as the Chulymskije tatary. They live today on the Chulym River near the town of Achinsk in Siberia. Chulym ethnicity originated with the Russian conquest of western Siberia, which drove many Baraba Tatars* east to the region of the Chulym River where they mixed with other Turkic-speaking people in the area. Until the nineteenth century, most of the Chulym Tatars were hunters and trappers, going after sable, fox, marten, ermine, bear, and wolf. When industrialization began to reach Siberia, some Chulym Tatars went to work in factories, tanneries, and sawmills. Since World War II, Russian ethnographers have classified the Chulym Tatars as Khakass*. The Chulym Tatars also include a small group of people known as Ketsiks, a Turkic-speaking people who settled south of Mariinsk in the nineteenth century. See TATAR.
REFERENCES: Shirin Akiner, *Islamic Peoples of the Soviet Union*, 1983; Alexandre Bennigsen and S. Enders Wimbush, *Muslims of the Soviet Empire: A Guide*, 1986; Ronald Wixman, *The Peoples of the USSR: An Ethnographic Survey*, 1984.

CHULYMSKIJE TATARY. See CHULYM TATAR.

CHUNZAL. See KHUNZAL and AVAR.

CHURKILI. See DARGIN.

CHUVAN. The Chuvan, also known as the Shelga, were a group of Yukagirs* who are now classified as a Chukchi* subgroup. See CHUKCHI and YUKAGIR.

REFERENCE: Ronald Wixman, *The Peoples of the USSR: An Ethnographic Handbook*, 1984.

CHUVASH. The Chuvash are a Turkic-speaking people whose homeland, the Chuvash Autonomous Republic, is located along the right bank of the middle Volga River in Russia. They are known to Russians* as the Chuvashi. According to the census of 1989, there were 1,839,228 Chuvash living in the Chuvash Republic, as well as in the adjoining regions of the Bashkir and Tatar Autonomous Republics and in the Kuybyshev and Ulyanovsk oblasts of the Russian Federated Republic. The Chuvash are divided into two main groups: the upper and northern Chuvash (Viryal* or Vir'ial), and the lower and southern Chuvash (or Anatri*). These divisions have both linguistic and historical antecedents.

The Chuvash language derives from the Bulgar group of the West Hunnic branch of Turkic languages and is related to ancient Bulgar and Khazar; the modern Chuvash dialects, however, are unlike and unrelated to any other modern Turkic dialect. Chuvash shows affinities to the language not only of the Volga Bulgars but also to Mongol* and Tungusic*. In addition, the Chuvash dialects have within them large numbers of loan words from both Slavic and Finno-Ugrian. The existence of both Finno-Ugrian and Turkic-speaking Bulgar strains within the Chuvash has stimulated controversy over their cultural base, which appears to center around the relative importance of either Finno-Ugrian or Turkic elements within the Chuvashian culture. For example, some scholars identify the Chuvash as the indigenous Finno-Ugrian population of Chuvashia, conquered by a small group of Turkic-speaking migrants, who then imposed their language and culture upon the native inhabitants. Others believe that a dominant, Turkic-speaking majority, the Bulgars, migrated into the area and assimilated the Finno-Ugrian natives. The Chuvash themselves can shed no light on the subject, as they can claim descent only from the ancient Bulgarians*, who were part of the Hunnic Confederation and whose state in the Volga region lasted from the seventh to the fifteenth centuries.

The difficulty with Chuvash ethnogenesis stems from the paucity of early source material mentioning them. Nothing conclusive or free of interpretational disputes can be said of pre-sixteenth-century sources. Thus, the questions about the early history of the Chuvash may never be completely resolved. For example, the Chuvash may have been mentioned by earlier chroniclers under another name or may have developed into a culturally distinct group at a relatively late date. The first clear mention of the Chuvash by that name comes from a Russian chronicle dated 1521, when the Chuvash were already a well-established and culturally distinct group in the region between the Sura and Sviiaga Rivers. In spite of the fragmentary and often contradictory evidence, however, a general history of the Chuvash prior to the sixteenth century can be outlined.

Possibly the earliest mention of the Chuvash dates from 922, when the Arab* traveler Ahmad ibn Fadlan identified a people called the Suvas or Savas whom he encountered on his trip through the Volga River region. Fadlan's Suvas (also known as Suvars or Savirs), along with the Bulgars, were the first Turkic* groups to appear in Chuvashia. The Suvas may be the ancestors of the Chuvash, or at least, have lent them their name. The histories of these two peoples, the Bulgars and the Chuvash, are extremely difficult to separate and may even be coterminous at this early date. Khazar expansionism into the south Russian steppes in the 670s, followed by Arab expansionism into the Caucasus region in the 730s, caused the Bulgars and later the Suvas, respectively, to migrate to the middle Volga. There they eventually established a Volga Bulgar state that was, until the tenth century, under the suzerainty of the Khazars. Some Chuvash may have begun, under Arab influence, to convert to Islam toward the end of the ninth century. Gaining independence upon the break-up of the Khazar Khanate, the Bulgars and Suvas established a Volga Bulgar empire that dominated the middle Volga region until the Mongol conquest of 1236. The migration of these two Turkic peoples into the region has been used to explain the existence of the two main contemporary Chuvash groups: the Bulgars are identified with the northern Chuvash, while the later Suvas are linked with the southern Chuvash. Although the question is subject to scholarly dispute, these two groups appear to have assimilated the native Finno-Ugrian peoples of this area.

In the thirteenth century, the Chuvash were conquered by the Mongols of the Golden Horde and forced to pay tribute. In addition, the Mongols' adoption of Islam as a state religion encouraged its spread among the Chuvash. Still, there is no historical indication of the degree to which the Chuvash accepted Islam or of its subsequent strength in their culture. Upon the break-up of the Horde into smaller subdivisions in the early fifteenth century, the Chuvash came under the control of the Khazan Khanate, which had appeared by the 1440s. Waves of disruptive Tatar* raiding into Chuvashia then forced the Chuvash to migrate northward out of their homelands, abandoning southern Chuvashia almost entirely from the fourteenth to the late sixteenth centuries. During those years, while southern Chuvashia reverted to the ''Wild Field,'' an influx of new settlers strengthened the Turkic element in northern Chuvashia. By the sixteenth century, the Chuvash had developed their own unique identity. Under Bulgar and Mongol suzerainty, the Chuvash made the transition from semi-nomadic cattle raising to more settled agriculturalism. And, while there may have been some degree of social stratification, in the form of a native landowning aristocracy that partially cooperated with the Khazars, Mongols, and Khazans, the historical evidence for a fully developed, feudal class structure simply does not exist.

The Chuvash came under Muscovite Russian control when the Khazan Khanate was defeated by Ivan the Terrible in 1552. When the Chuvash came under Russian rule, their status changed radically; they became an integral part of the Russian state and have participated in all the major developments of that state since the mid-sixteenth century. Further, the Chuvash, unlike the Tatars, were subjected to intensive baptism and Christianization, particularly during the eighteenth and nineteenth centuries. The Russians experienced much less success with the Tatars, who were wont to cling tenaciously to Islam. As the Chuvash are now overwhelmingly Christian, they bear little contemporary cultural resemblance to their Muslim Turkic cousins in the region. The forced conversions, together with a policy of russification, led to a considerable amount of unrest. Russian rebellions, such as those led by Stenka Razin in 1667–1671 and Emelyan Pugachev in 1773–1775, found ready support among the Chuvash. As a result, Muscovy was obliged to establish a capital at the village of Cheboksaray in 1555 and to empower a *namestnik* (local Muscovite governor) five years later. In addition, the Russians built other towns in the region throughout the 1570s and 1580s and established a string of forts throughout Chuvashia, as much to keep the natives quiescent as to guard the area from Tatar depredations. These villages and outposts not only encouraged migration into Chuvashia, but also made possible the resettlement of the southern Chuvashian "Wild Field," leading Chuvashia to fill out once again to its present-day boundaries.

The Chuvash national identity was advanced by the development of a written language, since the Chuvash had previously had no native written alphabet. The first Chuvash grammar was published in 1769, other texts, primarily the Scriptures and other religious texts, appeared soon after. Kazan University's Faculty of Oriental Languages (founded in 1804) pioneered work on the Chuvash language, while V. P. Vishnevskii's grammar and dictionary appeared in 1836. In 1868, the first Chuvash secondary school, later converted into a seminary, was opened in Simbirsk. In 1872, I. Y. Yakovlev compiled a Chuvash alphabet that stood unaltered until 1938. Some local primary schools taught students in the vernacular toward the end of the nineteenth century. Yakovlev was part of the steady stream of young boys who were trained in Russian schools, russified, and sent back to their homeland to work as teachers and priests. These people became champions of Russian culture. Yakovlev, in particular, was considered a national hero among his people, a sentiment that was discouraged by the Soviet authorities because of his "reactionary views," his opposition to the 1905 Revolution, and his ties to the Russian Orthodox church. After World War II, however, the Soviet government relaxed its attitude toward Yakovlev when they recalled that he had been encouraged in his work by V. I. Lenin's father, I. N. Ulyanov, who served as a school inspector in Simbirsk (today known as Ulyanovsk).

Their isolation from particularistic cultural ties has led the Chuvash to develop a unique nationalism that is neither pan-Finnic nor pan-Turkic. Instead, the Chuvash have harked back to their Volga Bulgar heritage, stressing the Bulgarian state and its stabilizing and civilizing influence on that area of Inner Russia. In pressing their nationalist claims, the Chuvash have, from time to time, resorted to violence. The Chuvash became particularly restless during the period of Soviet ascendency between 1905 and 1917. One anti-government uprising in the Jadrin district in 1913 was especially serious. Chuvashia also became the setting for a number of major confrontations between Red and White forces during the civil war.

After Soviet power was established in Cheboksaray in March 1917 and had spread throughout Chuvashia by May 1918, the Chuvash became especially vociferous nationalists and took the opportunity to make demands upon the new government. The government established the Chuvash Autonomous Province in June 1920, changing its name to the Chuvash Autonomous Soviet Socialist Republic within the Russian federation, in 1925. Along with sovietization, the Central Committee had been allowing the various nationalities to change their names if they wished. It was forced to deny this privilege to the Chuvash, however, when they insisted upon assuming the name "Bulgars" and renaming their homeland "Bulgaria." The Soviet leadership believed that such a move would be inconsistent with its nationalities policy, since it would strengthen a separatist Chuvash nationalism, lead to endless confusion with the Balkan Bulgarians, and cause resentment among other inner Russian Turkic peoples, such as the Kazan Tatars* who were likewise descended from the Volga Bulgars. The Chuvash also made the practical demand for the incorporation of the predominantly Russian town of Simbirsk (Ulyanovsk), the birthplace of Lenin, which they considered an important cultural center where many of the first books in the Chuvash language had been printed. The Central Committee reacted to both demands with outrage against their Chuvash comrades for displaying such nationalism. The committee deduced that the cause of these demands lay in the predominantly "reactionary" agrarian character of the region. The central government therefore responded by changing the republic's boundaries in 1926 to include a strong working-class district that did not share the Chuvash's romantic, "nationalist" notions. This move raised the percentage of proletarian workers in the Communist Party of Chuvashia from 9 to 40 percent within a matter of months.

In spite of this case of obvious gerrymandering and other changes to the party in Chuvashia, its peasantry remained very conservative and anti-Communist. In the 1930s, they violently resisted the introduction of collectivization, even to the point of attempted assassinations of the Communist propagandists stationed in Chuvash villages. The Provincial Committee, located in nearby Gorky, was finally forced to step in to restore order. Unlike other nationalities within the Russian Soviet Federated Socialist Republics (RSFSR), the Chuvash constituted a numerical majority in their own homeland, in spite of their proximity to Moscow and the Soviet's active encouragement of Russian immigration to Chuvashia. Since the break-up of the Soviet Union, this situation does not seem likely to change. As of 1979, the Chuvash made up 68.4 percent of the total population of Chuvashia, which represents only a 2 percent drop since 1959 and a 6 percent drop since 1926. That percentage had only dropped to 67.8 percent of the population in 1991.

REFERENCES: Walter Kolarz, *Russia and Her Colonies*, 1953; Charles Quelquejay, "Cuwash," *Encyclopedia of Islam*, 1965; Azade-Ayse Rorlich, *The Volga Tatars*, 1984.

Lee Brigance Pappas

CHUVASHI. See CHUVASH.

CHVARSHI. See KHWARSHI and AVAR.

CHVARSHIN. See KHWARSHI and AVAR.

CHWARSHI. See KHWARSHI and AVAR.

CHVARSHIN. See KHWARSHI and AVAR.

CHYSH. See SHOR.

CHYURKILI. See DARGIN.

CHYURKILIN. See DARGIN.

CIGAN. See GYPSY.

CIRCASSIAN. Much confusion attends the use of the English-language name Circassians (formerly Abazgo-Circassians*), which is applied to a number of related groups and tribes of the northwest Caucasus mountains. The Russian* name for these people is "Cherkess," but that is now applied to only one group of Circassians, those who live in the Karachai-Cherkess Autonomous Oblast. There are actually four officially designated nationalities in the Soviet Union that can be considered Circassians: the Adyghes*, the Cherkess*, the Kabards*, and the Abazas*. A fifth group, the Abkhazians* of the Georgian Republic, is linguistically related but culturally distinct.

The Circassians may at one time have occupied the entire area between the Don River and the Caucasus mountains, and between the Black Sea and the Stavropol plateau. But, as they found themselves overrun in turn by the Sarmatians, Mongols*, Turks*, and Russians, they are now reduced in number and are everywhere a minority population. The Circassians chiefly inhabit three territorial units: 1) the Adyghe Autonomous Oblast of Krasnodar krai, with its capital at Maikop; 2) the Karachai-Cherkess Autonomous Oblast of Stavropol krai, with its capital at Cherkessk; and 3) the Kabardino-Balkar Autonomous Republic, with its capital at Nalchik. The 1989 census counted 124,941 Adyghes, 54,000 Cherkess, 394,651 Kabards, and 33,801 Abazins. Thus, if we consider these people as a single ethnic group (which the Soviet government does not), there were 607,393 Circassians in the Soviet Union in that year. A large but indeterminate number live abroad, mostly in the Middle East. These are the descendants of Circassians expelled from Russia in 1864.

The Circassian homeland is a warm and fertile part of the former Soviet Union, with open grassland, rich soil, and numerous rivers carrying Caucasus snowmelt to the Black Sea. The terrain is eminently suitable for agriculture and thus has attracted many Russian and Ukrainian* settlers. The area contains coal, oil, and natural gas. Because of this geographic base, the traditional Circassian economy has revolved around animal husbandry. Circassians have a well-earned reputation throughout Central Asia and the Middle East for their skills in breeding horses, cattle, and sheep. They are also well-known for unrivaled horsemanship and marksmanship. Another important feature of the Circassian economy involves textiles, and their sheepskins and leathers are highly prized throughout Central Asia and the Middle East.

Circassian tribes spoke many dialects of a single language, but, because of their turbulent history, different tribes adopted various loan-words from Russian, Turkish, Georgian*, Persian*, and Arabic. Today, the Russian government recognizes Adyghe, Abkhazian, and Kabardino-Cherkess as official languages. They are mutually intelligible. All belong to the northwest group of the Caucasian language family.

What chiefly distinguishes Circassians from other Caucasian nations is the simple geographic fact that their rivers drain to the Black Sea, not the Caspian. Thus, from earliest times, they were peripherally in touch with the Mediterranean ecumene, by contrast with their inward-looking, xenophobic, eastern neighbors, the Ossetians*, Karachais*, and Chechens*. Greek* and Roman authors described tribes in the northwest Caucasus as particularly noted for their fine horsebreeding and horsemanship. Circassian women were considered especially beautiful; many were sold into Turkish and Arabian harems. Circassian men often hired out as mercenaries, and one particularly successful group ruled Egypt for centuries as the Mameluke dynasty. The Circassians traded with Byzantium in horses, honey, furs, and filigreed jewelry. Some converted to Christianity, which, however, blended with rather than displaced their pagan beliefs. Contact with Byzantium was interrupted in the thirteenth century by the Mongol conquest. In the fifteenth century, Circassians resumed trade with the West through Genoese merchants. Islam gradually penetrated Circassia in the sixteenth and seventeenth centuries, although this religion, too, only marginally affected their traditional beliefs and customs. The Circassians seem never to have imitated the fanatical excesses of eastern Caucasians such as the Chechens and Daghestanis*. Their social structures varied widely, from the loosely organized western tribes (Adyghes) to the elaborately hierarchical Kabardian kingdom. Many of their customs, including the vendetta, mandatory hospitality, and bride purchase, are pan-Caucasian.

The Circassians found themselves in a state of perennial war with the Tatar* Khanate of Crimea and with Turkic groups such as the Karachais, Kumyks*, and Nogais* who had been driven into the Caucasus by the wars of Genghis Khan. Since the western part of the Caucasus range is relatively low and gentle, the Circassians could not retreat into the mountains as did the Chechens and Ossetians. For protection, they alternately sought alliances with Turkey and Russia. Three diplomatic missions to Muscovy in the 1550s resulted in what the Circassians called an "alliance" and the Russians called a "voluntary union" with Russia. Ivan the Terrible took a Kabard princess as one of his wives. As Russian settlers followed the Cossacks* into the region between the lower Don and the Kuban, friction with the native Circassians developed.

The Circassians' fate was sealed by the Russo-Turkish wars. The Russians could not tolerate an independent Muslim Kabarda to the rear of their lines, and they forced Turkey to cede that territory (which it had never owned) in 1774.

The Kabards rebelled in 1778 but were defeated. There were more battles between 1787 and 1791. Russian troops defeated the Ottoman forces of Batal Pasha on the upper Kuban River in 1790, and founded the *stanitza* (fortress) of Batal-pashinsk (now the city of Cherkessk) in 1804. From there, the Georgian Military Road still winds through the mountains down to Sukhumi. General Aleksei Yermolov carried out vicious reprisals against Circassians and other Caucasians who resisted Russia. In 1829, the Turks gave up any claim to Circassia by the Treaty of Adrianople, but this was hardly the end of warfare between Russians and Circassians. Rebellions and reprisals continued in the 1840s and 1850s. The Circassians, although not direct participants in the Murid Wars, did take advantage of the Russians' preoccupation with suppressing the Imam Shamil and his followers to raid and harass the west Caucasus forts repeatedly. Shamil capitulated in 1859, and the Russians completed their conquest of the Circassians in 1864.

Those Circassians who survived the war were the given a choice of settling on the plains amidst Russians under Russian control or emigrating to Turkey. The number who went to Turkey is variously estimated at between 200,000 and 500,000. Conditions were horrible, and many died. Of those who survived, some were assimilated, and some went on to Syria, Jordan, Palestine, and Lebanon. Russians, Ukrainians, and Armenians* now poured into the depopulated Circassian lands. Economic development of the Caucasus accelerated in the last decade of the nineteenth century and the first decade of the twentieth, but it was strictly a Russian affair. The Circassians remained overwhelmingly rural.

Russian workers established a Kuban-Black Sea Soviet Republic in 1918, but the area was soon taken by White Guards. When the civil war ended with a Bolshevik victory, the Circassians were subjected to a seemingly endless round of administrative manipulations designed to keep them separate and always outnumbered by other groups. The Karachai-Cherkess Autonomous Oblast, for example, artificially joined the Turkic Karachais with the Caucasian Cherkess. The Kabardino-Balkar Autonomous Soviet Socialist Republic did the same, for the Balkars* are another Turkic group. It would have made more sense to create one region for the Balkars and Karachai, and another for the Cherkess and Kabards, but this did not suit V. I. Lenin, Josef Stalin, or their successors.

Soviet policy in the 1920s and 1930s affected the Circassians in three ways: First, the region's economy became heavily industrialized, and thus its value to the Soviet Union increased. Second, Soviet scholars devised three separate written languages (first using Latin and then Cyrillic script) for the Adyghes, Cherkess, and Kabards, where one common written language might have sufficed. Few publications ever appeared in those languages, and Circassian children were encouraged to learn Russian instead (most did so, but strictly as a second language). Third, the Bolsheviks tried to erase Islam, closing religious schools in 1922.

In World War II, the Germans* occupied the Adyghe Autonomous Oblast and its capital, Maikop, and the Karachai-Cherkess Autonomous Oblast and its capital, Nalchik. In 1944, Stalin decided that the Turkic people had been disloyal, so all Balkars and Karachais were deported to Central Asia. From then until 1957, when the punished nations were rehabilitated, the Karachai-Cherkess Autonomous Oblast was simply the Cherkess Autonomous Oblast.

Today ethnic separatism and local nationalism, so strong in the eastern Caucasus and the Transcaucasian republics, is far less threatening in the Circassian regions. Russians outnumber Adyghes three to one in the Adyghe Autonomous Oblast, and the Cherkess constitute a mere 10 percent of the population of the Karachai-Cherkess Autonomous Oblast. Only in the Kabardino-Balkar Autonomous Republic do Circassians outnumber Russians, and, even there, more than one-third of the population is Russian. The tiny Abazan population has no literary language and is being assimilated by the Cherkess.

REFERENCES: W.E.D. Allen and Paul Muratoff, *Caucasian Battlefields*, 1953; Maxim Kim, *The Soviet Peoples: A New Historical Community*, 1974; Louis J. Luzbetak, *Marriage and Family in Caucasia*, 1966; Hugh Seton-Watson, *The Russian Empire, 1801–1917*, 1967; R. T. Trakho, "Literature on Circassia and the Circassians," *Caucasian Review*, 1 (1955), 145–62.

Ross Marlay

COIBAL. See KOIBAL and KHAKASS.

COJLA CHEREMISS. See KOZHLA MARI.

COLIMCHAN. See KOLYMCHAN and RUSSIAN.

COLVA IURAK. See KOLVA NENETS and NENETS.

COLVA NENET. See KOLVA NENETS and NENETS.

COLVA SAMODI. See KOLVA NENETS and NENETS.

COLVA SAMOED. See KOLVA NENETS and NENETS.

COLVA SAMOIED. See KOLVA NENETS and NENETS.

COLVA SAMOYED. See KOLVA NENETS and NENETS.

COLVA YURAK. See KOLVA NENETS and NENETS.

COLVIN IURAK. See KOLVA NENETS and NENETS.

COLVIN SAMODI. See KOLVA NENETS and NENETS.

COLVIN SAMOED. See KOLVA NENETS and NENETS.

COLVIN SAMOIED. See KOLVA NENETS and NENETS.

COLVIN SAMOYED. See KOLVA NENETS and NENETS.

COLVIN YURAK. See KOLVA NENETS and NENETS.

COLYMCHAN. See KOLYMCHAN and RUSSIAN.

COMI. See KOMI.

COMI IJEM. See IZHMI and KOMI.

COMI IJMI. See IZHMI and KOMI.

COMI IZHEM. See IZHMI and KOMI.

COMI IZHMI. See IZHMI and KOMI.

COMI PERMIAK. See KOMI.

COMI PERMYAK. See KOMI.

CONDOMA TATAR. See KONDOMA TATAR and SHOR.

COREL. See KARELIAN.

CORELIAN. See KARELIAN.

CORIAK. See KORYAK.

CORYAK. See KORYAK.

COURS. See LATVIAN.

COSSACK. The Cossacks were truly a unique phenomenon in world history. They consisted of several bands of free warriors who roamed the vast expanse of the steppe north of the Black and Caspian seas. The origins of the Cossacks are very vague both because of a lack of records and because they have often been the focus of political propaganda by competing empires wishing to control the steppe. The Cossacks developed a militaristic society, borrowing traits from surrounding cultures and developing their skills at warfare through piracy, brigandage, and mercenary service. They survived in the power vacuum created by the tensions among the Russians*, Poles*, Lithuanians*, Tatars*, and Turks*—often playing one empire against another to gain wealth and maintain their freedom. But once the Russian Empire achieved its unassailable control of the steppe, the Cossacks were gradually reduced to the role of obedient servants of the tsar.

Throughout their history the Cossacks lived difficult lives. For centuries, they survived by constant warfare against the Tatars and the Turks and later by warfare on behalf of whoever paid them. For two centuries, they made war at the will of the tsar, who dismantled their society and turned them into ordinary soldiers. An old saying among the Cossacks was "Cossack glory means a dog's life." Still, long before these "dogs" accepted the tsar as their master, they had lived wild and free lives on the steppe. For many years, writers have been at a loss to explain Cossack origins. Although their beginnings are "shrouded in mist," it appears that the Cossacks were in fact fugitive peasants from several countries—primarily Russians, Ukrainians*, and Poles—who fled to the steppe to escape taxation, punishment, or oppression. There they adopted the life-style of the Turkic Tatars who had preceded them on the steppe. To understand the Cossacks, one must begin with these Tatars.

In the thirteenth century, the Tatars of the steppe were a part of the Golden Horde, which ruled the area from the Black Sea to Siberia and held Russia in vassalage. They in turn were ruled by Ghengis Khan's son, Batu Khan, and they spoke a Turkic* language. Tatar military structure was based on tens: ten men to a section, ten sections to a squadron, ten squadrons to a regiment, and ten regiments to a division. A leader was called an *ataman*, and his deputy an *esaul*; leaders at the lower levels were chosen by election. These words, among many others, and the election practices of the Tatars were adopted by the later Cossacks. Among the Tatars, there was no distinction between a soldier and a civilian. They were merciless in war, but saw no disgrace in fleeing from an enemy when the battle turned against them. They fought on horseback with sabers, bows and arrows, and lances complete with a hook for unseating enemy horsemen. By the late fourteenth century, the Mongol Khanates were beginning to break up because of strife among the hordes. This development allowed Russia to refuse payment of tribute in the fifteenth century and enabled both Russia and Lithuania to expand into Ukraine. But the Mongols did not give way quickly. Dispersion of the Golden Horde brought more active raiding by both the Mongols and the independent Tatars who lived around the Don, Donets, and Dnieper rivers. In these raids, the Tatars would capture goods, livestock, and slaves to trade in the Black Sea markets. In one raid, the Crimean Tatars* reportedly carried off 130,000 Russians.

The Russians and Lithuanians found themselves defenseless against these Tatar raids. It became apparent that Tatars could be defeated only by other Tatars, so the Russians began to hire Tatars for their defense. The first Tatars in Russian service were the Ryazan Cossacks, who, while attempting a raid on Ryazan, came to terms with the grand duke and entered his service. These Tatars then gave their service to the Russian tsar. Emigrant Tatars provided Russia with soldiers for border defense, becoming known as service Cossacks or town Cossacks. They were responsible to border barons, instead of to a Tatar prince, and were paid by the state. The majority of border town populations were Great Russian or Little Russian, but the outpost and regimental units that guarded the border were largely Tatar.

Beyond the border lay a 400-mile stretch of rich land controlled by no country but roamed by nomads and Tatar marauders. From the mid-fifteenth century on, Slavic peasants from Little and Great Russia began to migrate to this land, preferring to brave the dangers of the open steppe to facing their debts or the oppression of the Poles and Lithuanians. These peasants banded together in military colonies to defend themselves against Tatar raids and elected their own leaders. Those living on the frontier began to call themselves Cossacks. As Lithuania expanded, these Cossacks pushed further into the steppe, and some were hired by the Lithuanians for defense, just as the Tatars had been hired. Confronting the Tatars of the "wild country" the Russian frontiersmen began to adopt Tatar ways. They too used words such as *ataman* and *esaul*; they likewise adopted Tatar weapons and their style of warfare. They also began to practice the piracy of the Tatars. By the middle of the sixteenth century these Slavic Cossacks outnumbered the Tatars and the other tribes on the steppe. Moreover, they attacked and raided the Tatars just as the Tatars had raided the Slavs for centuries.

Because of the frequency of raids, agriculture was not possible for the Cossacks. They lived by fishing, hunting, and piracy. All of the Cossack communities were formed along most of the rivers that flow into the Black and Caspian seas: the Dniester, Dnieper, Don, Donets, Volga, and Yaik (Ural). The Cossacks of each river basin developed certain characteristics that distinguished them from each other. These communities were called hosts, or *voisko*, and each had its own government. All Cossacks hosts were originally democratic and egalitarian. The early Cossacks would return to the border towns where they held assemblies that often concluded in bloody fighting. "This was democracy in action," historian Philip Longworth has written.

The Don valley was entirely vacant in 1520, but complaints very soon began to arise over marauding bands that were attacking Turkish, Tatar, and Nogai* merchants. These marauders were Moscovite Russians who had fled to the steppe to escape servitude. The bands also included fugitives from Little Russia, Lithuania, Finland, and Turkey, but the largest portion of them were Tatar and Great Russian. The number of Muscovites fleeing to the Don Valley increased greatly during the reigns of Ivan the Terrible and his two immediate successors. Those with families settled in the upper regions, but those without families ranged from the Russian to the Tatar border and from the Crimea to the Volga in search of plunder. In 1551, the Don Cossacks attacked Azov. Believing them to be pawns of Moscow, the Sultan described them as "a creeping disaster." In 1570, Ivan the Terrible began employing Don Cossacks to escort envoys and caravans and, later, to raid the Tatars and recapture Russians taken by them. In the 1580s, Cossacks under Yermak Timofeyev were used to conquer the Tatar khanate of Sibir, which allowed the Russians to push through Siberia and reach the Pacific by 1640.

The Don Cossacks were originally divided into upper and lower groups along the river, but they gradually united. In the mid-seventeenth century, they lived in thirty villages on the Don and its tributaries. They were described as having a "swarthy or ruddy complexion," and they liked to drink. Their dress and their language was a mixture of Great Russian and Tatar. They lived by plunder, as well as by raising animals, hunting, fishing, and salt-farming. The Don Cossack assembly was called the *krug*, and, in imitation of the Tatars, it elected an *ataman* and his two *esaul* deputies. The *ataman* controlled the judging and punishing of crimes, except for the most serious cases when the *krug* would be called to confirm judgment. To the Cossacks, the worst crimes were treachery, cowardice, and theft from each other. The death penalty was frequent. When an *ataman* left office, he was designated as an elder; the elders then formed an advisory body for the new *ataman*. Their seat of government was at Cherkassk, where representatives from the outlying areas were sent when important matters had to be discussed in the *krug*.

The Don Cossacks maintained two types of settlements. One was a year-round settlement, called *gorodki*, made up of huts or semi-basement dugouts and surrounded by wattle fences or moats. The other were the *zimovishchi*, which were huts or dugouts that provided only winter quarters for homeless Cossacks who had spent their summers on campaign. The Don Cossacks maintained some of the shamanistic superstitions of the Tatars, but they adhered primarily to the Russian Church. They were tolerant of people of other faiths, except for Jews*, taking into their communities Old Believers, Muslims, Lamaists, and heathens. Like the Tatars, the Don Cossacks were organized by tens, and their military groups were given a mixture of Russian and Tatar names.

By the end of the 1600s Russians had moved closer to the Don Cossack territories; these newer populations had become more settled and begun to practice agriculture extensively. Agriculture had long been banned by the Cossacks, and, in 1690, the *krug* sent out its last prohibition of agriculture. Nonetheless, farming continued out of necessity. With agriculture came the personal holding of land, which had formerly been open communal property, and then private ownership. Some Cossacks acquired vast estates, and disparities in class were created. Poor Cossacks and newly arrived peasants worked as laborers for the richer Cossacks. Restrictions were placed on entry into the Don Host, and the Cossacks developed into a privileged class.

For more than a century, the tsars of Russia employed the Cossacks but took no responsibility for their actions. Tsars directed Cossack action but dealt with them as a foreign country through the Muscovite Foreign Office. The Cossacks were vital to Russia's defense against the Turks and the Tatars. Because of this situation, the Russians would not encroach on the Cossacks for fear that they might accept employment with Russia's enemies. Once Peter the Great sent the Don Cossacks against Azov, however, the Turkish threat to Russia was removed. This allowed the tsar to make greater demands on the Cossacks and to exert greater control over them. Russia then expanded farther into Don territory. Peter ordered the Cossacks to stop fishing in the lower Don and to give their entire stock of dried fish to the state. Needy Cossacks were ordered to take allotted work. Peter revoked the Cossack privilege of not returning escaped serfs and demanded the return of refugees who had arrived since 1695. To this last order, the Don Cossacks refused to comply. Many Don Cossacks moved to the Terek and Yaik rivers, and soon uprisings began in reaction to Peter's demands. These uprisings occurred among several Cossack hosts. In 1709, the tsar began to control the appointment of the *ataman* and, by mid-century, the elders (or *starshinas*) were appointed from St. Petersburg. At the end of the eighteenth century, serfdom was initiated on the Don, and the military of the Don Cossacks was separated from their civil government. Don Cossacks were even used against Zaporozhe Cossacks* in 1775. By this time, the Don Cossacks were no longer a frontier force, since the border had been pushed to the Kuban and Terek rivers. The number of Don Cossacks continued to increase from 19,000 troops in 1763, to over 50,000 in the Napoleonic Wars, in which 20,000 of them died.

Several other Cossack groups evolved out of the original collection of Don Cossacks. The Ural Cossacks*, who have also been called the Yaik, first emerged in the late sixteenth century as an identifiable Cossack group. Like the Don Cossacks, they also had a cultural mix in their ethnogenesis, with substantial Tatar and Kazakh* elements intermingling with the Russian background. The Ural Cossacks lived primarily between the Volga and the Ural rivers. The Greben Cossacks*, who were also called the Skoi, were another offshoot. Like the Ural Cossacks, they emerged as an identifiable group in the late sixteenth century, when they appeared in the southern reaches of Don Cossack territory. Greben Cossack culture is laced with North Caucasian elements, which reflect the contributions of the Chechens* and the Nogais*. The steppe of the eastern North Caucasus was the homeland of the Greben Cossacks. A third group to emerge from the Don Cossacks in the sixteenth century were the Terek Cossacks*. Like the Greben Cossacks, Terek Cossack culture contained many North Caucasian elements. In their case, however, the contributing cultures were those of the Ossetians*, Circassians*, and Nogais. The Terek Cossacks lived in the steppes of the central North Caucasus.

Two other Cossack groups also originated with the Don Cossacks, although their historical connections were indirect. The Transbaikal, or Zabaikal, Cossacks were descended from the Ural Cossacks. They first appeared as a distinct group in the late eighteenth century, and their ethnic roots were Russian, Buryat*, and Evenk*. The Transbaikal Cossacks* lived in the Transbaikal area of southern Siberia. Early in the nineteenth century, the Amur-Ussuri Cossacks* emerged from the Transbaikal Cossacks, especially after the addition of many Tungusic* and Manchu* peoples. The Amur-Ussuri Cossacks claimed the Amur and Ussuri river valleys of southeastern Siberia as their homeland.

All of these Cossack groups derived from the Don Cossacks. The second-largest Cossack host, and perhaps the most unusual, was the Zaporozhe (or Zaporozhian) Cossacks who lived along the Dnieper river in Ukraine. "Zaporozhe" comes from a Ukrainian word meaning "beyond the rapids." With Lithuania expanding into Ukraine, a number of Cossacks sought refuge on islands in the Dnieper beyond twenty-five miles of unnavigable cataracts. On one of these islands, they built a hide-away called a *sich*. The place was safe because it was difficult to reach from the north, provided an excellent position from which to observe the Tatars in the east, was partly covered by forest, and was hidden by reeds. According to one authority, "it was an ideal hide-out, a perfect nest for would-be robbers, a stronghold easy to hold against attack." The inhabitants of the Zaporozhe Sich were exclusively male and, until the seventeenth century, probably numbered fewer than 3,000 inhabitants. The population grew, and eventually the Sich developed a suburb of traders, along with tailors, boot-makers, bakers, brewers, coopers, blacksmiths, gunsmiths, and carpenters. The Zaporozhes became pirates on the Dnieper and in the Black Sea. They raided towns and villages along the coasts, and, by 1600, even Constantinople was in danger of attack by the Zaporozhe Cossacks.

The Zaporozhe pirates sailed river craft that were sixty feet long, twelve feet wide in beam, and sat low in the water. They had to be buoyed up with bundles of reeds to cope with the waves of the Black Sea. The boats had sails to use in fair weather, but were normally propelled by twenty or thirty oars with two men on each oar. These vessels were called seagulls, and one could be built by sixty Cossacks in about two weeks. They were swift and could easily out-maneuver the bulky Turkish galleys. Because of their small draught, the boats could also be sailed into waters too shallow for the galleys to follow. Armed with fauchards, pistols, muskets, and sabers, thousands of Cossacks in hundreds of these boats would set out on pirating expeditions, typically approaching their targets under cover of night and attacking at dawn. The Turks became so desperate to stop the Cossacks that they tried holding them back by stretching a great chain across the mouth of the Dnieper. This was unsuccessful, and the Zaporozhe Cossacks pushed on through. Sometimes, to avoid the Turks, Cossacks would carry their boats overland to other rivers flowing into the Black Sea.

The Polish government refused to recognize the existence of a Cossack community, but it hired Cossacks on an individual basis, placing their names in a register and paying them a regular sum. Ukrainian Cossacks were enrolled into Polish service as early as 1524, and, by 1625, there were six regiments of 1,000 men each registered as "Polish Cossacks." The registry was a means by which the Poles hoped to gain control of the Cossacks by offering rewards and special privileges only to registered Cossacks. But the 6,000 registered Cossacks amounted to only about one-tenth of all Ukrainian Cossacks in 1625. Many others fled to the Zaporozhe Sich, beyond the reach of Poland. Moscow also hired Ukrainian Cossacks, sending 500 of them against the king of Poland in 1581. As their reputation for fighting the Turkish infidels grew, the Zaporozhe Cossacks became idealized in the eyes of others as a brotherhood of knights, and, because women were excluded from the Sich, these men were described as a ''monkish military community.'' But, in reality, the Zaporozhes would fight for whoever paid them, including the Muslims, and they were anything but monkish.

The Zaporozhes' popular assembly was called the *Rada*, and only males were allowed to attend. Like the Don Cossacks, the Zaporozhe Cossacks elected their leaders. A newly elected *ataman* was expected to refuse the appointment at least twice, and he was spattered with mud by the elders to teach him humility. The *ataman* was responsible for administering justice, and their punishments were as severe as those of the Don Cossacks. In the Sich, murderers were tied to the corpses of their victims and buried alive with them. Gradually, the Zaporozhe Cossacks were influenced by the Polish military organization and began appointing officers as the Polish army did. The Cossacks created commanders of artillery and ordnance, as well as officials for collecting taxes, regulating trade, maintaining weights and measures, and guarding river crossings.

The Cossacks relied on immigration to increase their numbers and willingly accepting foreigners in the Sich. Among the Zaporozhes, ''the Russian element predominated, but Poles, Wallachians, Germans*, and Spaniards* found their way to the Sech, and the Zaporozhians would even accept a renegade Jew . . . despite [*sic*] their virulent anti-Semitism.'' New entrants into the Sich often had to prove their physical fitness and were required to be at least nominal Christians.

In the seventeenth century, the Zaporozhes sported huge mustaches and shaved their heads except for a top-knot. They wore colorful oriental clothing with baggy trousers, broad golden galloons (decorative braids), silk cummerbunds, and tall hats of sheepskin or turbans with ostrich feathers in them. By contrast, the early Zaporozhe Cossacks had been so poorly dressed that their word for launching a raid actually meant to ''find a coat for one's back.'' In the *Sich*, they had lived in huts, called *kish*, made of reeds and ''covered with horses' hide to keep out the rain.'' After a successful raid, they would celebrate wildly, getting drunk, singing, and performing very athletic dances. These celebrations might last for days.

During the ''time of troubles'' (1605–1613), many Zaporozhe and Don Cossacks fought on behalf of a pretender to the Russian throne, ''False-Dimitri.'' Later they fought against each other, as the Poles and the Russians vied for control of Moscow. Through the registry, the Poles offered the Ukrainian Cossacks regular pay, the officers even enjoyed certain privileges and status similar to that of the Polish nobility. Many Cossacks found this to be attractive and settled down into Polish service. They also began to farm land granted to them by the government. Over the registered Cossacks, the Polish government appointed a leader called the *hetman*. At the same time, the Poles would not recognize any rights for unregistered Cossacks, who were expected to fulfill certain feudal obligations to the Polish-Lithuanian landlords in Ukraine. Many Cossacks escaped to the Sich, which remained independent, and from there fought frequently with the Poles. In the mid-seventeenth century, a rebellion broke out among the Zaporozhe Cossacks against Polish rule. This revolt was led by Bogdan Khmelnyts'kyi and eventually led to the Russian acquisition of the eastern Ukraine.

The son of a wealthy registered Cossack, Khmelnyts'kyi was given a good education as a warrior in the Zaporozhe Sich. In 1646, a local Polish officer destroyed Bogdan's estate, killed his son, and stole his mistress. Bogdan could get no redress through the law and was forced to flee for his life. To other registered Cossacks he presented a document, claiming that it had been issued by the king, requesting the Cossacks to attack the Crimean Tatars*. The Cossacks were reluctant, and, after escaping arrest Khmelynts'kyi fled to the Zaporozhe Sich where he encouraged rebellion. He then went to the khan of the Crimean Tatars, Islam Girei III, presented him with the same document that he had shown earlier, and asked the Tatars to join him in an attack on the Poles. The khan agreed to send 4,000 men to Khmelnyts'kyi's aid. Dressed as monks and spreading Bogdan's call to arms, emissaries from the Sich moved secretly around Ukraine. Khmelnyts'kyi attacked and defeated the Polish fortress at Kodak. Cossacks from all over Ukraine began flooding into the Sich, which numbered 5,000 men by March of 1648. In April, Khmelnyts'kyi elected *hetman* over 8,000 Cossacks and 4,000 Tatars. When he met a Polish force sent to suppress the rebellion at Zheltyye Vody, the registered Cossacks in the Polish force threw down their banners and joined the rebels. Khmelnyts'kyi's victory over the Poles at Korsun sparked a tremendous uprising among serfs and peasants in Ukraine, White Russia, Galicia, Poland, the Don, Moldova, and Wallachia. Thousands rampaged toward the Sich to join the Cossack army, carrying whatever weapons could be found, including "forks, flails, scythes, even the jawbones of animals fixed to staves." The Jews were a particular target. Hundreds of thousands were slaughtered, perhaps "as much as 90 percent of the Ukrainian Jewish population."

The king of Poland agreed to negotiate with the Cossacks, but the negotiations in 1649 ended in a stalemate. Khmelnyts'kyi then raised 20,000 more men, and the Crimean khan brought him a host of Nogai warriors. Khmelnyts'kyi met a Polish force at Zbarazh and tried to starve them out, he then forced the king into the Treaty of Zborow when the king's relief force became bogged down while crossing a river. The Cossacks thereby gained a much improved position of independence in Ukraine.

When Khmelnyts'kyi tried to form a confederacy with Moldova, Wallachia, and Transylvania, the Poles again sent a force against the Cossacks. This time, they were more successful. The Tatars abandoned Khmelnyts'kyi's force in the field, and he was forced to retreat. Later he signed another treaty with the Poles on less advantageous terms. This treaty was unpopular with his followers, and hostilities broke out again. Unable to support their independence alone, the

Ukrainian Cossacks turned to the tsar for help. In October 1653, Russia recognized the Ukrainian Cossacks as a "free people" who were not bound to the
king of Poland. In January 1654, the Cossacks gave their loyalty to the tsar.
The Russian tsar allowed 60,000 Cossacks to be registered and gave them ownership of lands and towns, but he gave nothing to their peasant followers. He
also claimed the right to confirm their elected *hetman*.

Together, Cossack and Russian troops marched on Lithuania and to the west.
The Poles sued for peace, but the Cossacks were not allowed at the conference
table. Struggles continued for another decade until 1667, when Poland and Russia
divided Ukraine. Eventually, "under Muscovy all vestige of Cossackdom in the
Ukraine was to disappear."

Frightened by a revolt of the eastern Cossacks under Stenka Razin in 1671,
the Muscovite authorities began to take steps to prevent similar rebellions in the
future. Cossacks were ordered to swear oaths of loyalty to the tsar. Several
artificial regiments of "Cossacks" that had been set up by Tsar Alexei in the
1650s in the Slobodskaya Ukraine were eventually converted into regular hussars.
The Cossacks were no longer needed in Ukraine, so the tsar began to dismantle
their regiments. "Despite a succession of risings, the old Cossack traditions
gradually disappeared in the Ukraine, and in 1699 the Tsar felt able to abolish
registration altogether." The Zaporozhe Cossacks remained fairly independent
to the end of the seventeenth century, but were growing closer to the tsar, fighting
for him more frequently than anyone else. The government under Peter the Great
began to move Cossack settlers out so Russian landowners could expand their
holdings. After the revolt of Kondrati Bulavin was suppressed in 1708, the
territory of the Don Host was made a part of the Russian province of Azov.
Ivan Mazepa then became *hetman* of the Russian Ukraine. Stratification along
class lines accelerated under Mazepa. Rank-and-file Cossacks became either
landowning gentlemen or virtual serfs. Mazepa presided "the final liquidation
of Ukrainian Cossackdom." He was bought off by the Swedes to join their war
against Russia, and he persuaded the Zaporozhe Cossacks to follow him. Tsar
Peter defeated the Swedes and punished the Zaporozhe Cossacks by burning
their Sich to the ground. The tsar then began to relocate the Cossacks to the
rapidly expanding borders of the empire. While the military burdens on the
Cossacks continually increased, their supplies and pay were frequently inadequate. With the Zaporozhe, Don, and Yaik Cossacks all firmly under his control
by 1721, the tsar ceased to deal with the Cossacks through the College of Foreign
Affairs and placed their administration in the College of War, thereby doing
away with even the symbolic notion that the Cossacks were independent of
Russia. "The old institutions of self-government survived but they were gradually
sterilized of all real content." The *ataman* became merely a servant of the tsar,
and the assemblies, when they met at all, merely rubber-stamped decisions made
in St. Petersburg. Over the next fifty years, the Zaporozhe Cossacks turned to
trading, and some made vast fortunes, but poorer Cossacks often became thieves
or vagabonds. These would form gangs called *gaidamaks*, and they terrorized

much of Ukraine. In 1775, the government destroyed the Sich that had been rebuilt, declared the Zaporozhe land to be a part of the "New Russia," and relocated the Cossacks.

That relocation eventually led to the emergence of two new Ukrainian Cossack groups. Many of the disbanded Zaporozhe Cossacks fled across the Danube River into territory controlled by Turkey. They became known as Transdanubian Cossacks. Those who remained in Russian-controlled territory evolved into the Black Sea Cossacks.* When the Russo-Turkish War ended in 1791, they were relocated to the Kuban region where they became known as Kuban Cossacks.* In 1828, most of the Transdanubian Cossacks began returning to Russian-controlled territory where they officially became classified as Kuban Cossacks as well. They lived on the steppes of the eastern North Caucasus region, particularly near the Kuban River.

After the defeat of Emelyan Pugachev's revolt, the last vestiges of democratic government among the Cossacks was stamped out. The very name of the Yaik Cossacks was destroyed, the Cossacks of the Volga were moved to the Caucasus, and the Don Cossacks were placed under the direct rule of Grigori Aleksandrovich Potemkin, Catherine II's favorite. Only their skills as warriors allowed the Cossacks to continue as a group distinct from the general population. But now, the Cossacks constituted a warrior class within Russian society and not an independent society of their own. They were called the "martial estate," and their role in society was defined by their military organizations. They were frequently uprooted by the government and sent to colonize new lands. They were sent to the Terek, Astrakhan, the Kuban, Siberia, and the Mongolian border. When the government ran short of Cossacks, it merely gave other segments of the population Cossack status, including immigrants, orphans, exiles, and Kalmyk* and Bashkir* tribesmen. There would eventually be some fifteen different Cossack hosts, most of which were created at the command of the tsar. In 1775, senior Cossack officers were given rank and privileges similar to those of the minor Russian nobility; "from 1796 their children were allowed to inherit." Junior officers received gentry status in 1798, and peasants living on Cossack elders' land were tied to their estates as serfs.

More than 50,000 Cossacks fought against Napoleon. They were dressed in uniform and provided for by the government and the nobility. Ataman Platov led them through the war, and they fought side by side with the Russian army. Platov had called for volunteers among the Cossacks, saying it was their obligation "to sacrifice everything for the defense of . . . the August Throne." Nicholas I appointed Russian generals who had never been Cossacks as deputy *atamans*. Male Cossacks were obligated to perform military service "as long as they were fit to sit a horse or shoulder a rifle." As opposed to their earlier privileges, they were now required to pay taxes on land and a poll tax when not under arms. Alexander II believed the Cossacks to be of little use in the future. He began a number of policies to bring the Cossacks under Russian common law and Russian civil administration. In April 1869, a Russian statute provided

Cossack officers and officials with landed property rights, a move that helped to undermine the Cossack social order, because the lower classes, who remained under Cossack communal institutions, felt betrayed and demanded equal treatment. In imitation of the German army, the Cossacks were transformed in 1875 from long-service to short-service engagement, for the purpose of creating large reserves of trained men. Other reforms continued the process of converting the Cossacks into a regular force within the Russian military.

Total loyalty to the tsar became a tradition among the Cossacks, and they maintained it to the last. Their ancestors' pride in being completely free was replaced by pride in soldierly service. The Cossack regiment by World War I had become virtually indistinguishable from the Russian cavalry, except for their uniforms and traditional Cossack names. During the revolution, Cossacks at the front remained largely immune to the influence of the revolutionists, although Cossacks in the cities often sided with them. Cossacks had long been used by the tsars to suppress dissent, but, at the beginning of the revolution, Cossack guards in St. Petersburg ignored orders to attack a crowd of protesters. In the confusion of the years that followed, the Cossacks were divided among those who supported the revolution, those who still supported the tsar, and a few who attempted to set up an independent Cossack state.

Two statutes, in 1917 and 1918, reduced the Cossacks to the status of other Russian peoples. The collectivization campaigns of the late 1920s constituted another blow to the Cossacks. They resisted, but Josef Stalin mercilessly crushed them. The Bolsheviks wiped out the Cossacks by simply murdering a great many of them. Historians estimate that more than 1.25 million Cossacks met their deaths at Stalin's hands. Those who survived blended with the rest of the population, emigrated, or moved to the cities. In 1936, several "Cossack" regiments were re-created, but there was almost no connection between the new "Cossacks" and the Cossacks of earlier days. These regiments fought in World War II, and some so-called "Cossacks" were recruited by the German* army. Even if they had been true Cossacks, they would have been of little use. The age of cavalry and of Cossackdom had passed.

In recent years, there has been a revival of Cossack identity. The Cossack revival is rooted in the *perestroika* policies of Mikhail Gorbachev and the burst of Russian nationalism that spread through the Soviet Union and then the Commonwealth of Independent States (CIS) in the late 1980s and early 1990s. When Gorbachev called for a restructuring of the Soviet economy, increased entrepreneurial activity, and private incentives, the descendants of the Cossacks began arguing that they were uniquely suited for that role. The long tradition of Cossack economic success in the nineteenth and early twentieth centuries equipped their descendants for economic success today, so they argued, and they demanded exemption from all taxes throughout the 1990s as a form of reparation for what Soviet authorities had done to them in the 1920s and 1930s.

In addition to these economic issues, the Cossack revival has revolved around the protection of the Russian identity. During the 1980s and 1990s, Cossack groups appeared in places like Moldova, Azerbaijan, Armenia, Siberia, and the Baltics to protect ethnic Russian minorities there against persecution by local ethnic groups. They claimed that Russia needed a Cossack revival in order to revitalize the military service and resurrect the prosperous Cossack private farms of an earlier era. Yuri Averyanov, an ethnologist and leader of the Consultative Council on Problems of the Revival of Russian Cossacks, proposed the creation of an All-Cossack Bank, the revival of specialized Cossack military service, the restoration of Russian Orthodoxy as the Cossack religion, special representation for Cossacks in the Supreme Soviet, and, in areas where Cossacks constitute the majority of the population, the replacement of the local soviets with *hetman* boards of government. Cossack leaders have also called for restrictive measures against non-Russians in the CIS. The Don Cossacks have re-established their traditional Great Circle, or council, and they selected Mikhail Sholokhov, son of the Don Cossack writer Mikhail Aleksandrovich Sholokov, as their *hetman*. Ethnologists and political scientists have debated whether the Cossack revival was really an ethnic issue or not, but, for the first time in nearly seventy years, the Cossacks were a visible presence in Russia again.

REFERENCES: W. P. Cresson, *The Cossacks: Their History and Country*, 1919; *Current Digest*, 3 (November 16, 1991), 21; 43 (August 7, 1991), 9–10; 43 (September 23, 1991); 44 (April 8, 1992), 18; 44 (June 17, 1992), 13–14; W. G. Glaskow, *History of the Cossacks*, 1972; Linda Gordon, *Cossack Rebellions*, 1983; Henry Krasinski, *The Cossacks of the Ukraine*, 1848; Philip Longworth, *The Cossacks: Five Centuries of Turbulent Life on the Russian Steppes*, 1969; Robert H. McNeal, *Tsar and Cossack, 1855–1914*, 1987; James W. Redhouse, ed., *A Turkish and English Lexicon*, 1890; Albert Seaton, *The Horsemen of the Steppes: The Story of the Cossacks*, 1985; D. Mackenzie Wallace, *Russia*, 1878; Ronald Wixman, *The Peoples of the USSR: An Ethnographic Handbook*, 1984.

COURLANDER. See LATVIAN and LITHUANIAN.

COURONIAN. See LATVIAN.

COVA TUSH. See BATSBI and GEORGIAN.

COVA TUSHIN. See BATSBI and GEORGIAN.

COYBAL. See KOIBAL and KHAKASS.

COZHLA CHEREMISS. See KOZHLA MARI and MARI.

CRESHEN. See KRJASHEN TATAR and TATAR.

CREVIN. See LATVIAN.

CREVINGI. See LATVIAN.

CRIASHEN. See KRJASHEN TATAR and TATAR.

CRIEVIN. See KRIEVINI and VOD.

CRIEVINGI. See KRIEVINI and VOD.

CRIM TATAR. See CRIMEAN TATAR.

CRIMCHAK. See KRYMCHAK and JEW.

CRIMEAN. The 1989 census of the Soviet Union listed a population of 1,312 people who were identified as Crimeans. By this definition, those people claiming to be Crimeans were not Crimean Tatars* nor Slavic inhabitants of the Crimean Peninsula. Instead, they were descendants of the original Genoese, Venetian, Armenian*, and French* merchants who settled in the coastal cities of the Crimean Peninsula in the thirteenth century. Such towns as Kaffa, Evpatoria, and Tana had been inhabited primarily by these merchant families from the time of the Middle Ages, and they focused their economic energies on the exchange of goods among Asia, Europe, and the Middle East. In the subsequent centuries, the Crimea experienced a vast in-migration, first by Tatars*, who became known as the Crimean Tatars, and later by Russian* and Ukrainian* peasants attracted by the fertile soil of the steppes. Despite the intense social pressures of living in an alien ethnic environment, several thousand of those original Greeks*, Armenians, Genoese, French, and Venetians managed to maintain a distinct identity. As late as 1989, more than 1,300 still identified themselves as Crimeans and as Christians who were distinct from the surrounding Slavic as well as Muslim populations.
REFERENCE: Alan Fisher, *The Crimean Tatars*, 1987.

CRIMEAN JEW. See JEW.

CRIMEAN TATAR. The Crimean Tatars—also known as Kyrym (Krym) Tatars and Krym-Turks—are an ethnic group of 268,739 people, according to the 1989 census of the Soviet Union. They have been referred to historically as the Tavricheskije tatary and the Tauride tatary; Russians* call them the Krymskije tatary. Until 1944, they lived on the Crimean Peninsula, but, during World War II, they were deported to Central Asia, where they still remain today. Most of the Crimean Tatars live in or near Tashkent and are scattered throughout Uzbekistan. The Crimean Tatars first emerged as a self-conscious ethnic group in the thirteenth and fourteenth centuries. At the time, the coastal cities of the Crimean peninsula were controlled by Greek*, Armenian*, Jewish*, Italian*, and French* merchants; the vast steppes north of the mountains were inhabited by nomadic tribes that were Turkish in terms of language and Islamic in religion. In the mid-thirteenth century, when the Golden Horde invaded the region, Turkish* tribes established political control over the coastal cities. Large-scale Turkish immigration began in the late thirteenth century. Haci Giray became the first khan of an independent Crimean Khanate at the end of the fourteenth century. He was the first of the Giray dynasty.

In 1453, the Ottomans finally achieved their centuries-old dream of seizing Constantinople. The Ottomans proclaimed their sovereignty over the Crimea, but Giray continued to attract substantial Tatar* immigration. He managed to forge an alliance with the major Crimean Tatar clans, and, although the Ottomans claimed sovereignty, the Crimean Khanate enjoyed considerable independence. For the Ottomans, the presence of the Crimean Khanate, which had effective military resources, prevented Muscovy and Poland-Lithuania from expanding southward into the steppes. The Crimean Khanate enjoyed financial stability because of support grants from the Ottomans (in return for military service) and tribute payments from Muscovy and Poland. The khanate developed its own administrative bureaucracy, codified legal system, and hierarchical political institutions. The hereditary clans—Sirins, Argins, Barins, and Kipchak—owned large amounts of land and enjoyed real political power. Later Soviet claims that the Crimean Tatars were no more than nomadic brigands is false.

During the years of the independent Crimean Khanate, the Crimean Tatars played a key role in Eastern European politics. The Tatars provided tens of thousands of well-trained soldiers for Ottoman military campaigns. They also helped to defend the empire's northern flank against attack and encroachment by Muscovy and Poland-Lithuania. In other words, it was a buffer state. Moreover, the Crimean Tatars supplied slaves, salt, fish oil, grain, and meat to the Ottoman economy. Finally, the presence of the Crimean Tatars in the Crimea kept Slavic settlers from migrating to the rich soil of the steppes; such settlers therefore headed east to Siberia instead of south into Central Asia.

The decline of the Ottoman Empire gave Muscovy the opening it needed in the Crimea. Muscovy first invaded the Crimea in the 1680s, and, in 1696, Peter the Great captured Azov and gained Russian access to the Black Sea. Tatar slave raids then ended. In 1736, Russia invaded again. With access to the Mediterranean, Russia could play a more effective role in European politics; by stabilizing the southern frontier, Russia could also turn its attention to Poland. In addition, because of centuries of slave raids and military incursions by the Tatars, there was a deep Slavic hostility toward them. Catherine II saw the Russian campaign to its conclusion, conquering the Crimean Tatars and annexing the Crimea in 1783.

During the next century, a russification process went forward in the Crimea. Catherine II and subsequent Russian rulers respected the influence of the Muslim clergy, but they destroyed Tatar architecture and encouraged the large-scale immigration of Russian Slavs. Russian political and administrative institutions were imposed, and taxes were collected. The Russians also encouraged Tatar emigration to Turkey, which proceeded by the tens of thousands. The Crimean

War in the 1850s and then the Russian-Ottoman War of 1879 accelerated this emigration.

Late in the nineteenth century, a Crimean Tatar national awakening began to take place. After 1860, Russia encouraged the enrollment of Tatar children in Russian schools, and eventually a Tatar intelligentsia, separate from the traditional Muslim clergy, emerged. An early intellectual leader was Ismail Bey Gaspirali (Gasprinskii). He supported pan-Turkism, the modernization of Russian Islam, female equality, and an educated Turkish elite. Education was the key. Other groups, such as the Young Tatars and the Tatar Nationalists, soon followed, and more radical members among them demanded Crimean independence.

When World War I broke out, Russia went to war against Germany, Austria-Hungary, and the Ottoman Empire, and the Russians quickly grew suspicious of possible Tatar connections with the Ottomans. Russian worries about a Muslim fifth column drove a wedge between the Russians and the Tatars, and a strong Tatar independence movement emerged as an act of self-defense. People like Celebi Cihan and Cafer Seidahmet formed the Committee for the Defense of the Rights of Muslim Turko-Tatar Peoples of Russia and fled to Turkey to avoid arrest by Russian authorities. From there and later from Switzerland, they began to side with any group opposed to the tsar and that might be willing to remove Russian institutions and state authority from the Crimea. In 1917, the Tatar National Constituent Assembly, known as the Kurultay, convened and called for Crimean independence. Its program included national self-determination, a Tatar parliament, universal manhood suffrage, and separation of powers.

After the Bolshevik Revolution, the Crimean Tatars saw the imposition of Communist rule as just another form of Slavic oppression. Several Tatar leaders were executed, and groups of guerrilla resistance to Soviet authority appeared. In 1921, the Soviet Union decided to reach an accommodation with Tatar nationalists. Amnesty was extended to anti-Soviet Tatar leaders, and the Crimean Autonomous Soviet Socialist Republic (ASSR) was created. The central government did not, however, give in to Tatar demands that all political and economic institutions in the new republic be under Tatar control. The Tatar alphabet was latinized, and nationalist Tatar leaders were accused of ''bourgeois nationalism,'' imprisoned, or executed. Collectivization led to starvation in much of the Crimea in 1921, especially after Crimean foodstuffs were shipped to the ''more important'' central regions of the Soviet Union. More than 100,000 Tatars in the Crimea starved to death, and tens of thousands of others fled to Turkey and Romania. During the collectivization campaigns of 1928–1929, thousands of Crimean Tatar peasants were deported or slaughtered. Many Tatar peasants rebelled against Soviet authorities or engaged in passive resistance, which included killing their herds rather than turning them over to the collectives. The collectivization campaign led to another famine from 1931 to 1933. Between 1917 and 1933, approximately 150,000 Crimean Tatars—half of their population—had either been killed or deported from the Crimea. Between 1933 and

1939, those Crimean Tatar leaders who tried to stop the slaughter, or even to protest it, became part of Josef Stalin's "Great Purge." In 1938, the Latin alphabet of Tatar was replaced by a Cyrillic alphabet, and most Tatar literature was banned. No other Soviet nationality suffered as much under Soviet control as did the Crimean Tatars.

The disaster engulfing the Crimean Tatars only worsened during World War II. The invading German* armies established complete political control over the Crimea, and they organized the Tatars into military bands that fought against pro-Soviet partisan groups. Other Tatar groups fought against the Nazi occupation. In the spring of 1944, when the Red Army re-occupied the Crimea, the Crimean Tatars were targeted for persecution because of their "cooperation" with the Nazis. On the night of May 18, 1944, all Crimean Tatars were rounded up by the Soviet army, and the deportations began. The Crimean Tatars were scattered throughout Uzbekistan. On June 30, 1945, the Crimean ASSR was abolished and replaced by the Crimean Oblast of the Russian republic. Throughout the Crimea, Soviet authorities obliterated all historical, cultural, and linguistic traces of Tatar ethnicity. Place names were changed, and Tatar history was rewritten. Finally, on February 19, 1954, the Crimean Oblast was removed from Russia and given to Ukraine. Since the population of the Crimea at that time was largely ethnic Russian, this decision proved to be a point of ethnic and national competition in subsequent years.

Not until after the death of Stalin in 1953 did circumstances begin to change even marginally for the Crimean Tatars. In 1957, Nikita Khrushchev began to condemn Stalin's nationality policies and to rehabilitate some of the deported groups. In Tashkent, the Crimean Tatar newspaper, *Lenin Bayragi*, began publication. Restrictions on the movement of the Tatar people in Uzbekistan were lifted, and Tatar organizations began to appear. They wanted to be rehabilitated and allowed to return to the Crimea. For the next ten years, Tatar leaders and organizations kept up the pressure, even when leaders like Sevket Abduramanov ended up in prison because of their demands. Finally, on September 9, 1967, the Soviet government officially rehabilitated the Crimean Tatars, denied that they had collaborated with the Nazis, and condemned the anti-Tatar actions of the state.

But the Soviet Union did not provide for the return of the Crimean Tatars to their homeland. From the late 1960s through the 1980s, Tatar leaders continued their insistence that true rehabilitation meant the restoration of their lands and residences. Tatar newspapers, publishing houses, and university groups continued the revival of Tatar national culture, while Tatar leaders encouraged Tatar families to return to the Crimea, with or without the permission of the government. Several hundred families succeeded in this effort. A permanent lobby appeared in Moscow during the 1970s, and major cities in Uzbekistan were marked by repeated demonstrations on the part of Tatar groups. Groups such as the Representatives of the Crimean Tatar People to the World Public tried to make a case for their return to their traditional homeland. They also joined forces in the 1970s with other human rights advocates in the Soviet Union. Leading Tatar intellectuals like Esref Semizade and B. S. Gafurov pressed claims for restoration, even though Moscow authorities persecuted the most outspoken Tatar nationalists.

During the 1980s, the *glasnost* policies of Mikhail Gorbachev opened the debate dramatically. By that time, there were 64,000 Crimean Tatars living in the city of Tashkent, with another 139,000 in the Tashkent Oblast. Other Uzbekistan cities with major Crimean Tatar populations included Samarkand with 70,000, Andijan with 54,000, and Fergana with 51,000. There were 38,000 Crimean Tatars in the Kyrgyz area and 38,000 in the Osh oblast. Nonetheless, during the 1970s and 1980s, approximately 15,000 Crimean Tatar families managed to make their way back to the Crimea. Under Gorbachev, Tatar nationalists could speak more openly than ever before, and their hopes of actually achieving a return to the Crimea increased. But when the Soviet Union disintegrated in 1991, those hopes received a setback. By the end of that year, Russia and Ukraine were independent, sovereign nations, but the Crimea was still Ukrainian territory, and Ukrainian leaders were not inclined to permit the return of more than a quarter of a million Tatar settlers. They estimated that as many as 350,000 Crimean Tatars wanted to return to their homeland, but, of the 2.4 million people already living in the Crimea, more than 100,000 families were in dormitories because of a lack of housing, while another 159,000 families were on housing waiting lists. Ethnic Ukrainians* and ethnic Russians already in the Crimea bitterly opposed any proposals for the repatriation of another 350,000 homeless people. After widespread rioting in Uzbekistan against Meskhetians* and, to a lesser extent, against ethnic Russians and Crimean Tatars, the desire to return to the Crimea only intensified.

Throughout 1992, both Russia and Ukraine disputed the question of sovereignty over the Crimea, and Tatar hopes for a return to their homeland became complicated by that diplomatic struggle. Nevertheless, they started returning to the Crimea in 1992, creating tension among the ethnic Russians and Ukrainians there who had long since taken control of the Crimean Tatars' former lands. Conflict erupted between Crimean Tatars, who desperately wanted to return to their traditional homeland, and the Committee on the Affairs of Deported Peoples—a Ukrainian administrative group that opposed their return.

REFERENCES: *Current Digest*, 41 (November 1, 1989), 25–26; 42 (June 20, 1990), 27–28; and 44 (August 5, 1992), 25–27; Alan W. Fisher, *The Crimean Tatars*, 1987; Chantal Lemercier-Quelquejay, "The Crimean Tatars: A Retrospective Summary," *Central Asian Review*, 16 (1968), 15–25; Ann Sheehy, *The Crimean Tatars and Volga Germans: Soviet Treatment of Two National Minorities*, 1971; Osman Turkay, "The Tragedy of the Crimean Tatars," *Index on Censorship*, 3 (1974), 67–78.

CRIMEAN TATAR JEW. See KRYMCHAK and JEW.

CRIVISHI. See BELARUSIAN.

CROAT. The Croats are a South Slavic people who settled in the northwestern Balkan peninsula in the era of Slavic migrations from the sixth to the tenth centuries A.D. They maintained tributary relations with the Holy Roman Empire and the Byzantine Empire until the development of their own independent kingdom in the early eleventh century. The Croats were converted to Roman Christianity, and, between the eleventh to the thirteenth centuries, the Croatian Kingdom constituted one the most important Christian states in the Balkans. With the expansion of the Hungarian Kingdom in the twelfth and thirteenth centuries much of the Croatian Kingdom, especially the areas of Croatia and Slavonia, was subsumed into the Hungarian Kingdom. Between the thirteenth and fifteenth centuries, most of Croatian Dalmatia came under the control of the Republic of Venice.

The rise of the Ottoman Empire and the demise of Hungary in the fifteenth and sixteenth centuries led to the incorporation of most inland Croatian areas into the Ottoman realm. A belt of Croatian territory became the Austrian Military Frontier, defended by Serbian and Croatian military refugees, but most of the Dalmatian coastal regions of Croatia remained under Venetian control. In some areas, such as the city state of Dubrovnik, the Uskok areas of Senj and Kotar, and the Austrian Military Frontier, Croats maintained varying degrees of autonomy, due to the inaccessability of the regions, the usefulness of Croats' military services, or the proximity to Venetian and Hapsburg lands. As Ottoman power receded in the seventeenth and eighteenth centuries, most Croats living in inland areas came under Hapsburg rule as part of the Kingdom of Hungary. The fall of the Venetian republic during the Napoleonic wars brought the Dalmatian Croats under Austrian rule as well. Throughout most of the nineteenth century, Croats developed their modern national movement in attempts to achieve self-determination within the Hapsburg realm in the face of rival Magyar, Italian, Serb, and Slovene nationalisms. Two strains of Croatian nationalism developed, one favoring an exclusively Croatian national destiny and another calling for the unification of all South Slavs (Croats, Serbs, and Slovenes); the latter was known as Illyrism and later Yugoslavism. After the First World War, when the Allied powers attempted to have national frontiers reflect broad ethnic interests, Croatia, along with Serbia, Montenegro, Slovenia, Bosnia-Herzegovina, and Vardar Macedonia, became the new country of Yugoslavia, the land of the South Slavs.

The Second World War brought traumatic consequences to the new Yugoslav state. The Axis armies overran and dismembered Yugoslavia. These actions resulted in a brutal occupation and a multifaceted civil war that pitted South Slav nationalities and political groups against one another. The Communist-led partisans, under Josef Broz Tito had won out over rival forces (Chetniks, Ustashi, etc.) by 1945. Yugoslavia, reorganized into a federation of socialist republics, became one of the most important Communist states in Eastern Europe in the immediate postwar era. A falling out between the Soviet and Yugoslav Communist parties in 1948, however, led to the first serious rift in the Communist world, known commonly as the Tito-Stalin split. This schism made Yugoslavia a pariah among Communist states, and, in the late 1940s and early 1950s, Yugoslavia went its own way in domestic development (self-management over central planning) and international relations (nonalignment). Except for periods of tension in 1956 and 1968, Yugoslav-Soviet relations improved, and closer cultural, economic, and political ties developed. Nonetheless, Yugoslavia never joined the economic (CMEA) or military (Warsaw Pact) organizations of the Soviet bloc. As in the case of the former Soviet Union, the Yugoslav Socialist Federated Republic began to unravel in the late 1980s and early 1990s, with separate Slovenian, Croatian, Bosnian, and Macedonian states developing between 1990 and 1992. The Serbian and Montenegrin republics constituted the smaller Yugoslav state. The break-up of Yugoslavia has sparked civil wars in Croatia and Bosnia that make conflicts in the former Soviet Union dwarf in comparison.

The Croats had developed ties with the Russian Empire, but not to the same extent as the Balkan Orthodox Christians—the Bulgarians*, Greeks*, Orthodox Albanians*, Romanians*, and Serbs*. Because the Croats' religious and cultural orientation was Roman Catholic and Western, their relations with Orthodox Russia were more limited. Nevertheless cultural-religious relations between Croats and Russians did exist. The most important instance of these relations was the career of Iuri Krizhanich (Juraj Krizanic). Krizhanich was a Croatian Catholic priest sent to Russia to further the cause of union between the Catholic and Orthodox churches in the early seventeenth century. Having been trained as a Uniate missionary at the Greek College in Rome, Krizhanich served as a political adviser and diplomatic representative of Michael Romanov. He advocated not only the ecclesiatical union of the eastern and western churches, but also the political union of all the Slavic peoples under the sovereignty of the Muscovite tsar. As such, Krizhanich was a precursor to the Pan-Slavism of the nineteenth century.

During the eighteenth and nineteenth centuries, Croats emigrated to Russia in limited numbers. One factor was military and naval service. The development of the Russian navy under Peter I and Catherine II led to a number of Croats serving as officers and seamen in the Baltic and Black Sea fleets. In the 1740s and 1750s, the Russian imperial government under Tsarina Elizabeth viewed the Austrian Military Frontier (*militärgrenze*) as a model for frontier defenses in the recently conquered areas of the southern Ukraine. Russian agents were dispatched to the Croatian and Slavonian military frontier to entice some frontiersmen into Russian service. While these activities caused diplomatic problems with Austria, it also resulted in the settlement of over 10,000 *grenzers* to frontier regions of the southern Ukraine. While the overwhelming majority of these settlers were Serbs, there were probably some Croats included in the immigration. The areas of settlement became known as Novaia Serbiia and Slaviano-Serbiia, and the units in which they served were called the Serbian, Bulgarian, Macedonian, and Moldavian Hussar regiments. The ethnic composition of these and the other Balkan units was mixed and belied their nomenclature. The descendants of these settlers, together with those of later individual Croat immigrants in the eighteenth and nineteenth centuries have been assimilated over the years into the society and culture of the respective republics in which they reside. Through intermarriage, education, and other means, some Croats have entered the mainstream of the politics, society, culture, and economy of the former Soviet Union.

According to the 1989 Soviet census, Croats number some 1,100 within the Commonwealth of Independent States (CIS); the 1989 census was the first Soviet census in which Croats were counted. Most of those identified as Croats were nominally Roman Catholic, while others were Muslim South Slavs who declared themselves to be Croatian. The present Croatian population of the CIS probably has four separate origins. A proportion may be descendants of those Croats who immigrated to Russia prior to 1917. Another segment may be descendants of the interwar Yugoslav Communist immigration that survived the purges of the 1930s. Still others may have been part of the small Cominformist emigration following the Tito-Stalin Split of 1948; in the late 1940s and early 1950s, some Yugoslav supporters of Soviet Communism made it to the Soviet Union and served as cadres of opposition against Tito's "deviation," and probably a portion of today's Croatian population in the CIS comes from this group. Finally, most of the present Croatian population in the former Soviet Union no doubt entered in the 1970s and 1980s, as Yugoslav-Soviet relations improved and a number of Yugoslav firms became engaged in projects and joint ventures in the Soviet Union; others were students and political/military officials. The changes of the last few years, in both the former Soviet Union and Yugoslavia, may affect the Croatian population in the CIS and the relations between the Croats and the Russians as well as other CIS nationalities.

REFERENCES: Ivo Banac, The National Question in Yugoslavia: Origins, History, Politics, 1984; Ivo Banac, With Stalin Against Tito: The Cominformist Splits in Yugoslav Communism, 1988; Ivo Banac, "Yugoslav Cominformist Organizations and Insurgent Activity, 1948–1954," in At the Brink of War and Peace: The Tito-Stalin Split in Historic Perspective, Wayne S. Vucinich, ed., 1982; I Krizhanich, Politika, M. I. Tikhomirov, ed., and A. L. Goldberg, tr., 1965; James S. Olson, Catholic Immigrants in America, 1987; V. I. Picheta, "Iuri Krizhanich i ego otnoshenie k Russkomo gosudarstvu," Slavianskii Sbornik, V. I. Picheta and Zhelezhnov, eds., 1947, 202–40; G. V., "Juraj Krizanic," Mladost, 6 (1950), 804–19; N. M. Tikhomirov, "Istoricheskie sviazi russkogo naroda s iuzhnymi slavianami s drevneishikh vremen do poloviny XVII v.," Slavianskii Sbornik, V. I. Picheta, ed., 1947, 125–201.

Nicholas C. J. Pappas

CRYASHEN. See KRJASHEN TATAR and TATAR.

CRYM TATAR. See CRIMEAN TATAR.

CRYMCHAK. See KYRMCHAK and JEW.

CRYZ. See KRYZ and SHAH DAGH.

CUANADI. See BAGULAL and AVAR.

CUANADY. See BAGULAL and AVAR.

CUBACHI. See KUBACHI.

CUBAN. Cubans were listed in the 1989 Soviet census for the first time. At that point there were 5,113 people of Cuban descent living there. Before 1959, only a handful of Cubans lived in the Soviet Union, but Fidel Castro's takeover of the country from Fulgencio Batista changed those demographic patterns. Castro's own political persuasion was somewhat imprecise, but, when he nationalized large numbers of American-owned industries and properties in Cuba, the United States reacted with an embargo of the island. President Dwight D. Eisenhower terminated all American trade with Cuba until Castro either returned the properties or paid for them. Castro refused to do so and turned to the Soviet Union for assistance. Over the course of the next several years, Cuba became an intimate political partner with the Soviet Union. That close relationship prompted a number of Cubans to travel there. Many of them were students studying at Soviet universities, while others were military officials working with the Red Army.

When Mikhail Gorbachev implemented his policies of *glasnost* and *perestroika* in the late 1980s, Castro became an inveterate opponent of the liberal reforms. He remained an uncompromising Communist. Early in the 1990s, however, when the Communist Party collapsed in the Soviet Union, the billions of dollars in assistance that Moscow had sent to Cuba annually began to decline dramatically. The number of Cubans living in the Soviet Union dropped as well.
REFERENCE: Raymond E. Zickel, *Soviet Union: A Country Study*, 1989.

CUBAN ABHAZ. See ABAZA.

CUBAN ABKAZ. See ABAZA.

CUBAN ABKHAZ. See ABAZA.

CUBAN NOGAI. See NOGAI.

CUBAN NOGAY. See NOGAI.

CUBAN NOGHAI. See NOGAI.

CUBAN NOGHAY. See NOGAI.

CUMANDA. See KUMANDIN and ALTAI.

CUMANDIN. See KUMANDIN and ALTAI.

CUMARCHEN. See EVENK.

CUMIK. See KUMYK.

CUMUK. See KUMYK.

CUMYK. See KUMYK.

CUNDROV TATAR. See KUNDROV TATAR and TATAR.

CUNDROVSKIY TATAR. See KUNDROV TATAR and TATAR.

CURAMA. See KURAMA and UZBEK.

CURD. See KURD.

CURIAN. See LATVIAN.

CURIK CHEREMISS. See KURYK MARI and MARI.

CURIL. See AINU.

CURILIAN. See AINU.

CURISH. See LATVIAN and LITHUANIAN.

CURISHE. See LATVIAN and LITHUANIAN.

CURMANDJ. See KURD.

CURMANDZH. See KURD.

CURMANJ. See KURD.

CURONIAN. See LATVIAN.

CURYK CHEREMISS. See KURYK MARI and MARI.

CURZEME. See LATVIAN and LITHUANIAN.

CURZEMIAN. See LATVIAN and LITHUANIAN.

CUZNETS TATAR. See KUZNETSKI TATAR and SHOR.

CVANADI. See BAGULAL and AVAR.

CVANADY. See BAGULAL and AVAR.

CVANALI. See ANDI and AVAR.

CVANALY. See ANDI and AVAR.

CWANADI. See BAGULAL and AVAR.

CWANADY. See BAGULAL and AVAR.

CYPCHAK. See KYPCHAK and UZBEK.

CYPSHAK. See KYPCHAK and UZBEK.

CYRGHYZ. See KYRGYZ.

CYRGYZ. See KYRGYZ.

CYZL. See KYZYL and KHAKASS.

CYZYL. See KYZYL and KHAKASS.

CZECH. The 1989 census of the Soviet Union listed ethnic Czechs as a separate group for the first time, claiming that there were 16,355 people of Czech extraction living in the country. Religious conflict had characterized Czech history since the fifteenth century. The old Bohemian kingdom became the first Protestant country in Europe when Jan Hus led his revolt against the church. His execution for heresy in 1415 gave Czech nationalists a martyr, and Czech nationalism became intricately entwined with a Protestant, rather than a Roman Catholic, spirit. When the German-Catholic Hapsburgs took over Bohemia after the Battle of White Mountain in 1620, Roman Catholicism was imposed on every village. Peasants came to see the parish priest as an agent of the Hapsburgs. In parts of southern Bohemia, the church owned vast amounts of property and acted as landlord for many peasants.

A tradition of liberal "free thought" also permeated Bohemia in the nineteenth century. They wanted nothing to do with organized religion, especially with the Roman Catholicism they associated with German oppression. Committed to separation of church and state, freedom of thought, and scientific rationalism, they helped undermine the Roman Catholic emphasis on authoritarian control, conservatism, and corporate society. By the late nineteenth century, the Roman Catholicism professed by most Czechs had become compromised by nationalism, liberalism, and rationalism.

The Czech community in Russia has a number of origins. During the nineteenth century, some Czech intellectuals resentful of German control in the Holy Roman Empire looked to Russia and hoped in pan-Slavism to find the route to Czech liberation. There were also Bohemian farming communities in the Ukraine which had their origins in the late-eighteenth-century invitation the tsar sent out to German farmers to come to Russia. During the twentieth century, especially in the post–World War II years when Soviet authority took control in Czechoslovakia, there were several thousand Czech students, military officers, and political officials who took up residence in the Soviet Union. Since the collapse of the Soviet Union in 1991, the decline of the Russian economy, and the 1993 division of Czechoslovakia, the numbers of Czechs in Russia has declined. Many of them are now trying to relocate to the new Czech Republic, where they anticipate better economic and political fortunes.

REFERENCE: Raymond Zickel, *The Soviet Union: A Country Study*, 1991.

D

DAG CHUFUT. See MOUNTAIN JEW and JEW.

DAGESTANI. See DAGHESTANI.

DAGESTINI JEW. See MOUNTAIN JEW and JEW.

DAGH CHUFUT. See MOUNTAIN JEW and JEW.

DAGHESTANI. The term "Daghestani" is a generic reference to all of the peoples living in the Daghestan Autonomous Republic of Russia. These include the Avars*, Dargins*, Lezgins*, Laks*, Tabasarans*, Rutuls*, Kumyks*, Nogais*, Tsakhurs*, and Aguls.* Up to and including the Soviet census of 1926, the term also included the Akhwakhs*, Andis*, Archis*, Bagulals*, Botligs*, Chamalals*, Didois*, Godoberis*, Kapuchins*, Karatais*, Khunzals*, Khwarshis*, and Tindis*; these peoples are today included with the Avars. The 1926 census also listed the Kaitaks and Kubachis as separate peoples. Since then, they have been listed as Dargin subgroups.

Their geographic isolation in the mountains has protected the Daghestanis from outside depredations. It has also confined them to an economy based on animal husbandry, particularly sheep raising. Until the eighth century, the region was primarily Christian because of its cultural roots in the Albanian* empire, but Islam spread rapidly under the impact of the Arab* conquest. The conversion of the Daghestani peoples from their animistic religions to Islam was not complete, however, until the sixteenth century. Today, within the Commonwealth of Independent States, Daghestanis are recognized as the most anti-Communist, anti-Russian, and pro-Muslim people in the entire country. Their hatred for the state is legendary. Long after Russia annexed Daghestan, the Daghestani people resisted Russian control. The most sustained anti-Russian* rebellion—the Murid Uprising—lasted for over thirty years, from 1828 to 1859. It embodied a powerful anti-foreign, anti-Christian, and anti-Russian mentality. During the late 1980s and into the 1990s, the Daghestanis remained most adamant in their support for the dissolution of the Soviet Union and the end of Mikhail Gorbachev's centralized control.

REFERENCES: Shirin Akiner, *Isamic Peoples of the Soviet Union*, 1983; Alexandre Bennigsen and S. Enders Wimbush, *Muslims of the Soviet Empire: A Guide*, 1986; Ronald Wixman, *Language Aspects of Ethnic Patterns and Processes in the North Caucusus*, 1980; Ronald Wixman, "Daghestani," in Richard V. Weekes, *Muslim Peoples*, 1984, 211–19; Ronald Wixman, *The Peoples of the USSR: An Ethnographic Handbook*, 1984.

DAGHESTANI JEW. See MOUNTAIN JEW and JEW.

DAGHUR. See DAUR and BURYAT.

DAGUR. See DAUR and BURYAT.

DARGAN. See DARGIN.

DARGHIN. See DARGIN.

DARGIN. The Dargins are one of the Daghestani* peoples of the former Soviet Union. Their contemporary population approaches 300,000 people, and they live in the Southern and Central regions of what used to be the Daghestan Autonomous Soviet Socialist Republic. They are especially concentrated in the Sergokala Rayon and the Dakhadajev Rayon. The Dargins are surrounded by the Caspian Sea to the east, the Tabasarans* and Aguls* to the south, the Laks* and Avars* to the west, and the Kumyks* to the north. They call themselves the Dargwa or Dargan and are also known as the Dargva. Russians* refer to them as the Dargintsy. Their language is part of the northeastern Caucasic linguistic family and is divided into three independent, mutually unintelligible dialects. In the highlands of Dargin territory, people speak the Khurkili or Urakhi dialect. Dargins living in the eastern plains speak the Tsudakhar dialect. Most of the Dargin people, however, speak the Akusha dialect. The city of Akusha has historically dominated the economic and cultural life of the Dargin community, and, as a result, this dialect became the most prominent. The Dargin written language uses the Akusha dialect as its base. Most Dargins are also bilingual in either Avar or Kumyk*, primarily because, until the 1920s, the highland Dargins were being incorporated slowly into the Avar community while the Tsudakhar and Akusha-speaking Dargins were being heavily influenced by the Kumyks.

Historians believe that the Dargins are an indigenous people of the Caucasus. Islam was not introduced to their region until the beginning of the great Arab* conquests in the eighth century. The Kaitaks*, who are now considered a subgroup of the Dargins, established political control over the Dargins in the fourteenth century. That situation ended in 1820, when Russia assumed political dominance and administrative control. Russia created a Dargin District in 1860.

Like other ethnic groups in southern Daghestan, most Dargins are Sunni
Muslims loyal to the Shafi theological school, although a few thousand are Shiite
Muslims, most of whom live in the communities of Kurush and Miskindzha.
Until the fifteenth century, the Dargins were primarily animists with their own
folk religions, but Zoroastrianism, Judaism, and Christianity were making inroads. Persian* traders introduced Islam into southern Daghestan in the fifteenth
century, while the Golden Horde brought Islam into the northern region in the
sixteenth and seventeenth centuries. The occupation of the region by the Ottoman
Turks in the sixteenth century also helped to consolidate Islam. By the nineteenth
century, all but a few of the Dargin had been converted to Sunni Islam. They
are extremely devout, and, like other Muslim people in the Near East, Middle
East, and Central Asia in the 1970s and 1980s, they have been influenced by
the increasingly strident religious fundamentalism that has dominated the cultural
landscape. In spite of more than seventy years of anti-religious state policy, their
fundamental religious institutions and traditions—such as endogamous marriages, family mosques, religious marriages and burials, observance of Ramadan,
and faithful devotion to the teachings of the Koran—still flourish.

A profound anti-Russian* sentiment also permeates Dargin culture. Just after
the Russian Revolution, the government in Moscow established the Mountain
Autonomous Republic, with Arabic as the official language of the government
and schools. Dargins, along with many other highland ethnic groups, opposed
the policy and rebelled against it. The government then set up the Daghestan
Autonomous Soviet Socialist Republic in 1921; in 1925, it launched an anti-
Islamic campaign that included closing all Islamic schools, eliminating the use
of Arabic, and executing many local imams. At that point, state policy shifted
in favor of the Turkic people*, and Azerbaijani* became the official language
of the region. That policy ended in 1928, when the government declared that
Dargin, Avar,* Lezgin*, and Azerbaijani were all official languages. The government also began to create a Latin alphabet for the Dargin language in 1928,
but shifted back to the Cyrillic alphabet in 1938. Gradually, over the next twenty
years, the Russian language was imposed on all schools and government offices
in Daghestan.

The constant policies of cultural manipulation by the Soviet government only
increased Dargin resentment of Russian culture. The Dargin resisted the russification of their culture and also refused to participate in government programs
to relocate them out of the highlands and into lowland towns and collective
farms. As a result, all but a handful of the Dargin people retain a traditional
rural life-style. Economic life still revolves around animal husbandry (sheep and
goats in the highlands, cattle in the lowlands), gold and silver smithing, weaving,
pottery, and rug manufacturing. Because of their geographic isolation and their
resentment of state educational policies, Dargin education levels are among the
lowest in the former Soviet Union.

In addition to the Dargin proper, there are two other ethnic groups that Russian
ethnologists today classify as Dargin. The Kaitak* people, who call themselves

the Qaidaqlan, are also known as the Kaidak, Karakaitak, and Karakaidak. Although their language is now classified as a Dargin dialect, it is quite distinct and unintelligible to Dargin speakers. The Kaitaks live in the highland region of south-central Daghestan. They are Sunni Muslims who are divided into two dialect groups: the northern Kaitaks speak Magalis-Kaitak, while the southern Kaitak speak Karakaitak. Their total population is approximately 20,000 people. The other ethnic group linked to the Dargins is the Kubachi*. The Kubachis call themselves the Ughbug and are known to other Russians as the Kubachin or Zirekhgeran (Zerekhgeran). They too are Sunni Muslim in religion. The Kubachis number only several thousand people, and they live in the village of Kubachi in central Daghestan. Like the Kaitaks, the Kubachis are gradually being assimilated by the Dargins.

In the wake of the collapse of the Soviet Union in 1991, the anti-Russian elements of Dargin nationalism have only intensified. Dargin religion has been affected by the wave of Islamic fundamentalism sweeping through Central Asia, and their resentment of Communism's treatment of them over the previous seventy years is even more intense. Many Dargin leaders now talk openly of secession, membership in a pan-Islamic community, or the political reunification of the highland peoples in an entity resembling the older Mountainous Autonomous Republic of the 1920s.

REFERENCES: Alexandre Bennigsen, "Muslim Conservative Opposition to the Soviet Regime: The Sufi Brotherhoods in the North Caucasus," in Jeremy R. Azrael, ed., *Soviet Nationality Policies and Practices*, 1971; Alexandre Bennigsen and S. Enders Wimbush, *Muslims of the Soviet Union: A Guide*, 1986; Bruce Geiger, et al., *Peoples and Languages of the Caucasus*, 1959; T. S. Halasi-Kun, "The Caucasus: An Ethno-Historical Survey," *Studia Caucasia*, 2 (1956), 7–16; Brian Silver, "Language Policy and Linguistic Russification of Soviet Nationalities," in Jeremy R. Azrael, ed., *Soviet Nationality Policies and Practices*, 1971; Ronald Wixman, *Language Aspects of Ethnic Patterns and Processes in the North Caucasus*, 1980; Ronald Wixman, *The Peoples of the USSR: An Ethnographic Handbook*, 1984; Ronald Wixman, "Daghestanis," in Richard V. Weekes, ed., *Muslim Peoples*, 1984, 209–19.

DARGINTSY. See DARGIN.

DARGVA. See DARGIN.

DARGWA. See DARGIN.

DAUR. The Daur are a former Mongol* tribe that over the centuries has been steadily assimilated by the Buryats*. Today the people who identify themselves as Daur live along the upper Amur River. See BURYAT.

REFERENCE: Ronald Wixman, *The Peoples of the USSR: An Ethnographic Handbook*, 1984.

DERBENT. The Derbent people are a Kalmyk* subgroup. Their dialect is the basis of the Kalmyk written language. They live in the northern and western reaches of the Kalmyk Autonomous Republic. See KALMYK.
REFERENCE: Ronald Wixman, *The Peoples of the USSR: An Ethnographic Handbook*, 1984.

DETKIL'. See YUKAGIR.

DIDO. The term "Dido" refers to one of the tribal groupings of the Avar* people. The Dido proper, who call themselves the Qwanal and who have been referred to as the Didur, Didoi*, and Tsez, are Sunni Muslims. They are isolated in the high mountainous valleys of southwestern Daghestan close to Georgia. See DIDO PEOPLES or AVAR.
REFERENCE: Ronald Wixman, *The Peoples of the USSR: An Ethnographic Handbook*, 1984.

DIDO PEOPLES. Unlike "Dido," "Dido peoples" refers to the Dido group of the Avar* peoples. The Dido group includes the Didos proper as well as the Bezhetas, Ginugs*, Khwarshis*, and Khunzals*. See AVAR.
REFERENCE: Ronald Wixman, *The Peoples of the USSR: An Ethnographic Handbook*, 1984.

DIDOI. The Didoi, who call themselves the Tsez and who are known to Russians* as the Didoitsy or Tsezy, are an indigenous people of the Caucasus who today are classified with the Avars* for demographic purposes. Like the other Avar peoples, the Didoi are Sunni Muslims. They live in the Tsuntin Region of the Daghestan Republic. Although it is difficult to come up with current population estimates for the Didoi, primarily because of their census designation with the Avars, demographers estimate that there are approximately 15,000 people who either consciously identify themselves as Didoi or who are aware of their Didoi ancestry. See AVAR.
REFERENCES: Shirin Akiner, *Islamic Peoples of the Soviet Union*, 1983; Ronald Wixman, *The Peoples of the USSR: An Ethnographic Handbook*, 1984.

DIDOI PEOPLES. See DIDO PEOPLES.

DIDOITSY. See DIDOI and AVAR.

DIDOY. See DIDOI and AVAR.

DIDOY PEOPLES. See DIDO PEOPLES.

DIDUR. See DIDO and AVAR.

DIEDIDI. See JEW.

DIGOR. The Digor, who call themselves the Digoron, are today considered part of the larger Ossetian* community. More particularly, they are Sunni Muslims who have come under the cultural influence of the Kabards*. During World War II, the Digors were accused of collaborating with the Germans*, and they became part of Josef Stalin's mass deportation scheme that sent hundreds of thousands of Muslims of the North Caucasus to exile in Central Asia. The Digor were rehabilitated in the mid–1950s, and many began returning to their homeland in the North Ossetian Autonomous Republic. See OSSETIAN.
REFERENCE: Ronald Wixman, *The Peoples of the USSR: An Ethnographic Handbook*, 1984.

DIGORI. See DIGOR and OSSETIAN.

DIGORON. See DIGOR and OSSETIAN.

DIGORY. See DIGOR and OSSETIAN.

DJAVAHI. See DZHAVAKHI and GEORGIAN.

DJAVAKHI. See DZHAVAKHI and GEORGIAN.

DJEK. See DZHEK, SHAH DAGH, and AZERBAIJANI.

DJEMSHID. See DZHEMSHID and TAJIK.

DJUNGAR. See OIROT and ALTAI.

DJUNGARIAN. See OIROT and ALTAI.

DOLGAN. The Dolgans, who call themselves the Dulgaans, are a Yakut*-speaking people living in the Dolgano-Nenets Autonomous Oblast of the Krasnojarsk Territory of Russia, north of the Arctic Circle in northern Siberia. Russian* ethnologists view the Dolgans as a people with Tungusic* origins who were assimilated by the Yakuts. Their Yakut dialect is heavily laced with Evenk* words, indicating their mixed origins. They are divided into four subgroups: the Dolgans proper, the Edzhens, the Karyntuous, and the Dongots. Although the Dolgans adopted some elements of Eastern Orthodox Christianity, they have kept much of their original indigenous, animist faith. Although their culture has been largely subsumed by Yakut culture, they nevertheless retain a sense of Dolgan identity, and most still speak the Dolgan language. Most of the Dolgans live in collective farming arrangements and breed reindeer, hunt, and fish for a living. Their population is approximately 6,000 people.

Soviet collectivization schemes were first applied to the Dolgans in the 1930s. Although some Dolgans managed to keep their nomadic ways as late as the

1950s, most of them had to accept settled life in state villages. Industrial development in the region had a dramatic effect on the Dolgans after World War II. Coal mines, nickel mines, and natural gas projects created a huge demand for transportation, meat, and fish and helped to commercialize Dolgan economic life, converting many Dolgans into menial wage laborers. Moreover, the arrival of numerous ethnic Russians had powerful social consequences. By the 1960s, the number of single mothers had skyrocketed in the Dolgan communities, and many of the children were part-Dolgan, part-Russian. Finally, environmental destruction has compromised Dolgan life. The Dolgan-Nenets Autonomous Region was one of the most isolated in the Soviet Union, until the 1980s when state economists created the huge non-ferrous metal plants at Noilsk. Air pollution and the ravaging of hundreds of thousands of acres of reindeer pasturage destroyed the Dolgan economy. Tuberculosis, alcoholism, mental retardation, unemployment, and extreme poverty characterized Dolgan life there in the late 1980s.

Like other far northern peoples in Russia, the Dolgans became increasingly concerned during the 1960s and 1970s about the economic development of their homelands and the environmental damage that was occurring there. Dolgan leaders began to express that concern hesitantly in the 1970s, when environmental issues became more public in the Soviet Union. Because of the pressures of economic development and state resettlement policies, the Dolgans found themselves advancing deep into the Taimyr tundra of the western Arctic. Their territory included the land from Lake Pyasina and Norilsk to the Khatanga estuary. They lived in increasing proximity with the Nganasans*, although little intermarriage took place between the two groups. During the years of Mikhail Gorbachev's leadership, they became more vocal, joining such interest groups as the Association of Small Peoples of the Far North to demand the restoration of land rights and more environmentally sensitive development policies. After the collapse of the Soviet Union in 1991, the real threat faced by the Dolgans was that Russia, desperately seeking to extract itself from the economic catastrophe created by seven decades of Communist rule, might actually accelerate the development and mineral extraction programs in Siberia, further compromising the Dolgan habitat.

REFERENCES: Shirin Akiner, *Islamic Peoples of the Soviet Union*, 1983; James Forsyth, *History of the Peoples of Siberia*, 1992; Ronald Wixman, *The Peoples of the USSR: An Ethnographic Handbook*, 1984.

DOLYSHNIANY. See CARPATHO-RUSYN.

DON COSSACK. See COSSACK.

DON KALMUK. See KALMYK.

DON KALMYK. See KALMYK.

DON QALMAQ. See KALMYK.

DON QALMUK. See KALMYK.

DONGGAN REN. See DUNGAN.

DONGOT. See DOLGAN.

DOOLOS. See ICHKILIK and KYRGYZ.

DREVELIAN. See UKRAINIAN.

DREVELIANE. See UKRAINIAN.

DREVLYAN. See UKRAINIAN.

DREVLYANE. See UKRAINIAN.

DULEB. See UKRAINIAN.

DULEBIAN. See UKRAINIAN.

DULEBIANE. See UKRAINIAN.

DULGAAN. See DOLGAN.

DUNGAN. The Dungans are a Chinese* ethnic group who are relatively recent arrivals in Russia. They call themselves the Zhongyuan-ren, Huizo, Lao Hui Hui, Donggan Ren, Lao Khuei Khuei, or Yuan' Zhyn. To neighboring Russians*, they are known as the Dungane or Tung-an. Scholars disagree on Dungan origins. Russian ethnographers argue that they are ethnic Chinese who converted to Islam because of their sustained contact with Arab*, Persian*, and Turkic* traders over the centuries. Chinese ethnographers claim that the Dungan are Arab, Persian, and Turkic Muslims who first came to China as prisoners of the Mongol* rulers and who then assimilated, except for their religious loyalties, into the surrounding population.

The Dungan arrived in Russia in several migrations during the late nineteenth century. Beginning in 1867, after a series of ethnic altercations between the Dungans and the Taranchi*, some Dungans began leaving the Ili River valley in Xinjiang, China. Thousands fled with Po Yen-hu to the Semirech'e in 1877 after the collapse of the Muslim Emirate of Kashgaria, and thousands more crossed from the Ili Valley into Russia in 1881 after the signing of the Treaty of St. Petersburg. Most of the Dungan immigrants were poor and illiterate peasants, but they flourished in Central Asia and Kazakhstan. The vast majority of ethnic Dungan people remained behind, however, and today live in north-eastern China.

Ethnolinguists classify the Dungan language as part of the Sinitic branch of the Sino-Tibetan linguistic family. Within the Dungan language, there are three dialects that divide the Dungans into three subgroups. The Hansu (Gansu, Khan-suitsy) dialect is the official language for all the Dungan people but it is spoken mainly by the Hansu Dungans* living in the Kyrgyz Republic. The Shaanxi (Shensi, Shensiytsy) dialect is spoken by the Shensi Dungans* living in the Chu Valley of Kazakhstan. A third and much smaller group of Dungans are the Yage Dungans,* who settled in the villages of Aleksandrovka, Sokuluk, and Chilik. Finally, there is a small group of Dungans living in the Osh Oblast of the Kyrgyz Republic who have abandoned use of the Hansu dialect and speak only Uzbek*. Some Dungans live in the Uzbek Republic, and others dwell in such cities as Frunze and Alma-Ata. Demographers estimate that the Dungan population col-lectively exceeded 60,000 people by 1990. Most Dungans are trilingual. They speak their own Dungan dialect, along with Russian and either Kazakh* or Kyrgyz*. They are linguistically adept enough to switch almost unconsciously from one language to another. The Dungan dialects are published using a Cyrillic alphabet.

In terms of their religious faith, the Dungans are devout Sunni Muslims and pride themselves on the depth of their spirituality. They are faithful to the Hanafi law with the Sunni tradition. In fact, the Dungans commonly look down upon other Muslims for being less committed to the faith. According to Dungan tradition, older people are much more religiously devoted than the young, but the presence of Islamic mosques, religious holidays, and active mullahs praying and blessing the people attest to the power of religion among them, even though Soviet state policy was decidedly anti-religious. Many Dungan intellectuals, however, are openly critical of the impact of Islamic beliefs on Dungan society.

Not surprisingly, Dungans maintain a sense of ethnic separation from sur-rounding groups; when possible, that separateness assumes a physical dimension as well. They are essentially a rural people who prefer to live in all-Dungan villages. When they dwell in cities, they live essentially in Dungan ghettoes—sections of the city unofficially reserved for them. As a Sunni Muslim people, they also identify themselves as Chinese Muslims. Because of the Dungans' spirituality, Soviet anti-religious propaganda was quite intense in their com-munities. They do not interact socially with other people, except occasionally with the Uigurs*, and exogamous marriages are still quite rare. The Dungans also continue to live in extended family households of up to thirty members.

Economic life among Dungans is dominated by state policy. Dungans in rural areas live on collective farms that the state has designated as "Dungan farms." As many as 7,000 to 10,000 people live on these huge farms, which are essentially small cities. Most of these farms produce sugar beets, cattle, milk, and cheese products. The state also allows Dungan farmers to maintain private plots, where they raise vegetables, flowers, garlic, and tobacco. Dungans in the cities work at a variety of jobs, mostly in the blue-collar sector of the economy.

Although the Dungans maintain a strong sense of ethnic identity, which even includes those Dungans still living in China, their presence in Russia, Kazakhstan, and Kyrgyzia has nevertheless brought about a process of acculturation and, for groups like the Osh Valley Dungans, the beginning of assimilation. Although most Dungans still eat their food with chopsticks, they no longer eat as much rice as in the past. The Dungan community continued to bind women's feet in the Chinese tradition until the late 1940s, but that practice has been largely abandoned. Most Dungans have taken to Western clothes, although Shensi women still wear Chinese dresses. Nevertheless, they still have a strong sense of identity as Dungans. They view themselves as quite distinct from Chinese Dungans, eat with chopsticks, observe traditional symbols at weddings, funerals, and holidays, and are very careful about marrying exogamously, even with other Dungan subgroups. The Shensi Dungans are especially conservative.

REFERENCES: Alexandre Bennigsen and S. Enders Wimbush, *Muslims of the Soviet Empire: A Guide*, 1986; Svetlana Rimsky-Korsakoff Dyer, "Muslim Life in Soviet Russia: The Case of the Dungans," *Journal of the Institute of Muslim Minority Affairs*, 3 (1981), 42–54; Svetlana Rimsky-Korsakoff Dyer, *Soviet Dungan Kolkhozes in the Kirghiz SSR and the Kazakh SSR*, 1979; Svetlana Rimsky-Korsakoff Dyer, "Dungans," in Richard V. Weekes, ed., *Muslim Peoples*, 1984, 239–44; Svetlana Rimksy-Korsakoff Dyer, "Soviet Dungan Nationalism: A Few Comments on Their Origin and Language," *Monumenta Serica*, 33 (1977–1978), 363–78; Paul Wexler, "Zhunyanese (Dungan) as an Islamic and Soviet Language," *Journal of Chinese Linguistics*, 8 (1980), 294–304; Ronald Wixman, *The Peoples of the USSR: An Ethnographic Handbook*, 1984.

DUNGAN IAGE. See DUNGAN.

DUNGAN YAGE. See DUNGAN.

DUNGANE. See DUNGAN.

DUTCH. Until its 1989 census, the Soviet Union did not track, or at least did not publish, the number of foreign residents by nationality group. The 1989 census did provide these figures, and it indicated that in 1989 there were 964 Dutch citizens living in the Soviet Union. Ever since the Bolshevik Revolution, there had been a few Dutch living in the Soviet Union. Over the years, other expatriates infatuated with Marxism and the Communist experiment also took up residence there. There was never any significant movement of Dutch natives to change their citizenship and live their lives in the Soviet Union. There had also been other Dutch who, for economic reasons, were very interested in improving the business relationship between the Netherlands and Soviet Union. As disillusionment with the Communist Party, in both the Soviet Union and Holland, mounted during the Brezhnev era in the 1970s, the numbers of expatriates

declined. As Mikhail Gorbachev welcomed Western capital and technological expertise, however, the number of Dutch permanently residing in the Soviet Union increased. Of the 964 Dutch living in the Soviet Union in 1989, most of them were business people hoping to establish an economic foothold there.
REFERENCE: Raymond E. Zickel, ed., *Soviet Union: A Country Study*, 1991.

DZHAMSHID. See DZHEMSHID.

DZHAVAHI. See DZHAVAKHI and GEORGIAN.

DZHAVAKHI. The Dzhavakhi are one of the Kartvelian* ethnic groups that today are considered to be a subgroup of the Georgians*. They are Eastern Orthodox in their religious loyalties. See GEORGIAN.
REFERENCE: Ronald Wixman, *The Peoples of the USSR: An Ethnographic Handbook*, 1984.

DZHEK. The Dzhek, who have also been known historically as the Kryz* and the Gek, are today considered to be one of the Shah Dagh* peoples. Russians* call them the Dzhektsy. They are demographically concentrated in northeastern Azerbaijan, especially in the vicinity of Mt. Shah Dagh in the Konakhkend Rayon. They are Sunni Muslims in religion and are being assimilated by the surrounding Azerbaijani* community. See SHAH DAGH or AZERBAIJANI.
REFERENCE: Ronald Wixman, *The Peoples of the USSR: An Ethnographic Handbook*, 1984.

DZHEKTSY. See DZHEK, SHAH DAGH, or AZERBAIJANI.

DZHEMSHID. The Dzemshid are today considered to be a subgroup of the Tajiks*. Most Russian* ethnologists identify them as the descendants of immigrants from Afghanistan and Iran who arrived in the region during the reign of the Nadir Shah in the mid-eighteenth century. They were sent to western Afghanistan to act as a buffer against the expanding Turkmen* tribes. Most Dzhemshids now live in western Afghanistan, but a small number are across the border in the Turkmen Republic. They are Shiite Muslims. See TAJIK.
REFERENCES: Shirin Akiner, *Islamic Peoples of the Soviet Union*, 1983; Ronald Wixman, *The Peoples of the USSR: An Ethnographic Handbook*, 1984.

DZHUGI. See CENTRAL ASIAN GYPSY or GYPSY.

DZHUGUR. See TAT and JEW.

DZHUKHUR. See TAT and JEW.

DZHUNGAR. See OIROT and ALTAI.

DZHUNGARIAN. See OIROT and ALTAI.

DZUKAI. See LITHUANIAN.

DZUNGAR. See OIROT and ALTAI.

DZUNGARIAN. See OIROT and ALTAI.

E

EASTERN EVEN. See EVEN.

EASTERN FINN. See FINN.

EASTERN MARI. See MARI.

EASTERN SLAV. The term "Eastern Slav" is a generic linguistic reference to Russians*, Ukrainians*, and Belarusians*. Together, they constituted more than 70 percent of the population of the Soviet Union at the time of its dissolution in 1991.
REFERENCE: Ronald Wixman, *The Peoples of the USSR: An Ethnographic Handbook*, 1984.

EBRAELI. See JEW.

EDISAN. See NOGAI.

EDISHKUL. See NOGAI.

EESTI. See ESTONIAN.

EESTLASED. See ESTONIAN.

EGERUKAI. The Egerukai are an Adyghe* subgroup. Most ethnic Egerukai today live in Turkey after having migrated there in the 1860s. Those still in what used to be the Soviet Union are concentrated in the western reaches of the North Caucasus. See ADYGHE.

REFERENCE: Ronald Wixman, *The Peoples of the USSR: An Ethnographic Handbook*, 1984.

EGERUKAY. See EGERUKAI and ADYGHE.

EGERUQAI. See EGERUKAI and ADYGHE.

EGERUQAY. See EGERUKAI and ADYGHE.

EHERIT. See EKHIRIT and BURYAT.

EHRIT. See EKHIRIT and BURYAT.

EHSTI. See ESTONIAN.

EKHIRIT. The Ekhirit are a small group that today lives along the upper Lena River in Siberia. They are considered to be one of the major subgroups of the Buryats*. See BURYAT.
REFERENCE: Ronald Wixman, *The Peoples of the USSR: An Ethnographic Handbook*, 1984.

ELEKE BEYE. See EVENK.

EL'KAN. See EVENK.

ELLINO. See GREEK.

ELLINY. See URUM and GREEK.

EMRELI. The Emreli today live in the Turkmen Republic, primarily in the western part of the Khorezm Oasis. They are classified as a Turkmen* subgroup. See TURKMEN.
REFERENCE: Ronald Wixman, *The Peoples of the USSR: An Ethnographic Handbook*, 1984.

ENET. See ENT.

ENETE. See ENT.

ENISEI. See KET.

ENISEIAN. See KET.

ENISEIAN OSTYAK. See KET.

ENISEY. See KET.

ENT. Like the Nenets*, Nganasans*, and Selkups*, the Ents are a Samoyedic* people who speak a Uralian language—part of the Uralic-Altaic linguistic family. They call themselves the Enete (which means ''man'') and have also been known as the Enets, Yeinsei Samoyeds, Khantaika*, Tundra Yenisey Samoyeds, and Karasa Samoyeds*. The Karasa (Yuchi) Samoyeds were actually the Forest Ents, while the Khantaika were the Tundra Ents. Anthropologists believe that the Ents, who were once part of the larger Samoyedic people, split away from other Finno-Ugrian* groups around 3000 B.C. and migrated east, where they began to mix with Turkish-Altaic people around 200 B.C. The Samoyedic people who remained in Europe came under Russian* control around 1200 A.D., but those who settled farther east did not experience that control until the mid-fourteenth century. By the early seventeenth century, all of the Samoyedic people were under Russian control. The Ents have traditionally been a nomadic people, wandering on the tundras between the left bank of the Yenesei River and the Pyasina River in the western Taymyr Peninsula. During the winter, they stayed on the groved tundras near Pyasina Lake.

The traditional Ent economy revolved around reindeer herding and breeding. The reindeer provided the Ent with meat, lard, and blood, which they consumed, as well as with skins for clothes, shoes, tents, rope, harnesses, and strings; the Ent also used the tendons and horns. For their transportation, the Ents harnessed reindeer and attached them to sleds. Fishing was important, especially to the Forest Ents living in the Taz and Turukhan basins and along the lower reaches of the Yenesei River. The fish they mainly relied on was the sturgeon, although they regularly fished for and caught whitefish, salmon, ide, navaga, and trout as well. The Ents hunted and trapped the fox, silver fox, hare, ermine, wolverine, beaver, otter, and polar and brown bears. Western Ent groups also hunted sea mammals, especially the seal, bearded seal, white whale, Greenland seal, and walrus.

During the sixteenth and seventeenth centuries, the central government under the tsars practiced a policy of indirect rule from Moscow. They treated the native peoples of Siberia like the other peoples they had conquered. Forts were established to collect and forward to Moscow the *yasak*, or fur tax; actual administration of native peoples was left in the hands of local rulers. Moscow authorized the granting of citizenship to any native who converted to Christianity. This process led to forced baptisms and enserfment by local rulers, who then used their native serfs to increase fur trapping. For the Ents, the conversions were nominal at best. As the numbers of fur-bearing animals decreased, Moscow lost interest in the area and in the well-being of its natives. The Ents were part of this entire administrative process.

The indigenous people of Siberia suffered from their commercial and political contact with ethnic Russians*. Over the centuries, ethnic Russians penetrated the commercial activities in the region, enticing the Ents with iron and steel tools, firearms, and a variety of other trade goods. Large numbers of Ents adopted the use of alcohol as well, much to their harm. Ethnic Russians also brought diseases to the native peoples, especially venereal diseases, which had spread throughout Europe after the New World conquests in the late fifteenth and sixteenth centuries. After the completion of the Trans-Siberian Railroad in 1905, the arrival of ethnic Russians in Siberia increased dramatically, and the pressure on the Ents grew proportionately. The Ent population, which had exceeded 3,000 people in 1800, fell to only about 400 people by 1920.

After the Bolshevik Revolution and civil war, a debate over native policy proceeded throughout the 1920s. The Committee of the North, a government agency, proposed creating large reservations for the indigenous peoples of Siberia where they could be left alone to pursue their traditional life-styles. V. I. Lenin and a number of other Bolsheviks opposed this, "arguing it would prevent Native People from catching up educationally, politically, and economically with other Soviet nationalities." Instead, the Soviet government made the decision to incorporate the native peoples into the larger social, political, and economic body of the country. Between 1929 and 1932, the government created "national districts," which were small territorial administrative units named after each of the native peoples. Late in the 1920s and throughout the 1930s, the government also collectivized the indigenous economic activities. Because of their small numbers and isolation in the northern tundra, the Ents were not really affected until the 1930s. For the Ents, this meant the collectivization of their traditional reindeer-herding economy. The government also established "cultural bases" for the indigenous people—settlements complete with boarding schools, hospitals, day-care centers, veterinary dispensaries, and clubs, and they lumped the Ents together with the more numerous Nenets and Nganasans.

In essence, the Soviet government had embarked on an all-out effort to destroy Ent culture—to acculturate Ent children to Russian values and to eliminate the traditionally nomadic, subsistence economy of the Ent people. During the late 1930s, 1940s, and 1950s, the government also launched an assault on the Ent religion. Like most indigenous peoples, Ent religion was polytheistic and animist. There were many gods and spirits in the Ent pantheon, and they believed that the natural environment was a living, breathing place full of invisible ghosts and spirits. All phenomena in life were intricately related; nothing happened accidently or capriciously. During the tsarist era, Russian Orthodox Christianity had been superimposed on the native religion, creating a syncretic, mixed faith. Beginning in the late 1930s, the Soviet government began prohibiting both native and Russian Orthodox religious services among the Ent. In their place, the government worked to create almost a religious faith in Communism among the native people.

The biggest change in Ent life, however, came from the combined effects of industrialization and increased immigration by ethnic Russians into Siberia. During World War II, when the Soviet government relocated much of its industry east of the Ural Mountains to keep it out of German hands or protected from German artillery bombardment, large numbers of ethnic Russian workers suddenly moved into Siberia. State development plans accelerated that process in the 1950s and 1960s. In the process, the few surviving Ents found themselves herding reindeer on ever smaller amounts of land. The collapse of the Soviet economy in the 1970s and 1980s actually slowed that process somewhat, but, even then, the long-term changes being brought to Ent life were irreversible. Government economic policies were rapidly changing the natural environment, and the surviving Ents were being rapidly acculturated by the surrounding Nenets, Selkups, and Dolgans*. As late as the early 1990s, the Ent language was still being spoken by most Ents, and all of them were aware of their Ent heritage.

The *glasnost* policies of Mikhail Gorbachev had an empowering effect on Ent consciousness and political activism, even though their numbers were too small to give them any real voice in state affairs. But, in March 1990, the Ents joined the Association of Peoples of the North (APN), a lobbying organization of twenty-six small ethnic groups from the northern and northeastern reaches of the Soviet Union. Like the other ethnic groups in the APN, the Ents were concerned about the continuing migration of ethnic Russians and ethnic Ukrainians* into their homelands (a movement that reduced what little political and economic power that the indigenous people possessed), the lack of a specifically Ent national autonomous political unit, the lack of Ent representation in the Supreme Soviet, the continuing exploitation of Ent land and resources for the benefit of the rest of the country, especially since fair market prices were not paid for those resources, and the Ents' inability to assume sovereign ownership of those resources. The APN became the most significant organization representing Ent interests in the Soviet Union.

Ironically, the collapse of the Communist Party and the disintegration of the Soviet Union in 1991 actually guaranteed the destruction of Ent identity. More than anything else, the implosion of the Soviet economy explains the destruction of the Soviet Union. One of the major goals of people like Boris Yeltsin in Russia was the acceleration of economic development. Since huge quantities of natural resources exist in Siberia, the exploitation and exportation of those resources—especially coal, iron ore, natural gas, timber, and petroleum—would be a relatively quick way of earning hard currency to develop the rest of the economy. Russians therefore began importing Western technology to develop Siberia. In the process, the traditional Ent economy became even more threatened. If, during the rest of the 1990s, the development of the Siberian economy accelerates, the pressure on traditional Ent ways will become inexorable. Even by the early 1990s, there were no more than a few hundred people in Siberia who were still aware of their Ent background.

REFERENCES: Alice Bartels and Dennis Bartels, "Soviet Policy Toward Siberian Native People," *Canadian Dimension*, 19 (1985), 36–44; *Current Digest*, 41 (July 12, 1989), 24–26, and 42 (May 12, 1990), 34; Mike Edwards, "Siberia: In From the Cold," *National Geographic*, 177 (March 1990), 2–49; James Forsyth, *A History of the Peoples of Siberia*,

1992; Péter Hajdú, *Samoyed Peoples and Languages*, 1962; Constantine Krypton, "Soviet Policy in the Northern National Regions After World War II," *Slavic Review*, 13 (October 1954), 339–53; Piers Vitebsky, "Perestroika Among the Reindeer Herders," *Geographical Magazine*, 61 (June 1989), 23–34; Ronald Wixman, *The Peoples of the USSR: An Ethnographic Handbook*, 1984.

ENZEBI. See KHUNZAL and AVAR.

EREVAN. See AZERBAIJANI.

ERMEN. See ARMENIAN.

ERMENI. See ARMENIAN.

ERSARI. The Ersari are a Turkmen* group. They are concentrated demographically along the Amu Darya River, between the settlements of Kelif and Chardzhou, in the Turkmen Republic. See TURKMEN.
REFERENCE: Ronald Wixman, *The Peoples of the USSR: An Ethnographic Handbook*, 1984.

ERSARY. See ERSARI and TURKMEN.

ERZIA. See ERZYA and MORDVINIAN.

ERZIA MORDOVA. See ERZYA and MORDVINIAN.

ERZIA MORDOVIAN. See ERZYA and MORDVINIAN.

ERZIA MORDVIN. See ERZYA and MORDVINIAN.

ERZIA MORDVINIAN. See ERZYA and MORDVINIAN.

ERZYA. The Erzya constitute a major Mordvinian* subdivision and they are by far the larger of the two groups. Approximately 70 percent of Mordvinians are Erzya. They live throughout the middle Volga region. See MORDVINIAN.
REFERENCE: Ronald Wixman, *The Peoples of the USSR: An Ethnographic Handbook*, 1984.

ERZYA MORDOVA. See ERZYA and MORDVINIAN.

ERZYA MORDOVIAN. See ERZYA and MORDVINIAN.

ERZYA MORDVIN. See ERZYA and MORDVINIAN.

ERZYA MORDVINIAN. See ERZYA and MORDVINIAN.

ESKIMO. The Eskimos are a widely scattered ethnic group occupying a more than 3,500-mile-long territory that stretches from Greenland across the Arctic reaches of North America to eastern Siberia. They call themselves the Inuit, Yugut, Yugyt, Yupigut, or Yuit, which literally translates as the "real people." They have also been identified as Onkilon, Namol, and Yuity. The Eskimo language is part of the Paleo-Asiatic group, and today they are divided into two distinct dialects. Inupik speakers live from Greenland in the east to the area around Nome, Alaska, in the west. The other Eskimo language—Yupik—is spoken in southern Alaska and in eastern Siberia. It has four dialects: Mainland Yupik, Nunivak, Pacific Yupik, and Siberian Yupik. The Siberian Yupik language is closely related linguistically to that of the Chukchi* people of Siberia. The largest group of Eskimos lives in Alaska and Canada, while those in Russia number no more than 2,000 people. The Siberian Eskimos live on the coast of the Chukchi Peninsula in an area reaching from the Bering Strait in the north to Kresta Bay in the west. There are also Siberian Eskimos living on Wrangel Island.

Eskimo religious life is similar to that of other aboriginal people around the world. An animistic, polytheistic people, the Eskimos believe that all aspects of creation—animals, plants, insects, lakes, mountains, rivers, oceans, stars, the sun, the moon, and the wind—have souls of their own, a spiritual essence imparted from the source of all life. Human beings are not unique and transcendent but part of a larger, eternal whole. Not only do all things have spirits that give them life, but all spirit is fundamentally of the same essence, different only in degree and not in kind. Through discipline, observation, and personal tranquility, individuals can learn from the world and make contact with the soul of the universe or any of its creations. Among the Siberian Eskimos, the souls of the animals they hunt are particularly significant, and Eskimo ceremonial life is heavily laced with rituals devoted to whales, walruses, and seals. They also worship to propitiate Migim, the sea goddess.

Most anthropologists view the aboriginal Eskimo economy as one of the most extraordinary environmental adaptations in human history. Life for human beings in the Arctic regions is difficult at best, but the Eskimos have made a successful adaptation. Traditionally, the economy of the Siberian Eskimos has revolved around the hunt for great bowhead whales, seals, walruses, caribou, and polar bears. They have also practiced ice-fishing as another protein source. Their clothing, food, housing, and life-style have revolved around the great animals they hunt. Although the first European contacts with Eskimos occurred in the tenth century, it was not until the early eighteenth century that systematic economic contacts began. Systematic contact with the Siberian Eskimos by Russians* did not really begin until the early 1800s. The Eskimos then experienced a wave of epidemic diseases—influenza, mumps, smallpox, chicken pox, and so forth—and underwent a population decline.

Eskimos suffered under Soviet economic policies. The Committee of the North established its first cultural base at St. Lawrence Bay in 1928, and Eskimo boat crews were soon organized into seasonal hunting cooperatives. Many Eskimos who owned their own whale boats protested this collectivization, but it was to no avail. After World War II, many Eskimos were actually forced to live in Chukchi* villages after their own villages were forcibly dissolved. Soviet hunting collectives monopolized the Arctic waters and over-harvested the whales and walruses, making it impossible for Eskimos to support themselves. Between 1953 and 1967, fifty villages in the Chukchi National Region were reduced to only twelve villages, and they were all grouped into a few state-administered "farms." The construction of roads, pipelines, airfields, radar stations, and military installations permanently altered Eskimo life; the huge nuclear power facility at Bilibino in the Lesser Anyui Basin was the most famous example. Most Eskimos were soon reduced to menial labor.

Institutions of Russian government and education did not reach the Siberian Eskimos until the early twentieth century, but they exacted a toll on Eskimo life. During Josef Stalin's years of power, attempts were made to settle the Eskimos in permanent villages and to incorporate them into the economic life of the larger society. During the 1950s, when the Cold War between the United States and the Soviet Union escalated, Soviet authorities grew nervous about the presence of Eskimos in Naukan and on Big Diomede Island. Those Eskimo communities were close to the Soviet-American border and in occasional contact with Eskimos in Alaska, with whom they shared a language and culture. To prevent American-inspired espionage among the Eskimos, the Soviets forcibly removed them from Naukan and Big Diomede Island. In more recent years, as the regional economy and the Russian educational system have extended more deeply into Eskimo territory, there have been adjustments in Eskimo economic life. Wage labor to earn the money to purchase trade goods has become more and more important, and social and cultural integration with the surrounding Chukchi people is accelerating. Along with a number of other Siberian peoples, the Eskimos have joined the Association of Peoples of the North (APN) to promote their political and economic rights in Russia. Nevertheless, the Siberian Eskimos maintain a distinct ethnic identity today.

The collapse of the Soviet Union in 1991 has brought changes in Eskimo life and has the potential for still more in the future. It inspired some of the Eskimos who had been removed from Naukan and Big Diomede to return to their traditional homeland in 1992. Even more important, regular contact between Alaskan and Russian Eskimos was re-established early in 1992, allowing families that had been separated for more than a half-century to make contact with one another once again. The Soviet Union's collapse has also relieved them of the pressures of hunting for collective agencies and allowed them to resume traditional economic patterns.

REFERENCES: "A Chukchi Writer's View Then and Now," *Soviet Life*, (December 1990), 24, 35; Bryan Hodgson, "Hard Harvest on the Bering Sea," *National Geographic*, 182 (October 1992), 72–104; Richard K. Nelson, *Shadow of the Hunter: Stories of the Eskimo Life*, 1980; Dorothy J. Ray, *Ethnohistory in the Arctic: The Bering Strait Eskimo*,

1983; David Riches, *Northern Nomadic Hunter-Gatherers*, 1982; Carson Ritchie, *The Eskimo and His Art*, 1974.

ESKIMOE. See ESKIMO.

ESKIMOSY. See ESKIMO.

ESTI. See ESTONIAN.

ESTON. See ESTONIAN.

ESTONIAN. The Estonians are an ethnic group of approximately 1,027,000 people. They call themselves the Tallopoeg or Maames and live primarily in Estonia, Latvia, and Russia. The first permanent settlements in what is today Estonia appeared around 100 A.D. when migrating tribes crossed over from the south side of the Gulf of Finland. They were part of the Finno-Ugrian peoples* who had originated in Central Asia and eventually evolved into such groups as the Finns*, Estonians, Magyars*, Mordvinians*, Lapps*, and Permians. Over the course of several centuries, the Estonians' trading relationships strengthened with the Swedes and Finns in the west and weakened with the Slavs in the east. Those trading connections eventually gave the Estonians an orientation more toward northern and western Europe than to eastern Europe.

The economic relationships soon evolved into political ties. The more highly centralized Swedes gradually established political control over the Finns and Estonians. With Swedish military protection, Roman Catholic missionaries brought Christianity to the polytheistic, animist Finns and Estonians in the thirteenth century. In the sixteenth century, when Lutheranism swept through Sweden and displaced Roman Catholicism, Swedish missionaries carried the new religion to Finland and Estonia as well.

Estonian is part of the western, Balto-Finnish* branch of the Finno-Ugrian linguistic family. It is divided into several dialects, each of which is quite distinct from the others. The Tallinn dialect is spoken in the northern part of Estonia, where the capital city of Tallinn is located; this dialect is also known as Northern Estonian. The Tartu, or Southern Estonian dialect, is spoken in and around the city of Tartu in the south. Coastal Estonian, which is very close to Finnish, is spoken in the northeast. The literary language of the Estonians is based on the Tallinn dialect, and the Latin script is used.

A fourth Estonian dialect, known as Setu, is spoken among the Setu* people who live around Lake Peipus near the Estonian-Russian border. Historically, most Estonians had come under the influence of the Swedes, adopted the Lutheran religion, and maintained a thoroughly Western perspective, but there was a small group of Estonians whose ties were more Eastern, closer to the Karelians* and the Russians*. The Karelians are a Finnish group who had historically been heavily influenced by Russian culture. They live in Karelia, a region bounded by Finland to the west, the Murmansk region to the north, the White Sea and the area near Archangel to the east, and the Leningrad region to the south. Because of their proximity to Novgorodian Russians, the Karelians adopted the Eastern Orthodox religion instead of Lutheranism. The Setu became Eastern Orthodox as well, and their Estonian dialect is laced with Russian words. The Setu are in a state of assimilation with the Russians who surround them.

Finally, there is a Setu subgroup in Russia that still maintains a unique identity. They are known to ethnologists as the Krasnyy Estonians,* but they call themselves the Kraasna Maarahvas. In the seventeenth century, they migrated to the area of Krasnyy, a market town in what used to be the Pskov Gubernia. Like other Setu, they are Eastern Orthodox in religion, but they are unique in the extent to which their traditional animistic, folk values have survived. During the twentieth century, the Krasnyy Estonians have been completely assimilated linguistically by ethnic Russians, but they are still aware of their Estonian roots and separate identity.

Much of Estonia fell under Danish control in the thirteenth century, and, in 1346, after a great Estonian rebellion against the Danes, King Waldemar IV sold Estonia to the Knights of the Sword, a powerful, militaristic group of German* crusaders. German landlords gradually reduced the Estonians to peasant status. In 1521, Estonia came under Swedish control, but, 200 years later, King Charles XII ceded the country to Peter the Great of Russia. During the nineteenth century, Estonian peasants rose up in rebellion against their economic plight a number of times, and, after 1881, when the tsar began to impose harsh russification programs to wipe out the Estonian language and Lutheran religion, the Estonians began to acquire a sense of national identity. That identity gained in intensity during the first two decades of the twentieth century. After the Bolshevik Revolution of 1917, Russia pulled out of World War I, and the Allied Powers, in retaliation, awarded independence to Estonia in 1921. The Soviet Union recognized that state of affairs with considerable reluctance.

Recognition by the Soviet Union, however, did not imply Soviet acceptance or acquiescence in the status quo. The Soviet Union still wanted unfettered access to the Baltic Sea because of a new political imperative. World War I had made the Russians paranoid about Germany, and Soviet leaders were intent on creating a buffer zone in eastern and northeastern Europe between the "motherland" and the Germans. The Baltic states of Latvia, Lithuania, and Estonia were prime candidates for a Russian takeover when the time was right.

That time was 1939. In the summer of 1939, Germany and the Soviet Union signed the infamous Molotov-Ribbentrop, or Non-Aggression, Pact, agreeing to forgo military operations against one another and to divide Poland between them. On September 1, 1939, when German troops drove into western Poland, Soviet soldiers occupied eastern Poland. A month later, the Soviet Union forcibly acquired military bases in Estonia. A Soviet-staged *coup d'état* took place in 1940, and the new pro-Soviet regime in Tallinn voted to incorporate Estonia into the Soviet Union that August. When Germany invaded the Soviet Union in

June 1941, it also took over Estonia. That occupation lasted until 1944, when the Soviet army expelled the Germans. Hundreds of thousands of Estonians died during the fighting at the hands of both the Russians and the Germans. The Estonian population had stood at nearly 1.5 million people on the eve of World War II; as late as 1959, the population was only 988,616. During the first five years or so of the postwar period, Estonian guerrillas kept up the fight for independence, but, by 1950, the last vestiges of resistance had been destroyed.

For the next thirty-five years, the Soviet Union ruled Estonia with an iron hand. Agriculture was collectivized, and centralized bureaucratic controls were imposed on the entire economy. At that point, the Estonian economy began its long decline into the malaise that affected the entire Soviet economy in the 1980s and 1990s. After World War II, an in-migration of ethnic Russians began, primarily because the Soviet Union had designated Estonia for industrial development; tens of thousands of Russian workers and their families arrived. The repressive apparatus of the Soviet state became ever-present, and civil liberties were savagely circumscribed. Soviet troops were stationed permanently on Estonian soil, with young Estonian men drafted into the Soviet army. In 1939, ethnic Estonians had constituted 97 percent of the population. By 1970, those numbers had changed to 65 percent for the Estonians and 25 percent for the Russians. Belarusians and Latvians, among others, made up the remaining 10 percent. By 1990, the Estonians represented only 61 percent, while the Russians were almost a third. As the numbers of ethnic Russians increased, the intensity of nationalist sentiment, particularly separatist sentiment, in Estonia became diluted, at least compared to Lithuania, where ethnic homogeneity had remained stronger.

World War II and its immediate aftermath were devastating to Estonia. More than a quarter of the Estonian population perished during the conflict. After the war, Josef Stalin saw to the deportation of tens of thousands of Estonians whom he considered a threat to his regime. He was ruthless in suppressing the anti-Russian guerrilla campaigns that started up against collectivization in 1949. Stalin also began a massive campaign of russification throughout Estonia, forbidding the use of Estonian in public schools and governmental institutions and outlawing Estonian-language publications. The construction of heavy-industry plants on Estonian soil brought large numbers of ethnic Russians and Ukrainian* workers, who were given preferential treatment about housing. What emerged was a society in which Estonians constituted a high percentage of white-collar and service workers, while Russians and Ukrainians tended more toward blue-collar work. During the Leonid Brezhnev era in the 1970s, the russification campaign intensified, especially after Karl Vaino, a man of Russian-Estonian descent, was appointed first secretary of the Estonian Communist Party.

From 1945 to the mid–1980s, Estonian nationalism functioned mostly on a clandestine basis. Outspoken advocates of Estonian independence were quickly hustled off to the Siberian *gulags*, where they disappeared. Other Estonian nationalists fled to the West, where they kept up the campaign for independence from small offices in London, New York, and Washington, D.C. During the 1950s, 1960s, and 1970s, occasional, small, pro-Estonian demonstrations took place, and people surreptitiously displayed Estonian colors. Still, Estonian nationalists could accomplish little more than these symbolic acts, since bolder actions meant imprisonment and death. The winds of real change did not begin to blow until Mikhail Gorbachev came to power in Moscow in March 1985. Gorbachev announced his policies of *glasnost* and *perestroika* to stimulate Soviet economic and social life. The disastrous war in Afghanistan during the 1980s had exposed severe weaknesses in Soviet military policy, and it was clear to most inside observers that the Soviet economy, shackled by seventy years of Communist bureaucratic red tape, was imploding. Gorbachev understood the challenge that the Soviet Union faced: No nation could maintain superpower military status so long as it had a Third-World economy. Without dramatic social and economic change, the Soviet Union would not be able to hold its grip on Eastern Europe or continue to support its client states throughout the world. Looking to the Baltic states as an economic window to the West, Gorbachev began in 1987 to discuss the possibility of more political and economic freedom—perhaps even internal autonomy—in Lithuania, Latvia, and Estonia. Only through radical political and economic reform, as embodied in *glasnost* and *perestroika*, could Gorbachev hope to maintain the Soviet Union as a first-class world power.

What Gorbachev did not realize, however, was the extraordinary weakness inherent in what the Soviets called "union." For seventy years, Soviet internal unity and hegemony in Eastern Europe had been maintained by brutal military power and strong economic inducements. As the Soviet economy faltered in the 1980s, especially after the collapse of world oil prices in the mid–1980s and the sharp reductions that brought Soviet hard-currency earnings, Gorbachev's ability to provide economic assistance to the nations of Eastern Europe eroded. His ability to finance a strong military presence there vanished as well. By the late 1980s, Gorbachev had given the non-Soviet nations of Eastern Europe more freedom. With breathtaking speed, the Warsaw Pact fell apart, Communist governments collapsed throughout the region, and steps began to bring about the re-unification of Germany, all within a few months in 1989. German re-unification was complete late in 1990.

Gorbachev had not anticipated the impact of the liberation of Eastern Europe on other nationality groups within the Soviet Union. Internally as well as externally, the Soviet Union had been held together for seventy years by terror and military force, not by any sense of national loyalty among most of the non-Russian nationalities. New political freedoms in Poland, Hungary, Czechoslovakia, Romania, Yugoslavia, Germany, and Bulgaria only strengthened the national aspirations of many groups inside the Soviet Union. The political unrest appeared first in the Baltic region.

After taking control of the Soviet government in the mid–1980s, Gorbachev had decided that large-scale reform—political, economical and social—was the only way to prevent the complete collapse of the country. He therefore launched the policies of *glasnost* and *perestroika*. *Glasnost*, or openness, would permit a freer atmosphere for political debate while *perestroika* would facilitate economic restructuring. These policies unleashed political and social forces over which Gorbachev had no control. One of his greatest mistakes was his refusal or inability to take the nationality question seriously and develop workable policies to deal with it. In the Baltic countries, where independence and political freedom had prevailed between World War I and World War II, *glasnost* was almost certain to liberate pent-up feelings of nationalism and to generate demands for reform at least and complete independence at most. The fact that much of Estonia was able to receive television broadcasts from Finland made Estonians even more ripe for change. When Eastern Europe began its drive for liberation in 1988 and 1989, it was only a matter of time before Estonians also demanded the withdrawal of all Soviet troops and secession from the Soviet Union.

The beginning of Estonia's outright political rebellion against the Communist Party and Soviet rule came over the issue of the environment. Throughout 1987 and early 1988, an extraordinary debate had taken place in Estonia over government plans to launch a huge phosphate-mining industry in north-central Estonia, an industrial development whose scale was so enormous that it threatened to pollute air and water throughout the entire country. Over the previous six decades, Soviet economic planners had often pushed a mindless agenda of economic development without consideration of the environmental costs. Estonians had long nurtured a love for their country and its physical beauties, and they were frightened that the phosphate project would become an environmental nightmare, as so many other development projects had become since World War II. Ethnic Estonians also worried that such a huge industrial development would bring thousands more ethnic Russians into the country. Opposition to the project took its usual clandestine forms, but Soviet authorities were astonished when Tartu University and the Estonian Academy of Sciences—both establishment institutions—also publicly opposed the project. Moscow then backed down and tabled the project. The significance of this victory was not lost on Estonian nationalists, who felt emboldened to try for more.

Soon Estonian nationalists were testing just how far Gorbachev's *glasnost* policies would go. In August 1987, nearly 5,000 Estonian protesters gathered at Hirvepark in Tallinn to condemn the Molotov-Ribbentrop Pact (German-Soviet Non-Aggression Pact) of 1939 that had led to the destruction of Polish and Baltic independence. The dissidents were astonished when the demonstrations were allowed to continue unimpeded by arrests or police harassment. In April 1988, a variety of Estonian intellectuals began writing letters to Soviet authorities, praising the merits of "socialist democracy" and "socialist federalism." Later in the month, Edgar Savisaar organized the Estonian Popular Front to promote the virtues of political pluralism and an end to one-party rule. Gorbachev even endorsed the idea, and his consent led to the reluctant support of Vaino Valjas, the new head of the Estonian Communist Party.

Estonian nationalists were also enjoying the cross-fertilization of ideas from other Baltic groups. In May 1989, representatives from the Estonian Popular Front, the Latvian Popular Front, and the Lithuanian Sajudis met in Tallinn for the so-called Baltic Assembly, at which they openly talked of Lithuanian, Latvian, and Estonian autonomy. In August 1989, on the fiftieth anniversary of the Molotov-Ribbentrop Pact, nearly 2.4 million Lithuanians*, Estonians, and Latvians* simultaneously held hands in a human chain stretching 400 miles across all three Baltic countries and passing through their capital cities. By May 1990, public opinion polls indicated that more than 96 percent of ethnic Estonians favored complete independence.

The Estonian Popular Front constituted a grass-roots movement. In the beginning, Savisaar had taken the middle ground, condemning the excesses of Stalinism but at the same time rejecting the claims of the ''restorationists,'' who demanded an immediate return to the pre–1940 state of political affairs. Savisaar thought the restorationists were politically unrealistic and that, if the reform movement adopted their position, it was sure to invite a Soviet crackdown. The restorationists developed the Estonian National Independence Party, led by Lagle Parek and Tunne Kelam, which insisted on immediate independence. What Savisaar did not know was that events would soon destroy the moderate position, and ''extremist'' demands for independence became the majority popular opinion.

Soon other groups appeared. The Internationalist Movement, also known as Intermovement, represented the interests of ethnic Russians and other non-Estonians, who wanted to maintain their relationship with the Soviet Union. At their founding congress in 1989, they demanded the repeal of all language laws, the outlawing of independent Estonia's flag, continued Soviet management of the Estonian economy, and annexation of Estonia's heavily russified northeastern sector to the Leningrad Oblast of Russia. A few speakers at the meeting called for the mass deportation of ethnic Estonians. The leader of Intermovement was Yevgeny Kogon.

The political consciousness of the Estonian population received another major boost in 1989 and early 1990 because of the series of free elections held throughout Estonia. In March and April 1989, Estonians voted for delegates to the new Congress of People's Deputies in Moscow. Local government elections were held in December 1989. Another dramatic change occurred in June 1989 when Valjas became first secretary of the Estonian Communist party. He was the first Estonian native to hold the post, replacing Karl Vaino, a Brezhnev appointee who was the hardest of the hardliners. Valjas immediately called for local management of the Estonian economy and the negotiation of a new union treaty with the Soviet Union. In October 1989, the Estonian Popular Front openly announced, in no uncertain terms, that its avowed political objective was complete independence from the Soviet Union. The flag of independent Estonia—the blue, black, and white tricolor—was resurrected. One month later, the Supreme Soviet of the Estonian Soviet Socialist Republic (SSR) declared Estonian sovereignty, a move that Moscow immediately condemned. It also passed a two-year residency requirement for voting, in order to exclude recent Russian immigrants from the franchise. The Supreme Council declared Estonian the official language of Estonia. That was not enough for some radicals, who did not trust the Supreme Soviet of the Estonian SSR. In February 1990, dissident groups like the Estonian National Independence Party held elections for the non-Soviet Congress of Estonians, an alternate parliament. Finally, elections to the Supreme Soviet of the Estonian SSR were held in March 1990.

There was a powerful cultural imperative inherent in the Estonian nationalist movement. Estonians had long resented the russification process at work in Soviet educational and political policies. They also worried that since ethnic Estonians constituted only 61.5 percent of the Estonian population in 1989, they might not have enough support to guarantee a clear, overwhelming majority for independence. Early in 1989, representatives of the Estonian National Independence Party, the Estonian Citizens' Committees, the Estonian Heritage Society, and the Estonian Christian Union—in the name of strict legal continuity from the pre-World War II republic—began registering all individuals who had been born in independent Estonia or who could trace their lineage directly to independent Estonia. By February 1990, more than 700,000 people were claiming to be "pure Estonians." That month, the Supreme Soviet of the Estonian SSR declared that the Estonian Communist Party no longer had a "leading role" in Estonian political life. During the rest of the year, the Estonian Communist Party lost membership and strength.

In March 1990, the Congress of Estonia declared itself "the vehicle for reinstating the legal authority of the [pre–1940] Republic of Estonia's parliament" with the power to negotiate with the Soviet Union on the question of Estonian independence. On March 30, 1990, the Supreme Soviet of the Estonian SSR voted seventy-three to zero to proclaim that Soviet power in Estonia was illegal and that a transition period during which Estonia would move toward independence had begun. The twenty-seven non-Estonian delegates boycotted the vote, claiming that it was completely illegal. In April 1990, the Supreme Soviet, now called the Supreme Council, abolished the name "Estonian Soviet Socialist Republic" in favor of the "Republic of Estonia." Savisaar, who had been selected as prime minister by the Supreme Council, then asked the Soviet Union to open negotiations concerning Estonian independence.

At the end of 1990, Gorbachev made a sudden shift toward the right and decided to crack down on the Baltic independence movements. Soviet troops occupied strategic locations in Latvia and Lithuania, but Estonia escaped the violence because its political leaders had been more circumspect in the previous months than had the nationalist leaders in Latvia and Lithuania. Boris Yeltsin, the populist leader of the Russian Republic, visited Tallinn in December 1990 and expressed his own support for Estonian independence. During the spring of 1991, Gorbachev decided to hold an all-Union referendum on the future of the Union of Soviet Socialist Republics. An intense debate took place in Estonia

over whether even to participate in the election, since Estonia had already proclaimed Soviet rule illegal. Estonian leaders decided to hold a preemptive referendum of their own. When the results were in, 77.83 percent of the voters
answered the question of independence in the affirmative.

During the next seven months, a tense calm descended on Estonian-Soviet
relations. Because of its catastrophic economic problems, the Soviet Union was
preoccupied with internal problems, and Gorbachev had neither the time nor the
inclination to make a major investment of energy and resources in retaining the
loyalty of Estonia. The Estonians had not projected themselves toward independence with quite the intensity of the Latvians and Lithuanians, no doubt because
the size of its ethnic Russian minority was so much larger; after all, as of 1990,
only 61 percent of the population of Estonia consisted of ethnic Estonians, while
nearly a third were ethnic Russians. Independence for Estonia stirred up divisive
opinions among the Russians, and Estonian political leaders therefore had to
chart a more cautious course.

They threw caution to the winds in August 1991, however, when hardliners
in the Soviet Union launched their *coup d'état* against Gorbachev. The attempt
to overthrow the Soviet government began on Sunday, August 19, 1991, with
the arrest of Gorbachev by special KGB troops. At the time, Gorbachev was
vacationing with his family in the Crimea. By late in the afternoon on the first
day of the coup, elite Soviet troops invaded Latvia to seize control of its communications facilities and borders. Engineered by a small but powerful group
of people in the KGB, the Communist Party, the Soviet defense ministry, and
two major trade unions, the coup was poorly planned, carelessly executed, and
quickly over. Yeltsin, president of the Russian Republic, openly defied the
conspirators from the very beginning, and, when Soviet troops refused to carry
out the plotters' orders, the coup collapsed.

During the coup, on August 20, 1991, the Supreme Council of Estonia again
affirmed the reality of Estonian independence and drew up a plan for a constitutional transition. They decided to create a Constitutional Assembly consisting
of representatives of the Supreme Council and the Congress of Estonia. This
body would then draft a new constitution and take it to the voters in a referendum
in 1992. The Supreme Council selected thirty members for the Constitutional
Assembly, and the Congress of Estonia selected thirty as well.

The coup proved to be the death knell of the Communist Party, the KGB,
and the Soviet Union. Gorbachev returned to Moscow from the Crimea. He
quickly resigned from the Communist Party himself, arrested the conspirators,
and began an investigation to determine the depth of the rebellion within the
major political institutions of the country. Within weeks, one republic after
another, including all of the Baltic countries, Moldova, Belarus, and Ukraine,
had declared independence. Most of the Western nations began extending diplomatic recognition to Estonia and the other Baltic countries. The Soviet Union
was distintegrating, and, on September 5, 1991, the Supreme Soviet voted itself
out of existence, surrendering sovereignty to the republics and beginning work

on the construction of a new, loose confederation system. On September 6, 1991, the Soviet Union extended full independence to Estonia.

REFERENCES: Tonu Parming, "Population Processes and Nationality Issues in the Soviet Baltic," *Soviet Studies*, 32 (July 1980), 398–414; Tonu Parming and E. E. Jarvesco, eds., *A Case Study of a Soviet Republic: The Estonian SSR*, 1978; Toivo U. Raun, *Estonia and the Estonians*, 1987; Toivo U. Raun, "The Re-Establishment of Estonian Independence," *Journal of Baltic Studies*, 22 (Fall 1991), 251–57; Mare Taagepera, "The Ecological and Political Problems of Phosphate Mining in Estonia, *Journal of Baltic Studies*, 20 (Summer 1989), 165–74; Rein Taagepera, "Estonia in September 1988: Stalinists, Centrists and Restorationists," *Journal of Baltic Studies*, 20 (Summer 1989), 175–90; Rein Taagepera, "National Differences Within Soviet Demographic Trends," *Soviet Studies*, 20 (1968), 478–89; Rein Taagepera, "Soviet Collectivization of Estonian Agriculture: The Deportation Phase," *Soviet Studies*, 32 (July 1980), 379–97; Arveds Trapans, *Toward Independence: The Baltic Popular Movements*, 1990.

EVEN. Since the time of the Russian Revolution of 1917, the Evens (Ewens) of eastern Siberia have been recognized as a distinct ethnic group, but they have extremely complex origins and only the vaguest sense of identity as a single people. Before the revolution, they were known as the Lamuts. In fact, there is no single word that they have used to identify themselves as a group until very recently, and that word is the "Even." They have also been known as the Orochen, Tungus, Tongus, Birar, Manegir, and Manegry. The Even are scattered over a vast area of eastern Siberia, primarily east of the Lena River, and on the Kamchatka Peninsula. They are more likely to identify themselves regionally or by clan than by any sense of nationality. In the Okhotskiy Rayon, for example, the name "Even" or "Oven" is common, as it is in the Chukchi National Okrug. But those Evens living in the northern part of the Okhotsk coastal area call themselves the Oroch (Orochen, Orochel). Evens who are former members of the Tyugasir clan in what was once the Yakut Autonomous Soviet Socialist Republic call themselves Tyuges; those who know they are descended from Yukagirs* call themselves the Dutkil', and those living along the coast of the Sea of Okhotsk call themselves the Mene or Menel. That sense of ethnicity has been weakened over the years by the mixing of the Evens with other Siberian ethnic groups. The Evens living on the Kamchatka Peninsula have been heavily influenced culturally by the neighboring Koryaks*, while those in Yakutia have come under Yakut* influence. Most Evens there were bilingual in both their Even dialect and Yakut. There were approximately 7,000 Evens in 1926, and that number has increased slowly to 9,121 in 1959, 12,029 in 1970, 12,286 in 1979, and approximately 12,500 people today.

Ethnographers surmise that the Evens have descended from a mixture of Tungus and Yukagir culture over the centuries. Their language is part of the Tungusic* group of the Tungus-Manuchu division of the Uralic-Altaic languages. The speakers of the ancient Tungusic languages roamed over the vast Kolyma, Yana, and Indigirka river basins and, in the process, absorbed a great deal of Yukagir* culture. By the eighteenth century, people identified as "Lamut Yu-

kagirs'' were migrating east toward the Sea of Okhotsk; it was not until the
1840s that these people, who became the Evens, reached the Kamchatka Peninsula. There are two main Even dialects, and each is divided into a number of
subdialects, reflecting the complex identities of the Even people. The Eastern
Even dialect consists primarily of the Kolyma-Omolon, Ola, and Kamchatka
subdialects, while Western Even is made up of the Indigirka, Tompon, and
Allaika subdialects. Although there is a written Even language that is based on
the Ola dialect and uses Cyrillic characters, it is hardly used at all.

The traditional Even economy revolved around herding and hunting reindeer.
Evens were especially adept at hunting squirrels and selling their furs, but they
also hunted wild reindeer, bear, elk, and mountain sheep. They fished in mountain
streams for grayling. The Evens along the coast of the Sea of Okhotsk also fished
for salmon and hunted sea mammals, particularly seals. Except for the settled
sea-mammal hunters of the Okhotsk coast, most Evens were a nomadic people
who raised a breed of reindeer known for its large size and strength. They lived
in portable birch bark tents. Their social life revolved around patriarchal clan
systems, and their religion reflected that economic and social life-style. It was
a shamanistic, animist religion with cults based on the ''masters of the universe''—fire, water, and sunshine—as well as on such animals as the bear, the
reindeer, and the seal.

Russian* contact with the Even began in the seventeenth century. They treated
the Even like other peoples whom they had conquered, building forts and imposing the *yasak*, or fur tax, upon them. Moscow granted Russian citizenship
to Evens who agreed to baptism into the Russian Orthodox Church. But it was
a superficial conversion. The Evens still believed in their three-world cosmology:
the upper world, where the supreme god lived; the middle earth, where people
lived; and the underworld, where the spirits of the dead lived. Along with the
Russian government and Christian missionaries came Russian merchants, Russian settlers, European diseases, and vodka. The Evens suffered badly from
smallpox, chicken pox, mumps, and influenza. As a result, they underwent a
severe population decline that did not stabilize until the early nineteenth century.

The Russian Revolution of 1917 brought dramatic changes to Even life. Beginning in 1929, the Soviet government began the forced collectivization of Even
economic activities, but the plans encountered fierce resistance. Many Even
destroyed their reindeer herds rather than turn them over to the state. Others fled
with their herds to the most inaccessible areas where they were out of reach.
The Evens north of Okhotsk were extremely difficult to collectivize, not only
because of their resistance to state organization schemes but because of their
isolation. They wandered through the larch forests and across the tundra in the
Kolyma and Omolon basins, consciously avoiding any contact with ethnic Russians. Only in the summers, when some Evens migrated to the coastal areas,
did they attend state schools and seek medical treatment. It was not until 1930
that the Soviets succeeded in establishing a cultural base at Nagayevo, and a
number of poor Evens from the Ola subgroup came into permanent contact. But

when gold was discovered in the region in 1931–1932, ethnic Russians began requisitioning Even reindeer for transport and the Evens themselves for laborers. Many Even retreated still farther into the tundra to avoid contact with Russians. It was not until the early 1960s that the last of the Even class—the Rassokha and the Beryozov—were finally collectivized.

Many nomadic Even eventually settled down into permanent communities, complete with schools, day-care centers, clubs, and medical facilities. Those Even who continued to migrate often found their children required to remain in the settled communities where they could attend school. The state also collectivized Even hunting and fishing activities. The Ola dialect with a Latin alphabet had been developed by the early 1930s, but the alphabet was changed to Cyrillic in 1937. The vast majority of Even, however, never learned to read the language. Those who did read usually read Yakut- or Russian-language documents. Russian soon became the *lingua franca* of Siberia.

During World War II, the Evens were affected by the relocation of much Soviet industry to areas east of the Ural Mountains. The industrial relocation brought a huge influx of Russians. The arrival of so many Russians placed new pressures for assimilation on the Even, but they survived ethnically because of their relatively remote locations. In spite of the abundance of new industrial jobs, most Even remained tied to the fur trade, reindeer breeding, hunting, and fishing. Few Russians engaged in these economic activities because of the harsh environment and the special skills required. The greatest problem that the Even faced in the postwar years, however, was economic development. The Soviet government had a bias for large-scale industrial production schemes. These often resulted in severe damage to the environment, a development that seriously affected Even life. During the Stalin, Khrushchev, and Brezhnev years, native peoples protested such problems only at their peril.

The *perestroika* and *glasnost* policies of Mikhail Gorbachev after 1985 gave the Even more political freedom and ended the heavy-handed cultural repression they had experienced for fifty years. Unlike many other nationality groups in the Soviet Union, the Even had no interest in nationalism or political independence. Their concerns were much more economic, cultural, and environmental, because they wanted to be able to preserve their way of life—to maintain fish and animal populations, to protect the reindeer pastures, and the preserve water and air quality. In the late 1980s and early 1990s, Even leaders protested government plans to reverse the flow of several Siberian rivers so that they would flow into the Caspian Sea instead of the Arctic Ocean, thereby providing new water resources for hydroelectric power and agriculture. The Even also became active in such groups as the Association of the Peoples of the North (APN), in order to secure more political representation in the organs of government, to protest the continuing settlement of ethnic Russians and Ukrainians* on their land, to demand fair prices for the extraction of resources from their land, and to stop what they considered environmentally harmful development projects.

Although the Soviet government and, after 1991, the Russian government of

Boris Yeltsin were more amenable to the concerns of the Evens and other Siberian native peoples, these groups actually found themselves under increasing cultural pressure. The Evens had not developed any real sense of political nationalism, so no demands for Even independence emanated from Siberia in the late 1980s and early 1990s. The Even leaders were most interested in preserving their indigenous culture, especially their economic way of life. They therefore protested the petroleum and natural gas development policies that were causing the loss of their aboriginal land. They resented the construction of roads, highways, railroads, and pipelines that disrupted traditional reindeer migration routes and herding routines.

REFERENCES: Alice Bartels and Dennis Bartels, "Soviet Policy Toward Siberian Native People," *Canadian Dimension*, 19 (1985), 36–44; Mike Edwards, "Siberia: In From the Cold," *National Geographic*, 177 (March 1990), 2–49; James Forsyth, *A History of the Peoples of Siberia*, 1992; Constantine Krypton, "Soviet Policy in the Northern National Regions After World War II," *Slavic Review*, 13 (October 1954), 339–53; Piers Vitebsky, "Perestroika Among the Reindeer Herders," *Geographical Magazine*, 61 (June 1989), 23–34; Ronald Wixman, *The Peoples of the USSR: An Ethnographic Handbook*, 1984.

EVENK. The Evenk, also known as the Evenki, Ewenk, Tungus (Tongus), Lamut, Birars, Manegry, and Orochen, are one of the largest ethnic groups in northern Siberia. Most of the above names refer to earlier subgroups of the Evenks. Evenks are closely related to the Even*, who were once simply an Evenk subgroup. They are scattered over a huge expanse of territory, from the Yenesei River to the Sea of Okhotsk. They are also one of the most widely scattered nationalities in the former Soviet Union, their territory ranging over three million square kilometers of the Russian Far East. They border on the Evens, Yakuts*, and Dolgans* to the north; their southern boundary reaches as far south as Lake Baikal and the Amur River. Smaller groups of Evenks also live in the northwestern reaches of the People's Republic of China and in the Mongolian People's Republic. Russian* demographers placed the Evenk population at 64,000 people in 1987, and it has fallen since then. In 1926, there was a total of approximately 34,000 Evenks; that number had fallen to 24,151 by 1959. At that point, the Evenk population stabilized and began to increase slightly, to 25,149 in 1970 and 27,531 in 1979. The 1989 Soviet census listed the Evenk population at 29,000 people.

Ethnographers surmise that the Evens were descended from a mixture of Tungus and Yukagir* culture over the centuries. Their language is part of the Tungusic* group of the Tungusic-Manuchu division of the Uralo-Altaic languages. The speakers of the ancient Tungus languages roamed over the vast Kolyma, Yana, and Indigirka river basins and, in the process, absorbed a great deal of Yukagir culture. By the eighteenth century, people identified as "Lamut Yukagirs" were migrating east toward the Sea of Okhotsk; it was not until the 1840s that these people, who became the Evens, reached the Kamchatka Peninsula. Those left behind were the Evenks. They were first identified as an ethnic group as early as the fourteenth century. Archaeologists suspect that the most dominant people who mixed to become the Evenks had their origins in the region of Lake Baikal and the Amur River.

Russian Cossacks* constructed the Ket Fortress in 1602 and then began moving up the Yenesei River, where they confronted the Evenks for the first time in 1606 or 1607. By the mid–1620s, most of the Evenks living near the Yenesei River were paying the Russian fur tax on sable, fox, ermine, and squirrel. Russians made sure the taxes were paid by taking hostages from each Evenk clan and holding them for a tax ransom. The Evenks suffered a rapid population decline because of the diseases carried by the Russian settlers and because of the effects of alcohol. Russian Orthodox missionaries moved into Evenk land in the late seventeenth century, and, over the years, they made thousands of converts; these conversions were superficial at best, and, even today, the Evenks are only nominally Christians. The animistic tribal religion still exerts a strong pull on their spiritual and cultural loyalties. Christianity mingled with that sha- manistic faith, producing such religious fusions as a local version of St. Nicholas, the Russian Orthodox saint who functions in the Evenk pantheon as the deputy to the master-spirit of the upper world. The Evenk resented their Russian ov- erlords and resisted them, passively most of the time, but also violently between 1825 and 1841 when Evenk rebellions were common.

The Evenk economy was regionally divided. The "Foot" or "Sitting" Evenks lived along the Sea of Okhotsk and Lake Baikal, where they fished and hunted large sea mammals. The "Horse" Evenks lived in the southern Baikal, the Transbaikal, and the Upper Amur River regions. The Evenks living near the Yakuts* or Russians on the Lena, Lower Tunguska, Kirenga, and Amur rivers learned to raise cattle and also became settled farmers. Most of these Evenk supplemented their economic life by hunting elk and wild reindeer and capturing fur, which they sold for cash or used to pay their taxes. The Evenk living in the northern reaches of their territory turned to breeding reindeer as the basis of their economy. The Evenk economy still remains divided. The northern Evenk are primarily hunters, fishermen, and reindeer breeders, while the southern Evenk raise horses and cattle.

The Bolshevik Revolution in 1917 brought dramatic changes to Evenk life. In 1917, V. I. Lenin issued the "Declaration of Rights of the Peoples of Russia," guaranteeing sovereignty and equality to each ethnic group; Josef Stalin was named Commissar for Nationalities. Native rights, including those of the Evenk, to land, pasture, and hunting and fishing preserves were supposedly guaranteed in 1919. The civil war prevented the implementation of these lofty objectives, and, in 1924, the Commissariat of Nationalities was abolished, and jurisdiction over the Evenk shifted to a newly organized Committee of Assistance to the Peoples of the North. That committee was abolished in 1934, and jurisdiction was handed over to the Northern Sea Route Administration.

In 1927, the Soviet Union began establishing "cultural bases" in Evenk territory. The first opened at the mouth of the Tura River in October 1927 and included a boarding school for Evenk children, a health clinic, a bathhouse, and a community center. A library and theater were quickly added, and more cultural bases were soon established for the Evenk. In order to move the Evenks from clan-based government to a more modern society, small-scale soviets were established among them, beginning in the mid–1920s. By 1927, there were thirty-six functioning in the broader Yenesei River basin, and half of them were among the Evenk. In 1930, the government established the Evenk National Okrug, with 287,600 square miles of territory. That same year, the first Congress of Evenk Soviets convened.

The Soviet government began the forced collectivization of Evenk economic activities in 1929. The government declared all fur-bearing animals and all reindeer to be state property and subject to state regulations. Like the Evens, many Evenks destroyed their reindeer herds rather than turn them over to the state; others fled with their herds to the most inaccessible areas where they were out of reach. In spite of Evenk resistance, most of them had been collectivized into small cooperative villages by the time of World War II. Even then, those Evenks in the more remote areas of the Okhotsk region and Yakutia managed to maintain their nomadic freedom. Some of them were still living in their portable tepees as late as the mid–1960s. But those Evenks who had moved into the collectives by World War II found their lives still disrupted after the war. Soviet policy kept amalgamating smaller collectives into larger ones, and repeatedly relocated Evenks from outlying settlements into more centralized communities. Further, construction of the Baikal-Amur Mainline Railroad, mineral development, and construction of hydroelectric projects dramatically increased the demand for horse and reindeer transport; Evenk teamsters were forced to leave their herds and work for the state moving construction materials and people. The railroad, the diamond mines at Mirnyy in Yakutia, and the huge hydroelectic power project on the Vilui River disrupted Evenk lands and drove many Evenks farther to the north. By the early 1980s, there were more than 3,000 mineral deposits of various kinds being extracted from Evenk land.

Collectivization had a very negative effect on Evenk society. Evenk fathers and mothers often had to leave the collectives for extended periods of time to go to the reindeer pastures and hunting areas. Evenk children were thus left at home to be raised by Russian teachers and sitters. Also, because the Evenk were so scattered demographically, the arrival of many ethnic Russians compromised their language loyalties. By the 1980s, the use of the Evenk language was in a state of decline in Siberia.

More than anything else in their history, the devastation of the environment by economic development generated a budding spirit of nationalism among the Evenk. The greatest threat of all emerged in the 1980s when the government began plans to construct a huge dam across the Lower Tunguska River. The project would have raised the water level some 650 feet and flooded most of the Evenk National Okrug, including the capital at Tura. The Evenk way of life depended upon the preservation of the pastures and hunting grounds of the valley.

The Evenks began protesting the proposal, and Alitet Nemtushkin, an Evenk writer, put their protests into memorable prose, charging that "technocrats don't care about ethics." Representatives of other Siberian peoples, through the Association of the Peoples of the North, supported the Evenk claim that the project amounted to ecological catastrophe. Ethnic Russians prominent in the environmental movement joined the protest as well, and eventually the government cancelled the project.

By the early 1990s, three of the traditional clan-territorial Evenk groups still retained a local identity. The Negidal*—also known historically as the El'kan, Beyenin, Eleke Beye, Negda, Niyegda, Neidal, Nizhdal, and Negeden—are Evenks who have mixed with the Nivkhis*, Nanais*, and Ulchis* on the lower Amgun and Amur rivers. Most of them live in two settlements in Khabarovsk Krai in southeastern Siberia. The Manegirs (Manyagir, Manegri, and Kumarchan) live primarily along the Kumara River. Finally, there are still several thousand Evenks who identify themselves as the Orochen.

REFERENCES: Alice Bartels and Dennis Bartels, "Soviet Policy Toward Siberian Native People," *Canadian Dimension,* 19 (1985), 36–44; Mike Edwards, "Siberia: In From the Cold," *National Geographic,* 177 (March 1990), 2–49; Walter Kolarz, *Russia and Her Colonies,* 1952; Constantine Krypton, "Soviet Policy in the Northern National Regions After World War II," *Slavic Review,* 13 (October 1954), 339–53; William J. Pomeroy, "The Evenks: Affirmative Action in the USSR," in Marilyn Bechtel and Daniel Rosenberg, eds., *Nations and Peoples of the Soviet Union,* 1981, 101–12; Piers Vitebsky, "Perestroika Among the Reindeer Herders," *Geographical Magazine,* 61 (June 1989), 23–34; Ronald Wixman, *The Peoples of the USSR: An Ethnographic Handbook,* 1984.

EVENKI. See EVENK.

EVREI. See JEW.

EVREY. See JEW.

EVRIMEISET. See AYRAMOISET, FINN, and KARELIAN.

EWEN. See EVEN and EVENK.

EWENK. See EVEN and EVENK.

F

FARSI. See PERSIAN.

FEAPP. See FEAPPI and INGUSH.

FEAPPI. The Feappi are one of the two major subgroups of the Ingushes*; the subdivisions are based on former clan designations. See INGUSH.
REFERENCE: Ronald Wixman, *The Peoples of the USSR: An Ethnographic Handbook*, 1984.

FEPI. See KIST, FEAPPI, and INGUSH.

FERGANA TURK. See UZBEK.

FERGHANA TURK. See UZBEK.

FINN. The Finns are one of the former Soviet Union's smaller ethnic groups, and, within the ethnic category are a number of subdivisions. The Finns call themselves the Suomi or Suomalaiset. The first permanent settlements in what is today Finland appeared around 100 A.D., when migrating tribes crossed over from the south side of the Gulf of Finland. They were part of the Finno-Ugrian peoples*, who had originated in Central Asia and eventually evolved into such groups as the Finns, Estonians*, Magyars*, Mordvinians*, Lapps*, and Permians. Over the course of several centuries, the Finns' trading relationships strengthened with the Swedes in the west and weakened with the Slavs in the east. Those trading connections eventually gave the Finns an orientation more toward northern and western Europe than to eastern Europe.

Those economic relationships soon evolved into political ties. The more highly centralized Swedes gradually established political control over the Finns. Roman Catholic missionaries, with Swedish military protection, brought Christianity to the polytheistic, animist Finns in the thirteenth century. In the sixteenth century, when Lutheranism swept through Sweden and displaced Roman Catholicism, Swedish missionaries carried the new religion to Finland as well. At the same time, the Finns acquired the beginnings of a national consciousness and a literary language. Finnish is part of the western, Balto-Finnish* branch of the Finno-Ugrian linguistic family. In the early sixteenth century, Michael Agricola became the first writer to publish in the Finnish vernacular, but the cultural dominance of Sweden retarded the literary development of the language in Finland. It was not until the nineteenth century that Finnish became a truly literary language with an increasing volume of compositions.

By that time, most of Finland had also come under Russian* control. As early as 1710, Peter the Great decided to take control of Finland as a way of giving Russia an outlet on the Baltic Sea. By 1716, he had succeeded in this goal. The Russian-Swedish struggle for control of Finland raged on and off throughout the eighteenth century. In 1807, Napoleon and Tsar Alexander I discussed the Finnish question, and, at the conclusion of another Russo-Swedish war in 1809, Finland and the Aland Islands were ceded to Russia. Alexander I granted Finland status as a semi-independent grand duchy. In 1811, the province of Viborg was added to Finland.

The Finnish experience at the hands of the Swedes and Russians* had stimulated a growing sense of nationalism. Finland had been part of Sweden from the twelfth through the eighteenth centuries, and the language of the state bureaucracy was Swedish. Swedes controlled the political system and looked down upon the Finns as narrow-minded provincials. Russian control proved to be no better. By the end of the nineteenth century, Russia had abolished the Finnish army, drafted Finns into the Russian army, tried to impose Russian as the official language of Finland, and persecuted the Lutheran church in an attempt to impose Russian Orthodoxy. Under Tsar Alexander III, the Russian motto of "one law, one church, one tongue" became particularly obnoxious to the Finns, who began to resist russification actively. Tsar Nicholas II virtually eliminated the power of the Finnish legislature in 1899, and, within a few years, the office of the Russian governor of Finland had become a virtual dictatorship, complete with spies, a police state, deportations, censorship of the press, and the arrest of Finnish nationalists.

World War I and the Russian Revolution led quickly to Finnish independence. During the early stages of the war, the tsar was too preoccupied with the German* threat to worry much about Finland, and, when the Bolshevik Revolution erupted in 1917 and quickly evolved into a civil war, Finnish independence received another boost. The Soviet Union withdrew from World War I with the Treaty of Brest-Litovsk. The angry Allied Powers committed themselves to Finnish independence as a way of both getting back at the Russians and fulfilling President Woodrow Wilson's desire for the unification of ethnic and political boundaries in Europe. Finland declared itself a republic on June 17, 1919, and, on October 14, 1920, Finland signed a peace treaty with Soviet Russia. Finland was admitted to the League of Nations in 1921.

During their more than a century as part of the Russian Empire, the Finns had evolved into two distinct ethnic communities. Historically, the western Finns had come under the influence of the Swedes, adopted the Lutheran religion, and maintained a thoroughly Western perspective. The western Finns are located primarily in Finland proper, but sizable numbers of them also live in the Leningrad Oblast. Beginning in the seventeenth century, some western Finns from Savo and Ayrapaa had begun migrating to the Leningrad area in search of work and settling primarily along the Gulf of Finland. By 1900, there were approximately 120,000 Finns living there. They were Lutheran in religion, spoke a Finnish dialect, and referred to themselves either as Savakot* or Ayramoiset.*

The eastern Finns, who are known as Karelians* (Korela, Karyala) and call themselves the Karjala (Karjalainen), historically were heavily influenced by Russian culture. They live in Karelia, a region bounded by Finland to the west, the Murmansk region to the north, the White Sea and the area of Archangel to the east, and the Leningrad region to the south. Because of their proximity to Novgorodian Russians, they adopted the Eastern Orthodox religion instead of Lutheranism. They speak three dialects of Finnish, all of which have been strongly influenced by Russian. Karelians living in southern Karelia are known as Livviki* and speak the Livvi dialect. Karjala is spoken by Karelians proper who live in northern and central Karelia. The Lyydiki* people, who live in Kondopozhskiy and the Olonets Rayon, speak the Lyydiki dialect. During the medieval period, Karelia was an independent kingdom, but, in the early seventeenth century, it came under Swedish domination. Russia annexed Karelia in 1721, and the Soviet Union established Karelia as an autonomous republic in 1923.

When Finland became formally independent of the Soviet Union in 1919, Karelia remained under Russian control. Despite their cultural ties to the Russians, most Karelians expressed the desire to become part of Finland. When that did not materialize, Karelian nationalists rebelled against Moscow, but Soviet troops quickly crushed the rebellion. Finland then petitioned the League of Nations for sovereignty over Karelia. The League decided not to intervene, and the region remained Soviet territory. When the Soviet Union went to war and invaded Finland in 1939, Finns and Karelians resisted the aggression. For months, they put up a heroic struggle, but the superior numbers and resources of Soviet forces eventually prevailed. On March 13, 1940, Finland signed a peace treaty. The provisions of the treaty forced Finland to cede about 10 percent of its territory to the Soviet Union, which included the Karelian isthmus and the Finnish shore of Lake Ladoga. On March 31, 1940, the Soviet Union created the Karelo-Finnish Soviet Socialist Republic. When Germany invaded the Soviet Union in 1941, the Finns joined the Germans, but they were crushed in 1944, at which time the 1940 borders were restored. The Karelo-Finnish Soviet Socialist Republic was dissolved in 1956. Not until the 1980s, when Mikhail Gorbachev's policies of *glasnost* and *perestroika* gave such a boost to Soviet ethnic identity, did Karelian nationalism strongly reassert itself.

By that time, however, both the Karelian population of the Soviet Union in particular and the Finnish population in general had declined from its high around 1920. At the time of Finnish independence in 1919, there were approximately 380,000 Finns in the Soviet Union. Nearly 250,000 of them were Karelians, while 115,000 were Finns living in the Leningrad Oblast and perhaps 20,000 were western Finns living on the Soviet side of the border with Finland. During the twentieth century, substantial numbers of the Leningrad Finns assimilated into the larger Russian society, and, ever since World War II, there has been an emigration of Finns and Karelians from the Soviet Union to Finland. By the mid–1980s, the Karelian population had dropped to approximately 130,000 people, while the western Finns, along the Finnish border as well as in the Leningrad region, numbered only about 70,000 people. By 1990, Finland was preparing for a large-scale immigration of Finns and Karelians fleeing the economic collapse of the Soviet Union.

REFERENCES: Paul M. Austin, "Soviet Karelia," *Slavic Review*, 51 (Spring 1992), 16–35; George Maude, *The Finnish Dilemma: Neutrality in the Shadow of Power*, 1976; Ronald Wixman, *The Peoples of the USSR: An Ethnographic Handbook*, 1984.

FINNIC PEOPLES. The Finnic peoples of the former Soviet Union included those who speak any of the Finnic languages: Finns*, Izhoras*, Karelians*, Veps*, Estonians*, Lapps*, Mordvinians*, Maris*, and Komis*.

REFERENCE: Ronald Wixman, *The Peoples of the USSR: An Ethnographic Handbook*, 1984.

FINNO-UGORIAN PEOPLES. See FINNO-UGRIAN PEOPLES.

FINNO-UGRIAN PEOPLES. The term "Finno-Ugrian Peoples" is a generic reference to all of the groups in central and eastern Europe and Russia who speak a language that is part of the Finno-Ugrian group within the larger Uralic-Altaic linguistic family. Included in this large group of people are the Finns*, Izhorans*, Karelians*, Veps*, Estonians*, Vods*, Livs, Lapps*, Mordvinians*, Maris*, Udmurts*, Komis*, Komi Permyaks, Khants*, Mansi*, and Magyars*.

REFERENCE: Ronald Wixman, *The Peoples of the USSR: An Ethnographic Handbook*, 1984.

FIVE MOUNTAIN SOCIETIES OF KABARDA. See BALKAR.

FIVE MOUNTAIN TATARS. See BALKAR.

FOREST CHERKESS. See KOZHLA MARI and MARI.

FOREST ENISEI SAMODI. See KARASA SAMOYED and ENT.

FOREST ENISEI SAMOED. See KARASA SAMOYED and ENT.

FOREST ENISEI SAMOIED. See KARASA SAMOYED and ENT.

FOREST ENISEI SAMOYED. See KARASA SAMOYED and ENT.

FOREST ENISEY SAMODI. See KARASA SAMOYED and ENT.

FOREST ENISEY SAMOED. See KARASA SAMOYED and ENT.

FOREST ENISEY SAMOIED. See KARASA SAMOYED and ENT.

FOREST ENISEY SAMOYED. See KARASA SAMOYED and ENT.

FOREST ENT. See KARASA SAMOYED and ENT.

FOREST IENISEI SAMODI. See KARASA SAMOYED and ENT.

FOREST IENISEI SAMOED. See KARASA SAMOYED and ENT.

FOREST IENISEI SAMOIED. See KARASA SAMOYED and ENT.

FOREST IENISEI SAMOYED. See KARASA SAMOYED and ENT.

FOREST IURAK. See KHANDEYAR and NENET.

FOREST MARI. See MARI.

FOREST NENET. See NENET.

FOREST SELKUP. See SELKUP.

FOREST YENISEI SAMODI. See KARASA SAMOYED and ENT.

FOREST YENISEI SAMOED. See KARASA SAMOYED and ENT.

FOREST YENISEI SAMOIED. See KARASA SAMOYED and ENT.

FOREST YENISEI SAMOYED. See KARASA SAMOYED and ENT.

FOREST YENISEY SAMODI. See KARASA SAMOYED and ENT.

FOREST YENISEY SAMOED. See KARASA SAMOYED and ENT.

FOREST YENISEY SAMOIED. See KARASA SAMOYED and ENT.

FOREST YENISEY SAMOYED. See KARASA SAMOYED and ENT.

FOREST YURAK. See KHANDEYAR and NENET.

FRENCH. Until its 1989 census, the Soviet Union did not track, or at least did not publish, the number of foreign residents by nationality group. The 1989 census did provide these figures, and it indicated that in 1989 there were 964 French citizens living in the Soviet Union. Ever since the early eighteenth century, there had been French citizens living Russia. Upper-class Russians worshiped French culture and frequently sent their children to Paris for their educations; they also hired French tutors to teach their children in Russia. Further, French diplomats and military officials were frequently in Moscow providing advice and often leadership to the Russian diplomatic corps and army. After the Bolshevik Revolution, a new breed of French citizens took up residence in the Soviet Union. Most were expatriates infatuated with Marxism and the Communist experiment who decided to take up residence there. Still, there was never any significant movement of the French to change citizenship and live their lives in the Soviet Union. There had also been other people of French descent who, for economic reasons, were very interested in improving their business relationship with the Soviet Union. As disillusionment with the Communist Party in the Soviet Union and in France mounted during the Brezhnev era in the 1970s, the numbers of expatriates declined. As Mikhail Gorbachev welcomed European capital and technological expertise, however, the number of French citizens permanently residing in the Soviet Union increased. Of the 946 French living in the Soviet Union in 1989, most were business people hoping to establish an economic foothold there.
REFERENCE: Raymond E. Zickel, ed., *Soviet Union: A Country Study*, 1991.

FRONTIER KALMUK. See TELEUT and ALTAI.

FRONTIER KALMYK. See TELEUT and ALTAI.

FRONTIER QALMUQ. See TELEUT and ALTAI.

FRONTIER QALMYQ. See TELEUT and ALTAI.

G

GAGAUZ. The Gagauz are a small Turkic* tribe who do not currently possess their own homeland within the Commonwealth of Independent States (CIS). Instead, they have settled mainly in the following areas: the southwestern regions of the Moldovan Republic, where they occupy the districts of Komrat, Cadir-Lunga, Kangaz, Tarkliya, and Vulkanesti; the south of the Ukrainian Republic in the district of Zaporozh'e in Odessa; and the district of Rostov in the Russian Republic. There are additionally small Gagauz settlements in Central Asia in the Kokpekti, Zarma, Carskiy, Aksuat, and Urdzar districts of the Semipalatinsk region, as well as the eastern Kazakh and Pavodar region of Kazakhstan, in the region of Frunze in Kyrgyzistan, and in the Tashkent region of Uzbekistan. The total number of Gagauz in the CIS was 197,164 as of 1989. There are some scattered Gagauz villages numbering about 5,000 persons in Bulgaria in the districts of Varna, Yanbol, Topolovgrad, and in the Dobrudja, as well as in Romania, where there are only a few Gagauz villages left, most of those also in the Dobrudja.

The Gagauz speak a Turkic language called Gagauz that belongs to the South Turkic, Oguz group, or Oguz-Bulgar subgroup of Uralic-Altaic languages. There are two main dialect groups in Gagauz, the central and the southern, the former being more widespread and therefore the basis of their literary language; still, there are certain phonetic features from the southern that have been incorporated into the central dialect. Although Russian* is generally used for all official proceedings, Gagauz can be used if necessary. There is no indication that Gagauz is taught in the schools, and only a small handful of books are written in the language. The earliest Gagauz alphabet, a Cyrillic one, dates from 1895, and was created by Russian Orthodox missionaries in order to translate theological texts. As of 1980, there were no newspapers published in Gagauz nor any indication of its use in broadcasting to the people. Gagauz is unique among Turkic languages for both the large and increasing number of Slavonic (Bulgarian*, Russian, and Ukrainian*) and Romance (Moldovan* and Romanian*) loan words and the tenacity and persistence of its speakers to maintain their own language. Most recently, the Moldovan Republic has planned and introduced a written language for the Gagauz and has opened schools for instruction in their native language.

The origins of the Gagauz people are unclear, and there are a number of hypotheses for their ancestry. One apocryphal tale places their origins with a tribal chieftain named Gagavuz, who was granted a fiefdom in northeastern Bulgaria by the Seljuk sultan. According to one current hypothesis, the Gagauz derive from the Turkic-speaking Oguz, Uzy, and Kumans (or Polovtsy) who played an important role in the history of the south Russian steppes until 1237. These Gagauz may have migrated from the Black Sea region to the Dobrudja in eastern Bulgaria during the Middle Ages. The Gagauz may also have been joined by groups of Slavs (Bulgars) who adopted the Turkic language while retaining their Christian religion, thus introducing the Gagauz to Eastern Orthodoxy, which they profess today. Yet another hypothesis claims that the Gagauz are descended from forcibly turkified Bulgarians who managed to retain their Orthodox faith.

During the Russo-Turkish wars of the eighteenth and nineteenth centuries, the Gagauz, together with thousands of Bulgars, migrated to the Russian Empire to escape Ottoman rule. They settled in the rural, southern part of Bessarabia when that region became part of Russia after 1812. Thus, in their cultural traits, the Gagauz naturally most closely resemble the Bulgarians*, but they also share cultural affinities with the Moldovans and the Ukrainians, their neighbors. The Gagauz tended to assimilate into the dominant Romanian culture. The success of this policy is indicated in the 1926 Soviet Census, which listed only 844 Gagauz in Bessarabia, which was under Romanian rule from 1918 through 1940. After the Soviet annexation of Bessarabia in 1940, this "undesirable" (by Soviet standards) merging was frowned upon. The Gagauz were then encouraged either to retain their Gagauz culture or to russify.

The Soviets also followed a policy of organizing the Gagauz into collectives, primarily in agriculture, but also in animal husbandry and some industry. The majority continue to work on the land as peasants and, as a result, they maintain one of the highest birthrates in the republic. By early 1990, the Gagauz in the Moldovan Soviet Socialist Republic (SSR) began a movement for cultural and political autonomy, in response to the growth of the Moldovan majority's national movement. The Gagauz demand for self-rule, together with Russian and Ukrainian moves to set up a "Trans-Dneister" republic, constitute the most serious ethnic problem within the new Moldovan Republic. In July 1989, the Moldovan SSR established a commission to study the issue of political nationalism among the Gagauz. Gagauz representatives met in an extraordinary congress at Komrat at the end of 1989 and proposed the establishment of the Gagauz Autonomous Soviet Socialist Republic within the Moldovan Republic. Moldova did not sustain the Gagauz action. Less than a year later, Gagauz representatives met again in Komrat and adopted a "Declaration on the Gagauz People's Freedom and Independence From the Republic of Moldova." The Gagauz claimed that the

Molotov-Ribbentrop Pact of 1940, which initially established the Moldovan SSR, was an illegal act and that therefore the Gagauz had no obligation to observe it. They renounced their Moldovan citizenship, demanded a fair distribution of government financial resources, and asked the Soviet Union to recognize their independence from Moldavia and their federation with the larger country.

REFERENCES: *Current Digest*, 41 (December 13, 1989), 35, and 42 (September 19, 1990), 31–32; E. M. Hoppe, "I Gagauzi, populazione turco-cristiana della Bulgaria," *Oriente Moderno*, 14 (1934); Bill Keller, "The Gagauz People: A Soviet Mouse is Roaring, Hoping to Become a Republic," *New York Times*, August 7, 1989; Walter Kolarz, *Russia and Her Colonies*, 1953; A. I. Manov, *Gagauzlar*, 1940; Paul Wittek, "Yazijioglu Ali on the Christian Turks of the Dobrudja," *Bulletin of the School of Oriental and African Studies*, 14 (1952); Wlodzimierz Zajaczkowski, "Gagauz," *Encyclopedia of Islam*, 1965, vol. 2, 971–72.

Lee M. Pappas

GAGAVUZ. See GAGAUZ.

G'AKHEVALAL. See AKHWAKH.

GAKWARI-GAIDARI. See CHAMALAL and AVAR.

GALCHA. The Galcha are a small ethnic group living in the Darvaz and Karategin Mountains of the Tajik Republic. Russian* ethnologists classify them with the Tajiks*, but the Galcha are not of Iranian origins. Nonetheless, some of their religious beliefs are similar to ancient Zoroastrian concepts. See TAJIK.

REFERENCE: Ronald Wixman, *The Peoples of the USSR: An Ethnographic Handbook*, 1984.

GALCHAH. In addition to referring to the Tajik* subgroup living in the Parvaz and Karategin Mountains, the term "Galchah" has also been used as a generic, collective reference for the various Pamir* peoples. See PAMIR PEOPLES or TAJIK.

REFERENCE: Shirin Akiner, *Islamic Peoples of the Soviet Union*, 1983.

GALGAI. Along with the Feappi* clan federation, the Galgai clan federation constitutes one of the two constitutent groups comprising the Ingushes*. See INGUSH.

REFERENCE: Ronald Wixman, *The Peoples of the USSR: An Ethnographic Handbook*, 1984.

GALGAY. See GALGAI and INGUSH.

GANDZHA. See AZERBAIJANI.

GANSU DUNGAN. See DUNGAN.

GAPUT. The Gaput, who are also known as the Gaputlin, Ghaput, Ghaputlin, Khaput, and Khaputlin, are a subgroup of the Dzhek*, who themselves are part of the Shah Dagh* peoples. The Azerbaijanis have all but assimilated the Gaputs. See DZHEK, SHAH DAGH, and AZERBAIJANI.
REFERENCE: Ronald Wixman, *The Peoples of the USSR: An Ethnographic Handbook,* 1984.

GAPUTLIN. See GAPUT, DZHEK, SHAH DAGH, and AZERBAIJANI.

GATJUKAI. See CHERKESS.

GATJUKAJ. See CHERKESS.

GAZI KUMUK. See LAK.

GAZI KUMUKH. See LAK.

GAZI QUMUKH. See LAK.

GAZI QUMUQ. See LAK.

GEK. See DZHEK, SHAH DAGH, and AZBERBAIJANI.

GEORGIAN. The Georgian nation, with its long history and rich culture, holds a unique place among the former Soviet nationalities. Because of its strategic location between East and West, Georgia was frequently invaded by foreign armies, its lands devastated, and its people subjugated to foreign rule and quarreling native feudatories. The Georgians accepted features of other cultures, but they were able to maintain their own culture throughout. In Georgia, ethnicity always outlived its enemies. To understand the current nationality crisis in the Georgian Republic, it is necessary to trace the formation of the Georgian state and to show how history has shaped the Georgians into a self-conscious nationality and nation.

Georgia consists of three main geographical regions: 1) the southwestern slopes of the Caucasus; 2) the southern mountains that line the northern rim of the Armenian plateau; and 3) the central lowlands. Georgia is bordered by Russia to the north, Azerbaijan to the east, Armenia and Turkey to the south, and the Black Sea to the west. The climate is warm and humid in the western region and warm but drier inland. The climate in the mountainous regions ranges from subalpine up to the timberline and cold and alpine above it.

Georgian is the collective name for the closely related peoples and tribes inhabiting the mountains and plains of southwest Caucasia. The Georgians are divided into four main groups: 1) the Georgians, inhabiting East Georgia; 2) the Mingrelians* of central West Georgia; 3) the Lazes* in the southwestern mountains, now largely in Turkey; and 4) the Svanetians* in the southwest Caucasus, north of Mingrelia. The traditional occupations of the Georgians have been farming, stock breeding, gardening, viticulture, and various arts and crafts. They are generally Greek Orthodox with their own self-governing church. There are, however, a small number of converts to Islam and Roman Catholicism. The Mingrelians' traditional occupations have included farming, gardening, the cultivation of vineyards, and the production of silk. They too are members of the Georgian Orthodox Church. The Lazes have traditionally been farmers, fishermen, or traders, known outside of their homeland especially as professional cooks; they are Sunni Muslims. The traditional occupations of the Svanetians were agriculture, stock breeding, bee-keeping, and hunting; they belong to the Georgian Orthodox Church.

The first group, the Georgians, are subdivided into a variety of ethnic groups. Each of them has a distinct identity, although their languages are mutually intelligible. As a whole, the Georgians refer to themselves as the Kartveli or Kartvelians*, although they have been referred to by Russians* and Turks* as Gruzin, Gurcu, and Gruzian. The eastern Georgians are composed of the Kartlis*, Kakhetians*, Mesketians*, Dzhavakhis*, Ingilois*, Tushetians*, Khevsurs*, Pshavs*, Mokhevs*, and Mtiulis*. The Kartlis (Kartveli) are the core ethnographic group around which the Georgian nation was formed. The Kartli dialect became the foundation for the modern Georgian literary language; the Kartli are Eastern Orthodox in religion. Today they are scattered throughout the Georgian Republic. The Kakhetians (K'akheli) are also Eastern Orthodox, but they are demographically concentrated east of the Kura and Aragvi rivers in far eastern Georgia. The Meskhis (Meshi) are a complex group. Historically, some of them came under Turkish influence and converted to Sunni Islam, while others remained faithful to Eastern Orthodoxy. The Muslim Meskhis were deported to Central Asia in 1944, while the Christians were allowed to remain in southwestern Georgia. The Dzhavakhis (Dzhavahi) are all Eastern Orthodox in religion. The Ingilois (Inkiloi) are a Georgian subgroup with strong cultural and linguistic ties to the Azerbaijanis*. Unlike the vast majority of Georgians, the Ingilois are Shiite Muslims in their religious loyalties and are in a state of rapid assimilation by the Azerbaijanis. They are geographically concentrated between the Alazani River and the Cacausus Mountains near the border between Georgia and Azerbaijan. the Tushetians (Tush, Tushin, Tushuri) are Eastern Orthodox and live in the Tushetian region of Georgia. The Khevsurs (Khevsuri) are quite distinct from other Georgians. They claim to be the descendants of twelfth-century European crusaders. Their religion, though nominally Eastern Orthodox, retains heavy animistic influences. They live on the upper Eastern Aragvi and Argun rivers. The Pshavs (Pshaveli) are Eastern Orthodox and live to the south of the Khevsurs. The Mokhevs (Mokhevi) are Eastern Orthodox, as are the Mtiulis (Mtuili).

The western Georgians are composed of the descendants of the Imereli*, Racha*, Lechkum*, Guri*, and Adjar* peoples. The Imerelis (Imeretian) are

Eastern Orthodox and live between the Suram and Adjaro-Akhaltsikh mountain ranges and the Tskhenis-Tskali River. The Rachas (Rachin, Rach'veli) are also Eastern Orthodox and live in the upper Riono River Valley. The Eastern Orthodox Lechkums (Lechhumi, Lechkumi, Lechkhumeli) live along the middle Rioni River. The Guris (Guruli) live south of the Rioni River toward the Black Sea. The Adjars (Ach'areli, Achar) constitute another unique Georgian group. Like the Meskhis, they are Sunni Muslims in their religion, and they speak the Guri dialect, although it is laced with Turkish words. They live in the Adjar Autonomous Republic. Finally, there is a distinct body of Georgian Jews* who speak the Georgian language, rather than Hebrew, and identify themselves with Georgians.

Two other small groups have historically been closely related to the Georgians. The Laz (Lazi, Chan, Zan, Megrelo-Chan) people, mentioned above, live primarily in northeastern Turkey near the coast of the Black Sea. The Laz language is closely related to Mingrelian. The Laz are Sunni Muslim in religion, and only a few hundred live in the Soviet Union. Most of those who do are concentrated on the Chorokh River in the Adjar Autonomous Republic. The other group that has been classified with the Georgians is the Batsbi* (Batsaw). They are closely related to the Chechen* and Ingush* groups who migrated into the Tushetia region of Georgia. There are only a few hundred people left in the area who identify themselves as Batsbis.

Georgians are descended from some of the earliest inhabitants of the Caucasus Mountain region. The ethnic formation of the Georgian people appears to have taken place in Georgia itself, in the first half of the first millenium B.C., through a mixture of the native inhabitants and the incoming Anatolian peoples. The West Georgian tribes united into a kingdom that was called Colchis by the Greeks* who colonized its coast. The capital of this kingdom lay at Kutaisi. After the death of Alexander the Great, the East Georgian state of Kartli emerged. Both states became Roman vassals in 64 B.C., with Colchis becoming a Roman province from 64 A.D. until the fifth century. Byzantium and Iran quarreled over Kartli until the seventh century when the Arabs* came. Both states were quite civilized in antiquity and enjoyed high standards of housing and culture. Kartli had an elaborate social structure that was based on a tension between the largely autonomous princes and the kings who attempted to reduce them to obedience.

Kartli became a Christian state under King Mirian in 337. The Lazians, who had seized control of Colchis during a temporary decline in Roman power in the fifth century, accepted the new faith in about 520. The history of Kartli and of Colchis-Lazica is tied to that of the neighboring states of Armenia and Caucasian Albania and can be understood only within the framework of the wider Caucasian civilization. Kartli and Lazica became deeply involved in the struggle between Byzantium and Iran over Caucasia. Several campaigns were waged on their territory between the fifth and seventh centuries.

Caucasia was overrun by the Arabs in the seventh century A.D., and a Muslim governor was installed at Tbilisi. The Georgian kings and princes ruled under

Arab suzerainty. The rule of the Ummayad Caliphs was heavy and that of the Abbasids heavier still, especially in regard to taxation. Numerous revolts took place against the Arabs in Kartli and Armenia. In the resulting reprisals, Byzantine-Arab wars, and Khazar invasions between the seventh and ninth centuries, Caucasia was devastated.

By the eighth century, Byzantine rule over Lazica had become tenuous. During the same period, West Georgia was seized by Leon II of Abkhazia, who founded the greater Abkhazian state of Abasgia. In the east, Kakhetia emerged as a separate state, while Tbilisi remained under an Arab emir. In the ninth century, however, the might of the Bagratid dynasty gave rise to the unification of Georgia. Supported by the church, the peasants, and the merchant and craft classes, the Bagratids acquired the thrones of both Abasgia and Kartli. In 1008, Bagrat III succeeded in uniting East and West Georgia into one kingdom (Sak'art'velo) for the first time in history. Under his successors, a Turkish invasion had to be repulsed. Nevertheless, under David III, "The Builder" (reigned 1089–1125), Demetrius I (reigned 1125–1156), George III (reigned 1156–1184), and Queen Tamara the Great (reigned 1184–1212), Georgia became the most powerful state in Caucasia. The capital of the united kingdom, originally at Kutaisi, was transferred to Tbilisi in 1122. Tbilisi soon grew to be a cosmopolitan center of close to 100,000 inhabitants. Unprecedented wealth and prosperity characterized this period. Georgian art, architecture, and literary creativity reached their highest levels.

Unfortunately, this golden age was abruptly terminated by the Mongol* invasions. By 1243, the entire country had succumbed to them. Georgia remained autonomous but paid heavy tribute and rendered military aid. The rural population was ruined by heavy taxation, and the towns entered a period of decline. In the fourteenth century, the Mongols weakened and Georgia entered into highly profitable trade relations with Venice and Genoa. A revival occurred, but this period too was cut short by the eight devastating invasions of Tamerlane in the years 1386–1403. Moreover, the fall of Constantinople cut the Georgians off from the rest of Christendom, as well as from lucrative trade and ties with the Mediterranean. In the decades that followed, Georgia disintegrated into three separate Bagratid kingdoms and five virtually independent principalities. From the sixteenth to eighteenth centuries, Georgia was ravaged in the Turko-Persian wars. Thousands of its people were deported to the Ottoman Empire or to Safavid Iran as slaves, many as part of the "slave-soldier" systems of the Ottomans (*devşirme*) and Safavids (*gulams*). The Persians* sacked Tbilisi as late as 1795— the fortieth time that the city had been taken by force since 627. With trade at a standstill and the country ruined and depopulated, the Georgians turned their eyes increasingly toward the growing might of Russia, especially in the wake of Peter I's Persian expedition of 1721. In 1783, King Heraclius II placed his country under Russian protection with the Treaty of Georgievsk. Upon the death of his successor, George XII, Russia annexed the main Georgian state. Further annexations by Russia quickly followed, and soon all of the Georgian lands were acquired (Imeretia in 1810, Guria in 1829, Svanetia in 1858, Abkhazia in 1864, and Mingrelia in 1866).

Under Russian* rule, peace and prosperity returned to Georgia. The population increased fivefold by 1913. Western progress and intellectual currents reached the country, industrialization began, and serfdom was abolished in between 1864 and 1871. Tbilisi became not only the center of Russian rule in Transcaucasia and the seat of its viceroy, but also the focal point for the Georgian and Armenian* cultural revivals of the nineteenth century. Construction of oil pipelines, a railroad connecting Baku with Tbilisi, and the ports of Batum and Poti in the 1870s and 1880s hastened industrial development and the rise of the working class. Russian socialism reached Georgia early, and the Marxist Russian Social Democratic Party was active.

After a century within the Russian empire, the Georgians recovered the possibility of shaping their own future. Transformed by the Russian "gathering" of Georgian lands, the economic and social integration of diverse Georgian territories through the rise of market relations and easier communication, and the intellectual awakening, Georgia had acquired many of the attributes of nationhood. Both urban workers and peasants had created political institutions of their own and were a mobile force in society. The national awakening and social development in the country had taken place in a particular multinational context, one in which Russians occupied the administrative hierarchy and Armenians controlled the economy. Georgians were numerically dominant in Tbilisi and Kutaisi, but, in terms of political and economic power, they were the least powerful nationality.

The century of Russian rule had prepared Georgians for statehood, but its full realization presented dangers and difficulties. Aware of the risks of becoming independent, the social democratic leadership refrained from declaring Georgian independence in the first year of the Russian Revolution and sought the best solution to its political dilemmas within the new revolutionary Russia.

At the outbreak of the Russian civil war in March 1918, the leaders of the three major South Caucasian peoples seceded from the Russian Empire to form the Transcaucasian Republic. In May, however, this state broke up into the separate republics of Georgia, Armenia, and Azerbaijan. For the next three years, the Georgian government, dominated by Menshevik Social Democrats, introduced various socialist reforms, courted the Germans*, and signed a peace treaty with Soviet Russia in May 1920. This treaty proved to be short-lived, as the Red Army moved into Georgia in February 1921 and established a Soviet government dominated by Bolsheviks. Georgia was then merged into a Transcaucasian Socialist Federal Soviet Republic (SFSR) that included Armenia and Azerbaijan. The Transcaucasian SFSR entered into the Soviet Union in 1922. This arrangement lasted until December 5, 1936, when the Georgian Soviet Socialist Republic (SSR) was formally established as a constituent unit of the Soviet Union. From that time until the death of Josef Stalin, the Georgian Republic was dominated by Lavrenty Beria. After the death of Stalin in 1953,

Beria fell, and his followers were purged and executed. Vasilii Mzhavanadze was then put in the position of First Secretary of the Georgian Communist Party for the next nineteen years. Accused of laxness in dealing with local corruption, Mzhavanadze fell in 1972. Under the new First Secretary, Eduard Shevardnadze, a new but bloodless purge took place.

Under the Soviet regime, Georgia experienced rapid industrialization and urbanization. The population more than doubled between 1913 and 1970, and its population density is now one of the highest in the former Soviet Union. In 1970, 66.8 percent of the population of Georgia was Georgian, with Armenians and Russians forming just under 10 percent each and Azerbaijanis nearly 5 percent. The rest of the population is made up largely of Abkhazians*, Ossetians*, and Adjars. The Georgian Republic consists of approximately 70,000 square kilometers and includes the Abkhazian Autonomous Republic, the Adjar Autonomous Republic, and the autonomous province of South Ossetia. Of the Georgian Republic's population, 90 percent lives in the lowlands and 10 percent in the mountains.

In 1970, industry formed 40 percent of the Georgian gross national product and accounted for 34 percent of the labor force. Nearly half of the industry is devoted to food processing; the rest involves the production of iron, steel, rolled metal and machinery, and hydroelectric power. In 1978, a major dam was under construction on the Ingur River. Agriculture, which occupies 38 percent of the labor force, consists largely of the production of tea, citrus fruits, and cereals in the lowlands and grapes for the manufacture of wines and cognacs in the warm, dry central and eastern regions. Mosquito control and the draining of swamps has done much to improve the health of the East Georgian population and to increase the amount of soil available for cultivation.

The Georgians represent one of the most distinctive and highly individualistic peoples of the Soviet Union. They are a proud people with a great love of music and wine. While they are generally warm, friendly, and easy-going, they are also heavy drinkers, hot-tempered, and quick to take offense. The Georgians had a written language in pre-Christian times. Upon their conversion to Christianity, they created a new writing system in the fifth century A.D. The earliest known Georgian book is *The Martyrdom of St. Shushanik*, written in the fifth century. Along with translations, hagiography, church chronicles, and other historical texts, the Georgians developed a rich secular literature. The Golden Age of the eleventh and twelfth centuries saw the rise of both epic and lyric poetry. *The Knight in the Panther's Skin* by Shota Rustaveli was produced at this time and remains one of the great epics of world literature.

After the Russian occupation of Georgia, literature and cultural life revived in spite of the oppressive censorship. The Georgian language has received serious scientific study by modern linguists, who have been fascinated by the fact that Georgian is not related to any of the major language groups either in Europe or the Near East. Prince Il'ia Tchavtchavadze (1837–1907) founded the modern Georgian nationalist movement and devoted his life to the revival of Georgian national consciousness. He established a school of nationalist thinkers, referred to as the "first group," in 1869. This group was succeeded by the more radical "second group," which gave way to the young Georgian Marxists of the "third group" (1892). Among this group who turned to Bolshevism was Josef Dzhugashvili (later known as Stalin). By the turn of the twentieth century, Georgian literature and intellectual life, which had been profoundly influenced by romanticism, nationalism, socialism and other Western currents entering by way of Russia, had reached heights unknown since the Golden Age of Queen Tamara.

This sense of nationalism has remained and grown among Georgians in recent years. Georgians see themselves and their culture as older and superior to that of the Russians. In comparison to the materialistic Soviet ideology, the Georgians believe they practice a life of honor, chivalry, and ancient tradition. There is a split in opinion regarding the future of the republic. There are both those who want independence and those who would prefer to maintain the status quo. Tensions between Georgia, Abkhazia, South Ossetia, and Adjar could produce great conflicts that would transform the Georgian nation once again.

The peoples of the Soviet Union were greatly affected by the social revolution of the Stalin years, as well as by the political changes since Stalin. Still, the emphasis of most analysts of the recent Soviet past has been on the Russian heartland and the ruling Communist elite. When attention has been given to the non-Russian periphery, it has usually focused on the treatment of the minority nationalities as a separate aspect of Soviet policy, as "nationality policy," or the "national question." This approach usually neglects to examine the underlying indigenous social developments taking place in the ethnic areas.

The experience of the Georgian Republic has not been shaped to any great extent by the practices of official nationality policy. Instead, Georgia's development has been the product primarily of indigenous social and political trends and of local resistance. Modernizing forces from outside the Caucasus and nationalizing forces within Georgia have been in an intense struggle since Stalinist police rule loosened its grip.

In the 1950s, the nationality question was seldom in the spotlight. In 1961, however, Nikita Khrushchev set the official theory of national development: Soviet nationalities were to continue to evolve through the "flourishing" of their ethnic cultures, but this process would lead dialectically to a "drawing together" of these nations until their "complete merger" was achieved with the creation of a new Soviet people. With the fall of Khrushchev in 1964, some slight changes were introduced into Soviet nationality policy. The term "complete merger" was eliminated from official statements about the future of Soviet minorities. Although the term "drawing together" was retained, Leonid Brezhnev stressed that this process would occur through social forces, not as the result of artificial prodding by the party. In 1965, the government once again began to publish the laws of the Supreme Soviet in the national languages of the republics. These fluctuations in official policy seem to have had less effect on the development of Georgian society than did the long-term, underlying dynamics that began in the Stalin years and even earlier.

The new Communist party leadership basically adopted a policy of "benign neglect" toward the nationalities. This policy would soon prove to be inadequate. Two developments occurred in the years that followed: first, local national elites, with a base of support in their republics, gained independent attitudes and practices with nationalist implications; second, a new nationalism with oppositional overtones came to be articulated more and more openly. Although the 1977 Soviet constitution affirmed the successful construction of socialism in the Soviet Union, the leadership insisted that separate national identities were being maintained. Three days before the constitution was ratified by the Supreme Soviet, Brezhnev declared (*Pravda*, May 24, 1977):

The Soviet people's social and political unity does not in the least imply the disappearance of national distinctions. . . . The friendship of the Soviet peoples is indissoluble, and in the process of building communism they are steadily drawing ever closer together and their spiritual life is being mutually enriched. But we would be taking a dangerous path were we artificially to step up this objective process of national integration. That is something Lenin persistently warned against, and we shall not depart from his precepts.

The basic realization regarding nationalities was that no program of political, social, and economic reform in the Soviet Union could succeed unless it took into account the needs and aspirations of the nationalities. After the Helsinki Accords, watch-dog groups pressed for national rights within the context of human rights, as guaranteed by the Soviet Union under the international treaty. Periodic crackdowns and arrests continued, however, and, by the end of the 1970s, the KGB had put a virtual end to all dissident activities.

In the spring of 1978, the issue of adopting new constitutions in the Union republics, based on the 1977 Soviet Constitution, came up. An attempt was then made to remove the anomaly of the three Transcaucasian republics, where Georgian, Armenian, and Azerbaijani had the status of state languages. The omission of articles stipulating them as the official languages caused an outcry. Demonstrations broke out throughout Georgia. Thousands protested in the streets of Tbilisi until Shevardnadze assured Georgians that the official status of the Georgian language would be retained. The articles were restored.

The situation became more complicated with the addition of the Abkhaz question. In December 1977, Abkhaz intellectuals protested against Georgian infringement of the national rights of the Abkhazian people. The Abkhaz case brought to light another factor in the nationalities problem in the Soviet Union. The question was not one of Russian control and russification but of the domination of a small national group by a larger one. The Abkhaz requested to be transferred from the Georgian SSR to the Russian Soviet Federated Socialist Republic (RSFSR), but the request was denied. Their grievances were recognized, however, and they were granted several cultural and economic concessions.

In the early 1980s, the Abkhaz question was raised once again. Georgians living in Abkhazia protested about discrimination against them at the hands of the Abkhazians. Georgian intellectuals petitioned Shevardnadze and Brezhnev to address the situation. During 1981, at least five demonstrations are known to have taken place in Georgia at which the Abkhaz question figured alongside broader issues connected with the defense of the Georgian language, history, and culture. March 1981 saw over 1,000 students at the University of Tbilisi protest against the dismissal of Akaki Bakradze, a popular professor who taught a course on Georgian literature. Another protest took place when the Ninth Congress of Georgian Writers met later that month. Large groups of students and intellectuals demonstrated in defense of Georgian national rights. Shevardnadze agreed to meet with their representatives. A Georgian activist, Zviad Gamsakhurdia, presented the Georgian party leader with a document entitled ''The Demands of the Georgian People.'' The document included proposals to protect the status of the Georgian language, improve the teaching of Georgian history and preservation of Georgian historical monuments, and protect the Georgians in Abkhazia. Other Georgian protests took place in Mtskheta in October 1981; there 2,000 people protested, again, in defense of the Georgian language. Unrest continued, and, in 1982, intellectuals protested against the arrest of dissenters on trumped-up charges.

Protests in 1924, 1956, and 1978 had usually ended with bloody consequences. For the first few years of Mikhail Gorbachev's new policy of *glasnost*, there was little organized opposition to the authorities. In 1987, however, tensions began to mount again. There were concerns regarding the Caucasian railway, the environment, the destruction of historical monuments, and blank spots in Georgian history. At the end of 1987, several prominent dissidents formed the Il'ia Tchavtchavadze Society. They demanded that all matters concerning the future of Georgia be settled in accordance with the wishes of the Georgian people, that major projects be submitted to the public for approval, that Georgian become the state language, that Georgian history and geography be taught at school, and that Georgians be allowed to perform their military service in Georgia.

Another influential and more radical group split off from the mainstream in early 1988. This group rejected any compromise with the authorities and saw its main task as the moral regeneration of the Georgian nation. All the independence movements, no matter how radical or conservative, recognized the importance of a close association between the future independent state and the Georgian Orthodox church. This belief is demonstrated by the thousands of young Georgians who have recently been christened in mass baptisms in different parts of the country.

By the end of 1988, the number and intensity of demonstrations had increased. Large numbers of peasants and workers began to voice their demands. Complaints against corrupt government officials involved in the illegal sale of land to the Azerbaijanis constituted a major issue. Ethnic tensions between Abkhazians and Georgians spilled over into violence. An anti-Abkhazian protest evolved into a massive demonstration for independence. On April 9, 1989, Soviet troops broke up this demonstration with tanks, shovels, and poison gas; twenty people were killed. One year later, residents gathered in the streets to mark the anniversary of this bloody crackdown and to mourn the dead. One young speaker added that they were celebrating "a great victory on the difficult road to freedom and complete independence."

Lacking any coherent policy and bereft of moral authority, the Georgian Communist Party became increasingly confused in light of the growing challenge to its authority. Repression widened the gap between the state and the people, while reforms were viewed as concessions to popular pressure. If the policies were meant to intimidate the Georgians, this was clearly not happening. The 5.4 million people of the Georgian republic have never forgotten the brief period of independence that they enjoyed between 1918 and 1921, before the invading Bolshevik forces imposed Bolshevik rule. The Georgians contended that they were then illegally forced into the union, in violation of the 1920 "non-interference" treaty with Moscow. They had no intention of backing off at that point, insisting that Soviet Russia forcibly annexed Georgia, thereby violating the 1920 treaty recognizing Georgia's independence.

In 1990, protests continued at a steady rate. In a swift and unprecedented concession to public pressure, the Georgian Academy of Sciences Institute of Nuclear Physics decided to close down its experimental nuclear reactor in Mtskheta, north of Tbilisi. This decision was made on March 21, the day after a mass demonstration in Mtskheta. Concessions were made in part because of the extremely volatile political situation in Georgia.

On May 23, 24, and 25, 1990, approximately 6,200 delegates assembled in Tbilisi for the first congress of the National Forum. The forum was an umbrella organization intended to coordinate the ambitions of the numerous political groups and parties that had developed over the previous year. By an overwhelming majority, the congress voted to elect a National Congress that would perform the role of an alternative parliament, form a transitional coalition government, and open negotiations with Moscow on Georgia's secession from the Soviet Union. Although their demands were not likely to be acknowledged, the congress chose this course of action after watching Lithuania's failed attempt to achieve independence by legal means. On September 30, unofficial elections were held for Georgian National Congress. The final results of the election were announced on October 22 by TASS, the Soviet news service. Somewhat surprisingly, the greatest number of seats were won by radical Georgian National Independence Party, which advocated a campaign of mass civil disobedience in order to expedite Georgia's secession. Many Georgians, however, have remained vigorously opposed to mass civil disobedience, fearing the fragmentation of the democratic forces. Within the national movement, disquieting trends were perceived to be emerging: compromised elements were said to be infiltrating the various political parties, and demagogues were allegedly conducting witch hunts, intimidating students, and alienating the intelligentsia. There was also a risk that factionalism would again erupt into open violence, as it had in April, when members of rival organizations had shot at each other on Tbilisi's main boulevard. Some observers concluded that Georgia was on the verge of becoming "a second Lebanon" or plunging into civil war.

The Georgian drive for independence sparked ethnic tensions among the republic's minority peoples, who make up a substantial 30 percent of the population. For example, on November 10, 1990, members of the South Ossetian Oblast Soviet and "Ademon Nykhas" demanded that the Georgian Supreme Soviet upgrade the oblast to the status of an autonomous republic. The response of the Georgian authorities was to fire the oblast's first secretary. After being elected as chairman to the new Supreme Soviet, Gamsakhurdia said, "We intend to preserve the autonomy of the national minorities." Nonetheless, the Georgian parliament voted to abolish South Ossetian autonomy. Georgian troops have reportedly been deployed in South Ossetia, presumably in anticipation of protests or violence from the local population.

Many have become concerned about the Georgia-for-Georgians tone that was pervading the political debate. Gamsakurdia stated that Moscow was "fighting against us through the hand of other nationalities." "We're hoping to avoid civil war here," one Georgian, fretting over recent developments, said; "but yes, it's a possibility." "The nations of the Caucasus should not fight each other but rise up together against Moscow," another speaker said, "Don't let anything distract you from independence."

The history of Georgia reveals a pattern of resistance to foreign domination and alien cultural inputs that have threatened its national integrity. Nevertheless, Georgia's identity is in part the product of successive foreign impositions. Its unique "Georgian-ness" can never be separated from the complex exchange that has gone on with its neighbors. Georgian history began with various tribes speaking related languages and forming a loose confederation under a primitive state. They were seen by outsiders as a single people. In the classical age, a social hierarchy was created and evolved over the next thousand years. Orthodox Christianity provided an identity and ideology that distinguished Georgians from their Muslim and Armenian neighbors. The development of a market economy broke down the isolation of Georgia's villages, bringing peasants and nobles into closer contact with Russian officials and with entrepreneurs from other countries. A secular national awareness later developed among Georgians, first among the intelligentsia and later, through the Marxists, among workers and peasants. By the early twentieth century, Georgians were a self-conscious nationality under the leadership of the Mensheviks. The consolidation of the Georgians as a nation came during the first seventy years of Soviet power. Even though the thrust of Marxism seemed opposed to the creation of a separate Georgian nation, the result was a conscious Georgian nation that was prepared to act in its own interest, whether on its own or not. The recent developments toward Georgian independence exemplify the self-conscious nature of the Georgian people.

The drive for independence continued during 1990 and 1991. Although Gamsakhurdia seemed to be the answer to the Georgian independence movement in 1990, by mid–1991, he had begun to hamper the cause. Factionalism erupted into open violence as ethnic tensions spread throughout the republic. Gamsakhurdia maintained his belief that Gorbachev was scheming to create a civil war, using Shevardnadze as a "provocateur." As the Gamsakhurdia's paranoia grew, he came to see his prime minister, Tengiz Sigua, as a "liar and criminal," plotting a coup against the new government. In response to these accusations, thousands took to the streets, demanding Gamsakhurdia's resignation. In addition, his prime minister and foreign minister quit the cabinet, accusing him of dictatorial practices.

Gamsakhurdia was quick to prove his critics right. To quell the protests, he resorted to authoritarian tactics, such as firing on protesters and jamming all Soviet and Russian broadcasts to the Georgian Republic. After police arrested opposition leaders, angry Georgians occupied the state's radio and television center, cutting off Gamsakhurdia as he made his presidential address.

In March 1991, a referendum was held on the question of Georgian independence. The vote was overwhelmingly favorable, and independence was declared on April 9. That May, Gamsakhurdia carried 87 percent of the vote to become the republic's first democratically elected president. By September, however, some polls showed his popularity as low as 20 percent. Gamsakhurdia continued to derail Georgia's independence movement by curbing the press and making statements such as "We cannot tolerate collaborationalists." He also announced that it was a criminal offense to insult him or his office. In addition, there were several military clashes between opposition forces and government troops, the latest after Gamsakhurdia barricaded himself inside the Georgian Parliament building and insisted that he would hold out until he was dead.

Ethnic tensions grew as the new government was formed. Georgian treatment of minorities (Armenians, Abkazians, Kurds*, Ossetians, and Adjaris) was compared with the Kremlin's treatment of minorities within the Soviet Union. Gamsakhurdia went so far as to say that "mixed marriages threaten the purity of the Georgian race." Conditions became so severe as to bring a threat from the parliament of the Russian Republic to impose sanctions if steps were not taken to resolve ethnic fighting in the region. Violence between government forces, opposition forces, and ethnic groups continued throughout 1991. In September, police tried to remove forty hunger strikers who were protesting outside the parliament. In the scuffle, at least two were injured and one anti-government protester set himself on fire. Heavy fighting continued until late December, when Gamsakhurdia was finally overthrown.

In spite of the constant upheaval in Georgia, the republic's representatives have continued to search for economic independence and international recognition. In October 1991, Temur Gamtsemlidze, the counselor to the prime minister, presented Georgia's future plans to the United Nations. Georgia was planning to wean itself from Soviet economic ties and to rid itself of old Communist restrictions on international trade and investment. Counselor Gamtsemlidze described Georgia as open for free business. He promoted the opportunities for tourism, skiing, agricultural production, and mineral reserves. Since then, Georgia has been promoting new markets, new products, and new industries, and the counselor specifically asked the United States and the United Nations for recognition of its independence and sovereignty.

Ethnic fighting and an unstable government are nothing new to the people of the Georgian Republic, but the self-conscious nature of the Georgian people prevails. With the dissolution of the Soviet Union at the end of 1991, Georgia has gained its best opportunity to establish itself as a democratic, independent nation. If internal fighting does not destroy the republic, it may again be one of the most notable nations of the Caucasus. But the demise of the Soviet Union has not really solved any of the major issues. A Russian-Georgian rivalry has simply replaced what had formerly been a Soviet-Georgian rivalry.

Internecine conflicts have intensified in Georgia in the wake of the independence movement. While Gamsakhurdia won an overwhelming majority (87 percent) in the presidential poll of May 1991, opposition to his government grew during the year as his political rivals accused him of dictatorial tendencies. Their accusations were borne out in August 1991, when Gamsakhurdia took personal control of the ministries of Justice, Interior, and Foreign Affairs. Opposition to his personal rule kept growing, especially since Gamsakhurdia was equivocal in his opposition to the August coup in Russia. By late September 1991, Gamsakhurdia had declared a state of emergency, and, by the end of the year, civil war had broken out between his supporters and opponents. His opponents got the upper hand in the conflict in January, 1992 and announced that the president had been deposed and replaced by a military council. Gamsakhurdia and his supporters withdrew to the western regions of Mingrelia and Abkhazia. In March, a Georgian State Council was formed from the military council and the opposition parties. The new council chose Eduard Shevardnadze, formerly first secretary of the Georgian Communist Party and Soviet foreign minister, as chairman.

Intermittent fighting continued between pro- and anti-Gamsakhurdia forces in 1992, especially in western Georgia, but these clashes were overshadowed by ethnic strife between the Georgian government on one side and the Ossetian and Abkhazian separatist movements on the other. In both Ossetia and Abkhazia, fighting had broken out *before* August 1991. The supreme soviet of the South Ossetian Autonomous Region of Georgia had in fact declared its sovereignty as early as September 1990, while the separatist movement in Abkhazia organized itself in the late 1980s. Fighting in Ossetia has eased, due to the formation of a joint Russian-Georgian peace-keeping force agreed upon by Shevardnadze and Boris Yeltsin in June 1992. In Abkhazia, by contrast, the fighting has not subsided but has intensified. The military situation, which has allowed the Abkhazians, a minority of 17 percent in their own republic, to break from Gcorgia, has strained Russian-Georgian relations, with the Georgians accusing Russian forces remaining in the area of supporting the rebels and the Russian accusing the Georgians of mistreating ethnic Russians in Abkhazia and elsewhere in Georgia.

Because of the turmoil in 1991 and 1992, Georgia did not join the Commonwealth of Independent States (CIS). Nevertheless, it did receive diplomatic recognition from the United States and other nations, in part due to the reputation of its head of state, Shevardnadze. Georgia was also admitted into the Conference of Security and Cooperation in Europe, the North Atlantic Cooperation Council, and the United Nations in 1992. Georgia has also developed notably good relations with its southern neighbors, Turkey and Iran.

REFERENCES: W.E.D. Allen, *A History of the Georgian People*, 1936; Nora Beloff, *Inside the Soviet Empire: The Myth and the Reality*, 1979; Stephen Cohen, Alexander Rabinowitch, and Robert Sharlet, *The Soviet Union Since Stalin*, 1980; Elizabeth Fuller, "Georgia Edges toward Secession," *Radio Liberty Reports on the USSR*, 2: 22 (June 1, 1990), 14–18; David M. Lang, *The Georgians*, 1966; David M. Lang, *A Modern History of Soviet Georgia*, 1962; Ronald Suny, *The Making of the Georgian Nation*, 1988.

Leigh Range

GEORGIAN JEW. Scholars, as well as Georgian Jews themselves, disagree on their origins, some arguing that the Georgian Jews immigrated to Georgia from Iran and the Caucasus in ancient times and, others claiming that Georgian Jews are descended from indigenous people who converted to Judaism during the reign of the khazars between the eighth and twelfth centuries. They are unique among most of the Jews* of the Commonwealth of Independent States in that their written language does not have a Hebrew script. Beginning in the 1970s, the number of Georgian Jews steadily declined because of emigration to Israel. That emigration accelerated after the collapse of the Soviet Union in 1991. See JEW.

REFERENCES: Lionel Kochan, ed., *The Jews in Soviet Russia since 1917*, 1970; Benjamin Pinkus, *The Jews of the Soviet Union: The History of a National Minority*, 1988; Solomon N. Schwarz, *The Jews in the Soviet Union*, 1951.

GERMAN. The most complex nationality in what used to be the Soviet Union are the Germans. As a result of the history of the area, Germans do not constitute a cohesive nationality in the Commonwealth of Independent States (CIS). Rather, their presence in this region evolved through three major historical events that are both separate and intertwined. Now numbering more than 2,000,000 people, the Germans are scattered over an area extending from the extreme western oblast of the Russian Republic (Kaliningrad) to many areas of Kazakhstan and Siberia.

When the Communists took control of the Russian Empire in 1917, Germans were concentrated in the Volga Valley, particularly around Saratov, and in Ukraine, largely in the west (Volhynia) and the south (Crimea). These Germans were descendents of settlers who had been invited by Catherine the Great to populate territories that the tsarist armies had conquered in their wars against the Tatars* and Ottoman Empire from the sixteenth to the eighteenth centuries.

During the tsarist period, the central government also employed a small but politically powerful group of German advisers. Indeed, many Romanov family members were ethnic Germans, the best known of whom was Catherine the Great herself, a native of Mecklenburg. There was, however, a distinct class difference between the handful of Germans in the tsar's court and the frontiersmen in the south.

A second German population lived in the Baltic provinces—Estonia, Livonia, and Courland. These provinces were separated from the Russian Empire shortly after the October Revolution of 1917: Courland became Latvia, and Livonia was divided between Estonia and Latvia. These provinces—later republics—evolved from early German bishoprics (Dorpat, Reval, Riga, and Dunaburg), that had been founded in the thirteenth century during the Christianization of the Baltic littoral by German missionaries. Interestingly, the official name for these Germans was "Balts," a term now used as a generic name for ethnic Estonians*, Latvians*, and Lithuanians*. The German-Balt community was largely eliminated during World War II as a consequence of the German-Soviet (Non-Aggression Pact) Treaty of 1939, which stipulated Estonia and Latvia to be in the Kremlin's sphere of influence. Germans living in the area were transferred and settled in the General-Government (areas of Poland proper that were acquired by Berlin in September 1939). After World War II, they were again uprooted and now live largely in western Germany and Austria. Many have since migrated from Europe to countries in the Western and Southern Hemispheres.

The third German-populated area acquired by the Soviet Union was the northeastern tip of Germany proper (northern East Prussia), which was annexed in 1945, when Josef Stalin violated the Atlantic Charter's prohibition against boundary changes. Subsequently, the Soviets expelled the Germans from the province, which was then partitioned. Its northernmost area—Memelland—was given to the Lithuanian Soviet Socialist Republic (SSR), while the remainder was converted into an oblast of the Russian Soviet Federated Socialist Republic (RSFSR).

The language spoken by the various German groups reflects the dialects of the regions in Germany from whence they had emigrated. In East Prussia, the Salzburg and Obersteiermark dialects predominated, while in Memelland, a Rehenish dialect was heard (the town was originally named Neudortmund). Rhenish dialects, including those from Strassburg and Metz, were also common among the Balts, while Swabian (Schwabisch), Bavarian, Danubian, and northern dialects were trademarks of the settlements in Ukraine and Russia.

Confessional divisions formed the primary distinction among the German colonies established in Russia and Ukraine. These distinctions were the residue of the fierce religious wars that had shaken Germany in the years following the Reformation. In these colonies, there were thirty-one Catholic settlements and seventy-one Lutheran settlements, which also accepted Mennonites (from West Prussia) and other Reformist sects. Only two colonies were inter-denominational—Katharanienstadt and Borgard. The latter had been founded by French Huguenots and was originally called Beauregard.

An industrious people, the Germans were a civilizing factor wherever they settled. In an epic adventure bearing many similarities to the European colonization of North America, the German migration along the Baltic shore, the Volga Valley, and in Ukrainian areas established farms, towns, castles, mines, and new avenues of commerce uniting Eastern and Western Europe. Many towns, particularly those set up along the Baltic coast from East Prussia to Estonia, were granted charters along the lines of those given to Lubeck and Magdeburg by the Holy Roman Empire during the tenth century.

Initial German settlement in the part of Eurasia eventually known as the Soviet Union originated in the thirteenth century, when colonies were established along the Baltic littoral. The founders were bishops, supported by knights belonging to the Teutonic and Livonian Crusading orders. Beginning these settlements at the end of the Crusades, the knights brought with them a centralized type of government first developed by them in the Near East. The newly conquered territories were therefore organized as military districts, in which the religious and secular life were combined. In creating this type of government, the Germans wished to avoid the internecine warfare so rampant in their homelands further west. Feuding, for example, was outlawed in the new provinces. And finally, since the districts were beyond the political control of the Holy Roman Empire, a centralized government gave the settlers a greater sense of security.

The first knightly organization to attract German participation was the Brothers of the Militia of Christ (often called the Livonian Knights), which was created by Bishop Albert and consisted of volunteers from Germany. Bishop Albert offered free land to people who took part in what is popularly called the Northern Crusade. The original purpose was to Christianize the Letts (Latvians), Estonians, and Semgalians (Lithuanians). The winning of the North was chronicled in excellent detail by a parish priest of the period, Henry of Livonia.

A second organization, the Teutonic Knights, who were originally organized to assist the papel forces in the Near East, also attracted adherents. At the close of the Crusades, the Teutonic Knights obtained papal authority to Christianize the Old Prussians, a Baltic people living at the mouths of the Nieman, Pregel, and Vistula rivers. In 1237, this order of knights expanded northward into Courland by uniting with the Livonian Order of the Bishop of Riga. At its greatest extent (1404), the territory of the Teutonic Knights extended from the Vistula to the Gulf of Bothnia and included Gotland (a large island off Sweden) and Neumark (a German province south of Pomerania and east of the Oder River). Though successful, the order failed to see the need for reform in the post-Crusade era; such reform would have widened the corporate state to include new urban elements. This mistake led to military misfortune, and, during the fifteenth century, the Teutonic Knights were eclipsed by their neighbors. Sweden acquired Estonia, Livonia, and Courland, while East Prussia, including Memelland, became Polish fiefs.

German culture in the northern Baltic flourished under Swedish rule, since Stockholm permitted local control in the provinces, but Swedish power waned in the seventeenth century. In 1720, at the conclusion of the Northern Wars, these lands were ceded to Russia. Thus, the Germans in these provinces were the first to come under Russian* rule. St. Petersburg continued the Swedish practice of giving the German-Balts quasi-autonomy, exempting them from certain taxes and allowing them to remain in control of their estates. Shortly thereafter, Russia was victorious in conflicts against the Tatars and the Ottoman Empire, acquiring territories along the Volga and in Ukraine. The need to colonize these areas prompted the Russian government to solicit German immigration. Thus, a second group of Germans came under Russian rule. For the Germans, immigration to Russia meant an escape from the miserable living conditions, caused by overpopulation and crop failures in Germany. Consequently, Russian agents were sent throughout Germany soliciting settlers. Their task was made easy by a special 1,350-word manifesto by Catherine II, which granted Germans religious freedom, self-government, local control of schools, and freedom from both military service and impressment into other state services. The peak years of settlement were 1764 through 1774. The German towns established along the Volga were placed under the control of a new *Tutle-Kanzlei* or Chancellery for the Guardianship of Foreign Germans (a phrase that acknowledged the distinction between the immigrants and the long-established German populations in Russia's Baltic provinces).

Since the chief purpose of this German colonization was to build up the new frontier territories bordering Turkey, the manifesto gave the settlers a thirty-year exemption from taxes, if they settled on previously undeveloped land, as well as a ten-year interest-free loan for homes and farm machinery. Other benefits included free transportation from their point of embarkation and board money. The settlers also had the right to return to Germany at any time. Although the document did not specify how much land a family was to be granted, the subsequent Colonial Law of 1764 allocated thirty *desiatins* (about eighty acres) per family. Despite great hardships encountered as they trekked eastward, the Germans made a success of the program. Indeed, the government used identical programs to encourage German migration into Ukrainian* areas acquired from Poland in 1772. This area, Volhynia, received more immigrants from 1830 to 1870 as Germans fled the unrest in Russian-ruled Poland proper. The settlement policy was used again after 1804 for areas along the Black Sea acquired from the Ottoman Empire (principally Odessa and Crimea).

Many immigrants were members of distinct religious groups, such as the Moravian Brethren; hence, the stipulation on religious freedom. As part of the religious fervor of the colonists, the Moravian Brethren community from Herrnhut, Saxony, established their colony, Serepta, at the eastern extreme of the Volga region, in an area inhabited by Lamaistic Kalmyks*, a Mongol* people. Though the brethren failed to Christianize them, the colony offered an example of German industry. Many villages were named after the towns from whence the Germans had migrated, such as Strassburg, Danzig, Holstein, Salzburg, Zug, and so forth. Other towns used the family name of the mayor or the first person to settle the area. Three notable exceptions were Katharanienstadt, named for Tsarina Catherine II; Drolovskaya, named in honor of the president of the special chancellery; and Paulskoye, named for Tsar Peter.

The German immigrants suffered great hardships as they tried to tame the steppes of southern Russia and Ukraine. One major problem they encountered was the lack of trees, a far cry from the shady valleys of the Rhine, Inn, Danube, Weser and Oder. For housing, the Germans developed the famous sodhouse— homes that were literally built into the ground. Originally, the sodhouse was simply a hole dug in the ground and covered with a cone of twigs, with a smokehole for ventilation. Eventually, construction evolved into a technique using sod ''bricks.'' Another severe problem facing the settlers was that their immigration came just at the beginning of a drought cycle. This caused many crop failures in the first several years. The determination of Russian authorities to turn the land into a ''breadbasket,'' coupled with contemporary misunderstandings of climatic conditions, caused the government to declare, in September 1767, that the Germans were forbidden to engage in any craft other than agriculture. This decree violated the 1764 law, which had specifically stated that the oldest son was to learn a trade. The Saratov settlements, for example, were prohibited from mining salt at Lake Elton, an endeavor that would have brought wealth. Those in violation of the declaration, such as artisans, were sentenced to hard labor or lashing with a knout (a Russian leather whip), and the mayors of the German towns had to enforce this decree. The German immigrants thus became serfs in all but name.

Crop failures were worsened by the inability of the Russian government to deliver seeds on time each spring. Often plantings were made as late as May or June. The mixture of privation, homesickness, poor economy, harsh winters, and torrid summers, along with raids by outlaws and Tatars*, took their toll on the settlers. It is estimated that at the outbreak of the October 1917 Revolution, the schools in the Saratov region were among the most backward in all of Russia. The economic hardships caused many Germans to emigrate. Some went back to Germany, while others fled to Russia's Baltic provinces or to the St. Petersburg area. Many eventually went to North America, founding settlements in Colorado, North Dakota, Kansas, Saskatchewan, and elsewhere.

Those who stayed persevered. The first good harvest occurred in 1775 (at the close of the drought cycle) and production improved markedly when the Germans replaced Russian plows with improved farm machinery. By 1940, the year prior to Stalin's decree expelling Germans from Saratov, the region had in fact become Russia's breadbasket, despite the earlier sufferings. Along with wheat, the farmers grew rye, millet, barley, oats, hemp, flax, sunflowers, potatoes, and tobacco.

When the Bolshevik Revolution broke out, the German population in the Russian Empire was divided as to whether to support the Reds or the Whites. In the western (Baltic) provinces, the Germans generally supported the White Army, since the Germans were largely merchants and landholders, two classes of people who stood to lose the most if the Communists were to take control.

Much of this became a moot issue after Estonia and Latvia obtained their sovereignty. During the subsequent period of Baltic independence from the new Soviet Union, the Germans enjoyed cultural autonomy in the two new republics. The only difficulty experienced by Germans during the interwar period was an attempt at lithuanization of Memelland from 1923 until the mid–1930s.

In Russia proper and in Ukraine, the Bolsheviks won significant support from the German minority. This was due partly to the increased privations caused by World War I and partly to Bolshevik promises of land. In 1918, workers established communes under the banner "Autonomous Communes of Volga German Workers." During the civil war between the Red and White forces, the German lands along the Volga experienced much destruction. German support for V. I. Lenin proved to be a blessing. The wartime commune in the Saratov region evolved into the first autonomous ethnic region of the Soviet Union, established in 1924 as the Volga German Autonomous Republic of the RSFSR. More than 25 percent of the Soviet Germans lived in this republic, which, by 1940, included over a thousand colonies. Its creation reflected the Soviet realization that national differences cannot be papered over with calls to "worker solidarity."

The Volga German Autonomous Republic suffered great oppression during the 1930s when Stalin instituted forced collectivation. Many Germans fell victim to the extermination campaign against "counter revolutionaries" and other real or presumed opponents of Communism. The most cataclysmic event to affect Germans in the Soviet Union was the outbreak of hostilities between Nazi Germany and the Soviet Union in 1941. The Red government reacted with a decree declaring all Germans living in the Soviet Union to be a fifth column. Subsequently, the Germans were subject to internal deportation to areas further east, primarily to the Central Asian republics and Siberia. The deportations began in August 1941, when the Germans in Volhynia and the Crimea were "evacuated" (the Stalinist euphemism for deportation). The evacuations and "transfers" (another euphemism) continued during 1942. The areas were then populated with Russians and Ukrainians.

Prior to these deportations, there was already a sizable German population in the west and central Asian portions of the Soviet Empire, since Germans had migrated there during the tsarist period as frontiersmen, entrepreneurs, and government employees. In fact, according to the 1926 census, there were 79,000 Germans in southwestern Siberia and 51,000 in Kazakhstan. During and after World War II, the general disarray in Siberia, caused by the influx of new settlers and the huge numbers of political prisoners, afforded some German prisoners of war the opportunity to avoid recapture after fleeing from forced labor camps. They simply acquired the identity papers of Volga Germans who had died in the migration but whose deaths had never been officially recorded.

After the war, the Soviet government began a denationalization program, whereby Germans were denied the opportunity to maintain their language and culture. By the mid–1960s, enforced russification had taken its toll. According to both Soviet and independent German sources, the cultivation of the German language by the Soviet Germans had deteriorated to such an extent that many German refugees to Germany and Austria lack fluency in German. The most serious decline occurred in the areas under direct Russian control, whereas in the other republics, notably Kazakhstan, the decline was less severe. According to Soviet census reports, the lowest level of use of the German language by German ethnics was reported in 1959, when only 43 percent stated that they spoke German at home.

Life for the Germans began to improve in the mid–1950s as an adjunct of the Kremlin's foreign policy goals. The watershed year was 1955, when the Soviet Union and West Germany exchanged ambassadors. Eager to wean West Germany from the Western alliance, the Khrushchev regime began to loosen or abolish some of the restrictions that had been placed on Germans by Stalin. One of the first to be eliminated was the one requiring special settlements. Nonetheless, the Germans were still not permitted to return to their original villages in the Volga region or Ukraine. Northern East Prussia, including Memelland, likewise remained off limits to internal migration.

Indeed, the need to find a suitable place for a German homeland within the Soviet Union was the major development after Stalin's death. This issue was compounded by the lack of civil and human rights throughout the Soviet Union. Pressure for re-creating a German republic began to mount in earnest during the 1960s. In 1964, Premier Nikita Khrushchev lifted the Stalinist decree, freeing Germans from the government-imposed stigma of being a "fifth column." In addition, the Soviet Union's foreign obligations to the German Democratic Republic had a subtle influence on improving the conditions of Germans in Moscow's realm.

The first known effort by a postwar Soviet government to establish a republic for Germans appeared in a statement by Leonid Brezhnev in 1972. At that time, Brezhnev issued a decree permitting Germans to migrate back to the Volga area. These documents were discovered in 1988 by Konstantin Ehrlich, the editor of a German magazine in Kazakhstan, when he took advantage of new liberties instituted by *glasnost*. By then, however, the Volga area had become populated by ethnic Russians, invited there by Stalin. The territory had been reincorporated into the Russian Republic as a direct administrative district. Each time the government has issued a statement implying or clearly stating an intention to re-establish a German Republic in the Volga region, it has been met with strong opposition. The German people themselves are lukewarm to the decision to re-establish a German Republic. At the summer 1990 meeting of German ethnics in Moscow, for example, they showed little enthusiasm for the proposal.

The Kremlin also toyed with the idea of creating a German republic in the northeast corner of Kazakhstan, an area of the Soviet Union with a large concentration of Germans. This areas was part of Siberia until the 1930s when it was united to Kazakhstan. In April 1988, at Tselinograd, the Soviet government read a declaration of intent to establish a German state, with Yermentau as the capital. This action led to severe rioting throughout the region, and thus the plan was shelved indefinitely. It is doubtful that the plan will ever come to fruition. Not only are the Kazakhs* opposed to it, but Germans themselves show little enthusiasm for the project. Now that Alma Ata has greater control of its destiny, as a result of the reforms following the abortive coup in 1991, the so-called Tselinograd variant is a dead letter.

The need for a German homeland in the Soviet Union was discussed on March 18, 1991, during a meeting between President Mikhail Gorbachev and the German foreign minister, Hans-Dietrich Genscher. Besides touching on the homeland question, Gorbachev totally abrogated Stalin's anti-German declaration by noting that "they [the Germans] have done nothing to discredit themselves in two centuries" of settlement in Russia. In May 1991, the State Commission on the Problems of Soviet Germans met with President Gorbachev to review the Volga question. It was stressed that any policy should be accompanied by meshing the interests of all the people in the region. The proposed republic would be created on a step-by-step basis. Another agreement was reached with O. I. Lobov, First Vice Chairman of the RSFSR Council of Ministers, to discuss jurisdictional problems with the Congress of Soviet Germans.

Meanwhile, the Commission advised Kazakhstan, Kyrgyzia, and Russia to give specific consideration to proposals restoring German national districts, especially in the Altai, the Omsk region, and around Orenburg (the only major town in the Soviet Union whose German name was not altered by the Stalinists). On July 4, 1991, the Russian parliament approved a decision made by the Altai Autonomous Region in western Siberia near northeastern Kazakhstan to establish a German autonomous district there. The Altai*, however, have also expressed an interest in independence from Russia.

Support for establishing a German Republic in the Kaliningrad Oblast (KO) also gained momentum; the area includes the former East Prussian city of Königsberg. Kurt Wiedmeier has identified the KO as "the most logical place" for a German homeland. In an interview with *Der Spiegel* in 1990, he further noted that if the Soviet Union founded a German Soviet Socialist Republic in northern East Prussia, "Germans could not be accused of taking foreign land." A barometer of the popularity of this idea was first revealed in the October 1989 issue of *Literatura Gazetty*, a German-language magazine serving ethnic Germans in Russia and Ukraine. According to a poll of its German readers, 80 percent indicated a preference for moving to northern East Prussia rather than migrating to West Germany. Additional support was garnered at the 1990 Convention of USSR Germans in Moscow. In *Sovietskaya Rossiya* (August 11, 1990), Hugo Wormsbecher, a member of *Wiedergeburt*, an umbrella organization for ethnic Germans in the Soviet Union, commented that KO should become an autonomous region for Germans in the Soviet Union and that plans to settle Germans in the Volga area should be scuttled.

Moscow also encouraged German migration to this westernmost oblast of the RSFSR, with support from the oblast's governor, Yuri Semyonov, and the mayor of Kaliningrad, Nikolai Chromenko. One of the earliest examples of Kremlin support was the 1989 suggestion by Gorbachev to rename the capital Kantgrad, in honor of Immanual Kant, the well-known German philosopher who lived his entire life in Königsberg. Currently, the German population of the KO is on the rise. The city of Kaliningrad, for example, now has more than 4,000 German residents, up from 200 in 1989. Viktor Hoffman, chairman of the 2,000 member *Eintracht* (a German cultural organization in the KO) has received numerous inquiries about relocation. In addition, Governor Semyonov wanted more "industrious and reliable German workers" in the KO, according to a report in *Der Spiegel*. Support by the mayor was best exemplified by his stern rebuke in 1990 to Alexander Savkin, an old-line Russian Communist, who not only objected to the influx of Germans but also demanded a referendum on the question. Chromenko dismissed Savkin's demands as "discrimination nonsense," further noting that all two million Germans were full Soviet citizens.

Indeed, the growing pressure to establish a German state in the KO prompted *Time Magazine* to identify the oblast as "Free Königsberg" in a list of new nations to debut during the 1990s. The effects of renewed German migration to northern East Prussia include the use of German as the language of instruction in an elementary school and the fact that German has now replaced English as the foreign language of choice in the oblast's schools. Even souvenirs bearing the word "Königsberg" and the Prussian/German eagle are now sold in the KO. Other signs include a new museum honoring German architects and artists Simon Dach, Julius Rupp, and Käthe Kollwitz. A Goethe Institute will open soon, and the famous cathedral where the Hohenzollern kings were crowned is slated for reconstruction. A consortium of the Russian Orthodox and German Evangelical churches is coordinating the project. Mayor Chromenko would like to tear down the Stalinist-style Senatorial House, built in 1966 on the site of the royal castle. When the castle was destroyed by the Communists, local Russians protested bitterly, according to reports in the *Moskauer Nachrichten* during the 1960s. Yuri Ivanov, chairman of the Soviet Cultural Fund of Kaliningrad, is trying to rebuild the cultural heritage of northern East Prussia, a task which includes contacting the Germans who were expelled by the Communists after World War II. One result has been the erection of a new pedestal for the statue of Kant. This was a gift from *Die Zeit*, a liberal German daily published in Hamburg.

Since the KO is separated from Russia by Lithuania, the Russians living in the oblast seem to support sovereignty for the area. Beyond local government support for German in-migration, Ivanov noted in early 1991 that "sometime soon we will establish our own Baltic republic." He further noted that such a republic could be a bridge between Russia and Germany. At present, the oblast is still best described as a military reserve. Indeed, prior to the August 1991 coup, Mayor Chromenko had worried that "as long as the oblast remains a military province, a strong dogmatic wind could condemn everything." One of the military factors is the homeporting of much of the Baltic fleet in KO. During elections in the RSFSR, the Germans largely supported Boris Yeltsin, whose reform programs resemble those of *Wiedergeburt*.

A major change in the KO occurred in June 1991, when President Yeltsin authorized the creation of a free-trade zone. Plans for this had begun in June 1989, during the Kohl-Gorbachev summit, when both agreed that a special economic zone would facilitate economic assistance to the Soviet Union. Local leaders such as Chromenko and Semyonov supported this plan. More support came from Friedrich Wilhelm Christians, a German banking expert on Eastern Europe. He also expressed the view that the oblast could be a linchpin for understanding between Russians and Germans. With the new status came a new name—the Amber Free Trade Zone. Although the term officially referred to the fossilized resin found in great abundance along the Baltic shore, the term carried political overtones as well. The German translation, "Bernstein," could also refer to Eduard Bernstein, the famous Social Democrat who spurned Marxism during the nineteenth century.

As in other areas of Russia, KO is also planning to return cities to their original names. The decision on renaming the capital of this gestating fourth Baltic state will be resolved by a referendum, the date of which has not been decided. The voters will have four options: Königsberg (supported by Mayor Chromenko, the oblast's government, and the Germans); Kaliningrad, the Stalinist term; Kantgrad, the term suggested by Gorbachev; and Baltic Seaport (in German, Ostseehafen; in Russian, Baltisyk). The last option is a sign that other towns will soon regain their original names. Baltisyk was the name given by Stalinists to Pillau, the deepwater port for Königsberg.

The question of restoring German statehood in an area formerly known as the Soviet Union will apparently be resolved through a combination of high-level study and consent by the governed. At present, the German community has widely varying views on its fate. Many, such as those now moving to the Kaliningrad Oblast/Amber Free Trade Zone, want an autonomous entity, including sovereignty. There is, however, still disagreement as to where the German autonomous region should be established—in the Volga or in northeastern Kazakhstan. Others, specifically those who have put down roots in the areas to which they were exiled, prefer to remain where they are. This group strives for cultural autonomy, similar to that granted in the Altai. A third group cherishes dreams of returning to Ukraine, the Volga area, Crimea, the Caucasus, and the St. Petersburg area, from whence they were exiled during the 1940s. A fourth group, hopelessly frustrated by over a half century of injustices, simply wants to emigrate.

The interests of the Germans have to do with satisfying their national needs, the revival and development of their language and culture, and the preservation of themselves as a distinct people. If statehood is not attained, the Germans in Russia may evolve into a stateless limbo similar to that of Palestinians in the Mideast. The Germans in the former Soviet Union receive moral and financial support from Germany and from emigré communities throughout the world. The German government funnels $110 million annually to assist in the construction of schools, hospitals, and social centers for Germans, not only in the KO, but in Russia proper, Kazakhstan, and elsewhere.

At present, the largest populations of Germans in the Commonweatlh of Independent States lie in a broad area stretching from the Altai Autonomous Region, which borders on the Republics of Mongolia and Kazakhstan, to the city of Orenburg on the west slope of the Ural Mountains. A significant population remains in northeastern Kazakhstan, specifically between Tselinograd and Ust'-Kamenogorsk. A smaller German population lives along the Kazakhstan-Kyrgyzia frontier, as well as in eastern Uzbekistan. In Ukraine, German communities are located in the Dnepropetrovsk, Zaporozhe, and Odessa regions. Small German populations live in the three newly independent Baltic republics. In Lithuania, for example, Germans comprise 6 percent of the population in Memelland; German minorities still exist in Estonia and Latvia. Their chief cultural centers are Tallinn and Tartu in Estonia, Riga and Dobele in Latvia. As indicated above, the extreme western oblast of the RSFSR, Kaliningrad, has a German minority whose numbers are increasing through migration from other areas of the former Soviet Union.

With the collapse of Communism and the introduction of meaningful reforms, life for Germans in the territory of the former Soviet Union will begin to improve once the reforms take effect. The creation of a homeland for Germans may be considered one of the more important reforms, since it would assure their identity as a people.

REFERENCES: Alexander Dallin, *German Rule in Russia, 1941–1945: A Study of Occupation Policies*, 1957; Christian Dueval, "An Unprecedented Plenum of the CPSU Central Committee," *Radio Liberty Dispatch* (May 3, 1972), 3–4; Ann Sheehy and Bohdan Nahaylo, *The Crimean Tatars, Volga Germans, and Mesketians: Soviet Treatment of Some National Minorities*, 1980.

John A. Fink

GERMAN OF BESSARABIA. See BESSARABIAN GERMAN and GERMAN.

GERMAN OF THE BALTICS. See BALTIC GERMAN and GERMAN.

GERMAN OF THE VOLGA. See VOLGA GERMAN and GERMAN.

GERMAN OF UKRAINE. See UKRAINIAN GERMAN and GERMAN.

GHAPUT. See GAPUT, DZHEK, SHAH DAGH, and AZERBAIJANI.

GHAPUTIN. See GAPUT, DZHEK, SHAH DAGH, and AZERBAIJANI.

GHAZI KUMUQ. See LAK.

GHIBDITLI. See GODOBERI and AVAR.

GIDATL. See CHAMALAL and AVAR.

GIDATL-ANDALALAY-KARKH. See CHAMALAL and AVAR.

GILIAK. See NIVKHI.

GILYAK. See NIVKHI.

GINUG. The Ginug are a Sunni Muslim people who are classified as an Avar*
subgroup. They are an extremely isolated people geographically, dwelling in the
high valleys of southwestern Daghestan. See AVAR.
REFERENCE: Ronald Wixman, *The Peoples of the USSR: An Ethnographic Handbook*,
1984.

GINUGH. See GINUG and AVAR.

GINUKH. See GINUG and AVAR.

GLAZOV TATAR. The Glazov Tatars live near the Cheptsa River in the Middle
Volga River area. See TATAR.
REFERENCE: Ronald Wixman, *The Peoples of the USSR: An Ethnographic Handbook*,
1984.

GLAZOVSKIY TATAR. See GLAZOV TATAR and TATAR.

GODOBERI. The Godoberi, who call themselves the Ghibditli, are today considered to be a subgroup of the Avar*. Russians* refer to them as the Godoberintsy. They are Sunni Muslim in religion, are being assimilated by the Avar,
and live primarily in Godoberi village and Zibirkhali village in the Botlikh region
of west-central Daghestan. Like many other groups among the small, geographically isolated Caucasian peoples, the Godoberi identity is more local than generic. Ethnic identity revolves more around village than around a sense of
Godoberi consciousness. Although it is difficult to come up with current population estimates for the Godoberi, primarily because of their census designation
with the Avars, demographers estimate that there are approximately 2,000 people
who either consciously identify themselves as Godoberi or who are aware of
their Godoberi ancestry. See AVAR.
REFERENCES: Shirin Akiner, *Islamic Peoples of the Soviet Union*, 1983; Ronald Wixman, *The Peoples of the USSR: An Ethnographic Handbook*, 1984.

GODOBERIN. See GODOBERI and AVAR.

GODOBERINTSY. See GODOBERI and AVAR.

GOGOBERI. See GODOBERI and AVAR.

GOKLEN. The Goklen are a subgroup of the Turkmen*. They live along the coast of the Caspian Sea at the western edge of the Turkmen Republic. See TURKMEN.
REFERENCE: Ronald Wixman, *The Peoples of the USSR: An Ethnographic Handbook*, 1984.

GOLCHA. See TAJIK and PAMIR PEOPLES.

GOLD. See NANAI.

GOLDI. See NANAI.

GOLDY. See NANAI.

GOLEND. See BELARUSIAN.

GOLENDRY. See BELARUSIAN.

GOLIAD. See BELARUSIAN.

GOLIADY. See BELARUSIAN.

GOLJAD. See BELARUSIAN.

GOLJADY. See BELARUSIAN.

GOLYAD. See BELARUSIAN.

GOLYADY. See BELARUSIAN.

GORETS. See CAUSASIAN MOUNTAINEER.

GORNIY TADZHIK. See MOUNTAIN TAJIK and TAJIK.

GORNO-BADAGHSHANI. See PAMIR PEOPLES and TAJIK.

GORNO-BADAGSHANI. See PAMIR PEOPLES and TAJIK.

GORNO-BADAHSHANI. See PAMIR PEOPLES and TAJIK.

GORNO-BADAKHSHANI. See PAMIR PEOPLES and TAJIK.

GORNY KALMUK. See ALTAI.

GORNY KALMYK. See ALTAI.

GORNY QALMUK. See ALTAI.

GORNY QALMYK. See ALTAI.

GORNEY SHOR. See SHOR.

GORNY TADJIK. See MOUNTAIN TAJIK and TAJIK.

GORNY TADZHIK. See MOUNTAIN TAJIK and TAJIK.

GORNY TAJIK. See MOUNTAIN TAJIK and TAJIK.

GORNY TATAR. See BALKAR.

GORNYY. See ALTAI.

GORNYY KALMUK. See ALTAI.

GORNYY KALMYK. See ALTAI.

GORNYY QALMUK. See ALTAI.

GORNYY QALMYK. See ALTAI.

GORNYY SHOR. See SHOR.

GORNYY TADJIK. See MOUNTAIN TAJIK and TAJIK.

GORNYY TADZHIK. See MOUNTAIN TAJIK and TAJIK.

GORNYY TAJIK. See MOUNTAIN TAJIK and TAJIK.

GORNYY TATAR. See BALKAR.

GORSKIY EVREI. See MOUNTAIN JEW and JEW.

GORSKIY IEVREI. See MOUNTAIN JEW and JEW.

GORSKIY YEVREI. See MOUNTAIN JEW and JEW.

GORSKIY YEVREY. See MOUNTAIN JEW and JEW.

GORTSY. See MOUNTAINEER and CAUCASIAN MOUNTAINEER.

GORUNYA. See RUSSIAN.

GORYUN. The Goryun are a subgroup of the Polekh*, who are themselves a subgroup of the Russians*. The Goryun live in the Kursk Gubernya in far western Russia. That region was long under Ukrainian* control, and the Goryun, although ethnically Russian, exhibit many Ukrainian cultural traits. See POLEKH or RUSSIAN.
REFERENCE: Ronald Wixman, *The Peoples of the USSR: An Ethnographic Handbook*, 1984.

GORYUNY. See GORYUN.

GREAT RUSSIAN. See RUSSIAN.

GREEK. In the modern context, the term ''Greek'' has had three connotations. First, until the nineteenth century, it applied to adherents of the Orthodox church in the Near East. Since then, the term has applied mostly to those people who speak variants of modern Greek and whose homelands are in the southern Balkan peninsula, the Aegean and Ionian Islands, Asia Minor, and Cyprus. Included in the appelation are both Greek-speakers and those who consider themselves Greeks while residing in diaspora communities throughout the world. This last element would include the 357,957 inhabitants of the former Soviet Union who were listed as Greeks in the last Soviet census of 1989. The Greek element of the population of the former Soviet Union includes those individuals who speak Greek as their mother tongue (approximately 125,000), as well as those who speak Turkish, Tatar*, Russian*, and other languages but claim to be Greek (over 200,000). In addition to the Russian term ''Greki,'' the words ''Elliny,'' ''Romioi,'' ''Rum,'' and ''Urum'' are used to denote Greeks in territories of the Commonwealth of Independent States (CIS). The traditional areas of settlement and the largest concentrations of Greeks are found around the Black Sea in Ukraine, the Russian Republic, and Georgia; scattered groups also live in other areas, especially Armenia and the Central Asian Republics. Although Greeks have constituted a very small group in Russian and Soviet census reports in the nineteenth and twentieth centuries, they have played a role in Russian and Soviet history far beyond the number of current inhabitants of the CIS. They now account for about 0.1 percent of the CIS population and have no officially sanctioned homeland or population concentration. Nonetheless, Greeks and Greek-speakers have probably had longer recorded historical ties to the area of what constitutes the CIS than any other non-indigenous people.

Greeks have been involved in the lands of the Black Sea region of the CIS for nearly two-thousand years, to before the foundation of the first Russian* state. The origins of this involvement are in the mists of myths and legends. These include the myths about the punishment of Prometheus in the Caucasus and the voyage of Jason and the Argonauts to the legendary Kingdom of Colchis. The first historical mentions of the Black Sea region come from the early Greek historian Herodotus, who chronicled the development of the steppe peoples of his era (the Cimmerians and the Scythians) and their relations with the Persian Empire.

Ancient sources and modern authorities have shown that Greeks developed trade relations with the Scythians in the years between 750 and 500 B.C. Trade between the Greek city states and the Scythians usually consisted of the Greeks trading luxury goods, wine, olive oil, and art objects for salt, fish, wheat, honey, beeswax, and slaves. In time, a number of Greek city states established colonies along the Black Sea coast, including Tyras, Borysthenes (Olbia), Kerkinitis, Chersonesus, Theodosia, Pantikapaion, Myremkion, Tiritaka, Nymphaion, Phanagoria, Hermonassa, Tanais, Phasis, and Dioskourias. There is archaeological evidence that Greeks may have resided among the Scythians in the interior as commercial wayfarers or settlers. These Greek communities coexisted peacefully with the steppe peoples and maintained lively trade with them. The grain trade became so important in the fifth and fourth centuries B.C. that the rupture or maintenance of that trade became a strategic objective for warring Greek city states, during, for example, the Peloponnesian War.

Following the conquests of Alexander and the ushering in of the Hellenistic age, many of the Greek city states along the Black Sea came under the control of hellenized eastern rulers, such as Mithradates, until the conquest of the East by the Romans during the third to the first century A.D.; at that point, many of the Greeks in Hellenized settlements came under Roman authority. Those in the eastern Crimea and the Taman Peninsula were part of the hellenized kingdom of Cimmerian Bosporus, an ally of Rome. Corresponding to the establishment of Roman rule in the coastal regions was the development of new steppe polities under an Iranian-speaking people known as the Sarmatians, and later under the Germanic Goths and the Turkish Huns and Khazars. While many of the former Greek colonies declined and disappeared under pressure from the steppe peoples, the southern coastal settlements under Roman and later Byzantine rule were able to maintain themselves as outposts of the Roman state and of Mediterranean civilization well after the dissolution of the Roman Empire in the West. Enduring raids and invasions from Sarmatians, Goths, Huns, Khazars, Alans, and other migratory peoples, the Black Sea provinces of the Roman Empire and its successor, the Byzantine Empire, maintained active trade relations with the interior regions to the north and east for centuries.

Trade from Cherson province in the Crimea increased in importance with the transfer of the Roman capital to Byzantium. The relative proximity of Cherson to the new imperial capital of Constantinople ensured a continual influx of Greek speakers into the region, especially as the eastern Roman Empire became more Greek than Latin in its official character in sixth and seventh centuries. The Byzantines' loss of Egypt and Syria to Islam in the seventh century made the Black

Sea trade even more important, since the empire now had to depend upon Anatolian agriculture and imports from the north for its salt, fish, honey, wax, and grain. Some Roman and Byzantine towns in the region, such as Kaffa, Bosporus (Kerch), Hermonassa (Tmutorakan), and Sebastopolis (Sukhumi), came under the rule of the various steppe peoples and eventually under Genoese control. Nonetheless, a Greek element continued to be active in these settlements as well.

The Byzantines' relations with the peoples of the north, such as the Alans and the Khazars*, continued to be intimate, as attested by the works of Theophanes and Constantine Porphyrogenitus. Attempts at Christian missionary work among the Alans and the Khazars were made by Byzantine missionaries, notably Cyril and Methodius of Thessalonica, who later became known as Saints Cyril and Methodius, the apostles of the Slavs.

The status of the remnants of the old Greco-Roman settlements of the Byzantine province of Chershon changed greatly as a result of the founding of the Kievan Rus' principality. Initially, in its pagan stage, the Kievan Rus' raided Byzantine Black Sea possessions and made at least two seaborne attacks on Constantinople in the ninth and tenth centuries. In time, the relationship changed from one of raiding to trading, with agreements between the Kievan Rus' and the Byzantine Empire on commercial questions. In addition to trade, many Kievan Rus' entered Byzantine military service. Whether these raiders, traders, and mercenaries were Scandinavians or Slavs in ethnicity has been open to dispute, as part of the general "Normanist Controversy" in the historiography of early medieval Russia. Suffice it to say that these individuals came from the lower terminus of the Great Eastern or Varangian route between the Baltic and the Black Sea, which eventually became known as the Kievan Rus' principality. These people, whether of Scandinavian or Slavic origin, were initially from Kievan Rus' lands. It is interesting to note that Greeks did not go to the northern Black Sea to trade; rather, northerners went south. The change in trade relations and power in the Black Sea region weakened the Byzantine outpost of Cherson in the north, to the extent that it was captured by the Kievan Rus' under Prince Vladimir in 985. The town and province were returned to Byzantium, however, in return for the hand of an imperial princess. In the later Middle Ages, the Crimea became a crossroads and an area of rivalry among Rus', Polovtsy, Byzantines, Genoese, Mongols*, and Tatars*. Nonetheless, a Greek/Byzantine presence remained in the area, as evidenced by the Byzantine principality of Theodoro (Mankoup), which survived as an autonomous or independent entity from the thirteenth to the fifteenth centuries. Greeks have made up a significant segment of the population of the Crimea into modern times.

While the Byzantines lost their predominance in trade and power in the northern Black Sea, they gained tremendously in cultural and political influence with the baptism of Vladimir and the subsequent Christianization of his realm. Since Vladimir and the Kievan Rus' opted for Byzantine Christianity, the principality became an ecclesiastical province of the patriarchate of Constantinople, with a prelate known as a metropolitan. While most of the bishops and clergy were native, the metropolitan was, with few exceptions, a Byzantine Greek until the fifteenth century. Aside from the metropolitan, other Byzantines, including scholars, artists, and artisans, who were either attached to the metropolitan's court or to imperial embassies, came to Kievan Rus' lands between the tenth and fifteenth centuries. Other Byzantines were employed by Rus' princes or affiliated themselves to the great monasteries.

In the thirteenth century, Byzantine-Kievan Rus' relations were affected by the break-up of the unified Byzantine state following the Fourth Crusade in 1204 and the Mongol invasion of Russia in the 1240s. While a truncated Byzantine state reemerged in 1266 and had a precarious existence for another 188 years, the Kievan Rus' state was succeeded by the new unified principality of Muscovy, which was based upon monarchic principles adopted from both the Mongols and the Byzantines. In the period from 1200 to 1450, Byzantine Greeks continued to emigrate to Russian lands and to participate in Russian and Ukrainian* cultural life. One such figure was Feofan Grek (Theophanes the Greek), a unique Byzantine iconographer of the fourteenth century who influenced the Russian iconographic school of Andrei Rublev.

From the thirteenth to the fifteenth centuries the decline and fall of the Byzantine Empire led to an exodus of Greeks to Russia as well as the West. The Byzantine contribution to the Italian Renaissance, in the form of the introduction of Greek studies to the West, is well known. The Byzantine influence on the development of culture in Muscovy is less well recognized. One of the most important figures in Russian letters in the late fifteenth and early sixteenth centuries was Maxim Grek (Michael Trivolis, or Maximos the Greek), an Epirote exile who spent a number of years in Florence and Mount Athos before going to Russia. In addition to scholars like Maxim, Byzantine courtiers and artists came to Muscovy in the entourage of Sophia Palaeologos, the niece of the last Byzantine emperor. As a result of Sophia's marriage to Ivan III, a number of former Byzantine officials became chancery and diplomatic officials of the Muscovite prince. It is significant that the marriage of Sophia to Ivan introduced Byzantine court ceremonials and symbols to the Muscovite principality. The fall of Byzantium and the theoretical transfer of the imperium accomplished by the marriage of Sophia and Ivan provided a historical precedent for the Muscovite political theory of the Third Rome. This theory posited Moscow as the legitimate successor to Rome and Byzantium.

From the time of Ivan III to Peter I, Greeks continued to come to Russia for three reasons: religious refuge and aid, diplomatic and military service, and commercial immigration. Since most of the Greeks and other Orthodox Christians of the Near East were under the Islamic rule of the Ottoman Empire and since Muscovy was the only major independent Orthodox realm in existence in the early modern era, Greeks and other Orthodox Christians gravitated toward Russia for protection, aid, and livelihood.

In ecclesiastical relations, Orthodox hierarchs, including the patriarchs of Alexandria, Antioch, and Jerusalem, made journeys to Russia for alms and support from the Muscovite tsar. They also traveled to Ukraine in the seventeenth century to re-establish an Orthodox episcopate in the wake of the defection of most of the Ukrainian hierarchy to the Uniate movement after the Council of Brest in 1592. A number of Greek clerics found employment in Russia and Ukraine as instructors in ecclesiastical schools, as manuscript correctors, and as scholars. Among the latter were Paisius Ligarides, the Likoudes brothers, and Arsenios of Elasson.

Other Greeks went to Russia to find service in the military and diplomatic service of the Muscovite tsar. For example, in the late sixteenth and early seventeenth centuries, during the Time of Troubles, a number of Greeks served as cavalrymen in Muscovite service. Some entered the diplomatic service; an example is Nicholas Spatharios-Milescu, who led a Muscovite embassy to China and negotiated the treaty of Nerchinsk in 1693.

Finally, some Greeks settled in Russia in the Muscovite era for economic reasons. Trade between Muscovy and the Near East did not develop until Muscovy absorbed the eastern Ukraine in the seventeenth century. The Greek merchants of the Ukrainian towns of Kiev, Kharkov, and Nezhin were granted privileges of the Muscovite-Ottoman trade by the Cossacks*, the Ottomans, and Muscovy. Greeks became involved first in the fur trade between Russia and the Near East; later they also dealt in other commodities. Greek involvement in the fur trade continued into the eighteenth and nineteenth century. An indication of this is the fact that the first chief representative of the Russian-American Company in Alaska in the 1790s was one Efstratios Delarof, a Greek from the Peloponnesus.

The reign of Peter I brought more Greeks into Russian military, naval, and diplomatic service. The trend of increasing numbers of Greeks in Russian service continued under Peter's immediate successors. It was not until the reign of Catherine II, however, that large numbers of Greeks were either absorbed into the Russian state or settled within its boundaries. This increase of Greeks in Russia was brought about by the military operations in Greek lands during the two Russo-Turkish wars of 1769–1774 and 1787–1791. The Russian operations in the first conflict included the fomenting of uprisings in the Peloponnesus and other Greek areas. Although these insurrections failed, large numbers of refugee rebels entered into service with Russian naval forces in the Aegean and the Levant in the years 1770–1774. Following the war and the treaty of Kucuk Kainarci in 1774, many of the Greeks who had collaborated with Russians emigrated to Russia, chiefly to newly conquered territory in the southern Ukraine.

In addition, Russian expansion toward the Black Sea absorbed Greeks living in previously Ottoman and Crimean Tatar* territory. A large number of Greeks of the Crimea were resettled in Russian territory in and around the town of Mariupol (whose Soviet name was Zhdanov). Balkan and Aegean Greeks, as well as Orthodox Albanians*, were colonized in the area around Kerch and Yenikale as military settlers known as the Albanian Force. With the Russian annexation of the Crimea in the 1780s, these military colonists were reorganized into a unit known as the Greek Infantry Regiment and resettled on the southern coast of the Crimean Peninsula at Balaklava. In addition to the southern Russian settlements, Catherine's government organized a Greek gymnasium to educate refugee boys. Eventually, this school became known as the Cadet Corps of Foreign Co-Religionists and trained over 200 officers in Russian naval and military service. Besides army and navy service, significant numbers of Greeks, together with other Balkan Christians, entered Russian diplomatic and consular service in the late eighteenth and early nineteenth centuries, holding the majority of posts in the Near East and the Mediterranean. One of their number, Ioannes Capodistrias, became Foreign Minister under Tsar Alexander I.

The general Greek population in Russia grew prodigiously from the late eighteenth through the nineteenth century. In part, this population growth was caused by refugee settlers, in the wake of the Russo-Turkish wars of that era. The rapid development of Greek merchant communities in southern Russia and of the Greek merchant fleet likewise had their origins in the aftermath of these wars. As Russia's southern provinces developed, however, the most important factors in Greek immigration were trade, shipping, and economic opportunity. Throughout the nineteenth century, Greek merchant communities in southern Russia contributed to the economic growth of the Black Sea and Caucasus regions, while Greek shipping, under Russian and other registries, played an important role in the development of Russian trade in the Mediterranean.

Russia continued to be a center of Greek settlement into the twentieth century. The Greek communities in Russia remained the largest concentration of Greeks outside of Greece and the Ottoman Empire until the period of mass immigration to the United States in the early twentieth century. According to Greek sources, there were 515,000 Greeks in Russia prior to the Bolshevik Revolution. These included, according to area, 75,000 in Kars and Ardahan (present-day Turkey); 52,000 in Tbilisi and Chalia (Georgia); 25,000 in Batum (Georgia); 55,000 in Sukhumi (Georgia); 15,000 in Baku (Azerbaijan); 25,000 in the Black Sea Guberniia (Taman Peninsula); 80,000 in the Kuban region; 10,000 in the Terek region; 20,000 in Stavropol; 70,000 in the Crimea (Ukraine); 35,000 in Cherson (Ukraine); 15,000 in Rostov-on-Don and Taganrog (Russia); 30,000 in Marioupol (Russia); and 8,000 elsewhere.

An indication of the comparative size of these Greek communities is the fact that, by the turn of the century, Greek consular representatives in Russia outnumbered those from most other European countries. Greece maintained a larger consular service in Russia, including two consulates-general (in Odessa and Kiev), seven consulates (in Baku, Batum, Helsinki, Kishinev, Moscow, Sevastopol, and Taganrog), and thirteen vice-consulates (in Akkerman, Berdyansk, Feodosia, Ismail, Kerch, Mariupol, Nikolayev, Poti, Reni, Rostov-on-Don, Yeisk, and Yenicheisk).

The numbers and general condition of Greeks in Russia changed drastically with the Russian Revolutions of 1917 and the subsequent civil war. Since a significant segment of the Greeks were engaged in trade, commerce, crafts, and business, most were perceived as bourgeois or petit-bourgeois. They were thus "class enemies" of the new Bolshevik government. In addition, Greece was called upon by the Entente powers (Russia, France, and Great Britain) to participate in a military/naval intervention in the Black Sea region during the Russian civil war in early 1919. Greece sent an expeditionary force of 23,351 men, which was supposed to become an army corps of 42,000 troops. The Greek troops, together with Polish units, were the most effective forces deployed against the Bolsheviks and were the least influenced by war-weariness and Bolshevik propaganda. After three months, however, the allied intervention could not be maintained, and the Greek force's positions proved to be untenable. The expeditionary force was withdrawn to Bessarabia. The Greek role in the intervention produced a good deal of official and unofficial anti-Greek sentiment within Russia, which resulted in the emigration of tens of thousands of Greeks. Between 1919 and 1924, 47,091 Greeks emigrated from Russia and settled in Greece.

In the same year, 1924, Greece and the Soviet Union established diplomatic relations. The resettlement of Russian Greeks in Greece soon became a diplomatic issue. The Soviets raised the question of the repatriation of Greeks from Russia, claiming that "on the territory of the USSR there reside about 300,000 Greek citizens, a considerable part of whom is engaged in private trade and cannot adapt itself to our laws." This statement, made in the late 1920s, may indicate that Greeks in Russia were taking advantage of the limited privatization authorized under the New Economic Policy to re-establish businesses. The Greek government responded that such a mass repatriation would be an intolerable burden, in light of the more than 1.5 million recent Greek refugees from Turkey whom Greece was then trying to absorb. Nevertheless, repatriation was begun, in exchange for Armenian* refugees in Greece who wished to settle in Soviet Armenia. By 1928, about 70,000 Greeks from Russia had resettled in Greece. These included large numbers of Greek refugees from the eastern Black Sea regions of Turkey, who had fled to Soviet territory in the wake of World War I and the Greco-Turkish War of 1919–1922. Even more Greeks desired to emigrate to Greece, as shown by demonstrations at the Greek embassy in Moscow in 1929. Only limited numbers could be resettled after 1928, however, due to policies of the Greek government that restricted immigration to those with family members already living in Greece. The onset of the Great Depression and the tightening of Soviet emigration policy under Josef Stalin also limited emigration. Still, some Greeks were deported by the Soviets to Greece, as was the case with a number of former merchants from the Crimea in 1932.

Unfortunately, during the Stalin era, many more Greeks were arrested and deported to remote parts of the Soviet Union. Reports of Soviet arrests of Greeks appeared in Greek newspapers as early as 1931. Beginning in late 1937 and throughout 1938, Greeks not living in established Greek communities were subjected to mass arrest, on the pretext that they were foreign agents; soon after, all males over seventeen within the large Tatar-speaking Greek community of Mariupol were rounded up. These mass arrests eventually spread to other Greek communities, while Greek Orthodox churches, Greek-language schools, and other cultural institutions were closed. The Greek government attempted to respond to the problem by offering visas to more Greeks in Russia, but it had to act cautiously to avoid spurring on more purges of Greeks. According to one source, upwards of 150,000 Greeks were jailed and exiled between 1937 and 1939. In 1938, 20,000 Russian Greek refugees, mostly women and children, arrived in Greece. The purges eased after 1939.

The coming of World War II to the Soviet Union, following the Axis invasion of 1941, issued in a new era of trials for the Greeks in Russia. Most of the areas where the majority of Greeks still resided (Ukraine, the Crimea, the Black Sea coast, and the northern Caucasus) came under Axis occupation. According to both later Soviet and Greek sources, many Greeks in the Crimea suffered under Nazi rule. During the war, Greeks outside of the occupied areas participated in the Soviet war effort. Although there was no evidence of collaboration with the Axis occupation, most of the Greek population of the Crimea was exiled to Kazakhstan, along with the Crimean Tatars, upon the liberation of the Crimea in 1944. Most of the Greeks in Ukraine, southern Russian, and the Caucasus were subsequently exiled to Siberia and the Central Asian republics beginning in June 1949. This massive deportation was not officially mentioned nor explained. In *The Gulag Archipelago*, Aleksandr Solzhenitsyn postulated that Stalin might have ordered the Russian Greeks' removal in his rage over the Communist failure in the Greek civil war in the Balkans.

Following this forced movement eastward of around 200,000 Greeks, the last major immigration of Greeks to Russia and the Soviet Union began in 1950. As an aftermath of the Communist defeat in the Greek civil war in late 1949, a major portion of the Democratic Army of Greece, the Greek Communist Party, and their supporters became political refugees in the Soviet Union. While other Greek guerrillas were settled in Poland, Hungary, East Germany, Czechoslovakia, and Romania, most were eventually sent to the Soviet Union. The political refugees who came to the Soviet Union numbered over 10,000. They were initially feted upon their arrival in Odessa but were soon sent to Central Asia. Some were placed in leadership positions in the exiled Greek communities there, while others were tried and purged for various crimes against the party and sent to prison and/or exile.

With the advent of de-Stalinization under Nikita Khruschev in 1956, Greeks who wished to return to their original homes on the Black Sea coast and in the Caucasus were allowed to do so. The only exceptions were the Greeks of the Crimea, who were allowed to return somewhat later. By the late 1950s, many Greeks had returned, but much difficulty arose over their resettlement. Evidence of these changes are found in population figures given in the *Great Soviet Encyclopedia*. The first edition, published in the interwar period, noted that 72,032 Greeks lived in Ukraine and 52,654 in the Caucasus, but there is *no* mention of Greeks living in those regions in the second edition, published in the early 1950s. The updated English version of the third edition, published in the 1970s, showed that there were 106,900 Greeks in the Ukraine (including the Crimea), 89,000 in Georgia, 5,000 in Armenia, and 57,800 in the Russian Soviet Federated Socialist Republics (RSFSR), according to the 1970 census.

Besides returning to their home areas along the Black Sea, significant numbers of Soviet Greeks have emigrated to Greece since 1956. Although Soviet authorities have pressured Soviet Greeks to renounce their Greek citizenship, between 50,000 and 60,000 maintained their Greek citizenship as late as the 1970s. In the decade between 1965 and 1975, over 15,000 Greeks from the Soviet Union, both Greek and Soviet citizens, emigrated to Greece; the trend continued into the 1980s. Along with many Greeks born in Russia and the Soviet Union came many political refugees (and their families) from the 1940s, after the announcement of amnesty for participants in the Greek civil war.

While emigration has been an option for some, most Greeks or persons of Greek descent will probably remain in the republics of the CIS, barring total economic and political turmoil. Over the years, many Greeks have been assimilated into the society and culture of the republics in which they reside, especially because of the cultural and religious ties that Greeks have with Russians, Ukrainians*, Georgians*, and other nationalities. Through intermarriage, education, and other means, many Greeks have entered the mainstream of the politics, society, culture, and economy of the former Soviet Union. Probably the most notable figure of Greek origin in recent times is the reform mayor of Moscow, Gavril Popov.

Since 1985, the changes in the former Soviet Union have brought about a flowering of Greek cultural, religious, and ethnic institutions among the Greeks in the new republics of the CIS that mirror similar developments among other ethnic groups. An example of this is the Cultural Enlightenment Society of Crimean Greeks, which, by early 1991, had nearly 20,000 members. If and when general political, social, economic, and cultural opportunities widen in the new CIS, Greek communities may actually flourish with an influx of Greeks seeking such opportunities, as they had in the nineteenth century.

REFERENCES: G. Alef, "Diaspora Greeks in Moscow," *Byzantine Studies*, 6 (1979), 26–34; R. P. Bartlett, *Human Capital: The Settlement of Foreigners in Russia, 1762–1804*, 1979; S. K. Batalden, *Eugenios Voulgares in Russia, 1771–1806*, 1982; Robert Conquest, *The Nation Killers*, 1970; Robert Conquest, *The Soviet Deportation of Nationalities*, 1960; J. V. Haney, *From Italy to Muscovy: The Life and Works of Maxim the Greek*, 1973; P. Herlihy, "The Ethnic Composition of the City of Odessa in the Nineteenth Century," *Harvard Ukrainian Studies*, 1 (1977), 53–78; P. Herlihy, "Greek Merchants in Odessa in the Nineteenth Century," *Harvard Ukrainian Studies*, 3–4 (1979–1980), 399–420; V. A. Karidis, "The Formation of Greek Communities in Southern Russia, 1774–1821," *Newsletter of the Study Group on Eighteenth-Century Russia*, 5 (1977), 7–9; Walter Kolarz, *Russia and Her Colonies*, 1952; G. B. Leon, "The Greek Merchant Marine, 1453–1850," in G. B. Leon, ed., *The Greek Merchant Marine*, 1969, 469–83; W. K. Medlin and C. G. Patrinelis, *Renaissance Influences and Religious Reforms in Russia*, 1971; E. H. Minns, *Scythians and Greeks*, 1913; A. M. Nekrich, *The Punished Peoples*, 1978; D. Obolensky, *The Byzantine Commonwealth*, 1971; D. Obolensky, "Byzantium and Russia in the Late Middle Ages," in J. R. Hale, *et al.*, eds., *Europe in the Late Middle Ages*, 1965, 248–65; D. Obolensky, "Byzantium, Kiev, and Moscow: A Study in Ecclesiastical Reltions," *Dumbarton Oaks Papers*, 11 (1957), 248–65; D. Obolensky, "The Crimea and the North Before 1204," *Archivium Ponticum*, 35 (1978), 123–33; N. Pappas, *Greeks in Russian Military Service in the Late Eighteenth and Early Nineteenth Centuries*, 1991; S. Petsalis-Diomidis, "Hellenism in Southern Russia and the Ukrainian Campaign," *Balkan Studies*, 13 (1972), 221–58; D. T. Rice, *The Scythians*, 1957; M. Rostovtseff, *Iranians and Greeks in South Russia*, 1922; J. Smedley, "Archaeology and the History of Cherson," *Archivium Ponticum*, 35 (1978), 172–92; A. Solzhenitsyn, *The Gulag Archipelago*, vols. 1 and 2, 1974, 1976; T. Stoianovich, "The Conquering Balkan Orthodox Merchant," *Journal of Economic History*, 20 (1960), 234–313; Andrew L. Zapantis, *Greek-Soviet Relations, 1917–1941*, 1982.

Nicholas C. J. Pappas

GREKI. See URUM and GREEK.

GREKO. See GREEK.

GRUZIAN. See GEORGIAN.

GRUZIN. See GEORGIAN.

GRUZINSKIY EVREI. See GEORGIAN JEW and JEW.

GRUZINSKIY IEVREI. See GEORGIAN JEW and JEW.

GRUZINSKIY YEVREI. See GEORGIAN JEW and JEW.

GRUZINSKIY YEVREY. See GEORGIAN JEW and JEW.

GUDAUT. The Gudaut are a subgroup of the Bzyb*, who themselves are one of the constituent groups of the Abkhaz* peoples. See ABKHAZ.
REFERENCE: Ronald Wixman, *The Peoples of the USSR: An Ethnographic Handbook*, 1984.

GUDAUTI. See GUDAUT and ABKHAZ.

GUDAUTY. See GADAUT AND ABKHAZ.

GUNEI. See LEZGIN.

GUNZEBI. See KHUNZAL and AVAR.

GUNZIB. See KHUNZAL and AVAR.

GUNZIBI. See KHUNZAL and AVAR.

GUNZIBTSY. See KHUNZAL and AVAR.

GURANI. See KURD.

GURI. The Guri, who call themselves the Guruli, are a subgroup of the Georgians*. The Guri are Eastern Orthodox and are concentrated demographically near the lower Rioni River in Georgia. See GEORGIAN.
REFERENCE: Ronald Wixman, *The Peoples of the USSR: An Ethnographic Handbook*, 1984.

GURIAN. See GURI and GEORGIAN.

GURULI. See GURI and GEORGIAN.

GUTSUL. See HUTSUL, CARPATHO-RUSYN, and UKRAINIAN.

GYPSY. The Gypsies are a unique ethnic group. They are often known as Tsiganes. Although anthropologists continue to debate their origins, the dominant interpretation holds that they emerged from northern India, that they spread out to the north and west, and that their language—Romany—has ancient ties to Sanskrit. Today, Gypsies can be found all over the world, and most of them retain a remarkable sense of identity. The ancestors of those who ended up in Europe spent extended periods of time in Afghanistan and Turkey. Europeans first recorded the presence of Gypsies in Crete in 1322, Corfu in 1346, and Germany in the early 1400s. The name "Gypsies" was attached to them because some of the earliest Gypsies claimed to be Christians from "Little Egypt." Other names have also been applied to the Gypsies, depending upon which part of North Africa, Europe, the Near East, the Middle East, or Asia they were living in. Even the earliest records from the fourteenth century comment on the powerful sense of identity that the Gypsies maintain, as well as their exaggerated sense of self-protection and self-preservation as a cultural group.

Among the most remarkable characteristics of the Gypsy life-style is their nomadism of a very unusual sort. Although other nomadic ethnic groups tend to confine their wanderings to a particular economic habitat and overwhelmingly to rural areas, Gypsy nomadism has assumed global dimensions and has been adapted to urban, industrial settings. In terms of language and religion, the nomadic Gypsies tend to adopt the religion and language of their host society, but most of them still speak Romany and maintain an elaborate Gypsy folk culture. Historically, the Gypsies earned their living trading horses, manufacturing violins, working as coppersmiths and blacksmiths, training animals, telling fortunes, and selling trade goods. Socially, the Gypsies are divided into tribal groups, each with its own dialect and individual sense of identity.

In the former Soviet Union, approximately half of the Gypsies are Muslim and half are Eastern Orthodox. The Muslims are Sunnis of the Hanafi school. Whether Christian or Muslim, the Gypsies are only superficially loyal to organized, institutional religion, and they preserve many of their pre-Christian and pre-Islamic rites and beliefs. For the most part, Gypsies tend to keep their own company, preferring to marry endogamously and confine intimate social contacts only to other Gypsies.

Because of their powerful ethnic identity, unique language, nomadism, and economic life-style, the Gypsies have aroused considerable hostility among non-Gypsy groups; indeed they still do. That suspicion of and dislike for Gypsies reached genocidal proportions during World War II when Nazi Germany targeted the Gypsies as undesirables, in the same category as the mentally ill, the retarded, homosexuals, and Jews.* While more than six million Jews died in the Holocaust, approximately 500,000 Gypsies suffered the same fate. The Gypsies in the Soviet Union were not spared. When the German* armies swept into the Soviet Union in 1941, Gypsies were shot alongside Jews; later in the war, when the Germans constructed the death camps in Poland, Gypsies were shipped there along with Jews. Those who survived did so by fleeing Nazi-held territories or blending into the surrounding population.

The Central Asian Gypsies* call themselves Mugi or Mughat. That term is often qualified by a regional location, such as Mughat Samarkandi or Mughat Bukhori. They are known as Dzhugi or Mazang to the Tajiks*, Luli to the Uzbeks*, and *Sredneaziatskije tsygany* to Russians*. Unlike Gypsy groups located farther to the west, the Central Asian Gypsies have lost their Romany language and speak either Tajik or Uzbek. Most of them are also devout Sunni Muslims. The Central Asian Gypsies continued their migratory ways, making their living by peddling, fortune-telling, begging, singing, and dancing, until the 1930s, when Soviet policies insisted on settling them. Most of them settled into Gypsy quarters in major cities. As a result increasing numbers of Central Asian Gypsies were incorporated into the larger industrial economy. They number approximately 12,000 people.

Today there are approximately 225,000 Gypsies in what used to be the Soviet Union; this figure represents a large increase from roughly 130,000 people in 1959. Although they are widely scattered throughout the republics, from the European West to Siberia and down into the southern reaches of the country, they live primarily in the major cities. They call themselves the Rom, Tsygan, or Mugi/Mughat. They tend to divide into subgroups or tribes based on clan affiliations, geographic loyalties, or occupational groupings. Each of those groups, except for the Central Asian Gypsies, speaks a peculiar Romany dialect. In addition to these mainline, Romany-speaking Gypsies, there are two more distantly related Gypsy groups. In Armenia, the Bosha* Gypsies speak Armenian* instead of Romany and are far more assimilated; they live on the border between the Azerbaijan and Armenia. The Tajik-speaking Central Asian Gypsies retain some Romany words but are still very distinct from mainline Gypsy groups.

They have adopted Tajik or Uzbek as their first language. Those who speak Tajik are identified as Jugis. Because of the power of the state in the former Soviet Union and its need to control population movements, official government policy discouraged Gypsy nomadism and worked to concentrate them into permanent urban life-styles.

The political and economic instability that characterized life in the Soviet Union and then the Commonwealth of Independent States in the late 1980s and early 1990s brought new problems to Gypsies. Nationalistic rivalries erupted all over the country, and older ethnic rivalries and resentments were revived. As people began looking for scapegoats to explain their economic plight, the Gypsies again became targets for renewed rounds of hostility and persecution. Anti-Gypsy rioting spread from place to place, with the most serious occurring in Odessa in mid–1992; there the local officials labeled the Gypsies "dirty vermin."
REFERENCES: Shirin Akiner, *Islamic Peoples of the Soviet Union*, 1983; Zoltan Barany, "Democratic Changes Bring Mixed Blessings for Gypsies," *RFE/RL Research Report*, 1 (May 15, 1992), 40–47; Konrad Bercovici, *The Story of the Gypsies*, 1975; *The Current Digest* 44 (June 17, 1992), 23; Rena C. Gropper, *Gypsies in the City: Cultural Patterns and Survival*, 1975; Denis Harvey, *The Gypsies: Wagon Time and After*, 1980; Charles G. Leland, *The English Gypsies and Their Language*, 1980; Judith Okely, *The Traveller-Gypsies*, 1983; Ronald Wixman, *The Peoples of the USSR: An Ethnographic Handbook*, 1984; Jan Yoors, *The Gypsies*, 1983.

GYPSY OF CENTRAL ASIA. See CENTRAL ASIAN GYPSY and GYPSY.

H

HAI. See ARMENIAN.

HAIDAK. See KAITAK and DARGIN.

HAIDAQ. See KAITAK and DARGIN.

HAITAK. See KAITAK and DARGIN.

HAITAQ. See KAITAK and DARGIN.

HAKASS. See KHAKASS.

HALHA. See KHALKHA.

HALHA MONGOL. See KHALKHA.

HANDISEW. See ANDI and AVAR.

HANSU. See HANSU DUNGAN and DUNGAN.

HANSU DUNGAN. The Hansu Dungan, who call themselves the Khansui, are one of the subgroups that comprise the Dungan* people of the Commonwealth of Independent States. They originally migrated from Hansu Province in China, and they speak a Hansu dialect of Mandarin Chinese. They are Sunni Muslim in their religious loyalties and live in the Osh Oblast of Kyrgyzia. See DUNGAN.
REFERENCES: Svetlana Rimsky-Korsakoff Dyer, "Muslim Life in Soviet Russia: The Case of the Dungans," *Journal of the Institute of Muslim Minority Affairs*, 3 (1981), 42–54; Ronald Wixman, *The Peoples of the USSR: An Ethnographic Handbook*, 1984.

HANSUI. See HANSU DUNGAN and DUNGAN.

HANSUY. See HANSU DUNGAN and DUNGAN.

HANT. See KHANT.

HANTAIKA. See KHANTAIKA SAMOYED.

HANTAIKA SAMODI. See KHANTAIKA SAMOYED.

HANTAIKA SAMOED. See KHANTAIKA SAMOYED.

HANTAIKA SAMOIED. See KHANTAIKA SAMOYED.

HANTAIKA SAMOYED. See KHANTAIKA SAMOYED.

HANTAYKA. See KHANTAIKA SAMOYED.

HANTAYKA SAMODI. See KHANTAIKA SAMOYED.

HANTAYKA SAMOED. See KHANTAIKA SAMOYED.

HANTAYKA SAMOIED. See KHANTAIKA SAMOYED.

HANTAYKA SAMOYED. See KHANTAIKA SAMOYED.

HANTE. See KHANT.

HAPUT. See GAPUT, SHAH DAGH, and AZERBAIJANI.

HAPUTLIN. See GAPUT, SHAH DAGH, and AZERBAIJANI.

HAQASS. See KHAKASS.

HARDURI. See KHARDURI and TAJIK.

HASIDIC JEW. See JEW.

HATUKAI. See KHATUKAI, ADYGHE, and CIRCASSIAN.

HATUKAY. See KHATUKAI, ADYGHE, and CIRCASSIAN.

HATUQAI. See KHATUKAI, ADYGHE, and CIRCASSIAN.

HATUQAY. See KHATUKAI, ADYGHE, and CIRCASSIAN.

HAYDAK. See KAITAK and DARGIN.

HAYDAQ. See KAITAK and DARGIN.

HAYTAK. See KAITAK and DARGIN.

HAYTAQ. See KAITAK and DARGIN.

HAZARA. See KHAZARA and TAJIK.

HEMSHIL. See KHEMSIL, ARMENIAN, MESKHETIAN, and AZERBAI-JANI.

HEMSHILI. See KHEMSIL, ARMENIAN, MESKHETIAN, and AZERBAI-JANI.

HEMSHIN. See KHEMSIL, ARMENIAN, MESKHETIAN, and AZERBAI-JANI.

HEVSUR. See KHEVSUR and GEORGIAN.

HIGHLAND MARI. See MARI.

HINALUG. See KHINALUG, SHAH DAGH, and AZERBAIJANI.

HINALUGH. See KHINALUG, SHAH DAGH, and AZERBAIJANI.

HINALUKH. See KHINALUG, SHAH DAGH, and AZERBAIJANI.

HITRI. See KHITRI and CHUVASH.

HIURKILI. See DARGIN.

HOLAM. See KHOLAM and BALKAR.

HOLAMCHI. See KHOLAM and BALKAR.

HOLAMCHILI. See KHOLAM and BALKAR.

HOLAMCHY. See KHOLAM and BALKAR.

HOLAMCHYLY. See KHOLAM and BALKAR.

HOLAMLI. See KHOLAM and BALKAR.

HOLAMLY. See KHOLAM and BALKAR.

HONGODOR. See KHONGODOR and BURYAT.

HORA. See KHORIN and BURYAT.

HORIN. See KHORIN and BURYAT.

HORVAT. See UKRAINIAN.

HOSHEUT. See KHOSHEUT and KALMYK.

HUF. See KHUF, RUSHAN and TAJIK.

HUFIDJ. See KHUF, RUSHAN, and TAJIK.

HUFIDZH. See KHUF, RUSHAN, and TAJIK.

HUFIJ. See KHUF, RUSHAN, and TAJIK.

HUIZU. See DUNGAN.

HULAM. See KHOLAM and BALKAR.

HULAMCHI. See KHOLAM and BALKAR.

HULAMCHILI. See KHOLAM and BALKAR.

HULAMCHY. See KHOLAM and BALKAR.

HULAMCHYLY. See KHOLAM and BALKAR.

HULAMLI. See KHOLAM and BALKAR.

HULAMLY. See KHOLAM and BALKAR.

HUNGARIAN. See MAGYAR.

HUNZAL. See KHUNZAL and AVAR.

HURKILI. See DARGIN.

HUTSUL. The Hutsuls, who call themselves the Hutsuly and who are known to Russians* as Gutsul, are a subgroup of Carpatho-Rusyns*. They are Christian in religion but divided between Eastern Orthodox and Uniate Catholic. The Hutsuls live in the highlands of Ivano-Frankovsk, Chernovits, and Zakarpatskaya oblasts in western Ukraine. They still speak their dialect as a native language, and, unlike the other groups of western Ukrainians, the Hutsuls still identify themselves as Hutsuls, not as Rusyns. See UKRAINIAN and CARPATHO-RUSYN.

REFERENCES: Alexander Bonkalo, *The Rusyns*, 1990; Paul Robert Magocsi, *The Rusyn-Ukrainians of Czechoslovakia*, 1983, and *The Shaping of a National Identity: Subcarpathian Rus', 1848–1948*, 1979; Ronald Wixman, *The Peoples of the USSR: An Ethnographic Handbook*, 1984.

HVARSHI. See KHWARSHI and AVAR.

HVARSHIN. See KHWARSHI and AVAR.

HWARSHI. See KWARSHI and AVAR.

HWARSHIN. See KHWARSHI and AVAR.

HYURKILI. See DARGIN.

I

IAGE. See YAGE DUNGAN and DUNGAN.

IAGE-DUNGAN. See YAGE DUNGAN and DUNGAN.

IAGNOB. See YAGNOB and TAJIK.

IAKUT. See YAKUT.

IAKUTIANE. See YAKUTYAN and RUSSIAN.

IARA. See YARA, KACHA, and KHAKASS.

IARIN. See YARA, KACHA, and KHAKASS.

IARKENDLIK. See YARKENLIK and UIGUR.

IARKENLIK. See YARKENLIK and UIGUR.

IASTA. See YASTA, KACHA, and KHAKASS.

IASTIN. See YASTA, KACHA, and KHAKASS.

IATVIAG. See BELARUSIAN.

IATVIG. See BELARUSIAN.

IATVIGIAN. See BELARUSIAN.

IATVING. See BELARUSIAN.

IATVINGIAN. See BELARUSIAN.

IAZGUL. See YAZGULEM and TAJIK.

IAZGULEM. See YAZGULEM and TAJIK.

IAZGULIAM. See YAZGULEM and TAJIK.

IAZVA. See YAZVA, KOMI-PERMYAK, and KOMI.

IAZVA KOMI PERMYAK. See YAZVA, KOMI-PERMYAK, and KOMI.

IAZVA ZIRIAN. See YAZVA, KOMI-PERMYAK, and KOMI.

IAZVA ZYRIAN. See YAZVA, KOMI-PERMYAK, and KOMI.

IAZVA ZYRYAN. See YAZVA, KOMI-PERMYAK, and KOMI.

IAZVIN. See YAZVA, KOMI-PERMYAK, and KOMI.

IAZVIN KOMI PERMYAK. See YAZVA, KOMI-PERMYAK, and KOMI.

IAZVIN ZIRIAN. See YAZVA, KOMI-PERMYAK, and KOMI.

IAZVIN ZYRIAN. See YAZVA, KOMI-PERMYAK, and KOMI.

IAZVIN ZYRYAN. See YAZVA, KOMI-PERMYAK, and KOMI.

IAZVINSKY. See YAZVA, KOMI-PERMYAK, and KOMI.

IAZVINSKY KOMI PERMYAK. See YAZVA, KOMI-PERMYAK, and KOMI.

IAZVINSKY ZIRIAN. See YAZVA, KOMI-PERMYAK, and KOMI.

IAZVINSKY ZYRIAN. See YAZVA, KOMI-PERMYAK, and KOMI.

IAZVINSKY ZYRYAN. See YAZVA, KOMI-PERMYAK, and KOMI.

ICHIGE. See SAGAI and KHAKASS.

ICHKILIK. The Ichkilik, who have also been known as the Pamir-Alai Kyrgyz, are today considered a subgroup of the Kyrgyz*, although their identity is very decentralized. Those people, who collectively call themselves Ichkilik, are actually very conscious of their sub-Ichkilik identities. The tribes who make up the Ichkilik are the Kypchak*, Naiman, Teut, Kesek, Zhoo Kesek, Kangdy,

Boston, Noigut, Avagat, and Tooloos. Most of them breed yaks in the Pamir-Alai Mountains of Kyrgizia. See KYRGYZ.

REFERERNCE: Ronald Wixman, *The Peoples of the USSR: An Ethnographic Handbook*, 1984.

IDARAW HEKWA. See TINDI and AVAR.

IDARI. See TINDI and AVAR.

IDERA. See TINDI and AVAR.

IDERIN. See TINDI and AVAR.

IDERINTSY. See TINDI and AVAR.

IENISEI. See KET.

IENISEI OSTYAK. See KET.

IENISEI SAMODI. See ENT.

IENISEI SAMOED. See ENT.

IENISEI SAMOIED. See ENT.

IENISEI SAMOYED. See ENT.

IENISEI TATAR. See KHAKASS.

IEZID. See YEZID and KURD.

IGIN. See KYZYL and KHAKASS.

IGUANI. See ESTONIAN.

IJEM. See KOMI.

IMBAT. See KET.

IMERELI. The Imereli are one of the tribal groups that consolidated into the Georgian* people. They maintain a distinct identity with an identifiable dialect and live along the Tskhenis-Tskali River as well as in the Caucasus, Suram, and Adzharo-Akhaltsikh mountain ranges in Georgia. See GEORGIAN.

REFERENCE: Ronald Wixman, *The Peoples of the USSR: An Ethnographic Handbook*, 1984.

IMERETIAN. See GEORGIAN.

IMERLIAN. See GEORGIAN.

INARI. See LAPP.

INBAK. See KET.

INDIAN. Until its 1989 census, the Soviet Union did not track, or at least did not publish, the number of foreign residents by nationality group. The 1989 census did provide these figures. It indicated that in 1989 there were 2,614 Indians and Pakistanis living in the Soviet Union; Indians constituted approximately half of that group. Ever since the Bolshevik Revolution, there had been Indians living in the Soviet Union. Most were expatriates infatuated with Marxism and the Communist experiment, but there was never any significant move by Indians to change their citizenship and live their lives in the Soviet Union. After World War II, with the Cold War between the United States and the Soviet Union gaining momentum, the Soviet Union provided financial aid to bring Indian students to Moscow to study in an attempt to build its power base in South Asia. More recently, there have also been a few Indians who, for economic reasons, were strongly interested in improving their business relationship with the Soviet Union. Most Indians living in the Soviet Union in the late 1980s were students and businessmen.
REFERENCE: Raymond E. Zickel, ed., *Soviet Union: A Country Study*, 1991.

INDIGIRKA. See EVEN.

INGERMANLAND. See IZHORA.

INGERMANLAND FINNS. See IZHORA.

INGERMANLANDIAN. See IZHORA.

INGHILOI. See INGILOI, GEORGIAN, and AZERBAIJANI.

INGHILOY. See INGILOI, GEORGIAN, and AZERBAIJANI.

INGILO. See INGILOI, GEORGIAN, and AZERBAIJANI.

INGILOI. Since 1926, the Ingiloi (Inkiloi) have been listed as a subgroup of the Georgians* by Soviet and Russian* ethnologists. They call themselves the Ingilo and are known to Russians as Ingilojtsy. They speak the Kakhetian* dialect of the Georgian language, but they have borrowed heavily from Azeri for their vocabulary. The main difference between the Georgians and the Ingiloi is religion. Early in the seventeenth century, Shah Abbas I of Persia introduced Islam into the region, and the Ingiloi became loyal Shiites. The Ottomans later occupied Transcaucasia and converted some Ingilois to the Hanafi school of the Sunni Muslim faith. Since then, the Ingilois have fallen under Azerbaijani* influence and are now overwhelmingly loyal to the Shiite tradition. Still, when Russia formally took control of eastern Georgia in 1801, some of the Ingilois converted back to Christianity.

Today, the Ingilois number approximately 5,000 people and live in the Kasum, Ismailly, Tauz, and Shamkhor districts of the Azerbaijan republic. Most of them work in the silk and canning industries. The Ingilois are becoming increasingly assimilated with Azerbaijanis. They now use Azeri as their literary language and have high rates of intermarriage with Azerbaijanis. See GEORGIAN and AZERBAIJANI.

REFERENCES: Shirin Akiner, *Islamic Peoples of the Soviet Union*, 1983; Alexandre Bennigsen and S. Enders Wimbush, *Muslims of the Soviet Empire: A Guide*, 1986; Ronald Wixman, *The Peoples of the USSR: An Ethnographic Handbook*, 1984.

INGILOJTSY. See INGILOI, GEORGIAN, and AZERBAIJANI.

INGILOY. See INGILOI, GEORGIAN, and AZERBAIJANI.

INGRIAN. See IZHORA.

INGUSH. The Ingush are an Islamic people of the north-central Caucasus who are very closely related to the Chechens*. Like the Chechens, they identify themselves as the Nakhchuo people, although they have also been known historically as the Galgai*, Lamur, Mountaineers*, and Kist*. According to Soviet authorities, the Ingush have been designated merely a "sub-nationality," even though the Chechens are considered a "nation." Like the Chechens, the Ingush are indigenous to the Caucaus range and speak a dialect of the Nakh group of the Caucasian language family. They describe themselves as members of the Galgai tribe of the Nakh people.* Ingushetia, as their region is informally called, constitutes the westernmost part of the Chechen-Ingush Autonomous Republic in Russia.

The main differences between the Chechens and the Ingush arose because of their different experiences with Russian* colonization. The Ingush are descendants of the western Nakh people, primarily the Galgai and Feappi* clan federations, who were more peacefully inclined toward the Russians than were the Chechens, who are the eastern Nakh people. The Fortanga River has traditionally been the dividing line between them. Another difference is that many Ingush were still Christian in the late eighteenth century, when they were brought into the orbit of the expanding tsarist empire (though all are Sunni Muslim now). During the 1860s, when large-scale ethnic Russian penetration of the Caucasus began, the western Nakh were passive about the arrival of the newcomers, while the eastern Nakh resisted violently. At that point, the Russians began referring to the eastern and western Nakh as different peoples. The western Nakh became known as Ingush, while the eastern Nakh became known as Chechen. Russian historians claim that the Ingush "voluntarily became Russian subjects," which probably indicates their lack of resistance rather than any genuine enthusiasm for the tsar. Whereas the Chechen were driven off the plain and into the mountains, the Ingush were encouraged to come down from the mountains and settle on the plain. The Ingush took little part in the bitter Imam Shamil uprising from 1834 to 1858, which stamped a permanent mark on the Chechens.

The Ingush were treated as poorly by the Soviets as their Chechen relatives. Ingushetia was merged into the Mountain (Gorskaya) People's Autonomous Republic in 1920, then hived off as the Ingush Autonomous Oblast in 1924, and then merged into the Chechen-Ingush Autonomous Soviet Socialist Republic in 1934. During the great Stalinist purges of the 1930s, most Ingush intellectual leaders were slaughtered and the Ingush literary language was outlawed. Bolshevik attempts to suppress Islam backfired. In response to government attempts to close mosques, deport Islamic leaders, outlaw arranged marriages, and prohibit Muslim funerals, the Ingush simply became more closely identified, both personally as well as politically, with their own Islamic faith and with the loyalties of the anti-Russian Chechen. Josef Stalin's crude collectivization campaigns in the late 1920s and 1930s only reinforced those feelings.

When Nazi Germany invaded Soviet Russia and German* troops neared the Caucasian oilfields, the Ingush were found on both sides. Their less-than-perfect record of loyalty to the Soviet homeland resulted in the mass deportation of Ingush and Chechens in February 1944. The 1939 census had counted 318,000 Chechens and 74,000 Ingush, but, in 1944, they were all taken by train to scattered locations across the steppes of northern Kazakhstan, where their culture and language were supposed to die out. Their autonomous region was abolished, without a word appearing in the press until two years later. At that time, the Supreme Soviet announced that many Chechens had joined volunteer units organized by the Germans while the "main population took no counter-action against the betrayers of the Fatherland." More recent Russian scholars estimate that the number of Chechen and Ingush who were actually deported was probably around 478,000 people.

The Ingush internal exile lasted thirteen years, until, along with seven other deported nations, they were rehabilitated in 1957 at the Twentieth Party Congress. The deportations and mass suffering that they experienced during World War II and in the late 1940s and early 1950s sharpened their anti-Russian sentiments, making them almost as anti-Russian as the Chechen had long been. Even in their diaspora, the Ingush had clung to their language, religion, and customs, and their birthrate was sufficiently high that their population more than doubled, from 74,000 in 1926 to 158,000 in 1970. The 1989 Soviet census placed the Ingush population at 237,557 people. Chechen-Ingush was declared to be once again a literary language, and newspapers in the Chechen-Ingush language reappeared. Resettlement to their homeland proceeded gradually, but, naturally, there were problems. Daghestani* families (Avars* and Dargins*) had in the meantime been moved into Ingush and Chechen villages; now those people in turn had to be expelled. Moscow again arbitrarily redrew the borders of Chechen-Ingushetia, so that its land area would henceforth be 19,300 square kilometers. The Ingush had clung tenaciously to Islam during their exile. Official Soviet sources estimated in 1975 that fully half the Chechen and Ingush population belonged to Sufi brotherhoods. Mosques were reopened in 1978. Many Chechens and Ingush have openly defied Soviet authorities by making pilgramages to the tombs of past religious and military heroes.

Glasnost encouraged Chechens and Ingush to demand increased autonomy. Mikhail Gorbachev was far more willing than any of his predecessors to tolerate political questioning and even political protest. Many Soviet nationalities therefore began demanding more information about Stalin-era excesses or protesting what they did know about what had happened. In 1989, the Chechen-Ingush Regional Committee in the Soviet Union began openly protesting the tragedy that had befallen them under Stalin, and Soviet authorities tolerated their public demands. In the turmoil that followed the failed military coup in Moscow in August 1991, they declared independence. This represented a direct threat to the territorial integrity not only of the Soviet Union but also of the Russian Federation itself, of which the Chechen-Ingush Autonomous Republic is a constituent part. Demonstrators knocked down a statue of V. I. Lenin in Grozny, blockaded KGB headquarters, and seized radio and television stations. A retired Chechen bomber pilot named General Dzhokhar Dudayev arose as a political strongman. He seized control of Chechenia on September 6, 1991, and was elected president on October 27. Dudayev claimed the support of 5,000 soldiers and 62,000 volunteers. The old enmity between Chechens and Russians reappeared as a high-stakes showdown between Dudayev and Russian President Boris Yeltsin, who declared emergency rule and sent 1,000 Interior Ministry troops to Grozny, only to have them withdrawn a few days later. In November 1991, Dudayev threatened to sever the Moscow-Baku highway and to launch terrorist attacks on Russian nuclear power stations, unless Chechen independence were recognized. Dudayev's words would have sounded familiar to Kunta Haji or Sheikh Mansur: "Why should our mothers cry, our old people cry, why should our children cry and live in so much fear? Why shouldn't Russia, which is where this evil is coming from, feel fear?" Dudayev raised the prospect of a Caucasian Federation to unite all the north Caucasus mountaineers from the Black Sea to the Caspian, and he appealed to Iran and Turkey for support.

It is questionable whether the Ingush feel nationalistic yet. Their self-identification tends to be either sub-national (tribal or clan loyalties) or supra-national (Muslim faith), but this may change. In 1989, an Ingush deputy to the Congress of People's Deputies presented an appeal that he claimed had 60,000 signatures—an absolute majority of the Ingush people—for full rehabilitation and "all national rights." If the Chechens should succeed in their drive for independence from Russia, the Ingush might seek their own homeland as well, so as not to be dominated by Chechens, who outnumber them four to one. There was some movement in that direction in 1991, when the Soviet Union agreed to divide Chechen-Ingushetia into two separate regions—Chechenia and Ingushetia.

There is some friction between the Ingush and their neighbors to the West, the Ossetians*, because when the Ingush returned from their internal exile in the 1960s, they found that Ossetians had occupied former Ingush land. In fact, the Ingush lay claim to half of the North Ossetian capital of Vladikavkaz. They also argue that the Prigorodny region of North Ossetia is their historic homeland. Ossetians do not accept that claim, and, throughout 1992, there was sporadic fighting in the region between Ossetian and Ingush militiamen. Several hundred people were killed in the fighting during 1992.

REFERENCES: Nikolai Fedorovich Bugai, "The Truth About the Deportation of the Chechen and Ingush Peoples," *Soviet Studies in History*, 30 (Fall 1991), 22–30; Robert Conquest, ed., *Soviet Nationalities Policy in Practice*, 1967; Bernhard Geiger, et al., *The Russian Conquest of the Caucasus*, 1908; Oleg Glebov and John Crowfoot, eds., *The Soviet Empire: Its Nations Speak*, 1989; *New York Times*, November 6, 1992; Hugh Seton-Watson, *The Russian Empire, 1801–1917*, 1957; Bohdan Nahaylo and Victor Swoboda, *Soviet Disunion: A History of the Nationalities Problem in the USSR*, 1989.

Ross Marlay

INKAROISET. See IZHORA.

INKERI. See IZHORA.

INKERIKOT. See IZHORA.

INKEROISET. See IZHORA.

INKHIES. See KHWARSHI and AVAR.

INKHOKARI. See KHWARSHI and AVAR.

INKILOI. See INGILOI, GEORGIAN, and AZERBAIJANI.

INKILOY. See INGILOI, GEORGIAN, and AZERBAIJANI.

INUIT. See ESKIMO.

INVEN. See KOMI.

IOKANG. See LAPP.

IOMUD. See YOMUD and TURKMEN.

IOMUT. See YOMUD and TURKMEN.

IR. See IRON and OSSETIAN.

IRANI. See PERSIAN.

IRANTSY. See PERSIAN.

IRKIT. See SAGAI and KHAKASS.

IRON. The Iron are a small ethnic group who are part of the larger group of Ossetian* peoples. They speak one of the three Ossetian dialects, and the Iron dialect is used as the Ossetian literary language. The Iron live primarily in the central and eastern regions of the North Ossetian Autonomous Republic. Unlike the Digor*, who are Muslim North Ossetians, the Iron are Eastern Orthodox in their religious loyalties. These Iron should not be confused with another group of people sometimes known as Iron—the Ironis*, who are Shiite Muslims and live in such Central Asian cities as Bukhara. See OSSETIAN.
REFERENCES: Alexandre Bennigsen and S. Enders Wimbush, *Muslims of the Soviet Empire: A Guide*, 1986; Ronald Wixman, *The Peoples of the USSR: An Ethnographic Handbook*, 1984.

IRONI. The Ironis are a small ethnic group of approximately 35,000 people who today live primarily in Uzbekistan and Turkmenistan. In 1785, Emir Shah Murad of Bukhara seized a number of Persian*-speaking Iranians in the area of Mary in southeast Turkmenistan and placed them into Bukharan* slavery. Over the years, their descendants mixed with merchant colonies that had originated in Iran but settled in Central Asia to do business. These communities also absorbed some Beluchi* people and other Shiites. They all became known generically as Ironis. For them, their religious consciousness as Shiite Muslims of the Ja'farite rite is far more important to their ethnic identity than any sense of political nationalism.
   Until 1910, the Shiite Ironis functioned comfortably in the larger Sunni Muslim communities of Central Asia. That year, a series of mutual massacres took place between Sunnis and Shiites in Bukhara; in response, the Ironis isolated themselves physically and socially, condemning marriages between Sunnis and Shiites and confining their contacts to those required for commercial and political exchanges. That strong sense of identity still survived in the 1980s, although some assimilation by neighboring Uzbeks* and Turkmen* was occurring. Most of the Ironis living in Uzbekistan speak Uzbek, while only a minority in Turk-

menistan speak Turkmen. These Ironis should not be confused with the Irons who live in the North Caucasus and are Eastern Orthodox North Ossetians*.
REFERENCES: Shirin Akiner, *Islamic Peoples of the Soviet Union*, 1983; Alexandre Bennigsen and S. Enders Wimbush, *Muslims of the Soviet Empire: A Guide*, 1986.

IRONTSY. See IRON.

IRONY. See OSSETIAN.

IRTISH TATAR. See IRTYSH TATAR and TATAR.

IRTYSH TATAR. The Irtysh Tatars are part of the larger collection of Siberian Tatars* and live in settlements along the Irtysh River in southern Siberia. The Siberian Tatars originated with the Mongol* invasion of Russia in the thirteenth century. They were converted to the Sunni Muslim faith, Hanafi school, by Islamic merchants in the fourteenth and fifteenth centuries. That conversion process among the Siberian Tatars continued for the next five centuries. Incoming Russian settlers drove the Irtysh Tatars off the best lands in the sixteenth century, and they then resettled at their present location. Until the nineteenth century, most of the Irtysh Tatars were hunters and trappers, going after sable, fox, marten, ermine, bear, and wolf. When industrialization began to reach Siberia, some Irtysh Tatars went to work in factories, tanneries, and sawmills. After the 1930s, most of the Irtysh found themselves living and laboring on collective farms. They numbered approximately 20,000 people in the 1970s they were in a state of rapid assimilation with surrounding Russians. See TATAR.
REFERENCE: Shirin Akiner, *Islamic Peoples of the Soviet Union*, 1983.

IRTYSH-KONDA. See KHANT.

IRY. See OSSETIAN.

ISHIM. See TARA TATAR.

ISHKASHMI. The Ishkashmi (Ishkashimi), who call themselves the Shikoshumi (Shikomshi), are one of the collective group known as Pamir peoples*. Russians* refer to them as the Ishkashimtsy. Like most other Pamir, they are Ismaili Muslim in religion. They are concentrated in one village in the Gorno-Badakhshan Autonomous Oblast in southeastern Tajikistan. See TAJIK or PAMIR PEOPLES.
REFERENCES: Shirin Akiner, *Islamic Peoples of the Soviet Union*, 1983; Ronald Wixman, *The Peoples of the USSR: An Ethnographic Handbook*, 1984.

ITALIAN. Until its 1989 census, the Soviet Union did not track, or at least did not publish, the number of foreign residents by nationality group. The 1989 census did provide these figures, and it indicated that in 1989 there were 1,942 Italians living in the Soviet Union. Ever since the Bolshevik Revolution, there had been Italians living in the Soviet Union. Most were expatriates infatuated with Marxism and the Communist experiment, but there was never any significant movement of Italians to change their citizenship and live their lives in the Soviet Union. There were other Italians who, for economic reasons, were very interested in improving their business relationship with the Soviet Union. As disillusionment with the Communist Party mounted during the Gorbachev era in the 1980s and early 1990s, in the Soviet Union as well as in Italy, the numbers of expatriates declined. As Mikhail Gorbachev welcomed European capital and technological expertise, however, the number of Italians permanently residing in the Soviet Union increased. Of the 1,942 Italians living in the Soviet Union in 1989, most were business people hoping to establish an economic foothold there.
REFERENCE: Raymond E. Zickel, ed., *Soviet Union: A Country Study*, 1991.

ITELMEN. The Itelmen are a tiny ethnic group located primarily on the Kamchatka Peninsula in Russia. They call themselves the Itel'men, although some Russians* refer to them as the Kamchadals*. Neighboring groups like the Chuchkis* or Koryaks* have referred to the Itelmen as the Khonchalo or the Nymylan*. In terms of their ethnic ancestry, the Itelmen are closely related to the Chukchi and Koryak people. In fact, the Itelmen language is mutually intelligible with Chukchi and Koryak; the three languages together constitute the Chukotic language group, which is part of the larger Paleo-Asiatic family of languages. Although the Itelmen population was listed at more than 4,000 people in the Soviet census of 1920, it has steadily declined since then, primarily because of high rates of intermarriage with ethnic Russians. By the late 1980s, the Soviet census bureau listed the Itelmen population at approximately 1,400 people.

The first Russian contact with the Itelmen came in 1697, when the Atlasov expedition contacted them and managed to collect a fur tax. At the time, the Itelmen were in a neolithic stage of development and lived in villages located in the southern reaches of the Kamchatka Peninsula. They fished along the major rivers, especially along the Kamchatka River, and they hunted seal, fur seal, and sea beaver. Some of the Itelmen, especially the southernmost ones, also hunted whales. Although meat from fish and game animals provided the bulk of their caloric intake, the Itelmen also ranged widely on foraging expeditions in search of berries, nuts, and herbs. In terms of their social and political life, the Itelmen lived a communal existence, with each village being inhabited by a single clan. They practiced a polytheistic, animist religion, in which the primary deities were extensions of the animals that they hunted. The Itelmen also worshiped a variety of mountain, forest, and ocean spirits, all of whom, they believed, had to be appeased in order to maintain balance and harmony in life.

The indigenous Itelmen life-style began to end in the early eighteenth century when the Russian government decided to exploit the fur potential of the Kamchatka Peninsula. At the time, the Itelmen were located throughout much of the Kamchatka Peninsula, as well as on the Kurile Islands and on Cape Lopatka. They constituted three specific groups, based on modest linguistic differences. The northern Itelmen lived on the Kamchatka River and the east coast of the peninsula south to the Nalachevaya River. The southern Itelmen lived in villages stretching from the Nalachevaya River down the coast to Cape Lopatka. Finally, the western Itelmen lived on the west coast of the Kamchatka Peninsula. They were divided into two subgroups—the Sedanka and the Khayryuzovo. Russian traders and Russian Orthodox missionaries soon entered Itelmen territory.

The influx of government officials, merchants, and Christian missionaries destabilized Itelmen society. Like many other indigenous people in their first encounters with Western Europeans, the Itelmen suffered from both epidemic diseases and the effects of the widespread distribution of alcohol. Between 1737 and 1781, the Itelmen population declined from more than 7,000 people to fewer than 3,000. Because far more Itelmen men than women died during those decades and because the rape of Itelmen women by Cossack* troops and government officials was so common, the surviving Itelmen were increasingly of mixed Russian-Itelmen ancestry. Large numbers of Russian peasant settlers married Itelmen women and "went native," living like other Itelmen while retaining their use of the Russian language. By 1800, there were relatively few full-blood Itelmen still alive. By 1820, only 1,900 people claimed to be Itelmen, and their life-style based on log cabins and dried fish was virtually the same as that of the surrounding Russians.

Because of the structure of Itelmen society, Russians had found it relatively easy to subdue them. The Itelmen had no chiefs, tribal governments, or organizations, so it was virtually impossible for them to sustain any type of political resistance. The rebellions in 1706, 1711, 1731, and 1742 were violent, but the Russians easily managed to suppress them. The Itelmen also suffered from the destruction of their environment. Russian hunters and their Itelmen employees hunted the sables, foxes, and sea otters to near extinction, destroying a traditional part of Itelmen economic life. The presence of fur trappers and merchants also introduced the Itelmen to a commercial economy and to metal trade goods; in the process, the Itelmen were slowly incorporated into a larger economy.

After the Russian Revolution of 1917 and the subsequent civil war, the Itelmen were even more intimately integrated into the workings of the new Communist state. Itelmen villages were organized into fishing and hunting cooperatives in the 1920s, and, by the 1930s, most Itelmen children were attending state schools in which Russian was the language of instruction. Increasing numbers of Itelmen began to raise cattle and produce potatoes and hay on communal farms, using equipment belonging to the state.

The distinctive Itelmen populations in northern and southern Kamchatka and on the Kurile Islands did not survive. Beginning in the late eighteenth century, the Russian government relocated thousands of Cossacks and ethnic Russian soldiers and peasants to the Kamchatka Peninsula. A good number of them married Itelmen women, and their offspring became known as Kamchadals. Similarly, the Itelmen on the Kurile Islands and on the east coast at Cape Lopatka intermarried with the Ainu* people, and their offspring became known as Near Kurilers*.

In the post-World War II years, Itelmen society continued to lose its indigenous trappings. Their original homeland in the Kamchatka River Valley was completely overrun by ethnic Russians, and the Itelmen themselves had become overwhelmingly mixed-blood Russian speakers (Kamchadals). Only 350 Itelmen even spoke their native language anymore, and they were concentrated near Tigil on the west coast of the Kamchatka Peninsula. More than 96 percent of those claiming to be Itelmen or Kamchadals in the 1980s were fluent in Russian or used Russian as their native language. Soviet policy also declared a number of Itelmen villages to be "non-viable" in the 1950s and relocated the Itelmen residents to larger communities. Hundreds of Itelmen became migrant workers, to whom Russians derisively referred as "state welfare pensioners"—burdens to socialist society. In spite of the cultural and linguistic assimilation, however, the Itelmen retained a distinct sense of identity in the 1980s.

The cataclysmic political events that shook the Soviet Union in 1991 had only a slight effect on the Itelmen. The Itelmen had not developed any identifiable sense of political nationalism in the twentieth century, so Mikhail Gorbachev's policies of *glasnost* and *perestroika* did not unleash any groundswell of sentiment for independence. The assimilation of the Itelmen had proceeded far past that issue. In fact, the likelihood of an accelerated process of assimilation was quite high because of the premium that President Boris Yeltsin of the Russian Republic placed on economic development in the wake of the collapse of the Soviet Union. In order to earn desperately needed hard currency, Russia began importing Western technology and Western engineers, and ethnic Russians began pouring into Siberia to exploit its natural resources. The increasing pace of industrial development doomed the Itelmen to complete assimilation.

In spite of the pressures for assimilation, however, the Itelmen did try to organize to promote their interests in the early 1990s. They joined such interest groups as the Association of Peoples of the North (APN) to try to achieve environmental protection and control over natural resources. Itelmen leaders began proposing tribal control over the Kamchatka Peninsula and requiring the Soviet Union (and, after 1991, Russia) to sign lucrative, short-term leases before any new extractive industries could be developed in the region.

REFERENCES: V. V. Antropova, "The Itel'mens," in M. G. Levin and L. P. Potapov, *The Peoples of Siberia*, 1964, 876–82; Alice Bartels and Dennis Bartels, "Soviet Policy Toward Siberian Native People," *Canadian Dimension*, 19 (1985), 33–47; James Forsyth, *A History of the Peoples of Siberia*, 1992; Walter Kolarz, *Peoples of the Soviet Far East*, 1954; Andrew Steiger, "Stone Age Peoples in the Age of the Airplane," *Pacific Affairs*, 14 (June 1941), 207–14; Ronald Wixman, *The Peoples of the USSR: An Ethnographic Handbook*, 1984; Alan Wood, ed., *Siberia: Problems and Prospects for Regional Development*, 1987.

ITEL'MEN. See ITELMEN.

ITKAN. The Itkan are one of the many Koryak* subgroups. They are concentrated on the east side of the Taigonos Peninsula in the Koryak Autonomous Oblast of eastern Siberia. See KORYAK.
REFERENCE: Ronald Wixman, *The Peoples of the USSR: An Ethnographic Handbook*, 1984.

ITKANA. See KORYAK.

ITKANSKY. See KORYAK.

IUG. See KET.

IUGO OSET. See OSSETIAN.

IUGO OSETIN. See OSSETIAN.

IUGRI. See UGRIAN PEOPLES and FINNO-UGRIAN PEOPLES.

IUGRIAN. See UGRIAN PEOPLES and FINNO-UGRIAN PEOPLES.

IUIT. See ESKIMO.

IUITI. See ESKIMO.

IUITY. See ESKIMO.

IUKAGHIR. See YUKAGIR.

IUKAGIR. See YUKAGIR.

IURAK SAMODI. See NENETS.

IURAK SAMOED. See NENETS.

IURAK SAMOIED. See NENETS.

IURAK SAMOYED. See NENETS.

IZHEM. See IZHMI and KOMI.

IZHEMTSY. See IZHMI and KOMI.

IZHMI. The Izhmi, who call themselves the Izva Tas and who have also been known as the Izhem or Izhmy, are one of the Komi* subgroups. They possess a distinct sense of identity and their own distinctive dialect. Approximately 11,000 Izhmi live in the Yamalo-Nenets Autonomous Oblast and the Tjumen Oblast. See KOMI.

REFERENCE: Ronald Wixman, *The Peoples of the USSR: An Ethnographic Handbook*, 1984.

IZHMY. See IZHMI and KOMI.

IZHOR. See IZHORA.

IZHORA. The Izhora are one of the Soviet Union's smallest ethnic groups. They call themselves the Karjala or Karjalainen (Karyala or Karyalainen) and have also been known historically as the Ingrian, Inkeri, Ingermanlandian, Inkeroiset, Inkaroiset, and Inkerikot. The Izhoras were once part of the Finno-Ugrian peoples* who had originated in Central Asia and eventually evolved into such groups as the Finns*, Estonians*, Magyars*, Mordvinians*, Lapps*, and Permians. Over the course of several centuries, most Finns developed trading relationships which were stronger with the Swedes in the west than with the Slavs in the east. Those trading connections eventually gave the Finns an orientation more toward northern and western Europe than to eastern Europe. The more highly concentrated Swedes gradually established political control over the Finns. Roman Catholic missionaries, with Swedish military protection, brought Christianity to the polytheistic, animist Finns in the thirteenth century. In the sixteenth century, when Lutheranism swept through Sweden and displaced Roman Catholicism, Swedish missionaries carried the new religion to Finland as well.

There were a smaller group of Finns, however, who were located farther to the east who came under Russian* Slavic influence. The eastern Finns, who are known as Karelians* (Korela, Karyala) and call themselves the Karjala (Karjalainen), historically were heavily influenced by Russian culture. They live in Karelia, a region bounded by Finland to the west, the Murmansk region to the north, the White Sea and the area of Archangel to the east, and the Leningrad region to the south. Because of their proximity to Novgorodian Russians, they adopted the Eastern Orthodox religion instead of Lutheranism. During the eleventh and twelfth centuries, a small group of Karelians left the main region of Karelian settlement and migrated south to lands along the Izhora River. They still referred to themselves as Karelians and spoke their Balto-Finnic* language. It was not until the twentieth century that they came to call themselves the Izhoras, after the river where they had settled; they are also sometimes known as Ingermanland Finns. By that time the Izhoras were beginning a rapid decline. There were more than 21,000 Izhoras in 1890, but those numbers dropped to 16,000 in 1926, 1,062 in 1959, and only 750 by the early 1980s. See FINN and KARELIAN.

REFERENCE: Ronald Wixman, *The Peoples of the USSR: An Ethnographic Handbook*, 1984.

IZVA TAS. See KOMI.

J

JAGNOB. See YAGNOB and TAJIK.

JAGNOBI. See YAGNOB and TAJIK.

JAGNOBTSY. See YAGNOB and TAJIK.

JALUTOROVSKI TATAR. The Jalutorovoski Tatars are part of the larger collection of Siberian Tatars*. They live today near the towns of Jalutorovsk in southern Siberia. They were converted to the Sunni Muslim faith, Hanafi rite, by Islamic merchants in the beginning of the fourteenth century, and that conversion process continued for the next five centuries. Russians finally conquered the region late in the sixteenth century. Incoming Russian* settlers drove the Jalutorovski Tatars off the best lands, and they resettled at their present location. Until the nineteenth century, most of the Jalutorovski Tatars were hunters and trappers, going after sable, fox, marten, ermine, bears, and wolves. When industrialization began to reach Siberia, some Jalutorovski Tatars went to work in factories, tanneries, and sawmills. After the 1930s, most of the Jalutorovski Tatars found themselves living and laboring on collective farms. They are in a state of rapid assimilation with the surrounding Russians. See TATAR.
REFERENCE: Shirin Akiner, *Islamic Peoples of the Soviet Union*, 1983.

JAMBULAK. See NOGAI.

JAMSHID. See DZHEMSHID.

JAPANESE. Soviet census takers did not begin separating out foreign residents by ethnic group until the 1989 census. At that time, they listed the number of Japanese residents at 691. Ever since the eighteenth century, the Russian* government had been interested in expanding the Russian Empire at the expense of the Japanese, and Japan was just as interested in guaranteeing that its geo-political interests were not compromised by Russia. At the beginning of the nineteenth century, there were 2,061 ethnic Japanese living in the region of Vladivostok; that number had increased to over 4,000 by 1909. The Bolshevik Revolution in 1917 created such economic and political turmoil in Siberia that most of the ethnic Japanese soon returned home to Japan. Those left behind were primarily students or political revolutionaries anxious to learn about Marxism-Leninism. The number of Japanese residents fell dramatically during World War II.

As a result of the Yalta and Potsdam conferences in 1945, the Soviet Union secured the right to annex the southern portion of Sakhalin Island and the Kurile Islands, which they did when the war ended. That action brought several hundred-thousand Japanese peasants, workers, and fisherman under Soviet control. Russians and Japanese had been disputing control of those areas for more than a century. With Sakhalin under Soviet control, Josef Stalin's government insisted on the evacuation of the Japanese residents of the area. Russian, Ukrainian*, Belarusian*, and Kazakh* workers were imported to replace the evacuating Japanese. A similar demographic phenomenon occurred in the Kurile Islands and on the Kamchatka Peninsula. Soviet-Japanese relations remained strained after the war, since the Japanese continued to lay claim to the southern portion of Sakhalin Island, which had been granted to them in 1905 after the Russo-Japanese War but given back to the Soviet Union in 1946.

Not until the 1970s and 1980s did the Japanese population of the Soviet Union begin to increase, and then it was primarily an economic phenomenon. Japanese corporations were interested in exploiting Siberian natural resources, and the Soviets were increasingly willing to consider Japanese financial assistance. Most of the Japanese businessmen living in the Soviet Union resided in Moscow, St. Petersburg, and Vladivostok; a few Ainu* from Japan periodically visited in Sakhalin as well. When the Soviet Union disintegrated in 1991, Japanese hopes for the return of their former possessions in the Kuriles and Sakhalin escalated, but ethnic Russians on the Kurile Islands began reviving Cossack* groups to defend Russian interests there.

REFERENCES: Walter Kolarz, *The Peoples of the Soviet Far East*, 1969; Raymond E. Zickel, *Soviet Union: A Country Study*, 1989.

JATVIG. See BELARUSIAN.

JATVIGIAN. See BELARUSIAN.

JATVING. See BELARUSIAN.

JATVINGIAN. See BELARUSIAN.

JATVJAG. See BELARUSIAN.

JAZGULAMTSY. See YAZGULEM, TAJIK, and PAMIR PEOPLES.

JAZGULEMTSY. See YAZGULEM, TAJIK, and PAMIR PEOPLES.

JEKOS. See YAKUT.

JERERUKOI. See CHERKESS.

JERERUKOJ. See CHERKESS.

JEW. This entry discusses various groups of Jews who all had a fully developed Jewish identity and inhabited parts of what became the Russian Empire and the Soviet Union. Discussing the groups chronologically, it covers Caucasian Jewry (including Georgian Jews* Daghestani or Mountain Jews*), Crimean Jews, the Khazars, the Karaites (or Karaim*), Central Asian/Bukharan Jews, and finally, Ashkenazic Jews. Once these Jews became part of the Russian Empire, the entry covers policies commonly applied to Jews up through the demise of the Soviet Union at the end of 1991.

Caucasian Jewry

For present purposes, the Caucasus includes the mountainous region between the Black and Caspian seas and regions to the north: Azerbaijan, Armenia, Georgia, and the oblasts and guberniias of Daghestan, Kutaisk, Tersk, Kuban, Elizavetopol, Kersk, and the Black Sea.

Although the history of Caucasian Jewry is over 2,000 years old, it is difficult to date its origin with certainty. Traditions among Caucasian Jews claim descent from the ten tribes of Israel, some of whom came to the area after the defeat of Israel by the Assyrians* in the eighth century B.C. Others believe that Jews came to the area after the Babylonian destruction of Judah and the First Temple in 586 B.C.; still others date the Jewish presence from the destruction of the Second Temple in 67 A.D. Jews were definitely in the area in pre-Christian times. Both in Armenia and Georgia, certain important aristocratic families (such as the Bagratuni in Armenia) considered themselves descendants of earlier Jewish settlers. The Sassanid Persians* also played a role; it is believed that, in the 400s A.D., Jewish immigrants came from northern Persia, adding to the Jews who had settled in the region earlier.

From these migrations ultimately emerged two main types of native Caucasian Jews—Georgian and Mountain (or Daghestan) Jews. The Georgian Jews, called Ebraeli, spoke a slightly archaic Georgian and were scarcely distinguishable from other Georgians* in appearance or manners. Aside from a collection of rabbinical decisions, the Georgian Jews produced no real literature. As their name indicates, they were found mostly in Georgia.

Mountain Jews (also called Dag Chufut) lived in the areas of Daghestan, Tersk, the Kuban, Baku, and Elizavetopol. Their language was Judeo-Tat (or Hebrew-Tat), a variant of a Tatar* tongue from Persia; it was similar both phonetically and morphologically to Persian, though influenced both by Hebrew and Turkish over time. Judeo-Tat was written with Hebrew letters.

Religiously, the Mountain Jews appear to have picked up certain un-Jewish ideas on demonology (as Muslims in the area apparently did). Thus, they believed in good and evil spirits that waged constant warfare and held power over people and nature. (The struggle between good and evil was central to Persian Zoroastrianism, whence these ideas may have reached the Caucasus.) Among the spirits, some visible and others invisible, were Ozhdegoe-Mar (the home spirit), Ser-Ovi (water), Shegadu (uncleanliness), Kessen-boi (autumn and spring), Zemirei (rain), and Idor (the spirit of government). The Mountain Jews produced some liturgical and cabalistic manuscripts, although the first printed book in Judeo-Tat appeared only in 1909.

The Mountain Jews were noted for their hospitality. Their homes (*sakli*) usually had three rooms, one for men, another for women and children, and the third—the most highly decorated—for guests. Women were considered distinctly subordinate to males, similar to the Muslims. Mountain Jews engaged mostly in agriculture, petty trade, and handicrafts.

In the seventh to the tenth centuries, the Khazar state included the northern part of the Caucasus. Some scholars speculate that the Khazar ruling elite may have gotten their Judaism from the Mountain Jews. Still a third type of Jews in the Caucasus were known as Subbotniki, or Sabbatarians. Apparently few in number (in 1897, there were only thirty such families in Tbilisi and some additional families in the area), they were perhaps descendants of the Khazars. While very traditional religiously, they later used Russian instead of Hebrew once the Russians* had conquered the Khazar state. Other Caucasian Jews disdained marriage with the Subbotniki.

The rise of Islam had an impact on the Caucasus and its Jews, who came under Muslim influence. Many Caucasian Jews apparently were compelled to convert to Islam, and, once the Khazar state fell, it no longer served as a refuge for oppressed Jews. In the process of conversion and intermarriage, the Jews left their mark on the area. Some native tribes, such as the Khevsurs*, Svanetians*, and Lezgins*, are believed to be of Jewish descent, and the Muslim Tats* included families who had preserved Hebrew books as family heirlooms. Some Ossetian* villages bore Hebrew names, and their marriage and funeral rites resembled those of Jews. The same may also be said of the Chechens*. Not all Jews converted, however. Guillaume de Rubrique found a ''large'' Jewish population in the eastern Caucasus in 1254, and Benjamin of Tudela reported in the preceding century that the Caucasian Jews were under the religious authority of the exilarch in Baghdad.

Little information on Caucasian Jews is available from the coming of the Mongols* in the thirteenth century to that of the Russians at the end of the eighteenth. Travelers who reported on the Jews said that their position was difficult and characterized by poor treatment from both Muslims and Christians, leading to additional conversions. The appearance of the Russians in the late eighteenth and early nineteenth centuries increased pressure on the Jews by the Muslims. That the pressure was greater from the Muslim side can be seen in politics. Mountain Jews increasingly sided with the Russians, obviously hoping for better treatment. Georgian Jews, on the other hand, were always pro-Georgian.

After 1799, the Caucasus increasingly came under Russian control. In 1804, the government permitted Jewish residence in the Caucasus Guberniia and the right to own land, but the rabidly anti-Semitic Nicholas I (reigned 1825–1855) decreed in 1827 that no Jews could live in the Caucasus. Local authorities appealed the policy, at first to no avail, arguing that the Jews were "people who are so useful here, and so . . . necessary both for the military and civilian officials as well as the natives themselves." Finally, in 1837, the government decreed that native Jews (i.e, Georgian and Mountain Jews) could reside in the Caucasus. Still, Caucasian Jews could live in no other part of the empire, and Jews from other parts of the empire could not move to the Caucasus.

Conditions changed under Alexander II (reigned 1855–1881). After 1860, Jewish merchants were permitted to reside in the Caucasus, as could Jews from elsewhere in the empire. Jewish merchants played an important role in the development and marketing of Baku oil. The Rothschilds founded the Caspian-Black Sea Company, and 44 percent of kerosene production and at least as large a share in the marketing of oil products was in Jewish hands in 1913–1914.

The influx of non-native Jews was such that, by the 1897 census, most of the Jews in the Caucasus were Ashkenazim. Of the 56,773 Jews then in the Caucasus, 7,038 (12.4 percent) were Mountain Jews, 6,034 (10.6 percent) were Georgian Jews, and almost all the rest (43,390, or 76.4 percent) were Ashkenazim, listing Yiddish as their native language. The largest concentrations of Jews were in Baku Gubernia (12,753), Daghestan Oblast (10,056), Tbilisi Gubernia (9,710), Kutaisk Gubernia (8,864), and Tersk Oblast (6,576). Of Jews in the Caucasus, most were engaged in trade (39.7 percent), industry (22.8 percent), the army (10 percent), and agriculture (6.5 percent, mostly in Daghestan).

The Soviet period saw a crackdown on all religions, including Judaism. As late as 1959, before the two post–1967 waves of Jewish emigration, there were 125,000 Jews in the Caucasus, of whom 35,000 were Georgian Jews and 25,000 Mountain Jews. The largest concentrations of Jews in that year were in Baku (26,623) and Tbilisi (17,311). The Jewish religion fared best in Georgia; around 1960, it was estimated that sixteen of the remaining sixty or so synagogues in the Soviet Union were in Georgia.

Crimean Jewry

Crimean Jewry's origins also extend back at least 2,000 years and are equally subject to debate. Local Jewish legend says the Crimean Jews are descendants of the Ten Tribes of Israel and reached Crimea after the Assyrian conquest of Israel in 722 B.C. This is unlikely. The earliest documented settlement is of Hellenized Jews in the first century B.C.; it is possible that some Jews fled to the Crimea after the defeat of the Bar Kochba revolt in the second century A.D. Other Jews probably arrived in the following centuries from other parts of the Near East, especially from Byzantium.

Whatever their origins, these Jews and their later Khazar co-Jews formed the so-called Krymchak*, the first of three types of Jews who would live in the Crimea. The Krymchaks came to speak a Chagatai/Tatar* dialect written with Hebrew letters, into which they may have translated parts of the Bible and some prayers. In most ways, they became indistinguishable from other Tatars* in later times.

The Krymchaks were traditional rabbinical/Talmudic Jews. Over the centuries, however, they used different liturgies, which led to religious disputes. In the sixteenth century, Rabbi Moses ben Jakob Hagole, originally brought from Kiev as a prisoner, convinced the various Krymchak groups to accept a liturgy used by the "Roman" (i.e., Byzantine) Jews, as opposed to that of the Babylonian Jews.

A second group of Jews associated with the Crimea were the Karaites. Although the nineteenth-century Karaite historian A. Firkovich tried to show that the Karaites had been in the Crimea from earliest times, in reality they probably came to the Crimea from Byzantium in the twelfth and thirteenth centuries. Although Karaites also spoke the Jagatai dialect and were similar to other Crimeans, Jews and non-Jews, they were different religiously and, under the Russians and Nazis, faced a fate different from that of the traditional Jews.

Third, after the Crimea became part of the Russian Empire in 1783, there was an influx of Ashkenazic Jews. By the late nineteenth century, these Jews formed a majority of Crimea's Jewish population.

At the beginning of the seventh century, when the Khazars secured a foothold in the eastern Crimea, they found many Jews already there. The Byzantine chronicler Theophanes the Confessor noted in 671 that numerous Hebrews lived near Phanagoria, east of the straits, and were a majority of the population in and about Sam-Karsh, an important trading center located west of the straits. Most of the Crimea was part of the Khazar kingdom from the seventh to the tenth centuries. Some historians have speculated that the Khazars accepted their Judaism from the Krymchaks (or, again, from the Caucasian Jews). It is likely that the toleration of the Jewish Khazars led to an influx of more Jews into the Crimea, most likely escaping oppression in the Byzantine Empire.

The Khazar kingdom began to decline in the tenth century, and a combined Byzantine-Russian attack led to the end of Khazar rule in the Crimea in 1016. There is little information about Jews in these centuries. It is probable, however, that the Jewish population declined and that some of the Jews might have gone or been taken to Russia. In Western Europe, the area continued to be known as Khazaria, or Gazaria, into the fifteenth and sixteenth centuries.

The Mongols* took most of the Crimea in 1236, but the western shore remained under the control of Genoa from 1263 until 1475. There were Jews in each portion. The largest Crimean Jewish community under Genoese rule was Kaffa;

one fifteenth-century traveler may have exaggerated when he said there were 4,000 Jewish homes there. The Mongols were at first tolerant about religion, and evidence of some conversions to Judaism among the Mongol elite would explain the strategic strongholds that the Mongols gave to Jews (especially to Karaites) in the Crimea. Most prominent of these was the unfortified "Jews' Fortress" at the new capital of Bagche-Saray (Bakhchisarai). The third Mongol/Tatar ruler, Berke, converted to Islam in 1258, beginning the Islamicization of the Crimea.

The process continued in 1475, when the Ottoman Turks* conquered the entire Crimea, which they held for the next 408 years. Both Krymchaks and Karaites were treated the same by the Ottoman Turks, and the Jewish communities received various charters (in 1598, 1608, 1625, 1682, and 1728) from the Muslim rulers confirming their rights. The Turks changed the trading routes, however, and Crimean Jews increasingly turned to agricultural pursuits. The Krymchak and Karaite Jewish communities survived under the Muslims, and, despite their religious differences, recognized their common heritage. There is some speculation that the so-called "Judaizer heresy" at the court of Ivan III in the late fifteenth century had its origins with Crimean Jews.

It is likely that Muslim persecution and conversions reduced the Jewish population over the centuries. Some Krymchaks may have moved to the Polish-Lithuanian kingdom when Ashkenazic rule was at its apogee there (1500–1648). In any case, when Russians acquired Crimea in 1783, there was a total of 469 families (Karaite and Krymchak) on the peninsula. In 1791, the authorities included Crimea in the Pale of Settlement, although major centers of development were forbidden to Jews, such as the military port of Sevastopol. This policy was eased somewhat, especially for wealthier merchants, in the second half of the nineteenth century. Most other Crimean Jews earned their livelihood as artisans/handicraftsmen or as agriculturalists.

One major change under Russian rule was the differentiation that the Russians made between Krymchaks and Karaites. The Russians clearly favored the Karaites. This led to a deep split in the Crimean Jewish community that had never before existed. A second change, especially after 1860, was the influx of Ashkenazi Jews from elsewhere in the empire, although the Krymchaks did not intermarry with them until the twentieth century.

The total number of Jews in the Crimea remained small. In 1897, there were 28,703 Jews, or 5.1 percent of the total population. Of these, 5,400 (19 percent) were Karaites, 3,300 (11.5 percent) were Krymchaks, and almost all the remainder (almost 70 percent) were Ashkenazim. The largest Jewish communities were in Simferopol (8,951), Kerch (4,774), Sevastopol (3,910), Karasubazar (also called Belogorsk; 3,144, nearly all Krymchaks), and Feodosiia (3,109).

Under Soviet rule, there were a few key developments. First, the Crimean Jews were included with other Soviet Jews, but in the first decade that did not lead to a decline in numbers. Indeed, the Jewish population of the Crimea was 39,921 in 1926, or 6.1 percent of the total. The largest community by far was Simferopol, with 17,364 Jews. Second, the Communists sought to place more

Jews on the land, at times with aid from the American Jewish Joint Distribution Committee. Although Birobidzhan (see below) replaced the idea of a Jewish Soviet Socialist Republic in the Crimea by 1931, the government had allocated 845,000 acres of land for Jews, on which 5,150 Jewish families had already settled. By 1938, there were eighty-six Jewish collective farms, with 20,000 Jews farming 392,000 acres.

The Nazis occupied the Crimea in 1941, destroyed the Jewish collectives and communities, and annihilated Ashkenazim and Krymchaks, but not Karaites. A Nazi report of early 1942 stated that 20,149 Jews from the western Crimea had been annihilated. On April 16, 1942, the Nazis declared the Crimea *Judenrein* (free of Jews).

Jewish life returned somewhat after World War II. By 1959, there were 26,374 Jews in the Crimea, although they now represented only 2.2 percent of the total population. Of these, 11,200 lived in Simferopol. In 1970, there were estimated to be 15,000 Jews in Simferopol and 8,000 to 10,000 Jews in Evpatoriia. It is not possible to break this down into Krymchak, Karaite, and Ashkenazic communities.

Khazars

The ethnic and religious origins of the Khazars are unclear. Nevertheless, the medieval Khazar Jewish state was the only Jewish state in the world between the fall of the Second Temple in 67 A.D. and the formation of Israel in 1948. It is therefore of great interest and significance in Jewish history.

The Khazars were probably a Turkish people who may have been related to the Volga Bulgars* and may have been an admixture of various peoples from the Volga region or further east. The first mention of them was in 627 by Theophanes, who wrote of "the Turks from the East whom they call Khazars." They might earlier have been called Akatsiri, a group that was allied with Byzantium against Attila the Hun as early as the fifth century. Later, the Khazars fought alongside Byzantium against the Persians and then the Arabs.* In the latter 500s, the Khazars moved westward, establishing themselves on the Sea of Azov, the Don, the lower Volga, the Caspian Sea, and the northern Caucasus.

Arab expansion pushed the Khazars northward in 725. Although the extent of the Khazar state between the seventh and tenth centuries has been disputed, generally their territory is believed to have included the Crimea, Caucasus, Volga, and Caspian regions. According to the Russian chronicles, however, tribes further west—the Poliane, Severiani, and Viatichians—paid tribute to the Khazars as late as 859, and the Viatichians at least until 964. The Khazars may even have occupied Kiev for a while. The Khazars called their king *chagan* and their queen *chatoun*. Their capital by the tenth century was Atel or Itel, located about eight miles from modern Astrakhan on the right bank of the Volga. For a long time, the kings remained semi-nomadic, wintering in the capital and spending the remainder of the year on the move. The Khazar state played a major role in the politics of the area, entering into marriage alliances even with

Byzantium. A Khazar princess, for instance, married the Byzantine Emperor Constantine V; their son was Leo IV the Khazar (reigned 775–780). Although long an ally of the Byzantines, it appears that the Khazar conversion to Judaism, combined with the anti-Jewish policy of various Byzantine rulers, hastened the end of that alliance.

Although one scholar has dated the conversion of the Khazar elite to Judaism as early as 620, it appears to have occurred later, probably between 740 and 809 A.D. Since the Khazar state included both the Crimea and the Caucasus, most scholars surmise that Khazar Judaism came from one or both of these areas. Although much evidence makes it clear that the Khazar state did become a Jewish state, the main source of information for the conversion itself is the so-called "Khazar Correspondence" of the tenth century, first published in 1577. It consists of two letters. The first is from the well-known Hisdai ibn Shaprut, the Jewish foreign minister of the Sultan of Córdoba, asking King Joseph about the Jewish Khazars, about whom he had heard. The second is a response from King Joseph, answering Hisdai's questions and discussing the conversion to Judaism. Although some scholars consider the letters, both written in Hebrew, a later forgery, others point out references to the letters in Jewish books beginning in the eleventh century, and the very different style of the two letters supports their veracity.

According to King Joseph, the conversion took place at an undated time under the Khazar King Bulan. Judaism remained weak in the state until the time of King Obadiah, who, by inviting in Jewish scholars and founding synagogues and schools, reinvigorated the religion, so that all subsequent Khazar rulers were Jewish. The Khazar Jewish religion was probably never very strong, nor is the claim that the Khazars were Karaites likely. Karaism did not become strong in the Crimea until a later date and was never strong in the Caucasus, which are the most likely sources of Khazar Judaism. The extent of the conversion is also subject to debate. Some Muslim writers have claimed that only the king and upper nobility were Jewish and that the vast majority of the Khazar people were Christians, Muslims, and heathens. Other historians have argued that most of the population was Jewish. The truth is probably in between. In any event, it seems likely that, in the ninth century, as the religion took hold among the ruling elite, a goodly number of at least the heathens probably followed their rulers and converted.

The Khazar state was apparently a rare example in history when three major faiths—in this case Judaism, Christianity, and Islam—seem to have cohabited peacefully for a considerable period of time. Hedged in by Muslims, Byzantium, and the rising new state of Kiev Rus', the Khazar kingdom went into decline in the tenth century. In 965, the Grand Prince of Kiev, Sviatoslav, attacked the Khazars and conquered their territory west of the Sea of Azov; four years later, the Russians took the Khazar lands east of that sea. The Khazars held on to the Crimea until 1016, when a joint Byzantine-Russian expedition expelled them, ending the Khazar state altogether.

But Khazar influence outlasted their state. The Khazars seem to have played an important role in the magyarization of Hungary. The Russian chronicles, for instance, refer to the Khazars as "White Ugrians" and to the Magyars* as "Black Ugrians." The Magyars were originally subjects of the Khazars, who may have encouraged them and accompanied them westward. Magyar towns such as Kozarvar (Khazar Castle) and Kozard apparently reflect this influence, and, under the Arpad kings, from the tenth to the fourteenth centuries, the prominent Kozarvari family was probably of Khazar origin. These western Khazars mostly converted to Christianity, although, as late as 1309, the council of the Hungarian clergy forbade Christians to marry those "described as Khazars."

In what later became Russian lands, the Jews in Kiev Rus' were likely of Khazar origin. Perhaps some had settled there before the end of the Khazar state, and others after 965. The presence of Jews is attested to by the so-called Jewish Gate in Kiev. It also seems clear that there was some connection between the Khazars on the one hand and the Mountain Jews in the Caucasus and the Karaites in the Crimea on the other. This is not to say, however, as Arthur Koestler argued in the 1980s, that the Khazars were the source of Eastern European Ashkenazic Jewry, a view that has received little support.

In psychological terms, the existence of a Jewish state, at a time when Jews were scorned by both Christians and Muslims, was very heartening to Jews. The Khazar state, for instance, served as the inspiration for the famous twelfth-century work by one of the greatest medieval Jewish poets and philosophers, Judah Halevi (1075–1141). Originally written in Arabic as *Kitab al Khozari*, translated into Hebrew as *Sefer ha-Kuzari* and later into English as *The Kuzari*, this work is a defense of Judaism in the form of a debate and dialogue between a Khazar ruler and other believers.

There have never been any firm population figures for the Khazar Jews, and the disappearance of the Khazar state means that any remaining Khazar Jews became part of other Jewish groups.

Karaites/Karaism

Karaites and Karaism represent not an ethnic group so much as a religious sect within Judaism that arose in the eighth century. Founded by Anan ben David, the older brother of the Babylonian exilarch (the religious head of the large Jewish community in Babylonia/Persia), its followers were known at first as Ananites. The outstanding ninth-century representative of this new movement, often considered second in importance only to Anan, was Benjamin ben Moses Nahawendi, the first writer to use the term "Kara'im/Benei Mikra" (Scripturalists/Sons of the Scripture). In positive religious terms, Karaism represents the recognition of Scripture as the sole source of Judaism and Jewish law. In negative terms, however, Karaism rejected the Talmudic oral law, which was well in place by the eighth century and which, as rabbinism, would dominate Jewish religious life until well into the nineteenth century.

Arising in Babylonia/Persia, Karaism was at its intellectual and literary zenith there and in Arab Muslim lands in the tenth and eleventh centuries. Karaism began to decline in the East in the twelfth century. By then, the center of Karaite Judaism had shifted to Europe. A new, albeit temporary, flourishing of Karaism arose in the Byzantine Empire in the thirteenth century, connected with the Karaite scholar Aaron ben Joseph ha-Rofe (Aaron the Elder), the most important Karaite biblical exegete, who also arranged the hitherto unstable Karaite liturgy into the organized ritual still used by Karaites.

Karaite Jews probably arrived in the Crimea from Byzantium; the earliest mention of them in the Crimea dates from 1170. Additional Karaites moved to the peninsula after the Mongol conquest. According to Karaite tradition, Karaism spread to Lithuania at the end of the fourteenth century, when Prince Vitovt, having defeated the Tatars in battle in 1392, took back to Lithuania many Tatar prisoners. Among them were some Karaites, whom the prince settled in Troki (near Vilna), Lutsk, and Halicz. Apparently, these Jews continued to speak Tatar.

Although very small numerically, the Polish-Lithuanian Karaite center flowered through its connection with the vastly larger and spiritually highly developed Polish-Lithuanian rabbinic community, and it soon developed its own literary tradition. The first important Lithuanian* Karaite author was Isaac ben Abraham Troki (1533–1594), author of the anti-Christian work *Hizzuk Emunah (The Strengthening of Faith)*. After the Hmelnitsky massacres, a Karaite apologist literature developed. Around 1700, at the request of Swedish scholars, the Karaite Solmon ben Aaron Troki wrote *Appiryon Asah Lo (Appiryon Does for Him)*, on the major differences between Karaism and rabbinism. The preceding year (1699), Mordechai ben Nisan Kukizow had also written a book on Karaism, *Dod Mordechai (Mordechai's Uncle)*, at the request of a Dutch scholar, Jacob Trigland. He also wrote *Levush Mordechai (Mordechai's Garment)*, in response to questions about Karaism asked by Sweden's King Charles XII.

Crimean Karaism, which had meanwhile been intellectually and spiritually stifled under Muslim rule, revived in the eighteenth century, when a group of Karaite scholars from Lutsk (in Volhnyia) moved to the Crimea to serve as religious leaders and teachers. Best known among them was Simhah Isaac ben Moses Lutzki, a writer whose works included an apologist history of Karaism entitled *Orah Zaddikim (The Way of the Righteous)*.

Karaites, always few in number, could never have gained ascendancy over the large Polish-Lithuanian (i.e., Ashkenazic) community, whose rabbinic and Hasidic masters were extraordinarily influential and powerful. In the Crimea, by contrast, there was no similar religious elite, and Karaism flourished. Although Tatars and Polish*-Lithuanian rulers made no distinctions in their treatment of Karaites and Rabbinites, and although both groups faced the same fate in the Polish-Lithuanian state during the Hmelnitsky massacres, the incorporation of the Crimea (in 1783) and of much of the former Polish-Lithuanian state (by 1795) into the Russian Empire led to fundamental changes. These occurred over the course of seventy years, starting in 1795, when Catherine II relieved Karaite

Jews of the double tax imposed on Jews. More changes occurred under the anti-Semitic Nicholas I, who decreed in the late 1820s that Jews were liable to military service; Crimean Karaites (like the Crimean Tatars) and Polish-Lithuanian Karaites were exempted, however.

Although the 1795 decree had set up a wall between Karaites and other Jews, and although the Karaites sought greater legal rights, for a few decades the Karaites refrained from attacking rabbinite Jews. During the 1830s, however, the Karaites began to stress their differences from other Jews in direct appeals to the Russian government. Important in these efforts were such Karaites as Simhah Bobovich, the first Karaite religious leader to be recognized as such by the Russian government; the Karaite scholar Joseph Solmon ben Moses Lutzki; and especially the most eminent Karaite scholar of the nineteenth century, Abraham Firkovich (1784–1874).

Firkovich has been widely praised and condemned. On the one hand, he unearthed valuable materials on both the Karaite and rabbinic traditions that had been considered lost and that might otherwise never have come to light. On the other, he also distorted the historical truth and fabricated forgeries to promote the Karaite cause for greater legal rights and distinctions from other Jews. He was certainly the last Karaite author of distinction. The work of these Karaites was designed to convince the Russian government that Karaism itself was older than the Jewish religion (a patent falsehood); that Karaites had lived in the Crimea since the seventh century B.C. (impossible, since Karaism did not exist then); that the Karaites, therefore, had nothing to do with the murder of Jesus (correct, but other Jews could say the same); that the Jews owed their culture and Hebrew language to the Karaites (false); and that the Karaites had nothing to do with the Talmud that was so despised by anti-Semites (correct). As absurd as most of these claims were, the tsarist government accepted them, perhaps in part because the Karaites in the Crimea tended to be much wealthier and therefore represented a different socio-economic class than the Krymchaks.

In any case, the Crimean Karaites were put on an equal religious footing with Crimean Muslims in 1840 and were granted the status of an independent church. At first, there was one diocese, in Feodosiia (Crimea); a second jurisdiction was established in Troki (Polish Russia) in 1863. The Karaite clergy now had the same rights as other clergymen in the empire. The Karaites sought further distinctions in terms of their appellation. At first listed as "Jews-Karaites," they persuaded the government to rename them "Russian Karaites of the Old Testament Faith" and simply "Karaites" in 1863. The Pale of Settlement no longer applied to Karaites after 1852, and, after 1855, they could be civil servants, unlike the "Jews." Nonetheless, after the new law on universal military training was decreed in 1874, the Karaites, like all other subjects of the tsar, were liable to military service.) During World War II, the Nazis too bought into this deception, saving Karaite lives. A decree of the Nazi Ministry of Interior in January 1939 said the Karaites were not part of the Jewish religious community, because their "racial psychology" was non-Jewish. When the Nazis captured the Crimea during World War II, Karaite scholars, to save their lives, told the Nazis that they were not Jews. The Nazis not only did kill the Karaites, but even gave them favorable treatment, and some Karaites actually collaborated with the Nazis.

The Karaites always made up but the tiniest numerical portion of the Russian Empire's Jews. When Russia took the Crimea in 1783, the population included 2,400 Karaite Jews. Over a century later, in 1897, the census enumerated 12,894 Karaites in the entire empire. It is estimated there were 10,000 Karaites in the Soviet state in 1932, mostly in the Crimea, and perhaps another 2,000 Karaites elsewhere in the world.

Central Asian/Bukharan Jewry

Geographically, the area under discussion lies between the Amu-Darya and Syr-Darya rivers and is bounded by Russia, Afghanistan, and India. Once part of the Persian and Bactrian Empires, it became Muslim in the eighth century and remained so after the Mongol conquest in the thirteenth. The Russian Empire took it over in the second half of the nineteenth century and called it Russian Turkestan. In the Soviet period, it became the Bukhara Oblast of the Uzbek Soviet Socialist Republic (SSR), though the Turkmen and Tajik republics absorbed part of what had formerly been extended Bukhara.

The terms "Bukharan" and "Central Asian Jews" are roughly synonymous. The term Bukharan Jews, however, was given to these Jews later by the Ashkenazim; Central Asian Jews referred to themselves as Hebrews, Jews, or Sons of Israel. The local Muslims referred to them as Dzhugur, a term of contempt.

Although, once again, local tradition dates the origins of these Jews to the Ten Tribes of Israel, in reality, they arrived on the scene much later. Some scholars have considered Bukharan Jews to be heirs of the Babylonian Jews who migrated there after the Roman conquest of Jerusalem in the first century B.C. via Merv and Khiva/Khorezm. Others have argued that these Jews came from Persia much later, during the reign of the Sassanid Persian King Peroz (reigned 459–484 A.D.), who persecuted Jews (and Christians). Finally, according to a tradition of Bukharan Jews, they came from Persia at the beginning of the fourteenth century, which may indicate that any earlier communities had died out. Whatever the date, scholars agree on the Persian origins of Central Asian Jewry. Family names show a definite Persian influence and their language, Tajiki-Jewish, is a Persian dialect with a Turkic* admixture, similar to that spoken by other peoples in the area.

Scholars do not know the size of the Central Asian Jewish community, but it probably declined after the rise of Islam as a result of the persecution of Jews reported by numerous travelers. The Jews had to wear clothing in public that distinguished them from Muslims, often lived in ghettos, could not occupy new buildings even inside the ghetto, had to hoist rags over their homes to distinguish them from Muslim homes, had to live in homes lower than those of the Muslims, could ride donkeys but not horses or mules, could not have their evidence admitted in court cases dealing with a Muslim, and paid extra taxes. At times, there were forced conversions; these produced crypto-Jews (like the Marranos in Iberia) called "chola" or Djedidi, who were shunned by both the Muslim and Jewish communities.

Despite persecutions, Jewish communities continued to exist. They had assessors who dealt with taxes, and they elected a *nasi*, or head of community, who was confirmed by the emir, to serve as both judge for the Jews and as their representative to the emir. The rabbi, called a *hakam*, was appointed; often the rabbi also served as the *nasi*. The Russians later retained this social structure. Like their Muslim neighbors, the Jews practiced polygamy until the Russians outlawed it. At home, Jewish women could mingle freely with the men, but out of doors they dressed like Muslim women.

Central Asian Jews were rabbinate/Talmudic Jews who used the Persian liturgy. Over the centuries, their religious practices deteriorated sharply. A fundamental change occurred at the end of the eighteenth century. Joseph Maman al Maghribi (also known as Joseph ha-Ma'aravi, 1752–1823), born in Tetuan, Morocco, but living in Safed, was sent on a mission to Jewish communities to seek funds for victims of a famine in Safed. He wound up spending thirty years in Bukhara, where he revived Jewish life, introduced Jewish schools and books, replaced the old Persian liturgy with the Sephardic one, and set the stage for what would become the Bukharan Jewish spiritual center in Jerusalem at the end of the nineteenth century. As to numbers, one European missionary, J. Wolff, wrote in 1844 that there were about 10,000 Bukharan Jews, who worked mostly as dyers and silk traders.

The Russians captured Tashkent in 1866; Samarkand and much of the Bukharan Khanate then became part of the Russian Empire. Jews began to receive better treatment. Since Bukhara remained directly under the control of the emir, however, many Bukharan Jews sought to move to those parts of Turkestan that were directly under Russian control. The Russian government tried to stop that movement in 1889, decreeing that those who had moved after the Russian conquest had to live in the frontier towns of Osh, Kata-Kurgan, and Petro-Aleksandrovsk. They later extended this list to include Samarkand, Margelan, and Khokand. The government permitted other Jews of certain classes to move to Central Asia as well, though they would not dominate the Jewish population there until World War II. Most Jews grew cotton and grapes; Jews in fact dominated the trade in cotton.

The total number of Bukharan/Central Asian Jews was small. In 1897, there were 18,868 "native" Jews in Central Asia, of whom 97.9 percent were urban. The native language for 93.9 percent was Tajiki. Approximately 10,000 Jews lived in Samarkand and another 4,000 to 5,000 in Bukhara.

A distinct feature of Central Asian Jewry was its Palestinian offshoot. Begun in 1868 by wealthier Bukharan Jews who sought a spiritual center in Palestine, the movement flourished. The Bukharan Quarter was in the Rehovat section of Jerusalem. It became a publishing center for books in the Tajiki-Jewish dialect that were sent back to Bukhara; about 170 such works had been published by 1939. In 1914, there were about 1,500 Bukharan Jews (still technically Russian subjects) in Jerusalem; that number increased to 2,500 after World War I.

The Bolshevik Revolution brought many changes. In February 1917, all legal restrictions were lifted from Bukharan Jews. In March 1918, however, after the Bolsheviks came to power but before Bukhara was under their control, there were pogroms in the area. By 1921, Central Asia was pretty much in the Soviet fold. Bolshevik economic policies adversely affected the trade-oriented Central Asian Jews. The Bolsheviks sought to settle more Jews on the land; by 1932, about 3,500 had done so, though they later abandoned the villages. The Bolsheviks also formed cooperatives of Jewish artisans, which were disbanded by the late 1930s. In terms of religion, the Bolsheviks abolished Hebrew as a "dead" language and insisted that the Jews use Tajiki. At first, this was written with Hebrew letters, but later, as with other Central Asian tongues, it came to be written with Latin letters.

Although the Jewish religion suffered during the Soviet period, the number of Central Asian Jews held steady and then expanded with the resettlement of some Ashkenazic Jews to Central Asia during World War II. The 1926 census enumerated 18,698 Bukharan Jews, with 7,740 in Samarkand, 3,343 in Bukhara, 1,347 in Tashkent, and 746 in Khokand. By 1959, there were 94,344 Jews in Uzbekistan with 50,445 in Tashkent alone. Of these, however, only 19,266 (20 percent) listed Tajiki as their native language while 27,560 (29 percent) listed Yiddish; most of the remainder were also probably Ashkenazi Jews who no longer spoke Yiddish. In 1970, before the main post–1967 waves of emigration, there were 103,000 Jews in Uzbekistan.

Ashkenazic Jewry

Like the other Jewish communities that became part of the Russian Empire, Ashkenazic Jewry was also fully developed before large numbers of Ashkenazic Jews became subjects of the Russian tsar. In the Jewish world, the term "Ashkenazic Jewry" refers in general to "European" Jews, in contradistinction to "Sephardic Jews," who are associated with the Muslim world and are often considered Eastern Jews, although the large medieval Spanish Jewish community was clearly Sephardic as well.

Some have argued that the origins of the Ashkenazic community, which numerically dominated the Jewish world by the eighteenth century, were in the East. We have seen that Khazar Jews played a role in the magyarization of Hungary, and Jews remained there. It is also clear that Jews from the Crimea and Caucasus on occasion probably lived in the area that was later associated with Ashkenazic Jewry, including Kiev Rus'. Karaite Jews began the development of the Karaite community in Lithuania; this was eventually a very Ashkenazic area. Still, it seems inaccurate to attribute the rise of the large Ashkenazic community to this small number of Jews.

Rather, the origins of the Ashkenazic community were in the West, in Europe proper. In addition to the very large Jewish community in Muslim and later Christian Spain, there were Jewish communities elsewhere in Christian Europe. The expulsion of the Jews from England (1290), France (1306 and 1394), various parts of the Holy Roman Empire, and finally Spain and Portugal (1492, 1497) led some Jews to move eastward to the rising Polish-Lithuanian state, where they were welcomed by the rulers for primarily economic reasons. One important feature of this group, which testifies to its Western origin, was its unique language that became the common tongue of Central and Eastern European Ashkenazic Jewry—Yiddish. Yiddish is a language that originated in High German dialects and integrated additional vocabulary from Hebrew and Slavic tongues; it is written with Hebrew letters.

Between 1500 and 1648, the increasingly large Jewish community in the Polish-Lithuanian state replaced Spain as the demographic and spiritual center of the Jewish world. By 1650, there may have been as many as 1.5 million Jews in the new center. These Jews had a great deal of internal autonomy. Unlike the East, where Jews were concentrated largely in towns and cities, in the Polish-Lithuanian state (which included a large part of Ukraine), Jews more frequently lived in little towns called *shtetls*, which were another characteristic feature of Eastern European Ashkenazic Jewry. Finally, rabbinic Judaism and scholarship were at their zenith in the Polish-Lithuanian community. That community fell into decline—economic and spiritual—after the Hmelnitsky massacres of 1648–1654 in the Polish-Lithuanian state and its Ukrainian parts. Estimates of the number of Jews killed in these massacres range from 100,000 to 500,000; the actual number of deaths is probably closer to the lower figure, but, in any case, Polish-Lithuanian Jewry never recovered fully from this disaster.

The decline led to another development in Judaism that became characteristic of the East European Ashkenazic Jewish Community as well—Hasidism. Founded by Israel ben Eliezer (1700–1760), Hasidism is a variant of traditional Judaism but originally differed in its attitude toward the Talmud. While not rejecting the Talmud, the bedrock of rabbinic Judaism, as the Karaites did, the Hasidism believed that heartfelt emotion and faith were equally as important as Talmudic study, since the latter was not readily available to observant Jews who were in desperate economic straits after the Hmelnitsky massacres. Although it did not deviate from the rules of rabbinic Judaism, the Hasidic movement was more concerned with a joyous approach to faith and life. This philosophy spread like wildfire throughout the East European Ashkenazic world that was soon to become part of the Russian Empire.

In demographic terms, the vast majority of the Russian Empire's Jews were Ashkenazim from the moment that large numbers of Polish-Lithuanian Jews came into the Empire. The Ashkenazim comprised at least 98 percent of the empire's Jews. Thus, both tsarist and Bolshevik policy toward the Jews was essentially aimed at this Ashkenazic community.

Jews in the Russian Empire, 1783–1917

Jews had lived on territory controlled by Russians prior to the partitions of Poland, most likely the descendants of the Khazar state. Although few in number and facing the hostility of Christian clergy, they apparently encountered fewer disabilities in Kievan Rus and Mongol Russia than did Jews elsewhere in medieval Europe. That changed with the so-called "Judaizer Heresy," which reputedly tried to introduce certain Jewish practices into the Russian Orthodox church, in the late fifteenth century. By the early sixteenth century, Jews were barred from entering Russia. When Russia acquired the right bank of Ukraine in the 1670s, Jews residing there were permitted to remain. Some even moved to Moscow, establishing the nucleus of Moscow Jewry.

But, generally speaking, the ban on Jews remained until the first partition of Poland in 1772. In addition, the state began persecuting Jews. In 1727, Catherine I ordered all Jews to leave Russia without their possessions. In 1739, the Russian Senate expelled all Jews from Little Russia (i.e., Ukraine), although this totaled only 573 people. The three partitions of Poland brought almost one million (Ashkenazic) Jews into the empire. At first, Catherine II did not discriminate against the Jews and left them with the same privileges that they had enjoyed in the Polish state. Even Simon Dubnow has admitted that "in the first two decades after the occupation of White Russia the Russian government observed a comparatively liberal, at least a well-intentioned, attitude towards the Jewish question."

This policy changed toward the end of Catherine II's reign, after which conditions deteriorated for over a century, in ways that touched upon every aspect of Jewish life. First, faced with new competition, Russian merchants complained to the government, resulting in a 1791 ukase or decree establishing the Pale of Settlement, limiting Jewish domicile to the newly acquired areas, and barring Jewish settlement from traditional Russia (i.e., pre-partition Russia). The Pale of Settlement, with adjustments, remained in force until 1917; in 1897, for instance, 93.9 percent of the empire's Jews lived in the Pale, and only 208,000 out of 5.2 million Jews lived in the interior of Russia or in Finland.

Second, tsarist rule not only sought to change the structure of Jewish economic life but also led to the further economic degradation of most of the empire's Jews. Even as early as Catherine's reign, in those areas open to them, Jewish merchants had to pay taxes twice as high as those paid by non-Jews. Alexander I (reigned 1801–1825) established a committee for the amelioration of the Jews in 1802. This committee issued a report in 1804, the key section of which (Clause 34) said that after 1806 "no one among the Jews in any village or hamlet shall be permitted to hold any leases on land or to keep taverns, saloons or inns, whether under his own name or under a strange name, or to sell wine in them, or even to live in them, under any pretext whatever, except when passing through." This was the economic death knell to Jews, since upwards of 500,000 Jews made their living, directly or indirectly, from participation in the liquor, tavern, or hostelry business. Begun in 1808, the expulsions were soon stopped. Alexander established another commission, which reported in 1812 that the economic role of the Jew in the villages was not negative. Jews were not guilty of the alcoholism of the peasants, the report said, because "the root of the drinking evil is not to be found with the saloon-keeper, but in the right of distilling . . . , which constitutes the prerogative of the squires and their main source of income." The tsar, however, rejected the report and, in 1824, began to enforce Clause 34. A government report of 1837 said that "while it [that policy] has ruined the Jews, it does not in the least seem to have improved the condition of the villagers." Economic conditions did not improve. A government report of the 1880s stated that 90 percent of the Jews constituted "a proletariat living from hand to mouth, in poverty, and under the most unhygenic conditions." The 1897 census found that 23.4 percent of the Jews were unemployed.

Third, the Russian state deprived the Jews of the social and religious autonomy they had enjoyed in the Polish-Lithuanian state. Although the Kahals—Jewish communal organizations—existed, they were forced to carry out the discriminatory policies of the state. Thus, in 1827, Nicholas decreed that Jews (except for Karaites), who had heretofore been exempt, were liable to military service, and Kahals were expected to deliver the recruits. Life in the military was long (twenty-five years), totally incompatible with Jewish life, and fraught with tremendous pressure to convert to Orthodoxy. Many young Jews physically mutilated themselves to avoid military service. In 1827, Nicholas narrowed the Pale by expelling Jews from Kiev; henceforth only certain Jews could reside there, for up to six months. Nicholas decreed laws against traditional Jewish dress, against women shaving their heads before marriage, against men wearing the hairlock (or *peies*). Finally, in 1844, he even abolished the Kahals themselves.

There was a temporary reprieve under Alexander II (reigned 1855–1881). Conditions for Jews in the military were somewhat eased. After 1859, Jewish merchants of the First Guild (i.e., the richest) and foreign Jews "noted for their social position" could permanently reside in St. Petersburg and Moscow. After 1861, Jews having academic degrees *and* working for the government could reside anywhere in the empire, and, after 1879, any Jew with an academic degree, regardless of his employment, could do likewise. Merchants of the first two ranks were admitted to Kiev, and, after 1865, Jewish artisans, mechanics, and distillers could reside outside the Pale. The government permitted freer access to schools for Jews. Thus, while in 1835, only eleven out of 1,906 university students in Russia were Jewish (.005 percent), by 1881, almost 9 percent of Russian university students were Jews, higher than the Jewish percentage of the total population.

Even by the end of Alexander II's reign, however, the trend was reversed. Local government and judicial reforms had permitted Jews equal representation, but a law of 1870 said that no more than one-third of a local governing body could be Jewish, even in areas where Jews were a much larger percentage of the population. After 1880, Jews were totally excluded from those governing boards. The right of Jews to serve on juries was likewise restricted to nine western provinces with large Jewish populations.

The situation deteriorated further under the last two Romanovs, Alexander III (reigned 1881–1894) and Nicholas II (reigned 1894–1917). In 1887, the government introduced strict limits on Jewish educational access. Within the Pale, Jews could comprise no more than 10 percent of any student body, even if Jews made up 50 percent or more of the population. Outside the Pale, the limits were set at 5 percent, and in St. Petersburg and Moscow—which had the best schools—at a mere 2 percent. This policy forced Jews to become external (i.e., correspondence) students or to attend private schools where the quotas did not exist. But in the 1890s, the government extended the same percentage limits to private schools and correspondence students, a good portion of whom were Jewish.

The government also began enforcing residency requirements more rigidly and inhumanely. In 1891, the government expelled 20,000 of the 30,000 Jews living in Moscow, many of whom had lived there for decades or were sick, lame, or on stretchers, with only twenty-four to forty-eight hours notice. The list of restrictions on Jews was enormous. The Pahlen Commission, set up in 1883 to study the Jewish question, reported that "no less than 650 restrictive laws directed against the Jews may be enumerated in the Russian code, and the discriminations and disabilities implied in these laws are such that they have naturally resulted in making until now the life of an enormous majority of the Jews in Russia exceedingly onerous."

The decades after 1881 were also characterized by the fourth phenomenon typical of later Russian rule, which put Jews constantly in fear for their lives and property. These were pogroms—beatings and rioting against Jews and Jewish property. Pogroms first broke out in the spring of 1881, after the assassination of Alexander II. Government complicity was part of the phenomenon, which, over the next four decades, led to hundreds of riots by Slavs against Jews. The worst pogroms would come during the civil war in the 1918–1921 period. It is estimated that 180,000 to 200,000 Jews lost their lives in these anti-Jewish actions.

These anti-Jewish policies affected literally millions of people. Unlike other Jewish communities in the empire, whose numbers were quite small, the Ashkenazic community that had become "Russian" with the three partitions of Poland (1772, 1793, and 1795) was large from the start and increased rapidly in the nineteenth century. It is estimated that there were about 1 million Jews in the empire in 1800 (before the incorporation of the Caucasus and Central Asia, but after the incorporation of the Crimea in 1783), about 1.5 million around 1850, and 5.2 million in the 1897 census. Of that 5.2 million, 93.9 percent (4.875 million) lived in the Pale of Settlement (Ukraine, Bessarabia, Lithuania, Belarusia, and Russian Poland) and were almost exclusively Ashkenazic. That the community was increasing rapidly can be seen from the fact that, in 1897, 49.9 percent of the Jews were younger than age twenty (26.6 percent were aged one to nine, and another 23.3 percent were aged ten to nineteen).

Russian Jews reacted to these difficult conditions in a number of ways. The majority, of course, simply tried to live their lives as well as they could under difficult conditions. A second reaction, by a very large minority, was to leave the country—that is, to emigrate. Between 1881 and 1914, over 1.5 million Jews left the Russian Empire. They were responsible for the rise of modern Jewish communities in Canada, Argentina, South Africa, and the United States. They also represented the first great numeric loss to Russian Jewry, which, combined with the rise of an independent Poland after World War I, the terrible losses of the Holocaust during World War II, and the two waves of post–1967 emigration from the Soviet Union, would lead almost to the demise of Russian Jewry by the end of the twentieth century.

In 1880, there were about 250,000 Jews in the United States; forty years later, there were 3.5 million. Two-million Jews emigrated to the United States between 1880 and 1920; 1.4 million (70 percent) came from the Russian Empire. Of the 4.2 million Jews in the United States by 1928, 3.5 million (83 percent) were of Eastern European origin, and the vast majority of those were from the Russian Empire. Emigration from Russia to Ottoman Palestine, in conjunction with the rise of Zionism, was much smaller but equally important. Many Zionist leaders (such as Theodor Herzl's precursors, Perez Smolenskim and Leon Pinsker, and later leaders, such as Asher Ginzbug/Ahad Ha'am and Menachim Ussishkin) and almost all the major leaders of the state of Israel for decades after 1948 (Chaim Weizmann, David Ben-Gurion, Golda Meir, and Menachim Begin) were born in the Russian Empire.

Still a third response was to remain and actively seek reforms through political action. This was the revolutionary movement, in which Jews played an increasingly important role after 1881. Between 1880 and 1890, 579 out of 4,301 arrested revolutionaries (13 percent) were Jewish. By 1898, 19 percent of arrested revolutionaries were Jewish, and, by 1899, the figure was 25 percent (213 of 1,140 and 351 of 1,414, respectively). Jews played a prominent role in the Marxist movement that overthrew the tsarist regime in 1917. Two of the six founders of the first Russian Marxist group, the Emancipation of Labor, were Jewish: Lev Deutsch and Paul Akselrod. V. I. Lenin's closest ally at the beginning of his revolutionary career was Julius Tsederbaum, who as "Martov" would be a key leader of the Marxist Mensheviks. Leon Bronshtein (Trotsky) played a role second only to Lenin's in carrying out the Bolshevik Revolution in 1917. M. N. Pokrovsky, the leading Marxist Bolshevik historian after the revolution, estimated that 25 to 33 percent of all party organizers in the early years of the movement were of Jewish descent; none were practicing Jews, of course. The Russian Jewish minority, which the Russian government persecuted so harshly, thus had an important role in ending that repressive regime, in hopes of improving life for themselves and for non-Jews as well. It remains but to see whether those dreams materialized.

Jews in the Soviet State, 1917–1991

The Soviet period was in many ways the most paradoxical. On the one hand, the tsarist disabilities on Jews were removed, and Jews had a greater opportunity to participate in society than at any previous time in their history. And participate they did. On the other hand, many of these gains were later obliterated, and the Soviet period saw the greatest attack on the Jewish religion and Jewish life in Russian-Soviet history. This, combined with continuing anti-Semitism and tremendous demographic losses, left both the Jewish community and the Jewish religion very weak in this area by the end of Communist rule in 1991.

This paradoxical treatment reflected Lenin's and official Bolshevik views on issues such as religion, nationalism, and cultural autonomy. Lenin was certainly not anti-Semitic, but he was against the Jewish religion, against Zionism, and against Jewish cultural autonomy. Lenin opposed all three as forces that divided and embittered people; he preferred instead the concept of internationalism, of eliminating differences among people so that they could work together. All religions were sorely tested under the Communists. Zionism, a form of nationalism, also suffered, and, although the Bolsheviks initially had to make concessions in the area of cultural autonomy, within a few decades, they also rescinded this, at least for the Jews.

On the positive side, the revolution ended the Pale of Settlement and permitted Jews to reside anywhere. Although most Jews, for a variety of reasons, continued to live in the same areas, many moved on. Thus, after the expulsions of most Jews from Moscow in the early 1890s, there were only 8,473 Jewish residents of Moscow in 1897. By 1926, there were 131,000 Jews in Moscow, and, by 1940, 400,000. St. Petersburg/Leningrad, which had 17,251 Jews in 1897, had 175,000 Jews by 1940. In 1897, the 25,724 Jews in these two leading cities represented .5 percent of the Empire's Jews; by contrast the 575,000 Jews in Moscow and Leningrad in 1940 represented 19 percent of the Jews in the Soviet Union (before the inclusion of Eastern Poland and the Baltic areas at the beginning of World War II).

The tsarist period had greatly hindered educational access for Jews, and the quotas of the 1890s had especially limited their access to the best institutions. This changed dramatically after the revolution. By 1935, although Jews comprised only 1.8 percent of the total Soviet population, 13.3 percent of all students in Soviet institutions of higher learning were Jews. It is true that, by the late 1960s, Jews made up only 2.5 percent of university students, but the 2.5 percent of the late 1960s represented 110,000 Jews, while the 13.3 percent in 1935 represented only 75,000. Since the Jewish population had declined in the interim, these figures meant that an even higher percentage of Jews were attending universities in the late 1960s than had in the 1930s. To look at the figures another way, for every thousand Soviet citizens attending higher educational institutions in the late 1950s, there were seventy-two Russians but two-hundred-forty-two Jews.

Educational opportunity clearly stimulated greater participation by Jews in secular society. Within two decades of the revolution, Soviet Jews made up 10 percent of the country's professional engineers, 7.4 percent of its semi-professional engineers, 9 percent of university faculties, 10.3 percent of informational-cultural personnel (newspeople, librarians, etc.), 10.7 percent of personnel in the arts and theater, 7.7 percent of all accountants and bookkeepers, 7.7 percent of all nurses, and 15.9 percent of all physicians. This is clearly an impressive accomplishment since Jews comprised under 2 percent of the nation's total population. In 1963–1964, Jews participated as ''specialists in the national economy'' at seven times the national average rate, and as ''scientific workers'' at eight times the average rate.

With their slogan ''national in form, socialist in content,'' the Bolsheviks also extended much greater non-religious cultural autonomy to Jews. This made sense since 97 percent of the Jewish population in 1897 spoke Yiddish as its native tongue. By 1929, 56 percent of all Jewish children were studying in Yiddish-language schools, and, in the early 1930s, over 160,000 Jewish children attended the approximately 1,000 schools in which classes were conducted in Yiddish. This led to a Yiddish flowering in the arts. In 1928, 238 Yiddish-language books were published in the Soviet Union with a press run of 850,000 copies; the comparable figures for 1935 were 437 and 1,900,000. In the 1930s, there were about forty Yiddish-language journals published in the country. There was also a flowering of state-supported Yiddish theater and theater troupes.

There was even an attempt, perhaps a hope, to gather all Jews in one area. This led to the establishment of the Jewish Autonomous Region of Birobidzhan, located in a remote corner of Asia near the Manchurian border, in the Khabarovsk District. The regime encouraged Jews to settle there after 1928, and, in 1934, Birobidzhan was declared a ''Jewish Autonomous Region.'' It never developed into an important Jewish center, certainly not for all Soviet Jewry. Many Jews who came later left. Birobidzhan's Jews and Jewish life suffered the same fate as those in the rest of the Soviet Union. Not many people went there. In 1970, the entire Jewish Autonomous Region had 180,000 people, of whom only about 14,000 were Jewish.

Perhaps most noticeable was Jewish participation in politics. We have already noted Jewish participation in the revolutionary movement. This continued after the revolution. Three of the most powerful Bolsheviks in the early 1920s were of Jewish origin: Leon Trotsky (Lev Davydovich Bronshtein) Grigori Zinoviev (Hirsch Apfelbaum), and Lev Kamenev (Rosenfeld). Stalin's predecessor as General Secretary of the Bolsheviks was Yakov Sverdlov; had he not died prematurely in 1918, Stalin might never have become dictator. Other key figures of Jewish origin were Maxim Litvinov, the Deputy People's Commissar of Foreign Affairs in the 1920s and Commissar of Foreign Affairs in the 1930s, and L. M. Kaganovich, one of Stalin's closest allies.

Jewish activism was widespread. In 1927, Jews held 10.3 percent of all administrative posts in Moscow, 22.6 percent of all civil service posts in the

JEW   325

Ukraine (versus 5.5 percent of the population), and 30 percent of all civil service posts in White Russia (versus 8.2 percent of the population). Military opportunities also opened up. During World War II, there were several hundred Jewish officers at the rank of lieutenant-colonel or above, including over fifty Jewish generals.

Jews were also represented in the Communist Party in disproportionate numbers. In 1927, Jews made up 4.3 percent of the party, more than double their share of the general population. At higher echelons of the party, the percentage of Jews was even higher. Once the anti-Semitic Stalin became dictator, there were fewer Jews at the top, but, as late as 1969, there were over 210,000 Jews in the party, representing one in six adult members. The Australian expert T. H. Rigby has reported that there were, on average, fifty-one Soviet citizens per 1,000 in the party, but 80 Jews per 1,000. In other words, even that late, Jews were much more likely than non-Jews to be party members.

In some ways, then, there were advances, but there is another side to the story. In tsarist times, life was very difficult for Jews because they were unable to participate freely in society. Still, they had their religion and their way of life, and these sustained them. Under Communist rule, Jews were granted the right to participate fully in society, but they had to abandon their religion and their way of life. Thus, despite the advances, the Soviet period must still be considered, on balance, a disaster for Jews in a number of ways.

First, not all the advances under the Communists were sustained. Anti-Semitism certainly did not disappear. Stalin's successor, Nikita Khrushchev, wrote that "anti-Semitism grew like a growth inside Stalin's own brain." This may have resulted from Stalin's seminary experience, from his struggles for power with leaders who were of Jewish origin in the 1920s, or from his children's marriages to Jews of which he disapproved. For whatever reason, anti-Jewish activity in the Soviet Union increased greatly after the formation of the state of Israel in 1948, when Soviet Jews were suspected of double loyalties. In 1948, the remaining 800 Yiddish-language schools, still teaching 20 percent of Soviet Jewish schoolchildren, were closed. The regime also shut down the Soviet Yiddish publishing houses and journals. In 1949, the Jewish State Theater in Moscow was closed down. Leading Yiddish-language writers were arrested, tried, and executed in 1952; these included David Bergelson, Der Nister, Dovid Hofstein, Lev Kvitko, and Perets Markish. In January 1953, in what some think was a prelude to another massive purge, came the announcement of the so-called "Doctors' Plot": Nine Kremlin physicians, six of whom were Jewish, were accused of poisoning Soviet leaders. The charges were dropped soon after Stalin's death in March 1953. Also, despite a promising beginning, the combination of unrelenting attacks on Judaism, anti-Semitism, and human losses meant that Yiddish was dying out. Although 97 percent of Russian Jews had spoken Yiddish as their native tongue in 1897, that figure had dropped to 70 percent as early as 1926, and, by 1970, stood at less than 18 percent. Further, although Jews remained more likely to be party members, after the 1930s, Jewish participation at higher levels of government declined, and it became more difficult for Jews to gain acceptance at leading schools and institutes.

Second, the Jewish religion suffered catastrophically under Communism. As early as January 1918, the Communists decreed the complete secularization of the state, the confiscation of all religious property and funds, the withdrawal of the status of legal entities from religious organizations, and the prohibition of religious instruction. As regards Judaism specifically, a 1919 decree dissolved all remaining Kahal-type and charitable organizations. More importantly, Hebrew was officially declared a dead, reactionary language and was declared illegal, ending the publication of materials in Hebrew for about seven decades.

All religious officials, including Jewish ones, were deprived of their civil liberties, had to pay higher taxes on their income, and were harassed in numerous ways. By the early 1930s, very few rabbis remained. The state took over the synagogues, and religious organizations had to lease their premises from the government. Prayerbooks, prayer shawls, torahs, and other objects were periodically seized and not returned; Jews seldom received permission to replace them. The regime, in a manner reminiscent of medieval Europe, staged show trials to denigrate Judaism. These "trials" always ended with a verdict of guilty, after the state produced "witnesses" who testified to the reactionary nature of Judaism and its organizations. The regime instituted "Red Seders" at Passover, which consisted of nationalizing synagogues and their contents at that holy season. The Soviet regime used the school system, which required much course work in "scientific atheism," to attack all religions, including Judaism. The state-controlled media emitted a constant stream of anti-religious propaganda. In 1929, the Soviet constitution was amended to omit the previous guarantee of the right of religious propaganda, while retaining the right of anti-religious propaganda. Educating people in their religion became illegal simply because it was "religious propaganda." Admission to schools, obtaining good jobs, and advancement in society in general became increasingly difficult, if not impossible, for people who actively practiced their religion.

Judaism nonetheless continued to function. As late as 1926, there were still 1,000 functioning synagogues, though this was far fewer than earlier. Stalin's revolution from above after 1928 led to an expanded attack; most remaining synagogues were shut down by 1941. After World War II, the anti-religious, anti-Jewish campaign resumed, and Khrushchev continued it in the 1950s. By 1960, there were perhaps sixty synagogues in the entire Soviet Union, and only one in Moscow. Under Mikhail Gorbachev, there was a partial rebirth of religious activity. Jewish publications became legal. A school for training Jewish religious workers opened in Moscow. There was promise of a better Jewish life. But for whom? At last, it became necessary to confront the third negative change during the Soviet period—the sharp reduction in the number of Jews.

In 1897, with 5.2 million Jews, the Russian Jewish community was by far the largest in the entire world. Since 1914, that number has dwindled steadily. First, of course, there were the 1.5 million Russian Jews who emigrated between

1881 and 1914, many of them after 1897. Second, the resurrection of a Polish state after World War I returned 3,000,000 Jews to Poland who had formerly lived in the Russian Empire. The empire also lost Jews to the newly freed Baltic republics of Estonia, Latvia, and Lithuania, not to mention Bessarabia (Moldavia). Further, there was a tremendous loss of Jewish life, often from pogroms, in Ukraine during the civil war of 1918–1920, probably amounting to 180,000–200,000 Jews. As a result, the number of Jews recorded in the 1926 Soviet census was 2.66 million, slightly over half the previous census (1897).

The next great depletion in Soviet Jewry occurred during World War II as part of the Nazi Holocaust to exterminate all Jews. The Baltic areas were retaken by the Soviets soon after the war began, but, when the Nazis attacked, they quickly seized this area. Of its 253,000 Jews, 90 percent were killed, as were 65 percent of White Russia's 375,000 Jews, 60 percent of Ukraine's 1.5 million Jews, and 11 percent of the Russian Republic's 975,000 Jews. Altogether, of 3,103,000 Jews in the Soviet Union when hostilities commenced, 1,480,000, or 47 percent, were lost. Thus, the 1959 census reported only 2.2 million Soviet Jews.

Soviet Jewry did not replenish itself for two main reasons. First, their birth rate in the Soviet Union was very low. Second, over the decades, there had been a good deal of intermarriage between Jews and non-Jews. Many Jews used that opportunity of non-Jewish-sounding names to avoid listing themselves as Jews and escape the negative consequences of being Jewish in the Soviet Union. The result was that, by 1970, the number of listed Jews was down to 2.15 million.

Then there occurred the third great demographic loss—two waves of Jewish emigration. Soviet authorities had taken a very dim view of emigration from utopia. Although several thousand Zionists had emigrated to Palestine in the decade after 1917, after 1928, hardly anyone emigrated from the Soviet Union. The Arab-Israel War of 1967 rekindled Jewish yearnings in the Soviet Union and pressure on the government led it to permit emigration. The first wave began slowly, in the early 1970s, with 13,000 emigrating in 1971. That first wave reached its high point in 1979, when 51,000 Soviet Jews emigrated. Altogether, from 1971 through 1981, some 256,000 Soviet Jews emigrated. Approximately 145,000 of them went to Israel, and most of the remainder settled in the United States. The regime of Leonid Brezhnev cracked down on emigration in the early 1980s. Indeed, in the entire five-year period between 1982 and 1986, a total of only 7,000 Soviet Jews received exit visas.

Then, under Gorbachev, the floodgates opened again. Beginning with 8,000 émigrés in 1987, the figures increased to 19,000 (1988) 71,000 (1989), 185,000 (1990), and 147,000 (1991). In that five-year period, 437,000 more Soviet Jews emigrated, approximately 352,000 to Israel. In other words, in the 1971–1991 period, a total of 700,000 Soviet Jews emigrated. In addition, with the coming of independence to the Baltic republics in 1991, many Jews are no longer "Soviet." It appears, then, that the total number of Jews in Russia in 1992 was probably somewhat over one million but was declining with continuing emigration. In addition, despite increased opportunities for religious activities, the Jewish religion had been nearly extinguished in the seventy-four years of Communist rule that ended, along with the Soviet Union, in late 1991.

REFERENCES: In the past century, there have been several Jewish encyclopedias that contain excellent information on the Jews in the territory of the Russian/Soviet Empire. These include, chronologically: *The Jewish Encyclopedia*, 12 vols., 1901–1912; *Evreiskaia entsiklopediia* [*The Jewish Encyclopedia*], 16 vols., 1906–1913; *The Jewish Encyclopedia*, 10 vols., 1939–1943; and *Encyclopaedia Judaica*, 16 vols., 1972. Monographic literature includes Gregor Aronson, et al., eds., *Russian Jewry, 1917–1967*, 1969; S. M. Dubnow, *History of the Jews in Russia and Poland from the Earliest Times to the Present Days*, 3 vols., 1916–1920; D. M. Dunlop, *History of the Jewish Khazars*, 1954; Louis Greenberg, *The Jews in Russia*, 2 vols., 1944, 1945; Lionel Kochan, ed., *The Jews in Soviet Russia since 1917*, 1970; Benjamin Pinkus, *The Jews of the Soviet Union: The History of a National Minority*, 1988; Solomon N. Schwarz, *The Jews in the Soviet Union*, 1951.

                                                                    Samuel A. Oppenheim

JUGI. See GYPSY.

JUKAGHIR. See YUKAGIR.

JUKAGIR. See YUKAGIR.

JUNGAR. See OIROT.

JYKHI. See TSAKHUR.

K

KABARD. Before the Bolshevik Revolution, the Kabards were generally lumped together with the Adyghes* and Cherkess* as a Circassian* people. But since the early nineteenth century, the Kabards had finished one stage in the process of ethnogenesis by developing a Kabardian identity that transcended the identities of any of its subgroups. In the 1920s, the Soviet Union decided to divide the Circassians into three groups, and, in the process, the Kabards received official recognition as a nationality. Although the Kabards are, like other Circassians, Sunni Muslims in their religious faith, they were the last of Circassians to be converted, and their ties to Russian Orthodoxy in particular and Russian culture in general remain well developed. The only exception to that conversion process was a small number of Kabards living around Mozdok in the North Ossetian Autonomous Republic. They remained Christians loyal to the Armenian-Gregorian rite. The Kabards today live in the northern mountains and steppes of what used to be the Kabardino-Balkar Autonomous Soviet Socialist Republic. Some Kabards also live in the Adyghe Autonomous Province. The Kabards call themselves the Keberdei, and Russians* refer to them as the Kabardintsy.

The Kabard language is generally part of the northwestern group of Caucasian languages, and its more particular affiliation is with the Abkhazian-Adyghe subgroup of those languages. It is closely related to Abazan*, Abkhazian*, and Adygheian. The language is divided into four subgroups of dialects: Greater Kabard, Mozdok, Beslan, and Kuban'. Greater Kabard is the dialect group around which the Kabard literary language has developed.

Ethnologists believe the Kabards are descended from a cluster of Caucasian tribes who called themselves Adyghe. They originated in the Kuban' Basin, adopted Christianity in the eleventh and twelfth centuries, and became widely known for their commercial trading skills. Beginning in the twelfth century, the Adyghe began a slow migration eastward, arriving on the left bank of the Terek River by the fourteenth century. The thirteenth-century invasion by the Golden Horde accelerated the eastward migration. Some of the Adyghes mixed with the local Alan peoples and eventually became known as Kabards. By the fifteenth century, the region on the left bank of the Terek River was known as Greater Kabardia, while the region on the right bank was known as Little Kabardia. Those Kabardians who stayed in the west became known as the Cherkess.

Early in the sixteenth century, the Ottomans and their subject state, the Crimean Khanate, brought Islam to the Kabards and the conversion process began. That process was a slow one, but, by the early 1800s, the Kabards had become Sunni Muslims of the Hanafi school. Generally, the Kabards resented Tatar* control, and in 1557, they asked Tsar Ivan IV for protection. He granted it in 1561 and strengthened the relationship by marrying a Kabard princess. He then established military outposts on the Terek River in 1563 and 1567. Russian* penetration of the area increased steadily for the next half century. The Ottomans and Persians* also had interests there, however, and, in 1739, the Treaty of Belgrade established Kabardia as a neutral state, a buffer zone, between the Ottomans and Russia. That changed with the Treaty of Kuçuk Kainavci (1774), whereby Kabardia became Russian territory. During the mid-nineteenth century, when the Shamil Revolt against Russia spread throughout the Caucasus, the Kabards maintained neutrality. Nevertheless, after Russia had established control over the region in the 1860s, there was a mass exodus of Kabards to Turkey, reducing their total in Russia at the beginning of the twentieth century to perhaps only 90,000 people.

Soviet policy in the 1920s and 1930s affected the Kabards in three ways: First, the region's economy became heavily industrialized, and thus its value to the Soviet Union increased. Second, Soviet scholars devised three separate written languages (first using Latin, then Cyrillic script) for the Adyghes, Cherkesses, and Kabards, where one common written language might have sufficed. Few publications ever appeared in those languages, and Kabard children were encouraged to learn Russian instead (most did so, but strictly as a second language). Third, the Bolsheviks tried to erase Islam, closing religious schools in 1922. In the 1920s, the Soviet Union officially classified all Circassian peoples into two groups. The western group was designated as the Cherkesses and the eastern group as the Kabards. Late in the 1930s, the ethnic lines were officially redrawn, with Circassians now being subdivided into three groups: The Adyghes were the western Circassians, the Cherkesses the central Circassians, and the Kabards the eastern Circassians.

When the Bolsheviks took over Russia, the Kabards did not resist the way many other groups in the region did. Traditionally, the Kabard nobility had worked closely with the Russian nobility; as a result, the Kabards did not develop serious anti-Russian hostility in the eighteenth and nineteenth centuries. Moreover, because of the power of the Kabard nobility, Kabards did not convert so deeply or intensely to Islam as did other groups. The Kabards did not cooperate in the anti-Russian Shamil Uprising is the nineteenth century, nor in the anti-Soviet rebellions of the early 1920s. In fact, Russians viewed them as the most loyal people in the North Caucasus. During World War II, the Kabards maintained a strong pro-Russian, anti-German profile. They thus managed to avoid the deportations that affected such groups as the Chechens*, Ingushes*, Karachais*, and Balkars.* Finally, because of the relative weakness of their Muslim loyalties, the Kabards have not developed any strong sense of pan-Islamic identity.

But at the same time, the 370,000 Kabards have maintained their Kabardian identity. Approximately 95 percent of them still speak Kabard as their native language, and there is a powerful tradition against marrying exogamously. The Kabards are known as a highly civilized people who harbor distinct feelings of superiority to surrounding groups. That conviction has contributed to the maintenance of Kabard ethnicity. See CIRCASSIAN.

REFERENCES: Shirin Akiner, Islamic Peoples of the Soviet Union, 1983; Alexandre Bennigsen and S. Enders Wimbush, Muslims in the Soviet Empire: A Guide, 1986; Louis J. Luzbetak, Marriage and the Family in Caucasia, 1966; Ronald Wixman, "Ethnic Nationalism in the Caucasus," Nationalities Papers, 10 (1982), 137–56; Ronald Wixman, "Circassians," in Richard V. Weekes, ed., Muslim Peoples, 1984, 203–9; Ronald Wixman, The Peoples of the USSR: An Ethnographic Handbook, 1984.

KABARDIAN. See KABARD.

KABARDINIAN. See KABARD.

KABARDINTSY. See KABARD.

KABARTAI. See KABARD.

KABARTAY. See KABARD.

KACHA. The Kacha constitute one of the subgroups of the Khakass*. In terms of ethnogenesis, the Khakass are a mixture of Turkic and Kettic groups. The Kacha themselves evolved from a gradual consolidation of six Turkic* groups— two Shalosa groups, Mungat, Tatar*, Kuba, and Tuba*—and five Kettic groups—Tatysh, Yara*-Yasta*, Tin, Abalak, and Aboltai. The Kacha then became the nucleus of the groups that evolved into the Khakass. They are nominally Eastern Orthodox in religion, but their animist traditions are still very real and powerful. Most of the Kacha are concentrated on the Yenesei River in the Khakass Autonomous Oblast. See KHAKASS.

REFERENCE: Ronald Wixman, The Peoples of the USSR: An Ethnographic Handbook, 1984.

KACHIN. See KACHA and KHAKASS.

KACHINTSY. See KACHA and KHAKASS.

KADAES. See KHWARSHI and AVAR.

KADJAR. See KAJAR and AZERBAIJANI.

KADZHAR. See KAJAR and AZERBAIJANI.

KAHELI. See KAKHETIAN and GEORGIAN.

KAIBAL. See KOIBAL and KHAKASS.

KAIDAK. See KAITAK and DARGIN.

KAITAGTSY. See KAITAK and DARGIN.

KAITAK. The Kaitak (Kaidak), who call themselves the Qaidaqlan or Khaidak and who have also been known to Russians* as the Karakaidak, Karakaitak, Karakaitaki, Kaitagtsy, and Khaidaki, are today classified as a subgroup of the Dargins*. They are scattered among the Dargins in the south-central mountains of Daghestan, primarily in the Dakhadajev Region. Most of them live in the Kaitak and Levashi districts. There are two basic subgroups within the Kaitak, each with a distinct dialect and geographical concentration. The northern Kaitak speak a dialect known as Magalas-Kaitak, while southerners speak the Karakaitak dialect.

During the eighth century, under the influence of the Arab* invaders, the Kaitaks were among the first of the Caucasian peoples to accept Islam; the conversion process continued for several more centuries. The thirteenth-century conquest by the Mongols* reinforced Islamic traditions, as did Ottoman influence in the fifteenth century. Still, as early as the fifteenth century, Christian missionaries were working among the Kaitaks. During the fifteenth century, the Kaitaks established a semi-independent political entity known as the Kaitak Utsmiyat, which was able to bring large numbers of Laks*, Dargins, and Kumyks* under its control. The Kaitak confederation managed to survive politically by walking a diplomatic tightrope between the Ottomans and the Persians*. The Kaitak Utsmiyat remained powerful through the eighteenth century, but it could not resist Russian expansion in the nineteenth century; Russia established a protectorate there in 1802. In 1820, direct Russian administration went into effect in Lower Kaitak (the region bordering the Caspian Sea). The Kaitak Utsmiyat was abolished in 1844, and, in 1862, direct Russian administration went into effect in the mountainous areas, collectively known as Kara-Kaitak, as well.

Today most Kaitaks work as farmers, raising fruit, wheat, and vegetables and sheep. They are Sunni Muslims of the Shafi tradition. Although it is difficult to come up with current population estimates for the Kaitaks, primarily because of their census designation with the Dargins, demographers estimate that there are approximately 25,000 people who either consciously identify themselves as Kaitaks or who are aware of their Kaitak ancestry. See DARGIN.

REFERENCES: Shirin Akiner, *Islamic Peoples of the Soviet Union*, 1983; Ronald Wixman, *The Peoples of the USSR: An Ethnographic Handbook*, 1984.

KAITAK. See KUMYK.

KAIVAN. See VEP.

KAJAR. The Kajars are considered a subgroup of the Azerbaijanis*. Historically, they have been a Turkic* Tribe who lived in Armenia. In the seventeenth and eighteenth centuries, when the Safavids tried to conquer the region, the Kajars settled in the Karabakh Khanate of western Azerbaijan. Agha Mohammed, a Kajar leader, overturned the Zend dynasty in Iran and established Kajar control in the area. This arrangement lasted until Reza Shah came to power in Iran in 1925. The Kajar population today exceeds 35,000 people, the vast majority of whom live in Iran. See AZERBAIJANI.
REFERENCES: Shirin Akiner, *Islamic Peoples of the Soviet Union*, 1983; Ronald Wixman, *The Peoples of the USSR: An Ethnographic Handbook*, 1984.

K'AKHELI. See KAKHETIAN and GEORGIAN.

KAKHETIAN. The Kakhetians, who call themselves the K'akhelis, are one of the many ethnic groups that evolved into the larger Georgian* group. They are Eastern Orthodox and live in eastern Georgia. See GEORGIAN.
REFERENCE: Ronald Wixman, *The Peoples of the USSR: An Ethnographic Handbook*, 1984.

KALAMIED. See LIVONIAN.

KALCHA. The Kalcha are considered to be one of the Kyrgyz* subgroups, even though they have very distinct ethnic origins with non-Kyrgyz roots. See KYRGYZ.
REFERENCE: Ronald Wixman, *The Peoples of the USSR: An Ethnographic Handbook*, 1984.

KALCHIN. See KALCHA and KYRGYZ.

KALCHINTSY. See KALCHA and KYRGYZ.

KALMADZHIS. See KAMASIN.

KALMAK. The Kalmak are a group of 300 to 400 people who are classified as part of the larger Kyrgyz* group, even though their ethnic and linguistic roots are Kalmyk*. They are being assimilated today by the Kyrgyz. The Kalmak are Sunni Muslims and live in the Tien Shan Obast of the Kyrgyz Republic. See KYRGYZ.

REFERENCE: Ronald Wixman, *The Peoples of the USSR: An Ethnographic Handbook*, 1984.

KALMUCK. See KALMYK.

KALMUK. See KALMYK.

KALMYK. The Kalmyks, who have also been known as the Kalmuks, Kal-mucks, Khal'mgs, and Oirots*, were a semi-nomadic, Mongol-speaking people whose original homeland was in East Turkestan. At the end of the sixteenth century, to escape the political and economic pressures of Chinese*, Kazakh*, and Mongol* feudal lords, the Kalmyks began migrating slowly to the west, displacing the native Nogais* as they went. The Nogais ended up leaving the region and heading farther to the southwest. The Kalmyks eventually settled in the lower Volga River basin, between the Don and Ural rivers. That region, formerly part of the Astrakhan Khanate, had been incorporated into Russia in 1556. By the late sixteenth century, the region known today as Kalmykia was under the authority of the Kalmyk Khanate. By the early 1600s, the Kalmyks were coming under more direct Russian* authority, a political development that protected them from the ravages of the larger and more aggressive khanates. During the sixteenth and seventeenth centuries, they became even more loyal to the Lamaist tradition of Buddhism.

In 1771, however, the Kalmyks found themselves in a disastrous situation. Word reached them that the Oirots, their ethnic cousins still living in China, were undergoing intense persecution at the hands of the Chinese. The majority of Kalmyks decided to migrate back to China to rescue them, but the decision proved to be catastrophic. On their trip to Mongolia, the Kalmyks came under vicious attacks from Bashkirs* and Kazakhs, and, when they reached Dzungaria, they were attacked by the Chinese. Most of the migrating Kalmyks did not survive the migration. About 13,000 Kalmyk families, however, did not take the trip, preferring to remain in Kalmykia. Russia dissolved the Kalmyk Khanate in 1771 and placed the remaining Kalmyks under the administration of Astrakhan Province. The government resettled some of them along the Ural, Terek, and Kuma rivers, while other Kalmyks ended up in Siberia. Still another group of Kalmyks in the Don River region became Don Cossacks*.

As a result of their association with the Cossacks*, the Kalmyk social life developed a strong tribal-military tradition. They became divided into two groups distinguished by their geographical concentration and linguistic differences. The Derbent* Kalmyks spoke the Derbent dialect and lived in the northern and western reaches of Kalmykia. The Torgout* Kalmyks spoke the Torgout dialect and lived in southern and eastern Kalmykia. There was also a tiny group of people known as Khosheut* Kalmyks who lived on the lower Volga River. The vast majority of the Khosheut Kalmyks were slaughtered during the 1771 migration to China.

The basic Kalmyk language is one of the western languages of the Mongol division of the Uralic-Altaic family of languages.

During the nineteenth century, the settlement of the Kalmyk steppes by ethnic Russian farmers accelerated, and the tsarist government favored this movement. In 1806, the government decided to limit Kalmyk pasture lands to a region between the Caspian Sea and thirty kilometers from the Volga River. The decree severely limited the nomadic, livestock-breeding life-style of the Kalmyks. Kalmyk herds declined from 2,500,000 head in 1803, to 1,000,000 in 1863, and to only 453,000 in 1896. Many impoverished Kalmyks were forced off the land and into work as fishermen and salt miners. In spite of their economic situation, the Kalmyks were not enthusiastic supporters of the 1917 revolution. In fact, they actively supported the anti-Bolshevik South Eastern League, an organization of Cossacks and North Caucasian nomadic peoples. When some of the political instability ended in 1920, the Soviet government established the Kalmyk Autonomous Oblast within Russia, and, between 1922 and 1925, the Kalmyks living in other regions of Russia were resettled there. The 1926 Soviet census placed the total Kalmyk ethnic population at 129,321 people.

For a brief period in the 1930s, Soviet authorities tried to promote cultural interaction between the Kalmyks, Buryats*, and Khalkas*. In January 1931, a special conference—the "First Cultural Conference of Mongol Peoples" took place in Moscow. Government officials were trying to convert the Khalkas, Buryats, and Kalmyks to the Latin alphabet and promoted the development of a consistent scientific terminology for all three languages. Within a few years, however, Soviet authorities became more concerned about the development of a pan-Mongol national movement among Mongol peoples of the Soviet Union, Mongolia, and China, so they began actively discouraging interaction between Kalmyks, Khalkas, and Buryats.

By 1959, the Kalmyk population had declined to only 106,066 people. Late in the 1920s, when collectivization reached the Kalmyks, they resisted Josef Stalin's plans for them, and he ruthlessly crushed all opposition. Thousands of Kalmyks died in the process. In 1941, the German* army invaded the Soviet Union, it succeeded in taking over Kalmykia. When the Soviet Army regained the region in 1943, Stalin included the Kalmyks in the great deportations of people to Central Asia. The Kalmyk Autonomous Soviet Socialist Republic, which had been created in 1933, was dissolved. The relocation process to Central Asia also proved devastating, and, by the mid–1950s, Soviet ethnographers were claiming that the Kalmyks had all but been eliminated as an ethnic entity in the Soviet Union.

This was by no means so, but it was not until 1956 that the Kalmyks were rehabilitated. They began drifting back to Kalmykia between 1956 and 1960. Their population did not recover to its 1926 level until the late 1960s. That population growth accelerated during the 1970s and 1980s, reaching a total of 174,000 people in the 1989 Soviet census. The economy of the Kalmyk Autonomous Soviet Socialist Republic in the 1980s revolved around livestock, grain, and wool production, as well as agricultural processing industries.

The political and economic turmoil that engulfed the Soviet Union in the late 1980s and led to its dissolution in 1991 affected the Kalmyks as well. The *glasnost* policies of Mikhail Gorbachev permitted Kalmyk scholars, especially at Kalmyk University in Elista, to begin protesting the genocidal policies of the Stalin era. They also began demanding local control of the minerals in Kalmykia, instead of having the central government purchase those resources at controlled prices and then sell them at world market prices. Still, anti-Russian sentiment in Kalmykia was not so pronounced in all areas. Ethnic Russians outnumbered ethnic Kalmyks in the republic, and the long association of many Kalmyks with the Cossacks had instilled in them at least an appreciation for Russian culture. In March 1992, the Kalmyk Autonomous Soviet Socialist Republic changed its name to the Republic of Kalmykia-Khalmag Tangch and approved federation within Russia, on the condition that subsoil resources remain under local control.
REFERENCES: Current Digest, March 22, 1989, 23, and March 25, 1992, 5–7; *Great Soviet Encyclopedia*, 1973, vol. 11, 364–68, 1973; Walter Kolarz, *The Peoples of the Soviet Far East*, 1969; Ronald Wixman, *The Peoples of the USSR: An Ethnographic Handbook*, 1984.

KALPAK. See KARAKALPAK.

KAMASA SAMODI. See KAMASA SAMOYED and KHAKASS.

KAMASA SAMOED. See KAMASA SAMOYED and KHAKASS.

KAMASA SAMOIED. See KAMASA SAMOYED and KHAKASS.

KAMASA SAMOYED. The Kamasa Samoyed are today classified as part of the Koibal* subgroup of the Khakass*. In the twentieth century, they lost their original Samoyedic language and adopted a Turkic* dialect. The Kamasa Samoyeds live in the Sayan region of the Khakass Autonomous Oblast. See KHAKASS.
REFERENCE: Ronald Wixman, *The Peoples of the USSR: An Ethnographic Handbook*, 1984.

KAMASIN. See KAMASA SAMOYED and KHAKASS.

KAMASIN SAMODI. See KAMASA SAMOYED and KHAKASS.

KAMASIN SAMOED. See KAMASA SAMOYED and KHAKASS.

KAMASIN SAMOIED. See KAMASA SAMOYED and KHAKASS.

KAMASIN SAMOYED. See KAMASA SAMOYED and KHAKASS.

KAMASSIAN SAMODI. See KAMASA SAMOYED and KHAKASS.

KAMASSIAN SAMOED. See KAMASA SAMOYED and KAHKASS.

KAMASSIAN SAMOIED. See KAMASA SAMOYED and KHAKASS.

KAMASSIAN SAMOYED. See KAMASA SAMOYED and KHAKASS.

KAMCHADAL. The term ''Kamchadal'' is used in the Soviet Union today to describe a small group of people of ethnically mixed Russian*-Itelmen* descent who live in the Kamchatka Peninsula. They speak Russian and are integrated into the larger economy, but they still maintain a strong identification with Itelmen society. During the eighteenth century, there were bitter battles between the Kamchadals and Russian Cossacks* in the Kamchatka Peninsula; the Cossacks wiped out most of the Kamchadals. Before the Russian conquest, there had been more than 30,000 Kamchadals, but only 5,000 were still alive in 1900. At the time, they made up nearly half of the population of their region. The ambitious colonization schemes of the Soviet regime in the 1920s and 1930s changed all that, reducing the Kamchadals to only 25 percent of the population by 1928 and only 12 percent by 1940. Those demographic changes have vastly accelerated the assimilation process.
REFERENCES: James Forsyth, *A History of the Peoples of Siberia*, 1992; Walter Kolarz, *The Peoples of the Soviet Far East*, 1969.

KAMCHATKA. See EVEN.

KAMEN. The Kamen are one of the constituent groups making up the Koryak* people. They work as hunters and fishermen and live in the Koryak Autonomous Oblast along Penzhina Bay in eastern Siberia. See KORYAK.
REFERENCE: Ronald Wixman, *The Peoples of the USSR: An Ethnographic Handbook*, 1984.

KAMENSHCHIK. See RUSSIAN.

KAMENTSY. See KAMEN and KORYAK.

KAMLAR. See KYZYL and KHAKASS.

KANGDY. See ICHKILIK and KYRGYZ.

KAPSA. See LITHUANIAN.

KAPSAI. See LITHUANIAN.

KAPSAY. See LITHUANIAN.

KAPUCHA. See KAPUCHIN and AVAR.

KAPUCHIAS SUKO. See KAPUCHIN and AVAR.

KAPUCHIN. The Kapuchins, who call themselves the Kapuchias Suko, have also been known historically as the Kapucha, Kapuchin, Bezhta, and Bezhetin; they are today classified as one of the Avar* subgroups. Russians* refer to them as the Kapuchintsy or Bezhetintsy. They live in one of the most isolated areas in what used to be the Soviet Union—the upper reaches of the Avar River in the high mountains of southwestern Daghestan, particularly in the village of Kapucha (Bezheta) in the Tsuntin Region. The Kapuchin identity is highly decentralized, with village loyalties transcending those of the group as a whole. There are, for example, three dialects of Kapuchin—Kapuchin (Bezheta) proper, Tljadal, and Khochar-Khota—corresponding to the three villages in which almost all Kapuchins live. Like other Avars, the Kapuchins are Sunni Muslims. Although it is difficult to secure accurate figures of the current Kapuchin population, because of their census classification with Avars, demographers estimate that there are as many as 4,000 people who either identify themselves as Kapuchins or are aware of their Kapuchin ancestry. See AVAR.
REFERENCES: Shirin Akiner, *Islamic Peoples of the Soviet Union*, 1983; Ronald Wixman, *The Peoples of the USSR: An Ethnographic Handbook*, 1984.

KARA. See NOGAI.

KARA-AGACH. See NOGAI.

KARA NOGAI. The Kara Nogai, who call themselves the Qara Nogai and who also have been known as the Black Nogai, Chernyy Nogai, or simply the Kara, constitute one of the main subgroups of the Nogai* people. Most Kara Nogais live in the extreme northern reaches of the Daghestan Republic. See NOGAI.
REFERENCE: Ronald Wixman, *The Peoples of the USSR: An Ethnographic Handbook*, 1984.

KARA TATAR. The Kara Tatar call themselves the Qara Tatar and have also been known as the Nukrat Tatar. They are a small group of Volga Tatars* who dwell on the Cheptsa River. See VOLGA TATAR or TATAR.
REFERENCE: Ronald Wixman, *The Peoples of the USSR: An Ethnographic Handbook*, 1984.

KARABAG. See AZERBAIJANI.

KARACHAEV. See KARACHAI.

KARACHAI. The Karachais (Karachev, Karachaev), who call themselves the Qarachaili (Kiarachaly, Kiarchal), are a Sunni Muslim ethnic group of the former Soviet Union. They are known to many of their neighbors as the Alans. Russians* also call them the Karachajevtsy. The Karachais are closely related to the Balkars*; in fact, the Balkars and the Karachais are both Turkic* people who share the same spoken and literary language, but they live in different, geographically isolated regions of the Northern Caucasus highlands and in different national territories. The Karachais are part of the Karachai-Cherkess Autonomous Oblast in Russia, while the Balkars are assigned to the Kabardino-Balkar Autonomous Republic. Karachai is one of the Kypchak* languages of the Turkic branch of the Uralic-Altaic linguistic family. Karachai and Balkar are mostly closely related to Kumyk* and Nogai*. Although scholars disagree about the process of ethnogenesis that produced the Karachais, most believe that the group emerged from a mix of Kypchak Turks*, Bulgarians*, Khazars, Hunns, and Caucasians. It was the attacking Mongol* hordes of the thirteenth century who drove the Karachais into the Northern Caucasus highlands.

Ethnologists suspect that the Karachais descended from Kypchak tribes in the northern Caucasus and that there was substantial contact historically with the Alans. The Nogais arrived in the region in the seventeenth century. The Kabard* brought Islam to them in the eighteenth century, but the Karachais themselves attribute their conversion to the work of Ishak Efendi, an eighteenth-century Kabard* mullah. The Russian state first assumed control of the Karachais in 1828, but, along with other highland peoples of the North Caucasus, they resisted Russian expansion and colonialism. Throughout the 1830s, 1840s, and 1850s, tsarist policies were committed to subduing the Karachais, and, in the 1860s and 1870s, large numbers of Karachais migrated to Turkey to escape the oppression. The 1926 Soviet census placed the Karachai population at approximately 55,000 people. By that time, the government was bent on suppressing any sense of North Caucasus unity and destroying the resistance movement in the highland regions. Part of their solution was administrative. Instead of putting the closely related Karachais and Balkars into the same autonomous political unit, designed along ethnic and geographic lines, they practiced a ''divide and conquer'' administrative policy, placing the unrelated Central Circassians* (Cherkess*) and Karachais into the Karachai-Cherkess Autonomous Oblast and the equally unrelated Balkars and Eastern Circassians (Kabard) into the Kabardino-Balkar Autonomous Soviet Socialist Republic.

Traditionally, and even today, the Karachais have been a transhumant people, who seasonally move livestock from one pasture to another. During the summers, the Karachais would drive their herds into the mountains, where they could graze in alpine pastures; in the winters, they drove them down into warmer forest clearings and lowland pastures. Families often accompanied the men during these migrations. After the Russian Revolution, the government implemented a process of collectivization, but the Karachais continued to move their cattle, pigs, and sheep from the highlands to the lowlands and back again. During the summer months, they began to live on state or collective farms. Some Karachais now work in such light industries as meat processing, dairying, baking, and sewing; a very few work in heavier industries, like coal mining and rock quarrying. The vast majority, however, are still engaged in animal husbandry and directly related agricultural pursuits, such as producing hay and other feed crops.

The Karachais are Sunni Muslims of the Hanafi school of Sharia law, but they are somewhat less devoted to Islam than many of their ethnic neighbors. The Karachai conversion to Islam did not occur until the eighteenth century, as a result of contact with Kabards. Perhaps because of the late conversion, as well as their semi-nomadic economy, the Karachais did not become as devoted to Sunni Muslim rituals as did many other Soviet groups. They often resented the Kabard religious leaders who imposed tax penalties on Karachai families that failed to attend the mosque regularly. As a result, they maintained a cultural independence from many Islamic traditions. Karachai women did not veil themselves, nor did the Karachais follow Islamic dietary restrictions, particularly the prohibition of pork. So, although the Karachais clearly recognize themselves as a Muslim people, they have not fallen in with the often fervent Islamic revivals of recent years. The limited nature of their conversion to Islam has guaranteed the survival of more traditional, animist beliefs and rituals in Karachai culture. These include a polytheistic sense of many functioning deities, spirits, ghosts, and supernatural beings, as well as rituals to appease those spirits and the elements.

The Karachais also do not have a well-developed sense of ethnic nationhood. Because of the geographic isolation of the North Caucasus highlands, the Karachai are divided by a bewildering variety of distinct, if similar, dialects, according to the valley in which they reside. Moreover, Karachai social and political life tends to revolve around a powerful sense of patriarchal clan loyalty. They usually marry endogamously within existing clans and identify themselves ethnically by their clan relations. Those loyalties are to one of four clan groups: the Adurkhay, Budian, Nawruz, and Trama. There is little or no sense of Transcaucasian or pan-Turkic nationalism among the Karachais. The only real identity they maintain that transcends their clan and valley loyalties is a sense of being a highland, or mountaineering, people. On that level, they feel a certain kinship with other mountain-dwelling people, even if those people speak a different language and worship as Christians.

Although the Karachais have no real sense of nationalism, they do possess strong anti-Russian and anti-Soviet feelings. The nineteenth-century resentment of Russian expansionism nurtured their hostility, and World War II intensified it. The German* army entered the Karachai Autonomous Province in August 1942, but, in January 1943, the Russians regained military control there. In retaliation for alleged Karachai collaboration with the Nazis, Josef Stalin had the Karachais herded into freight cars and deported to Central Asia and Kazakhstan. Stalin abolished the Karachai-Cherkess Autonomous Oblast at the same time. Tens of thousands of Karachai died during their exile, which lasted until

1956, when Soviet Premier Nikita Khrushchev extended amnesty to them as part of his de-Stalinization campaign. They began returning to their homelands, and, in 1957, the Karachbai-Cherkess Autonomous Oblast was re-established.

Today, the Karachai population is approaching 150,000 people. As many as 85 percent of them live in the upper and middle valleys of the Kuban River and its various tributaries, particularly the Taberda, Zelenchuk, and Aksut rivers in the Karachai-Cherkess Autonomous Oblast. The rest of the Karachais are scattered throughout Russia or are still living in Kazakhstan and Kyrgyzia where they were deported during World War II.

REFERENCES: Alexandre Bennigsen and S. Enders Wimbush, *Muslims of the Soviet Empire: A Guide*, 1986; Robert Conquest, *The Nation Killers*, 1970; Louis J. Luzbetak, *Marriage and the Family in Caucasia*, 1966; A. M. Nekrich, *The Punished Peoples*, 1978; Ronald Wixman, *Language Aspects of Ethnic Patterns and Processes in the North Caucasus*, 1980; Ronald Wixman, "Ethnic Nationalism in the Caucasus," *Nationalities Papers*, 10 (1982), 137–54; Ronald Wixman, *The Peoples of the USSR: An Ethnographic Handbook*, 1984.

KARACHAIEV. See KARACHAI.

KARACHAILI. See KARACHAI.

KARACHAJEVTSY. See KARACHAI.

KARACHAY. See KARACHAI.

KARACHAYEV. See KARACHAI.

KARACHAYLY. See KARACHAI.

KARACHEV. See KARACHAI.

KARADASH. The Karadash, who call themselves the Qaradashly, are a Turkmen* subgroup. The Karadash homeland is in the Khorezm Oasis of the Turkmen Republic. See TURKMEN.

REFERENCE: Ronald Wixman, *The Peoples of the USSR: An Ethnographic Handbook*, 1984.

KARADASHLI. See KARADASH and TURKMEN.

KARADASHLY. See KARADASH and TURKMEN.

KARAGA. The Karaga are a Koryak* subgroup. They are concentrated demographically in southeastern Kamchatka. See KORYAK.

REFERENCE: Ronald Wixman, *The Peoples of the USSR: An Ethnographic Handbook*, 1984.

KARAGA. See TOFALAR.

KARAGACH. See NOGAI.

KARAGASH. See KARAGASH TATAR.

KARAGASH TATAR. The Karagash Tatars, who call themselves the Qaragashly, are part of the larger cluster of Astrakhan Tatars*. They originated with the Golden Horde invaders of the thirteenth century and are descended more directly from the Nogai* Tatars. They are also closely related to the Kundrov Tatars*. See ASTRAKHAN TATAR or TATAR.

REFERENCE: Ronald Wixman, *The Peoples of the USSR: An Ethnographic Handbook*, 1984.

KARAGASHLI. See KARAGASH TATAR.

KARAGASHLI TATAR. See KARAGASH TATAR.

KARAGASHLY. See KARAGASH TATAR.

KARAGASHLY TATAR. See KARAGASH TATAR.

KARAGASS. See TOFALAR.

KARAGIN. See KORYAK.

KARAGINTSY. See KORYAK.

KARAIM. The Karaims (Karaites), who call themselves the Karaj, are a Turkic*-speaking group of Jews* whose homeland is primarily in the Crimean Peninsula. The Karaims are non-Talmudic Jews who were originally Khazars converted by missionaries from Jerusalem. Their language, which is part of the West Turkic linguistic group, is closely related to Kypchak*. They were present in the Crimea as early as the fourteenth century, and nearly 500 Karaim families later relocated to the cities of Trakai and Vilnius in Lithuania and Lutsk and Halych in Ukraine. Until the period of World War II, they maintained a very strong sense of identity, marrying endogamously and preserving their language and religious traditions. Unlike the Krymchaks*, who were devastated by Nazi atrocities during the war, the Karaims were spared the Holocaust because they managed to convince German* authorities that their association with Judaism was exclusively religious, without any ethnic dimension. They also managed to escape the deportations to Central Asia and Kazakhstan that harshly affected the surviving Krymchaks and Crimean Tatars*. In recent years, some Karaims have settled in Warsaw, St. Petersburg, and Moscow. The current Karaim population in the former Soviet Union exceeds 4,500 people. See JEW.

REFERENCES. Lionel Kochan, ed., *The Jews in Soviet Russia since 1917*, 1970; Benjamin Pinkus, *The Jews of the Soviet Union: The History of a National Minority*, 1988; Solomon N. Schwarz, *The Jews in the Soviet Union*, 1951; Ronald Wixman, *The Peoples of the USSR: An Ethnographic Handbook*, 1984.

KARAISM. See KARAIM and JEW.

KARAIT. See KARAIM and JEW.

KARAITE. See KARAIM and JEW.

KARAJ. See KARAIM and JEW.

KARAKAIDAK. See KAITAK and DARGIN.

KARAKAITAK. See KAITAK and DARGIN.

KARAKALPAK. The Karakalpak, who call themselves the Qaraqalpak, are a relatively small ethnic group who live in the former Soviet Union, Iran, Turkey, and Afghanistan. Their name translates literally as "Black Caps." They are also known as the Karalpak, Kalpak, or the Chernye Klobuki, and they are known to Russians* as Karakalpaki. Today they live in the Karakalpak Autonomous Republic, as well as in the Khorezm and Fergana districts of the Uzbek Republic, the Tashauz District of the Turkmen Republic, and portions of the Kazakh Republic and the Astrakhan District of Russia. There is much scholarly controversy about the Karakalpak, with some ethnographers considering them simply a subtribe of the Uzbeks*. Russians first used the term "Karakalpak" in the twelfth century, to refer to a people with whom Kiev had formed an alliance in order to stave off Kypchak* raids. In terms of their origins, the Karakalpak emerged as an identifiable tribal entity in the sixteenth century, when a slow merger began to occur between the various Mongol* and Turkic* tribes living north of the Caspian Sea and the indigenous Iranian-speaking people of the region. At that time, the Karakalpak lived on the lower Syr Darya River and enjoyed considerable political independence. In the seventeenth and eighteenth centuries, the process of ethnogenesis continued, and they migrated to a region south of the Aral Sea, partly to escape the hostility of their Kazakh* neighbors.

Early in the 1800s, some of the Karakalpaks were still living on the Syr Darya River, while others had settled in the Amu Darya River delta. The Karakalpak Autonomous Republic now includes that area. These Karakalpaks came under the control of the Khanate of Khiva in 1811. They resented Khivan control and rebelled several times in the nineteenth century. In 1873, Russia annexed the region of the Khanate of Khiva on the right side of the Amu Darya River, which was then designated a Russian protectorate. In 1918, the protectorate was incorporated into the Turkmen Autonomous Soviet Socialist Republic; but in 1920, Soviet authorities abolished the Khanate of Khiva and proclaimed the Khorezm People's Soviet Republic. This in turn was dissolved four years later. The Karakalpak Autonomous Province was established within the Kyrgyz Autonomous Soviet Socialist Republic in 1925. The province was named an autonomous republic in 1932 and transferred from Kyrgyzia to Russia. It became part of the Uzbek Soviet Socialist Republic in 1936.

By the end of the nineteenth century, the Karakalpaks were identified as two separate federations: the Kongrat Arys, which consisted of fifteen separate tribes and clans, and the On Tort Urun Arys, which consisted of fourteen clans and tribes. The major surviving Karakalpak subdivisions are the Kongrat, Ktay, Kypchak, Keneges, and Mangyt. The Karakalpak language is part of the northwest Turkic branch of the Altaic linguistic family. There are two Karakalpak dialects, with the northeastern one being a close relative of Kazakh and the southwestern one a close relative of Uzbek. The Karakalpak are of Mongol extraction, and they are Sunni Muslim in their religious loyalties, primarily of the Hanafi school. Today more than 330,000 Karakalpaks live in the Soviet Union, with another 55,000 in Turkey, 25,000 in Iran, and several thousand in Afghanistan, although that number is very indefinite, since substantial numbers of Karakalpak fled to Pakistan during the years of the Soviet occupation of Afghanistan in the 1980s.

The Karakalpak living in the former Soviet Union reside primarily in the Karakalpak Autonomous Republic, which lies in the northern section of the Uzbek Republic, covering the eastern region of the Amu Darya delta and the Khorezm Oasis. Its borders to the west and east are the Ust Urt and Kyzyl Kum deserts.

Before the Russian Revolution, the Karakalpak were a semi-nomadic people who combined irrigated farming with herding. Since that time, however, government policy has brought about a series of profound economic changes, even though small numbers of Karakalpaks still engage in nomadic transhumant animal husbandry. Today, approximately 45 percent of the Karakalpaks are city dwellers, who work in grain milling, fish processing, and light industrial work. The rest of the Karakalpak still live a rural life-style, although they labor on state and collective farms where they grow cotton, rice, alfalfa, musk melons, hemp, and sorghum. The state has also collectivized the livestock business; since the Karakalpaks raise sheep, cattle, horses, and camels, this policy has affected them as well. Some Karakalpak also worked for fishing collectives on the Aral Sea, although most of that work has disappeared because of environmental problems.

The Karakalpak Autonomous Republic is the most religious and Islamic region of the Soviet Union. In the northern reaches of the territory, the Sufi orders are very influential. In spite of the consistently anti-religious policies of the state (such as prohibitions of polygamy, anti-Islamic propaganda campaigns, and rulings against religious holidays and festivals that upset daily work patterns), the Karakalpaks are more likely to observe religious customs (male circumcision, fasting during Ramadan, Islamic marriages and funerals, avoidance of pork in the diet, local pilgrimages, and weekly devotions) than any other Central Asian Islamic group. They are Sunni Muslims of the Hanafi school.

But although the Karakalpaks are quite religious, they are less likely than any other Central Asian group to nurture strong feelings of ethnic nationalism. In fact, the Karakalpak sense of loyalty to a tribe or a clan is far more intense than any generic sense of identity. They have never enjoyed any political independence as an ethnic community and have always maintained strong kinship ties with various tribes of the Nogais*, Crimean Tatars*, Bashkirs*, and Kazakhs. They do not really look on the Uzbeks and Kazakhs as an alien people. In that sense, the Karakalpaks maintain more of a pan-Turkic identity than a narrow sense of Karakalpak nationhood. They also have a sense of being part of the larger Muslim community in the Soviet Union. Because of the Soviet public school system, however, more than half of all Karakalpaks are now fluent in Russian as a second language.

During the last twenty years, the Karakalpaks have found themselves, like millions of Uzbeks, the victims of environmental disaster in the Soviet Union. Massive, intensive cotton cultivation in the region of the Aral Sea, combined with heavy irrigation, has reduced that huge body of water to only a shadow of its former self. The salt-laced former sea floor, now exposed to the heavy winds of the region, is producing dust storms that spread salt over hundreds of square miles and poison water supplies, soil, and human beings. The infant mortality rate among Karakalpak children now exceeds 10 percent, and the adult population is suffering from extraordinarily high rates of cancer, especially of the throat, lungs, and esophagus. Only dramatic reductions in cotton cultivation in the region of the Aral Sea can bring improvements to the health of the Karakalpak people. Their resentment about these health and economic problems has created a budding nationalist movement among some Karakalpaks, who are calling for the establishment of an independent Karakalpak Republic.

REFERENCES: Elizabeth Bacon, *Central Asian Russian Rule*, 1966; Alexandre Bennigsen and S. Enders Wimbush, *Muslims of the Soviet Empire: A Guide*, 1986; Sir Olaf K. Caroe, *Soviet Empire: The Turks of Central Asia and Stalinism*, 1967; Kh. T. Esbergenov, "On the Struggle Against Survivals of Obsolete Customs and Rites (The Karakalpaks 'As' Memorial Feast)," *Soviet Anthropology and Archaeology*, 3 (1964), 9–20; Konstantin Symmons-Symonolewicz, *The Non-Slavic Peoples of the Soviet Union*, 1972; L. S. Tolstova, "The Karakalpak of Fergana," *Central Asian Review*, 9 (1961), 45–52; Victor Mote, "Karakalpaks," in Richard V. Weekes, ed., *Muslim Peoples*, 1984, 385–90; Ronald Wixman, *The Peoples of the USSR: An Ethnographic Handbook*, 1984.

KARAKALPAKI. See KARAKALPAK.

KARAKAYDAK. See KAITAK and DARGIN.

KARAKAYTAK. See KITAK and DARGIN.

KARAKIRGHIZ. See KYRGYZ.

KARAKIRGHYZ. See KYRGYZ.

KARAKIRGIZ. See KYRGYZ.

KARAKIRGYZ. See KYRGYZ.

KARALPAK. See KARAKALPAK.

KARAMURZA. See NOGAI.

KARANOGAI. See KARA NOGAI and NOGAI.

KARANOGAY. See KARA NOGAI and NOGAI.

KARANOGHAI. See KARA NOGAI and NOGAI.

KARANOGHAY. See KARA NOGAI and NOGAI.

KARAPAPAH. See KARAPAPAKH.

KARAPAPAK. See KARAPAPAKH.

KARAPAPAKH. The Karapapakh are a small ethnic group who today live primarily in and around Tashkent in the Uzbek Republic. Russian* demographers and ethnologists trace the migration of the Karapapakh back to the early nineteenth century, when they moved from Iran to Turkey. By 1820, there was a small but nevertheless distinct community of Karapapakhs living in northern Turkey. Late in the nineteenth century, they moved again, this time to northern Armenia and southern Georgia. With the Russian Revolution and Soviet expansion south in the late 1910s and 1920s, the Karapapakhs became a new nationality group in the Soviet Union. In terms of their ethnic background, the Karapapakh speak a Turkish language that is very closely related to Azeri. They are a Turkmen* tribe. Unlike most of the Muslims of the Soviet Union, who are followers of the Sunni tradition, the Karapapakhs are primarily of the Shi'a branch and, more particularly, of the Ali Illahis tradition. Because of that background, there has traditionally been an element of secretiveness and fanaticism to Karapapakh religion. Historically, they viewed themselves as distinct from both ethnic Russians and Sunni Muslims.

Late in the 1930s, the Soviet Union stopped classifying the Karapapakhs as a separate people, and, in 1944, they were included in the mass deportation of

Turkish peoples from Georgia and Armenia to Central Asia. With that forced migration, the Karapapakhs began to acquire a somewhat different identity as Meskhetians*—people from Meskhetia, like the Turks*, Khemsils*, and Kurds*, who were also forcibly moved. Because Shi'a Islam is a highly structured, hierarchical organization, especially compared to the more decentralized Sunni faith, the Karapapakhs have tended to lose some of their identity as Shiite Muslims since the forced migration. In the process, they have come to see themselves as part of the larger Muslim community—Sunni as well as Shiite. Like the other Meskhetians, the Karapapakhs have become intensely devout, in large part because of the heavy-handed, oppressive, and violent anti-Islamic policies of the Soviet Union. Today the Karapapakh population exceeds 10,000 people, and, although most of them still reside in Central Asia, a small number of Karapapakhs were allowed to return to their traditional homeland in northern Armenia and southern Georgia in the 1980s. There are approximately 30,000 Karapapakhs in Iran and another 60,000 in Turkey.

REFERENCES: Alexandre Bennigsen and S. Enders Wimbush, *Muslims of the Soviet Empire: A Guide*, 1986; Ronald Wixman, *The Peoples of the USSR: An Ethnographic Handbook*, 1984.

KARAPZAPAKHI. See KARAPAPAKH.

KARASA SAMODI. See KARASA SAMOYED and ENT.

KARASA SAMOED. See KARASA SAMOYED and ENT.

KARASA SAMOIED. See KARASA SAMOYED and ENT.

KARASA SAMOYED. The Karasa Samoyed have also been known as the Forest Yenesei Samoyed and as the Forest Ents. They are composed of their own subgroups—the Muggadi, Bai, and Yuchi. All of them together make up one of the two subgroups of the Ent* people. See ENT.

REFERENCE: Ronald Wixman, *The Peoples of the USSR: An Ethnographic Handbook*, 1984.

KARASHI. See KARAGASH TATAR, ASTRAKHAN TATAR, and TATAR.

KARASIN SAMODI. See KARASA SAMOYED and ENT.

KARASIN SAMOED. See KARASA SAMOYED and ENT.

KARASIN SAMOIED. See KARASA SAMOYED and ENT.

KARASIN SAMOYED. See KARASA SAMOYED and ENT.

KARATA. The Karata, who call themselves the Kirtle or K'k'irdi and who have also been known as Karatai, Karatintsy, and K'j'aralal, are today considered to be a subgroup of the Avars*. They are part of the Andi* cluster of the Avar people. Like almost all other Avars, the Karatas are Sunni Muslims. They are concentrated demographically along the Andi River in the higher altitudes of southwestern Daghestan, primarily in the Akhwakh Region. Their main village is named Karata. Although it is difficult to estimate the current Karata population because of their census classification with Avars, demographers believe that there are approximately 10,000 people who identify themselves as Karatas or are aware of their Karata heritage. See AVAR.

REFERENCES: Shirin Akiner, *Islamic Peoples of the Soviet Union*, 1983; Ronald Wixman, *The Peoples of the USSR: An Ethnographic Handbook*, 1984.

KARATAI. See KARATA.

KARATAI. The Karatais (not to be confused with the Karata or Karatai people of the Caucasus) are a subgroup of the Mordvinians*. In recent years, because of settlement patterns in the Tetyushkiy Rayon of the Tatar Republic where most Karatais live, they have abandoned Mordvinian and taken up Tatar* as their primary language. See MORDVINIAN.

REFERENCE: Ronald Wixman, *The Peoples of the USSR: An Ethnographic Handbook*, 1984.

KARATAY. See KARATAI and MORDVINIAN.

KARATIN. See KARATA and AVAR.

KARATINTSY. See KARATA and AVAR.

KARELIAN. Karelians, who call themselves the Karjala (Karyala), Korela, or Karyalainen and who are known to Russians* as the Karely, are a group of eastern Finns* living in the former Soviet Union. They numbered approximately 130,000 people in 1990. The first permanent settlements in what is today Finland appeared around 100 A.D., when migrating tribes crossed over from the south side of the Gulf of Finland. These were part of the Finno-Ugrian peoples* who had originated in Central Asia and eventually evolved into such groups as the Finns, Estonians*, Magyars*, Mordvinians*, Lapps*, and Permians.

The Karelians are the Finns who were most heavily influenced by Russian culture. The vast majority of them live in Karelia, a region bounded by Finland to the west, the Murmansk region to the north, the White Sea and the area of Archangel to the east, and the St. Petersburg region to the south. Because of their proximity to Novgorodian Russians, they adopted the Eastern Orthodox religion instead of the Lutheran faith of other Finns. They speak three dialects of Finnish, all of which have been strongly influenced by Russian. Karelians living in southern Karelia are known as Livviki* and speak the Livvi dialect. Karjala is spoken by Karelians proper who live in northern and central Karelia. The Lyydiki* people, who live in Kondopozhskiy and the Olonets Rayon, speak the Lyydiki dialect.

Over the course of several centuries, the Finns' trading relationships strengthened with the Swedes in the west and weakened with the Slavs in the east. Those trading connections eventually gave the Finns an orientation more toward northern and western Europe than to the East. Those economic relationships soon evolved into political ties. The more highly centralized Swedes gradually established political control over the Finns. Roman Catholic missionaries, with Swedish military protection, brought Christianity to the polytheistic, animistic Finns in the thirteenth century, and, in the sixteenth century, when Lutheranism swept through Sweden and displaced Roman Catholicism, Swedish missionaries carried the new religion to Finland as well. At the same time, the Finns began to acquire the beginnings of a national consciousness and a literary language. Finnish is part of the western, Balto-Finnish* branch of the Finno-Ugrian linguistic family. In the early sixteenth century, Michael Agricola became the first writer to publish in the Finnish vernacular, but the cultural dominance of Sweden in Finland retarded the literary development of the language. It was not until the nineteenth century that Finnish became a truly literary language with an increasing volume of compositions.

By that time, most of Finland had also come under Russian control. As early as 1710, Peter the Great decided to take control of Finland, as a way of giving Russia an outlet on the Baltic Sea; by 1716, he had achieved this goal. The Russian-Swedish struggle for control of Finland raged on and off throughout the eighteenth century. In 1807, Napoleon and Tsar Alexander I discussed the Finnish question, and, at the conclusion of another Russo-Swedish war in 1809, Finland and the Aland Islands were ceded to Russia. Alexander I granted Finland the status of a semi-independent grand duchy, and, in 1811, the province of Viborg was added to Finland.

The Finnish experience at the hands of both the Swedes and the Russians had stimulated a growing sense of nationalism. Finland had been part of Sweden from the twelfth through the eighteenth centuries; the language of the state bureaucracy was Swedish. Swedes controlled politics and looked down upon the Finns as narrow-minded provincials. Russian control proved to be no better. By the end of the nineteenth century, Russia had abolished the Finnish army, drafted Finns into the Russian army, tried to impose Russian as the official language, and persecuted the Lutheran church in an attempt to impose Russian Orthodoxy. Under Tsar Alexander III, the Russian motto of ''one law, one church, one tongue'' became particularly obnoxious to the Finns, who began an active resistance to russification. Tsar Nicholas II all but eliminated the power of the Finnish legislature in 1899, and, within a few years, the office of the Russian governor over Finland had become a virtual dictatorship, complete with spies, a police state, deportations, censorship of the press, and arrests of Finnish nationalists.

The Peace of Tartu in 1920 established the boundary between Finland and the Soviet Union. The treaty also stipulated that the "language of administration, legislation and public education" in the Karelian Workers' Commune had to be the "local popular language"—the Finnish language. At that time, there were only about 1,000 Finnish-speaking people living in Karelia; most of them were Finnish Communists who had migrated to the area after the defeat of the Red Finnsk in the 1918 Finnish civil war. With the triumph of Bolshevism in the Soviet Union, those Finns had great influence. In 1923, the Soviet Union established the Karelian Autonomous Soviet Socialist Republic (ASSR). Throughout the 1920s and early 1930s, these Finnish Communists vigorously recruited other Finnish immigrants from Canada, the United States, and Finland to construct socialism in Karelia. Most of them settled in urban areas, but the countryside remained ethnic Russian. Nevertheless, the public schools taught in Karelian, and Karelian literary publications abounded. By the 1930s, the Karelian ASSR had been thoroughly "finnicized."

No sooner had the process of "finnicization" been completed than the Soviet Union launched an assault on Finnish culture and Finnish nationalism. On January 1, 1938, every trace of Finnish was banned within the Karelian ASSR, but the assault had actually started earlier. Between 1935 and 1938, Stalin had begun the purge of Karelian leadership, sending most prominent Finns to prison or to their deaths. By 1938, there were only a few Finns of any influence still living in Karelia. Also in 1938, the Soviet Union introduced a new written language— Karelian in Cyrillic letters. All publications in Finnish were prohibited, a campaign of burning Finnish books was launched, and all Finnish-language schools were closed. During the Russo-Finnish War of 1939–1940, the campaign only intensified, with Finnish being described as a "fascist language." Any published reference to Finland was prohibited. In 1940, the Karelian ASSR was dissolved and replaced by the Karelo-Finnish Soviet Socialist Republic, with Cyrillic Karelian as the official language. During the Finnish occupation of Russian Karelia from mid–1941 to mid–1944, Finnish again became the official language. When the Russians regained control of the region in 1944, it remained the official language, but Finnish publications were discouraged. In 1956, the Karelo-Finnish Soviet Socialist Republic was dissolved and replaced once more by the Karelian ASSR.

Since that time, the Karelians have been undergoing a rapid assimilation process with the neighboring Russian community. In 1989, barely half of the Karelians used Karelian as their native language, and fully 95 percent of them were bilingual in Karelian and Russian. Whether that process will continue is uncertain. In May 1988, the administration of Mikhail Gorbachev officially acknowledged the campaign of terrorism launched against the Karelians by Josef Stalin, and, in July 1990, a group calling itself the Karelian Republic declared autonomy from the Soviet Union and recognized Karelian and Vep* as official languages. Karelians have also formed a variety of associations to preserve their language and culture. See FINN.

REFERENCES: Paul M. Austin, "Soviet Karelian," *Slavic Review*, 51 (Spring 1992), 16–35; Ronald Wixman, *The People's of the USSR: An Ethnographic Handbook*, 1984.

KARELY. See FINN and KARELIAN.

KARGA. See SAGAI and KHAKASS.

KARIM. See RUSSIAN.

KARIN TATAR. See KARA TATAR and TATAR.

KARINSKIY TATAR. See KARA TATAR and TATAR.

KARJALA. See FINN and KARELIAN.

KARJALA. See IZHORA.

KARJALAINEN. See FINN and KARELIAN.

KARJALAINEN. See IZHORA.

KARJALAISET. See FINN and KARELIAN.

KARJALAN. See FINN and KARELIAN.

KARPATO-RUS. See CARPATHO-RUSYN.

KARPATO-RUSIN. See CARPATHO-RUSYN.

KARPATO-RUSSIAN. See CARPATHO-RUSYN.

KARPATO-RUSYN. See CARPATHO-RUSYN.

KARPATO-RUTHENIAN. See CARPATHO-RUSYN.

KARPATO-UKRAINIAN. See CARPATHO-RUSYN.

KARPATSKO-RUS. See CARPATHO-RUSYN.

KARPATSKO-RUSIN. See CARPATHO-RUSYN.

KARPATSKO-RUSSIAN. See CARPATHO-RUSYN.

KARPATSKO-RUSYN. See CARPATHO-RUSYN.

KARPATSKO-RUTHENIAN. See CARPATHO-RUSYN.

KARPATSKO-UKRAINIAN. See CARPATHO-RUSYN.

KARTLELI. See KARTLI.

KARTLI. The Kartli, who call themselves the Kartleli, are today considered a subgroup of the Georgians*. Some ethnographers believe, however, that the Kartli were actually the core group around which the process of ethnogenesis produced the Georgian ethnic group. The Kartli dialect provides Georgians with their literary language. The Kartli are Eastern Orthodox. See GEORGIAN.
REFERENCES: David M. Lang, *The Georgians*, 1966; David M. Lang, *A Modern History of Soviet Georgia*, 1962; Ronald Wixman, *The Peoples of the USSR: An Ethnographic Handbook*, 1984.

KARTLIAN. See KARTLI and GEORGIAN.

KARTLIN. See KARTLI and GEORGIAN.

KARTVELIAN. The term "Kartvelian" is a generic reference for people speaking such Kartvelian languages as Svanetian*, Laz*, Mingrelian*, Georgian*, and Adjar*, as well as the various subgroups of the Georgian nation.
REFERENCES: David M. Lang, *The Georgians*, 1966; David M. Lang, *A Modern History of Soviet Georgia*, 1962; Ronald Wixman, *The Peoples of the USSR: An Ethnographic Handbook*, 1984.

KARYALA. See FINN, KARELIAN, and IZHORA.

KARYALAN. See FINN and KARELIAN.

KARYM. See RUSSIAN.

KASHGAR. The Kashgar, who call themselves the Kashkarlik, are Sunni Muslims who today are considered to be a subgroup of the Uigurs*. They originated in the town of Kashgar in Chinese Turkestan and migrated to Central Asia— more specifically to the Fergana Valley—during the eighteenth and nineteenth centuries. See UIGUR.
REFERENCES: Shirin Akiner, *Islamic Peoples of the Soviet Union*, 1983; Ronald Wixman, *The Peoples of the USSR: An Ethnographic Handbook*, 1984.

KASHGARLUK. See KASHGAR and UIGUR.

KASHGARLYK. See KASHGAR and UIGUR.

KASHGARTSY. See KASHGAR and UIGUR.

KASHKARLIK. See KASHGAR and UIGUR.

KASHKILIK. See KASHGAR and UIGUR.

KASIMOV TATAR. During the fifteenth century, Prince Kasim emerged as the leader of the Kasimov Khanate, and the Tatars* who are descended from the people of this region are known as Kasimov Tatars. They were refugees from the Kazan Khanate who settled near Riazan. They soon came under the vassalage of Moscow. At the end of the 1980s, there were several thousand Kasimov Tatars living in the Riazan Oblast. See TATAR.
REFERENCES: Alexandre Bennigsen and S. Enders Wimbush, *Muslims of the Soviet Empire: A Guide*, 1986; Ronald Wixman, *The Peoples of the USSR: An Ethnographic Handbook*, 1984.

KASOG. See AZERBAIJANI.

KATTITTURDUR. See SHAH DAGH.

KAVKAZ EVREI. See MOUNTAIN JEW and JEW.

KAVKAZ EVREY. See MOUNTAIN JEW and JEW.

KAVKAZ IEVREI. See MOUNTAIN JEW and JEW.

KAVKAZ YEVREI. See MOUNTAIN JEW and JEW.

KAVKAZ YEVREY. See MOUNTAIN JEW and JEW.

KAVKAZSKIY EVREI. See MOUNTAIN JEW and JEW.

KAVKAZSKIY EVREY. See MOUNTAIN JEW and JEW.

KAVKAZSKIY IEVREI. See MOUNTAIN JEW and JEW.

KAVKAZSKIY YEVREI. See MOUNTAIN JEW and JEW.

KAVKAZSKIY YEVREY. See MOUNTAIN JEW and JEW.

KAVKHAZ EVREI. See MOUNTAIN JEW and JEW.

KAVKHAZ EVREY. See MOUNTAIN JEW and JEW.

KAVKHAZ IEVREI. See MOUNTAIN JEW and JEW.

KAVKHAZ YEVREI. See MOUNTAIN JEW and JEW.

KAVKHAZ YEVREY. See MOUNTAIN JEW and JEW.

KAVKHAZSKIY EVREI. See MOUNTAIN JEW and JEW.

KAVKHAZSKIY EVREY. See MOUNTAIN JEW and JEW.

KAVKHAZSKIY IEVREI. See MOUNTAIN JEW and JEW.

KAVKHAZSKIY YEVREI. See MOUNTAIN JEW and JEW.

KAVKHAZSKIY YEVREY. See MOUNTAIN JEW and JEW.

KAYBAL. See KOIBAL and KHAKASS.

KAYDAK. See KAITAK and DARGIN.

KAYTAK. See KAITAK and DARGIN.

KAYVAN. See VEP.

KAZAK. See KAZAKH and AZERBAIJANI.

KAZAKH. The Kazakhs are a Central Asian, Turkic*-speaking peoples whose vast homeland, Kazakhstan, is located between the Caspian Sea, the Urals, and the Tien Shan Mountains in northwestern China. It is bordered in the north by the Russian Federated Republic, and to the south by Turkmenistan, Uzbekistan, and Kyrgyzistan. Of all the Central Asian republics, Kazakhstan has the most widely varied landscape, together with extremes of temperature. During the existence of the Soviet Union, Kazakhstan was second in size only to the Russian Soviet Federated Socialist Republic (RSFSR) itself. According to the census of 1989, there were 8,137,878 Kazakhs living in Kazakhstan, forming a minority in their own homeland. Over a million Kazakhs may also be found in the Russian and Uzbek republics, while smaller numbers reside in Turkmenistan and elsewhere in the Commonwealth of Independent States (CIS). In addition, there are over 600,000 Kazakhs in the Sinkiang-Uigur Autonomous Region of the Peoples Republic of China, as well as smaller numbers in Mongolia (71,000) and Afghanistan (20,000).

Kazakh, a Turkic language, is from the Kypchak* group, Kipchak-Nogai subgroup, in the Altaic branch of Ural-Altaic languages. It is most closely related to the languages of the Nogais* and Karakalpaks*. The Kazakh language retains a base vocabulary of Turkic words but, mirroring the complex history of its speakers, it contains a large fund of loan words from Russian*, Mongol*, Persian*, Arabic, and Chinese*. There is no native Kazakh alphabet; instead, Kazakh was first written with the Arabic script, with the advent of Islam. That was abandoned in favor of Cyrillic in the 1920s. The Kazakhs place great emphasis on their oral literary tradition, which survives in the form of their epic poetry, the most highly evolved of that of any Turkic peoples. The Kazakhs also emphasize riddles and folk tales about their oral tradition, a trait they share with their Turkic cousins. Fortunately, modern Kazakh scholars have developed an abiding interest not only in collecting and preserving their traditional literature, but also in developing a contemporary literature as well.

The ancestry of the present-day Kazakhs is extremely mixed—and obscure— principally because of the lack of source material and because of their pre-literate culture for most of their history. The modern Kazakhs may be heirs to an extremely ancient culture, since the earliest unearthed artifacts can be dated to the early Stone Age, around 300,000 years ago. Many directly traceable physical and material artifacts found in Kazakhstan go back as far as the Bronze Age and belonged to tribes with names such as the Sacae, Usun, Kang-yueh, and Alani. Later infusions of other groups, such as the Karluks and Turgash in the sixth and seventh centuries, the Oguz, Kimaks, and Kypchaks in the eighth to the eleventh centuries, the Khitans in the twelfth century, and, finally, the Kerait and Naiman in the early thirteenth century all contributed to the ethnic Turkic base that make up the Kazakhs. The Mongol conquest of Central Asia in the early thirteenth century played a tremendous role in the intermingling and interbreeding of these various groups to produce the Kazakh people.

The etymological origins of the Turkic term "Kazakh," while engaging and worthy of analysis, serve only to confuse and obscure the possible origins of the Kazakh people. The term emerged in Russian sources around the fourteenth century and had a wide range of meanings—from someone with a "clean-shaven head except for a long topknot," to "independent, vagabond, freebooter, adventurer, free warrior, nomad," and so on. The latter definition was probably a description of the Kazakhs' fame throughout Central Asia for their equestrian abilities and their freedom of movement. Another source claims that the word is a derivative of the Mongol word *khasaq*, which means a wheeled cart used by the Kazakhs to transport their portable felt yurts (tents) and other belongings. A nineteenth-century explanation claims that "Kazakh" derives from two Turkic words: *kaz* (goose) and *ak* (white). According to Kazakh lore, a legendary white steppe goose turned into a princess and gave birth to the first Kazakh. The word "Kazakh" also denotes an old Turkic social institution, referring to tribes who broke away from their prince or kinsmen. At any rate, it is most likely that the Kazakhs derived their name from this final meaning and that they evolved into an historically distinct group.

After the break-up of the Golden and White Hordes and of the other Mongol successor states in the late fourteenth century, the most important group to emerge from their ruins was the Uzbek* tribal confederation led by Barak Khan. Upon his death, Abu'l Khayr of the Shayban family conspired with one of Barak's chief rivals for the title of khan, thereby dispossessing the legitimate heirs. Khan Abu'l Khayr (reigned 1428–1468) was able to consolidate and strengthen the Uzbeks against the first of many periodic onslaughts from the east by the Dzungarian Oirots* (Chinese-speaking Muslims, related to the Buddhist Kalmyk* Mongols) in 1456. Several military setbacks, however, opened the way for an insurrection led by Barak's disinherited sons. Princes Janibek and Girey (also called Kirai) broke away from their own tribe. Abu'l Khayr died in 1468 fighting against these breakaway, or "Kazakh," nomads, but his famous grandson, Muhammad Shaybani Khan, later went to found the Shaybanid dynasty of Samarkand and Bukhara. Official Soviet histories name Janibek as the first Kazakh khan, who was succeeded by Girey's son Buyunduk; other sources maintain that Girey was the first elected khan and was succeeded by Buyunduk upon his death. At any rate, warfare between the Uzbeks under Muhammad Shaybani and the Kazakhs under Buyunduk continued for the rest of the fifteenth century. Soon after the Kazakhs' capture of the most important of the Syr Darya cities, Yasi (later known as Turkestan) and two khans made peace in 1500, and the Kazakhs took control over a readily definable and economically viable territory.

Warfare between various tribes and competing khans was always a very disruptive problem to the Kazakhs. By the beginning of the sixteenth century, however, other tribes, such as the Kypchaks, Naimans, and Argyns, were willing to unite under the strong leadership of Buyunduk's successor, Kasim Khan (reigned 1509?–1518). Indeed, it was then, during Kasim's tenure, that a true "Kazakh" people—united by language, culture, social organization, and the desire for an independent life free of empire-building khans—emerged and initiated a period of peace and stability. After Kasim's death, internecine fighting broke out once again and the Kazakh state began to disintegrate. Around the same time (late fifteenth and early sixteenth centuries), the Kazakhs organized themselves into three independent hordes (from the Turkic *ordu*, or army): the Ulu Zhuz, Orta Zhuz, and Kichi Zhuz (the Great Hundred, the Middle Hundred, and the Small Hundred). These three hordes were also known as the Older, Middle, and Younger Hordes, while their populations were known as the eastern, middle, and western Kazakhs. The third of these hordes generated a fourth horde, the Bukei, or Inner Horde, in the nineteenth century. These hordes together comprised the Kazakh Khanate. Each of these hordes was made up of clan, tribal, and family units that had cultural and organizational features in common with neighboring Turkic tribes such as the Nogais, Karakalpaks, and the Teleuts*. The Older Horde, based in Semirech'e, coalesced in the early sixteenth century, taking over the lands previously occupied by the early Sacae and Usun tribes from the fourth to the second centuries B.C., and encompassing the Usun, Kangly, Dulat, Albani, Suan, Jalair, and other tribes. The Middle Horde emerged in the early sixteenth century, and its lands came to embrace the Kypchak, Argyn, Naiman, Kerait, Uak, and Kongrat tribes that lived in the area. The Younger

Horde consisted of three basic tribal confederations: the Zheti-Ru, Alim-Ulu, and the Bai-Uly.

Theoretically, each horde was headed by a great khan and was composed of tribal divisions led by lesser khans. In reality, the great khan was seldom able to command all the tribes of his horde and was forced instead to rule through coalitions. The constituent tribes followed his directives only when there was an external threat, such as a military invasion. The khans were responsible for representing their tribes or hordes in diplomatic contacts with outsiders. These hordes depended upon pastoral nomadism. Although a number of towns sprang up as centers for crafts and commerce, these were very widely scattered. Nonetheless, as a result of this urban influence, the tribes of the southern part of Kazakhstan began to adopt the Sunni branch of the Hanafi school of Islam around the eighth century, and the religion increasingly penetrated northward in subsequent centuries. The Kazakhs converted at a relatively late date and were never very strong practitioners of their faith. Numerous shamanistic practices and beliefs continued to survive within their syncretistic form of Islam, which included a host of local demons and spirits, while their mullahs often doubled as shamans. Socially, the Kazakhs were organized into two broad classes: the upper class, which consisted of sultans, khans, chiefs, and tribal elders, together with their families and retinues; and, the lower class, which consisted of the masses and the slaves. Governing everyone were diverse tribal laws, some elements of Sharia law, and the civil decrees of the Khanate.

Informal trading contacts between the Kazakhs and their Russian neighbors had begun as early as the late sixteenth century, but these contacts, though eventually formalized by 1738, remained limited until the Dzungarians once again swept into Kazakhstan around 1680. The three Kazakh hordes were unable to put up any concerted resistance, owing to their own political infighting. As a result, the Dzungarians were able to continue their periodic depredations until the early eighteenth century, at which time the Kazakhs were forced to seek Russian protection and at last came under a unified command. The Dzungarians were finally driven eastward into China where they were decisively defeated by the Manchus* in 1758. In addition to the Dzungarians, the Kalmyk Mongols had begun to move into Kazakh territory beginning in 1718. Their major offensive thrust westward in 1723 caught the Kazakhs completely by surprise, forcing the latter to abandon their flocks and possessions and to flee wildly. During their subsequent campaign, which lasted until 1725, the Kalmyks took over the territories of the Small and Middle Hordes in central Kazakhstan, including lakes Tengiz and Balkhash. The Kazakhs found themselves completely unable to manage a defense of their homeland against these nomadic incursions. These external threats, coupled with the Kazakhs' debilitating internal conflicts, convinced them of the necessity of swearing an oath of loyalty to the Russian crown and of forming a defensive alliance with Russia; the latter was in the process of expanding eastward into Siberia and Central Asia. The Small Horde, led by another Khan Abu'l Khayr (reigned 1718–1749), formed such an alliance with

Russia in 1731; the Middle Horde joined in 1740, and part of the Greater Horde finally joined in 1742. Together, the Russians and the Kazakhs were able to fend off the Kalmyk menace, but in so doing, Kazakhstan ceased to exist as an independent state. The Russians were so weakened from fighting that their advance into Kazakhstan was retarded for some time. Despite such temporary setbacks, however, the Kazakhs very quickly became subject to Russian influence and control.

The tsarist government began to construct a series of forts at key locations and to station large contingents of soldiers in the area. In addition, the Russians encouraged European and Russian immigration to Kazakhstan, where these groups expelled the natives and competed for the most productive agricultural lands. As part of their oath of fealty to the Russian throne, the Kazakhs had been obliged to accept Russian apportionment of their hunting grounds. Therefore, by the provisions of the ukase (decree) of 1756 (a settlement between the Russians and the Bashkirs*), the Kazakhs were prohibited from using the fertile pasturelands, known as the "Inner Side," between the Ural and Volga rivers. This ban placed tremendous pressure on the Kazakhs' already shrinking pasturage and started a vicious cycle of economic deprivation and hardship and has characterized their relationship with Russia up to the present day. The Kazakhs' continued use of the pasturage brought Russian reprisals, in the form of herd reductions that further strained their economy. For the Kazakhs, this period in their history is called the *Aqtaban Shubirindi*, or the "Great Retreat." In addition to the punitive herd reductions, the tsarist government, upon the death of Abu'l Khayr, began a policy of disruptive meddling in the political affairs of the three hordes.

Abu'l Khayr's son and successor in the Small Horde, the unpopular Nur Ali Khan (reigned 1748–1786), came to the throne with Russian backing. He became a virtual puppet of the Russians, since he was otherwise unable to consolidate his position against his main rival, Sultan Batir Janibek. In spite of this political handicap, Nur Ali was able, at times, to pursue an independent policy toward Russia and to strike an equilibrium between both Russia and China. Since the Russians considered their relationship with the Small Horde as a showcase that had the potential for making inroads against the other Kazakh hordes, they were careful to treat Nur Ali with due considerations. In order to treat the nomadic Kazakhs in a more rational diplomatic manner, the Russian government built a fixed residence for Nur Ali in 1767, just as they had earlier built sheds and stables for his herds. In spite of Russian solicitousness, however, major friction between the Russians and the Small Horde continued. The conflicts centered around the use of the Inner Side pasturage (which the Russians had granted to Bashkir claimants), Nur Ali's perception of a conspiracy between his own brothers and Catherine II to prevent the succession of his son Ishim, and the mysterious deaths at Orenburg of two successive sons whom Nur Ali had entrusted to the Russians as hostages.

It was during this period of high tension between the Russian government and the Small Horde that the Pugachev Revolt of 1772–1774 flared up. It became the main channel for Kazakh dissatisfaction with the Russians and ultimately involved the Cossacks* against the Kazakhs. Emelyan Pugachev was an illiterate Don Cossack* who, wanting revenge for the mistreatment of his people by the Russian government, took advantage of the widespread rumor that Catherine II's husband, Peter III, had not actually been murdered. Pugachev, claiming to be Peter, soon found himself at the head of an army of rebellious malcontents and dispossessed serfs. Pugachev and his rabble eventually fought their way to the Ural Mountains, to a territory adjacent to that of the Small Horde. While the Russians were preoccupied with fighting Pugachev, especially during the unsuccessful siege of Orenburg in 1774, the Kazakhs were able to raid the Russian settlements and to take their herds into the forbidden pasturage of the Inner Side. In addition, the Small Horde entrusted 200 Kazakhs to Pugachev as security, granted 400 rebels protection in Kazakh territory, and committed a few thousand Kazakh troops to the siege of Orenburg.

More serious, however, was the Kazakh Rebellion of 1773–1776, which had been touched off by Pugachev's revolt and which continued beyond his defeat and execution. The goal of the Kazakh Rebellion was to gain access and control of the Inner Side, but internal discord among competing factions against Nur Ali's rule rendered success nearly impossible. Those allied against Nur Ali were led by an anonymous warrior identified in Kazakh folk tales only as the Invisible Man. After Pugachev's surrender, Nur Ali quickly allied himself with the Russians, a situation that only reinforced the opposition's resistance to him as a puppet of the Russians. Outright civil war threatened the Small Horde as the khans were unable to control the opposing clans. Eventually, in February 1775, the Russians were compelled to send a detachment of 300 Cossacks and 500 Bashkirs to restore order. The Cossacks were able to quash the rebellion by the summer of 1776, for which the Russian rewarded them with grants of land in Kazakhstan's already shrinking pasturage. The loss of large amounts of pasturage to the Cossack and Russian colonizers, coupled with the general brutality of the Cossack advance, provoked a tremendous amount of hostility and guerrilla resistance from the beleaguered Kazakhs. Nur Ali's quickly diminishing authority continued to evaporate.

Throughout this same period, the Russians were also making separate attempts to strengthen their ties with the Middle Horde. In 1731, the Russian government sent an emissary to Semeke Khan of the Middle Horde, offering him official recognition and suzerainty. Semeke, like the other Kazakh khans, was wont to treat his relationship with the Russians as an expedient to minimize the threat posed by the Dzungarians. For this reason, his relationship with the Russians appeared capricious and undependable. Semeke died in 1733 before the patents of investiture, naming him khan of the Middle Horde, could be conferred upon him. His son and successor, Abu'l Muhammad, was obliged to share power with another leader, Ablai Khan, who was the stronger of the two. In 1740, as a result of renewed hostilities with the Dzungarians, the two leaders went to

Orenburg to swear fealty to the Russians, and so came, albeit very loosely, into the Russian orbit. For about twenty years, Ablai shared rulership with Abu'l Muhammad, gradually easing the latter out of the seat of power by the year 1750. From then until his death in 1781, Ablai skillfully vacillated between the Russians and the Chinese, manipulating both powers to his horde's benefit. For example, Chinese sources claim that Ablai became a tributary to the Manchus, something that the Russian sources vigorously deny. Ablai led his tribe across the borders to pasturage in both empires and attacked border settlements at will. He flouted his relationship with the Russian border authorities while simultaneously claiming that his submission to China had been involuntary. For its part, Catherine's government attempted to woo Ablai firmly back into the Russian fold by building him a permanent palace and village, granting him an annual allowance of grain, and so forth. But Ablai was able to spurn these offers and to snub others at will. He thus maintained a good measure of tribal unity and political independence for the rest of his tenure. Following Ablai's death in 1781, however, his son Vali, like Nur Ali Khan of the Small Horde, soon came under the domination of the Russians. He controlled only a few of the clans, while the majority of the elders elected their own nominee, who ruled with the support of the Chinese. By the end of the eighteenth century, Vali had dissipated his power to the Russians, who made the position of the khan largely honorary.

The history of the Greater Horde was significantly different from those of the other two Kazakh hordes. Instead of gradual assimilation and a dissipation of political power to the encroaching Russian state, the Greater Horde experienced a progressive break-up and diaspora away from its traditional base in the Semirech'e region around the southern end of Lake Balkhash. The majority of the Greater Horde Kazakhs had been under the political control of the Dzungarian khanate. In the 1730s, however, when the other hordes were swearing their fealty to the tsarist government, one group of the Greater Horde Kazakhs broke off and joined with Er Ali, the son of Abu'l Khayr of the Small Horde. When the Chinese defeated the Dzungarians in 1758, the remaining majority of the Greater Horde Kazakhs came under Chinese control and obtained the right to move into former Dzhungar territories. Those Kazakhs who wanted to take advantage of the opportunity to claim these rich pasturelands migrated into Dzhungaria, while others moved to the Tashkent area east of the Aral Sea. This third group mixed with the native Karakalpak population and settled down to a semi-sedentary existence. Those Kazakhs who remained encamped in the traditional homelands in Semirech'e, abutting as it did Dzungaria, managed to establish their independence from China.

By the early nineteenth century, the Greater Horde Kazakhs of the Tashkent and Semirech'e region were subject to expansionist incursions not only by the Russians but by the Khokand Khanate of the Uzbeks, led by Shaybanid Omar Khan (reigned 1809–1822) and his successor Muhammad Ali Khan (reigned 1822–1840), as well. Sultan Suiuk, son of Ablai Khan of the Middle Horde, decided in 1818 to cast his lot with the Russians. This move was responsible for bringing 55,000 Kazakhs under Russian rule and for establishing a Russian foothold in the area for future penetration. Nonetheless, many of the ruling-class Kazakhs in these two regions recognized the suzerainty of the Khokand Khanate because it allowed them to retain their former social status and taxation privileges; the herder and farmer classes vacillated between Russia and Khokand as their tax burdens dictated. For their part, the Khokand khans persuaded the Kazakhs to support them because of their shared Islamic heritage, arguing that the Russians, as infidels, were illegitimate rulers of Muslims. The Russians constructed the Siberian military line, which not only demarcated Russian possessions from those of the Chinese but also constituted the frontier outposts of the struggle against Khokand and its allies, the khanates of Kiva and Bukhara. The Great Horde Kazakhs recognized Russian suzerainty in 1844 and were finally incorporated into the Russian Empire by 1865, following Russia's conquest of Tashkent, Aulie-Ata, Turkestan, Merke, and Chikment, which had cut the Kazakhs off from Khokand. The final annexation of the Khokand Khanate itself was accomplished in 1876.

From the end of the Pugachev Revolt until well into the twentieth century, the Kazakhs put up an almost continuous resistance to the Russian government. In turn, the Russians came to distrust Nur Ali and the Kazakhs and were thus increasingly motivated to rule the Kazakhs directly, allowing the khan to devolve into a mere figurehead. The questions of pasturage in the Inner Side and of land tenure remained paramount in Kazakh dealings with the Russians and often brought them into direct confrontations with the Cossacks, who had been awarded those Inner Side lands that had not previously been allocated to the Bashkirs. The Russians also began to refer to the Kazakhs as the "Kyrgyz Kazakhs" or the "Siberian Kyrgyz," to distinguish them from the Slavic Cossacks in whose midst many Kazakhs lived. In 1782, the Russians gave permission for Nur Ali and his family to use the Inner Side. This situation only created more problems, as it fueled the popular view of Nur Ali as a selfish opportunist and encouraged other clans to flout the ban. Armed clashes broke out between Kazakhs and Cossacks and also among the Kazakhs themselves throughout 1782–1783. Discontent flared into open revolt on numerous occasions, beginning with Sirim Batir's revolt of 1783, which involved part of the Middle Horde against the Cossacks. In response, the Russians were compelled to tighten their grip on political developments in Kazakhstan. Since Nur Ali was unable to control the Kazakhs as the Russians had demanded of him, the leading Kazakh elders met in 1785 to depose Nur Ali in favor of his brother, Er Ali. Other measures, such as the Igel'strom Reform of 1787–1790, which was initiated to pacify the warring clans, actually called for the abolition of the khanate and the division of the Small Horde into three different administrative units. The result was a virtual Russian protectorate over the Kazakhs, through which the former began actively to assimilate the Kazakhs into the Russian Empire.

In 1801, the Russian government created the Bukei, or Inner Horde, named for Nur Ali's son Sultan Bukei, in response to the perennial Kazakh need for more pastureland. This horde was allowed to take up residence in the area between the Volga and Ural rivers, in nominally Russian land. It was hoped that the creation of the Bukei Horde would alleviate the land problem, as indeed it did for the next twenty-five years. But the Horde prospered and grew so large that the old land problem surfaced again, becoming worse than ever. The Russians then embarked on a two-pronged program of acculturation in order to domesticate the Kazakhs. First, Russian schools were founded, beginning in 1789, which not only taught the Russian language to Kazakh children but inculcated them with the fundamentals of Western-style civilization. Second, throughout the nineteenth century, the Russians encouraged the practice of Islam. Compared to other Muslims who came under Russian rule, such as the Crimean Tatars* and Volga Tatars*, the Kazakhs did not reach the levels of economic, social, political, and cultural development of these other, more sedentary Muslims. As a result, they were more susceptible to economic and cultural influence, but less prone to social and political control. The policy of promoting Islam generally proved to be a long-term failure from the Russian perspective, since it encouraged conservatism and exclusivity among the Kazakhs. The Russians also tried other measures, such as providing free seed, loans, and tax exemptions to certain Kazakhs and permitting the Kazakhs to graze their herds in Cossack lands. Nonetheless, the anarchy engendered by the paralysis of the khan's authority, the virtually continuous state of warfare in Kazakhstan, and the encroachments of the Khivan Uzbeks into the Greater Horde all threatened the future of Russian trade and expansion in Kazakhstan. Finally, in 1824, the Russians were compelled to abolish the khanate completely in the Middle Horde, to modify it in the Small Horde, and to annex the territory of the Greater Horde entirely.

From then until the 1860s, the Speransky Reforms (formally known as the *Rules on the Siberian Kyrgyz*, promulgated in 1822), together with other reforms, were responsible for sweeping changes in the political and economic organization of the Small and Middles Horde Kazakhs. Ruling the Middle Horde from Omsk, the Russians divided the Kazakhs into administrative units, the smallest being the clan or *aul* (*rodavia uprava*), consisting of approximately fifteen homogeneous families. In turn, ten to twelve auls were organized into *volosts* (*inorodnaia uprava*); eighty-seven volosts made up four *okrugs* (districts), of which there were eventually seven. The Russians introduced a representative assembly into each okrug, which contained not only Kazakh representatives but Russian ones as well, sent by the Orenburg authorities. Still the overall administration of the Kazakhs remained in the hands of the Orenburg Frontier Commission. The reforms also attempted to induce the Kazakhs to become sedentary and to engage in farming, for which they were given plots of land, tools, and seed. The pomp and ceremony of the Kazakh nobility were maintained, while their powers were drastically curtailed; for example, they could use their hereditary titles and own land but were prohibited from owning serfs. The Orenburg Kyrgyz (formerly, the Small Horde Kazakhs) were ruled by a sultan-administrator, whose regularized duties gave him the use of an assistant, a secretary (scribe), a staff of five messengers, and a detachment of 100 to 200 Cossacks. This set-up was later extended to the Inner Horde as well. The Russians envisioned the functioning of the Kazakh civil service class as resembling that of an up-to-date, bureaucratic machine that could efficiently process tsarist mandates among the local natives. In practice, the Kazakh bureaucracy never functioned as well as the traditional political structures had. Indeed, it sometimes even exacerbated crisis situations, as the masses were wont to lump their own native rulers in with the Russian enemy. The political problem, in short, was that the Russians effectively destroyed the Kazakh aristocracy in the first half of the nineteenth century without creating anything to replace it.

The political reorganization of the Small and Middle Hordes, while far-reaching and thorough, surprised the tsarist government by its failure to ameliorate the continuing resistance among the clans. As always, the crux of Kazakh discontent was the need for more grazing land, the pressures for which resulted in two major uprisings. First, the hard winter of 1826–1827 forced many Kazakhs to risk the confiscation of their herds as a result of their search for pasturage across the Ural River. The Inner Horde Kazakhs made similar attempts to cross the Ural with their herds again in 1827–1828 and in 1829; each time, they were met with Russian armed force. This political and economic disruption, combined with frequent, localized violence, the continuing tax burden in the face of economic crisis, and the coercive presence of the Cossacks, provided the perfect pre-conditions for the revolt of Kenisary Qasimov, grandson of Ablai Khan of the Middle Horde. He is viewed by many Kazakhs as the first Kazakh nationalist. The revolt, lasting from 1837 to 1846, had as its most immediate cause the abolition of the rank of khan, but this issue soon became a lightning rod for all manner of discontents. Kenisary's movement excited mass support and alarmed the Russian authorities because his prestige and charisma threatened to bring the other hordes into what could have evolved into a full-scale Kazakh war. At any rate, Kenisary's revolt, with over 20,000 warriors at his command, was significant as the last concerted action by the horde. In the face of continuing resistance, the Russians attempted further political measures, land reforms, and social recombinations throughout the rest of the nineteenth century. All of these failed to pacify the essentially nomadic, herding culture of the Kazakhs.

A second and more violent revolt in July 1916 was centered in the Semirech'e region. In order to cope with the demands of World War I, the Russians issued edicts to the already overburdened Kazakhs, increasing their taxes and animal quotas and, for the first time, obliging them for military service through the draft. The Kazakhs, who had traditionally been exempted from military service by the tsars, interpreted the edicts as heralding a change in the policy toward the people of the steppes. They responded by attacking Russian and Cossack villages indiscriminately, killing some 2,500 Russians and Cossacks. The Russians responded by organizing a military force that drove some 300,000 Kazakhs either to flee into the mountains or else across the border into Chinese Sinkiang. Most of the Kazakhs' livestock, including 60 percent of their cattle, and their immovable belongings were looted by the colonists living among them. When they returned in the summer of 1917, around 83,000 starving and defenseless Kazakhs were slaughtered and, in some instances, burned alive by vengeful colonists. An additional million would later die of starvation during the 1921–1922 famine after losing their cattle to the Slav settlers, the White forces, and the Bolsheviks.

With relief and optimism, the Kazakh people welcomed the news of the February 1917 Revolution in Russia, which installed a provisional government under Premier Alexander Kerensky. The few intellectuals in Kazakh society at the time enthusiastically set about creating a Kazakh nationalist party, the *Alash Orda*, founded by Bukei Khan-uli; this organization was intended to represent the Kazakhs in the Russian parliament. The Kazakhs believed that the new government would work to rectify their long-standing grievances and perhaps even afford them a measure of autonomy. They were quickly disappointed, however, when the Bolsheviks took over in November and disbanded the constitutional government. For their part, the Kazakhs were bitterly divided into pro- and anti-Bolshevik camps that were too preoccupied with feuding among themselves to present a united front against the Communists. Those unable to support the new regime turned to the Alash Orda, transforming the party into an autonomous government that fought beside the tsarist White forces against the Bolsheviks. After the defeat of the Whites, the Bolsheviks created the Kyrgyz (Kazakh) Autonomous Soviet Socialist Republic (ASSR) within the RSFSR on August 26, 1920. Many Kazakhs then began to look toward accommodation with the new Soviet government, while the Alash Orda began to take on the character of a powerful nationalist movement.

Kazakh nationalism was fueled by the Stalinist policy of forced collectivization. The Soviet government appointed Filip I. Goloshchokin as Kazakhstan Party Secretary; in this capacity, he was responsible for encouraging the resumption of the colonization of Kazakhstan, a process facilitated by the opening of the Turkestan-Siberian Railway line, which cut across the eastern part of Kazakhstan, in 1930. In addition, Goloshchokin attempted to settle and collectivize around 400,000 Kazakh nomads. Kazakh nationalists, seeing the forced collectivization as an attempt both to russify the Kazakhs and to confiscate their cattle, resisted the policy bitterly. Nearly 70 percent of the collectives collapsed in 1932 when the Kazakhs fled into Chinese Sinkiang rather than submit to collectivization. The total Kazakh population declined by 22 percent, or roughly 1,500,000 persons, between 1926 and 1939, while towns and cities became predominantly Russian centers. Some of the drop can be attributed to the out-migration of Kazakhs to Sinkiang and Uzbekistan, but most of it was due to the violence of their resistance and to starvation.

In the same period, the Kazakhs slaughtered up to 80 percent of their herds, at first to prevent their nationalization but later to prevent the animals' starvation. This action proved to be the greatest hardship on the livestock-oriented Kazakh economy. By 1939, Kazakhs made up less than 50 percent of the population of their own republic. For his mistakes, Goloshchokin was removed shortly after the collectivization debacle, but the abrupt depopulation of Kazakhstan had an adverse effect on the long-term political and economic health of the region. Agricultural output fell to one-third of its pre-war level. Soviet concessions to encourage the Kazakhs' return and allegiance (in the form of allowing some private ownership of livestock) only served to stimulate the activities of Trotskyists, Bukharinists, and Kazakh "nationalist deviationists." For their part, Kazakh nationalists countered the tightening of the Soviet grip with active measures to halt further Russian colonization of the steppe and to drive out the ones already there. They envisioned a Kazakhstan that was for the Kazakhs; the Russian, Cossack, and Ukrainian* peasants would receive their share of land only after the Kazakhs themselves had been satisfied. The Soviet government, declaring these acts illegal, immediately eliminated the Kazakh nationalists from the Communist Party of Kazakhstan, a political blow from which the Kazakh nationalist wing never fully recovered. Soviet authorities in Kazakhstan were also obliged to deal with the Alash Orda, which they first courted, then actively persecuted, and eventually succeeded in suppressing.

The Stalinist political purges of the late 1920s and again in the late 1930s completed the process of breaking down the Kazakhs' resistance toward integration into the Soviet state. Those who voiced opposition to Moscow's policies were criticized for "bourgeois nationalism" and were, in many cases, purged. Some leading Kazakhs were removed in 1925, while others—even opponents of the Alash Orda—disappeared in 1927. The local ruling elite was liquidated, beginning in 1935, the Kazakh Communist Party was created in 1937, and the Kazakh national leadership had virtually disappeared by 1938. They were replaced in many cases by handpicked Russians, but native Kazakhs did assume political positions when their political loyalty was beyond question. These factors worked to change entirely the social and political complexion of the Kazakh people.

In spite of—or perhaps because of—these drastic political and cultural changes, the Kazakh economy remained stagnant until the early 1950s. But, in 1953, Nikita Khrushchev decided to transform the tremendously fertile but "under-utilized" lands of southern Siberia and northern Kazakhstan into a new breadbasket region for the Soviet Union. This so-called "Virgin Lands" policy not only required of the Kazakhs yet another economic shift, this time from grain-growing state farms (*sovkhoz*) to livestock-breeding state farms, but also a whole new bureaucratic apparatus, including the young Leonid Brezhnev, handpicked by Moscow to ensure the success of the new venture. These changes drew the two governments closer together and led to the integration of the Kazakh economy and party more fully into the Soviet administration. In addition to the Virgin Lands policy, the Soviets worked from World War II onward to transform Kazakhstan into a major industrialized center. For example, the third-largest coal-producing center in the Soviet Union was located in central Kazakhstan; the space exploration center is also located there. Oil production and copper mining were stimulated, and large numbers of Russian and Ukrainian technicians and skilled workers were imported into the region to staff the various enterprises. By their very concentration, they contributed to the urbanization of Kazakhstan.

After Brezhnev became General Secretary, he appointed a Kazakh party hack named Dinmukhamed Kunaev to fill his vacated position as first party secretary back in Kazakhstan. Kunaev held the position until December 1986, when he was removed by President Mikhail Gorbachev and replaced by an ethnic Russian. The news of his dismissal led to growing dissatisfaction among nationalist elements within Kazakh society, resulting in rioting, in which several persons were killed, and compelling Gorbachev to act with more sensitivity during the *perestroika* ("restructuring") era. Other indications that the Kazakhs were heeding the nationalist call were to be found in Soviet publications issued from Kazakhstan since the 1970s. For example, one letter published in the *Sotsialistik Kazakhstan* criticized the seemingly deliberate bad spelling of Kazakh language signs, the nonsensically literal translations from Russian, and the use of Russian loan words, even when Kazakh equivalents were available; all were signs of passive resistance on the part of the Kazakhs. Other editorial comments in newspapers included lectures on the need to rebuff nationalistic epidemics and the scolding of writers and artists for "enthusiasm and distortion." In the rural areas, nationalism was manifested by the maintenance of traditional customs and attitudes.

The Kazakhs became champions of reform of the Soviet system through their attempts to secure greater autonomy from Moscow. Gorbachev's *perestroika* appeared to offer them that opportunity. For example, a 1987 law abolished all restrictions on the number of animals that a farmer could maintain, resulting in a boom in the sheep, goat, and cattle populations. This, in turn, spurred a tremendous growth in meat sales. Kazakh nationalists also supported Gorbachev, maintaining that dangerous degree of support even through the coup attempted by Soviet hardliners against Gorbachev on August 19, 1991. Kazakh President Nursultan Nazarbayev came to international attention by publicly condemning the coup attempt and calling for Gorbachev's restoration. After the failed coup, Nazarbayev pressed his country's advantage by severing all ties with the discredited Communists and with the Kazakh Communist Party, which was compelled to disband. The politically astute Nazarbayev did not call for an immediate declaration of independence from Moscow; indeed, he strongly supported some form of continued union until it became obvious that the old union was dead. This move was necessary because Kazakhstan's economy, society, and culture are still strongly linked with those of Russia.

Since the failed coup of 1991, the citizens of Kazakhstan have created a presidential-parliamentary system of government that closely resembles that of Russia. Nazarbayev ran unopposed for its presidency. He continues to lack political opposition from his constituency, probably because he has not acted in a dictatorial manner, appears to be in favor of political pluralism, and enjoys the support of Russians as well as of ethnic Kazakhs. Nazarbayev has also taken an active role in international relations by joining with Boris Yeltsin in a mediation effort between Azerbaijan and Armenia and with the presidents of Russia, Ukraine, and Belarus to create the Commonwealth of Independent States (CIS), in a treaty signed in Alma-Ata. U.S. diplomatic concern centers around the continued presence of nuclear weapons in Kazakhstan; the United States is attempting to persuade the Kazakhs to return those weapons to the Russians. When Nazarbayev paid a visit to Washington in May 1992, he gave assurances that he would not oppose the withdrawal of those weapons within seven years and indicated a willingness to sign the Non-Proliferation Treaty, but only because American policymakers pledged to protect Kazakhstan in the event of a threat by a nuclear power. Most recently, the Kazakhs have been assembling a constitution that guarantees human rights to its citizens.

REFERENCES: Shirin Akiner, *Islamic Peoples of the Soviet Union*, 1983; W. Barthold, "Kazak," in *Encyclopedia of Islam*, 1983, 848–49; René Grousset, *The Empire of the Steppes: A History of Central Asia*, 1970; Martha Brill Olcott, *The Kazakhs*, 1987; Richard Pipes, *The Formation of the Soviet Union: Communism and Nationalism, 1917–1923*, 1980; Michael Rywkin, ed., *Russian Colonial Expansion to 1917*, 1988; M. Wesley Shoemaker, ed., *Russia, Eurasian States, and Eastern Europe, 1992*, 1992; Wayne S. Vucinich, *Russia and Asia: Essays on the Influence of Russia on the Asian Peoples*, 1972; Joseph L. Wieczynski, *The Modern Encyclopedia of Russian and Soviet History*, 1984, vol. 38.

Lee Brigance Pappas

KAZAN TATAR. The Kazan Tatars, who call themselves the Qazanlyk and who have been known as the Kazanlik, are perhaps the largest and most significant of the Tatar* groups in what used to be the Soviet Union. They are the descendants of Volga Bolgars, Volga Finns*, and Kypchak* Turks*, and their language reflects that diverse ancestry. The literary language of Tatar groups is based on the Kazan dialect. Most of the time, when people refer to the Tatars, they are actually describing the Kazan Tatars. See VOLGA TATAR and TATAR.

REFERENCE: Alexandre Bennigsen and S. Enders Wimbush, *Muslims of the Soviet Empire: A Guide*, 1986.

KAZANIS. See VOLGA TATAR.

KAZANLIK. See KAZAN TATAR and TATAR.

KAZANLUK. See KAZAN TATAR and TATAR.

KAZANLYK. See KAZAN TATAR and TATAR.

KAZI KUMUH. See LAK.

KAZI KUMUK. See LAK.

KAZI KUMUKH. See LAK.

KAZIKUMUH. See LAK.

KAZIKUMUK. See LAK.

KAZIKUMUKH. See LAK.

KAZYM. See KHANT.

KEBERDEI. See KABARD.

K'EBERDEI. See KABARD.

KEDAES. See KHWARSHI and AVAR.

KEDAES HIKWA. See KHWARSHI and AVAR.

KELDIKE. The Keldike are today considered to be a subgroup of the Kyrgyz*, even though their ethnic and linguistic roots are non-Kyrgyz. See KYRGYZ. *REFERENCE:* Ronald Wixman, *The Peoples of the USSR: An Ethnographic Handbook,* 1984.

KEMGOI. See CHERKESS.

KEMGOJ. See CHERKESS.

KEMIRGOI. See ADYGHE, CIRCASSIAN, and TEMIRGOI.

KEMIRGOY. See ADYGHE, CIRCASSIAN, and TEMIRGOI.

KEREK. The Kerek are a subgroup of the Koryak* who live along the coast of the Bering Sea. See KORYAK. *REFERENCE:* Ronald Wixman, *The Peoples of the USSR: An Ethnographic Handbook,* 1984.

KERJAK. See KERZHAK.

KERKETIAN. See CIRCASSIAN.

KERZHAK. The Kerzhak are ethnic Russians* who moved from their original homeland along the Kerzhenets River in the Nizhegorodskaya Gubernia. They are Russian Old Believers who fled persecution from the Russian Orthodox Church. As Old Believers, the Kerzhak are collectively classified as Starozhily*. See RUSSIAN or STAROZHILY.

REFERENCE: Ronald Wixman, *The Peoples of the USSR: An Ethnographic Handbook*, 1984.

KET. The Kets (Kett) are a tiny Siberian group whose long-range presence in the former Soviet Union as a functional ethnic group is highly threatened. They have also been known historically as the Eniseian Ostyaks*, Eniseians, Tingiyet, Kanacket, Din, Yenesei Ostyaks, and Yeniseis. Today the Ket population barely exceeds 1,000 people. They live in the Yenesei River Basin of western Siberia, particularly along the middle and lower Yenesei River in Turukhan Rayon and Yartsevskiy Rayon in the Krasnoyarsk Krai of the Russian Soviet Federated Socialist Republic (RSFSR). The Ket language is still spoken by most of the Kettish people, but ethnolinguists have had a difficult time classifying it. Some Soviet linguists categorize it as the last surviving language of the Yeneseian language family. More particularly, they see it as part of the Ket-Pumpokol' group of such languages. There are two surviving dialects of Ket: Imbat, which is spoken in the northern reaches of the Yenesei River Valley, and Sym (Iug), which is spoken by only three or four people in the southern part of the valley.

Historically, the Kets were a hunting and fishing tribe who migrated regionally in search of deer, bear, and other game animals. They lived in relatively small clan groupings and in semi-permanent dwellings, usually birch-bark tents. The Kets traveled up and down the Yenesei River and its tributaries in dugout birch canoes. Many ethnologists consider the Kets to be descendants of the original inhabitants of Siberia, which explains the unique structure of their language. They do not have the Asian physical features of most other Siberian inhabitants, and their complexions are much fairer. Their own points of origin are probably in the Tom basin.

Because of their location in western Siberia, the Kets were among the first Siberian peoples to be contacted by ethnic Russians* expanding east of the Ural Mountains. At the time of the arrival of the first Russians, early in the seventeenth century, there were several major Ket subgroups: the Kets proper, Kotts, Asans, Aras, Yaras*, and Baikots. The Kotts were already paying fur tribute to the Kyrgyz*, and Kott resistance to the Russians often had Kyrgyz support. But the presence of large numbers of Russians, as well as the economic changes that their presence brought to other Siberian groups, precipitated a process of assimilation among the Kets. By the late 1800s, the Kotts had been absorbed by ethnic Russians. The Asans had merged with the Evenks*, while the Ara, Yara, and Baikot had been absorbed by the Khakass*. Only the northernmost Ket group survived as self-conscious ethnic entity.

With increasingly large numbers of ethnic Russians in the region, some of the northernmost Kets gradually adopted reindeer breeding as the mainstay of their economy; hunting and fishing assumed only a secondary, supplemental importance. The reindeer, with their hides, meat, and milk, became central to the Ket economy, and Ket life revolved around the herds. Even the Ket religion changed. It remained, of course, animistic and shamanistic, but to the pantheon of deer and bear gods were added rituals and prayers to protect the reindeer herds. Russian Orthodox missionaries built churches and schools among the Kets as well, so Ket religious beliefs became a curious conglomeration of Christianity and the indigenous tribal faith.

Those Kets less willing to submit to Russian acculturation began a migration toward the Arctic. By the end of the seventeenth century, some Kets had reached the confluence of the Yenesei and Lower Tunguska rivers. Separated from other Ket clans, these Kets found themselves increasingly marrying Selkup* peoples; in the process, they lost some of their Ket identity. The Kets who remained in the south became an extremely oppressed, exploited people whom Russian settlers considered to be inferior. But even though they adopted a number of Russian institutions, they remained aware of their Ket identity.

The Russian Revolution brought about another series of dramatic changes in Ket life. Josef Stalin's preoccupation with collectivization forced the Kets into reindeer-breeding collective farms called *kolkhozes*. During the 1940s and 1950s, the Kets added gardening, dairy livestock, and fur farming to the list of collective activities. The Soviet scholar N. K. Karger tried to develop a writing system for the Kettish language in the 1930s, but the Kets never really adopted it. Those who became literate now use Russian as their literary language. In more recent years, as the industrialization and economic development of Siberia have accelerated, some Kets have found a variety of other types of employment. In the process, their interaction with ethnic Russians and other Siberian groups has become more extensive. Practically all Kets are bilingual in Ket and Russian, and increasingly large numbers of them are marrying non-Kets. The facts that they are no longer nomadic and that their children attend public schools are also stimulating assimilation. By the early 1990s, some Ket leaders were calling for a revival of Kettish culture, national autonomy, and self-determination. Because their numbers were so limited, they were convinced that only the establishment of some type of autonomous national territory for Kets would give them the ability to resist russification and preserve what remained of their national culture.

REFERENCES: Violet Conolly, *Siberia Today and Tomorrow: A Study of Economic Resources*, 1975; B. O. Dolgikh, *Kety*, 1934; *The Soviet Encyclopedia*, 1973, vol. 17, 426–27; Erwin C. Lessner, *Cradle of Conquerors: Siberia*, 1955; Piers Vitebsky, "Perestroika Among the Reindeer Herders," *Geographical Magazine*, 61 (June 1989), 23–24; Ronald Wixman, *The Peoples of the USSR: An Ethnographic Handbook*, 1984.

KETSH KHALKH. See KHINALUG, SHAH DAGH, and AZERBAIJANI.

KETSIK. See CHULYM TATAR.

KETT. See KET.

KEZEK. See ICHKILIK and KYRGYZ.

KHAAS. See KHAKASS.

KHAIDAK. See KAITAK and DARGIN.

KHAIDAKI. See KAITAK and DARGIN.

KHAIDAQ. See KAITAK and DARGIN.

KHAIRYUZOVO. See ITELMEN.

KHAITAK. See KAITAK and DARGIN.

KHAITAQ. See KAITAK and DARGIN.

KHAKASS. The Khakass, who call themselves the Khaas, are perhaps the most unusual ethnic or nationality group in the former Soviet Union. Almost all of them live in the southern reaches of the Krasnojar Territory of Russia. Before the Russian Revolution in 1917, they were not even known as the Khakass and did not identify themselves as a distinct people. Russians* referred to them as the Minusinsk (Minusa), the Turki, Yenesei Tatars*, or the Abakan Tatars*, but the Khakass did not identify themselves with any name. They are still much more likely to identify themselves by regional geographic identities. Those territorial groups are further subdivided by powerful clan loyalties, which themselves are grouped into strong family systems. The five main territorial groupings of the Khakass are the Kacha*, Kyzyl*, Sagai*, Beltir*, and Koibal*. The name "Khakass" was not used until after 1923 when Soviet authorities decided to replace the term "Minusinsk Tatars" to describe the tribes.

Ever since the late seventeenth century, a process of ethnogenesis has been at work creating the Khakass people. The Kacha (Kachin) tribe of the Khakass people developed from a fusion of Ket* and Uigur* peoples in south-central Siberia. The Kettish groups that went into the Kacha ethnogenesis were the Tatysh, Yara*-Yasta*, Abalak, Tin, and Aboltai, while the Uigur groups were the Shalosa, Mungat, Tatar*, Kuba, and Tuba*. The Kets are animists in terms of their religious loyalties, while the Uigur are Sunni Muslims. This combination rendered Kacha beliefs rather syncretic in nature. The Kachas lived on the east bank of the Abakan River, worked as semi-nomadic cattle breeders, and were known widely for their poetry. The Kyzyl tribe also represents a fusion of Uigur and Ket peoples, primarily from Melet, Acha, Argun, Kurchik, Basagar, Igin, Kamlar, and Shusty groups. The Beltir tribe is of primarily Tuvinian* extraction—that is, from the people who occupied the Abakan steppes and worked as farmers and cattle breeders. The Tuvinians are primarily Buddhists, with a good admixture of animist traditions, so Beltir beliefs are also quite eclectic. The Koibal are thoroughly Turkified linguistically today, and they are descendants of Samoyedic* and Kettish people, especially the Tarazhak, Kol, Abugach, the

Greater and Lesser Baikot, Kandyk, and Arsh. They originated in the Sayan Mountains and migrated to the Upper Yenisei River on the Abakan steppes. The Sagai are descended from an extremely complex mix of ancestors, including such Shor* groups as the Sebecha, Sai, Aba, Chetti Puri, Koby, Kyzylgaya, Karga, Shor, Kyy, Tom, and Tay clans; the Kyrgyz* and Pyuryut peoples, who are Yenesei Kyrgyz in origin; and such groups of Siberian Uigur as the Ichige, Turan, Choda, Irkit, and Sargyl. Their religious beliefs are also animist. Superimposed on all of these religious beliefs, however, was a veneer of Eastern Orthodox Christianity, which Russian* settlers and missionaries brought to Siberia in the eighteenth and nineteenth centuries.

The language of the Khakass people is primarily derived from the Uigur group of the Eastern Hun languages of the Turkic* language family. The Khakass language has also borrowed heavily, in terms of vocabulary, from other languages, especially Russian, Persian*, Arabic, and Mongolian. The three primary Khakass dialects are Kacha, Sagai, and Kyzyl. The Kacha dialect forms the heart of the Khakass language, and it is the basis of literary Khakass. The Soviet government formally established the language in 1922 on the basis of the Cyrillic alphabet. An attempt was made in 1929 to switch that alphabet to a Latin base, but Cyrillic was restored in 1939.

Before the arrival of Russian settlers in the seventeenth century, the Khakass were semi-nomadic hunters, fishermen, and livestock raisers. They also practiced a primitive form of agriculture. In 1759, the region of Khakassia was conquered by the Uigurs, but their rule was short-lived. Within a century, the Khakassians had reasserted themselves politically, brought an end to Uigur domination, and emerged as the most powerful state in Siberia. They became widely known because of their commercial interactions with Central Asia and China. The area of Khakass settlement began the process of incorporation into Russia when Russian forts and trading posts were constructed at Tomsk in 1604 and Krasnoiarsk in 1628. The increasing presence of Russians brought an end to the periodic Mongol* incursions into Khakassian land, and the Khakassians recognized the value of the Russian presence. Khakassians leaders asked Tsar Alexei Mikhailovich to annex their region in 1664, as a means of permanently protecting them from Mongol depredations, but it was not until the reign of Peter the Great that the annexation was complete. He constructed a fort on the Abakan River and sent a Cossack* regiment to man it.

But the Russians brought their own forms of imperialism, including tribute payments, seizure of the best agricultural land, and the imposition of Christianity. The whole area also became a place of formal exile for opponents of the various tsars. In the 1890s, the Trans-Siberian Railroad cut through Khakass land and brought increasing numbers of ethnic Russians, making Khakassians a small minority (in the 1980s, ethnic Khakassians constituted 12 percent of the population there, while Russians were more than 78 percent).

The Russian Revolution brought a dramatic change to the Khakass after 1917. The Khakass National Okrug was established in 1923 with the capital at Abakan.

The Khakass Autonomous Oblast (AO) was created in 1930. Josef Stalin collectivized Khakass agriculture in the early 1930s, forcibly ending the semi-nomadic hunting and foraging practices of those Khakass still engaged in that type of economy. In 1935–36, Soviet authorities crushed a budding pan-Turkic national movement in which the Khakass, Altais, and Kazakhs were to become part of a new Turkic Soviet republic. Industrialization of the economy of the Khakass Autonomous Oblast accelerated after World War II, with an emphasis on such extractive industries as coal, iron ore, and timber. In the 1960s, such light industries as textiles, building materials, and food processing became increasingly prominent. More and more Khakass abandoned life on the collective farms for industrial jobs. The collective farms in Khakass territory raise spring wheat, oats, potatoes, sheep, cattle, and hogs.

The Khakass sense of national identity is quite weak, at least compared to many other groups in what was formerly the Soviet Union. Powerful centrifugal forces still divide the Khakass into Kachi, Kyzyl, Sagai, Koibal, and Beltir tribes, with each of those groups fractured into powerful clan and family systems. The Kacha today live on the steppes on the left bank of the upper Yenesei River in the Khakass AO. The Kyzyl, for their part, are concentrated demographically in the White and Black Iyus river valleys and around Lake Bozhe in the Khakass AO. The Beltir live on the middle and upper Abakan River, while the Sagai live on the steppes between the Kuznets Alatau Spur and the Kamyshta and Abakan rivers in the Khakass AO; the Koibal live on the steppes between the Abakan River, the Yenesei River, and the Sayan foothills. Khakassian religion is now a complicated mixture of animism, Islam, Eastern Orthodoxy, and Buddhism, eclectic enough to prevent religious identities from contributing to any sense of nationalism. The Khakass are increasing rapidly, from 45,608 in 1926 to 56,584 in 1959, 66,725 in 1970, 70,776 in 1979, and more than 81,000 in 1989. The presence of so many Russians around the Khakass, however, has introduced powerful assimilationist forces among them. Nearly 70 percent of the Khakass are fluent in Russian, and more than half of the Khakass are marrying ethnic Russians. In recent decades, Russian ethnologists have also included several Tatar* groups within the larger Khakass category, including the Abakan Tatars, Chulym Tatars*, Meletski Tatars*, Minusinsk Tatars*, and Yenesei Tatars.

Mikhail Gorbachev's policies of *glasnost* and *perestroika* unleashed powerful nationalist forces in the Soviet Union in the 1980s, and the Khakass people were no exception. Groups such as the Khakass Cultural Center and the Tun Association of the Khakass People began asserting themselves, working to reduce Communist political power in the Khakass AO and to promote Khakass cultural institutions. A few radical Khakass activists talked of secession from the Soviet Union, but more moderate voices simply called for Khakassian sovereignty within the Soviet Union. The ethnic Khakass constitute only 11 percent of the population of the province, while ethnic Russians total nearly 80 percent. In August 1990, the provincial soviet proclaimed a Khakass Republic, but ethnic

Russians protested any attempt to secede from the Soviet Union. The Khakass Council of Elders then began demanding that the most influential positions in the provincial government be set aside for ethnic Khakass, a proposal that ethnic Russians resented and opposed. Ethnic Russians also opposed the formation of special Khakass militias. The proposal triggered the formation of special military units of ethnic Russians who claimed to be Cossacks. After the dissolution of the Soviet Union in 1991, these debates between the Khakass and the Russians in Khakassia continued.

REFERENCES: *Current Digest*, 42 (January 22, 1992), 26–27; James Forsyth, *A History of the Peoples of Siberia*, 1992; Mikhail Sarazhakov, "Khakassia: Birthplace of the American Indian?" *Soviet Life* (May 1989), 16–17; *Soviet Encyclopedia*, 1973, vol. 28, 548–51; Ronald Wixman, *The Peoples of the USSR: An Ethnographic Handbook*, 1984.

KHALKHA. The Khalkhas, also known as Mongols* or Khalka Mongols, are a small ethnic group whose cultural ties are to the people of the Mongolian People's Republic (MPR). Their language, known as Khalkha Mongolian, is the official language of the MPR. Historically, Russia and the Soviet Union have been very interested in the Khalkhas because of their strategic concerns about Mongolia. Russian and Soviet policymakers have long wanted to influence the nominally sovereign, huge, and sparsely populated MPR. The MPR had been supervised far more closely and allowed less independence than any of the former East European satellites. It was considered by some to be virtually a sixteenth republic of the former Soviet Union.

The Khalkhas are closely related—culturally, linguistically, politically, and religiously—to the much more numerous Buryats* of the Soviet Union. The Buryat language is a dialect of Mongolian, but different enough from the standard Khalkha Mongolian of the MPR so that speakers of the two dialects cannot really understand one another. Like Buryat society, Khalkha social organization is based on the family, clan, and tribe. Their favorite sports include wrestling, horse racing, and archery. Their epics consist of enormously long *uligers*, or poems. Marriages are exogamous and arranged. The Khalkha economy was traditionally based on sheep, horses, and cattle. Hence, their diet featured domesticated meat and milk products, supplemented by hunting and trapping. Whole tribes hunted together, sending beaters into the woods to flush out game and to slaughter Siberian stags, reindeer, foxes, and wolves.

The original Khalkha religion was shamanism, a belief that the world is permeated by good and bad spirits who can be propitiated through chants and rituals performed by shamans (witches). Lamaism (Tibetan Buddhism) spread north from Tibet to Mongolia, reaching the Khalkhas in the seventeenth century, at the very same time that Russians* were bringing Eastern Orthodoxy Christianity from the west. The result is that, among the western Buryats, about half are shamanist and half are Christian, while the Buddhism of the Transbaikal Buryats is syncretically mixed with shamanism. The Khalkhas also became Buddhists. By the time of the first Russian contacts, Khalkha society had evolved into a theocracy in which every family gave sons to the monkhood. The *datsans* (Buddhist monasteries) controlled much of the best land.

Russian explorers, trappers, and later settlers reached Lake Baikal in the 1600s. The territory and its people were taken into the Russian state by the treaties of Nerchinsk (1689) and Kyakhta (1728), which delineated spheres of influence between tsarist Russia and Manchu China. Typically, Soviet historians have described the russification of the Khalkhas as "progressive" and the anti-Russian uprisings of 1695 and 1696 as "anti-feudal." Historically, Russian imperialism had a religious tone, and Khalkhas were sometimes baptized forcibly. When the Trans-Siberian Railway reached Irkutsk in 1898, it seemed that Khalkha culture in Russia might vanish entirely, especially since government officials gave Khalkha and Buryat land to Slavic immigrants. During the Russo-Japanese War of 1904–1905, Japanese* agents spread a "pan-Mongol" ideology, in an effort to woo Buryats and Khalkhas from their allegiance to Russia. Russia lost the war and ceded certain Far Eastern territories to Japan, but a secret agreement in 1907, followed by a formal treaty in 1912, recognized Outer Mongolia as a Russian sphere of influence. Therefore, pan-Mongolism might now be used as a positive weapon to keep all Mongols within the Russia empire.

Buryats and Khalkhas did not play an important role in the Russian civil war of 1918–1922, but Japanese military forays deep into Siberia revived Russian fears of Mongol disloyalty. To many Russians, all Asians looked alike and were untrustworthy. To keep the Japanese at bay, the Bolsheviks used Buryats and Khalkhas to make Mongolia the first Soviet satellite. Buryat radicals, Khalkha followers, and Soviet agents promoted a Mongolian "revolution" in 1921, and a clique of Soviet Buryats actually ran Mongolia until 1928, dominating the indigenous Khalka Mongols. At times, they pursued pan-Mongol, not exclusively pro-Russian, policies.

V. I. Lenin created the Buryat-Mongol Autonomous Soviet Socialist Republic (BMASSR) in 1923. Of course, it was really a sub-unit of the Russian Federation of the Soviet Union, autonomous in name only. The first six years of Soviet power were peaceful. Then, on May 27, 1929, the Party Central Committee decreed the "socialist re-organization" of Buryat agriculture. The subsequent collectivization was an unmitigated disaster. Buryats and Khalkhas slaughtered their livestock rather than see them confiscated. Nomads were forcibly settled on collective cattle and sheep farms. Hunters were forced to live in what the Communist Party called "well-equipped hunting stations," and trappers were made to rear sable in captivity. Many Buryats and Khalkhas fled to Mongolia, but things were no better there, for the MPR politburo was no less faithful in carrying out Josef Stalin's wishes. Outright rebellion in the MPR in 1931 and 1932 forced Stalin to relent, but only because fresh Japanese aggression in Manchuria raised the value of Mongol loyalty.

Japanese encroachments fueled Stalin's suspicion of all Asians, especially since Japan posed as the defender of Buddhists worldwide. The Communists accused Buryat and Khalkha lamas of sabotage and used that as a pretext to destroy monasteries and to defrock monks in Buryatia and Mongolia. Buryats and Khalkhas had already been removed from power in the MPR; now treason was found in the BMASSR as well. Mikhail Yerbanov, the Buryat party boss, was suddenly discovered to be a bourgeois nationalist; he was shot, along with fifty-three others, on October 12, 1937. Then Stalin carved up Buryatia, transferring the eastern steppe to Chita Oblast and the four western counties to Irkutsk Oblast. The Mongolian script was banned. To dilute the Buryat and Khalkha population, special privileges were decreed for Russian and Ukrainian* settlers. In 1943, Stalin dissolved the autonomous republic of a different Mongol people, the Kalmyks*, and scattered them around the Soviet Union. In 1944, he incorporated the formerly Mongolian Tannu Tuva region into Russia as the Tuva Autonomous Oblast. These bizarre territorial manipulations continued after Stalin's death. In 1958, when Mao Zedong's overtures to the MPR aroused old Russian fears, the name ''Mongol'' was taken away from Buryatia: The Buryat-Mongol ASSR became simply the Buryat ASSR.

Along with an assault on Buryat culture, the Soviet government worked diligently to russify Khalkha culture. Publication of Khalkha epic poems was banned in the 1950s, regulations were passed prohibiting the public display of Buddhist symbols, many Buddhist monasteries were closed, and Khalkha children were forced to attend public schools where the language of instruction was Russian. Between 1959 and the late 1980s, the Khalkha population of the Soviet Union declined from more than 5,000 people to fewer than 3,000. The real reason for the decline, however, was less the oppressiveness of the Soviet state than the omnipresence of Buryat culture. Khalkha culture and identity are rapidly disappearing into the larger Buryat culture.

REFERENCES: Walter Kolarz, *The Peoples of the Soviet Far East*, 1954; William O. McCagg and Brian D. Silver, eds., *Soviet Asian Ethnic Frontiers*, 1979; Robert Rupen, *How Mongolia is Really Ruled*, 1979; Robert Rupen, *Mongols of the Twentieth Century*, 1964; K. V. Vyatkina, ''The Buryats,'' in M. G. Levin and L. P. Potapov, eds., *The Peoples of Siberia*, 1964, 203–42; Pyotr Zubkhov, ''Buryatia: A Republic on Lake Baikal,'' *Soviet Life*, 378 (1988), 41–46.

                                                                            Ross Marlay and James S. Olson

KHALKHA MONGOL. See KHALKHA.

KHALKA MONGOLIAN. See KHALKHA.

KHAL'MG. See KALMYK.

KHAMSHENLY. See KHEMSIL.

KHANAG. See TABASARAN.

KHANDEIAR. See KHANDEYAR and NENETS.

KHANDEYAR. The Khandeyar, who are also known as the Forest Nenets and the Forest Yurak, are one of the main sub-divisions of the Nenets* people. See NENETS.
REFERENCE: Ronald Wixman, *The Peoples of the USSR: An Ethnographic Handbook*, 1984.

KHANSUITSY. See DUNGAN.

KHANT. The Khants, or Khanty, are a people of the Russian Far East who number approximately 21,000. Russians* traditionally refer to the Khants as Ostyaks*, sometimes calling them Ob Ostiaks, Obdor, Berezov, and Surgut Ostiaks as well. The area in which the Khants make their home is located on northwestern Siberia along the lower reaches of the Ob River. The majority of the Khants live in the Khanty-Mansi Autonomous Area of the former Soviet Union. The Khanty-Mansi Autonomous Area became part of the present-day Russian Republic following the collapse of the Soviet Union after the failed coup of August 1991. Some Khants are also found in the neighboring Yamalo-Nenets Autonomous Area; others inhabit the northern portions of the Tomsk Oblast.

The Khanty tongue belongs to the Ugrian* division of the Finno-Ugrian group of languages. Other languages within the Ugrian division are Mansi*, the language of a small neighboring tribe in northwestern Siberia, as well as Magyar*. The Khanty and the Mansi tongues are grouped together as the Ob-Ugrian languages, a term reflecting the location of the two groups in the basin of the Ob River in the Western Siberian Plain. Similarly, the Khants and Mansi are often referred to collectively as the Ob-Ugrian peoples. The Khant language is divided into ten dialects. Four of the dialects—Obdor, Shuryshkar-Berezov, Kazym, and Sherkaly—make up a northern dialect group. Three are contained in a southern dialect group—Altym, Leusha, and Irtysh-Konda; three others—Surgut, Salym, and Vakh-Vas'-Yugan—make up an eastern dialect group.

Historians have presented two sharply contrasting theories concerning the origins of the Khants. One view holds that their first homeland was in the valley of the Pechora River in the northeastern corner of European Russia. In this view, the Khants were the "Yugrians," mentioned in Russian chronicles as early as the twelfth century. This people subsequently moved eastward, crossing the Ural Mountains and resettling in the basin of the Ob River. The opposing view holds that the Khants were formed around 500 A.D. out of a mixture of peoples originally located east of the Urals. In this view, steppe peoples from the Irtysh basin migrated northward and blended with the old Uralic tribes that had been settled in the north since 2000 B.C.

The home of the Khants is located in the Arctic tundra and taiga. It is a region of deep northern forests and swampland that remains frozen during most of the year. Within this harsh environment, the Khants have developed a set of distinct social and economic practices and institutions. Similarly, Khanty religious beliefs have taken clear forms. Traditional Khanty religious belief stresses reincarnation.

Each new-born Khant is seen as the reincarnation of a deceased member of the tribe. Thus, the birth of a child is accompanied by ceremonies designed to establish the reincarnated identity within the newborn and to give the infant the suitable ancestral name. Before the Soviet period, shamans were openly called upon to perform religious ceremonies and to provide healing services. Khanty religion included the worship of wooden idols that represented sacred animals and deceased clan ancestors.

Until well into the twentieth century, the Khants were largely a nomadic hunting and fishing people. They also engaged in herding reindeer. Their social organization revolved around a system of patrilineal clans. The clans, in turn, were grouped into multi-clan phratries. The traditional Khanty social system stressed severe restrictions on women within the multi-family households common to Khanty life. The presence of women was thought to defile household idols and to offer dangerous temptation to male members of their husbands' families. Khanty women therefore covered their faces with veils. They were restricted from entering large areas of the family hut, and they were barred from the attic, where their presence would defile everything on the floor below.

The Khants came under Russian control during the closing decades of the sixteenth century and in the first portion of the seventeenth century. Following the first great Russian penetration of Siberia under the Cossack* leader Yermak in 1581, Russian fur traders established themselves in this region. They were soon followed by government officials. In 1595, a Russian administrative center was set up at Novosoy Gorodok (now Salekhard) at the mouth of the Ob River on the site of the Khanty town of Punovatvash.

Russian fur traders and government officials constituted only a minority of the population in this thinly inhabited region. Nonetheless, they used their monopoly of firearms and their links to friendly Khanty tribal leaders to assert control. A fur tax was imposed on the Khanty population, but the nature of the terrain made it possible for the Khants to escape serious exploitation by moving away from the Russian settlements. Thus, armed rebellion against Russian authority rarely occurred. The Khants were officially converted to the Russian Orthodox Church by the middle of the eighteenth century, but the conversion was only nominal. Traditional Khanty religious beliefs and social structures largely survived.

By the early years of the nineteenth century, Russian entrepreneurs had begun encroaching on native lands. Political leaders, notably Michael Speransky, the reforming governor-general of Siberia in the years 1819–1822, established laws to shield the Khants from exploitation. But the remoteness of the region and the scanty governmental presence there prevented effective enforcement. Marxist writers have stressed the sweeping way in which entrepreneurs stole Khanty land and fishing grounds.

Russian influence began to have its greatest effect on the Khants following the Bolshevik Revolution of 1917. An indication of the gap between Khanty and Russian society came in 1923: The government could not find a single literate member of the Khants to take part in an agricultural exhibition in Moscow. A special government body, the Committee of the North, was set up in 1924 to deal with peoples like the Khants. It introduced basic elements of modern civilization, such as scientific medical care and primary schools, and it campaigned against the subjugation of women. By the close of the 1920s, Russia's northern regions were organized on a territorial basis. As part of this process, the Khanty-Mansi National Area was formed in the years 1930 and 1931.

The Russian impact on the Khants intensified after 1929, as all of Soviet society was being reshaped under the leadership of Josef Stalin. The government developed a Khanty alphabet, and books were published for the first time in the Khants' language. Production units, such as fishing, hunting, and reindeer-breeding collectives, were formed. Russian settlers and officials in these northern regions conducted an active campaign against the traditional Khanty religion. Social practices, such as the role of shamans in treating disease and the abduction of brides, were also condemned. Deliberate efforts to modernize the Khants extended beyond Stalin's death in 1953. In the 1960s, for example, the government sponsored ''open face'' ceremonies to encourage Khanty women to abandon their veils.

The result, according to anthropologist Marjorie Mandelstam Balzer, has been a blend of indigenous and Russian ways. Khanty beliefs and cultural practices have survived most clearly among the minority of the Khants who continue to live a nomadic existence as reindeer herders in the extreme north. Still, the majority of Khants, who follow a settled life-style in fishing and agricultural villages, also cling to tradition in many ways. Balzer has pointed out that even Khants who speak Russian, own snowmobiles, and served as Communist Party officials preserve their ethnic identity via rituals connected to important life-cycle events. Thus, Khanty women continue to seclude themselves during and after giving birth. They no longer depart to a birth hut in order to deliver their infants apart from the male population, but deliveries in Soviet maternity hospitals serve the same purpose. More important, they avoid contact with men for the traditional period of two months following a birth. Many continue to cover their faces with the veil.

Balzer found that even Khants who held Communist Party offices participated in rituals, such as those reflecting a belief in reincarnation. Thus, she has noted Khants who demonstrate ''plural social identities.'' At the same time, older Khanty women have remained more isolated from the social change stimulated by the Soviet government. They are still less likely than male members of their families to speak Russian or to attend Russian films. This portion of the Khanty population is thus a particularly strong conservative influence pushing for the preservation of traditional beliefs and rituals. Nonetheless, Soviet influence has been a factor in permitting changes in the crucial area of male-female relationships. Balzer has concluded that Khanty women used Soviet disapproval of the tradition of separating menstruating women in isolated huts to end a practice to which they themselves had already come to object.

In the important burial ritual of the Khants, bodies are now washed and internment takes place in an atmosphere of silence; both these elements reflect Russian influence. Moreover, the practice of piling the possessions of the deceased on his grave has been modified. Miniature sleds are now used to symbolize the actual possessions of the deceased. Russian Orthodox crosses and Soviet military decorations are often seen on Khanty grave piles. Government pressure, based on economic needs, has curtailed the former sacrifice of reindeer and work animals.

The developments of the Soviet period have brought most of the Khants into a settled life-style in fishing and hunting villages. Most live and work alongside their Russian neighbors in such settings. The phenomenon of a common village cemetery, divided into Russian and Khanty sections, is a symbol of both the encroachments of the outside world and the continuing effort to preserve a Khanty identity. At the same time, the recent discovery of oil and natural gas deposits in the region of the Khants promises further challenges to Khanty traditions.

By the late 1980s, Soviet economic policies had left western Siberia in a shambles. Massive oil extraction projects, with the consequent oil and chemical spills, all but ruined the fish catches, and a variety of large-scale engineering projects had done similar damage to reindeer pasturages. The proposed construction of railroads, roads, and pipelines to move natural gas to markets promised even more damage. Khanty writers like Yeremey Aipin and Roman Rugin protested the environmental catastrophe engulfing their people. Many educated Khants have joined the interest groups representing indigenous peoples, and they support their demands for more cautious development policies that will permit the survival of indigenous peoples and their cultures.

REFERENCES: Terence Armstrong, *Russian Settlement in the North*, 1965; Boris Babanov, "The Khanty: In Harmony with Nature," *Soviet Life* (January 1989), 30–34; Marjorie Mandelstam Balzer, "Behind Shamanism: Changing Voices of Siberian Khanty Cosmology and Politics," *Social Science & Medicine*, 24 (1987), 1085–93; Marjorie Mandelstam Balzer, "Rituals of Gender Identity Markers of Siberian Khanty Ethnicity, Status, and Belief," *American Anthropologist*, 83 (December 1981), 850–67; Marjorie M. Balzer, "The Route to Eternity: Cultural Persistence and Change in Siberian Khanty Burial Ritual," *Arctic Anthropology*, 17 (1980), 77–85; James Forsyth, *A History of the Peoples of Siberia*, 1992; M. G. Levin and L. P. Potapov, eds., *The Peoples of Siberia*, 1956; Ilmari Manninen, *Die finnisch-ugrischen Volker*, 1932; Z. P. Sokolova, *Sotsial'naia organizatsiia Khantov i Mansi v XVIII-XIX vv.: Problemy fratrii i roda*, 1983; Z. P. Sokolova, *Strana Iugoriia*, 1976.

Neil M. Heyman

KHANTAIKA. See ENT.

KHANTAIKA SAMODI. See KHANTAIKA SAMOYED and ENT.

KHANTAIKA SAMOED. See KHANTAIKA SAMOYED and ENT.

KHANTAIKA SAMOIED. See KHANTAIKA SAMOYED and ENT.

KHANTAIKA SAMOYED. The Khantaika Samoyed, who are also known as the Tundra Yenesei Samoyed, are one of the major Ent* divisions. They are a nomadic people who wander across the open tundra. See ENT.
REFERENCE: Ronald Wixman, *The Peoples of the USSR: An Ethnographic Handbook,* 1984.

KHANTI. See KHANT.

KHANTY. See KHANT.

KHAPUT. See GAPUT, DZHEK, SHAH DAGH, and AZERBAIJANI.

KHAPUTLIN. See GAPUT, DZHEK, SHAH DAGH, and AZERBAIJANI.

KHAQASS. See KHAKASS.

KHARDURI. The Kharduri are today classified as a subgroup of the Tajiks*, although their ethnic and linguistic origins are non-Tajik. Most of them live in the Surkhan-Darya Oblast of the Uzbek Republic. See TAJIK.
REFERENCE: Ronald Wixman, *The Peoples of the USSR: An Ethnographic Handbook*, 1984.

KHASAVA. See NENETS.

KHASAV-JURT. See KUMYK.

KHASAVYURT. See KUMYK.

KHATUKAI. The Khatukai are one of the constituent subgroups of the Adyghe* people in the North Caucasus. During the 1860s, the vast majority of Khatukais migrated to Turkey, leaving behind only the small minority who still live between the Belaya and Pshish rivers. See ADYGHE.
REFERENCE: Ronald Wixman, *The Peoples of the USSR: An Ethnographic Handbook*, 1984.

KHATUKAY. See KHATUKAI and ADYGHE.

KHAYDAK. See KAITAK and DARGIN.

KHAYDAQ. See KAITAK and DARGIN.

KHAYRYUZOVO. See ITELMEN.

KHAYTAK. See KAITAK and DARGIN.

KHAYTAQ. See KAITAK and DARGIN.

KHAZAR. See JEW.

KHAZARA. The Khazara, who also call themselves the Berber or Barbari, are an ethnic group in Afghanistan who are divided between the Shiite Muslims in the east and the Sunni Muslims in the west. They were politically independent until 1884, when Amir Abdur Rahman of Kabul brought them under his control. Most of the Khazaras had become Shiite Muslims during the reign of Shah Abbas I, but, during the reign of Nadir Shah in the mid-eighteenth century, the Barbari, a Khazara subgroup, became Sunnis. Although the vast majority of Khazaras live in Afghanistan, a small number still living in the Tajik and Turkmen republics are aware of their Khazara roots. In both of those places, the surviving Khazara are in a state of advanced assimilation. They are classified as a Tajik* subgroup. See TAJIK.

REFERENCES: Shirin Akiner, *Islamic Peoples of the Soviet Union*, 1983; Ronald Wixman, *The Peoples of the USSR: An Ethnographic Handbook*, 1984.

KHEAK. See CHERKESS.

KHEMSHILY. See KHEMSIL and ARMENIAN.

KHEMSHINY. See KHEMSIL and ARMENIAN.

KHEMSIL. The Kehmsil (Khemshin, Armenian Muslims), who call themselves the Hemshili or Khamshenly, were once Armenian Orthodox Christians who came under the influence of the Ottoman Turks* in the eighteenth century. They have also been known historically as Khemshiny and Khemshily. The vast majority of them live in Turkey. They converted to the Sunni Muslim faith and became loyal to the Hanafi theological school. During the nineteenth century, a small number of Khemsils migrated across the Russian border into what is today the Adjar Autonomous Republic. Adjaria is part of the larger Georgian Republic and lies along the border of Turkey. By the time of the migration, the vast majority of the Khemsils had abandoned Armenian* as their native tongue and adopted Turkish. The 1926 Soviet census listed the Khemsil population at 629 people; in subsequent censuses, they were lumped together with Armenians or Azerbaijanis*. In 1944, the Soviet government forcibly relocated all Khemsils to Central Asia, primarily to the region around Tashkent. They have still not been permitted to return to Adjaria. Instead, they have become part of a process of ethnogenesis that has created a new Soviet ethnic group—the Meskhetians*. Soviet demographers estimate the contemporary Khemsil population—in terms of those who identify themselves as Khemsil or who are aware of their Khemsil heritage—at around 1,000 people. See MESKHETIAN, ARMENIAN, or AZERBAIJANI.

REFERENCES: Shirin Akiner, *Islamic Peoples of the Soviet Union*, 1983; Ronald Wixman, *The Peoples of the USSR: An Ethnographic Handbook*, 1984.

KHEMSIN. See KHEMSIL.

KHEVSUR. The Khevsur are today considered to be a subgroup of the Georgians*, and they are one of the Kartvelian* groups around which the Georgian nation formed. Khevsur mythology claims that they are descended from medieval European crusaders who tried to bring Christianity and conquer the Holy Land; their religion is a cultural fusion of indigenous animistic traditions and Eastern Orthodox Christianity. Most of the Khevsurs live along the upper Eastern Aragvi River and the upper Argun River in the Georgia Republic. See GEORGIAN.
REFERENCE: Ronald Wixman, *The Peoples of the USSR: An Ethnographic Handbook*, 1984.

KHEVSURI. See GEORGIAN.

KHEVSURIAN. See GEORGIAN.

KHIK. See WAKHAN, TAJIK, and PAMIR PEOPLES.

KHINALUG. The Khinalug, who call themselves the Kattitturdur or the Ketsh Khalkh, are one of the Shah Dagh* peoples; Russians* refer to them as the Khinalugtsy. They are Sunni Muslims and live near Mount Shah Dagh in the Azerbaijan Republic. They are especially concentrated in the village of Khinalug in the Konakhkend Region. Most Khinalugs today speak Azerbaijani and are assimilating with that surrounding majority group. Soviet demographers estimate the contemporary Khinalug population—in terms of those who identify themselves as Khinalug or who are aware of their Khinalug heritage—at around 2,000 people. See SHAH DAGH or AZERBAIJANI.
REFERENCES: Shirin Akiner, *Islamic Peoples of the Soviet Union*, 1983; Ronald Wixman, *The Peoples of the USSR: An Ethnographic Handbook*, 1984.

KHINALUGH. See KHINALUG and SHAH DAGH.

KHINALUGTSY. See KHINALUG, SHAH DAGH, and AZERBAIJANI.

KHINALUKH. See KHINALUG and SHAH DAGH.

KHITRI. The Khitri are a subgroup of the Anatri* people, who themselves are one of the constituent groups of the lowland Chuvashes*. The Khitri live in the southeastern portion of the Chuvash Autonomous Republic and are surrounded by Tatars* and Tatar culture. See CHUVASH.

REFERENCE: Ronald Wixman, *The Peoples of the USSR: An Ethnographic Handbook*, 1984.

KHIURKILI. See DARGIN.

KHIURKILIN. See DARGIN.

KHOLAM. The Kholam are one of the Balkar* subgroups. Most of them are concentrated demographically in the Cherek River Valley in the Kabardino-Balkar Autonomous Republic. See BALKAR.
REFERENCE: Ronald Wixman, *The Peoples of the USSR: An Ethnographic Handbook*, 1984.

KHOLAMCHI. See KHOLAM and BALKAR.

KHOLAMCHILI. See KOHLAM and BALKAR.

KHOLAMCHY. See KOHLAM and BALKAR.

KHOLAMCHYLY. See KHOLAM and BALKAR.

KHOLAMLI. See KHOLAM and BALKAR.

KHOLAMLY. See KHOLAM and BALKAR.

KHONCHALO. See ITELMEN.

KHONGODOR. The Khongodor are one of the constituent subgroups of the Buryats*. Most of them live on the banks of the upper Angara River. See BURYAT.
REFERENCE: Ronald Wixman, *The Peoples of the USSR: An Ethnographic Handbook*, 1984.

KHORA. See KHORIN.

KHORIN. The Khora are a Buryat* subgroup. Most of them are concentrated near Lake Baikal and on Olkhon Island in southern Siberia. See BURYAT.
REFERENCE: Ronald Wixman, *The Peoples of the USSR: An Ethnographic Handbook*, 1984.

KHORINTSY. See KHORIN and BURYAT.

KHORVAT. See UKRAINIAN.

KHORVATIAN. See UKRAINIAN.

KHORVATY. See UKRAINIAN.

KHOSHEUT. The Khosheut are one of the subgroups of the Kalmyks*. During the eighteenth century, they migrated to the Lower Volga River region, but most of them died on the journey. Only a small remnant still survives. See KALMYK.
REFERENCE: Ronald Wixman, *The Peoples of the USSR: An Ethnographic Handbook*, 1984.

KHUF. The Khuf, who call themselves the Khufidzh, are today classified as a subgroup of the Tajiks*. Actually, they are of Rushan* descent—one of the Pamir* cluster of people. They are rapidly being assimilated by the Tajiks. See RUSHAN or TAJIK.
REFERENCES: Shirin Akiner, *Islamic Peoples of the Soviet Union*, 1983; Ronald Wixman, *The Peoples of the USSR: An Ethnographic Handbook*, 1984.

KHUFI. See KHUF, TAJIK, and PAMIR PEOPLES.

KHUFIDZH. See KHUF, TAJIK, and PAMIR PEOPLES.

KHUFTSY. See KHUF, TAJIK, and PAMIR PEOPLES.

KHUGNON. See KHUF, TAJIK, and PAMIR PEOPLES.

KHUIKDERE. See AGUL.

KHULAM. See KHOLAM and BALKAR.

KHULAMCHI. See KHOLAM and BALKAR.

KHULAMCHILI. See KHOLAM and BALKAR.

KHULAMCHY. See KHOLAM and BALKAR.

KHULAMCHYLY. See KHOLAM and BALKAR.

KHULAMLI. See KHOLAM and BALKAR.

KHULAMLY. See KHOLAM and BALKAR.

KHUNAMI. See KHUNZAL.

KHUNINI. See SHUGNAN and TAJIK.

KHUNZAKH. See AVAR.

KHUNZAL. The Khunzal, who call themselves the Khunami and who have been known historically as the Enzebi, Gunzebi, Gunzibi, and Nakhada, are classified today as one of the Avar* peoples. Russians* refer to them as the Khunzaly or Gunzibtsy. They are part of the Dido* cluster of the Andi-Dido* group, and they are Sunni Muslims. The Khunzals live in one of the most geographically isolated regions in the world—near the Georgian border in the mountains of southwestern Daghestan, primarily in the Tsuntin Region. Soviet demographers estimate the contemporary Khunzal population—in terms of those who identify themselves as Khunzal or who are aware of their Khunzal heritage—at around 1,000 people. See AVAR.
REFERENCE: Ronald Wixman, *The Peoples of the USSR: An Ethnographic Handbook*, 1984.

KHUNZALY. See KHUNZAL and AVAR.

KHURKILI. See DARGIN.

KHUSHANDERE. See AGUL.

KHVARSHI. See KHWARSHI and AVAR.

KHVARSHIN. See KHWARSHI and AVAR.

KHVARSHINY. See KHWARSHI and AVAR.

KHWARSHI. The Khwarshi call themselves the Kedaes Hikwa or Khuani. They are known to Russians* as the Khvarshiny. Today they are classified as one of the Avar* peoples. The Khwarshi are Sunni Muslims who are part of the Dido* cluster of people in the Andi-Dido* group. There are two groups of Khwarshi who are distinguished by linguistic differences. The Khwarshi proper speak the Kedaes dialect, while the Inkhokari speak the Inkhies dialect. Before World War II, the Khwarshi were geographically isolated on the Ori-Tskalis River in southwestern Daghestan, primarily in the Tsumadin Region. Since that time, they have become more accessible after their migration to the Vedeno Rayon in Daghestan. Surrounded by Avars, the Khwarshi are being assimilated by the larger group, and they use Avar as their literary language. Russian demographers estimate the contemporary Khwarshi population—in terms of those who identify themselves as Khwarshi or who are aware of their Khwarshi heritage—at around 800 people. See AVAR.

REFERENCE: Ronald Wixman, *The Peoples of the USSR: An Ethnographic Handbook*, 1984.

KHWARSHIN. See KHWARSHI and AVAR.

KHWARSHINTSY. See KHWARSHI and AVAR.

KHYURKILI. See DARGIN.

KHYURKILIN. See DARGIN.

KIAKH. See ADYGHE.

KIARACHALY. See KARACHAI.

KIARCHAL. See KARACHAI.

KILDA. See LAPP.

KILE. The Kile are classified as one of the subgroups of the Nanais*, even though they are not of Nanai origin. Ethnologists trace their cultural and linguistic roots to the Evenk*. They are concentrated demographically along the Kur and Gorin rivers in Siberia, north of the Chinese border. See NANAI.
REFERENCE: Ronald Wixman, *The Peoples of the USSR: An Ethnographic Handbook*, 1984.

KIPCHAK. See KYPCHAK and UZBEK.

KIPSHAK. See KYPCHAK and UZBEK.

KIRGHIZ. See KYRGYZ.

KIRGHIZ KAISAK. See KYRGYZ KAZAKH and KAZAKH.

KIRGHIZ KAYSAK. See KYRGYZ KAZAKH and KAZAKH.

KIRGHIZ KAZAK. See KYRGYZ KAZAKH and KAZAKH.

KIRGHIZ KAZAKH. See KYRGYZ KAZAKH and KAZAKH.

KIRGIZ KAISAK. See KYRGYZ KAZAKH and KAZAKH.

KIRGIZ KAYSAK. See KYRGYZ KAZAKH and KAZAKH.

KIRGIZ KAZAK. See KYRGYZ KAZAKH and KAZAKH.

KIRGIZ KAZAKH. See KYRGYZ KAZAKH and KAZAKH.

KIRIM TATAR. See TATAR.

KIRIMCHAK. See KRYMCHAK and JEW.

KIRTLE. See KARATA.

KIST. The Kist are classified as part of the Ingush* people. They are also known as the Feappi*. The Kist live in the vicinity of the Pankis Gorge in the Tushetia region of northern Georgia. See INGUSH.
REFERENCE: Ronald Wixman, *The Peoples of the USSR: An Ethnographic Handbook*, 1984.

KIST'I. See KIST, FEAPPI, and INGUSH.

KISTIN. See KIST, FEAPPI, and INGUSH.

KISTINTSY. See KIST, FEAPPI, and INGUSH.

KIUERIK. See CHULYM TATAR.

KIURIN. See LEZGIN.

KIZIL. See KYZYL and KHAKASS.

K'J'ARALAL. See KARATA and AVAR.

KJUERIK. See CHULYM TATAR.

K'K'IRDI. See KARATA and AVAR.

KOBY. See SAGAI and KHAKASS.

KOIBAL. The Koibal have also been known historically as the Mator. They are of mixed Samoyedic* and Ket* origin, and they were Turkified during the sixteenth and seventeenth centuries. Today they are classified as a subgroup of the Khakass*, although their own separate identity remains strong, as do some of their own subgroup identities. Those identities are based on military and kinship groupings that had developed over the centuries. The major Koibal subgroups have been the Tarazhak, Kol, Abugach, Greater Baikot, Lesser Baikot, Kandyk, and Arsh. Their religious loyalties are formally Eastern Orthodox,

although they retain major elements of their ancestral animistic traditions. The Koibal live north of the Sayan mountains on the Abakan steppes. See KHAKASS.
REFERENCE: Ronald Wixman, *The Peoples of the USSR: An Ethnographic Handbook,* 1984.

KOJLA CHEREMISS. See KOZHLA MARI and MARI.

KOJLA CHEREMISS MARI. See KOZHLA MARI and MARI.

KOKHCHI. See CHECHEN.

KOLA. See LAPP.

KOLIMCHAN. See KOLYMCHAN and RUSSIAN.

KOLIN. See LAPP.

KOLINTSY. See LAPP.

KOLMY-OMOLON. See EVEN.

KOLVA. See NENETS.

KOLVA IURAK. See NENETS.

KOLVA NENETS. The Kolva Nenets (Kolva, Kolva Samoyed, Kolva Yurak) are today classified as a Nenets* subgroup, even though they have ethnic and linguistic origins that are both Nenets and Komi*. During the nineteenth century, some Nenets men married Komi women who came from the Izhmi* subgroup; the children ended up speaking the Izhmi dialect. The group is concentrated demographically along the Kolva River. See NENETS.
REFERENCE: Ronald Wixman, *The Peoples of the USSR: An Ethnographic Handbook,* 1984.

KOLVA SAMODI. See KOLVA NENETS and NENETS.

KOLVA SAMOED. See KOLVA NENETS and NENETS.

KOLVA SAMOIED. See KOLVA NENETS and NENETS.

KOLVA SAMOYED. See KOLVA NENETS and NENETS.

KOLVA YURAK. See KOLVA NENETS and NENETS.

KOLVIN. See KOLVA NENETS and NENETS.

KOLVINTSY. See KOLVA NENETS and NENETS.

KOLYMA YUKAGIR. See YUKAGIR.

KOLYMCHAN. The Kolymchan are classified today as ethnic Russians*, although their linguistic and cultural roots are both Russian and Yakut*. These ethnic Russians emigrated to Siberia, adopted the Yakut language and culture, but still maintained a Russian identity. Most of them live along the Kolyma River in eastern Siberia. See RUSSIAN and YAKUT.
REFERENCE: Ronald Wixman, *The Peoples of the USSR: An Ethnographic Handbook*, 1984.

KOLYMCHANE. See KOLYMCHAN, RUSSIAN, and YAKUT.

KOMI. The Komi, who call themselves the Komi Mort or Komi Voityr (also known historically as Zyryan and Komi Zyryan), totaled 345,007 people in the 1989 census of the Soviet Union. Although they all consider themselves to be one people, they are actually divided into three relatively distinct groups, separated by minor linguistic and geographic differences. Those three groups are the Komi proper, the Komi Permyak, and the Izhmi*. Their languages are mutually intelligible as parts of the Finnic division of the Uralic-Altaic language family. Likewise, all three groups inhabit the northeastern region of European Russia. In terms of their religious loyalties, the Komi are Eastern Orthodox, but their faith remains laced with the animistic traditions of their pre-Christian heritage. Late in the fourteenth century, St. Stephen of Perm' worked as a missionary priest among the Komi. He converted large numbers of them to Christianity, constructed a written alphabet for the Komi language, and translated parts of the Bible into Komi. There are also substantial numbers of Old Believers among the Komi, whose religious loyalties were shaped by the ethnic Russian* Old Believers who settled in the area to escape persecution. The expanding Muscovite state annexed the Komi territory in 1478, and the large influx of ethnic Russians began, making them the majority within a century.

The Komi proper, who were specifically called Zyryans for centuries, are descended from ancestors who originally inhabited the middle and upper Kama River region. The Zyryans were closely associated with the Udmurts*, whose ancestors lived nearby in the Viatka Basin. Some time in the first millenium before Christ, the ancestors of the Komi and Udmurts split, with the Komi continuing to live in the Kama River basin. Around 500 A.D., these Komi themselves divided, with some of them migrating from the upper Kama River region to the Vychegda Basin. There they mixed with other indigenous peoples and began acquiring a separate ethnic identity. Russians began calling them the Vychegda Perm', and they evolved into the contemporary Komi. Those who stayed behind in the Kama Basin became known as Komi Permyaks. Beginning in the mid–1500s, the Komi began their migration again, moving deeper into the upper Vychegda and Pechora river basins. At the time, their economy revolved around fishing, hunting, small-scale farming, and livestock breeding. They took to reindeer breeding late in the nineteenth century, especially in the northern reaches of their territory. After the arrival of large numbers of Russian settlers, the Komi also earned a reputation as shrewd commercial traders in northern Siberia. The Komi language is divided into three dialects, all of them mutually intelligible. Those dialects are known as Pechora, Udor, and Verkhne-Vyshegod.

Closely related to the Komi are the Izhmi (Ijem, Izhem, Izhmi, Izhmy). The Izmi, who call themselves the Izva Tas, are a Komi people who mixed closely with the Nenets* in northern Siberia. Like the Komi, they are Eastern Orthodox in religion, with a good admixture of Old Believers, but their shamanism has strong elements of Nenet belief. They are concentrated between the Pechora and Izhma rivers. Several thousand more Izhmi live in the Yamalo-Nenets Autonomous Oblast and the Tjumen Oblast. Their traditional economy, like that of the Komi, has revolved around fishing, hunting, livestock raising, small farming, and reindeer breeding.

The third major Komi group is the Komi Permyak, who are also known as Permyaks. The Komi Permyak population exceeds 155,000 people, most of whom live in the Komi Permyak Autonomous Oblast. They speak two primary dialects. The northern dialect is known as Kosinsko-Kama, while the southern dialect is called Inven. Two other groups of Komi Permyak live outside the Komi Permyak Autonomous Oblast; as such, they constitute a separate ethnographic group. The Yazva* dialect is considered a Komi dialect, while the Zyuzda* dialect is a transitional language between Komi and Komi Permyak.

For all three groups of the Komi peoples, the expansion of Russian society gradually absorbed them into larger market systems. Major trade routes that crossed Komi territory developed from Archangel to the Viatka-Kama Basin and on to Siberia. Exportation of fish, furs, and game animals increased in the seventeenth century. By the nineteenth century, the coal, timber, iron ore, and paper industries were beginning to develop. The Bolshevik Revolution of 1917 dramatically transformed Komi life. The Komi Autonomous Oblast was established in 1921, and it was raised to the status of the Komi Autonomous Soviet Socialist Republic in 1936. The Komi-Permyak National Okrug was created in 1929. Rapid industrialization forced large numbers of Komi to settle in cities and towns where they could work in the mills and factories. Beginning in the late 1920s, the state collectivized Komi agricultural labor.

Today there is only the most limited sense of nationalism among the Komi people. They are somewhat scattered geographically, and, for centuries, they have been surrounded by ethnic Russians and have been members of the Russian Orthodox Church. They constitute less than a third of the people of the Komi Autonomous Republic and the Komi-Permyak Autonomous Oblast. Assimilation between the Komi and ethnic Russians is continuing. There are also approximately 14,000 Komis living in the western Arctic, between Arkhangelsk Province and Taimyr, as well as in the Yamal national region.

REFERENCES: Walter Kolarz, *Russia and Her Colonies*, 1952; *Soviet Encyclopedia*, 1973, vol. 12, 598–608; M. P. Likachev, et al., *Komi Writers*, 1926; A. N. Federova, *Komi Soviet Writers*, 1968; Ronald Wixman, *The Peoples of the USSR: An Ethnographic Handbook*, 1984.

KOMI IJEM. See IZHMI and KOMI.

KOMI IJMI. See IZHMI and KOMI.

KOMI IZHEM. See IZHMI and KOMI.

KOMI IZHMI. See IZHMI and KOMI.

KOMI IZHMY. See IZHMI and KOMI.

KOMI MORT. See KOMI.

KOMI NENET. See KOMI and NENETS.

KOMI-PERMYAK. See KOMI.

KOMI-VOITYR. See KOMI.

KOMI-ZIRIAN. See KOMI.

KOMI-ZYRIAN. See KOMI.

KOMI-ZYRYAN. See KOMI.

KONDOMA TATAR. The Kondoma Tatars are part of the larger collection of Siberian Tatars* who originated with the Mongol* invasion of Russia in the thirteenth century. The term "Kondoma Tatar" is more a reflection of their location in the Kuznetsk Basin of southern Siberia than of any distinct identity as a special group of Tatars*. The Tatars were converted to the Sunni Muslim faith, Hanafi school, by Islamic merchants in the fourteenth and fifteenth centuries. Contact with Russians led to the Tatars' conversion to Eastern Orthodox Christianity, although the conversion was superficial at best. Strong elements of shamanistic animism survived among them. Since World War II, Russian ethnographers have classified them with the Shors*. See SHOR and TATAR.

REFERENCES: Shirin Akiner, *Islamic Peoples of the Soviet Union*, 1983; Alexandre Bennigsen and S. Embers Wimbush, *Muslims of the Soviet Empire: A Guide*, 1986.

KORAK. See KORYAK.

KOREAN. At least half a million Koreans live in the former Soviet Union. Census figures for Koreans are thought to be unreliable, however, for some have acculturated to Russian* and Uzbek* society and may identify with those groups. The real figure is thus undoubtedly higher than the official 1989 count of 437,335. Most Soviet Koreans have kept their language, their culture, and their distinctive religion, which is a mixture of Buddhist, shamanist and Confucian elements. The majority now live in what used to be Soviet Central Asia, where they were sent *en masse* by Josef Stalin, but more than 100,000 live in the Primor'ye (Maritime) Province and on Sakhalin Island. The latter group had been sent to Sakhalin as laborers by the Japanese* during World War II, and they found themselves inside the Soviet Union when the fighting ended. They call themselves the Koryosaram and are known to Russians as the Korei.

The largest group of Koreans lives on collective farms in Uzbekistan. Approximately 150,000 are found in Tashkent Oblast, south of the capital, and in the Lower, Central and Upper Chirchik Districts, northeast of the city. Others tend fertile farms and orchards in the Fergana Valley. About 10,000 Koreans live near Samarkand. A roughly equal number were sent to Kungrad Rayon, of the Karakalpak Autonomous Republic, to farm the banks of the Amu Darya (Oxus) River where it fans out into a delta before entering the south end of the Aral Sea. Another group of Koreans was sent to Gurlen District of Khorezm Oblast, where irrigation has made farming possible, even on the edge of the lifeless Kara Kum desert.

The second largest population of Koreans lives in Kazakhstan, where they began pioneer farming in 1924. They grow rice and cotton on collective farms along both banks of the Syr Darya (Jaxartes) River in Kyzl Orda Oblast. The city of Kyzl Orda—with its Korean-language newspaper, radio station, and theater—is a cultural center for Koreans. Korean settlements are also located in eastern Kazakhstan near the town of Kuygan, where the Chu River empties into Lake Balkhash, and on the Karatal River near Taldy-Kurgan. A scattering of Koreans is also found in Kyrgyzia, Turkmenistan, and Tajikistan.

Korean immigration to tsarist Russia began when the declining Chinese* Manchu* dynasty ceded the Ussuri region to Russia in the Treaty of Peking (1860). The tsar wished to encourage settlement of the cold, forested Pacific coast, which was then only lightly populated by native Siberian tribes. His offer of free land attracted Korean families, who came in 1863 across the Tumen River border and by sea to Pos'yet Bay, south of Vladivostok. The Korean government could not prevent the emigration, particularly when famine struck in 1869. For the rest of the nineteenth century, Koreans moved into the Vladivostok region. The 1907 census counted 46,000, but if illegal immigrants were included, the total might have been 30 percent higher.

From the Russian point of view, this situation posed both advantages and disadvantages. The Koreans seemed assimilable. Many took Russian names and

converted to Orthodox Christianity. They were also industrious and law-abid-
ing—just the kind of pioneers that the Russian government was seeking. On the
other hand, their very success aroused the envy of Russian settlers who, if they
could not hire cheap Korean labor, physically assaulted Koreans on account of
their strangeness. Fears of a "yellow peril," widespread in America at the time,
drove Russian policy too. To dilute the Korean population of the Maritime
Region, these families were sent to clear land in a frigid zone north of the Amur
River that later became the Jewish Autonomous Region.

Japan attacked Russia in 1904 and made a protectorate of Korea the following
year. The Japanese formally annexed Korea in 1910 and held it until 1945. This
humiliation generated a burning Korean nationalism among exiles in Russia.
They tried by all means, including armed attack and assassination, to oust the
Japanese from Korea. The Japanese-Russian *rapprochement* of 1907–1914, however, included a deal whereby Russian authorities cracked down on the Korean
nationalists in the Maritime Province in return for Japanese suppression of Russian revolutionaries in Tokyo.

Four thousand Koreans fought in the Russian army in World War I, a profoundly discouraging experience that sharpened their political awareness; some,
but not all, leaned toward Bolshevism. The point became moot when Japanese
troops took Vladivostok in 1918, perpetrating brutalities on Koreans there, just
as in Korea proper. The Koreans' hatred for the Japanese propelled them into
common cause with the Bolsheviks. When the Soviets finally expelled Japan
from Siberia in 1922, many Koreans joined the Communist party.

During the Japanese inter-regnum, imperial planners had envisioned large rice
farms along the Ussuri River, for the crop can be grown even that far north.
The Soviets implemented this scheme, establishing collective and state rice farms
that were worked exclusively by Koreans, who possessed unmatched skills in
cold-climate wet-rice agriculture. This very positive experience instilled in the
Koreans an enthusiasm for collective farming notably lacking among Russian
and Ukrainian* peasants.

Koreans were lured to Kazakhstan as early as 1924, with promises of a warmer
climate and free, irrigable land along the Syr Darya River. Their diligence and
success again aroused resentment, especially when the Koreans allowed themselves to be used by Stalin in his collectivization drive. They were seen as
usurping land from "kulaks" who were sent, ironically, to the Soviet Far East,
whence the Koreans had come. Incidents occurred in which Russian peasants,
resisting Stalin's decrees, killed Korean settlers. Stalin allowed Korean cultural
institutions to flourish in the first half of the 1930s. Korean newspapers were
published in both the Far East and Central Asia; Korean-language schools were
established. All this was swept away in a drastic policy reversal after 1936,
however. Henceforth, all non-Russian people were told to forget their native
languages and customs and to become like Russians. This policy was called
"proletarianization."

Stalin's increasingly paranoid mental state was not completely without cause:

Developments in Spain, Germany, and Japan foretold a coming world war. Traitors were "discovered" in the most unlikely places, and nationalities inhabiting borderlands were simply picked up by the NKVD (as the KGB was then known), put in freight cars, and sent thousands of miles into the interior of the Soviet Union. Such was the fate of the Soviet Koreans. Stalin correctly suspected that the Japanese would try to infiltrate spies from Korea and Manchuria into settled communities in the Soviet Pacific regions. Documentary details are lacking, but, by December 1937, all 180,000 Koreans who had lived in the Far Eastern Territory were simply gone—shipped westward on the Trans-Siberian Railway to start new collective and state farms in Kazakhstan and Uzbekistan.

The Koreans' agricultural talents proved most useful to the Soviet state. They turned marshes into rice farms in Khorezm and even pioneered rice and cotton farms in the arid, continental climate of Karakalpakia. As long as Stalin was alive, few details of their lives behind the Iron Curtain emerged, but an unusually large number of Koreans were recognized for their outstanding labor achievements. In the thaw that followed Stalin's death, it again became permissible to study national minorities. The Soviet ethnographer R. Sh. Dzharyglasinova reported in 1956 that most of the Central Asian Koreans had retained their language (albeit with some Russian and Uzbek loan-words), as well as their family custom, traditional foods, furniture, and even architecture. They were once again reading newspapers and listening to radio broadcasts in their own language, but they had adopted certain Uzbek clothes and farm implements.

There are two main reasons why the Central Asian Koreans have adjusted relatively well to Soviet culture: First, having no national area to call their own (unlike the Uzbeks, Kazakhs*, and many smaller groups), they have no formal political or administrative leader to fight for their separate identity. Thus assimilation, not separation, is their only realistic option. Second, as heirs to the Confucian tradition, they revere educational achievement and make sure their children attend higher schools and learn Russian. Many Koreans have become professionals and have moved from collective farms to the cities, where their talents and skills can be utilized in industries, institutes, and universities. Nevertheless, they are still victimized by Russian prejudices against Orientals. Indirect confirmation of this prejudice may be read into Yuri Andropov's cryptic remark, in a 1982 speech, that the Koreans were indeed "full-fledged Soviet citizens."

It might seem that a sizable population of loyal Soviet Koreans would make an ideal tool for Russian meddling in Korean politics, but this has never been the case. The Korean Communist Party before World War II was small, ineffective, and factionalized. Soviet Koreans enjoyed a brief period of moderated influence in the Democratic Republic of Korea (North Korea) after 1954, but soon fell victim to dictator Kim Il-Sung's intense suspicion of Russians. Soviet Koreans had changed too much to be accepted in either Pyongyang or Seoul.

Koreans living near the Aral Sea face a different challenge in the 1990s: The sea is drying up. Irrigation canals have taken nearly all the water from the Amu Darya and the Syr Darya rivers. In some years, no water at all enters the Aral.

The result is the dessication, shrinkage, and the eventual disappearance of that great inland sea. The receding waters leave behind barren salt flats. Desert winds whip up those salts, filling the skies of Uzbekistan and Kazakhstan with poisonous dust storms. Even a partial restoration of the Aral Sea would necessitate abandoning the irrigation canals that the Koreans had dug.

REFERENCES: R. Sh. Dzharyglasinova, "The Koreans in Central Asia," *Central Asian Review*, 15 (1967), 212–18; William S. Ellis, "The Aral: A Soviet Sea Lies Dying," *National Geographic*, 177 (1990), 73–92; Walter Kolarz, *The People of the Soviet Far East*, 1965; Bohdan Nahaylo and Victor Swoboda, *Soviet Disunion: A History of the Nationalities Problem in the U.S.S.R.*, 1989; Alexsandr M. Nekrich, *The Punished Peoples: The Deportation and Fate of Soviet Minorities at the End of the Second World War*, 1978; Dae-Sook Suh, ed., *Koreans in the Soviet Union*, 1987.

Ross Marlay

KOREANS OF CENTRAL ASIA. See KOREAN.

KOREI. See KOREAN.

KOREL. See FINN and KARELIAN.

KORELA. See FINN and KARELIAN.

KORELIAN. See FINN and KARELIAN.

KORELY. See FINN and KARELIAN.

KORELYAN. See FINN and KARELIAN.

KORIAK. See KORYAK.

KORYAK. The Koryaks are an indigenous people of northeastern Siberia in the former Soviet Union. Closely related ethnically and linguistically to the Chukchis* and ethnically to the Itelmen*, the Koryaks speak a Chukotic language, which is part of the larger Paleo-Asiatic family. They live in scattered villages throughout the Koryak Autonomous Oblast, south of the Chukchis. The Koryaks are subdivided into nine identifiable tribal groups, each with its own ethnic identity and distinguishable dialect. The largest of the Koryak subgroups is the Chavchuven*, who constitute approximately half of the Koryak people. The Chavchuven have also been referred to as the Nymylan*. Historically, the Chavchuven have been reindeer breeders, and, although they are scattered throughout the Koryak Autonomous Oblast, they are most concentrated in the interior. Another Koryak group is the Kamen*. The Kamen have a distinctly different dialect phonologically from the other Koryak groups and, therefore, a more distinctive ethnic identity. The Kamen have long been a sedentary people who live in coastal villages along Penzhina Bay. The Kamen economy revolved around the hunting of common seals, bearded seals, walruses, and white whales. The Paren*, like the Kamen, are a sedentary people who have traditionally hunted sea mammals for their livelihoods. They live along the Paren' River on the east coast of the Taygonos Peninsula. The Itkan*, or Itkana, share an economy similar to that of the Kamen and Paren; they live in several villages near the Paren on the Taygonos Peninsula. The other Koryak groups live in different economic habitats. The Apuka*, or Apukin, live at the mouth of the Apuka River and farther north along the Bering Sea coast. The mainstay of their economic life is fishing, especially the Siberian salmon. The Kereks*, who live northeast of the Apuka on the Bering Sea coast between Natal'ya Bay and Cape Navarin, are primarily fishermen as well, although they also hunt sea mammals. The second-largest Koryak group, in terms of population, is the Alyutor*. The Alyutor are a mixed group economically. Some of them are sedentary and live on the Kamchatka Isthmus, where they hunt sea mammals. Other groups of Alyutor are reindeer herders. The Karaga* are closely related in terms of their dialect to the Alyutor. They live on the east coast of the Kamchatka Peninsula between Tymlaty in the north to Uka in the south. The Karaga are hunters. The final Koryak group is the Palan*, who live along the coast of the Sea of Okhotsk, between Lesnaya in the north and Vayampolka in the south. The Palan hunt sea mammals, but they are also active fur trappers because of the abundance of the Kamchatka sable in their area. During the twentieth century, these regional identities among the Koryak have become progressively less significant, although they still survive. The Koryak are acquiring a more generic identity. Soviet demographers placed the Koryak population at approximately 7,500 people in 1926; by 1990, it had climbed only to approximately 8,000 people.

In addition to their dialect differences, the various Koryak groups are still divided by economics, particularly by the split between the nomadic and seminomadic reindeer groups and the sedentary hunters and fishermen. The differences between the two ways of life were distinct enough for anthropologists to claim that coastal Koryaks had more in common culturally with the coastal Chukchi than they did with the nomadic Koryaks. Coastal Chukchis and Koryaks primarily ate the meat and fat of walruses, common seals, and bearded seals. They also hunted white whales and other whales. The nomadic Chukchi and Koryak, by contrast, ate reindeer meat, fat, brain, intestines, and blood. The reindeer not only provided the Chukchi with food, but also with skins for clothes, shoes, tents, rope, harnesses, and strings; they used the tendons and horns as well. For their transportation, the nomadic Koryaks and Chukchis harnessed reindeer and attached them to sleds, while the coastal Chukchis and Koryaks traveled by dog sleds.

Koryak religious life is similar to that of other aboriginal people around the world. An animistic, polytheistic people, they believed that all aspects of creation—animals, plants, insects, lakes, mountains, rivers, oceans, stars, the sun, the moon, and the wind—had souls of their own. Not only did all things have spirits that gave them life, but all spirit was fundamentally of the same essence, different only in degree and not in kind. Through discipline, observation, and personal tranquility, individuals could learn from the world and make contact with the soul of the universe or any of its creations. Among the Koryaks, the souls of the animals they hunted and herded were particularly significant. In terms of religious rituals and festivals, the coastal Koryaks were different from the nomadic Koryaks. Coastal Koryak religious life was heavily laced with rituals devoted to whales, walruses, and seals. They sacrificed dogs annually to guarantee good hunts, while the nomadic Koryaks offered bits of entrails, meat, blood, and bone marrow to the gods to protect the reindeer herds.

Ethnic Russians* first encountered the Koryaks in 1642, when the Cossack* Ivan Yerastov met up with groups of Kamen herders. The Russians built Fort Nizhnekolymsk in 1644 and Fort Anaydir in 1649 among the Chukchi. Commercial traders, fur trappers, and hunters, using those forts as their base, then established permanent contact with the Koryaks. Systematic Russian contact brought a wave of epidemic diseases—influenza, mumps, smallpox, chicken pox, and so forth—and the Koryak population declined. The Palan became especially involved with Russian fur traders. As the numbers of fur-bearing animals decreased, Moscow lost interest in the area and in the well-being of its natives. The Koryaks were part of this entire administrative process. By the mid-eighteenth century, the Russians and Koryaks had been drawn together in an increasingly commercialized economy. They began holding annual fairs, in which the Koryaks would trade reindeer hides, furs, and walrus tusks for alcohol, iron tools, firearms, ammunition, and tobacco. In the nineteenth century, as increasing numbers of ethnic Russians settled in the region, the economic contacts strengthened. Completion of the Trans-Siberian Railroad in 1905 expanded those economic contacts even more.

The Bolshevik Revolution of 1917 had an effect on the Koryaks. The subsequent civil war, with its capricious twists and shifting loyalties, made the Koryaks still more suspicious of ethnic Russians. The Russians had a base at Gizhiga, on Penzhina Bay, from which they tried to implement new state policies. They started with the coastal Koryaks, establishing a fishing collective at Gizhiga in 1929. The experiment was a financial disaster. The government could not get transport ships to Gizhiga, so for two years the catch of the collective rotted. Nevertheless, within the next two years, the government established ten new fishing collectives. By 1934, nearly half of the coastal Koryaks had been organized into collectives where they lived in small villages of semi-subterranean houses. When the government established a school at Manily, a significant number of these coastal Koryaks migrated to work for those collectives so that their children could go to school there.

The collectivization of the nomadic, reindeer-herding Koryaks was a slower process. Early in the 1920s, there were sixty-five rich Koryaks who owned herds of more than 10,000 reindeer each. Approximately 400 families had 100 reindeer each. The rest of these Koryaks, owning only a few head each, often worked for the richer Koryaks. The government began an intensive effort to collectivize these Koryaks in 1932, but the Soviets encountered bitter resistance. State agents, backed by military authority, forcibly purchased reindeer for the collective herds; many Koryaks slaughtered their animals rather than turn them over to the government. The reindeer population of the Koryak National Region, an administrative unit that had been established in 1930, fell from 264,000 in 1926 to 127,000 in 1934.

The government also established "cultural bases" for the indigenous people—settlements complete with boarding schools, hospitals, day-care centers, veterinary dispensaries, and clubs. The government worked to minimize the nomadic nature of Koryak life. It was easier for the government to create those bases for the coastal-dwelling Koryaks than for the nomadic Koryaks, but the government encouraged the nomads to settle down as well. The Soviet government also created a Cyrillic alphabet for the Koryak language in 1932. In 1938, Russian became the language of instruction for all Koryak schoolchildren. Finally, the government launched an assault on Koryak religion. Russian Orthodox Christianity had been superimposed on the native religion under the tsars, creating a syncretic, mixed faith. Beginning in the late 1930s, the Soviet government prohibited both native and Russian Orthodox religious services among the Koryaks.

Dramatic changes in Koryak life have occurred since World War II. During the war, the Soviet government relocated much of its industry east of the Ural Mountains to keep it out of German hands or protected from German artillery bombardment. Large numbers of ethnic Russian workers suddenly moved into Siberia. State development plans accelerated that process in the 1950s and 1960s. In the process, the Koryaks found themselves herding reindeer on ever smaller amounts of land. More and more Chavchuvens and Alyutors moved into the settled coastal villages, and fewer and fewer herded reindeer. The collapse of the Soviet economy in the 1970s and 1980s actually slowed that process somewhat, but, even then, the long-term changes in Koryak life had become irreversible. Many Koryaks still followed the reindeer and lived in their *yaranga* tents, but increasingly large numbers abandoned the herds for jobs at construction sites, oil and natural gas wells, and mass-production factories.

After 1985, the *perestroika* and *glasnost* policies of Mikhail Gorbachev gave the Koryaks more political freedom and ended the heavy-handed cultural repression that they had experienced for fifty years. In 1988, along with other indigenous peoples, the Koryaks contacted Gorbachev shortly after the Communist Party of the Soviet Union (CPSU) established a special nationality commission to strengthen collective farms and other state businesses, including fur trade operations. They likewise participated in the creation of the Association of Peoples of the North (APN) on March 31, 1990, during a meeting in the Kremlin. This group was organized to defend the interests of twenty-six northern peoples by slowing the pace of economic development, the influx of ethnic Russian settlers, and the deterioration of the natural environment. The APN also wanted the government to ratify both the 1957 International Convention on Protection and Integration of Indigenous and Other Tribal and Semi-Tribal Populations in Independent Countries and the 1989 Convention on Indigenous and Tribal Peoples in Independent Countries, in order to affirm that the Koryaks have a right to the ownership and possession of lands that they have traditionally occupied. In 1990, some Koryak leaders declared the "autonomy" of the Koryak, a symbolic statement designed to promote Koryak interests.

Ironically, the collapse of the Communist Party and the disintegration of the Soviet Union in 1991 actually made the achievement of Koryak objectives less likely to occur. Once the idea of privately owned property was no longer considered a seditious concept, the Koryaks had a better chance than ever before of staking out some kind of property or territorial claims. The implosion of the Soviet economy was destined to undermine that hope. One of the major goals of people like Boris Yeltsin in Russia was the acceleration of economic development. Since huge volumes of natural resources exist in Siberia, the exploitation and exportation of those resources—especially coal, iron ore, natural gas, timber, and petroleum—represented a relatively quick way of earning hard currency to develop the rest of the economy. Russians began importing Western technology to develop Siberia. In the process, the traditional Koryak economy became even more threatened. If, during the rest of the 1990s, the development of the Siberian economy accelerates, the pressure on traditional Koryak ways will become even more intense.

REFERENCES: Alice Bartels and Dennis Bartels, "Soviet Policy Toward Siberian Native People," *Canadian Dimension*, 19 (1985), 36–44; Mike Edwards, "Siberia: In From the Cold," *National Geographic*, 177 (March 1990), 2–49; James Forsyth, *A History of the Peoples of Siberia*, 1992; Constantine Krypton, "Soviet Policy in the Northern National Regions After World War II," *Slavic Review*, 13 (October 1954), 339–53; Piers Vitebsky, "Perestroika Among the Reindeer Herders," *Geographical Magazine*, 61 (June 1989), 23–34; Ronald Wixman, *The Peoples of the USSR: An Ethnographic Handbook*, 1984.

KOSHAN. See AGUL.

KOSINSKO-KAMA. See KOMI.

KOTT. See RUSSIAN and KET.

KOYBAL. See KOIBAL or KHAKASS.

KOZHLA CHEREMISS. See KOZHLA MARI and MARI.

KOZHLA MARI. The Kozhla Mari constitute part of the eastern division of the Mari* people. They are closely related to the Olyk Mari, or Meadow Mari, who constitute the other branch of the eastern Mari. The Kozhla Mari have also been known as the Forest Mari. They have succeeded in resisting Christianization and retain a strong loyalty to their ancestral animistic faith. The Kozhla Mari

live in the Kari Autonomous Republic, primarily on the left bank of the Volga River. See MARI.
REFERENCE: Ronald Wixman, *The Peoples of the USSR: An Ethnographic Handbook*, 1984.

KOZHLA OLYK CHEREMISS. See KOZHLA MARI AND MARI.

KRAASNA MAARAHVAS. See KRASNYY ESTONIAN and ESTONIAN.

KRASNA MAAMEES. See KRASNYY ESTONIAN and ESTONIAN.

KRASNIY ESTONIAN. See KRASNYY ESTONIAN and ESTONIAN.

KRASNYY ESTONIAN. The Krasnyy Estonians are part of the larger group of Setu* Estonians*. They call themselves the Kraasna Maarahvas. In the 1600s. they migrated to the town of Krasnyy in the Pskov region, and their name was taken from that geographic reference. They have been assimilated by Russians* during the twentieth century, although there are still individuals who are aware of their Krasnyy background. See ESTONIAN.
REFERENCE: Ronald Wixman, *The Peoples of the USSR: An Ethnographic Handbook*, 1984.

KRESHEN. See KRJASHEN and TATAR.

KREVINGI. See KRIEVINI and LATVIAN.

KREVINI. See KRIEVINI and LATVIAN.

KRIASHEN. See KRJASHEN and TATAR.

KRIEVINGI. See LATVIAN.

KRIEVINI. The Krievini are today classified with the Latvians*, although some of them have managed to maintain a separate sense of identity. In the 1400s, a group of Vods* who had converted to Eastern Orthodoxy migrated to the Zemgale area in what is today Latvia. They became known as Krievini and have been steadily assimilated by the Latvians. That process of assimilation has been extremely slow, however, because the Krievini are Eastern Orthodox while the Latvians are Lutherans. The Krievini live in the Courland region of Latvia. See LATVIAN.

REFERENCE: Ronald Wixman, *The Peoples of the USSR: An Ethnographic Handbook*, 1984.

KRIEVINS. See LATVIAN.

KRIEVINSH. See LATVIAN.

KRIM TATAR. See CRIMEAN TATAR and TATAR.

KRIMCHAK. See KRYMCHAK and JEW.

KRIVICHI. See BELARUSIAN.

KRIVICHIAN. See BELARUSIAN.

KRIZ. See KRYZ, DZHEK, SHAH DAGH, and AZERBAIJANI.

KRJASHEN. The Krjashens (Kryashens), who call themselves the Chokngan or Kreshen, are Volga Tatars* who became Christians. They have also been identified historically as Christian Tatars. Soon after the Russian* conquest of the Kazan and Astrakhan khanates in the 1550s, Russian Orthodox missionaries arrived in the area and converted thousands of people. When the missionaries left, most of the Krjashens reverted to Islam. A second wave of conversions occurred in the eighteenth century, when Russians began their assault on Islam in the Volga region. When the pressure was off, thousands again reverted to Islam, but, by the early 1900s, there were more than 100,000 Krjashens in Russia. They spoke the same language as the Volga Tatars and made their livings in the same ways. During the Soviet period, when the government closed down churches and mosques, the Krjashens became almost indistinguishable from other Volga Tatars. Since that time, they have been classified as Tatars. See TATAR or VOLGA TATAR.
REFERENCE: Ronald Wixman, *The Peoples of the USSR: An Ethnographic Handbook*, 1984.

KRYASHEN. See KRJASHEN, TATAR, and VOLGA TATAR.

KRYMCHAK. The Krymchaks (Krimchaks) are Turkic*-speaking Jews* who lived on the Crimean Peninsula until World War II. They were Orthodox Jews whose written language was Hebrew; they believed in the Talmud and observed Orthodox rituals. They were farmers whose economic life was indistinguishable from surrounding non-Jewish groups, but they possessed a powerful sense of identity and married endogamously. German* armies reached the Crimea in the fall of 1941, and the liquidation of the Krymchaks began. Thousands of them were shot between November 1941 and January 1942. After the war, the survivors scattered throughout the Soviet Union or emigrated to the United States and Israel. Today there are several hundred people in what used to be the Soviet Union who are aware of their Krymchak origins, but most of them are being assimilated by the Crimean Tatars*. See JEW.

REFERENCES: Lionel Kochan, ed., *The Jews in Soviet Russia since 1917*, 1970; Benjamin Pinkus, *The Jews of the Soviet Union: The History of a National Minority*, 1988; Solomon N. Schwarz, *The Jews in the Soviet Union*, 1951.

KRYMSKIJE TATARY. See CRIMEAN TATAR.

KRYM-TATAR. See CRIMEAN TATAR.

KRYM-TURK. See CRIMEAN TATAR.

KRYTS'AR. See KRYZ and AZERBAIJANI.

KRYZ. The Kryz are today classified as a one of the Shah Dagh* peoples. They live in the village of Kryz and speak a distinct dialect. Russians* call them the Kryztsy. Although the Kryz call themselves Kryts'ar, they tend to use a village focus as their ethnic identity, so decentralized is their concept of community. Each Kryz village has its own dialect, but almost all Kryz speak Azerbaijani. They are Sunni Muslims. Soviet demographers estimate the contemporary Kryz population—in terms of those who identify themselves as Kryz or who are aware of their Kryz heritage—at around 8,000 people. See DZHEK, SHAH DAGH, or AZERBAIJANI.

REFERENCES: Shirin Akiner, *Islamic Peoples of the Soviet Union*, 1983; Ronald Wixman, *The Peoples of the USSR: An Ethnographic Handbook*, 1984.

KRYZTSY. See KRYZ and AZERBAIJANI.

KUBA. See KACHA and KHAKASS.

KUBA. See LEZGIN and AZERBAIJANI.

KUBACHI. The Kubachi call themselves the Ughbug or Urbughan. They have also been known as the Zirekgeran or Zerekhgeran. Russian* ethnographers today classify them as a subgroup of the Dargins*, but they retain a strong sense of Kubachi identity. For centuries, the Kubachi have enjoyed a reputation in the Near East and Central Asia as fine goldsmiths and silversmiths. They are known as well for their manufacture of daggers and chain mail. Like the neighboring Kaitaks*, with whom they share the Sunni Muslim religion and many other cultural characteristics, the Kubachis are being assimilated by the Dargins. They live in one village—Kubachi—in the Dakhadajev Region of central Daghestan. Although contemporary population estimates are difficult to achieve, because of

the classification of the Kubachi with the Dargins, demographers argue that there may be as many as 5,000 people who either identify themselves as Kubachi or who are aware of their Kubachi heritage. See KAITAK or DARGIN.
REFERENCES: Shirin Akiner, *Islamic Peoples of the Soviet Union*, 1983; Ronald Wixman, *The Peoples of the USSR: An Ethnographic Handbook*, 1984.

KUBACHIN. See KUBACHI and DARGIN.

KUBACHINTSY. See KUBACHI and DARGIN.

KUBAN ABHAZ. See ABAZA.

KUBAN ABKAZ. See ABAZA.

KUBAN ABKHAZ. See ABAZA.

KUBAN COSSACK. In 1775, the Russian* government officially dissolved the Zaporozhe Cossacks*. Many of them fled across the Danube River into Turkish-controlled territory, but those who remained behind in Russian-controlled territory evolved into the Black Sea Cossacks*. At the conclusion of the Russo-Turkish War of 1787–1791, when the tsar grew extremely suspicious of Black Sea Cossack connections with the Zaporozhe Cossacks across the Danube, the Black Sea Cossacks were relocated to the Kuban area, where they evolved into the Kuban Cossacks. In 1828, most of the Zaporozhe Cossacks moved from Turkish territory and joined up with the Kuban Cossacks, whose homeland was near the Kuban River on the steppes of the North Caucasus. Kuban Cossack culture has been strongly influenced by the Circassians*. See COSSACK.
REFERENCES: Philip Longworth, *The Cossacks*, 1969; Ronald Wixman, *The Peoples of the USSR: An Ethnographic Handbook*, 1984.

KUBAN NOGAI. See AK NOGAI and NOGAI.

KUBAN NOGAY. See AK NOGAI and NOGAI.

KUBAN NOGHAI. See AK NOGAI and NOGAI.

KUBAN NOGHAY. See AK NOGAI and NOGAI.

KUMANDA. See KUMANDIN and ALTAI.

KUMANDIN. The Kumandins—also known as the Kumandas, Kuvandy, Kuvandyg, Kuvandykh, Kuvanty, and Kumandy—live on the Bija, Isha, and Kozha rivers and speak one of the Altai* dialects. They represent a mixture over the centuries of Turkic* immigrants, indigenous peoples of southern Siberia, Shors*, and Russians*. Their dialect is also closely related to Tuba*, Chelkan*, Shor, and Khakass*. They divide themselves into two general groupings—the Lower Kumandins (Altyna Kumandy) and the Upper Kumandins (Oro Kumandy). Most of them today are farmers working on collectives. Although a few of the Kumandins are Sunni Muslims, most are Russian Orthodox Christians. See ALTAI. *REFERENCE:* Ronald Wixman, *The Peoples of the USSR: An Ethnographic Handbook*, 1984.

KUMANDINTSY. See KUMANDIN and ALTAI.

KUMANDY. See KUMANDIN and ALTAI.

KUMARCHAN. See EVENK.

KUMARCHEN. See EVENK.

KUMIH. See KUMYK.

KUMIK. See KUMYK.

KUMUK. See KUMYK.

KUMUKH. See LAK.

KUMYK. The Kumyks (Kumuk, Kumik, Kumih, Qumuq), who call themselves the Qumuq, are a very influential ethnic group in the Daghestan Autonomous Republic. Russians* call them the Kumyki. Their homeland is primarily in the lowlands of the northeast Caucasic Mountains between the Terek and Samur rivers. Most Kumyks live a rural agricultural and pastoral life-style, although, in recent years, increasing numbers of them have relocated to Daghestani cities, especially Makhachkala on the Caspian Sea, to work in industry. The Kumyk language is part of the Oghuz group of the Kypchak* division of Turkic languages, and today, because of extensive word exchanges over the centuries, it is mutually intelligible with Azerbaijani*; more than 6,000,000 Azerbaijanis border Kumyk land to the south. The Kumyk population today exceeds 250,000 people. In seven districts of lowland Daghestan (Khasavyurt, Babayurt, Kizilyurt, Buinaksk, Karabudakhkent, Kaiakent, and Kaitak), the Kumyk constitute the majority group in the population. They are also located in such cities as Makhachkala, Buinaksk, Khasavyurt, Izerbash, and Derbent, while a few are scattered throughout the Chechen-Ingush Autonomous Republic and the North Ossetian Autonomous Republic.

The Kumyks are divided into three traditional groups based on dialect and geography. The northern Kumyks—the people of the Kumyk Plain—speak the Khasavyurt dialect and live in the districts of Khasavyurt and Babayurt, with some in the Kizilyurt district. In the nineteenth century, the northern Kumyks participated in the anti-Russian Shamil movement, and they remain especially anti-Russian. The central Kumyks speak the Buinaksk (Bujnaksk) dialect and are particularly influential in the districts of Buinaksk, Karabudakhkent, and Kizilyurt. The central Kumyks are the largest and most influential of the Kumyk subgroups, and, during the nineteenth century, they sided with the Russians and opposed the Shamil movement, which put them at odds with the northern Kumyks. Finally, the southern Kumyks speak the Kaitak dialect; they are a highland people living in the districts of Kaiakent and Kaitak. During the nineteenth-century anti-Russian Shamil movement, they maintained their neutrality.

Ethnologists believe the Kumyks originated with the fifth-century migrations of Turkic* and Mongolian* people heading west across the steppes of Central Asia. They constitute a mixing of the indigenous Caucasus peoples with Turkic-speaking people, especially after the fall of the Khazar state in the tenth century. Most of those Turkic tribes were probably Kypchaks. Between the eleventh and thirteenth centuries, the Kumyks strengthened their sense of an independent identity and moved into the lowlands of the steppes in the North Caucasus. Under the pressure of the Golden Horde in the late thirteenth and fourteenth centuries, the Kumyk converted to the Sunni Muslim religion, Hanafi school. During the fifteenth and sixteenth centuries, the Kumyks established their own political entity—the Shamkhalat of Tarki. Within a century, they were in control of substantial numbers of Avars* and Dargins*. Because the Kumyks came to control the lowland winter pasture areas of that region, their language was adopted as a second language by large numbers of Chechen*, Avar, Dargin, Nogai*, Kaitak*, Ando-Didi*, and Kubachi* people. The Kumyk also became influential in such Caspian port cities as Makhachkala, Khasavyurt, and Buinaksk, and their language became a *lingua franca* there as well.

During the seventeenth century, the Kumyks found themselves trying to deal with the ethnic Russian expansion into steppes of Central Asia. Their sense of identity was sharpened even more because of the violent struggles for power that characterized political life in the Transcaucasia. To ward off Russian influence, the Kumyks declared their loyalty to the Safavid dynasty in Persia in the sixteenth and seventeenth centuries. Because of that historical experience, a minority of the Kumyks became Shiite Muslims. Those most likely to switch to Shiite practices were the urban workers in close contact with Azeri workers, who were also Shiite. The Kumyks were caught in the middle of the Russian-Ottoman wars of the seventeenth and eighteenth centuries. When Peter the Great occupied Derbent in 1722 and defeated the Safavid dynasty, it was the beginning of the end for Kumyk independence. With his defeat of the Ottoman Turks and the signing of the Treaty of 1724, Peter established Russian control over the western littoral of the Caspian Sea. The Kumyks managed to exercise a degree of autonomy for the next century, but in 1859, when the Russians finally crushed the Shamil rebellion, the Kumyks, as well as the other Daghestani* groups, were permanently brought under Russian sovereignty. Russia formally ended the

Shamkhalat in 1867. The Kumyk region was then incorporated into the Temir-Khan-Shura District and was directly administered by Russia.

When the revolutionary movement gained momentum in Russia in the early twentieth century, many Kumyks were involved. The port cities of the Caspian Sea had been undergoing industrialization for several decades, and thousands of Kumyk workers had acquired an identity as a laboring class. Although most Kumyks preferred an Islamic or Turkic nationalism to a Communist ideology, the urban Kumyks supported the Bolsheviks during the revolution.

Today the Kumyks remain one of the most influential of the Daghestani ethnic groups. The Kumyk language has a strong literary tradition, led by writers like Yirchi Kazak, Osmanov Muhammad, Nuray Batirnurzayov, and Zeyel-abid Batirnurzayov. Newspapers are published in Kumyk (Cyrillic alphabet), and radio and television programs broadcast in the language as well. In terms of economic life, the Kumyks have traditionally been farmers and fishermen, but, during the 1970s and 1980s, the nature of their work changed. Many Kumyk farmers switched to the large-scale production of cereals and cotton, while others manage large state collectives. Kumyk villagers are widely known for their handicrafts, especially gold, silver, and iron works, as well as woolen textiles and carpets. Increasingly large numbers of Kumyks can be found working in the oil industries (refineries and drilling rigs) of the Caspian region, as well as in the new chemical, machine tool, tool and die, and construction plants.

Although the rate of urbanization is high among the Kumyks, they have nevertheless maintained a strong sense of ethnic identity. The vast majority of Kumyks use the Kumyk language as their native tongue, and large numbers of Daghestanis, especially Dargins and Avars, are adopting it as their first language as well. Because of their population concentration, the urban and rural Kumyks are able to stay in close communication. They still emphasize strong family ties, endogamous marriages, and their Islamic religion, even though it is not quite as strong as that of other Caucasian Muslim groups.

As the forces of nationalism gathered momentum in the Soviet Union in the late 1980s and early 1990s, the Kumyks also began to acquire a heightened sense of ethnicity. They had long resented the anti-Muslim programs of the Russian and Soviet states, and, as the Soviet Union crumbled in 1991, Kumyk identity became even more pronounced. In 1990, a number of Kumyks founded Tenglik, or the Kumyk People's Movement, with Salav Aliyev as its leader. Aliyev began calling for a cultural revival of Kumyk values and for political self-determination. He also affiliated Tenglik with the Assembly of Turkic Peoples when it was formed late in 1991. Azerbaijanis, Balkars*, and Nogais soon joined with the Kumyks in promoting pan-Turkic values.

REFERENCES: Alexandre Benningsen, ''Muslim Conservative Opposition to the Soviet Regime: The Sufi Brotherhoods in the North Caucasus,'' in Jeremy R. Azrael, ed., *Soviet Nationality Policies and Practices*, 1978; Alexander Bennigsen and S. Enders Wimbush, *Muslims of the Soviet Empire: A Guide*, 1986; *Current Digest*, 44 (March 11, 1992), 25;

Bernhard Geiger, et al., *Peoples and Languages of the Caucasus*, 1959; K. H. Menges, *Turkic Languages and Peoples: An Introduction to Turkic Studies*, 1968; Robert Olson, "Kumyks," in Richard V. Weekes, ed., *Muslim Peoples*, 1984, 417–21; Ronald Wixman, *The Peoples of the USSR: An Ethnographic Handbook*, 1984.

KUMYKI. See KUMYK.

KUNDROV TATAR. The Kundrov Tatars are a Tatar* group who have adopted some of the characteristics of the surrounding Kalmyk* people. They are Sunni Muslims and live near Astrakhan. Along with the Karagash, they form the group known as the Astrakhan Tatars*. See ASTRAKHAN TATAR, VOLGA TATAR, and TATAR.
REFERENCE: Ronald Wixman, *The Peoples of the USSR: An Ethnographic Handbook*, 1984.

KUNDURSKIJE TATARY. See KUNDUR.

KUR. See LATVIAN.

KURAMA. The Kurama call themselves the Qurama and are known to Russians* as the Kuramintsy. Although Russian ethnographers describe them as a subgroup of the Uzbek*, they have decidedly non-Uzbek origins, with cultural and linguistic traits that are a mix of Kypchak*, Mongol*, and Iranian elements. By the early nineteenth century, they were living in the Fergana Valley. See UZBEK.
REFERENCES: Shirin Akiner, *Islamic Peoples of the Soviet Union*, 1983; Ronald Wixman, *The Peoples of the USSR: An Ethnographic Handbook*, 1984.

KURAMINTSY. See KURAMA.

KURCHIK. See KYZYL or KHAKASS.

KURD. The Kurds are one of the largest ethnic groups in the world that does not enjoy the protection of nation-state status. They call themselves the Kurmandzh. A few Kurds refer to themselves as Soran, while Russians* call them Kurdy. Kurdish nationalism, focusing on the dream of an independent Kurdistan, challenges the existing state structure of the Middle East. All Kurds, it seems, believe themselves to be part of the Kurdish nation, though they may be citizens of the Soviet Union, Turkey, Iraq, Iran, and Syria. Kurds are Indo-European by language and race, and thus are quite distinct from their Arab* and Turkish* neighbors. Census data on Kurds is wildly unreliable. In Iran, census categories are religious, not ethnic. Iraq greatly minimizes its count of (secessionist) Kurds. Turkey actually denies that they exist, claiming that they are "mountain Turks" who have forgotten their language. The following figures, therefore, must be considered as no more than estimates, but there are approximately 4,000,000 Kurds in Iran, 3,000,000 in Iraq, 8,000,000 in Turkey, 600,000 in Syria, and 153,000 in the Soviet Union. The figure for the Soviet Union, based on the 1989 census, is probably closer to the mark than the others, for Moscow has no particular axe to grind vis-à-vis the Kurds, and—except during the Stalin years—has not treated them badly. It must be noted, however, that Azerbaijanis* and Turkmen*, in their autonomous republics, might well wish to count Kurds as members of the eponymous group, thus minimizing the figures on Kurds. As a rule, Kurds marry only other Kurds, and so have not assimilated with the dominant ethnic groups of the six Soviet Republics where they currently live.

The Kurdish language is part of the general northwestern group of Iranian languages, and it is divided into a variety of dialect groups and subgroups. The two primary groups of dialects are Kurmandzhi, which is located in northwestern Kurdish territory, and Sorani, which is in the southwest. Other important dialect groups for Kurds are Gurani, Luri, and Zaza. Their language is also filled with a variety of Russian, Arabic, Turkish, Azerbaijani, and Turkmen words.

Most Soviet Kurds live south of the Caucasus Mountains, the largest concentration, about 68,000, dwelling in Armenia. Some 20,000 live in Yerevan, Armenia's capital, while the remainder live in two dozen compact Kurdish villages scattered across the mountainous countryside. Most Kurds in the world are Sunni Muslims of the Shafi school, but Kurds in what used to be the Soviet Union are primarily Shiite Moslems. About half the Kurds in Armenia are Yezidis* (Yazidis)—that is, practitioners of a secretive religion that mixes ancient cultic rites with elements of Zoroastrianiam, Judaism, Manichean dualism, Nestorian Christianity, and Islam. Muslim Kurds call them "devil-worshippers." The Yezidis speak Kurdish, but constitute a distinct endogamous subgroup. They were driven out of Turkey in nineteenth-century pogroms. Most of the 36,000 Kurds in the recently independent Georgian Republic live in Tbilisi (Tiflis), the capital city. Not many remain in the Meskhetian* border area, from where they were arbitrarily exiled to Central Asia in 1944. The historical record of the Kurds in Azerbaijan is filled with lacunae. Census data over the years show inexplicable rises and falls. The position of Azerbaijani Kurds in the 1990s is especially precarious, since virtual warfare between Armenians* and Azerbaijanis broke out as soon as Moscow's authority weakened. Most of the estimated 10,000 Azerbaijani Kurds are Shiite.

A cluster of Kurdish villages is found east of the Caspian Sea, in the Kopet Mountains, just north of the border between Iran and the Turkmen SSR. These are descendants of the so-called "Khorasan Kurds," who were sent in the early 1600s by a Persian* Safavid ruler, Shah Abbas, to guard the eastern frontiers of his empire against incursions by Central Asians. These Kurds preferred the northern slopes of the Kopet Dag, where lingering snows kept the pastures green all summer. Hence, when the Russo-Persian border was formally demarcated along the ridgeline in 1893, they stayed and became subjects of the tsar. Kurds in Turkmenistan today live in those same mountain settlements and also in the cities of Ashkabad, Mary, and Bayram Ali. Kurdish exile groups claim the actual population there is far higher than the 10,000 that the government counts. Finally, there are Kurdish settlements in Central Asia of deportees and their descendants, who have not been allowed to return to their Transcaucasian home. In Kazakhstan, 20,000 Kurds live in the Chimkent (Tchimkent), Jamboul (Dzhamboul), and Alma-Ata districts. In Kyrgyzia, about 14,000 Kurds live primarily around Osh (Oche).

The natural defensibility of their rugged homeland, centered on the Taurus and Zagros ranges and around lakes Van and Urmia, enabled Kurds to retain their distinct identity through at least 3,000 years of history. They have always been known as tenacious guerrilla fighters, men who would not yield to Xenophon, Richard the Lion-Hearted, or Saddam Hussein. At the same time, the mountain-and-valley topography of Kurdistan has engendered tribal rather than national loyalty, great religious diversity, and many regional dialects instead of a single Kurdish language. Kurdish nationalism, therefore, represents a triumph of the subjective (a feeling of shared identity) over the objective (great diversity). A fine literary and poetic tradition has been a source of pride for all Kurds.

In the nineteenth century, nomadic Kurds drifted north from Turkey and Persia at the same time as the Russian tsars were pushing the borders of their empire southward, fighting a series of wars with the Ottomans and Persians. The Treaty of Turkmanchai (1828) transferred territory north of the Araks River to Russia. The Congress of Berlin (1878) ceded Turkish territory, too. One result of Russian aggrandizement was that, when the Soviet Union was formed in 1922, 70,000 Kurds became citizens of "the world's first workers' and peasants' state."

Soviet Kurdish history then began to diverge from that of Kurds elsewhere. In the first place, certain hopeful developments during the first decade of Soviet power (literacy campaigns, industrialization, etc.) attracted Kurds from isolated mountain villages in Armenia and Georgia to the growing cities of Yerevan and Tbilisi. Moreover, nomadism was extinguished. The border was sealed too, completely cutting Soviet Kurds off from the political currents agitating the rest of Kurdistan in the aftermath of World War I. The Allies had promised the Kurds a homeland from the ruins of the Ottoman Empire but betrayed them with the Treaty of Lausanne (1923). Kurds have been engaged in separatist wars against Turkey, Iraq, and Iran ever since, but this has hardly affected the lives of Soviet Kurds at all.

In the 1920s and again in the 1940s, Moscow experimented with Kurdish puppet governments, as part of a divide-and-conquer strategy aimed at Turkey and Iran. An "Autonomous Republic of Kurdistan," with its capital at Lachin, was carved out of Azerbaijan in 1923, but it mysteriously vanished six years later, perhaps under strong pressure from the (Turkic) Azeris. The Soviets also sponsored a short-lived "Republic of Mahabad" in Iranian Kurdistan in 1946, probably hoping to establish a satellite on the Polish* model, but it did not survive the withdrawal of Soviet troops. Its Kurdish leaders were publicly shot by the angry Iranians.

Josef Stalin at first encouraged Soviet Kurds to develop their national culture. A Kurdish newspaper, *Ria-taze* ("New Way" or "New Road"), was published in Yerevan beginning in 1930. The Latin script was adapted to Kurdish. Kurdish schoolchildren were taught their own language, and institutes of Kurdish studies were established in Moscow, Leningrad, and Yerevan. The entire policy was swept away in 1937 by Stalin's deepening suspicion of everything non-Russian. The first deportation of Kurds to Central Asia occurred in that year, for reasons unknown. Two more waves of forced internal exile during World War II transferred Kurds from the Soviet Union's borderlands deep into Central Asia. The death toll is not known. Stalin seems to have feared that any ethnic group with kinsmen on the other side of the border was potentially subversive, no matter how unlikely Kurdish collaboration with Turks or Persians might actually have been. It made no difference that a Kurdish regiment fought to defend Minsk from the Germans*.

The deported Kurds were part of a larger multinational group of inhabitants of Meskhetia, an area on the Turkish-Georgian border. The Meskhetians included Turks, Azerbaijanis and Khemsils* (Turkized Armenians) as well as Kurds. All were classified first as Turks and later as Azerbaijanis. They made so much trouble for the authorities that the Supreme Soviet issued a special decree in 1968 recognizing their original ethnicities, but stating flatly that they had "settled permanently" in Central Asia.

Precious little information on Soviet Kurds has filtered out in recent decades. A Soviet ethnographic journal claimed in 1965 that those in Turkmenia were being assimilated into Turkmen culture, which in turn was melding into "Soviet culture." This claim was highly dubious. It might seem that loyal Communist Kurds would make an ideal tool for destabilizing neighboring countries. Since the 1960s, however, the Soviets have preferred to work within the existing state structure in the Middle East, even supplying Saddam Hussein with many of the weapons that he used to suppress Kurdish separatists. In fact, it was the United States, not the Soviet Union, that sought to use Kurdish nationalism for its own purposes. The Gulf War of 1991, in which Iraq invaded Kuwait and United Nations forces, led by the United States, counterattacked, made political life even more difficult for the Kurds. Saddam Hussein's forces harassed the Kurds throughout 1991. Thousands of them fled into the Soviet Union, only to find that whole country breaking up by the end of the year. At this writing, the situation in that troubled corner of the world is completely chaotic. No one can predict what the future will bring for the Kurds.

What the Gulf War achieved, however, was putting the Kurdish question before the world community in an unprecedented way. Their persecution and suffering at the hands of Saddam Hussein in Iraq has given them at least a modest voice in the world community, and some Kurdish nationalists have escalated their demands for Kurdish autonomy. They argue that, as the most populous people without a country in the world, the Kurds deserve their own nation state. That demand, of course, conflicts with existing political interests in Russia, Iran, Iraq, Turkey, and Syria, and the likelihood of a Kurdish state is extremely small. Still, Kurdish nationalism has acquired an urgency and an audience that are unprecedented.

Those feelings began to find some institutional expression in the late 1980s, particularly among the 60,000 or so Kurds who lived in Armenia. Kurdish-language radio broadcasts were inaugurated over Armenian radio in 1987, and the Armenian Writers' Union established a Kurdish section. The Institute of Oriental Studies in the Armenian Republic Academy of Sciences formed a Kurdish studies department, and, in September 1989, a Soviet Kurdish Society met in Moscow, announcing its goal of Kurdish political autonomy. Kurdish nationalism, however, has faced a major obstacle in the Armenian-Azerbaijan conflict, especially in Nagorno-Karabakh (Kavabagh). Both sides in the struggle are trying to use the Kurds to their political advantage. Armenians talk of reviving "Red Kurdistan," which existed between 1923 and 1930, because it would guarantee their control over the corridor to Karabakh. In 1992, Uakil Mustafayev, a leader in *Yakbun*, a Kurdish rights organization, demanded the return of Kelbadzhar, Zangelan, and Kobetlya from Azerbaijan and the restoration of a Kurdish state.

REFERENCES: Shirin Akiner, *Islamic Peoples of the Soviet Union*, 1983; T. F. Aristova and G. P. Vasil'yeva, "Kurds of the Turkmen SSR," *Central Asian Review*, 13 (1965), 302–9; Gerard Chaliand, ed., *People Without a Country: The Kurds and Kurdistan*, 1980; Robert Conquest, *The Nation-Killers: The Soviet Deportation of Nationalities*, 1970; *Current Digest*, 42 (April 11, 1990), 30, and 44 (July 22, 1991), 23–24; William Eagleton, *The Kurdish Republic of 1946*, 1979; Elizabeth Fuller, "Kurdish Demands for Autonomy Complicate Karabakh Equation," *RFE/RL Research Report*, 1 (June 5, 1992), 12–14; David McDowall, *The Kurds*, 1989.

Ross Marlay

KURDY. See KURD.

KURIK CHEREMISS. See KURYK MARI and MARI.

KURIK CHEREMISS MARI. See KURYK MARI and MARI.

KURIL. See AINU.

KURILIAN. See AINU.

KURILTSY. See AINU.

KURIN. See LEZGIN.

KURISCHE KONIGE. See KURSU KONINI, LATVIAN, and LITHUANIAN.

KURISH KENIGE. See KURSU KONINI, LATVIAN, and LITHUANIAN.

KURISH KING. See KURSU KONINI, LATVIAN, and LITHUANIAN.

KURKHDERE. See AGUL.

KURKUROO. The Kurkuroo are classified today as a subgroup of the Kyrgyz*, although they are not Kyrgyz in terms of their linguistic and cultural roots. See KYRGYZ.
REFERENCE: Ronald Wixman, *The Peoples of the USSR: An Ethnographic Handbook,* 1984.

KURMANDJ. See KURD.

KURMANDZH. See KURD.

KURMANDZHI. See KURD.

KURON. The Kuron are classified today as a subgroup of the Kyrgyz, although they are not Kyrgyz in terms of their linguistic and cultural roots. The Kuron are concentrated demographically in the Tyen Shan Oblast of the Kyrgyz Republic. See KYRGYZ.
REFERENCE: Ronald Wixman, *The Peoples of the USSR: An Ethnographic Handbook,* 1984.

KURONIAN. See KURSU KONINI, LATVIAN, and LITHUANIAN.

KURSENIEKI. See LATVIAN.

KURSHI. See KURSU KONINI, LATVIAN, and LITHUANIAN.

KURSI. See LATVIAN.

KURSIAI. See KURSU KONINI, LATVIAN, and LITHUANIAN.

KURSININKAS. See KURSU KONINI, LATVIAN, and LITHUANIAN.

KURSININKI. See KURSU KONINI, LATVIAN, and LITHUANIAN.

KURSU KENINI. See KURSU KONINI, LATVIAN, and LITHUANIAN.

KURSU KONINI. The Kursu Konini are a tiny group of ethnic Latvians* who distinguish themselves ethnically by their claim that they are descendants of a noble class who once enjoyed the protection and patronage of German* rulers, including legal recognition of feudal and land titles. See LATVIAN and LITHUANIAN.
REFERENCE: Ronald Wixman, *The Peoples of the USSR: An Ethnographic Handbook*, 1984.

KURT. See KURD.

KURURMUSKII. See MANCHU.

KURYK CHEREMISS. See KURYK MARI and MARI.

KURYK MARI. The Kuryk Mari constitute one of the major constituent groups of the Mari* people. They have also been known historically as the Highland Mari. During the seventeenth century, the Kuryk Mari superficially accepted some of Eastern Orthodox Christianity, but they also retained many of their ancestral religious beliefs and rituals. Their religion sets them apart from the lowland Mari groups, who rejected the Christian missionaries outright. The Kuryk Mari dialect is also distinct and mutually unintelligible from lowland Mari. See MARI.
REFERENCE: Ronald Wixman, *The Peoples of the USSR: An Ethnographic Survey*, 1984.

KURZEMIAN. See KURZEMNIEKI, LATVIAN, and LITHUANIAN.

KURZEMNIEKI. The term "Kurzemnieki" refers to ethnic Latvians* who are or know that their ancestors were from Kurzeme Province. See LATVIAN and LITHUANIAN.
REFERENCE: Ronald Wixman, *The Peoples of the USSR: An Ethnographic Handbook*, 1984.

KUVAKAN. See BASHKIR.

KUVANDY. See KUMANDIN and ALTAI.

KUVANDYG. See KUMANDIN and ALTAI.

KUVANDYKH. See KUMANDIN and ALTAI.

KUVANTY. See KUMANDIN and ALTAI.

KUZNETS TATAR. See KUZNETSKI TATAR and SHOR.

KUZNETSKI TATAR. The Kuznetski Tatars are part of the larger collection of Siberian Tatars*. The term ''Kuznetski Tatar'' is more a reflection of their location in the Kuznetsk Basin of southern Siberia than of any distinct identity as a special group of Tatars.* These Tatars were converted to the Sunni Muslim faith, Hanafi school, by Islamic merchants in the fourteenth and fifteenth centuries. Russians* finally conquered the region in the late sixteenth century. Contact with Russians led to the Tatars' conversion to Eastern Orthodox Christianity, although the conversion was superficial at best. Until the nineteenth century, most of the Kuznetski Tatars were hunters and trappers, but when industrialization reached Siberia, some Kuznetski Tatars went to work in factories, tanneries, and sawmills. After the 1930s, most of the Kuznetski Tatars found themselves living and laboring on collective farms. Since World War II, Russian ethnographers have classified them with the Shors*. See SHOR and TATAR.
REFERENCES: Shirin Akiner, *Islamic Peoples of the Soviet Union*, 1983; Ronald Wixman, *The Peoples of the USSR: An Ethnographic Handbook*, 1984.

KVANADI. See BAGULAL and AVAR.

KVANADIN. See BAGULAL and AVAR.

KVANADY. See BAGULAL and AVAR.

KVANALI. See ANDI and AVAR.

KVANALY. See ANDI and AVAR.

KWANADI. See BAGULAL and AVAR.

KWANADY. See BAGULAL and AVAR.

KWANALI. See ANDI and AVAR.

KWANALY. See ANDI and AVAR.

KWANTL HEKWA. See BAGULAL and AVAR.

KWARSHI. See AVAR.

KYPCHAK. See NOGAI.

KYPCHAK. The Kypchak, who call themselves the Qypshak, are classified today as a subgroup of the Uzbeks*. In terms of their linguistic origins, they have both Turkic* and Mongol* roots. Most ethnographers identify them as a transition group between the Uzbeks and the Kazakhs*. They are descendants of the Kypchak tribes who first came to the Fergana Valley in the thirteenth and fourteenth centuries. See UZBEK and KAZAKH.

REFERENCES: Shirin Akiner, *Islamic Peoples of the Soviet Union*, 1983; Ronald Wixman, *The Peoples of the USSR: An Ethnographic Handbook*, 1984.

KYPCHAQ. See KYPCHAK, KAZAKH, and UZBEK.

KYPSHAK. See KYPCHAK, LAZAKH, and UZBEK.

KYPSHAQ. See KYPCHAK, KAZAKH, and UZBEK.

KYRGHYZ KAISAK. See KYRGYZ KAZAKH.

KYRGHYZ KAYSAK. See KYRGYZ KAZAKH.

KYRGHYZ KAZAK. See KYRGYZ KAZAKH.

KYRGYZ. The Kyrgyz (also variously spelled Kirgiz, Khirghiz, Qyrqyz, and Khirgiz) are a Central Asian Turkic*-speaking people whose homeland, the Republic of Kyrgyzistan (or Kyrgyzia), is located at the western end of the Tien Shan Mountain Range of northwestern China, which is the republic's eastern neighbor. Kyrgyzistan is bordered in the north by the Republic of Kazakhstan and on the south by Uzbekistan and Tajikistan. Since over 85 percent of Kyrgyzistan is higher than 5,000 feet above sea level, the country is predominantly a cold, harsh, mountainous region of only marginally fertile land. According to the census of 1989, there were 2,530,998 Kyrgyz, out of a total population of 4.3 million, in Kyrgyzistan, forming a 52 percent majority in their own homeland. The next largest ethnic group in the country is the Russians*, who comprise 22 percent of the population. Other ethnic groups who live in the region include, in descending numbers, the Uzbeks*, Ukrainians*, Tatars*, Chinese* Muslims, Germans*, and Dungans*. For their part, some 120,000 Kyrgyz live in the Namangan, Andidzhan, and Fergana districts of Uzbekistan, in the Gorno-Badakhshan, Garm, and Pamir regions of Tajikistan, and in the neighboring regions of Kazakhstan. Another 110,000 Kyrgyz reside in the Xinjiang Uigur Autonomous Region in the People's Republic of China.

Kyrgyz, a Turkic language, belongs to the Nogai* subgroup, Kyrgyz-Kypchak* group, in the Eastern Hunnic branch of Uralic-Altaic languages. It is most closely related to the languages of the Kazakhs* and, to a lesser degree, of the Karakalpaks*, Tatars, and Kypchak Uzbeks. Indeed, the Kyrgyz are culturally very closely related to the Kazakhs and Karakalpaks. The only differences are that the Kyrgyz have more Mongolic and Altaic-Turkic elements in their culture and were predominantly transhumant nomads, as opposed to being steppe nomads like the Kazakhs. The Kyrgyz language has two major dialects that correspond to historical and cultural differences between northern and southern Kyrgyz. For example, the southern dialect contains a major fund of loan words from the Persian* language, due to the geographic proximity of Iran and Tajikistan to Kyrgyzistan. Some authors maintain that, until the twentieth century, the Kyrgyz language had been an unwritten one; others claim that the Kyrgyz used a written form of Uzbek and Uigur*, popularly known throughout Central Asia as "Turkii." Still others maintain that at the height of their power, around the ninth century, the Kyrgyz regularly used a Turkic "runic" script, which, together with their agricultural knowledge, was subsequently lost in the cultural disruptions following the Mongol* conquests of the thirteenth century. Until the 1920s, the Kyrgyz language was written in the Arabic script; from then until the 1940s, the Latin alphabet was used. The Cyrillic script, introduced by the Russians, has been in use since then. Like their Turkic cousins in Central Asia, the Kyrgyz place great emphasis on their oral epic poetry, the first example of which was published in 1910.

The etymological origins of the term "Kyrgyz" are derived, apparently, from two Turkic words: *girgh* (forty) and *giz* (girl, or daughter). Kyrgyz lore identifies the name as referring to "descendants of the forty maidens." The earliest Chinese sources, dating from the second century A.D., mention a group of people called the Kien-kuen (apparently derived from the Mongolic word *kirkun*), whose homeland lay to the northwest of the land of the K'ang Kiu (of Sogdiana). Another, less precise source names a people called the Kik-Kun, who may have lived in the area of the Yenesei River in Siberia as early as 201 B.C. The first reliable source naming the Kyrgyz as such appeared in the Turkic *Orkhon* inscriptions of the eighth century; these, together with the Chinese T'ang-shu annals, place the Kyrgyz homeland in the region of the Upper Yenesei River, north of the Kog-men or Sayan Mountains. Some Turkic inscriptions, dated from the fifth to the seventh centuries and found in the Yenesei region, have been attributed to the Kyrgyz. Interestingly, in these early sources, the Kyrgyz were described as a red-haired, white-skinned, yet already thoroughly turkicized people. These sources attributed their coloration to the alleged contacts of the Kyrgyz with the Slavs. Ethnographers and historians continue to disagree, however, about the continuity of relationship of the early Kyrgyz with their contemporary namesakes. The earliest records of the Kyrgyz of present-day Kyrgyzistan date back only to the early sixteenth century.

The Kyrgyz became politically important in history in 840 A.D., when they defeated the Uigur state in northwestern Mongolia and took over the lands between the Yenesei and Orkhon rivers. Between 840 and 925, the Great Kyrgyz State was the most powerful polity in Central Asia. Yet, in the early tenth century, the Kyrgyz themselves were defeated by the newly emergent Karakhitay Empire. The Kyrgyz resurfaced with the arrival of the Ghenghis Khanite

Mongols, to whom the Kyrgyz were finally compelled to submit in 1218. While the majority of Kyrgyz remained in the Upper Yenesei region, a group of them migrated southward, probably around this time, into the western Tien Shan region familiar as the modern Kyrgyz homelands. While a small residual number of the Yenesei Kyrgyz (those who failed to participate in the Mongol relocation) would eventually be absorbed by the Khakass* and Tuvinian* groups, the Kyrgyz of the Tien Shan region were themselves subject to successive waves of invasion and subjugation by a number of Turkic tribes, including the Turgesh, the Karluks, and the Karakhanids, groups that the Kyrgyz would themselves one day subjugate and absorb. The people of the Tien Shan region became part of the *Ulus* (*tribe*) of Chagatai, Ghenghis Khan's second son. The Mongols' depredations were responsible for the severe retrogression of Kyrgyz culture, including the loss of the art of writing, for the next century. Upon the break-up of the Golden and White Hordes and of the other Mongol successor states around the late fourteenth century, the Tien Shan region came under the control of the Khanate of Mo-golistan. With the exception of an obscure reference to an individual named Muhammad being invested as khan of the Kyrgyz by Sayid Khan of the Mongols in 1514, the Kyrgyz once again went into eclipse in contemporary sources until the seventeenth century.

In 1607, the Yenesei Kyrgyz concluded as alliance with the Kazakhs. Apparently recognizing Kazakh suzerainty only with great difficulty, the sources record the Kyrgyz killing of a Kazakh tax collector who was sent to them in 1609. For the most part, however, the Yenesei Kyrgyz did not come under the political control of the Kazakhs until the middle of the seventeenth century. In 1642, the Kalmyk* Mongol Khan Batur described the Yenesei Kyrgyz, whom he called the *Burut*, as being "Kalmyk." By 1646, the Russian plenipotentiary to Central Asia, Daniyil Arshinskiy, optimistically referred to these Kyrgyz as "Russian subjects." In 1683–1685, the Tien Shan Kyrgyz were forced to flee before a terrible onslaught by the Kalmyks (Mongolian Buddhists, related to the Dzungarian Oirots* who were Muslims). Nearly all the Tien Shan Kyrgyz were driven into neighboring eastern Turkestan (into Yarkand, Kashgar, Khotan, the Pamir, and Alay ranges, and the Fergana Valley). In 1703, the Kalmyks arranged with the Russians to transfer the bulk of the Yenesei Kyrgyz, numbering about 3,000 to 4,000 tents, outward into the Tien Shan region. Eventually, these Kyrgyz were reunited with the displaced Kyrgyz, who returned to their homelands after the Manchu* defeat of the Kalmyk/Oirot Federation in 1758. After this date, the Kyrgyz became Chinese subjects, but, in reality, their nomadic culture and life-style made them virtually independent.

During the period of struggle against the Mongols, the Kyrgyz began to convert to the Sunni branch of the Hanafi school of Islam under Sharia law. Their first *ulema*—religious leaders—came from Uzbekistan, and later as the Tatar influence in Central Asia grew, from the Volga River region. The Kyrgyz also became devout followers of at least six different orders of Sufism. As reflected in their epic poetry, they apparently viewed their struggle against the Mongols as a holy war. Typical of the syncretism of Turkic culture in general, however, the Kyrgyz were wont to meld Islam with their older shamanistic religion. The most significant socio-economic unit of Kyrgyz society was the *oy* (family household), which consisted of a man, his wife, or wives, their unmarried children, their married sons, and the sons' children. Also common to this group were other close blood relatives, adopted members, and sometimes even unrelated dependents. These *oy* were organized into clan and tribal units, which were, in turn, divided into two major "wings," the right (*Ong Kanat*) and the left (*Sol Kanat*), based on traditional Turkic military organization.

The nature of nomadic herding and the need for women's labor made the Islamic tradition of female seclusion an impractical luxury. Kyrgyz women enjoyed considerable status and rights; they did not wear the veil, and they were not compelled to avoid contact with non-kinsmen. They could and did become heads of household and property owners upon the death of their husbands (in the absence of an eldest adult male child), and they were considered active participants in family decision making. A highly unusual feature of Kyrgyz culture concerned one's ability to trace male ancestry back seven generations, an extreme form of patrilineage. All forms of kinship ties (i.e., blood, marriage, and fictive), memberships in particular clans and, by extension, Kyrgyz society as a whole were very exclusive and based on this ability. Those individuals who were unable to perform the genealogical ritual had the status of slaves (*kul*) and were considered unsuitable for marriage; the issue of mixed marriages were likewise looked upon as *kul*. As a result, exogamy with non-Kyrgyz was strongly discouraged.

The Kyrgyz increasingly came into contact with the expanding Russian Empire beginning in the mid-seventeenth century. Upon the destruction of the Kalmyk* empire in 1758, the Russian government began its ominous policy of interfering with Kyrgyz internal affairs. A prime example of this Russian meddling may be seen in the transfer of the "Kyrgyz" moniker to the Kazakhs, who were thereafter known to the Russians as the "Kyrgyz-Kazakhs," in distinction from the Cossacks*, who were in the process of being settled in Kazakhstan by the Russians. Then, in order to identify the true Kyrgyz, the Russians began to refer to them as the "Kara-Kyrgyz," or Black Kyrgyz, a name the Kyrgyz themselves have always thoroughly disclaimed. The extension of Russian influence over the Kyrgyz differed considerably from that imposed upon the Kazakhs. Unlike the Kazakhs, the Kyrgyz had never had a nobility of princes and aristocrats. Their only leaders were tribal elders, or *Manap*, and these individuals owed their position entirely to their personal influence. In addition, Kyrgyz society was prone to fragmentation, probably due to the almost continual state of war against the Kyrgyz. And finally, while the Kyrgyz came under the nominal suzerainty of China from 1758 until the mid-nineteenth century, they enjoyed during that time a *de facto*, though short-lived independence.

The first Kyrgyz to come under Russian rule were not defeated by the Russians but, instead, had appealed to the Russian government for help against other

Kyrgyz aggressors. In the 1830s, the Sarybagysh Kyrgyz, backed by the Uzbek Khanate of Khokand, had defeated the Kyrgyz, bringing them under the rule of the khan as tribute-paying vassals. Under Khokand's suzerainty, the Kyrgyz were taxed much more heavily, and alien elements were settled among them. It was during this period of upheaval that Islam became much more firmly established among the Kyrgyz. In 1854, the Bugu Kyrgyz of the northern Kyrgyz groups requested Russia's protection; the following year, their chief Borombai, together with 10,000 families under his leadership, applied to the Russian government for citizenship. In return, Borombai was granted the rank of lieutenant, and his people were exempted from Russian taxes. All Russian efforts at mediation between the Sarybagysh and Bugu Kyrgyz proved fruitless, however; therefore, in 1862, the Russians established a garrison in the town of Pishpek (which later became Soviet Frunze). The following year, the Bugus requested the permanent stationing of another Russian garrison on Lake Issyk Kul, not only to protect them from the Sarybagysh, but to shield them from Khokandian tax collectors as well. By 1867, the majority of northern Kyrgyz tribes joined the Bugus either in voluntarily requesting or, at least, in accepting, Russian rule. Those Kyrgyz tribes that could not submit to Russian rule migrated into the Pamir Mountains and Afghanistan.

The southern Kyrgyz launched a revolt against the Khokand Khanate in 1870. Pleading for Russian support, they withdrew into Russian-controlled territory in hopes of drawing the Russians into the conflict. When Khokand's Khan Khudayar was compelled to capitulate to the Russians during the interim, however, the southern Kyrgyz found themselves fighting for their independence against a different enemy. The southern Kyrgyz' struggle against Russian hegemony assumed the character of a Muslim holy war. The remaining northern Kyrgyz groups, together with the southern Kyrgyz, were finally forced to accept Russian rule by 1876. Following the conquest, the Russians established the government of Turkestan in 1867 and the so-called Government of the Steppes in 1882, a move that contributed to the destruction of the political and cultural unity of the Kyrgyz steppes.

The situation was exacerbated by the familiar Russian policy of encouraging Slavic, Cossack, and German* immigration into Kyrgyzistan. The first wave of colonists to the area competed for all the most productive agricultural lands, leading to the constriction of pasturage for the native Kyrgyz. In many cases, the amount of land allotted to a Kyrgyz herdsman was prohibited from exceeding the amount granted to the average agricultural colonist, whose needs were often far less. The Russian colonists were routinely incorporated into the Cossack army of Semirech'e, whose job it was to assign the most fertile lands. The western Russian famines of 1891 and 1898 were responsible for bringing in another wave of colonists, tripling the number of Russian settlers around the capital of Pishpek (Frunze) and marginalizing the native nomads to the mountains and steppes. The reduction of pasturage signalled the start of a vicious cycle of compensatory herd reductions, followed closely by ever-declining living standards. Beginning as early as 1866, northern Kyrgyzistan suffered tremendous economic hardships, becoming one of the most neglected and under-developed areas of Russian Central Asia.

A major revolt against Russian rule, involving both the Kyrgyz and the Kazakhs, took place in 1916, on the eve of the Bolshevik Revolution. Both groups, disaffected by their eroding cultural and living standards, erupted into open revolt when the Russian government introduced a general military conscription among the steppes peoples to fight in World War I. Thousands of Russian colonists and Kyrgyz were killed, while more than 150,000 nomads abandoned their possessions and fled into neighboring China. The Bolsheviks established control over Kyrgyzistan by first seizing power in Tashkent, the administrative center of Turkestan. After intense fighting with the Kyrgyz, who were allied with the tsarist White Army and interventionists against the Red Army, the Bolsheviks finally established control over Kyrgyzistan by 1919. The Bolsheviks failed to create an administrative unit for the Kyrgyz; instead, Kyrgyz lands were divided among the various provinces of the newly created Turkestan Autonomous Soviet Socialist Republic (ASSR).

During the early Soviet period, the Bolsheviks simply continued the tsarist policy of encouraging the colonization of Kyrgyzistan. As had been the case with Kazakhstan, the bulk of the Communist administration was, by necessity, recruited from the non-native or colonial element, since a sufficiently large Kyrgyz Communist element had not yet developed. The Bolsheviks ruthlessly suppressed or dissolved all competing, non-Communist political parties and nationalist groups, such as the Alash Orda and the Shura-i Islam, that advocated either nationalism or autonomy. Confronted by the continuation of nationalist resistance in the form of the Basmachi Revolt, the Bolsheviks were compelled to adopt a more conciliatory stand toward Turkestan after 1919. For example, the Soviet government instituted land reform in Kyrgyzistan, returning lands that had been given to colonists. In addition, the National Delimitation of 1924, which divided Central Asia by ethnicity, gave Kyrgyzistan autonomous oblast (province) status within the Russian Soviet Federated Socialist Republics (RSFSR). Later, in 1926, the area became the Kyrgyz ASSR. In 1936, the Kyrgyz ASSR evolved into a full constituent republic of the Soviet Union. The Communists also ensured that leading Kyrgyz leaders, such as Qasim Tinistan-Uulu, were given prominent positions in the government. Finally, traditional, nomadic, clan-oriented, *manap*-led Kyrgyz society was maintained virtually intact.

Two policies pursued by the Stalinist regime—the collectivization of the peasantry and the purges—were responsible for initiating the most far-reaching changes in Kyrgyz society. The brutal Stalinist policy of forced settlement and collectivization of the Kyrgyz herdsmen in 1927–1928 had consequences almost as tragic for the Kyrgyz as they had been for the Kazakhs. The policy was responsible for initiating widespread resistance among the Kyrgyz, who tended to slaughter their livestock and flee toward the Chinese border rather than submit.

The Basmachis, quiescent since the early 1920s, reappeared in armed opposition to collectivization. Some in Soviet ruling circles began to fear a native-led conspiracy to derail the collectivization program and even to overthrow, with the help of foreign powers, the Communist regime in Kyrgyzistan. Nevertheless, the collectivization of the Kyrgyz proceeded apace, and by 1933, 67 percent of peasant households had been collectivized.

In the political purges of the late 1920s and 1930s, leading individuals in both the intellectual and political life of Kyrgyzistan were removed, silenced, and, in some cases, executed. Tinistan-Uulu, a dominant figure in the intellectual and cultural life of Kyrgyzistan, was the leading individual from the intelligentsia to be purged. Others were also arrested. Still, it has been argued that the purges conducted against the intellectual elite were largely limited to the suppression of suspect literature rather than personalities. In the field of politics, three chairmen of the Kyrgyz Council of Ministers, three first secretaries of the Kyrgyz party organization, the chairman of the Kyrgyz Central Executive Committee, as well as numerous others from the party leadership, were also purged. The object in every case was to bring to the fore only those individuals who had demonstrated unqualified support of and ideological compatibility with Stalinist goals. Indeed, the ranks of the intelligentsia were decimated between 1934–1939, and party membership showed a 51 percent decline for the same period.

A great deal of change was instituted during the Soviet period. The largely nomadic life-style ended with the settling of Kyrgyz nomads on collectives and state farms. Although the Kyrgyz are no longer considered truly nomadic, the majority continue to live as closely as they can to the way their ancestors did: They live in the valleys, in mud or adobe permanent homes, for at least part of the year and spend the summer months living in the mountains in their traditional round felt *yurt* tents, tending their flocks. These changes have been accompanied by some agricultural mechanization and the introduction of irrigation projects to increase cultivation. Numerous Kyrgyz have been drawn away from their traditional ways and into cities for work and a more modern life-style, yet the overwhelming number of industrial jobs continue to be staffed primarily by non-Kyrgyz workers.

Soviet President Mikhail Gorbachev's *perestroika* had no effect on the republic until 1990, when ethnic rioting broke out along the Kyrgyz Republic's border with the Uzbek Republic; 200 people were killed. The Kyrgyz Communist Party leader, Absamat Masaliev, attempted to induce the republic's Supreme Soviet to create the office of president and to get himself elected to that position. An opposition group within the Soviet, calling itself *Democratic Kyrgyzstan*, elected Askar Akayev instead. The attempted coup against Gorbachev in August 1991 was mirrored by a simultaneous attempt by the local KGB chief to depose Akayev. Troops loyal to the Kyrgyz president surrounded the party headquarters and arrested the KGB chief. Afterwards, Akayev banned the Kyrgyz Communist Party from government office, and the party soon dissolved itself. The republic's Supreme Soviet modified the Kyrgyz constitution to create a presidential-parliamentary form of government, with an elective presidency and a prime minister responsible to the Supreme Soviet. In the subsequent elections on October 12, 1991, Akayev, with a reputation as a genuine democrat, much like Kazakhstan's Nursultan Nazarbayev, was virtually the guaranteed winner, since no other candidates bothered to oppose him.

REFERENCES: Shirin Akiner, *Islamic Peoples of the Soviet Union*, 1983; Edward Allworth, *Central Asia: A Century of Russian Rule*, 1967; Azamat Altay, "Kirghiziya During the Great Purge," *Central Asian Review*, 12 (1964), 97–107; Elizabeth E. Bacon, *Central Asia Under Russian Rule*, 1966; Alexandre Bennigsen and Chantal Lemercier-Quelquejay, *Islam in the Soviet Union*, 1967; René Grousset, *The Empire of the Steppes: A History of Central Asia*, 1970; Charles W. Hostler, *Turkism and the Soviets*, 1957; Lawrence Krader, *Peoples of Central Asia*, 1963; M. Wesley Shoemaker, ed., *Russia, Eurasian States, and Eastern Europe* (formerly *The Soviet Union and Eastern Europe*), 1992; Alec Nove and J. A. Newth, *The Soviet Middle East: A Communist Model for Development*, 1966; Alexander G. Park, *Bolshevism in Turkestan, 1917–1927*, 1957; Richard Pipes, *The Formation of the Soviet Union: Communism and Nationalism, 1917–1923*, 1980; Michael Rywkin, ed., *Russian Colonial Expansion to 1917*, 1988; Michael Rywkin, *Russia in Central Asia*, 1963; Wayne S. Vucinich, ed., *Russia and Asia: Essays on the Influence of Russia on the Asian Peoples*, 1972; Geoffrey Wheeler, *The Peoples of Soviet Central Asia*, 1966; Serge A. Zenkovsky, *Pan-Turkism and Islam in Russia*, 1960.

Lee Brigance Pappas

KYRGYZ KAISAK. See KYRGYZ KAZAKH.

KYRGYZ KAYSAK. See KYRGYZ KAZAKH.

KYRGYZ KAZAK. See KYGRYZ KAZAKH.

KYRGYZ KAZAKH. The term "Kyrgyz Kazakh" was used by the Russians* for a time to refer to the Kazakhs*. They used the term primarily as a way of distinguishing them from the Cossacks*, who were in the process of being settled in Kazakhstan by the Russians. See KAZAKH.

REFERENCE: Ronald Wixman, *The Peoples of the USSR: An Ethnographic Handbook*, 1984.

KYRYM TATAR. See CRIMEAN TATAR or TATAR.

KYURIN. See LEZGIN.

KYY. See SAGAI or KHAKASS.

KYZL. See KYZYL or KHAKASS.

KYZYL. The Kyzyl call themselves the Qyzyl. They have also been identified historically as the Kizil or the Chulym Tatars*. Today they constitute one of the major subgroups of the Khakass*. In terms of their ethnic origins, the Kyzyl have both Turkic* and Kett* roots, and they remain aware of their own subdivision into different identity groups: Kyzyl, Melet, Acha, Argun, Kurchik, Basagar, Igin, Kamlar, and Shusty. They are concentrated demographically in the Khakass Autonomous Oblast, especially along the White River, Black Iyus River, Serezh River, Pechishcha River, and Uryup River. See KHAKASS.
REFERENCE: Ronald Wixman, *The Peoples of the USSR: An Ethnographic Handbook*, 1984.

KYZYLGAYA. See SAGAI or KHAKASS.

L

LAHAMUL. See LAKHAMUL and SVANETIAN.

LAK. The Laks are a conservative Muslim ethnic group who today live in the Daghestan Autonomous Republic, particularly in the south-central reaches of the republic, wedged between the territory of the Avars* and the Dargins.* They are concentrated in the Lak, Kuli, and New Lak rayons. Although the Soviet government tried in recent years to relocate the Laks to more urban areas, they prefer their rural villages. They call themselves the Laq and have also been known historically as the Ghazi Kumuq, Kazi Kumukh, and Kazikumyk; Russians* refer to them as the Laktsy. Their language is closely related to Dargin, although they are mutually unintelligible; together they constitute a branch of the Caucasic language family. There are five mutually intelligible Lak dialects: Kumukh, Vitskh, Vikhli, Ashtikuli, and Balkar.* Of those dialects, Kumukh became the *lingua franca* for Lak traders and commercial enterprises. The Laks make their living as farmers, herders, and artisans, but the Lak economy is among the least developed in the Soviet Union. In the 1989 census, Soviet demographers placed the Lak population at 118,386 people.

The Laks are one of the indigenous peoples of the Caucasus, probably descendants of the Gumik tribe. Like most of the inhabitants of the region, the Laks are Sunni Muslim in their religious loyalties and devoted to the Shafi theological school. Islam came to the Laks from three directions. Arab* traders first began introducing the religion in the eighth century; Persian* traders brought it into the area again beginning in the fifteenth century; and thirdly, Mongol* invaders carried it in from the north in the sixteenth and seventeenth centuries. The Laks were slower than other Daghestani* peoples to adopt Islam. Nonetheless, by the mid-nineteenth century, the Laks had been thoroughly converted, both religiously and culturally, to Sunni Muslim values and beliefs. Today the Laks remain extremely devoted to the faith, attending mosque regularly, observing Ramadan, praying daily, circumcising male children, and conducting regular Muslim ceremonies for marriages and funerals.

The Laks emerged as a politically powerful group in Daghestan during the fourteenth century, when their principality, known as the Shamkhalat, became a semi-independent entity on the southern border of the Golden Horde. By the fifteenth century, they were expanding to the northeast, coming to control a substantial amount of Kumyk* land. They tried to resist the increasing power and presence of the Russians in the nineteenth century, but it was to no avail. In 1865, Russia abolished the Shamkhalat and brought Lak territory under direct Russian administrative control.

During the nineteenth and twentieth centuries, the policies of the tsars and then the Communist governments alienated the Laks and intensified their sense of ethnic solidarity. As large numbers of ethnic Russian settlers poured into Transcaucasus in the nineteenth and early twentieth centuries, the Laks found themselves confronted by an alien people who enjoyed the backing of the state. The Russian settlers managed to seize large areas of Lak land and brought commercialized forms of agriculture and animal husbandry. The arrival of so many ethnic Russians in the Daghestan region led to the Shamil Rebellion. Daghestanis in general, including the Laks, resented the Russians, and, in 1834, Imam Shamil, an Avar Muslim leader, declared independence for Daghestan and imposed the Koran as the law of the land. Older animistic beliefs were crushed, and the government fought the Russian Orthodox church. The Shamil Revolt collapsed in 1858, but, by that time, the hatred of the Daghestanis and Laks for everything Russian was complete.

Governmental pressures to russianize and then sovietize the Lak people continued during the twentieth century. Just after the Russian Revolution, the Soviet government tried to placate those who wanted to create a single Islamic state out of the entire Muslim population of the North Caucasus region. They established the Mountain Autonomous Republic in 1920, with Arabic as the official language, but most Laks, as well as other ethnic Daghestanis, had no love for Arabic and opposed the decision. They resisted the government, and, in 1921, the state created the Daghestan Autonomous Soviet Socialist Republic as an ethnic subdivision of the larger republic; a few years later, Arabic ceased to be the official language. In the late 1920s, the Soviet government conducted an intense anti-Islamic campaign that included widespread imprisonment and the execution of local religious leaders. The government tried to latinize the Lak language in the early 1930s, switching to the Cyrillic alphabet in 1938. At that time, Russian became the only language of instruction in the public schools. Early in the 1960s, state policy prohibited the teaching of Lak and other Daghestani languages in the public schools.

In addition to trying to russianize Lak culture, the government worked diligently at sovietizing the Lak economy. Traditionally, the Lak people had owned land and livestock herds communally. The Soviet government therefore assumed that the process of converting those ethnic communal arrangements into economic collectives—with the government owning the land and the herds—would be simple. The Laks resisted. They found they had to sell their produce to government collectives at state-mandated prices, and, in the end, the Lak community found itself in poorer economic circumstances. Because of the state-controlled economy and the heavy-handed attempts to change Lak culture, the Lak sense of ethnicity has only intensified over the years. The Laks are distinctly anti-Communist, anti-Soviet, anti-Russian, and anti-Christian. More than 95 percent of ethnic Laks still speak the native language and are intensely loyal to their Muslim faith.

Because of their historical experience, the Laks also enjoy high prestige among Daghestani peoples. They enjoy much greater internal cohesion than the other Daghestani groups, primarily because they have no tribal or clan subdivisions and because they enjoyed a single historical experience as part of the Kazi Kumukh Khanate. The Lak territory has also been widely recognized as the religious center of Islam for Daghestani Muslims.

REFERENCES: Alexandre Bennigsen, "Muslim Conservative Opposition to the Soviet Regime: The Sufi Brotherhoods in the North Caucasus," in Jeremy R. Azrael, ed., Soviet Nationality Policies and Practices, 1978; Alexandre Bennigsen and S. Enders Wimbush, Muslims of the Soviet Empire: A Guide, 1986; Vladimir Rogov, Languages and Peoples of the USSR, 1966; Ronald Wixman, Language Aspects of Ethnic Patterns and Processes in the North Caucasus, 1980; George Feizuillin, "The Persecution of National-Religious Traditions of the Moslems of the USSR," Caucasian Review, 3 (1956), 69–76; Ronald Wixman, "Daghestanis," in Richard V. Weekes, ed., Muslim Peoples, 1984, 211–19; Ronald Wixman, The Peoples of the USSR: An Ethnographic Handbook, 1984.

LAKHAMUL. The Lakhamul are considered to be a subgroup of the Svanetians*, although their ethnic origins are quite obscure. Until the late nineteenth century, they were Jews*, but most of them converted to Eastern Orthodox Christianity, at which point they became classified as Svanetians. There may be a handful of people in Georgia who are aware of their Lakhamul background. See JEW or SVANETIAN.

REFERENCES: S. T. Anisimov, Svanetia, 1940; Ronald Wixman, The Peoples of the USSR: An Ethnographic Handbook, 1984.

LAKHAMULTSY. See SVANETIAN.

LAKTSY. See LAK.

LAMUR. See INGUSH.

LAMUT. See EVEN and EVENK.

LAO HUI HUI. See DUNGAN.

LAO KHUEI KHUEI. See DUNGAN.

LAPP. The Lapps, or Laplanders, are a small ethnic group inhabiting the Arctic sections of Norway, Sweden, Finland, and the Soviet Union. They call themselves the Saami (Sameh, Sapme, Samek, Samelats) and are also known as the Lopar or Kola Lapps. Because their social and political organization has never transcended a tribal level, there have been no firm territorial boundaries to Lapland. Over the centuries, the Lapps have wandered, paying no attention to national frontiers. Nonetheless, the general area of what is known as Lapland includes the counties of Nordland, Troms, and Finnmark in Norway, the counties of Vasterbotten and Norrbotten in Sweden, the county of Lappi in Finland; and parts of the Kola Peninsula of the Soviet Union. The entire region consists of approximately 193,000 square miles, and about 50,000 ethnic Lapps live there. Of that total, approximately 26,000 live in Norway, 17,000 in Sweden, 4,000 in Finland, and perhaps 3,000 in Russia. For years, scholars believed that the Lapps were closely related to Siberian tribes, but more recent research by Russian* and Scandinavian ethnolinguists has placed the Lapp language clearly within the Finno-Ugrian* branch of the Uralic-Altaic language family. In other words, they are related to Finns*, Magyars*, and Estonians*, and not to the Samoyeds* or other such tribes of Siberia.

Historically, the Lapps once inhabited a huge expanse of territory that ranged from southeastern Norway all the way across Scandinavia and throughout the entire Kola Peninsula of the Soviet Union. Gradually, however, the expansion of Norwegian, Swedish, and Finnish populations from the south compressed them into their contemporary Arctic homeland. Most Lapps made their living from hunting and fishing, and they often practiced a rudimentary agriculture on small plots near the fjords in the summer forests. Only a small minority of Lapps ever lived a truly nomadic life of following the reindeer herds across the Arctic tundra, although that stereotype has become the dominant image of the Lapps. Most Lapps today are still hunters, fishermen, farmers, although the Lapps of Norrbotten County in Sweden are more likely to be iron miners. The Soviet Lapps are also hunters and farmers, and a substantial number of them still maintain reindeer herds in the heavily forested regions of the Kola Peninsula.

In terms of religion, the Lapps are in the midst of a cultural transition from their traditional tribal beliefs to Christianity. The Lapps of Norway, Sweden, and Finland have a syncretic religion mixing animism with Lutheranism, while the Soviet Lapps have combined Russian Orthodox beliefs and rituals with their earlier animism. For the Lapps, organized religion provides a form of supernatural intervention when folk beliefs seem inadequate. Their earlier animism united all of nature into a cosmic whole. Animals, plants, minerals, the sun, the moon, the stars, and the earth were alive, imbued with a measure of knowledge, individual consciousness, and awareness of the things around them. Lapps gave a name to every animal, tree, river, stream, meadow, mountain, hill, and valley. For them, all aspects of creation had a spiritual essence, and there was a balance to nature that human beings had to respect. Careful observation of the behavior of plants, animals, and the elements helped people predict the future, avoid danger and tragedy, and exercise some control over life. The Lapp religious world was full of spirits—mythological devils, witches, water spirits, ghosts, cloud-beings, and generalized spiritual entities, all of whom had to be respected and often appeased. Only in recent years, as the Lapps have become integrated into the regional economy and their children have attended public schools, have the traditional tribal beliefs entered a period of decline.

The Lapps of the Soviet Union are divided into several subgroups, each characterized by a Lapp dialect that is not intelligible to other Soviet Lapp groups. The Notozer Lapps live in the western region of the Kola Peninsula, the Kilda Lapps live in its northern and central reaches, and the Iokang Lapps live in its eastern part. The Lapp dialects of what used to be the Soviet Union are closely related to the Inari Lapp dialect of Finland. Together they constitute the Eastern Lapp group of Lapp dialects. Since Lapp has not been converted to a written language, the Soviet Lapps use Russian as their literary language.

REFERENCES: Roberto Bosi, *The Lapps*, 1960; Arthur Spencer, *The Lapps*, 1978; Nils-Aslak, *Greetings from Lappland*, 1983; Karl S. Wikstrom, *North of Skarv Island*, 1985; Ronald Wixman, *The Peoples of the Soviet Union: An Ethnographic Handbook*, 1984.

LAQ. See LAK.

LATGAL. See LATVIAN.

LATGALI. See LATVIAN.

LATGALIAN. The Latgalians, who call themselves the Latgolisi, are ethnic Latvians* who maintain a distinct sense of identity as Latgalians. Unlike most Latvians, the Latgalians are Roman Catholic rather than Lutheran, primarily because their historical roots included Lithuanian* and Polish* domination. Ethnolinguists have identified Latgalian as a transitional language between Latvian and Lithuanian. Most Latgalians live in eastern Latvia near the border with Russia and Lithuania. See LATVIAN.

REFERENCE: Ronald Wixman, *The Peoples of the USSR: An Ethnographic Handbook*, 1984.

LATGALIESI. See LATGALIAN and LATVIAN.

LATGALIS. See LATVIAN.

LATGOLISI. See LATVIAN.

LATVIAN. The Latvians, or Letts, who call themselves the Latviesi, are today an independent people, with a population of approximately 1,600,000. The vast majority of the Latvians live in Latvia, although approximately 100,000 are scattered throughout Russia and Belarusia, especially in St. Petersburg and Moscow. The Republic of Latvia is located on the Baltic Sea between Lithuania to the south, Estonia to the north, and Russia and Belarusia to the east. Russians* call them the Latyshi. Lativans are closely related linguistically to the Lithuanians* but culturally to the Finns* and Estonians*. Although the Lithuanians and Latvians were once a single people with common linguistic roots, their histories were quite different. While the people of Lithuania fell under the cultural influence of Slavic-Polish Catholics, the Latvians were ruled by the Teutonic Knights and Scandinavians. Thus, while the Lithuanians became devout Roman Catholics, the Latvians were converted to Protestantism, primarily Lutheranism.

The Latvian, or Lettish, language is clearly related to Lithuanian, but it has no common roots with Estonian. Like Lithuanian, Lettish is one of the Baltaic languages, which themselves are part of the larger Indo-European linguistic family. Although Lettish is not closely related to Russian, years of geographical proximity and political association have introduced large numbers of Russian words and phrases into the language. Unlike Russian, which uses the Cyrillic alphabet, Lettish employs the Latin alphabet. Contemporary Latvian has three active dialects. Central Latvian is spoken in and around Riga and claims the most Latvian speakers. Upper Latvian, also known as Augszemnieks, is spoken in eastern Latvia; Livonian*, also known as Tamnieks, is spoken in northwestern Latvia.

The contemporary people of Latvia are the descendants of four ancient Baltic tribal peoples. The most distinct of those tribes, and the one that retains a contemporary identity, is the Latgalians*, who call themselves the Latgolisi; they are also known as the Latgali, Latgalis, Letgal, Lettgal, and Letts. Ethnolinguists view the Latgalians as a transitional people between the Lithuanians and the Latvians. The majority of the Latgalians live in southeastern Latvia near the frontier with Lithuania and Russia. Although Lithuanians and Latvians cannot really understand one another's languages, both can, with some effort, understand Latgalian. Historically, unlike other Latvians, the Latgalians fell under Polish*-Lithuanian* cultural domination, and they emerged from that experience as devout Roman Catholics.

The second Baltic tribe that became part of ethnic Latvia was the Kursi (Kur or Cour), who long ago lived near the Courish Lagoon and on the coast of Latvia and Lithuania, south and west of the city of Riga. When the Teutonic Knights brought that region under their control, the Kursi began a long process that resulted in their assimilation by Lithuanians, Latvians, and, to a lesser extent, by Germans* in East Prussia. The Kursi have also been known by the designations Kursiai, Kursininkai, Kursininkas, and Kursenieki. There are still a few Latvians who are aware of their Kursi roots. Some Latvians call themselves Kursi and claim to be the descendants of the Kursi nobility. Some descendants of Kursi-speaking people fled the Courish Lagoon region during World War II. They assimilated with Latvians, Lithuanians, and Germans, but some of their descendants also remember their Kursi beginnings.

The third Baltic tribe from which the Latvians descend is the Zemgali, also known as the Zemgalietis, Zemgaliesi*, or Semigallian. They live in Zemgale, which is one of the traditional provinces of Latvia, located in the central part of the country. Although they speak Latvian and are overwhelmingly Protestant, the Zemgali nevertheless see themselves as a distinct people. The final Latvian tribe is the Seli. In addition to these four basic groups, the Latvians are also in the process of absorbing large numbers of Livonians, also known as Livs, Liivi, Libi, Livi, and Libiesi. Unlike the other Latvian subtribes, the Livonian language is part of the Finno-Ugrian* language group, and as such is related closely to Estonian and Finnish, and more distantly to Magyar*.

Historians and archaeologists know that representatives of the four Latvian tribes were living in the region as early as 800 A.D. During the thirteenth century, the Teutonic Knights steadily took more and more control of what is today Latvia and established a strong German influence there. They were still in control of Latvia in the sixteenth century when the Protestant Reformation took place. As a result, most of the people of Latvia became Lutheran. Over the centuries, the Latvians have also had to deal with periodic incursions by Swedes and Russians.

Indeed, the Latvians historically found themselves continuously harassed by Russians, primarily because of Russia's geo-strategic need for an outlet on the Baltic Sea. Peter the Great began the conquest of Latvia in 1721 when he expelled the Swedes from Livonia. The rest of the Latvian provinces came under Russian control later in the eighteenth century, when the partitions of Poland occurred. The Russians received control over Latgale in 1772 and over Courland and Zemgale in 1795. During their years of sovereignty over Latvia in the nineteenth and early twentieth centuries, Russia tried to implement a series of anti-Lettish, pro-Russian programs, including attempts at suppressing the Lutheran religion, prohibitions of the Lettish language in the public schools, and restrictions on the celebration of national holidays. That Russian dominance continued through World War I.

During the years of Russian control, the prominent German landowners of Latvia were able to maintain their estates, while large numbers of Latvians functioned in a status of near-serfdom. Against the backdrop of German economic control and Russian political and cultural domination Latvian nationalism grew steadily in the nineteenth century. Lettish became a modern literary language in the mid-nineteenth century through the writings of people like Juris Alunans, Janis Rainis, Andrejs Upitis, and Janis Endzelins. Of course, the increasingly strident Latvian demands for independence collided with the Russian need for Baltic port facilities.

The process of Latvian independence got its real boost during World War I. German troops occupied all of Latvia south of the Daugava River during the war. When the Bolshevik Revolution erupted in Russia in 1917, the upheaval and subsequent civil war led to the withdrawal of the Soviet Union from the Allied side. As a punishment for Russia and in recognition of the growing maturity of Latvian nationalism, the Allied powers pushed for Latvian independence. An independent Latvian Republic was proclaimed in 1918, and the peace conference at Versailles in 1919 gave tacit recognition to the proclamation. Most countries of Western Europe recognized Latvian independence, and, in 1920, Germany and the Soviet Union did so as well.

Recognition by the Soviet Union, however, did not imply Soviet acceptance or acquiescence in the status quo. Russia still wanted unfettered access to the Baltic Sea. In addition to that geo-political imperative, there was a new political imperative as well. World War I had made the Russians paranoid about Germany, so Soviet leaders were intent on creating a buffer zone in eastern and northeastern Europe between the "motherland" and the Germans. The Baltic states of Latvia, Lithuania, and Estonia were prime candidates for a Russian takeover when the time was right.

That time came in 1939. In the summer of 1939, Germany and the Soviet Union signed the infamous Non-Aggression Pact, agreeing to forgo military operations against one another and to divide Poland between them. Thus, on September 1, 1939, when German troops drove into western Poland, Soviet soldiers occupied eastern Poland. A month later, the Soviet Union forcibly acquired military bases in Latvia. A Soviet-staged coup d'état took place in 1940, and the new pro-Soviet regime in Riga voted to incorporate Latvia into the Soviet Union in August 1940. When Germany invaded the Soviet Union in June 1941, it also took over Latvia. German occupation lasted until 1944, when the Soviet army expelled the Germans. Hundreds of thousands of Latvians died during the fighting. During the first five years or so of the postwar period, Latvian guerrillas kept up the fight for independence, but, by 1950, the last vestiges of resistance had been destroyed.

For the next thirty-five years, the Soviet Union ruled Latvia with an iron hand. Agriculture was collectivized, and centralized bureaucratic controls were imposed on the entire economy. At that point, the Latvian economy began its long decline into the malaise that eventually affected the entire Soviet economy in the 1980s and 1990s. After World War II, an in-migration of ethnic Russians began, primarily because the Soviet Union had designated Latvia for industrial development. This policy led to the arrival of tens of thousands of Russian workers and their families. The repressive apparatus of the Soviet state became ever present; civil liberties were savagely circumscribed. Soviet troops were stationed permanently on Latvian soil, and young Latvian men were drafted into the Soviet army. In 1939, ethnic Latvians had constituted 75 percent of the population, while ethnic Russians were only 10 percent. In 1970, those numbers had changed to 57 percent for the Letts and 30 percent for the Russians, and, by 1990, the Letts were only 51 percent and the Russians almost a third. As the numbers of ethnic Russians increased, the intensity of Latvian nationalist sentiment, particularly of separatist sentiment, was diluted, at least as compared with Lithuania, where ethnic homogeneity was stronger.

From 1945 to the mid–1980s, Latvian nationalism functioned, for the most part, on a clandestine basis. Outspoken advocates of Latvian independence were hustled off to Siberian gulags, where they disappeared. Other Latvian nationalists fled to the West, where they kept up the campaign for independence from small offices in London, New York, and Washington, D.C. In 1933, during the period of their independence, Latvians had constructed the statue of a female figure, known as "The Lady of Liberty," in downtown Riga. Latvians revere it as their "Freedom Monument." It stands in the middle of what was then known as Lenin Boulevard. During the 1950s, 1960s, and 1970s, occasional pro-Latvian demonstrations took place at the monument, and people surreptitiously placed floral arrangements in the national colors of deep red and white at the base of the statue. But Latvian nationalists could do little more than these symbolic acts; bolder courses meant certain imprisonment and death.

The winds of real change did not begin to blow until Mikhail Gorbachev came to power in Moscow in March 1985. Gorbachev announced his policies of *glasnost* and *perestroika* to stimulate Soviet economic and social life. The disastrous war in Afghanistan during the 1980s had exposed severe weaknesses in Soviet military policy, and it was clear to most inside observers that the Soviet economy, shackled by seventy years of Communist bureaucratic red tape, was imploding. Gorbachev understood the challenge that the Soviet Union faced: No nation could maintain a superpower military status so long as it had a Third-World economy. Without dramatic social and economic change, the Soviet Union would not be able to maintain its grip on Eastern Europe or continue to support its client states throughout the world. Looking to the Baltic states as an economic window to the West, Gorbachev began in 1987 to discuss the possibility of more political and economic freedom—perhaps even internal autonomy—in Lithuania, Latvia, and Estonia. Only through radical political and economic reform—embodied in *glasnost* and *perestroika*—could Gorbachev hope to maintain the Soviet Union as a first-class world power.

What Gorbachev did not realize, however, were the extraordinary weaknesses inherent in what the Soviets called "union." For seventy years, Soviet internal unity and its hegemony in Eastern Europe had been maintained through brutal military power and strong economic inducements. As the Soviet economy faltered in the 1980s, Gorbachev's ability to provide economic assistance to the nations of Eastern Europe eroded away, especially after the collapse of world oil prices in the mid–1980s and the sharp reductions this meant for Soviet hard currency earnings. Gorbachev's ability to finance a strong military presence vanished as well. By the late 1980s, Gorbachev had given the non-Soviet nations of Eastern Europe more freedom. In a breathtaking matter of months in 1989, the Warsaw Pact fell apart, Communist governments collapsed throughout the region, and steps began to bring about the reunification of Germany, a process that was completed late in 1990.

Gorbachev had not anticipated the impact of the liberation of Eastern Europe on other nationality groups in the Soviet Union. Internally as well as externally, the Soviet Union had been held together by terror and military force, not by any sense of national loyalty among most of the non-Russian nationalities. New political freedoms in Poland, Hungary, Czechoslovakia, Romania, Yugoslavia, Germany, and Bulgaria only strengthened the nationalist aspirations of many groups inside the Soviet Union. The political unrest appeared first in the Baltic region, and the first rebellion against Soviet authority came, not surprisingly, in Latvia.

In 1986, a small group of Latvian radicals formed the so-called Helsinki–86, group (formally called the Organization for the Defense of Human Rights Helsinki–86). They wanted political and economic autonomy for Latvia, an avowed respect for human rights from the Soviet state, an end to the orchestrated russification of the population and culture, and a recognition of Lettish as the state language. When the KGB began arresting some of the leaders, other members held a successful rally at the Freedom Monument in Riga. In 1987, a number of Helsinki–86 leaders were deported to the West, but new radical groups soon began to appear. By 1989, the largest of these, with 10,000 dues-paying members, was the Latvian National Independence Movement (*Latvijas Nacionla Neatkaribas Kustiba*, or LNNK); its most distinguished leader is Eduards Berklavs. Modris Plate and Juris Rubenis founded the Renaissance and Renewal movement, designed to bring about a revival of the Lutheran Church in Latvia. By mid-August 1988, Visvaldis Brinkmanis had managed to register nearly 500,000 ethnic Latvians into a democratic organization that became known as the Citizens' Congress.

Other groups had political philosophies that more closely reflected Soviet wishes. The Interfront organization represented the interests of ethnic Russians and other non-Latvians who wanted to maintain at least some type of close relationship with the Soviet Union. They demanded the repeal of all language laws requiring the use of Lettish, called for criminal penalties for those displaying the flag of independent Latvia, opposed local management of the economy, and favored the annexation of border regions by Russia. A few extremists even called for the mass deportation of ethnic Latvians. But although Interfront received considerable support from the Soviet Union, it represented only a minority opinion.

Latvians participated in an enormous symbolic act of independence on August 23, 1989. More than 2.4 million Lithuanians, Latvians, and Estonians joined hands in a human chain that stretched 400 miles across the Baltic nations in protest of the fortieth anniversary of the Soviet takeover of the region. This was the largest mass demonstration in the history of the Soviet Union. The Communist Party of the Soviet Union condemned the demonstration as ''destructive, anti-Soviet, and anti-national,'' but it was only the beginning.

Because of widespread draft dodging in Latvia, as well as in a number of other Soviet republics, Gorbachev deployed Soviet paratroopers in January 1991 to capture the conscripted young men and forcible bring them into the Soviet army. By that time, of course, large numbers of Latvians already viewed the Soviet army as a foreign occupation force. Soviet troops also occupied the main newspaper-publishing building in Riga, the Latvian capital. All of Latvia's newspapers were and still are published in this building, but the Latvian Communist Party claimed ownership of it. The arrival of the troops precipitated an anti-

Soviet demonstration by 10,000 people in downtown Riga. On January 20, 1991, elite Soviet troops stormed the police headquarters building in Riga. In the process, four Latvian defenders of the building were killed.

During the next seven months, a tense calm descended on Latvian-Soviet relations. Because of its catastrophic economic problems, the Soviet Union was preoccupied with internal problems of its own, and Gorbachev had neither the time nor the inclination to make a major investment of energy and resources in retaining the loyalty of Latvia. The Latvians had not projected themselves toward independence with quite the intensity of the Lithuanians, no doubt because the size of its ethnic Russian minority was so much larger; after all, by 1990, only 51 percent of the population of Latvia were ethnic Latvians, while nearly a third were ethnic Russians. Independence for Latvia stirred up divisive opinions among the Russians, and Latvian political leaders therefore had to chart a more cautious course.

They threw caution to the winds in August 1991, however, when hardliners in the Soviet Union launched their *coup d'état*. The attempt to overthrow the Soviet government began on Sunday, August 19, 1991, with the arrest of Gorbachev by special KGB troops. At the time, Gorbachev was vacationing with his family in the Crimea. By late in the afternoon of the first day of the coup, elite Soviet troops invaded Latvia to seize control of its communications facilities and borders. Engineered by a small but powerful group of people in the KGB, the Communist Party, the Soviet defense ministry, and two major trade unions, the coup was poorly planned, carelessly executed, and quickly over. Boris Yeltsin, president of the Russian Republic, openly defied the conspirators from the very beginning, and, when Soviet troops refused to carry out the plotters' orders, the coup collapsed. In the midst of the coup, the Latvian parliament declared its independence from the Soviet Union.

The failed *coup d'état* had special significance for Latvia, since a particular conspirator was one of their own—the hated Boris K. Pugo. Pugo was born in the city of Kalinin in 1937. His father was a Latvian Bolshevik who had been imprisoned during the 1930s when Communism was outlawed in Latvia. His son Boris had graduated from the Riga Polytechnic Institute with an engineering degree, but he spent his career working for the Communist Party. In 1976, he became head of the KGB in Latvia. Pugo was an outspoken opponent of Latvian independence, and he became *persona non grata* in his own country. Gorbachev, hoping to appease some of the hardliners who feared the implications of *perestroika* and *glasnost*, appointed Pugo as head of the Interior Ministry in December 1990. Latvians were not surprised when it became clear that Pugo was one of the leaders of the coup. They were also delighted when the coup collapsed after a few days and more delighted still when news reached them two days later that Pugo had committed suicide. In the eyes of most Latvians, Pugo's ideological and then personal acts of self-destruction mirrored what was happening on a larger scale to the Soviet Union.

They were right. The coup proved to be the death knell of the Communist

Party, the KGB, and the Soviet Union. Gorbachev returned to Moscow from the Crimea. He quickly resigned from the Communist Party himself, arrested the conspirators, and began an investigation to determine the extent of the rebellion within the major political institutions of the country. Within weeks one republic after another, including all of the Baltic nations, Moldova, Belarus, and Ukraine, had declared independence. Most of the Western nations began extending diplomatic recognition to Latvia and the other Baltic countries. The Soviet Union was disintegrating. On September 5, 1991, the Supreme Soviet voted itself out of existence, surrendering sovereignty to the republics, and then beginning work on the construction of a new, loose confederation system. On September 6, 1991, the Soviet Union extended full independence to Latvia.

REFERENCES: Alfred Bilmanis, *History of Latvia*, 1969; Nadia Diuk and Adrian Karatnycky, *The Hidden Nations: The People Challenge the Soviet Union, From Lithuania to the Ukraine*, 1990; Juris Dreifelds, "Latvian National Rebirth," *Problems of Communism*, 38 (July-August 1989), 77–79; Nils Muiznieks, "The Daugavpils Hydro Station and 'Glasnost' in Latvia," *Journal of Baltic Studies*, 18 (Spring 1987), 56–70; Vito V. Simanis, *Latvia*, 1984; Darshan Singh, *Soviet Family of Nations: A Latvian Journey*, 1984; Jan Arveds Trapans, *Toward Independence: The Baltic Popular Movements*, 1990.

LATVIESI. See LATVIAN.

LATYSH. See LATVIAN.

LATYSHI. See LATVIAN.

LAZ. The Laz people call themselves the Lazi but have also been known historically as the Chan, Zan, and Megrelo-Chan. Russians* refer to them as the Laztsy. Ever since 1938, Soviet and Russian demographers have classified the Laz as a subgroup of the Georgians*. In terms of their ethnic origins, the Laz are an Ibero-Caucasian people who speak a Mingrelian* language. The vast majority of the Laz live in Turkey along the Black Sea coast between Trabzon and the Georgian border. Their total population is approximately 200,000 people, but perhaps only 1,500 of them live in what used to be the Soviet Union. Those 1,500 people live mostly on the Chorokh River in the Adjar Autonomous Republic of Georgia.

They have been located there for at least 2,000 years. They established the Kingdom of Lazica and adopted Christianity in the sixth century. Lazica was soon caught, however, between the dynastic rivalries of Persia and Byzantium, both of which wanted control of the southern shore of the Black Sea. Georgia incorporated Laz territory in the tenth century, but, in 1461, Mehmet II and the Ottomans conquered it. They then held the region for several centuries, during which time the Laz were converted to the Hanafi school of Sunni Islam. The Russo-Turkish War of 1877–1878 resulted in the transfer of Batumi, with its small Laz population, from Ottoman to Russian sovereignty. See GEORGIAN.

REFERENCES: Shirin Akiner, *Islamic Peoples of the Soviet Union*, 1983; Alexandre Bennigsen and S. Enders Wimbush, *Muslims of the Soviet Empire: A Guide*, 1986; Ronald Wixman, *The Peoples of the USSR: An Ethnographic Handbook*, 1984.

LAZI. See LAZ.

LAZTSY. See LAZ.

LECHHUMI. See LECHKHUMI and GEORGIAN.

LECHKHUM. See LECHKHUMI and GEORGIAN.

LECHKHUMELI. See LECHKHUMI and GEORGIAN.

LECHKHUMI. The Lechkhumi call themselves the Lechkhumeli. Their language is closely related to Imereli* (Imeretian), one of the western Georgian* dialects. They are concentrated along the middle Rioni River in Georgia. The Lechkhumi are Eastern Orthodox Christians. See GEORGIAN.
REFERENCE: Ronald Wixman, *The Peoples of the USSR: An Ethnographic Handbook*, 1984.

LECHKUM. See LECHKHUMI and GEORGIAN.

LECHKUMI. See LECHKHUMI and GEORGIAN.

LEMKI. See LEMKY or CARPATHO-RUSYN.

LEMKO. See LEMKY or CARPATHO-RUSYN.

LEMKY. The Lemky are one of the three groups that comprise the Carpatho-Rusyns*. Like the Boikis* and the Hutsuls*, the Lemky were Uniate Catholics until after World War II, at which time they came under Soviet authority. They then became Eastern Orthodox Christians because the Uniate church was abolished. Most of the Lemky live in Poland. Those living in Ukraine are concentrated in the far western reaches of the republic. See CARPATHO-RUSYN.
REFERENCE: Ronald Wixman, *The Peoples of the USSR: An Ethnographic Handbook*, 1984.

LENINGRAD FINN. Beginning in the seventeenth century, small numbers of Finns* began migrating to the region of Leningrad. During the nineteenth century, they assimilated large numbers of Vods* and Izhoras*. They live today primarily along the Baltic Coast. See FINN.

REFERENCE: Ronald Wixman, *The Peoples of the USSR: An Ethnographic Handbook,* 1984.

LESGHIAN. See LEZGIN.

LETGAL. See LATVIAN.

LETGALIAN. See LATVIAN.

LETT. See LATVIAN.

LETTGAL. See LATVIAN.

LETTGALIAN. See LATVIAN.

LETTO-LITHUANIAN. See LATVIAN and LITHUANIAN.

LEUSHA. See KHANT.

LEZG. See LEZGIN.

LEZGH. See LEZGIN.

LEZGHI. See LEZGIN.

LEZGHIAN. See LEZGIN.

LEZGHINIAN. See LEZGIN.

LEZGI. See LEZGIN.

LEZGIN. Until the time of the Russian Revolution, the term "Lezgin" was a generic description for all the ethnic groups of the highlands southwest of the Caspian Sea in what is today the Daghestan Autonomous Republic. Since then, ethnologists have grown more careful in making group identifications, and the once generic Lezgins have become the Lezgins proper, the Aguls*, Rutuls*, and Tabasarans*. The Lezgin refer to themselves as the Lezghi (Lezgi), but they are also known as Kurin, Akhta, and Akhtin. Russians refer to them as the Lezginy. Historians believe that their origins lie in the merger of the Akhty, Alty, and Dokuz Para federations. These were indigenous peoples of the Caucasus who spoke Lezgin dialects; the merger also included clans living among the Rutuls. The Lezgin language is part of the Samurian group of northeastern Caucasic languages and is divided into three distinct dialects. Kurin (Kiurin), or Gunei, is spoken by the majority of the Lezgins and forms the basis of the

Lezgin written language. The Lezgins living in the Azerbaijan Republic speak the Kuba dialect, while the remainder speak Akhty (Sumar).

Today there are more than 420,000 Lezgins in the former Soviet Union. The vast majority of them live in southeastern Daghestan, especially in the Kurakh, Kasumkent, Magaramkent, Akhty, and Dokuzpara rayons, and across the border in Azerbaijan, primarily in the Kuba and Kusar rayons. There are also substantial numbers of Lezgins living in the city of Baku in Azerbaijan. The Lezgins are surrounded by Tsakhur* people to the west; by Rutuls, Aguls, and Tabasarans to the north; and by Azerbaijanis* to the south. Until the time of the Russian Revolution, the Lezgins were being assimilated by the Azerbaijanis, and today practically all Lezgins are bilingual, speaking Azeri as a second language.

Like other ethnic groups in southern Daghestan, the Lezgins are Sunni Muslims loyal to the Shafi theological school. The only exception are the Lezgins living in the Dokuzpara Rayon, who are Shiites. Until the fifteenth century, the Lezgin people were primarily animists with their own folk religions, but Zoroastrianism, Judaism, and Christianity were making inroads. Persian* traders introduced Islam into southern Daghestan in the fifteenth century, while the Golden Horde brought Islam into the northern region in the sixteenth and seventeenth centuries. The Ottoman occupation of the region beginning in the sixteenth century helped to consolidate Islam there. By the nineteenth century, the Lezgins had all been converted to Sunni Islam. They are extremely devout in their religious devotions. Like other Muslim people in the Near and Middle East in the 1970s and 1980s, they have been influenced by the increasingly strident religious fundamentalism that has dominated the cultural landscape. In spite of more than seventy years of anti-religious state policy, their fundamental religious institutions and traditions—such as endogamous marriages, family mosques, religious marriages and burials, observance of Ramadan, daily prayers, circumcision of male children, and faithful devotion to the teachings of the Koran—still flourish.

The Lezgins differed politically from many other Daghestani peoples because they did not form their own principality or country. Instead, they maintained a loyalty based on internal tribal federations. The Lezgins in Azerbaijan were part of the Kuba Khanate, while the Lezgins in the Derbent region were under the control of the Derbent Khanate. The political principality of the Laks—the Kazi Kumukh Khanate—assumed control of the Lezgins for a time in the eighteenth century, but, beginning in 1812, Russia took them over, creating the Kiurin Khanate; this later became known as the Kiurin District.

A profound anti-Russian sentiment permeates Lezgin culture. Just after the Russian Revolution, the government in Moscow created the Mountain Autonomous Republic, with Arabic as the official language of the government and the schools. The Lezgin, along with many other highland ethnic groups, opposed this policy and rebelled against it. The government then created the Daghestan Autonomous Soviet Socialist Republic (ASSR) in 1921. In 1925, Moscow launched an anti-Islamic campaign, which included closing all Islamic schools, eliminating the use of Arabic, and executing many local imams. At that point, state policy shifted in favor of the Turkic* peoples, and Azeri became the official language of the region. That policy ended in 1928, when the government declared that Dargin*, Avar*, Lezgin, and Azeri were all official languages. The government also began to create a Latin alphabet for the Lezgin language that year, but changed back to the Cyrillic alphabet in 1938. Gradually, over the next twenty years, the Russian language was imposed on all schools and government offices in Daghestan.

The constant cultural manipulations by the Soviet government only increased Lezgin resentment of Russian and Soviet culture. The Lezgins resisted russification and also refused to participate in government programs to relocate them out of the highlands into lowland towns and collective farms. As a result, most Lezgin have retained a traditional rural life-style. Economic life still revolves around animal husbandry (sheep and goats in the highlands, cattle in the lowlands), gold and silver smithing, weaving, pottery, and rug manufacturing. Nonetheless, the government has collectivized Lezgin land and Lezgin herds, and government agents purchase Lezgin products at fixed prices, increasing popular resentment toward the state. Because of their geographic isolation and their resentment of state education policies, Lezgin education levels are among the lowest in the former Soviet Union.

Government attempts to suppress their Muslim religion, manipulate their language, alter their economy, and relocate them from their traditional homelands had clearly created powerful resentments among the Lezgin. Mikhail Gorbachev's policies of *perestroika* and *glasnost* in the late 1980s and early 1990s, as well as the internal collapse of the economy and then the Soviet Union itself, exacerbated nationalistic tensions throughout the country and unleashed centrifugal ethnic forces. The Lezgins are an intensely Muslim nationality group, and their leaders are becoming more and more strident in their demands for independence from Moscow and for self-determination.

The Lezgins have been especially concerned about the fact that their community has been divided between Azerbaijan and Daghestan. Robert Ramazanov, a Lezgin journalist, remarked in 1990 that:

Our people have been divided between an autonomous republic and a Union republic for many years, and because of this we were denied the opportunity to develop our culture and economy on a common basis. Moreover, whereas in Daghestan we were granted full constitutional rights, in the neighboring republic this was not the case. The movement's immediate goals are to devise acceptable ways to bring about Lezgin unification.

Lezgins have organized *Sadval* (Unity) to promote democracy, Lezgin unification, and independence. The Samur Movement, formed in Baku in 1991, has also opposed the division of the Lezgin community. In 1992, when Azerbaijan and Russia decided to draw a firm, formal boundary between the two republics, the Lezgins protested, fearing that such a step would permanently prevent their unification.

REFERENCES: Alexandre Bennigsen, "Muslim Conservative Opposition to the Soviet Regime: The Sufi Brotherhoods in the North Caucasus," in Jeremy R. Azrael, ed., *Soviet Nationality Policies and Practices*, 1971; Alexandre Bennigsen and S. Enders Wimbush, *Muslims of the Soviet Empire: A Guide*, 1986; *Current Digest*, 42 (August 22, 1990), 27, and 44 (August 19, 1992), 24; Bruce Geiger, et al., *Peoples and Languages of the Caucasus*, 1959; T. S. Halasi-Kun, "The Caucasus: An Ethno-Historical Survey," *Studia Caucasia*, 2 (1956), 7–16; Brian Silver, "Language Policy and Linguistic Russification of Soviet Nationalities," in Jeremy R. Azrael, ed., *Soviet Nationality Policies and Practices*, 1971; Ronald Wixman, *Language Aspects of Ethnic Patterns and Processes in the North Caucasas*, 1980; Ronald Wixman, "Daghestanis," in Richard V. Weekes, ed., *Muslim Peoples*, 1984, 211–19; Ronald Wixman, *The Peoples of the Soviet Union: An Ethnographic Handbook*, 1984.

LEZGINY. See LEZGIN.

LIBI. See LATVIAN.

LIBIESI. See LATVIAN.

LIETUVIAI. See LITHUANIAN.

LIIVI. See LATVIAN.

LITHUANIAN. Lithuania, a political subdivision of approximately 25,200 square miles, was one of the smallest republics of the former Soviet Union. It is located on the Baltic Sea, bordered by Latvia to the north, Belarus to the east and south, and Kaliningrad Oblast of the Russian Soviet Federated Socialist Republic (RSFSR) to the west (an area that was once the Konigsberg area of East Prussia), and Poland to the southwest. Its population in 1990 totaled more than 3.6 million people, of whom approximately 80 percent were ethnic Lithuanians. The largest non-Lithuanian group consists of ethnic Russians*; the second largest non-Lithuanian population consists of Poles*, most of whom came into Lithuania with the annexation of Vilnius and the surrounding area in 1939. There are also Latvians*, Belarusians*, and Jews*. Approximately 200,000 ethnic Lithuanians live in other parts of Russia, primarily in European Russia and in Siberia, and most of them still work diligently at maintaining their identity. Perhaps 70,000 live just across the Lithuanian border in Latvia, Belarus, and the Kaliningrad Oblast. Another 50,000 or so live in the environs of Moscow, St. Petersburg, and Kiev, while tens of thousands more are in Siberia, most of whom were relocated there during the terrorist reign of Josef Stalin.

There are four primary Lithuanian subgroups. They are the Aukstaiciai*, the Dzuki, the Suvalkieciai*, and the Zemaiciai*. The Aukstaiciai (Aukstaiti, Aukstai, Aukshtai, Aukshtay, Aukshtayty) today are known in Lithuania as "highlanders" and live primarily in southern and eastern Lithuania. Their dialect became the foundation for literary Lithuanian, which first emerged in the six teenth century. The Dzuki, considered by many a subgroup of the Aukstaiciai, live primarily in southeastern Lithuania, and their dialect has historically been heavily influenced by Polish. The Suvalkieciai (Uznemunieciai, Suval, Suval-kechai, Suvalkechay, and Suvalki) live southwest of the Nemunas River in Lithuania; some scholars have further divided the Suvalkieciai into two subgroups—the Kapsas and the Zanavykiai*. Finally, the Zemaiciai (Zhemaiti, Zhemoit, Samogit), known to Lithuanians as the "lowlanders," live in western Lithuania. The Zemaiciai are a major ethnographic subdivision of Lithuanians, like the Aukstaiciai.

Although Lithuania was one of the last places in Europe to adopt Roman Catholicism (a process that gained momentum after the union with Poland in 1385), the Catholic Church eventually came to play a central role in its national culture, helping people to establish a distinct national identity and to explain the mysteries of life, overcome uncertainty, and secure the future. Lithuanians have saints, such as St. Casimir, who are believed to intervene with God on behalf of peasant welfare. Lithuanians also believe that other specific saints perform lesser miracles. Lithuanians appeal regularly to St. George as the protector of animals, for example. They also have an intense devotion to the Virgin Mary, as seen in the veneration of the shrine of Our Lady of Siluva. During pilgrimages to the shrine, Lithuanians pray for divine protection, redemption, and blessings. Local parish priests play critical roles in interpreting the sacred world and guiding the peasant relationship with God. A minority of Lithuanians, primarily those who once lived under Prussian control, are Lutheran in religion, but they constitute only 4 percent of the Lithuanian population.

The Lithuanian language is related to ancient Sanskrit and features many archaic elements of the Indo-European linguistic family. Along with Latvian, it is part of the Baltic group. The earliest book to be written in Lithuanian was a Roman Catholic catechism published in 1547, and the first dictionaries and grammars in Lithuanian appeared in the seventeenth century. At the universities of Königsberg and Vilnius, historical, linguistic, and folkloric researchers provided the impetus to develop Lithuanian as a literary language. That language was primarily based on the Aukstaiciai dialect. In the nineteenth century, a nationalist literature developed in Lithuania, which helped to fuel demands for independence and self-determination.

By the mid–1300s, the Lithuanian empire in Europe stretched from the Baltic Sea in the northwest to the Black Sea in the southeast. But this movement had collided with Polish expansion by the end of the fourteenth century, and, on August 15, 1385, Poland and Lithuania signed the Union of Krevo, which created a dynastic coalition between them. Beginning in 1501, the two kingdoms were ruled by one sovereign; after 1569, they shared a common legislature. Over the years, however, Poland, with its larger population and strategic geographic location, became the more dominant of the two powers. Polish language, laws, and customs began to permeate both countries. The relationship between Lithuania and Poland became even closer with the Union of Lublin in 1572. Western

European intellectuals poured into Lithuania, and Polish became the first language of the Lithuanian nobility. The Lithuanian ethnic identity became subordinate to a Polish identity, although it never completely disappeared; rather, it was maintained primarily by the lower classes.

Lithuania remained within Poland's political and cultural orbit for the next 400 years, but, in 1795, much of Lithuania was ceded to Russia. At the time, the Russian Slavs were seeking cultural hegemony in Eastern Europe, another economic outlet on the Baltic Sea, and an improvement in their strategic position vis-à-vis East Prussia. Lithuania was an obvious target, for it gave Russia an outlet on the Baltic and flanked East Prussia. But Russian domination was completely inconsistent with the direction of Lithuanian history. Lithuania's orientation has historically been Western, not Eastern. Ethnically, the Lithuanians are more closely related to northern Europe and Poland, rather than to Russia. They are Roman Catholic rather than Eastern Orthodox in religion. Their language is written in Latin rather than Cyrillic script, and they are culturally more in tune with Scandinavia, Germany, and Hungary than with Russia. In terms of economic history, too, Lithuania has found itself located on trade routes that run down the Baltic Sea to Poland, Germany, the Low Countries, and Great Britain, rather than down the great Russian rivers to the Caspian and Black seas. Finally, Lithuanian politics has always had a powerful anti-authoritarian strain, while Russian political philosophy has been just the opposite. So although Russia technically took control of Lithuania in 1795, it was destined to be a difficult relationship at best. Lithuanian ethnic identity developed on the cutting edge of Russian oppression, and, in the process, it acquired a highly ethnocentric quality.

In Lithuanian culture, religious identity and political nationalism became closely connected. During the seventeenth and eighteenth centuries, the Russian and Prussian governments that surrounded Lithuania came to view Roman Catholicism as a form of political treason and a cultural intrusion. Lithuanian Catholicism thus was caught between the competitive intolerances of Prussian Lutheranism and Russian Orthodoxy. After taking control of Lithuania, Russian authorities tried in vain to restrict the Catholic Church and suppress the Lithuanian language throughout the nineteenth century. When a large number of the Lithuanian elite joined the Polish rebellion of 1830, Tsar Nicholas I reacted with a bitterly aggressive program of russification. He prohibited the use of the Lithuanian language, closed large numbers of Lithuanian schools and Roman Catholic monasteries, and forbade the use of the term "Lithuania." Nothing could be printed in Lithuanian, and serious attempts were made to convert the Lithuanians' written language to the Cyrillic alphabet. Russia became the official language. After the rebellion of 1863 in Poland and Lithuania, Tsar Alexander II ordered that all teaching of religion in public schools be conducted in Russian; shortly thereafter, he ordered that Russian be used as the language of instruction in all Lithuanian public and parochial schools. He outlawed crosses on Catholic churches, forbade devotional processions and parish temperance associations, demanded prior approval of all clerical appointments, eliminated clerical visitations with parishioners, banned the construction of new chapels or the repair of old ones, and censored all sermons. Alexander also fired large numbers of Lithuanian civil servants and imported Russians to fill the positions.

But instead of transforming Lithuanian Catholicism into Russian Orthodoxy, the Russian assault only intensified Lithuanians' local nationalism and Roman Catholic identity. Although Lithuanian literature had a long history, it was during the years of the Russian captivity in the nineteenth century that it really flowered. Jonas Maciulis was a typical example. His epic, lyrical poems, such as "Young Lithuania" and "Our Sufferings," celebrated Lithuanian history and culture, implicitly expressing a passion for independence and national self-determination. The struggle against Russian domination often seemed to go hand in hand with a defense of the church and the promotion of the faith during the nineteenth and early twentieth centuries. In the process, Roman Catholicism and Lithuanian national identity became inextricably connected. In 1883, Jonas Basanavicius began printing a nationalist journal, *Ausra*, and smuggled it into Lithuania from East Prussia. In spite of strict Russian prohibition, it was published in Lithuanian. Lithuanian national identity continued to strengthen, and, after the 1905 Russian revolution, tsarist authorities temporarily granted Lithuania freedom of speech and the right to convene a congress at Vilnius. Basanavicius headed up that congress. Its first order of business was to demand autonomy for Lithuania, the restoration of its frontiers to include ethnic Lithuanians living in Russia and Latvia, the declaration of Vilnius as the capital city, and the legalization of Lithuanian as the language of instruction in private and public schools. The tsar never acquiesced to those demands, but Lithuanian nationalism was galvanized by them nonetheless.

In September 1915, Lithuanian nationalists found themselves with a new enemy. The German* army occupied Lithuania, and, in addition to the death and destruction brought by World War I, Germany also tried to prohibit the use of the Lithuanian language and constantly suspected Lithuanians of sedition. Secret nationalist groups emerged and agitated against the German occupation. On February 16, 1918, Antanas Smetona, a leading Lithuanian nationalist, declared the independence of Lithuania. After the adoption of a provisional constitution in October 1918, Smetona became the president of Lithuania. Germany recognized Lithuanian independence in 1919, and the Soviet Union followed suit in 1920. France and Britain extended recognition in 1921, and the United States did so in 1922. The yellow, red, and green flag of an independent Lithuania waved throughout the country.

But Lithuanian independence was destined to be short-lived. The return of Germany to world-power status under Adolf Hitler intensified the Soviet geopolitical need to expand into the Baltic region. Stalin looked to Finland, Estonia, Latvia, and Lithuania as means of securing the northwestern Soviet border against German expansion. In August 1939, Germany and the Soviet Union signed the infamous Non-Aggression Pact, by which the two countries divided northeastern Europe between them. Germany acquired, at least from the Russians, the tacit acceptance of their sovereignty over western Poland, while the Soviets acquired control over eastern Poland and the Baltics. Hitler invaded Poland a month later, triggering World War II. In the summer of 1940, the Soviet Union invaded Lithuania, established a puppet Communist government there, and then saw to it that Lithuania requested annexation as the Lithuanian Soviet Socialist Republic, the fourteenth republic of the Soviet Union. The Soviet Union immediately began to impose Russian culture once again and deported tens of thousands of suspected Lithuanian nationalists. The programs of russification, deportation, and clerical persecution, so common under tsarist rule in the nineteenth century, were revived. The United States and Great Britain refused to recognize the annexation, and Lithuanian government groups functioned in London and Washington, D.C., lobbying for Western foreign policies that might eventually liberate their homeland.

When Germany invaded Lithuania, Latvia, Estonia, and the Soviet Union in June 1941, Lithuanian nationalists, hoping that the invasion would bring liberation from their Soviet masters, rose up and declared their independence. The Germans would have none of it, and, on July 17, 1941, Hitler announced creation of the "Ostland," a new political entity composed of Lithuania, Latvia, Estonia, and Belarus. Hitler was no more willing than the Russians to establish an independent Lithuania. Lithuanian partisans fought against German occupation forces, but as many as 300,000 Lithuanians, mostly Jews*, died at German hands in the early years of the war. In 1944, the Soviet counter-attack drove the German army out of Lithuania. The fact that Lithuanian nationalists had declared independence from the Soviet Union immediately after the German invasion did not endear them to Stalin, however. He quickly turned on Lithuanian nationalists, killing tens of thousands of them and sending several hundred thousand more to *gulag* prison camps. Some scholars estimate that during World War II and Stalin's reign of terror, as much as a third of the Lithuanian population was killed or deported.

The return of the Soviet Union to power also restored the traditional Lithuanian borders. In the partitioning of Lithuania in 1795, the port city of Klaipeda on the Baltic and its surrounding area had become part of Prussia, while the rest of the country became part of Russia and, after 1815, of the Kingdom of Poland. Although Lithuania achieved its independence after World War I, Poland seized Vilnius, the ancient Lithuanian capital city, in 1920. The Allies saw to it that Klaipeda and its surrounding district were restored to Lithuania in 1923, but the Germans took it back in 1940. As part of the partitioning of Poland in 1939 and 1940, however, Vilnius was restored to Lithuania, and, when World War II ended, the Klaipeda region on the Baltic was also restored.

Nonetheless, the restoration of the traditional frontiers did little to help Lithuania. During the next forty years, the Soviet Union managed to ruin the Lithuanian economy. In an outburst of ideological fervor, the Soviets outlawed private farm ownership and collectivized much of Lithuanian agriculture. In the wake of collectivization, productivity declined dramatically. Without the slightest environmental consideration, the Soviets clear-cut the Lithuanian forests and constructed heavy industries that polluted the countryside. Severe restrictions on foreign commerce cut Lithuania off from its traditional economic links to Western Europe. To limit the power of ethnic Lithuanians, the Soviet Union encouraged Russian immigration there, promising preferential treatment in acquiring jobs and housing. Some Lithuanian nationalists conducted a continuing guerrilla war against Soviet troops in the country, but most Lithuanians realized that there was little they could do to drive the Russians out. The Soviet invasion of Hungary in 1956 had been an object lesson to all of Eastern Europe. Like the rest of the Soviet bloc, the Lithuanian economy went into a tailspin from which there was no recovery. By the late 1980s, per capita income in Lithuania was only one-eighth of that of Finland and Denmark. In 1940, the per capita incomes of Finland, Denmark, and Lithuania had been the same.

The end of the Stalinist era and the rise of people like Nikita Khrushchev, Alexei Kosygin, and Leonid Brezhnev ended the overt terrorism of the 1920s, 1930s, 1940s, and early 1950s, but the modest easing of political repression immediately unleashed Lithuanian nationalism. Throughout the 1940s and 1950s, Stalin's heavy-handedness had forced Lithuanian political nationalism into a period of quiescence, since the only alternative to prudence seemed annihilation. But in the 1970s, more overt forms of political protest began to appear. On May 14, 1972, for example, Romas Kalanta, a nineteen-year-old Lithuanian man, set himself on fire in the name of Lithuanian independence. His burial two days later triggered several days of protests, rioting, and demonstrations in the city of Kaunas. Soviet security forces had to be called in to put down the rebellion. By the mid–1970s, an umbrella organization known as the Lithuanian National People's Front was holding clandestine meetings throughout the country and calling for independence.

The winds of real change did not begin to blow until Mikhail Gorbachev came to power in Moscow in March 1985. Gorbachev announced his policies of *glasnost* and *perestroika* to stimulate Soviet economic and social life. The disastrous war in Afghanistan during the 1980s had exposed severe weaknesses in Soviet military policy, and it was clear to most inside observers that the Soviet economy, shackled by seventy years of Communist bureaucratic red tape, was imploding. Gorbachev understood the challenge that the Soviet Union faced: No nation could maintain a superpower military status so long as it had a Third-World economy. Without dramatic social and economic change, the Soviet Union would not be able to maintain its grip on Eastern Europe or continue to support its client states throughout the world. Looking to the Baltic states as an economic window to the West, Gorbachev began in 1987 to discuss the possibility of more political and economic freedom—perhaps even internal autonomy—in Lithuania, Latvia, and Estonia. Only through radical political and economic reform—embodied in *glasnost* and *perestroika*—could Gorbachev hope to maintain the Soviet Union as a first-class world power.

What Gorbachev did not realize, however, were the extraordinary weaknesses inherent in what the Soviets called "union." For seventy years, Soviet internal unity and its hegemony in Eastern Europe had been maintained through brutal military power and strong economic inducements. As the Soviet economy faltered in the 1980s, Gorbachev's ability to provide economic assistance to the nations of Eastern Europe eroded away, especially after the collapse of world oil prices in the mid–1980s and the sharp reductions this meant for Soviet hard currency earnings. Gorbachev's ability to finance a strong military presence vanished as well. By the late 1980s, Gorbachev had given the non-Soviet nations of Eastern Europe more freedom. In a breathtaking matter of months in 1989, the Warsaw Pact fell apart, Communist governments collapsed throughout the region, and steps began to bring about the reunification of Germany, a process that was completed late in 1990.

Gorbachev had not anticipated the impact of the liberation of Eastern Europe on other nationality groups in the Soviet Union. Internally as well as externally, the Soviet Union had been held together by terror and military force, not by any sense of national loyalty among most of the non-Russian nationalities. New political freedoms in Poland, Hungary, Czechoslovakia, Romania, Yugoslavia, Germany, and Bulgaria only strengthened the nationalist aspirations of many groups inside the Soviet Union. The political unrest appeared first in the Baltic region, and one of the first rebellions against Soviet authority came, not surprisingly, in Lithuania.

A mild-mannered music professor, Vytautas Landsbergis, emerged as the leader of the Lithuanian independence movement. In mid–1988, Landsbergis, along with a number of enthusiastic supporters, organized the Initiative Group in Support of Perestroika. They began to demand autonomy from the Soviet Union, but the exhilaration of those demands created a momentum for complete independence, which Gorbachev was not ready to grant. Early in 1989, the supreme soviet of Lithuania voted to make Lithuanian, not Russian, the official language of the republic and to require all upper-level political officials to be fluent in Lithuanian. Ethnic Russians living in Lithuania vigorously protested the decision. On August 23, 1989, hundreds of thousands of Lithuanians participated in a protest against the fiftieth anniversary of the German-Russian Non-Aggression Pact of 1939, which had spelled the end of Lithuanian independence. Lithuanian nationalists joined hands—literally—with Latvian and Estonian nationalists in a human chain that extended 400 miles from Tallinn to Riga and then to Vilnius. Symbolically, those 2.4 million-plus people holding hands faced west toward Europe, with their backs to the Soviet Union, to express their political and cultural orientation. Although the Kremlin claimed that the Baltic states were being pushed into an "abyss . . . by nationalist leaders," the warning fell on deaf ears.

The drive for Lithuanian independence found political expression in the *Sajudis* movement. On February 25, 1990, multi-party elections were held in Lithuania, and the Communist Party was overwhelmingly rejected. The Sajudis Party won a majority in the Lithuanian parliament, and debate began immediately on leaving the Soviet Union altogether. Gorbachev found the debate unsettling, to say the least, and told the Lithuanians that they would be subject to a $33 billion payment and the surrender of the Baltic port of Klaipeda if they seceded. The Sajudis leaders were not about to be intimidated. On March 11, 1990, Sajudis declared Lithuanian independence and renamed the country the Republic of Lithuania, discarding the Lithuanian Soviet Socialist Republic designation by a vote of 124 to 0. In response, Gorbachev called the declaration of independence "illegitimate and invalid" and demanded its repeal. A week later, Gorbachev ordered the confiscation of all private firearms in Lithuania.

There were other groups whose political philosophy more closely reflected Soviet wishes. The *Yedinstvo* (Unity) organization represented the interests of ethnic Russians and other non-Lithuanians who wanted to maintain some type of close relationship with the Soviet Union. They demanded the repeal of all language laws requiring the use of Lithuanian, called for criminal penalties for those displaying the flag of independent Lithuania, opposed local management of the economy, and favored the annexation of border regions to Russia. A few extremists even called for the mass deportation of ethnic Lithuanians. But although Yedinstvo received considerable support from the Soviet Union, it represented only a minority opinion.

The crisis escalated later in March. Lithuanian soldiers began to desert the Soviet army with the express blessing of the Lithuanian parliament. Gorbachev sent troops into Lithuania on March 22. They secured the Communist Party headquarters and began rounding up and arresting the deserters. Gorbachev insisted that the Lithuanian parliament repeal the declaration of independence, and, when they refused, he decided early in April to cut off all shipments of oil, natural gas, sugar, and wood to Lithuania. The embargo affected the Lithuanian economy immediately, imposing severe hardships and forcing the government early in May to consider "suspending" the independence proclamation for a limited period while negotiations took place with the Soviet Union. On May 18, 1990, Gorbachev agreed to meet with Prime Minister Kazimiera Peunskiene of Lithuania to discuss the impasse. A week later, Gorbachev stated publicly that Lithuania could be independent in two years if it suspended the declaration of independence. At the end of June 1990, the Lithuanian parliament agreed to "freeze" the declaration for 100 days while negotiations on ultimate independence continued. Gorbachev responded by immediately reopening the oil pipelines and lifting the embargoes.

For the rest of 1990, the political crisis in Lithuania was overshadowed by the larger political and economic crisis in the Soviet Union. Although the Lithuanians raised Gorbachev's ire in late July 1990 by drafting all their young men into a new Lithuanian national defense army, which effectively sheltered them from service in the Soviet army, he did little more than protest because he was consumed by so many other problems. When Lithuanian citizens began to harass Soviet troops in Lithuania, Soviet Defense Minister Dimitry Yazov authorized the soldiers to defend themselves. The Lithuanian Parliament called his remarks incendiary, arguing that they "contained more than just hidden threats, threats which a neighboring country has escalated recently for reasons unknown to us." The 100-day suspension of the independence declaration came and went with no resolution. Political rebellions had also erupted in Estonia, Latvia, Moldova, Azerbaijan, and Armenia, and there was unrest in Belarus, Ukraine, and Russia as well. Worse for Gorbachev, however, was the imminent collapse of the Soviet economy. In December 1990, food rationing began in Moscow and Leningrad, and the prospect of starvation in the Soviet Union by early 1991 was very real.

For Lithuanian nationalists, the catastrophe engulfing the Soviet Union was both good news and bad news for their own chances of independence. As the economic deterioration of the Soviet Union continued and as ethnic rebellions spread throughout the country, the ability of the central government to keep everyone in line declined. As Gorbachev's own political position eroded, however, he had to shore up his support among conservatives and the military. These groups demanded the preservation of order. By late 1990 and early 1991, *perestroika* was coming to an end. Gorbachev stopped sending subsidized shipments of oil, metals, and natural gas to Lithuania on January 1, 1991, and, several days later, Soviet paratroopers were deployed inside Lithuania to enforce the military draft laws. Lithuanian young men were in fact avoiding the draft in record numbers, but President Landsbergis claimed that the Soviet objective was "not to catch a few thousand young men but to destabilize the situation and provoke clashes." The presence of Soviet troops in Vilnius precipitated mass demonstrations and rioting in mid-January 1991. On January 13, Soviet troops killed fifteen Lithuanians who were resisting. A series of similar, if less violent, confrontations took place during the spring and summer of 1991.

Independence finally came to Lithuania in the early fall of 1991. The poorly timed, abortive *coup d'état* that upper-echelon individuals in the KGB, the Communist Party, and the Soviet defense establishment staged against Gorbachev in August 1991 proved to be the death knell of the hardliners. President Boris Yeltsin of the Russian Republic openly defied the conspirators, as did large numbers of Soviet citizens and crucial elements of the military. Gorbachev quit the Communist Party and, with the support of Yeltsin and leaders in a number of other republics, restructured the Soviet Union as a loose confederation. The Baltic Republics, however, wanted no part of it. While the coup was occurring in August, Lithuania unilaterally declared its independence from the Soviet Union. It assumed control of its borders, organized a defense force, and began designing its own currency. At the outset of the coup, elite Soviet troops had invaded Lithuania, but they were withdrawn within a few weeks of the collapse of the conspiracy. As the *coup d'état* disintegrated, so did the Soviet Union. On September 6, 1991, Lithuania, after more than forty-two years, was finally independent again.

REFERENCES: A. M. Bendictsen, *Lithuania, the Awakening of a Nation*, 1924; Juozas Daumantas, *Fighters for Freedom: Lithuanian Partisans Versus the USSR*, 1975; Kestutis K. Girnius, "The Collectivization of Lithuanian Agriculture, 1944–1950," *Soviet Studies*, 40 (July 1988), 460–78; E. J. Harrison, *Lithuania Past and Present*, 1924; R. F. Leslie,

Reform and Insurrection in Russian Poland, 1856–1865, 1969; James S. Olson, *Catholic Immigrants in America*, 1987; Thomas Remeikis, "Communist Party of Lithuania: A Historical and Political Study," Ph.D. dissertation, University of Illinois, Urbana, 1973; K. V. Tauras, *Guerrilla Warfare on the Amber Coast*, 1962; V. Stanley Vardys, *The Catholic Church, Dissent, and Nationality in Soviet Lithuania*, 1978; V. Stanley Vardys, *Lithuania under the Soviets: Portrait of a Nation, 1940–1965*, 1965.

LITHUANIAN TATAR. The Lithuanian Tatars are descended from the Golden Horde invaders who arrived in what was then the Grand Duchy of Lithuania between the fourteenth and the mid-sixteenth centuries. They were Muslims. By the end of the 1500s, there were more than 200,000 Tatars* living there. Lithuanian Tatars soon were integrated into the surrounding Lithuanian communities, losing their native tongue but retaining their Muslim religion. The primary Tatar settlements were in Hrodno, Minsk, Trakai, and Vilna (Vilnius). It was relatively easy for them to maintain Islamic culture because of the close commercial relations between Lithuania and Muslim communities in the Near East.

Prior to the union with Poland, Lithuania was, in terms of religious composition, a pluralistic principality with its nobility comprising Orthodox and Catholics and its general population consisting of Jews, Muslims, and others. After the union between Poland and Lithuania in 1569, however, those contacts were severed. The Lithuanian Tatars then came under considerable persecution from Polish Catholics who viewed Islam as an alien, anti-Christian religion. Tatar emigration from the region began, and the numbers of Tatars steadily declined.

After World War I and the Russian Revolution, the former Western Belarus territories of Lithuania came under Polish authority while Eastern Belarus territories became part of the Soviet Union. During World War II, Germans* and Russians went after Tatar intellectuals. By 1945, virtually all of them had either been killed or deported. Most of Western Belarus territories were re-incorporated into the Soviet Union, which meant that the surviving Tatars had become either Lithuanian Tatars or Belarusian Tatars. Josef Stalin's anti-religious terrorism, however, had weakened the Tatar attachment to Islam in the Soviet Union. Since they had long since lost their native language, they gradually disappeared as an identifiable ethnic group. Still, there are people in Lithuania who know of their Tatar roots.

REFERENCE: Shirin Akiner, *Islamic Peoples of the Soviet Union*, 1983.

LITOV. See LITHUANIAN.

LITOV TATAR. See LITHUANIAN TATAR.

LITOVSKIY TATAR. See LITHUANIAN TATAR.

LITOVSKY. See LITHUANIAN.

LITTLE ANYUY CHUKCHIS. See CHUKCHI.

LITTLE RUSSIAN. See UKRAINIAN.

LIV. See LIVONIAN or LATVIAN.

LIVGILAINE. See KARELIAN.

LIVI. See LATVIAN.

LIVIAN. See LIVONIAN or LATVIAN.

LIVONIAN. The Livonians are a group of people in Latvia who are being assimilated by ethnic Latvians.* Historically, the Livonians living in westernmost Latvia were known as the Raandalists, while those to the east were known as the Kalamied. Today they live on the coast between the Gulf of Riga and the Baltic Sea. Livonian is a Finnish* language that is spoken by only a few hundred people.
REFERENCE: Ronald Wixman, *The Peoples of the USSR: An Ethnographic Handbook*, 1984.

LIVVIKEI. See KARELIAN.

LIVVIKI. The Livviki, who call themselves the Livgilaine, the Livvikei, and the Karjala, are ethnic Karelians*. They live in the southwestern region of the Karelian Autonomous Republic. See KARELIAN.
REFERENCE: Ronald Wixman, *The Peoples of the USSR: An Ethnographic Handbook*, 1984.

LOPAR. See LAPP.

LOWLAND MARI. See MARI.

LULI. See GYPSY.

LUORAVETLAN. See CHUKCHI.

LURI. See KURD.

LYG ORAVETLYAN. See CHUKCHI.

LYUDDIKI. See LYYDIKI, VEP, or KARELIAN.

LYUDIKI. See LYYDIKI, VEP, or KARELIAN.

LYUDINIKAD. See LYYDIKI, VEP, or KARELIAN.

LYYDIKI. The Lyydiki, who call themselves the Lyydilaine or the Lyydikoi, have also been known historically as the Lyudiki. They are an ethnically and linguistically distinct group of Karelians*. Most of the Lyydiki live in the Kondopozhskiy and Olonetskiy rayons in the Karelian Autonomous Republic. See KARELIAN.

REFERENCE: Ronald Wixman, *The Peoples of the USSR: An Ethnographic Handbook,* 1984.

LYYDINIK. See VEP.

M

MAARLULAL. The Maarlulal, who have also been known historically as the Magarulal, are one of the large clan federations that constitute the core of the Avar* people. The Avar people in general use the term Maarlulal as the term for themselves. See AVAR.
REFERENCE: Ronald Wixman, *The Peoples of the USSR: An Ethnographic Handbook*, 1984.

MADIAR. See MAGYAR.

MADJAR. See MAGYAR.

MADYAR. See MAGYAR.

MADZHAR. See MAGYAR.

MAGALIS-KAITAK. See DARGIN.

MAGARULAL. See MAARLULAL and AVAR.

MAGYAR. The Magyar, also known as Hungarians and Vengry people, are one of the smaller ethnic minorities in the Soviet Union. The Magyars first migrated from the steppes between the Volga and Kama rivers during the ninth century A.D. Historians are still uncertain exactly what caused the mass exodus from their homeland, but one possibility is that they left to escape incursions by the Mongol* tribes. The Magyars migrated into the Carpathian Basin, which was largely unpopulated at that time. What native peoples did exist in the area were easily overcome. The Magyar "horde," as it is often called, was actually a federation of ten tribes called the On-Ogur (Ten Arrows). Seven of the tribes were Magyar, and three were Turkic* Khazars (or Kavars in Magyar). Each of the tribes was led by a hereditary chieftan. Arpad, the leader of the most powerful tribe, allied the federation with the Carolingian emperor, Arnulf. In 892 A.D. Arnulf called on the Magyars to assist him in his campaign against Sviatopluk, a Moravian duke. In 896, the entire Magyar population crossed the Carpathians en masse. By 906, they had destroyed the Moravian empire, and, by 907, they had occupied Pannonia. For approximately sixty years, the Magyars acted as raiders and mercenaries in Central Europe. In 955, at the Battle of Lechfeld (outside Augsburg, Germany), the Magyars suffered a disastrous defeat at the hands of Otto I. This event was extremely important for two reasons. First, it effectively ended the Magyars' raiding way of life. Second, it allowed for a consolidation of power among Arpad's descendants.

Arpad's great-grandson, Geza, re-established central authority over the tribal chiefs in 972 A.D. One year later, he sent an embassy to Otto II at Quendlinburg. Realizing the importance of Christianity as an instrument of foreign policy, Geza and his family were baptized into the Roman Church in 975 and opened the country to foreign missionaries. He further strengthened his ties with the West when, in 996, he married his son, Istvan I, to the Bavarian princess, Gisella. After Geza's death in 997, Istvan I succeeded to the hereditary chieftainship. Like his father before him, Istvan continued to consolidate his power and subdued all his rivals. He further weakened the authority of the other hereditary chieftains by asking for and receiving a crown from Pope Sylvester II in the year 1000.

Though the process of Christianization had begun under Geza, it was under Istvan that all but a minority of the Magyars were converted to Roman Catholicism. Istvan simultaneously set up a feudal system that resembled, although not completely, the French and German systems. In the Hungarian feudal structure, all individuals, including the nobility, were the king's servants.

Following Istvan's death in 1038, Hungarian history was marked by almost 200 years of regicide, political revolt, and dynastic conflict. Sixteen different kings held the throne during this period, and there were two major pagan revolts against the Latin Church in 1047 and 1063. The lack of strong national leadership coupled with dynastic rivalries combined to cause severe political degradation and extensive loss of territory.

Despite the internal upheaval, several external factors benefited Hungary. Austria was in the process of expanding politically and territorially at the expense of the Holy Roman Empire. This activity critically weakened German claims of suzerainty over Hungary. At the same time, most of the other neighboring states were of approximately the same size and strength as Hungary. Moreover, Laszlo I (reigned 1077–1095), Hungary's sixth king, and Kalman (reigned 1095–1116), the seventh, did much to strengthen Hungary internally. Laszlo consolidated the northern frontier along the Carpathian crest and expanded into Transylvania. He then settled Transylvania with German* immigrants (called Saxons) and with the Szekely, a Magyar-speaking tribe. Kalman consolidated the southwestern flank and conquered Croatia, Bosnia, and Northern Dalmatia. Thus, despite almost two centuries of internal political strife and uncertainty, Hungary emerged in the thirteenth century as a large and powerful state with close to 2,000,000 inhabitants.

Hungary's prosperity did not last long, however. The first of Hungary's five "national tragedies" occurred in 1241, when the Tatars* under Batu Khan overran the eastern border. By 1242, Hungary had lost approximately half of its population. Losses ranged from 20 percent in the Dunantul to 100 percent in parts of the Alfold. Bela IV (reigned 1235–1270) managed to rebuild and refortify the nation. In 1301, however, the last Arpad king, Andrew III, died, and the throne passed to foreign claimants.

Hungary's second tragedy occurred in 1526 at the Battle of Mohacs, when the Ottoman Turks* destroyed the Hungarian army. From 1428 through 1526, Hungary had been menaced by the Ottomans. For nearly a century, both sides had fought pitched battles, all of which had resulted in stalemate. In 1521, the Ottomans, under Suleyman II, took and held all the major fortresses on the southern frontier. For five years, the Hungarian court did nothing, and factionalism ran rampant. Finally, in 1526, Suleyman II delivered the crushing blow. Hungary was divided into three parts. Transylvania became an independent, albeit subject, principality. The main part of Hungary fell under direct Ottoman control, and a narrow strip of Hungarian territory along the Austrian* frontier was incorporated into the Hapsburg Empire. Ironically, although Transylvania was subject to the Ottoman Empire, it was here that the idea of an independent Hungarian state was kept alive.

The third of Hungary's tragedies occurred with its inclusion into the Hapsburg Empire. In 1683, the Hapsburgs defeated the Ottomans at Vienna. Realizing that it was possible to defeat them, Austria went on the offensive and took Buda in 1686. By 1697, the Ottomans had been forced from all Hungarian lands except around Temesvar (Timisoara), and that was retaken in 1721. Hungary thus became a possession of the Hapsburgs. Hungary enjoyed mixed blessings under the Hapsburgs. Initially, Hungary was so thoroughly abused, economically and religiously, by the occupying Hapsburg forces that many Hungarians believed that they had been better off under the Muslim Ottomans. When Empress Maria Theresa ascended to the throne, however, she enacted modest reforms and opened Hungary to Western education, science, culture, and government. Her actions also opened Hungary to active germanization. Initially, germanization occurred passively, as the Hungarian aristocracy came to use the language more and more. Indeed, germanization was so thorough that many in the aristocracy and upper class "forgot they were Hungarian."

Passive germanization led to forced germanization under Joseph II. This, together with Leopold II's and Franz's foreign campaigns, censorship, and anti-reformist attitudes, fanned the flames of Hungarian resentment and nationalism. Hungarians increasingly saw themselves as an Austrian resource that was too often used and exploited for the benefit of German Austria. At the same time, an increased awareness of their own national identity led Hungarians to attempt forced magyarization on other minorities, particularly on the Saxons in Transylvania, the Slovaks*, the Serbs*, the Croats*, the Romanians*, and the Carpatho-Rusyns*.

German-Austrian chauvinism finally resulted in the failed Hungarian Revolution of March 1848. Led by Lajos Kossuth, a journalist and brilliant orator, the Hungarian diet established a national (i.e., Hungarian) government, which was responsible to a freely elected parliament; the parliament then declared Hungarian to be the national language. Other reforms were initiated soon after, the most important of which was a new constitution. In December 1848, Franz Joseph I was crowned emperor, but the Hungarians refused to recognize him, ostensibly because he had not been crowned with the Hungarian crown of St. Stephen (Istvan I). Kossuth called for a complete break with Austria and declared Hungary an independent republic.

The Hapsburg government refused to accept this situation and sent troops against the new government. Hungarian forces were at first routed, but, as the war progressed, they were able to force the Austrians out. In May 1849, Franz Joseph asked for and got Russian* military assistance. By August of 1849, the revolution had been crushed, and the Hungarian army surrendered to the Russians at Vilagos.

Following the war, the Hapsburg government was extremely vindictive. Any Hungarian government officials or army officers who did not leave Hungary were either put to death or imprisoned. By December 1865, however, Franz Joseph was forced to negotiate with the Hungarians out of political necessity. The Hungarian Diet was reopened, and the 1848 constitution was recognized. In 1867, Hungary was recognized as a state of at least equal constitutional standing with the other Hapsburg lands. Thus, it was now not so much the Hapsburg empire as the Austro-Hungarian Empire.

Hungary's fourth national tragedy occurred with the end of World War I. Hungary, through its association with Austria, found itself on the losing side and was severely penalized. With the signing of the Treaty of Trianon, Hungary lost approximately 60 percent of its territory and 30 percent of its Magyar-speaking population. Large Magyar minorities went to Czechoslovakia, Romania, and Yugoslavia. These irredenta would continue to be a focus for nationalistic aspirations and concerns down to the 1990s.

The end of World War I and the signing of the Treaty of Trianon did not signal a corresponding end to hostilities between Hungary and its neighbors, nor did it lead to a stable government. By 1919, the freely elected government, headed by Mihaly Karolyi, was on the verge of collapse. Karolyi handed the government over to a Communist party led by Bela Kun. Kun immediately proclaimed the establishment of a Hungarian Soviet Republic. He then launched a military offensive against the Czechoslovak armies that had mobilized along the Hungarian border. After winning a series of victories, Kun established a soviet republic in Slovakia. At this point, Romanian troops invaded Hungary, and Kun was forced to withdraw back to Hungary. The domestic situation there had deteriorated to the point of economic collapse, due to Kun's policies. By the time the Romanian army had reached Budapest, the government had collapsed. Kun fled to Moscow, where he was executed in 1939 during one of Josef Stalin's purges.

Although free elections were held in 1920 under Allied supervision, the government was dominated by a reactionary, Admiral Miklos Horthy. Hungarian nationalism was on the rise, due in part to the humiliating conditions of the Treaty of Trianon. The Horthy government developed close relations with both Benito Mussolini's Italy and Nazi Germany. With the German occupation of Czechoslovakia in 1938, Hungary was allocated part of Slovakia and all of Ruthenia. In January 1939, Hungary signed the Anti-Comintern Pact. When Romania surrendered in 1940, Hungary was granted a large portion of Transylvania. In April 1941, Hungarian troops occupied the territory that had been awarded to Yugoslavia by the Treaty of Trianon. The following December, Hungary declared war on the Soviet Union and suffered heavy casualties on the Russian front. Toward the end of the war, in February 1945, Soviet troops occupied Budapest. Although free elections were held in March 1945, the freely elected government of Zoltan Tildy was overthrown in January 1947 by Communists led by Matyas Rakosi. The territories that had been recovered during the war were again stripped from Hungary and returned to Czechoslovakia, Romania, and Yugoslavia. The only exception was Ruthenia, which was annexed by the Soviet Union in 1945.

Hungary was brutally oppressed by the Rakosi regime. The situation grew so critical that Rakosi was forced by Moscow to share power with Imre Nagy, a reform-minded Communist. Nagy was removed in 1955 after being denounced by Rakosi; he was replaced by Ernö Gerö, a staunch Rakosi supporter. The ensuing socio-political crisis resulted in the anti-Communist/anti-Russian Hungarian Revolution of 1956. Twelve days later, the revolution was crushed by Soviet military might, and between 200,000 to 400,000 Hungarians fled abroad. Janos Kadar was placed in power, and, although a committed Communist and staunch Moscow ally, he instituted the most benign regime in Eastern Europe.

Mikhail Gorbachev's program of *glasnost* and *perestroika* during the mid–1980s soon resulted in a third "revolution" in Hungary. Communist radicals, led by Imre Pozsgay, effectively split the Communist Party into "true" Communists (the conservatives) and the Socialists (the reform wing of the party). They also legalized true opposition parties, rewrote the constitution, opened Hungary's border with Austria, and led Hungary back toward a Western-oriented capitalist system.

Magyar is a branch of the Finno-Ugrian* group of the Uralic linguistic family and is related only to Finnish* and Estonian* among the languages of Europe. The earliest written remnant of Magyar is a one-page funeral oration, dating from around 1200 A.D. The first known poem, "Mary's Lament," dates from approximately 1300, and a biography of St. Francis of Assisi dates from about 1370. Matthias Corvinus (1458–1490) ushered in a "renaissance state," during which vernacular literature experienced a major upswing. Corvinus' influence continued after his death, and Hungarian literature flourished during the sixteenth century. A Magyar-Latin dictionary was published in 1538, followed by two Magyar grammars in 1539 and 1549. Gaspar Heltai was perhaps the most important translator, poet, historian, and writer of this time. Heltai did some Biblical translations into Magyar, but credit for translating the work goes to Gaspar Karolyi, a Lutheran minister. The first translation of the Bible in Magyar was printed in 1590.

With the advent of Hapsburg control in 1721 came a cultural and literary reawakening. Through Vienna, upper-class Hungarians were exposed to the French, German, and English concepts of the Enlightenment. French authors were particularly influential, to the extent that the Hapsburgs set up a strict censorship of all foreign literature. With Joseph II's edict declaring German to be the official language (1784), Hungarian intellectuals saw their primary duty as the cultivation of Magyar. Magyar authors began to work systematically on reforming and standardizing Magyar, and increasing numbers of the Hungarian elite began patronizing Magyar literature. Gyorgy Bessenyei was one of the major figures of this early literary awakening. The year 1840 marked the flowering of Magyar literature. Particularly influential were Sandor Petofi (who was not even a native Magyar) and his close friend, Janos Arany. It was through them that the language spoken by the common people became the vehicle for artistic expression, setting the norms for modern Magyar literature.

Historically, Hungary has been a Roman Catholic nation but with a significant Protestant population. The nation was opened to Catholic missionaries in 975, and, by 1000, most of the population had been converted, at least nominally. After the Battle of Mohacs in 1526, both Lutheranism and Calvinism spread quickly. In general, the Germans and Slavs preferred Lutheranism, while the majority of Hungarian Protestants were Calvinists. Interestingly enough, despite almost 200 years of occupation by the Ottoman Turks, Islam never gained any sizable number of converts in Hungary, as it did in Albania.

Following the expulsion of the Ottoman Turks from Hungary, Leopold I of Austria initiated a counter-reformation and ordered the persecution of the Protestants. There was considerable resistance on the part of the nobility (most of whom were Calvinists), and eventually Maria Theresa rescinded the edict and guaranteed basic religious freedom. A 1949 survey showed that 66 percent of the population were Roman Catholic, 22 percent were Calvinist, 5.2 percent were Lutheran, and 2.7 percent were Uniates (practically all of these were magyarized Ruthenes). The rest consisted of smaller numbers of Jews*, Greek Orthodox, and Unitarians.

Magyars in the Soviet Union are actually a mix of true Magyars, Slovaks, and Carpatho-Rusyns* (Ruthenians) who were "magyarized" before 1918, and Slovaks and Carpatho-Rusyns who were "magyarized" after 1918, and Slovaks who have continued to be assimilated since 1946. In 1979, there were 171,000 people in the Soviet Union who identified themselves as Magyars; this number was up from 157,000 in 1970. The 1989 Soviet census placed the Magyar population at 172,000. Those numbers had not increased much over 1979 because of assimilation and the migration of some Magyars back to Hungary after the collapse of the Iron Curtain in 1989. Some Magyar nationalists today are clamoring to have the Transcarpathian (Zakarpatskaya) Oblast transferred back from Ukraine to Hungary, where economic life is much better. There are, of course, large numbers of Ukrainians* who oppose such a move.

It was not until the late 1980s and early 1990s that the Hungarian media began reporting the mistreatment of the Magyars living in the Zakarpatskaya Oblast of the Ukrainian Soviet Socialist Republic. Most of them live in the towns of Uzhgorod, Mukachevo, Sevliush, and Beregovo. That region had belonged to Hungary until the end of World War I, but Czechoslovakia annexed it in 1919. The region was returned to Hungary in 1939, but then the Soviet Union annexed it in 1945. Because they had fought on Germany's side during World War II, the Hungarians now living in the Soviet Union suffered severe persecution. Not until 1952 was Hungarian permitted in public schools, and restrictions were placed on the Roman Catholic and on the Reformed (Calvinist) churches. Most of those restrictions were lifted late in the 1980s, and, after the fall of the Communist regime in 1989, the new government of Hungary demanded that the Soviet Union treat its Magyar citizens fairly.

REFERENCES: Scott Wm. Bumbaugh, *Soviet Reforms and the Case of Hungary*, 1990; Scott Wm. Bumbaugh, "Hungarian Situation Report/3," *Radio Free Europe Research*, March 21, 1988, Item 4; Andrew Janos, *The Politics of Backwardness in Hungary, 1825–1945*, 1982; Georges Jorre, *The Soviet Union—The Land and its People*, 1950; Robert A. Kahn, *A History of the Hapsburg Empire, 1526-1918*, 1974; Imre Lukinich, *A History of Hungary*, 1937; Carlile Aylmer Macartney, *Hungary*, 1962; Carlile Aylmer Macartney, *Hungary and Her Successors*, 1937; *Radio Liberty Research Bulletin*, July 8, 1988, 20–24; Robert Wm. Seton-Watson, *Racial Problems in Hungary*, 1972; Peter F. Sugar, *A History of Hungary*, 1990.

                                                            Scott Wm. Bumbaugh

MAHOSH. See MAKHOSH, ADYGHE, and CIRCASSIAN.

MAJAR. See MAGYAR.

MAKHOSH. The Makhosh are one of the constituent subgroups making up the Adyghes*. They are concentrated demographically between the Laba and Belaya rivers in the western reaches of the North Caucasus. See ADYGHE or CIRCASSIAN.

REFERENCE: Ronald Wixman, *The Peoples of the USSR: An Ethnographic Handbook*, 1984.

MALKAR. The Malkar, who call themselves the Malkarly, are a Balkar* subgroup. They constitute the core group around which the Balkar group formed. The Malkars live in the Malka River Valley in the Kabardino-Balkar Autonomous Republic. See BALKAR.
REFERENCE: Ronald Wixman, *The Peoples of the USSR: An Ethnographic Handbook*, 1984.

MALKARCHI. See MALKAR and BALKAR.

MALKARCHILI. See MALKAR and BALKAR.

MALKARCHY. See MALKAR and BALKAR.

MALKARCHYLY. See MALKAR and BALKAR.

MALKARLA. See MALKAR and BALKAR.

MALKARLAR. See MALKAR and BALKAR.

MALKARLY. See MALKAR and BALKAR.

MALKARLI. See MALKAR and BALKAR.

MALLQARLI. See MALKAR and BALKAR.

MALO RUS. See UKRAINIAN.

MALO RUSIN. See UKRAINIAN.

MALO RUSSIAN. See UKRAINIAN.

MALORUS. See UKRAINIAN.

MALORUSIN. See UKRAINIAN.

MALORUSSIAN. See UKRAINIAN.

MALQARCHI. See MALKAR and BALKAR.

MALQARCHILI. See MALKAR and BALKAR.

MALQARCHY. See MALKAR and BALKAR.

MALQARCHYLY. See MALKAR and BALKAR.

MALQARLI. See MALKAR and BALKAR.

MALQARLY. See MALKAR and BALKAR.

MAMKHEG. The Mamkheg, who call themselves the Mamkhegh, are one of the Adyghe* subgroups. Ever since the sixteenth century, the Mamkheg have lived along the middle Belaya River in the western region of the North Caucasus, but most of them left that area in the mid–1860s and emigrated to Turkey. See ADYGHE or CIRCASSIAN.
REFERENCE: Ronald Wixman, *The Peoples of the USSR: An Ethnographic Handbook*, 1984.

MAMKHEGH. See MAMKHEG, ADYGHE, and CIRCASSIAN.

MANCHU. The Manchus (Manchurians), who call themselves the Mandzhu, are an ethnic group of more than 5,000,000 people who live in northeastern China, particularly in southern Manchuria. They are descendants of the ancient Tungus people who were present in Manchuria as early as the third century B.C. The Tungus represented a consolidation of such local tribes as the Sushen, Ilu, Wochu, Wuchi, and Moho, as well as a variety of neighboring Turkic and Mongol* tribes. By the early seventeenth century, the Manchus had become a self-conscious ethnic entity. They were led by the Emperor Nurhatsi, who established an imperial capital at Mukden. The name "Manchu" by that time referred to the people of the region. Later in the seventeenth century, the Manchus established the Ch'ing Empire by conquering Korea, Mongolia, and China. They pushed into Dzungaria, Tibet, and other borderlands in the eighteenth century. The expansion eventually diluted Manchu culture, however, and the language entered a period of steady decline as more and more Manchus adopted Chinese.* Except for the Manchu people living in the villages of Heilungkiang Province, Manchu was dead as a spoken language by the early twentieth century. In the People's Republic of China, the Manchu today work primarily as farmers, raising grains, legumes, hemp, and vegetables; a number of highland Manchus work in the lumber industry. Only a handful of people living in what used to be the Soviet Union are even aware of their roots as Manchu people, although approximately 20,000 people speak one of the Manchu languages: the Nanais*, Oroks*, Orochis*, Ulchis*, and Udegeis*.
REFERENCES: Alice Bartels and Dennis Bartels, "Soviet Policy Toward Siberian Native People," *Canadian Dimension*, 19 (1985), 36–44; Mike Edwards, "Siberia: In From the Cold," *National Geographic*, 177 (March 1990), 2–49; Constantine Krypton, "Soviet Policy in the Northern National Regions After World War II," *Slavic Review*, 13 (October 1954), 339–53; Piers Vitebsky, "Perestroika Among the Reindeer Herders," *Geographical Magazine*, 61 (June 1989), 23–34.

MANCHU PEOPLES. The term "Manchu peoples" is a generic reference to those groups speaking one of the Manchu languages in the Uralic-Altaic linguistic family. The primary groups are the Nanais*, Oroks*, Orochis*, Ulchis*, and Udegeis*.
REFERENCE: Ronald Wixman, *The Peoples of the USSR: An Ethnographic Handbook*, 1984.

MANCHURIAN. See MANCHU and MANCHU PEOPLES.

MANDJU. See MANCHU and MANCHU PEOPLES.

MANDJURI. See MANCHU and MANCHU PEOPLES.

MANDJURIAN. See MANCHU and MANCHU PEOPLES.

MANDJURY. See MANCHU and MANCHU PEOPLES.

MANDZHU. See MANCHU and MANCHU PEOPLES.

MANDZHURI. See MANCHU and MANCHU PEOPLES.

MANDZHURIAN. See MANCHU and MANCHU PEOPLES.

MANDZHURY. See MANCHU and MANCHU PEOPLES.

MANEGIR. See EVENK.

MANEGRY. See EVENK.

MANGKYT. See NOGAI.

MANGU. See ULCHI.

MANGUN. See ULCHI.

MANIAGIR. See EVENK.

MANSI. The Mansi, once known as Voguls and Yugras, are a small ethnic group living in the Ob River basin, particularly along the Konda and Severnaia Sos'va rivers, in the Tjumen Oblast of the Khanty-Mansi National Okrug in Russia. Others live in the Sverdlovsk Oblast. The Mansi are closely related with the Khant*. Their two languages form the Ob-Ugrian group of the Ugrian cluster of languages, which are themselves part of the larger Uralian branch of the

Uralic-Altaic linguistic family. Russian* ethnologists argue that the Mansi first emerged from a process of ethnogenesis that occurred around the first century A.D.; they believe that migrating Ugrians* coming from the south mixed with the existing hunting and fishing tribes of the Trans-Ural mountain region. The Mansi were first identified as an independent group in written sources of the eleventh century, when they were called Yugras or Ugrians. By the fourteenth century, they had acquired the name of Voguls.

Beginning in the fifteenth century, when Muscovite imperial control reached their homeland, the Mansi came under Russian influence, and they stubbornly, sometimes violently, resisted russification up through the sixteenth century. The Mansi suffered from their contact with ethnic Russians. Over the centuries, Russians penetrated commercial activities in the region, enticing the Mansi first with iron and steel tools, and, later, with firearms and a variety of other trade goods. Large numbers of Mansi adopted the use of alcohol as well, much to their harm. The ethnic Russians also brought diseases to the native peoples, especially venereal diseases, which had spread throughout Europe after the New World conquests in the late fifteenth and sixteenth centuries. The Mansi population entered a long period of decline that did not stabilize until the mid-eighteenth century.

During the sixteenth and seventeenth centuries, the central government under the tsars practiced a policy of indirect rule from Moscow. They treated the native peoples of Siberia like other peoples they had conquered. Forts were established for the purpose of collecting the *yasak*, or fur tax, for Moscow. Actual administration of native peoples was left in the hands of local rulers. Moscow authorized the granting of citizenship to any native who converted to Christianity, a process that led to forced baptisms and enserfment by local rulers, who then used their native serfs to increase fur trapping. As the numbers of fur-bearing animals decreased, Moscow lost interest in the area and in the well-being of its natives. The Mansi were part of this entire administrative process. Missionaries from the Russian Orthodox Church began working among the Mansi in the late 1700s. Although most of the Mansi converted, they retained powerful elements of their indigenous religious beliefs, making their Christianity an eclectic mix of formal, institutional religion and a vast, rich folk culture that revolved around the environment, flora, and fauna of western Siberia.

The Bolshevik Revolution brought great changes to Mansi life. Although the Soviet government ostensibly offered some political recognition in the establishment of the Khanty-Mansi National Okrug in 1930, the policies were actually designed to assimilate the Mansi. The traditional Mansi economy revolved around fishing, hunting, and reindeer breeding, and Josef Stalin's policies tried to collectivize those activities beginning in the late 1920s. Early in the 1930s, the government created a literary language for the Mansi; this written language used a Latin alphabet, but, in 1939, it was changed to Cyrillic. Compulsory attendance at public schools where Russian was the language of instruction introduced Mansi children to Russian culture. The Mansi population stood at approximately 5,754 people in 1926; it had grown to nearly 8,000 people by the late 1980s.

Up through the 1960s, the Mansi still managed to maintain much of their traditional culture. Although the capital city of the Khanty-Mansi National Region—Khanty-Mansiysk—was only 1,200 miles east of Moscow, the region did not undergo the same accelerated development as many other regions of Siberia. Although the region was rich in potential resources, there were severe impediments to their extraction. The area was densely forested and marked by hundreds of low watershed rivers. Moreover, a huge marshland extended from the Baraba Steppe in the south to the Arctic Circle in the north, between the Urals and Tomsk. The Mansis, despite the collectivization programs of the 1930s, managed to keep hunting and fishing in a nomadic manner. Their shamanistic religion, complete with bear worship, still thrived. Perhaps most crucially, their economy supported the state economy. Mansis played a key role in fish production on the Ob and Irtysh rivers. Typically, Mansi families left the collective settlements in the spring and migrated upriver, where they fished in nomadic communities. In the autumn, they returned to their permanent settlements to begin the hunting season.

This relative isolation began to change quickly in the 1960s. Soviet geologists discovered huge deposits of oil and natural gas all over the Mansi homeland. Pipelines were laid throughout the Khanty-Mansi National Region to deliver the petroleum products to Perm and Tjumen. The Urals and the Ob River were connected by the construction of a railroad right across the Khanty-Mansi National Region. Oil and gas wells appeared throughout the region, and enormous numbers of ethnic Russians and Ukrainians swarmed to the area. Roads, highways, and railway trunk lines were constructed. In the process, the Mansis were often pushed off the land and abused by the newcomers. Worse yet, the state made no provision for assisting them in dealing with the effects of modern industrialization.

By the 1980s, Mikhail Gorbachev's policies of *perestroika* and *glasnost* were having an enormous impact. The region had great geo-strategic and economic significance to the Soviet Union because of its oil and natural gas deposits, which supplied more than half of the Soviet Union's annual production. Khanty and Mansi leaders began demanding local control over those assets, because the Soviet Union was extracting them at a fixed price and then selling them at world prices, thereby cheating the local populations of the true wealth of their region. Late in 1991, Khanty and Mansi leaders proclaimed the sovereignty and independence of the region, but local soviets refused to recognize the change, primarily because the ethnic Russian delegates worried about its implications. The Russians were willing, however, to discuss the matter and consider remaining within the Soviet Union (and, after 1992, in Russia), as long as some type of local control over natural resources was provided.

REFERENCES: *Current Digest*, 42 (January 16, 1991), 23–24; *Great Soviet Encyclopedia*, 1973, vol. 15, 436; James Forsyth, *A History of the Peoples of Siberia*, 1992.

MANSUR. See NOGAI.

MANYAGIR. See EVENK.

MARI. The Maris, who were formerly called the Cheremiss (Cheremis), are an ethnic group in the former Soviet Union who live in their own autonomous republic (the Mari Autonomous Republic). The Mari population totaled 428,192 people in 1926, and it has increased since then to 504,205 in 1959, 598,628 in 1970, 621,961 in 1979, and 670,277 in 1989. Historians have argued that the Mari first appeared as an identifiable ethnic group in the sixth century. They fell under the rule of the Khazar empire in the eighth century, surviving economically through slash-and-burn agriculture, hunting, fishing, and small-scale, local commerce. By the mid-ninth century, the expanding cultural and political influence of the Volga Bulgarians* had displaced Khazar influence among the Maris, and they remained under Bulgarian control until the mid-twelfth century. At that point, the Mongol Tatars* took over, reaching Mari land in the 1230s and rapidly bringing them under subjugation. Tatar control of the Mari continued until the middle of the sixteenth century, when the Russian* Empire established control over their territory. Significant Russian cultural and economic contact with the Mari had actually begun as early as the twelfth century.

Ethnographers and ethnolinguists identify the Mari as a Finnic* people. Their language is part of the Mari group of the Finnic branch of the Uralic-Altaic language family. Their territorial homeland stretches throughout the Middle Volga region, though they live in the Mari Autonomous Republic, the Bashkir Autonomous Republic, the Udmurt Autonomous Republic, and the Tatar Autonomous Republic, as well as in the Kirov, Gorky, Perm', and Sverdlovsk autonomous oblasts of Russia. There are three basic divisions to the Mari people, each distinguished from the other two by a distinct dialect. The Kuryk Mari*— also known as the Mountain Mari, Forest Mari, and Highland Mari—live on the right bank of the Volga River and are by far the largest of the Mari subgroups. The second largest Mari subgroup is the Olyk Mari, also known as the Meadow Mari and the Lowland Mari; they dwell on the left bank of the Volga River. The smallest of the Mari groups is the Upo Mari*, or Eastern Mari. They live in the Bashkir Autonomous Republic, the Tatar Republic, and the Sverdlovsk Oblast. The Upo Maris first began their eastern migration in the sixteenth century; it gained momentum in the seventeenth and eighteenth centuries, by which time they had acquired a distinct identity.

Mari religion traditionally reflected their nomadic, subsistence economic life and resembled that of other aboriginal peoples around the world. They were an animistic, polytheistic people. Mari religious life revolved around a shaman leader who propitiated the powers of the universe. Nothing in life occurred capriciously, accidentally, or inadvertently. All phenomena were connected in complex inter-relationships that human beings had to try to understand if they were to survive.

Russian Orthodox missionaries first reached the Maris in the sixteenth century and began a long, difficult attempt to convert them to Christianity. The missionary work became especially intense in the early 1800s, when Russian nationalists began to worry about the other distinct nationalities among them. Since Christianization and education went hand-in-hand, the missionaries worked to develop a literary language for the Maris. In 1803, Russian Orthodox linguists developed a Cyrillic alphabet for Kuryk Mari, and they published a Russian Orthodox catechism that same year. The four Gospels of the New Testament were first published in the Olyk alphabet and appeared in Cyrillic two decades later, the Eastern Maris used the Olyk alphabet as their written language. Missionary work was difficult among the Mari. Most of the Kuryk Mari accepted Russian Orthodoxy, but, on the other side of the Volga River, the Olyk and Upo Mari were more resistant to change and retained most of their animist faith. As they migrated into Bashkir* and Tatar regions, some of the Maris converted to Islam or at least incorporated elements of Islam into their existing religion.

Mari identity first emerged more than a thousand years ago, but it did not really take on the form of an overt political nationalism until the nineteenth century. In the 1870s, a number of Mari leaders began openly resisting the attempts of the Russian Orthodox Church to convert them. That resistance erupted in full-scale rebellion in the 1870s, when a religious-nationalistic sect, known as the Kugu Sorta (Great Candle), openly campaigned against the church. The Kugu Sorta was especially influential among the Olyk Maris and the Upo Maris. This fact explains why today both of those subgroups retain substantially more of their religious traditions than do the Kuryk Maris. The Mari literary languages developed in the nineteenth century; such Mari writers as S. G. Chavain, M. S. Gerasimov-Mikai, and N. S. Mukhin were producing an ethnic literature in the early 1900s.

The Bolshevik Revolution in 1917 changed Mari life. In 1920, an autonomous oblast was established for the Maris, and this was elevated to the Mari Autonomous Soviet Socialist Republic (ASSR) in 1936. Most of the Mari ASSR's 8,900-square-mile territory was located on the left bank of the Volga River. The collectivization of Mari agriculture began in the late 1920s and, by the late 1930s, the process had been virtually completed. The Soviet government also launched a drive to industrialize the area rapidly. Public schools dictated the use of Russian as the medium of instruction late in the 1930s. In spite of these efforts to acculturate the Mari, the Mari have maintained a cohesive sense of identity. Even in the early 1990s, more than 80 percent of the Mari people still spoke Mari as their native tongue, and less than two-thirds of them understood Russian. They also have remained faithful to many elements of their animistic religion.
REFERENCES: *Great Soviet Encyclopedia*, 1973, vol. 15, 468–74; Ronald Wixman, *The Peoples of the USSR: An Ethnographic Handbook*, 1984.

MARKOV. The Markov are ethnic Russians* who, beginning in the seventeenth century, migrated east to the polar region of northern Siberia and settled among the local Chuvash* and Yukagir* peoples. Culturally and economically, they adopted the life-styles of those people, making their livings by hunting, fishing, and breeding reindeer, but they retained their use of the Russian language while adopting many words from local tribes. They still view themselves as Russians

and distinct from the surrounding people. Most of the Markov live in the village of Markovo on the Anadyr River. See RUSSIAN.
REFERENCE: Ronald Wixman, *The Peoples of the USSR: An Ethnographic Handbook*, 1984.

MARKOVTSY. See MARKOV.

MATOR. See KOIBAL and KHAKASS.

MAZANG. See GYPSY.

MEADOW MARI. See MARI.

MEDNY ALEUT. See ALEUT.

MEGRELI. See MINGRELIAN and GEORGIAN.

MEGRELIAN. See MINGRELIAN and GEORGIAN.

MEGRELO-CHAN. See LAZ, MINGRELIAN, and GEORGIAN.

MEGRELO-LAZ. The term "Megrelo-Laz" is an old one that used to refer to the Mingrelian* and Laz* peoples. Although they speak similar languages, their ethnic identities are very different, since the Mingrelians are Eastern Orthodox Christians and the Laz are Sunni Muslims.
REFERENCE: Ronald Wixman, *The Peoples of the USSR: An Ethnographic Handbook*, 1984.

MEGRELO-ZAN. See MEGRELO-LAZ.

MELET. See KYZYL and KHAKASS.

MELETSKI TATAR. The Meletski Tatars are part of the larger collection of Siberian Tatars*. The term "Meletski Tatar" is more a reflection of their location in the Meletski region of the Khakass Autonomous Oblast in southern Siberia than of any distinct identity as a special group of Tatars. Russians* finally conquered the region in the late 1500s. Contact with Russians led to their conversion to Eastern Orthodox Christianity, although the conversion was superficial at best. Strong elements of shamanistic animism survived among them. Until the nineteenth century, most of the Meletski Tatars were hunters and trappers, and when industrialization began to reach Siberia, some Meletski Tatars went to work in factories, tanneries, and sawmills. Since World War II, Russian ethnographers have classified them with the Khakass. See KHAKASS and TATARS.

REFERENCE: Shirin Akiner, *Islamic Peoples of the Soviet Union*, 1983.

MENE. See EVEN.

MENEL. See EVEN.

MESHCHERA. The term "Meshchera" is a generic reference to Mordvinian* people who have undergone a process of assimilation. Those who were assimilated by ethnic Russians* and became Christians are known as Meshcheryak, while those who adopted Islam and the Tatar* language became known as Mishars.* See MISHAR, MESHCHERYAK, and MORDVINIAN.
REFERENCE: Ronald Wixman, *The Peoples of the USSR: An Ethnographic Handbook*, 1984.

MESHCHERIAK. See MESHCHERYAK and MORDVINIAN.

MESHCHERJAKI. See MESHCHERYAK and MORDVINIAN.

MESHCHERYAK. The Meshcheryak, who sometimes call themselves the Russiky, are a people of mixed ethnic origin. They were originally Mordvinians*, who intermarried over the years with ethnic Russians* living in their vicinity. They adopted the Russian language and the Eastern Orthodox religion. Their Russian dialect, however, is distinguished by its Mordvinian elements. Most Meshcheryaks live in the Oka River basin in the Ryazan Oblast and the Tambov Oblast in the Volga River region. See RUSSIAN, MORDVINIAN, or MESHCHERA.
REFERENCE: Ronald Wixman, *The Peoples of the USSR: An Ethnographic Handbook*, 1984.

MESHETIAN. See GEORGIAN and MESKHETIAN.

MESHI. See GEORGIAN and MESKHETIAN.

MESKHETIAN. Historians and anthropologists now consider the Meskhetians of the Commonwealth of Independent States (CIS) as a contemporary example of ethnogenesis. There was no such thing as a Meskhetian ethnic group in the Soviet Union until the 1950s and 1960s. To be sure, there was a group of Turks* living in Georgia who were known as the Meskhi, but the emergence of today's Meskhetian people in the Soviet Union is a post-World War II phenomenon. Late in 1944, after charging them with collaborating with the Nazi army of occupation, Josef Stalin decided to deport large numbers of people forcibly from southwestern Georgia and northern Armenia, a region commonly known as Meskhi. These people were relocated to southern Kazakhstan and Central Asia— primarily Uzbekistan, Tajikistan, and Kyrgyzia—and forbidden to return to Meskhi. At the time (1944), approximately 170,000 people lived in Meskhetia. Stalin then relocated land-starved peasants from the highlands of the Caucasus to settle the region. During their sojourn in exile, the original inhabitants were required to report every two weeks, almost like prisoners on parole, to Soviet authorities.

Although it is difficult for historians to come up with reliable population figures, most demographers believe that the relocation involved between 100,000 and 150,000 people who came from a number of ethnic communities. The largest group were the Meskhi Turks who had lived in the Kura River valley of the Georgia Soviet Socialist Republic. These rural people were conservative, deeply religious Sunni Muslims of the Hanafi school. In addition to the Meskhi Turks, Stalin deported the Karapapakhs,* an Ali Illahi Muslim group living in northern Armenia close to the border with Georgia. Some ethnologists viewed the Karapapakhs as a Turkmen* subtribe speaking an Azeribaijani*-like language. The third group from the Meskhi region was the Khemsils*, another Sunni Muslim group of the Hanafi school. Stalin also deported two groups of Kurds*, one Sunni Muslim and the other Ali Illahi, from southern Georgia and from the Adjar Autonomous Republic. Finally, small numbers of southern Georgian,* Azeri-speaking Turkmen, as well as Muslim Abkhaz* and Adjars*, were also deported.

By early 1945, these disparate groups found themselves living in poverty in Central Asia, the victims of one of Stalin's acts of terrorism. Thousands of them had died during or as a result of the deportation. Their suffering only made them more anti-Soviet, anti-Russian, and anti-Communist than they had been before; in the process, they had become even more religious. Because they spoke Turkish languages and were all Muslims, they were soon able to overcome differences over dialect or religious dogma. The Sunni/Hanafi Muslims and the Ali Illahis were able to come together. Consequently, a new ethnic group of Meskhetian Turks began to emerge. The term ''Meskhetian'' is thus a collective reference for the Sunni and Ali Illahi Muslim groups from southwestern Georgia and northern Armenia who were deported to Central Asia late in 1944. They have become militantly Muslim and increasingly nationalistic in perspective. They number approximately 100,000 people. Unlike the other North Caucasians, who were rehabilitated in 1956 and allowed to return to their homelands, the Meskhetians are still confined to Central Asia.

On a number of occasions since the late 1950s, the Meskhetians have appealed for United Nations (UN) support for their desire to return to their homelands, but the UN has not responded because of Soviet opposition. Not until the late 1980s, with the regime of Mikhail Gorbachev, were some Meskhetians allowed to return to south Georgia, and that permission was more informal than official. The large majority of Meskhetians still live in Uzbekistan, Tajikistan, and Kyrgyzia. The Meskhetians' opportunity to return to southwestern Georgia and take up farming, however, clashed directly with the wishes of those Caucasian peasants and their descendants who had been living on the land for the previous forty-five years. Meskhetians therefore began forming political action groups to promote their desire to return to Georgia. The most active of those groups, headed by Yuri Sarvarov, is the Temporary Organizing Committee on Returning Home.

During the late 1980s and early 1990s, the Meskhetians suddenly found themselves in a tenuous social and political situation. In June 1989, Meskhetians living in the Fergana Valley of Uzbekistan became the targets of intense Uzbek* frustration. Rumors began circulating in the spring of 1989 that the new Congress of People's Deputies in Moscow was going to make amends for the forced relocation of the Meskhetians and allow them to return at last to their homeland in the north Caucasus; supposedly, the Meskhetians would be awarded individual homesteads. Local Uzbeks, who were themselves suffering from high unemployment rates and living in crowded, delapidated housing, became enraged over the rumors. There was also considerable local resentment about the refusal of the Meskhetians to join a radical pan-Islamic group committed to driving ethnic Russians out of the region. In an incident arising out of the cost of a basket of strawberries, thousands of Uzbek youths went on a rampage, burning and looting entire Meskhetian settlements, killing more than a hundred Meskhetians, and wounding thousands of others. The ethnic riot and similar, though less serious, forms of discrimination in Tajikistan and Kyrgyzia have only reinforced the desire of the Meskhetians to return to their homeland.

REFERENCES: Alexandre Bennigsen and S. Enders Wimbush, *Muslims of the Soviet Empire: A Guide*, 1986; *Current Digest*, 41 (February 22, 1989), 3–4, (July 5, 1989), 16–19, and 42 (March 28, 1990), 26; Martha Brill Olcott, "The Slide into Disunion," *Current History*, 90 (1991), 338–44; Ann Sheehy and Bohdan Nahaylo, *The Crimean Tatars, Volga Germans and Meskhetians: Soviet Treatment of Some National Minorities*, 1980; Ronald Wixman, *The Peoples of the USSR: An Ethnographic Handbook*, 1984.

MESKHI. The Meskhi are a group of Turks* who went into the ethnogenesis of the Georgians*. During World War II, those Meskhi who were Sunni Muslims were deported to Central Asia, where many of them went into the making of the Meskhetian* group. Those who were Eastern Orthodox in religion were allowed to stay behind in Georgia, however, where they assimilated into the larger Georgian group. See MESKHETIAN, GEORGIAN, and TURK.

REFERENCE: Ronald Wixman, *The Peoples of the USSR: An Ethnographic Handbook*, 1984.

MICHIGIZ. See MICHIKIZ and CHECHEN.

MICHIK. See MICHIKIZ and CHECHEN.

MICHIKIZ. The Michikiz are one of the constituent groups making up the Chechen* people. See CHECHEN.

REFERENCE: Ronald Wixman, *The Peoples of the USSR: An Ethnographic Handbook*, 1984.

MINGRELIANS. The Mingrelians (Megrelians) are the inhabitants of western Georgia who have traditionally dwelt in a region north of the Rioni River along the Black Sea coast to the north of the Adjar Autonomous Republic, to the south of Svanetia and Abkhazia, and to the west of Imeretia and Georgia proper. Mingrelia is a sub-tropical area of the eastern Black Sea littoral, originally consisting of marshes, forests, and wooded foothills, but today mostly under cultivation, producing citrus fruits, grapes, tobacco, and tea. Problems from malarial swamps affected the development of the area until the late nineteenth and twentieth centuries. The inhabited regions of Mingrelia range from sea level to 500 meters above it. Historical Mingrelia can be considered to consist of the contemporary governing districts of Zugdidi and Senaki.

The Mingrelians have been considered part of the Georgian nation since 1930 and have many cultural affinities with the Georgians.* The most important factors distinguishing the Mingrelians from the other components of the Georgian nation have been their different languages as well as local historical developments.

According to linguistic authorities, the Mingrelian language is part of a separate branch of the southern Caucasian group of the Ibero-Caucasian family. It is also spoken by the Muslim Laz* (who live in the extreme southwestern territory of the Adjar Autonomous Republic and the Trabzon region of the Turkish Republic). The Mingrelian language consists of two dialects: Samuzakan*-Zugdid in the west and Senaki in the east. Mingrelian has not developed into a literary language, so Georgian is used as the official language in education, government, business, and the media.

Together with Svanetia, Abkhazia, and Guria, Mingrelia was part of the legendary Kingdom of Colchis, which became a tributary state of Persia between the sixth and fourth centuries B.C. Colchis later had intermittent periods of independence and autonomy under Hellenistic kingdoms like that of Mithradates. In 64 B.C., the Romans made client kingdoms out of Colchis and Iberia, the eastern Georgian kingdom that consisted of Kartvelia, Imeretia and Kakhetia. By 64 A.D., Colchis, including Mingrelia, had become a Roman province, while control over the Iberian kingdom was contested by Rome and the Parthians. In late antiquity, the whole Transcaucasus region became an area of rivalry between the Roman Empire (later Byzantium) and the revived Persian* Empire of the Sassanids, with both empires attempting to maintain native surrogate states. From the fourth to the sixth centuries A.D., Mingrelia vacillated between being a tributary principality under the Byzantine client kingdom of Lazica (west Georgia) and the Sassanid client kingdom of Kartli (east Georgia). The rise of Islam in the seventh century, the subsequent destruction of Sassanid Persia, and the weakening of Byzantium led to the formation of an independent kingdom known as Abazgia or Abkhazia, of which Mingrelia was a part.

Later, Mingrelia was included in the united Georgian kingdom of the Bagratids, from the tenth to the thirteenth century. The turmoil caused by the Mongol* invasions of the thirteenth century, however, as well as the Timurid invasions of the late fourteenth and early fifteenth centuries and the rise of Ottoman and

Safavid power in the sixteenth century, shattered the delicate feudal unity of the Georgian state. Georgia became divided into feudal kingdoms and principalities. One of these was Mingrelia, which was ruled by a dynasty known as the Dadiani. Between the sixteenth and the eighteenth centuries, Mingrelia was a vassal principality under Ottoman suzerainty and had to pay both monetary and human tribute (slaves) to the sultan. Unlike the Lazes, the Adjars*, and the Abkhazians*, the Mingrelians did not undergo Islamization during this period, perhaps because of the strong organizational presence of the Eastern Orthodox church in the area. The Mingrelians had adopted Byzantine Christianity as early as the fourth century and a strong episcopal see existed in Zugdidi. The bishops of Zugdidi maintained ties with other Orthodox prelates at Kutaisi (Imeretia) and further east.

As early as 1638, the Dadiani princes of Mingrelia had sworn feudal allegiance to the Russian tsar. In reality, this was a symbolic gesture, made to offset the feudal authority of the Bagratid king of Imeretia to the east. Both Imeretia and Mingrelia were tributary states under the Ottomans until the nineteenth century. The expansion of Russia into the Transcaucasus in the eighteenth and early nineteenth century led to the establishment of a Russian* protectorate over the principality of Mingrelia in 1803, although the Dadiani were allowed to rule Mingrelia under Russian authority until 1867. During the Crimean War (1854–1856), Mingrelia was invaded by Ottoman forces, and Mingrelians joined Russians to repel this incursion. The hostilities caused a great deal of economic hardship on the Mingrelian population, especially on the enserfed peasantry. After the war, attempts by the Mingrelian gentry to return the peasantry to their prewar status led to an uprising in 1857. The Russian authorities from Imeretia intervened and imposed a commission to oversee the governing of the principality for the minor prince Nicholas Dadiani. When Prince Nicholas reached the age to rule on his own in 1867, the Russian government pressured him to pass his sovereignty over to the tsar in exchange for estates in Russia. Mingrelia thus became part of the Russian Empire. In the same year of 1867, the Russian government abolished serfdom and emancipated the peasantry of Mingrelia.

The period of Russian imperial rule saw the first steps toward the modernization of Mingrelia, with the integration of the area's economy into the rest of Georgia and the Russian Empire. Agricultural produce, wine, tobacco, tea, and silk from Mingrelia began to be sold in a wider market, and industrial goods and services were introduced. In addition, the draining of malarial swamps and the reclamation of land began to bring about an increase in the area's population, both from natural growth and from immigration. The population in Mingrelia had grown to about 300,000 by 1897. Nonetheless, the social and economic problems of Mingrelia, in its transition from a serf-based agricultural economy to a modern land-tenure system and market economy, led to revolutionary activity in the region. Integration with the Russian Empire brought not only official tsarist ideology but also the revolutionary ideology of the radical intelligentsia, especially the *narodniks* or populists. Georgian populists viewed Mingrelia as having ideal conditions for agrarian revolution. A populist conspiracy in Mingrelia in

1876 ended in failure, but it portended future events in 1905. During the revolutionary disturbances that racked all of Georgia that year, many Mingrelians participated in national and social revolutionary movements.

World War I, the Russian Revolution, and the subsequent civil war brought tremendous changes to Mingrelia, as to all of the Caucasus region. Politically, Mingrelia successively became part of the independent Republic of Georgia between 1918 and 1921, the Transcaucasian Federated Soviet Socialist Republic between 1922 and 1936, and the Georgian Soviet Socialist Republic from 1936 until 1991. Socially and economically, Mingrelia went through the same traumatic developments that other parts of Georgia endured under Soviet rule. Forced collectivization and industrialization were initiated under Josef Stalin and carried out by the local Communist leader Lavrenty Beria, who himself was of Mingrelian origin and had been born in Abkhazia. Armed force and widespread arrests had to be used to enforce collectivization in Mingrelia between 1930 and 1932.

As of 1930, Mingrelians were no longer counted as a separate ethnic or linguistic group by Soviet authorities. The last Soviet census to count them as a separate people was that of 1926. In that census, 243,999 people declared themselves to be Mingrelian, while 284,834 stated that Mingrelian was their mother tongue. Mingrelian does not exist as a written or official language in Georgia, so, by 1970, over 99 percent of all Georgians (including "former Mingrelians") declared Georgian to be their native language. The homogenization of Mingrelians and Svanetians* into the Georgian nationality was a process that was helped along by Soviet policies.

Political repression through purges of the native party apparatus and the use of police terror were hallmarks of the regime of Beria in Georgia in general and in Mingrelia in particular; he personally supervised purges throughout Georgia. Mingrelia was implicated in one of the last purges of the Stalin era. In 1951, Stalin claimed that a Georgian nationalist movement that was plotting to wrest Georgia from the Soviet Union with the aid of western powers had been discovered in Mingrelia. Beria, by then the head of the whole Soviet secret police, carried out mass arrests, liquidating thousands of Mingrelians and other Georgians in 1951 and 1952.

The socialist economic policy in the postwar Stalin years emphasized the agricultural development of the lowlands of Mingrelia. From the end of World War II to the death of Stalin, thousands of immigrants from highland areas of Georgia, such as Svanetia, were obliged to resettle in the lowlands of Mingrelia. It is open to speculation whether this forced postwar resettlement had political as well as economic motivations. Since 1953, in-migration to Mingrelia has continued, so that today the proportion of Mingrelians within the territory of historical Mingrelia is difficult to access.

The economic modernization of Mingrelia continued in the Khrushchev and Brezhnev eras with the construction of food-processing and other industrial facilities, the introduction of new methods for agriculture, and the establishment of tourism. Tied in with this economic modernization have been attempts to modernize and secularize the Mingrelians through education, the media, and travel. These developments have no doubt hastened the cultural assimilation of Mingrelians with the rest of Georgia, especially through the use of Georgian as the official and literary language. It is unclear whether the dissolution of the Soviet Union and the establishment of an independent Georgian Republic will alter this process of assimilation, but it will certainly not result in the types of ethnic problems that have been seen in Abkhazia and Ossetia. Although the Mingrelians are different from the other Georgians in their spoken language, their religious/cultural affinities and their use of Georgian as a literary language will probably continue to affiliate them with the Georgian nation.

REFERENCES: On the Mingrelians within Georgian history, see W.E.D. Allen, *A History of the Georgian People from the Beginning Down to the Russian Conquest in the Nineteenth Century*, 1936; K. A. Borozdin, *Zakavkazskiia vospominaniia: Mingrelia i Svanetia s 1851 po 1861 god*, 1885; D. M. Lang, *A Modern History of Soviet Georgia*, 1962; D. M. Lang, *The Georgians*, 1966; Ronald Suny, *The Making of the Georgian Nation*, 1988; Cyril Toumanoff, "Christian Caucasia between Byzantium and Iran: New Light from Old Sources," *Traditio*, 10 (1954); Cyril Toumanoff, "Introduction to Christian Caucasian History," *Traditio*, 15 (1959) and 17 (1961).

Nicholas C. J. Pappas

MINGRELO-CHAN. See MINGRELIAN and GEORGIAN.

MINGRELO-LAZ. See MINGRELIAN and GEORGIAN.

MINGRELO-ZAN. See MINGRELIAN and GEORGIAN.

MINKIZ. See MICHIKIZ and CHECHEN.

MINUSA. See KHAKASS.

MINUSA TATAR. See MINUSINSK TATAR and KHAKASS.

MINUSIN. See MINUSINSK TATAR and KHAKASS.

MINUSINSK. See MINUSINSK TATAR and KHAKASS.

MINUSINSK TATAR. The Minusinsk Tatars are part of the larger collection of Siberian Tatars* who originated with the Mongol* invasion of Russia in the thirteenth century. The term "Minusinsk Tatar" is more a reflection of their location in the town of Minusinsk at the confluence of the Abakan and Yenesei rivers in southern Siberia than of any distinct identity as a special group of Tatars*. They were Sunni Muslims. Contact with Russians beginning in the late 1500s led to the Tatars' conversion to Eastern Orthodox Christianity, although the conversion was superficial at best. Strong elements of shamanistic animism survived among them. After the 1930s, most of the Minusinsk Tatars found themselves living and laboring on collective farms. Since World War II, Russian ethnographers have classified them with the Khakass*. See KHAKASS and TATARS.

REFERENCE: Shirin Akiner, *Islamic Peoples of the Soviet Union*, 1983.

MISHAR. The Mishars are Mordvinians* who fell under Volga Tatar* influence, adopted the Tatar* language, converted to the Sunni Muslim religion, and intermingled and intermarried with the Finnic-Ugrian* Mordvinians. Their conversion came at the time of the Bulgarian* kingdom and Golden Horde, but they managed to retain a Finnic ethnic identity. They are distinguished from the Volga Tatars by the fact that the vast majority of the Mishar are peasant farmers. They have a strong, distinct sense of ethnic identity and usually live in purely Mishar villages. Russians* refer to them as Mishari. Today those people who identify themselves as Mishars live primarily in the Tatar Autonomous Republic, the Chuvash Autonomous Republic, the Mordvinian Autonomous Republic, the Bashkir Autonomous Republic, and Russia. See MORDVINIAN, MESHCHERA, and MESHCHERYAK.

REFERENCE: Alexandre Bennigsen and S. Enders Wimbush, *Muslims of the Soviet Empire: A Guide*, 1986.

MISHARI. See MISHAR.

MISHER. See MISHAR.

MIZHOLZHEGI. See CHECHEN.

MOHEV. See MOKHEV or GEORGIAN.

MOKHEV. The Mokhev are today classified as a subgroup of the Georgian* nation. See GEORGIAN.

REFERENCE: Ronald Wixman, *The Peoples of the USSR: An Ethnographic Handbook*, 1984.

MOKHEVI. See MOKHEV and GEORGIAN.

MOKSHA. The Moksha constitute one of the two main Mordvinian groups. Theirs is a distinct language. Although the Moksha are scattered throughout the Middle Volga River valley, they tend to be concentrated in the Penza and Orenburg oblasts of the Mordvinian Autonomous Republic. See MORDVINIAN.

REFERENCE: Ronald Wixman, *The Peoples of the USSR: An Ethnographic Handbook*, 1984.

MOKSHA MORDOVIAN. See MOKSHA and MORDVINIAN.

MOKSHA MORDVA. See MOKSHA and MORDVINIAN.

MOKSHA MORDVIN. See MOKSHA and MORDVINIAN.

MOKSHA MORDVINIAN. See MOKSHA and MORDVINIAN.

MOLDOVAN. The terms ''Moldavians'' or ''Moldovans'' refer to a people of Romanian* language and origin who inhabit the historical region northeast of the Carpathians and southwest of the Pruth River in the Republic of Romania and the territory of the adjacent Moldovan Republic between the Pruth and Dniester rivers. From the fourteenth to the nineteenth centuries, the people of these two regions were united in a single principality, Moldova, under Ottoman suzerainty. Since 1812, the territory between the Pruth and Dniester, often referred to as Bessarabia, has come under intermittent Russian*, Romanian, and Soviet rule. The territory to the southwest remained the Principality of Moldova, which in 1858 combined with Wallachia into the united principalities of Moldova and Wallachia. In 1862, these became known as the Principality of Romania, attaining independence and the status of a kingdom in 1878. In the 180 years since the first Russian annexation of Bessarabia, most of the territory of Moldova between the Pruth and the Danube rivers has been under Russian or Soviet administration three times, for a total of 132 years. It was a part of Romania twice, for a total of 57 years, and has been an independent republic twice, once for two months in 1918, and since August 1991. The modern Republic of Moldova includes most of the traditional territory of Bessarabia, except for the Bugeac coastal region, which has been part of the Ukraine since 1944. Moldova also includes a strip of territory north of the Dniester river, known as the Trans-Dniester region.

Within the Commonwealth of Independent States (CIS), Moldovans number 3,355,240 persons, according to the Soviet census of 1989. About 80 percent of this number, or 2.7 million, reside in the Moldovan Republic proper and constitute about 65 percent of its population. Ukrainians* and Russians make up the next largest ethnic groups there, comprising about 14 percent and 12 percent of the population, respectively; the East Slavic minorities are concentrated in towns and in the Trans-Dniester region. The fourth largest ethnic group (5 percent) are the Gagauz*—Orthodox Christian Turks.* There are also Bulgarians*, Jews*, and others. The bulk of Moldovans outside of the Republic of Moldova (13 percent, or about 380,000) reside in the Ukrainian Republic, especially in the territories adjacent to Moldova and in the former Bukovina. The other 7 percent live in other republics. One problem in estimating the population is that included in Soviet census records is a registered Romanian nationality with a population of 145,918 in 1989. These were probably ethnic Romanians* who could prove that they were not from the territory of the Moldavian Soviet Socialist Republic (SSR). This problem is a result of the Soviet policy of attempting to establish a Moldavian nationality separate from the Romanian one.

The Moldovans of Russia and the Soviet Union are so closely related to the Romanians in language, ethnicity, and historical development, however, that they can be considered one and the same people. Indeed, one of the keystones of the recent Moldavian national movement has been the desire for the unification of Moldova with Romania. The language of the Moldovans, like that of the Romanians, makes up the easternmost branch of the Romance language group. Like French, Italian, Spanish, Portuguese, and Romanche, it evolved from vulgar Latin as spoken in the later years of the Roman Empire and in early medieval times. While both Moldovan and Romanian have many Slavic, Greek*, and Turkish loan words, the core of the languages indicates a Latin origin. Any divergent development of the Romanian and Moldovan languages has to do mostly with the different language policies of the Soviet and Romanian governments and perhaps with the proximity of the Moldovans to Ukrainian*, Russian, and Bulgarian* speakers. Moldovan diverges from Romanian only in a dialectical sense, due to its greater number of Slavic loan words, some introduced under Russian and Soviet rule. Still, many of these loan words have long existed in Romanian dialects without becoming part of the Romanian literary language, while they have been kept or reintroduced into the Moldovan literary language under the Soviets. Up until recently, the most distinct difference between the Romanian and Moldovan languages has been their alphabets. The principalities of Moldavia and Wallachia used Old Church Slavonic, Greek, and Old Romanian as their official languages until the early nineteenth century. Old Romanian used a modified Cyrillic script. In the early nineteenth century, a modified Latin alphabet was adopted by Romanians in Transylvania, in the autonomous principalities of Moldavia and Wallachia, and in Bessarabia. This became the standard alphabet for speakers of Romanian in the Russian and Hapsburg Empires, as well as those in the emerging Romanian state. Under the Soviets, however, Romanian speakers in Moldova were forced to revert to a Cyrillic script.

Two main opposing views exist regarding the ethnogenesis of the Romanian and Moldovan people. Romanian national historians assert that the origins of their people can be found in the amalgamation of the Dacian people with Roman colonists during the existence of the Roman province of Dacia between 106 and 238 A.D. According to this Romanian national view, the Dacians, a Thraco-Illyrian people who inhabited the area of present-day Romania in ancient times, were subdued by the Romans under the Emperor Trajan. The Romans then transformed the former Dacian kingdom into the Roman province of Dacia. During the 130-odd years of Roman rule, a process of latinization occurred in Dacia, which was very similar to what happened in Gaul and the Iberian peninsula under Roman rule. The Romanian national historiography also asserts that during the era of migrations, when Danubian lands were occupied by Goths, Huns, Avars*, Bulgars, Slavs, Pechenegs, Uzes, and others, the Romanian people survived as a separate entity by retreating into the vastness of the Carpathian mountains until the thirteenth century. At that point, they descended and re-entered history as the Wallachians and Moldovans.

The main opposing view of Romanian ethnogenesis, held by some Hungarian and Western scholars, is that the Romanians are descended from the romanized population of the Balkan Peninsula *south* of the Danube, which survived the era of migrations by retreating to the Pindus, Rhodope, Dinaric, and Balkan mountains. According to this view, the latinized population of the Balkans known as Vlachs (*Vlachoi* or *Koutsovlachoi* in Greek, *Eflak* in Turkish, *Vlasi* in Slavic, and *Aromuni* in Vlach) participated in the forming of the Second Bulgarian Empire in the late twelfth and early thirteenth centuries and then dispersed. The bulk of the Balkan Vlachs migrated north of the Danube and settled in present-day Romanian lands, including Bessarabia, in the thirteenth century. Pockets of these Vlachs remained in the Balkans and today constitute the Aromuni or Vlach minorities in Albania, Bulgaria, Greece, and Macedonia.

The development of these conflicting views of Romanian origins have much to do with the development of modern Romanian nationalism and conflicting ethnic claims between Romanians and Hungarians in Transylvania. Due to the paucity of evidence, neither of these opposing views can be conclusively proved or discounted. Soviet Moldovan historians, in contrast, have attempted to fabricate a separate ethnogenesis for the Moldovans by over-emphasizing the Slavic component in the development of the Moldovan nation from earliest times to the present. They have, in other words, attempted to transform a regional history into a national history.

The territory of the present Republic of Moldova was the northeastern part of the principality of Moldavia from the fourteenth century to the early nineteenth century. The principality of Moldavia was organized by Prince Bogdan after the settlement of the region between the Carpathians and the Dniester River by Romanian speakers (from either Transylvania or the Balkans, depending on the historical point of view). The region between the Pruth and the Dniester rivers was absorbed by the Moldovan principality after intermittent conflicts with Tatar* and other steppe tribes. Part of that region—the coastal area between the Danube and the Dniester—was under the authority of a princely dynasty from Muntenia known as the Basarabs, whose progenitor was the founder of Wallachia. The Moldovan princes were able to acquire the coastal region from the Basarabs in the 1400s.

The Moldovan principality maintained a precarious independence in the fifteenth and sixteenth centuries, struggling to meet threats from the north and west by the Hungarians and the Poles*, from the northeast by the Crimean Tatars*, and from the south by the Ottoman Turks. Moldova reached its highest position as a state under Stephen the Great (Stefan Viatul) in the second half of the fifteenth century and the first years of the sixteenth. Continuing Turkish incursions into the southern territories of Moldova and occupation of its southern territories under Sultan Selim the Grim forced Stephen's son and successor, Bogdan II, to submit to the Ottoman overlordship and become a vassal principality. Subsequently, the principality of Wallachia also entered into tributary relations with the Ottomans.

The Ottomans had not only forced the Moldovan princes to recognize Ottoman suzerainty by the sixteenth century, but they also annexed the coastal territory between the Danube and Dniester. Later in the century, that region was placed under the authority of the vassal Girei Khan when the Crimean Tatar Khanate likewise became a vassal of the Ottomans under Suleiman the Magnificent; this area became known as Bujak or Bugeac. The Turks* also called the coastal region Bessarabia, after the Wallachian ruler Basarab and his family who had settled the region. During the sixteenth and seventeenth centuries, Moldova continued under Ottoman rule, either directly (as in the case of the Bugeac region) or under the tributary princes (the inland regions between the Carpathians and the Dniester). In those centuries, both the principalities of Moldova and Wallachia intermittently attempted to throw off Turkish suzerainty by exploiting the wars between the Ottomans and the Hapsburgs, the Poles, and, later, the Russians.

In the late seventeenth and early eighteenth centuries, the Danubian principalities became the focal point of armed conflict and diplomatic rivalry among the Turks, Austrians*, and Russians. Turkish power had begun to retreat from the region as a result of both internal dysfunctions within the Ottoman state and defeats at the hands of the Hapsburgs. By 1699, the principality of Transylvania, with its mixed Romanian, Hungarian, and German* population, was annexed by the Hapsburgs in the Treaty of Karlowitz. Under Peter I (the Great), Russia began its expansion into the Black Sea littoral with a successful expedition against the Turkish fortress town of Azov in 1695–1696. Later, in the wake of his victory over the Swedes at Poltava in 1709, Peter made plans for a campaign against the Turks in southern Ukraine and the principalities. He negotiated with the princes of Moldova and Wallachia for Romanian support, in return for liberation from their increasingly onerous tributary status under the Ottomans. He was successful in concluding an agreement with the Prince of Moldova, Dmitrie Cantemir, whereby Moldova would become an independent principality under the protection of Russia and Cantemir would rule as a hereditary prince with authority over the restive Moldovan nobility. But Peter's campaign in Moldova was far from a success. The Prince of Wallachia, Constantine Brincoveanu, did not support the operation, and the Russian-Moldovan force was defeated by the Turks at the Pruth River. Peter was able to salvage his army only by bribing the Ottoman Grand Vizier to allow a withdrawal of the Russian army from the Pruth.

Cantemir withdrew with the Russians, received an estate as a pension, and spent his retirement writing a history of the Ottoman Empire, among other works. Following the short Russo-Turkish War, the Ottomans initiated a policy of replacing native princes with Phanariotes. The Phanariotes were prominent

Greeks* in Constantinople who had traditionally held administrative positions in the Greek Orthodox patriarchate in the Lighthouse (*fener* or *phanar*) district of the Ottoman capital. The Ottoman government believed that these bureaucrats, with family and other connections in Constantinople, would be more reliable than native princes.

Because the principalities of Moldova and Wallachia were located along the direct invasion route to the Ottoman capital, they became areas of warfare and occupation in subsequent Russo-Turkish wars. Russian forces again occupied most of the principality of Moldova, including the capital of Iasi, in the Russo-Turkish War of 1737–1738. A lack of a coordinated effort between Russian and Austrian forces, however, as well as various military reverses, necessitated the ultimate withdrawal of the Russian army under General Münnich. In the Russo-Turkish War of 1769–1774, Russian forces under General Rumiantsev occupied both principalities. Russian diplomats negotiated the treaty of Kuçuk Kainarca, which allowed Russia to intervene diplomatically on behalf of the principalities in Constantinople and established Russian consular representation in Iasi and Bucarest. In the interlude between the first (1769–1774) and second (1787–1791) Russo-Turkish wars under Catherine II, the empress corresponded with the Austrian Emperor Joseph about their plans to partition the Ottoman Empire. Part of that project included the formation of the Russian-dominated buffer state to be known as the Kingdom of Dacia in place of the Danubian principalities.

In the Russo-Turkish War of 1787–1791, the Russians scored significant victories against the Ottomans in Moldova and again occupied Iasi. Nonetheless, the withdrawal of Austria from an allied effort at Sistovo in mid–1791, a new war with Sweden, and the hostile neutrality of Britain and France forced the Russians to conclude a less ambitious peace treaty at Iasi. Still, Russia annexed the territory between the Bug and Dniester Rivers, established new naval and trade center at Odessa, and became a powerful new neighbor of Moldova.

In the interim between Peter I's abortive efforts in Moldova and the later Russian drives to the Dniester, Russia's policies in the newly captured areas of southern Ukraine included the settlement of Balkan and other European immigrants in military installations and colonies. The settlers included Germans*, Jews*, Greeks,* Serbs*, and Bulgarians; Moldovans and Wallachians also immigrated and settled in areas of what was then known as New Russia. In the 1740s, Russian authorities organized special regiments in the new regions named after Balkan territories in order to attract military settlers. One of these units was the Moldavian Hussar Regiment. The ethnic composition of this and the other Balkan units (Serbian, Bulgarian, Macedonian) was mixed, despite their name. Nevertheless, between 1763 and 1782, upwards of 23,000 Moldovans settled in New Russia, chiefly in Yelizavetgrad province, but also in the Crimea. When Russia's border reached the Dniester, Moldovan immigration to Russian territory continued and intensified. In the Ochakov district, Moldovans made up 49 percent of the total population of 23,743. By 1799, Moldovans constituted 39 percent of a population of 46,700 in the same district.

Finally, in the Russo-Turkish war of 1806–1812, Russian forces again occupied the Pruth-Dniester region of Moldova. By the Treaty of Bucharest in 1812, they annexed the territory and named it Bessarabia, using the old Turkish name for the coastal reaches as the nomenclature for the whole territory. From then until the twentieth century, the area was known in European diplomatic parlance as the province of Bessarabia. The Russians initially gave Bessarabia the status of an autonomous province. Its autonomy was revoked under Nicholas I in 1829, however, because it had been an area of intrigue during the Greek Revolution of 1821 and the Decembrist uprising of 1825. Russian and Soviet scholars have looked upon the annexation of Bessarabia as a progressive move in Moldova's history, in that it "led to accelerated development in farming, handicrafts, and trade." By contrast, Romanian national scholars have taken a much dimmer view of the Russian incorporation of Moldova; as one writer asserted: "The eagle of the Urals had sunk its talons deep in her bleeding body and had ravished from her five great fortresses, 17 cities, and 685 villages, with a population of about half a million souls."

Russian rule of a portion of Bessarabia was interrupted by the Crimean War. At the Peace of Paris, Russia, as the defeated power in 1856, had to cede southern Bessarabia along the Danube and Black Sea to the Principality of Moldova. This portion remained with Moldova when it united with Wallachia to become the United Principalities (later Romania). The status of this area changed again during the Eastern Crisis of 1875–1878. According to the Treaty of Berlin, which ended the crisis, Romania was given full independence and the status of a kingdom but was forced to cede southern Bessarabia to Russia in return for the less desirable province of Dobrudja in the southern bend of the Danube near the Black Sea.

Russian rule of Bessarabia thus continued. According to Romanian nationalist historians, the Russian administration was deleterious to Moldovans, in that it encouraged immigration by Ukrainians, Russians, Bulgarians, Gagauzi, Germans, and Ashkenazi Jews, and thereby weakened the native Moldovan element in the population. According to one Romanian source, the Moldovan population of Bessarabia declined from 86.7 percent of the total population in 1817 to 47.6 percent in 1897. These historians also assert that Russian rule did not result in the progressive social and economic development claimed by Russian and Soviet historians, but rather the opposite. Bessarabia continued to be one of the most backward provinces of the Russian empire, with a population that had the highest mortality rate in Europe—twice that of the Russian average. In addition, ethnic tensions arose in the province in the late nineteenth and early twentieth centuries, as evidenced by the notorious pogroms at Kishinev (Chisinau).

The period of Russian imperial administration of Bessarabia ended during World War I with the collapse of the Russian war effort and the revolutions of February and October 1917. After the abdication of Nicholas II and the formation of the provisional government, a Moldovan National Committee was organized in Kishinev in April 1917, which called for autonomy, land reform, and the use of the Romanian language for the province of Bessarabia within the projected new Russian state. The overthrow of the provisional government in October 1917 by the Bolsheviks brought about the formation of a provisional government in Kishinev, called the State Council (*Sfatul Tarii*). This Moldovan national council of soldiers, workers, and peasants, modeled after the soviets in Russia and the rada in Ukraine, was dominated by nationalist Moldovans, rather than Bolsheviks, and it declared the formation of an autonomous republic within a federation of Russian republics on December 2, 1917. A month later, Bolsheviks were able to occupy Kishinev, the capital, but were forced out two weeks later. The State Council then declared Bessarabia the independent Republic of Moldova on January 24, 1918.

Facing increased civil strife and fearing a return of the Bolsheviks or encroachments by Ukrainian nationalists, the State Council resorted to a call for military support from Romania, and, on March 27, 1918, the state council voted for a provisional unification with Romania. On December 9, 1918, the State Council voted for unconditional union, which recognized the full sovereignty of the Romanian monarchy; the former Austrian province of Bukovina entered into union with Romania as well. In 1919, the newly united Romanian province of Bessarabia continued to be threatened by the burgeoning power of the Bolshevik Red Army, which was in the process of eliminating its domestic enemies. The Dniester river line was defended by Moldovan, Transylvanian, and Bukovinian volunteers who had served in the Russian Imperial Army, as well as by newly formed Polish forces, regular Romanian army units, and a Greek expeditionary corps recently withdrawn from Odessa.

The Allied powers recognized the Romanian acquisition of Bessarabia and Bukovina at the Paris Peace Conference on March 9, 1920, establishing the Dniester as the Romanian frontier with whatever government would be established in that part of the former Russian Empire in the wake of the Russian civil war. The Bessarabian-Romanian union was formally sanctioned by the Treaty of Paris on October 28 of the same year. The union and the Romanian annexation of Bessarabia were not recognized by the Bolshevik government in Russia, however, which had emerged victorious in the civil war by 1921.

Two years after the establishment of the Ukrainian Soviet Socialist Republic within the new Union of Soviet Socialist Republics (USSR, or Soviet Union), a Moldovan Autonomous Soviet Socialist Republic (ASSR) was formed along the Soviet side of the Dniester in October 1924. This republic was organized to conduct a propaganda campaign against Romanian possession of the former Bessarabia and to develop an effective Romanian Communist cadre. The Soviet regime initially recognized no difference between Moldovans and Romanians; the first publications within the autonomous republic were printed in Romanian with the Latin script, and the first Soviet census in 1926 registered Moldovans as Romanians. Later documentation of the 1926 census "adjusted" the terminology to describe the overwhelming majority of Romanians in the census as Moldavians. According to the 1926 census, there were 283,556 Romanians in the Soviet Union (278,905 Moldavians and 4,651 Romanians in later versions). Of these, only 60 percent of Romanian speakers in the Soviet Union resided in the Moldovan ASSR. The republic consisted of over 8,000 square kilometers, with a capital at Tiraspol; out of the population of 568,984, only 172,419 or 30.3 percent were Romanians or Moldovans. The largest ethnic group in the republic were Ukrainians, who comprised 48.8 percent (277,515) of the population. Russians, Jews, Germans, Bulgarians, and Poles made up the remaining 20 percent of the autonomous republic's inhabitants. Of the Romanian/Moldovan population in the Moldovan ASSR, only 6,260, or 3.5 percent, were urban dwellers, so that very few of them participated in the governing of their own republic. The autonomous republic was run mostly by Russian and Ukrainian party officials in a heavy-handed and brutal manner, especially in the 1930s. In the late 1920s, the Cyrillic alphabet was introduced as the official script of the "native" language of the Moldovan ASSR.

With the coming of the Second World War, the international situation created conditions for the Soviet annexation of Romanian Bessarabia and its incorporation into a larger Moldovan Soviet Socialist Republic. The Ribbentrop-Molotov Agreement (Non-Aggression Pact) of August 1939 established spheres of influence in Eastern Europe. Nazi Germany recognized Romanian Bessarabia as being within the Soviet Union's sphere of influence. The Soviet Union revived its claim to Bessarabia, in spite of the fact that it had renounced such claims upon the establishment of diplomatic relations between the Soviet Union and Romania in 1934. Romania rebuffed the Soviet claims until the fall of France in June 1940. The Soviet Union then demanded that Romania cede Bessarabia and northern Bukovina. Without foreign support, Romania had to accept the annexation and allowed Soviet forces to enter Bessarabia. By August 1940, most of Bessarabia had been amalgamated with a small part of the Moldovan ASSR and formed into Moldavian Soviet Socialist Republic. The Ukrainian SSR, which lost a bit of territory from its former autonomous republic, received the coastal region of Bugeac (Ismail and Cetata Alba), as well as the Khotin district, in exchange. In the same month, the Vienna awards had forced Romania to cede northern Transylvania to Hungary and Dobrudja to Bulgaria. By October of 1940, after some internal problems, Romania joined the Axis in order to retake Bessarabia and Bukovina.

During their first annexation of Bessarabia in 1940–1941, the Soviets began a rapid "sovietization" of the new Moldovan SSR. They sent 13,000 specialists and party activists from Russia, Ukraine, and Belarus to incorporate Bessarabia into the Soviet system. Most industrial and commercial enterprises were socialized, a significant portion of the land was confiscated and redistributed in preparation for the collectivization of agriculture, and over 100,000 Moldovans were relocated to other Soviet republics. With the Axis invasion in 1941, some 300,000 inhabitants of former Bessarabia and vast quantities of capital goods and livestock were "evacuated" to republics away from the border. Throughout the eleven-month period of Soviet rule, upwards of 150,000 inhabitants of Bessarabia and Bukovina were deported to Siberia and Central Asia, and thousands were summarily executed. Romanian occupation authorities in 1942 and 1943 reported discovering the mass graves of thousands of executed individuals.

In June 1941, Romanian forces joined in the Axis invasion of the Soviet Union and, by 1942, Romania had reclaimed Bessarabia and Bukovina and was administering the region between the Dniester and the Bug rivers, including Odessa, which was called the Transnistria. By the summer of 1944, the fortunes of war had reversed. The Axis war effort on the eastern front had collapsed, and Soviet forces had occupied not only Bessarabia, but also all of Romania. The new National Front government of Romania cooperated with the Soviet forces in operations against the Germans, but was forced to recognize Soviet reannexation of Bessarabia. The Paris Peace Treaty between the Soviet Union and the Communist-dominated Romanian government restored northern Transylvania to Romania but transferred Bessarabia and Bukovina to the Soviets and southern Dobrudja to the Bulgarians.

The return of Soviet administration to Bessarabia brought about a revival of the Moldavian SSR with its 1940–1941 boundaries. The process of sovietization was renewed. Those who had cooperated with the Romanian authorities in 1941–1944 were eliminated, and a greater effort was made to eliminate the republic's linguistic, ethnic, and cultural affinities to Romania. It can be said that this policy was pursued because, and not in spite of, the fact that Romania proper had become a people's republic by 1948. The Soviets could no longer use political and ideological differences to keep Moldova separate from Romania, so they had to do more and sever any ethnic, linguistic, and cultural ties between Moldova and Romania.

The Cyrillic script was imposed in all Moldovan schools, government organs, businesses, publications, and media, while many Russian loan words were introduced into the Moldovan vocabulary. In addition, Old Church Slavonic loan words were also reintroduced while Romance neologisms and adoptions from French and other Romance languages were eliminated. These "reforms" were justified as efforts to rid the language of "national-bourgois" influence. Theories were propounded that claimed that the Moldovan language was of Slavic or composite Slavic-Latin origin. Nonetheless, since the death of Josef Stalin, even some Soviet scholars had to concede that Romanian and Moldovan are basically the same language, which had been artificially altered for political considerations.

Moldovan history was likewise rewritten to show that the Moldovans' ties to the rest of Romania were non-existent or tenuous, while those with Ukraine and Russia were frequent and close. Folk culture—art, music, and dance—was cleansed of any "national deviation," bowdlerized, and controlled through official clubs, organizations, troupes, and ensembles. As throughout the Soviet Union, party and state organs attempted to discourage religious activities among the Moldovans. When this could not be done, efforts were made to amalgamate the Moldovans, who are overwhelmingly Eastern Orthodox, with the Russian

Orthodox Church organization, to which all Orthodox believers (Russians, Ukrainians, Gagauzi, Bulgarians) in the republic belonged.

Questions about the ethnicity of the Moldovans and the status of Moldova vis-à-vis the Soviet Union and Romania became international issues in the late 1950s and early 1960s. De-Stalinization in the People's Republic of Romania, following the death of Stalin, did not take the forms of liberalization and internal reforms that it did in other bloc countries; rather it took the form of a revival of nationalism. Romanian opposition to Nikita Khrushchev's call to make Romania an agricultural component in an integrated Communist economic union, known as the Council of Mutual Economic Assistance (CMEA or COMECON), led to some tensions between the Soviet Union and Romania. The Romanian Communist Party continued the Stalinist policy of autarchic economic development. During the early 1960s, Russian place names for Romanian towns were dropped, the teaching of Russian in Romanian schools was halted, and certain Soviet-Romanian cultural institutions were dissolved. The Sino-Soviet split afforded the Romanian Communists a chance to assert some limited self-initiative in foreign relations with the West, but they maintained a rigid, unreformed, one-party system at home. It was during this period that the question of the Moldovans and Moldova was secretly debated among the party leaders of the Soviet Union, China, and Romania, as indicated by the reputed memoirs of Khrushchev.

The fall of Khrushchev in 1964 and the death of Romanian leader Gheorghe Gheorghiu-Dej in 1965 led to further apparent strains between the Soviet Union and Romania over COMECON, the Warsaw Pact, relations with the West, *and* the issue of Moldova. Nicolai Ceaucescu, Gheorghiu-Dej's successor, attempted to maintain a vicious totalitarian regime and create a cult of personality around himself by exploiting Romanian nationalist sentiment. On the issue of Moldova, Romanians began to publish works by Karl Marx and Friedrich Engels that substantiated Romanian claims to the area and refuted Soviet ones. Romanian history books began to describe the Republic of Moldova as a historical part of Romania. Nevertheless, the Romanians did not press the issue in inter-party and diplomatic circles, especially after the Warsaw Pact invasion of Czechoslovakia in 1968. During the invasion, Romanian forces did not participate, and Romania initiated mutual defense plans with Marshall Tito's Yugoslavia. Khrushchev's successor, Leonid Brezhnev, had served as party chief of Moldova in 1950–1952 and was adamant about maintaining Soviet Moldova. The Soviets began to respond with their own propaganda campaign. Party leaders and ''official intellectuals'' in Moldova challenged Romanian historical claims to Moldavia and characterized Romanian historiography as having returned to the bourgois-nationalist school of pre-socialist Romania, which was reactionary and anti-Soviet. The progressive aspects of Moldova's incorporation into the Russian Empire and later the Soviet Union were stressed. Attempts were likewise renewed to describe Moldovan as a separate nationality. Correspondingly, any manifestation of Romanian national sentiment among the Moldovans was suppressed.

In the years between Stalin's death in 1953 and Brezhnev's ascendancy in 1964, Moldovans had begun to re-establish some cultural and personal ties with Romania. Soviet authorities allowed the importation of books, periodicals, and motion pictures from Romania, together with some controlled travel and commerce, but this limited intercourse began to get out of hand. Importation of books and magazines from Romania became so widespread that bookstores and libraries maintained special areas for Romanian publications in Latin script. By the early 1960s, there were two to three times as many Moldovans subscribing to Romanian newspapers and periodicals as to Moldovan publications. By the late 1960s, the importation of Romanian publications and films had been severely curtailed, and it was fully done away with by 1970. In addition, cultural exchanges of folkloric and popular entertainers were also halted. The ban on Moldovan-Romanian cultural contacts continued until the era of Mikhail Gorbachev, with the exception of the uncontrolled media of radio and television broadcasts.

While the Soviet Union and Romania renewed their Friendship Treaty in 1970, which pledged recognition of the existing boundaries, clashes on the propaganda front continued. Romanian publications renewed their views on the Romanian character of Soviet Moldova, just as some Soviet works began to claim that *all* of Moldova had wished to be united with Mother Russia in 1812, thus hinting at a threatened Soviet annexation of Moldova to the Pruth. The signing of the Helsinki Accords in 1975, which guaranteed the post–1945 frontiers of European nations, did not settle the issue. Nonetheless, it is evident that, by 1976, the Soviets had pressured the Romanians to ease up on the nationalist assertions. In that year, Ceaucescu claimed that Romania had no territorial ambitions, but did question the validity of Soviet historiography on Moldova and the Moldovans. In the summer of 1976, however, Ceaucescu visited Moldova and studiously evaded the nationality question. Nonetheless, the national issue between Moldova and Romania would continue, especially, in Romania, into the Gorbachev era.

The initiation of *glasnost* and *perestroika* under Gorbachev reopened the nationality issue among Moldovans. Calls for national self-determination, linguistic reform, and unification with Romania became widespread, although the reported depredations of the Ceaucescu regime initially cooled the ardor for unification among many Moldovans. One of the first important Moldovan national issues to be addressed in the Gorbachev era was that of the Moldovan language. Between 1987 and 1989, a tremendous debate arose within the Moldovan party, government, and cultural institutions, as well as among scholars and officials, over the official adoption of Latin script for the Moldovan language. Attempts by the party and state to halt or moderate the movement met with widespread opposition. By early 1989, the presidium of the Moldovan Supreme Soviet issued legislation that replaced Cyrillic characters with the Latin script for the Moldavian language and tacitly recognized "that Moldavian and Romanian are identical."

In the wake of the language issue, an opposition movement known as the Moldovan People's Front or the Popular Front of Moldova became prominent, demonstrating about such issues as the use of Moldovan or Russian as an inter-ethnic language and Soviet military conscription in Moldova. The nationalist activities of Moldovans, together with labor unrest, led to divisions within the Moldovan Communist Party leadership. By mid–1989, Mircea Snegur, a leader of the democratic-nationalist faction of the party, was elected president of the republic. Snegur began to distance himself from the party as disturbances continued to rise in frequency and intensity. In November 1989, riots broke out in Kishinev, which led to further splits within the Communist party leadership. The bloody events of the Romanian revolution of December 1989, which overthrew the Ceaucescu regime, had the effect of intensifying Romanian nationalism within Moldova.

By June 1990, the Supreme Soviet of the Moldavian SSR declared their republic to be a sovereign state and officially changed its name to Moldova. Even after this declaration of sovereignty, difficulties arose over the status of non-Moldovan ethnic groups within the republic, especially of the Ukrainians and Russians in the Trans-Dniester region and the Gagauzi of the southwest. These groups began their own national movements in response to the rise of Moldovan/Romanian nationalism. One of the demands of the growing Popular Front of Moldova movement was eventual reunification with Romania—an idea that became increasingly popular with the downfall of Ceaucescu. Fear of this prospect led to the development of separatist movements among these minorities within the republic.

The government of Snegur increasingly allied itself with the Moldovan Popular Front and asserted its freedom of action with regard to the Soviet Union. Together with the Georgian Republic, Moldova participated in neither the plebiscite on the continuation of the Soviet Union in March 1991 nor in the later negotiations for a new union treaty. During the coup against Gorbachev on August 19, 1991, the Soviet regional military commander had his units surround Kishinev. Snegur responded by calling for mass demonstrations against the coup, in which over 100,000 people in the city participated. Three days after the collapse of the coup in August, Moldova was declared an independent republic.

Almost immediately after the declaration of independence, certain areas broke off from the new republic. The Turkic-speaking, Orthodox Christian Gagauzi, numbering 150,000 and concentrated in settlements in the extreme southwest corner of Moldova along the Pruth, had declared themselves to be a separate republic as early as 1990. The Trans-Dniester area had a population of about 600,000 of mixed ethnic composition, of which less than half were Moldovans. In September 1991, a plebiscite held within that area reputedly showed that a majority opted for independence for Moldova.

The issue of these mini-republics, the ethnic problem in general, and the question of unification with Romania have been the main political dilemmas that have plagued Moldova since independence. Fighting broke out in the Trans-Dniester region when the Moldovan government tried to reassert its authority there. President Snegur and the legislature split over the use of armed forces to re-establish the republic's authority across the Dniester. Fearing reprisals from Ukraine and Russia, Snegur opposed military action and urged negotiation. In October 1991, Igor Smirnov, the head of the Trans-Dniester government, offered to join a federal Moldova, if it would adopt a cantonal system for Trans-Dniester, Gagauzi, and Moldova.

Realizing that one of the main stumbling blocks in re-integrating the breakaway mini-republics with Moldova was the prospect of Moldova's unification with Romania, Snegur declared that he was ultimately in favor of an independent Moldova. Indeed, before the August coup, Snegur stated that "Both we and the government of Romania are committed to the idea of the existence of two states speaking the same language." Such a stance against unification addressed other considerations as well. Snegur and the Moldovan political establishment would lose their power with such a unification. In addition, the prospect of unification with a post-Ceaucescu Romania, which was experiencing even more economic turmoil than Moldova, did not seem appealing to many Moldovans. In backing off from unification, Snegur came to a parting of ways with the Moldovan Popular Front, which firmly supported unification.

In elections held on December 8, 1991, Snegur ran as a candidate for president without a party. The two opposing candidates withdrew from the contest, and Snegur ran unopposed. The Popular Front could not field an eligible candidate in time and called for a boycott of the elections. Nonetheless, Snegur won an overwhelming victory, with over 80 percent of the registered voters participating. Perhaps the Popular Front's boycott failed because of voter fears over union with a politically unstable and economically weak Romania. Another more telling factor may be that the Moldovan political system, while moving toward pluralism, still maintained elements of a one-party system.

The impasse with the breakaway mini-republics was not resolved by the election. Indeed, both Trans-Dniestria and Gagauzia held rival elections on December 1, 1991, and prohibited voting in the republican elections of December 8. The Moldovan legislature then declared on December 11 that the elections in the mini-republics were not legitimate and therefore void. Snegur subsequently attempted to compromise with the Trans-Dniesterian Republic by offering it the status of a free-trade zone in return for its nullifying its declaration of independence. This attempt was to no avail, and both the mini-republics have continued to resist incorporation into the Moldovan Republic. Fighting between the militia of the Trans-Dniesterian Republic, supported by former Soviet troops and Cossack* volunteers, and the newly formed Moldovan army continued intermittently but with more intensity in 1992, especially in the Bendery area. Ethnic strife has also been reported elsewhere in the republic, particularly in and around Gagauzia. There have been attempts to settle the problems through negotiations and mediation by the new Russian and Ukrainian governments. Another problem that may arise in the future is the status of the Bugeac coastal region between the Danube and the Dniester, which has been a part of Ukraine since 1944. Although the Ukrainians and Bulgarians in the region make up a majority of the population, the Moldovan ethnic presence is considerable, and, historically, the area was part of Moldova and the province of Bessarabia.

Moldova under President Snegur joined the Commonwealth of Independent States (CIS) on December 21, 1991, in a shift from its previous policy of remaining aloof from other former Soviet republics. While the Moldovan Republic has decided to form its own armed forces and not establish a CIS military command, the ties with the CIS may be the only avenue that the Republic of Moldova can use to solve the ethnic problem of the mini-republics, short of war.

As in the case of the other newly independent republics of the CIS, Moldova is experiencing difficulty in transforming itself from a command economy to a market economy, from a one-party state to a multi-party state, and from a Soviet republic to an independent state. Since the question of a separate Moldovan ethnicity has been settled in favor of a common national identity with Romanians, the question of unification with Romania, the problem of other ethnic minorities and their enclaves, and the issue of Moldova's future relations with the republics of the CIS, especially Ukraine and Russia, will remain on the horizon in the future.

REFERENCES: On Bessarabia, Moldova, and the Moldovans, consult N. Dima, *Bessarabia and Bukovina: The Soviet-Romanian Territorial Dispute*, 1982; N. Dima, *From Moldavia to Moldova: The Soviet-Romanian Territorial Dispute* (second edition of work above), 1991; N. Dima, "Moldavians or Romanians?" in R. S. West, ed., *The Soviet West*, 1975; S. Fischer-Galati, "Moldavia and the Moldavians," *Attitudes of Major Soviet Nationalities*, 1973; J. Gold, "Bessarabia: The Thorny 'Non-Existent' Problem," *East European Quarterly*, 13 (1979); J. F. Jewsbury, *The Russian Annexation of Bessarabia: 1774–1828*, 1976; L. Kristof, "Russian Colonialism and Bessarabia: A Confrontation of Cultures," *Nationalities Papers*, 2 (1974); G. Nandris, *Bessarabia and Bukovina*, 1968; "Moldavia: Dealing with the Language Issue," *Current Digest of the Soviet Press*, 41 (March 15, 1989); I. Nistor, *Bessarabia and Bukovina*, 1939.

Nicholas C. J. Pappas

MOLDOVEN. See MOLDOVAN.

MONGOL. The term "Mongol" has been used in Russian* history to describe the thirteenth-century invasion of Russia and Transcaucasia by the Golden Horde. Today, the ethnic group within the former Soviet Union that is mostly closely related to those Mongol invaders is the Khalkas*, who linked themselves to the Buryats*. See KHALKA, BURYAT, and KALMYK.

REFERENCE: Walter Kolarz, *The Peoples of the Soviet Far East*, 1954.

MONTENEGRIN. The Montenegrins are a South Slavic people who settled in the western Balkans in the era of Slavic migrations from the sixth to the eleventh centuries A.D. They are usually identified with the Serbs*, with whom they share a common religious, cultural, and historical heritage. Their homeland is located to the west of Serbia and Kosovo, north of Albania and south/southeast of Bosnia-

Herzegovina. Through their tribal chieftains, the Montenegrins (known as Crno-gorci in Serbian, Chernogortsy in Russian) maintained tributary relations with the First Bulgarian Empire and the Byzantine Empire until the development of their own independent principality of Deocleia in the tenth century. They were converted to the Eastern Orthodox branch of Christianity and became part of the independent Serbian kingdom in the late twelfth century. Since then, they have been considered part of the Serbian nation, in spite of their later divergent development. From the eleventh to the fourteenth centuries, the Serbian kingdom grew into the most powerful Christian state in the Balkans until the rise of the Ottoman Empire. With the expansion of the Ottoman Empire in the fourteenth and fifteenth centuries, most of the Serbs lost their independence; their ethnic base shifted northward and westward to what is today Serbia proper. The Mon-tenegrins, however, were able to maintain a precarious autonomy, due to the inaccessibility of their homeland, their clan and tribal organization, their military skills, and their proximity to Venetian territories. The Montenegrins were or-ganized into a confederation of tribes under *vladika*, their prince bishop.

In the late seventeenth and eighteenth centuries, Montenegro became virtually independent of Ottoman rule and developed close ties with the Russian Empire. With the rise of Russia as a European power under Peter the Great and his successors, military and political relations between Russia and the Montenegrins intensified. Montenegrins organized and participated in uprisings against the Ottomans during the Russo-Turkish Wars of the eighteenth and early nineteenth centuries. In particular, the Russo-Turkish Wars of 1769–1774, 1787–1791, 1806–1812, 1828, and the Crimean War (1853–1857) brought about the emi-gration of individuals and small groups of Montenegrins to the Russian Empire. As the Ottoman Empire disintegrated in the eighteenth and nineteenth centuries, the Serbs and Montenegrins achieved first *de facto*, and then, in 1878, *de jure* independence. After World War I, as part of the Allied Powers' attempt to make national frontiers reflect broad ethnic interests, Montenegro became—along with Croatia, Serbia, Slovenia, Bosnia-Herzegovina, and Vardar Macedonia—the new country of Yugoslavia, the land of the South Slavs. With the Communist ascendancy after World War II, Montenegro became a constituent republic of the Socialist Federated Republic of Yugoslavia. Since the breakup of Yugoslavia, Montenegro has joined Serbia to form a smaller Yugoslavia.

There is no separate Montenegrin nationality listed in the 1989 Soviet census. The Montenegrins are counted among the 3,100 Serbs within the Commonwealth of Independent States (CIS). While there have been attempts, particularly in Josef Broz Tito's Yugoslavia to develop a separate Montenegrin national identity, most Montenegrins consider themselves to be Serbs; as such, Montenegrins are considered part of the Serbian nation. See SERB.

REFERENCES: Ivo Banac, *The National Question in Yugoslavia: Origins, History, Politics*, 1984; N. M. Tikhomirov, "Istoricheskie sviazi russkogo naroda s iuzhnymi slavianami s drevneishikh vremen do poloviny XVII v.," *Slavianskii Sbornik*, V. Picheta, ed., 1947, pp. 125–201; Wayne S. Vucinich, "Who are the Montenegrins," in *Festschrift in Honor of Ferdo Sisic*, 1975; Wayne S. Vucinich, "Serbian Military Tradition," in *War and Society in East Central Europe*, B. Kiraly *et al.*, eds., 1979, vol. 1, pp. 311–14.

Nicholas C. J. Pappas

MORDOVIAN. See MORDVINIAN.

MORDVA. See MORDVINIAN.

MORDVA ERZIA. See ERZYA and MORDVINIAN.

MORDVA ERZYA. See ERZYA and MORDVINIAN.

MORDVA MOKSHA. See MOKSHA and MORDVINIAN.

MORDVIN. See MORDVINIAN.

MORDVINIAN. The Mordvinians, who call themselves the Mordva, Erzya*, or Moksha*, and who are also known as the Mordovians and Mordvins, are an ethnic group living throughout a broad area of the Middle Volga region of Russia. Their population stood at 1,340,415 people in 1926, and it has been in a state of steady decline ever since, primarily because of their assimilation by ethnic Russians*. Their population had dropped to 1,285,116 in 1959, 1,262,670 in 1970, 1,191,765 in 1979, and 1,153,516 in 1989. In terms of their ethnic ancestry, the Mordvinians are part of the Finnish* family, and their language is of the Finnic group of the Uralian branch of the Uralic-Altaic family. They are scattered in relatively small clusters among the Russian population between Nizhny Novgorod and Ryazan in the west and the Ural Mountains in the east, especially in the Gorky, Orenburg, Saratov, Penza, Ul'ianovsk, and Kuybyshev oblasts. Others live in the Tatar, Chuvash, and Bashkir autonomous republics. Their largest concentration is in the Mordvinian Autonomous Republic, a political subdivision of 10,100 square miles, whose principal town and capital city is Saransk.

At the present time, there are five main groups of Mordvinians, the two largest of which are the Moksha and the Erzya. The Moksha live particularly in the western reaches of the Mordvinian Republic in the Penza and Orenburg oblasts, and in the Tatar Autonomous Republic. The Erzya live in the northeastern reaches of the Mordvinian Republic, in the Tatar and Bashkir autonomous republics, and in the Gorky, Kuybyshev, Saratov, and Orenburg oblasts. Located in the southern part of the Mordvinian Republic are the Tengushev*, a group of Mordvinians who constitute a transitional group between the Erzya and the Moksha. The Erzya and Moksha dialects of Mordvinian are mutually unintelligible to one another, and the two peoples constitute distinct ethnic groups. The Teryukhan are a small group of Mordvinians living near the city of Nizhny Novgorod. They are a Mordvinian group who no longer speak Mordvinian, either privately or publicly. Instead, they speak Russian, although they remain aware of their Mordvinian roots. The final group of Mordvinians are the Karatai*, who live in a few villages in the Tatar Autonomous Republic. Those villages are located in the Tetyushkiy Rayon. They have completely given up Mordvinian in favor of Tatar*.

There are also two other groups in the region who are conscious of their Mordvinian roots, although they no longer maintain a particularly Mordvinian identity. During the Russian conquest of the Volga area, large numbers of Mordvinians were assimilated into Russian society. Others were absorbed by Tatar society. Generically, these assimilated Mordvinians are known as Meshchera*. More particularly, those who converted to Russian Orthodox Christianity and adopted the Russian language became known as Meshcheryak*. Those who fell under Tatar influence, adopted the Tatar language, and converted to the Sunni Muslim religion became known as the Mishars*.

The first literary reference to the Mordvinians came in the sixth century when they were located in villages between the Oka and Middle Volga rivers. Ethnologists believe that between the seventh and the twelfth centuries, as agriculture took hold among the Mordvinians, their patriarchal and clan social system gave way to a more village-oriented political and social system. The city of Nizhni Novgorod was the capital of the Mordvinians before its conquest in 1172 by troops of three Russian principalities—Suzdal, Ryazan, and Murom. For the next two centuries, the conquest of the Mordvinians continued, with Muscovy joining the assault. By the thirteenth century, Russians were referring to the Mordvinians as the Purgasova Volost' or Purgasova Rus', because so many ethnic Russian peasants had settled near the lower Moksha River among the Mordvinians. The area was incorporated into the Russian political subdivisions of Ryazan and Nizhni Novgorod. From the thirteenth to the fifteenth centuries, the Mordvinians fell under the control of the Mongols* and Tatars, and they joined with Russians in the resistance movement against Mongol rule. When the Khanate of Kazan fell in 1552, the Mordvinians voluntarily became part of the Russian state.

During the late sixteenth and early seventeenth centuries, Russians built a strong line of military fortifications and settlements in the southeastern reaches of Mordvinia to provide a defensive perimeter against attacks from nomadic tribes. At the same time, increasing numbers of ethnic Russians poured into the area, and, in the process, the Mordvinians became a second-class people. They lost huge amounts of land and experienced heavy-handed proselytizing from Russian Orthodox missionaries. Tens of thousands of Mordvinians fled their native lands and headed east of the Sura and Volga rivers, out into the Ural Mountains and southern Siberia. Russian history during the eighteenth and nineteenth centuries is replete with Mordvinian uprisings against ethnic Russian landlords and the authority of the Russian state.

The Mordvinian economy remained overwhelmingly agricultural well into the twentieth century. Most Mordvinian farmers functioned on a subsistence level until the completion of the Moscow-Kazan Railroad in the 1890s, which integrated the region more completely into the larger commercial economy. The commercial production of beef increased, as did the timber industry, but most Mordvinians remained tied to the land. Commercial connections with Russia were accompanied by cultural links as well. Public schools in which the language of instruction was Russian proliferated in Mordvinian territory, and the process of assimilation began to accelerate.

The Bolshevik Revolution in 1917 had a dramatic impact on Mordvinian life. In 1919, a Mordvinian section was established in the People's Commissariat for Nationalities in Russia, and, in 1921, a Congress of Communists of Mordvinian Nationality met in Samara. The Mordvinian Okrug was established in 1928, and it became the Mordvinian Autonomous Oblast in 1930; in 1934, the Mordvinian Autonomous Soviet Socialist Republic was created. The government established a Cyrillic alphabet for the Erzya dialect in 1922 and for the Moksha dialect in 1926. State economic planning led to diversification and collectivized farming. There were some resistance to collectivization on the part of Mordvinian *kulak* peasants in the late 1920s, and Josef Stalin liquidated most of them. During World War II, when the Soviet Union relocated most Russian industry east of the Urals, in order to escape Nazi destruction, Mordvinia underwent dramatic economic change. Subsequent economic developments gave rise to heavy and chemical industries and machine tool enterprises. For the last five decades, the Mordvinians have become more and more russified. Each new census reveals a smaller number of people who identify themselves as Mordvinians, and, in 1989, more than a third of all those who called themselves Mordvinian no longer spoke the Mordvinian language. Another third of Mordvinians are completely bilingual in Mordvinian and Russian.

REFERENCES: *Great Soviet Encyclopedia*, 1973, vol. 15, 560–65; Isabelle Kreindler, *The Mordvinians: A Doomed Soviet Nationality?*, 1984; Ronald Wixman, *The Peoples of the USSR: An Ethnographic Handbook*, 1984.

MOTOR. See KOIBAL and KHAKASS.

MOUNTAIN JEW. The Mountain Jews*, who have also been known historically as the Daghestani Jews, the Dag Chufut, and the Tati Jews, are a unique Jewish group in what used to be the Soviet Union. Ethnologists are uncertain about their origins, because they are not related to the Ashkenazic Jewish population. They have roots in Azerbaijan and have for centuries spoken the Tat* language, which has an Iranian base. Most of the Mountain Jews, over the centuries, assimilated into the Georgian* Christian community or the Azerbaijani* Muslim community. The Mountain Jews who did not convert tended to be geographically isolated in the eastern mountains. They speak a Tat dialect, which is laced with Hebrew and Daghestani* words. Since the late 1970s, the Mountain Jewish community has been steadily declining in size because of emigration to Israel and the United States. Those remaining behind live primarily

in such towns as Derbent and Buinaksk in Daghestan, Baku and Kuba in Azerbaijan, Nalchik in the Kabardino-Balkar Autonomous Republic, and Groznyy in the Chechen-Ingush Autonomous Republic. See TAT or JEW.
REFERENCE: Ronald Wixman, *The Peoples of the USSR: An Ethnographic Handbook*, 1984.

MOUNTAIN KALMUK. See KALMYK.

MOUNTAIN KALMYK. See KALMYK.

MOUNTAIN MARI. See MARI.

MOUNTAIN QALMUQ. See KALMYK and ALTAI.

MOUNTAIN QALMYQ. See KALMYK and ALTAI.

MOUNTAIN SHOR. See SHOR.

MOUNTAIN SHORIAN. See SHOR.

MOUNTAIN TADJIK. See MOUNTAIN TAJIK and TAJIK.

MOUNTAIN TAJIK. The Mountain Tajiks, whom Russians* call the Gorniy Tajik, constitute one of the two constituent groups of the Tajiks. Unlike lowland Tajiks, who are very closely related to Uzbeks*, the Mountain, or highland, Tajiks are linked culturally to the Pamir* groups. They are Sunni Muslims. See TAJIK and PAMIR PEOPLES.
REFERENCE: Ronald Wixman, *The Peoples of the USSR: An Ethnographic Handbook*, 1984.

MOUNTAIN TATAR. See BALKAR.

MOUNTAINEER. The term ''Mountaineer'' generally refers to the indigenous peoples of the North Caucasian highlands, who are sometimes known as North Caucasian Mountaineers. Russians* have called them the Gortsy or Tavlintsy. The term is more geographic than linguistic or religious, and it includes the Karachais*, Balkars*, Ossetians*, Ingush*, Chechens*, Avars*, Dargins*, Laks*, Tabasarans*, Aguls*, Rutuls*, Tsakhurs*, and Lezgins*.
REFERENCE: Ronald Wixman, *The Peoples of the USSR: An Ethnographic Handbook*, 1984.

MRASS TATAR. The Mrass Tatars are part of the larger collection of Siberian Tatars* who originated with the Mongol* invasion of Russia in the thirteenth century. The term ''Mrass Tatar'' is more a reflection of their location in the Mrass region of the Kuznetsk Basin of southern Siberia than of any distinct identity as a special group of Tatars. The Tatars were converted to the Sunni Muslim faith, Hanafi school, by Islamic merchants in the fourteenth and fifteenth centuries. Russians* finally conquered the region in 1581 and established forts at Tjumen in 1586, Tobolsk in 1587, Tara in 1594, and Tomsk in 1604. Contact with Russians led to the Tatars' conversion to Eastern Orthodox Christianity, although the conversion was superficial at best. Strong elements of shamanistic animism survived among them. Until the nineteenth century, most of the Mrass Tatars were hunters and trappers, going after sable, fox, marten, ermine, bear, and wolf. When industrialization began to reach Siberia, some Mrass Tatars went to work in factories, tanneries, and sawmills. After the 1930s, most of the Mrass Tatars found themselves living and laboring on collective farms. Since World War II, Russian ethnographers have classified them with the Shors. See SHOR and TATARS.
REFERENCE: Shirin Akiner, *Islamic Peoples of the Soviet Union*, 1983.

MRASSA TATAR. See SHOR and TATAR.

MRASSIN. See SHOR.

MRASSIN TATAR. See MRASS TATAR.

MRASSINSKIY TATAR. See MRASS TATAR.

MRASSINY. See SHOR.

MTIULI. The Mtiuli are one of the constituent groups of the Georgian* nation. See GEORGIAN.
REFERENCE: Ronald Wixman, *The Peoples of the USSR: An Ethnographic Handbook*, 1984.

MTUILI. See GEORGIAN.

MUGAT. See GYPSY.

MUGHAT. See CENTRAL ASIAN GYPSY and GYPSY.

MUGHAT-BUKHORI. See CENTRAL ASIAN GYPSY and GYPSY.

MUGHAT-SAMARKANDI. See CENTRAL ASIAN GYPSY and GYPSY.

MUGI. See GYPSY.

MULTANI. See GYPSY.

MUNGAT. See KACHA or KHAKASS.

MUNIB-KVANKHIDATL'. See ANDI and AVAR.

N

NADKHOKUADZH. See CHERKESS.

NAGAIBAK. The Nagaibaks (Nogaibaks) call themselves the Nogaibaks and are referred to by Russians* as Nagaibaki. When large numbers of Russian settlers reached their area in the eighteenth century, the Nagaibaks were Muslims who converted to Christianity. During the nineteenth and early twentieth centuries, however, most of them reverted to Islam and intermarried with Tatars* and Bashkirs*, with whom Russian ethnographers classify them. See BASKHIR or TATAR.
REFERENCE: Ronald Wixman, *The Peoples of the USSR: An Ethnographic Handbook*, 1984.

NAGAIBAKI. See NAGAIBAK.

NAGAIBAQ. See NAGAIBAK and BASHKIR.

NAGAYBAK. See NAGAIBAK and BASHKIR.

NAGAYBAQ. See NAGAIBAK and BASHKIR.

NAGHAIBAK. See NAGAIBAK and BASHKIR.

NAGHAIBAQ. See NAGAIBAK and BASHKIR.

NAGHAYBAK. See NAGAIBAK and BASHKIR.

NAGHAYBAQ. See NAGAIBAK and BASHKIR.

NAH PEOPLES. See NAKH PEOPLES.

NAHADA. See KHUNZAL and AVAR.

NAHADIN. See KHUNZAL and AVAR.

NAIMAN. See ICHKILIK and KYRGYZ.

498   NAKH PEOPLES

NAKH PEOPLES. The term "Nakh peoples" (Veinakh peoples), is an older, generic, linguistic reference to people who speak one of the Nakh languages in the Caucasic group. The term is only rarely used anymore. The languages include in the Nakh group are Chechen*, Ingush*, Kist, and Batsbi*.
REFERENCE: Ronald Wixman, *The Peoples of the USSR: An Ethnographic Handbook*, 1984.

NAKHADA. See KHUNZAL and AVAR.

NAKHADIN. See KHUNZAL and AVAR.

NAKHADINTSY. See KHUNZAL and AVAR.

NAKHCHUO. See CHECHEN.

NAKHICHEVAN. See AZERBAIJAN.

NAMOL. See ESKIMO.

NAMOLI. See ESKIMO.

NAMOLY. See ESKIMO.

NANAI. The Nanai, who call themselves the Nani, are closely related to the Ulchis*, Oroks*, and Orochis*, all of whom consider themselves to be part of the larger Nani* group, since their languages are mutually intelligible. They speak one of the Manchu languages.

By the mid-nineteenth century, the Nanais were caught between Chinese and Russian expansion. Ethnic Russians had entered Nanai land from the north, while Chinese farmers were entering from the south. In order to avoid being surrounded by the Chinese, large numbers of Nanais left their homes and settled in more isolated forest areas. Those Nanais who stayed behind often became enslaved or dependent because of debts to Chinese traders and large farmers. To pay their debts, many Nanais were forced to give their wives and daughters as concubines to wealthy Chinese businessmen and landowners. Smallpox and other diseases reduced the Nanai population. Nanai culture was hard pressed to survive because of pressures to assimilate. By 1900, there were fewer than 3,000 Nanais still living in the Sungari-Ussuri region of China.

To the north, the large-scale immigration of ethnic Russians* and Ukrainians* placed similar pressures on the Nanais. By 1915, the Nanais there were out-numbered more than one-hundred to one. Russian and Ukrainian farmers used slash-and-burn techniques to farm, and, because they used wood as a fuel, they deforested much of the Nanai homeland. They also hunted the sable to extinction and pushed the Nanai off the best fishing grounds. Large numbers of Nanais thus found themselves working as servants and wage laborers in the Russian commercial economy. Increasingly large numbers of Nanais adopted Russian as their primary language.

After the Bolshevik Revolution, the pace of change accelerated for the Nanais. The government collectivized their economic activities and forced the Nanais into ever larger settlements. During World War II, Russian industry actively recruited young Nanais, and this trend continued after the war. By 1970, more than 25 percent of Nanais lived in cities. By the late 1980s, less than half of the Nanais spoke Nanai as their primary language. That change in linguistic allegiances was due in part to a concentrated government effort to eliminate Nanai as the language of instruction in public schools.

In spite of these changes, however, much of the traditional Nanai religion survived, even though it incorporated elements of Russian Orthodoxy, Buddhism, and Confucianism. They believe in the god Sangi, ruler of the skies, who intervenes in human affairs to prevent sadness or to punish people for damaging the environment. The Nanais often relied on shaman healers for medical care, and the bear feast was still being celebrated in many Nanai communities in the late 1980s.

Because Nanai religion had such a powerful environmental dimension to it, the ecological destruction that accompanied Soviet development policies profoundly affected the Nanais. During the 1960s, 1970s, and 1980s, local oil refineries and pulp and paper mills badly polluted the Amur River, destroying much of the fish population and depriving many Nanais of their livelihood. Plans to construct a nuclear power plant near Lake Evoron, where the Nanais believe Mudur, the heaven dragon, lives, have precipitated a bitter protest movement. Nanai activists such as Yevdokia Gayer, who was elected to the Supreme Soviet in Moscow in 1988, and Pongsa Kile, are demanding a reduction in economic development so that the Nanai can preserve a semblance of their traditional lifestyle.

The Nanai people today total approximately 12,000 and are of mixed origins. They reside in the lower Amur River basin. Another 2,000 or so Nanais live across the border in the People's Republic of China. Ironically, the collapse of the Communist Party and the disintegration of the Soviet Union in 1991 actually made their retention of Nanai identity less likely. More than anything else, the implosion of the Soviet economy explained the destruction of the Soviet Union. One of the major goals of people like Boris Yeltsin in Russia was the acceleration of economic development. Since huge volumes of natural resources exist in Siberia, the exploitation and export of those resources—especially coal, iron ore, natural gas, timber, and petroleum—represented a relatively quick way of earning hard currency for developing the rest of the economy. Russians began importing Western technology to develop Siberia, and, in the process, the traditional Nanai economy became even more threatened. If, during the rest of the 1990s, the development of the Siberian economy accelerates, the pressure on traditional Nanai ways will become even more intense.

REFERENCES: Alice Bartels and Dennis Bartels, "Soviet Policy Toward Siberian Native People," *Canadian Dimension*, 19 (1985), 36–44; Alina Chadayeva, "Land of the Ancient Mangbo," *Soviet Life* (December 1990), 25–28; Mike Edwards, "Siberia: In From the Cold," *National Geographic*, 177 (March 1990), 2–49; James Forsyth, *A History of the Peoples of Siberia*, 1992; Constantine Krypton, "Soviet Policy in the Northern National Regions After World War II," *Slavic Review*, 13 (October 1954), 339–53; Piers Vitebsky, "Perestroika Among the Reindeer Herders," *Geographical Magazine*, 61 (June 1989), 23–34; Ronald Wixman, *The Peoples of the USSR: An Ethnographic Handbook*, 1984.

NANAY. See NANAI.

NANI. The term "Nani" is a generic description of the Nanai*, Ulchi*, Orok*, and Orochi* peoples, all of whom speak very similar languages and consider themselves part of the same group. See NANAI, ULCHI, OROK and OROCHI.
REFERENCE: Ronald Wixman, *The Peoples of the USSR: An Ethnographic Handbook*, 1984.

NARIM. See NARYM SELKUP and SELKUP.

NARIMI. See NARYM SELKUP and SELKUP.

NARIMY. See NARYM SELKUP and SELKUP.

NARIM SELKUP. See NARYM SELKUP and SELKUP.

NARODY DAGESTANA. See DAGHESTANI.

NARYM. See NARYM SELKUP and SELKUP.

NARYM SELKUP. The Narym Selkup constitute one of the two Selkup* divisions. They have also been called the Taiga Selkup, Forest Selkup, and Narym Ostyak*. They are quite distinct from the Tundra Selkup and are culturally closer to the Ket* people who live near them in the Ob Basin. The Narym Selkup are themselves divided into two different groups, based on dialect. The Narym Selkup living in the Kargasokskiy Rayon speak a dialect known as Tym*, while those in the Verkhne Ketskiy Rayon speak Ket. Today most of the Narym Selkups live in the Yamalo-Nenets Autonomous Oblast and in the Tomsk Oblast, where Russians* are assimilated by them. See SELKUP.
REFERENCE: Ronald Wixman, *The Peoples of the USSR: An Ethnographic Handbook*, 1984.

NARYMY SELKUP. See NARYM SELKUP and SELKUP.

NATKI. See NANAI.

NATKI. See MANCHU.

NATUHAI. See NATUKHAI, ADYGHE, and CIRCASSIAN.

NATUHAY. See NATUKHAI, ADYGHE, and CIRCASSIAN.

NATUKAI. See NATUKHAI, ADYGHE, and CIRCASSIAN.

NATUKAY. See NATUKHAI, ADYGHE, and CIRCASSIAN.

NATUKHAI. The Natukhai are an Adyghe* subgroup. They are concentrated demographically near the coast of the Black Sea, between the Dzhuba and Kuban rivers. See ADYGHE or CIRCASSIAN.
REFERENCE: Ronald Wixman, *The Peoples of the USSR: An Ethnographic Handbook*, 1984.

NATUKHAY. See NATUKHAI, ADYGHE, and CIRCASSIAN.

NATUQAI. See NATUKHAI, ADYGHE, and CIRCASSIAN.

NATUQAY. See NATUKHAI, ADYGHE, and CIRCASSIAN.

NAWRUZ. See KARACHAI.

NEAR KURILER. The term ''Near Kuriler'' refers to a small group of Itelmen* on the Kurile Islands and on Cape Lopatka who have settled among the Ainu*, with whom they have largely assimilated. See AINU or ITELMEN.
REFERENCE: Ronald Wixman, *The Peoples of the USSR: An Ethnographic Handbook*, 1984.

NEAR KURILIAN. See NEAR KURILER, AINU, and ITELMEN.

NEGDA. See NEGIDAL and EVENK.

NEGEDEN. See NEGIDAL and EVENK.

NEGIDAL. The Negidal—also known as the El'kan, Beyenin, Eleke Beye, Neidal, Iizhdal, and Negeden—are a subgroup of the Evenks*, one of the largest ethnic groups of northern Siberia. The Negidals emerged as a mix of Evenks with the surrounding Nivkhi*, Nanai*, and Ulchi* peoples. They are concentrated demographically in two villages along the Amgun and Amur rivers in Khabarovsk Kray in southeastern Siberia.

By the late 1800s, there were approximately 500 Negidals living on the Amgun River near the mouth of the Amur River. They supported themselves by fishing and by hunting seals and large game animals. Like the other people of the Amur River, the Negidals used plank boats, birch bark canoes, fish-skin robes, and conical tepees. After the Bolshevik Revolution, the Soviet government had considerable success in ending the nomadic life-style of the Negidals and in settling them in permanent communities. The state tried to organize hunting and herding collectives, assisted many Negidals in making the transition to farming, and secured the services of other Negidals as industrial workers. By 1934, there were primary schools for Negidal children, and the language of instruction was Russian. Today, ethnographers doubt that the Negidals can long survive as an independent ethnic group. They are completely surrounded and vastly outnumbered by ethnic Russians, and the acculturation process is well under way.

The Negidals had not developed any real sense of political nationalism, so no demands for Negidal independence emanated from Siberia in the late 1980s and early 1990s. Negidal leaders were really interested in preserving indigenous culture, especially their economic way of life. They protested the petroleum and natural gas development policies that were taking over their aboriginal land. The construction of roads, highways, railroads, and pipelines disrupted traditional reindeer migration routes and herding routines. Since huge volumes of natural resources exist in Siberia, the exploitation and export of those resources—especially coal, iron ore, natural gas, timber, and petroleum—represented a relatively quick way of earning hard currency for developing the rest of the economy. Russians began importing Western technology to develop Siberia. In the process, the traditional Negidal economy became even more threatened. If, during the rest of the 1990s, the development of the Siberian economy accelerates, the pressure on traditional Negidal ways will become even more intense. In that sense, capitalism may bring about the assimilation that Communism failed to achieve.

REFERENCES: Alice Bartels and Dennis Bartels, "Soviet Policy Toward Siberian Native People," *Canadian Dimension*, 19 (1985), 36–44; Mike Edwards, "Siberia: In From the Cold," *National Geographic*, 177 (March 1990), 2–49; James Forsyth, *A History of the Peoples of Siberia*, 1992; Walter Kolarz, *Russia and Her Colonies*, 1952; Constantine Krypton, "Soviet Policy in the Northern National Regions After World War II," *Slavic Review*, 13 (October 1954), 339–53; William J. Pomeroy, "The Evenks: Affirmative Action in the USSR," in Marilyn Bechtel and Daniel Rosenberg, eds., *Nations and Peoples of the Soviet Union*, 1981, 101–12; Piers Vitebsky, "Perestroika Among the Reindeer Herders," *Geographical Magazine*, 61 (June 1989), 23–34; Ronald Wixman, *The Peoples of the USSR: An Ethnographic Handbook*, 1984.

NEIDA. See NEGIDAL and EVENK.

NEIDAL. See NEGIDAL and EVENK.

NEIDEN. See NEGIDAL and EVENK.

NEMETS. See GERMAN.

NEMTSY. See GERMAN.

NENETS. The Nenets—also known historically as the Nentsy, Khasava, Yurak, Yurak Samoyeds, or Samoyeds*—are one of the Soviet Union's most populous northern ethnic groups. They are a Samoyedic people, like the Ents*, Ngana- sans*, and Selkups*, and their language is part of the Samoyedic group of the Uralian languages, which are part of the larger Uralic-Altaic linguistic group. Anthropologists believe that the Nenets split away from other Finno-Ugrian* groups around 3000 B.C. and migrated east, where they began to mix with Turkish-Altaic people around 200 B.C. The Samoyedic people who remained in Europe came under Russian* control around 1200 A.D., but those who had settled farther east did not experience that domination until the mid-fourteenth century. By the early seventeenth century, all of the Samoyedic people were under Russian control.

There are two distinct groups of Nenets, and they are divided by both regional location and dialect. Far to the north are the Tundra Nenets*, and, in the southern reaches of Nenets territory, there are the Forest Nenets, also known as the Khandeyar*. A third group of people, known as Komi Nenets, are actually an example of relatively recent ethnogenesis, since they are the descendants of a mixture of Nenets and Komi* ancestors. This third group lives in the Komi Autonomous Republic as well as in the Nenets Autonomous Oblast. Historically, they consisted of Nenets who married into the Izhmi* tribe of the Komi. They identify themselves as Nenets, although they speak the Komi dialect. Today, the Nenet population exceeds 32,000 people, up from 23,000 in 1959 and 15,400 in 1926. The vast majority of the Nenets live in the Nenets Autonomous Oblast, the Yamalo-Nenets Autonomous Oblast, and the Dolgano-Nenets, or Taimyr, Autonomous Oblast in northwestern Siberia. Smaller groups of Nenets live on the islands of Kolguev and Novaya Zemlaya in the Arctic Ocean.

The traditional Nenets economy revolved around herding and breeding rein- deer. The reindeer provided the Nenets with meat, lard, and blood, which they consumed, as well as skins for clothes, shoes, tents, rope, harnesses, and strings; they also made use of the tendons and horns. For their transportation, the Nenets harnessed reindeer and attached them to sleds. The Tundra Nenets grazed their herds all year round on the tundra land between the forests and the sea coast. In the spring, they avoided the mosquitos and gadflies by driving the herds north to the Arctic Ocean coast. Trained dogs managed the herds, which sometimes numbered in the thousands. Fishing was important to the Nenets, especially to the Forest Nenets living along the lower reaches of the Ob, Nadym, Pur, Taz, and Yenesei rivers. They relied particularly on the sturgeon, although they regularly fished for and caught whitefish, salmon, ide, navaga, and trout. The Nenets also hunted and trapped the fox, silver fox, hare, ermine, wolverine, beaver, otter, and polar and brown bears. The western Nenets groups also hunted sea mammals, especially the seal, bearded seal, white whale, Greenland seal, and walrus. The Forest Nenets engage in the same breeding, hunting, and fishing activities, but they are not so nomadic as the Tundra Nenets.

Nenets society was carefully organized into well-defined clans that had their own grazing, hunting, and fishing lands, as well as nomadic routes. The clans maintained mutual aid societies, burial grounds, common sacrificial ground, signs, and symbols. Marriages were forbidden within clans. The clan system was so well organized that, when collectivization began in the 1930s, the Soviet government used the existing clans as the organizational basis. Family life was patriarchal in nature.

During the sixteenth and seventeenth centuries, the central government under the tsars practiced a policy of indirect rule from Moscow. They treated the native peoples of Siberia as they did the other peoples they had conquered. Forts were established to collect and forward to Moscow the *yasak*, or fur tax, but actual administration of native peoples was left in the hands of local rulers. Moscow authorized the granting of citizenship to any native who converted to Christianity, a process that led to forced baptisms and enserfment by local rulers, who then used their native serfs to increase fur trapping. As the numbers of fur-bearing animals decreased, Moscow lost interest in the area and in the well-being of its natives. The Nenets were part of this entire administrative process.

The indigenous peoples of Siberia suffered from their commercial and political contact with ethnic Russians. Over the centuries, ethnic Russians penetrated commercial activities in the region, enticing the Nenets first with iron and steel tools, and later with firearms and a variety of trade goods. Large numbers of Nenets adopted the use of alcohol as well, much to their harm. In addition, ethnic Russians brought diseases to the native peoples, especially venereal diseases, which had spread throughout Europe after the New World conquests in the late fifteenth and sixteenth centuries.

The Bolshevik Revolution of 1917 and the subsequent civil war changed the Nenets life. The new Soviet government issued the "Declaration of the Rights of the Peoples of Russia" in 1917, which guaranteed the "equality and sovereignty of the peoples of Russia; the right of self-determination, including separation and the formation of independent states; abolition of all national and national-religious privileges or restrictions; and free development of national minorities and ethnic groups inhabiting the territory of Russia." Under Josef Stalin, who served at the time as Commissariat for Nationalities, the program was implemented. When the Commissariat for Nationalities was abolished in 1924, a new Committee of Assistance to the Peoples of the North, or Committee of the North, took over.

A debate over native policy proceeded throughout the 1920s. The Committee of the North proposed creating large reservations for the indigenous peoples of Siberia, where they could be left alone to pursue traditional life-styles. But Lenin and other Bolsheviks opposed this, "arguing it would prevent Native People from catching up educationally, politically, and economically with other Soviet nationalities." Instead, the Soviet government decided to incorporate the native peoples into the larger social, political, and economic body of the country. Between 1929 and 1932, the government created "national districts," which were small territorial administrative units named after each of the natives peoples, including the Nenets. Late in the 1920s and throughout the 1930s, the government also collectivized indigenous economic activities. For the Nenets, this meant the collectivization of their traditional reindeer-herding economy. Collectivization inspired considerable resistance among Nenets leaders, but it was to no avail. The government also established "cultural bases" for the indigenous people— settlements complete with boarding schools, hospitals, day-care centers, veterinary dispensaries, and clubs. The government sought to minimize the nomadic nature of Nenets life.

During the 1930s, the Soviet government developed a written language for the Nenets. It created a Latin alphabet for Nenets in 1933, changing it to a Cyrillic alphabet in 1937. Between 1930 and 1957, more than fifty schools were established for Nenets children. In 1938, Russian became the language of instruction in all government schools. In essence, the Soviet government had embarked on an all-out effort to destroy Nenets culture—to acculturate Nenets children to Russian values and to eliminate the traditional, nomadic, subsistence economy of the Nenets people. During the late 1930s, 1940s, and 1950s, the government also launched an assault on Nenets religion. Nenets religion, like that of most indigenous peoples, was polytheistic and animist. The Nenets believed that the natural environment was a living, breathing place, full of invisible ghosts and spirits. Many of those spirits were malevolent and could be appeased only through the blood sacrifice of dogs, reindeer, or other animals. God, in the Nenets religion, was not directly approachable by human beings. Instead, they had to go through mediating spirits called *tadepco*. Nenets religion maintained a cult of the dead, in which deceased clan ancestors were worshipped. The Nenets religious leader in each clan was a shaman, who was believed to be endowed with supernatural powers. Nenets folklore maintained elaborate heroic epics and lyrical songs celebrating Nenets origins. All phenomena in life were intricately related, and nothing happened accidentally or capriciously. During the tsarist era, Russian Orthodox Christianity had been superimposed on the native religion, creating a syncretic, mixed faith. Beginning in the late 1930s, the Soviet government began prohibiting both native and Russian Orthodox religious services among the Nenets. In their place, the government worked to create an almost religious faith in Communism.

The Nenets resented and resisted the cultural imperialism that came to them as a result of Stalin's policies. During the early 1950s, several Nenets rebellions erupted in the Arkhangelsk area, where Nenets fought violently against government officials. The uprisings were ruthlessly suppressed by Soviet troops, and the rebel leaders were either executed or shipped to Siberian prison camps where they lingered and died.

The biggest change in Nenets life, however, came from the combined effects of industrialization and the increased immigration of ethnic Russians into Siberia. During World War II, when the Soviet government relocated much of its industry east of the Ural Mountains to keep it out of German* hands or protected from German artillery bombardment, large numbers of ethnic Russian workers suddenly moved into Siberia. State development plans accelerated that process in the 1950s and 1960s. As a result, the Nenets found themselves herding reindeer on ever smaller amounts of land. The collapse of the Soviet economy in the 1970s and 1980s actually slowed that process somewhat, but, even then, the long-term changes being brought to Nenets life were irreversible. Many Nenets still followed the reindeer and lived in tepee shelters made of reindeer hides, but increasingly large numbers abandoned the herds for jobs at construction sites, oil and natural gas wells, and mass-production factories. Soviet economists and ethnologists have estimated that the Nenets lost more than 20,000,000 acres of prime grazing land in the post-World War II era.

The primary culprit in the land alienation was the huge natural gas field in the Yamalo-Nenets National Region. Development of these resources required massive deforestation for road and pipeline construction and earth-moving engineering projects. Oil and natural gas discoveries in the region became commonplace in the 1960s and 1970s, as did the damage to the tundra and the forests because of site preparation and oil spills. Roads were constructed connecting sites with Tjumen, Tobolsk, Surgut, and Urengoi. Pipelines running from the wells to Tjumen, Omsk, Tomsk, the Urals, and Kuznetsk Basin cut across Nenets land. A series of gold-dredging projects also eroded river beds in the area. Tens of thousands of Russian workers poured into the region. In the process, Nenets life was completely disrupted.

The Nenets had never developed any real sense of political nationalism, so no demands for Nenets independence emanated from Siberia in the late 1980s and early 1990s. Instead, Nenets leaders were really interested in preserving their indigenous culture, especially their economic way of life. They protested the policies on petroleum and natural gas development that were despoiling their aboriginal land. Furthermore, the construction of roads, highways, railroads, and pipelines disrupted traditional reindeer migration and herding routines. Early in the 1990s, the Nenets organized many public demonstrations against government development projects. Some Nenets, for example, formed a boat chain across the Sop River to protest the pollution produced by a sand and gravel plant on the river. Nenets leaders also joined the recently formed Association of Peoples of the North. Several of them are pushing for a Nenets cultural revival. One of these is Anastasia Lapsui, a broadcast journalist who translates and publishes Nenets texts and who broadcasts news and culture in the Nenets language.

Ironically, the collapse of the Communist Party and the disintegration of the

Soviet Union in 1991 actually made the achievement of Nenets objectives less likely. More than anything else, the implosion of the Soviet economy explained the destruction of the Soviet Union. One of the major goals of people like Boris Yeltsin in Russia was the acceleration of economic development. Since huge volumes of natural resources exist in Siberia, the exploitation and export of those resources—especially coal, iron ore, natural gas, timber, and petroleum—represented a relatively quick way of earning hard currency for developing the rest of the economy. Russians began importing Western technology to develop Siberia, and, in the process, the traditional Nenets economy became even more threatened. If, during the rest of the 1990s, the development of the Siberian economy accelerates, the pressure on traditional Nenets ways will become even more intense.

REFERENCES: Alice Bartels and Dennis Bartels, "Soviet Policy Toward Siberian Native People," *Canadian Dimension*, 19 (1985), 36–44; Mike Edwards, "Siberia: In From the Cold," *National Geographic*, 177 (March 1990), 2–49; Péter Hajdú, *Samoyed Peoples and Languages*, 1962; Constantine Krypton, "Soviet Policy in the Northern National Regions After World War II," *Slavic Review*, 13 (October 1954), 339–53; Alexander Tropkin, "Yamal: What Price Progress?" *Soviet Life* (December 1990), 16–20; Piers Vitebsky, "Perestroika Among the Reindeer Herders," *Geographical Magazine*, 61 (June 1989), 23–34.

NENTSY. See NENETS.

NEYDA. See NEGIDAL and EVENK.

NEYDAL. See NEGIDAL and EVENK.

NEYDEN. See NEGIDAL and EVENK.

NGANASAN. The Nganasan are the northernmost people of the former Soviet Union; they have been known historically as the Nya and the Tavgi Samoyeds. The Nganasan are scattered throughout the enormous Taymyr Autonomous Oblast of northwestern Siberia, which comprises 860,000 square kilometers of territory. Their most immediate neighbors are the Nenets*, Dolgans*, and Yakuts*. The Nganasan are divided into two main tribal groups. The Avam people live in the western reaches of the Taymyr Peninsula, while the Vadeev* are located on the tundra of the eastern part of the peninsula, between the Kheta River, Taymyr Lake, and Khatanga Bay. The northern border of Nganasan territory is a line running from the shores of the Yenesei Gulf, out along the ridges of the Byrranga and Northeastern plateaus, down to the Gulf of Khatanga. The southern boundary consists of the edge of the forested tundra. Linguistically, the Nganasan are most closely related to the Nenets, who possess a very similar Samoyedic* language in the Uralic-Altaic family.

Ethnologists suspect that the ancestors of the Nganasan were Samoyedic tribes living in the area of the Sayan Mountains in southern Siberia. In the seventeenth century, before the Dolgans arrived in the region, the Nganasan lived farther south than they do today. By the seventeenth century, however, the Avam were living on the Tundra. Russians* first reached the Nganasan in 1610, when Mangazeya Cossacks* reached the Pyasina River. By the mid–1620s, most of the Nganasans living near the Yenesei River were paying the Russian fur tax on sable, fox, ermine, and squirrel. Russians made sure the taxes were paid by taking Nganasan hostages and holding them for a tax ransom. The Nganasans suffered a rapid population decline because of the diseases carried by the Russian settlers and because of the deleterious effects of alcohol.

Russian Orthodox missionaries reached Nganasan territory in the late seventeenth century. Over the years, they made many converts, but the conversions were superficial; even today, the Nganasan are only nominally Christians, for the animistic tribal religion still exerts a strong pull on their spiritual and cultural loyalties. A polytheistic people, the Nganasan believed that all aspects of nature have individual souls. Nganasan shamans could propitiate the powers of nature in order to minimize some of its capriciousness. The Nganasan attributed life and consciousness to such naturally occurring phenomena as rivers, caves, and mountains, and even to diseases (such as smallpox and dysentery) and to man-made objects (such as tools, sledges, and housing).

Because of their remote location on the Taymyr tundra in the far north, the Nganasan escaped many of the depredations that other Siberian peoples endured, at least until the twentieth century. They hunted wild reindeer as their staple food. They followed the herds and also fished, hunted fowl (especially goose, duck, and partridges), and trapped foxes and other fur-bearing animals. Because of their interest in Western tools, the Nganasans were seduced into the Russian fur economy from the mid-eighteenth century on, and they did hunt some sable for cash. For the most part, however, Nganasan social, economic, and religious life remained intact until the Bolshevik Revolution.

In 1930, however, the pace of change began to accelerate. Soviet authorities declared the entire Tymyr tundra to be one large collective. The Nganasan resisted, refusing to sell fish and fur to the collective and also refusing to settle in permanent villages. Because of the austere environment of the tundra, Soviet authorities in the 1930s did not make much of an effort to enforce compliance. Still, the Nganasans could not avoid being affected by government activities. By the late 1940s, they abandoned their annual migration to the Yenesei estuary for summer grazing because of the presence of so many ethnic Russians there.

In the 1970s and 1980s, however, Soviet industrial development caught up with the Nganasans. The entire economy of the remote Tymyr region became dominated by the massive non-ferrous metal plants of the city of Norilsk. The surrounding reindeer pastures became lifeless because of vehicular traffic. Corrupt Russian officials profited from the collectives, and the Nganasans were reduced to menial labor. Alcoholism and tuberculosis became endemic, and the rates of infant mortality and mental retardation rose extremely high. The Nganasan life-style had been all but destroyed.

Like many other northern peoples in Russia, the Nganasan are extremely concerned about damage to the environment, which has been such a serious problem in the Soviet Union and Russia. In 1991, the Nganasan joined the Association of Peoples of the North (APN), an interest group of indigenous Siberian peoples that has campaigned for environmental protection and the restoration of ancient tribal land rights. One of the Nganasan demands involves returning sovereign control of the land to the tribe and requiring the Russian government to lease it back—but only with prior Nganasan approval—for industrial development projects. As an individual group of 900 people, of course, the Nganasan have no political leverage, but, as part of the APN, they hope to wield more influence.

REFERENCES: Alice Bartels and Dennis Bartels, "Soviet Policy Toward Siberian Native People," Canadian Dimension, 19 (1985), 36–44; Mike Edwards, "Siberia: In From the Cold," National Geographic, 177 (March 1990), 2–49; James Forsyth, A History of the Peoples of Siberia, 1992; Péter Hajdú, Samoyed Peoples and Languages, 1962; Constantine Krypton, "Soviet Policy in the Northern National Regions After World War II," Slavic Review, 13 (October 1954), 339–53; A. A. Popov, The Nganasan: The Material Culture of the Tavgi Samoyeds, 1966; Piers Vitebsky, "Perestroika Among the Reindeer Herders," Geographical Magazine, 61 (June 1989), 23–34; Ronald Wixman, The Peoples of the USSR: An Ethnographic Handbook, 1984.

NIEGDA. See NEGIDAL and EVENK.

NIJDA. See NEGIDAL and EVENK.

NIJDAL. See NEGIDAL and EVENK.

NIMILAN. See NYMYLAN and KORYAK.

NIVKHI. The Nivkhi, numbering approximately 400 individuals are a Paleo-Asiatic people living on the northern half of Sakhalin Island, along the western coast (from Cape Sakh-Kotan to Cape May) and the east coast (south to Cape Delisle de la Croyere), along the Tym River, and, in the southern part of the island, at Cape Patience and the Poronyo River. They also live on the Asian mainland, astride the Amur River as far inland as Geri and south along the coast of the Tatar Sound to the Choma River. Some live as well on islands in the Bay of Ud, north of the Amur Delta.

Until the 1917 Revolution, they were commonly known as Gilyaks. The formal name change from "Gilyak" to "Nivkh" occurred in 1922, when the nation came under Kremlin occupation. Nivkh is the people's own name for their nationality. This official name change was in accord with the nationality policies of the Leninists. A Tungus*-Manchurian* people, the Nivkhi are related to the

Ainu* of southern Sakhalan Island and the Goldi, another small nationality on
Sakhalin Island, who are often called "Fishskin Tatars" because of their use of
salmon skins for clothing. The Nivkhi speak a unique Tungusian language, akin
to those spoken by Native American nations along the north Pacific coast of
North America, although specific generic ties have yet to be confirmed. There
are two dialects, Amur and Sakhalin.

A seafaring people, the Nivkhi fish principally for two species of salmon as
well as hunt for sea mammals. Indeed, until the October Revolution, the Nivkhi
had a subsistence economy based on these items. Their diet is supplemented
with bear and other land mammals, and dog is eaten during religious ceremonies.
Although nominally members of the Russian Orthodox church, most Nivkhi still
practice a traditional religion centered around a shaman. The bear is worshipped
as a sacred animal. A major religious custom is the use of an *inao*, which is a
willow stick finely whittled until it has a mane of long slender shavings. A fence
of *inaos* is often built to hold a bear cub, which is fattened for sacrifice. One
of the first Westerners to attend a bear festival was the German anthropologist,
Berthold Laufer, during the years 1898–1899. Nivkhi clothing is quite colorful
and is made from local materials, including birch-bark hats, salmon-skin coats,
eagle-feather fans, and embroidered silk. Clothing decorations reflect both Chinese* and Russian* influences.

Until recently, Nivkhi lived chiefly in semi-underground houses known as
yurtes. These resemble the homes of the Kamchadals* and Koryaks* but have
side doors. Entry to these homes, though, is often via smokeholes in the roofs.
During the summer, the Nivkhi reside in tents erected on stilts, to allow for
better ventilation and to escape local flooding. The Amur Nivkhi live in mud
huts. The dog is their only domesticated animal. It is used to power the traditional
means of transportation, a birchwood sled known as a *narte*. Like the sleds
employed by the Kamchadals, Nivkhi *nartes* have driver seats, and the dog is
attached to the sled by means of a neck harness. Their staple food is dried fish
called *ma* (a word that also means bread). Reflecting their contact with Chinese,
Japanese*, and Manchurians*, the Nivkhi use chopsticks.

Nivkhi life is centered around tribal clans, which still survive, albeit with little
official recognition, after seventy-odd years of Communist oppression. The only
custom to have vanished is that of group marriage, which was widespread as
recently as 1905.

Little is known of the ancestors of the Nivkhi. Current Russian scholarship
suggests that the Nivkhi are descended from early Neolithic inhabitants, although
most evidence for this is admittedly extrapolated from the histories of neighboring
peoples. The history of Sakhalin Island prior to Russian occupation is full of
many wars between area nations. The Nivkhi and the Ainu were the major
belligerents, and Nivkhi folklore contains many reports of bloody battles. Remains of Ainu dwellings, known as *kugi-tulkch*, can still be seen in Nivkhi areas
on north Sakhalin. The first known contact between the Nivkhi and Western
explorers occurred in 1645, when a Russian expedition led by a Cossack*, V. D.

Poyarkov, camped in a Nivkhi settlement at the mouth of the Amur River. Subsequent explorations were made by Russian, Dutch*, and French* adventurers.

Russia's first annexations of Nivkhi lands occurred in 1850, when the government annexed the Amur Delta. The first Russian settlement was established in the same year at Nikolayevsk-na-Amure, at the mouth of the Amur River. Russia's eastward thrust occurred at the same time that Japan was extending its influence northward. Both powers eyed Sakhalin Island, and, in 1855, a Russo-Japanese condominium was reached, establishing dual control of the 29,000-square-mile island. This agreement was dissolved in 1875, when Russia ceded the Kurile Islands to Japan. Sakhalin Island then became part of the Russian Empire and was used primarily as a penal colony until 1905. After ceding southern Sakhalin to Japan following the Russo-Japanese War, the Romanovs tried to develop the northern portion of the island by encouraging Russian settlements.

The power vacuum, caused by the collapse of the tsarist government and the Russian civil war, prompted local people to invite Japanese forces to occupy the region in August 1918, thereby bolstering the influence of the local Japanese minority who were opposed to the Bolsheviks. Unrest between the Bolsheviks and the Japanese culminated in the infamous Nikolayevsk Massacre of March 11–15, 1920, when Red forces murdered countless "reactionaries," primarily the Japanese minority. Gradually, the Japanese presence was replaced by the Far Eastern Republic, a Leninist creation based in Chita. By 1922, this republic had annexed all the Nivkhi territories; later the same year, the republic was merged into the Soviet Union. As part of the Soviet Union, the Nivkhi areas were re-incorporated into Russia, which was renamed the Russian Soviet Federated Socialist Republics (RSFSR).

From 1922 until 1988, the Nivkhi lived in relative isolation from the outside world yet endured many dramatic changes in their life-style. Although the Nivkhi were granted three small national areas (two on the island and one at the delta), they were subjected to collectivization and the destruction of their traditional forms of self government. A Nivkhi national revival can be said to have begun in 1988 when, along with other small nations, they contacted Mikhail Gorbachev shortly after the Communist Party of the Soviet Union (CPSU) established a special nationality commission to strengthen the collective farms and other state businesses, including fur-trade operations. The Nivkhi were alarmed at these suggestions because they signaled more control by the Kremlin.

Mounting conflicts between Moscow and the peoples of the Far North, including the Nivkhi, culminated in the creation of the Association of Peoples of the North (APN) on March 31, 1990, during a meeting in the Kremlin. Organized to defend the interests of twenty-six northern nations, the APN elected Vladimir Sangi, a Nivkhi, as president. The APN hoped to help the northern nations tackle such problems as economic expansion by various bureaucracies, flaws in Soviet nationality policies, and the ecological deterioration in northern areas.

In an interview with *Izvestia* on July 12, 1990, Sangi condemned the collective farms because they have been a means of Russian colonization and because the Nivkhi have been forced to relocate to cities where there is neither work nor housing. Sangi also expressed his fear that Kremlin phrases, such as "ensuring the development of areas in which the people of the north live," are just code-words to prevent the Nivkhi from mastering their own destiny. He noted that Communism must be changed, because current practice did not respect Nivkhi traditions. By encouraging the immigration of foreigners, chiefly Russians, the character of the land was being changed. For example, according to Sangi, electoral reforms in the RSFSR had eliminated Nivkhi representation in the Supreme Soviet, even though the Nivkhi did present candidates. The problem was that the Nivkhi are few in numbers and have no homeland of their own.

To rectify this situation, Sangi has stated that the Nivkhi must have their own homeland, despite their numerical size, as a way to protect their local interests. Ministries could then lease land from them, following a Nivkhi referendum, thereby giving the small nation a say in development. The Nivkhi would have the first say about the use of their natural resources. Reforms of the command economy are also necessary. Currently, the state pays the Nivkhi twenty-six kopeks per kilogram of salmon but resells the fish at a price hundreds of times higher. These state monopolies must be abolished because they favor outside interests. An example of successful economic reform among the Nivkhi is a hunting and fishing cooperative organized in the Noglicki District on Sakhalin Island where members earn 1,500 rubles monthly.

Another goal of the Nivkhi has been to have the Soviet Union, and now Russia, ratify both the 1957 International Convention on Protection and Inte-gration of Indigenous and Other Tribal and Semi-Tribal Populations in Inde-pendent Countries and the 1989 Convention on Indigenous and Tribal Peoples in Independent Countries, in order to affirm that the Nivkhi have a right to the ownership and possession of lands that they have traditionally occupied. In July 1990, free economic zones were declared for Sakhalin Island and the Maritime Territory, the two areas of the RSFSR where the Nivkhi live. While welcoming the possibility of better contacts with the outside world, Nivkhi leaders are concerned that unbridled development could cause ecological problems. A major concern is the development of oil shale deposits in the sea off Sakhalin Island. Nevertheless, the Nivkhi do welcome visits by foreign delegations expressing an interest in establishing contacts.

As part of their goal of autonomy, the Nivkhi want to reestablish clan, tribal, and elder councils as their form of government. Better health care is also nec-essary. The average life expectancy has declined by twenty years between 1960 and 1990, according to the APN. With the introduction of more personal freedom in the Nivkhi territories, crime has increased alarmingly. For instance, between 1988 and 1989, there was a 60.7 percent increase in reported crimes, including a 44.7 percent jump in serious crimes. A major cause for this has been the influx of outsiders. In fact, so many foreigners have come to Sakhalin Island that the infrastructure is being severely taxed; for example, native islanders are unable to obtain plane tickets, according to Valerie Mosolewski. Currently, an autonomous homeland is the main Nivkhi goal. The dissolution of the Soviet Union in 1991 and the increasing ethnic centrifugal forces in Russia will most likely only stimulate their demands for political autonomy.

REFERENCES: Alice Bartels and Dennis Bartels, "Soviet Policy Toward Siberian Native People," *Canadian Dimension*, 19 (1985), 36–44; *Current Digest*, 41 (May 3, 1989), 8–9, and 42 (August 22, 1990), 20–21; Mike Edwards, "Siberia: In From the Cold," *National Geographic*, 177 (March 1990), 2–49; James Forsyth, *A History of the Peoples of Siberia*, 1992; Constantine Krypton, "Soviet Policy in the Northern National Regions After World War II," *Slavic Review*, 13 (October 1954), 339–53; Piers Vitebsky, "Perestroika Among the Reindeer Herders," *Geographical Magazine*, 61 (June 1989), 23–34.

John A. Fink

NIYEGDA. See NEGIDAL and EVENK.

NIYEGDAL. See NEGIDAL and EVENK.

NIZHDA. See NEGIDAL and EVENK.

NIZHDAL. See NEGIDAL and EVENK.

NOGAI. The Nogai (Nogailar, Nogaitsy, and Mangkyt), also known as the Volga Muslims, are an ethnic group numbering approximately 125,000 people. They call themselves the Noghai. As many as 50,000 of them reside in Bulgaria, Romania, and Turkey, with the majority living today in the former Soviet Union. Most of the Nogai in what was the Soviet Union reside in the vast steppe region west of the Caspian Sea. They are particularly concentrated between the Terek and Kuma rivers and, down in the Crimea, near the town of Perekop. Other Nogais can be found in the Achikulak Rayon of the Stavropol Krai and in the Chechen-Ingush Autonomous Republic. Smaller numbers live in the Karachai-Cherkess Autonomous Province. They have been generically included as one of the Daghestani* peoples. The Nogai first emerged as an ethnic group in the late thirteenth century. Soviet ethnologists identify them as descendants of the Golden Horde invasion, specifically linking them to the Emir Nogai, a prominent Mongol* general. The emir was essentially the war lord of a vast region that included the steppes between the Caspian Sea and Dobrudja rivers. Emir Nogai died in 1300, and the political unity of his region disintegrated. The sense of ethnic identity among the Nogai, however, survived his death.

The Nogai tribes wandered the vast steppes between northern Kazakhstan and southern Siberia until the sixteenth century, when Tsar Ivan IV of Russia conquered Astrakhan and Kazan. The Nogai Horde then split in two. One group was known as the Great Horde and lived in the Lower Volga region, which came under Russian* rule in 1557. The Little Horde occupied the land around the right bank of the Kuban' River, the Sea of Azov, and the southern Ukraine. The Great Horde reunited with the Little Horde after being driven south by the expanding Kalmyks* in 1634. At that point, the reunited Nogai Horde came under the political control of the Crimean Tatars*.

Although the Nogai are divided by a variety of regional dialects, they generally speak a language that is part of the Kypchak* group of Turkic* languages, which are themselves part of the larger Uralic-Altaic linguistic family. Most of the Nogai people speak one of three basic dialects. The Ak* dialect is spoken by the Nogai who live in the northern reaches of the Karachai-Cherkess Autonomous Oblast. They are sometimes referred to as the White Nogai. The Achikulak* speakers live in the northern part of the Chechen-Ingush Autonomous Republic. The third group—the Kara*, also known as Black Nogai—live in the northern part of the Daghestan Autonomous Republic. The Kara constitute the largest of the Nogai groups. Because of their close historical ties with the Turkish khanates of the Crimean Peninsula and with the Ottoman sultans, the Nogai became converts to the Sunni Muslim religion. Unlike most of the Daghestani peoples, however, who are Sunni Muslims of the Shafi school, the Nogais adhere to the Hanafi school, because of their association with the Ottomans.

The Nogai economy has traditionally been based on animal husbandry, especially sheep and goats in the highlands and cattle in the lowlands. Some of them participate in gold and silver smithing, weaving, pottery, and rug manufacturing. The Nogais living near Perekop also work in a variety of blue-collar occupations. During the 1950s and 1960s, the Nogai economy changed as state cooperative enterprises and collective farms became the norm, thus reducing the semi-nomadism that had characterized Nogai life for so long. Most Nogai children attended public schools where Russian was the language of instruction, and most Nogai workers became employees of the state.

The economic integration of the Nogai has been accompanied by their increasing social assimilation. During the last 140 years, Nogai ethnic identity has been gradually eroded in the Soviet Union. During the 1860s, when significant Russian expansion into Nogai territory began, there was a large-scale emigration of Nogai. The emigrants went to Turkey, the Crimea, and Romania. By the late nineteenth and early twentieth centuries, the Nogai were being assimilated by the surrounding Russians, Circassians*, Kumyks*, and the Crimean* and Astrakhan Tatars.*

Although the forces of ethnic nationalism have had a powerful influence on recent Soviet and Russian history, the Nogais have not been as deeply affected, primarily because their identities as members of subgroups are more powerful than their identity as Nogais. They are divided into four major tribes—Bujak, Edisan, Jambulak, and Edishkul—and five minor tribes—Mansur, Kypchak, Karamurza, Tokhtam, and Novruz. Feelings of ethnic kinship remain extremely powerful within these tribal groupings.

REFERENCES: Alexandre Bennigsen, *The Evolution of the Muslim Nationalities of the USSR and Their Linguistic Problems*, 1961; Bernhard Geiger, et al., *Peoples and Languages of the Caucasus*, 1959; Karl H. Menges, *The Turkic Languages and Peoples*, 1968; Aleksandr J. Neikrich, *The Punished Peoples*, 1978; N. A. Smirnov, *Islam and*

Russia, 1956; Stefan Wurm, *Turkic Peoples of the USSR*, 1954; Serge A. Zenkovsky, *Pan-Turkism and Islam in Russia*, 1960; Ronald Wixman, *The Peoples of the USSR: An Ethnographic Handbook*, 1984.

NOGAIBAK. See NAGAIBAK and BASHKIR.

NOGAIBAK. See NOGAI.

NOGAIBAQ. See NAGAIBAK and BASHKIR.

NOGAILAR. See NOGAI.

NOGAITSY. See NOGAI.

NOGAJTSY. See NOGAI.

NOGHAI. See NOGAI.

NOGHAIBAK. See NAGAIBAK and BASHKIR.

NOGHAIBAQ. See NAGAIBAK and BASHKIR.

NOGHAY. See NOGAI.

NOGHAYBAK. See NAGAIBAK and BASHKIR.

NOGHAYBAQ. See NAGAIBAK and BASHKIR.

NOIGUT. See ICHKILIK or KYRGYZ.

NOKHCHO. See CHECHEN.

NORTH CAUCASIAN. The term "North Caucasian" is a geographic reference describing the indigenous peoples of the North Caucasus. Included in this grouping are the Circassians*, Abazas*, Karachais*, Balkars*, North Ossetians*, Ingush*, Chechens*, Avars*, Dargins*, Kaitaks*, Kubachis*, Kumyks*, Nogais*, Laks*, Lezgins*, Tabasarans*, Aguls*, Rutuls*, and Tsakhurs*.
REFERENCE: Ronald Wixman, *The Peoples of the USSR: An Ethnographic Handbook*, 1984.

NORTH OSETIAN. See NORTH OSSETIAN, IRON, DIGOR, and OSSETIAN.

NORTH OSETIN. See NORTH OSSETIAN, IRON, DIGOR, and OSSETIAN.

NORTH OSSETIAN. The term "North Ossetian" is a geographic reference to the Iron* and Digor* peoples who live north of the Great Caucasian Mountains.

516   NORTH OSSETIN

REFERENCE: Ronald Wixman, *The Peoples of the USSR: An Ethnographic Handbook*, 1984.

NORTH OSSETIN. See NORTH OSSETIAN, IRON, DIGOR, and OSSETIAN.

NORTHERN ALTAI. See ALTAI.

NOTOZER. See LAPP.

NOVOSELETS. The term "Novoselets" is no longer used in Russia as a ethnological term, but, since around the 1920s, it referred to Eastern Slavs (Russians*, Ukrainians*, and Belarusians*) who had settled in Siberia. Before then, they were known as the Sibiryaks.
REFERENCE: Ronald Wixman, *The Peoples of the USSR: An Ethnographic Handbook*, 1984.

NOVOSELTSY. See NOVOSELETS.

NOVRUZ. See NOGAI.

NUKHA. See AZERBAIJANI.

NUKRAT TATAR. See KARA TATAR and TATAR.

NUKRATSKIY TATAR. See KARA TATAR and TATAR.

NYA. See NGANASAN.

NYMYLAN. The term "Nymylan" refers to those Koryaks* who do not work as nomadic reindeer herders but who are settled hunters and fishermen along the coastal area of Siberia. See KORYAK.
REFERENCE: Ronald Wixman, *The Peoples of the USSR: An Ethnographic Handbook*, 1984.

NYMYLUN. See ITELMEN, KORYAK, and NYMYLAN.

NYMYLYN. See ITELMEN, KORYAK, and NYMYLAN.

O

OB OSTIAK. See KHANT.

OB OSTYAK. See KHANT.

OB UGOR. See KHANT and MANSI.

OB UGORTSY. See KHANT and MANSI.

OB UGRIAN. See KHANT and MANSI.

OBDOR. See KHANT.

ODUL. See YUKAGIR.

OIRAT. See OIROT.

OIRAT. See KALMYK.

OIROT. See ALTAI.

OIROT. The Oirots, who call themselves the Dzungars or Mongols*, are western Mongols who have common cultural roots with the Buryats* and Kalmyks*. The vast majority of them are Buddhists. See BURYAT and KALMYK.
REFERENCE: Ronald Wixman, *The Peoples of the USSR: An Ethnographic Handbook*, 1984.

OKHOTSK. See EVEN.

OKO NGANASAN. The Oko Nganasan are members of the Oka clan of the Dolgan* people who, during much of the nineteenth century, settled among the Nganasan* and became virtually a subgroup of them. See NGANASAN or DOLGAN.
REFERENCE: Ronald Wixman, *The Peoples of the USSR: An Ethnographic Handbook*, 1984.

OLA. See EVEN.

OLCHI. See ULCHI.

OLET. See BURYAT.

OLIK CHEREMISS. See KOZHLA MARI and MARI.

OLIK CHEREMISS MARI. See KOZHLA MARI and MARI.

OLYK CHEREMISS. See KOZHLA MARI and MARI.

OLYK CHEREMISS MARI. See KOZHLA MARI and MARI.

OLYK MARI. See KOZHLA MARI and MARI.

OMOK. See YUKAGIR.

OMOLEN CHUKCHI. See CHUKCHI.

ONKILON. See ESKIMO.

ONMYLEN. See CHUKCHI.

ORO KUMANDY. See KUMANDIN and ALTAI.

OROCH. See EVEN.

OROCHEL. See EVEN.

OROCHEN. See EVEN and EVENK.

OROCHI. Along with the Ulchis*, Oroks*, Nanais*, and Udegeis*, the Orochis (Oroki) are one of the closely related Nani* peoples. In fact, some ethnographers consider them, as they do themselves, a single people occupying different geographical areas. They speak a Manchu* language.

In terms of religion, the Orochis retain many beliefs of their indigenous, animist religion. Although they have incorporated many elements of Russian Orthodoxy, Buddhism, and Confucianism (because of their contact with Russians* and Chinese*), they still believe in a world of spirits and deities, all related to their environment. They have a sense of obligation that leads them to propitiate those spirits in order to maintain balance in their lives and to prevent, or at least contain, capricious natural disasters.

But almost everything else about their world has changed as a result of Soviet ideological policies and economic development. Beginning in the 1930s, Soviet officials have pressured the Orochis to relocate and settle permanently. Most of the Orochis eventually gravitated to the village of Uska in the Sovetskaia Gavan' Rayon of the Russian Soviet Federated Socialist Republic. The government also organized the Orochi into fishing collectives. It also established several schools for Orochi children in the 1930s, and, although the children were allowed to speak Orochi in school, they were also forced to learn Russian. Orochi has no written language, so literacy meant the ability to read and write Russian. By the mid–1980s, less than 40 percent of the Orochis claimed Orochi as their mother tongue. Russian had displaced it as the language of most Orochis.

Economic development also pushed the Orochis closer to extinction as a distinct ethnic group. The construction of oil and natural gas wells, hydroelectric and nuclear power plants, mines, and pulp and paper mills have devastated the Orochi environment while also bringing tens of thousands of ethnic Russians and Ukrainians* to their homeland. By the mid–1980s, the Orochis were completely surrounded by Russians and constituted less than one-tenth of one percent of the population of their region.

Some Orochis are protesting what has happened to them over the last several decades. The Association of the Orochi is a lobbying group designed to protect the environment where the surviving Orochi live. Lyudmila Grishina, president of the Association of the Orochi in Khabarovsk Territory, has stated that ''over the past twenty years my people's numbers have steadily declined. The reason—being forced to resettle in other regions. We've already been moved five times from our ancestral lands. That's why we don't have any fishermen or hunters in our villages, and we are losing our native language and culture. Poor health services and unfit housing conditions have taken their toll too.'' Other Orochi leaders are trying to teach the Orochi language to teenagers. Survival of Orochi culture, however, will be difficult.

REFERENCES: Alice Bartels and Dennis Bartels, ''Soviet Policy Toward Siberian Native People,'' Canadian Dimension, 19 (1985), 36–44; Mike Edwards, ''Siberia: In From the Cold,'' National Geographic, 177 (March 1990), 2–49; James Forsyth, A History of the Peoples of Siberia, 1992; Constantine Krypton, ''Soviet Policy in the Northern National Regions After World War II,'' Slavic Review, 13 (October 1954), 339–53; Alexander Tropkin, ''Congress of Hope,'' Soviet Life, (December 1990), 10–15; Piers Vitebsky, ''Perestroika Among the Reindeer Herders,'' Geographical Magazine, 61 (June 1989), 23–34; Ronald Wixman, The Peoples of the USSR: An Ethnographic Handbook, 1984.

OROK. Along with the Ulchis*, Orochis*, Nanais*, and Udegeis*, the Oroks are one of the closely related Nani* peoples. In fact, some ethnographers consider them, as they do themselves, a single people occupying different geographical areas. They speak a Manchu* language. The Oroks (Ul'ta, Ul'cha) people, who total approximately 200 individuals, are of mixed origins. They consist of a mixture of Udegei, Nanai, Ulchi, Negidal*, Nivkhi*, and Evenk* peoples. They live primarily in the northern reaches of Sakhalin Island.

Orok life has been dramatically affected by political and economic events in the twentieth century. During the 1930s, state policy succeeded in bringing most Oroks into reindeer collectives, limiting their nomadism in order to augment state transportation needs. World War II proved to be devastating to many Oroks. At the outbreak of the war, there were about 300 Oroks in southern Sakhalin Island. Because of Japanese* control of southern Sakhalin, these Oroks faced assimilationist pressures from Japanese culture; many were conscripted into the Japanese army. After the war, Soviet officials killed a significant number of these Oroks as punishment for "collaborating" with the Japanese. Many of the survivors migrated to the island of Hokkaido between 1947 and 1955, leaving the rest of the Orok community confined to northern Sakhalin Island, where they became part of a single reindeer-herding collective.

REFERENCES: Alice Bartels and Dennis Bartels, "Soviet Policy Toward Siberian Native People," *Canadian Dimension*, 19 (1985), 36–44; Mike Edwards, "Siberia: In From the Cold," *National Geographic*, 177 (March 1990), 2–49; James Forsyth, *A History of the Peoples of Siberia*, 1992; Constantine Krypton, "Soviet Policy in the Northern National Regions After World War II," *Slavic Review*, 13 (October 1954), 339–53; Piers Vitebsky, "Perestroika Among the Reindeer Herders," *Geographical Magazine*, 61 (June 1989), 23–34; Ronald Wixman, *The Peoples of the USSR: An Ethnographic Handbook*, 1984.

OROSHOR. Most ethnographers classify the Oroshor today as a subgroup of the Rushan*, who are one of the Pamir* peoples. They are Ismaili Muslims in their religious loyalties and, like many of the Pamir peoples, they are being rapidly assimilated by the Tajiks*. See PAMIR PEOPLES or TAJIK.

REFERENCE: Ronald Wixman, *The Peoples of the USSR: An Ethnographic Handbook*, 1984.

OS. See OSSETIAN.

OSET. See OSSETIAN.

OSETIAN. See OSSETIAN.

OSETIN. See OSSETIAN.

OSETINY. See OSSETIAN.

OSETY. See OSSETIAN.

OSI. See OSSETIAN.

OSMAN TURK. See OSMANLY TURK, MESKHETIAN, and AZERBAIJANI.

OSMANLY TURK. The term ''Osmanly Turk'' is an archaic reference to Turks* living in what used to be the Soviet Union. Several decades ago, the term ''Turk'' was used to refer to Azerbaijanis*, especially to those of the Shiite Muslim faith. By contrast, Turks who were Sunni Muslims were described as Osman, or Osmanly, Turks. The vast majority of the Osman Turks lived in Georgia, along the Turkish border. During World War II, most of them fell victim to Stalin's purges and deportations. They have since disappeared into the new ethnic group known as Meskhetians*. See MESKHETIAN, AZERBAIJANI, or TURK.
REFERENCE: Ronald Wixman, *The Peoples of the USSR: An Ethnographic Handbook*, 1984.

OSMANSKIY TURK. See OSMANLY TURK, MESKHETIAN, and AZERBAIJANI.

OSSET. See OSSETIAN.

OSSETE. See OSSETIAN.

OSSETIAN. The Ossetians (also spelled Ossetins, Oselty) are an ethnic group of the central Caucasus Mountains who, though different from Russians* in language, religion, and customs, have, under both tsars and commissars, maintained a mutually beneficial relationship with their Slavic colonizers. The Ossetians call themselves Ir or Digor*, based on tribal loyalties, and Russians refer to them as the Osetiny, Digory, Ironi*, or Iry. Today, most Ossetians live in the North Ossetian Autonomous Republic, which used to be the North Ossetian Autonomous Soviet Socialist Republic (Severnaia Osetiia ASSR). Located on the north slope of the great mountain range, the North Ossetian Autonomous Republic is within the Russian Soviet Federated Socialist Republic (RSFSR, or ''Russia''). A smaller number of Ossetians live on the south slope of mountains in the South Ossetian (Iuzhnaia Osetiia) Autonomous Oblast of the Georgian Republic or in neighboring regions. In the 1979 census of the Soviet Union, 299,022 Ossetians, or 55.2 percent of the total population, lived in the North Ossetian ASSR, while 65,077, or 12 percent, lived in the South Ossetian Autonomous Oblast. Another 18 percent lived in the Georgian SSR, while the rest were scattered throughout the Kabardino-Balkar ASSR, the Stavropol Krai, Moscow, the Chechen-Ingush Autonomous Soviet Socialist Republic, the Rostov

Oblast, the Krasnodar Krai, the Daghestan ASSR, and the Tajik, Uzbek, Kazakh, Azerbaijan, and Turkmen republics.

There was a total of 170,000 Ossetians counted in the 1897 census; 272,000 in 1926, 410,000 in 1959, and 542,000 in 1979. In the 1989 Soviet census, the total number of Ossetians was 597,802. Their political power has been diluted by the fact that Russians constitute one-third of the population of North Ossetia and Georgians* constitute almost a third of the population of South Ossetia. The autonomy of both regions has in fact been nominal.

The Ossetian homeland straddles one of the world's most forbidding mountain ranges, so there is tremendous environmental diversity according to altitude. From north to south, there are first the Mozdok and Ossetian Plains, which are steppe lands drained by the Terek River. These areas are suitable for farming, and have attracted Russian settlers. Then come the foothill zones of mixed pasture and beech-oak forest. Further into the Caucasus, the inhabitants are squeezed into narrow river valleys. Only a very few passes between the glaciated peaks allow movement south into climatically mild Georgia, and these have naturally assumed great strategic importance in Russia's wars with the Turks* and Persians*. The Ossetians' relatively undeveloped sense of nationhood may be attributed to the extreme difficulty of travel and communication: Most villages can be reached only by footpath.

Ossetians speak an Indo-European language of the Iranian group, somewhat influenced by the Turkic languages of their neighbors. Dialects originally followed tribal lines, but, over the years, one dialect, called Iron*, has been recognized as correct Ossetian. There are two other functioning Ossetian dialects—Digor and Taul (Tuallag). There is also a geographical dimension to the linguistic differences. The Ossetians speaking the Iron dialect are concentrated in the eastern region of the North Ossetian Autonomous Republic, primarily on the slopes of the Great Caucasian mountain chain, while the Digor live in the Digor Valley of the western North Ossetian Autonomous Republic; the Taul live in the South Ossetian Autonomous Oblast. The gradual extinction of the archaic Digor dialect was accelerated by Josef Stalin's dislike for that group. He formally declared Digor not to be a literary language. Most Ossetians speak Russian as a second language.

Finally, there is a profound religious division in the Ossetian community. The Iron- and Taul-speaking Ossetians are Christians—Eastern Orthodox in their religious orientation. The Iron were converted to Christianity in the twelfth and thirteenth centuries by the Georgians. The Taul are Ossetians who crossed the Caucasus Mountains and settled on their southern slopes. They too are Eastern Orthodox and heavily influenced by Georgians. The Digor-speaking Ossetians are Sunni Muslims of the Hanafi school. Islam came to them in the seventeenth and eighteenth centuries from Kabarda, but, until World War II, the Muslim Ossetians were at best lukewarm in their religious commitment. In 1944, however, Stalin had the Digors deported, along with the Chechens*, Ingushes*, Karachais*, and Balkars*. Since then, their religious identity has become more intense. Radical Islamic Sufism is penetrating the Ossetian community from neighboring Ingush areas.

Ossetians trace their ancestry back to the Scythians, but this is conjectural. They are definitely descended from one tribe of the Sarmatians, the Alans. The Alans were pushed out of the plain and into the foothills by the Huns in the fourth century. Waves of Tatar* and Mongol* invaders then pushed the Alans (Ossetes) further back into the mountain gorges, and effectively destroyed their material culture. The most prominent remaining structures from that period are tall stone watchtowers inside of which all the people of a village could barricade themselves from raiders. Ossetians who remained on the north slope lived in perpetual conflict with the warlike Kabards*, but only the Digor Ossets were culturally influenced by the Kabards and converted by them to Islam. Ossetians who migrated to the south slope have retained their language and culture in medieval and modern Georgia.

Russian imperial expansion reached the Caucasus during the reign of Catherine the Great. By contrast with local Muslim tribes, who resisted fiercely, the Ossetians welcomed the Russians, since they offered protection from the Kabards and actually permitted Ossetian resettlement of the plains. Russian missionaries worked unsuccessfully to eradicate the many indigenous practices that pervade Ossetian Christianity. The monotheism of Muslim Ossetians is similarly compromised by animist beliefs and deities.

From the Russian point of view, the Ossetians were the only Christians in a sea of hostile Muslin mountain tribes. Furthermore, they occupied both ends of the strategic Darial pass. From 1774, when North Ossetia was absorbed into Russia, to the present, Russian policy has therefore been to cultivate the Ossetians. The most important Russian town in Ossetia is Vladikavkaz (meaning "Authority over the Caucasus"). The Georgian Military Road was completed in 1799, facilitating the Russian conquest of Georgia in 1801. A parallel Ossetian Military Highway was hacked through a 9,000-foot pass in 1889. Neither road is usable in the winter. Soviet historians somewhat exaggerate the "historic relations of friendship between the Russian and Ossetian peoples," but it is true that Ossetians have enlisted in the Russian army to help defeat Poles*, Turks, and, later, Nazis.

North Ossetia's economy was transformed by industrialization and urbanization in the nineteenth century. Zinc and lead mines were opened, and natural gas was discovered. The vital railroad to the oil boomtown of Baku passed through Ossetia, and a branch line reached Vladikavkaz. Social Democrats and Bolsheviks recruited Ossetian workers for revolutionary activity. In the civil war following the Russian Revolution in 1917, Ossetia saw fighting between Bolsheviks, Mensheviks, and General Anton Denikin's counterrevolutionary armies. The official Soviet appraisal is that, on balance, the Ossetians helped the Bolsheviks.

A South Ossetian Autonomous Oblast was carved out of Georgia in 1922. North Ossetia was incorporated into an "Autonomous Mountain Soviet Socialist

Republic'' that was supposed to bring together all the North Caucasus tribes, but this experiment was quickly abandoned and the North Ossetian Autonomous Oblast was formed in July 1924. The next year, a delegation of Ossetians unsuccessfully petitioned Stalin for unification of the two Ossetias.

Bolshevik policy in Ossetia aimed to 1) eliminate social practices deemed feudal, such as clan warfare and bride-stealing; 2) encourage literacy in Ossetian, first utilizing Cyrillic script, then Latin, then Cyrillic again; and, 3) develop the economy on the basis of farming and sheep-herding collectives. These efforts were moderately successful, despite the natural resistance of independent mountaineers to collectivization. In many villages, Ossetians used Stalin's purges to carry on old vendettas. The name of North Ossetia's capital was changed from Vladikavkaz to Ordzhonikidze in 1932, to honor a leading Bolshevik and onetime collaborator of Stalin's. In 1936, North Ossetia was formally upgraded from an autonomous oblast to an autonomous republic, but, of course, the distinction was meaningless in practice. Stalin's mother was part Ossetian, but that fact probably was unimportant to the unsentimental dictator. The Ossetians were relatively well-treated mainly because it was in the Russian national interest to do so.

In World War II, a prime German* objective was the oil fields of Baku and Grozny. Ordzhonikidze was occupied in December 1942, but Ossetians remained loyal to the Soviet Union, harassing the Germans from behind the lines. Their sentiments contrasted sharply with those of the Chechens, who welcomed any deliverer from Russian bondage. The Ossetians were duly rewarded with many "Hero of the Soviet Union" medals. Their republic was arbitrarily enlarged at the expense of the Chechen-Ingush ASSR and the Stavropol Territory of Russia. In addition, the capital was renamed once again: For ten years (1944–1954), it was called Dzaudzikau, the Ossetian pronunciation of Vladikavkaz. One group of Ossetians, however, the Muslim Digors, received the same treatment as other anti-Russian, Muslim mountaineers, such as the Chechen and Ingush. Once the Germans were driven back, the Digors were rounded up and deported wholesale to Central Asia. There are small colonies of Ossetians scattered across that region even today. Despite Soviet support for Ossetian "nationhood," most Ossetians identify with their religion (either Christian or Muslim) or with their tribe. Traditional customs, including polygamy, continue. Women are subordinated to their husbands and in-laws.

Literary and artistic expressions of Ossetian culture received encouragement from the Soviet government. After 1954, the writing system of South Ossetia, which has been based on the Georgia alphabet, was made identical to that in North Ossetia, which is based on the Russian alphabet. There are Ossetian-language newspapers and some Ossetian broadcasting on radio, but not on television. In Ordzhonikidze, there is a university, as well as institutes for medicine, agriculture, and mining.

The industrial development of Ossetia has done more than any deliberate government policy to alter traditional ways. New roads have been built into the mountains, including the mammoth Transcacuasian Highway and its four-kilometer tunnel at the Rok Mountain Pass. There is heavy industry, including machine-building, textile mills, glassware factories, and a substantial food-processing sector. These enterprises tend to be concentrated in Ordzhonikidze, however, and so are of more benefit to Russian settlers in that city than to Ossetians in the countryside. Timber is the most important industry in south Ossetia.

Chaotic conditions in the Soviet Union after 1989 brought great misery to the South Ossetians. They sensed danger in rising Georgian nationalism, which perforce had an undertone of hatred for the Russians, and, by extension, for any pro-Russian group. The South Ossetians demanded unification with North Ossetia, which Georgians saw as part of a Russian plot. In November 1989, thousands of Georgians marched on Tskhinvali (formerly Staliniri), the South Ossetian capital, which had to be defended by Interior Ministry troops dispatched by Moscow. In December 1990, the Georgian Supreme Soviet declared that South Ossetia was no longer autonomous and gave the Georgian Military commander there authority to suppress newspapers and ban demonstrations. Fighting commenced in January 1991; by August of that year, more than 200 South Ossetians had been killed. In a plebiscite in March 1991, Georgians voted overwhelmingly (98.9 percent) for secessions from the Soviet Union, but Ossetians wished to remain part of it. As the newly elected president of Georgia, Zviad Gamsakhurdia, veered toward one-man rule, he began referring to Ossetians as unwanted guests who should "go back" to North Ossetia. Gamsakhurdia proposed limiting Georgian citizenship to those who could prove that their ancestors had lived in Georgia before 1801. The Georgian militia surrounded Tskhinvali, cut off the city's heat and electricity, and began an artillery bombardment. In September 1991, an American congressional committee on human rights canceled a planned visit to Tskhinvali because of incoming mortar fire. In the countryside, Ossetian homes were burned and looted. The Ossetians gave as good as they got, for most villages in the region were in fact composed of a mixed population of Georgians and Ossetians. At the end of 1991, a flood of refugees from South Ossetia crossed the Caucasus, seeking safety in North Ossetia, and the Russian parliament warned Georgia of economic sanctions unless the fighting was brought to an end.

There is also some friction between the Ossetians and the Ingushes, their neighbors to the east. When the Ingushes returned from their internal exile in the 1960s, they found that Ossetians had occupied former Ingush land. In fact, the Ingush lay claim to half of the North Ossetian capital of Vladikavkaz and also argue that the Prigorodny region of North Ossetia was their historic homeland; Ossetians do not accept that claim. Throughout 1992, there was sporadic fighting in the region between Ossetian and Ingush militiamen, and several hundred people were killed.

REFERENCES: W.E.D. Allen and Paul Muratoff, *Caucasian Battlefields*, 1953; Elizabeth Fuller, "Georgian Parliament Votes to Abolish Ossetian Autonomy," *Radio Liberty Reports on the USSR*, 2:51 (December 21, 1990), 8–9; *New York Times*, November 6,

1992; Michael Pereira, *Across the Caucasus*, 1973; Walter Kolarz, *Russia and Her Colonies*, 1952; Richard V. Weekes, ed., *Muslin Peoples: A World Ethnographic Survey*, 1984.

Ross Marlay

OSSETIN. See OSSETIAN.

OSTIAK. See OSTYAK.

OSTIAKO-SAMODI. See SELKUP.

OSTIAKO-SAMOED. See SELKUP.

OSTIAKO-SAMOIED. See SELKUP.

OSTIAKO-SAMODI. See SELKUP.

OSTYAK. The term "Ostyaks" was used historically in Russia to describe a large number of indigenous peoples who lived in the Ob basin in western Siberia. Included in the Ostyak grouping were the Tatars*, Khants*, Bashkirs*, Kets*, and Selkups.*
REFERENCE: Ronald Wixman, *The Peoples of the USSR: An Ethnographic Handbook*, 1984.

OSTYAKO-SAMOED. See SELKUP.

OSTYAKO-SAMOIED. See SELKUP.

OSTYAKO-SAMOYED. See SELKUP.

OSTYAKO-SAMOYED. See SELKUP.

OSY. See OSSETIAN.

OTIAKI. See UDMURT.

OVEN. See EVEN.

OYRAT. See OIROT.

OYROT. See ALTAI.

OZBEK. See UZBEK.

OZBEQ. See UZBEK.

P

PADAR. The Padar are considered to be a subgroup of the Azerbaijanis*, and are concentrated demographically in Azerbaijan. They make their living raising livestock. The Padar are Sunni Muslims in religion, speak a distinct dialect, and maintain a strong sense of ethnicity. See AZERBAIJANI.
REFERENCES: Shirin Akiner, *Islamic Peoples of the Soviet Union*, 1983; Ronald Wixman, *The Peoples of the USSR: An Ethnographic Handbook*, 1984.

PAKISTANI. Until its 1989 census, the Soviet Union did not track, or at least did not publish, the number of foreign residents by nationality group. The 1989 census did provide these figures, and it indicated that in 1989 there were 2,614 Indians* and Pakistanis living in the Soviet Union, of whom Pakistanis constituted approximately half. Ever since the Bolshevik Revolution, there had been a few Pakistanis living in the Soviet Union. Most were expatriates infatuated with Marxism and the Communist experiment, but there was never any significant movement by Pakistanis to change their citizenship and live their lives in the Soviet Union. After World War II, as the Cold War between the United States and the Soviet Union gained momentum, the Soviet Union provided financial aid to bring Pakistani students to Moscow to study. More recently, there have also been a very few Pakistanis who, for economic reasons, were much interested in improving their country's business relationship with the Soviet Union. Most Pakistanis living in the Soviet Union since the late 1980s have been students and businesspeople.
REFERENCE: Raymond E. Zickel, ed., *Soviet Union: A Country Study*, 1991.

PALAN. The Palan are a Koryok subgroup. They are distinguished from other Koryaks by their distinct dialect and by their territorial concentration near the Sea of Okhotsk coast in the Koryak Autonomous Oblast. See KORYAK.
REFERENCE: Ronald Wixman, *The Peoples of the USSR: An Ethnographic Handbook*, 1984.

PALANTSY. See PALAN and KORYAK.

PALEO-ASIATIC PEOPLES. The term "Paleo-Asiatic peoples" has long been used as a generic reference to all the people of Siberia who do not speak one of the languages in the Uralic-Altaic linguistic family. Included in the Paleo-Astiatic group have been the Eskimos*, Aleuts*, Chukchis*, Koryaks*, Itelmen*, Nivkhis*, and Yukagirs*.

REFERENCE: Ronald Wixman, *The Peoples of the USSR: An Ethnographic Handbook*, 1984.

PALEO-SIBERIAN PEOPLES. See PALEO-ASIATIC PEOPLES.

PAMIR PEOPLES. The term "Pamir peoples" is an older, generic designation for the Shugnans* (Shugni, Shugnantsy), Rushans* (Rushani, Rushantsy), Bartangs* (Bartangi, Bartangtsy), Yazgulem* (Yazgulemi, Jazgulemtsy, Jazgulamtsy), Ishkashmis* (Ishkashimi, Ishkashimtsy), Wakhans* (Vakhans, Vakhantsy, Wakhis, Wakhanis), Bajui* (Badzhujtsy), and Kufs* (Khuftsy) groups. They have also been known collectively as Mountain Tajiks*, Pamirian Tadjiks, and Galchahs. The Yazgulems live in the Yazgulem River Valley and call themselves the Zgamig. The Rushans, who call themselves the Rykhen, inhabit the Pyanzh Valley between the Yazgulem and Bartang rivers. The Khufs call themselves the Khufidzh and are classified as a Rushan subgroup. The Bartangs refer to themselves as the Bartangidzh and live in the Bartang River Valley. South of the Rushans are the Shugnans, whose self-designation is Khugnon and who live in the Middle Pyanzh Valley and along the Gunt and Shah-Dara rivers; the Shugnans are the most numerous of the Pamirian peoples. The Bajui call themselves the Badzhuwedzh and are today classified as a subgroup of the Shugnan. The Ishkashimis refer to themselves as the Shikomshi, live south of the Shugnans and are the southernmost of the Pamir groups. The Wakhans, who call themselves the Khik, live in the highlands of the Pyanzh Valley and on the Pamir River.

Although local tradition among the Pamirian peoples holds that they are descended from the leaders of Alexander the Great's invasion army, who reached the area in the fourth century B.C. and decided to live in the inaccessible mountain valleys, the Pamir peoples first appeared historically in the second century A.D. when Chinese* chroniclers mentioned the Rushans, Shugnans, and Wakhans. Although they enjoyed brief periods of independence over the years, the Pamir peoples were usually under the political control of some foreign power. In the mid-eighteenth century, Ahmad Shah Durrani established an independent Afghan* state, and, by the late nineteenth century, during the reign of Abdur Rahman, most of the Pamir peoples were controlled politically from Kabul. The Emir of Bukhara, which was part of a Russian* protectorate, was expanding to the south. At the same time, the British* were expanding toward the Hindu Kush. In 1895, to prevent a collision, Britain and Russia agreed to place the border between Russia and Afghanistan at the Pyanzh River. The Emir of Bukhara controlled the land on the northern side, while Afghanistan controlled the land to the south. Russia annexed all of the Pamir possessions of the Emir of Bukhara in 1904.

The Pamir peoples speak Iranian languages and live in the Gorno-Badakhshan Autonomous Oblast in Tajikistan. They are Ismaili Muslims of the Nizarit rite, except for the Yazgulems, and Wakhans, and some Bartangs, who are Sunnis of the Hanafi school. Russian and then Soviet ethnologists long viewed them as distinct peoples, but, for the past sixty years, they have been included as Tajik* subgroups. The Shugnan dialect is the *lingua franca* for the Pamir peoples. There are also Pamir groups living in Afghanistan and in China. As of the early 1990s, the population of all of the Pamir groups together was just below 100,000 people. The Shugnans have a population of nearly 50,000 people, the Rushans approximately 15,000 people, the Wakhans 14,000, the Bartangs 7,000, the Yazgulems 5,000, the Khufs 3,000, and the Ishkashmis 1,000.

REFERENCES: Shirin Akiner, *Islamic Peoples of the Soviet Union*, 1983; Alexandre Bennigsen and S. Enders Wimbush, *Muslims of the Soviet Empire: A Guide*, 1986; Yuri Kushko, ''The Pamirs,'' *Soviet Life*, (June 1990), 28–35; Ronald Wixman, *The Peoples of the USSR: An Ethnographic Handbook*, 1984.

PAMIR TADJIK. See TAJIK and PAMIR PEOPLES.

PAMIR TADZHIK. See TAJIK and PAMIR PEOPLES.

PAMIR TAJIK. See TAJIK and PAMIR PEOPLES.

PAMIR-ALAI KIRGHIZ. See ICHKILIK and KYRGYZ.

PAMIR-ALAI KIRGIZ. See ICHKILIK and KYRGYZ.

PAMIR-ALAI KYRGHIZ. See ICHKILIK and KYRGYZ.

PAMIR-ALAI KYRGYZ. See ICHKILIK and KYRGYZ.

PAMIR-ALAI QIRGHIZ. See ICHKILIK and KYRGYZ.

PAMIR-ALAI QIRGIZ. See ICHKILIK and KYRGYZ.

PAMIR-ALAI QIRGYZ. See ICHKILIK and KYRGYZ.

PAMIR-ALAI QYRGHYZ. See ICHKILIK and KYRGYZ.

PAMIRI. See PAMIR PEOPLES and TAJIK.

PAMIRIAN TADJIK. See TAJIK and PAMIR PEOPLES.

PARABA. See BARABA TATAR.

PAREN. The Paren are one of the Koryak* subgroups. They are distinguished from other Koyraks by their distinct dialect and by their territorial concentration on the Paren River in the Koryak Autonomous Oblast. See KORYAK.
REFERENCE: Ronald Wixman, The Peoples of the USSR: An Ethnographic Handbook, 1984.

PARENTSY. See PAREN and KORYAK.

PASHTANIS. See AFGHAN.

PECHORA. See KOMI.

PEOPLES of DAGESTAN. See DAGHESTANI.

PEOPLES OF DAGHESTAN. See DAGHESTANI.

PEOPLES OF MOUNT SHAHDAG. See SHAHDAGH and AZERBAIJANI.

PEOPLES OF MOUNT SHAH DAGH. See SHAH DAGH and AZER-BAIJANI.

PEOPLES OF MOUNT SHAHDAG. See SHAH DAGH and AZERBAIJANI.

PEOPLES OF MOUNT SHAKHDAG. See SHAH DAGH and AZER-BAIJANI.

PEOPLES OF MOUNT SHAKHDAGH. See SHAH DAGH and AZER-BAIJANI.

PEOPLES OF SIBERIA. The term ''Peoples of Siberia'' is an older reference used in nineteenth- and twentieth-century Russia to describe all of the indigenous peoples of Siberia.
REFERENCE: Ronald Wixman, The Peoples of the USSR: An Ethnographic Handbook, 1984.

PEOPLES OF SIBERIA AND THE FAR EAST. The term ''Peoples of Siberia and the Far East'' is an older reference used in nineteenth- and twentieth-century Russia to describe the indigenous people living in Siberia, and, in that sense, it is synonymous with the term ''Peoples of Siberia.''
REFERENCE: Ronald Wixman, The Peoples of the USSR: An Ethnographic Handbook, 1984.

PEOPLES OF SOUTHERN SIBERIA. The term "Peoples of Southern Siberia" is an older reference used in nineteenth- and twentieth-century Russia to describe the nomadic livestock herders of southern Siberia. It included the Altais*, Buryats*, Khakass*, Tuvinians*, West Siberian Tatars*, Shors*, Tofalars*, and Yakuts*.
REFERENCE: Ronald Wixman, *The Peoples of the USSR: An Ethnographic Handbook*, 1984.

PEOPLES OF THE BALTIC. See BALTIC PEOPLES, LATVIAN, ESTONIAN, and LITHUANIAN.

PEOPLES OF THE CAUCASUS. See CAUCASIAN.

PEOPLES OF THE EAST. The term "Peoples of the East" is an older reference used in nineteenth- and early twentieth-century Russia to describe all of the indigenous peoples living in Siberia, Central Asia, the Middle Volga basin, and Transcaucasia.
REFERENCE: Ronald Wixman, *The Peoples of the USSR: An Ethnographic Handbook*, 1984.

PEOPLES OF THE GORNO-BADAGSHAN. See PAMIR PEOPLES and TAJIK.

PEOPLES OF THE GORNO-BADAKHSHAN. See PAMIR PEOPLES and TAJIK.

PEOPLES OF THE MIDDLE VOLGA. The term "Peoples of the Middle Volga" is an older reference used in nineteenth- and early twentieth-century Russia to describe the Finnic*- and Turkic*-speaking groups of the region. Generally, the term included the Maris*, Udmurts*, Mordvinians*, Tatars*, Chuvashes, and Bashkirs*.
REFERENCE: Ronald Wixman, *The Peoples of the USSR: An Ethnographic Handbook*, 1984.

PEOPLES OF THE NORTH. The term "Peoples of the North" is an older reference used in nineteenth- and early twentieth-century Russia to describe the indigenous peoples living in the far northern reaches of Russia and in Siberia. Included in the terminology are the Khants*, Mansis*, Lapps*, Nenets*, Ents*, Nganasans*, Selkups*, Evens*, Evenks*, Negidals*, Nanais*, Ulchis*, Oroks*, Orochis*, Udegeis*, Eskimos*, Aleuts*, Chukchis*, Koryaks*, Itelmen*, Nivkhis*, Yukagirs*, Dolgans*, Tofalars*, and Yakuts*.
REFERENCE: Ronald Wixman, *The Peoples of the USSR: An Ethnographic Handbook*, 1984.

PEOPLES OF THE PAMIRS. See PAMIR PEOPLES and TAJIK.

PEOPLES OF THE SOVIET EAST. The term ''Peoples of the Soviet East'' is a generic reference used earlier in the twentieth century, primarily by Western scholars, to describe the indigenous peoples living at the southern and eastern extremities of the Russian and Soviet empires. The term usually included all of the Muslim groups and the southern Siberians.
REFERENCE: Ronald Wixman, *The Peoples of the USSR: An Ethnographic Handbook*, 1984.

PEOPLES OF THE SOVIET WEST. The term ''Peoples of the Soviet West'' is a generic reference used earlier in the twentieth century, primarily by Western scholars, to describe the indigenous peoples living in European Russia. The term usually included the Ukrainians*, Belarusians*, Latvians*, Estonians*, Lithuanians*, Finns*, Karelians*, Moldovans*, Jews*, and Poles*.
REFERENCE: Ronald Wixman, *The Peoples of the USSR: An Ethnographic Handbook*, 1984.

PEOPLES OF THE VOLGA. The term ''Peoples of the Volga'' is a generic reference used earlier in the twentieth century, primarily by Western scholars, to describe the indigenous peoples living along the Volga River. These included the Maris*, Mordvinians*, Udmurts*, Tatars*, Bashkirs*, Chuvashes*, and Kalmyks*.
REFERENCE: Ronald Wixman, *The Peoples of the USSR: An Ethnographic Handbook*, 1984.

PEOPLES OF TRANSCAUCASIA. The term ''Peoples of Trascaucasia'' is a generic reference used earlier in the twentieth century, primarily by Western scholars, to describe the indigenous peoples living in the region of the Caucasus Mountains. Usually included in the term were the Georgians*, Armenians*, Azerbaijanis*, Mingrelians*, Svanetians*, Lazes*, Ossetians*, Udis*, Tats*, Talysh*, and Shah Daghs*.
REFERENCE: Ronald Wixman, *The Peoples of the USSR: An Ethnographic Handbook*, 1984.

PEOPLES OF TURKESTAN. The term ''Peoples of Turkestan'' is a generic reference used earlier in the twentieth century, primarily by Western scholars, to describe the indigenous peoples living in what used to be Turkestan. The term generally included the Uzbeks*, Tajiks*, Kyrgyz*, Turkmen*, and Karakalpaks*.

REFERENCE: Ronald Wixman, *The Peoples of the USSR: An Ethnographic Handbook*, 1984.

PERMIAK. See KOMI.

PERMIAN. See KOMI.

PERMYAK. See KOMI.

PERMYAN. See KOMI.

PERSIAN. The Persians are a small ethnic group of approximately 25,000 people who today live primarily in Uzbekistan and Turkmenistan. They call themselves Farsi and are known to Russians* as Persy. In 1785, Emir Shah Murad of Bukhara seized a number of Persian-speaking Iranians in the area of Mary and placed them into Bukharan* slavery. Over the years, their descendants mixed with merchant colonies that had originated in Iran but settled in Central Asia to do business. These communities also absorbed some Beluchi* people and other Shiites. They all became known generically as Persians or Iranis. For them, their religious consciousness as Shiite Muslims of the Ja'farite rite is far more important as an ethnic identity than is any sense of political nationalism.

Until 1910, the Shiite Persians functioned comfortably in the larger Sunni Muslim communities of Central Asia, but, in 1910, a series of mutual massacres occurred between Sunnis and Shiites in Bukhara. In response, the Persians isolated themselves physically and socially, condemning marriages between Sunnis and Shiites and confining contacts to required commercial and political exchanges. After 1926, Soviet census officials classified the Persians and Iranis as one group, even though they had distinct origins and identities. That sense of identity still survived in the 1980s, although some assimilation by neighboring Uzbeks* and Turkmen* was occurring. Most of the Persians living in Uzbekistan speak Uzbek, while only a minority in Turkmenistan speak Turkmen.

REFERENCES: Shirin Akiner, *Islamic Peoples of the Soviet Union*, 1983; Alexandre Bennigsen and S. Enders Wimbush, *Muslims of the Soviet Empire: A Guide*, 1986.

PERSY. See PERSIAN.

PIATIGORSKIE OBSHCHESTVA KABARDY. See BALKAR.

PINCHUKI. See BELARUSIAN and POLESHCHUK.

POLE. By the early 1990s, Soviet enthologists estimated that there were approximately 1,135,000 people of Polish descent living in the Soviet Union. Like their counterparts in Poland, the Poles of the Soviet Union possess a strong sense of ethnic identity. Poland was an independent state for centuries until the 1790s when Prussia, Russia, and Austria-Hungary partitioned the country among themselves. Throughout the nineteenth century, some Poles migrated into the western part of Belarusia and Ukraine in search of jobs and land. When World War I ended and the Allied Powers decided to redraw the map of Europe, they reestablished Poland as a sovereign nation. The Austro-Hungarian Empire was dissolved, Germany lost much of Prussia, and Russia lost what had been known as Congress Poland. The nation of Poland existed once again, and, this time, it controlled substantial amounts of land in western Ukraine, western Belarus, and southeastern Lithuania, including the city of Vilnius. In 1926, there were approximately 780,000 Poles in the Soviet Union. Over the next twenty years, large numbers of Poles migrated to southeastern Lithuania, Polish-controlled areas of Belarus, and Ukraine, especially to the cities, where they worked as bureaucrats and political administrators. By 1940, as a result of the Soviet annexation of these areas, there were more than 1,500,000 Poles in the Soviet Union. Most of the contemporary Polish population of the Soviet Union consists of the descendants of those interwar migrants.

Poland's independent status was short-lived. When Adolf Hitler came to power in Germany in 1934, he was intent on recovering for Germany the land that had been lost as a result of the Treaty of Versailles in 1919, and the German-speaking region of Prussia was foremost on his mind. At the same time, Josef Stalin and the Soviet Union also wanted to recover those parts of Ukraine, Belarusia, and Lithuania that had been theirs until 1919. Moreover, the Russians were paranoid about German* intentions in eastern Europe and believed that repossession of eastern Poland would give them a buffer zone against Hitler. In 1939, the two powers signed the Non-Aggression Pact, which, among other things, authorized them to invade and carve up Poland once again. The invasion took place on September 1, 1939.

The temporary rapprochement between Germany and the Soviet Union and the eventual war between them proved to be disastrous for the Poles of the Soviet Union. Stalin knew that the Poles were a proud, nationalistic people. He also knew that the partition of Poland would not sit well with them. Therefore, to forestall any rebelliousness among the Soviet Union's new Polish population, Stalin launched a massive deportation program, which sent hundreds of thousands of Polish leaders to Siberia, the Urals, and Kazakhstan. When Germany invaded the Soviet Union in 1941, the remaining Poles in Belarus and Ukraine suffered at the hands of Hitler's stormtroopers. At the end of World War II, with massive numbers of Soviet troops occupying Belarus, Lithuania, Poland, and Ukraine, thousands of Polish citizen emigrated across the Soviet frontier into Poland.

After the war, the Soviet Union's Poles still found themselves in difficult circumstances. Their own ethnic identity was decidedly nationalistic and Roman Catholic, but they were living under the political control of a centralized, officially atheistic state. During the next forty years, the Polish population of the Soviet Union steadily declined, primarily as a result of the assimilation of Polish young people into the surrounding Ukrainian*, Belarusian*, and Lithuanian* populations. Their numbers declined from approximately 1,500,000 people in

1940 to 1,380,282 in 1959, 1,167,000 in 1970, 1,151,000 in 1979, and 1,140,000 in 1990. It was not until the rise of Mikhail Gorbachev in the Soviet Union and Lech Wałesa in Poland during the late 1980s that the Poles of the Soviet Union were able to recapture their own ethnic heritage.

Historically, Poles have been among the most devoutly Roman Catholic people in Eastern Europe. Catholicism bound peasants into a unified moral community. They lived in a world of religious and social consensus, circumscribed by the church and supervised by the priest, making up a system of values revolving around the intimacy of language, culture, and tradition.

During the nineteenth and twentieth centuries, Russia and then the Soviet Union sharpened the Polish sense of identity by relentlessly attacking the Roman Catholic church and the Polish language. During the seventeenth and eighteenth centuries, Russia looked upon Roman Catholicism in Poland as both a political threat and a cultural intrusion. After taking control of Poland in the 1790s, Russia tried in vain to restrict the church and suppress the Polish language. In 1864 and 1865, the tsar ordered that all teaching of religion in public schools be conducted in Russian; shortly thereafter, he ordered that Russian be used as the language of instruction in all public and parochial schools. Russian authorities even injected their language into Roman Catholic liturgies. They outlawed crosses on Catholic churches, devotional processions, and parish temperance associations. They demanded prior approval of all clerical appointments, eliminated clerical visitation with parishioners, forbade the construction of new chapels or the repair of old ones, and censored all sermons. But instead of wiping out Roman Catholicism, Russian oppression only succeeded in making the church the premier symbol of Polish ethnicity.

After the brief interlude of Polish independence between 1919 and 1939, the Soviet Union, now in the guise of its officially atheistic political culture, continued to suppress Roman Catholicism in Ukraine, Belarus, and Lithuania. The Communist government of Poland did the same, even going so far as to murder nationalistic priests in the 1980s. But just as in the nineteenth and early twentieth centuries, persecution only made the Poles "more Polish and more Catholic." During the 1970s, there was a powerful resurgence of Polish nationalism, and the Roman Catholic church was widely viewed, by Russians as well as Poles, as the main vehicle of that revival. The election of Pope John Paul II, the first Polish pope, intensified the Polish Catholic identity. During the late 1980s and early 1990s, Poles in the Soviet Union overwhelmingly favored the rise to power of Wałesa in Poland, and they thrilled to the new independence of Poland and the withdrawal of Soviet troops from their ancestral homeland in 1990. When Pope John Paul II visited Ukraine in 1990, tens of thousands of Soviet Poles attended his outdoor Masses and wept at their ability, after so many decades, to worship openly.

But the changes sweeping through Eastern Europe and the Soviet Union in the late 1980s and early 1990s were not an unmixed blessing for Poland. The transition from a state-controlled to a market economy was a difficult one for

Poland. Although the Poles were committed to making those changes, they suffered from major economic problems. Even worse off was the Soviet economy, which virtually imploded in the early 1990s. Polish authorities have feared that a Soviet economic collapse, combined with less restrictive emigration policies, might lead to a mass movement of Soviet Poles to Poland, just when the Polish economy is least able to absorb them.

These changes have, however, permitted a more open look at the plight of Poles living in the Soviet Union. Between 1939 and 1941, and again from 1944 to 1953, as many as 1.8 million Poles were deported to Siberia, ostensibly because they opposed the Soviet takeover of eastern Poland in 1939, assisted the Nazis during World War II, or participated in the Home Army, an anti-Communist resistance movement. More than 500,000 Poles perished in the deportations to Siberia. In 1988, a number of human rights groups in Poland began to protest what had happened, and, late in 1988, some of them formed a group known as the Siberian Union with Ryszard Reiff as its leader. The headquarters were in Warsaw but branches also formed in the Soviet Union, demanding information about what had happened to those who had been deported.
REFERENCES: Norman Davies, *God's Playground: A History of Poland*, 1982; M. K. Dziewanowski, *Poland in the Twentieth Century*, 1977; J. S. Karski, *The Great Powers and Poland, 1919–1945*, 1985; R. F. Leslie, *Reform and Insurrection in Russian Poland, 1856–1865*, 1969; "New Association Focuses on Poles Repressed in the USSR," *Radio Free Europe Research*, 14 (No. 912), March 23, 1988, 21–26; Norman J. Pounds, *Poland Between East and West*, 1964; George W. Simmonds, ed., *Nationalism in the USSR and Eastern Europe in the Era of Brezhnev and Kosygin*, 1977; Ray Taras, *Poland: Socialist State, Rebellious Nation*, 1986; P. S. Wandycz, *The Lands of Partitioned Poland, 1795–1918*, 1974.

POLEH. See POLEKH and RUSSIAN.

POLEHI. See POLEKH and RUSSIAN.

POLEKH. The Polekh are ethnic Russians* who live so far to the west among Belarusians* and Lithuanians*, in the Seim and Desna river valleys of western Russia, that they have acquired a distinct identity. Those Polekhi who live in the Kurk Gubernya, which was formerly Ukrainian* territory, also exhibit Ukrainian cultural characteristics. See RUSSIAN.
REFERENCE: Ronald Wixman, *The Peoples of the USSR: An Ethnographic Handbook*, 1984.

POLEKHI. See POLEKH and RUSSIAN.

POLESHAN. See POLISHCHUK and UKRAINIAN.

POLESHCHUK. The Poleshchuk are a Belarusian* subgroup. Over the centuries, they have maintained a sense of separation from other Belarusians because of their geographic isolation in the swampy lowlands of the Pinsk Oblast and in southwestern Brest Oblast. The Poleshchuk are thus divided into two subgroups. The Poleshchuk who live in Pinsk are known as the Pinchuki, while those from the Brest Oblast are designated the Breshyki. See BELARUSIAN.
REFERENCE: Ronald Wixman, *The Peoples of the USSR: An Ethnographic Handbook*, 1984.

POLESHUK. See POLESHCHUK and BELARUSIAN.

POLESIAN. See POLESHCHUK, POLISHCHUK, BELARUSIAN, and UKRAINIAN.

POLESYAN. See POLESHCHUK, POLISHCHUK, BELARUSIAN, and UKRAINIAN.

POLIAK. See POLE.

POLIAN. See POLISHCHUK and UKRAINIAN.

POLIESHAN. See POLESHCHUK, POLISHCHUK, BELARUSIAN, and UKRAINIAN.

POLIESIAN. See POLESHCHUK, POLISHCHUK, BELARUSIAN, and UKRAINIAN.

POLIESHCHUK. See POLESHCHUK, POLISHCHUK, and UKRAINIAN.

POLISHAN. See POLISHCHUK and UKRAINIAN.

POLISHCHUK. The Polishchuk, who have also been known historically as the Polyan, are a subgroup of Ukrainians*. Like the neighboring Poleshchuk*, who are Belarusian*, the Polishchuk are distinguished by their geographic isolation in the swampy lowlands of Polesie in northwestern Ukraine. Their own Ukrainian dialect is mutually intelligible with the Belarusian dialect of the Poleshchuk; therefore, ethnolinguists classify both groups as transitional between Belarusian and Ukrainian. See UKRAINIAN.
REFERENCE: Ronald Wixman, *The Peoples of the USSR: An Ethnographic Handbook*, 1984.

POLISIAN. See POLISHCHUK and UKRAINIAN.

POLISYAN. See POLISHCHUK and UKRAINIAN.

POLUVERTSY. See SETU and ESTONIAN.

POLUVERTSY. The Poluvertsy should not be confused with the Setu* Estonians*, who have sometimes also been referred to as Poluvertsy. The term "Poluvertsy" refers properly to ethnic Russians* living north of Lake Peipus in Estonia who converted to Lutheranism. Although the Estonians* have assimilated them, there are still people in the area who are aware of their Poluvertsy roots. See ESTONIAN or RUSSIAN.
REFERENCE: Ronald Wixman, *The Peoples of the USSR: An Ethnographic Handbook*, 1984.

POLYAK. See POLE.

POLYAK. In addition to referring to ethnic Poles*, the term "Polyak" also describes a group of ethnic Russians* who are Old Believers of the Russian Orthodox Church. During the persecution of the Old Believers in the seventeenth and eighteenth centuries, the Polyaks emigrated to Poland, but their stay there was only temporary. When Poland was partitioned late in the eighteenth century and the Polyaks found themselves once again under Russian control, they fled to Siberia where they settled among the Altais* and Buryats*. Those living among the Buryats became known as Semeiki*. See ALTAI, BURYAT, or RUSSIAN.
REFERENCE: Ronald Wixman, *The Peoples of the USSR: An Ethnographic Handbook*, 1984.

POLYESHCHUK. See POLESHCHUK and BELARUSIAN.

POLYESHUK. See POLESHCHUK and BELARUSIAN.

POLYAKI. See RUSSIAN.

POLYAN. See UKRAINIAN.

POMORY. The Pomory are ethnic Russians* who maintain a distinctly separate identity. Beginning in the eighteenth century, Russian emigrants from the Novgorod area settled in the region of the White Sea, where they became hunters and fishermen. They retained their use of the Russian language and their sense of being Russian, but they also developed a distinct sense of being Pomory as well. See RUSSIAN.
REFERENCE: Ronald Wixman, *The Peoples of the USSR: An Ethnographic Handbook*, 1984.

PONTIC. See GREEK.

PORUBEZHNIY KALMUK. See ALTAI and TELEUT.

PORUBEZHNIY KALMYK. See ALTAI and TELEUT.

PORUBEZHNIY QALMUQ. See ALTAI and TELEUT.

PORUBEZHNIY QALMYQ. See ALTAI and TELEUT.

PORUBEZHNIYY KALMUK. See ALTAI and TELEUT.

PORUBEZHNIYY KALMYK. See ALTAI and TELEUT.

PORUBEZHNIYY QALMUQ. See ALTAI and TELEUT.

PORUBEZHNIYY QALMYQ. See ALTAI and TELEUT.

PSHAV. The Pshav, who call themselves the Pshaveli, are a Kartvelian* group that evolved into the Georgian* nation. They speak a Georgian dialect and are Eastern Orthodox. Most of the Pshav live along the Aragvi River and the lower Iori River in Georgia. See GEORGIAN.
REFERENCE: Ronald Wixman, *The Peoples of the USSR: An Ethnographic Handbook*, 1984.

PSHAVELI. See GEORGIAN.

PYATIGORSKIE OBSHCHESTVA KABARDY. See BALKAR.

PYURYUT. See SAGAI and KHAKASS.

Q

QABARD. See KABARD.

QABARDIAN. See KABARD.

QABARDIN. See KABARD.

QABARDINIAN. See KABARD.

QABARTAI. See KABARD.

QABARTAY. See KABARD.

QACHA. See KACHA and KHAKASS.

QACHIN. See KACHA and KHAKASS.

QADJAR. See KAJAR and AZERBAIJANI.

QADZHAR. See KAJAR and AZERBAIJANI.

QAIBAL. See KOIBAL and KHAKASS.

QAIDAQ. See KAITAK and DARGIN.

QAIDAQLAN. See KAITAK and DARGIN.

QAITAQ. See KAITAK and DARGIN.

QAJAR. See KAJAR and AZERBAIJANI.

QALCH. See KALCHA and KYRGYZ.

QALMUQ. See KALMYK.

QALMYK. See KALMYK.

QAMASA SAMODI. See KAMASA SAMOYED, KOIBAL, and KHAKASS.

QAMASA SAMOED. See KAMASA SAMOYED, KOIBAL, and KHAKASS.

QAMASA SAMOIED. See KAMASA SAMOYED, KOIBAL, and KHAKASS.

QAMASA SAMOYED. See KAMASA SAMOYED, KOIBAL, and KHAKASS.

QAMASIN SAMODI. See KAMASA SAMOYED, KOIBAL, and KHAKASS.

QAMASIN SAMOED. See KAMASA SAMOYED, KOIBAL, and KHAKASS.

QAMASIN SAMOIED. See KAMASA SAMOYED, KOIBAL, and KHAKASS.

QAMASIN SAMOYED. See KAMASA SAMOYED, KOIBAL, and KHAKASS.

QAPUCHA. See AVAR.

QAPUCHIN. See AVAR.

QARA NOGAI. See KARA NOGAI and NOGAI.

QARA NOGAY. See KARA NOGAI and NOGAI.

QARA NOGHAI. See KARA NOGAI and NOGAI.

QARA NOGHAY. See KARA NOGAI and NOGAI.

QARA QIRGHIZ. See KYRGYZ.

QARA QYRGHYZ. See KYRGYZ.

QARA QIRGIZ. See KYRGYZ.

QARA QYRGYZ. See KYRGYZ.

QARA TATAR. See KARA TATAR and TATAR.

QARACHAI. See KARACHAI.

QARACHAILI. See KARACHAI.

QARACHAILY. See KARACHAI.

QARACHAY. See KARACHAI.

QARACHAYLI. See KARACHAI.

QARACHAYLY. See KARACHAI.

QARADASH. See KARADASH and TURKMEN.

QARADASHLI. See KARADASH and TURKMEN.

QARADASHLY. See KARADASH and TURKMEN.

QARAGASH. See KARAGASH TATAR, ASTRAKHAN TATAR, and TATAR.

QARAGASHLI. See KARAGASH TATAR, ASTRAKHAN TATAR, and TATAR.

QARAGASHLY. See KARAGASH TATAR, ASTRAKHAN TATAR, and TATAR.

QARAIM. See KARAIM and JEW.

QARAIT. See KARAIM and JEW.

QARAITE. See KARAIM and JEW.

QARALPAQ. See KARAKALPAK.

QARANOGAI. See KARA NOGAI and NOGAI.

QARANOGAY. See KARA NOGAI and NOGAI.

QARANOGHAI. See KARA NOGAI and NOGAI.

QARANOGHAY. See KARA NOGAI and NOGAI.

QARAPAPAKH. See KARAPAPAKH, MESKHETIAN, and AZERBAIJANI.

QARAPAPH. See KARAPAPAKH, MESKHETIAN, and AZERBAIJANI.

QARAPAPAQ. See KARKAPAKH, MESKHETIAN, and AZERBAIJANI.

QARAQAIDAQ. See KAITAK and DARGIN.

QARAQAITAQ. See KAITAK and DARGIN.

QARAQALPAQ. See KARAKALPAK.

QARAQIRGHIZ. See KYRGYZ.

QARAQYRGHIZ. See HYRGYZ.

QARAQIRGIZ. See KRYGYZ.

QARAQYRGYZ. See KYRGYZ.

QARASA SAMODI. See KARASA SAMOYED.

QARASA SAMOED. See KARASA SAMOYED.

QARASA SAMOIED. See KARASA SAMOYED.

QARASA SAMOYED. See KARASA SAMOYED.

QARASHI. See KARAGASH TATAR, ASTRAKHAN TATAR, and TATAR.

QARASIN SAMODI. See KARASA SAMOYED.

QARASIN SAMOED. See KARASA SAMOYED.

QARASIN SAMOIED. See KARASA SAMOYED.

QARASIN SAMOYED. See KARASA SAMOYED.

QARATA. See KARATA and AVAR.

QARATAI. See KARATAI and MORDVINIAN.

QARATAY. See KARATAI and MORDVINIAN.

QARIM. See RUSSIAN.

QARIMI. See RUSSIAN.

QARYM. See RUSSIAN.

QARYMY. See RUSSIAN.

QARIN TATAR. See KARA TATAR and TATAR.

QASHGAR. See KASHGAR and UIGUR.

QASHGARLIK. See KASHGAR and UIGUR.

QASHGARLUK. See KASHGAR and UIGUR.

QASHGARLYK. See KASHGAR and UIGUR.

QASHQAR. See KASHGAR and UIGUR.

QASHQARLIK. See KASHGAR and UIGUR.

QASHQARLUK. See KASHGAR and UIGUR.

QASHQARLYK. See KASHGAR and UIGUR.

QASIMOV TATAR. See KASIMOV TATAR.

QASOQ. See AZERBAIJANI.

QAUDAQLAN. See DARGIN.

QAYBAL. See KOIBAL and KHAKASS.

QAYDAQ. See KAITAK and DARGIN.

QAYTAQ. See KAITAK and DARGIN.

QAZAN TATAR. See KAZAN TATAR and TATAR.

QAZANLIK. See KAZAN TATAR and TATAR.

QAZANLUK. See KAZAN TATAR and TATAR.

QAZANLYK. See KAZAN TATAR and TATAR.

QAZAQ. See AZERBAIJANI and KAZAKH.

QAZI QUMUH. See LAK.

QAZI QUMUKH. See LAK.

QAZI QUMUQ. See LAK.

QAZIQUMUH. See LAK.

QAZIQUMUKH. See LAK.

QAZIQUMUQ. See LAK.

QIPCHAQ. See KYPCHAK and UZBEK.

QIPSHAQ. See KYPCHAK and UZBEK.

QIRGHIZ. See KYRGYZ.

QIRGHIZ QAISAQ. See KAZAKH.

QIRGHIZ QAYSAQ. See KAZAKH.

QIRGHIZ QAIZAKH. See KAZAKH.

QIRGHIZ QAZAQ. See KAZAKH.

QIRGIZ. See KYRGYZ.

QIRGIZ QAISAQ. See KAZAKH.

QIRGIZ QAIZAKH. See KAZAKH.

QIRGIZ QAYSAQ. See KAZAKH.

QIRGIZ QAZAQ. See KAZAKH.

QIRIM TATAR. See CRIMEAN TATAR and TATAR.

QIRIMCHAQ. See KRYMCHAK and JEW.

QIZIL. See KYZYL and KHAKASS.

QOIBAL. See KOIBAL and KHAKASS.

QONDOMA TATAR. See SHOR.

QOYBAL. See KOIBAL and KHAKASS.

QRIM TATAR. See CRIMEAN TATAR and TATAR.

QRIMCHAQ. See KRYMCHAK and JEW.

QRIZ. See KRYZ, SHAH DAGH, and AZERBAIJANI.

QRYZ. See KRYZ, SHAH DAGH, and AZERBAIJANI.

QUBACHI. See KUBACHI and DARGIN.

QUBAN ABHAZ. See ABAZA.

QUBAN ABKHAZA. See ABAZA.

QUBAN NOGAI. See AK NOGAI and NOGAI.

QUBAN NOGAY. See AK NOGAI and NOGAI.

QUBAN NOGHAI. See AK NOGAI and NOGAI.

QUBAN NOGHAY. See AK NOGAI and NOGAI.

QUMANDA. See KUMANDIN and ALTAI.

QUMANDIN. See KUMANDIN and ALTAI.

QUMUQ. See KUMYK.

QUMYQ. See KUMYK.

QUNDROV TATAR. See KUNDROV TATAR, ASTRAKHAN TATAR, and TATAR.

QURAMA. See KURAMA and UZBEK.

QURD. See KURD.

QURD QURMANDJ. See KURD.

QURD QURMANDZH. See KURD.

QURD QURMANJ. See KURD.

QURT. See KURD.

QWANADI. See BAGULAL and AVAR.

QWANADIN. See BAGULAL and AVAR.

QWANALIN. See BAGULAL and AVAR.

QWANALY. See BAGULAL and AVAR.

QWANNAL. See ANDI.

QYPCHAQ. See KYPCHAK and UZBEK.

QYPSHAQ. See KYPCHAK and UZBEK.

QYRGHYZ. See KYRGYZ.

QYRGHYZ QAISAQ. See KAZAKH.

QYRGHYZ QAYSAQ. See KAZAKH.

QYRGHYZ QAZAKH. See KAZAKH.

QYRGHYZ QAZAQ. See KAZAKH.

QYRGYZ. See KYRGYZ.

QYRGYZ QAISAQ. See KAZAKH.

QYRGYZ QAYSAQ. See KAZAKH.

QYRGYZ QAZAKH. See KAZAKH.

QYRGYZ QAZAQ. See KAZAKH.

QYZYL. See KYZYL and KHAKASS.

R

RAANDALIT. See LIVONIAN.

RACHA. The Racha, who call themselves the Rach'veli and who have been known as the Rachin, are a subgroup of the Georgians*. Like other Georgians, they are Eastern Orthodox in religion. The Racha live in the upper Rioni River valley of Georgia. See GEORGIAN.
REFERENCE: Ronald Wixman, *The Peoples of the USSR: An Ethnographic Handbook*, 1984.

RACHIN. See RACHA and GEORGIAN.

RACHINTSY. See RACHA and GEORGIAN.

RACH'VEL. See RACHA and GEORGIAN.

RACH'VELI. See RACHA and GEORGIAN.

RANDAL. See LIVONIAN and LATVIAN.

ROM. See GYPSY.

ROMANIAN. Romanians are one of the peoples who inhabit the historical region northeast of the Carpathians and southwest of the Pruth River in the Republic of Romania and the territory of the adjacent Moldovan Republic between the Pruth and Dniester rivers. From the fourteenth to the nineteenth centuries, the people of these two regions were united in a single principality called Moldova under Ottoman suzerainty. Since 1812, the territory between the Pruth and Dniester, often referred to as Bessarabia, has come repeatedly under Russian*, Romanian, and Soviet rule. The territory to the southwest remained the principality of Moldova. In 1858, it joined with Wallachia, forming the united principalities of Moldova and Wallachia, which, in 1862, became known as the principality of Romania. Romania, in turn, attained independence and the status of a kingdom in 1878. In the 180 years since the first Russian annexation of Bessarabia, most of the territory of Moldova, between the Pruth and the Danube, has been under Russian or Soviet administration three times (for a total of 132 years); the territory was part of Romania twice (for a total of 57 years), and has also been an independent republic twice (once for two months in 1918, and again since August 1991). The modern Republic of Moldova includes most of the traditional territory of Bessarabia, except for the Bugeac coastal region, which has been part of Ukraine since 1944. It also includes a strip of territory north of the Dniester river known as the Trans-Dniester region.

The Moldovans* of Russia and the Soviet Union are so closely related to the Romanians in language, ethnicity, and historical development that they can be considered one and the same people. Indeed, one of the keystones of the recent Moldovan national movement has been the desire for the unification of Moldova with Romania. The language of the Moldovans, like that of the Romanians, makes up the easternmost branch of the Romance language group. Like French, Italian, Spanish, Portuguese, and Romanche, it evolved from the vulgar Latin spoken in the later years of the Roman Empire and early medieval times. While both Moldovan and Romanian have many Slavic, Greek*, and Turkish loan words, the core of the two languages indicates a Latin origin. Any divergent development of the Romanian and Moldovan languages has to do mostly with the different language policies of the Soviet and Romanian governments and perhaps with the proximity of the Moldovans to Ukrainian*, Russian, and Bulgarian* speakers. Moldovan diverges from Romanian only in a dialectical sense, due to a greater number of Slavic loan words, some introduced under Russian and Soviet rule. Many of these loan words, however, have existed in Romanian dialects without becoming part of the Romanian literary language. They have been kept or re-introduced into the Moldovan literary language under the Soviets. Up until recently, the most distinct difference between the Romanian and Moldovan languages has been their alphabets. The principalities of Moldova and Wallachia used Old Church Slavonic, Greek, and Old Romanian as official languages until the early nineteenth century; Old Romanian used a modified Cyrillic script. In the early nineteenth century, a modified Latin alphabet was adopted by Romanians in Transylvania, the autonomous principalities of Moldova and Wallachia, and in Bessarabia. This became the standard alphabet for speakers of Romanian in the Russian and Hapsburg empires, as well as those in the emerging Romanian state. Under the Soviets, Romanian speakers in Moldova were forced to revert to a Cyrillic script.

Two main views exist regarding the ethnogenesis of the Romanian and Moldovan people. Romanian national historians assert that the origins of their people can be found in the amalgamation of the Dacian people with Roman colonists during the existence of the Roman province of Dacia between 106 and 238 A.D. According to this Romanian national view, the Dacians, a Thraco-

Illyrian people who inhabited the area of present-day Romania in ancient times, were subdued by the Romans under the Emperor Trajan. The Romans transformed the former kingdom into the Roman province of Dacia. During the 130-odd years of Roman rule, a process of latinization occurred in Dacia, which was very similar to what happened in Gaul and the Iberian peninsula under Roman rule. Romanian national historiography also asserts that during the eras of migrations, when Danubian lands were occupied by Goths, Huns, Avars*, Bulgars, Slavs, Pechenegs, Uzes, and others, the Romanian people survived as a separate entity by retreating into the vastness of the Carpathian mountains until the thirteenth century, when they descended and re-entered history as the Wallachians and Moldovans.

The second view of Romanian ethnogenesis, held by some Hungarian and Western scholars, is that the Romanians are descended from the Romanized population of the Balkan Peninsula *south* of the Danube, who survived the era of migrations by retreating to the Pindus, Rhodope, Dinaric, and Balkan mountains. According to this view, the latinized population of the Balkans, known as Vlachs (*Vlachoi* or *Koutsovlachoi* in Greek, *Eflak* in Turkish, *Vlasi* in Slavic, and *Aromuni* in Vlach), participated in the formation of the First Bulgarian Empire in the late twelfth and early thirteenth centuries and then dispersed. The bulk of the Balkan Vlachs migrated north of the Danube and settled in present-day Romanian lands, including Bessarabia, in the thirteenth century. Pockets of these Vlachs remained in the Balkans and today constitute the Aromuni, or Vlach, minorities in Albania, Bulgaria, Greece, and Macedonia.

The development of these conflicting views of Romanian origins have to do with the development of modern Romanian nationalism and the conflicting ethnic claims between Romanians and Hungarians in Transylvania. Due to the paucity of evidence, neither view can be conclusively proved or discounted. Soviet Moldovan historians, by contrast, have attempted to fabricate a separate ethnogenesis for the Moldovans by over-emphasizing the Slavic component in the development of the Moldovan nation from earliest times to the present. In other words, they have attempted to transform a regional history into a national history.

The last Soviet census of 1989 registered 145,918 people of Romanian ethnicity in the Soviet Union, but this number does not tell the whole story. Soviet authorities have classified the Moldovans, who speak essentially the same language and have the same ethnic roots as the Romanians, as a separate nationality since the late 1920s. Before the annexation of Bessarabia and the formation of the Moldavian Soviet Socialist Republic, the first Soviet census of 1926 had registered all Romanian speakers in the Soviet Union as Romanians. Later documentation of the 1926 census "adjusted" the terminology to describe the overwhelming majority of Romanians in the census as Moldovans. According to the 1926 census, there were 283,556 Romanians in the Soviet Union (278,905 Moldovans and 4,651 Romanians). While a majority (60 percent) of Romanian speakers resided in the Moldavian Autonomous Soviet Socialist Republic (ASSR), they constituted only about 30 percent of the region's total population. This mini-republic consisted of over 8,000 square kilometers along the Dniester River bordering Romanian Bessarabia. The largest ethnic group in the republic were Ukrainians, who comprised 48.8 percent (277,515) of the population. Russians, Jews,* Germans*, Bulgarians, and Poles* made up the remaining 20 percent of the autonomous republic's inhabitants.

Of the Romanian population in the Moldavian ASSR, only 6,260 were urban dwellers; the rest were villagers, so that very few of them participated in the governing of their own republic. The autonomous republic was governed by non-Romanian party officials in an uncompromising and oppressive manner, especially in the 1930s. In the late 1920s, the Cyrillic alphabet replaced Latin as the official script of the "native" language of the Moldavian ASSR. When the Soviets annexed the Romanian territory between the Dniester and the Pruth during World War II, the Romanian inhabitants of that era were declared to be a separate nationality known as Moldovans.

Soviet censuses expressed the population categorized as "Romanian" this way: 1926: 4,651; 1959: 106,366; 1970: 119,292; 1979: 128,792; 1989: 145,918. These post–1926 numbers probably represent those individuals who could prove that they originally came from areas of Romania outside the territory of the Moldavian SSR and were bold enough to declare themselves Romanians. Besides those in the new Moldovan Republic, Romanians or Moldovans in other parts of the Commonwealth of Independent States (CIS) are found chiefly in Ukraine, Russia, and Kazakhstan. They number about 300,000 to 400,000 in Ukraine, 90,000 to 100,000 in Russia, and 30,000 in Kazakhstan. The Romanian-speaking population outside the Moldovan Republic includes the descendants of refugees and settlers from the Danubian principalities of Moldavia and Wallachia. During the Russo-Turkish Wars of the nineteenth and twentieth centuries, significant numbers of Romanians settled in Ukraine, especially in the region between the Bug and the Dniester rivers. Some of these settlers later migrated to other parts of the Russian Empire, including the Crimea. Another portion of the Romanians in the other republics are those Moldovans/Romanians sent into exile during the Stalin era, especially during the annexations of Romanian Bessarabia (which became the Moldavian SSR) in 1940–1941 and after 1945. Other groups and individuals found in other republics of the CIS are no doubt part of some natural migration patterns within the former Soviet Union.

Since the advent of *glasnost*, Moldovans in and out of the Moldovan Republic have increasingly identified themselves as Romanians. In addition, the new Moldovan Republic has declared in 1991 that its Romanian-speaking majority are Romanians with close ties to Romania. It is not yet known whether the governments of the new post-Soviet successor states of Ukraine, Russia, and Kazakhstan will count their Romanian-speaking inhabitants as Romanians or Moldovans. See MOLDOVAN.

REFERENCES: N. Dima, *Bessarabia and Bukovina: The Soviet-Romanian Territorial Dispute*, 1982; N. Dima, *From Moldavia to Moldova: The Soviet-Romanian Territorial Dispute*, 1991; N. Dima, "Moldavians or Romanians?" in R. S. West, ed., *The Soviet West*, 1975.

Nicholas C. J. Pappas

ROMEI. See URUM and GREEK.

ROMEO. See GREEK.

ROEMEOI. See GREEK.

RUMANIAN. See ROMANIAN.

RUMYN. See ROMANIAN.

RUMYNY. See ROMANIAN.

RUSAKI. See KRIEVINI and LATVIAN.

RUSHAN. The Rushans, who call themselves the Rykhen, constitute one of the groups making up the Pamir Peoples*. Russians* refer to them as the Rushantsy. They are classified today as a subgroup of the Tajiks*. Rushan is an Iranian language, more specifically a member of the Shugnano-Rushan group of East Iranian languages; speakers of Shugnan* understand Rushan. Rushan is divided in its own right into two dialects—Rushan proper and Khuf. Most of the Rushan are Ismaili Muslims who live in the Pyanzh River valley. They are being assimilated by the surrounding Tajiks. See TAJIK.

REFERENCES: Shirin Akiner, *Islamic Peoples of the Soviet Union*, 1983; Ronald Wixman, *The Peoples of the USSR: An Ethnographic Handbook*, 1984.

RUSHANI. See RUSHAN.

RUSHANTSY. See RUSHAN.

RUSIN. See CARPATHO-RUSYN.

RUSNAK. See CARPATHO-RUSYN.

RUSNIAK. See CARPATHO-RUSYN.

RUSNYAK. See CARPATHO-RUSYN.

RUSSIAN. Ethnic Russians, who call themselves Russkie and who are also known as Velikorussians, are by far the largest ethnic group in the Commonwealth of Independent States (CIS). Their population in the 1989 Soviet census was listed as 145,071,550 people. They constituted approximately one-half of the population of the country at that time. Russians are primarily Eastern Orthodox in their religious loyalties, and they are the core ethnic group around which imperial Russia and later the Soviet Union were created. Like Belarusians* and Ukrainians*, the Russians are Eastern Slavs in their tribal origins. Over the course of several centuries, a number of smaller ethnic groups emerged within the larger community of Great Russian Slavs. Their identity as Russians was complicated by unique geographical, linguistic, and religious factors.

Smaller Ethnic Groups

The Meshcheryaks*, for example, are a people of mixed ancestry who consider themselves Russians. They are descendants of the Meshchera*, a group of Volga Finns* who migrated to the Oka River basin in the Ryazan and Tambov oblasts and mixed with ethnic Russians there. They adopted the Russian Orthodox faith, and their language is a Russian dialect loaded with Mordvinian* terms.

In the far western reaches of the Russian ethnographic region, along the Seim and Dena rivers, one group of Russian settlers mixed with local Belarusians and Lithuanians*. They called themselves the Polekh*. Some of the Polekhs* became Roman Catholics, but most of them retained their Russian Orthodox faith and the Russian language, even though they saw themselves as a distinct group within the larger Russian community. The Goryuns* were a subgroup of the Polekhs, who lived in the Kursk Gubernya that for years was part of Ukraine. They adopted many Ukrainian cultural characteristics, even though, like the Polekhs, they kept a separate sense of identity.

Another subgroup of Russians was known as the Starozhily*, which literally translates as "Old Inhabitants." The Starozhily were ethnic Russians who migrated east from central Russia in the sixteenth and seventeenth centuries to isolated areas in southern Siberia. They went there in search of work or land, scattering widely throughout Siberia. Another reason for their migration was a split that occurred in the Russian Orthodox Church in 1667. Over the years, because of its isolation from Constantinople, the liturgies of the Russian Orthodox Church had changed, slowly and subtly, through the infusion of Russian words and cultural themes into the Greek* texts. Patriarch Nikon of the Russian Orthodox Church decided to reform those texts by restoring them to the originals, but, in the process, he alienated many members who viewed the reforms as foreign intrusions. Those people who rejected the changes became known as Old Believers and often found themselves the object of intense persecution. Many of them headed east to escape the power of both the church and the state.

As time passed, the Starozhily became divided into several subgroups who still saw themselves culturally as Russians but whose ethnic identities were particularly narrow. One of the Starozhily subgroups was the Bukhtarmans*, or

Kamenshchiki. The Bukhtarmans were Old Believers from Nizhegorodskaya Gubernya who specialized in the stonemason craft and lived along the Kerzhenets River. To avoid persecution and start a new life, the Bukhtarmans headed east and settled in southern Siberia, predominantly in the Gornyi Altai. The Polyaks* were another Starozhily group. They were also Old Believers who fled central Russia to avoid persecution, but they first headed west to Poland in the late seventeenth and early eighteenth centuries. When Polish independence died with the partitions in the 1790s, the Polyakis moved again, this time east to Siberia. Those who settled in the Altai region retained their identity as Polyaks, but those who ended up in the Transbaikal region came under heavy Buryat* influence. Because of their strong commitment to extended family clans, they became known as Semeikis* (Semeyki). The Kerzhak* people, like the Bukhtarmans, originated in Nizhegorodskaya Gubernya near the Kerzhenets River and scattered throughout Siberia in order to escape religious persecution and find new land.

There was another group of Old Believers who were not part of the larger Starozhily group. They originally left central Russia in the seventeenth century to escape religious persecution and became associated with the Ural Cossacks*. They headed down to Central Asia where they settled in what are today Kazakhstan and the Karakalpak Autonomous Soviet Socialist Republic (ASSR). These Russian immigrants became known as Urals* after settling along the Amu-Darya and Syr-Darya rivers and on islands in the Aral Sea. Even though they were surrounded by large numbers of Muslims, the Urals retained the Russian language and their Old Believer religion. Most of them traditionally worked as fishermen, but their livelihoods have been disrupted by Soviet agricultural policies that have diverted rivers for cotton cultivation and, in the process, dried up much of the Aral Sea. Like surrounding Karakalpaks*, the Urals suffer from high rates of disease, especially cancer, because of their polluted environment.

Several groups of ethnic Russians have cultural identities based on their geographical isolation and their relationships with surrounding people. One of these groups is the people known as Kamchadals*, who are ethnic Russians living on the Kamchatka Peninsula and closely related to the Itelmen*. The Itelmen are a tiny ethnic group located primarily on the Kamchatka Peninsula; they call themselves the Itel'men, although some Russians refer to them also as the Kamchadals. Although the Itelmen population was listed at more than 4,000 people in the Soviet census of 1920, it has steadily declined since then, primarily because of high rates of intermarriage with ethnic Russians. Several thousand people have Itelmen-Russian ancestry, and they are known as Kamchadals. Although they speak Russian as their native language, identify themselves as ethnic Russians, and are loyal to the Russian Orthodox Church, they also retain significant elements of Itelmen culture in their daily lives.

The Zatundren* are another mixed Russian ethnic group. Today they live in the northern tundra region of Russia, primarily along the Dudinka and Khatanga rivers in what was formerly known as the Dolgano-Nenets Autonomous Oblast in central Siberia. When they first arrived in the region, they found themselves surrounded by the local Dolgan* people, who, at the time, were heavily influenced by the Yakut* people. The Russian settlers mixed with the Dolgans and Yakuts, adopting their economic life-style and a variety of their folk traditions. They became known as the Zatundren, and they retained their sense of being Russian as well as their use of Russian as the native language. Similarly, the Sayans* are a group of eighteenth-century Russian immigrants to the area of the Kursk Oblast. Although differing only slightly from other Russians who have arrived more recently, they nevertheless constitute a distinct ethnographic entity.

Still another group of Russians of mixed ancestry are the Karym people of the Transbaikal region. Russian explorers, trappers, and later settlers reached Lake Baikal in the 1600s. The territory and its people—the Buryats—were taken into the Russian state by the Treaties of Nerchinsk (1689) and Kyakhta (1728), which delineated spheres of influence between tsarist Russia and Manchu* China. Russian imperialism had a religious tone, and the Buryats, most of whom were Buddhists loyal to the Dalai Lama of Tibet, were sometimes forcibly baptized. Soon the Irkutsk Buryats took Russian names, began wearing Russian-style clothes, and abandoned nomadism for agriculture. They planted wheat, buckwheat, rye, and barley. Soon, too, the Buryats were victimized by Russian land policies, including serfdom. Russians settled along the Siberian riverbanks and around the shores of Lake Baikal, eventually outnumbering Buryats in the region. The descendants of this Russian-Buryat mix are known as the Karyms. Although they speak Russian and identify with ethnic Russians, strong elements of Buryat tradition remain in their system of values.

The Kolymchans* are also the descendants of an ethnic mix, this time between ethnic Russians and native Yakuts. Ethnographers believe that the Yakut people originated in the Transbaikal region and then moved farther north to escape Buryat persecution. Beginning in the seventeenth century, ethnic Russians began to settle in Siberia, and several thousand of them eventually ended up on the Kolyma River. During the next 300 years, they were virtually absorbed by the Yakuts, adopting the Yakut language and Yakut culture. Nevertheless, they continued to see themselves as distinct from other Yakuts and referred to themselves as Russians. Others in the area began to call them Kolymchans. Closely related to the Kolymchan are the Yakutyans* (Yakutians), another group of ethnic Russians who settled among the Yakuts. These Russians placed their homes along the Lena River and mixed heavily with the local Yakuts, retaining the Russian language but having many cultural characteristics of the Yakut. Nevertheless, they still identify themselves as ethnic Russians.

Another group of ethnic Russians migrated north into the polar regions of Siberia in the eighteenth century, where they became closely associated with the Yukagirs* and Chuvash*. Because of the inhospitable environment, they never became involved in a larger commercial economy. Over time, they adapted to the elements and supported themselves by hunting, fishing, and breeding reindeer and dogs. Along with economic connections to the Siberian tribes came cultural connections. Many of these Russians, who came to be known as Markovs*, adopted local festivals and even some religious beliefs. At the same time, however, the Markovs retained the use of Russian as their native tongue, even though most of them were bilingual or trilingual in Chuvash and Yukagir as well. They live today in the village of Markovo on the Anadyr River. They also continued to identify themselves as ethnic Russians, not as Chuvashes or Yukagirs. Closely related to the Markovs are the Russkoustins*, who live in the village of Russkoe Uste on the Indigirka River in the polar area. They too fish, hunt, and raise reindeer and dogs, and they have retained the Russian language and Russian identity. The Russkoustin, however, have mixed more intimately with Chuvash and Yukagir culture than have the Markovs.

The Pomory* are a group of Russians living along the coast of the White Sea. Like so many other Russian settlers moving north and east, they migrated into the area in the eighteenth century. Most of them were from the Novgorod region. They adapted to the local economy and became fishermen and hunters; a good number of them also took up maritime occupations. They retained the Russian language as their native tongue and their ties to the Russian Orthodox Church, but, because of their geographical isolation, they developed a separate identity as Pomory as well.

Early History and Territorial Expansion

In the pre-Christian era, the region that is today called Russia was inhabited by a variety of nomadic tribes. Characterized by vast, open plains, the country was subject to a series of migratory invasions by such groups as the Scythians, Goths, Avars*, Magyars*, and Khazars. The Slavic tribes resided in the northern regions of Russia, northeast of the Carpathian Mountains. Their migrations began in the sixth century, and they gradually evolved into three basic groups. The western Slavs became known as Poles*, Czechs*, and Slovaks*, while the southern Slavs became the Serbians*, Croatians*, Slovenes, and Bulgars (or Bulgarians*). The eastern Slavs evolved into the people known as Belarusians, Russians, and Ukrainians. Because of the relatively simple river portages over the plains of western Russia, the eastern Slavic expansion, as well as trade and commerce, flowed easily from the Baltic Sea to the Black Sea. The Russians, or Great Russian Slavs, became by far the largest group, in terms of population, of any Slavic people. Kiev on the Dnieper River and Novgorod on the Volkhov River became the two primary Russian commercial centers.

According to Russian tradition, in 862 the warring Slavic tribes invited Rurik, a Scandinavian leader, to come to Novgorod and consolidate them politically. Under Rurik and his dynastic successors in the ninth and tenth centuries, Russia expanded northeast and northwest. Rurik's successor, Prince Oleg, also brought Kiev under his control and led his armies as far south as Constantinople, where he signed a treaty with Byzantium in 911. By the middle of the tenth century, Kiev had become the most prominent Russian city, and the Kievan Rus' had conquered much Khazar land in the southeast, Pecheneg land on the Black Sea steppes, and Bulgar territory to the southwest. The confederation Kievan Rus' principalities reached its imperial peak in the middle of the eleventh century.

With the sack of Constantinople by the Crusaders in 1204, the decline of the Kievan principalities began. The fall of Constantinople triggered a disastrous decline in trade and commerce, and large numbers of Kievan Russians began migrating north. Dynastic struggles among the prince weakened the solidarity of the House of Rurik, and Russia disintegrated into a variety of competing political entities—Galicia, Volhynia, Suzdal, Chernigov, Polotsk, Smolensk, and Novgorod—which nonetheless had linguistic, cultural, and historical affinities. Beginning in 1223 and continuing intermittently for the next generation, the Mongol* invasion changed the course of Russian history. Because of the region's forests and swamps, the invasion stopped short of Novgorod in the northeast, but the Mongols then headed south, destroying the city of Kiev in 1240 and extending their conquests as far west as Poland and Hungary. At the same time, a succession of Swedish, Teutonic Crusades, and Lithuanian armies invaded Russia from the west. Prince Alexander Yarolavevich eventually decided to subject himself to Mongol rule rather than continue to fight on two fronts.

The Mongol invasion destroyed the embryonic institutions of representative government that had appeared in several Russian cities. The Mongols imposed their own laws and Asian culture all over Russia, producing major demographic changes. The westernmost Russians fled farther to the west to escape; these people eventually became known as Belarusians, or White Russians. The people of Kiev evolved into Ukrainians. In northern Russia, the people became known as Great Russian Slavs, Velikorussians, or, simply, Russians. Those people, free of Mongol domination, became the political heart and soul of Russian nationalism.

These events in medieval Russian history had essentially succeeded in cutting Russia off from the West. When Prince Vladimir decided, around 990 A.D., to convert to Byzantine Orthodox Christianity instead of Roman Catholicism, he sowed the seeds of independent cultural development. When the schism between the two churches occurred in 1054, Russia became involved in the feud between Catholicism and Orthodoxy, and its loyalties were decidedly anti-Catholic. When the Ottomans conquered Constantinople in 1453, bringing most of the Orthodox churches under their control, only Russian Orthodoxy survived independently. This circumstance made the Russians self-centered and extremely isolated culturally. The Mongol invasion in 1237 only served to isolate Russian culture further from the West. During the two centuries when the Renaissance, the Reformation, and the commercial revolution spread across Western Europe, breaking the bonds of traditionalism and unleashing powerful new social, economic, and political forces, the Mongols controlled Russia.

During the thirteenth and fourteenth centuries, the city of Moscow gradually rose to a position of dominance as the main Russian vassal principality within the Mongol empire, primarily because of its favorable position on the major trade routes and its collaboration with the Mongols. Ivan I became Prince of Muscovy in 1328, and the Mongols recognized him as the Grand Prince collector of their tribute from all of Russia. Ivan saw to it that Moscow became the metropolitan see of the Russian Orthodox Church, and he began to refer to himself as the ruler "of all Russia." In 1380, as Mongol rule was falling prey to internal political dissension, Muscovy rose up in rebellion and began the century-long process of casting off Mongol rule. Muscovy then began a steady expansion of its size and power. When Constantinople fell to the Ottoman Turks in 1453, Russian Orthodox church leaders proclaimed Moscow as the "third Rome." Under Ivan III, Muscovy took control of the state of Novgorod in 1471, terminated Mongol tribute payments in 1480, and seized the state of Tver in 1485. The princes of Rostov and Yaroslavl' also came under the control of Ivan III. As a result of a series of wars with Lithuania in the 1490s and early 1500s, Muscovy acquired Pskov in 1510, Smolensk in 1514, and Ryazan in 1517. By the early 1500s, Muscovy was in control of all territory that was ethnically Russian. Ivan III also laid claim to parts of Belarusia and Ukraine, which were under Lithuanian control. He also married a niece of the last Byzantine Emperor and introduced imperial symbols and court ceremonials into Muscovite government.

Muscovy expansion accelerated during the reign of Ivan IV, or "Ivan the Terrible," who became known as "tsar." Ivan's armies annexed Kazan in 1552 and Astrakhan in 1554, giving Muscovy access to the entire Volga River basin and Central Asia. He encouraged military colonists, known as Cossacks*, to settle along the lower Dnieper, Volga, and Don rivers in Central Asia as a way of protecting Muscovy's frontiers on the south and southeast. Some of those Cossacks headed northeast, crossing the Ural Mountains into western Siberia and defeating the armies of the Siberian Khanate in 1581. Ivan IV then laid claim to all land west of the Ob' and Irtysh rivers. In terms of political philosophy, Ivan III and Ivan IV both made autocracy the fundamental principle of government.

Following a protracted succession crisis in the early seventeenth century, known as the "Time of Troubles," the territorial aggrandizement of Muscovy accelerated even more, with major gains achieved in the southwest and east. In 1648, a combined group of Ukrainians and Ukrainian Cossacks revolted against Polish rule and asked to be placed under the suzerainty of Muscovy. The rebellion led to a protracted war between Poland and Muscovy. The conflict was not settled until the Treaty of Andrusovo in 1667, which split Ukraine along the Dnieper River, with the western Ukraine remaining under Polish control and eastern Ukraine coming under Muscovite control.

Muscovy had already acquired Siberian territory west of the Ob' and Irtysh rivers, but, in the seventeenth century, large numbers of Russian traders, merchants, and explorers pushed farther east toward the Yenisei River. By the middle of the seventeenth century, they had crossed the Yenisei River and had reached the Lena River. It was not long before these Russians had reached the Amur River Valley, which constituted the westernmost part of the Chinese* empire. The collision of these two empires resulted in war, but with the Treaty of Nerchinsk (1689), Muscovy surrendered all claims to the Amur River Valley.

That treaty essentially confined Russia to the region north of the Amur Valley. Nevertheless, the expansion to the east during the seventeenth century gave Muscovy a territorial base that extended from Eurasia almost to the Pacific Ocean. The descendants of those Russian settlers in Siberia came to be known as "Old Inhabitants."

It was not until the reign of Peter I, the Great, that Muscovy made its major gains in the west. Peter became convinced that Russia would remain a backward nation until it adopted the military and economic values of Western Europe. He built a Western-style army for Russia, using Prussian and other military advisors; with English help, he constructed the first Russian navy. He streamlined the government, brought the Russian Orthodox Church under strict political control, dramatically raised government revenues and introduced Western educational models to Russia. He fought a long war with Charles XII of Sweden, which finally resulted in victory. In 1721, Sweden signed the Treaty of Nystadt, surrendering to Peter the territories of Livonia, Estonia, and Ingria. Peter had finally given Russia an outlet on the Baltic Sea. That same year, Peter proclaimed Muscovy to be the Russian Empire.

Later in the eighteenth century, under the rule of Catherine II, Russia made major territorial gains in the south and west. Russia went to war with the Ottoman Empire in 1768, and, with the Treaty of Kuchuk-Kainarji in 1774, Catherine separated the Crimean Tatars* from Ottoman control and gave Russia an outlet on the Black Sea. She annexed the Crimea in 1783. A second Russian-Turkish War took place between 1787 and 1792. It ended with the Treaty of Jassy. By the end of the eighteenth century, the Ottoman Empire no longer constituted a serious threat to Russia.

The disintegration of Poland also gave Russia new opportunities to the west. Late in the eighteenth century, Poland found itself threatened on all sides by the Prussians, Austrians, and Russians. The first partition of Poland occurred in 1772, and Russia received parts of Livonia and Belarus. The second partition occurred in 1793, when Russia secured most of Belarus and Ukraine west of the Dnieper River. An anti-Russian rebellion then arose in Poland, and the three powers moved in and finished off Poland as an independent nation. The Napoleonic Wars also gave Russia, under Alexander I, territorial opportunities in the west and south. Alexander seized the Grand Duchy of Finland from Sweden in 1809, took Bessarabia from Turkey in 1812, created the Russian Kingdom of Poland, and secured the region of Baku from the Persians in 1813. Russian settlers had by then crossed the Bering Straits and settled in Alaska. The Russian expansion in the Caucasus began with the annexation of Georgia in 1804. With all these expansions, Russia had acquired large numbers of Jews*, Ukrainians, Belarusians, Poles, Germans*, Finns*, Latvians*, Estonians*, Georgians*, Armenians*, Lithuanians, and assorted Muslim peoples.

The acquisition of so many non-Russian nationalities triggered a nativist reaction among the ruling elites. During the reign of Tsar Nicholas I, the slogan

"Autocracy, Orthodoxy, and Nationality" was promulgated as expressing the fundamental principles of political loyalty. They involved unquestioning fidelity to the authority of the tsar, the sovereignty of the Russian Orthodox Church as the religion of the whole society, and the use of Russian as the language of government, education, and literature. In a burst of Russian nationalism, Nicholas I and his successor Alexander II heavy-handedly launched an assault on non-Russian institutions. In 1839, Nicholas I suppressed the Uniate (Greek Catholic) Church of the Ukraine and Belarusia. In 1864 and 1865, the state ordered that all teaching of religion in public schools be conducted in Russian and shortly thereafter ordered that Russian be used as the language of all instruction in public and parochial schools. The state prohibited the publication of newspapers and magazines in non-Russian languages. In Poland it outlawed crosses on Catholic churches, devotional processions, and parish temperance associations; demanded prior approval of all clerical appointments; eliminated clerical visits with parishioners; forbade the construction of new chapels or the repair of old ones; and censored all sermons in non-Orthodox churches.

Later in the nineteenth century, Russian expansion in Asia began again. Russian troops moved into the central Caucasus in the late 1850s. Like dominos, the great centers of Central Asian Muslim civilization came under Russian control. Russians seized Tashkent in 1865, Bukhara in 1868, Khiva in 1873, Geok-Tepe in 1881, and Merv in 1884. Russia freed more than 10,000 slaves in Central Asia, constructed a number of railroads that helped to integrate the region into the larger commercial economy, and introduced cotton cultivation to the area.

The Opium War of 1839–1842 in China piqued Russian interest in the Far East again. The British* victory in the war and its annexation of Hong Kong forced Russia to consider a new move to gain access to the Pacific Ocean by controlling the entire length of the Amur River. China was inclined to cooperate with the Russians, in hopes of forestalling British penetration of the region. Therefore, in the treaty of Aigun in 1858, Russia acquired the left bank of the Amur River to the Ussuri River, and Russia and China agreed to joint sovereignty over the rest of the Amur River all the way to its Pacific outlet.

In 1860, Count Nikolai Muraviev, governor-general of Eastern Siberia, established the city of Vladivostok (Queen of the East) on the coast near the Korean* border. At the same time, a combined Anglo-French force occupied Beijing. Under Russian diplomatic auspices, the British and French* agreed to withdraw their forces, and, in gratitude, the Chinese signed the Treaty of Beijing with Russia in 1860. As a result of the treaty, Russia secured control of both the Amur and Ussuri river valleys and the right to build a port and naval base at Vladivostok. The treaty also gave Russia the entire coastal area from the Amur River to the Korean border. Because of the cost of these acquisitions and programs, the tsar sold Alaska to the United States for $7 million in 1867. Late in the 1870s, Russian troops occupied Turkmen* land along the borders of Iran and Afghanistan. In 1895, Japan recognized the Russian presence on the Liaotung

Peninsula and in Port Arthur in southern Manchuria, but Russia lost those concessions in the disastrous Russo-Japanese War of 1904–1905. The peace treaty gave Japan southern Sakhalin Island and control over Korea and southern Manchuria.

World War I and the Bolshevik Revolution brought about a shrinking of the empire that the Russians had constructed over the previous 600 years. By late in 1917, Russia was in the midst of revolution and civil war, and it became clear to V. I. Lenin that Russia could not both continue to fight World War I and even hope to succeed in the Communist revolution. He decided that peace must be secured at virtually any cost. Therefore, on March 3, 1918, Russia signed the Treaty of Brest-Litovsk, surrendering control of Poland, Estonia, Latvia, Lithuania, Finland, Ukraine, and part of the Caucasus. As they gained the upper hand in 1919, the Bolsheviks militarily established Soviet republics in Belarus in January 1919, Ukraine in March 1919, Azerbaijan in April 1920, Armenia in November 1920, and Georgia in March 1921. They tried but failed militarily to regain control of Finland, Poland, Estonia, Latvia, and Lithuania, all of which became independent republics after World War I. Russia proper became known as the Russian Soviet Federated Socialist Republic.

It was not until World War II that the Soviet Union regained what it had lost. Concerned about German expansion on its western frontier, the Soviet Union signed the Non-Aggression Pact with Germany and promptly seized eastern Poland in September 1939 while the Germans were taking western Poland. In October 1939, Soviet troops occupied Estonia, Latvia, and Lithuania. In a surprisingly difficult war, the Soviets forced Finland to cede some of its eastern territories between November 1939 and March 1940, and they annexed Bessarabia and Bukovina from Romania in June 1940. Within two years of the end of World War II, Soviet troops and pro-Soviet puppet governments had pushed the Soviet sphere of influence farther west than ever before, all the way across Poland into eastern Germany, and including Czechoslovakia, Hungary, Romania, Bulgaria, Yugoslavia, and Albania. This was the high point of the Russian and Soviet empires.

During the regimes of Josef Stalin, Nikita Khrushchev, and Leonid Brezhnev, the process of russification—the elimination of non-Russian cultural institutions—became state policy. This policy was nothing new; indeed, it had been a Russian goal for over a century. Nevertheless, the Slavic peoples of Europe never united because the factors holding them together—common origins, hatred of the Germans, fear of the Turks*—never overcame the political, geographic, religious, and linguistic forces dividing them. By 1840, pan-Slavic nationalism had emerged in central and eastern Europe. Slavic intellectuals attended pan-Slavic congresses in Prague in 1848 and Moscow in 1867; they talked of political unity, proclaimed the existence of a unique Slavic culture, and extolled the superiority of Slavic values. But pan-Slavism always foundered on Slavic nationalisms. Each Slavic group possessed its own history and cultural identity, and the Belarusians, Czechs, Slovaks, Poles, Carpatho-Rusyns*, Ukrainians, Slovenes, Croats, Serbs, and Bulgarians* all had ideas different from those of the Russians. They envisioned pan-Slavism as a loose confederation of independent subcultures, while the Russians longed for an empire with the throne at Moscow. Other Slavs shuddered at that thought. Early in the 1920s, Lenin had warned against what he called "Great Russian chauvinism." He had hoped instead to create a revolving leadership for the Soviet Union that would respect ethnic diversity. Lenin's premature death in 1924 aborted that dream, and, under Josef Stalin, the dual processes of centralization and russification proceeded unabated.

The Russian Orthodox Church

During the 1960s, 1970s, and 1980s, as ethnic nationalism intensified in the Baltics, Georgia, and the Central Asian Republics, Russian nationalism gained momentum as well. Central to the historical Russian identity was the Russian Orthodox Church. Patriarch Photius of Constantinople first began sending Christian missionaries to Russia in the ninth century, but they met with little success. Because Kiev was located near the Dnieper River, a thoroughfare between the upper Slavic regions of Europe and Constantinople, there was, however, a constant flow of Christians and Christian ideas into the region. Princess Olga of Russia was baptized a Christian, but her decision had little impact on other Russians. Russian Christianity had its real beginnings in Kievan Rus', when, in 987, Prince Vladimir accepted Christianity and declared the Byzantine Rite to be the state religion. Vladimir's conversion was more political than religious. He was baptized in 987, prior to his marriage to the Byzantine Princess Anna; he then forced the Russian nobility, middle classes, and peasants to join the new religion. Vladimir's son Yaroslav then invited Bulgarian Christian missionaries to come into Russia, and they brought with them liturgies that had been translated into Old Slavonic. As a result, Russian Christianity, almost from its inception, was oriented toward liturgical, canonical, theological, and spiritual works that had been translated from the original Greek into Old Slavonic for use in Bulgaria. The head of the church at Kiev usually was a Greek, since the patriarch at Constantinople had the right, until 1458, to nominate the leading bishops of the church.

Russians looked to the patriarch of Constantinople as the leader both of the Byzantine Rite and of all of Eastern Orthodox Christianity. The Orthodox Church had been the religious arm of the Byzantine Empire since the fourth century. It was the state religion: The emperor, as first layman of the church, selected the patriarch from three candidates chosen by a church council, and the church was often considered part of the political bureaucracy. Unlike the pope, who was expected to be independent of nationalism, the patriarch of Constantinople was clearly subordinate to the emperor. Church and state were one, and state was supreme in matters of church government, but not doctrine.

The process of separatism between Eastern and Western Christianity began in the fourth century. At that point, the popes began to call Rome the apostolic center of the church on the grounds that St. Peter had given the keys of the kingdom to the bishop of Rome. All other bishoprics were secondary, since juridical authority flowed from the papacy through the priesthood; sovereignty resided in Rome. Emperor Theodosius of Constantinople, accustomed to controlling church and state, was unwilling to share power with anyone. In 381, he rejected papal claims and declared that there were two centers of Christianity; the patriarchs of Rome and Constantinople were given precedence in prestige over those patriarchs in Alexandria, Antioch, and Jerusalem.

Political relations between the two centers slowly deteriorated, and the split deepened during the iconoclastic controversy of the eighth century. Emperor Leo III of Constantinople decided that Muslims were right in condemning images as superstitious idolatry. He therefore removed icons (painted or mosaic representations of Christ or of saints) from churches throughout the empire. Riots erupted immediately. Troops crushed the rebellion, and Pope Gregory II bitterly condemned the decision. Not until 843 were the images restored, and, by then, the ill will between the two churches had become permanent. Subsequent schisms were short-lived until the mid-eleventh century. In 1054, the pope and the patriarch excommunicated each other, and the Fourth Crusade of 1204, when Catholic crusaders sacked Constantinople, completed the split.

Eastern Orthodoxy then evolved into several independent exarchates and patriarchates. The Ecumenical Patriarchate remained in Constantinople, but older patriarchates existed in Alexandria, Antioch, and Jerusalem. After the fall of Constantinople to the Ottoman Turks in 1453, the Metropolitan, later patriarch, of the Russian Orthodox Church assumed actual leadership, and several other independent churches emerged in Serbia, Bulgaria, Greece, Romania, Georgia, Cyprus, and elsewhere, all with power to consecrate priests and mediate ecclesiastical disputes. This was Orthodoxy—an autonomous association of the eastern patriarchates and autocephalous churches that recognized the patriarch of Constantinople as its honorary leader.

Beyond this major controversy over power, other differences divided the eastern and western churches. Rome insisted on a celibate priesthood, while the eastern churches permitted priests to marry. They also argued about the procession of the Holy Spirit; Catholics believed that the Holy Spirit went from the Father and the Son to man, while Orthodox theologians claimed the Spirit came only from the Father. Still other differences were cultural and demographic. Populations in the West were relatively contiguous, and Catholicism was comparatively homogeneous—the pope was the acknowledged head of the church, and Latin was the liturgical language everywhere. But in the East, where ethnic groups were isolated, religious pluralism developed; in each region, the church had its own liturgies, usually in a local language understood by the congregation. In the West, religion and nationality were distinct, but in the East, the church was part of nationhood and the nation an expression of the church. The Western dualism between church and state gave rise to the idea that all power did not rest in the state and that other segments of the society could criticize and even transcend the political establishment. In the East, however, a more authoritarian tradition developed: Since the hierarchy was closely affiliated with the state, the church could play no role in criticizing national policies.

Over the centuries, the Russian clergy became increasingly disgruntled about the control wielded over them by the patriarch at Constantinople. After Constantinople was overrun by the Turks in 1453, clerical resentment turned into absolute antipathy. Prominent Russian clergymen began to demand their own patriarch at Moscow and described Moscow as the "Third Rome"—a new headquarters for Christianity in Europe. The Greek Patriarch Jeremias II visited Moscow in 1589 and agreed to their requests. On January 23, 1589, Job was named the first Russian patriarch. The Greek church vehemently protested the action and subsequently demanded that all of Job's successors receive their investiture from Constantinople. The Russians would have none of it. Although the Greeks considered the Russian patriarch subordinate to those of Constantinople, Alexandria, Antioch, and Jerusalem, the Russians claimed that Moscow was third in honor, behind only Constantinople and Alexandria.

During the seventeenth century, the Russian Orthodox Church was divided by a schism of its own. When Nikon was elected patriarch in 1652, he was determined to bring about liturgical reforms and to assert his ecclesiastical powers against the tsar. Over the centuries, as the old Greek texts had been translated and re-translated into Old Slavonic, errors and misinterpretations had increasingly appeared. Since those translations were often made independently at different churches and monasteries, the liturgies varied from region to region and even from village to village. Constantinople had frequently condemned such changes and had demanded the reform of the Russian texts. Patriarch Nikon called a special council in 1654 and ordered the correction of the Old Slavonic texts to make them consistent with the Greek texts used in Constantinople. The proposal raised a storm of protest among many Russians who had come to view their texts as sacred and unchangeable. Those who refused to accept the changes became known as Old Believers, and they were soon subject to intense persecution.

Patriarch Nikon's attempt to break the hold of the tsar over the church resulted in both short-term and long-term problems for the church. He was personally stripped of his holy office and exiled for life to a monastery. Moreover, the ruling families of Russia decided to make sure that the church remained under their strict political control. That process continued throughout the seventeenth century, and Peter the Great completed it. Adopting an ecclesiastical organization similar to Lutheran Prussia, Peter established the Most Holy Synod, a council of eleven clergymen, appointed by him, to govern the church; he thereby substantially eliminated the office of the patriarch. From that point until the Russian Revolution in 1917, the church essentially became an arm of the state.

The fall of the Romanov dynasty in 1917 brought an end to the Holy Synod and, for Russian Orthodox conservatives, raised hopes that the centuries of state-controlled religion would also come to an end. Patriarch Tikhon emerged as the leader of the church, but, when civil war erupted between the Bolsheviks and their opponents, he worked hard not to take sides, claiming that he simply represented all believers, regardless of their political opinions. Once the war was over and the Bolsheviks had consolidated their power, however, they turned on the church, imprisoning Tikhon, closing churches, and plundering Russian Orthodox treasures. Under international pressure, Lenin and the Communists released the patriarch from jail, and, until his death in 1925, Tikhon openly condemned the state assault on the church. Karl Marx had contemptuously described religion as the "opiate of the masses," and Lenin, as well as his successors, were concerned about the political and economic influence of the church. They were certainly not willing to tolerate a belief system to rival the supremacy of the Communist Party.

During the 1920s, persecution of the church intensified. Prominent clerics were imprisoned or executed, churches were closed or turned into museums, monasteries were vacated, and clerical appointments, even at the level of bishop and patriarch, were ignored. By 1930, only seventeen Russian Orthodox churches were still open in Moscow, compared to more than 500 before 1917. Only three were open in Leningrad. The persecution did not stop until World War II, when the government sought to rally all segments of Soviet society against the Nazi invaders. Because of the state commitment to atheism, however, the persecution started up again once the war ended and continued throughout the rest of the Stalin, Khrushchev, and Brezhnev years. Even during the first few years of Mikhail Gorbachev's administration, the persecution continued. Anti-religious propagandists were encouraged to continue their rhetorical assaults on the church, and every year several hundred more churches were closed. By the early 1980s, membership in the Russian Orthodox Church totaled approximately 45,000,000 people, down from a membership of 115,000,000 members in 1917. Russian Orthodoxy, once the centerpiece of ethnic Russian identity, was badly debilitated.

Russification and the New Soviet Man

Nonetheless, there were powerful continuities between the Russian and Soviet empires. In terms of national boundaries, the Soviet Union by 1930 was very similar to the Russian empire of the late nineteenth and early twentieth centuries. Each was imbued with a powerful religious ideology—the Russian empire with the Russian Orthodox Church, the Soviet empire with Marxism-Leninism. Both empires were autocratic states with strong suspicions about democratic thought. Just as the Russians had come to view themselves as the "third Rome," the spiritual center of Christianity, so the Soviets saw themselves as the heart and soul of international Communism. Both empires were militaristic and expansionist, and both were committed to russification—the Russians in the name of Tsar, Church, and Pan-Slavism and the Soviets in the name of Communism and the "Soviet man."

During the Brezhnev administration in the 1970s, the Soviet Union officially added a new wrinkle to their notion of nationalism, promoting the idea of the "Soviet man." According to Marxist theory, history was marching inexorably toward Communism. Especially in the Soviet Union, where capitalist obstacles had been eliminated, society would change as well, becoming international in outlook and Communist in ideals. Parochial perspectives, which were sustained by ethnic nationalisms and misguided religious loyalties, would steadily decay. Stalin had long described such a process, but, under Brezhnev and his ideological "tsar," Mikhail Suslov, it reached new highs. Suslov called for a "merger of nations," asserting that state policy could accelerate the elimination of such parochial nationalities. The key to the merger, Suslov argued, was russification— mandatory learning of the Russian language and the exclusive use of Russian as the language of government throughout the country. Suslov was especially heavy-handed in pushing russification in Ukraine and Belarusia, where he thought the process would be easy, since the people there were also Eastern Slavs. Moreover, if he could bring Belarusia and Ukraine into a merger with Russia, the smaller, non-Slavic nationalities would have no choice but to follow. Brezhnev and Suslov pushed this goal with missionary zeal.

Not surprisingly, Russians came to dominate the governing institutions of the Soviet Union. In June 1990, the Soviet Union's ruling Politburo had eighteen members, and fourteen of them were ethnic Russians. The general staff of the Soviet military machine was overwhelmingly Russian, as was the Council of Ministers of the Soviet Union. Indeed, more than 80 percent of the heads of central state committees in the late 1980s were ethnic Russians. Unwritten rules dictated that in the non-Russian republics, a highly russified indigenous leader headed the Communist party apparatus as first secretary, while the second secretary had to be ethnic Russian.

There were also powerful economic and cultural reasons for pushing russification. Most Russians were convinced that, since non-Russian nationalities were backward and somewhat uncivilized, the imposition of the Russian language would make for a more modern, advanced society. In economic terms, they believed that the entire country needed a single language for economic transactions to avoid a severe problem of inefficiency. Suslov also argued that linguistic diversity was a liability in the Red Army and that scientific research and the promotion of scientific skills would be much more efficient if Russian were the country's first language. Finally, Suslov insisted that centralized political control of the state would work much more efficiently if Russian were the only language used in governmental affairs. Those policies, of course, only caused more resentment among the non-Russian nationalities, and, in the 1980s, when Mikhail Gorbachev eased some of the heavy-handedness, ethnic nationalisms soon surfaced again.

For years, a silent resentment had existed just below the surface of Russian culture, a feeling that the politics and society of the Soviet Union had somehow subsumed Russian culture, that Russia and the Soviet Union had fused into a single whole while the other nationalities had been able to maintain separate identities. Many Russians even had a sense of envy toward the republics, because they at least enjoyed the symbols of nationhood: individual parliaments, learned societies, national histories, Communist parties, cultural traditions, and languages. Russians often felt that their culture was completely obscured by the Soviet shadow. One example was the portraits of children that the Soviet Union frequently printed and distributed throughout the country. The posters showed children from the fourteen other republics wearing traditional ethnic garb, while Russian children were dressed in the uniform of the Soviet Komsomol.

There was also a growing sense of alarm among the Russians about the non-Russian nationalities. The high birth rate of many of the non-Russian groups was startling. Between 1959 and 1970, the numbers of Central Asians and Azerbaijanis* had increased by 50 percent, and the Uzbeks* had surpassed the Belarusians to become the third largest group in the Soviet Union. The Muslim peoples were increasing in the population at a rate of 3.5 times as fast as the Russians. The non-Russians also seemed fanatically loyal to their native languages, indicating that the so-called "Soviet man" was a long way from emerging.

Most Russians had been extremely ethnocentric in the first place, looking down on non-Russians as inferior people who needed training and uplifting. Ethnic epithets were popular throughout the Russian Soviet Federated Socialist Republic (RSFSR). Ethnic Russians derisively referred to Armenians, for instance, as *Armyashka*, or "little Armenians." The term *Chernozhopy*, or "black asses," was used to describe Central Asians and dark-skinned Georgians, Armenians, and Azerbaijanis. Russians called Ukrainians *Khokhly*, which translated as "stupid" or "stubborn," and *Makaronniki* (macaronis). Mongols, Buryats, and other Asians were known as *Kosoglazy* ("slant eyes"), *Ploskomordy* ("flat snouts"), or *Zhopomordy* ("ass faces"). Jews* were referred to as *Zhids* ("yids" or "kikes"). Ethnic Russians used the term *natsmen* ("colonial wog") in everyday conversation to describe non-Russian minorities.

Of course, all of the other nationalities had their own resentments too, seeing in Soviet policies only a barely veiled attempt to russify their cultures. Russian nationalists, however, were not convinced of this. For them, Russia had more than half of the Soviet Union's population and two-thirds of its land mass; Russia was the glue of the Soviet Union. All of the other republics, in the words of Yuri Prokofyev, were simply "dwarf governments." They therefore resented the russophobia sweeping across the country. As Russian writer Valentin Rasputin said, "We are tired of being the scapegoats, of enduring the slurs and the treachery. . . . Live with us or not, just as you like, but do not behave arrogantly toward us."

Aspects of New Russian Nationalism

But Russian nationalism was far more complicated than the nationalisms of the Lithuanians, Latvians, Estonians, Georgians, Azerbaijanis, and Armenians. For each of those groups, Russian culture and the Communist Party had become the targets that unified their nationalist aspirations. Their goals thus revolved around the ideas of secession, independence, and cultural and linguistic revival.

Although Russian nationalists were similarly resentful of Communism and of what the Soviet Union had done to Russian identity, their own movement was divided by intense cultural and political differences. By the 1980s, there were actually three movements for Russian nationalism—one based on liberal democracy, another revolving around a conservative revival of Russian culture, and a third, more radical, model based on political authoritarianism.

The moderate wing of Russian nationalism first emerged in the 1970s with very limited goals, primarily because overt anti-Soviet political activity would have inspired a crackdown by the Brezhnev regime. Moderate nationalism revolved around the ideas of cultural revival, environmental protection, market economics, and political democracy. Still, they focused their activities on the restoration of long-neglected monuments to Russian history, especially churches in cities as well as in villages. The ostensible reasons they gave for the restorations were cultural, historical, and architectural, rather than religious, but, during the 1970s and 1980s, several thousand churches were either rebuilt or refurbished. The neglect of the churches had for years left a void in Russian culture and compromised the Russian identity. Even non-religious Russian nationalists viewed the cultural revival in religious terms; that is, they saw the restoration of Russian Orthodoxy to being a mainstream institution relatively free of political oppression as an important step in revival of Russian nationalism. The leading group pushing the restorations was the All-Russian Society for the Preservation of Monuments.

A budding environmental movement also appeared in the 1970s. To even the most casual observer, Soviet economic policies had been so growth-oriented, so committed to rapid industrialization, that environmental disasters had occurred throughout the country. In fact, the Soviet Union's emphasis on steel production and chemical manufacturing, traditionally the most polluting industries, made these problems even worse. The virtual drying up of the Aral Sea and the Chernobyl nuclear accident in 1986 were only the most notorious examples. A total of 103 Russian cities have air pollution levels more than ten times higher than what is considered safe; sixteen cities suffer pollution levels more than fifty times as high. Because of untreated sewage, agricultural run-off, and industrial discharges, most rivers, lakes, and seashores in the Soviet Union are badly contaminated. Fish production in the Black, Caspian, and Baltic seas is falling drastically because of pollution. Landfills, hazardous waste sites, and disposal of nuclear waste have all been handled for decades without the slightest concern for the environment. Pesticides and fertilizers have been improperly used. The pollution has become so bad that it has actually contributed to a decline in the gross national product. Some Western economists estimated that, by 1990, the degradation of natural resources and pollution were costing the Soviet Union more than 17 percent of its GNP every year.

Russian environmentalists were initially quite cautious in their approach, selling environmental protection as good economics, but the idea of protecting Mother Russia from pollution was a powerful one among Russian nationalists.

The so-called Green Movement faced serious obstacles, however, since independent, non-governmental political movements were strictly prohibited and data on the environment were heavily classified. Back in the nineteenth century, such Russian writers as Vladimir Vernadsky became environmental philosophers, praising the virtues of Mother Russia and demanding humane care for the environment. During the 1930s, Stalin imprisoned and executed outspoken environmentalists. The modern environmental movement nonetheless struck a real chord in Russian nationalism. At Moscow State University a student movement appeared in the 1960s, calling for the protection of the environment; a movement among intellectuals arose to protect Lake Baikal, the world's largest supply of fresh water. Early in the 1980s, still another group appeared in the Soviet Union. They opposed a grandiose state scheme to reverse the flow of Siberian rivers so that they would water the dry Central Asian republics rather than go "uselessly" into the Arctic Ocean.

Other liberal Russian nationalists, many of whom were academics, began to suggest tentatively that one way out of the country's economic malaise was to build incentives into the production process. They too had to be very careful about not upsetting hardline Communist ideologues, but they nevertheless began to venture out with such simple suggestions as allowing workers on collective farms to keep the proceeds from the small plots of land specifically assigned to their families. In addition, they also suggested that if the state imposed certain profit requirements on major state industries, this policy would spur growth and actually improve productivity and environmental protection. Finally, the liberal Russian nationalists hoped to lift the heavy-handed oppression of the state in order to encourage political debate, academic and artistic freedom of expression, and more democratic political institutions.

For these liberal Russian nationalists, the advent of Mikhail Gorbachev and his policy of *glasnost* in the 1980s was a seminal event, exactly what they had been waiting and hoping for over a decade. Their dream of liberal democracy received a dramatic boost when Gorbachev permitted rival political parties to function openly. Likewise, their hopes for the development of a more market-oriented economy received strong encouragement when Gorbachev began to permit the establishment of profit-oriented cooperatives to compete with state industries. A spontaneous Green Movement developed in the late 1980s to lobby for a more sane environmental policy, and Gorbachev responded to their demands. In 1986, he blocked the program to change the course of the Siberian rivers and, in 1988, established the State Committee for the Protection of Nature. The moderates hated the oppression of the Stalin years and wanted democracy and multicultural tolerance. In short, liberal Russian nationalists saw in Gorbachev an opportunity to bring Russia into the modern twentieth-century Western world.

But it was that very idea of making Russia into a liberal democracy that struck fear into more conservative Russian nationalists. For centuries, Russian conservatives had been suspicious of the West, and every Russian leader who has looked westward, whether Peter the Great in the seventeenth century or Gorbachev in the twentieth, has had to deal with a ferocious backlash from the right. Contemporary Russian writers like Vladimir Soloukhin and Valentin Rasputin have evoked images of "Old Russia" and "Great Russia"—a land of clean open spaces, comfortable peasant villages, proud extended families, stable but authoritarian governments, and the Russian Orthodox Church, complete with its spires and its bearded patriarchs and priests. Many of these people have found a political home in the Russian Patriotic Society, established in 1989, or in such organizations as the Association of Russian Artists and the Fund for Slavic Writing and Slavic Cultures. They believe that the Soviet state and Communist ideology had suppressed Russian culture, dirtied the countryside, collectivized the villages, assaulted the churches, and destabilized the polity. They have only one thing in common with Communism: a strong commitment to political authority, to rule with an iron hand; unlike the Communists, however, they want authority to be vested in ancient institutions. In the name of Russian purity, they want to cast off the alien republics, particularly the Muslim fanatics of Central Asia. They want nothing to do with the liberal democracy or modern, industrial economies of the West. Instead, they desire a return to the village economies of the peasant years. They also want Russian Orthodoxy restored as the central institution of Russian life. Finally, they wish to abandon the secular values of the West and turn inward, as so many Russian nationalists have wanted to do, and have succeeded in doing, over the past five centuries. These conservative nationalists have formed other groups, such as the Union for the Spiritual Revival of the Fatherland, to oppose liberal democratization.

In short, conservative Russian nationalists have seen no panacea in the liberal democracies of the West. For them, Gorbachev was taking Russia down the wrong path, a path that would lead to secularism, materialism, and spiritual death for Mother Russia. Central to the conservative nationalists' program has been the restoration of the Russian Orthodox Church to its rightful place at the heart of national life. For a thousand years, the church, Russian culture, and Russian identity had been inseparable; the starting point of Russian nationalism was love of Mother Russia and reverence for the Orthodox Church. Even for non-believers, the church represented the best in Russian art, music, and architecture. Gorbachev tried to please these conservatives by ending the decades-old persecution of the church. In 1988, he met with a group of prominent Russian Orthodox leaders, including Patriarch Pimen, re-opened hundreds of previously closed churches, returned a number of important monasteries to clerical control, transferred thousands of religious relics from state museums to the church, and permitted Russians to participate in the festivals celebrating the millenium of the Russian Orthodox Church. By the end of 1988, nearly 100 or more Russian Orthodox parishes were functioning than there had been one year earlier. Between 1985 and 1990, 4,100 Russian Orthodox parishes were either established or re-opened. Even more interesting, many Russian Orthodox clergymen ran for office as "people's deputies," including Metropolitan Aleksii of Leningrad and Novgorod. He later succeeded Patriarch Pimen as head of the church. In the March 1990 elections, 190 Russian Orthodox clerics were elected as deputies. Another major development was the open adoption of a social mission by Russian Orthodox parishes around the country. They began sponsoring hospitals, day-care centers, orphanages, workshops, and shelters; that same year, Gorbachev removed legislation from the books that had prohibited churches from undertaking such social missions. The Communist Party had long denied the need for this kind of activity since these types of problems were endemic only in capitalist countries. The 1990 Law on Freedom of Conscience and Religious Organizations explicitly permitted churches to undertake social missions and to sponsor charitable work. Finally, the government authorized state printing offices to begin printing Bibles in Russian and allowed Russian Orthodox churches to sponsor Sunday schools and other forms of religious instruction.

Of course, Gorbachev's reasons for liberating the church were not simply to satisfy conservative Russian nationalists. Rather, he worried that his dreams of *perestroika* and *glasnost* would go up in the flames of ethnic nationalism, that the centrifugal forces of religion and ethnicity would bring about the break-up of the Soviet Union. Gorbachev knew that the Russian Orthodox Church was firmly planted in Russia, Belarusia, Ukraine, Latvia, Moldova, and Estonia, and he hoped that the church might provide enough cultural glue to maintain the political unity of the country.

In addition to liberal nationalists, committed to democratic political institutions, environmentalism, and the market economy, and conservative nationalists, calling for the resurrection of Russian Orthodoxy and the restoration of an authoritarian, stable government, there was yet a more radical, indeed reactionary, movement of Russian nationalists. Gorbachev felt comfortable dealing with the liberals and the conservatives; the radical nationalists, however, were more frightening. It was not just the Communist Party that they hated; they also despised modernization, urbanization, industrialism, modern technology, and Western popular culture. One of the leading figures in radical Russian nationalism was Aleksandr Solzhenitsyn, even though he was in exile in the United States. For the Nobel Prize winner, life in the United States was like ''spiritual castration.'' Capitalism and materialism made life more comfortable physically, but there was no reason for life in the United States. Solzhenitsyn still saw the meaning of life in Mother Russia, but the Soviet Union and Communist Party had all but eviscerated it.

The radicals rejected democracy and demanded authority; they disdained the West and called for the development of the Russian interior. They hated large-scale economies and demanded the return of land to peasants and the reconstruction of Russian village life. They blamed Communism for the destruction of the environment, the mindless plunder of natural resources, the pandemic of alcoholism, and the incredible number of abortions (which in 1990 averaged six in the lifetime of every adult woman), which threatened the country with population decline. Radical nationalist groups, bearing such nostalgic names as Fatherland,

Memory, Fidelity, Patriot, and Renewal, popped up around the country during the 1980s, and they frequently turned to anti-Semitism, also blaming Jews for much of the country's plight. Because Leon Trotsky and other prominent Bolsheviks were Jewish, many of the radical nationalists have seen the Russian Revolution of 1917 as a kind of Jewish plot to destroy the country. Some of them have even called for the restoration of the monarchy as an answer to the chaos surrounding them in Russia.

By far the most extreme group of Russian nationalists is Pamyat ("Memory"), an organization that first emerged in 1979 in the Soviet Ministry of the Aviation Industry and which by 1987 had taken control of the All-Russian Society for the Preservation of Historical and Cultural Monuments. Its leader was Dmitri Vasiliyev, a charismatic photographer and journalist. At first, Pamyat was interested simply in preserving the cultural and architectural artifacts of the Russian past, but, by the mid–1980s, it had acquired a new ideology—an almost mystical, religious devotion to all things Russian and the strong conviction that there was an international conspiracy to destroy the Russian people and Russian culture. There has also been a strong temperance strain in Pamyat, growing out of the belief that one of the ways that Jews and Freemasons were attempting to destroy Russia was by creating a nation of alcoholics. The true enemies of ethnic Russians, they decided, were thus international Zionists and Freemasons. By 1987, Vasiliyev had given Pamyat a new ideology—the secession of Russia from the Soviet Union and the restoration of the monarchy. His followers took to wearing black T-shirts, jack boots, and military great coats; they carried banners displaying the double eagle of the Romanov family as well as lightning bolts shaped something like Nazi swastikas. They took to public demonstrations and even mugged known Jewish intellectuals. Pamyat's brand of Russian nationalism had a strong strain of fascism in it.

By the early 1990s, Pamyat was organized throughout Russia—in Moscow, St. Petersburg, Kaliningrad, Kursk, Taganrog, Riga, Ermak, Novosibirsk, and Yuzhno-Sakhalinsk. But there was a rival to Pamyat in Sverdlovsk, where a literary society known as Otechestvo ("fatherland") appeared in 1987. They too have detected Zionist, Nazi, and Freemason conspiracies in Russia, blamed the ponderous bureaucracy on those conspiracies, and also roundly condemned rock music, Western values, and all forms of liberalization. They likewise have demanded the restoration of state authority—enough power to maintain the political order that is so traditionally Russian.

This burst of Russian nationalism found political expression in 1990, when the Russian Congress began to debate the question of state sovereignty. At a meeting of the congress in June, delegates debated a Declaration on the State Sovereignty of the Russian Federation. This was extremely controversial, with delegates from the autonomous republics objecting to provisions in the declaration that indicated that Russian sovereignty took precedence over their own. The debate revealed the potential for ethnic fracturing within Russia as well as within the larger Soviet Union.

The great concern that Gorbachev and other Russian moderates faced in the late 1980s was the political and economic disarray spreading throughout the country. The most conservative elements of the Russian power structure—the Communist Party, the military, and the KGB—all had a vested interest in the maintenance of the status quo. The collapse of the Communist parties throughout Eastern Europe in 1989 and 1990 struck fear into the hearts of Russian Communists. Similarly, the withdrawal of Russian troops from those areas angered many military leaders, who found the Russian army—which they had considered an almost sacred institution—suffering from severe morale problems. Gorbachev's hints at democratization likewise undermined confidence among members of the KGB. At the same time, the great worry of liberal Russian nationalists was that conservative opponents of Gorbachev (conservative Russian nationalists, the military, the KGB, and the Communist Party bureaucrats) might form a right-wing coalition and take the Soviet Union back into the dark ages of authoritarianism. The abortive *coup d'état* of August 1991 amounted to just that kind of political backlash.

The coup failed for a variety of reasons, not the least of which was the fact that the liberal wing of Russian nationalism enjoyed by far the most support in the country at large. When Boris Yeltsin took to the barricades in defiance of coup leaders, he enjoyed the support of tens of millions of ethnic Russians who did not want to turn back the clock. He had been democratically elected as the president of the Russian Federation, and his star soon eclipsed Gorbachev's. The demise of the Soviet Union at the end of 1991 left Yeltsin as the premier leader of the country.

Even so, Yeltsin still faced the same threat that Gorbachev had faced, although Yeltsin's nemesis was economic rather than political. Gorbachev had worried about conservative elements organizing politically to prevent their own loss of power. Yeltsin's greatest concern was that the economic collapse of the Soviet Union would soon erode the support he had among the Russian masses. The seventy-four years of Communist control of the Soviet Union constituted the greatest example of economic mismanagement in the history of the world. By 1990, the economic infrastructure—cultural as well as physical—was incapable of supporting a modern economy. The ruble could not be converted into other world currencies; goods could not be delivered to market; and people were spending most of their time waiting in lines for bread rather than working on their jobs. Shortages were so severe that malnutrition and hunger were becoming commonplace. What struck terror into Yeltsin and other liberals was that, if faced with starvation, the Russian masses would opt for the "iron hand" of despotism again, as they had so many times in the past.

REFERENCES: *Current Digest*, 42 (June 13, 1990), 4–15, and 42 (July 11, 1990), 13–14; Nadia Diuk and Adrian Karatnycky, *The Hidden Nations: The People Challenge the Soviet Union from Lithuania to Armenia, the Ukraine to Central Asia*, 1991; Hilary F. French, "Environmental Problems and Policies in the Soviet Union," *Current History*, 90 (October 1991), 333–37; Anthony Jones and William Moskoff, *Ko-ops: The Rebirth of Entrepreneurship in the Soviet Union*, 1991; Anthony Jones, Walter D. Connor, and David E. Powell, eds., *Soviet Social Problems*, 1991; Bohdan Nahaylo and Victor Swoboda, *Soviet Disunion: A History of the Nationalities Problem in the USSR*, 1989; Roger Portal, *The Slavs*, 1969; David E. Powell, "The Revival of Religion," *Current History*, 90 (October 1991), 328–33; Hugh Seton-Watson, *The East-European Revolution*, 1956; Hedrick Smith, *The Russians*, 1972; Hedrick Smith, *The New Russians*, 1990.

RUSSIKY. See RUSSIAN.

RUSSKIY. See MESHCHERYAK or RUSSIAN.

RUSSKOUSTIN. Beginning in the late seventeenth and early eighteenth centuries, small groups of Russians* began migrating east toward Siberia. Some of them settled in the polar region, where they adopted the economic life-styles—hunting, fishing, and breeding reindeer and dogs—of the surrounding Chuvash* and Yukagir* peoples. They have managed to retain use of the Russian language, however, and continue to identify themselves as ethnic Russians. Most of them live in Russkoe Uste on the Indigirka River. See RUSSIAN.
REFERENCE: Ronald Wixman, *The Peoples of the USSR: An Ethnographic Handbook*, 1984.

RUSSKOUSTINTSY. See RUSSIAN, CHUVAN, and YUKAGIR.

RUSYN. See CARPATHO-RUSYN.

RUTHENIAN. See CARPATHO-RUSYN.

RUTUL. Until the time of the Russian Revolution, the Rutul people were generally classified as the Lezgin*, itself a generic term used to describe all of the ethnic groups of the highlands southwest of the Caspian Sea in what is today the Daghestan Autonomous Republic. Most Rutuls are concentrated on the upper Samur River in the Rutul rayon of Daghestan. A much smaller number live across the border in Azerbaijan. Russians* refer to the Rutul as the Rutul'tsy, but the Rutuls have no general name for themselves. Instead, they identify themselves by the name of the village in which they live. Since the revolution, ethnologists have been more careful in making group identifications, and the once generic Lezgins have today become the Lezgins proper as well as the Aguls*, Rutuls, and Tabasarans*. The Rutul language, which has no written equivalent, is part of the Samurian* group of the Caucasic languages. Between the 1920s and the 1950s, Azerbaijan* and Lezgin served as the literary language for the Rutuls. That practice was terminated by state policy in the 1950s, after which Russian became the Rutuls' written language.

Ethnologists believe that the Rutuls have lived in the region ever since the fifth century. At that time, they were most likely animists. Some Rutuls converted to Islam with the Arab* invasions of the eighth century, but until the fifteenth century, most Rutuls were primarily animists with their own folk religions, though Zoroastrianism, Judaism, and Christianity were making inroads. Persian* traders accelerated the Rutul conversion to Islam in the fifteenth century, as did the Golden Horde invasions of the northern region in the sixteenth and seventeenth centuries. By the nineteenth century, the Rutuls had all been converted to the Sunni faith of Islam. The Rutuls remain extremely devout in their religious devotions, and, like other Muslim people in the Near East and Middle East in the 1970s and 1980s, they have been influenced by the increasingly strident religious fundamentalism that has dominated the cultural landscape. In spite of more than seventy years of anti-religious state policy, fundamental religious institutions and traditions—such as endogamous marriages, family mosques, religious marriages and burials, observance of Ramadan, and faithful devotion to the teachings of the Koran—still flourish.

From the sixteenth through the eighteenth centuries, the Rutuls constituted a powerful political confederation known as the Rutul Mahal. Each village had a civil and military leader who interacted with counterparts in other villages to develop common policies. Ethnic Russians began arriving in the early nineteenth century, and the Rutuls resisted their expansion. In 1838, the Rutul Aga-Bek led a widespread uprising against Russia; within a few years, Russia had crushed the movement and annexed the Rutul Mahal. The Rutul Mahal was formally annexed by Russia in 1844.

A profound anti-Russian sentiment permeates Rutul culture. Just after the Russian Revolution, the government in Moscow created the Mountain Autonomous Republic with Arabic as the official language of the government and the schools. The Rutul, along with many other highland ethnic groups, opposed the policy and rebelled against it. The government then created the Daghestan Autonomous Soviet Socialist Republic in 1921. In 1925, it launched an anti-Islamic campaign, which included closing all Islamic schools, eliminating the use of Arabic, and executing many local imams. At that point, state policy shifted in favor of the Turkic* peoples, and Azeri became the official language of the region. That ended in 1928, when the government declared that Dargin*, Avar*, Lezgin, and Azerbaijani were all official languages. The government also decided at that time that the Aguls were to merge with the Lezgins, while the Rutuls, as well as the Tsakhurs*, were to merge with the Azerbaijanis. Gradually, over the next twenty years, the Russian language was imposed on all schools and government offices in Daghestan.

The constant policies of cultural manipulation by the Soviet government only increased Rutul resentment of Russian culture, and many Rutuls did not want to merge with the Azerbaijanis. The forced assimilation policy of the government had the effect of reducing the Rutul population from approximately 10,500 people in 1929 to only 6,700 in 1959. Since then, however, the Rutul population has started to rise again, with an estimated population in 1990 of approximately 19,000 people. Economic life still revolves around animal husbandry (sheep and goats in the highlands and cattle in the lowlands), gold and silver smithing, weaving, pottery, and rug manufacturing. Because of their economic need to trade goods within the region of Daghestan, many Rutuls also speak Azeri and Lezgin. Traditionally, the Rutuls were governed by rigid, endogamous, patriarchal clan systems, in which young people were encouraged to marry their first or second cousins. That sense of clan cohesion was strengthened by the fact that all land was owned communally by the extended family unit. During the 1960s and 1970s, the Soviet state succeeded in establishing government cooperatives and collectivizing many Rutul cattle herds and pasture lands, much to the resentment of the local people.

REFERENCES: Alexandre Bennigsen, "Muslim Conservative Opposition to the Soviet Regime: The Sufi Brotherhoods in the North Caucasus," in Jeremy R. Azrael, ed., *Soviet Nationality Policies and Practices*, 1971; Alexandre Bennigsen and S. Enders Wimbush, *Muslims in the Soviet Empire: A Guide*, 1986; Bruce Geiger, et al., *Peoples and Languages of the Caucasus*, 1959; T. S. Halasi-Kun, "The Caucasus: An Ethno-Historical Survey," *Studia Caucasia*, 2 (1956), 7–16; Helmut Liely, "Shepherds and Reindeer Nomads in the Soviet Union," *Soviet Studies*, 31 (July 1979), 401–16; Brian Silver, "Language Policy and Linguistic Russification of Soviet Nationalities," in Jeremy R. Azrael, ed., *Soviet Nationality Policies and Practices*, 1971; Ronald Wixman, *Language Aspects of Ethnic Patterns and Processes in the North Caucasus*, 1980; Ronald Wixman, "Daghetanis," In Richard V. Weekes, ed., *Muslim Peoples*, 211–19; Ronald Wixman, *The Peoples of the USSR: An Ethnographic Handbook*, 1984.

RUTULIS. See RUTUL.

RUTUL'TSY. See RUTUL.

RYKHEN. See RUSHAN, TAJIK, and PAMIR PEOPLES.

S

SAAMI. See LAPP.

SABBATARIAN. See JEW.

SABMI. See LAPP.

SAGAI. The Sagai constitute one of the Khakass* subgroups. A complex process of ethnogenesis produced the Sagai. They have roots in the Shor*, Yenesei Kyrgyz*, and various Siberian clans. Not surprisingly, their religious loyalties are a complex mix of Eastern Orthodox and traditional animistic beliefs. The Sagai live between the Kuznets Alatau Spur and the Kamyshta and Abakan rivers in the Khakass Autonomous Oblast. See KHAKASS.
REFERENCE: Ronald Wixman, *The Peoples of the USSR: An Ethnographic Handbook*, 1984.

SAGAY. See SAGAI and KHAKASS.

SAI. See SAGAI and KHAKASS.

SAIAN. See SAYAN and RUSSIAN.

SAKA. See YAKUT.

SAKHA. See YAKUT.

SALIR. See SALYR and TURKMEN.

SALYM. See KHANT.

SALYR. The Salyr call themselves the Salyrly. They are a Turkmen* subgroup. The Salyr speak a distinct dialect and maintain a separate sense of identity. Most of them live in the Chardzhou Oblast in the Turkmen Republic. See TURKMEN.
REFERENCE: Ronald Wixman, *The Peoples of the USSR: An Ethnographic Handbook*, 1984.

SALYRLY. See SALYR and TURKMEN.

SAMAGAR. See SAMOGIR and NANAI.

SAMEH. See LAPP.

SAMEK. See LAPP.

SAMELATS. See LAPP.

SAMODI. See NENETS, ENT, and NGANASAN.

SAMODI TAVGI. See NGANASAN.

SAMODIN. See SAMOYED.

SAMODIN TAVGI. See NGANASAN.

SAMOED. See NENETS, ENT, and NGANASAN.

SAMOED TAVGI. See NGANASAN.

SAMOEDIC PEOPLES. See SAMOYED.

SAMOGIR. The Samogir are today considered a subgroup of the Nanais*, even though their ethnic origins are probably Evenk*. See NANAI.
REFERENCE: Ronald Wixman, *The Peoples of the USSR: An Ethnographic Handbook*, 1984.

SAMOGIT. See ZEMAICIAI and LITHUANIAN.

SAMOGITIAN. See ZEMAICIAI and LITHUANIAN.

SAMOIED. See SAMOYED.

SAMOIED TAVGI. See NGANASAN.

SAMOYED. The term "Samoyed" is a generic description of five groups of people in the former Soviet Union: the Nenets*, Ents*, Nganasans*, Selkups*, and Kamas, who became part of the Khakass*. They are scattered widely across Asia, from the White Sea in the west, across the tundra of the Kara Sea and the Arctic Ocean, to Khatanga Bay in the east. Their southern boundary is primarily the Sayan Mountains. Their economic life has traditionally revolved around hunting, fishing, and reindeer breeding, with livestock raising and farming increasingly common among the southern Samoyedic groups.
REFERENCE: Péter Hajdú, *The Samoyed Peoples and Languages*, 1962.

SAMOYED TAVGI. See NGANASAN.

SAMURIAN PEOPLES. The term "Samurian peoples" is basically a generic linguistic reference to those people who speak one of the Samurian languages, which are part of the larger Caucasic family. Included in this linguistic classification are the Lezgins*, Rutuls*, Aguls*, Tabasarans*, Tsakhurs*, Udis*, and Shah Daghs*. Most of them are Sunni Muslims, except for the Budugs*, who are Shiites, and the Udis, who are Christians.
REFERENCE: Ronald Wixman, *The Peoples of the USSR: An Ethnographic Handbook*, 1984.

SAMURZAKAN. The Samurzakans are an Abkhaz* subgroup. Historically, they have had a close relationship with the Mingrelians*, and their language reflects that relationship, since it carries a large Mingrelian vocabulary. Most of them live along the Inguri River in southeastern Abkhazia. See ABKHAZ.
REFERENCE: Ronald Wixman, *The Peoples of the USSR: An Ethnographic Handbook*, 1984.

SAMURZAKAN-ABKHAZ. See SAMURZAKAN.

SAMURZAKAN-ZUGDIDI. See MINGRELIAN.

SAPME. See LAPP.

SARIK. See SARYK and TURKMEN.

SART. The term "Sart" is used to refer to a group of several thousand Uzbek* merchants who settled in the cities of Samarkand, Bukhara, and Khiva. Today they are bilingual in Uzebk and Tajik, while retaining a unique identity. See UZBEK and TAJIK.
REFERENCE: Ronald Wixman, *The Peoples of the USSR: An Ethnographic Handbook*, 1984.

SART KALMUK. See SART KALMYK and KALMYK.

SART KALMYK. The Sart Kalmyks are listed as a Kyrgyz* subgroup, but they have unique origins. In the mid–1980s, they settled in the Issyk-Kul area of what is now the Kyrgyz Republic and became Sunni Muslims. They then began a slow process of assimilation, adopting the Kyrgyz language while retaining many Kalmyk* cultural characteristics. Today there are approximately 2,700 people who identify themselves as Sart Kalmyks, and 90 percent of them speak Kyrgyz as their native language. See KALMYK.
REFERENCE: Ronald Wixman, *The Peoples of the USSR: An Ethnographic Handbook*, 1984.

SART OZBEK. See SART, UZBEK, and TAJIK.

SART OZBEQ. See SART, UZBEK, and TAJIK.

SART QALMUQ. See SART KALMYK.

SART QALMYQ. See SART KALMYK.

SART UZBEK. See SART, UZBEK, and TAJIK.

SARTOL. The Sartols are a Buryat subgroup who were originally Khalkhas* from Mongolia. See BURYAT.
REFERENCE: Ronald Wixman, *The Peoples of the USSR: An Ethnographic Handbook*, 1984.

SARYG. See SAGAI and KHAKASS.

SARYK. The Saryk call themselves the Saryqly and are one of the ethnic groups making up the Turkmen* people. The Saryk have a distinct sense of identity, speak a separate dialect, and live in the Murgab River Valley in the Turkmen Republic. See TURKMEN.
REFERENCE: Ronald Wixman, *The Peoples of the USSR: An Ethnographic Handbook*, 1984.

SARYQLY. See SARYK and TURKMEN.

SASIGNAN. See ALEUT.

SAVAKKO. See SAVAKOT and FINN.

SAVAKOT. Along with the Ayramoiset*, the Savakots are ethnic Finns* who settled in Ingermanland, in what is now the St. Petersburg Oblast, in the seventeenth century. They are Lutherans and retain a sense of distinct ethnic identity. Most of the Savakots live south of the Kovasha River on the coast of the Gulf of Finland. See FINN.

REFERENCE: Ronald Wixman, *The Peoples of the USSR: An Ethnographic Handbook*, 1984.

SAYAN. The Sayans are ethnic Russians* who settled in the Kursk Oblast. See RUSSIAN.
REFERENCE: Ronald Wixman, *The Peoples of the USSR: An Ethnographic Handbook*, 1984.

SAYANY. See SAYAN and RUSSIAN.

SEBECHA. See SAGAI and KHAKASS.

SEDANKO. See ITELMEN.

SELENGA. The Selengas are a Buryat* subgroup. See BURYAT.
REFERENCE: Ronald Wixman, *The Peoples of the USSR: An Ethnographic Handbook*, 1984.

SELENGIN. See SELENGA and BURYAT.

SELI. See LATVIAN.

SEL'KUP. See SELKUP.

SELKUP. The Selkup, also known as Sel'kup or Ostyako-Samoyed, are a small indigenous tribal people of Siberia. They are closely related to other Samoyedic* peoples, such as the Nenets*, Ents*, and Nganasans*. Their language is one of the southern Samoyedic languages, which are part of the Uralian division of the Uralic-Altaic linguistic family. Ethnologists divide the Selkup into two general cultural groups. The northernmost Selkup are called the Taz Turukhan Selkup* or the Tundra Selkup. They speak the Taz* dialect. The Selkups living farther to the south are known as the Narym, or Forest Selkup. They speak one of two dialects, either Tym Selkup* or Ket*, because of their close relationship with Kettish people in the region.

Anthropologists believe that the Nenets, who were then part of the larger group of Samoyedic people, split away from other Finno-Ugrian* groups around 3000 B.C. and migrated east, where they began to mix with Turkish-Altaic people around 200 B.C. The Samoyedic people who remained in Europe came under Russian* control around 1200 A.D., but those who had settled farther east did not experience Russian domination until the mid-fourteenth century. By the early seventeenth century, all of the Samoyedic people were under Russian control. The Selkup population now totals approximately 3,000 people, and the vast majority live in the Yamalo-Nenets Autonomous Oblast and in the Tomsk Oblast.

The traditional Selkup economy revolved around herding and breeding reindeer. The reindeer provided the Selkups with meat, lard, and blood, which they consumed, as well as skins for clothes, shoes, tents, rope, harnesses, and strings; they also used the tendons and horns. For their transportation, the Selkups harnessed reindeer and attached them to sleds. Fishing was especially important to the Forest Selkups. The fish they relied on most heavily was the sturgeon, although they regularly fished for and caught whitefish, salmon, ide, navaga, and trout. The Selkups also hunted and trapped the fox, silver fox, hare, ermine, wolverine, beaver, otter, and polar and brown bears.

The Selkup suffered from the commercial and political contact with ethnic Russians, beginning in the sixteenth century. Ethnic Russians penetrated commercial activities in the region, enticing the Selkups first with iron and steel tools, and later with firearms and other trade goods. Large numbers of Selkups adopted the use of alcohol as well, much to their harm. In addition, the ethnic Russians brought diseases to the native peoples, especially venereal diseases, which had spread throughout Europe after the New World conquests in the late fifteenth and sixteenth centuries.

The Bolshevik Revolution set in motion a series of disastrous changes in Selkup life. At the time of the revolution, the northern Selkups lived in the Taz River Valley near the Arctic Circle, while the southern Selkups resided on both sides of the Ob River. The southern Selkups had already had prolonged contact with Russians and were well on the way to assimilation. The northern Selkups were more isolated. When collectivization plans were implemented in the late 1920s and early 1930s, the territory of the southern Selkups was flooded with ethnic Russians and Ukrainians*, most of whom were "kulak" peasants Stalin had displaced from their homes and lands in southern Siberia, European Russia, and Ukraine. Selkup land was parceled out and designated for the new settlers. Those settlers immediately set to clearing the forests, plowing ground, and building homes.

Because of the vast expanses of marsh and the inclement weather, agriculture was a difficult proposition. Most of the new settlers had to support themselves by hunting, fishing, and lumbering. The government launched timber and chemical projects and cleared more land. By 1938, nearly 500 square miles of Selkup forests had been leveled. The state created the Selkup National District in the Tym River Valley and began resettling the Selkups there. Russian settlers had also begun to kill bears indiscriminately, because they believed they were harmful to cattle. To the Selkups, the bear was a sacred animal. Cedar nuts were also sacred to Selkup cosmology, but the Russian settlers began harvesting them commercially. The southern Selkups began to flee the Russians, leaving the Bachkara, Chaya, Kenga, Ob, and Parabel river valleys for the more isolated Ket and Tym river valleys in the north.

The northern Selkups managed to stay somewhat more isolated for a longer period of time, even though Soviet agents tried to collectivize them in the late 1930s. Large-scale development of oil and natural gas fields in the Yamalo-Nenets National Region in the 1960s finally affected the northern Selkups. Development brought tracked vehicles, oil spills, site construction, and the building of pipelines, roads, and railroads, all of which badly damaged the homeland of the northern Selkups, even as the influx of ethnic Russians and Ukrainians imposed new cultural pressures on them. In the process, Selkups found themselves herding reindeer on ever smaller amounts of land. The collapse of the Soviet economy in the 1970s and 1980s actually slowed that process somewhat, but, even then, the long-term changes coming to Selkup life were irreversible. Many Selkups still followed the reindeer and lived in tepee shelters made of reindeer hides, but increasingly large numbers abandoned the herds for jobs at construction sites, oil and natural gas wells, and mass-production factories. Soviet economists and ethnologists estimate that the Selkups lost more than 8,000,000 acres of prime grazing land in the post-World War II era.

Although the *perestroika* and *glasnost* policies of Mikhail Gorbachev after 1985 gave Selkups more political freedom and ended the heavy-handed cultural repression that they had experienced for fifty years, the Selkups, unlike many other Soviet nationality groups, actually found themselves under more cultural pressure. The Selkups had not developed any real sense of political nationalism, so no demands for Selkup independence emanated from Siberia in the late 1980s and early 1990s. Selkup leaders were really interested in preserving indigenous culture, especially their economic way of life. They protested the petroleum and natural gas development policies that were taking their aboriginal land. The construction of roads, highways, railroads, and pipelines disrupted traditional reindeer migration routes and herding routines.

Mounting conflicts between Moscow and the peoples of the Far North, including the Selkups, culminated in the creation of the Association of Peoples of the North (APN) on March 31, 1990, during a meeting in the Kremlin. Organized to defend the interests of twenty-six Northern nations, the APN elected Vladimir Sangi, a Nivkhi*, as president. The APN hoped to help the nations tackle such problems as economic expansion by various bureaucracies, flaws in Soviet nationalities policies, and the ecological deterioration in northern areas. The APN condemned the collective farms as a means of Russian colonization that forces Siberian peoples to relocate to cities where there is neither work nor housing. Moreover, industrial development changes the character of the land, by encouraging the immigration of foreigners, chiefly Russians. To protect the indigenous environment and economy, the Selkup want the Soviet government to ratify both the 1957 International Convention on Protection and Integration of Indigenous and Other Tribal and Semi-Tribal Populations in Independent Countries and the 1989 Convention on Indigenous and Tribal Peoples in Independent Countries, in order to affirm that the Selkup have a right to the ownership and possession of the lands that they have traditionally occupied.

The division of the Selkup between the Tundra Selkup in the north and the Narym, or Forest Selkup, to the south is cultural as well as geographical. The Forest Selkup are far more assimilated into Russian culture than the more isolated Tundra Selkup. While the Tundra Selkup speak exclusively their own Selkup dialect, the Narym are bilingual in Russian and Tym or Ket. Indeed, many of the Narym have abandoned their indigenous language altogether in favor of Russian. While the Narym have been largely integrated into the local commercial economy, the Tundra Selkup continue to pursue more indigenous economic pursuits, especially hunting, fishing, and reindeer herding. The Tundra Selkup also maintain strong loyalties to their indigenous religion, while the Narym are more likely to mix Christianity with their native animism, or, if they are highly educated, to have largely abandoned formal religion. And, while the Tundra Selkup population is stable, the population of the Narym is rapidly declining because of intermarriage with ethnic Russians. Between 1970 and 1990, the total Selkup population declined from 4,300 people to 3,000 people, and most of the drop was among the Narym.

REFERENCES: Alice Bartels and Dennis Bartels, "Soviet Policy Toward Siberian Native People," *Canadian Dimension*, 19 (1985), 36–44; Mike Edwards, "Siberia: In From the Cold," *National Geographic*, 177 (March 1990), 2–49; James Forsyth, *A History of the Peoples of Siberia*, 1992; Constantine Krypton, "Soviet Policy in the Northern National Regions After World War II," *Slavic Review*, 13 (October 1954), 339–53; Alexander Tropkin, "Congress of Hope," *Soviet Life*, (December 1990), 10–11; Piers Vitebsky, "Perestroika Among the Reindeer Herders," *Geographical Magazine*, 61 (June 1989), 23–34; Ronald Wixman, *The Peoples of the USSR: An Ethnographic Handbook*, 1984.

SEMEIKI. Late in the seventeenth century, after the modernization reforms in the Russian Orthodox Church, the tsarist government began to persecute the Old Believers (individuals who refused to accept the reforms). The Semeiki are Old Believers who fled to Poland to escape persecution. They were subsequently expelled from Poland and relocated to the Lake Baikal region of south-central Siberia. See RUSSIAN.

REFERENCE: Ronald Wixman, *The Peoples of the USSR: An Ethnographic Handbook*, 1984.

SEMEYKI. See SEMEIKI and RUSSIAN.

SEMIGALLIAN. See LATVIAN.

SENAKI. See MINGRELIAN.

SERB. The Serbs are a South Slavic people who settled in the south-central and western Balkans in the era of Slavic migrations from the sixth to the eleventh centuries. Through their tribal chieftains (*zupans*), they maintained tributary relations with the First Bulgarian Empire and the Byzantine Empire until the development of their own independent kingdom in the eleventh century. They were converted to the Eastern Orthodox branch of Christianity and developed their own autocephalous, autonomous church at the time of the foundation of their kingdom. From the eleventh to the fourteenth centuries, the Serbian Kingdom grew into the most powerful Christian state in the Balkans until the rise of the Ottoman Empire. With the expansion of the Ottoman Empire in the fourteenth and fifteenth centuries, most of the Serbs lost their independence, and their ethnic base shifted northward and westward to what are today Serbia proper, Montenegro, and parts of Bosnia-Herzegovina and Croatia. In some areas, such as Montenegro, Brda, and the Austrian Military Frontier, Serbs maintained varying degrees of autonomy, due to the inaccessibility of the regions, the clan and tribal organization of the Serbs, the Serbs' military skills, and the proximity of Venetian and Hapsburg lands. In other areas, peasants paid modest taxes and the Serbian Orthodox Church functioned as a government, which shared powers with village headmen known as *knezes*. As the Ottoman Empire disintegrated in the eighteenth and nineteenth centuries, the Serbs and Montenegrins achieved first autonomy and then independence. After World War I, as part of the Allied Powers' attempt to make national frontiers reflect broad ethnic interests, Serbia and Montenegro became—along with Croatia, Slovenia, Bosnia-Herzegovina, and Vardar Macedonia—the new country of Yugoslavia, the land of the South Slavs.

World War II brought traumatic consequences to the new Yugoslav state. The Axis forces overran and dismembered Yugoslavia. These actions resulted in a brutal occupation and a multifaceted civil war that pitted south Slav nationalities and political groups against one another. The Communist-led partisans, under Josef Broz Tito, had won out over rival forces (Chetniks, Ustashi, etc.) by 1945. Yugoslavia, reorganized into a federation of socialist republics, became one of the most important Communist states in Eastern Europe in the immediate postwar era. A falling out between the Soviet and Yugoslav Communist parties in 1948, however, led to the first serious rift in the Communist world, known commonly as the Tito-Stalin split. This schism made Yugoslavia a pariah among Communist states, and, in the late 1940s and early 1950s, Yugoslavia went its own way in domestic development (self-management over central planning) and international relations (nonalignment). Yugoslav-Soviet relations improved, except for periods of tension in 1956 and 1968, and closer cultural, economic, and political ties developed. Nonetheless, Yugoslavia never joined the economic (CMEA) or military (Warsaw Pact) organizations of the Soviet bloc. As in the case of the Soviet Union, the Yugoslav Socialist Federated Republic began to unravel in the late 1980s and early 1990s, with separate Slovenian, Croatian*, Bosnian, and Macedonian states developing between 1990 and 1992. The Serbian and Montenegrin* republics constituted the smaller Yugoslav state. The break-up of Yugoslavia has sparked civil wars in Croatia and Bosnia that make conflicts in the former Soviet Union dwarf in comparison.

Like the other Balkan Orthodox Christians—the Bulgarians*, Greeks*, Orthodox Albanians*, and Romanians*—the Serbs maintained significant ties with Russia. Relations between Serbs and Russians began in the thirteenth century with the formation of the independent Serbian Kingdom and the Serbian Orthodox Church. Initial Russian-Serb relations were primarily ecclesiastical and cultural. These ties really developed in the late fourteenth century as medieval Serbia was increasingly absorbed into the Ottoman Empire. Significant numbers of

Serbs emigrated to Russia and participated in the monastic and literary revival in Russia. Some of these Serbs were followers of Euthymius of Tmovo, the last Bulgarian patriarch and a leading exponent of the mystical quietistic movement known as hesychasm. These Serbian and other South Slav exiles were instrumental in the introduction of the new literary forms and styles to Russian Old Church Slavonic; this was known as "the second South Slav influence" to distinguish it from the initial introduction of Old Church Slavonic in the tenth century. This "second South Slav influence" saw the revival of early South Slavic forms in Russian Old Church Slavonic and the development of a style known as ornamental formalism. This style included the use of rare words, "caulks" consisting of three or more words, rhyme, and the repetition of sounds, which became known as the "weaving of words." This literary style developed among Byzantine, Bulgarian, and Serbian writers who were influenced by hesychasm. It was spread to Russia by South Slavic émigrés in the fifteenth century and remained the dominant literary style in Muscovy up to the seventeenth century.

During the period of Ottoman rule, from the fourteenth to the nineteenth centuries, significant numbers of Serbians emigrated to Russia, especially in the eighteenth and nineteenth centuries. One of the most important factors that impelled Serbian immigration was military service. As early as the late sixteenth and early seventeenth centuries, during the "Time of Troubles," a number of Serbs served as cavalrymen in Muscovite forces. With the rise of Russia as a European power under Peter the Great and his successors, military and political relations between Russia and the Serbs intensified. Serbs and Montenegrins organized and participated in uprisings against the Ottomans during the Russo-Turkish Wars of the eighteenth and early nineteenth centuries. In particular, there was close cooperation between Russia and the warrior community of Montenegro in this period.

A large-scale migration of Serb military settlers to Russia was organized in the mid-eighteenth century. In the 1740s and 1750s, the Russian imperial government under Tsarina Elizabeth viewed the Austrian Military Frontier (*militärgrenze*) as a model for frontier defenses for the recently conquered areas of the southern Ukraine. Since a significant segment of the Hapsburg frontier troops were Serbs, Russian agents were dispatched to the Croatian and Slavonian military frontier to entice Serbs into Russian service. While these activities caused diplomatic problems with Austria, it also resulted in the settlement of some 10,000 Serbs to frontier regions of the southern Ukraine. Their areas of settlement became known as Novaia Serbiia and Slavianoserbiia; the units in which they served were called the Serbian, Bulgarian, Macedonian, and Moldavian Hussar regiments. The ethnic composition of these and the other Balkan units was mixed and belied their nomenclature.

Three other factors played a role in later Serbian emigration to Russia. The first was the common religious and linguistic ties between Serbians and Russians, which prompted sporadic emigration of Serbian clergy and others in search of aid and asylum in Russia. The second was the growth of a Balkan merchant class in the eighteenth century, which, although dominated by Greeks*, included Serbians and other Balkan peoples; some Serbs thus emigrated to the Russian Empire in search of commercial opportunities. The third and most significant factor was the series of Russo-Turkish wars in the eighteenth and nineteenth centuries, in which South Slav lands often became areas of operations. The vagaries of war, revolt, and reprisal caused emigrations of Serbs seeking asylum in Russian-controlled areas of the Southern Ukraine and Crimea. In particular, the Russo-Turkish Wars of 1769–1774, 1787–1791, 1806–1812, 1828, and the Crimean War (1853–1857) brought about emigrations of individuals and groups of Serbs to the Russian Empire, but not on the larger scale of Bulgarians* and Greeks in the same period.

The descendants of these settlers have for the most part been assimilated over the years into the society and culture of the respective republics in which they reside, especially because of the cultural, linguistic, and religious ties that Serbs have with Russians, Ukrainians, and other nationalities. Through intermarriage, education, and other means, many Serbs entered the mainstream of the politics, society, culture, and economy of the former Soviet Union.

According to the 1989 Soviet census, Serbs number some 3,100 within the Commonwealth of Independent States (CIS); the 1989 census was the first Soviet census in which Serbs were counted. Most of those identified as Serbs are nominally Serbian Orthodox Christians, while others are Muslim South Slavs who declared themselves to be Serbian. The present Serbian population of the CIS probably has four separate origins. A proportion of the number may be descendants of those Serbs and Montenegrins who immigrated to Russia prior to 1917. Another segment may be descendants of the interwar Yugoslav Communist immigration that survived the purges of the 1930s, while others may have been part of the small Cominformist emigration following the Tito-Stalin Split of 1948; in the late 1940s and early 1950s, some Yugoslav supporters of Soviet Communism made it to the Soviet Union and served as cadres of opposition against Tito's "deviation." A portion of today's Serbian population in the CIS probably comes from this group. Finally, another part of the Serbian population in the former Soviet Union no doubt entered in the 1970s and 1980s, Yugoslav-Soviet relations had by then improved, and a number of Yugoslav firms were engaged in projects and joint ventures in the Soviet Union. Others came as students and political/military officials. Considering the historical ties of the Serbs and Montenegrins with Russia, the changes of the last few years, in both the former Soviet Union and Yugoslavia, may affect the Serbian population in the CIS and the relations of the Serbs with the Russians and other CIS nationalities.

REFERENCES: Ivo Banac, *The National Question in Yugoslavia: Origins, History, Politics*, 1984; Ivo Banac, *With Stalin Against Tito: The Cominformist Splits in Yugoslav Communism*, 1988; B. N. Floria, "Vykhodtsy iz Balkanakh stran na russkoi sluzhbe," *Balkanskie issledovaniia 3, Osloboditel' nie dvizheniia na Balkanakh*, 1978, 57–63; N. D.

Polon'ska-Vasylenko, *The Settlement of the Southern Ukraine (1750–1775)*, 1955; Wayne S. Vucinich, "Serbian Military Tradition," in *War and Society in East Central Europe*, B. Kiraly *et al.*, 1979, vol. 1, 311–14.

Nicholas C. J. Pappas

SETU. The Setu, who have also been known as the Polouvetsy* or the Setukesian, are a subgroup of the Estonians* who have been heavily influenced historically by the Russians*. The Setu live along the Estonian-Russian border and have converted to the Eastern Orthodox religion; this sets them apart from most other Estonians who are Lutherans. The Setu dialect of Estonian contains many Russian words. See ESTONIAN.
REFERENCE: Ronald Wixman, *The Peoples of the USSR: An Ethnographic Handbook*, 1984.

SETUKESIAN. See SETU and ESTONIAN.

SEVERO KAVKAZ. See NORTH CAUCASIAN.

SEVERO KAVKAZTSY. See NORTH CAUCASIAN.

SEVERO OSETIN. See NORTH OSSETIAN and OSSETIAN.

SEVERO OSETINTSY. See NORTH OSSETIAN and OSSETIAN.

SHAANXI DUNGANS. See DUNGAN.

SHADAG. See SHAH DAGH.

SHAH DAGH. The term "Shah Dagh" (Shakhdag, Shakhdagh, Shadag) is a generic description of several small ethnic groups living in the vicinity of Mount Shah Dagh in the Azerbaijan Republic; in particular, they live in three major villages of the district of Konakhkent near the Daghestani border. The name of each village has historically corresponded to the name of one ethnic group. In the 1926 Soviet census, there were approximately 2,000 Budugs* (Budukh, Budugh) living in the village of Budug. Like the rest of the Shah Dagh peoples, the Budugs were Muslims; unlike the others, the Budugs were faithful to the Shiite Muslim movement, which had its roots in Persia and Iran. Budugs also lived in the villages of Deli Gaya and Guney Budug in the district of Konakhkent; there are scattered groups of Budugs as well in the districts of Khudat, Ismailly, Khachmass, Kuba, Kutkashen, and Zardob in Azerbaijan. According to the 1926 Soviet census, a second group, consisting of 2,600 Dzhek* (Get) people, was living in the village of Kryz, in addition to Dzheks in the villages of Alik, Jek, and Gapuk in Konakhkent district. Like the Budugs, Dzheks could also be found in the districts of Khudat, Ismailly, Khachmass, Kuba, Kutkashen, and Zardob. Ethnolinguists have identified three subgroups of the Dzhek: the Dzhek, Kryz*, and Gaput*. The Dzhek are Sunni Muslim in religion, with their theological loyalties in favor of the Shafi school. The third Shah Dagh group are the Khinalug* (Khinalugh, Khinalukh), who numbered only 100 people in the 1926 census and lived in Khinalug village in the district of Konakhkent. They call themselves the Kattitturdur. The Khinalugs are Sunni Muslims of the Shafi school.

The Shah Dagh language is one of the Samurian* group, itself part of the northeastern branch of Caucasic languages. Economic life in the Konakhkent district still revolves around animal husbandry (sheep and goats in the highlands, cattle in the lowlands), gold and silver smithing, weaving, pottery, and rug manufacturing. Because of the need to trade goods within the region of Daghestan, many Shah Daghs had to learn to speak Azeri. Traditionally, the Shah Daghs were governed by rigid endogamous patriarchal clan systems, in which young people were encouraged to marry first or second cousins. That sense of clan cohesion was strengthened by the fact that all land was owned communally by the extended family unit. During the 1960s and 1970s, the Soviet government also succeeded in establishing government cooperatives and collectivizing many Shah Dagh herds and pasture lands; this policy aroused much resentment among the local people.

Although many people in the Soviet Union are still aware of their Shah Dagh heritage, the Budugs, Khinalugs, and Dzheks did not appear in the Soviet censuses of 1959, 1970, and 1979. Ever since the 1920s, they have listed their nationality as Azerbaijani*, even though they spoke their own native dialects. The fact that they were bilingual in Azeri and were surrounded and vastly outnumbered by Azerbaijanis* contributed to their assimilation. Most Russian ethnologists today believe that the Shah Daghs have been all but completely assimilated by Azerbaijanis.

REFERENCES: Alexandre Bennigsen, "Muslim Conservative Opposition to the Soviet Regime: The Sufi Brotherhoods in the North Caucasus," in Jeremy R. Azrael, ed., Soviet Nationality Policies and Practices, 1971; Alexandre Bennigsen and S. Enders Wimbush, Muslims of the Soviet Union: A Guide, 1986; Bruce Geiger, et al., Peoples and Languages of the Caucasus, 1959; T. S. Halasi-Kun, "The Caucasus: An Ethno-Historical Survey," Studia Caucasia, 2 (1956), 7–16; Brian Silver, "Language Policy and Linguistic Russification of Soviet Nationalities," in Jeremy R. Azrael, ed., Soviet Nationality Policies and Practices, 1971; Ronald Wixman, Language Aspects of Ethnic Patterns and Processes in the North Caucasus, 1980; Ronald Wixman, The Peoples of the USSR: An Ethnographic Handbook, 1984.

SHAHSEVEN. The Shahseven are a subgroup of the Azerbaijanis*. They are a transhumant people who live near the Iranian border in southern Azerbaijan. During the seventeenth century, some of their traditional grazing lands in southern Azerbaijan came under Russian* control, but, until 1884, this change did not hinder them because they were able to move freely across the border between Russia and Persia. Most of the Shahseven live in Iran today, but there are probably several thousand living in Azerbaijan. The Shahseven are Shiite Moslems. See AZERBAIJANI.

REFERENCES: Shirin Akiner, *Islamic Peoples of the Soviet Union*, 1983; Alexandre Bennigsen and S. Enders Wimbush, *Muslims of the Soviet Empire: A Guide*, 1986; and Ronald Wixman, *The Peoples of the USSR: An Ethnographic Handbook*, 1984.

SHAKHDAG. See SHAH DAGH.

SHAKHDAGH. See SHAH DAGH.

SHAKHSEVEN. See SHAHSEVEN and AZERBAIJANI.

SHALOSA. See KACHA and KHAKASS.

SHAPSUG. The Shapsugs, who call themselves the Shapsugh, are an Adyghe* subgroup. They have been concentrated demographically between the Dzhuba River and the Shakhe River along the coast of the Black Sea. See ADYGHE or CIRCASSIAN.

REFERENCE: Ronald Wixman, *The Peoples of the USSR: An Ethnographic Handbook*, 1984.

SHAPSUGH. See SHAPSUG, ADYGHE, and CIRCASSIAN.

SHELGA. See CHUVASH and YUKAGIR.

SHEMEKHA. See AZERBAIJANI.

SHENSI. See SHENSI DUNGAN and DUNGAN.

SHENSI DUNGAN. The Shensi are a Dungan* subgroup. They originated in Shensi Province in China and speak the Shensi dialect. The Shensi have settled in the Chu Valley in the eastern reaches of the Kazakh Republic. See DUNGAN.

REFERENCE: Ronald Wixman, *The Peoples of the USSR: An Ethnographic Handbook*, 1984.

SHENSIYTSY. See SHENSI DUNGAN and DUNGAN.

SHERKALY. See KHANT.

SHESHEN. See CHECHEN.

SHIKOMSHI. See ISHKASHMI, TAJIK, and PAMIR PEOPLES.

SHIKOSHUMI. See ISHKASHMI, TAJIK, and PAMIR PEOPLES.

SHKHARAWA. See ASHKHARAWA and ABAZA.

SHOR. The Shor—also known historically as the Mountain Shor, Mrassa, Kondoma, Aba (Abin), Chysh, and Kuznets Tatars—are a small group of Turkic-speaking people who live in the south of the Kuznetsk Basin in southern Siberia. The Shor are the product of a long-term process of ethnogenesis that brought together various tribes of Samoyedic*, Kettic*, and turkified Ugrian* peoples who were living in south-central Siberia. Their language is part of the Old Uigur* subgroup of the eastern division of the Turkic branch of the larger Altaic language family; it is divided into two basic dialects, one spoken in the region of Mrass and Tomsk and the other in Kondoma and the Lower Tom' region. The first sustained contact between Shors and Russians* began in the seventeenth century, when Russian settlers began arriving in large numbers and the tsarist government established its political authority there. At the time, the Shor economy revolved around hunting, fishing, and gathering cedar nuts.

The influx of Russian settlers into the valleys of the upper Tom' River in the late eighteenth and early nineteenth centuries changed Shor economic life. Traditionally, the Shors had supplied finished iron products to the Oirots*, Kyrgyz*, and Teleuts*. They were widely known as the "Blacksmith Tatars." But Russian merchants brought more sophisticated iron tools, and the Shor blacksmiths could not compete—not in terms of price, quality, or diversity. Russian officials also forced the Shors to pay the *yasak* fur tax, so large numbers of Shors left their homes around the town of Kuznetsk and headed into the forests to hunt sable and other fur-bearing animals. The Shors developed feelings of hatred toward the Russians who had so dramatically changed their lives.

When the Russians first arrived, the Shor religion was similar to the shamanistic-animistic beliefs of the other indigenous peoples of Siberia. For the Shor, religion and their geographical environment were inseparable. The world was inhabited by invisible spirit beings of all sorts, whose interaction with human beings was constant and whose control over the elements was absolute. For the Shor, no natural phenomenon was accidental or coincidental. Everything—from disease to natural disasters—could be attributed to the invisible powers of the universe, so human beings were obligated to treat those forces with respect and submission. Shamans were central figures in Shor culture because they propitiated the invisible forces. Missionaries from the Russian Orthodox Church began working actively among the Shor in the eighteenth century. They made superficial progress, but what ultimately emerged was an eclectic fusion of Shor folk beliefs and Christian doctrine.

The Bolshevik Revolution and the subsequent full-scale economic development of the Shor homeland had a dramatic and ultimately devastating impact on Shor ethnicity. The Kuznetsk Basin contains some of the world's richest iron ore and coal deposits, which Soviet industry desperately needed. At first, the new Soviet government worked hard at paying due respect to Shor culture. They established the Mountain Shor (Gorno-Shorskiy) National Rayon in 1929 and developed a literary language for the Shor, using a Cyrillic alphabet (in 1930, the government switched to a Latin alphabet). At the time, there were approximately 12,600 Shorian people living there, and they constituted the majority of the population.

By that time, however, there were already problems between the Shor and the government. For centuries, Shor hunters had known of the iron ore deposits in their homeland; they called it the "red stone." In the late 1920s, however, they refused to cooperate with Soviet geologists in locating the deposits, fearing the impact that economic development would have on their life-styles. Their fears were well-founded. When the iron ore deposits were eventually located, the Soviet government began importing thousands of Russian and Ukrainian* miners to extract the metal. By 1931, the Shor constituted only 40 percent of the population of the Mountain Shor National Rayon; by 1938, their percentage had dropped to only 13 percent. In 1939, the Soviet government dissolved the Mountain Shor National Rayon and required all Shor publications to employ the Cyrillic alphabet again.

Since World War II, the Shor have been in a long ethnic decline. By the 1980s, their population exceeded 16,000 people, but they represented less than 5 percent of the local population. They lived on the middle Tom, Kondoma, and Mrassa rivers. Less than half of the people who identified themselves as Shor in the 1989 Soviet census actually spoke the Shor language, and virtually all of the Shor are bilingual in Russian. Russian is the language of commerce, education, and the media. Virtually nothing is published in the Shor language any longer, and there is no sense of Shor nationality, either politically or culturally. Today most Shors live on collective farms and work as farmers and breeders, although a few still work as trappers and hunters. There is also a contingent of Shors who work as miners in the huge coal fields of the Kuznetsk Basin. In recent years, Russian ethnographers have placed several Tatar* groups in the larger Shor category, including the Kuznetski Tatars*, Kondoma Tatars*, and Mrass Tatars.

REFERENCES: Alexandre Bennigsen and S. Enders Wimbush, *Muslims of the Soviet Empire: A Guide*, 1986; Walter Kolarz, *The Peoples of the Soviet Far East*, 1969; Ronald Wixman, *The Peoples of the USSR: An Ethnographic Handbook*, 1984.

SHQARAWA. See ASHKHARAWA and ABAZA.

SHQIPETAR. See ALBANIAN.

SHUGHNAN. See SHUGNAN and TAJIK.

SHUGNAN. The Shugnan (Shugnani, Shugni), who call themselves the Khunini or Khugnon, are one of the Pamir* peoples. Russians* refer to them as the Shugnantsy. Historically, they are related to the Mountain Tajiks*. They are Ismaili Muslims in religion. One group of Shugnans—the Bajui*—speak a dialect distinct enough to give them a separate and powerful sense of identity. They are concentrated demographically in the Gorno-Badakhshan Autonomous Oblast in Tajikistan. They are the most numerous of the Pamir groups. See PAMIR PEOPLES, MOUNTAIN TAJIK, or TAJIK.
REFERENCES: Shirin Akiner, *Islamic Peoples of the Soviet Union*, 1983; Ronald Wixman, *The Peoples of the USSR: An Ethnographic Handbook*, 1984.

SHUGNANI. See SHUGNAN, TAJIK, and PAMIR PEOPLES.

SHUGNANTSY. See SHUGNAN, TAJIK, and PAMIR PEOPLES.

SHUGNI. See SHUGNAN, TAJIK, and PAMIR PEOPLES.

SHURYSHKAR-BEREZOV. See KHANT.

SHUSTY. See KYZYL and KHAKASS.

SHWAN. See SVANETIAN and GEORGIAN.

SIBERIAN TATAR. Traditionally, the term ''Siberian Tatars'' has been used to refer to two distinct groups of people: first, the Turkic-speaking peoples who arrived in Siberia between the sixth and eighth centuries and mixed with the indigenous Kettic* and Samoyedic* peoples, and, second, the descendants of the White Horde Mongols who reached Russia in the thirteenth century. Today the term is used to refer to the latter group, since the former peoples are identified by separate nationality terms. The Abakan Tatars*, Chulym Tatars*, Meletski Tatars*, Minusinsk Tatars*, and Yenesei Tatars* are today classified with the Khakass*; the Kuznetski Tatars*, Kondoma Tatars*, and Mrass Tatars* are classified with the Shors*; and the Chernevyje Tatars* are part of the Altais*. The group known today simply as Siberian Tatars includes the Baraba Tatars*, Irtysh Tatars*, Tara Tatars*, Tobol Tatars*, Tomsk Tatars*, Tura Tatars*, Tjumen Tatars*, and Jalutorovski Tatars*.

The Siberian Tatars originated with the Mongol* invasion of Russia in the thirteenth century. Although the Mongol Horde eventually disintegrated, they brought about the turkicization of the steppes between the southern Urals and the Ob River, driving such indigenous peoples as the Selkups*, Mansis*, and Khants* farther north. The Siberian Tatar khanate emerged, as did a number of distinct Tatar communities. The economy of the region changed from nomadic hunting and herding to more settled occupations, and the Siberian Khanate became linked by caravan routes to Islamic Central Asia. Beginning in the late fourteenth century, Islamic merchants started the Siberian Tatars on the long road to conversion to the Sunni Muslim faith, Hanafi school. That conversion process among the Siberian Tatars continued for the next five centuries. Most Siberian Tatars, however, remained loyal to their indigenous, shamanistic religion. Those living in northern Turkestan were separated from the Islamic centers and trade routes by vast expanses of desert; they remained faithful to their religion, with its emphasis on animal sacrifice and ancestor worship, well into the 1900s. During the fifteenth century, the region came under Ibak Khan and his Siberian Khanate, which reached north from present-day Kazakhstan to the Arctic Ocean.

Under Ivan the Terrible, Russia conquered the Kazan Khanate in 1552, threatening the Siberian Tatars who lived beyond the Ural Mountains and the Volga River. Russians* finally conquered the region in 1581 and established forts at Tjumen in 1586, Tobolsk in 1587, Tara in 1594, and Tomsk in 1604. Some Siberian Tatars who had fought with the Russians during the conquest were rewarded for their services, but most were subjected to the *yasak* fur tax and treated as a servile class. A few native Tatar leaders, known as *mirzas*, were absorbed into the gentry after they converted to Russian Orthodoxy in the early 1700s, and the Tatars in Bukhara became a prosperous merchant middle class. The other Siberian Tatar groups supported themselves in traditional ways. The Tobol Tatars, for example, lived in the swamps north of Tobolsk and lived on fish, waterfowl, elk, and some farming. The Baraba Tatars were nomadic herders, raising cattle, sheep, and horses. The Chulym Tatars gathered cedar-pine nuts, hunted, and fished.

Still, most Siberian Tatars enjoyed relative isolation, except for those living in the major river valleys, areas that had attracted Russian settlement. In the eighteenth century, the Russian government decided that river transportation was inadequate for development, since it existed only on a north-south axis. They decided to develop east-west transportation routes as well, first with a series of forts in the 1740s and then with the Moscow-Siberian Highway in the 1760s. The new road cut across Siberia, from Tjumen all the way to Krasnoyarsk on the Yenesei River. Russian settlers followed the road, and, by 1800, ethnic Russians outnumbered the Siberian Tatars in Western Siberia by 400,000 to 39,000. Russian settlers used slash-and-burn farming techniques, and the Siberian Tatars thereby lost their hunting lands and their cedar-pine nut forests, which the Russians commercialized. The Siberian Tatars were reduced to poverty as manual laborers in the lumbering and gold-mining industries. The rates of loss of culture and of exogamous marriage increased.

The Bolshevik Revolution brought even more change to the lives of the Siberian Tatars. Although Bolsheviks in the early 1920s talked about self-determination for non-Russian peoples, their real concerns were with class divisions, not with ethnicity, so even the most liberal Bolsheviks viewed ethnic self-determination as a transitional stage toward assimilation. The fact that so many ethnic Russians lived in the region and so vastly outnumbered the Siberian Tatars made that assimilation process all but inevitable. Yet, even as late as the 1980s, the Tatar sense of ethnicity still survived, even though their traditional language, costumes, and ethnic traditions had fallen into disuse. Although their clan loyalties largely disintegrated after World War II, they did acquire a larger sense of being Tatars. See TATARS.

REFERENCES: Shirin Akiner, *Islamic Peoples of the USSR*, 1983; Alexandre Bennigsen and S. Enders Wimbush, *Muslims of the Soviet Empire: A Guide*, 1986; James Forsyth, *A History of the Peoples of Siberia*, 1992.

SIBERIAN YUPIK. See ESKIMO.

SIBIRIAK. See SIBIRYAK, RUSSIAN, UKRAINIAN, and BELARUSIAN.

SIBIRYAK. ''Sibiryak'' is a Russian term used to describe the Eastern Slavs—Russians*, Belarusians*, and Ukrainians*—who settled in Siberia during the era of the Russian Empire.

REFERENCE: Ronald Wixman, *The Peoples of the USSR: An Ethnographic Handbook*, 1984.

SKOI. See GREBEN COSSACK and COSSACK.

SLAV. The Slavs are a diverse group of people originating in Central Asia who slowly pushed into Eastern Europe during the Middle Ages. Around 400 A.D., they reached a frontier running from the Adriatic Sea to the Elbe River, but the Germans stalled their further expansion west. Two-hundred years later, the Slavic fringe penetrated the Balkans. During the long migration, Slavic communities developed into many political, religious, and linguistic groups. The Eastern Slavs consist of Ukrainians*, Belarusians*, and Russians*. Poles*, Czechs*, and Slovaks* make up the Western Slavs. The Southern Slavs consist of Bulgarians*, Croats*, Serbs*, Macedonian Slavs, and Slovenes.

Slavs never united because the factors holding them together—common origins, hatred of the Germans*, and fear of the Turks*—could not overcome political, geographic, religious, and linguistic forces dividing them. By 1840, pan-Slavic nationalism had emerged in central and eastern Europe, but it foundered because of the strength of individual group loyalties. Each Slavic group possessed its own history and cultural identity, and the Czechs, Slovaks, Poles, Carpatho-Rusyns*, Ukrainians, Slovenes, and Croatians always worried about domination at the hands of Russian Slavs. Moreover, the Slavs did not enjoy territorial integrity. Western and Eastern Slavs were separated geographically from the Southern Slavs by Germans, Austrians*, Magyars*, and Romanians*.

Only the Russians and Poles had ever been independent in modern history. Ukrainians were under Russian domination. Poland was divided three ways: Western Poles in West Prussia and Posen were controlled by Prussia; Southern Poles in Galicia technically lived in Austria-Hungary; and Eastern Poles were under Russian sovereignty. Czechs, Slovaks, Croatians, and Slovenes were also included in Austria-Hungary, while the Bulgarians were part of the Ottoman Empire. Religious allegiances divided the Slavs as well. While the Poles, Czechs, Slovaks, Slovenes, and Croatians were Roman Catholic, the Russians, Bulgarians, and Serbs were Eastern Orthodox. Carpatho-Rusyns and Ukrainians were "Greek Catholics" within Uniate churches; these churches were loyal to Rome but retained a married clergy and insisted on Slavic, rather than Latin, liturgies. Finally, there were isolated pockets of Slavic Muslims throughout the Balkans. Linguistic differences further undermined pan-Slavism. Although Slavic languages are Indo-European and share similarities in morphology, syntax, and phonetics, major divisions appeared in Slavic dialects and alphabets as early as the seventh century. By 1500, Slavs were using either Glagolithic, Cyrillic, or Latin alphabets, and individual Slavic groups were speaking separate dialects. The Serbs and Croatians, for example, could understand each other's spoken but not written words, because the two alphabets were different.

During the 1980s, after seventy years of Russian domination in Eastern and Southern Europe, those Slavic differences asserted themselves with a vengeance. Poland broke out of the Russian orbit in 1989. Under the severe pressures of economic collapse, the Soviet Union disintegrated. Belarusians created the new nation of Belarus, and Ukrainians finally enjoyed an independent Ukraine. Czechoslovakia broke up into the Czech Republic and Slovakia, two independent nations, on January 1, 1993. And, tragically, Yugoslavia disintegrated into independent Slovenia, Croatia, Bosnia, Macedonia, and Serbia, with vicious ethnic civil wars bringing catastrophe to the entire region.
REFERENCES: Roger Portal, *The Slavs*, 1969.

SLOVAK. The Slovak people constitute one of the smaller ethnic minorities in the former Soviet Union, and that number is declining rapidly through processes of assimilation. In 1959, there were 14,674 people in the Soviet Union who identified themselves as Slovaks; that number had declined to 11,658 by 1970 and to 9,409 by 1979. The 1989 Soviet census placed the Slovak total at 10,107, but the economic collapse of the Soviet Union in the early 1990s resulted in an exodus of Slovaks to Czechoslovakia (later Slovakia). Like the Czechs, the Slovaks are a western Slavic people. They first migrated to Slovakia from the Carpathian Mountains in the fifth century. Until the ninth century, the Czechs and Slovaks were united under the Great Moravian Empire, but, in 896, Magyar* armies invaded and conquered Slovakia, separating it from Czech Bohemia and Moravia. In Bohemia and Moravia, the Czechs struggled to maintain their independence from German-speakers to the west, Prussians on the north, and Austrians on the south. In 1620, the Hapsburgs brought Bohemia and Moravia into their empire, reducing the Czechs to second-class status. At the same time, the Slovaks were suffering under Magyar domination. For Czechs and Slovaks, power and prestige were in Vienna and Budapest, not Prague or Bratislava, and the elites in those cities were Austrians and Hungarian Magyars. Over the centuries, Slovak ethnicity was cut by the edge of Magyar oppression.

The overwhelming majority of Slovaks are Roman Catholics. Slovakia accepted Christianity in response to the missionary endeavors of Saints Cyril and Methodius, who came from Byzantium in the ninth century, converted the population, and then declared their loyalty to Rome, leaving Roman Catholicism as the spiritual heritage of the Slovaks. A mountainous country lying between the plains of Hungary and Poland, Slovakia was generally able to avoid the cyclical warfare between Tatars*, Turks*, Swedes, Russians*, Germans*, Poles*, and Lithuanians*, and it enjoyed the stability and conservatism common among people tied to the same isolated region for generations. The Slovaks were a highly traditional people, devoted to their families, parishes, and villages.

From the fall to the Great Moravian Empire in the tenth century until the creation of Czechoslovakia in 1918, the Slovaks were under Magyar domination. Geography was much of the problem. The major rivers of Slovakia drain out of the mountains onto the Hungarian plains, creating a powerful commercial and economic link between Slovaks and Magyars. The Slovaks developed only the most limited sense of ethnic nationalism. Late in the eighteenth century, Roman Catholic priest Anton Bernolák tried to develop a Slovak literary language; his mostly unsuccessful efforts had some success a half century later in the work of Ludovít Stúr. Slovakia became part of the Hapsburg regime in 1526, and, in 1867, as part of the Austro-Hungarian Compromise known as the *Ausgleich*, Slovakia came under complete Hungarian control within the Austro-Hungarian Empire. An intense program of magyarization was then implemented. Magyars in Hungary tried to eradicate the Slovak language, which took refuge in Roman Catholic churches. There the people openly used it in their songs, prayers, and confessions. Slovak nationalism and Roman Catholicism thus became intimately connected.

The Austro-Hungarian Empire was beset by enormous ethnic and religious divisions, and World War I delivered its death blow. Out of the former empire and its surrounding regions came Poland, Hungary, Austria, Czechoslovakia, and Yugoslavia. The new nation of Czechoslovakia brought Bohemia, Moravia, and Slovakia together after more than 900 years of separation; the Paris Peace Conference also included sub-Carpathian Ruthenia to the east of Slovakia. This region had previously been part of Russia, but, because the Bolsheviks had taken the Soviet Union out of World War I, the Allies retaliated at Paris by seizing the region and incorporating it into Czechoslovakia. Although the Ruthenians were Catholics, they were Eastern Rite, or Uniate, Catholics. Uniate Catholics had once been Eastern Orthodox but had realigned themselves with Rome. They acknowledged the pope in Rome as the head of the world church but used their own vernacular in church liturgies, allowed their priests to marry, and received both the bread and the wine during the Eucharist. The Uniate tradition also had some adherents in eastern Slovakia.

When Czechoslovakia was created in 1918, there were already some Slovaks living in Ruthenia; between 1918 and 1945, thousands more migrated to the east to live there. At the end of World War II, however, Soviet troops occupied eastern Czechoslovakia and refused to return Ruthenia to Czechoslovakia. At that point, the Slovaks living in Ruthenia became a Soviet ethnic minority. The vast majority of them lived just across the Czechoslovakian border in the western Ukraine; they live there still. In 1945, they still spoke the Slovak language, although their dialect had been strongly influenced by Magyar and Ukrainian*; most of them remained Roman Catholics faithful to the Uniate tradition.

The number of Slovaks in the Soviet Union is declining because of assimilation. By the 1970s, more Soviet Slovaks spoke Magyar than Slovakian as their primary language, and even those who used Slovakian as their primary language were bilingual in Magyar. Their literary language is Magyar. The collapse of the Soviet bloc in eastern Europe and the subsequent disintegration of the Soviet Union in the late 1980s and early 1990s have stimulated Slovak nationalism. In 1992, advocates of Slovak independence succeeded in launching the break-up of Czechoslovakia, and Slovaks in Russia and Ukraine welcomed the news.

REFERENCES: Robert A. Kann, *A History of the Hapsburg Empire, 1526–1918*, 1974; Carlile Macartney, *Hungary*, 1934; Andrew Janos, *The Politics of Backwardness in Hungary, 1825–1945*, 1982; Robert Seton-Watson, *A History of the Czechs and Slovaks*, 1965; Peter Brock, *The Slovak National Awakening: An Essay in the Intellectual History of Modern Slovakia*, 1955; Joseph M. Kirschbaum, *Slovakia in the 19th and 20th Century*, 1973; Ludvic Nemec, *Church and State in Czechoslovakia*, 1955; Joseph A. Mikus, *Slovakia and the Slovaks*, 1977.

SOGDIAN. See YAGNOB and TAJIK.

SOIOT. See SOYOT and BURYAT.

SOLON. See BURYAT.

SOR. See SHOR, SAGAI, and KHAKASS.

SORAN. See KURD.

SORANI. See KURD.

SOUTH OSET. See TUALLAG and OSSETIAN.

SOUTH OSETIAN. See TUALLAG and OSSETIAN.

SOUTH OSETIN. See TUALLAG and OSSETIAN.

SOUTH OSSET. See TUALLAG and OSSETIAN.

SOUTH OSSETIAN. See TUALLAG and OSSETIAN.

SOUTH OSSETIN. See TUALLAG and OSSETIAN.

SOUTHERN ALTAI. See ALTAI.

SOYON. See TUVINIAN.

SOYOT. The Soyots have Tuvinian roots but are a subgroup of the Buryats*. They have also been known historically as the Tunka Soyots. Most of them live in the Oka Aimak Rayon of the Buryat-Mongol Autonomous Republic. See BURYAT.
REFERENCE: Ronald Wixman, *The Peoples of the USSR: An Ethnographic Handbook*, 1984.

SOYOT. See TUVINIAN.

SPANIARD. Until its 1989 census, the Soviet Union did not track, or at least did not publish, the number of foreign residents by nationality group. The 1989 census did provide those figures, and it indicated that, as of 1989, there were 3,737 people of Spanish descent living in the Soviet Union. Ever since the Bolshevik Revolution, there had been Spaniards living in the Soviet Union. Most were expatriates infatuated with Marxism and the Communist experiment. After the victory of Generalissimo Francisco Franco in the Spanish Civil War brought the Fascists to power in Spain in the 1930s, several thousand of the vanquished leftists, Communists, and Socialists fled to the Soviet Union for safety. Nonetheless, there was never any significant movement of Spaniards to change their citizenship and live their lives in the Soviet Union. There have also been other Spaniards who, for economic reasons, were very interested in improving their business relationship with the Soviet Union. As disillusionment with the Communist Party, in both the Soviet Union and Spain, mounted during the Brezhnev era in the 1970s, the numbers of expatriates declined, but, as Mikhail Gorbachev welcomed European capital and technological expertise, the number of Spanish citizens permanently residing in the Soviet Union increased. The 3,737 Spaniards living in the Soviet Union in 1989 were primarily students, descendants of the Civil War immigrants, and business people hoping to establish an economic foothold there.
REFERENCE: Raymond E. Zickel, ed., *Soviet Union: A Country Study*, 1991.

SREDNEAZIATSKIJE TSYGANY. See CENTRAL ASIAN GYPSY and GYPSY.

STAROZHILY. The term ''Starozhily'' is a generic reference for those ethnic Russians* who, beginning in the seventeenth century, migrated to Siberia. Most of them were trying to escape religious persecution because of their status as Old Believers. Although most of them were eventually assimilated into the surrounding Siberian populations, some maintained distinct identities as ethnic Russians, especially groups like the Bukhtarmen*, Polyakis*, and Semeikis*. See RUSSIAN.
REFERENCE: Ronald Wixman, *The Peoples of the USSR: An Ethnographic Handbook*, 1984.

STAVROPOL TRUHMEN. See TRUKHMEN and TURKMEN.

STAVROPOL TRUKHMEN. See TRUKHMEN and TURKMEN.

STAVROPOL TURKMAN. See TRUKHMEN and TURKMEN.

STAVROPOL TURKMEN. See TRUKHMEN and TURKMEN.

STAVROPOL TURKOMAN. See TRUKHMEN and TURKMEN.

STAVROPOL TURKOMEN. See TRUKHMEN and TURKMEN.

STEPPE KAMASIN. See KAMASIN.

SUBBOTNIKI. See JEW.

SUDAVI. See LITHUANIAN and BELARUSIAN.

SUG KARGA. See SAGAI and KHAKASS.

SUMAR. See LEZGIN.

SUNGARI. See MANCHU.

SUOMALAISET. See FINN.

SUOMI. See FINN.

SURA'I. See ASSYRIAN.

SURGUT. See KHANT.

SURGUT OSTIAK. See KHANT.

SURGUT OSTYAK. See KHANT.

SUVAL. See SUVALKIECIAI and LITHUANIAN.

SUVALKECHAI. See SUVALKIECIAI and LITHUANIAN.

SUVALKECHAY. See SUVALKIECIAI and LITHUANIAN.

SUVALKECHIAI. See SUVALKIECIAI and LITHUANIAN.

SUVALKI. See SUVALKIECIAI or LITHUANIAN.

SUVALKIECIAI. The Suvalkieciai, who have also been known as Uznemu-nieciai and Zanemantsy, are a subgroup of the Lithuanians*. They are concentrated southwest of the Nemunas River. Eastern Suvalkieciais are called the Kapsai, while those in the west are the Zanavykiai. See LITHUANIAN.
REFERENCE: Ronald Wixman, *The Peoples of the USSR: An Ethnographic Handbook*, 1984.

SVAN. See SVANETIAN and GEORGIAN.

SVANETIAN. The Svanetians live in the mountains of northwestern Georgia, inhabiting a region inland and to the east of the Abkhazian Autonomous Republic, north of the Mingrelian* areas of Georgia proper, and west of Ossetia. Svanetia is a high mountain region on the southern rim of the Caucasus, consisting of Alpine meadows, snow-capped peaks, coniferous forests, and rapid streams flowing into the Inguri and Kodori rivers. The inhabited regions of Svanetia range from 500 to 2,000 meters above sea level and are accessible only through mountain passes, ravines, and gorges. The inaccessibility of Svanetia from both the mountain territories to the north and the foothills and lowlands to the south have both protected and isolated the Svanetians. Svanetia consists of Lower Svanetia in the uplands of the Tskhenis Tsquali Mountains (Lentekhi region); Upper Svanetia (Mestia region), along the upper reaches and tributaries of the Inguri River; and Abkahazian Svanetia (Gulripsh region of the Abkhazian Autonomous Republic). Lower and Upper Svanetia are traditional areas of Svanetian settlement, while Abkhazian Svanetia was settled by Svanetians in the 1890s and 1900s.

Although they are now considered a part of the Georgian* nation, the Svanetians have their own unique language, a radically different social and economic development, and a separate political history dating from ancient times. The most important factors in the difference between the Svanetians and the other components of the Georgian nation, such as the Kartvelians* and Mingrelians, have been their isolated homeland (described above), their unique language, and their archaic social structure.

According to most linguists, the Svanetian language developed into a separate branch of the Southern Caucasian division of the Ibero-Caucasian family of the Caucasian group in the second millenium B.C., diverging from Georgian and Zan (Mingrelian and Lazian*). The Svanetian language is so different from the Laz, Mingrelian, and Kartvelian today that it has eighteen vowel sounds, as opposed to five vowels for Georgian. Up until recently, Svanetian has not been allowed to develop into a literary language, since education, government, business, and the media all use Georgian.

The other distinguishing feature of the Svanetians is their societal organization and customs, which point to a form of polity that can be called a warrior community. A significant portion of the Svanetian people was able to maintain autonomy until modern times through the geographical inaccessibility of their homeland, the martial ability of the inhabitants, and a social organization based upon a clan system. Authorities from ancient times to the present have described the Svanetians as a fierce warrior race who defended their mountain fastnesses with a tenacious independence. According to Strabo, the "Svaneti" had a rough and ready militia of archers; later authors from the seventeenth through the nineteenth centuries described them as deadly musketeers who crafted their own firearms. Into the twentieth century, the Svanetians, especially those in the more remote areas of "Free Svanetia," were organized socially and politically into tightly knit extended families and clans. Each extended family had a large house with a tower for defense, similar to towers found among clan societies in Greece, Albania, and Corsica. Members of the clan were obliged to support the clan in mutual defense and in blood feuds. Inter-clan problems were settled in accordance with customary law. Often a single clan would make up an entire hamlet or village, which would hold assemblies to elect clan/village leaders and discuss local problems. Regional or "national" assemblies, involving representatives from most or all the clans, would meet to deal with broader issues of internal peace and external security.

While Svanetians adopted Byzantine Christianity between the sixth and ninth centuries, the Eastern Orthodox church had no episcopal organization in Svanetia. The Svanetians therefore had to depend upon clergy brought in from Mingrelia or Kartvelia, and, in long periods of isolation, certain areas had to depend upon itinerant or unordained priests. In many cases, Christianity was merely a veneer over pre-Christian beliefs and customs. An interesting feature of Christianity in Svanetia has been the proliferation of small family or clan chapels, which is also seen in some Orthodox clan areas in the Balkans, such as Montenegro and Cheimarra. The Svanetians' celebration of the Christian feastdays were often events that reconciled blood feuds and other clan disputes. As late as the 1970s, Soviet authorities were still attempting to discourage these feasts of reconciliation by blocking off access to remote shrines. The fact that the Svanetians adopted and maintained their allegiance to the Orthodox Church in its Georgian liturgical form was important in their integration into the Georgian nation.

These singular features of Svanetia and the Svanetians can be explained to a great extent by looking at the history of the region and its people. Svanetia has a separate history going back to the late bronze age, when it was under the influence of the fabled kingdom of Colchis. According to the ancient geographer Strabo, the legend of the Golden Fleece of Colchis was traced to Svanetia, where gold deposits from the upland streams had been exploited from early times. Writing in the first century A.D., Strabo described the Svanetians as dominating the mountain regions north and east of the Greek* trade outpost of Dioscuriada near Sukhumi in Abkhazia. Svanetia in that period was tribal kingdom with a warlike population. In late antiquity, the Transcaucasus became a region of contention between the Eastern Roman Empire and Sassanid Persia; Svanetia became embroiled in the conflict. In the fourth and sixth centuries, Svanetia vacillated between being a tributary principality under the Byzantine client kingdom of Lazica (west Georgia) and the Sassanid client kingdom of Kartli (east Georgia). Christianity in its Byzantine form entered Svanetia sometime in this era, although the earliest extant Christian sites in Svanetia date from the late ninth century.

With the rise of Islam in the seventh century, the subsequent destruction of Sassanid Persia, and the weakening of Byzantium, the area of western Georgia became independent of Byzantine suzerainty and formed a kingdom known as Abazgia, or Abkhazia, of which Svanetia was a *eristavate* (vassal principality). Around 1000 A.D., Svanetia became a principality of the united Bagratid Kingdom of Georgia and remained so until the Mongol* invasions in the mid-thirteenth century. With the break-up of the Bagratid kingdom, Svanetia had a brief period of independence under the Vardanidze dynasty. The Bagratids were able to restore the unity of the Georgian kingdom in the mid-fourteenth century and overthrew the Vardanidze clan.

Soon after this restoration of Georgian power in Svanetia, the western Transcaucasus was convulsed by feudal conflicts and later foreign invasions by the Ottoman Turks* and Safavid Persians*. Georgia was fragmented into several regional principalities and ethnic/confessional enclaves. Western Georgia came under Ottoman rule, with the bulk of Abaza, the Laz, and the Abkhazians* embracing Islam and with Mingrelia becoming a vassal principality under Ottoman suzerainty. Svanetia became increasingly isolated and fragmented in this period of turmoil between the fourteenth and nineteenth centuries. Lower Svanetia came under the rule of the Dadiani nobles as part of the principality of Mingrelia. This area became known as Princely Svanetia. The western part of Upper Svanetia was ruled by princes of the Dadishkeliani family. The eastern part of Upper Svanetia, known as Free Svanetia, was not ruled by nobles. Free Svanetia was, by the nineteenth century, a confederation of clans that had all the earmarks of a warrior society similar to those of Montenegro and Mani in the Balkans.

The Russian* annexation of Kartlia and part of Mingrelia in the early 1800s brought the Dadiani and Dadishkeliani nobles to allegiance to the Tsar. Civil strife among the Dadishkeliani and their vacillation during the Crimean War

(1854–1856), however, led to direct Russian rule in 1858 and eventual Russian annexation of Dadishkeliani Svanetia in 1869. The clans of Free Svanetia recognized Russian suzerainty in the 1830s but did not allow Russian officials or church missions into the area until the late 1840s. Russian envoys, backed by military force, were able to open the region to further Russian influence by the 1850s. The imposition of a detachment of Cossacks* in one village, together with an attempt at a Russian livestock and land survey, led to an uprising in 1875, which was put down by a combination of Russian diplomacy and military action.

Russian rule weakened the clan system through introduction of Russian-appointed clan and village leaders and the suppression of blood feuds and banditry. A significant number of Svanetians from Upper Svanetia were settled in a territory vacated by Muslim Abkhazians who had been forced to emigrate to Turkey in the late nineteenth and early twentieth centuries. This transfer of population produced the third region of Svanetia, known as Abkhazian Svanetia, which is now within the Abkhazian Autonomous Republic.

World War I, the Russian Revolution, and the civil war affected all parts of Svanetia, as old clan rivalries were transformed into a struggle between Whites and Reds. Some Svanetians formed a small Communist cadre in these years and were opposed by the bulk of Svanetians, who mostly supported an independent Georgia. Uprisings against Soviet rule broke out in 1921–1922 and again in 1924. The Svanetians were pacified militarily by the Red Army; their leadership was purged and eliminated, and their lands and flocks were collectivized.

Because Svanetia was considered such a backward region, Soviet authorities attempted to make it a model of socialist modernization in the 1930s. In the field of transportation, they established air service to Svanetia and constructed dirt automotive roads in Lower and Upper Svanetia in the 1930s. In industry, the Soviets attempted to develop mining, gold prospecting, and lumbering there. In agriculture, the Soviets attempted to wean the Svanetians from their traditional ways of life by collectivizing agriculture and livestock breeding, constructing more modern homes without towers, and introducing electricity to some villages. Svanetia became such a model for development that the Soviets produced a motion picture in 1930 entitled *Salt for Svanetia* to illustrate its progress.

Nevertheless, the socialist development in Svanetia seems to have been ephemeral, since, in the postwar period, development policy was reoriented toward the lowlands of Mingrelia and Kartvelia. From the end of World War II to the death of Stalin, thousands of Svanetians were obliged to resettle in the lowlands of Georgia. It is unclear whether this forced postwar resettlement had political as well as economic motives. Since 1953, voluntary migration out of Svanetia has continued, but not at the same rate as from other mountain regions in Georgia. Today the population of Svanetians is about 40,000 within the Georgian Republic and about 4,000 in the Abkhazian Autonomous Republic.

Economic modernization of Svanetia continued in the Nikita Khrushchev and Leonid Brezhnev eras, with the construction of paved automobile roads to Upper

Svanetia, the development of the Inguri River Hydroelectric Power Plant, the introduction of new machinery and techniques for highland agriculture, and the establishment of tourism. Tied in with this economic development have been attempts to modernize and secularize the Svanetians through education, the media, and more convenient transportation. These efforts have increasingly opened Svanetia to the outside world. Some Svanetians have migrated out of their homeland while outsiders, mostly Georgians, have moved in. These developments have brought about a certain amount of cultural assimilation with the rest of Georgia, especially with the use of Georgian as an official and literary language. The heavy-handed attempts to root out traditional religion, culture, and societal customs have not been so successful, however, and have led to resistance movements for religio-cultural revival. The break-up of the Soviet Union and the emergence of an independent Georgian Republic will no doubt change the relationship between the Svanetians and the Georgian government but will probably not result in the severe ethnic strife that has been seen in Ossetia and Abkhazia. Although the Svanetians are distinct from the Georgians and Mingrelians in their language and historical development, their religious and cultural affinities, as well as their use of Georgian as literary language, will probably keep them within the Georgian nation.

REFERENCES: For the history of Svanetia within Georgia, see W.E.D. Allen, *A History of the Georgian People from the Beginning Down to the Russian Conquest in the Nineteenth Century*, 1936; D. M. Lang, *The Georgians*, 1966; R. G. Suny, *The Making of the Georgian Nation*, 1988; Cyril Toumanoff, "Christian Caucasia between Byzantium and Iran: New Light from Old Sources," *Traditio*, 10 (1954) and "Introduction to Christian Caucasian History," *Traditio*, 15 (1959) and 17 (1961). On Svanetia and the Svanetians, see S. Anisimov, *Svanetia*, 1940; I. Bartolomei, "Proezdka v Vol'nuiu Svanetiiu," *Zapiski Kavkaskago Otdela Imperatorskago Russkago Georgraficheskago Obshchestva*, 3 (1855); D. Bakradze, "Svanetia," *Zapiski Kavkaskago Otdela Imperatorskago Russkago Georgraficheskago Obshchestva*, 6 (1864); K. A. Borozdin, *Zakavkazskiia vospominaniia: Mingrelia i Svanetia s 1851 po 1861 god.*, 1885; B. Degen-Kovalevskii, "Svanskoe selenie kak istoricheskii istochnik," *Sovetskaia Etnografiia*, 4–5 (1936); D. Freshfiel, *The Exploration of the Caucasus*, vol. 2, 1896; A. Kuznetsov, *Verkniaia Svanetia*, 1974; F. Sobol, *Verkniaia Svanetia*, 1974.

Nicholas C. J. Pappas

SVANY. See SVANETIAN and GEORGIAN.

SWAN. See SVANETIAN and GEORGIAN.

SWANETE. See SVANETIAN.

SYM. See KET.

T

TABARASAN. See TABASARAN.

TABASARAN. Until the time of the Russian Revolution, the Tabasaran people were generally classified as the Lezgins*, which was a generic term used to describe all of the ethnic groups of the highlands southwest of the Caspian Sea in what is today the Daghestan Republic. Since then, ethnologists have been more careful in making group identifications; the once generic Lezgins have become the Lezgins proper, the Aguls*, the Rutuls*, and the Tabasarans. The Tabasaran people live near the border of Daghestan and Azerbaijan, east of the Aguls and between the Dargins* to the north and the Lezgins to the south. They are concentrated primarily in the Khiv and Tabasaran rayons of Daghestan. The Tabasarans call themselves the Tabasaran or the Tabasaran Zhvi. The Tabasaran language is part of the Samurian* group of the Caucasic languages. There are two basic Tabasaran dialects, which are mutually unintelligible. The Khanag dialect is used by the northern Tabasaran people, while in the south the Tabasaran dialect proper is spoken. In the late 1980s, the Tabasaran population exceeded 85,000 people.

Although there is little information about the origins of the Tabasarans, ethnologists believe them to be an indigenous people of the Caucasus. They came under the direct control of the Arabs* in the eighth century. Like other ethnic groups in southern Daghestan, the Tabasarans are now Sunni Muslims loyal to the Shafi theological school. They are extremely devout, and, like other Muslim people in the Near and Middle East in the 1970s and 1980s, they have been influenced by the fervent religious fundamentalism that has increasingly dominated the cultural landscape. In spite of more than seventy years of anti-religious state policy, fundamental religious institutions and traditions—such as endogamous marriages, family mosques, religious marriages and burials, observance of Ramadan, the circumcision of male babies, and faithful devotion to the teachings of the Koran—still flourish.

In terms of their political history, the Tabasarans developed a powerful principality of their own in the fifteenth century. This was known as the Maisumat of Tabasaran, and it made up one of the three great political states in Daghestan; it came under Russian* domination in the early nineteenth century. The Tabasarans have been uncomfortable under the Russian yoke, however, and a profound anti-Russian sentiment permeates Tabasaran culture. Just after the Russian Revolution, the government in Moscow created the Mountain Autonomous Republic with Arabic as the official language of the government and the schools. The Tabasarans, along with many other highland ethnic groups, opposed the policy and rebelled against it. The government then created the Daghestan Autonomous Soviet Socialist Republic in 1921 and, in 1925, launched an anti-Islamic campaign that included closing all Islamic schools, eliminating the use of Arabic, and executing many local imams. At that point, state policy shifted in favor of the Turkic* peoples, and Azerbaijani* became the official language of the region. That ended in 1928, when the government declared Dargin, Avar*, Lezgin, Tabasaran, and Azerbaijani all to be official languages. That year, the government also began to create a Latin alphabet for the Tabasaran language, but that program was changed back to the Cyrillic alphabet in 1938. Gradually, over the next twenty years, the Russian language was imposed on all schools and government offices in Daghestan.

The constant policies of cultural manipulation by the Soviet government only increased Tabasaran resentment of Russian culture. The Tabasarans resisted the russianization of their culture and also refused to participate in government programs to relocate them out of the highlands and into lowland towns and collective farms. As a result, all but a handful of the Tabasaran people retain their traditional rural life-style. In addition to trying to russianize the culture, the government worked diligently to sovietize the Tabasaran economy. Traditionally, the Tabasaran people had owned land and livestock herds communally, so the Soviet government converted those ethnic communal arrangements into economic collectives, with the government owning the land and the herds. The Tabasarans thus had to sell their farm produce, livestock, and manufactured goods to government collectives at state-mandated prices, and, in the end, the Tabasaran community found itself in a poorer economic situation. Because of the state-controlled economy and the heavy-handed attempts to change Tabasaran culture, the Tabasaran sense of ethnicity, which is distinctly anti-Communist, anti-Russian, and anti-Christian, has only intensified over the years. More than 95 percent of ethnic Tabasarans speak the native language and are intensely loyal to their Muslim faith. Economic life still revolves around animal husbandry (sheep and goats in the highlands, cattle in the lowlands), gold- and silver-smithing, weaving, pottery, and rug manufacturing. Because of their geographic isolation and their resentment of state educational policies, Tabasaran education levels are among the lowest in the Soviet Union.

REFERENCES: Alexandre Bennigsen, "Muslim Conservative Opposition to the Soviet Regime: The Sufi Brotherhoods in the North Caucasus," in Jeremy R. Azrael, ed., *Soviet Nationality Policies and Practices*, 1971; Bruce Geiger, et al., *Peoples and Languages of the Caucasus*, 1959; T. S. Halasi-Kun, "The Caucasus: An Ethno-Historical Survey,"

Studia Caucasia, 2 (1956), 7–16; Brian Silver, "Language Policy and Linguistic Russification of Soviet Nationalities," in Jeremy R. Azrael, ed., *Soviet Nationality Policies and Practices*, 1971; Ronald Wixman, "Daghestanis," in Richard V. Weekes, ed., *Muslim Peoples*, 1984, 211–19; Ronald Wixman, *The Peoples of the USSR: An Ethnographic Handbook*, 1984; Ronald Wixman, *Language Aspects of Ethnic Patterns and Processes in the North Caucasus*, 1980.

TABASARAN ZHVI. See TABASARAN.

TABASARANTSY. See TABASARAN.

TABUNUT. The Tabunut are a Buryat* subgroup. Most of them live along the Selenga River. See BURYAT.
REFERENCE: Ronald Wixman, *The Peoples of the USSR: An Ethnographic Handbook*, 1984.

TADJIK. See TAJIK.

TADJIK CHAGATAI. See CHAGATAI and TAJIK.

TADJIK CHAGATAY. See CHAGATAI and TAJIK.

TADJIK CHAGHATAI. See CHAGATAI and TAJIK.

TADJIK CHAGHATAY. See CHAGATAI and TAJIK.

TADZHIK CHAGATAI. See CHAGATAI and TAJIK.

TADZHIK CHAGATAY. See CHAGATAI and TAJIK.

TADZHIK CHAGHATAI. See CHAGATAI and TAJIK.

TADZHIK CHAGHATAY. See CHAGATAI and TAJIK.

TAG KARGA. See SAGAI and KHAKASS.

TAIGA KAMASIN. See KAMASIN.

TAJIK. The Tajiks, also sometimes called Sarts* or Sarjkolis, are a Central Asian, Iranian-speaking people whose homeland, the Republic of Tajikistan, is bordered on the north by Kyrgyzistan, on the northeast by the Republic of Uzbekistan, on the east by Sinkiang Province in western China, and on the south by Afghanistan. Over 90 percent of Tajikistan is covered by mountains, and almost half of the republic lies at elevations of more than 10,000 feet in three mountain systems: the Tien Shan in the north, the Hissar-Alay in the center, and the Pamirs in the southeast. According to the Soviet census of 1989, there were 4,216,693 Tajiks out of a total population of 5,112,000 in Tajikistan, forming an 82 percent majority in their own homeland. The next largest ethnic group in the country is the Uzbeks* at 23 percent of the population, and next come the Russians*, who make up 7 percent. Other ethnic groups that live in the region include, in descending numbers, Ukrainians*, Tatars*, Germans*, Kyrgyz*, and Jews*. Some 3,000,000 Tajiks also live in Afghanistan, but this figure is unreliable, since the term "Tajik" is used to denote all Persian* speakers; in addition, there are some 20,000 Tajiks in China, and other small Tajik groups in northern Iran and Pakistan. The etymological origin of the term "Tajik" is derived from Taz or Taiy, an Arabic tribal appelation; an early form of this was Tazik or Tezik, which came to mean either "an Arab" or an Iranian subject of the Arabs*. Later, the Russians widened the meaning of the term to include "trader from Central Asia." By definition, traders usually came from urban, settled locales; hence, the other name for the Tajik (and other settled peoples, such as some of the Uzbeks) was Sart, a Turkic* word meaning sedentary.

Tajik belongs to the southwest division of the Iranian branch of the Indo-European family of languages and is very closely related to Persian. This fact sets the Tajiks apart from their other Central Asian neighbors, the majority of whom speak a variety of Turkic languages. The Iranian language, often called Farsi, is also spoken in the Hindu Kush area of northeast Afghanistan. The Tajiks speak a variety of dialects that are determined, in large part, by where in Tajikistan they live and their country's difficult terrain. The four most important dialect groups of Tajik are the northern (which includes the Samarkand-Bukhara, east and west Fergana, Ura-Tjube, and Pendzhikent regions); the central (Seravshan, Rishtan, and Sokh regions); the southern (Badakhshan, north and south Kulab, Karategin, and other regions); and the southeastern (Darwaz group). The main differences among the dialects are mainly phonetic. The northern group appears to be the educated standard against which usage is judged.

The present-day Tajiks are apparently the descendants of one of the early, proto-Indo-European civilizations that entered Central Asia as early as 2000 B.C. Since the Bronze Age, the indigenous tribes of the Tajikistan region had been subject to numerous waves of conquest from the south and the east, due primarily to the position of Tajikistan as a natural corridor to the plains of Transoxiana. Although the inaccessibility of most of Tajikistan has affected the Tajiks' assimilation with foreign cultures, they have never been immune to the cyclic ebb and flow of the empires in the region. For that reason, the history of Tajikistan has long been bound up with that of Uzbekistan to the west, since both regions were often conquered together and governed by the same ruler. For example, in the sixth century B.C., Tajikistan, within the region then known as Bactria (an area lying south of the eastern end of the Amu Darya River, which today roughly corresponds to the southeastern portion of Uzbekistan and the western half of Tajikistan), formed part of the empire of the Achaemenid King Cyrus I;

later, in the fourth century B.C., the same area became known as Sogdiana, and was conquered by Alexander the Great. These two empires, the Bactrian and the Sogdian, provide the first recorded links to the Tajiks' Iranian heritage. Around the beginning of the current era, invading Scythians briefly controlled the area, until they themselves were driven southwards into India by an Indo-European people whom the Chinese* called the Yueh-Chih, or the Tokharians. The area, for a time completely under the control of the Tokharians, even came to be known as Tokharistan and formed the geographical base of the powerful Tokharian Kushan Empire.

By the fifth century, A.D., the last of the weak Tokharian Kushans was driven out of Bactria by the nomadic Ephthalite Huns, possibly the earliest of many subsequent waves of Turkic* invasion into Central Asia. With the exception of the Arab* conquest of Central Asia in the mid-eighth century, the Turkic influx into the region remained steady until the arrival of the Karakhanids of the tenth century. The arrival of these Turkic nomads, together with that of the Seljuks of the eleventh and twelfth centuries and the Genghis Khanite and Timurid Mongol invasions of the thirteenth through the fifteenth centuries, all worked to turkicize the bulk of Central Asia thoroughly, including large portions of Tajikistan. Only the Pamir* peoples of the remote Pamir Mountain region, (speakers of one of the East Iranian languages) and the ancestors of the Tajiks (speakers of a West Iranian language) would remain as the two enclaves of Indo-European speakers able to resist the turkification process successfully.

From this small ethnic nucleus, the Tajiks evolved, perhaps as early as the eighth century, into three distinct cultural groups: the lowland Tajiks of the valleys and oases, who are similar in culture and life-style to the sedentary Uzbeks; the "Mountain" Tajiks*, who share a common religion with the lowland group; and, the Pamiri Tajiks, who appear to be the descendants of the Pamiri tribes and the Farsi-speaking mountain-dwellers of northern Afghanistan. These three cultural groups are still extant today. In addition, there are two other ethnographic offshoots of the Tajiks: the Chagatais* (the name of one of Genghis Khan's grandsons; not to be confused with the Turkic, Uzbek clan also called Chagatai), who are Farsi speakers of possibly Turkic origin; and, the Kharduris*, a formerly semi-nomadic Tajik group of unknown origin. Currently, the Tajiks are in the process of assimilating various Iranian and non-Iranian peoples living in Tajikistan. The most unusual and intriguing of these groups are the Yagnobis*, currently numbering about 2,000 people, who speak the ancient and primitive Sogdian language, which possesses a vocabulary of only 2,500 words, has no written form, and contains a "secret language" of cryptic substitutes to mislead outsiders.

Islam, which was brought to Tajikistan in the wake of the Arab conquests of the eighth century, supplanted various older religions, such as Zoroastrianism, Buddhism, Nestorianism, and Manichaeanism, and played a vital role in establishing the distinctiveness of Tajik culture. The majority of the Tajiks, of both the lowland and mountain groups, became Sunni Muslims of the Hanafi school of Sharia Law. In addition, a few groups of Imami Ithna-Ashari (or "Twelver") and Ismaili ("Sevener") Shia were established primarily among the small Pamiri Tajik tribes dwelling in the Pamir Mountains of the south. Under Islamic influence, the Tajiks established peace among themselves and encouraged the rise of local dynasties, such as the short-lived but spectacularly successful Perso-Arabic Samanid Empire (903–999 A.D.), which became the one expression of Tajik statehood until the Soviet period. Bukhara, the Samanid capital, became a glittering center of commerce and learning in the expanding Islamic world. For example, the scientific discoveries of the great encylopedist Ibn Sina (Avicenna) are a part of the Tajik heritage. The Tajiks fostered the caravan trade with southeastern Europe, China, Mongolia, India, Afghanistan, Iran, and the Caucasus. They also mined precious metals to facilitate commerce; Samanid coins found in Moscow, Novgorod, and as far north as the Baltic coast attest to strong commercial ties with Russia even this early. The Tajik ethnicity and language, which probably evolved out of one of the regional dialects and came to replace Sogdian, were most likely permanently established at this time.

The strength of the Tajiks' commitment to Islam undoubtedly aided them in their maintaining cultural unity in the face of further Turkic incursions, particularly those of the Mongols*, Timurids, and Uzbeks. Throughout the period of the Turkic and Mongolic invasions, from the eleventh through the fifteenth centuries, the Tajiks tenaciously maintained literary Persian as their official language. From the fifteenth until the early twentieth century, urban Tajiks were obliged to employ two languages, Persian and Turkic, with Persian heavily predominant. The Mongol conquest of the thirteenth century was responsible for the disruption of the Tajiks' culture and the isolation of their homeland from outside influences. It is possible that the Mongol-Tatar invading armies never fully enveloped the rural and mountain Tajiks; the cities, however, typically located in highly accessible valleys, were often leveled, their populations massacred, and their works of material and spiritual culture looted or destroyed. In the late fourteenth century, with the waning of the Mongols and their successor states throughout Central Asia, the Tajik ruling classes cast their allegiance with the Turkic warrior Timur, known to the West as Tamerlane, who launched a series of predatory wars against neighboring lands and created a vast state with Samarkand as its capital. Once again, Tajikistan was able to enjoy briefly the cosmopolitanism and commerce that its proximity to the Timurid empire afforded. After Tamerlane's death, his empire crumbled into mutually hostile minor feudatories, and Tajikistan sank into obscurity.

From the sixteenth to the mid-nineteenth centuries, the Tajiks' relations with their powerful and expansionistic neighbors, the Turkic Uzbeks, helped deliver the weakened Tajik state to the expanding Russian Empire. At the beginning of the sixteenth century, the Uzbeks, a minor branch of Genghis Khan's Mongols, led by the famous Muhammad Shaybani Khan, conquered former Timurid domains along the southern shore of the Aral Sea, where they established a lasting Uzbek presence in the region. The Uzbek khans immediately began to bring the Tajiks to the east under their rule, creating a number of small, semi-independent Tajik border states along the frontier between the Uzbek Khanate and China. With the conquest of the Shaybanid Bukharan Khanate by a re-invigorated Persia in the eighteenth century, the northwestern portion of Tajikistan, in particular the fertile, strategic, and heavily populated Fergana Valley oasis, declared its independence for a short time in the 1760s and recognized Chinese suzerainty. This region was soon incorporated into Bukhara's rival, the rising Khokand Khanate (Bukhara, Khiva, and Khokand, the three Uzbek power centers located between the Amu and Syr Darya rivers, resembled city-states more than khanate empires). Nonetheless, internal dissension between the sedentary Sart population and the semi-nomadic Uzbek tribesmen, coupled with continuous warfare with Bukhara and other northern tribes, had severely weakened the Khokand Khanate by the 1850s, rendering it susceptible to Russian incursions.

By the middle of the nineteenth century, the tsarist government had begun to accelerate its conquest of Central Asia because of continued Khokand hostilities against Russia's Kazakh* subjects. Russia's southward expansion toward Afghanistan, during which it annexed the Tajik areas of Ura-Tjube and Khodzhent, and the simultaneous British* expansion northward from India to Afghanistan generated friction and rivalry between the two imperial powers for possession of southeastern Central Asia. In 1867, a governor-generalship of Russian Turkestan was formed under direct military administration. The next year, Russian forces conquered and extended full protectorate status over the Emirate of Bukhara to gain back some lost territory following a minor renaissance of Bukharan expansionism.

In sum, by the end of the nineteenth century, all of the territory in northern Tajikistan was under direct Russian rule, while the territory in the south came under Russian-dominated Bukharan control. The second of the three Uzbek khanates, Khiva, fell to Russians in 1873. Finally, after Russia's suppression of the Khokand Uprising of 1873–1876 (a revolt of Khokandian nationalists against their khan's pro-Russian policies), the tsarist government felt justified in abolishing the Khokand Khanate entirely. Its territory, including the Tajiki portion of the Fergana Valley, was merged into the Fergana Oblast as part of Governor-Generalship of Turkestan. Thus, with the Bukharan and Khokandian annexations, the entire territory of Tajikistan became incorporated, either directly or indirectly, into the Russian Empire. The intense rivalry between the British and the Russians in Central Asia was settled by an 1895 Anglo-Russian agreement, whereby the boundary between Afghanistan and Tajikistan was established along the Pyanzh river. The southwestern and central portions of Tajikistan and western Pamirs remained within the Bukharan Khanate until after the Bolshevik Revolution; until then, this area was not considered a separate polity but simply one of the constituent parts of Russian Turkestan.

After the conquest, the Russians established a colonial government over the entire region, called the Turkestan Governor-Generalship, based in the ancient city of Tashkent in eastern Uzbekistan. The tsarist and colonial governments followed their habitual policy of encouraging immigration to Turkestan by settlers who were then given preference in acquiring the most productive agricultural lands. Naturally, the influx of homesteaders to the area fostered the colonial relationship between Russia and Tajikistan. Tajik society soon consisted of a politically privileged, elite Russian minority dominating a large, silent, and inert native population that was bound by religious and cultural traditionalism. The Tajiks shared these and similar problems with their Central Asian neighbors. The Russians retained as much native administration as possible in order to reduce the cost of government. Yet, as has often been the case with colonial administration, such governance was arbitrary, illogical, grossly wasteful, mismanaged, and undertaken to suit the interests and convenience of the central government, not of Tajiks or other natives.

The Muslim natives in these protectorates were classed as *inorodtsy*, or aborigines, possessing neither the full rights nor the obligations of Russian citizenship, a situation that would have explosive repercussions during World War I. Russian attempts to conscript native peoples to participate in the war led to widespread rioting among Sarts and nomads throughout Central Asia. The natives believed that they were becoming subject to obligations without compensatory rights. In addition, they were often treated with contempt by the Russian administrator and other bureaucrats. Most bureaucrats had never bothered to learn the local language and believed that their "civilizing mission" consisted solely of replacing native cultures with their own, certain that natives would cheerfully abandon their own cultures for that of the "superior" Russians, once they had been exposed to it. The natives proved far more loyal to their culture than the Russians had thought they would be. In spite of these obvious problems, the incorporation of Tajikistan into tsarist Russia was valuable in encouraging economic development among the sedentary, commerce-oriented Tajiks. Once again, as the result of their association with a large imperial polity, Tajik commerce and crafts flourished and found a ready market in the Russian cities of the north.

When the Bolshevik Revolution took place in October 1917, the Bolsheviks, with the help of the colonial Communist cadres, undertook a brutal, repressive campaign to consolidate power and restructure the Tajik government, in an effort to incorporate the Tajiks into the Soviet regime. Indeed, soon after the Bolshevik Revolution, the Communist bureaucracy in the various Central Asian republics was staffed almost entirely by Russians, either of necessity or as a result of Russian ethnic exclusiveness. In April 1918, the Communists incorporated part of the Tajik homeland into the newly created Turkestan Autonomous Soviet Socialist Republic (ASSR). By 1920, the Soviet takeover of Bukhara included claims against the remainder of Tajikistan. Paradoxically, in the early years of Soviet rule, the largely sedentary Tajiks—with the greatest claim to an ethnic homeland—found theirs liquidated by fiat, while the nomadic peoples of Central

Asia were in the process of having homelands created for them. The Soviets did not redress this embarrassing inequity until 1924.

The Tajiks and Uzbeks, unlike their neighbors, the Kazakhs and Kyrgyz, did not actively collaborate with the White and interventionist forces in fighting against the Bolsheviks during the civil war. Instead, after the Communists seized power, Tajikistan became the locus of a major uprising, which was as much anti-Russian as it was anti-Communist. In Bukhara, Muslim reformers known as Jadidists or "Young Bukharans" (recalling the "Young Turks" of the contemporaneous Ottoman Empire) had been petitioning their reactionary emir, Sa'id Mir 'Alim, for liberal reforms; these he granted as long as Russian power induced him to do so. When Russia was plunged into civil war, the emir perceived his opportunity to end the reforms and executed large numbers of Young Bukharans; the remaining Young Bukharans were then obliged to turn to the Bolshevik government. In 1920, with Red Army assistance, the Young Bukharans were able to drive the emir into Tajikistan. There he organized a following around a local bandit organization, whose name, the Basmachi (from the Turkic *basmak*, meaning to attack or raid, but more generally translated as bandit), he adopted for his movement. The Basmachis attracted support from all manner of disaffected groups—conservative Muslims, nationalists, anti-Russians, and anti-Communists, as well as the usual assortment of freebooters, mercenaries, and terrorists. Like latter-day Central Asian Robin Hoods, the Basmachis received their greatest assistance from the peasantry, at whose hands they were often clothed, fed, and hidden from the authorities. The Basmachis maintained guerrilla resistance against the Soviet government for another decade before the latter was able to stamp out completely the appeal of "Basmachism."

In 1924, as part of the National Delimitation of Turkestan, which divided up Central Asia along ethnic lines, the Soviets finally established the Tajik ASSR within the Uzbek SSR. Communist party leaders hoped that this concession to nationalism might mollify the Tajiks, yet this one positive step was followed by many negative ones: frequent political changes at the all-Union level; Josef Stalin's ruthless consolidation of power, the continuing Basmachi problem; and finally, the effects of forced collectivization and industrialization. All of these measures served only to renew and exacerbate the Tajiks' resistance to sovietization. Even Tajikistan's promotion to full union status in 1929 proved insufficient to quell the natives' bitterness and discontent. The majority of Tajiks continued to view Soviet authority as brutal and repressive, and they refused the enticements offered by Communist agitation and propaganda. In the face of such resistance, the nurturing of a native cadre was an excruciatingly slow, taxing affair, but Stalin made the situation worse. He responded rashly and perversely, with a decade-long cycle of purges, beginning in 1927, initiated against what he called the "bourgeois-nationalist elements" of Tajikistan's native party leadership. Ironically, the Soviets were never able to rebuild the native Tajik presence in the Communist Party hierarchy of Tajikistan. Indeed, as late as 1990, Tajiks were still a minority in the party, obliging Moscow to send out officials to run the Tajik government.

The Tajiks managed to resist pressure from the central government with regard to religious and social change, as well. Once again, the Tajiks' strong commitment to Islam appears to have protected them from the more deleterious effects of alien cultural incursions, in this case, Communism. The Central Committee Congresses regularly bemoaned and criticized the Tajiks' reactionary and seemingly unreasonable attachment to their religion. For their part, however, the Tajiks, still confined largely to rural areas and isolated mountain regions, have continued to live within their traditions. Even among the elite, the customary way of life survives. For example, all segments of society participate in the traditional move to the *kishlak*, or village winter quarters, located in the relatively warm valley regions. In addition, most Tajiks make the distinction between "public" life, which is more modern, and "private" life, which still conforms significantly to traditional forms. The Tajik reaction to the sovietization of their culture has likewise been ambivalent. They have embraced the nationalist tendencies of pride in the revival of their ancient heritage while still resisting the pressures to view this heritage from a unified Soviet perspective.

In the mid–1980s, Mikhail Gorbachev's programs of *glasnost* and *perestroika* became the one window of opportunity for the natives to implement uniquely Tajik solutions to local problems. Nonetheless, the natural outcome of such ideological independence from Moscow could only be actual independence; the Tajik Supreme Soviet therefore declared Tajikistan's sovereignty in August 1990. After the abortive coup against Gorbachev in 1991, the Soviets' political hold over Tajikistan quickly began to loosen. Tajik party leader and chairman of the local supreme soviet, Kakhar Makhkamov, was forced to resign for his support of the coup attempt. His successor, Kadriddin Aslonov, was responsible for effecting Tajikistan's break with Moscow. He resigned from the Tajik Communist Party and promptly issuing a decree banning its activities.

Angry at being upstaged and marginalized, the Tajik Supreme Soviet, whose membership was over 95 percent Communist, immediately ousted Aslonov in favor of Rakhmon Nabiyev, a loyal party hack. It also declared a state of emergency in the capital city of Dushanbe, in the wake of the civil unrest caused by the ouster of an apparently sympathetic party leader there who had given permission to tear down a statue of Lenin. The rioters became angry over the apparent assumption of dictatorial powers by the supreme soviet. Shortly afterwards, the membership of the Tajik Communist Party dissolved its organization and established, in its stead, the euphemistically named Socialist Party. On September 30, 1991, after continued protest rallies in Dushanbe, the supreme soviet was compelled to lift the state of emergency and, two days later, to suspend the activities of both the officially dissolved Tajik Communist Party and the Socialist Party.

Presidential elections, held on November 24, included the participation of a number of newly formed political parties, including the Democratic Party of Tajikistan and the Popular Movement *Rastokhez* (or Revival). A number of religiously based parties, from which the Supreme Soviet had recently lifted its ban, also fielded a candidate, Akbar Turadzhonzoda, who subsequently declined to run. Party hack Nabiyev, running against several other candidates, finally won, but his election to the presidency is considered illegitimate by a segment of Tajik society. The groups opposed to Nabiyev have organized themselves into an armed, rebel faction operating around the city of Dushanbe. Nabiyev's prime minister, Akbar Mirzoyev, is the former chair of the Kulyab Region Executive Committee and is a builder by profession. Since the majority of seats in Tajikistan's parliament are still controlled by former Communists, these deputies have attempted to re-impose leftist control by re-invoking a state of emergency to deal with the rebels who are creating disturbances around Dushanbe. The rebels are calling for Nabiyev's resignation and his replacement by a council comprised, in part, by members from the opposition parties.

Tajikistan appears to be evolving toward institutionalized pluralism, which some scholars believe may be facilitated by its traditional political factionalization based on regional clans. This typically Tajik approach to politics even manifested itself to some degree in the apparently monolithic Tajik Communist Party during the height of Soviet power. The current scholarly debate seems to center on the outcome of such clan-based political parties. If the trend continues, Tajikistan's pluralism might be unique and bear little resemblance to Western-style democracies. At the same time, it is more likely that the Tajiks' reliance on familiar traditions and cultural patterns may again be helping them through the crises resulting from the passing of yet another regional empire.

REFERENCES: Shirin Akiner, *Islamic Peoples of the Soviet Union*, 1983; Edward Allworth, ed., *Central Asia: A Century of Russian Rule*, 1967; René Grousset, *The Empire of the Steppes: A History of Central Asia*, 1970; Richard Pipes, *The Formation of the Soviet Union: Communism and Nationalism, 1917–1923*, 1980; Teresa Rakowska-Harmstone, "The Dialects of Nationalism in the USSR," *Problems of Communism* (May-June 1974); Barry M. Rosen, "An Awareness of Traditional Tadzhik Identity in Central Asia," in Edward Allworth, ed., *The Nationality Question in Soviet Central Asia*, 1973; Michael Rywkin, ed., *Russian Colonial Expansion to 1917*, 1988; Emmanuel Sarkisiyanz, "Russian Conquest in Central Asia: Transformation and Acculturation," in Wayne S. Vucinich, ed., *Russia and Asia: Essays on the Influence of Russia on the Asian Peoples*, 1972; M. Wesley Shoemaker, ed., *Russia, Eurasian States, and Eastern Europe*, 1992; Wayne S. Vucinich, ed., *Russia and Asia: Essays on the Influence of Russia on the Asian Peoples*, 1972; Joseph L. Wieczynski, ed., *The Modern Encyclopedia of Russian and Soviet History*, 1984.

Lee Brigance Pappas

TAJIK CHAGATAI. See CHAGATAI and TAJIK.

TAJIK CHAGATAY. See CHAGATAI and TAJIK.

TAJIK CHAGHATAI. See CHAGATAI and TAJIK.

TAJIK CHAGHATAY. See CHAGATAI and TAJIK.

TALISH. See TALYSH and AZERBAIJANI.

TALUSH. See TALYSH and AZERBAIJANI.

TALYSH. The Talysh are a small ethnic group who call themselves the Tolish or Talush and are known to Russians* as Talyshi. Ethnographers identify them as an ancient people whose roots, thousands of years ago, were in the Talysh Mountains in the southeastern Caucasus, along the border between Iran and what was formerly the Azerbaijani Soviet Socialist Republic. In that sense, their ancestors were Caucasian as well as Iranian. They are concentrated particularly on the southeastern shores of the Caspian Sea. Their language belongs to the northwestern group of Iranian languages, and it is spoken in both southern Azerbaijan and across the border in northern Iran. There are approximately 200,000 Talysh-speaking people living in Iran.

In the mid-eighteenth century, Seid Abbas established the Talysh Khanate in Azerbaijan and northern Iran; his son inherited the throne in 1747, ruling until 1786. By that time, both Russia and Persia were competing for control of the area. The khanate's ruling family found Persian* inroads especially irritating, and the Talysh Khanate developed a Russian* orientation. The Talysh leader, Mir-Mustafa, began appealing to Russia for protection from Persia in 1795, and Russia established a protectorate over Talysh in 1802; the Persians unsuccessfully contested this. In 1828, with the Treaty of Turkmanchai, the Talysh Khanate became Russian territory, and its own political sovereignty was dissolved. By then, the British* were already contesting both Russian and Persian control of the area, siding with the Afghans* in their boundary struggles with Persia. Under constant British pressure, the borders of Iran were delineated in the nineteenth century. In 1881, Iran ceded half of Sistan Province to Afghanistan. In 1884, Iran lost Merv (Mary) to Russia, and, in 1893, the British set the boundaries between Iran and British India at British Baluchistan.

Traditionally, the Talysh economy revolved around cattle raising, and livestock remains a prominent economic activity today. In the twentieth century, especially after the Bolshevik Revolution, the Talysh became heavily involved in agriculture and horticulture, raising vegetables, citrus fruits, and rice; today they raise tea, bamboo, and eucalyptus as well. The Talysh are also skilled carpet weavers. Finally, the Talysh are known throughout Azerbaijan for their intellectual abilities and literacy. They tend to be more highly educated and more literate than the surrounding groups, usually being bilingual, in Azeri and Talysh, and sometimes even trilingual, in Azeri, Russian, and Talysh.

Ethnographers assumed that the Talysh were rapidly disappearing in the twentieth century, being absorbed by the far more numerous Azerbaijanis*. The state in fact encouraged that process, replacing the Talysh Latin alphabet with Cyrillic script in 1939 and thereby forcing those Talysh who were literate to turn to Azeri publications. But the Talysh have proved to be far more ethnically resilient than the Soviet government anticipated. They are a completely rural people, with fewer than 200 of the Talysh living in cities, and they prefer physical as well as cultural separation from other groups. Talysh material culture closely resembles that of the Azerbaijanis, and both groups are Shiite Muslims. In the 1959 Soviet census, relatively few people identified themselves as Talysh, and the Soviet Union did not even try to count them in the censuses of 1970 and 1979. In the 1980s, however, it became increasingly clear that there was a core of Talysh who still clung to their mother tongue and refused to speak either Russian or Azeri. The Soviet Union decided to count them in the 1989 census and identified the 21,914 Talysh. Most of them live in the far southern districts of Azerbaijan—Astara and Lenkora—on the border with Iran. They constitute the majority population in Astara, Lenkora, Lerik, and Masally.

REFERENCES: Shirin Akiner, *Islamic Peoples of the Soviet Union*, 1983; Amin Banani, *The Modernization of Iran, 1921–1941*, 1961; Alexandre Bennigsen and S. Enders Wimbush, *Muslims of the Soviet Empire: A Guide*, 1986; Richard N. Frye, *Iran*, 1954; Walter Kolarz, *Russia and her Colonies*, 1952; *Great Soviet Encyclopedia*, 1980, vol. 25, 345–46; Ronald Wixman, *The Peoples of the Soviet Union: An Ethnographic Handbook*, 1984.

TALYSHI. See TALYSH.

TAMNIEK. See LATVIAN.

TAPANTA. See ABAZA.

TARA TATAR. The Tara Tatars are part of the larger group of Siberian Tatars* who emerged from the Siberian Khanate. They call themselves the Tarlyk, and Russians* refer to them as Tarskije Tatary. The traditional homeland of the Tara Tatars was on the shores of the Irtysh River near the mouth of the Tara River. The city of Tara was the primary communications link between Russian Siberia and Central Asia. The Tara Tatars were first introduced to the Muslim faith by Islamic merchants traveling that trade route in the fourteenth and fifteenth centuries.

The Tara Tatars have had a strong sense of identity, and they resisted the onslaughts of Russian culture. In 1722, when Peter the Great ordered all subjects to take an oath of allegiance to the tsar, the Tara Tatars rose up in rebellion. Peter savagely crushed the rebellion, destroying hundreds of Tatar homes and executing the rebel leaders through decapitation and impalement. The subsequent construction of Russian forts across Siberia in the 1740s and the completion of the Moscow-Siberian Highway in the 1770s brought hundreds of thousands of Russians* to Siberia. In the process, the Tara Tatars were reduced to a tiny minority in their homeland. Since then, the processes of assimilation have brought a russification of Tatar culture, although there are still 10,000 people who identify themselves as Tara Tatars. See TATAR.

REFERENCES: Shirin Akiner, *Islamic Peoples of the Soviet Union*, 1983; James Forsyth, *A History of the Peoples of Siberia*, 1992.

TARANCHI. The Taranchi call themselves the Taranchy and today are considered to be a subgroup of the Uigur*; specifically they are Uigurs who originated in the region of eastern Turkestan, which is in China. In the mid-eighteenth century, the Chinese* government relocated 6,000 families from Kashgaria to the Ili Valley. Approximately two-thirds of those families settled on the right bank of the Ili River and the others on the left bank. There they all became settled farmers and developed into a semi-independent political entity over the next century. In 1871, Russia occupied the Ili Valley. When it was returned to China in 1882, most of the more than 50,000 Taranchis moved voluntarily to the Semirech'e district of Russia. See UIGUR.

REFERENCES: Shirin Akiner, *Islamic Peoples of the Soviet Union*, 1983; Alexandre Bennigsen and S. Enders Wimbush, *Muslims of the Soviet Empire: A Guide*, 1986; Ronald Wixman, *The Peoples of the USSR: An Ethnographic Handbook*, 1984.

TARANCHY. See TARANCHI and UIGUR.

TARLIK. See TARA TATAR and TATAR.

TARLUK. See TARA TATAR and TATAR.

TARLYK. See TARA TATAR and TATAR.

TARSKIJE TATARY. See TARA TATAR.

TAT. The Tats, also known as the Tati or Taty, constitute one of the most unusual of all ethnic groups in the former Soviet Union, for some are Jewish, some Muslim, and some Christian. Tat origins are obscure, and all theories of how they acquired their varied religions are based on supposition. They are an overwhelmingly urban people. The term "Tat" was first used by Turks* to describe any people of non-Turkish origin, but, by the 1920s, it more specifically described the Tat people proper. Muslim Tats are both Shiite and Sunni, although the majority are Shiites of the Ja'farite school. Christian Tats follow the Armeno-Gregorian rite. Western and Soviet authorities differ on whether the Tati-speaking Jews* (also called Mountain Jews*) should be classified as Jews or Tats. Unfortunately, census figures reflect this fundamental confusion. The three Tat communities live in distinct geographical regions. The Jewish Tats live primarily in southern Daghestan, especially in the villages of Krasnaya Sloboda and Vartashen, as well as in the city of Baku in Azerbaijan. The Christian Tats are concentrated in Matrosa village in the Shemakha district and Kilvan village in Divichi district; other Tats call them the Dzhukhur. The Muslim Tats live in the city of Baku, on the Apsheron Peninsula, and in the districts of Siazan, Divichi, Kuba, Konakhkent, Shemakha, and Ismailly in northern and northeastern Azerbaijan. Other Tats are scattered throughout the Georgian Republic, the Armenian Republic, and Chechen-Ingushetia.

The most widely accepted theory of Tat origins argues that they are descendants of ancient Iranian groups that lived in Azerbaijan. The eastern Caucasus has throughout history been a frontier region between the world of the steppes and that of the Middle East. The Tats may have lived there since the fourth century A.D. One commonly proposed explanation of their origin is that they were originally a community of martial Jews assigned to guard the northern reaches of the Sassanian Persian empire. The Tats do not differ in appearance from their neighbors. Their region has been ruled successively by Persians*, Armenians*, Arabs*, the Seljuk Turks, the Mongols*, the Ottomans, the Persians again, and finally the Russians*.

The 22,000 Tats officially counted in the 1979 Soviet census inhabit the most easterly part of the Caucasus mountains, where the climate is generally hot and dry. Many live and work in the oil city of Baku on the Apsheron Peninsula in the Azerbaijan Republic, while others live in towns below sea level along the western shore of the Caspian Sea in the Daghestan Republic in Russia. A smaller number of Tats live in the other Transcaucasian Republics (Armenia and Georgia) and other North Caucasus regions (Chechen-Ingushetia and Ossetia). Despite their rural origins, more than 97 percent of all Tats live in cities today.

The Tati language belongs to the southwest branch of the Iranian family of languages. It thus is closely related to Persian, Kurdish, and Ossetian* but quite unrelated to the Caucasian and Turkic languages of neighboring peoples. The Tati language is a central focus of Tat identity, because their identity has developed a political dimension and because of their religious diversity. The dialect of the Jewish Tats contains many loan-words from Hebrew, as that of the Muslim Tats contains some from Azeri Turkish. Beyond that, individual villages speak sub-dialects. Only Jewish Tati is written; Muslim Tats write in Azeri, and the small number of Christian Tats write in Armenian. The Soviet government half-heartedly promoted Jewish Tati as a literary language utilizing the Cyrillic script; it sponsored a Tati newspaper and published some Tati paeans to collectivization. About one-fourth of Tats claimed Russian as their first language in the 1959 census, but these may have been Jewish Tats seeking to avoid official anti-Semitic discrimination. Muslim Tats speak Azeri as a second language.

Tats follow the general way of life common to the Caucasus mountain peoples: they have a strong orientation toward clan and village, a distrust of outsiders that is paradoxically combined with extravagant hospitality, vendettas that are treated as sacred obligations to be passed down for generations, and domination of women by men. They have practiced diverse occupations; some have been farmers, merchants, and artisans. They have traditionally placed a premium on endogamous marriage, but the assimilation process in recent years has diluted that emphasis.

Jewish Tats endured official anti-Semitism in the tsarist empire, and many were therefore attracted to Zionism. In the early twentieth century, some sent their children to Europe and Palestine for study. By all accounts, their Judaism was most unorthodox, for it included the worship of many pagan deities and some fire rituals that are thought to indicate Zoroastrian influence. Jewish Tats were initially more enthusiastic about the Bolshevik regime than most other Caucasian peoples, and they greeted the final defeat of White Russian forces in 1920 with relief. Subsequently, things did not go well for them, however. An official investigation into Tati complaints in 1926 found that local authorities discriminated against them shamelessly.

Collective farms were established for Jewish Tats, while the majority of Muslim Tats became oil workers. There is little reason to think that the Tats, small in number as they are, can much longer maintain their separate identity. Those Tats in the Daghestan Republic adhere most closely to the Tat language, while Tats living elsewhere are slowly adopting Russian as their first language. They have, however, little or no sense of political nationalism. Jewish Tats, particularly in the late 1980s and early 1990s, when Mikhail Gorbachev's policies of *perestroika* and *glasnost* provided more mobility to Soviet Jews, may emigrate to Israel; those who stay are likely to be assimilated into Russian culture. Muslim Tats are already well on their way to being assimilated into Azerbaijani* society, while Christian Tats are moving slowly into Armenian society.

REFERENCES: Shirin T. Akiner, *The Islamic Peoples of the Soviet Union*, 1983; Alexandre Bennigsen and S. Enders Wimbush, *Muslims of the Soviet Empire: A Guide*, 1986; W. J. Johelson, *Peoples of Asiatic Russia*, 1928; R. S. Komarov, *Taty*, 1879; B. V. Miller, *Taty*, 1929.

Ross Marlay

TAT EVREI. See MOUNTAIN JEW and JEW.

TAT EVREY. See MOUNTAIN JEW and JEW.

TAT IEVREI. See MOUNTAIN JEW and JEW.

TAT JEW. See MOUNTAIN JEW and JEW.

TAT YEVREI. See MOUNTAIN JEW and JEW.

TAT YEVREY. See MOUNTAIN JEW and JEW.

TATAR. Over the years, the term "Tatar" has been used in a variety of ways in Russia, the Soviet Union, and the Commonwealth of Independent States (CIS). For centuries, many Russians* used it as a generic reference to anybody of Muslim or Turkic descent who was living in European Russia; sometimes the term was used to describe anybody of Asian descent. More specifically, however, the term "Tatar" describes the descendants of the Kypchak* and other Turkic* tribes who migrated west out of southern Siberia between the tenth and the thirteenth centuries. Much of the Mongol* armies that invaded Russia in the thirteenth century was composed of these Turkic-speaking peoples. These people tended to mix with the indigenous groups wherever they settled—with Finnic*, Slavic, and Bulgarians peoples in the Volga River Valley and in the Crimea, with Caucasic people in the eastern reaches of the North Caucasus, and with various Siberian peoples in West Siberia.

During that process of ethnogenesis, the peoples who retained their Kypchak dialects and converted to Islam (the Hanafi school of the Sunni faith) became known more particularly as Tatars. By the 1500s, the Golden Horde had fallen under the control of its Turkic elements, and the terms "Tatar" and "Golden Horde" had become essentially synonymous. When the Golden Horde disintegrated, several new Tatar states emerged, such as the Astrakhan Khanate and the Kazan Khanate. Russia conquered Kazan in 1552 and Astrakhan in 1556. Eventually, the Tatars spread from the Polish border in the west to Siberia in the east and, in the process, became divided into a variety of tribal and territorial groups. The Volga Tatars*, or Kazan Tatars, were considered the main group of Tatars, but there were also the Astrakhan Tatars*, which included the Kundrov Tatars* and the Karagash Tatars*; the West Siberian Tatars*, which included the Baraba Tatars*, the Tam Tatars, the Tara Tatars*, the Tobol Tatars*, and the T'jumen Tatars*; and the Belarusian Tatars*, Chulym Tatars*, Crimean Tatars*, Glazov Tatars*, Kara Tatars*, Kasimov Tatars*, Krjashen* Tatars, Lithuanian Tatars*, and Mishar* Tatars*. The Tatar population is one of the most rapidly growing in the CIS. Soviet census takers placed the Tatar population at 2,916,536 in 1926, 4,967,701 in 1959, 5,930,670 in 1970, 6,317,468 in 1979, and 6,645,588 in 1989.

The *glasnost* and *perestroika* policies of Mikhail Gorbachev, as well as the centrifugal ethnic forces operating in Russia and the Soviet Union in the late 1980s and early 1990s, set in motion an increasingly strident variety of Tatar nationalism. Groups such as the Mardzhani Society, *Tugan Yak* (Our Father's Land), *Bulgar el jadid* (New Bulgar), Society of Cultural Ecology, Tatar Public Center, and *Ittifak* (Alliance) National Independence Party, and the *Suverenitet* (Sovereignty) Committee appeared. The most radical Tatar leaders, such as Fauzia Bairamova, called for an independent Tatar Republic in 1991. They also wanted to expand Tatar political reach well beyond the boundaries of the Tatar Autonomous Republic to include all lands ever controlled historically by Tatars— more than half of Russia. But, in 1990, only half of the Tatar Autonomous Republic was ethnic Tatar; most of the others were ethnic Russians who controlled the cities and opposed Tatar independence.

Other groups advocated the creation of a Greater Tataria to unite the Tatar Autonomous Republic with the Mari Autonomous Republic, and Chuvash Autonomous Republic, the Udmurt Autonomous Republic, and portions of Ulyanovsk, Kuybyshev, and Orenburg. Between 1917 and 1919, many Tatar nationalists had campaigned for creation of a Volga-Urals state, which would have included the Tatars, Maris*, Chuvashes*, and Bashkirs*, but the Bolsheviks opted for the smaller Tatar Autonomous Soviet Socialist Republic, which they established in 1920. Dreams of a more expansive Tatar political entity revived in the late 1980s and early 1990s.

Tatarstan began taking formal steps toward independence in August 1990, when its supreme soviet adopted the ''Declaration on the State Sovereignty of the Republic of Tatarstan.'' In February 1992, Tatarstan stopped sending tax revenues to Russia, and, in March 1992, leaders of Tatarstan held a referendum on sovereignty. More than 61 percent of the 2,132,000 people who voted approved the resolution for state sovereignty and absolute control of natural resources, especially the huge oil and natural gas reserves in the Tatar Autonomous Republic. Mintimer Sharimiyev, president of Tatarstan, also refused to sign the union treaty in 1992. To do so, he argued, would be tantamount to denying the Tatar right to sovereignty. The supreme soviet of Tatarstan also began debating secession from Russia, primarily because it resented the loss of 30,000,000 tons of their own oil to Russia each year. Russian President Boris Yeltsin denounced all plans for an independent Tatarstan, since Russia's loss of the region would be a strategic and economic disaster.

REFERENCES: Alexandre Bennigsen and S. Enders Wimbush, *Muslims of the Soviet Empire: A Guide*, 1986; *Current Digest*, 41 (February 22, 1989), 1–2; 43 (December 25, 1991), 1–6; 44 (April 15, 1992), 24–25; and (April 22, 1992), 6–8; Alan W. Fisher, *The Crimean Tatars*, 1987; Chantal Lemercier-Quelquejay, ''The Crimean Tatars: A Retrospective Summary,'' *Central Asian Review*, 16 (1968), 15–25; Azade-Ayse Rorlich, *The Volga Tatars: A Profile in National Resilience*, 1986; and Ann Sheehy, *The Crimean Tatars and Volga Germans: Soviet Treatment of Two National Minorities*, 1971.

TATAR OF TRANSCAUCASIA. See AZERBAIJANI.

TATARY. See TATAR.

TATI. See TAT.

TATI JEW. See MOUNTAIN JEW and JEW.

TATSKIY EVREI. See MOUNTAIN JEW and JEW.

TATSKIY EVREY. See MOUNTAIN JEW and JEW.

TATSKIY IEVREI. See MOUNTAIN JEW and JEW.

TATSKIY YEVREI. See MOUNTAIN JEW and JEW.

TATSKIY YEVREY. See MOUNTAIN JEW and JEW.

TATY. See TAT.

TATY JEW. See JEW.

TATYSH. See KACHA and KHAKASS.

TAUL. See OSSETIAN.

TAULLAG. See OSSETIAN.

TAULU. See MOUNTAINEER.

TAURIDE TATARY. See CRIMEAN TATAR.

TAVARICHESKIJE TATAR. See CRIMEAN TATAR.

TAVAS. See CHUVASH.

TAVGI SAMODI. See NGANASAN.

TAVGI SAMOED. See NGANASAN.

TAVGI SAMOIED. See NGANASAN.

TAVGI SAMOYED. See NGANASAN.

TAVLIN. See MOUNTAINEER and CAUCASIAN MOUNTAINEER.

TAVLINTSY. See MOUNTAINEER and CAUCASIAN MOUNTAINEER.

TAYA. See SAGAI or KHAKASS.

TAZ. The Taz are one of the two groups comprising the Taz Turukhan Selkups*, who constitute the northern, or tundra, branch of the Selkups*. The Taz live in the tundra of the Yamalo-Nenets Autonomous Oblast. See SELKUP.
REFERENCE: Ronald Wixman, *The Peoples of the USSR: An Ethnographic Handbook*, 1984.

TAZ SELKUP. The Taz Selkup are one of the groups making up the northern, or tundra, Selkups*. That group has also been called the Taz Turukhan Selkup. See SELKUP.
REFERENCE: Ronald Wixman, *The Peoples of the USSR: An Ethnographic Handbook*, 1984.

TAZ TURUHAN SELKUP. See TAZ TURUKHAN SELKUP.

TAZ TURUKHAN SELKUP. The Taz Turukhan Selkup are the northern or Tundra Selkups*. They live in northwestern Siberia, in the Yamalo-Nenets Autonomous Oblast and are ethnically distinct from the Narym Selkups*, who live in the forests farther to the south. The Taz Turukhan Selkup are themselves divided by dialect into the Taz* and the Turukhan. See SELKUP.
REFERENCE: Ronald Wixman, *The Peoples of the USSR: An Ethnographic Handbook*, 1984.

TEKEINTSY. See TEKKE and TURKMEN.

TEKIN. See TEKKE and TURKMEN.

TEKKE. The Tekke are the largest subgroup of the Turkmen*, constituting more than a third of the Turkmen population. During the 1920s, the Tekke violently resisted the incorporation of Turkmenistan into the Soviet Union. At the time, large numbers of the Tekke fled across the border into Afghanistan. Those who stayed behind live primarily in the Murgab and Tedzhen river basins and in the foothills of the Turkmen Republic, especially between Kopet Dagh and Kyzyl-Armavat to the west and Zangezur Karakum to the north. See TURKMEN.
REFERENCE: Ronald Wixman, *The Peoples of the USSR: An Ethnographic Handbook*, 1984.

TELENGIT. The Telengits—also known as the Tolos, Telesy, Chui, Uryankhai Kalmyk, and Chui-kizhi—are classified as a subgroup of the Altais*. As early as the sixth century, they were present in the Turkish Khanate of southern Siberia. Today most of them live along the Chulyshman, Chuja, and Argut rivers of the Gorno-Altai Autonomous Province. Most of them still work in animal husbandry on collective farms, although a few also labor as miners. They speak a southern Altai dialect and are nominally Christians. See ALTAI.
REFERENCES: Shirin Akiner, *The Islamic Peoples of the Soviet Union*, 1983; Alexandre Bennigsen and S. Enders Wimbush, *Muslims of the Soviet Empire: A Guide*, 1986; Ronald Wixman, *The Peoples of the USSR: An Ethnographic Handbook*, 1984.

TELENGUT. See TELEUT.

TELESI. See TELESY and ALTAI.

TELESY. The Telesy are considered to be a subgroup of the southern Altais*. They are of Turkish origin. See ALTAI.
REFERENCE: Ronald Wixman, *The Peoples of the USSR: An Ethnographic Handbook*, 1984.

TELEUT. The Teleuts, who call themselves the Telenguts and are also known as White Kalmyks*, are a Turkic-speaking people who live along the Great Bachat River and the Little Bachat River in the Kemerovo region of Russia. They speak a southern Altai* dialect that is closely related to Kyrgyz*. Russian* ethnographers have long classified them as Altais. From the sixth to the eighth centuries, the Teleuts were under the control of the Turkish Khanate of southern Siberia, where they lived between the Irtysh and Ob' rivers and were vassals of the Kalmyks and Altais. Today they are heavily russified, although most of them are Sunni Muslims. See ALTAI.
REFERENCES: Shirin Akiner, *The Islamic Peoples of the Soviet Union*, 1983; Alexandre Bennigsen and S. Enders Wimbush, *Muslims of the Soviet Empire: A Guide*, 1986; Ronald Wixman, *The Peoples of the USSR: An Ethnographic Handbook*, 1984.

TEMIRGOI. The Temirgoi have also been known historically as the Kemirgoi and the Chemgui. They are one of the major subgroups of the Altai* people. Since the years of the great migration to Turkey after the failed Shamil rebellion in the 1850s, most Temirgoi have lived in Turkey. Those who remained in what is now the Commonwealth of Independent States are concentrated demographically between the lower Laba and Belaya rivers in the western reaches of the North Caucasus. See ADYGHE, CHERKESS, and CIRCASSIAN.
REFERENCE: Ronald Wixman, *The Peoples of the USSR: An Ethnographic Handbook*, 1984.

TEMIRGOJ. See TEMIRGOI.

TEMIRGOY. See TEMIRGOI, ADYGHE, and CIRCASSIAN.

TENGUSHEV. See TENGUSHEV MORDVINIAN and MORD-VINIAN.

TENGUSHEV ERZIA. See TENGUSHEV MORDVINIAN and MORD-VINIAN.

TENGUSHEV ERZYA. See TENGUSHEV MORDVINIAN and MORD-VINIAN.

TENGUSHEV MORDOVIAN. See TENGUSHEV MORDVINIAN and MORD-VINIAN.

TENGUSHEV MORDVA. See TENGUSHEV MORDVINIAN and MORD-VINIAN.

TENGUSHEV MORDVIN. See TENGUSHEV MORDVINIAN and MORD-VINIAN.

TENGUSHEV MORDVINIAN. The Tengushev Mordvinians are actually a group of Erzya* Mordvinians who migrated out of the Middle Volga region in the seventeenth century to the southern part of the Mordvinian Autonomous Republic. Over the decades, they have evolved into a third Mordvinian* group. See MORDVINIAN.
REFERENCE: Ronald Wixman, *The Peoples of the USSR: An Ethnographic Handbook,* 1984.

TEPTER. See BASHKIR and TEPTYAR.

TEPTIAR. See BASHKIR and TEPTYAR.

TEPTJAR. See BASHKIR and TEPTYAR.

TEPTJARI. See BASHKIR and TEPTYAR.

TEPTYAR. Originally, the term "Teptyar" (Teptjar, Teptiar) was not really an ethnic classification. Instead, it was an administrative term used by Bashkirs* to describe the rents paid to them by the Turkic* and Finno-Ugrian* peoples—Tatars*, Chuvashes*, Maris*, Mordvinians*, and Udmurts*—who had relocated to the Volga region after the fall of the Kazan Khanate in 1552. More specifically, the Teptyars were Volga Tatars* who had made the migration eastward after 1552. They settled as peasants among the Bashkirs and had to pay the special tribute that earned them their name. Most of them were converted to Islam by the Bashkirs and assimilated to the Bashkir language and culture. Nevertheless, they maintained a distinct identity in Bashkiria and called themselves Tipters. Their language is a mix of Tatar and Bashkir. Ever since the early 1930s, Russians* have classified them as Bashkirs, although they still refer to them as the Teptjari. See BASHKIR.
REFERENCE: Alexandre Bennigsen and S. Enders Wimbush, *Muslims of the Soviet Empire: A Guide,* 1986.

TEREK COSSACK. The Terek Cossacks emerged from the Don Cossacks* in the sixteenth century. Like the Greben Cossacks*, Terek Cossack culture contained many North Caucasian elements, although in their case, the contributing cultures were the Ossetian*, Circassian*, and Nogai*. The Terek Cossacks lived in the central steppes of the North Caucasus. See COSSACK.
REFERENCES: Philip Longworth, *The Cossacks,* 1969; Ronald Wixman, *The Peoples of the USSR: An Ethnographic Handbook,* 1984.

TERIUHAN MORDOVIAN. See TERYUKHAN MORDVINIAN and MORDVINIAN.

TERIUHAN MORDVA. See TERYUKHAN MORDVINIAN and MORDVINIAN.

TERIUHAN MORDVIN. See TERYUKHAN MORDVINIAN and MORD-VINIAN.

TERIUHAN MORDVINIAN. See TERYUKHAN MORDVINIAN and MORD-VINIAN.

TERIUKHAN MORDOVIAN. See TERYUKHAN MORDVINIAN and MORD-VINIAN.

TERIUKHAN MORDVA. See TERYUKHAN MORDVINIAN and MORD-VINIAN.

TERIUKHAN MORDVIN. See TERYUKHAN MORDVINIAN and MORD-VINIAN.

TERIUKHAN MORDVINIAN. See TERYUKHAN MORDVINIAN and MORD-VINIAN.

TERYUHAN MORDOVIAN. See TERYUKHAN MORDVINIAN and MORD-VINIAN.

TERYUHAN MORDVA. See TERYUKHAN MORDVINIAN and MORD-VINIAN.

TERYUHAN MORDVIN. See TERYUKHAN MORDVINIAN and MORD-VINIAN.

TERYUHAN MORDVINIAN. See TERYUKHAN MORDVINIAN and MORD-VINIAN.

TERYUKHAN MORDOVIAN. See TERYUKHAN MORDVINIAN and MORD-VINIAN.

TERYUKHAN MORDVA. See TERYUKHAN MORDVINIAN and MORD-VINIAN.

TERYUKHAN MORDVIN. See TERYUKHAN MORDVINIAN and MORD-VINIAN.

TERYUKHAN MORDVINIAN. The Teryukhan Mordvinians are a tiny group of Mordvinians* who live near the city of Nizhni Novgorod in Russia. Although they no longer speak Mordvinian and have been assimilated, culturally and linguistically, by the surrounding Russian* population, many of them are still aware of their Mordvinian roots. See MORDVINIAN.

REFERENCE: Ronald Wixman, *The Peoples of the USSR: An Ethnographic Handbook*, 1984.

TEUT. See ICHKILAK and KYRGYZ.

TIIN. The Tiin are a subgroup of the Kacha*, who are themselves a subgroup of the Khakass*. See KHAKASS.
REFERENCE: Ronald Wixman, *The Peoples of the USSR: An Ethnographic Handbook*, 1984.

TIM. See TYM SELKUP and SELKUP.

TIM KARAKON. See TYM SELKUP and SELKUP.

TIM KARAKON OSTIAK. See TYM SELKUP and SELKUP.

TIM KARAKON OSTYAK. See TYM SELKUP and SELKUP.

TIN. See TINN and KHAKASS.

TINDAL. See TINDI and AVAR.

TINDALY. See TINDI.

TINDI. The Tindi, who call themselves the Idaraw Hekwa, have also been known historically as the Idari, Idera, Iderin, and Iderintsy. Today they are classified by ethnologists as a subgroup of the Avars*, but their identity as members of a village in the high valleys of southwestern Daghestan is actually stronger than their sense of being generically Tindi. Like the Avars, they are Sunni Muslims. Although it is difficult to provide a contemporary population estimate for the Tindis, demographers believe that there are as many as 10,000 people in western Daghestan who identify themselves as Tindi or are aware of their Tindi heritage. See AVAR.
REFERENCES: Shirin Akiner, *Islamic Peoples of the Soviet Union*, 1983; Ronald Wixman, *The Peoples of the USSR: An Ethnographic Handbook*, 1984.

TINDIGYET. See KET.

TINDII. See TINDI.

TIPTER. See TEPTYAR and BASHKIR.

TIUMEN TATAR. See TJUMEN TATAR.

TIURK. See AZERBAIJANI, TURK, UZBEK, and TURK OF FERGANA AND SAMARAKAND.

TIURK OF FERGANA AND SAMARKAND. See AZERBAIJANI, TURK, UZBEK, and TURK OF FERGANA AND SAMARAKAND.

TIURK OF FERGHANA AND SAMARKAND. See AZERBAIJANI, TURK, UZBEK, and TURK OF FERGANA AND SAMARAKAND.

TIURKI. See AZERBAIJANI, TURK, UZBEK, and TURK OF FERGANA AND SAMARAKAND.

TIVER. See UKRAINIAN.

TIVERIAN. See UKRAINIAN.

TIVERTSY. See UKRAINIAN.

TJUMEN TATAR. The Tjumen Tatars are part of the larger collection of Siberian Tatars*. They live today near the towns of Tjumen and Jalutorovsk. They were converted to the Sunni Muslim faith, Hanafi school, by Islamic merchants in the fourteenth and fifteenth centuries. The Tjumen Tatars were affected only slightly by the arrival of Russians* and the Russian conquest in the late sixteenth and early seventeenth centuries, but eventually, the Russian settlers pushed some Tatars off the land. That process accelerated after the 1760s, when the Moscow-Siberian Highway brought hundreds of thousands of Russian settlers. The city of Tjumen boomed, and the Tjumen Tatars were quickly absorbed into a commercial economy. The completion of the Trans-Siberian Railroad in the early 1900s brought large numbers of Ukrainian* and Belarusian* settlers as well. The Tjumen Tatars abandoned their traditional economic habits and became workers in new commercial enterprises. Because of the presence of so many Russians, Ukrainians, and Belarusians, the Tjumen Tatars lost much of their culture, even though they managed to retain their sense of being Tatar. They numbered approximately 20,000 people in the 1980s, but they were in a state of rapid assimilation with surrounding Russians. See TATAR.
REFERENCE: Shirin Akiner, *Islamic Peoples of the Soviet Union*, 1983; James Forsyth, *A History of the Peoples of Siberia*, 1992.

TLISI. See BAGULAL and AVAR.

TOBOL TATAR. The Tobol Tatars are part of the larger collection of Siberian Tatars*. They live today on the Tobol River and on the Irtysh River between Tara and Tobolsk. The origins of the Tobol Tatars go back to the Mongol* invasions of Siberia in the thirteenth century. The Siberian Khanate developed in the region, and the Tatars in Tobolsk were one of the constituent groups.

Islamic merchants working the trade routes between Russian Siberia and Central Asia introduced Islam to the people of Tobolsk in the late fourteenth century; the conversion of the Tobol Tatars took place slowly over the next several centuries. They gradually became loyal to the Hanafi school of the Sunni Muslim faith. Russia conquered Tobolsk in 1587, and, throughout the seventeenth century, a steady if small stream of ethnic Russians* reached the region. It was not until the 1760s, however, when Russians completed construction of the Moscow-Siberian Highway, that a mass influx of Russians took place, setting in motion the gradual loss of the more overt aspects of Tobol Tatar culture. That process has continued. Today, there are approximately 30,000 people who are aware of their Tobol Tatar roots, even though they have been thoroughly russified. See TATAR.

REFERENCES: Shirin Akiner, *Islamic Peoples of the Soviet Union*, 1983; James Forsyth, *A History of the Peoples of Siberia*, 1992.

TOBOLIK. See TOBOL TATAR and TATAR.

TOBOLIQ. See TOBOL TATAR and TATAR.

TOBOLUK. See TOBOL TATAR and TATAR.

TOBOLUQ. See TOBOL TATAR and TATAR.

TOBOLYK. See TOBOL TATAR and TATAR.

TOBOLYQ. See TOBOL TATAR and TATAR.

TODJAN. See TODZHAN, TUVINIAN, and TOFALAR.

TODZHAN. The Todzhan consist of several hundred people of Tuvinian* extraction who settled in the Irkutsk Oblast. They are surrounded by Tofalars* and have adopted many Tofalar cultural characteristics. See TUVINIAN or TOFALAR.

REFERENCE:Ronald Wixman, *The Peoples of the USSR: An Ethnographic Handbook*, 1984.

TOFA. See TOFALAR.

TOFALAR. The Tofalars (Tofas), who call themselves the Tubalar, are a tiny Russian* ethnic group who live primarily in the Irkutsk Oblast in south-central Siberia. They were formerly known as the Karagas*. Collectively, the Tofalars have roots among a variety of Turkic*, Mongol*, Samoyedic*, and Kettic* peoples. Historically, the Tofalars roamed widely across the northern slopes of the Eastern Sayan Mountains and, because of the steppe and mountain-steppe geography of the region, had a long history of contact with one another. Their original home was in the foothills of the Sayan Mountains, but they migrated to their present homeland beginning in the seventeenth century. The upper Yenesei River valley is characterized by three distinct economic life-styles. The groups dwelling in the mountainous forests make their living by hunting and herding reindeer. Those living in the high forests and meadows are more likely to support themselves by raising horses and cattle, as well as by hunting. People on the steppes pursue a full-fledged pastoral life-style, primarily raising horses, cattle, goats, and sheep. The Tofalar language is heavily Turkic in its base. Ethnolinguists classify it as belonging to the Old Uigur* group of the eastern division of the Turkic branch of the Uralo-Altaic linguistic family.

The Tofalars are related culturally, linguistically, and ethnically to the Tuvinians*. Another prominent Tuvinian subgroup, the Todzhans*, today lives among the Tofalars and has adopted the Tofalar language. The Tuvinian Autonomous Oblast, which is located in south-central Siberia, sits on the northern border of Mongolia and was not incorporated into the Soviet Union until 1944. Until 1911, the Tuva region was politically part of Outer Mongolia, which was controlled by the Ch'ing Empire out of Beijing, China. Although Tuva declared its independence from China in 1912, a tripartite agreement between China, Russia, and Tuva in 1915 left the region autonomous but still within Beijing's sphere of influence. During the Russian Revolution and the subsequent civil war, control of Tuva frequently changed hands between various Red and White armies. When the dust settled after the revolution, Tuva was known as the Tuva People's Republic, an autonomous state under Soviet sovereignty; its capital was Kyzyl. Of course, it was really a sub-unit of the Russian Federation of the Soviet Union, autonomous in name only. In 1961, it became known as the Tuvinian Autonomous Soviet Socialist Republic.

What separated the Tofalars from the Tuvinians more than anything else was their willingness to adapt to Russian cultural influences in the eighteenth and nineteenth centuries. While the Tuvinians held fast to their Lamaist Buddhist traditions, most Tofalars converted to Russian Orthodox Christianity. Likewise, the Tuvinians resisted speaking Russian, even as a second language, while the Tofalars readily adopted it. Not surprisingly, the Tofalars are far more likely to intermarry with ethnic Russians than are the Tuvinians. With the establishment of Soviet control after the Bolshevik Revolution came Soviet economic and cultural models; collective farming and herding were imposed on Tofalar pastoralists. The herdsmen resisted the collectivization process, however, and the Stalin regime liquidated many of them, which explains the decline in the Tofalar population from nearly 3,000 people in 1926 to only 620 in 1979. The Tofalar population had increased to nearly 700 people in the 1989 census, but most of that growth was in the Todzhan group. The Tofalars themselves are in an advanced state of assimilation with ethnic Russians. Many of them still pursue traditional economic activities, primarily hunting, trapping, and reindeer herding.

REFERENCES: Sevyan Vainshtein, *Nomads of South Siberia: The Pastoral Economies of Tuva*, 1985; A. S. Stein, *Innermost Asia*, 1928; H. H. Vreeland, *Mongol Community and Kinship Structure*, 1957; Ronald Wixman, *The Peoples of the USSR: An Ethnographic Handbook*, 1984.

TOJAN. See TODZHAN, TUVINIAN, and TOFALAR.

TOKHTAM. See NOGAI.

TOLISH. See TALYSH and AZERBAIJANI.

TOLO. See TELENGIT and ALTAI.

TOM. See SAGAI and KHAKASS.

TOM SAGAI. See SAGAI and KHAKASS.

TOMPON. See EVEN.

TOMSK TATAR. The Tomsk Tatars are part of the larger collection of Siberian Tatars*. They live today near Tomsk in southern Siberia. The Tomsk Tatars descend from the Siberian Tatars who themselves began with the Mongol* invasion of Russia in the thirteenth century. Russians* established a fort at Tomsk in 1604, and with the assistance of Khants* and Tobol Tatars*, they conquered the region. By that time, Islamic merchants working the trade routes between Russian Siberia and Central Asia had already introduced Sunni Muslim beliefs of the Hanafi school to the Tomsk Tatars. The Islamic conversion process was aided by the arrival of Muslim refugees from the Kuchum Khanate in the mid-eighteenth century. In spite of the arrival of hundreds of thousands of Russians to the Tom River Valley, the Tomsk Tatars managed to retain their religion, language, and national culture into the twentieth century. Soviet authorities collectivized the Tomsk Tatars in the 1930s. The assimilation process has continued throughout the twentieth century, but there are still several thousand people in and around Tomsk in western Siberia who are aware of their Tomsk Tatar roots.
REFERENCES: Shirin Akiner, *Islamic Peoples of the Soviet Union*, 1983; James Forsyth, *A History of the Peoples of Siberia*, 1992.

TONGUS. See EVENK and BURYAT.

TOOLOO. See ICHKILIK and KYRGYZ.

TORGOUT. The Torgout are one of the subgroups of the Kalmyk*. Their identity has both a tribal and a territorial dimension. For the most part, they live in the southeastern region of the Kalmyk Autonomous Republic. See KALMYK.

REFERENCE: Ronald Wixman, *The Peoples of the USSR: An Ethnographic Handbook*, 1984.

TRAMA. See KARACHAI.

TRANSBAIKAL BURIAT. See BURYAT.

TRANSBAIKAL BURYAT. See BURYAT.

TRANSBAIKAL COSSACK. The Transbaikal, or Zabaikal, Cossacks are descended from the Ural Cossacks*. They first appeared as a distinct group in the late eighteenth century, and their ethnic roots were Russian*, Buryat*, and Evenk*. The Transbaikal Cossacks lived near Lake Baikal in southern Siberia. See COSSACKS.
REFERENCES: Philip Longworth, *The Cossacks*, 1969; Ronald Wixman, *The Peoples of the USSR: An Ethnographic Handbook*, 1984.

TRANSBAYKAL BURIAT. See BURYAT.

TRANSBAYKAL COSSACK. See TRANSBAIKAL COSSACK and COSSACK.

TRANSCAUCASIAN. See PEOPLES OF TRANSCAUCASIA.

TRANSCAUCASIAN TATAR. See AZERBAIJANI.

TRANSDANUBIAN COSSACKS. See COSSACK.

TRUCHMEN. See TRUKHMEN.

TRUCHMENY. See TRUKHMEN.

TRUKHMEN. The Trukhmen are today considered a subgroup of the Nogais*, although their origins are in Turkmenistan. They call themselves the Turkpen. In the seventeenth century, they left the Mangyshlak Peninsula in Turkmenistan and settled among the Nogais in the North Caucasus. At the time, they belonged to the Chaudor tribe; like the Turkmen*, they are Sunni Muslims. Since then, they have been steadily assimilated by the Nogai, although they still speak a Turkmen dialect—one loaded with Russian*, Nogai, and Kalmyk* words. The Trukhmen live primarily in the Stavropol Krai in the Nogai steppes of the North Caucasus. They number today approximately 10,000 people and are sometimes referred to as Stavropol Turkmen. See TURKMEN or NOGAI.

REFERENCES: Shirin Akiner, *Islamic Peoples of the Soviet Union*, 1983; Ronald Wixman, *The Peoples of the USSR: An Ethnographic Handbook*, 1984.

TRUKHMEN OF STAVRAPOL. See TRUKHMEN.

TSAHUR. See TSAKHUR.

TSAKHIGHALI. See TSAKHUR.

TSAKHUR. The Tsakhur, who call themselves the Tsakhighali, are a small Daghestani* ethnic group in the former Soviet Union; Russians* refer to them as the Tsakhury. They are typically included by ethnologists as one of the many small Samurian groups of southern Daghestan. They live in thirteen villages in the district of Rutul in the highest reaches of the Samur Valley in the Daghestan Soviet Socialist Republic. Smaller groups of Tsakhur live in the districts of Zakataly, Kakh, and Belokany in the Azerbaijan Republic. Those Tsakhur living in Azerbaijan are being assimilated by Azeri-speaking people, while those in Daghestan continue to be linguistically independent. Although demographers disagree about the size of the Tsakhur population, it today numbers approximately 15,000 people.

Ethnologists believe that the Tsakhurs are an indigenous people of the Caucasus mountains. Historically, they have lived in the most geographically remote valleys in the mountains; consequently, they have been isolated from the larger world. During the Arab* invasion of the Caucasus in the eighth century, however, the Tsakhurs adopted Islam. By the 1400s, the Tsakhurs had undergone a process of political consolidation, establishing a confederation of the various Tsakhur groups led by a sultan. Russian expansion reached the Tsakhurs in 1803, but government policy allowed the Tsakhur Sultanate to exist officially and to enjoy a limited autonomy.

During the nineteenth and twentieth centuries, the policies of the tsars and then of the Communist governments alienated the Tsakhur and intensified their sense of ethnic solidarity with other highland and Muslim peoples in the Soviet Union. As large numbers of ethnic Russian settlers poured into the Transcaucasian region in the nineteenth and early twentieth centuries, the Tsakhurs found themselves confronted by an alien people who enjoyed the backing of the state. The Russian settlers brought commercialized forms of agriculture and animal husbandry, and they managed to seize large areas of land from native Daghestanis, including the Tsakhur. The presence of these ethnic Russians in the Daghestani region led to the Shamil Rebellion between 1834 and 1858. Daghestanis in general resented the Russians, and, in 1834, Imam Shamil, an Avar* Muslim leader, declared independence for Daghestan and imposed the Koran as the law of the land. He thus sought to crush out older animistic beliefs and fought the Russian Orthodox Church. When the Shamil Revolt reached the Tsakhurs in 1844, Sultan Daniel-Bek supported the rebels against the Russian government.

In retaliation, Russia forcibly deported the entire Tsakhur population to Azerbaijan in 1852; there they remained until 1860. The Shamil Revolt collapsed in 1858. By that time, Daghestani and Tsakhur hatred for everything Russian was complete.

Like most other inhabitants of the region, the Tsakhurs are Sunni Muslim in their religious loyalties. Within that Sunni faith, most are devoted to the Shafi theological school. Islam came to the Tsakhur from three directions. Arab traders first began introducing the religion in the eighth century; Persian* traders then brought it into the area beginning in the fifteenth century; finally, Mongol* invaders carried it in from the north in the sixteenth and seventeenth centuries. By the mid-nineteenth century, the Tsakhurs had been thoroughly converted, religiously and culturally, to Sunni Muslim values and beliefs. They remain devoted to the faith, attending mosque regularly, praying daily, circumcising male children, and conducting regular Muslim ceremonies for marriages and funerals.

Governmental pressures first to russianize and then to sovietize the Tsakhur people continued during the twentieth century. Just after the Russian Revolution, the Soviet government tried to placate those who wanted to create a single Islamic state out of the entire Muslim population of the North Caucasus region. They established the Mountain Autonomous Republic in 1920, with Arabic as the official language. Most Tsakhurs, as well as other ethnic Daghestanis, however, had no love for Arabic and opposed the decision. They resisted the government, and, in 1921, the state created the Daghestan Autonomous Soviet Socialist Republic as an ethnic subdivision of the larger republic. Policy changed again a few years later, and Arabic ceased to be the official language. In the late 1920s, the Soviet government conducted an intense anti-Islamic campaign that included widespread imprisonment and the execution of local religious leaders. The government tried to develop a literary language for the Tsakhurs in 1932, but this policy was soon abandoned. Avar was then declared to be the Tsakhur written language, but, in 1938, Russian became the only language of instruction in public schools. Early in the 1960s, state policy prohibited the teaching of Tsakhur, as well as of the other Daghestani languages, in the public schools.

In addition to trying to russianize Tsakhur culture, the government worked diligently at sovietizing the Tsakhur economy. Traditionally, the Tsakhur owned their land and livestock herds communally, so the Soviet government converted those ethnic communal arrangements into economic collectives, with the government owning the land and the herds. The Tsakhurs had to sell their produce to government collectives at state-mandated prices, and, in the end, the Tsakhurs came to feel that their economic situation was deteriorating. Because of the state-controlled economy and the heavy-handed attempts to change Tsakhur culture, the Tsakhur sense of ethnicity has only intensified over the years, becoming distinctly anti-Communist, anti-Russian, and anti-Christian. More than 99 percent of ethnic Tsakhurs speak the native language and are intensely loyal to their Muslim faith. Today they are among the Soviet Union's most nationalist people and are clamoring for independence from Moscow, although that sense of nationality is not confined to just their own people. Indeed, the Tsakhurs feel a trans-ethnic kinship with other Muslims, as well as with other Daghestani mountaineers.

REFERENCES: Alexandre Bennigsen and S. Enders Wimbush, *Muslims of the Soviet Empire: A Guide*, 1986; Alexandre Bennigsen, "Muslim Conservative Opposition to the Soviet Regime: The Sufi Brotherhoods in the North Caucusus," in Jeremy R. Azrael, ed., *Soviet Nationality Policies and Practices*, 1978; Vladimir Rogov, *Languages and Peoples of the USSR*, 1966; Ronald Wixman, *Language Aspects of Ethnic Patterns and Processes in the North Caucusus*, 1980; George Feizuillin, "The Persecution of National-Religious Traditions of the Moslems of the USSR," *Caucasian Review*, 3 (1956), 69–76; Ronald Wixman, "Daghestanis," in Richard V. Weekes, ed., *Muslim Peoples*, 1984, 211–19; Ronald Wixman, *The Peoples of the USSR: An Ethnographic Handbook*, 1984.

TSAKHURIS. See TSAKHUR.

TSAKHURY. See TSAKHUR.

TSATSAN. See CHECHEN.

TSES. See DIDOI and AVAR.

TSEZ. See DIDOI and AVAR.

TSEZY. See DIDOI and AVAR.

TSIGAN. See GYPSY.

TSIGAN SREDNEI AZII. See CENTRAL ASIAN GYPSY.

TSIGANE. See GYPSY.

TSIGANE SREDNEI AZII. See CENTRAL ASIAN GYPSY.

TSORDZH. More than 1,000 people live in the village of Tsordzh in the Pamir Mountains of Tajikistan. Their language is so unusual that some ethnolinguists consider them a distinct ethnic identity, even though they are officially classified as a Pamir* people, who are themselves classified as Tajiks*. See PAMIR PEOPLES or TAJIK.

REFERENCE: Yuri Kushko, "The Pamirs," *Soviet Life* (June 1990), 28–35.

TSOVA. See GEORGIAN.

TSOVA TUSH. See BATSBI and GEORGIAN.

TSOVA TUSHIN. See BATSBI and GEORGIAN.

TSOVA TUSHINTSY. See BATSBI and GEORGIAN.

TSUDAKHAR. See DARGIN.

TSYGAN. See GYPSY.

TSYGAN SREDNEI AZII. See CENTRAL ASIAN GYPSY.

TSYGANE. See GYPSY.

TSYGANE SREDNEI AZII. See CENTRAL ASIAN GYPSY.

TUAL. See TUALLAG and OSSETIAN.

TUALLAG. The Tuallags have their ethnic origins among the Iranian Ossetians*
who were driven into the Caucasus region by Turks* and Mongols*. They are
Eastern Orthodox in religion, closely related culturally and linguistically to the
Iron*, and are being assimilated by the Georgians*. See OSSETIAN or
GEORGIAN.
REFERENCE: Ronald Wixman, *The Peoples of the USSR: An Ethnographic Handbook*,
1984.

TUALTSY. See TUALLAG and OSSETIAN.

TUBA. See KACHA and KHAKASS.

TUBA. See SHOR.

TUBALAR. The term ''Tubalar'' is used by the Tofalars* to describe themselves. It also, however, describes a small subgroup of the Tofalars who eventually became a constituent group of the Altais*. See ALTAI.
REFERENCE: Ronald Wixman, *The Peoples of the USSR: An Ethnographic Handbook*,
1984.

TUBULAR. See TUBALAR.

TUMA. See TUBA.

TUMAN. See CHUKCHI.

TUMEN TATAR. See TJUMEN' TATAR and TATAR.

TUNDRA ENISEI SAMODI. See KHANTAIKA SAMOYED and ENT.

TUNDRA ENISEI SAMOED. See KHANTAIKA SAMOYED and ENT.

TUNDRA ENISEI SAMOIED. See KHANTAIKA SAMOYED and ENT.

TUNDRA ENISEI SAMOYED. See KHANTAIKA SAMOYED and ENT.

TUNDRA ENISEY SAMODI. See KHANTAIKA SAMOYED and ENT.

TUNDRA ENISEY SAMOED. See KHANTAIKA SAMOYED and ENT.

TUNDRA ENISEY SAMOIED. See KHANTAIKA SAMOYED and ENT.

TUNDRA ENISEY SAMOYED. See KHANTAIKA SAMOYED and ENT.

TUNDRA ENT. See KHANTAIKA SAMOYED and ENT.

TUNDRA IENISEI SAMODI. See KHANTAIKA SAMOYED and ENT.

TUNDRA IENISEI SAMOED. See KHANTAIKA SAMOYED and ENT.

TUNDRA IENISEI SAMOIED. See KHANTAIKA SAMOYED and ENT.

TUNDRA IENISEI SAMOYED. See KHANTAIKA SAMOYED and ENT.

TUNDRA IURAK. See TUNDRA NENETS and NENETS.

TUNDRA NENETS. The Tundra Nenets are a Nenets* subgroup. They are
concentrated demographically along the coast of the Arctic Ocean in the Yamalo-
Nenets Autonomous Oblast, the Taymyr Autonomous Oblast, and the Nenets
Autonomous Oblast. See NENETS.
REFERENCE: Ronald Wixman, *The Peoples of the USSR: An Ethnographic Handbook*,
1984.

TUNDRA SELKUP. See SELKUP.

TUNDRA YENISEI SAMODI. See KHANTAIKA SAMOYED and ENT.

TUNDRA YENISEI SAMOED. See KHANTAIKA SAMOYED and ENT.

TUNDRA YENISEI SAMOIED. See KHANTAIKA SAMOYED and ENT.

TUNDRA YENISEI SAMOYED. See KHANTAIKA SAMOYED and ENT.

TUNDRA YENISEY SAMODI. See KHANTAIKA SAMOYED and ENT.

TUNDRA YENISEY SAMOED. See KHANTAIKA SAMOYED and ENT.

TUNDRA YENISEY SAMOIED. See KHANTAIKA SAMOYED and ENT.

TUNDRA YENISEY SAMOYED. See KHANTAIKA SAMOYED and ENT.

TUNDRA YUKAGIR. See YUKAGIR.

TUNDRA YURAK. See TUNDRA NENETS and NENETS.

TUNG-AN. See DUNGAN.

TUNGAS. See EVENK, EVEN, and NEGIDAL.

TUNGAS. See YAKUT.

TUNGUS. See EVENK, EVEN, and NEGIDAL.

TUNGUS. See YAKUT.

TUNGUSIC PEOPLES. The term "Tungusic Peoples" is an older, linguistic reference to those indigenous people in the former Soviet Union who speak a language belonging to the Tungusic branch of the Tunguso-Manchu* group within the Uralic-Altaic language family. The term includes the Evens*, Evenks*, and Negidals*.
REFERENCE: Ronald Wixman, *The Peoples of the USSR: An Ethnographic Handbook*, 1984.

TUNKA SOIOT. See SOYOT, TUVINIAN, and BURYAT.

TUNKA SOYOT. See SOYOT, TUVINIAN, and BURYAT.

TURAN. See SAGAI and KHAKASS.

TURFAN. See TURPAN and UIGUR.

TURFANLIK. See TURPAN and UIGUR.

TURFANLUK. See TURPAN and UIGUR.

TURFANLYK. See TURPAN and UIGUR.

TURK. See AZERBAIJANI.

TURK. The Soviet census of 1926 listed a number of "Ottoman Turks" residing within the Soviet Union, but a major difficulty appears to be in the meaning of the term "Turk" as used by both the census officials and the respondents. Earlier in the twentieth century, when the Ottoman Empire had but recently been liquidated, some individuals could still claim to be Ottoman Turks. The terms "Ottoman" and "Osmanli" were self-conscious and class-bound, rather than technical ethnic appellations; thus, many of the Ottoman ruling class had chosen self-imposed exile rather than life in Kemal Ataturk's republic. Some of these Ottomans retired to a life of relative ease in other Muslim lands, such as Egypt; a few chose instead to live among other closely related Turks, such as the Crimean Tatars*. In the latter years of the empire, the Tatars* had figured heavily in the Ottoman bureaucracy and were considered honorary Ottomans. Individuals claiming to be "Ottoman Turks" in the 1926 census did so, in all likelihood, with full knowledge of the unspoken implications of their actions. The Ottoman Turks are no longer listed separately in the census, so presumably they have either been assimilated or have left the country.

Nonetheless, the more recent census of 1989 counted 207,369 Turks in what is today the Commonwealth of Independent States (CIS). Again, there appears to be little distinction in what is an otherwise generic term. In certain cases, the term "Turk" could denote any inhabitant of the CIS who speaks a Turkic language. For example, some members of the Uzbek* population, who are descended from Turkic tribes that settled in Central Asia from the eleventh to the thirteenth century, were called Turks prior to the Soviets' National Delimitation of 1924, which established homelands for minorities based on their ethnicity. Most modern scholars, such as Bennigsen, believe that the term "Turk" in the Soviet census relates specifically to the Meskhetians*, formerly of the Georgian Republic and now residing in Kazakhstan. This group was deported to Central Asia after World War II. Bennigsen has noted that Soviet literature treating the Turks has been careful to make a distinction between "Turki," or the Turks of modern Turkey; and "Tiurki," a general appellation referring to all Turkic-speaking peoples. The latter term was used before 1935 to refer specifically to Azeri and Transcaucasian Turks. Probably also included in the appellation Turk are some Karapapakhs*, who are Alevi Turkmen* in eastern Armenia; Khemsils*, who are Muslim Armenians* who also speak Turkish; as well as some Kurds*, Crimean Tatars, Azerbaijanis*, Adjars*, and Laz*, who may have declared themselves to be Turks. These groups may have been motivated by the search for national identities under Mikhail Gorbachev's policy of *glasnost*. Two common denominators appear to be the closeness of their spoken or literary languages with modern Turkish and their affinities with the former Ottoman Empire. There is also probably a proportion of the Turkish population of the CIS who emigrated from Turkey for political reasons (e.g., Turkish Communists). Interestingly, there are far more Muslim émigrés (Turks, Cherkesses*, Abkhazians*, Tatars, and others) from the former Russian Empire and Soviet Union living in the Republic of Turkey today than Turkish émigrés in the CIS.

REFERENCES: Shirin Akiner, *Islamic Peoples of the Soviet Union*, 1983; Alexandre Bennigsen and S. Enders Wimbush, *Muslims of the Soviet Empire: A Guide*, 1986.

Lee Brigance Pappas

TURK. The term "Turk" has had a variety of meanings in Russian and Soviet ethnology. It has been used to describe residents of Turkey, Azerbaijanis* in the early decades of the twentieth century, Meskhetians* during the process of their ethnogenesis, the semi-nomadic Uzbeks* living in Fergana and Samarkand, and a few hundred Turkish-speaking people living with Kurds* in Firyuz and Germab in Turkmenistan.

REFERENCE: Ronald Wixman, *The Peoples of the USSR: An Ethnographic Handbook*, 1984.

TURK OF FERGANA AND SAMARKAND. The Turks* of Fergana call themselves the Turki. They are semi-nomadic people who are subdivided into smaller tribes that each maintains a strong sense of identity. They are all Sunni Muslims in religion, and most of them live in the Fergana and the Samarkand oblasts of Uzbekistan. Although Russian* demographers have classified them as an Uzbek* subgroup ever since 1926, they actually have non-Uzbek origins. They are descended from Turkic tribes that arrived in the Fergana Valley long before the Uzbeks. See UZBEK.

REFERENCE: Shirin Akiner, *Islamic Peoples of the Soviet Union*, 1983; Ronald Wixman, *The Peoples of the USSR: An Ethnographic Handbook*, 1984.

TURK OF FERGHANA AND SAMARKAND. See TURK OF FERGANA AND SAMARKAND or UZBEK.

TURKESTANI. The term "Turkestani" is an older, generic reference to the indigenous peoples living in what used to be known as Turkestan—today's Uzbekistan, Tajikistan, Turkmenistan, and Kyrgyzia. Included in this group are the Uzbeks*, Tajiks*, Pamir* peoples, Turkmen*, Kyrgyz*, and Karakalpaks*.

REFERENCE: Ronald Wixman, *The Peoples of the USSR: An Ethnographic Handbook*, 1984.

TURKI. See KHAKASS and TURK OF FERGANA AND SAMARKAND.

TURKI. See UZBEK.

TURKIC PEOPLES. The term "Turkic Peoples" is widely used in what used to be the Soviet Union to describe the indigenous peoples of the country who spoke a Turkic language. Included in this large group are the Bashkirs*, Tatars*, Kumyks*, Karachais*, Balkars*, Kazakhs*, Kyrgyz*, Karakalpaks*, Nogais*, Altais*, Gagauz*, Azerbaijanis*, Chuvashes*, Khakass*, Tuvinians*, Tofalars*, Yakuts*, Turkmen*, Uigurs*, Turks*, Karaims*, Dolgans*, Shors*, and Uzbeks*. Most scholars believe that the Turkic peoples originated in Mongolia and then fanned out across Asia and into Europe. They first appeared as an identifiable group in the sixth century. Their arrival in the former Soviet Union came in three stages. They had appeared in Central Asia and Siberia by the sixth century, in Transcaucasia by the eleventh century, and west of the Volga River by the thirteenth century. For the most part, the Turkic peoples became ethnically dominant in the areas that they conquered, and the Turkic languages spread widely.

The Turkic presence in Central Asia was signified by the rise of the Götürk Empire, or "khaganate," in the sixth century, when nomadic Semirech'e tribes consolidated politically. This empire survived until the eighth century, when the Uigurs seized control; they eventually succumbed in turn to the Kyrgyz. By that time, various Turkic-speaking peoples had penetrated southern Siberia. In the eleventh century, the Seljuk-Oghuz tribes established an empire that reached from the Amu Darya River in the east to the Euphrates River in the west. Turkic speakers spread throughout Transcaucasia. The Mongol* Tatar invasions of the thirteenth century constituted the final stage in the Turkic penetration of what later became the Soviet Union.

REFERENCES: Shirin Akiner, *Islamic Peoples of the Soviet Union*, 1983; Ronald Wixman, *The Peoples of the USSR: An Ethnographic Handbook*, 1984.

TURKMAN. See TURKMEN.

TURKMAN OF STAVROPOL. See TRUKHMAN and TURKMEN.

TURKMEN. The Turkmen are a Central Asian, Turkic-speaking people whose homeland, the Republic of Turkmenistan, is located along the southeastern shore of the Caspian Sea. It is bordered on the northwest by the Republic of Kazakhstan, on the north and northeast by Uzbekistan, on the south by Iran, and on the southeast by Afghanistan. Turkmenistan is primarily a land of deserts. The largest of these is the low-altitude Kara Kum or Black Sand Desert, which occupies four-fifths of the entire country and is the fourth-largest desert in the world. Annual rainfall averages around three to four inches, making Turkmenistan's strong continental climate stiflingly hot and dry in the summer and bitterly cold in the winter. It is not uncommon for the winter temperatures to fall below $-25°$ Farenheit. Since the Kara Kum is too arid to support any significant population, the majority of Turkmen reside in its marginal oases, enjoying foothills and mountains only in the extreme south and southeast. According to the census of

1989, there were 2,718,297 Turkmen in Turkmenistan, out of a total population of 3.6 million, forming a 68 percent majority in their own homeland. The next largest ethnic group in the country is the Russians*, who comprise 13 percent of the population. Other ethnic groups that live in the region include Kazakhs*, Tatars*, Ukrainians*, Armenians*, Karakalpaks*, and Azerbaijanis*. For their part, a small number of Turkmen live in the western regions of Uzbekistan, as well as in Karakalpakia, Tajikistan, Armenia, Azerbaijan, and Turkey. In the seventeenth and eighteenth centuries, a group of Turkmen migrated from the Mangyshlak Peninsula on the Caspian Sea to the Nogai steppes in the northern Caucasus; there they are known as Trukhmen* and form a significant enclave in the Stavropol region.

Turkmen, a Turkic language, belongs to the Oghuz-Turkmen group, in the southwestern (or Oghuz) branch of Uralic-Altaic languages. It is most closely related to the Turkish spoken by the Turks* of Anatolia in the modern Republic of Turkey and to Azerbaijani, as well as to Crimean Tatar*, Gagauz* (Balkan Turkish), Kashgai (southern Iran), and Karaim*. This makes sense because the medieval Oghuz tribes were the direct ancestors of the Turkmen, the Seljuks, the Ottoman Turks, and the Ottomans' descendants, the Anatolian Turks. The main difference between the Anatolian Turks and the Turkmen is that the latter have retained strong tribal and clan divisions, in keeping with the other Central Asian Turkic cultures; this fact manifested itself in the unique political organization of their homeland under Soviet rule. The Turkmen language is divided into numerous distinct but mutually intelligible dialects that correspond to the seven major and twenty-four minor tribal divisions in Turkmen society. The modern literary language of the country is derived from an amalgam of the dialects. In addition, the Turkmen language contains a fund of loan words from Arabic and Persian*, and, to a lesser extent, from the Russian language, due to Turkmenistan's geographic proximity to each of these areas. Some authors maintain that, until the twentieth century, the Turkic peoples of Central Asia had not developed a native alphabet; others claim that they used a written form of Uzbek* and Uigur* popularly known throughout Central Asia as "Turki"; still others insist that they regularly used an unusual Turkic "runic" script that was abandoned when the Turkic peoples converted to Islam. In any case, until the late 1920s, the Turkmen language was written in the Arabic script; from then until 1940, the Latin alphabet was used. The Cyrillic script, introduced by the Russians, has been in use since then. The language of the Trukhmen of the North Caucasus is basically Turkmen that has been influenced by the neighboring Nogai*.

The etymological origins of the term "Turkmen" are unclear. Some surmise that the word was used to distinguish between Muslim and non-Muslim Oghuz peoples, the base stock from whom the Turkmen evolved. To modern Anatolian Turks, however, the word "Turkmen" is used more to identify nomadic, as opposed to sedentary, Turks. The alternate (and archaic) Western spellings, "Turkoman" or "Turcoman," were probably derived from the Persian spelling

"Turkuman"; the "-men" or "-man" suffixes, which resemble English words, are entirely coincidental.

The area familiar as the modern homeland of the Turkmen had been inhabited since prehistoric times by numerous waves of Indo-European peoples, such as the Iranian-speaking Massagetes (Scythians). In the sixth century B.C., the area became part of the empire of the Achaemenid King Cyrus I, and later, in the fourth century B.C., part of the Pathian empire. By the ninth century A.D., Turkmenistan had been successively invaded by the Persian Sassanids (226–651), the Ephthalite Huns (fifth and sixth centuries), and the Perso-Arabic Samanid Empire (903–999).

Turkic tribes had been migrating into western Central Asia, to the area between the Ural Mountains and the Aral Sea, since at least the fifth and sixth centuries A.D. By the end of the seventh century, some of these Turkic tribes were trading with and accepting missionaries from the expanding Islamic empire of the Arabs*. But, most significantly the Oghuz Turks were driven westward by Mongol* and Chinese* pressure, entering the region from their original homelands in Mongolia between the eighth and tenth centuries. The Oghuz very quickly consolidated their hold on the territories to the north of the Syr Darya River, coming to dominate and largely supplant the native Iranian cultures in southern Central Asia. As their culture came into increasingly frequent contact with the Islamic empire, the Oghuz pressed southward into the area between the Caspian Sea and the left bank of the Amu Darya River—the general area of what is modern Turkmenistan. The Oghuz tribes lost no time in establishing trading, religious, and cultural contacts with the highly cosmopolitan, Perso-Arabic, Islamic empire to the south. These Oghuz Turks were mentioned for the first time in chronicles at the end of the tenth century, when the Arab historian Makhdisi referred to them, in connection with their recent conversion to Islam, as "Turkmen." The Turkmen had become Sunni Muslims of the Hanafi school of Sharia law. Even today, the Turkmen have a reputation for a passionate and charismatic, albeit unorthodox, attachment to their faith.

In 1037, two brothers of the dominant Seljuk clan, Chagri and Tughril Bek, led—and sometimes followed—a group of Oghuz Turkmen into the Caucasus region, Mesopotamia, and Asia Minor in the never-ending search for fresh pasturage. After conquering these territories, the brothers established the Seljuk Empire with its capital at Isfahan. In 1040, the Seljuks defeated the Ghaznavids, who themselves had conquered the Samanid Empire to the east. By 1055, they were strong enough to march into western Iran to defeat the Buwayhids, the *mamluk* slave-soldiers who stood between the Seljuks and the caliphal throne in Baghdad. Turkic peoples had been extensively employed throughout Islamic lands as administrators, mercenaries, and mamluks, over predominantly Arab* and Persian* populations well before the eleventh century. But, in the year 1055, Tughil offered his services to the Abbasid Caliph and was appointed Sultan—the secular ruler of a new Middle Eastern empire, with the authority to command the mamluk armies and conquer new territories in the name of Islam. The golden age of Arab-Persian ascendancy was effectively over. The Abbasids became the distinguished but powerless hostages of the Turkmen warriors who purported to serve them.

In 1071, Tughril Bek's nephew, Alp Arslan, defeated the Byzantine army under the emperor Romanus Diogenes at the momentous Battle of Manzikert, opening the way for the conquest of Anatolia. In his wake, the nomadic Oghuz Turkmen drifted across northern Iran and into Anatolia, occupying much of the central Anatolian Plateau region. Later, in 1280, the Seljuks granted a *gazilik* (or march fiefdom) in northwestern Anatolia to another small, obscure Oghuz tribe under the leadership of a chieftain named Osman, instructing him to raid and make holy war against the neighboring Byzantine infidels. The Osmanlis (or "Ottomans," a Western corruption) established a fabulous sprawling empire that had supplanted that of the Seljuks by 1300 and that lasted until the twentieth century. Only two other Oghuz-Turkmen states were founded: the Kara Koyunlu or "Black Sheep" Turkmen (in existence from 1378 to 1469), and the Ak Koyunlu or "White Sheep" Turkmen, 1387–1502, both centered in Azerbaijan and neighboring Armenia.

The Oghuz-Turkmen who migrated westward eventually lost their nomadic life-style and ethnic identity. Those who remained in Central Asia, however, established themselves at Khorasan (the former Ghaznavid capital) and Khwarizm (the Transoxiana region) in the eleventh and twelfth centuries, retained their tribal customs, and came to form the basis of the Turkmen nation. The Turkmen capital of Merv became an important center of commerce and learning. Nonetheless, the Turkmen were by no means effectively united against invaders. In many ways, they were little more than a disparate assortment of feuding tribes, held together only by a shared language and common traditions. As a result, the Mongols had little difficulty in dividing the native Turkmen tribes against one another and conquering their territories. The Mongols' invasion and destruction of Khwarizm in 1219–1223 had as disastrous an effect on Turkmen unity as their invasions had had on other nomadic cultures across Central Asia, a situation on which the Mongols capitalized in their distribution of the Turkmen homelands. The northern Turkmen of the Mangyshlak Peninsula and Khwarizm became part of the *ulus* (tribe) of Jochi, Genghis Khan's first son and founder of the Golden Horde, while the southern Turkmen groups were divided up between the *ulus* of Chagatai and of Hulagu (reigned 1256–1265), grandson of Genghis Khan and founder of the Ilkhanid Empire of Persia and Iraq. It was during the Mongol period that the term "Oghuz" was finally discontinued; since the Turkmen had long ago converted to Islam, little remained of the original shamanistic tribe, and other illustrious Turkmen empires had arisen claiming descent not from the Oghuz but from the Turkmen.

Upon the break-up of the Mongol Empire throughout Central Asia in the fourteenth century, southern Turkmenistan, including the area of Khorasan, came under the control of an ambitious Ilkhanid vizier. This was the Turkic warrior Timur, known to the West as Tamerlane, who launched a series of predatory wars between 1380 and 1387, overrunning Khorasan, Jurjan, Mazandaran, Sijistan, Afghanistan, Fars, Azerbaijan, and Kurdistan, and creating a vast state of these domains with Samarkand as its capital. After Tamerlane's death in 1405, the Azerbaijan region quickly fell, first to the Black Sheep and then to the White Sheep Turkmen. Tamerlane's son and successor, Shah Rukh, carried out several successful campaigns against Kara Yusuf (1390–1420), the leader of the Black Sheep Turkmen and ruler of Azerbaijan, Shirvan, and other regions in the northwest. At length, Yusuf was obliged to recognize the suzerainty of the Timurids, but his successors, Kara Iskender (1420–1437) and Jehan Shah (1437–1467), became rulers over all of northwestern Persia. The Timurid dynasty managed to outlast its Kara Koyunlu (Black Sheep) nemesis by only two years; the last Timurid Shah, Abu Said, died in 1469. The Turkmen soon became involved in empire-building of their own, albeit indirectly.

Turkmenistan had always been susceptible to invasion from the south and had been part of Persian empires since ancient times. In 1501, a Persian nobleman named Ismail, the son of a Persian Sufi mystic of the Safavid order and a White Sheep Turkmen princess, defeated the White Sheep chieftain Alwand. He took Tabriz, the White Sheep capital, and had himself proclaimed shah. In the process, he gained revenge for the murder of his father and brothers by the previous White Sheep leader. He also founded the first native Persian dynasty in centuries. Shah Ismail (1501–1524) had recruited the bulk of his military from Turkmen tribes; they were converts to Shia Islam and known as the *Kizilbash* or "Redheads" after their distinctive red headdresses. These Kizilbash were fanatical followers of Ismail in his role as the head of the Safavid Sufis. Modern scholars surmise that Ismail may have had in mind the creation of a Turkmen state. Certainly, his conquests to the north brought the whole southern portion of Turkmenistan into his empire. During the same period, however, the Turkic Uzbeks had erupted southward into the plains of Transoxiana, laying claim to the northern portions of Turkmenistan for the establishment of their Khanates of Khiva and Bukhara. Meanwhile, to the west, the rise of the Ottomans effectively barred Ismail from extending control into eastern Anatolia, from which he had drawn his most fervent Turkmen supporters. As a result of these external political pressures, the Safavid state was compelled to assume its geographical boundaries, basically those of the modern state of Iran, though somewhat larger, becoming not a Turkmen state as envisioned, but a Persian one.

Turkmenistan, the frontier territory between Safavid Persia and the Uzbek khanates, was the scene of constant warfare between the sixteenth and eighteenth centuries. Paradoxically, it was during this time that the territories of the Turkmen tribes became clearly defined and began vaguely to resemble modern Turkmenistan. Shah Abbas (1585–1626) settled a large Kurdish* population, known for their prowess in battle, in the Kopet Dag region, in order to protect the northeastern borders of his empire. Nadir Shah of the revitalized Afsharid state invaded Turkmenistan in the early eighteenth century and conquered the city-states of

Khiva and Bukhara in 1740. Later in the eighteenth century, the resurgent Bukharan Khanate, under the leadership of the Emir Ma'sum, conquered and leveled the city of Merv in southern Turkmenistan, deporting its entire population to Bukhara and destroying its famous irrigation canals. The Turkmen, for their part, became ingenious at vacillating between the conflicting parties. Together with their martial skills and their pastoral nomadism, this tactic allowed them to maintain their independence. Unfortunately, the Turkmen were not able to use these talents to create a lasting state of their own during this turbulent period, since they came to attach a greater value to tribal, clan, and family loyalties than to any sedentary (hence distant) king or ruler. Only in the nineteenth century would the Turkmen begin the arduous process of unifying under a central government in the face of accelerating Russian expansionism from the north.

Traditionally, all Turkmen lived in round, felt-covered, and highly portable *yurts*, whether they were migratory or not. They used the independence thus gained to maintain their freedom from taxation, conscription, manipulative bureaucrats, and the ever-present threat of land rent. The political organization of Turkmen society evolved to fit their absolute reluctance to submit to outside authority. Even today, the Turkmens' political and cultural life is organized around tribes and clans. For example, although the majority of Turkmen are Sunni Muslims, the Sufi mystical orders are as popular today as the Safavid Shi'a order had been in the sixteenth century. Yet in Turkmenistan, more than in any other territory of Central Asia, the Sufi orders were, and continue to be, closely bound with the tribal structure of the nation. In social organization, patrilineage has always been the norm, with genealogies traced through the male lines, so that all Turkmen in a particular tribe were expected to be able to trace their lineage back to a common ancestor. When an external military threat was considered too great for smaller, less inclusive descent groups, the Turkmen united with several other closely related descent groups to form one large group based on more distant ancestry.

The nature of nomadic herding and the necessity of women's labor made the Islamic tradition of female seclusion, including the wearing of the veil, an impractical luxury. Turkmen women have a reputation for ferocity, working and at times fighting alongside their men. In domestic arrangements, however, the wife will, through custom, politeness, and good breeding, defer to her husband. Extended families—consisting of a man, his wife, their unmarried children, their married sons with their sons' wives and children, all living communally in several tents—continue even today to be the norm in Turkmen society. The head of a household married his daughters off in the order of their birth, collecting a bride price on each one. The young brides then went away to become part of their husbands' households. Likewise, young, married men, upon reaching the age of thirty-five or forty, moved away from their father's tent, again in order of birth, to set up their own households. Indeed, other groups descended from the Turkmen, such as modern Anatolian Turks, who have not been nomadic for hundreds of years and who live in an industrialized, urbanized, politically developed society, still attempt to maintain the extended family relationship, even if they now live in only a three-bedroom apartment.

By the middle of the nineteenth century, the Turkmen tribes were finally beginning to unite, for the first time in their history, under a central government led by the most powerful of their tribes, the Tekke Turkmen. Although this was a positive step, it naturally destabilized the Turkmen polity, rendering it susceptible to the Russian Empire's accelerating advance from the north. The simultaneous British* expansion northward from India into Afghanistan also generated friction and rivalry between the two imperial powers for the possession of southern Central Asia and further destabilized the nascent Turkmen state. In 1868, Russian forces conquered and extended full protectorate status over Turkmenistan's northern and eastern neighbors, the Emirate of Bukhara and the region of Tajikistan. The second of the three Uzbek khanates, Khiva, fell to the Russians in 1873. Finally, after Russia's suppression of the Khokand Uprising of 1873–1876, the tsarist government felt justified in abolishing the Khokand Khanate entirely. With the annexations of the Uzbek khanates and Tajikistan completed, the conquest and subjugation of the Turkmen tribes and their lands became the next Russian objective. The Turkmen tribes never had a chance to form a nation-state or even to coalesce into a confederation before their takeover by the Russians.

The ties with Russia actually went back as early as 1677. The Caspian Trukhmen came under Russian rule, not because they had been defeated by the Russians but because they had encouraged the relationship by declaring themselves to be Muscovite subjects. Other Turkmen tribes followed suit on three different occasions in 1745, 1802, and 1811. Yomud Turkmen fought on the side of Russia against Persia in 1826–1828 and appeared to prefer the Russians to the Uzbek Khivans; they reversed themselves in 1877, however, and resisted the Russian army's attempt to force requisitions from them. By 1850, around 115,000 Turkmen had voluntarily submitted to Russian rule, and, by the 1870s, the entire Tekke Turkmen tribe had applied to become Russian subjects. On the other hand, Peter the Great's first attempted military expedition from the Caspian to the city of Khiva in 1717 ended in its complete annihilation by the Turkmen, who were famous as ferocious warriors. Russian penetration into the area was delayed for over a century because of Turkmen resistance. The Turkmen apparently attempted to engage in the same highly advanced art of vacillation in their dealings with the Russians that they had earlier used against the Persians and Uzbeks. By the mid-nineteenth century, however, the Russians had learned how to deal efficiently with idiosyncratic nomadic peoples in their conquest of Central Asia and hence were wise to the Turkmen's ploy. The Russians began their conquest of the Turkmen in 1877 and had subdued the Turkmen by 1881–1884, but only after fighting one of the bloodiest campaigns—including the Battle of Gok Tepe in 1881—of Russian colonial history.

In 1899, Turkmenistan was organized into the Transcaspian Oblast, becoming a part of the Governor-Generalship of Turkestan, which had been established in Transoxiana in 1867. Under Russian colonial rule, the Turkmen were fortunate to avoid the most troublesome problems that their neighbors of the steppes experienced. For example, since the greater part of Turkmenistan is desert and could not immediately support any appreciable agriculture, the Turkmen tribes did not experience the overnight division of their pasturage into farming plots, nor were they immediately forced to accept alien hordes of colonial peasants living in their homelands. Almost as soon as the Russians had taken over Turkmenistan, however, the tsarist government set to work on plans to irrigate and cultivate the salvageable portions of the desert, using canals to the Aral Sea. Turkmenistan's cotton boom of the 1890s was the result of the Russians' success. With cotton came the establishment of Russian fortress towns like Ashkhabad, increased regulation, the institution of private landed property, and the alienation of the Turkmen from their traditional lands.

On the eve of the Bolshevik Revolution in 1916, a major nationalist revolt against Russian rule took place, involving the Turkmen and other Central Asian cultures as well. Disaffected by their eroding cultural and living standards, the Turkmen erupted into open revolt when the Russian government introduced general military conscription among the steppes peoples to fight in World War I. The Turkmen, participating in the general revolt under their leader Junayid Khan, succeeded in overthrowing the Khan of Khiva. They set themselves up in power in 1918. Thousands of Russian colonists and Central Asian natives were killed while more than 150,000 nomads abandoned their possessions and fled into neighboring China.

The Russian Revolutions of 1917 and the subsequent civil war greatly affected the Turkmen, who were still suffering from the consequences of the Revolt of 1916. The Russian colonial population of Turkmenistan coalesced into three competing organizations in 1917–1919, based on their own political leanings: the "Whites," comprised of former tsarist bureaucrats and military officials; a Social-Revolutionary (S-R) organization of Central Asian Railway workers; and a small cadre of Bolsheviks ("Reds") operating on instructions received from Tashkent. The "Whites," who refused any dealings with the natives or the S-Rs, managed to form a government in Ashkhabad known as the Provisional Government of Transcaspia in the summer of 1917. For their part, the railroad workers set up an S-R soviet in Ashkhabad. But, in the spring of 1918, upon hearing of the Bolshevik Revolution, a small Bolshevik faction from the Tashkent soviet took over the Ashkhabad soviet and attempted to supplant the provisional government. By the summer of 1918, the "Whites," with the active assistance of the S-Rs and Turkmen, were able to dislodge the Bolsheviks by organizing and establishing the Provisional Revolutionary Government of Transcaspia, which was compelled to guarantee Turkmen and S-R representation.

In the meantime, native Turkmen forces were also coalescing in Turkmenistan and elsewhere with the object of resuming the unification plans cut short by the Russian conquest at the end of the previous century. In early 1918, a number of native residents of Ashkhabad organized a Provisional Turkmen Congress as an expression of the developing Turkmen national movement. This embryonic nationalist group could not unilaterally challenge Russian authority in Ashkhabad, be it tsarist, S-R, or Bolshevik. Therefore, in February 1918, the Provisional Turkmen Congress attempted to create a national armed force, based upon the Turkmen cavalry regiments of the Imperial Army; this effort was immediately suppressed by Bolshevik forces. Finding themselves stymied in that direction, the Turkmen Congress subsequently rejected Bolshevik offers of coalition, because these offers did not include important leadership positions for Turkmen. The Turkmen Congress was obliged instead to make common cause with the Whites' Provisional Revolutionary Government of Transcaspia. Oraz Serdar, a Turkmen military officer, headed the Transcaspian government's defense forces. In order to fend off the Bolsheviks, Serdar and the Transcaspian government were compelled to begin impressing Turkmen into their army. This decision had the disastrous effect of causing widespread desertions to the Bolsheviks, who did not practice impressment.

Some Turkmen tribal leaders, such as Junayid Khan, were also active in the desert countryside in opposing the Bolsheviks' assumption of power. Junayid Khan, however, became embroiled in a struggle for the khanate of Khiva, which caused many Khivan Uzbeks to join Bolshevik ranks in subduing Turkmenistan. The hard-pressed Transcaspian government, unable to ward off the growing Bolshevik forces from Tashkent and Khiva, appealed for aid from the British Military Mission in northeastern Persia, which sent a token force of 1,000 troops to aid the Transcaspian government's efforts to stop the Bolshevik advance. By June 1919, the British force was withdrawn, and, shortly thereafter, Ashkhabad fell to the Red Army. By early 1920, Junayid Khan's tribal forces were driven by the Bolsheviks into the desert, where they were joined by elements of Oraz Serdar's forces. These leaders and their combined units continued to resist Bolshevik rule for a few more years in the Turkmens' own version of the Basmachi Revolt.

Initially, the territory of Turkmenistan came under the authority of the Bolshevik People's Republics of Khiva and Bukhara. The Communists soon did away with these polities and their leadership with the National Delimitation of 1924, which established national homelands for the Central Asian peoples based on ethnicity; they therefore created the Uzbek and Turkmen Soviet Socialist Republics (SSR). A Turkmen Communist Party was formed, and the Turkmen SSR became part of the Soviet Union in 1925. One of the first decrees of the Bolshevik government in 1920 caused the tsarist period's privately owned tracts of land to revert to the traditional communal land tenure system of the Turkmen tribes, on the assumption that communal lands would lend themselves to collectivization. This tribal land tenure was then abolished in favor of the collectivization of livestock breeding and the placement of the "excess" population on collective farms engaged in cotton cultivation. The Soviet attempts at forced collectivization and settlement of nomads led to several very violent and bloody revolts against the Soviet government in the late 1920s and early 1930s. These, in turn, brought in Soviet armed force, arrests, liquidations, and party purges.

According to Soviet sources, a clandestine Turkmen nationalist movement existed between 1922 and 1927, with the goals of throwing off Soviet rule, with British aid, and establishing an independent Turkmenistan. Soviet sources also uncovered another subversive Turkmen organization, known as Turkmen Azatlygi (Turkmen Liberty), in the early 1930s. The revelations about this organization brought about large-scale purges and persecution of Turkmen political and cultural leaders. It is still unclear how much of this information was valid and how much was fabricated for the purge trials of the Turkmen Communists in 1937–1938. In 1946–1948 and again in 1959, smaller purges occurred over "nationalist deviationism" in Turkmen political and cultural institutions. Aside from these, there have been no other large-scale repressions of Turkmen since the late 1930s. The number of native Turkmen in the Communist party and government has increased over the years. In 1938, only 55 percent of the members of the Turkmen Supreme Soviet were natives, whereas, by 1947, 65.8 percent were Turkmen. In 1958–1959, much of the Turkmen leadership of the Communist Party of Turkmenistan advocated that all leading posts in the party and government ought to be held by Turkmen; the Russian elements in the party, backed by the Communist Party of the Soviet Union (CPSU), were able to purge these leaders. Since that time, native discussion of the need for more autonomy has increased, especially in the economic sphere. Nonetheless, some sources insist that the Turkmen SSR was the least restive of the Soviet republics in the post-Stalin years. Perhaps this assumption is held because the Turkmen SSR was based not on concepts of a modern nation-state but on tribal affiliations. Indeed, Turkmenistan was the only republic explicitly established on this basis.

The Soviets continued the tsarist policy of developing Turkmenistan for cotton production as well as for Russian colonization. In the 1950s, the Soviets completed work on the Great Kara Kum Canal, the world's largest irrigation and shipping channel, running from Kerki on the Amu Darya River to the cities of Merv and Ashkhabad. Other elaborate plans to reclaim more of the desert included the construction of another transportation waterway and widespread irrigation projects, based on the Kara Kum Canal, to be built from the Amu Darya to the Caspian Sea near Krasnovodsk. These projects, completed in the 1960s, brought about a rise in cotton production. They are also in part responsible for the ecological disaster caused by the unchecked use of chemical fertilizers and pesticides. These not only contributed to the dessication of the fresh-water Aral Sea but to its poisoning, as well. Industrial development, while lagging behind that of other republics, also grew in the Soviet period, especially with the exploitation of oil and gas reserves.

This sedentary agricultural and industrial development has altered both the ethnic composition of Turkmenistan and the traditional Turkmen way of life. In 1926, the Turkmen in Turkmenistan comprised 77.9 percent of the overall population; by 1959, this figure had dropped to 60.9 percent. Correspondingly, the

Russian part of the population grew from 5.8 percent to 17.3 percent. Today, as a result of disparities in birth rates and the slowing of immigration, the Turkmen portion of the population has grown to about 68 percent while the Russian segment has declined to about 13 percent. Soviet efforts to modernize Turkmenistan, while meeting resistance, have nonetheless introduced a general system of education, a written language based first upon the Latin, then Cyrillic, scripts, and a system of mass media. In spite of these changes, however, many aspects of Turkmen culture, particularly Islam and tribal affinities, have remained resilient and have even displayed a revival since 1985.

With the development of *glasnost* and *perestroika* under Mikhail Gorbachev, increased autonomy has fostered economic, social, cultural, and political changes in Turkmenistan. Economically, the republic's government and party began to reverse the deleterious effects of cotton production, chemical fertilizers, and pesticides. The government quota of Turkmen cotton was lowered, and more land was allocated for food crops and livestock breeding. An increase in media attention to traditional Turkmen culture and society has led to the beginnings of a revival of the traditional Turkmen allegiances to Islam and tribe, as well as to the open growth of Turkmen nationalism. In August 1990, the Supreme Soviet of the Turkmen SSR declared the republic to be a sovereign state. Soon after, in October, Saparmurad Niyazov, first secretary of the Turkmen Communist Party, emulated Gorbachev by having himself elected to the newly created office of President of the Republic.

Following the collapse of the coup against Gorbachev in August 1991, Niyazov proclaimed the independence of the Republic of Turkmenistan. A plebiscite was held on October 26, 1991, on the issue of independence; 94 percent of the population reportedly voted for independence. After this referendum, Niyazov confiscated all assets of the CPSU within the republic but maintained the structure and name of the Communist Party of Turkmenistan until December 1991. In that month, the Turkmen Communist Party changed its name to the Turkmen Democratic Party and declared itself to be in favor of market reforms and the privatization of state property. Niyazov became not only the head of the new party but also the president and prime minister of the new Republic of Turkmenistan. The government and political system of Turkmenistan still maintain many aspects of the Soviet one-party regime. Nonetheless, the new constitution of Turkmenistan includes features of a traditional presidential republic, with a strong president who is also the prime minister, a parliament known as the *majlis*, and constitutional and supreme courts. The constitution also includes an institution known as the People's Supreme Council, which is to be a broad-based, consultative body to the parliament and president.

As the least industrialized of the Central Asian republics and with one of the least reformed governments in the Commonwealth of Independent States (CIS), Turkmenistan looked as if it would probably be in for political, social, and economic instability in coming years. However, a number of sources in 1993 reported that Turkmenistan was among the most stable and prosperous of the

CIS republics. Its growing ties with the outside world, especially with the Republic of Turkey, may bode well for the future. Attraction to the Islamic Republic of Iran is limited to neighborly relations because of the fact that most Turkmen are staunchly Sunni Muslim. One significant economic asset is Turkmenistan's partially developed oil and natural gas industry. Agreements have been made between Turkmenistan and Turkey to foster the production and introduction of Turkmenistan's oil and gas reserves to the world market. It is hoped that this policy will aid Turkmenistan in its metamorphosis from a command to a market economy. The political future of Turkmenistan, as of the other Central Asian republics, will depend upon the events and trends in the CIS, the Middle East, and South Asia.

REFERENCES: Shirin Akiner, *Islamic Peoples of the Soviet Union*, 1983; Edward Allworth, ed., *Central Asia: A Century of Russian Rule*, 1967; Vladimir N. Basilov, ed., *Nomads of Eurasia*, 1989; Leslie Dienes, "Pastoralism in Turkestan: Its Decline and Its Persistence," *Soviet Studies*, 27 (July 1975), 343–65; René Grousset, *The Empire of the Steppes: A History of Central Asia*, 1970; Aman Berdi Murat, "Turkmenistan and the Turkmen," in Zev Katz, ed., *Handbook of Major Soviet Nationalities*, 1973; Richard Pipes, *The Formation of the Soviet Union: Communism and Nationalism, 1917–1923*, 1980; Michael Rywkin, ed., *Russian Colonial Expansion to 1917*, 1988; Emmanuel Sarkisiyanz, "Russian Conquest in Central Asia: Transformation and Acculturation," in Wayne S. Vucinich, ed., *Russia and Asia: Essays on the Influence of Russia on the Asian Peoples*, 1972; M. Wesley Shoemaker, ed., *Russia, Eurasian States, and Eastern Europe*, 1992; Wayne S. Vucinich, ed., *Russia and Asia: Essays on the Influence of Russia on the Asian Peoples*, 1972; Joseph L. Wieczynski, ed., *The Modern Encyclopedia of Russian and Soviet History*, 1984.

Lee Brigance Pappas

TURKMEN OF STAVROPOL. See TRUKHMEN and TURKMEN.

TURKOMAN. See TURKMEN.

TURKOMAN of STAVROPOL. See TRUKHMEN and TURKMEN.

TURKPEN. See TRUKHMEN.

TURPAN. The Turpan call themselves the Turpanlyk. Their origins are in the village of Turfan in the eastern Turkestan region of China. The Turpan migrated to Russia in the eighteenth century. They are classified today as a subgroup of the Uigur*. See UIGUR.

REFERENCE: Ronald Wixman, *The Peoples of the USSR: An Ethnographic Handbook*, 1984.

TURPANLYK. See TURPAN and UIGUR.

TURQOMAN. See TURKMEN.

TURQOMAN of STAVROPOL. See TRUKHMEN and TURKMEN.

TURUHAN SELKUP. See TURUKHAN SELKUP and SELKUP.

TURUKHAN SELKUP. The Turukhan Selkup, who have also been known as the Baikha Ostyak*, are a subgroup of the Taz Turukhan*, or northern, Selkups*. They live in the Yamalo-Nenets Autonomous Oblast, especially near the Turukhan and Yelogui rivers. See TAZ TURUKHAN SELKUP or SELKUP.
REFERENCE: Ronald Wixman, *The Peoples of the USSR: An Ethnographic Handbook*, 1984.

TUSH. See GEORGIAN.

TUSHETIAN. The Tushetians call themselves the Tushuri. They are a Kartvelian* group that became one of the Eastern Orthodox peoples who evolved into the Georgian* nation. See GEORGIAN.
REFERENCE: Ronald Wixman, *The Peoples of the USSR: An Ethnographic Handbook*, 1984.

TUSHIN. See TUSHETIAN and GEORGIAN.

TUSHURI. See TUSHETIAN and GEORGIAN.

TUVA TODJAN. See TODZHAN, TUVINIAN, and TOFALAR.

TUVA TODZHAN. See TODZHAN, TUVINIAN, and TOFALAR.

TUVAN. See TUVINIAN.

TUVIN. See TUVINIAN.

TUVINIAN. The Tuvinians, who call themselves the Tuva (Tuvan), Tuwa, and Tyva, and who were known historically as the Soyons, Soyots*, and Uriankhais, are a small ethnic group who live in a large area on both sides of the Yenesei River in the Tuvinian Autonomous Oblast. The Tuvinians first emerged from the process of ethnogenesis into an identifiable cultural group by the early eighteenth century. They were divided into two primary groups. The Western Tuvinians, who constitute the majority of the population, lived in the steppes and mountain steppes of central, southeastern, southern, and western Tuva. The Eastern Tuvinians, also known as Todja or Todja-Tuvinians, inhabit the taiga-steppe zones of Tuva, primarily in Todja and the upper Kaa-Khem River basin. Collectively, the Tuvinians come from a mixture of Turkic*, Mongol*, Samoyedic*, and Kettic* peoples. The Turkic groups included the Kuular, Tyu-lyush, Uigur*, Kyrgyz*, Baiyryk, Deleg, Saryglar, and a number of other groups; they evolved into the Western Tuvinians. The Mongol groups consisted of people like the Olet, Urat, Duyrbet, Salchak, Mongush, and Mingat; except for the Urat, they too became Western Tuvinians. The Samoyedic peoples who evolved into Tuvinians were primarily the Maady, Khaazut, and Choodu, who became part of both the Western and Eastern Tuvinians. Finally, the Kettic group was the Toduts, who became Eastern Tuvinians.

The process of Tuvinian ethnogenesis was assisted by the geography of Tuva. Most of the component groups lived in the steppe and mountain-steppe regions of Tuva, and they had had a long history of conflict with one another within the geographic isolation of Tuva. Tuva consists of a series of high mountain valleys at the headwaters of the Yenesei River; rugged mountains cut the region off from the rest of Siberia and Mongolia. These peoples also came from similar economic backgrounds. The upper Yenesei River valley is characterized by three distinct economic life-styles. The groups living in the mountainous forests make their livings by hunting and herding reindeer. Those living in the high forests and meadows are more likely to support themselves by raising horses and cattle, as well as by hunting. People on the steppes pursue a full-fledged pastoral life-style, primarily raising horses, cattle, goats, and sheep. The Tuvinian economy still reflects those divisions. Finally, the groups spoke similar versions of Turkic languages. Even the Mongolian, Samoyedic, and Kettic groups who went into the development of the Tuvinians had long since spoken variants of Turkic languages. The Tuvinian language, therefore, was heavily Turkic in its base. Ethnolinguists classify it as belonging to the Old Uigur group of the eastern division of the Turkic branch of the Uralic-Altaic linguistic family.

The Tuvinian Autonomous Oblast, which is located in south-central Siberia, sits on the northern border of Mongolia and was not incorporated into the Soviet Union until 1944. The Turkish Khanate conquered what is today Tuvinian ter-ritory in the sixth century, and it was in turn conquered by the Chinese* in the seventh century. The Uigurs took control in the eighth century, but their dom-ination gave way to rule by the Yenesei Kyrgyz in the ninth century. The Mongols controlled the region from 1207 to 1368, when a series of Eastern Mongolian rulers established dominance there. The Altyn khans took over in the sixteenth century and the Dzungarians in the last half of the seventeenth century. The Manchus* overthrew the Dzungarians in 1758, at which point the entire region came under Chinese control. After the Treaty of Peking between Russia and China in 1860, trade relations arose in the region, and a small colony of Russian settlers developed.

Until 1911, the Tuva region was politically part of Outer Mongolia, which was controlled by the Ch'ing Empire out of Peking China. When the Chinese Revolution erupted in 1911, the subsequent instability provided Russia with the opportunity it needed, and, in 1914, they established a protectorate over Tuva. Although Tuva declared its independence from China in 1912, a tripartite agreement in 1915 between China, Russia, and Tuva left the region autonomous but still within Beijing's sphere of influence. During the Russian Revolution and subsequent civil war, control of Tuva frequently changed hands between various Red and White armies. When the dust settled after the revolution, Tuva was known as the Tannu-Tuva People's Republic, an autonomous state under Soviet sovereignty. Its capital was Kyzyl. Of course, it was really a sub-unit of the Russian Federation of the Soviet Union, autonomous in name only. Mongolia tried briefly to re-establish control over the region in the 1920s, but the Soviet Union successfully resisted. The Soviets real fear about the region was Japanese* military forays deep into Siberia. These revived Russian* fears of Asian disloyalty. To many Russians, all Asians looked alike and were untrustworthy. It thus became important for Josef Stalin to establish permanent control over the region. In 1944, he dissolved the Tuva People's Republic and included the area in the Russian Soviet Federated Socialist Republic (RSFSR) as the Tuvinian Autonomous Oblast. In 1961, it became known as the Tuvinian Autonomous Soviet Socialist Republic.

With the establishment of Soviet control came Soviet economic and cultural models. Collective farming and herding were imposed on Tuvinian pastoralists, and many of them resisted by destroying their livestock rather than turning the animals over to the state. Soviet troops forcibly settled many Tuvinians on collective cattle and sheep farms. Most Tuvinians were Buddhist in their religious faith, and the Soviet government worked diligently at destroying monasteries and defrocking monks. Tuvinian artists were enjoined from using their traditional Buddhist symbolism because, they were told, it would stifle their creativity; instead, they were to learn realistic art from the "rich legacy of Russian painting." Likewise, Tuvinian songs were henceforth to tell of the struggle to build a socialistic society. The Tuvinian literary language, which had once used classical Mongol and Tibetan, was forced to employ the Cyrillic alphabet in all publications. Despite these economic and cultural hardships, the Tuvinian population grew steadily during the Stalin era. Between 1931 and 1959, the number of ethnic Tuvinians increased from approximately 40,000 to 100,000 people.

The Tuvinian population has continued to increase in recent years. Between 1959 and the late 1980s, the number of ethnic Tuvinians went from 100,000 to nearly 180,000 people. Growing numbers of Tuvinians found themselves working in industrial jobs and settling in small towns in the region. Until the 1970s, the Tuva homeland remained one of the most isolated regions of the Soviet Union. Siberian railroads did not penetrate the area, and the only paved roads were blocked by ice for much of the year. The surrounding mountains heightened the Tuva sense of isolation. But, in the 1970s, huge asbestos deposits were discovered in Tuva, and the Soviet Union launched a crash program to develop them. Not surprisingly, they did so without considering the ecological and health consequences. Huge open-pit asbestos mines polluted the air and will, no doubt, have long-term consequences for those Tuva who live nearby, particularly producing high rates of mesothelioma, a deadly form of lung cancer.

Although Soviet tolerance for Buddhism has traditionally been quite low, to say the least, a relaxation occurred in the 1970s and 1980s. Only a few hundred Tuvinian Buddhist lamas remain, but, during the Brezhnev years, the government tried to use Buddhism as part of its worldwide peace propaganda. Buddhism was declared to be a "peace religion" that was "struggling for peace and tranquility on the planet." A small number of Tuvinian seminarians were sent to Mongolia for study. By the early 1990s, anti-Buddhist persecution had been drastically reduced under Mikhail Gorbachev. Tuvinian nationalism also found new expression in the era of *glasnost*. Tuvinians are pushing for expanded Tuvinian-language education, while a few Tuvinian radicals are calling for the independence of Tuva or for its formal affiliation with Mongolia.

REFERENCES: Sevyan Vainshtein, *Nomads of South Siberia: The Pastoral Economies of Tuva*, 1985; A. S. Stein, *Innermost Asia*, 1928; H. H. Vreeland, *Mongol Community and Kinship Structure*, 1957.

TUWA. See TUBA.

TYM KARAKON OSTIAK. See TYM SELKUP, NARYM SELKUP, and SELKUP.

TYM KARAKON OSTYAK. See TYM SELKUP, NARYM SELKUP, and SELKUP.

TYM KARAKON SELKUP. See TYM SELKUP, NARYM SELKUP, and SELKUP.

TYM OSTYAK. See TYM SELKUP, NARYM SELKUP, and SELKUP.

TYM SELKUP. The Tym Selkup, who have also been known as the Tym Karakon Selkup, are one of the subgroups of the Narym*, or forest, Selkups, who are themselves a subgroup of the Selkups*. See SELKUP.

REFERENCE: Ronald Wixman, *The Peoples of the USSR: An Ethnographic Handbook*, 1984.

TYUGE. See EVEN.

TYUMEN TATAR. See TJUMEN TATAR and TATAR.

TYURK. See TURK and AZERBAIJANI.

TYURK OF FERGANA AND SAMARKAND. See TURK OF FERGANA AND SAMARKAND and UZBEK.

TYURK OF FERGHANA AND SAMARKAND. See TURK OF FERGANA AND SAMARKAND and UZBEK.

TYURKI. See TURK.

TYURKI OF FERGANA AND SAMARKAND. See TURK OF FERGANA
AND SAMARKAND and UZBEK.

TYURKI OF FERGHANA AND SAMARKAND. See TURK OF FERGANA
AND SAMARKAND and UZBEK.

U

UBIH. See CIRCASSIAN.

UBIKH. See CIRCASSIAN.

UBYH. See CIRCASSIAN.

UBYKH. See CIRCASSIAN.

UDEE. See UDEGEI.

UDEGEI. The Udegeis, who call themselves the Udee, are closely related to the Nanais*, Ulchis*, Oroks*, and Orochis*, all of whom consider themselves to be part of the Nani* group since their languages are mutually intelligible. The Udegeis live east of the Amur and Ussuri rivers near the Pacific Ocean, inland from the port of Sovetskaya Gavan. They speak a Manchu* language. The Udegeis number approximately 2,400 people.

The Udegeis living in the Sikhote-Alin Mountains and on the coast of the Sea of Japan enjoyed relative freedom from Russian cultural and political pressure until the nineteenth century. They were nomadic hunters who lived in bark tepees and traveled on skis. The Udegeis demonstrated their difference from other Manchu groups by wearing their hair in two plaits instead on one. Their society was organized around powerful clans. Udegei religion was shamanistic and animistic, and it incorporated elements of Buddhism and Confucianism. They were known for the amulets and effigies that they carved out of wood and placed in trees to propitiate the unseen spirits of the world. Udegei decorative art reflected their Chinese* roots. Udegei ceremonial robes combined the Chinese dragon with their own favorite geometrical renditions of fish scales.

In the nineteenth century, the Udegeis found themselves facing intense pressures from the arrival of Russian* and Chinese settlers. The Chinese came in from the south into Ussuri and Sikhote-Alin. The Udegeis resisted pressures to become farmers, since they preferred their hunting ways, but many of them were unable to avoid falling into debt to Chinese creditors, who often forcibly took Udegei wives and daughters as payment. The Udegeis also suffered from epidemics of smallpox and other diseases. Their population fell, and many of them disappeared into Chinese culture in the twentieth century.

After the completion of the Trans-Siberian Railroad in 1907, other Udegeis suffered from massive Russian and Ukrainian* immigration. Russian and Ukrainian farmers cleared huge tracts of land in the Amur-Ussuri region; they planted crops and used the wood for fuel. In the process, they badly damaged Udegei hunting lands, forcing the Udegei to migrate farther north for game animals.

The Bolshevik Revolution added new burdens to Udegei life. The violence of the civil war made them even more suspicious of Russians, and they tried to avoid all contact with them. Soviet agents went deep into the forests to find the Udegei. In 1934, the first of the Udegei hunting collectives was established, but inter-clan rivalries among the Udegei completely disrupted collective operations. The state tried to force the Udegeis in the Bikin Valley to become farmers, but, after fifteen years of problems, the experiment was abandoned and the Udegeis there were allowed to return to hunting. Coastal Udegeis were forced to establish fishing collectives on the coast.

During the rest of the twentieth century, the Udegei population held steady, but the influences of Russian culture proved to be unavoidable. By the 1970s, more than 70 percent of all Udegeis spoke Russian as their native language, and almost all of them had been absorbed into the industrial economy. Soviet economic policies in the 1980s laid waste the Udegei forests, leveling hundreds of square miles of their old hunting grounds. Udegei leaders protested the fate of their homeland, and the more enlightened political environment of the Gorbachev era gave them some leverage. In March 1990, the State Forestry Committee of the Soviet Union gave the Udegeis absolute economic control over the entire Samarga River Valley, and the Udegeis quickly put a stop to the wholesale destruction of the forests.

REFERENCES: Alice Bartels and Dennis Bartels, ''Soviet Policy Toward Siberian Native People,'' *Canadian Dimension*, 19 (1985), 36–44; Mike Edwards, ''Siberia: In From the Cold,'' *National Geographic*, 177 (March 1990), 2–49; James Forsyth, *A History of the Peoples of Siberia*, 1992; Walter Kolarz, *The Peoples of the Soviet Far East*, 1969; Constantine Krypton, ''Soviet Policy in the Northern National Regions After World War II,'' *Slavic Review*, 13 (October 1954), 339–53; Piers Vitebsky, ''Perestroika Among the Reindeer Herders,'' *Geographical Magazine*, 61 (June 1989), 23–34.

UDEGEY. See UDEGEI.

UDEHE. See UDEGEI.

UDEKHE. See UDEGEI.

UDI. The Udis are also known as the Udins, Utis, Utins, and Utiis. The Udi language is part of the Samurian* group of northeastern Caucasic languages. Ethnohistorians consider them to be one of the most ancient ethnic groups in the former Soviet Union—descendants of the earlier inhabitants of Azerbaijan. During the seventh and eighth centuries, when the Udis were a large group of people scattered widely throughout Azerbaijan, many of them were converted to the Shiite Muslim faith by Arab* tradesmen and warriors, who were expanding into Central Asia. The Udis had been Christians, and most of them belonged to the Church of Arran, a Caucasian Albanian group (not to be confused with the Albanians* of the Balkans), when the Arabs arrived. A minority of the Udis remained loyal to their Christian origins, in spite of intense Shiite pressure. Since that time, however, the Udi group steadily shrank in size as its members were assimilated by Azerbaijanis*, Persians*, and Armenians*. In the eighth century, the remaining Udis were converted to the Monophysite Christian tradition of the Armenians, who believed that elements of deity and humanity were both combined in the living figure of Jesus Christ.

By 1800, there were two distinct groups of Udi. The majority group consisted of Udi Shiites—the descendants of the Muslim converts of a thousand years before. The smaller group were Armeno-Gregorian Christians, who were strongly influenced by the Armenians living in Azerbaijan and still loyal to the Monophysite tradition. During the course of the nineteenth century, most of the Udi Shiites were assimilated by the much larger, neighboring communities of Azerbaijani Shiites. That process continued during the twentieth century, eventually making the Muslim Udis a minority group among Udis. The Armeno-Gregorian Christian Udis who lived in Vartashen and Nidz in the Azerbaijan Soviet Socialist Republic became the largest group. A second group of Christian Udis moved to the region of Oktomberi in the eastern reaches of the Georgian Soviet Socialist Republic in the 1920s. Over the years, they abandoned their Monophysite tradition and converted to Russian Orthodoxy. Significant numbers of Udi Christians were also assimilated by Armenians during the nineteenth and early twentieth centuries, but, in the 1950s, the Soviet government banned the use of Armenian as a language of instruction for Udis in public schools; the use of Russian* slowed the assimilation process.

Today, the Udi population of the former Soviet Union totals approximately 8,800 people. Most are farmers, raising a variety of products, especially fruit, cattle, and sheep. They are divided into three groups. The largest consists of the Armeno-Gregorian (Monophysite) Christians who live in Vartashen in the Vartashen Rayon of Azerbaijan and in Nidzh in the Kutkashen Rayon of the same republic. A small Udi Shiite group lives with the Udi Christians in this area. Finally, a small group of Russian Orthodox Udi lives in Oktomberi, Kvareli Rayon, in eastern Georgia.

REFERENCES: Alexandre Bennigsen and S. Enders Wimbush, *Muslims of the Soviet Empire: A Guide*, 1986; Sir Olaf Caroe, *The Soviet Empire: The Turks of Central Asia and Stalinism*, 1953; Ronald Wixman, *The Peoples of the USSR: An Ethnographic Handbook*, 1984.

UDIN. See UDI.

UDINY. See UDI.

UDMORT. See UDMURT.

UDMURT. The Udmurts, who were formerly called the Votyaks (Votiaks), Ary, Ariane, and Otiaki, are an ethnic group in the former Soviet Union who live in the Udmurt Autonomous Republic in Russia. The Udmurt population totaled 504,187 people in 1926, and it has increased since then, to 624,794 in 1959, 704,328 in 1970, 713,696 in 1979, and 746,522 in 1989. Historians argue that the Udmurt first appeared as an identifiable ethnic group in the sixth century. They fell under the Khazars in the eighth century, surviving economically through slash-and-burn agriculture, hunting, fishing, and small-scale, local commerce. By the mid-ninth century, the expanding cultural and political influence of the Volga Bulgarians* had displaced Khazar influence among the Udmurts, and they remained under Bulgarian control until the mid-thirteenth century. At that point, the Mongol* Tatars* took over, reaching Udmurt land in the 1230s and rapidly bringing them under subjugation. Tatar domination of the Udmurts continued until the middle of the sixteenth century. At that point, the Russian* Empire established control over their territory, although significant Russian cultural and economic contact with the Udmurts had started as early as the twelfth century. Beginning in 1489, the area along the Middle and Upper Viatka River was incorporated into Russia as Viatka Land. In 1552, the Kama Udmurts voluntarily accepted annexation by Russia, within six years, all Udmurts were effectively under Russian jurisdiction.

Ethnographers and ethnolinguists identify the Udmurt as a Finnic* people. Their language is part of the Permian group of the Finnic branch of the Uralic-Altaic language family. Their territorial homeland stretches throughout the Middle Volga region. They live in their own autonomous republic as well as in the Bashkir Autonomous Republic, the Tatar Autonomous Republic, and in the Kirov, Perm', and Sverdlovsk autonomous oblasts of Russia. There are two basic divisions to the Udmurt people—northern and southern. Each has a distinct dialect, although the dialects are mutually intelligible. The Udmurts are closely related to the Komis* and Komi Permyaks.

Another group is closely related to the Udmurts and is being rapidly assimilated by them. The Besermen* (Besermyan) are a Turkish people from the Middle Volga who came under Udmurt influence. Besermen culture was extremely close to Tatar and Chuvash* cultures, and their language is loaded with Tatar words. Until the 1930s, the Besermen were treated as a separate ethnic group in the Soviet Union. At that time, their population exceeded 10,000 people; since then, they have been classified as Udmurts. Those who have not been completely assimilated by the Udmurts live in the Glazovskiy and Balezinskiy rayons of the Udmurt Autonomous Republic.

Udmurt religion traditionally reflected their nomadic, subsistence economic life. It resembled the animism of other aboriginal peoples. Udmurt religious life revolved around a shaman leader who propitiated the powers of the universe. Nothing in life occurred capriciously, accidentally, or inadvertently. All phenomena were connected in complex inter-relationships that human beings had to try and understand if they were to survive. Russian Orthodox missionaries first reached the Udmurt in the sixteenth century and began the long, difficult attempt to convert them to Christianity. The missionary work became especially intense in the early 1800s, when Russian nationalists began to worry about all the distinct nationalities among them. Since Christianization and education went hand-in-hand, the missionaries worked to develop a literary language for the Udmurt. In the eighteenth century, Russian Orthodox linguists developed a Cyrillic alphabet for them, based on an Udmurt dialect that was transitional between the northern and southern dialects. Missionary work among the Udmurts was difficult. Most of them superficially accepted Russian Orthodoxy, but strong elements of their original animist faith survived. Those Udmurts living in close proximity to the Tatars also adopted elements of Islam.

The Bolshevik Revolution in 1917 brought great changes to Udmurt life. In 1920, an autonomous oblast, known as the Votyak Autonomous Oblast, was established for the Udmurts; it was renamed the Udmurt Autonomous Oblast in 1932 and was elevated to the Udmurt Autonomous Soviet Socialist Republic (ASSR) in 1934. Most of the Udmurt ASSR's 16,400 square miles were located between the Kama and Viatka rivers. The collectivization of Udmurt agriculture began in the late 1920s and, by the late 1930s, the process had been virtually completed. The Soviet government also launched a drive to industrialize the area rapidly. Public schools dictated the use of Russian as the medium of instruction late in the 1930s. In spite of these efforts to acculturate the Udmurts, however, the Udmurts have maintained a cohesive sense of identity. Even in the early 1990s, more than 80 percent of the Udmurt people still spoke Udmurt as their native tongue, and less than two-thirds of them understood Russian. They have also remained faithful to many elements of their animistic religion.

REFERENCES: *Great Soviet Encyclopedia*, 1973, vol. 26, 541–48; Ronald Wixman, *The Peoples of the USSR: An Ethnographic Handbook*, 1984.

UDOR. See KOMI.

UGHBUG. See DARGIN.

UGLICH. See UKRAINIAN.

UGLICHI. See UKRAINIAN.

UGOR. See UGRIAN PEOPLES.

UGORIAN. See UGRIAN PEOPLES.

UGRI. See UGRIAN PEOPLES.

UGRIAN PEOPLES. The term ''Ugrian Peoples'' is used generically to refer to people who speak a language that is part of the Ugrian division of the Uralian branch of the larger Uralic-Altaic family. Normally included in this descriptive term are Khants*, Mansis*, and Magyars*.
REFERENCE: Ronald Wixman, *The Peoples of the USSR: An Ethnographic Handbook*, 1984.

UGRO-RUSIN. See CARPATHO-RUSYN and UKRAINIAN.

UGRO-RUSSIAN. See CARPATHO-RUSYN AND UKRAINIAN.

UGRO-RUSYN. See CARPATHO-RUSYN and UKRAINIAN.

UGRO-RUTHENIAN. See CARPATHO-RUSYN and UKRAINIAN.

UHRO-RUSIN. See CARPATHO-RUSYN and UKRAINIAN.

UHRO-RUSSIAN. See CARPATHO-RUSYN and UKRAINIAN.

UHRO-RUSYN. See CARPATHO-RUSYN and UKRAINIAN.

UHRO-RUTHENIAN. See CARPATHO-RUSYN and UKRAINIAN.

UIGHAR. See UIGUR.

UIGHUR. See UIGUR.

UIGUR. The Uigurs (Uighur, Uyghur, Uighar) are a Turkic* people who today are concentrated in the Xinjiang-Uigur Autonomous Region of the People's Republic of China. Russians* call them the Uigury. Their total population may exceed 12,000,000 people, of whom 262,199 live in what used to be the Soviet Union, according to the 1989 Soviet census. Other Uigurs live in Afghanistan, Pakistan, and India. Those who live in the former Soviet Union are concentrated in Uzbekistan and Kyrgyzia; smaller numbers are scattered throughout Turkmenistan. The largest urban concentration of Uigurs is in the city of Tashkent, where more than 30,000 live and work. Along with Uzbek*, Uigur is a member of the Karluk division of the Turkic family of the Uralic-Altaic languages. Today, the Uigurs of the former Soviet Union are divided into two basic cultural groups, based on differences in dialect and history. The southern or Fergana Uigurs, live in the Fergana Valley of Uzbekistan. Most of them are in an advanced state of assimilation with the larger body of Uzbeks, and their dialect of Uigur, when they speak it, is laced with Uzbek words. The northern or Semirech'e Uigurs, live in the Semirech'e region of Kazakhstan. They have maintained a strong sense of Uigur identity, retaining their language and culture and marrying endogamously.

The Uigurs are one of the oldest of the Turkic-speaking peoples of Central Asia. They originated with the nomadic tribes of eastern Turkestan in the third and fourth centuries, and, until the eighth century, they were part of the Juan-Juan Khanate. They then became part of the Turkic Khanate. When that polity disintegrated in the eighth century, the Uigurs underwent a process of ethnic consolidation and formed an Uigur state on the Orkhon River in the Tuva Region. That action made them the rulers of the Mongol* steppes. The Yenesei Kyrgyz* overran the Uigur in 840, expelling them from Mongolia, which precipitated a migration of some Uigurs to eastern Turkestan and Kansu, where they formed two independent states. Both of those Uigur states later fell victim to the Tanguts, Karakitais, and Mongols. During the era of Mongol domination, the Uigur language was a *lingua franca* in the area. By the fourteenth century, the term "Uigur" had fallen into disuse, and the Uigurs instead identified themselves by their place of residence, such as the Kashgarlik*, or people of Kashgar, or by their occupations, such as the Taranchi*, meaning "farmers."

In the mid-eighteenth century, the Manchus* of China established control over the Uigur and a long period of oppression and exploitation began. In the mid–1700s, the Chinese* resettled approximately 6,000 Uigur families to the Ili Valley. Most of them were farmers—the Taranchis. The Uigurs rebelled several times against Manchu domination in the eighteenth and nineteenth centuries. Russia seized the Ili Valley in 1871, and, although it was returned to China in 1882, most of the Taranchis moved farther west to remain under Russian* control. The southern Uigurs came in relatively small numbers, and Russian authorities settled them in the Fergana Valley among local Uzbeks and Kyrgyz. Much smaller numbers of them were also settled in Tajikistan and Turkmenistan. The northern Uigurs, who ended up in the Semirech'e region, came primarily from the Ili Valley in Xinjiang. Between 1881 and 1883, nearly 50,000 Ili Uigurs, fleeing after their abortive Muslim revolt against the Manchus, came to Russia, and Russian authorities settled them in isolated regions where they maintained their distinct identity.

The Uigurs often migrated as whole villages; as a result, they have retained that decentralized identity. For instance, the Aksulak came from the village of Aksu, while the Kashgarlik migrated from the town of Kashgar in Chinese Turkestan. The Turpanlik*, or Turfanlik, came from the town of Turfan, and the Yarkenlik* (Yarkendlik) traced their roots back to the town of Yarkend, also in Chinese Turkestan. After the victory of Mao Zedong in China in 1949, a second wave of Uigur emigrants settled in the Soviet Union to escape the political turmoil at home.

The eighteenth-century migration from Chinese Turkestan to Semirech'e and the Fergana Valley led to dramatic changes in the Uigur life-style. For centuries, they had practiced a pastoral nomadism that kept them on the move from oasis to oasis. After the great migration, they began to make the transition to settled agriculture. Uigur farmers settled permanently around the oases and worked on small farms, raising melons, cotton, maize, peaches, plums, and wheat. In the cities and towns of the region, they became shopkeepers, merchants, and craftsmen. The more settled life-style also helped to produce a more sophisticated Uigur literature. Such poets as Shair Akhun, Khislat Kashgari, Turdy Garibi, and Abduraim Nizari rose to prominence, and Uigur writers, in reaction to the years of Manchu and Chinese oppression, developed a literature of social protest.

Over the centuries, the Uigurs underwent a series of religious transformations, from Shamanism to Buddhism to Manichaeanism. Beginning in the tenth century, however, as Islam penetrated Central Asia and Turkestan, the Uigurs began a conversion process that was complete by the fourteenth century. They were and still are Sunni Muslims of the Hanafi rite, and, like many other Muslim groups of Central Asia, the Uigurs have been heavily influenced by the Sufi orders. The eighteenth- and nineteenth-century migrations to Uzbekistan and Kyrgyzia served to intensify the Muslim devotions of the Uigur people.

The Bolshevik Revolution had a dramatic impact on Uigur identity. Because of their location on the border between the Soviet Union and China, as well as the interest both countries had in maintaining the political loyalties of their border minorities, the Soviet Union encouraged, rather than discouraged, the development of Uigur national identity. They were not given an autonomous region, but, at the All-Uigur Congress in Tashkent in 1921, the Soviet Union allowed them to use the term "Uigur" to identify themselves. That was surprising, given the fact that many Uigurs had joined in the Kazakh* rebellion against Russian authority in 1916. The Uigurs underwent the collectivization of their farming in the 1920s and 1930s, and several thousand of them fled back to China to escape those political and economic pressures.

Like other Central Asian groups, the Uigurs have been affected by the centrifugal forces of nationalism and political disintegration, although not so directly as several other groups. During the ethnic violence in the Fergana Valley in 1989 and 1990, many Uigurs joined Uzbeks, with whom they are rapidly assimilating, in their attacks on the Meskhetians* and ethnic Russians. Unemployment in the region was severe, and the economic hopelessness bred social unrest. The more northern Uigurs, whose sense of ethnic identity has always been more pronounced, revived the idea of an All-Uigur movement in the late 1980s and began trying to make contact with Uigur groups scattered throughout Tajikistan, Kazakhstan, Kyrgyzia, and Uzbekistan, as well as with the much larger Uigur community of the People's Republic of China. It is unlikely, however, that Uigur nationalism will ever find expression in statehood. The southern Uigur in the Fergana Valley are too far along the road to assimilation with the Uzbeks, while the northern Uigur in Semirech'e, although more overtly aware of their identity, have neither the historical experience nor the political infra-structure necessary for independence.

REFERENCES: Elizabeth E. Bacon, *Central Asia Under Russian Rule*, 1966; Alexandre Bennigsen and S. Enders Wimbush, *Muslims of the Soviet Empire: A Guide*, 1986; *Current Digest*, 41 (July 5, 1989), 16–18; *Great Soviet Encyclopedia*, 1973, vol. 26, pp. 553–54; David Lu, *Moslems in China Today*, 1964; Colin Mackerras, ed., *The Uighur Empire According to the T'ang Dynastic Histories: A Study in Sino-Uighur Relations*, 1973; H. H. Wiens, "Change in the Ethnography and Land Use of the Ili Valley and Region, Chinese Turkestan," *Annals of the Association of American Geographers*, 59 (1969), 753–75; I-fan Yang, *Islam in China*, 1957.

Lee Brigance Pappas

UIGURY. See UIGUR.

UKLICH. See UKRAINIAN.

UKRAIN. See UKRAINIAN.

UKRAINIAN. Ukraine (until 1991, the Ukrainian Soviet Socialist Republic or Ukrainian SSR) has an area of 233,100 square miles (603,700 square kilometers) and a population of 51,704,000, according to the January 1989 census. Of these, 36,488,951 officially consider themselves ethnic Ukrainians; the remainder consists of 10,471,600 Russians*, 406,000 Belarusians*, and various other minorities (Moldovans*, Poles*, Jews*, Greeks*, etc.). Extensive intermarriage between Ukrainians and Russians complicates the ethnic composition. Prolonged russification, both tsarist and Soviet, has also taken a great toll. Moreover, an additional 11,000,000 Ukrainians live outside Ukraine, particularly in Russia (around 4,500,000) and in various Western countries (Canada, United States, Great Britain, Brazil, etc.). Territorially, Ukraine is the second-largest country in Europe (after Russia), and it is often compared with France. The territory of Ukraine was significantly increased by the incorporation of Western Ukraine in 1939 (Molotov-Ribentropp Pact) and the incorporation of Crimea in 1954. Ukraine is strategically located on the northern shores of the Black Sea (654 miles of coast), and it has common land borders (4,018 miles long) with Russia, Belarus, Poland, Czechoslovakia, Hungary, Romania, and Moldova. Ukraine is subdivided into twenty-five oblasts. It lacks natural borders and lies on the historical trade and invasion routes between Europe and Asia. With the exception of the western regions, most of Ukraine (around 95 percent) is open country, a great plain rising from the flat eastern steppes at the gates of Asia toward the mountains in the west. This vast plain is one of the most fertile in the world, renowned for its famous black soil (*chernozem*). The richness of the soil has historically rendered Ukraine the "bread basket of Europe" and decisively shaped the ancestral agrarian civilization of the Ukrainians. The country is well watered by numerous rivers, the most important being the Dnieper (Dnipro, Dnipr, or Dniepr; in Greek, Boristhenes), which is 2,285 kilometers long and divides Ukraine into more or less equal parts. Dnieper—the "Father"—is closely associated with the steppe ethos of boundless freedom and amplitude; it thus plays a pre-eminent role in Ukrainian history, culture, and national psyche (the song "The Mighty Dnipr Moans and Bellows," with lyrics written by the national poet, Taras Shevchenko, has become an unofficial national anthem). Other major rivers are the Danube (Dunai), Dniester, Boh, Don, and Kuban'. The only significant mountain chains are the Carpathians in Western Ukraine and the Crimean Mountains, both geologically old and worn out. Ukraine has the following vegetation zones: forest, forest-steppe, steppe, and mountain belts. The country enjoys a temperate continental climate, with only occasional temperature extremes.

Ukraine is rich in minerals, including iron, manganese, titanium, aluminum, and coal, although some of these are becoming more inaccessible after a century of intense mining. The region has inadequate petroleum and natural gas resources, which it must therefore import from increasingly unreliable sources. Ukraine was a vital industrial center of both the former Russian Empire and the former Soviet Union. In the late nineteenth century, the·Donets'-Krivyi Rih (Krevoi Rog) district, rich in coal and iron deposits, became the first major center of industrialization in the tsarist state. The industrial output of Ukraine, together with the food resources, made it indispensable for the economic might of the Soviet Union from its inception. In more recent times, Ukraine's economy accounted for nearly 25 percent of the total Soviet agricultural output, 22 percent of its industrial output, and an ever greater percentage of its arms production. It still controls the majority of the Soviet strategic highways, railroads, and pipelines connecting Russia with Europe and Central Asia, all of which complicates the present post-Soviet environment. Ukraine's economy thus continues to remain closely intertwined with that of Russia and the former Soviet republics.

Ukrainians (*ukraintsi*) have also been known in history as "Ruthenians" (*rus'ki, rusyny*) and as "Little" or "Lesser-Russians" (*malorosy*). The term *Malo* ("lesser") *Rus'* originated with the Byzantine ethno-geographical categorization, whereby areas closer to Byzantium were labeled as "lesser" or "little," while more remote regions were "great" or "greater" (comparable to the nomenclatures of "Minor" and "Magna Graecia"). Hence, the terms "Little" or "Great" Russia do not denote value judgment, relative importance, or power. The term "Ukraine" (*Okraina, Ukraina*) means "frontier" or "borderland" and appeared for the first time in twelfth-century chronicles, when it was used in reference to a relatively small region (Galicia-Dniester district). By the late sixteenth century, when much of Ukraine was incorporated by the Polish-Lithuanian* Commonwealth, the term had come into vogue, serving to denote the borderlands of Poland rather than of Muscovy (the historical predecessor of present-day Russia). This shift coincided with several trends: conflicts based on nationality (Poles vs. Ukrainians), creed (Catholics vs. Orthodox), and class (gentry vs. peasantry); the rise of the Zaporozhe Cossacks* (Kozaks); and the emergence of a purely ''Ukrainian'' (rather than the previous *rus'ian*) identity.

Ethnically, Ukrainians belong, along with the Russians and Belarusians, to the Eastern Slavic branch of the Indo-European peoples. Ukraine's geographical location at the ''crossroad of nations'' on the Eurasian plain, however, proved conducive to complex racial and cultural mixture. Anthropologically, Ukrainians are composed of at least six subgroups: Dinaric, Mediterranean, Alpine, Nordic, Sub-Nordic, and Lapp*. Evidence suggests the human habitation there goes back some 300,000 years to the Lower Paleolithic Era, which is associated with Neanderthal culture. During the Upper Paleolithic Era (around 40,000 B.C.), the Neanderthals were replaced by a fair, long-skulled Nordic type—the Cro-Magnon or Aurignacian race. These proved to be the celebrated Ice-Age hunters of Ukraine. Later, during the Mesolithic Era (8000–5000 B.C.), there was an influx of the Armenoid round-headed types from the Caucasian regions. Their arrival coincided with the advent of an early agriculturalist way of life, perhaps the oldest in Europe. During the Neolithic period (5000–1800 B.C.), in the region extending from the Dnieper to the Carpathians, the sophisticated Trypilian culture flourished. This culture is best illustrated by its exquisite pottery, with symbolic motifs of spirals and whorls painted on a sepia, black, and white background, as well as by clay figurines of a Mother-Goddess. For some time, this was the most advanced culture in all of Europe and, in the opinion of some scholars, it influenced the early Greek (pre-Mycenaean, pre-Minoan) and Aegean civilizations.

During the Bronze, the Iron, and the Middle Ages, there were numerous nomadic incursions into the steppe regions of Ukraine. The most important newcomers were the Scythians (seventh century B.C.), whose way of life was splendidly described by the fifth-century Greek historian Herodotus. Some scholars believe that the ''Scythian-plowmen'' that Herodotus described were actually Ukrainians or proto-Slavs. Scythian royal tombs contained exquisite gold jewelry favoring a horse motif. Under the Scythians, Ukraine again became associated, albeit distantly, with the Aegean world. In the third century B.C., the Sarmatians, a branch of the Iranian people, invaded southern Ukraine and prevailed for five centuries. The first Slavic elements (Sclaveni) appear in first-century A.D. Roman chronicles. Some modern scholars believe that Ukraine was the original homeland of all Slavic peoples, but the evidence is incomplete. By the sixth century, the Slavs were already subdivided into three linguistic subgroups. The Ukrainians emerged from the East-Slavic groups associated with the proto-Slavic Antes (Antae). The Antes were a large tribal society of peasants, artisans, and merchants, maintaining trade relations with Greeks and Romans. They also had an urban culture, and it appears that the present city of Kiev was their trading center and capital city. Moreover, in the south, along the shore of the Black Sea, there were extensive Greek colonies and important cities (Olbia, Chersonesus, Pantipacaeum, Theodosia, etc.). Indeed, there is still a significant Greek presence in Ukraine. Modern Ukrainians are clearly products of considerable ethnic mixture going back for millennia. Nevertheless, the dark, round-headed, Dinaric type constitutes the largest group (approximately 45 percent of the population).

For historical and geo-political reasons, Ukrainians are further subdivided into three major ethnographic and dialectic categories: Central-Eastern (or Southeastern), Northern, and Western (or Southwestern). The Central-Eastern subgroup, centered in the mid-Dnieper region (Chernihiv-Kiev-Poltava areas), is where the modern Ukrainian nation was formed; the Kiev-Poltava dialect became the literary language in the nineteenth century. Here the legacy of the medieval Kievan Rus'ian culture collided with the steppe ethos of the nomadic steppe peoples and Tatars* oo Crimea, giving rise to the Cossacks of Zaporozhia (literally meaning ''beyond the cataracts'' of the Dnieper). The Cossacks' sense of boundless freedom and heroic military exploits are a central part of the Ukrainian identity. Renowned for its grain farming and animal husbandry, this region gravitated into the Russian political and religious sphere of influence. This is particularly true of the extreme eastern areas, which are still heavily russified. Kiev, Kharkiv, Dnipropetrovsk, and Donetsk are the main cities.

The Northern regions (Sumy, Zhytomyr, Rivno, Volyn, and portions of the Kiev and Chernihiv districts) are predominantly dairy and grain-producing areas. Historically, they were less influenced by the steppe nomads and more by their proximity to Russia and Belarus. One particular ethnographic group of Ukrainians, the Polischuk*, reside in the Polisia marshes and are culturally and linguistically associated with the neighboring Belarusians.

Finally, the Western regions are quite distinct from the other two as a result of their culture and history. A significant portion of this region—Galicia (Halchyna), Bokovyna (Bukovina), Transcarpathia—was formerly associated with the Austrian Empire and Poland, being incorporated into the Ukrainian SSR only in 1939. Historically, politically, and psychologically, this region belongs to the ''Middle European'' milieu. The heart of this region is the city of L'viv (Lvov, Lemberg), Ukraine's second capital. The southeastern regions, centered on the large port city of Odessa, is rather cosmopolitan in ethnic composition. Much of the population consists of fairly late arrivals from elsewhere, particularly from Russia. Hence, the population in this district is also quite russified.

The history of Ukraine, like that of most East European nations, is marked by a high degree of discontinuity between its major epochs. Not surprisingly, the central themes in Ukrainian history have been the preservation of national identity, foreign domination, the quest for statehood, and modernization. The latter involved the transformation from a traditional agrarian society to a more diversified and pluralistic one; the other themes are all related to state-building imperatives. Because of its peculiar inability to forge a stable and cohesive national state, Ukraine has been relegated by some state-oriented scholars, such as Ivan Lesiak-Rudnytsky, to the category of ''non-historical'' nations. By ''non-historicity'' Lesiak-Rudnytsky does not mean that Ukraine lacks a rich and diverse historical past; rather, the concept simply indicates a ''rupture in historical continuity through the loss of a traditional representative class'' and of national state structures. Indeed, statelessness and loss of elites has often led the Ukrainian people, like the Hebrews, to political and cultural captivity, to becoming strangers in their own land, to being a large yet amorphous and exploited mass. Nowhere is this more evident than in the present terminological and historical confusion over the nature of "Ukrainian-hood," which outsiders often assume is a modern invention. Ukrainians believe that they are descended directly from the Rus', but there is a fundamental difference between "Rus' " and "Russia." The first evokes the medieval Kievan state, which the Ukrainians claim as their historical legacy. By contrast, the term "Russia" (*Rossiia*) was formally adopted by Tsar Peter the Great to denote his empire, comprised of what used to be known as 'Muscovy'' or the "Muscovite State" (*Moskovskoe gosudarstvo*) and the various later territorial acquisitions, such as Ukraine. The customary association of "Rus' " with "Russia" has thus, in a practical sense, deprived the Ukrainians of a historical name and clouded their national origins. This problem is also manifest in the conflict between Russians and Ukrainians over the medieval Kievan legacy, which has been formally incorporated as part of the Muscovite-Russian state. The foremost historian of Ukraine, Mykhailo Hrushevs'kyi wrote an article, "The Traditional Scheme of 'Russian' History and the Problem of a Rational Organization of the History of the Eastern Slavs" (1904), that boldly challenged the traditional interpretation and has even been supported by some Russian historians (such as A. E. Presniakov).

Nevertheless, due to a lack of institutional or national support (itself the result of centuries of Russian and Soviet domination), this concept has proved too radical. The problem is that "Ukrainian-hood" has been perceived as either a quixotic variation on "Great-Russianness" or a form of rabid yet historically unsubstantiated nationalism. Even Ukrainians themselves often see their history as one of the extension of foreign power and national ennui. In his monumental *Istoriia Ukrainy-Rusy*, Hrushevsky attributed this situation to "unfavorable historical circumstances" that:

dimmed the glorious and brilliant moments in the life of the Ukrainian nation, together with its expressions of action and creative energy, and cast it [Ukraine] upon the crossroads of political life as a defenseless booty for the insatiable appetites of its neighbors, an ethnographic mass without a national countenance, without traditions, and even without a name.

Hrushevsky's characterization of Ukrainian statelessness and submerged national identity, though somewhat melodramatic, nevertheless reflects accurately the vicissitudes of state- and nation-building in the Ukrainian historical process. This process was marked by a horizontal rather than a vertical progression, with periods of relative ascendancy followed by nearly complete decline. There have been at least three distinct historical epochs in Ukraine: the medieval Kievan Rus' era (tenth through thirteenth centuries), the Cossack period (sixteenth through early eighteenth centuries), and the period of tsarist-Soviet domination. Both the Kievan and the Cossack epochs resulted in the creation of distinct yet short-lived states. The third attempt at statehood was made in the period from 1917 through 1921, prior to Ukraine's incorporation into the Soviet Union. In 1991, Ukraine launched yet another bid for statehood by formally seceding from the Soviet Union.

The formation of the medieval Kievan state goes back to at least the sixth century. It was not until the famous "arrival" of the Varangian (Viking) Rurikid dynasty in the ninth century, however, that this state gained prominence. Its center was Kiev, the "mother-city of Rus'," an important link in the overland eastern trade route. Kiev also occupied a strategic position on the vital river route that stretched "from Varangians to the Greeks" (Scandinavia to Byzantium). Hence, Kiev's *raison d'être* was trade, complemented by sporadic plunder of the Byzantine littoral. Indeed, in 860, the Kievans launched a major attack against Constantinople, and, as the Byzantine chronicles reported, it took a miracle from the Virgin to save the city. Such Kievan rulers as Oleg (reigned 882–912), Igor (913–945), Olga (945–964), and Sviatoslav (964–972) distinguished themselves not only by their incessant warfare against the steppe nomads, but also by their relations with the Byzantines. Sviatoslav, the last representative of Varangian "heroic barbarism" in Kiev, dreamed of a Danubian empire that would eclipse even Byzantium.

The age of Varangian barbarism ended with Prince Volodymyr (Vladimir) the Great (980–1015). In 988, he ordered the conversion of his people to Christianity, stating that "He who refuses to be baptized will become my enemy." He married a Byzantine princess and presided over a loose confederation of principalities (Kiev, Novgorod, Chernihiv, etc.). He was subsequently canonized by the church. His choice of Byzantine, rather than Latin, Christianity proved fateful, in that it determined the culture of Ukraine for the next centuries. Byzantine influence was strongly manifest in the Cyrillic alphabet, as well as in the literature, art, architecture, and world-view of the Kievan Ukrainians. While it is true, as Dmimitry Obolensky has succinctly observed, that Kievan Rus' was an integral part of the "Byzantine Commonwealth," it was never a political or administrative outpost of the Byzantine empire. During the tenth and eleventh centuries, Kiev became a great center in its own right, completely independent from Byzantine meddling (except in church affairs). Its rulers maintained close trade, political, and personal relations with the ruling dynasties of Latin Europe. For example, a Kievan princess, Anna, became the queen of France and was apparently one of the few in the French court who could read and write. Another princess, Elizabeth, was married to the Norwegian king Harold (Hardraada), who invaded England in 1066. It must be noted that Kievan princes did not emulate the Byzantine brand of autocracy (caesaro-papism), which, some scholars believe, was revived later by Muscovite rulers. Rather, they ruled with the consent of their retainers.

The Kievan state reached its apogee of power and prestige under Yaroslav the Wise (1019–1054), nicknamed the "father-in-law of Europe" for having married his daughters and sons into foreign ruling houses. He introduced a rota system for succession to avoid dynastic conflicts, but it failed. Following his death, intense internecine strife sapped the vitality of the Kievan state and speeded its political atomization. Continuous pressure from the steppe nomads also contributed to the deepening crisis. The city of Kiev was particularly vulnerable to external threats. In 1169, the Suzdalian prince, Andrei Bogoliubskii, sacked and burned Kiev. But it was the Mongol* conquests, led first by Genghis Khan in 1123 and then by Batu Khan, in 1236, that sealed the fate of Kiev and the Kievan state. The city fell to the Mongols in 1240 and was completely devastated. The remaining principalities fell one by one to the Golden Horde.

The center of princely power shifted first to the western Galician-Volhynian state and later to the northern Vladimir-Suzdal principalities. Galician princes such as Danylo (reigned 1238–1262) and Lev (reigned 1264–1301) maintained relations with the Latin West (Danylo was awarded a crown and the title "King of Rus' " by the pope). When the dynasty died out, Galicia-Volhynian territories were parceled out among Lithuania (which received Volhynia, eastern Podolia, and Kiev), Poland (Galicia, Kholm, and western Podolia), Muscovy (Chernihiv-Siveria), Hungary (Trans-Carpathia), and Moldova (Bukovina). When the Union of Lublin (1569) united Poland and Lithuania into a single commonwealth, significant Ukrainian lands fell under direct Polish rule. Repressive Polish policies led to the national, economic, cultural, and confessional persecution of the Ukrainian minorities. Cities such as L'viv (Lvov) were placed under the Magdeburg Law, which favored Polish and German* elements. The crown made vast land grants to the Polish magnates (gentry), who in turn systematically enserfed the Ukrainian peasantry. The Ukrainian upper classes, in order to maintain their privileges, quickly emulated Polish ways and converted to Catholicism.

Only a few Ukrainian notables resisted the pressure for de-nationalization. Among them was Prince Konstantyn Ostrozh'skyi (1527–1608), who played a major role in Ukrainian political and cultural life in the sixteenth century. He founded the Ostroh Academy, the first intellectual center of Ukraine. Another important center of Ukrainian learning was established by the L'viv Brotherhood. The pivotal event of this period, however, was the Union of Brest of 1596. Ukrainians declared loyalty to the Church of Rome while preserving Byzantine (Orthodox) rites. This created the Ukrainian Greco-Catholic (Uniate) Church and the permanent division of Ukrainians along confessional lines.

By the the late sixteenth and early seventeenth centuries, there was a shift away from the western regions to the steppe frontier of central and southwest Ukraine. For reasons of over-population and the spread of serfdom, pioneers were attracted by the relative freedom and abundance of the steppe. Life on the steppe, however, was compromised by threats from the Crimean Tatars*, who sent annual plundering expeditions against settled communities. Hence, military forays into the steppe regions against the Tatars became common. In the spring, armed detachments would venture into the steppe or down the Dnieper River to trap, fish, or hunt. This activity was called going *na ukhody* ("to freeboot"). The *ukhodnyky* ("freebooters") would often clash with Tatar expeditions. This struggle over the steppe frontier gave rise to the famous Cossacks of the Zaporozhia.

The origins of the organized Zaprozhe Cossack host go back to the mid-sixteenth century, when Dmytro Baida Vyshnevets'kyi (d. 1564), a former chief administrator of the Kaniv and Cherkasy districts, built the first Cossack stronghold on the Dnieper island of Khortytsia in 1552. Known subsequently as *Sich* (the term derives from *sikty*, "to cut"), this stronghold was moved numerous times, but it became forever associated with the Cossack ethos. The Cossack host itself constituted a democratic military association of freemen, bound to a strict code of honor and vows of brotherhood. Their military exploits (often associated with plundering raids) became legendary, while their avowed defense of faith and nationality have provided a source of identification for Ukrainians. Superb horsemen, they excelled in lightning attacks and encircling tactics. Albeit often hired as mercenaries (they participated, for example, in the Thirty Years' War), the Cossacks owed allegiance to no one. Sworn enemies of the Tatars and their masters, the Ottoman Turks, the Cossacks would send armed flotillas down the Dnieper, break through the Tatar fortifications in the Crimea, and prey upon the Turkish coast around the Black Sea. These campaigns seriously undermined Tatar and Turkish power in the region.

The Cossack host would have little significance to Ukrainian history had it not become the main opponent to Polish expansionism into the heart of Ukraine. The Polish government naturally grew concerned about the growth of Cossack power and tried to keep their numbers down. Polish landlords also were troubled by the flight of many indentured serfs to the Cossack Sich. Polish authorities therefore resorted to the practice of registering Cossacks. Registered Cossacks were given revenues and special privileges for not waging war on Poland. This created tensions among unregistered Cossacks, to the extent that, beginning in 1591, there were several Cossack rebellions. Petro Sahaidachnyi (d. 1621), the first major Cossack *hetman* (elected supreme leader of the Cossack host), reorganized the Cossacks and transformed them into a highly disciplined army. Tensions between Poles and Ukrainians increased on many levels. In 1648, Ukrainian discontent exploded into a war of national liberation.

The Ukrainian-Cossack war against Poland was led by Bohdan Khmelnyts'kyi (Khmelnitsky) (ca.1595–1657). A well-educated military captain from Chyhyryn and a member of the petty nobility, he had suffered some personal grievances that the Polish courts refused to rectify. In 1647, he fled to Zaporozhia, where he was elected *hetman* and organized the uprising against Poland. Khmelnyts'kyi led an alliance of Cossacks, dissatisfied peasants, and Crimean Tatars to early brilliant victories against the Poles in 1648. In the course of the struggle, Khmelnyts'kyi founded the Ukrainian hetmanate, a Cossack state divided into military regiments administered by colonels, with the capital temporarily set in Chyhyryn. But the war with Poland dragged on for years. In 1654, Khmelnyts'kyi made a fateful decision that set the course of Ukrainian history: he signed the Treaty of Pereiaslav, which placed Ukraine under the protectorate of the tsar of Muscovy.

Khmelnyts'kyi's decision was prompted by the continuous yet inconclusive war with Poland, which seriously weakened both sides. Fearing further Polish expansionism, he turned to Muscovy. After protracted negotiations, the treaty was formally sworn at the town of Pereiaslav, against the express wishes of many of Khmelnyts'kyi's lieutenants. The precise terms of the treaty have become a source of great dispute, largely because the original documents have disappeared and the only extant texts are Muscovite drafts.

The official Russian view is that the Pereiaslav agreement was nothing less than a "reunion" of Ukraine with Muscovy. Ukrainians too agree that Khmelnyts'kyi tied Ukraine's fortunes to Russia, but only militarily, thereby allowing the preservation of an independent Cossack state headed by a *hetman*. Both sides agree that Russia has repeatedly violated the agreement by its subsequent incorporation of Ukraine into the Russian Empire. Khmelnyts'kyi himself, just prior to his death in 1657, began to reconsider his decision, but the treaty had given Muscovy a political and military foothold in Ukraine. Subsequent *hetmans*, such as Ivan Vyhovs'kyi (reigned 1657–1659) and Dmytro Doroshenko (1665–1676) sought to preserve the integrity of the hetmanate, but without success. In 1667, Ukraine was partitioned between Muscovy and Poland, marking the beginning of a long period of fratricidal conflicts known as the "Ruin." A truncated hetmanate maintained a precarious existence on the Left-Bank of the Dnieper Ukraine. Under Hetman Ivan Mazepa (reigned 1687–1709), the Ukrainians made their most dramatic attempt to break free from Moscow's grasp.

Mazepa was a man of exceptional ability and refinement. Under him, Left-Bank Ukraine experienced a great cultural revival. He built churches (Kiev's St. Sophia Cathedral was restored to its present "Cossack Baroque" style), patronized the arts, and endowed schools. The center of intellectual activity in Mazepa's Ukraine was the Kiev-Mohyla Academy (founded in 1632), the first institution of higher learning in Ukraine. At first, Mazepa believed that Ukraine could remain independent by cooperating with Peter I's Russia. As tsarist decrees became increasingly oppressive, however, he grew convinced that Ukrainian autonomy was becoming a mere technicality. Thus, in 1707, he entered into secret negotiations with the Swedish King Charles XII, but Mazepa then engaged in the Great Northern War against Russia. The Swedish-Cossack forces were defeated at the decisive Battle of Poltava (1709), which, in effect, established the Russian Empire. Mazepa's capital, Baturyn, and its entire population were savagely wiped out by tsarist armies, while Mazepa, for his "betrayal" of Peter I, was officially anathematized by the Russian Orthodox Church. Subsequently, the term "Mazepist" became synonymous with "traitor" in Russian parlance.

Poltava settled the fate of Ukraine. Mazepa's immediate successor in exile, Hetman Pylyp Orlyk (reigned 1710–1742) engaged in extensive diplomacy with the European powers to promote the restoration of an autonomous hetmanate but met with no success. In 1775, the last Zaporozhian Sich was destroyed by an order from Empress Catherine II, and, in 1781, the hetmanate itself was officially abolished. Left-Bank Ukraine was directly incorporated as an integral part of the Russian Empire. With the second and third partitions of Poland in 1793 and 1795, the remaining Ukrainian lands were also brought under direct Russian rule. Only Galicia escaped Russian domination, falling under Austrian control, where it remained from 1772 until 1918. Russian expansion under Catherine II also included the seizure of Crimea and the Black Sea coast from the Tatars. For all practical purposes, Ukraine had ceased to exist as a separate entity.

Indeed, the reign of Catherine II (1762–1796) established the traditional Russian policies of russification, national and cultural oppression, and economic exploitation. Despite her reputation as an enlightened despot, she institutionalized serfdom in Ukraine and parceled out huge landed estates to her legion of favorites. Understandably, Ukrainians are not great admirers of this "Northern Semiramis." Shevchenko, the national poet, reflected the general sentiment when he called her "an evil hag." The policies of other tsars, such as the reactionary Nicholas I (reigned 1825–1855) and even the reformer Alexander II (reigned 1855–1881), proved equally repressive; Alexander II's infamous "Ems Ukase" of 1873 totally banned the use of the Ukrainian language in print, for example.

While the majority of the privileged Ukrainian elites remained content with tsarist de-nationalizing policies, some resisted. Enlightened nobles (aptly called by one historian "Peoples of Old Ukraine"), such as Count Alexander Bezborod'ko, Hvyhorii and Vasyl' Poletyka, Vasyl' Kapnist, and others, longed for the Cossack past and believed that an autonomous Ukrainian hetmanate could still be revived with Russian blessings. Their hopes proved naive, but they were instrumental in preserving a national consciousness through their studies and research into Ukrainian history and ethnography. Perhaps one of the first "awakeners" was the philosopher Hrygorii Skovoroda (1722–1794), a worldly former student of the Kiev-Mohyla Academy who is sometimes called the Ukrainian Socrates. His populist ideals, tinged with baroque spirituality, found wide appeal among Ukrainians. Widespread nostalgia for the Cossack past was further aroused by *Istoriia Rusov* (History of the Rus'), which was written in Russian around 1800 by an unknown author and circulated in hundreds of manuscript copies for many years. The profound significance of this work, however, was that, for the first time, the traditional defense of Cossack liberties was fused with liberal ideas of the European Enlightenment—a synthesis between local patriotic ideals and mainstream Western political theories. In 1796, Ivan Kotliarevs'kyi, a member of the Poltava region gentry, published *Eneida* (Aeneid). This was a travesty of the famous Virgilian epic, in which a Cossack Aeneas romps through a pagan yet Ukrainianized antiquity with groups of ribald Zaporozhians. The poem was written in the vernacular, and its publication marked the birth of a purely Ukrainian literature. These and other developments not only lent legitimacy to Ukrainian aspirations but also provided a kind of artistic and cultural "investment" for a genuine Ukrainian cultural renaissance. After all, the early writings of the Ukrainian-born Nikolai Gogol (Hohol') did not germinate in a cultural void.

The beginning of the modern Ukrainian revival, however, dates from 1840, when Taras Shevchenko (1814–1861) published a small anthology of poetry, titled the *Kobzar* (The Bard), in St. Petersburg. Born a serf, Shevchenko was a painter by training but proved to be an extraordinarily gifted poet. In his poetry, which was clearly inspired by *Istoriia Rusov*, he sang of Cossacks, hetmans, and rebels and lamented the fate that had befallen Ukraine. While his imagery was both nostalgic and romantic, the message was uncompromisingly revolutionary. He was unforgiving of those who gravitated into the Russian imperial milieu (of Gogol, he wrote "while you laugh, I weep"). As a poet, Shevchenko did not produce a systematic political program, but, in later works ("The Dream," "The Epistle," "The Testament," etc.), he called for a national uprising against tyranny and foreign rule. Naturally, the tsarist authorities could not tolerate this and sent Shevchenko into a forced ten-year exile in Central Asia; Nicholas I personally ordered that he be "forbidden to write or to paint." Still, Shevchenko became both the prophet and the father of the Ukrainian national renaissance. The expanded version of Shevchenko's *Kobzar* has become a mandatory possession for every conscious Ukrainian.

In 1845, a group of Ukrainian intellectuals in Kiev founded a secret society, known as the "St. Cyril and Methodius Brotherhood." Its aims was the liberation of the Ukrainian people and the unification of all Slavs into a general federation. While Shevchenko was a founding member, the leading figures in the Brotherhood were two scholars, Panteleimon Kulish and Mykola Kostomarov. Its program was outlined in Kostomarov's *Knyhy byttia ukrains'koho narodu* (Book of Genesis of the Ukrainian People), which also provided a legal basis for Ukraine's independence from Russia. In 1847, the government disbanded the society and sent its leaders (including Shevchenko) into exile.

In 1861, a branch of *Hromada*, a St. Petersburg association of Ukrainians, was opened in Kiev; more branches soon appeared in other cities. Hromada's journal, *Osnova*, provided a forum for Ukrainian writers, poets, and scholars. This and similar periodicals began to shape a civil, nationally conscious society, led not only by poets and writers but also by distinguished scholars. Ethnography (reflecting the contemporary Cossack nostalgia and tsarist strictures) was the early favorite field of scholarly activity, but it was soon supplanted by the development of formal national history. From Kostomarov and Alexander Lazarevskyi to Volodymyr Antonovych, the first genuine historian of Ukraine, history became not only the repository of the national consciousness but also an instrument of a national-populist agenda—the so-called *khlopomany* (peasant-lovers) movement of the 1860s, with an emphasis on the "people."

Western Ukrainian lands, under relatively benevolent Austrian rule, also underwent a comparable national movement. Among the first awakeners of

Galicia was the "Ruthenian Triad," Markian Shashkevych (1811–1843), Ivan Vahylevych (1811–1866), and Iakiv Holovats'kyi (1814–1888), who published a literary collection, called *Rusalka Dnistrova* (Dniester's Nymph, 1837) in Ukrainian. Like *Eneida* in Left-Bank Ukraine, this collection was instrumental in the emergence of a literary tradition in Western Ukraine. With the abolition of serfdom in 1848, Galician Ukrainians entered the volatile Austrian political arena. They elected thirty-nine deputies to the first Austrian Diet. Shortly thereafter, they established a Ukrainian studies department at the L'viv University, published various popular and scholarly works in Ukrainian, and promoted cultural and educational activities through regional branches of the *Prosvita* (Enlightenment) Society (established in 1868). The most important scholarly-cultural organization, however, was the Shevchenko Scientific Society (established in 1873), whose members spanned both Russian and Austrian Ukraine. Indeed, contact between the two regions increased significantly.

Toward the end of the nineteenth century, a true Ukrainian political movement developed. To a large degree, the modern Ukrainian political movement began with Mykhailo Drahomanov (1841–1895), who produced the first systematic program. He believed that the solution of the Ukrainian problem lay in the democratization of both Austria-Hungary and Russia, whereby the Ukrainians would enter into an alliance with all progressive forces in Eastern Europe, Great Russians not excluded. The tsarist government responded with Alexander II's Ems Ukase of 1876, which temporarily stifled further national activities in Russian Ukraine. For a time, the focus of Ukrainian nationalist activities became Galicia, where the historian Mykhailo Hrushevs'kyi (1866–1934)—along with the poet Ivan Franko (1856–1916), the writer Vasyl' Styfanyk (1871–1936), and others—transformed the Shevchenko Scientific Society into a national institution.

Three developments in Russian Ukraine had a profound effect on subsequent developments: the abolition of serfdom in 1861, the progressive weakening of the tsarist system, and the modernization of the society by means of rapid industrialization and accelerated economic development. This last also included the rapid politicization of earlier cultural and literary movements. In the 1890s, the first true political parties, such as the "Revolutionary Ukrainian Party" (RUP), came into existence. RUP originated in the industrial city of Kharkiv (Kharkov) adopted a Marxist program, and soon became the Ukrainian Social-Democratic Labor Party. Other parties emerged as well, reflecting diverse programs and constituencies. There was also significant Ukrainian participation in the first two imperial dumas in St. Petersburg. The most important developments, however, were the political reconciliation between the Ukrainian elites and the masses, the spread of literacy, and the growth of Ukrainian political consciousness among the agrarian elements. As a result of these changes, the unveiling of a statue of Kotliarevs'kyi in Poltava in 1903, for example, became in effect a massive all-Ukrainian demonstration. Indeed, by about 1905, ideas for the complete restructuring of the Ukrainian society had been formulated by Viacheslav Lypyns'kyi (1882–1931), who called upon the russified and polonized Ukrainian nobility to return to the Ukrainian cause. Many did.

When World War I came in 1914, the Ukrainian movement was still in its early stages. The Ukrainian press, though not entirely banned, still suffered from steady repression by the tsarist authorities. Cultural and educational organizations invariably folded under official pressures. The peasantry remained largely illiterate and thus politically inarticulate. Regional differences, notably between Eastern and Western Ukrainians, were still pronounced.

The advent of the Russian Revolution in March 1917, however, changed the Ukrainian political landscape. On March 19, 1917, a mere week after the abdication of Tsar Nicholas II, a Ukrainian assembly, the Central Rada (council), was established in Kiev. It was headed by the historian Hrushevs'kyi, who had returned from exile in Moscow. In June, the Central Rada issued its "First Universal," declaring that Ukraine would seek independence. The Central Rada also created an executive organ, the General Secretariat, with Volodymyr Vynnychenko (1880–1951) as president. This action immediately created a conflict with the Russian Provisional Government of Prince Lvov. When V. I. Lenin and the Bolsheviks seized power in November 1917, they set up a rival Ukrainian government, called the "Ukrainian Soviet Republic," in the eastern provinces, with the city of Kharkiv (Kharkov) as its capital. Pressured by the Bolsheviks (who had declared war on the Kiev government), the Central Rada hastened to conclude a separate peace treaty with Germany at Brest-Litovsk (February 9, 1918). In December, Red Guards set forth on a bloody march on Kiev, destroying towns and villages along their way. With the Bolsheviks approaching, the Central Rada issued its "Fourth Universal" on January 22, 1918, proclaiming complete Ukrainian independence. A week later, 300 students died at Kruty, in a vain effort to defend Kiev. The capital fell, and the Central Rada fled to Zhytomyr.

Intent on securing the extensive food supplies provided by the Treaty of Brest-Litovsk, units of the German* and Austrian* armies relieved Kiev from Bolshevik control. Essentially an army of occupation, the Germans disbanded the Central Rada shortly thereafter and replaced it with a puppet regime, a hetmanate under Pavlo Skoropads'kyi (1873–1945), the scion of a distinguished Cossack family. Under Skoropads'kyi's rule, a degree of normality was established and widespread Ukrainianization occurred. Yet the hetman was unpopular, especially among the peasants, who bore the heavy burdens of provisioning the German military, and among the nationalists, who resented his association with former tsarist officials and with the German occupiers. Political opposition to his rule grew, and, when the German troops left Ukraine, Skoropads'kyi was forced to surrender his powers to the Directory in December 1918. The Directory was composed of members of the Central Rada, including Vynnychenko and Symon Petliura (1877–1926), the chosen supreme commander; in early 1919, Petliura became the head of the government. But the new government was surrounded by enemies: Bolsheviks, Whites (anti-Communist Russians), Poles, Allied intervention forces, peasant anarchists, and so forth. Ukraine became the arena for a complex and bloody struggle of diverse interests.

In October 1918, Western Ukraine also declared its independence from Austria-Hungary, and a Ukrainian National Council (UNR) was established in L'viv. To defend this independent entity, the Ukrainian Galician Army was created. The Poles claimed Galicia as their own and immediately resisted. As they had done centuries ago, the two sides entered into a protracted conflict. This led to negotiations between the UNR and the Kiev government, and, on January 22, 1919, in a massive ceremony in St. Sophia Square in Kiev,the formal unification of Western and Eastern Ukraine took place. Nevertheless, Ukraine found itself still at war with both Poland and Soviet Russia. The struggle was desperate and uneven, and by 1921, it was all over. Once again, Ukraine was divided by foreign powers—the lion's share going to the Soviets and Galicia to Poland. Petliura himself was forced into exile, and, in 1926, he was assassinated in Paris by a Jewish nationalist for his alleged persecution of Jews in Ukraine.

During the period of "War Communism," Bolsheviks in Ukraine for a time maintained the facade of a sovereign Ukrainian Soviet state. Indeed, in 1919, an official "Constitution of the Ukrainian SSR" was promulgated, and there were even formal treaties between the Russian and Ukrainian Soviet republics. In 1922, by means of such a "treaty," Ukraine was incorporated into the newly former Soviet Union as an "independent founding republic"; a separate Ukrainian constitution was issued in 1925. In reality, however, Ukraine had become an industrial and economic colony ruled from Moscow. Mass terror was instigated against the peasants almost from the outset, while systematic purges were conducted against the "enemies of the people" (the intelligentsia). Only the Communist Party was permitted to exist. Curiously, although the Ukrainian Communist Party was essentially controlled by Moscow, it was not ideologically homogeneous, particularly during the period of the New Economic Policy (NEP). A fundamental debate was taking place between the advocates of "international" (Russian) communism and the "national" (Ukrainian) variation. In 1923, during a temporary halt in Bolshevik-sponsored terror, a policy of "ukrainianization" was formally introduced by People's Commissar Oleksander Shums'kyi and continued by his successor Mykola Skrypnyk (1872–1933). While the policy was meant to promote the Ukrainian language, it also resulted in a major cultural and artistic revival. There was even talk of an autonomous Soviet Ukrainian state.

The rise of Josef Stalin, however, changed the political atmosphere in Ukraine. The brief revival of Ukrainian culture, subsequently labeled "the executed renaissance", was brutally terminated. The relatively liberal NEP gave way to the first Five Year Plan, which imposed strict controls over agriculture, industry, technology, education, and culture. In 1930s, the forced collectivization of the agricultural sector was launched, along with open state warfare against independent peasants, known as the *kurkuls* (*kulaks* in Russian). Hundreds of thousands of peasants were sent to die in the vast Soviet gulag. As agricultural production plummeted in 1932–1933, Stalin punished the peasants by forcibly requisitioning food from them. Special brigades would comb the villages, looking for hidden food. Most of the gathered grain rotted away at railways depots for lack of storage facilities and transportation. By the spring of 1933, a terrible famine had swept through Ukraine, killing somewhere between 7,000,000 to 10,000,000 people. No outside relief was allowed to enter, even as foreign correspondents, such as Walter Duranty of the *New York Times*, wrote glowing accounts denying the famine stories. To many modern Ukrainians, the famine of 1933, along with the Chernobyl disaster of 1986, stand as symbols of the Russian historical imperative to destroy the Ukrainian nation.

The famine was accompanied by systematic purges of the Ukrainian elites. The campaign began in 1929–1930, when forty-five leading scholars, writers, and intellectuals were accused of belonging to a secret nationalist organization, the Union for the Liberation of Ukraine. Thousands of others were then either executed outright or sent to certain death in the Siberian labor camps. This period became known as *Yezhovshchyna* (after M. Yezhov, the commissar of internal security). The previous policy of ukrainianization gave way to systematic russification, with ethnic Russians (including Nikita Khrushchev) brought from the outside to fill key positions vacated by the purges. Some notable Ukrainians, such as writer Mykola Khvyliovyi and commisar of education Mykola Skrypnyk, committed suicide. Stalin's new Constitution of 1936 guaranteed on paper impressive individual and national rights (including the right of secession). In reality, it proved but a cover for the new totalitarian order. During the same period, the pace of industrialization in Ukraine reached fever pitch.

During the interwar years, Western Ukraine was part of the Polish state. Poland never granted autonomy to the Ukrainians and promoted a policy of assimilation. Still, Ukrainians were allowed to participate in the political system through legally recognized parties, such as the Ukrainian National Democratic Union. At the same time, harsh Polish measures stimulated secret political activities on both the left and the right. The Organization of Ukrainian Nationalists (OUN), founded in 1929, aspired to independence and practiced acts of political terrorism against Polish officials. The 1939 Nazi-Soviet Non-Aggression Pact, which allowed the Soviet Union to annex Western Ukraine directly into the Ukrainian SSR, proved a severe blow to the OUN and its goals. The Soviets immediately implemented mass terror against the local population. In the ensuing crises, the OUN split into two warring factions: a radical wing, led by Stephen Bandera, and a moderate one, led by Andrii Mel'nyk. Both factions continued their internecine feud but also carried out an underground struggle against the Nazis, the Soviets, and the Poles to the end of World War II and even beyond. In 1940, the Soviets also "liberated" Bokovyna (Bukovina) and Bessarabia from Romania, the Ukrainian regions were incorporated directly into the Ukrainian SSR, with the remainder organized into the Moldovan SSR.

On June 22, 1941, the Nazis broke the Non-Aggression Pact and invaded the Soviet Union. Their march across Ukraine was rapid. On June 30, L'viv was taken; on September 19, Kiev fell, and, on October 24, Kharkiv (Kharkov). In their retreat, the Soviets carried out mass executions of the political prisoners; extensive Soviet killing fields have already been opened to the public. At first, some Ukrainians received the Germans as liberators and even volunteered for military service against the Red Army. The Germans, however, chose to continue the Soviet-style repressions and harsh colonial policies toward the Ukrainians. In the fall of 1941, the Germans began a mass extermination of Jews, intellectuals, and prisoners of war. Babi Yar, on the outskirts of Kiev, became but the most infamous mass-killing center. Some 3,000,000 Ukrainians were sent to Germany as "East-workers." Partisan resistance grew, and, in 1942, the OUN was re-organized into the Ukrainian Insurgent Army (UPA), commanded by General Taras Chuprynka (known as Roman Shukhevych prior to the revolution). The army fought against both the Germans and the advancing Soviets. In 1943, the Germans began their retreat, systematically destroying towns and villages and driving the civilian population westward. Many Ukrainians ended up in the numerous "displaced persons" camps in Germany. At war's end, some returned home (to receive automatic ten-year labor-camp sentences for their "betrayal of the Fatherland"), but the majority eventually emigrated to far-flung corners of the world.

The war had devastated Ukraine. Its major cities (Kiev, Kharkiv, etc.) lay in ruins, and some 80 percent of its industry had been either destroyed or transferred elsewhere. Its human losses were among the highest in Europe, compounded by the mass terror of the 1930s, emigration, and the massive repressions and deportations of the postwar period. All concessions to Ukrainian culture and nationality made during the war (to woo Ukrainians into the Soviet camp) were abolished. Campaigns against "bourgeois nationalism" were resumed in 1946, and counter-insurgency activities, directed mostly against UPA, were intensified (Chuprynka himself fell in battle in 1950).

Nonetheless, while the Soviet army and the secret police were battling the UPA in Western Ukraine, Stalin granted all Soviet republics, Ukraine included, the right to establish direct relations with foreign states. This proved but a paper technicality, but, in 1945, Ukraine (along with the Soviet Union and Belarus) became a charter member of the United Nations, although without direct diplomatic relations. (English efforts to establish direct diplomatic relations with Ukraine in 1947 and 1950 were ignored.) In 1949, the Ukrainian SSR received its own state emblem and flag (red, with a narrow horizontal blue stripe, adorned with hammer, sickle, and five-pointed gold star). At the same time, however, the Uniate (Ukrainian Catholic) Church was formally dissolved in 1946. Young Ukrainians were "voluntarily" sent to Siberian and Central Asian settlements, while Ukrainian cities, particularly Kiev, received a heavy infusion of Russians.

Stalin's death in 1953 brought a period of relative relaxation. Russification was temporarily halted, and the Ukrainian government, hitherto powerless, received a modicum of authority over economic, financial, and educational initiatives. In his famous "Secret Speech" denouncing Stalin's crimes in 1956, Nikita Khrushchev catalogued some of the crimes committed against the Ukrainians in earlier periods. The ensuing policy of "de-Stalinization" and attacks on the "cult of personality" allowed additional concessions to Ukrainian cultural identity, albeit not in matters of education and language, where russification continued unabated. Stalin's demise also brought immediate changes in the leadership of the Ukrainian Communist Party. In 1957, an ethnic Ukrainian, A. P. Kirichenko, became general-secretary; he was soon replaced by another native, N. Podgorny (or Pidhirnyi). When Podgorny was made president of the Soviet Union in 1963, he was replaced in Ukraine by Petro Shelest. At first, Shelest proved a loyal executor of Moscow's policies, but eventually he rebelled against the economic exploitation of his republic. In 1972, Leonid Brezhnev accused Shelest of "latent nationalism" and removed him from power, appointing the more compliant Volodymyr Shcherbyts'kyi to have charge of the Ukrainian apparatus.

The early 1960s witnessed a Ukrainian renaissance, brought forth by the "Sixties" (Shistydesiatnyky)—young intellectuals, poets, writers, critics, and publicists. At first, their goals were not overtly political, in that they wished merely to promote and safeguard Ukrainian culture and language. But in the Soviet context, language and culture were dangerous political issues, and the authorities resorted to repressive measures. This in turn brought about demands for political and national rights within the framework of the existing laws and constitutional guarantees.

In 1964, the last remnants of the "Khrushchev Thaw" ended with the sudden removal of its architect from power. In September 1965, some twenty-five members of the Ukrainian intelligentsia were arrested in diverse parts of the republic. They included the historian Valyntyn Moroz, the literary critic Ivan Svitlychnyi, and others. They were accused of nationalism, anti-Soviet activities, and other crimes against the state. For this, they were sentenced, after closed trials, to various terms in labor camps. The trials, however, provoked an unprecedented wave of protests. The journalist Viacheslav Chornovil gathered and publicized documents pertinent to the trials in a collection, called *The Chornovil Papers*, which circulated widely in manuscript form; for this, he himself was arrested in 1967. The dissenters then resorted to *samizdat* ("self-publishing") and, in 1970, the *Ukrainian Herald*, which was printed surreptitiously, documented Soviet violations of civil rights regularly.

In 1972, when Shelest was removed from office, the Soviet crackdowns on Ukrainian dissent intensified under the direction of the KGB chief Yuri Andropov. A new wave of arrests followed. Among those arrested were the most prominent dissenters, including the following: Iurii Shukhevych (the son of the UPA genreral Taras Chuprynka), poets Vasyl' Stus and Vasyl' Kalynets', critic Ievhen Svers'tiuk, artist Stefaniia Shabatura, philologist Nadia Svitlychna, and many others. A new twist was the internment of dissenters, including cyberneticist Leonid Pliushch and war hero General Petro Grigorenko, in psychiatric clinics for their "sluggish schizophrenia." The fall of Shelest also encouraged Shcherbyts'kyi's crackdown on further cultural and linguistic reforms.

The Helsinki Accords of 1975, which guaranteed various international civil rights, led to the formation of "Helsinki Watch" groups throughout the Soviet Union. The Ukrainian group was headed by writers Mykola Rudenko and Oleksii Tykhyi; both were subsequently arrested and sent to Siberia. The Ukrainian Helsinki group, however, was an unprecedented phenomenon, in that it was an open civic organization and that it established contacts with similar groups throughout the Soviet Union. Its membership was diverse and included committed Marxists. Indeed, dissent took many forms. The government's fierce persecution of Ukrainian Uniates had failed to obliterate the Ukrainian Greek Catholic Church ("the church in catacombs"). Thus, in 1982, Iosyf Terelia organized the Committee for the Defense of the Ukrainian Catholic Church to demand outright legalization. Ukrainian Orthodox Christians also began to resist their domination by the Moscow patriarchate. The most vocal and dynamic religious dissent came from Ukrainian Baptists and other evangelicals, who continued to grow in numbers despite extremely harsh governmental repression.

The death of Brezhnev in 1982 and the emergence of Mikhail Gorbachev in 1985 once again altered the situation in Ukraine. Gorbachev's rise marked the emergence of a new generation of Soviet *apparatchiki*—younger, more sophisticated, and committed to change. Gorbachev's policy of *perestroika* (restructuring) of the moribund Soviet economy entailed *glasnost* (openness) of the hitherto secretive Soviet society. To what extent this policy was meant to apply beyond the rarefied atmosphere of Moscow is a matter of speculation. In any case, Gorbachev's *glasnost* was severely tested by the Chernobyl disaster of April 26, 1986. The events of the nuclear power complex, a mere sixty miles from Kiev, proved to be the worst atomic accident in history, blanketing vast regions in Ukraine and Belarus with radioactive fallout. In typical Soviet fashion, the authorities attempted to cover up the tragedy, to the extent that officials did not even deem it necessary to cancel planned festivities in Kiev or to evacuate the people from the nearby town of Prypiat. Many people were therefore exposed to massive radiation. Resentment not only over the handling of the disaster but also over the decision to build obsolete and unsafe nuclear power plants so close to densely populated regions was widespread. Moreover, tension between the Ukrainian and Soviet Union governmental agencies, who blamed each other, mounted. To Ukrainians, Chernobyl, more than any other event in recent memory, has become both a symbol of Russian imperial disdain for Ukraine and a catalyst for renewed national unity.

Fueled by Gorbachev's somewhat incoherent reforms and the relative weakening of the party and government structures, events were rapidly unfolding in Moscow and the Baltic republics. Nonetheless, most Ukrainians seemed strangely reluctant to press their case against the besieged Kremlin. Gorbachev, sensing an awakening giant to the south, made a trip to Ukraine in February 1989. There he suggested that "We Slavs must stick together; the future of the Soviet Union depends on our unity." In the ensuing elections for the Congress of Peoples' Deputies on March 26, the Communist candidates suffered major setbacks, including the humiliating defeat of five regional party bosses at the polls. Even more significantly, the election campaign opened the floodgates of public debate on a wide variety of topics. Something of a civil society was beginning to emerge.

The momentum for Ukrainian autonomy had already experienced a quantum leap with the emergence in 1988 of the Ukrainian Peoples' Movement for Restructuring, better known as *Rukh* (literally, "movement"), in Kiev. In September 1989, it held its first congress in L'viv, the historic center of modern Ukrainian nationalism. The congress proved to be an eclectic event—part political, part cultural, and part funk. This was particularly evident during the second congress in October 1990. It attracted huge crowds, in open defiance of the authorities. Young men dressed as Cossacks mingled with the crowd, while Sister Vika, a post-punk band, entertained the crowd with such sardonic ditties as "I don't want sausage, don't want butter, don't want fancy dining;/All I want is for the Kremlin's star to keep on shining." Despite the theatrics, Rukh became the Ukrainian version of Poland's Solidarity or Czechoslovakia's Civic Forum—an umbrella organization for all progressive forces, including even reformed and reform-minded Communists. Indeed, its founder was poet Ivan Drach (b. 1936), a card-carrying member of the Communist Party, now cast in the mold of a classic nineteenth-century literary nationalist like Giuseppe Mazzini or Adam Mickiewicz. Important support was also lent by the outlawed Uniate Church. Within a short period, Rukh had become a powerful force, with some 700,000 dues-paying members and millions of fellow travelers. Its policies were pluralistic, including significant Jewish participation; one of its founding members was Alexander Burakovsky, while the commission on national minorities was headed by Yosif Zisels. Dmytro Pavlychko, another Rukh leader, summarized the general consensus when he stated that "the idea of Ukraine just for Ukrainians is unacceptable."

There were other forces gathering strength as well. By 1989, other independent groups had also emerged to challenge the primacy of the Ukrainian Communist Party (CPU). They included the environmentalist organization *Zelenyi Svit* (Green World, better known as the "Greens"), the Democratic Union, and the Memorial Society. Equally ominous for the government were the independent workers' movements, particularly in the Donbass and other heavily russified regions of Eastern Ukraine. Although the grievances of the Donbass workers were predominantly economic and social in character, the workers became rapidly politicized, joined the democratic movement, and called for Ukrainian autonomy. In 1989, they launched a series of local strikes and in July joined the striking miners of western Siberia. Among their demands were the abolition of Article 6 from the Soviet Constitution (which gave a monopoly of power to the Communist Party) and the immediate resignation of the CPU boss, Shcherbyts'kyi. Against all expectations, an intense hatred of the "partocrats" roused the national consciousness of hitherto inarticulate and apolitical miners. A popular slogan among the Donetsk miners was *Komuniaky na hiliaky* ("Commies to the gallows").

Shcherbyts'kyi's political impotence with regard to Rukh and the miners' movement led to his dismissal in September 1989. He was replaced in the CPU by Volodymyr Ivashko, widely perceived as a Kremlin stooge. Indeed, Ivashko was instrumental in sabotaging Rukh's nominations for the local and republican elections that took place on March 4, 1990. Yet, despite the obstructionist tactics of the CPU, the newly constituted Democratic Bloc won 108 of the 450 seats in the Ukrainian Supreme Soviet. With the addition of sixty seats won by various independent candidates, the opposition could count on 170 votes to challenge the Communist-led majority in the parliament. Indeed, in Western Ukraine, the Rukh supporters nearly swept the elections.

In June 1990, when Ivashko was elected Chairman of the Supreme Soviet (which was the highest governmental office), the Democratic Bloc in the parliament launched a strong protest, objecting to the party chief's also becoming head of state. The conflict was resolved when Ivashko, on Gorbachev's invitation, resigned first as CPU chief and then as head of state in July to become the Deputy Chairman of the Soviet Communist Party in Moscow. His departure was marked by joyous celebrations in Kiev, with the crowd chanting in derision *Proshchay Ivashko, pereletna ptashko*! ("Farewell Ivashko, the itinerant birdie"). Stanislav Hurenko then became the CPU chief; a former Brezhnev crony, Vitalyi Masol, was re-elected (after considerable opposition) as premier, and Leonid Kravchuk, the former second secretary of the CPU in charge of ideology, became chairman of the supreme soviet.

A remarkable event took place on July 16, 1990, when the Ukrainian Supreme Soviet, with Kravchuk presiding, formally adopted a four-point declaration. The document proclaimed Ukrainian sovereignty, its rights to a national army and security forces, the supremacy of republican authority over Ukraine's territories, and an intent to transform Ukraine into a nuclear-free zone. These represented an affirmation of general principles rather than immediate goals, an apparent concession to pressures from the independent parties. Perhaps only a few really understood their significance. Protests, however, continued. In October, 100,000 students marched on Kiev. A tent city housing some 500 hunger-striking students arose in the center of the city. The student hunger strike received wide publicity throughout Ukraine, apparently with the blessing of certain officials in the government. Masol was forced to resign, and Vitold Fokin (a native Ukrainian, despite the Russian surname) came in as the compromise choice for premier. The arrest of Stepan Khmara, a fervent nationalist, stirred up another round of demonstrations and protests. This incident smacked of KGB provocation, and, as the case dragged on, it began to assume a surreal quality, involving numerous people and bizarre incidents.

By October 1990, disillusionment with *perestroika* and Gorbachev's sudden shift to the right radicalized Rukh, which had originally been pressing only for a measure of autonomy. At its second congress in October 1990, it called for the outright independence of Ukraine. At the same time, the Ukrainian government was engaged in the negotiations for a new Union treaty, which was to be put to a popular referendum in the spring of 1991. The ballot also included a referendum on the sovereignty declaration. The results proved ambivalent. The election drew 84 percent of all eligible voters. Of these, 70 percent voted to support Gorbachev's "renewed federation" to preserve the integrity of the Soviet Union, but 80 percent also voted for sovereignty. Some of the democratic forces interpreted the results as a mandate for Ukrainian independence. Demands for complete Ukrainian independence by parliamentary means were advocated by various factions, including new political parties, like the Ukrainian Republican Party and the Ukrainian Peasant Democratic Party. Some recognized the legitimacy of the U.S.-based Ukrainian "exile government." Even the CPU split into "national" and "pro-empire" factions.

The initial Ukrainian response to the attempted coup of August 19, 1991, by the nefarious Committee for the State of Emergency was cautious. On August 20, the Presidium of the Ukrainian Supreme Soviet issued a mild rebuke of the plotters, but the situation in Kiev remained calm. The collapse of the coup and the subsequent banning of the Communist Party by Boris Yeltsin, however, brought an immediate response. On August 24, the Ukrainian Supreme Soviet passed a resolution for Ukrainian independence, pending a national referendum on December 1, when presidential elections would also take place.

Although some sixty candidates were nominated for the post of the president of Ukraine, Kravchuk clearly had the lead from the start. Despite his Communist past and relative silence during the Moscow coup (just one month before the coup, he was still advocating the idea of a "renewed union"), he had the experience and the proper pro-independence credentials to satisfy even the skeptics. Moreover, the opposition was split among five separate candidates. Only Chornovil, a former dissident and mayor of L'viv (Lvov), was a viable opponent for the politically sagacious Kravchuk. In the end, with some 84 percent of the electorate participating, Kravchuk received a clear majority of 62 percent of the vote, while Chornovil could muster only 23 percent of the total. More importantly, an astonishing 90 percent voted in favor of independence. Even heavily russified districts voted in favor. The Ukrainian referendum, both symbolically and practically, spelled the end of the once mighty empire known as the Soviet Union. On December 8, 1991, Kravchuk, together with Yeltsin of Russia and Shushkevich of Belarus (formerly Belarusia), met in Minsk to sign the obituary. Urging the world community to withdraw recognition of the former Soviet Union, they called for the immediate recognition of new Commonwealth of Independent States (CIS). Shortly thereafter, the CIS became composed of eleven members. This loose confederation was forged primarily to satisfy Ukrainian concerns about possible Russian aggression. It is ironic, therefore, that Ukraine has been instrumental in deconstructing the CIS. From the outset, Ukrainians had seen it as a transitional structure (an "instrument of civilized divorce"), whereas others, most notably Russia, had interpreted it as a unified, supra-national structure. Kravchuk has consistently pressed for weak ties among the members and blocked any efforts to create permanent CIS structures. Instead, he has insisted on bilateral relations, reminding everyone that CIS was not a state and was not subject to international law.

There were other difficulties. When Yeltsin, through a spokesman, stated that the results of the Ukrainian referendum would require Russia to reconsider the present borders, the Ukrainians reacted with great alarm. Yeltsin immediately defused the crisis by sending a delegation headed by Vice-President Rutskoi and the mayor of St. Petersburg, Anatolii Sobchak, to Kiev to offer explanations. Other sources of discord have included the reapportionment of the Soviet national assets, the external debt, currency and customs regulations, and so forth. But it is the military situation that has proved exceedingly complex. The most immediate concern has been control over the vast arsenal of strategic and tactical nuclear weapons on Ukrainian soil. Eventually, Ukraine, abiding by its earlier resolution to become a nuclear-free zone, relinquished the tactical weapons to Russian command. Still, the nuclear weapons dispute demonstrated the volatility of the military situation. With great reluctance, Ukraine originally agreed to a CIS unified military command, with the provision that Ukraine also be allowed to have an independent national guard. Steps to form an independent Ukrainian army, however, had preceded the formation of the CIS. At one time, Kravchuk formally announced that all land, air, and naval forces in Ukraine were to be nationalized. Although this declaration proved too sweeping and somewhat premature, the territorial forces were quickly ''Ukrainianized'' by Minister of Defense Konstantyn Morozov. At present, Ukraine has an army of approximately 700,000, with plans to reduce it eventually to between 200,000 and 300,000.

A dispute continues to fester over the control of the Black Sea fleet and the status of Crimea, both of which remain potential sources of conflict between Russia and Ukraine. The confrontation is more than a mere show of inflated sovereignty or the opening gambit for the inevitable deal between two former ''brethren'' nations. It symbolizes a much larger and more unpleasant reality for Russia and challenges its sense of historical destiny. Psychologically, the loss of Ukraine is painful (Lenin had said that ''to lose Ukraine would be to lose one's head''), since, for Russia, this event is tinged with a sense of betrayal by a ''younger brother.'' Beyond the imperial syndrome, there remains Russia's historical, strategic, and geo-political thrust toward Constantinople and the Dardanelles, warm water ports, and great power status. An independent Ukraine, in full control of the Black Sea fleet and its Crimean bases, presumably would force Russia to abandon the centuries-old expansionist dream of the Russian tsars.

Thus, the Crimean Peninsula, with its strongly ethnic Russian population (the original Tatar inhabitants having been dispersed under Stalin), has become a symbol for the increasingly vocal Russian conservatives and neo-fascist ideologues of ''one and indivisible Russia.'' Vladimir Lukin, a member of the Russian parliament, circulated a memo in January 1992, urging a re-examination of the legality of the transfer of Crimea to Ukrainian jurisdiction in 1954. This action outraged the Ukrainians, who believed that any Russian action on the issue of Crimea constituted a violation of the CIS charter. The situation worsened after the much-publicized trip of Vice-President Rutskoi to Sevastopol in April 1992, when, hugging the huge gun barrel of a warship, he claimed both Crimea and the Black Sea as Russia's property. Ukraine responded by giving Crimea greater autonomy, but the situation was complicated by a May resolution for independence; this was subsequently rescinded by the Crimean parliament. There have since been repeated incidents and confrontations between the Ukrainians and the Russian Black Sea fleet. In July 1992, Kravchuk and Yeltsin agreed to postpone any decision on the fate of the fleet for three years, which means that the issue will continue to simmer. Ukrainians remain apprehensive about Russian motives. They perceive the presence of the Russian military on the Black Sea as a threat to Ukrainian sovereignty and an obstacle to their economic well-being. Many also believe that even a democratic Russia will never be reconciled to the loss of Ukraine, its prize colonial possession. Viewing Ukrainian independence not as a final act but as a historical aberration, Russia will continue to work to influence events in Ukraine, both from beyond the borders and from within, by inciting anti-Ukrainian sentiment among the sizable Russian minority. This policy is also apparent in the continuing crisis in Moldova, where Russia seems intent on a land-grab. Although the scenario for an all-out conflict appears somewhat farfetched, relations with their former Russian masters, fraught with the memory of centuries of oppression, make Ukrainians weary.

Hence, Ukrainians are intent on separating themselves from the Russian sphere as quickly as possible. Ukraine has refused to be part of the "ruble zone" and, after a mixed experiment with a coupon system, it is about to introduce its own currency, the *hryvnia*. Ukrainians are determined to join the European "common home," from which they believe they were torn by unfavorable historical circumstances. Even before the formal act of independence, Ukraine began to establish economic and political links with other countries. Prime attention was given to its immediate western neighbors, to Hungary, Czechoslovakia, and—ironically—to its old historic foe, Poland. Beyond that, Germany is perceived as Ukraine's most important potential economic and political partner. Canada, which has a significant Ukrainian minority, is likewise becoming a major economic and cultural partner. By contrast, the United States, insofar as Ukrainians are concerned, is still "Russo-centered" (thanks largely to President Bush's famous "chicken Kiev" speech to the Ukrainian Parliament on the eve of the Soviet coup in August 1991, in which he advised Ukrainians to refrain from "suicidal nationalism") and has not yet become a reliable ally. Ukrainians are still trying to convince Washington and the European governments that an independent and strong Ukraine is the best guarantee against any future Russian aggression. They point out that Russia has neither fully renounced its imperial heritage nor completely accepted the inviolability of present borders. Moreover, there has been a blurring of CIS and Russian concerns, in that the huge CIS strategic forces and centralized command still remain under strict Russian control.

Hence, when Americans or Europeans express concern about the reluctance of Ukrainians to give up their strategic weaponry, their claim to the Black Sea fleet, or their determination to maintain a viable national army, they show that they do not understand that Russia, by sheer force of contiguity and historical weight, is and will always be Ukraine's most important strategic concern. For now, Russia is too preoccupied with its internal restructuring and too dependent upon the West to revert to its historical expansionism. But should Russia put its house in order or should its current experiment with democracy give way to authoritarianism, then all bets are off. Ukrainians are keenly aware that the West will prove unwilling or unable to guarantee Ukrainian sovereignty, as demonstrated by the Yugoslav example, forcing Ukraine to stand alone against great odds.

In the meantime, Ukrainians, with the notable exception of the Crimean and Black Sea fleet issue, have been extremely careful not to antagonize the Russian bear on their northern, eastern, and (at least for now) southern flanks. So far, there have been no significant inter-ethnic conflicts within the borders of Ukraine, and the euphoria over independence has not translated into chauvinism. Ukrainian authorities have ruled out any form of discrimination in matters of language, culture, and political organization; thus, the rights of Ukrainian citizenship are not contingent upon ethnic or linguistic conditions. Even the much-publicized loyalty oath for armed forces units is offered in both Ukrainian and Russian. Moreover, the government of Kravchuk (unlike that of Yeltsin) has not been drawn into the Moldovan quagmire, despite historic territorial claims and the presence of a significant Ukrainian population in the Trans-Dniester region.

The issue of what exactly constitutes a "Ukrainian" nowadays is still a matter of considerable ambiguity. Historically, Ukrainians have defined their uniqueness in contradistinction with "Muscovism" or "Russianness." To a larger extent, this has been a matter of language; hence, the urgent pleas for the "ukrainian-ization" of politics and culture by the intelligentsia in the 1930s and the 1960s. Thus, the father of Ukrainian linguistic exceptionalism, poet Taras Shevchenko, remains a powerful symbol in the national consciousness. His *Kobzar*, in a true sense, has become the repository of Ukrainian existential exclusivity. The same may be said of the Cossack legacy, the Ukraine's most enduring myth and symbol of resourcefulness and democratic ideals. Outsiders today may be amused by the sight of young men rigged out in Cossack dress and paraphernalia, sporting the Zaporozhian *osyledyts'* (a traditional Cossack scalplock hairpiece) and swords. But the Cossack epoch, separated from the current uncertain realities by long centuries of "non-historicity," is actually the most immediate collective memory of an independent national existence. Other potent symbols are the once-forbidden blue and yellow flag and the trident emblem, a legacy of the Kievan era. It should be noted that the revival of Cossack traditions has emerged among Russians as well.

The problem of national character, however, remains complicated. Historically, Ukrainians have been a nation of peasants struggling with modernity; consider Ivan Franko's celebrated declaration that "I am a peasant—prologue, not epilogue.'' Lacking a clearly defined, middle-class, political culture, Ukrainians have devised political philosophies based both on the Cossack's extreme individualism and on peasant fatalism. In the Cossack tradition, the *hetman* was democratically elected and subject to recall, but, once chosen, he exercises absolute power; some may perceive Kravchuk's political proclivities in these terms. At the same time, modern efforts to introduce militancy into the peasant ethos and thus to create a new order (exemplified by Viacheslav Lypyns'kyi's *Letters to My Brother Farmers* in 1921–1922) have met with only partial success. Nevertheless, the stoic fatalism and inherent conservatism of peasants have preserved the identity of the entire nation during some of the bleakest periods of Ukrainian history. Indeed, the nineteenth-century national movement was village-based, whereas the present national consciousness is predominantly urban and professional in origin.

The Ukrainian world view rests mostly on idealism. Not objective reality but the ''ideal'' sustains the quest for fulfillment. This idealization begins with the Ukrainian attachment to the soil and the *prostor* (open-spaces), a veneration of the female sex, a belief in human goodness and dignity, and boundless optimism. While Ukrainians have failed to produce a philosophical system based on the ego principle, individualism is nonetheless central to the Ukrainian psyche; any encroachment upon individualism, even if it benefits the entire community, will be resented. This extreme, almost anarchistic, individualism tends to reject all manner of authority and communal life when obedience and compromise are required. The Ukrainian will regard individualism as an end in itself, while the *hromada* (community) is merely the sum or union of individuals. This is particularly striking when compared with the Russian *mir* (commune) tradition, whose collectivist and subservient tendencies, in the view of some observers, are central to Russian socio-political culture. Hence, in the Ukrainian mentality, there is the assumption that extreme tsarism is a natural extension of the Muscovite character and that the Marxist-Leninist idea is its natural by-product. Yet both Russians and Ukrainians demonstrate a preponderance of feeling over reason (perhaps characteristics of all Slavs), whereas boundless enthusiasm may be followed by total apathy and despair. These emotional extremes create a psychological imbalance, which has been reflected in high and low points of Ukrainian history.

Still, the Ukrainian worldview is characterized by optimism. Despite the crushing catastrophes and cruel vagaries of history, the centuries of servitude and persecution, the man-made famines and totalitarian terror, the displacement and de-nationalization, hope for a better future was ever present. Indeed, the recent collapse of the Soviet Union and the emergence of an independent Ukraine had always been an item of faith with the Ukrainians; the only surprise was in the matter of timing and method. Most believed that it could happen only through violent means. That independence came with apparent Russian ''consent'' proved somewhat unsettling.

The effect of seven decades of Soviet rule upon the new Ukraine remains to be seen. The present government of Kravchuk has often been dismissed as an oligarchy composed of the old Communist (Brezhnevite) *apparat*. Radical economic reform has been widely discussed but not implemented. Similarly, laws on privatization have been passed and immediately ignored. Concurrent inflation and the collapse of production have become disastrous. Indeed, the recent dismissal of Volodymyr Lanovyi, the reform-minded deputy prime minister in charge of economics, was widely criticized as a step backward. Lanovyi was an advocate of the "market system" and was considered by many observers to be the best hope for meaningful economic reform. He had pushed through a privatization measure that was almost immediately shelved. He also criticized the system of coupons introduced as a preliminary Ukrainian currency, in the spring of 1991; Lanovyi believed that the imperative for a separate Ukrainian currency was motivated purely by political, rather than economic, reasons. He was replaced by a trusted member of the old *nomenklatura*. Yet, at the center of this raging storm is Kravchuk, who, for all his notoriety, remains something of an enigma.

Originally a faithful *apparatchik*, Kravchuk, at age fifty-seven, has become a fierce advocate of Ukrainian independence. Many perceive this transformation as cynical opportunism, while others have hailed him as a response to Shevchenko's timeless query, "Where is our Washington?" All agree that he is a *khytryi lys* (wily fox) with superb skills of self-promotion. A Communist since his youth, Kravchuk rose quickly to become a member of the CPU's Central Committee, where he excelled, according to one of his detractors, in "closing churches and exposing 'Ukrainian bourgeois nationalists.' " In 1979, he was put in charge of agitation and propaganda and, in 1988, he became the chief ideologist of the CPU. Writer Abraham Brumberg has stated that Kravchuk's recent conversion to democratic principles represents nothing less than a "triumph of calculation." Yet, to Kravchuk's credit, he has been unique among the old partocrats in his grasp of the tenor of the times, which led him into an early dialogue with the emerging Rukh. To those critical of his timidity during the 1991 coup, he has responded that, by keeping Ukraine calm, he shielded it from bloodshed. It is clear that Kravchuk (unlike his predecessor Ivashko, who left for Moscow's uncertain political currents) has understood the great power base inherent in a nation of 52 million people. He clearly enjoys the trappings of independent statehood, and the power and recognition that derive from popular support. Nonetheless, he has placed an overwhelming emphasis on political stability and state-building at the expense of economic reforms. At times, he seems to equate loyalty to the state with respect for his own presidential authority. Thus, when Ukrainians from the diaspora criticized him during the World Congress of Ukrainians, held in August 1992 to commemorate the first anniversary of Ukrainian independence, he reacted autocratically, suggesting that, in the future, such critics would be summarily deported and their privilege for other visits to Ukraine permanently withdrawn; still, he also suggested that they might consider taking Ukrainian citizenship, upon which they could freely criticize whomever they wished. This mixture of democratization and authoritarianism has confounded his most vocal critics and neutralized the forces against him. This has been particularly true of the two most significant independent parties, Rukh and New Ukraine.

Kravchuk has managed to split Rukh into two camps: The Chornovil faction (named for his main opponent during the presidential elections), which stands for the rapid development of civil society in a democratic Ukraine and thus remains antagonistic to Kravchuk's present policies of caution and consensus politics; and a majority faction which supports the *bublyk* (bagel) concept, whereby democracy is viewed as a hole with a strong state structure around it. Curiously, Chornovil has maintained a certain unity between the two factions by means of "constructive opposition"; that is, he has supported the president when he promotes Ukrainian statehood and criticized him when he opposes democratic or economic reforms. In the recent past, both Rukh and Kravchuk have actually exploited each other—Rukh in its promotion of Ukrainian independence as the primary objective and Kravchuk in his drive to consolidate and legitimize his executive power. Kravchuk still needs the Rukh umbrella to protect him against the possible revival of the old Communist Party (renamed the "Socialist Party"), which may or may not represent a real threat; some see the revived party as the proverbial bogy-man that Kravchuk has devised to frighten his more vociferous opposition. With consummate skill, however, he has neutralized Rukh by adopting its nationalist platform, to the extent that some observers are convinced that Rukh has already played out its historical role and should disband.

The other party, the New Ukraine, essentially follows Chornovil's ideals. The difference is that New Ukraine is largely based on the Democratic Platform, a progressive faction that split from the Ukrainian Communist Party in 1990. Since many of its members are not ethnic Ukrainians, this party has tended to emphasize economic and democratic reforms. In contrast to Rukh, it has stressed a federative system of governance rather than a unitary centralized state. Led by Volodymyr Filenko, the party combines business, industrial, academic, and professional interests. Like Rukh, it tends to be somewhat regional, drawing its membership largely from eastern and southern Ukraine, while Rukh draws from central and western districts.

Fear of Russia indeed unites the opposition in support of Kravchuk and his policies of cautious change. Mykhailo Horyn, one of Rukh's co-founders who now represents the Ukrainian Republican Party, has even involved the diaspora community to promote national unity behind Kravchuk. While he denies the existence of a "presidential party," he nevertheless believes that "it is very important to protect the office of the president." But even Horyn has suggested that "from time to time we may bite at Kravchuk's ankles." Such "biting," for example, produced a semi-secret conclave between Kravchuk and the opposition and the eventual resignation in October 1992 of Prime Minister Fokin, who had been deflecting much of the criticism directed at Kravchuk. Fokin was forced out by a "no confidence" parliamentary vote, in clear defiance of Kravchuk. The main issue was Fokin's (and, by implication, Kravchuk's) timid economic reforms. Fokin was then replaced by Leonid Kuchma, former director of a large industrial-military conglomerate. Kuchma's pragmatic economic policies ran afoul with the disruptive parliament and he resigned in the fall of 1993. As inflation skyrocketed and the economic crisis worsened, the parliament abolished itself. New parliamentary elections were called for March of 1994. The need for fundamental reforms persists.

By the fall of 1993, Ukraine had had just over two years of heady independence. Now the sobering socio-economic realities and geo-political complexities have begun to set in. There is a tendency to see the current situation in Ukraine in terms of a glass that is either half empty or half full. Certain segments see the present emphasis on statehood, at the expense of economic and democratic reforms, as a preamble to a new authoritarianism, perhaps even some sort of neo-fascism. There is a view that, so far, the price of this drive for total independence has been economic disaster, national and intra-national tensions, and growing popular disillusionment. The economic situation in 1993 has deteriorated dramatically; combined industrial and agricultural production has fallen by 25 percent, and both unemployment and the crime rate have risen. The government still controls the medium of television, which seems to promote the official line. While press censorship has been abolished, the state is the sole distributor of newsprint. There are also some signs of latent chauvinism. Organized political opposition remains weak. These internal conditions, along with the potential problems with Russia, render the future uncertain. In a worst-case scenario, a "Chilean solution" will be adopted to cope with the continuing malaise. Worse still, the lack of foresight by the present leadership will mean that the bid for independence will once again fail and Ukraine will be plunged into another long night of non-historical existence.

Conversely, the half-full perception subscribes to a cautious optimism. For instance, it may be pointed out that Ukraine's independent existence and the processes of state building and democratization have been remarkably peaceful, at least when compared with the situations in some of the other former republics, including Russia itself. The economic situation is daunting, but Ukraine is not alone in struggling to overcome the legacy of the previous command economy. Inevitably, there will be greater decentralization in both the economic and administrative spheres, brought about by pressures not only from below but also from outside players, such as the International Monetary Fund. Moreover, with only the Crimean drama as an exception, Ukraine has few of the ethnic, political, and cultural divisions that will plague Russia for the foreseeable future. Ukrainian politics is dominated by Western-minded elites. Communist die-hards are relatively weak and incompetent, mostly because the best and the brightest have been taken for service in Moscow; the durability of those left behind, even when they masquerade as "born-again democrats," is far less than that of their counterparts in Russia. Even the wily Kravchuk must be viewed as a transitional figure, who will either entirely embrace the democratization processes or be pushed aside by the inexorable march of events. Ukrainians are intent on being part of the European community of nations. Civil society is gradually emerging everywhere, but it probably has a much greater chance of success in Ukraine than in Russia, where the Westernizing democratic forces find themselves in conflict with imperialist Slavophiles (exemplified by Vladimir Zhirinovsky's Liberal-Democratic Party and the anti-Semitic Pamyat organization). In Ukraine, the emerging structures of civil society point toward political pluralism and multi-ethnic accommodation. Even Crimea has received autonomous status from the Kiev government. Extremist and irredentist nationalist groups do exist, but they are relatively weak, even in Western Ukraine. Recent public polls suggest that Ukrainians have no stomach for extremism of any kind.

Much of this development is contingent upon Russia, with which Ukraine must continue to maintain an almost symbiotic relationship. It is a paradoxical situation. A vulnerable and politically unstable Ukraine will continue to incite Russia's imperial ambitions; at the same time, these imperial ambitions have forced Ukraine to put a premium on state-building, to the extent that the inevitable neglect of internal conditions may render Ukraine politically even more unstable. Ukrainians have been sobered by the realization that, as demonstrated by the unfolding Yugoslav crisis, they may not be able to count on the West's assistance, should Russia resort to aggression to reclaim some of its "historical" territories. They are all too aware that the West is still fixated on Russia and sees it as the successor to the now-defunct Soviet Union. Still, they are convinced that time is on the Ukrainian side, in that Ukraine may well consolidate its political, military, social, and economic structures before Russia does. They will thus integrate Ukraine into the European community of nations. This, in turn, will facilitate Russia's final reconciliation with the concept of an independent Ukraine (which means the end of the empire) and will help Russia to redefine its own national identity and to bury its authoritarian and xenophobic legacy. It may be that Ukraine will prove instrumental in Russia's own Europeanization.

REFERENCES: V. Kubijovic, ed., *Ukraine: A Concise Encyclopedia*, 2 vols., 1963–1971; P. Kardash, *Ukraine and Ukrainians*, 1988; I. Mirchuk, *Ukraine and Its People*, 1946; H. Petrenko, *Soviet Ukraine*, 1969; N. Chirovsky, *An Introduction to Ukrainian History*, 3 vols., 1981–1986; D. Doroshenko, *A Survey of Ukrainian History*, 1975; M. Hrushevsky, *A History of Ukraine*, 1941; C. Manning, *The Story of Ukraine*, 1957; Orest Subtelny, *Ukraine: A History*, 1988; S. Horak, "Periodization and Terminology of the History of the Eastern Slavs: Observations and Analyses," *Slavic Review*, 31 (1972), 853–62; N. Polonska-Vasylenko, *Two Conceptions of the History of Ukraine and Russia*, 1968; I. Rudnytsky, *Rethinking Ukrainian History*, 1984; L. Wynar, *Mykhailo Hrushevsky: Ukrainian-Russian Confrontation in Historiography*, 1988; P. Potichnyj, ed., *Poland the Ukraine: Past and Present*, 1980; Ivan L. Rudnytsky, *Essays in Modern Ukrainian History*, 1987; D. Cizevsky, *A History of Ukrainian Literature*, 1975; N. Chirovsky, *Old Ukraine*, 1966; B. Grekov, *Culture of Kievan Rus'*, 1947; N. Polonska-Vasylenko, *Ukraine-Rus' and Western Europe in the 10th and 13th Centuries*, 1964; G. Vernadsky, *The Origins of Russia*, 1959, and *Kievan Russia*, 1948; J. Basarab, *Pereiaslav*

1654: A Historiographical Study, 1982; M. Braichevsky, *Annexation or Reunification: Critical Notes on One Conception*, 1974; T. Chyznewska-Hennel, "National Consciousness of Ukrainian Nobles and the Cossacks from the End of the Sixteenth to the Mid-Seventeenth Century," *Harvard Ukrainian Studies*, 10 (1986), 377–92; L. Gordon, *Cossack Rebellions: Social Turmoil in Sixteenth-Century Ukraine*, 1983; T. Hunczak, "The Politics of Religion: The Union of Brest 1596," *Ukrains'kyi istoryk*, 2–4 (1972), 97–106; Z. Kohut, *Russian Centralism and Ukrainian Autonomy: Imperial Absorption of the Hetmanate, 1760s–1830s*, 1988; L. Lewitter, "Poland, Ukraine, and Russia in the Seventeenth Century," *Slavonic and East European Review*, 27 (1948), 157–71; J. Serech, "Stefan Yavorsky and the Conflict of Ideologies in the Age of Peter the Great," *Slavonic and East European Review*, 30 (1951), 40–62; O. Subtelny, "Mazepa, Peter I, and the Question of Treason," *Harvard Ukrainian Studies*, 2 (1978), 158–83; A. Sydorenko, *The Kievan Academy in the Sixteenth Century*, 1977; M. Bohachevska-Khomiak, *The Spring of a Nation: The Ukrainians in Eastern Galicia in 1848*, 1967; P. Herlihy, *Odessa: A History, 1794–1914*, 1986; J. Kozik, *The Ukrainian National Movement in Galicia, 1815–1849*, 1986; G. Luckyj, *Shevchenko and the Critics*, 1980; D. Saundes, *The Ukrainian Impact on Russian Culture, 1750–1850*, 1985; A. Adams, *The Bolsheviks in Ukraine: The Second Campaign 1918–1919*, 1963; J. Borys, *The Sovietization of Ukraine, 1917–1923*, 1960; T. Hunczak, ed., *The Ukraine, 1917–1921: A Study in Revolution*, 1977; I. Nahayevsky, *History of the Modern Ukrainian State, 1917–1923*, 1966; O. Pidhainy, *The Formation of the Ukrainian Republic*, 1966; T. Prymak, *Mykhailo Hrushevsky*, 1987; J. Reshetar, *The Ukrainian Revolution, 1917–1920: A Study in Nationalism*, 1952; M. Khvylovy, *The Cultural Renaissance in Ukraine*, 1986; R. Sullivant, *Soviet Politics in the Ukraine 1917–1957*, 1962; B. Krawchenko, *Social Consciousness in Twenteith-Century Ukraine*, 1985; M. Carynyk, "The Famine the 'Times' Could Not Find," *Commentary*, (November 1983), 32–40; B. Krawchenko and R. Serbyn, *Famine in Ukraine, 1932–33*, 1986; J. Armstrong, *Ukrainian Nationalism, 1939–1945*, 1963; I. Kamenetsky, *Hitler's Occupation of Ukraine, 1941–1944*, 1956; Y. Bilinsky, *The Second Soviet Republic*, 1964; B. Lewytskyj, *Politics and Society in Soviet Ukraine, 1953–1980*, 1984; B. Krawchenko, *Ukraine After Shelest*, 1983; D. Marples, *Chernobyl and Nuclear Power in the USSR*, 1986; P. Potichnyj, *Ukraine in the Seventies*, 1975; G. Shevelov, "The Language Question in Ukraine in the Twentieth Century," *Harvard Ukrainian Studies*, 10 (1986), 71–170 and 11 (1987), 118–224; K. Farmer, *Ukrainian Nationalism in the Post-Stalin Era*, 1980; V. Chornovil, *The Chornovil Papers*, 1968; I. Dzyuba, *Internationalism or Russification: A Study of Soviet Nationality Policy*, 1968; D. Marples, *Ukraine Under Perestroika: Ecology, Economy, and the Workers' Revolt*, 1991; S. Blank, "Russia, Ukriane, and the Future of the CIS," *The World and I* (October 1992), 589–609; A. Brumberg, "The Road to Minsk" and "Not So Free at Last," *The New York Review of Books* (January 30, 1992), 21–26, and (October 22, 1992), 56–63; K. Johnstone, *National Identity and Relations in Lvov: A Survey of Ukrainians, Russians, and Jews*, 1992; A. Karatnycky, "The Ukrainian Factor," *Foreign Affairs*, 71 (Summer 1992), 90–107; A. Karatnycky, "The Minsk Meet," *American Spectator* (February 1992), 27–33; "Ukraine," N. Stone, "The Mark of History," G. Urban, "The Awakening," and I. Brzezinski, "The Geopolitical Dimension", *The National Interest*, 27 (Spring 1992), 29–52; R. Solchanyk, *Ukraine: From Chernobyl to Sovereignty*, 1992.

Alexander Sydorenko

UKRAINIAN GERMAN. The term "Ukrainian German" refers to those ethnic Germans* who migrated to the lower Dnieper region during the reign of Catherine the Great. They lived there until World War II, when the German invasion of Ukraine led to their deaths or deportation. Most of those who survived retreated with the German army back into Germany in 1945. There are still people living in Ukraine who are aware of their German ancestry. See GERMAN.
REFERENCE: Ronald Wixman, *The Peoples of the USSR: An Ethnographic Handbook*, 1984.

UKRAINTSY. See UKRAINIAN.

UL'CHA. See MANCHU.

ULCHI. The Ulchis, also known historically as the Mangu and the Olchi, are closely related to the Udegeis, Nanais*, Oroks*, and Orochis*, all of whom consider themselves to be part of the Nani* group, since their languages are mutually intelligible. The Ulchis live primarily along the Lower Amur River in the Khabarovsk Krai of southeastern Siberia. They speak a Manchu* language. The Ulchis are descended from the Ilou, Mohe, and Pohai, a group of Tungus tribes who were important in Chinese* history from 100 B.C. to 1000 A.D., and from the Jurchens, ancestors of the sixteenth century Manchus. In the nineteenth century, the Ulchis totaled approximately 1,500 people and lived in the Amur basin, north of the Nivkhis*, and east to the coast. Their main food source was the salmon, which spawned along the Amur and its tributaries. The Ulchis also fashioned clothing from the skins of larger salmon and hunted game animals, particularly elk and deer. The Ulchis were a relatively settled people, occasionally shifting locations along the rivers and moving back and forth between summer and winter homes. Clan and tribal loyalties were relatively weak in the lower Amur River basin. Such peoples as the Ulchis, Negidals*, Nanais, Oroks, and Ainus* lived in close proximity to each other and often intermarried.

Russia's first annexations of Manchu land occurred in 1850, when it seized the Amur Delta. The first Russian* settlement was established that year at Nikolayevsk-na-Amure, at the mouth of the Amur River. Russia's eastward thrust occurred at the same time that Japan was extending its influence northward. Both powers eyed Sakhalin Island, and, in 1855, a Russo-Japanese condominium was reached, establishing dual control of the 29,000-square-mile island. This agreement was dissolved in 1875, when Russia ceded the Kurile Islands to Japan. Sakhalin Island then became part of the Russian Empire and was used primarily as a penal colony until 1905. After ceding southern Sakhalin to Japan following the Russo-Japanese War, the Romanovs tried to develop northern Sakhalin and encouraged Russian settlements there.

The Bolshevik Revolution and subsequent civil war devastated the Ulchis and the other peoples of the Lower Amur River. The region became a battleground for White Cossacks*, Japanese* soldiers, partisans, and the Red Army. The native peoples, including the Ulchis, were subjected to acts of incredible violence—rape, destruction of herds and property, deforestation, and murder. Peace did not come to the region until 1925. By that time, the Ulchis were terrified of Russian officials. Soviet authorities immediately began their collectivization schemes, and the semi-settled life-style of the Ulchis made the process relatively quick. By 1930, the Ulchis had all become part of fishing and hunting collectives; there were no individual Ulchi hunters or fishermen left. By 1934, there were seven schools teaching Ulchi children, and the language of instruction was Russian.

During World War II, government agents actively recruited Ulchi men to work in the timber, mining, and petroleum industries. This policy set in motion a gradual migration process that brought more and more Ulchis to towns and cities. The demographic shift continued after the war, leading to the demise of the Ulchi extended family and its cooperative institutions. Exogamous marriages became more common. In the 1960s and 1970s, a generation gap emerged between younger Ulchis, who had been educated in state schools, and their parents and grandparents, who still adhered to the traditional shamanistic religion. By the early 1980s, only one-third of Ulchis spoke Ulchi as their mother tongue; the others spoke Russian. In the ethnically mixed settlements, Russian had become a *lingua franca* in the 1940s and 1950s; by the 1970s and 1980s, it had become the native language. The Ulchi population exceeds 2,500 people, but ethnologists doubt the survival of the Ulchis as an ethnic group.

REFERENCES: Alice Bartels and Dennis Bartels, "Soviet Policy Toward Siberian Native People," *Canadian Dimension*, 19 (1985), 36–44; Mike Edwards, "Siberia: In From the Cold," *National Geographic*, 177 (March 1990), 2–49; James Forsyth, *A History of the Peoples of Siberia*, 1992; Constantine Krypton, "Soviet Policy in the Northern National Regions After World War II," *Slavic Review*, 13 (October 1954), 339–53; Piers Vitebsky, "Perestroika Among the Reindeer Herders," *Geographical Magazine*, 61 (June 1989), 23–34; Ronald Wixman, *The Peoples of the USSR: An Ethnographic Handbook*, 1984.

UL'TA. See MANCHU.

UNANGAN. See ALEUT.

UNANGUN. See ALEUT.

UNGA. The Unga are a Buryat* subgroup. Their separate identity is based primarily on their territorial consciousness. See BURYAT.
REFERENCE: Ronald Wixman, *The Peoples of the USSR: An Ethnographic Handbook*, 1984.

UNGIN. See UNGA and BURYAT.

UPO CHEREMISS. See UPO MARI and MARI.

UPO MARI. The Upo Mari, who have also been called the Upo Cheremiss or Eastern Mari, are a Mari* subgroup. Over the centuries, the Upo Mari have come under direct Tatar* influence. Their religion mixes Islamic with animistic rituals and beliefs. They are concentrated demographically in the Bashkir Autonomous Republic, the Tatar Autonomous Republic, and the Sverdlovsk Oblast of Russia. See MARI.
REFERENCE: Ronald Wixman, *Peoples of the USSR: An Ethnographic Handbook*, 1984.

URAKHI. See DARGIN.

URAL. The Urals are ethnic Russians* who live along the lower Amu Darya and lower Syr Darya rivers. Some are also located on Aral Sea islands. That location places them inside the Karakalpak Autonomous Republic and in Kazakhstan. They migrated to the area in the nineteenth century and became fisherman. In spite of the surrounding populations, they have maintained a sense of being ethnic Russians. Because of the environmental disaster that has overtaken the Aral Sea region in the past three decades, especially the virtual drying up of the Aral Sea itself, they have suffered both the loss of their livelihoods and high disease rates. See RUSSIAN.
REFERENCE: Ronald Wixman, *The Peoples of the USSR: An Ethnographic Handbook*, 1984.

URALIAN. The term "Uralian" is a linguistic reference describing the indigenous peoples of the former Soviet Union who speak one of the languages in the Uralian branch of the Uralic-Altaic family. The term thus includes the Finns*, Izhoras*, Karelians*, Veps*, Estonians*, Vods*, Livonians*, Lapps*, Mordvinians*, Maris*, Udmurts*, Komis*, Komi Permyaks, Khants*, Mansis*, Magyars*, Nenets*, Ents*, and Nganasans*.
REFERENCE: Ronald Wixman, *The Peoples of the USSR: An Ethnographic Handbook*, 1984.

URALTSY. See RUSSIAN.

URANGHAI SAHA. See YAKUT.

URANGHAI SAKHA. See YAKUT.

URANGHAY SAHA. See YAKUT.

URANGKHAI SAKHA. See YAKUT.

URANGKHAY SAKHA. See YAKUT.

URIANHAI. See TELENGIT, ALTAI, and TUVINIAN.

URIANHAI KALMUK. See TELENGIT, ALTAI, and TUVINIAN.

URIANHAI KALMYK. See TELENGIT, ALTAI, and TUVINIAN.

URIANHAI QALMUQ. See TELENGIT, ALTAI, and TUVINIAN.

URIANHAI QALMYQ. See TELENGIT, ALTAI, and TUVINIAN.

URIANHAY. See TELENGIT, ALTAI, and TUVINIAN.

URIANHAY KALMUK. See TELENGIT, ALTAI, and TUVINIAN.

URIANHAY KALMYK. See TELENGIT, ALTAI, and TUVINIAN.

URIANHAY QALMUQ. See TELENGIT, ALTAI, and TUVINIAN.

URIANHAY QALMYQ. See TELENGIT, ALTAI, and TUVINIAN.

URIANKHAI. See TELENGIT, ALTAI, and TUVINIAN.

URIANKHAI KALMUK. See TELENGIT, ALTAI, and TUVINIAN.

URIANKHAI KALMYK. See TELENGIT, ALTAI, and TUVINIAN.

URIANKHAI QAIMUQ. See TELENGIT, ALTAI, and TUVINIAN.

URIANKHAT QALMYQ. See TELENGIT, ALTAI, and TUVINIAN.

URIANKHAY. See TELENGIT, ALTAI, and TUVINIAN.

URIANKHAY KALMUK. See TEKENGIT, ALTAI, and TUVINIAN.

URIANKHAY KALMYK. See TELENGIT, ALTAI, and TUVINIAN.

URIANKHAY QALMUQ. See TELENGIT, ALTAI, and TUVINIAN.

URIANKHAY QALMYQ. See TELENGIT, ALTAI, and TUVINIAN.

URUM. The Urums, who refer to themselves as the Greki, Elliny, Romei, or Urumchi, are ethnic Greeks* who speak Turkish and live primarily in the Abkhazian Autonomous Republic within Georgia or in Armenia. They were first attracted to Georgia in the late eighteenth century by the prospects of finding jobs in the mining industry. In the late nineteenth century, a second wave of Greeks left Turkey for Abkhazia to replace the emigrating Circassians*. The vast majority of the Urums are farmers, raising tobacco on collective farms. They are Eastern Orthodox in their religious affinities. See GREEK.

REFERENCE: Nicholas Pappas, *Greeks in Russian Military Service in the Late Eighteenth and Early Nineteenth Centuries*, 1991; Ronald Wixman, *The Peoples of the USSR: An Ethnographic Handbook*, 1984.

URUMCHI. See URUM and GREEK.

URUSBI. See KARACHAI.

URUSBIEV. See BALKAR.

URUSBIEVTSY. See KARACHAI.

URUSPI. See KARACHAI.

URUSPIEVTSY. See KARACHAI.

URYANHAI. See TELENGIT, ALTAI, and TUVINIAN.

URYANHAI KALMUK. See TELENGIT, ALTAI, and TUVINIAN.

URYANHAI KALMYK. See TELENGIT, ALTAI, and TUVINIAN.

URYANHAI QALMUQ. See TELENGIT, ALTAI, and TUVINIAN.

URYANHAI QALMYQ. See TELENGIT, ALTAI, and TUVINIAN.

URYANHAY. See TELENGIT, ALTAI, and TUVINIAN.

URYANHAY KALMUK. See TELENGIT, ALTAI, and TUVINIAN.

URYANHAY KALMYK. See TELENGIT, ALTAI, and TUVINIAN.

URYANHAY QALMUQ. See TELENGIT, ALTAI, and TUVINIAN.

URYANHAY QALMYQ. See TELENGIT, ALTAI, and TUVINIAN.

URYANKHAI. See TELENGIT, ALTAI, and TUVINIAN.

URYANKHAI KALMUK. See TELENGIT, ALTAI, and TUVINIAN.

URYANKHAI KALMYK. See TELENGIT, ALTAI, and TUVINIAN.

URYANKHAI QALMUQ. See TELENGIT, ALTAI, and TUVINIAN.

URYANKHAI QALMYQ. See TELENGIT, ALTAI, and TUVINIAN.

URYANKHAY. See TELENGIT, ALTAI, and TUVINIAN.

URYANKHAY KALMUK. See TELENGIT, ALTAI, and TUVINIAN.

URYANKHAY KALMYK. See TELENGIT, ALTAI, and TUVINIAN.

URYANKHAY QALMUQ. See TELENGIT, ALTAI, and TUVINIAN.

URYANKHAY QALMYQ. See TELENGIT, ALTAI, and TUVINIAN.

UTI. See UDI.

UTII. See UDI.

UTIIN. See UDI.

UTIN. See UDI.

UYGHUR. See UIGUR.

UYGUR. See UIGUR.

UZBEK. The Uzbeks are the largest ethnic group in Uzbekistan, and they make up the largest Muslim community within the Commonwealth of Independent States (CIS). Prior to the demise of the Soviet Union, the Uzbeks ranked third in number among the major nationality groups, being outnumbered only by Ukrainians* and ethnic Russians*. According to the Soviet census of 1989, the population of Uzbekistan then stood at 19,906,000, representing an increase of 29 percent since 1979, most of which may be attributed to the high Uzbek birth rate. Approximately 70 percent of Uzbekistan's population is Uzbek, and sizable numbers of Uzbeks live in the surrounding nations of Kazakhstan, Kyrgyzistan, and Turkmenistan. In addition, more than 1.5 million Uzbeks occupy regions of northern Afghanistan and adjoining sections of China, bringing the total Uzbek population of Central Asia close to 20,000,000.

Literary Uzbek is a Turkic* language belonging to the Uralic-Altaic language family and is heavily influenced by Persian* (Farsi). Numerous spoken dialects exist, most lacking the vowel harmony of Kazakh* and other related Turkic tongues. Dialects in the northern part of Uzbekistan, traditionally the domain of nomads, are almost devoid of Persian influence, however. The modern literary language is based on the Tashkent dialect and is derived from Chaghatai*, the literary language of the Timurid empire. Uzbek was written in the Arabic script until 1927, when it was replaced by the Latin script, which was in turn discarded for the Cyrillic script in 1940. Recently, a movement once again to latinize the script has surfaced in Uzbekistan, while others there promote the return of the Arabic alphabet.

The Uzbeks have traditionally been divided into clans or tribes, but have also developed cultural distinctions based on geographic location (i.e., sedentary peoples versus nomadic tribes). Many sources refer to the urbanized segment of the Uzbek people, especially those living in the southern reaches of Uzbekistan, as Sarts*. Historically, the Sarts were a merchant class composed of Tajiks*, who adopted the Turkic tongue of their nomadic neighbors while roaming the northern steppes of Uzbekistan. At least two other major ethnic divisions may be identified within the Uzbek people: the Turkis and Kypchaks*. Both of these groups display some Mongolian as well as Persian influence, and the Kypchak have preserved most of their clan divisions.

In terms of religion, the great majority of Uzbeks are Muslims, belonging to the Sunni branch of Islam. Because of restrictions and repression during the Soviet period, many Uzbeks do not observe all of the traditional rituals and ceremonies of Islam, including the month of Ramadan, the *haj* (pilgrimage to Mecca), and others. In addition, Islam in Uzbekistan and elsewhere in Central Asia has been deeply influenced by both Sufism and local folk beliefs, especially in rural districts. Ironically, "folk Islam," as it is sometimes called, was probably reinforced by Soviet policies, which resulted in a dearth of mosques, copies of the Koran, and Muslim teachers. These deficiencies led the Uzbek faithful to ascribe religious significance to various local sites, such as the graves of deceased mullahs, and natural features, such as springs or trees.

Pre-Islamic Antecedents

The historical origins of the Uzbeks are obscure. The name "Uzbek" appears to be derived from Ghiyath ad-Din Muhammed Uzbek, a Tatar* Khan of the Golden Horde, who ruled the lower reaches of the Volga basin in the fourteenth century. A determined Muslim proselytizer, Uzbek Khan was evidently so admired by many of his followers that they adopted his name as a clan designation. Some of their descendants eventually drifted eastward to occupy parts of Central Asia, but this branch of what Edward Allworth has termed the "Modern Uzbeks" is only one thread in the complex ethnic tapestry of the people we know as the Uzbeks.

The land that the ancient Greeks* called Transoxiana, which corresponds roughly to today's modern state of Uzbekistan, has been occupied by various peoples for millennia. The first residents of the region may have been the Massagetae, a nomadic people closely related to the Scythians, whom Herodotus described in the fifth century B.C. Upon arriving in Transoxiana some one hundred years after Herodotus wrote his account, Alexander the Great encountered the prosperous and culturally advanced Sogidan civilization, which had already established the cities known today as Samarkand and Bukhara, as well as other settlements in the Fergana Valley. The Sogdians were master traders on the Silk Road and eventually became crucial middlemen between the Chinese* Empire to the east and the Persian and Byzantine empires to the west. Although Alexander's influence on the region was ephemeral, succeeding invasions by a variety of groups left a lasting impression on the cultural, racial, and ethnic composition of the modern Uzbek people.

By 552 A.D., a new power had arisen in Central Asia and controlled the territory of modern Uzbekistan: the Turks*. The Turks were of Mongolian origin and may have been ethnically related to the enigmatic peoples whom the ancient Chinese called the Juan-juan; the actual origins of the Turks, however, are quite unclear. In 583, the Turkic empire was partitioned in half, with the western portion controlling the territory stretching between the Aral Sea and the Altai mountains. For the next century, the Western Turks played a pivotal role in the balance of power between the Persian and Byzantine empires, as well as serving as a conduit between the Chinese and the civilizations to the west and south. Most inhabitants of the Western Turkish Empire were Buddhists, although Zoroastrianism and Manichaeanism both appear to have been widely observed as well; in addition, small communities of Nestorian Christians could be found in urban areas. By the close of the seventh century, new forces were entering Central Asia and would profoundly alter the region's cultural composition for the next 1,200 years.

The Impact of Islam

In order to understand the role of Islam in Central Asia today, one must have a grasp of what that role has been in the past. Islam is not simply a religion: It is a way of life. Islamic dogma penetrates much more deeply into the lives of its devotees than is the case for many, if not most, Christian believers. As Michael Rywkin has noted:

Islam, which bears on the identity, behavior, attitudes, and way of life of the peoples of Soviet [sic] Central Asia, permeates all the social, political, and economic aspects of their lives. Even when one discusses each aspect of these lives, separately, . . . religion remains an indispensable ingredient.

In Central Asia, Islam has for centuries been an aspect of the culture that served to cement disparate tribes and clans together. These groups were distinguished by their settlement patterns (nomadic peoples vs. urban merchants and agriculturists), their language differences (distinct Turkic languages as well as Iranian dialects), and their tribal animosities—a situation that continues to hold true for Central Asia today.

Islam first penetrated into the territory of what is today known as Uzbekistan in the eighth century. Conquering Arab* armies brought Islam to the area. By 705 A.D., the Arab warrior Khotaiba ibn Muslim had expanded the Arabian

Empire toward the borders of the Chinese state. In 711, Khiva fell to the invading Arabs, and the remainder of the region succumbed rapidly, due to internal disputes that had seriously weakened the remaining Turkic forces. Khotaiba was relatively successful at converting the inhabitants of Central Asia to Islam, albeit sometimes at the point of a sword. The grip of Islam on the local populace was solidified by the stationing of an Arab "missionary" in every household.

At the same time that Arab influence was gaining strength in Transoxiana, the Chinese Empire was expanding westward. This occurred in response to the growing threat posed by an aggressive Tibetan Empire on China's southern flank, as well as by Chinese desires to consolidate territorial gains that had already been achieved in Central Asia. Conflict between the Chinese and Arab empires was inevitable, and tensions culminated in a major battle at the Talas River, not far from modern Tashkent, in 751. A combined force of Arabs, Tibetans, and Turks defeated a Chinese army, thereby securing Arab control over most of Central Asia. This in turn established Islam as a permanent feature of Central Asian culture, and, following the Chinese defeat, the conversion of the Turkish population continued apace. When Arab influence waned at the end of the ninth century, the void was filled by the Persian Samanid dynasty, which continued the proselytizing policies of its precursor.

Over the next few centuries, the region again fell under Turkic hegemony, following the establishment of a succession of smaller states that often engaged in internecine warfare with neighboring tribes. Eventually, an Islamic empire (Khivan) was created with Samarkand as its capital city. In the early years of the thirteenth century, the leader of the Khivan state had the poor judgment to execute the envoys of Genghis Khan, thus inciting the Great Khan to embark on a "punitive raid" toward the west. He did not cease punishing the perpetrators until he had conquered most of the Asian continent, even bringing the city-states of Kiev and Muscovy under the Mongol aegis. In Central Asia, the Mongols* sacked and destroyed most of the major settlements, although there and in other Islamic regions, the indigenous religious establishment was successful in converting many of their Mongol overlords.

The Mongols retained their hold on Transoxiana until the rise of yet another of history's great conquerors—Timur (Tamerlane). Timur was born in what is now Uzbekistan, not far from the ancient city of Samarkand. Claiming descent from Genghis Khan, he quickly set out early in life to build an enormous empire that, at its height, stretched from the Black Sea to the Indus River, with Samarkand as its capital. Timur's exploits brought Central Asia into much closer contact with both the Arab and Persian cultures, a situation that led to an intellectual and literary renaissance in Transoxiana. This was the beginning of a "Golden Age" of Central Asian culture, which lasted for a century and a half. Elements of Islamic architecture were adopted, and these eventually spread northward to Russia. The art of calligraphy was greatly advanced, and the cities of Bukhara and Samarkand were renowned throughout the Islamic world for the achievements of their universities and scholars. In Samarkand, a grandson of

Timur, Ulugh Beg, founded an observatory as advanced as any in Europe. Similarly, the physician Avicenna, a resident of Bukhara, published his *Canon of Medicine*, which was employed as a medical text in Europe for several hundred years. This was also the era of Ali Shir Navai, who may rightly be considered the "Chaucer" of Central Asian literature. Not only did Navai contribute a sizable body of his own work, he was also the patron of a number of other writers and poets. Although they wrote in Persian or Arabic, not in a Turkic dialect, Navai and his contemporaries are viewed by modern Uzbeks as part of their cultural heritage; they are being rediscovered in Uzbekistan today, along with more modern writers who were denounced and banned during the Soviet period. Many of the Uzbek intelligentsia have discovered that, when their cultural flourishing was at its peak, the Russian state was in its infancy, and Russian civilization was primitive by comparison.

At the beginning of the sixteenth century, the dynastic legacy of Timur came to an end with the arrival of the Uzbeks, a warlike confederation of Turkic tribes migrating into Transoxiana from the northeast. The Uzbeks captured Samarkand in 1512 and soon controlled most of the territory of modern Uzbekistan. The territory thus conquered was subsequently divided into three distinct states that were ruled autocratically by Uzbek emirs or khans (the title depending on the particular polity). These states took their names from principal cities located in each of them: Bukhara, Khiva, and Khokand. All three soon developed trade links with the increasingly powerful Muscovite state to the north, and Ivan the Terrible's conquest of the Muslim khanates of Kazan and Astrakhan only served to strengthen these ties. For the next 300 years, the Uzbek states functioned as conduits for trade between Russia and China, in addition to conducting reciprocal commerce with Russian merchants.

The Russian Empire continued to expand southward during the sixteenth and seventeenth centuries, eventually spreading into the steppe lands of Kazakhstan at the beginning of the 1800s. Simultaneously, Uzbek colonists were pressuring Kazakh nomads from the south. Russian expansion toward the southwest having been checked in the Crimea, the tsars turned their attention to the Muslim lands located to the southeast. By the middle of the nineteenth century, the St. Petersburg regime had embarked on a program of military conquest of Central Asia. Khokand, situated in the fertile Fergana Valley, fell to Russian forces in 1853. Twelve years later, Tashkent, the major metropolis of the Khokand Khanate, surrendered to a besieging Russian army. Khokand subsequently became, along with much of present-day Kazakhstan, "Russian Turkestan." Bukhara and Khiva successfully resisted incorporation into the Russian Empire proper, only to become vassal states under the suzerainty of the tsar. In this capacity, they functioned as buffer states against the encroachment of British* influence from the south.

Thus, by the end of the nineteenth century, the Russian Empire governed a large portion of its Central Asian realm directly and held considerable sway in the remainder. The Russian conquest brought with it an influx of Russian settlers, along with a more advanced infrastructure in the form of rail development. Islamic institutions were not abolished or persecuted, although, at least in Turkestan, the Russian Orthodox Church was allowed to pursue prospective converts with the same zeal that it had earlier displayed among the Volga Tatars* and other subjugated Islamic peoples. Within the borders of the two vasal states (Bukhara and Khiva), Orthodox activities were much more difficult and limited.

At the same time, massive changes in the economic structure of the region were occurring. Agricultural emphasis was shifted from grain production to cotton, principally to supply the growing demand in European Russia. This trend was continued by the Soviets, eventually having catastrophic consequences for Uzbekistan's environment, especially in the Aral Sea region.

The Uzbeks and other Central Asians living in Russian Turkestan did not accept Russian rule readily. In 1898, a revolt broke out in the Fergana Valley, centered around the town of Andijan. The leader of this rebellion, Muhammed Ali Khalfa, was a Sufi adept, and he was able to rouse his followers against the Russian infidels in a *jihad* (holy war). More than a score of Russian troops were killed, but the movement failed to spread to other cities in Turkestan. Khalfa was eventually caught and hanged by the imperial authorities, and the revolt was crushed. This would not be the last attempt to expel the Russians from the region under the banner of jihad, however.

While most of the important events connected with the 1905 revolution took place in European Russia, those events had an important impact on Central Asia as well. The reformers in Russia proper had as their counterparts in Bukhara and Khiva a group of young radicals known as the Jadids, an appellation derived from the Uzbek for "new method." Initially, the Jadids desired only to reform the Islamic educational system, but their goals soon expanded to include reform throughout Islamic society—in particular, religious reform. Neither the emir in Bukhara nor the khan in Khiva greeted the Jadid movement with enthusiasm, so the Jadids functioned underground in both states. In the 1920s, many Jadid intellectuals joined forces with the new Communist regime, only to be executed or exiled during the purges of the late 1920s and early 1930s.

In 1916, during the height of World War I, the tsar attempted to increase Russian troop strength by instituting a military draft in Central Asia. This represented a reversal of the former policy of exempting Muslims from military service. To add insult to injury, the edict advised the Islamic draftees that they would be deployed only in a support role and would not engage in combat. For a culture whose men prided themselves on their prowess in battle, this decree was unbearable, and the Muslims of Turkestan indicated their displeasure by once again attacking their Russian overlords. Another jihad was declared, this time with considerably more casualties than in 1898. The violence was also more widespread, occurring in Samarkand, the Fergana Valley, and other parts of Turkestan. The uprising was still being suppressed at the time of the Bolshevik Revolution.

The Soviet Period

It is a little-known fact that the Bolshevik Revolution actually began within the present borders of Uzbekistan, not in St. Petersburg. On September 12, 1917, a coalition of Bolsheviks, Mensheviks, and Socialist Revolutionaries took power in Tashkent, more than a month before the Bolsheviks occupied the Fortress of Peter and Paul in the Russian capital. The soviets established in Tashkent, Samarkand, and other cities in Turkestan had few Muslims among their members. Nonetheless, the change of leadership was welcomed by many if not most of the Uzbek intelligentsia, since the Bolsheviks had been quite explicit in enunciating their position toward the constituent nations of the Russian Empire. For example, in April 1917, at the Seventh All-Russia Conference of the Bolshevik Party, the following resolution had been passed:

The right of all nations forming part of Russia freely to secede and to form independent states must be recognized. To deny them this right, or to fail to take measures guaranteeing its practical realization, is equivalent to supporting a policy of seizure or annexation.

Muslim leaders accepted these pronouncements at face value, and, in November of the same year, the Fourth Conference of Muslims of Central Asia, meeting in the city of Khokand, proclaimed the independence of Turkestan. A local government composed mostly of Muslim leaders took power there. Muslims soon learned how shallow the Bolshevik assertions were, however, and, early in 1918, Bolshevik forces attacked Khokand and overthrew the Muslim government that had been established there. A soviet formed of Bolsheviks was granted control of the city, and Bolshevik soldiers continued to occupy the region. The Bolsheviks managed to alienate the local people further by failing to provide sufficient food supplies. This neglect sowed the seeds of resentment that later grew into the most serious challenge to Soviet authority in Central Asia—the Basmachi revolt.

The Basmachi Revolt

Throughout the 1920s and into the 1930s, the Soviet authorities in Soviet Central Asia had to contend with an insurgency that at times threatened to destroy Communist hegemony in the region, the so-called Basmachi movement. ''Basmach'' is the Uzbek word for bandit, and, initially, many members were brigands who preyed on local merchants. With the Bolshevik takeover of the Khokand administration, however, the ranks of the Basmachi started to swell with disaffected Muslims. Some of these were Muslim clerics who opposed the atheistic Bolsheviks on religious grounds; others were Muslim nationalists fighting Russian domination, and still others were Jadids who understandably felt betrayed by the Bolsheviks. Even Muslim units of the Red Army defected to the Basmachi side. Regardless of their origins, the Basmachi represented even a more serious threat than the White Army had in Central Asia. By the fall of 1920, the Basmachi ruled the Fergana Valley, with the exception of the larger cities; those remained under Soviet control.

Soviet imperialist policy in the region did nothing to reduce sympathy for the Basmachi among the local population. In March 1921, the Soviets deposed the government of Khiva, which had recently been established by the Young Khivans (a group who patterned themselves after the Young Turks in Turkey), and what had once been an independent nation was absorbed into the Soviet state. Khiva became a Soviet republic, and its Communist Party was purged. This action only intensified Muslim nationalism and support for the Basmachi cause. By the winter of 1921–1922, the revolt was at its height. Estimates of the number of rebel troops during this period reach as high as 20,000, and the city of Bukhara was nearly taken by the rebels in early 1922.

V. I. Lenin and his associates rather belatedly realized that armed force was not a fruitful approach toward the Basmachi uprising and began to institute a series of reforms roughly concurrent with the New Economic Policy (NEP). These included the return of land that had formerly been owned by Muslim religious institutions (*Waqfs*), the re-instatement of Islamic courts in the Fergana Valley (*kazi*), and increased deliveries of food to the area. This shift in policy, along with internal feuding among the Basmachi, resulted in the decline of the insurrection. Pockets of armed resistance remained in Soviet Central Asia until the mid–1930s, however, when the movement was finally crushed by Josef Stalin.

The current political geography of former Soviet Central Asia was created in the mid–1920s and 1930s, when the Communist Party of the Soviet Union (CPSU) instituted a program to divide Central Asia into administrative units based on nationality. In 1924, Uzbekistan and Turkmenistan were the first two socialist republics created there, along with autonomous republics and oblasts for other Central Asia national groups. Since the incorporation of the Karakalpak Autonomous Soviet Socialist Republic (ASSR) in 1936, the borders of Uzbekistan have remained relatively constant. Thus, the geographic configuration of Uzbekistan and the remainder of the nascent states in Central Asia continue to reflect Soviet policy, not necessarily the realities of current ethnic distribution.

The Stalinist Period

The impact of Stalinist rule in Uzbekistan, as elsewhere in the Soviet Union, was profound and devastating, especially with regard to the indigenous culture. In terms of Islam, the Stalin era may be divided into two periods: from 1928 to 1941 and from World War II to Stalin's death in 1953. From the late 1920s and to the early 1940s, Soviet Islam suffered from severe persecution administered by Stalin's regime, with many leading Uzbek figures, both Communist and non-Communist, vanishing into the gulag. Starting in 1928 and continuing for two decades, many prohibitions and limitations concerning Islam were enacted by the Communist Party. One of the most pernicious of these was the outlawing of the Arabic script and its replacement first with the Latin and then the Cyrillic alphabet. This move effectively isolated the Islamic population in two ways. First, it inhibited communication with the rest of the Muslim world, since Arabic functions as a *lingua franca* among many Islamic believers. Secondly, it created a rift between Soviet Muslims and their Islamic heritage, since many copies of the Koran that were available to Uzbeks and other Central Asians were written in Arabic.

In addition, two of the so-called "pillars of Islam" were eliminated: the haj, or pilgrimage to the holy city of Mecca, which every devout Muslim must make at least once if health and finances permit, and the Muslim practice of giving alms. To the Soviets, the second "pillar" was obviously superfluous—in a Communist society, where all are "equal," charity is clearly unnecessary. Beyond these penalties, Islam within Soviet borders suffered from a massive closing of mosques. Available figures indicate the awesome extent of the war waged against Islam by the authorities. In 1910, there were 26,000 mosques in the Russian Empire; by 1928, only 1,300 remained open. These data are even more startling when one considers that the drive to extirpate Islam did not reach full throttle until the late 1920s. Public burnings of the Koran then became common, and, during the Stalinist purges of the 1930s, the native Communist elite was decimated, including, ironically, many former Jadids. In most cases, the void left in the Uzbek Party leadership was filled by ethnic Slavs.

The pressures brought to bear on his regime during World War II forced Stalin to adopt a more conciliatory attitude toward religion. This new approach took several forms in relation to Islam. Between 1942 and 1944, Muslim leaders in the Soviet Union were allowed to convene a number of meetings, which formerly had been prohibited. At the end of the war, an additional *medresse* (Islamic seminary) was opened in Tashkent. Some mosques were opened during the war years as well, although the exact number of these is unknown. At any rate, judging from estimates made at the start of Nikita Khrushchev's anti-religious campaign, the number could not have been very large. Stalin also made token accommodation by allowing a small group of Muslims to make the haj, but the number was insignificant. The number of devotees permitted this privilege during most of the Soviet period was consistently below forty each year.

Stalin's most important concession to Islam during the Second World War was a *de jure* recognition of Islam and the creation of what is commonly termed "official Islam" in the Soviet Union. This came about as a result of the establishment of four "Muslim Spiritual Boards," which functioned as regional administrative centers within the Islamic areas of the Soviet Union. These boards were officially sanctioned by the Communist Party and considered the only legitimate administrative apparatus for Islam in the Soviet Union. The Muslim Spiritual Board for Central Asia was headquartered in Tashkent, the Uzbek capital; during the Soviet period, it was held to be the most influential of the four. While appearing to grant Muslims some degree of autonomy, the establishment of an "official" Islamic structure also gave the Soviet regime leverage with Islamic leaders that it had previously lacked.

After the Nazi menace was repelled, Stalin retained his moderated position. Closures of mosques continued, but not with the same speed as in the pre-war years, and, although Islam was still viewed as antithetical to the building of socialism, it was tolerated as an anachronist residue of tsarist times that would soon die out. Considerable resources were still devoted to eradicating Islam, but these measures were mostly propagandistic and not physical.

Post-Stalin Policy

Although initially greeted as a "reformer," the last years of Khrushchev's regime were marked by bitter repression of religion in the Soviet Union. At this time, a larger number of mosques were shut down, dropping the figure of around 1,500 to about 400. The causes of this abrupt reversal of policy by the Soviet government are still debated; Islam does not appear to have fared any better or worse than the Russian Orthodox Church or other groups. In any case, antireligious propaganda and atheistic work among the population increased up to 1964, when Khrushchev was ousted.

Leonid Brezhnev discontinued Khrushchev's harsh attack and instead began to employ Islam as an effective tool of Soviet foreign policy, especially among Middle Eastern countries. Muslim authorities from within the hierarchy of "official Islam" were allowed to travel abroad as envoys, and numerous conferences were held in Tashkent and other Central Asian cities. These attracted Islamic leaders from around the world. A few new mosques were opened during this period, but, like Stalin's wartime concessions, they amounted to little in comparison with pre-Soviet figures.

By the early 1980s, geo-political events, such as the Iranian revolution in 1979 and the Soviet invasion of Afghanistan in the same year, had engendered a return to a harsh anti-Islamic approach in Moscow. At first following the policy of his predecessors, Mikhail Gorbachev came to a more moderate position toward Islam in the final years of his administration, and much of the vicious anti-Islamic rhetoric gradually disappeared from the Uzbek and Russian-language press in Uzbekistan.

The Gorbachev policies of *glasnost* and *perestroika* were implemented quite slowly in Uzbekistan. Likewise, a much tighter rein was kept on unofficial political movements there than in many other republics of the Soviet Union. The Uzbek Communist Party retained control of the government through three different first party secretaries in the years 1988–1989, even in spite of a massive cotton production scandal that had rocked the republic in the mid–1980s.

The Soviet Legacy

The Soviet era had a disastrous effect on Uzbekistan's environment and on the health of Uzbeks and other ethnic groups there. The obsessive drive to produce cotton at the expense of other crops, including the excessive use of chemical agents and the over-use of the waters of the Syr Darya and Amu Darya rivers for irrigation, have resulted in epidemics of hepatitis A and other infectious diseases. In some rural districts in western Uzbekistan, as much as 80 percent of the population suffer from cancer and various blood disorders; the infection rate for hepatitis approaches 40 percent. According to statistics released in the late 1980s, infant mortality in many parts of Uzbekistan exceeds 10 percent.

Due to shoreline retreat, caused by the over-use of the rivers that replenish it, the fishing industry of the Aral Sea has been obliterated, destroying the livelihood of thousands who live (or lived) along its margins.

Mostly exploited for cotton production and natural resources while under Soviet sway, the Uzbek economy now suffers from severe imbalances. The lack of investment in infrastructure and industry by authorities in Moscow has left the new nation of Uzbekistan with an agriculture-based economy, in a region where more than 40 percent of the population is under the age of sixteen. Unemployment levels stand at 40 percent in some parts of the Fergana Valley of eastern Uzbekistan, and some surveys indicate that more than 50 percent of the population in 1990 lived below the official poverty line. The combination of ethnic rivalries, economic hardship, and the disintegration of Soviet authority has led to violent confrontations, notably in June 1989, when Uzbeks and Meskhetian* Turks clashed in the Fergana Valley.

Uzbekistan declared independence in June 1990 and reaffirmed its sovereignty on August 31, 1991, in the wake of the attempted coup in the Soviet Union. The government, however, remains in the hands of former Communist Party members, who have simply renamed their organization the People's Democratic Party (PDP). The former first party secretary and now president, Islam Karimov, has steadfastly blocked the empowerment of alternative political parties and has disrupted the formation of any of an Islamic nature.

Nevertheless, in spite of official repression, a number of alternative political parties have been established in Uzbekistan over the last several years. Of these, the largest appears to be Birlik (Unity), led by the cyberneticist Adurrhakim Pulatov; this party claims over 100,000 members. A second, much smaller party of the intelligentsia is Erk (Will), a splinter party from Birlik that is headed by the well-known Uzbek poet, Muhammed Solih. In the presidential election of 1991, Birlik, considered the more radical of the two, was prevented from participating; Erk was allowed to field Solih as a candidate only a few weeks before the election. Karimov was thus able to garner 86 percent of the popular vote and declare himself a "democratically elected" leader.

Although political parties of a religious character have been outlawed in Uzbekistan, some Islamic political organizations have been established. The most powerful of these is the Uzbek wing of the Islamic Renaissance Party (IRP), which is sometimes called the Islamic Revival Party. Driven underground when security forces disrupted its founding congress in January 1991, the IRP in Uzbekistan continues to command significant support, although the number of its followers is difficult to ascertain. The fact that the Karimov administration has gone to considerable lengths to limit the activities of the party is perhaps indicative of IRP's potential strength in Uzbekistan.

In the wake of the disintegration of the Soviet Union, Karimov has attempted to build ties to other nations throughout the Muslim world, making official visits in 1991 to Turkey, Egypt, and other nations, with the hope of creating trade linkages and establishing his credentials as a "moderate" whom Western nations can trust. Attracting investment capital from abroad is essential to Uzbekistan's economic survival. Toward that end, Uzbekistan, along with other Central Asian nations, has joined the revived Economic Cooperation Organization, a trade organization originally composed of Pakistan, Turkey, and Iran.

Uzbek culture was subsumed by Russian culture for nearly seventy-five years during the Soviet period. It should thus come as no surprise that independence has released a powerful drive to recapture and preserve as much of the Uzbek culture as possible, especially among the Uzbek intelligentsia. The effort to establish Uzbek as the country's official language, the move to return to the Latin or Arabic script, and the desire to reclaim the region's storied Islamic heritage all point to the fact that these elements are key components or the *raison d'être* for the Uzbek state.

At the same time the Uzbeks and other groups living in Uzbekistan face enormous challenges as they strive to build their nation. The lack of capital for economic development and the catastrophic environmental damage sustained during the last forty years are obstacles that will require years, if not generations, to overcome. Ethnic tensions between Uzbeks and some minority groups (including Russians) remain high. As the Uzbeks continue to assert their new-found authority and recover their cultural history, the potential for conflict remains great.

REFERENCES: Edward Allworth, *The Modern Uzbeks*, 1990; Wilfrid Blunt, *The Golden Road to Samarkand*, 1973; James Crithlow, *Nationalism in Uzbekistan: A Soviet Republic's Road to Sovereignty*, 1991; Hélène Carrère D'Encausse, *Islam and the Russian Empire: Reform and Revolution in Central Asia*, 1988; René Grousset, *The Empire of the Steppes: A History of Central Asia*, 1970; Karl H. Menges, "People, Languages and Migrations," in Edward Allworth, ed., *Central Asia: 120 Years of Russian Rule*, 1989; Michael Rywkin, *Moscow's Muslim Challenge*, rev. ed., 1990; Denis Sinor, ed., *The Cambridge History of Early Inner Asia*, 1990; Paul D. Steeves, *Keeping the Faiths: Religion and Ideology in the Soviet Union*, 1989; Ronald Wixman, *The Peoples of the USSR: An Ethnographic Handbook*, 1984.

Reuel R. Hanks

UZBEQ. See UZBEK.

UZNEMUNIECIAI. See LITHUANIAN.

V

VAD. See VOD.

VAD'D'ALAISET. See VOD.

VADEEV NGANASAN. The Vadeev Nganasan are a subgroup of the Nganasans*. They are actually the descendants of Evenks* who settled on Nganasan land on the Taymyr Peninsula in the eighteenth century and have since been largely assimilated. See NGANASAN.
REFERENCE: Ronald Wixman, *The Peoples of the USSR: An Ethnographic Handbook*, 1984.

VADEYEV. See NGANASAN.

VAHAN. See WAKHAN, PAMIR PEOPLES, and TAJIK.

VAKHAN. See WAKHAN, PAMIR PEOPLES, and TAJIK.

VAKHANTSY. See WAKHAN, PAMIR PEOPLES, and TAJIK.

VAKH-VAS'-YUGAN. See KHANT.

VELIKO RUS. The term "Veliko Rus" is of Byzantine origin and refers to Great Russian* Slavs. See RUSSIAN.
REFERENCE: Ronald Wixman, *The Peoples of the USSR: An Ethnographic Handbook*, 1984.

VELIKO RUSSKIY. See VELIKQ RUS and RUSSIAN.

VELIKORUSSIAN. See VELIKO RUS and RUSSIAN.

VENGER. See MAGYAR.

VENGERTSY. See MAGYAR.

VENGRY. See MAGYAR.

VEP. With a contemporary population of fewer than 8,000 people, the Veps are one of the former Soviet Union's smallest ethnic groups. They are closely related to the Finns*, and more particularly to the Karelians*. They call themselves the Vepsa or Lyudinikad; the Veps have also been known historically as the Chud, Chudin, Lyydinik, Chukhar, Chukhon, Kaivan, and Vepsya.

The Veps are closely related to the Karelians—culturally, linguistically, and religiously—and were once part of the larger Karelian population. Their language is a Baltic one and thus part of the larger Uralic-Altaic language family. They are largely Russian Orthodox in religion. The Veps live in three areas. The northern Veps live near Lake Onega in the Karelian Autonomous Republic. They call themselves the Lyudinikad, and their dialect is mutually intelligible with Karelian. The central Veps, who also call themselves the Lyudinikad, live in the Vologda and Leningrad oblasts; their dialect is not easily understandable to Karelians. The southern Veps, who refer to themselves as Veps, are located primarily in the Efimovskiy Rayon in what used to be the Leningrad Oblast.

The in-migration of so many ethnic Russians, as well as the russification process implemented by the tsars in the nineteenth century and the Soviet government in the twentieth, has accelerated the assimilation process for the Veps. The ethnic Vep population has steadily declined since the Bolshevik Revolution. There were nearly 35,000 Veps in 1917, but that number had decreased to fewer than 8,000 in the early 1990s. Like nearly everyone else in the Soviet Union, Vep workers and farmers suffered horribly from the collapse of the Soviet economy in the 1980s and early 1990s. Indeed, public officials in Finland were greatly concerned that many Veps, Karelians, and ethnic Finns would flee the Soviet Union for Finland in order to feed themselves. Whether by flight to Finland or through continued assimilation by ethnic Russians, the Vep population in the former Soviet Union is destined to continue to decline. In 1989, barely half of the Karelians used Karelian as their native language, and fully 95 percent were bilingual in Karelian and Russian; the numbers were similar for the Veps. It is uncertain if that process will continue. In May 1988, the Mikhail Gorbachev administration officially acknowledged the Stalinist terrorism campaign against the Veps, and, in July 1990, a group calling itself the Karelian Republic declared its autonomy from the Soviet Union and recognized Karelian and Vep as official languages. Veps, along with Karelians and Izhorans*, also formed a variety of associations to preserve their language and culture. The chances for the survival of Vep culture, however, are extremely remote.

REFERENCES: Paul M. Austin, "Soviet Karelian," *Slavic Review*, 51 (Spring 1992), 16–35; George Maude, *The Finnish Dilemma: Neutrality in the Shadow of Power*, 1976; Ronald Wixman, *The Peoples of the USSR: An Ethnographic Handbook*, 1984.

VEPSA. See VEP.

VEPSYA. See VEP.

VERKHNE-VYSHEGO. See KOMI.

VERKHOVYNTSI. See CARPATHO-RUSYN.

VIDZEMIAN. See VIDZEMIESI and LATVIAN.

VIDZEMIESI. The Vidzemiesi are a subgroup of the Latvians*. They live in Vidzeme Province. See LATVIAN.
REFERENCE: Ronald Wixman, *The Peoples of the USSR: An Ethnographic Handbook*, 1984.

VIDZEMNIEK. See VIDZEMIESI and LATVIAN.

VIDZEMNIEKI. See VIDZEMIESI and LATVIAN.

VIDZEMNIEKS. See VIDZEMIESI and LATVIAN.

VIETNAMESE. The 1989 Soviet census claimed that a total of 16,752 Vietnamese were living in the country. The origins of the Vietnamese community there went back to the early 1920s when Ho Chi Minh, the father of Vietnamese independence, lived in Moscow for several years after his conversion to Marxism-Leninism. He had long been searching for a way to liberate Vietnam of its French* imperial masters and the Vietnamese elite who did their bidding. When Ho Chi Minh learned from reading V. I. Lenin that capitalism and imperialism just represented different sides of the same coin, he found his answer. Throughout the 1920s and 1930s, other Vietnamese Communists also found refuge in the Soviet Union, where they studied and prepared themselves to overthrow the French. Success finally came in 1954, when Ho Chi Minh's Vietminh defeated the French at the Battle of Dienbienphu. The Geneva Accords divided Vietnam at the seventeenth parallel, creating the Democratic Republic of Vietnam under Ho Chi Minh in the north and the Republic of Vietnam under Ngo Dinh Diem in the south.

The Soviet Union then began supplying military advisers and financial assistance to North Vietnam. During the 1950s and 1960s, the Vietnamese community in the Soviet Union—consisting of students, party officials, military officers, and technicians—grew substantially. Those numbers increased throughout the rest of the 1960s and 1970s, when the American war in Vietnam was taking place. The North Vietnamese victory in 1975 finally united all of Vietnam under Communist control, and the Soviet Union provided large-scale economic assistance to the whole country.

REFERENCES: James S. Olson and Randy Roberts, *Where the Domino Fell: America and Vietnam, 1945–1990*, 1991; Raymond Zickel, *The Soviet Union: A Country Study*, 1991.

VIKHLI. See LAK.

VIRIAL. See VIRYAL and CHUVASH.

VIROLAISET. See ESTONIAN.

VIRYAL. The Viryal are a Chuvash* subgroup and are sometimes called the upper Chuvash. They live in the northern Chuvash Autonomous Republic. See CHUVASH.

REFERENCE: Ronald Wixman, *The Peoples of the USSR: An Ethnographic Handbook*, 1984.

VITSKH. See LAK.

VOD. Most ethnologists view the Vods as the ancient ancestors of the Setu Estonians* and the Livonians*. They were a large and powerful group in the eleventh and twelfth centuries, when they lived between the Neva and Narva rivers. As the Novgorod state began its expansion, however, they came more and more under Russian* influence, eventually becoming slavicized. The Vod language is mutually intelligible with Estonian. Like the Setu*, the Vods are Eastern Orthodox. The 1959 census of the Soviet Union listed only twenty-three people who claimed to be Vods, and a handful of people of that ancestry are still alive.

REFERENCE: Ronald Wixman, *The Peoples of the USSR: An Ethnographic Handbook*, 1984.

VOGUL. See MANSI.

VOJAN. See VOD.

VOLGA FINN. The term ''Volga Finns'' is a generic reference to those people living along the Volga River who speak a Finnic language. Included in this grouping are the Maris*, Udmurts*, and Mordvinians*.

REFERENCE: Ronald Wixman, *The Peoples of the USSR: An Ethnographic Handbook*, 1984.

VOLGA GERMAN. The Volga Germans are ethnic Germans* who migrated to the Volga region of Russia in the eighteenth century. They were devastated by World War II, when German armies invaded the Soviet Union. At the beginning of the war, they were deported to Kazakhstan and southwestern Siberia. Unlike the Baltic Germans*, Bessarabian Germans*, and Ukrainian Germans*, they did not flee with the German armies in 1944 and 1945. Most remain in Kazakhstan today, although, since the disintegration of the Soviet Union in 1991, emigration to Germany has dramatically increased. By the early 1990s, some nationalists had emerged in the Volga German community, advocating the establishment of an autonomous Volga German Republic. Russian president Boris Yeltsin worked hard at discouraging such proposals. When Boris Peters, chairman of the Volga Society of Russian Germans, demanded such an autonomous republic in 1992, Yeltsin argued that it would be a possibility only if the regional population were at least 90 percent ethnic German. When Yeltsin offered to allow Volga Germans to settle on 300,000 hectares of land in Volgograd, they protested because that area was a former artillery firing range full of undetonated shells. See GERMAN.

REFERENCES: *Current Digest*, 44 (February 12, 1992), 18–19; Ann Sheehy and Bohdan Nahaylo, *The Crimean Tatars, Volga Germans, and Meskhetians: Soviet Treatment of Some National Minorities*, 1980; Ronald Wixman, *The Peoples of the USSR: An Ethnographic Handbook*, 1984.

VOLGA MUSLIM. See NOGAI.

VOLGA TATAR. The Volga Tatars, also known historically as the Kazanis, Mishars*, and Bulgars, are an ethnic group in the former Soviet Union who numbered more than 5,000,000 people in 1990. Also known as Kazan Tatars*, they are by far the largest of the Tatar* groups. Volga Tatars can be subdivided into three groups based on language and religion. The Mishars, or Mishar Tatars, are descendants of Finnic-speaking Meshchera* groups who adopted the Sunni Muslim faith of the Tatars and became Tatarized; nonetheless, the Mishar still maintain several identifiable Finnic* cultural and linguistic traditions. They are separated from the other Volga Tatar groups by their dialect. The Kazanis, or Kazan Tatars, are the largest of the Tatar groups, and they have become known basically as Tatars. They are the descendants of Volga Bulgarians, Volga Finns*, and Kypchak* Turks*; the Kazanis are also Sunni Muslims. Finally, there are the Krjashen*. Unlike the Kazanis and the Mishars, the Krjashen converted to Eastern Orthodox Christianity. During the twentieth century, the Krjashen have become more and more oriented toward ethnic Russian* culture.

The Kazan Tatars lived in what became known as the Kazan Khanate during the fifteenth and sixteenth centuries and had emerged as an identifiable, self-conscious ethnic group by the sixteenth century. Some of them were descended from Kypchak peoples who had originated with the Tatars of the Golden Horde. The Kypchak tribes had come out of Siberia from the tenth to the thirteenth centuries. Other Kazanis were descended from Bulgars—Turkic-speaking peoples who had moved into the Middle Volga and Lower Kama river areas during the eighth century, after Magyar* invaders had driven them from the Azov steppes. The five major Bulgarian tribes were the Suvars, Esegels, Bersulas, Barandzhars, and Bulgars proper. By the twelfth century, the Bulgars had formed a state whose political power extended over a broad area, reaching as far as the Zai river to the east and to Samara to the south. The Kypchak and the Bulgar groups mixed together to form the Tatars, who at the time spoke the Kazan dialect.

In 1236, Mongol* armies under Batu Khan devastated Bulgar lands. Four years later, the Mongols were west of Moscow and had captured Kiev. They then moved still farther west, into Poland and the Pannonian Plains of Hungary. There were decades of rebellion against the Mongols of the Golden Horde, but, eventually, the Bulgars adopted the Sunni Muslim faith of their conquerors and accepted indirect administrative rule by the Mongols. By the mid-fifteenth century, the Kazan Khanate had emerged as the political heir of the former Bulgar state. Tempestuous economic and political relations began with Ivan III of Muscovy in the 1450s, and it was no secret that the Russians* had imperial designs on the Kazan Khanate. Kazan soon became a wealthy, prosperous state, and the Kazan Tatar language flourished.

But the Kazan Khanate drew Muscovy's envy and, in 1552, Ivan IV and his Russian armies conquered the Kazan Tatars. After the conquest, at the request of the Russian Orthodox Church, Ivan IV set out to convert the Tatars to Christianity and to russify them. When the Tatars did not convert voluntarily, forcible conversions began. The Tatars rebelled in 1556, but they failed to throw off the Russian yoke. By the seventeenth century, the government was executing any Muslim found to be proselytizing Islam. Measures of economic coercion were also imposed. For instance, Christian Tatars could pass their land on to heirs, but the land of deceased Muslim Tatars went to their nearest Christian relatives. Likewise, Tatars could not rent land from Russians. New Tatar revolts, led by Stenka Razin, occurred in 1669 and 1670, and large numbers of Tatars left the Middle Volga River region for Bukhara, the Kazakh steppes, and Central Asia. The best of their land went to Russian nobles, immigrating Russian peasants, and Russian Orthodox monasteries. Early in the eighteenth century, Peter the Great added new coercive measures, exempting Christian Tatars from certain taxes and military service. Finally, in the mid-eighteenth century, the Russian government launched an attack on Muslim mosques in the Middle Volga region, destroying 418 of 536 of them between 1740 and 1743.

The reign of Catherine II brought a temporary respite for the Tatars, who were nonetheless proving most difficult to convert. Catherine's imperial designs looked southeast to the Kazakh steppes and Central Asia, and she decided that the Volga Tatars could be useful to the Russian state in its expansion. The Volga Tatars were an enterprising people with contacts throughout the Muslim world, and she hoped to exploit those relationships. She therefore put an end to the heavy-handed conversion campaigns, allowed the Volga Tatars to form their own businesses, encouraged them to accumulate wealth, and established the Muslim Ecclesiastical Council as the final authority in purely religious disputes. But when Nicholas I assumed the Russian throne in 1825, the conversion campaigns began anew, complete with economic coercion and the ideas of N. I. Il'minskii, who believed that the best way of converting the Tatars was through education. By the mid-nineteenth century, government schools for Tatar children taught Russian, mathematics, Muslim religion, and the Tatar language in the curriculum.

At the same time, however, a reform movement within Tatar society was creating secular institutions capable of allowing them to survive—economically, politically, and culturally—in Russian society. The Tatars set up farm cooperatives to market their crops more profitably and credit associations to give them access to capital. By the early twentieth century, various benevolent associations were serving Tatar social and economic needs. The Volga Tatars had remained loyal to their Islamic faith but had also managed to establish successful secular institutions as well. Tatar literary and historical societies appeared, as did Tatar books, newspapers, and magazines. Moreover, they became more politically active, forming such groups as Shakirdlk and Hurriyet and electing Tatar representatives to the early twentieth century Dumas. These Tatar institutions played a leading role in the modernist movement among the Muslims of Russia in the early twentieth century.

After the Bolshevik Revolution, the Volga Tatars played a similarly important, indeed dominant, role in the All-Russian Muslim Council, which supported the provisional government. The Tatars then spent several years campaigning for the establishment of a single, autonomous Volga-Urals state that would include the Tatars, Bashkir*, Chuvash*, and Mari*, but the government never went along with the idea, primarily because of Bashkir opposition. Instead, the Tatar Autonomous Soviet Socialist Republic was established in 1920 in the lowlands between the Middle Volga and Kama rivers. It had a territory of more than 26,000 square miles.

The positive relationship between the Tatar people and the Soviet state was short-lived. During the 1920s, people like Mirsaid Sultangaliev worked to build Tatar nationalism, organizing and leading underground nationalist societies and campaigning for Tatar political autonomy; he was part of the Tatar Communist National movement. Soon, however, his calls for such things as the "Republic of Turin," an independent, ethnically homogeneous state to include the Middle Volga, Azerbaijan, Daghestan, Turkestan, and the North Caucasus, offended Josef Stalin and brought on a vicious purge in the late 1920s and 1930s. Tatars were purged from the Communist Party leadership. Tatar institutions, like the Society of Tatarology and the Tatar State Publishing House, were shut down. From the intellectual elite to the most humble peasant, Tatar nationalist loyalties were rigidly suppressed.

But Volga Tatar national identity survived. Even though the Soviet Union would not permit the flourishing of an overt political nationalism, they have proved to be culturally resilient. Over the centuries, there had been a substantial mixing of the Tatar and Russian populations, and today more than half of the Tatars live in cities. Increasing numbers of Tatar children are bilingual (in Tatar and Russian) and are going on to institutions of higher education. Nevertheless, more than 85 percent of Tatars still use Tatar as their native language. They marry endogamously most of the time. Most Tatars still observe Muslim rituals for birth, circumcision, marriage, and burial, as well as the dietary code. In recent years, there has been a revival of interest in Islam among Tatar intellectuals. Simultaneously, intellectual interest in Tatar history and Tatar literature has never been stronger.

In the 1970s and 1980s, signs of more radical political nationalism appeared among the Volga Tatars. Some Volga Tatars began speaking of a pan-Turkic nationalism and condemning the Russian language sections on civil service and university entrance examinations. They demanded changes of programming on state radio and television to reduce the inordinately large volume of Russian language programs. They also pressed for an end to government practices that encouraged Russian-Tatar marriages by rewarding the couples with trips or good apartment assignments. They condemned the disrepair of Islamic mosques around the country and the decades of anti-religious propaganda. Nevertheless, most of the Volga Tatars in the 1980s rejected the radical initiatives, preferring instead to maintain the bicultural accommodation that had served them so well for so long.

The *glasnost* and *perestroika* policies of Mikhail Gorbachev, as well as the centrifugal ethnic forces operating in Russia and the Soviet Union in the late 1980s and early 1990s, stirred up an increasingly strident variety of Tatar nationalism. Groups such as the Mardzhani Society, *Tugan Yak* (Our Father's Land), *Bulgar el jadid* (New Bulgar), the Society of Cultural Ecology, the Tatar Public Center, the *Ittifak* (Alliance) National Independence Party, and the *Suverenitet* (Sovereignty) Committee appeared. The most radical Tatar leaders, such as Fauzia Bairamova, called for an independent Tatar Republic in 1991. They also wanted to expand Tatar political reach well beyond the boundaries of the Tatar Autonomous Republic to include all lands ever controlled historically by Tatars—more than half of Russia. But only half the population of the Tatar Autonomous Republic was ethnic Tatar in 1990; most of the others were ethnic Russians, who controlled the cities and opposed Tatar independence.

Other groups advocated the creation of a Greater Tataria to unite the Tatar Autonomous Republic with the Mari Autonomous Republic, the Chuvash Autonomous Republic, the Udmurt Autonomous Republic, and portions of Ulyanovsk, Kuybyshev, and Orenburg. They harked back to the campaign for a Volga-Urals state after the Bolshevik Revolution. At that time, the Bolsheviks had opted for the smaller Tatar Autonomous Soviet Socialist Republic, which was established in 1920. Dreams of a more expansive Tatar political entity revived in the late 1980s and early 1990s.

Tatarstan began taking formal steps toward independence in August 1990, when its supreme soviet adopted the "Declaration on the State Sovereignty of the Republic of Tatarstan." In February 1992, Tatarstan stopped sending tax revenues to Russia, and, in March 1992, leaders of Tatarstan held a referendum on sovereignty. More than 61 percent of the 2,132,000 people who voted approved the resolution for state sovereignty and for absolute control of natural resources, especially their huge oil and natural gas reserves. Mintimer Sharimiyev, president of Tatarstan, refused to sign Gorbachev's union treaty in 1991. To do so, he argued, would be tantamount to denying the Tatar right to sovereignty. The supreme soviet of Tatarstan also began debating formal secession from Russia, primarily because they resented the loss of 30,000,000 tons of their own oil to Russia each year. Russian President Boris Yeltsin denounced all plans for an independent Tatarstan, since Russia's loss of the region would be a strategic and economic disaster.

REFERENCES: *Current Digest*, 41 (February 22, 1989), 1–2; 43 (December 25, 1991), 1–6; 44 (April 15, 1992), 24–25, and (April 22, 1992), 6–8; and Azade-Ayse Rorlich, *The Volga Tatars: A Profile in National Resilience*, 1986.

VOLGA TURK. The term "Volga Turk" is a generic reference to people living along the Volga River who speak a Turkic* language. Included in this grouping are the Tatars*, Bashkirs*, and Chuvash*.

REFERENCE: Ronald Wixman, *The Peoples of the USSR: An Ethnographic Handbook*, 1984.

VOT. See VOD.

VOTES. See VOD.

VOTIAK. See UDMURT.

VOTYAK. See UDMURT.

VOYTAK. See UDMURT.

VOZHAN. See VOD.

VOZHANE. See VOD.

W

WAHAN. See WAKHAN or TAJIK.

WAKHAN. The Wakhan call themselves the Khik; they are also known as Wakhani and Vakhan. Today ethnologists classify the Wakhan as one of the Pamir peoples*. Their linguistic roots are Iranian. Like other Pamir groups, the Wakhan are Ismaili Muslims. Because they are surrounded by Tajiks, they are gradually being assimilated by them. Most Wakhans live in remote valleys of the Gorno-Badakhshan Autonomous Oblast of Tajikistan. They are especially concentrated at the headwaters of the Pyandzh, Darshai, Boibar, and Pamir rivers. See PAMIR PEOPLES or TAJIK.
REFERENCE: Ronald Wixman, *The Peoples of the USSR: An Ethnographic Handbook*, 1984.

WEST SIBERIAN TATAR. The term ''West Siberian Tatar'' has been used in the past as a generic reference to the Tobol*, Tjumen*, Tara*, and Baraba Tatars*. See TATAR.
REFERENCE: Ronald Wixman, *The Peoples of the USSR: An Ethnographic Handbook*, 1984.

WESTERN EVEN. See EVEN.

WESTERN FINN. See FINN.

WESTERN FINNIC PEOPLES. See BALTO-FINNIC PEOPLES.

WESTERN TUNDRA CHUKCHI. See CHUKCHI.

WHITE KALMUK. See TELEUT and ALTAI.

WHITE KALMYK. See TELEUT and ALTAI.

WHITE NOGAI. See AK NOGAI and NOGAI.

WHITE NOGAY. See AK NOGAI and NOGAI.

WHITE NOGHAI. See AK NOGAI and NOGAI.

WHITE NOGHAY. See AK NOGAI and NOGAI.

WHITE QALMUQ. See TELEUT and ALTAI.

WHITE QALMYQ. See TELEUT and ALTAI.

WHITE RUSSIAN. See BELARUSIAN.

WHITE RUTHENIAN. See BELARUSIAN.

Y

YAGE. See YAGE DUNGAN and DUNGAN.

YAGE DUNGAN. The Yage Dungans are a subgroup of the Dungan* people who live in Aleksandrovka, Sokuluk, and Chilik in the Kazakh Republic. Most of these Dungans originated in Hansu and Shensi provinces in China. Most Dungans speak either the Hansu or the Shensi dialect, but the Yage Dungans speak a dialect known as Ninsya-Lanchzhou. The Yage Dungans maintain an identity quite separate both from other Dungans and from non-Dungans; other Dungans tend to look down on them. See DUNGAN.
REFERENCE: Ronald Wixman, *The Peoples of the USSR: An Ethnographic Handbook*, 1984.

YAGHNOB. See YAGNOB.

YAGNOB. The Yagnob call themselves the Yaghnob or Yagnobi. They have roots in Iranian culture, particularly the old Sogdian population that became a constituent part of the Uzbeks* and the Tajiks*. The Tajiks are gradually assimilating them. Their language is part of the Eastern Iranian group of languages and has western and eastern dialects. Most Yagnob are Sunni Muslims, although a few are Ismaili Muslims. Today they are classified as a subgroup of the Tajiks and live along the upper Yagnob River in the Pamir Mountains of Tajikistan; a smaller number live along the Varzob River. The Yagnobi population exceeds 4,000 people. See TAJIK.
REFERENCES: Shirin Akiner, *Islamic Peoples of the Soviet Union*, 1983; Ronald Wixman, *The Peoples of the USSR: An Ethnographic Handbook*, 1984.

YAGNOBI. See YAGNOB and TAJIK.

YAIK. See URAL COSSACK and COSSACK.

YAKUT. The Yakuts (Iakuts), who call themselves the Sakha (Saka), have also been known historically as the Tungus, Jekos, and Urangkhai Sakha. They are numerically the largest of the ethnic groups in Siberia. The Yakut population has increased from 296,244 people in 1970, to 328,018 in 1979, to 382,255 in 1989. Most Yakuts live in what used to be the Yakut Autonomous Soviet Socialist Republic (ASSR) and in immediately adjacent areas. Their language is part of the northeastern branch of the Turkic* languages, although its vocabulary is laced with Mongol* and Tungusian* words. Such Yakut clan names as Osekuji, Ontuls, Kokui, Kiriks, Kyrgydays, and Orgots indicate their Siberian origins, while other clan names reveal a Turkish background. Within that Turkic language branch, however, Yakut is somewhat isolated, which is the natural result of the Yakuts' demographic isolation from other Turkic speakers since the fourteenth century. There are also relatively few regional differences in Yakut dialects; all are mutually intelligible. Most Russian* ethnographers suspect that the Yakuts are descended from a mixture of peoples from the area of Lake Baikal, Turkish tribes from the steppe and Altai Mountains, and indigenous peoples of Siberia, particularly the Evens* and Evenks*.

The Yakuts themselves are divided into two primary groups, based on geography and economics. Agriculture is possible only in the southern areas, along the middle stretches of the Lena River, although the Yakuts did not make the transition to sedentary farming until the nineteenth century. The Yakut groups farther north in what was once the Yakut ASSR are semi-nomadic hunters, fishermen, and reindeer breeders, like many other northern peoples of Siberia. They have traditionally been poorer than their southern neighbors. Yakut fishermen caught carp, mundu, muksun, and salmon in the rivers and lakes of the region, while Yakut hunters took squirrels, hares, elk, foxes, bear, deer, ermine, partridge, geese, wild reindeer, and ducks. They smoked the meat and transformed the hides into pelts, which they used for clothing or as trade items. The reindeer-breeding Yakuts used the animals primarily for transportation, milk products, and sale.

Farther to the south, where temperatures were slightly more moderate, the Yakuts were pastoralists who raised horses and cattle. Their livestock-oriented pursuits have traditionally distinguished them from the other ethnic groups of Siberia. These Yakuts were semi-nomadic, using their horses and cattle for hides, meat, milk, and transportation. During the late eighteenth and early nineteenth centuries, the Yakut pastoralists went through a transition when raising cattle became more economically important then breeding horses. Some of these Yakuts also engaged in breeding reindeer. The Yakuts who worked in animal husbandry were also familiar with the range grasses of Siberia and harvested them with scythes in order to feed their animals during the long winter months. Because of their skill working with horses, these southern Yakuts also developed sophisticated blacksmithing skills, extracting iron ore and smelting it in primitive forges.

When ethnic Russians* first arrived in the region of Yakutia in the 1620s, the

Yakuts were living along the Lena and Amga rivers, the lower Viliui and Olekma rivers, and the upper Iana River. They functioned in a semi-nomadic, subsistence economy, moving their cattle herds twice yearly between summer and winter pastures. The more northerly Yakuts groups engaged primarily in hunting, fishing, and breeding reindeer. At the time of the Russian arrival, the Yakuts were divided into about eighty patriarchal clans, with strong nuclear families as the focus of social life. Even at that point, however, the clan-tribal loyalties were beginning to break down as the Yakuts acquired a broader sense of ethnic identity. That new identity led to the creation of the *toyon* class, an elite group of Yakuts with extensive holdings of land, cattle, and horses and who kept other Yakuts in slavery or other forms of bondage. Much of Yakutia was in an essentially feudal state when the Russians began arriving.

Russia annexed Yakutia in the 1620s and quickly imposed the fur tax. Soldiers and merchants poured into the area to crush the Yakut. The tribute taxes, which the Yakut paid in sable and fox furs, were oppressive, requiring the Yakuts to ignore their cattle herds in order to secure enough pelts for the tax. The Yakuts rose up in rebellion against the Russians several times between 1634 and 1642, but the revolts were all crushed. The violence, along with the introduction of a variety of European diseases, took its toll on the Yakut population. Large numbers of Yakuts tried to escape Russian influence by migrating. The solution became more common as the fur resources of the region were depleted in the eighteenth century. By the end of the eighteenth century, there were new Yakut settlements on the Kolyma, Indigirka, Olenek, and Anabar rivers.

During the eighteenth century, Russian annexed more territories to the east—Kamchatka, the Chukchi Peninsula, the Aleutian Islands, and Alaska. Yakutia became a thoroughfare between eastern and western Siberia. More ethnic Russians settled in the area, and the Yakuts were increasingly incorporated into the regional cash economy. The completion of the mail route in 1773 brought in still more Russians, as did the construction of the convict camps to which the tsars sent their political opponents. In 1846, gold was discovered in Yakutia, bringing a new deluge of Russian settlers. Construction of the Siberian Railroad in the 1880s and 1890s, as well as the development of commercial shipping on the Lena River, accelerated the commercialization of the region. Southern Yakuts made the transition to sedentary agriculture, maintaining their cattle herds and turning to the production of oats, rye, barley, potatoes, and vegetables.

Along with the transition to a Russian commercial economy, the Yakuts found themselves subject to cultural change as well. Russian Orthodox missionaries began working among the Yakuts at the end of the seventeenth century. By the end of the eighteenth century, most Yakuts had at least been baptized as Christians. By the early 1800s, virtually all of the Yakuts were registered as Eastern Orthodox Christians, although substantial elements of their traditional folk religion survived. Upper-class *toyons* were far more likely than peasants to be truly converted Christians, and the surviving Yakut shamans still believed in an invisible world of spirits. The spirits living in the ''upper world'' received sacrifices of Yakut horses, while those in the "lower world" received cattle sacrifices. The primary spirit worshipped by animistic Yakuts was Uluu-Toyon, who governed the upper world. Less powerful deities also occupied the Yakut pantheon. The Yakuts believed that all plants, animals, and natural objects possessed their own spirits and that human beings had to be careful to appease and propitiate those spirits. Evil spirits and gods had to be controlled through the magic of the shaman. During the twentieth century, however, the indigenous faith has gradually decayed, especially among the southern, agricultural Yakuts, whose interaction with ethnic Russians has been more constant. Only remnants of the old faith still exist.

The Bolshevik Revolution had a dramatic impact on Yakut life. The new Soviet government issued the "Declaration of the Rights of the Peoples of Russia" in 1917, which guaranteed the "equality and sovereignty of the peoples of Russia; the right of self-determination, including separation and the formation of independent states; abolition of all national and national-religious privileges or restrictions; and free development of national minorities and ethnic groups inhabiting the territory of Russia." Under Josef Stalin, who served at the time as Commissar for Nationalities, the program was implemented. Because the Yakuts were by far the largest of the northern peoples, there was little doubt that at least the appearance of ethnic autonomy would be extended to them. In 1922, the Soviet Union established the Yakut ASSR, consisting of 3,103,200 square miles carved out of the Russian Republic. When the Commissariat for Nationalities was abolished in 1924, a new Committee of Assistance to the Peoples of the North (or Committee of the North) assumed responsibility for indigenous affairs, and the Yakuts were part of that jurisdiction.

Over the centuries, the Russians had been less heavy-handed with the Yakuts than with any of the other native peoples, probably because the Yakuts were so numerous. After the creation of the Yakut ASSR, the Soviet government established dozens of national districts there for the Evens, Evenks, and Yukagirs*, but, in most cases, they still placed Yakuts in the most politically powerful positions. Moreover, the Russians recognized the power of the Yakut identity. The Yakuts were absorbing such surrounding ethnic groups as the Dolgans*, Evens, and Evenks, and even some Russian immigrants had been assimilated. The Yakutyans* were ethnic Russians who settled in the area of the Lena River and adopted Yakut customs while maintaining the Russian language. The Kolymchans* were ethnic Russians who eventually adopted the Yakut language as well, even while retaining a sense of their Russian roots.

The Russians, tsars as well as commissars, were also aware that the Yakuts had developed a strong sense of ethnic nationalism before the Bolshevik Revolution. Yakut as a written literature began to appear in the late 1800s and early 1900s from the pens of people like A. E. Kulakovskii, A. I. Sofronov, and N. D. Neustroev. Yakut nationalists formed the Yakut Union in 1906 and demanded that all Yakut lands that had been seized by the state, the Russian Orthodox Church, and ethnic Russians be returned to the Yakut people. Tsarist forces arrested and imprisoned leaders of the Yakut Union in an attempt to crush budding Yakut nationalism. The Bolsheviks did not trust Yakut nationalists either, with good reason. During the civil war, substantial numbers of Yakuts fought on behalf of the Whites. Still, the Bolsheviks, for a time at least, tolerated groups like the Yakut People, a cultural organization, and such literary publications as *The Morning Star*. Yakut writers like Kulakovskii got away with warning the Yakut people that Russian culture and Bolshevism were threats to their way of life. Altan Saryn spread ideas of Pan-Turkism among the Yakuts in the 1920s.

The tolerance came to an end in 1928. Stalin launched his collectivization campaign against Yakut pastoralists, breeders, and hunters, and the Yakuts violently resisted the loss of their property and the imposition of new life-styles. The Soviet government, however, ruthlessly implemented the decree, and tens of thousands of Yakuts disappeared. In 1926, on the eve of the campaigns, there had been 240,709 ethnic Yakuts in the Soviet Union. While demographers do not know exactly how many Yakuts Stalin eliminated, the Yakut population had not recovered to its pre-collectivization level even by 1963. It was an enormous purge, a bloodletting from which the Yakuts did not recover for decades. In 1928, the Central Committee of the All-Union Communist Party purged the local Yakut leaders of the Yakut ASSR, dissolved all ethnic Yakut organizations, and prohibited Yakut publications. Subsequent purges during the 1930s wiped out another level of Yakut leadership. Public schools in the Yakut ASSR were prohibited from using Yakut as a language of instruction. Moreover, the rapid industrialization of the region—especially to extract gold, coal, and timber— brought large numbers of ethnic Russians and Ukrainians* to the Yakut ASSR, making the Yakuts an ethnic minority in their own country. That trend continued in the post-World War II years.

During the 1960s and 1970s, Soviet policies continued to discourage overt expressions of Yakut nationalism, and relatively few Yakuts were willing to resist that pressure. Nevertheless, they resented the attempts at russification that characterized government policy and remained fanatically loyal to their native language and sense of peoplehood. When the *glasnost* and *perestroika* policies of Mikhail Gorbachev opened the door to political and cultural debate in the 1980s, Yakut nationalism soon found expression. Mounting conflicts between Moscow and the peoples of the far north, including the Yakut, culminated in the creation of the Association of Peoples of the North (APN) on March 31, 1990, during a meeting in the Kremlin. Organized to defend the interests of twenty-six northern peoples, the APN hoped to help them tackle such problems as the economic expansion promoted by various bureaucracies, flaws in Soviet nationalities policies, and the ecological deterioration of northern areas.

The failed *coup d'état* against Gorbachev in August 1991 unleashed nationalist sentiments across the Soviet Union, and the Yakut ASSR was no exception. The Yakut population was growing, the memories of the hardships and mass deaths of the collectivization campaigns of the 1920s and 1930s were still quite clear, and anti-Russian sentiment was strong. Yakuts also realized that they were rich in natural resources and would become, no doubt, a prime target of the cash-starved, poverty-stricken Soviet Union. On August 15, 1991, the Supreme Soviet of Yakutia declared the sovereignty of the "Yakut Republic." They expressed a willingness to remain politically affiliated with the Soviet Union, but they declared their exclusive control over all of the gold, diamonds, timber, coal, oil, and tin in the republic. They also made clear their intention to sell their resources at market prices around the world.

The Yakut declaration of sovereignty was opposed by both Soviet leader Gorbachev and Russian leader Boris Yeltsin. The last thing they needed was the secession of resource-rich republics. Demography was on the Russian side in the dispute. Although there were more than 382,000 Yakuts in 1989, they were actually a minority in Yakutia, with ethnic Russians outnumbering them two to one. Russian leaders appealed to the ethnic loyalties of the Russians in Yakutia, and the Yakut Supreme Soviet was unable to follow up on its declaration of sovereignty. When the Soviet Union broke up at the end of 1991 and Russia became independent, Yeltsin launched the country on a series of economic reforms that promised the resource-rich republics that they would not be looted by the resource-poor areas.

REFERENCES: Alice Bartels and Dennis Bartels, "Soviet Policy Toward Siberian Native People," *Canadian Dimension*, 19 (1985), 36–44; Mike Edwards, "Siberia: In From the Cold," *National Geographic*, 177 (March 1990), 2–49; James Forsyth, *A History of the Peoples of Siberia*, 1992; Péter Hajdú, *Samoyed Peoples and Languages*, 1962; Constantine Krypton, "Soviet Policy in the Northern National Regions After World War II," *Slavic Review*, 13 (October 1954), 339–53; Walter Kolarz, *The Peoples of the Soviet Far East*, 1969; Piers Vitebsky, "Perestroika Among the Reindeer Herders," *Geographical Magazine*, 61 (June 1989), 23–34; Ronald Wixman, *The Peoples of the USSR: An Ethnographic Handbook*, 1984.

YAKUTIAN. See RUSSIAN, YAKUT, and YAKUTYAN.

YAKUTIANE. See RUSSIAN, YAKUT, and YAKUTYAN.

YAKUTYAN. The Yakutyans are a group of people with mixed ethnic Russian* and Yakut* origins. They are descended from Russian settlers who colonized Siberia and settled among the indigenous Yakut population beginning in the seventeenth century. Over the centuries, they have intermarried with the Yakuts and adopted many features of Yakut economic and cultural life. At the same time, however, they have retained the Russian language and still define themselves as Russians. Most of the Yakutyans live near the Lena River in the Yakut Autonomous Republic. See RUSSIAN or YAKUT.

REFERENCE: Ronald Wixman, *The Peoples of the USSR: An Ethnographic Handbook*, 1984.

YAKUTYANE. See RUSSIAN, YAKUT, and YAKUTYAN.

YARA. The Yara, who have also been known as the Yarin, are a small group of Kettic* people, who are part of the larger Kacha* cluster, which itself is now considered a Khakass* subgroup. See KACHA or KHAKASS.
REFERENCE: Ronald Wixman, *The Peoples of the USSR: An Ethnographic Handbook*, 1984.

YARA-YASTA. See KACHA, KHAKASS, and YASTA.

YARIN. See YARA and KHAKASS.

YARKENDLIK. See YARKENLIK and UIGUR.

YARKENDLYK. See YARKENLIK and UIGUR.

YARKENLIK. The Yarkenlik are a Uigur* subgroup. The Yarkenlik lived in Chinese* Turkestan, primarily in the village of Yarkend, until they migrated to Central Asia in the late eighteenth century. Their ethnic identification was typical of most Uigurs, who viewed themselves largely in terms of their village origins in China. That practice did not begin to fade until the twentieth century. See UIGUR.
REFERENCE: Ronald Wixman, *The Peoples of the USSR: An Ethnographic Handbook*, 1984.

YARKENLYK. See YARKENLIK and UIGUR.

YASTA. The Yasta, who have also been known as the Yastin, are a small group of Kettic* people who are part of the larger Kacha* cluster, which itself is now considered a subgroup of the Khakass*. See KACHA or KHAKASS.
REFERENCE: Ronald Wixman, *The Peoples of the USSR: An Ethnographic Handbook*, 1984.

YASTIN. See YASTA and KHAKASS.

YATVIG. See BELARUSIAN.

YATVIGIAN. See BELARUSIAN.

YATVYAG. See BELARUSIAN.

YATVYAGIAN. See BELARUSIAN.

YATVYING. See BELARUSIAN.

YATVYINGIAN. See BELARUSIAN.

YAZGHULEM. See YAZGULEM and TAJIK.

YAZGHULYAM. See YAZGULEM and TAJIK.

YAZGHULYIAM. See YAZGULEM and TAJIK.

YAZGUL. See YAZGULEM and TAJIK.

YAZGULEM. The Yazgulem call themselves the Zgamig. They are a Pamir* people who today are being assimilated by the Tajiks*. Yazgulem is an Iranian language, and the Yazgulem people are Sunni Muslims. Most of the Yazgulem today live in southeastern Tajikistan and across the border in Afghanistan. See PAMIR PEOPLES and TAJIK.
REFERENCES: Shirin Akiner, *Islamic Peoples of the Soviet Union*, 1983; Ronald Wixman, *The Peoples of the USSR: An Ethnographic Handbook*, 1984.

YAZGULIAM. See YAZGULEM and TAJIK.

YAZGULYAM. See YAZGULEM and TAJIK.

YAZID. See YEZID and KURD.

YAZIDIS. See YEZID and KURD.

YAZVA. See KOMI.

YAZVA KOMI PERMIAK. See YAZVA KOMI PERMYAK and KOMI.

YAZVA KOMI PERMYAK. The Yazva Komi Permyak, who have also been known as the Yazvin, are one of the subgroups of the Komi Permyak, who are themselves a part of the larger Komi* people. They live along the Yazva River. See KOMI.
REFERENCE: Ronald Wixman, *The Peoples of the USSR: An Ethnographic Handbook*, 1984.

YAZVA ZIRIAN. See YAZVA KOMI PERMYAK and KOMI.

YAZVA ZIRYAN. See YAZVA KOMI PERMYAK and KOMI.

YAZVA ZYRIAN. See YAZVA KOMI PERMYAK and KOMI.

YAZVA ZYRYAN. See YAZVA KOMI PERMYAK and KOMI.

YAZVIN. See YAZVA KOMI PERMYAK and KOMI.

YAZVIN KOMI PERMYAK. See YAZVA KOMI PERMYAK and KOMI.

YAZVIN KOMI PERMYAK ZIRIAN. See YAZVA KOMI PERMYAK and KOMI.

YAZVIN KOMI PERMYAK ZIRYAN. See YAZVA KOMI PERMYAK and KOMI.

YAZVIN KOMI PERMYAK ZYRIAN. See YAZVA KOMI PERMYAK and KOMI.

YAZVIN KOMI PERMYAK ZYRYAN. See YAZVA KOMI PERMYAK and KOMI.

YAZVINSKIY. See YAZVA KOMI PERMYAK and KOMI.

YAZVINSKIY KOMI PERMYAK. See YAZVA KOMI PERMYAK and KOMI.

YAZVINSKIY KOMI PERMYAK ZIRIAN. See YAZVA KOMI PERMYAK and KOMI.

YAZVINSKIY KOMI PERMYAK ZIRYAN. See YAZVA KOMI PERMYAK and KOMI.

YAZVINSKIY KOMI PERMYAK ZYRIAN. See YAZVA KOMI PERMYAK and KOMI.

YAZVINSKIY KOMI PERMYAK ZYRYAN. See YAZVA KOMI PERMYAK and KOMI.

YENESEI. See KET and ENT.

YENESEI OSTIAK. See KET.

YENESEI OSTYAK. See ENT.

YENESEI SAMODI. See ENT.

YENESEI SAMOED. See ENT.

YENESEI SAMOIED. See ENT.

YENESEI SAMOYED. See ENT.

YENISEI OSTYAK. See KET.

YENISEIAN. See KET.

YENESEI TATAR. See SIBERIAN TATAR and KHAKASS.

YENISEY. See KET and ENT.

YENISEY OSTYAK. See KET.

YEZID. The Yezids are a subgroup of the Kurds*, but their status as a subgroup is a function of religion rather than language. Specialists in Middle Eastern and Central Asian religions trace Yezid beliefs back to Zoroastrianism, the religion of Persia before the great conversion to Islam. The Yezid religion retains the Zoroastrian belief in an afterlife and the emphasis on a continuous struggle between good and evil in the universe. The Sunni Muslims in the region, who are the large majority, have viewed the Yezid faith as sacrilege and have been anxious to exterminate it. The Yezids faced intense persecution in Turkey and other regions of the Near East, so many of them began migrating to Armenia and Georgia in order to survive. Suspicion of the Yezids still survives in the region, even among the Sunni Muslim Kurdish majority. See KURD.
REFERENCES: Gerard Chaliand, ed., *People Without a Country: The Kurds and Kurdistan*, 1980; William Eagleton, *The Kurdish Republic of 1946*, 1979; David McDowall, *The Kurds*, 1989; Ronald Wixman, *The Peoples of the USSR: An Ethnographic Handbook*, 1984.

YEZIDIS. See YEZID and KURD.

YOMUD. The Yomud (Yomut) are a Turkmen* subgroup and live east of the Caspian Sea. They are Sunni Muslims. See TURKMEN.
REFERENCE: Ronald Wixman, *The Peoples of the USSR: An Ethnographic Handbook*, 1984.

YOMUT. See YOMUD.

YUAN' SHYN. See DUNGAN.

YUCHI. See ENT.

YUGO OSET. See TUALLAG and OSSETIAN.

YUGO OSSETIN. See TUALLAG and OSSETIAN.

YUGRA. See MANSI, UGRIAN, and KHANT.

YUGRI. See MANSI, UGRIAN, and KHANT.

YUGRY. See MANSI, UGRIAN, and KHANT.

YUGUT. See ESKIMO.

YUGYT. See ESKIMO.

YUIT. See ESKIMO.

YUITI. See ESKIMO.

YUITY. See ESKIMO.

YUKAGHIR. See YUKAGIR.

YUKAGIR. The Yukagir (Yukaghir, Jukagir, Jukaghir), who call themselves the Odul or Detkil', are one of the smallest identifiable ethnic groups still functioning in the former Soviet Union. At one time, the Yukagir wandered across a wide swathe of tundra and steppes in northeastern Siberia, but, in the past two centuries, their numbers have dwindled dramatically. They have recovered somewhat in the last several decades, however. The 1926 census of the Soviet Union listed the Yukagir population at 443 people, and that number had increased to 615 people in 1970 and 835 in 1979. Although reliable census information has not been available concerning the Yukagir, estimates placed the population at approximately 850 people in the late 1980s. Today there are two distinct Yukagir groups. One group lives in the tundra, right at the edge of the forest, in the Chukochei River Basin on the lower Kolyma and Alazeya rivers. They are sometimes known as Tundra Yukagirs. The second group dwells in the Upper Kolyma region, more specifically the Sredne-Kanskiy Rayon in the Magadan Oblast and the Verkhne-Kolmskiy Rayon in what was formerly the Yakut Autonomous Soviet Socialist Republic. They are sometimes called the Kolyma Yukagirs.

Yukagir is a Paleo-Asiatic language with close ties to the Uralic and Altaic languages, indicating a considerable linguistic mixing over the centuries. Yukagir is also loaded with Russian*, Even*, Yakut*, and Nenets* words. The two Yukagir dialects spoken today correspond to the geographical groupings of the Yukagir people and are mutually unintelligible. Neither one of the dialects is a written language, so those Yukagir who are literate read and write in the Russian and Yakut languages. Almost all of the Yukagir speak more than one language; the vast majority of the Kolyma Yukagir also speak Yakut, while the Tundra Yukagir speak Even as well as Chukchi* and Yakut.

Historically, the Yukagir economy was based primarily on nomadic hunting and fishing, with relatively few Yukagirs (mostly Tundra Yukagirs) tending reindeer herds. The Yukagir were widely scattered throughout northeastern Siberia and numbered in the thousands of people. They were especially concentrated from the Lena River to the mouth of the Anadyr' River. They were also divided into a number of subgroups, including the Omoks, Anauls, Chuvashes*, and Khodyns. Although they spoke similar languages, the Yukagir did not have a sense of common ethnic identity since their matrilineal clan loyalties were very powerful. Ethnic Russians* first encountered the Yukagir in the mid-seventeenth century. Russian commercial traders, fur trappers, and hunters then established permanent contact with them. Systematic Russian contact brought a wave of epidemic diseases—influenza, mumps, smallpox, chicken pox. As a result, the Yukagir underwent a rapid population decline, from approximately 10,000 people in 1700 to 2,350 in 1859. Moscow authorized the granting of citizenship to any native who converted to Christianity, a process that led to forced baptisms and enserfment by local rulers, who then used their native serfs to increase fur trapping. As the numbers of fur-bearing animals decreased, Moscow lost interest in the area and in the well-being of its natives. The Yukagir, along with many other Siberian peoples, were part of this entire administrative process. By the mid-eighteenth century, the Russians and Yukagirs were increasingly drawn together in a commercialized economy. They began holding annual fairs at which the Yukagir would trade reindeer hides and furs for alcohol, iron tools, firearms, ammunition, and tobacco. In the nineteenth century, as increasing numbers of ethnic Russians settled in the region, the economic contacts strengthened. Completion of the Trans-Siberian Railroad in 1905 expanded those economic contacts even more.

Before contact with ethnic Russians, Yukagir religious life was similar to that of other aboriginal peoples around the world. The souls of the animals they hunted and herded were particularly significant. The arrival of ethnic Russians—trappers, settlers, and missionaries—brought about the conversion of most Yukagir to Russian Orthodoxy, but the conversion was superficial at best. Yukagir religion became a syncretic mix of animism and Christianity, with tribal shamans retaining great spiritual influence over the lives of the Yukagir people.

The Bolshevik Revolution of 1917 had a dramatic impact on the Yukagir. Late in the 1920s and throughout the 1930s, the government also collectivized indigenous economic activities. For the Yukagir, this policy meant the collectivization of their hunting, trapping, and reindeer-herding economy. For the Soviet government, collectivization had a dual purpose. It would both help implement Communist economic ideology and aid in acculturating Yukagir children to Russian values while eliminating their traditionally nomadic, subsistence economy. The government established "cultural bases" for the indigenous people. These were settlements complete with boarding schools, hospitals, day-care centers, veterinary dispensaries, and clubs. The government worked in this way to minimize the nomadic nature of Yukagir life. The programs ended the continuing decline of the Yukagir population; because of poverty and disease, the Yukagir population had dropped from 2,350 in 1859 to only 443 in 1926, but it had increased to 615 in 1959 and to more than 800 in 1979.

After World War II, the changes in Yukagir life accelerated. Because of the German* threat in the west, Soviet authorities had relocated much of the country's industry east of the Ural Mountains during World War II, and that decision brought hundreds of thousands of ethnic Russian families out to Siberia. Soviet state development plans continued that process during the 1950s and 1960s; the Yukagir found themselves in a rapidly changing economy. Although some Yukagir continued to work on government hunting and reindeer-breeding collectives, more and more found work at construction sites, oil and natural gas wells, and mass-production factories. They interacted more consistently with other ethnic groups—especially Russians, Yakuts, Evens and Chukchis—and became even more acclimated to a broader cultural and economic world.

The *perestroika* and *glasnost* policies of Mikhail Gorbachev in the 1980s reduced some of the state-imposed pressure to assimilate to Russian culture and Communist political ideology. In 1990, the Yukagir joined twenty-five other native Siberian peoples in establishing the Association of Peoples of the North (APN). They wanted to slow the pace of economic development, the influx of ethnic Russian settlers, and the deterioration of the natural environment. They also wanted the government to ratify both the 1957 International Convention on Protection and Integration of Indigenous and Other Tribal and Semi-Tribal Populations in Independent Countries and the 1989 Convention on Indigenous and Tribal Peoples in Independent Countries, in order to affirm that the Yukagir have a right to the ownership and possession of lands that they have traditionally occupied. Uralo Ado, a Yukagir writer, lamented the environmental destruction and cultural loss his people were experiencing in the 1980s.

One political response to the problem of the independence and sovereignty of the peoples of the far north has involved the re-creation of nationality districts in places without autonomous regions. In the early 1990s, a number of Yukagir leaders demanded the re-establishments of those districts, many of which had existed in the 1920s and 1930s. The Yukagir also called for the establishment of national ethnic parks—vast regions that would be assigned to particular ethnic groups so that they could pursue the unrestricted development of their traditional life-styles and prevent outside economic interference. The Yukagir demands collided headlong with Russia's need to develop Siberia economically. Moreover, ethnic Russians in Siberia vastly outnumber the Yukagir, are desperate for jobs, and favor development. All these factors make the likelihood of Yukagir success remote at best.

REFERENCES: Alice Bartels and Dennis Bartels, "Soviet Policy Toward Siberian Native People," *Canadian Dimension*, 19 (1985), 36–44; *Current Digest*, 41 (May 3, 1989), 8–9; Mike Edwards, "Siberia: In From the Cold," *National Geographic*, 177 (March 1990), 2–49; Eric Green, *Ecology and Perestroika: Environmental Protection in the Soviet Union*, 1990; W. T. Jochelson, *The Jukaghir and the Jukaghirized Tungus*, 1926;

Constantine Krypton, ''Soviet Policy in the Northern National Regions After World War II,'' *Slavic Review*, 13 (October 1954), 339–53; Piers Vitebsky, ''Perestroika Among the Reindeer Herders,'' *Geographical Magazine*, 61 (June 1989), 23–34; Ronald Wixman, *The Peoples of the USSR: An Ethnographic Handbook*, 1984.

YUPIGUT. See ESKIMO.

YUPIK. See ESKIMO.

YURAK. See NENETS.

YURAK SAMODI. See NENETS.

YURAK SAMOED. See NENETS.

YURAK SAMOIED. See NENETS.

YURAK SAMOYED. See NENETS.

YURMATIN. See BASHKIR.

YURMATYN. See BASHKIR.

YUS SAGAI. See SAGAI and KHAKASS.

Z

ZABAIKAL COSSACK. See TRANSBAIKAL COSSACK and COSSACK.

ZAKARPATO-RUS. See CARPATHO-RUSYN and UKRAINIAN.

ZAKARPATO-RUSIN. See CARPATHO-RUSYN and UKRAINIAN.

ZAKARPATO-RUSYN. See CARPATHO-RUSYN and UKRAINIAN.

ZAKARPATSKO-RUS. See CARPATHO-RUSYN and UKRAINIAN.

ZAKARPATSKO-RUSIN. See CARPATHO-RUSYN and UKRAINIAN.

ZAKARPATSKO-RUSYN. See CARPATHO-RUSYN and UKRAINIAN.

ZAKARPATSY. See CARPATHO-RUSYN and UKRAINIAN.

ZAKATALO-KAZAK. See AZERBAIJANI.

ZAN. See MEGRELO-LAZ and GEORGIAN.

ZANAVYKIAI. The Zanavykiai are a subgroup of the Suvalkieciai*, who are themselves one of the primary Lithuanian* subgroups. They live southwest of the Nemunas River in the Suvalkiya region of Lithuania. See SUVALKIECIAI or LITHUANIAN.
REFERENCE: Ronald Wixman, *The Peoples of the USSR: An Ethnographic Handbook,* 1984.

ZANEMAN. See SUVALKIECIAI and LITHUANIAN.

ZANEMANE. See SUVALKIECIAI and LITHUANIAN.

ZAPORGIAN COSSACK. See ZAPOROZHE COSSACK and COSSACK.

ZAPOROZHE COSSACK. The Zaporozhe Cossacks first emerged in the late sixteenth and early seventeenth centuries when a process of ethnogenesis brought groups of Ukrainian* and Crimean Tatar* peasants together. When the Russian* government dissolved the Zaporozhe Cossacks in 1775, some of them migrated across the Danube River to lands controlled by the Ottomans. Those left behind evolved into the Black Sea Cossacks. See COSSACK.
REFERENCE: Philip Longworth, *The Cossacks,* 1969.

ZATUNDREN. The Zatundren are ethnic Russians* who began migrating to Siberia in the eighteenth century. They settled in the tundra between the Dudinka and Khatanga rivers, where they mixed with the existing Dolgan* population. Over the centuries, they adopted the Dolgan language but have managed to maintain a separate identity as Russians. See RUSSIAN and DOLGAN.
REFERENCE: Ronald Wixman, *The Peoples of the USSR: An Ethnographic Handbook,* 1984.

ZATUNDRENE. See ZATUNDREN, DOLGAN, and RUSSIAN.

ZAZA. See KURD.

ZEMAICIAI. The Zemaiciai constitute a Lithuanian* subgroup. They live in western Lithuania. Russians* refer to them as Zhmud. See LITHUANIAN.
REFERENCE: Ronald Wixman, *The Peoples of the USSR: An Ethnographic Handbook,* 1984.

ZEMAITI. See ZEMAICIAI and LITHUANIAN.

ZEMAITIS. See ZEMAICIAI and LITHUANIAN.

ZEMGAL. See ZEMGALIESI and LATVIAN.

ZEMGALI. See ZEMGALIESI and LATVIAN.

ZEMGALIAN. See ZEMGALIESI and LATVIAN.

ZEMGALIESI. The Zemgaliesi are a subgroup of the Latvians* who live in Zemgale Province. Some ethnographers classify Latvians into subgroups based on their provincial origins. See LATVIAN.
REFERENCE: Ronald Wixman, *The Peoples of the USSR: An Ethnographic Handbook,* 1984.

ZEMGALIETIS. See ZEMGALIESI and LATVIAN.

ZEMGALIS. See ZEMGALIESI and LATVIAN.

ZEREHGERAN. See ZIREKHGERAN, DARGIN, and KUBACHI.

ZEREKHGERAN. See ZIREKHGERAN, DARGIN, and KUBACHI.

ZGAMIG. See YAZGULEM.

ZHEMAIT. See ZEMAICIAI and LITHUANIAN.

ZHEMAITI. See ZEMAICIAI and LITHUANIAN.

ZHEMAITY. See ZEMAICIAI and LITHUANIAN.

ZHEMAYTY. See ZEMAICIAI and LITHUANIAN.

ZHEMOIT. See ZEMAICIAI and LITHUANIAN.

ZHID. The term ''Zhid'' is a Russian* epithet for an individual of Jewish descent. See JEW.
REFERENCE: Ronald Wixman, *The Peoples of the USSR: An Ethnographic Handbook*, 1984.

ZHMUD. See ZEMAICIAI and LITHUANIAN.

ZHMUT. See ZEMAICIAI and LITHUANIAN.

ZHONGYUAN-REN. See DUNGAN.

ZHOO KESEK. See ICHKILIK and KYRGYZ.

ZIREKHGERAN. In Persian*, the word for a maker of chains or jewelry is Zirekhgeran. Since the Kubachi* are widely known in Central Asia for their jewelry, they have often been called Zirekhgerans. See KUBACHI or DARGIN.
REFERENCE: Ronald Wixman, *The Peoples of the USSR: An Ethnographic Handbook*, 1984.

ZIRIAN. See KOMI.

ZIRIAN IJEM. See IZHMI and KOMI.

ZIRIAN IJMI. See IZHMI and KOMI.

ZIRIAN IZHEM. See IZHMI and KOMI.

ZIRIAN IZHMI. See IZHMI and KOMI.

ZIUZDA. See ZYUZDA KOMI PERMYAK and KOMI.

ZIUZDA KOMI PERMYAK. See ZYUZDA KOMI PERMYAK and KOMI.

ZIUZDA ZIRIAN. See ZYUZDA KOMI PERMYAK and KOMI.

ZIUZDA ZYRIAN. See ZYUZDA KOMI PERMYAK and KOMI.

ZIUZDIN KOMI PERMYAK. See ZYUZDA KOMI PERMYAK and KOMI.

ZIUZDIN ZIRIAN. See ZYUZDA KOMI PERMYAK and KOMI.

ZIUZDIN ZYRIAN. See ZYUZDA KOMI PERMYAK and KOMI.

ZYRIAN. See KOMI.

ZYRIAN IJEM. See IZHMI and KOMI.

ZYRIAN IJMI. See IZHMI and KOMI.

ZYRIAN IZHEM. See IZHMI and KOMI.

ZYRIAN IZHMI. See IZHMI and KOMI.

ZYRYAN. See KOMI.

ZYRYAN IJEM. See IZHMI and KOMI.

ZYRYAN IJMI. See IZHMI and KOMI.

ZYRYAN IZHEM. See IZHMI and KOMI.

ZYRYAN IZHMI. See IZHMI and KOMI.

ZYUZDA. See ZYUZDA KOMI PERMYAK and KOMI.

ZYUZDA KOMI PERMYAK. The Zyuzda Komi Permyak, who are also known as the Zyuzdin, are a subgroup of the Komi Permyaks. Their language is considered to be a transitional one between Komi* and Komi Permyak. They live in the Zyuzdinskiy Rayon of Kirov Oblast. See KOMI.
REFERENCE: Ronald Wixman, *The Peoples of the USSR: An Ethnographic Handbook*, 1984.

ZYUZDA ZIRYAN. See ZYUZDA KOMI PERMYAK and KOMI.

ZYUZDA ZYRYAN. See ZYUZDA KOMI PERMYAK and KOMI.

ZYUZDIN KOMI PERMYAK. See ZYUZDA KOMI PERMYAK and KOMI.

ZYUZDINSKIY. See ZYUZDA KOMI PERMYAK and KOMI.

ZYUZDIN ZIRIAN. See ZYUZDA KOMI PERMYAK and KOMI.

ZYUZDIN ZYRIAN. See ZYUZDA KOMI PERMYAK and KOMI.

Appendix A
Major Ethnic Groups of the Soviet Union by Republic, 1990

Republic	Ethnic Group	Percent of Population
Armenian	Armenian	89.7
	Azerbaijani	5.5
	Russian	2.3
	Kurd	1.7
Azerbaijan	Azerbaijani	78.1
	Russian	7.9
	Armenian	7.9
Belorussian (Belarus)	Belarusian	79.4
	Russian	11.9
	Polish	4.2
	Ukrainian	2.4
	Jewish	1.4
Estonian	Estonian	64.7
	Russian	27.9
	Ukrainian	2.5
	Belarusian	1.6
	Finnish	1.2
Georgian	Georgian	68.8
	Armenian	9.0
	Russian	7.4
	Azerbaijani	5.1
	Ossetian	3.3
	Abkhazian	1.7
Kazakh	Russian	40.8
	Kazakh	36.0
	Ukrainian	6.1
	Tatar	2.1
Kyrkyz	Kyrgyz	40.7
	Russian	22.0
	Uzbek	10.3
	Ukrainian	2.6
	Tatar	1.7
Latvian	Latvian	53.7
	Russian	32.8
	Belarusian	4.5
	Ukrainian	2.7
	Polish	2.5

Republic	Ethnic Group	Percentage of Population
Lithuanian	Lithuanian	80.1
	Russian	8.6
	Polish	7.7
	Belarusian	1.5
Moldavian (Moldova)	Moldovan	63.9
	Ukrainian	14.2
	Russian	12.8
	Gagauzi	3.5
	Jewish	2.0
	Bulgarian	2.0
Russian	Russian	82.6
	Tatar	3.6
	Ukrainian	2.7
	Chuvash	1.2
Tajik	Tajik	58.8
	Uzbek	22.0
	Russian	10.4
	Tatar	2.1
Turkmen	Turkmen	68.4
	Russian	12.6
	Uzbek	8.5
	Kazakh	2.9
Ukrainian	Ukrainian	73.6
	Russian	21.1
	Jewish	1.3
	Belarusian	0.8
	Moldovan	0.6
	Polish	0.5
Uzbek	Uzbek	68.7
	Russian	10.8
	Tatar	4.2
	Kazakh	4.0
	Tajik	3.9
	Karakalpak	1.9

Source: Michael Mandelbaum, ed. The Rise of Nations in the Soviet Union.
         New York: Council on Foreign Relations. 1991.

Appendix B
Ethnic Populations of the Soviet Union,
1926–1989

Group	1926	1959	1970	1979	1989
Abaza	13,825	19,591	25,448	29,497	33,801
Abkhaz	56,957	65,430	83,240	90,915	102,938
Adyghe	---	---	---	---	124,941
Afghan	---	---	---	---	8,951
Agul	7,653	6,709	8,831	12,078	19,936
Albanian	---	5,258	4,402	3,500*	4,085
Aleut	353	421	441	546	660*
Altai	39,062	45,270	55,812	60,015	71,317
American	---	---	---	---	746
Arab	28,978	---	---	---	11,599
Armenian	1,567,568	2,786,912	3,559,151	4,151,241	4,627,227
Assyrian	9,808	21,803	24,294	25,170	26,289
Austrian	---	---	---	---	731
Avar	158,769	270,394	396,297	482,844	604,202
Azerbaijan	1,706,605	2,939,728	4,379,937	5,477,330	6,791,106
Balkar	33,307	42,408	59,501	66,334	88,771
Bashkir	713,693	989,040	1,239,681	1,371,452	1,449,462
Belarusian	4,738,923	7,913,488	9,051,755	9,462,715	10,030,441
Beluchi	9,974	7,842	12,582	18,997	29,091
British	---	---	---	---	637
Bukharan	23,671	---	---	---	---
Bulgarian	---	---	---	---	378,790
Buryat	237,501	252,959	314,671	352,646	421,682
Chechen	318,522	418,756	612,674	755,782	958,309
Cherkess	---	30,453	39,785	46,470	54,000*

Group	1926	1959	1970	1979	1989
Chinese	---	---	---	---	11,418
Chukchi	12,332	11,727	13,597	14,000	14,000*
Chuvash	1,117,419	1,469,766	1,694,351	1,751,366	1,839,228*
Circassian	---	---	---	---	52,356
Crimean	---	---	---	---	1,312
Crimean Tatar	---	---	---	---	268,739
Croatian	---	---	---	---	1,100
Cuban	---	---	---	---	5,113
Czech	---	---	---	---	16,335
Dargin	108,963	158,149	230,932	287,282	365,797
Dolgan	656	3,932	4,877	5,053	5,400*
Dungan	14,600	21,928	38,644	51,694	69,686
Dutch	---	---	---	---	964
Ent	378	---	---	---	200*
Eskimo	1,293	1,118	1,308	1,510	1,700*
Estonian	---	988,616	1,007,356	1,109,851	1,027,255
Even	2,044	9,121	12,029	12,286	13,000*
Evenk	38,805	24,151	25,149	27,531	30,000*
Finn	134,791	92,717	84,750	77,079	67,318
French	---	---	---	---	798
Gagauz	844	123,821	156,606	173,179	197,164
Georgian	1,564,333	2,691,950	3,245,300	3,570,504	3,983,115
German	1,238,549	1,619,655	1,846,317	1,936,214	2,035,807
Greek	`213,765	309,308	336,869	343,809	357,957
Gypsy	---	---	---	---	261,956

Group	1926	1959	1970	1979	1989
Indian	---	---	---	---	1,300*
Ingush	74,097	105,980	157,605	186,198	237,557
Iranian (Persian)	---	---	---	---	40,510
Italian	---	---	---	---	1,942
Itelmen	4,217	1,109	1,301	1,307	1,300*
Izhora	16,137	1,062	781	748	829
Japanese	---	---	---	---	691
Jews	5,000,000*	2,267,814	2,150,707	1,810,876	1,376,910
Kabard	---	---	---	---	394,651
Kalmyk	129,321	106,066	137,194	146,631	174,528
Karachai	55,123	81,403	112,741	131,074	156,140
Karakalpak	146,317	172,556	236,009	303,324	423,436
Karapapakh	6,316	---	---	---	10,000*
Karelian	248,120	167,278	146,081	138,421	131,357
Kazakh	3,968,289	3,621,610	5,298,818	6,556,442	8,137,878
Ket	1,428	1,019	1,182	1,122	1,100*
Khakass	45,608	56,584	66,725	70,776	81,428
Khant	17,800	19,410	21,138	20,934	20,500*
Komi	226,383	287,027	321,894	326,700	345,007
Komi-Permyak	---	---	---	---	152,074
Korean	---	313,735	357,507	388,926	437,335
Koryak	7,439	6,287	7,487	7,879	8,500*
Kumyk	94,549	134,967	188,792	228,418	282,178
Kurd	69,184	58,799	88,930	115,858	152,952
Kyrgyz	762,736	968,659	1,452,222	1,906,271	2,530,998

Group	1926	1959	1970	1979	1989
Lak	---	---	---	---	118,386
Lapp	1,720	1,792	1,884	1,888	1,900*
Latvian	141,703	1,399,539	1,429,844	1,439,037	1,459,156
Lezghin	134,529	223,129	323,829	382,611	466,833
Lithuanian	41,463	2,326,094	2,664,944	2,850,905	3,068,296
Magyar	5,476	154,738	166,451	170,553	171,941
Manchu	---	---	---	---	20,000*
Mansi	5,754	6,449	7,710	7,563	7,400*
Mari	428,192	504,205	598,628	621,961	670,277
Meskhetian	---	---	---	---	100,000*
Moldovan	278,905	1,214,139	2,697,994	2,968,224	3,355,240*
Mordvinian	1,340,415	1,285,116	1,262,670	1,191,765	1,153,516*
Nanai	5,309	8,026	10,005	10,516	11,000*
Negidal	683	---	537	504	475*
Nenet	15,462	23,007	28,705	29,894	31,000*
Nganasan	867	748	953	867	850*
Nivkhi	4,076	3,717	4,420	4,397	4,300*
Nogai	36,274	---	51,784	59,546	75,564*
Orochi	647	782	1,089	1,198	1,250*
Ossetian	272,272	412,592	488,039	541,893	597,802
Pakistani	---	---	---	---	1,300*
Pole	782,334	1,380,282	1,167,523	1,150,991	1,126,255
Romanian	4,651	106,366	119,292	128,792	145,918
Russian	77,791,124	114,113,579	129,015,140	137,397,089	145,071,550
Rutul	10,495	6,732	12,071	15,032	20,672
Selkup	1,630	3,768	4,282	3,565	3,300*
Serb	---	---	---	---	3,100
Shor	12,601	15,274	16,494	16,033	16,572

Group	1926	1959	1970	1979	1989
Slovak	---	14,674	11,658	9,409	10,017
Spaniard	---	---	---	---	3,737
Tabasaran	31,983	34,700	55,188	75,239	98,488
Tajik	978,680	1,396,839	2,135,883	2,897,697	4,216,693
Talysh	---	---	---	---	21,914
Tat	28,705	11,463	17,109	22,441	30,817
Tatar	2,916,536	4,967,701	5,930,670	6,317,468	6,645,588
Tofalar	2,829	586	---	620	650*
Tsakhur	19,085	7,321	11,103	13,478	20,055
Turk	---	---	---	---	207,369
Turkmen	763,940	1,001,585	1,525,284	2,027,913	2,718,297
Tuvinian	---	100,145	139,388	166,082	206,924
Udegei	1,357	1,444	1,469	1,551	1,600*
Udi	---	---	---	---	8,849
Udmurt	504,187	624,794	704,328	713,696	746,562
Uigur	108,570	95,208	173,276	210,612	262,199
Ukrainian	31,194,976	37,252,430	40,753,246	42,347,387	44,135,989
Ulchi	723	2,055	2,448	2,552	2,700*
Uzbek	3,904,622	6,015,416	9,105,093	12,455,978	16,686,240
Vep	32,785	16,374	8,281	8,094	13,341
Vietnamese	---	---	---	---	16,752
Yakut	240,709	233,344	296,244	328,018	382,255
Yukagir	443	442	615	835	900*

*Estimated population.

Source: Ronald Wixman. The Peoples of the USSR: An Ethnographic Handbook (Armonk, NY: M. E. Sharpe, 1984); Michael Mandelbaum, ed. The Rise of Nations in the Soviet Union (New York: Council on Foreign Relations, 1991; Gosudarstvennyi komitet po statistike, Natsionalnyi sostav naseleniia, Chast' II (Moscow, 1989), 3-5.

Appendix C
A Brief History of Islam, with Special Reference to Russia and the Soviet Union

Islam is one of the three great monotheistic philosophies of the world. Those who adhere to the principles of Islam, called Muslims, include people from every racial group. Muslims make up approximately one-fifth of the world's total population. In the republics of the former Soviet Union, Muslims comprise approximately 16 percent of the people, and most of them are citizens of the Central Asian republics.

The Arabic term "Islam" means "submission," while "Muslim" means "he who submits." In Islam, submission to the will of God (Allah) is the single most important fact of human existence. The Western term "religion" is generally applied to Islam, but this word is inadequate to express what Islam means to its followers. Islam is an all-embracing world view—a manner of arranging one's life within the community as well as a vehicle for managing one's relationship with God.

Islam is the most recently established of the world's three great monotheisms, the other two being Judaism and Christianity. According to Muslims, the Word of God was first revealed to the Prophet Muhammed in a cave near Mecca, in the year 610 of the Christian era. Muhammed was an upright and honest man, a merchant by profession, who was troubled by the corruption and falsity he saw in the cosmopolitan trading centers he visited. He was acquainted with Hebrew and Christian traditions. Periodically, he withdrew from society to meditate. It was during one such period of meditation that he received the "Call to Prophecy," and the "Revelation of the Words of Allah."

The message of Islam was first preached to Muhammed's family members, and it was from among them that he gained his first adherents. Preaching to men of his town, Mecca, he met resistance and open defiance; only the prominence of his relatives in the tribe Quraysh protected him. Opposition did not disappear, however, it was just diverted from Muhammed personally to his less influential followers. Faced with increased persecution in Mecca and following the deaths of Muhammed's powerful uncle, Abu Talib, and his wife, Khadija, in 619, it was impossible for Muhammed and the Muslim community to remain in Mecca. This tension was relieved when a delegation from Yathrib, a town some 400 kilometers to the north, came to Mecca seeking Muhammed to mediate between opposing clans in their town. Muhammed agreed to come, provided that the town would accept his preaching of Islam and protect him. Once this stipulation was accepted, Muhammed sent his followers to Yathrib in small groups. He and Abu Bakr, one of his most stalwart companions, were the last to leave Mecca in September of 622. Ten years later, on the Prophet's death, Abu Bakr succeeded Muhammed as leader of the Muslim community.

The year of the Emigration (*Hijrah*) marks the beginning of the Muslim calendar: year one, Hijrah, began with the first day of the lunar year in which the Hijrah took place, July 16, 622 in the Christian era. The Muslim calendar uses a lunar month of twenty-nine or thirty days; therefore, a Muslim year of twelve lunar months is approximately eleven days shorter than a solar year. The lunar New Year, as well as every other event dated by the lunar calendar, rotates through the seasons.

Muhammed quickly achieved political as well as social and moral leadership in Yathrib, a town in which the atmosphere was far different from that of Mecca. Yathrib was an agricultural and herding town, while Mecca was a center of commerce and pagan religion. Muhammed settled the initial dispute and began to exercise administrative and political control of the town. The Quran (Koran) reflects this change in the shift of its revelations from moral topics in Mecca to more legal and political ones in Yathrib.

Yathrib, City of the Prophet (Yathrib, Medina an-Nebi), soon became known simply as "al-Medina." As the new home of the Muslim community and as the protector of Muhammed, Medina came into direct conflict with Mecca. In the tradition of the region, raids and skirmishes between Medina and Mecca began soon after the Hijrah. Many nomadic clans and tribes joined with the urban tribes of Medina under Muhammed's leadership to oppose Mecca, both to secure commercial advantage and to honor other ties.

Muhammed died in 632, without a male heir and without designating a successor in the Muslim community. Leading members of the Muslim community therefore met soon after Muhammed's death to select a successor. A strong successor (*khalif*) would be necessary both to continue community leadership and to retain or restore alliances with outlying tribes that considered their agreements to have been with Muhammed himself, not with the Muslim community. Muhammed's first successors were chosen by consensus (the traditional tribal method) from among his earliest converts. Abu Bakr, the Companion of the Prophet who had remained with Muhammed during the Hijrah, became the first of the khalifs.

Under the leadership of the first four khalifs, called the "Rightly Guided" (Rashidun) khalifs, the Arab Muslims began a course of Islamic conquest that lasted for a thousand years. Conquests begun within two years of the Prophet's death took Islamic warriors across North Africa to Spain, through South Asia and into the islands of Indonesia and the Philippines, north through the Balkans to the gates of Vienna, and northeast into Central Asia. People of many different cultures and languages, once defeated in battle, converted to the faith and became the cutting edge of further conquests.

Islam was an easy faith to adopt; it essentially demanded very little of the faithful. To be recognized as a Muslim, with all the privileges that such recognition eventually offered to members of a conquering and ruling society, all one had to do was be willing to recite the Profession of Faith, called in Arabic the Shahaddah: "There is no god but God, and Muhammed is the Messenger of God" (*La 'ila illa Allah, wa Muhammed rusuul Allah*). Since, according to the Quran, no one can know the human heart except God, no true Muslim could in good conscience doubt that one who had made the Profession of Faith was indeed a Muslim.

In addition, Islam has four more basic requirements—four things that a devout Muslim is expected to undertake for the good of his soul. Together with the profession, these are known as the Five "Pillars of Faith" in Islam: 1.) acknowledgment of the supremacy of One God (*Ash-Shahaddah*); 2.) prayers, five times daily (*As-Salat*); 3.) giving alms (*Az-Zakat*); 4.) fasting during the ninth month, Ramadan (*As-Sauvem*); and 5.) pilgrimage to Mecca (*Al-Hajj*). Of these, the Hajj (hadj) is expected of a Muslim only once during his lifetime, and then only if his health and circumstances permit it.

The Word of God, as revealed through the Prophet Muhammed, is contained in the Quran, the holy book of Islam. Muslims believe that the Quran was revealed in a "clear Arabic tongue" so that it would not be corrupted. According to Islamic belief, earlier monotheists had been given messages from God, but, over time, these messages had become corrupted by translation and interpretation. To the Muslims, the Quran cannot be translated. The words might be rendered into another language, but the essential, original meaning would thereby be lost.

The Quran mentions ninety-nine prophets whom God sent to man before Muhammed. Among these are Adam, Abraham, Moses, most of the Hebrew prophets, and Jesus. Abraham is considered to be the father of the Arabs, through his son Ishmael, whose mother, Hagar, was Abraham's concubine. As written in the Quran, Ishmael and Abraham together built the House of God at Mecca (the Ka'aba), which is the focal point of the Hajj and toward which Muslims face during their daily prayers. Moses is the prophet mentioned most often in the Quran; the story of God's call to rescue the sons of Israel, Ishmael's nephew, is found in the Quran. Jesus is recognized as the messiah, the special one of God, but not as the Son of God. Islamic tradition considers the concept of Jesus as Son of God to be blasphemy, since it associates another being with God and thus denies the validity of the Oneness of God.

According to Muslims, all these prophets brought the authentic message from God to humans, but their followers reinterpreted and revised the message until it was corrupted beyond true understanding. Later followers of these prior prophets may well be sincere, but they are following a corrupted message and are therefore, at best, misguided. The Holy Books of Jews and Christians, the Torah and the Bible Testaments, are thus considered by Muslims to be "just stories," while, in the Quran, one finds the true Word of God.

Two of the Muslims' holy cities, Mecca and Medina, are intimately associated with the life of Muhammed. The third Holy City of Muslims is Jerusalem. Jerusalem is a sacred city both because it is the city of the prophets, and because of the tradition of the Prophet Muhammed's dream vision. In this vision, he flew on the Angel Gabriel's horse from Medina to Jerusalem, ascended to view the afterlife, and returned to Medina in one night. The rocky outcropping now covered by the Dome of the Rock on the Temple Mount in Jerusalem is by tradition the place from which Muhammed made his ascent into Heaven. Jerusalem has ritual importance as well, for it was the original focus of prayer and the direction in which one faced when praying. The tribes that had called Muhammed to Medina included both Christians and Jews. The Prophet expected these monotheists, who shared with him the common background of a revealed religion and a Holy Book, to recognize the truth of his message immediately, but they did not. Muhammed was angered and therefore changed the direction of daily prayers toward Mecca and the traditional Arab holy place, the Ka'aba, to the south. Jerusalem, however, retained its importance in Islam as the third most holy city.

Prayer in Islam is a daily ritual for every individual. Muslims are expected to pray five times each day: at the first light, at noon, in the middle of the afternoon, at last light, and at dinner time. The tradition is flexible, however; just as Hajj is required only of those who are physically fit and whose circumstances allow it, those who miss one or more of the day's prayers can make them up by saying additional short prayers at times when daily prayer is possible. Although Muslims will generally recite these daily prayers in groups, the Islamic faith holds that each Muslim truly prays as an individual, standing separately before Allah.

Friday, the Islamic holy day, is marked by corporate prayer. All male Muslims in the community, as well as many of the older females, gather in the community mosque for the midday prayer and usually an address by the local prayer leader. The mosque need be no more than an unadorned open place with some indication of the direction toward

Mecca, a place from which the leader can address the group, and a facility in which Muslims can make their ablutions prior to prayer. Muslims must be clean when they stand before God; hence, the requirement that there be a place for cleaning hands, feet, and head near the mosque. In most places, this need is filled by a free-flowing fountain in the forecourt of the mosque, but, where water is lacking, clean sand performs the same ritual function. The ritual requirement for cleanliness also explains the tradition of the prayer rug, on which a Muslim stands, bare-footed, to pray.

Islam has no organized clergy as that term is understood in Christianity. No one stands between the individual Muslim and God. Prayer leaders, called "Imams" (meaning "in front"), are simply men who are respected by the group and who lead the community in the ritual prayers. The senior or most learned leader in the mosque normally gives the Friday sermon, which may be a commentary on verses from the Quran, a lecture on the Muslim's duty to his community, a specific call for community action, or any other topic for the benefit of the community. Traditionally, the imam of the mosque was not paid; either he was supported by the generous gifts of the Muslim community or maintained himself by a trade. Although there is no Quranic requirement that an imam attend any sort of training for his position, Muslims have come to expect their prayer leaders to be educated men.

Education has been important in Islam since the years of the first Muslim conquests. The strongest support for education has been the Quran itself. If one accepts the idea that the Quran is the Word of God, that no one can interpret the Word for anyone else, and that the Word is untranslatable, then the ability to read the Quran in Arabic is absolutely required. There is a tradition that written Arabic was developed in its present form specifically to ensure that those who learned the Quran were reciting it correctly, without any deviation from the original Word. The Quran quickly became the Muslim's style guide and grammatical text as well as his Holy Book. The first formal schools in Islam were founded in community mosques, where boys and young men could learn to read the Quran and study other useful knowledge. Groups of scholars, taught by older, respected men of the community, formed the nucleus around which great Islamic universities grew.

As conquests expanded the Muslim world, the original Arab warriors came into contact with older civilizations that had literate traditions of their own. Muslim scholars learned from these older traditions, preserved them, and carried forward their developments in science, philosophy, astronomy, art, and other areas of knowledge. Thus, in the halls of al-Azar University of Cairo in the tenth century of the Christian era, one might find Muslim scholars discussing the works of Plato and Socrates, while others experimented with the effects of herbal medicines, developed new mathematical treatises on architecture or music, or plotted more accurately the courses of celestial bodies.

The requirement for Hajj encouraged the curiosity in many men to see new places. Once having traveled a great distance to get to Mecca, many Muslim scholars did not return directly to their homes but continued to travel throughout the world. These scholars wrote of their travels, providing their contemporaries and later generations with vivid images of the world in which they lived. Among these traveling scholars was Ibn Khaldun, who wrote the first scientifically based studies of people and civilizations; he is therefore called the father of sociology and rational historiography. Another was Ibn Battuta, who visited China, Ceylon, Constantinople, and central Africa; a third, al-Masudi, visited and wrote about every country of Asia, Zanzibar, and most of North Africa.

Within a generation of the Prophet's death, Muslim traders and caravan merchants had penetrated far beyond the expanding borders of the Islamic empire, following the same trade routes that their fathers had followed but carrying Islam with them. Merchant-traders were among the first Muslims to be seen in Central Asia, moving along the Great Silk Road to China or north along the river systems to the amber-trading sites near the Baltic Sea. Merchants collected information as well as traded goods in their travels. They were therefore sought out by Muslim leaders planning expeditions into the House of War (*Dar al-Harb*)—those regions of the world not under Islamic control, or outside of the house of Islam (*Dar al-Islam*).

The first Muslim conquerors expanded the Dar al-Islam throughout the Arabian Peninsula, winning over other Arab tribes and converting them to Islam. The next expansion was to the north, against Byzantine and Sassanian forces. Muslim tradition has it that the Prophet sent messages to the three great rulers of the known world, calling on them to submit to the Will of Allah and become Muslims. The rulers of Byzantium, Persia, and Abyssinia declined to be converted and brought upon themselves the fate that Allah had decreed.

The Sassanian Empire, already weakened by lengthy conflict with the Eastern Romans, was the first to fall to the Arab conquerors. The collapse of the Sassanian Empire was due as much to internal decay as to external pressure, but it gave Arab Muslim rulers control over many non-Arab people for the first time. Subsequent political and social developments in Islam can be traced to the accommodations this conquest required.

Muslims are guided—socially, politically, and ethnically—by the life and teachings of the Prophet Muhammed. The collected set of customary procedures or habitual practices, which are based on the sayings and doings of Muhammed, are called the Sunna of the Prophet. Those Muslims who follow the Sunna exclusively are known as People of the Sunna, or Sunni Muslims. The Sunni may be considered the "orthodox" Muslims; they make up about 90 percent of Muslims worldwide, including most of the Muslims of the Central Asian republics.

The Shi'i (*Shi'ites*) comprise most of the remaining 10 percent of Muslims. The Shi'i derive from the political disputes surrounding the election of khalifs in the years following the Prophet's death. From the very beginning, a significant group of Muslims believed that the Prophet's successor should come from the family of the Prophet, following blood lines. The Prophet had no male heirs, but his daughter Fatima had been married to an early convert and cousin of Muhammed, 'Ali ibn Abu-Talib ('Ali, son of Abu-Talib, Muhammed's uncle and protector). 'Ali was subsequently selected as the last of the Rashidun khalifs, but he was never able to establish complete control over all the Muslims. It was 'Ali who moved the Muslim capital away from Medina to Kufa, in what is now Iraq. 'Ali was opposed politically by Mu'awwyia, a Muslim governor and military leader in Damascus, who eventually succeeded in eliminating 'Ali and subsequently ruled as khalif. After 'Ali's murder, his supporters raised additional forces to proclaim their disaffection from Damascene authority and to promote the sons of 'Ali (hence the grandsons of the Prophet) to leadership. As symbols of opposition to the ruling Arab Muslim hierarchy, these sons, Hassan and Hussein, came to represent the aspirations of non-Arab Muslims for equal shares in the benefits of the Islamic Empire. Mu'awwyia, the khalif, pensioned Hassan off to Medina; Hussein refused to be bought off and was martyred at Karbala, near Kufa.

This sequence of events confirmed the opposition of those Muslims who had supported 'Ali; they continued in opposition, calling themselves the Faction of 'Ali (*Shi'at 'Ali*) or Shi'ites. The Shi'i center remained in Iraq. Although all Muslims share a respect for 'Ali and his sons, the Shi'i consider that true Islamic leadership and authority is carried solely through the descendants of the Prophet. In the early centuries of Shi'ism, several disputes arose as to who the true descendants of 'Ali, Hassan, and Hussein were. These disputes have resulted in a division of Shi'ism into major subgroups.

The Isma'ili Shi'ites trace their origin to the eighth century of the Christian era; Isma'il was the eldest son of the sixth Shi'i imam; therefore, the group is sometimes called the Seveners. The Twelvers (*Ithna-Asheria*) Shi'i are followers of the twelfth imam. The Twelvers, also known as the Ja'farite rite, form the largest Shi'i sect. Twelvers agree with the Isma'ilis on the succession of the imamate up to Isma'il, but they claim that, since Isma'il died or was disowned prior to his father's death, the true imamate passed not to Isma'il, but to his younger brother, Musa al-Kazim. Twelvers believe that the last true imam of Shi'i Islam disappeared in a miracle or was "hidden from view" during the late ninth century and will return as the Mahdi or Muslim messiah in the future. Twelver Shi'ism became the state religion of Iran in the sixteenth century.

Islam provides Muslims with a pattern for political organization as well as for personal behavior. This pattern is contained in Muslim Law (*Shariah* or *Sharia*) and in the collected traditions of the Prophet (*Hadith*). As the Prophet became increasingly involved in the political life of Medina, the Revelation that he received from Allah had ever more to do with relationships within a just community. The Quran, as the means that God chose to transmit the Shariah, is the original Islamic legal text. For Muslims, the Quran is thus the primary source of law and unimpeachable.

The Hadith of the Prophet are statements that, at a certain time, in a certain place, the Prophet was noted to have said or done a specific thing, providing a precedent for other specific activities. In the legal sense, these traditions of the Prophet are used to soften the rigidity of Quranic law and are used where no clear Quranic legal example exists. Each particular hadith is accompanied by a list of the authorities who reported it (*isnad*), reaching from the most recent reporter who wrote it in a recognized text, back from person to person to the original witness of the event, who should be a known Companion of the Prophet. The evaluation of isnad and hadith criticism is one of the oldest Islamic sciences.

The Shariah and Hadith make up the basis for Muslim political science. This corpus of knowledge, however, is not without its Muslim critics. Various groups of Muslim scholars, from the seventh century on, have offered different opinions on what constitutes law in the Muslim community, and, more specifically, how Muslims are to adapt the canon of the law to changing circumstances. Among Sunni scholars, four main schools of jurisprudence and legal thought developed during the first four centuries of Islam. Adherents of each school consider theirs to be better than the others, but, generally speaking, Muslims have considered each school to be acceptable. The four schools of Sunni jurisprudence are:

1. Maliki, the oldest school, which puts the greatest emphasis on tradition;
2. Hanafi, which relies on judicial opinion more than on tradition and allows reasoning by analogy (*qiyyas*) to reach logical conclusions for legal questions;
3. Shafi'i, which places greatest reliance on logic and reasoning, thus providing the most flexibility in jurisprudence; the school makes use of authenticated hadith and accepts the consensus of the educated community as a legal guide; and
4. Hannabali, which offers the most fundamentalist approach to shariah and hadith, rejecting consensus as a legal tool and limiting the use of analogy.

The four schools were well established by the eleventh century, which may be considered the high point of classical Islamic civilization.

There are several official Islamic rites in the former Soviet Union. The vast majority are Sunni Muslims of the Hanafi school. In the region of Daghestan, there are nearly 2.5 million people who belong to the Shafi'i school, except for the Nogais*, who are Hanafi. There are other rites as well. More than 70 percent of the Azerbaijanis* are followers of the Ja'farite rite of the Shi'a creed. The Ironis* and the Muslim Tats* also adhere to the J'afarite rite, as do another 125,000 or so people in such Central Asian cities as Samarkand, Mary, Bukhara, Krasnovodsk, and Ashkhabad. Today there are more than 5,000,000 followers of the Ja'farite rite in the Commonwealth of Independent States (CIS). Approximately 125,000 Pamir* people of the Gorno-Badakhshan Autonomous Oblast in the Tajik Republic are Ismailis of the Nizarit rite. The Ismaili religion has a long tradition of clandestine activity, almost resembling a secret society, with no mosques and no public religious activity. Approximately 50,000 people, mostly Iranian émigrés scattered throughout Azerbaijan, the Turkmen Republic, and in Astrakhan, are Bahais. Finally, there are approximately 12,000 Karapapakhs* who are Shi'a extremists, known as the "Ali Illahis."

When European Crusaders invaded the Holy Lands to wrest them from the Saracens at the end of the eleventh century, they found much that was attractive and technologically advanced in comparison to the keeps and castles they had left behind. Returning Crusaders brought with them spices, unusual fruits, Eastern clothing, new habits such as frequent bathing, and medical and scientific knowledge that sparked a revival of learning in Europe, leading eventually to the European Renaissance. Intellectual and technological advances during the Renaissance, as well as the fall of Constantinople, led to European expansion both into the New World and across Asia.

Six-hundred years after the First Crusade, the various Muslim principalities, khanates, and emirates of Central Asia fell under the control of the expanding Russian Empire. The Khanate of Khiva, the Emirate of Bukhara, and other polities were border states in the poorly defined march regions of the Ottoman, Saffavid (Persian), and Russian Empires. As city-states that controlled considerable areas of surrounding agricultural and pasture land, these independent political units were often centers of Islamic learning and artistic endeavor, with wealth based on control of trade routes. Bukhara, in what is now Uzbekistan, was known as a center of Islamic scholarship; and its state library was once the scholastic home of the physician and philosopher Ibn Sina (Avicenna). Samarkand, also in Uzbekistan, had been Tamerlane's (Timur al-Leng) capital city, which he had embellished with palaces and mosques of glazed brick, marble, and mosaic work. The thirteenth-century sacking of such cities by Mongol* hordes was devastating. Nonetheless, these cities had revived sufficiently by the seventeenth and eighteenth centuries to provide significant obstacles to Russian imperial forces, in spite of the technological superiority of Europeans who were beneficiaries of the Renaissance.

In the middle of the fourteenth century, an energized Muscovy began to drive back the weakened heirs of the Golden Horde, and, in the process, they assumed control over more and more Muslims. A century later, Muscovy began its southern and eastern expansion. Kazan fell under Russian control in 1552, Astrakhan in 1556, and western Siberia in 1598. Russian authorities immediately launched programs of forced conversion, expulsion, and land expropriation against the Muslim population. The Russian conquest of Muslim lands continued in the sixteenth and seventeenth centuries. In the eighteenth century, Russians entered the North Caucasus region, where they encountered fierce resistance from the Muslim mountaineers there. The Russian conquest of Central Asia began in 1855. They took Chimkent that year and Tashkent in 1865, establishing protectorates in Bukhara and Khiva in 1873 and abolishing the Khanate of Khokand in 1876. Turkmen territory fell under Russian control between 1873 and 1884, and, at the turn of the century, the Russians occupied the land of the Pamirs.

With the beginning of the Bolshevik Revolution, Russian-Muslim relations entered a period characterized by complex shifting, and often contradictory political policies. During the years of the civil war, between 1917 and 1919, Bolsheviks launched indiscriminate anti-religious crusades against all the faiths of Russia, including Islam. In 1919, those crusades subsided, and government policy took a new direction. It recognized the possibility of Muslim National Communism, whereby Muslim leaders who joined the party were allowed to exercise political authority. For the most part, Soviet authorities avoided heavy-handed anti-religious campaigns among Muslims, but they did eliminate the economic power of many Muslim clerics, dissolved the ecclesiastical courts, and ended the confessional school system.

In 1928, however, Josef Stalin launched a wholesale assault on Islam within the Soviet Union. Thousands of mosques were closed or destroyed, and most Muslim clerics were killed or imprisoned. The state accused them of being spies and counter-revolutionaries, and they suffered severely from the consequent state terrorism. Throughout the 1930s, the Soviet government also produced a steady stream of anti-Muslim propaganda and distributed it throughout the country. That anti-Islam crusade ended only in 1941, when Germany invaded the Soviet Union. Soviet authorities needed the support of religious groups throughout the country, so the official attitude toward Islam changed dramatically.

During the postwar period, government policy continued to shift back and forth. The period of benign neglect, which had existed since 1941, continued until 1959, when Nikita Khrushchev launched a new assault on Islam. The number of mosques in country illustrates the trend. There had been 26,279 mosques in the Russian Empire in 1912. That number fell to only 1,500 in Stalin years, and Khrushchev saw to it that another 1,000 mosques were closed between 1959 and 1964. Between 1964 and 1982, Leonid Brezhnev stopped the crusade against Islam, ending all state-supported anti-Islamic propaganda and even allowing some new mosques to open in the 1970s. Muslim clerics were allowed to travel abroad and to bring visiting foreign delegations to the Soviet Union.

But, in the 1980s, anti-Muslim sentiments among ethnic Russians and Ukrainians* increased again. The fundamentalist revolution under the Ayatollah Khomeini threatened to spread into the Muslim communities of the Soviet Union, and the Soviet invasion of Afghanistan in 1979 exaggerated the hostilities further. Ethnic Russians preached about the high Muslim birth rate and how it threatened the country. Communist officials decried the religious fanaticism that seemed to be increasing in the Caucasus and Central Asia.

In the Gorbachev era of *glasnost* and *perestroika* (1985–1991), Soviet authorities eased restrictions on the profession and practice of Islam. This resulted in the phenomenal growth of Muslim institutions and activities in Central Asia, the Volga region, and the Caucasus. Between 1985 and 1991, functioning mosques were organized, built, or re-established at a rapid rate. Their number rose from 395 mosques in 1985 to 2,300 mosques in 1991. Likewise, Muslim religious schools opened or reopened in Baku, Kazan, and other traditional centers in Central Asia and the Caucasus. By 1989 a great deal of Muslim activism manifested itself in various republics. Muslims organized demonstrations to reopen mosques and other foundations, and to remove religious leaders who had collaborated with Soviet party authorities over the years. In addition, a number of Muslim students began studying in the Middle East. The continued growth of Islam brought about an increased interest among Muslims abroad. Since becoming independent, Turkey, Saudi Arabia, and Iran have aided in the revival of Islamic institutions in the former Soviet Union and have restored ties between Muslims in the new republics and the rest of the Islamic world. Indeed there has been a vying among these outside powers for influence in the new republics.

REFERENCES: Tor Andre, *Mohammed: The Man and His Faith*, 1955; A. J. Arberry, *The Koran Interpreted*, 1955; C. E. Bosworth, *Islamic Surveys 5: The Islamic Dynasties*, 1967; S. N. Fisher, *The Middle East: A History*, 1966; H.A.R. Gibb, *Studies on The Civilization of Islam*, 1962; A. Guillaume, *Islam*, 1954, 1956; J. R. Hayes, ed., *The Genius of Arab Civilization, Source of the Renaissance*, 1983; M.G.S. Hodgson, *The Venture of Islam*, 3 vols., 1974; J. Sabini, *Islam: A Primer*, 1983; F. Schuon, *Understanding Islam*, 1976; B. Spuler, *The Muslim World, Parts I, II and III*, 1969; J. A. Williams, ed., *Great Religions of Modern Man: Islam*, 1961.

Gary R. Hobin

Appendix D
A Chronology of the Russian and
Soviet Empires

6th–8th Centuries: The Slavic migration reaches the forest zone of Russia, and Turkic Khazars conquer the Black Sea steppes.

9th Century: Norse invaders enter Russia, moving down the Volga and Dnieper river basins toward Constantinople.

860	The Norse and Slavs launch their first attack on Constantinople.
862	The Ryurik Dynasty is established in Novgorod.
875	The Samanid Empire arises in Transoxiana and Khwarezm.
882	Novgorod unites with Kiev to become one nation, with its capital at Kiev. Prince Oleg, who is a Varingian, becomes the first historically verifiable ruler of Kievan Rus'.
907	Prince Oleg begins his military campaign against Byzantium.
911	A peace treaty is signed between Kiev and Byzantium.
930	The Karakhanid Empire arises in Central Asia.
941	Igor, prince of Kievan Rus', begins his expedition against Constantinople.
943	Kiev launches an assault on Persia.
944	Igor ends his expedition against Constantinople.
955	Princess Olga, the regent of Kievan Rus', converts to Christianity.
967	Svyatoslav destroys the Khazar state.
971	Svyatoslav, son of Prince Igor, conquers Bulgaria. Kievan Rus' signs a peace treaty with Byzantium, losing the Balkans and the Crimea.
980	The reign of Prince Vladimir of Kiev begins.
989	Prince Vladimir converts to Christianity, and he insists that all the people of Kievan Rus' do the same.
999	The Samanid Empire in Transoxiana and Khwarezm falls.
1015	Prince Vladimir of Kiev dies.
1019	Prince Jaroslav of Novgorod assumes the throne of Kiev.
1036	Prince Jaroslav codifies the laws of Kievan Rus'.
1037	Prince Jaroslav defeats the Pechenegs and begins the construction of St. Sofia Cathedral in Kiev.
1051	Ilarion becomes the first native leader of the Orthodox Church in Kievan Rus'.
1068	Polovtsians invade Kiev.
1113	Kievan Rus' begins its revival under the rule of Prince Vladimir Monomakh.

1136	The republic of Novgorod gains its independence from Kievan Rus'.
1137	The Kara Khitai Empire arises in Central Asia.
1147	The city of Moscow is established.
1156	Novgorod gains its first Christian bishopric.
1165	The Karakhanid Empire in Central Asia falls.
1169	Prince Vladimir Andrei Bogoliubskii of Vladimir-Sluzdal' and his army attack and sack Kiev; he then assumes the title "Grand Prince of Kiev and all Rus." Kiev ceases to be the center of the Kievan Rus' principalities.
1204	Crusaders capture Constantinople.
1206	Genghis Khan takes control of the Mongols.
1215	The Mongols begin their conquest of China.
1216	The Kara Khitai Empire in Central Asia falls.
1218	The Mongols begin their conquest of Central Asia.
1219	The Mongols begin their first raids into Kievan Rus'.
1221	The Mongols complete their conquest of Central Asia and begin their invasion of Transcaucasia.
1223	At the Battle of River Kalka, the Mongols begin their major incursions into Rus' lands.
1227	Genghis Khan dies.
1231	The Mongols complete their conquest of Transcaucasia.
1236	The medieval Mongol-Tatar state is formed.
1237	The Mongols, under Batu Khan, invade Russia.
1240	Kiev falls to the Mongol invaders.
1241	The Mongols conquer Rus'.
1242	The Mongols attack southern Russia, Poland, and Hungary. Aleksandr Nevsky successfully wards off a Teutonic attack on Novgorod.
1243	The Golden Horde is formed.
1244	The Mongols withdraw from southern Russia, Poland, and Hungary.
1252	Moscow becomes an independent, hereditary principality. The rule of Alexander Nevsky, Grand Prince of Muscovy, begins.
1253	Prince Daniil of Galicia-Volhynia is crowned monarch of Kievan Rus' by the pope.
1256	The Mongols begin their conquest of the Caucasus and Iran.
1259	The Mongols complete their conquest of the Caucasus and Iran.
1280	The Mongols complete their conquest of China.
1302	Moscow annexes Pereyaslavl, Kolomna, and Mozhaisk.
1325	Ivan I becomes Prince of Moscow.
1327	Ivan I is named "Grand Prince of Vladimir" by the Mongols. Moscow becomes the holy see of the metropolitan of the Russian Orthodox Church.

1341   Ivan I dies, and Simeon the Proud assumes control of Moscow.

1353   Simeon dies, and Ivan II assumes the throne.

1359   The rule of Ivan II ends, and the rule of Dmitry Donskoy as Prince of Moscow
        begins.

1368   Olgerd of Lithuania attacks Muscovy.
        Mongol power collapses in China.

1370   The reign of Timur (Tamerlane), the conqueror of Transoxiana, Khwarezm,
        Khorasan, Transcaucasia, and northern India begins; he founds the Timurid
        dynasty in Central Asia.

1380   Dmitry Donskoy defeats the Golden Horde at the Battle of Kulikovo.

1382   The Mongols attack and sack Moscow.
        Shirvanshah dynasty begins in northern Azerbaijan.

1386   Poland and Lithuania join in a dynastic union.
        Timur conquers southern Azerbaijan.

1389   Basil I assumes power in Moscow.

1402   Timur defeats the Ottoman sultan, Bayezit I, at the Battle of Ankara.

1405   The Reign of Timur ends.

1408   The Golden Horde destroys Moscow.
        Kara-koyunlu dynasty begins its reign over southern Azerbaijan.

1425   Basil I of Moscow dies, and Basil II assumes the throne.

1436   The Kazan Khanate is established.

1443   The Crimean Khanate is established.

1450   The Golden Horde begins to disintegrate.
        The Uzbek Astrakhan Khanates are established.

1451   The reign of Sultan Mehmet II begins in the Ottoman Empire.

1453   The Ottoman Turks capture Constantinople.

1462   The rule of Ivan III, the Great, begins.

1463   Moscow annexes Yaroslavl and the lands of the Mari.

1468   The Kara-koyunlu dynasty in southern Azerbaijan disintegrates.

1469   The Ak-koyunlu dynasty begins its rule over southern Azerbaijan.

1474   Moscow annexes Rostov.
        The Crimean Khanate falls under the political control of the Ottomans.

1477   Moscow annexes Novgorod.

1480   Ivan III overthrows Mongol/Tatar rule.
        The Siberian Khanate is established.

1485   Moscow annexes Tver'.

1500   Shirvanshah dynasty dies out in northern Azerbaijan.
        The Kazakh Khanate is established.

1502   Shah Ismail conquers Tabriz.
        The Safavid Empire is established.

1505	Tsar Ivan III dies, and Tsar Basil III assumes the throne as grand prince of Muscovy.
1506	The reign of Sultan Mehmet II ends.
1510	Moscow annexes Pskov.
1514	Moscow annexes the territories of Smolensk. At the Battle of Chaldiran, the Ottomans defeat the Safavids.
1520	The reign of Sultan Suleyman I begins in the Ottoman Empire.
1526	The Moghul Empire is established in India.
1533	Basil III dies, and Elena becomes regent until Ivan IV, who is then three years old, is ready to assume the throne.
1538	The regency of Elena ends, and the rule of Ivan IV, the Terrible, begins.
1547	Ivan the Terrible assumes the title of tsar.
1552	Russia captures and annexes the Khanate of Kazan, begins construction of a chain of stockades along the southern border, starts colonizing the steppes, and establishes control over the Maris.
1555	By the Treaty of Amasya, the boundary is established between the Ottomans and Safavids in Georgia and Armenia.
1556	Russia completes its conquest of the Khanate of Astrakhan, bringing the Volga Tatars and the Chuvashes under Russian control.
1557	Russia establishes control over the Bashkirs.
1558	Ivan the Terrible begins his long but unsuccessful Livonian War in hopes of establishing Russian access to the Baltic coast.
1565	Ivan the Terrible begins the Oprichnina Reign of Terror.
1566	The reign of Sultan Suleyman I ends.
1569	The Union of Lublin brings about the merger of Poland and Lithuania, creating the Polish-Lithuanian Commonwealth.
1571	The Crimean Tatars begin their invasion and destruction of Moscow.
1578	The Ottomans conquer Tbilisi in Georgia.
1581	Ermak begins his conquest of Siberia.
1582	Russia begins its conquest of Siberia by sanctioning Ermak's expedition.
1583	The Livonian War ends. The Ottomans conquer Shirvan, Daghestan, and Yerevan.
1584	Archangel is founded. Ivan IV dies, and the rule of Tsar Fedor Ivanovich begins.
1587	The reign of Shah Abbas I of Persia begins.
1589	The Patriarchate of Moscow is established.
1590	The Ottomans conquer Gandzha and Karabagh (Karabakh).
1596	The Uniate church is established in Poland and Lithuania by the Union of Brest.
1598	The Ryurik Dynasty ends with the death of Fedor, and Tsar Boris Gudunov comes to power. The Siberian Khanate falls under Russian sovereignty.

1599   The Astrakhanid dynasty begins its rule of Bukhara.

1605   Tsar Boris dies, and the ''Time of Troubles'' (virtual civil war) begins under the rule of Fedor II and then the First False Dmitrii.

1606   The rule of the First False Dmitrii ends, and the rule of Basil Shuiskii begins. The Bolotnikov Revolt occurs.

1610   A Polish occupation of Moscow begins.
The rule of Shuiskii ends, and the Second False Dmitrii comes to power.

1611   Kuzma Minin and Dmitrii Pozharskii begin the counter-attack against the Polish occupation.

1612   The Polish occupation of Moscow ends, and the Safavids regain portions of Azerbaijan and the Caucasus from the Ottomans.

1613   The ''Time of Troubles'' ends when Michael Romanov assumes the throne of Russia, beginning the Romanov dynasty.

1628   The reign of Shah Abbas I ends.

1637   The Don Cossacks capture Azov.

1639   By the Treaty of Kasr-i Shirin, the Ottomans recognize Safavid control over parts of Armenia and Caucasia.

1643   The reign of Abul-Ghazi Khan in Khiva begins.

1644   The Russian Cossacks first reach the Chukchis.

1645   Tsar Michael Romanov dies, and Alexis I assumes the Russian throne.

1648   The Ukrainian Cossacks rise up against Polish rule.

1649   Serfdom is formally established by law.

1654   The Ukrainian Cossacks swear allegiance to Moscow, a Russo-Polish War begins over Ukraine, and the Treaty of Pereyaslavl' places Ukraine under the control of the tsar.

1663   The reign of Abul-Ghazi Khan in Khiva ends.

1667   The Russo-Polish War ends, and Poland cedes Kiev and Smolensk to Russia in the Peace of Andrusovo.

1671   The revolt of Stenka Razin begins.

1672   Peter the Great is born.

1676   Alexis I dies, and Fedor III assumes the Russian throne.
War breaks out between the Ottoman Empire and Russia.

1681   The war with the Ottoman Empire ends.

1682   Fedor III dies, and the regency of Sophia begins. The half-brothers Ivan V and Peter I become co-tsars.

1687   Russia launches an unsuccessful military campaign against the Crimean Tatars.

1689   Russia signs the Treaty of Nerchinsk with China.
Peter the Great assumes the throne of Russia, ending the regency of Sophia.

1696   Ivan V dies, and Peter the Great becomes the only tsar.
Russian armies capture the port of Azov from the Ottoman Empire, which gives Russia control of the Black Sea.

1700	War breaks out between Sweden and Russia.
1703	The city of St. Petersburg is founded.
1705	The Bashkir Revolt begins.
1707	Charles XII of Sweden invades Russia. Cossack uprising begins in the Don River region.
1708	The Cossack uprising ends.
1709	Russia wins a decisive victory over Sweden at the Battle of Poltava.
1710	The Cyrillic alphabet is reformed.
1711	War breaks out between Russia and the Ottoman Empire. The Bashkir Revolt ends.
1713	Russian war with the Ottoman Empire ends. St. Petersburg becomes the capital of Russia.
1721	The Treaty of Nystad ends the Russo-Swedish War, giving Russia a foothold on the Baltic Sea. Peter the Great proclaims Muscovy as the Russian Empire and brings the Russian Orthodox Church under political control by establishing the Holy Synod.
1722	War breaks out between Russia and Persia. Peter the Great conquers Derbent.
1723	The Russo-Persian War ends. Table of Ranks is established.
1724	Catherine is crowned Empress of Russia. With the Treaty of Istanbul, Russia and the Ottomans divide Azerbaijan between them, and the Ottomans gain control over Georgia and Shirvan.
1725	Peter the Great dies, and Catherine I assumes the throne of Russia.
1727	Catherine I dies and is succeeded by Peter II.
1730	The rule of Peter II ends, and Empress Anna takes control of the government.
1731	Russia establishes control over the Little Kazakh Horde.
1732	The Araks River is designated as the northern boundary between the Safavids and the Ottomans; the Ottomans have control over the Caucasus, while the Safavids control Azerbaijan.
1734	Russia surrenders its possessions in Azerbaijan to Persia.
1735	The Nadir Khan conquers Daghestan, Shirvan, Georgia, and Armenia, overcoming Ottoman resistance. The Russo-Turkish War begins.
1736	Shah Abbas III, the last of the Safavid Dynasty, dies, and Nadir Khan becomes Shah of Persia.
1739	The Russo-Turkish War ends.
1740	The rule of Empress Anna ends, and the rule of Ivan VI begins. Russia completes the conquest of Aktyubinsk and establishes control over the Middle Kazakh Horde. Nadir Shah invades Central Asia.
1741	The rule of Ivan VI ends, and the rule of Empress Elizabeth begins.

1747   Nadir Khan, Shah of Iran, is assassinated.
        The Khanates of Azerbaijan, Baku, Gandzha, Karabagh (Karabakh), Kuba, Nakhichevan, Talysh, and Shemakha are established.

1753   The rule of the Astrakhanid Dynasty in Bukhara ends and is replaced by the Manghit Dynasty.

1762   The rule of Empress Elizabeth ends, and the rule of Peter III begins.
        Peter III is murdered, and Catherine the Great succeeds to the throne of Russia.

1768   Another Russo-Turkish War begins.

1772   Poland is partitioned for the first time.

1773   Emelian Pugachev begins the peasant revolt.

1774   The Treaty of Kuchuk Kainarji ends the war between the Russians and the Ottomans.

1783   Russia annexes the Crimea but the Ottoman Turks refuse to recognize the annexation.
        Eastern Georgia is granted Russian protection.

1784   Russia completes its conquest of the Kumyks.

1787   War again breaks out between Russia and the Ottoman Empire.

1791   The war between Russia and the Ottoman Empire ends with the signing of the Treaty of Jassy.

1793   The second partition of Poland occurs.

1794   Agha Mohammed Khan establishes the Kajar dynasty in Persia and invades the Caucasus.

1795   The third partition of Poland occurs.
        Russia completes the annexation of Belarus, which had begun in 1772.

1796   Catherine the Great dies, and Paul I assumes the throne of Russia.

1800   The rule of Alim Khan begins in Khokand.
        Eastern Georgia is formally ceded to Russia.

1801   Paul I dies, and Alexander I assumes the Russian throne.

1804   Western Georgia is ceded to Russia.
        The Kungrat dynasty begins its rule in Khiva.

1805   War breaks out between Russia and Persia.

1806   War breaks out between Russia and the Ottoman Empire.
        Russia annexes Baku, the major city of Azerbaijan.

1809   Russia completes its conquest of Poland.
        Russia annexes Finland from Sweden but extends autonomous status to Finland.
        The rule of Alim Khan in Khokand ends.

1810   Russia takes control of Abkhazia.

1812   France invades Russia and takes Moscow.
        Bessarabia is ceded to Russia when the Ottomans and Russians sign the Treaty of Bucharest, ending the Russo-Turkish War.

1813   The Russo-Persian War ends with the Treaty of Gulistan, which brings Dagh-

estan and the khanates in northern Azerbaijan (including the Talysh) under
Russian control.

1814   Alexander I triumphantly enters Paris.

1815   The Napoleonic Wars end with the Battle of Waterloo.

1817   Serfdom is abolished for peasants of the Baltic region.
       During the Caucasian War, Russia establishes control in the central Caucasus.

1825   Alexander I dies, and Nicholas I assumes the throne.
       The Decembrist Revolt occurs, led by liberal military officers who want to
       transform Russia into a constitutional monarchy or republic.
       Russia formally assumes sovereignty over Kabarda.

1826   Another Russo-Persian War begins.
       The Talysh Khanate is dissolved.
       With the Convention of Akkerman, the Ottomans recognize Russian sovereignty
       over the Caucasus.

1827   At the Battle of Navarino, the Ottoman fleet is destroyed.

1828   The Treaty of Turkmanchai ends the Russo-Persian War, and Persia cedes
       Northeastern Armenia and Nakhichevan to Russia.
       War breaks out between Russia and the Ottomans.
       Russia completes the establishment of sovereignty over Azerbaijan and conquers
       the Karachais.

1829   The Treaty of Adrianople ends the Russo-Turkish War.

1830   The Polish Revolt begins.

1831   The Polish Revolt is suppressed.

1832   The first Mohammed Ali crisis begins.

1833   The Treaty of Unkiar-Skelessi ends the first Mohammed Ali crisis.
       Tsar Nicholas I proclaims "Autocracy, Orthodoxy, and Nationality" as the
       guiding principles of Russian rule.

1834   The Imamate of Shamil begins in Daghestan and Chechenia. The Shamil Re-
       bellion begins.

1837   The first Russian railroad connects St. Petersburg with Tsarskoe Selo.

1838   The First Afghan War breaks out between the British and Afghans.

1839   The second Mohammed Ali crisis begins.

1840   The second Mohammed Ali crisis ends.

1842   The First Afghan War ends.

1846   The Khokand Khanate submits to Russian authority, and the Great Kazakh
       Horde comes under Russian control.

1848   Revolutions break out in France, Austria, Italy, and Germany.
       Karl Marx publishes the *Communist Manifesto*.

1849   Tsar Nicholas I intervenes to assist Austria in putting down the Hungarian
       Rebellion.

1851   The St. Petersburg-Moscow Railway opens.

1854　The Crimean War between Britain, France, Russia, and the Ottomans begins.
Russia establishes a fortress at Alma Ata.

1855　Nicholas I dies, and the rule of Alexander II begins.
Russia begins its gradual annexation of Kyrgyzia.
The large exodus of Muslim peoples from the Russian Empire to the Ottoman Empire begins.

1856　The Crimean War ends.
Shamil, the leader of the Avars, makes his last stand against Russian conquest.

1858　Russia begins its penetration of northeast Asia, which soon leads to the acquisition of the Amur and Maritime provinces from China with the signing of the Treaty of Beijing in 1860.
Russia also annexes Svanetia.
The Shamil Rebellion ends.

1859　Imam Shamil surrenders, and the Russian conquest of the Caucasus is complete, except for Circassia.
Southern Bessarabia is included in the newly established Romania.

1860　The city of Vladivostok is founded.

1861　Alexander II announces the emancipation of the serfs.

1863　The Polish Rebellion occurs.

1864　The conquest of Circassia is completed, and the conquest of Central Asia and Turkestan begins.
China cedes what later becomes the East Kazakhstan Oblast to Russia.
Russia takes control of the Fergana Valley and dissolves Abkhazia as a semi-independent principality.

1865　Russia conquers Tashkent.

1866　The conquest of Bukhara is complete.

1867　Russia sells Alaska to the United States for $7 million.
Russia establishes the Governor-Generalship of Turkestan.

1868　Russia conquers Samarkand and establishes protectorates over Bukhara and the Tajiks.
The Russian conquest of Central Asia is complete.

1873　Russia establishes a protectorate over the Khanate of Khiva.
Khokand Uprising begins.
Russia and Great Britain agree to spheres of influence in Central Asia.

1875　Russia gives the Kurile Islands to Japan and receives the southern half of Sakhalin in return.

1876　Russia completes the annexation of Kyrgyzia and of the Khokand Khanate after the rebellion is crushed.
The reign of Sultan Abdul Hamid II begins in the Ottoman Empire.

1877　Another Russo-Turkish War begins.

1878　The Treaty of San Stefano ends the Russo-Turkish War.
Bulgaria declares its independence.

In the Berlin Treaty, southern Bessarabia once again becomes part of Russia.
The Second Afghan War between the British and the Afghans begins.

1880 The conquest of Turkestan is complete.
The Second Afghan War ends.
The Young Turk Movement begins.

1881 Tsar Alexander II is assassinated, and the rule of Alexander III begins.
Russia establishes a settlement at Ashkabad.
Russia and China sign the Treaty of St. Petersburg.
Russia conquers the Turkmen at the Battle of Gok-Tepe.

1885 An Anglo-Russian crisis erupts over Afghanistan.
The Bulgarian crisis begins.
The Transcaspian Oblast is formed.
Russia completes its conquest of western Turkestan.
The large migration of Muslims from Russia to the Ottoman Empire comes to
an end.
The construction of the Transcaspian Railroad, from Krasnovodsk through Sa-
markand and Tashkent to the Fergana Valley, begins.

1887 The Bulgarian crisis ends.

1891 Construction begins on the Trans-Siberian Railway.

1894 Alexander III dies, and the rule of Nicholas II begins.

1895 Russia completes its takeover of East Pamir.
The Anglo-Russian Boundary Commission fixes the boundary between Afghanistan and Russia.

1896 Russia expands into Manchuria.

1899 The construction of the Transcaspian Railroad is completed.
Russia establishes the Transcaspian Oblast.

1900 The Boxer Rebellion erupts in China.

1901 A Russo-Iranian Treaty is signed.

1903 Construction of the Trans-Siberian Railroad ends.

1904 The Russo-Japanese War begins.

1905 The Russo-Japanese War ends in defeat for Russia, and the Revolution of 1905
erupts in Russia.

1906 The first Duma is elected.

1907 The Anglo-Russian Entente comes into being.

1909 The reign of Sultan Abdul Hamid II ends.

1911 Russian and British troops occupy Iran.

1914 World War I begins.
Tuva is declared to be a Russian protectorate.

1915 The Lake Baikal link to the Trans-Siberian Railroad is completed.
The Union for the Liberation of Ukraine is established.

1916 Rasputin is murdered.

Imanov leads an anti-Russian rebellion in Kazakhstan. Anti-Russian uprisings, inspired by military conscription laws, spread throughout Central Asia.

1917   Nicholas II abdicates the Russian throne.
The Bolshevik Revolution begins, and Vladimir I. Lenin becomes the leading political figure in Russia.
Russia withdraws from World War I.
The Ukrainian Soviet Republic is proclaimed, and the All-Russian Cossack Union is established.

1918   World War I ends.
Tsar Nicholas II and his family are murdered.
The Russian Soviet Federated Socialist Republic (RSFSR) is formed.
Ukraine, Armenia, Belarus, Azerbaijan, Estonia, Georgia, Latvia, and Lithuania declare independence.
In the Treaty of Brest-Litovsk with the Central Powers, Russia loses Poland, Finland, the Baltics, and Ukraine.
Civil war sweeps throughout Russia.
The Turkestan Autonomous Soviet Socialist Republic and the Volga German Autonomous Workers' Commune are formed.
The Transcaucasian Federation is proclaimed.
Romania occupies Bessarabia.

1919   The Allied Powers sign the Treaty of Paris, ending World War I. Russia loses its Polish territory as well as Finland, Latvia, Lithuania, and Estonia.
Belarus and Ukraine are established as theoretically independent republics.
Transcarpathia becomes a part of Czechoslovakia known as Sub-Carpathian Russia.
The Bashkir Autonomous Soviet Socialist Republic is established.
The Basmachi Movement gains momentum in Central Asia.

1920   The Kyrgyz Autonomous Soviet Socialist Republic and the Far Eastern People's Republic are established.
Peace agreements are signed with Estonia, Latvia, and Lithuania, giving them Soviet recognition.
The Bukhara People's Republic is established, ending the Manghit dynasty.
War begins between Russia and Poland.
Armenia is established as a theoretically independent republic.
The Chuvash Autonomous Oblast, the Daghestan Autonomous Soviet Socialist Republic, the Kalmyk Autonomous Oblast, the Tatar Autonomous Soviet Socialist Republic, and the Votyak Autonomous Oblast are formed.
Great Britain, France, Italy, and Japan give Bessarabia back to Romania.

1921   The civil war in Russia ends with the consolidation of power by Lenin and the Bolsheviks.
The Soviet Union signs friendship treaties with Afghanistan, Iran, and Turkey.
Lenin launches the New Economic Policy.
The Georgian Soviet Socialist Republic, the Abkhazian Autonomous Soviet Socialist Republic, and the Crimean Autonomous Soviet Socialist Republic are established.
The Mountain (Gorskaia) People's Autonomous Republic is established, with

authority over the Balkars, Chechens, Ingushes, Kabardians, Karachais, and Ossetians.

The Kabarda Autonomous Oblast, the Komi Autonomous Oblast, the Adjar Autonomous Soviet Socialist Republic, the Moldavian (Moldovan) Autonomous Soviet Socialist Republic, and the Tuva People's Republic are established.

1922   The Mountain-Altai Autonomous Oblast is established.

The Transcaucasia Soviet Federated Socialist Republic is formed, uniting Armenia, Azerbaijan, and Georgia.

Russia signs the Treaty of Rapallo with Germany.

The Union of Soviet Socialist Republics is established, composed of Russian, Belarusian, Ukrainian, and Transcaucasian republics.

The Adyghe Autonomous Oblast, the Chechen Autonomous Oblast, and the Oirot Autonomous Oblast are established.

Far Eastern People's Republic is dissolved.

The Kabarda-Balkar Autonomous Oblast, the Karachai-Circassian Autonomous Oblast, the South Ossetian Autonomous Oblast, and the Yakut Autonomous Soviet Socialist Republic are established.

1923   The Buryat-Mongol Autonomous Republic, the Karelian Autonomous Soviet Socialist Republic, and the Nagorno-Karabakh Autonomous Oblast are established.

1924   Lenin dies, and Josef Stalin, Nikolai Bukharin, Lev B. Kamenev, Leon Trotsky, and Grigorii V. Zinov'ev begin their struggle for power.

The Mountain Peoples Autonomous Soviet Socialist Republic and the Bukhara People's Republic are dissolved.

Turkmenistan and Uzbekistan are raised to republic status.

The National Delimitation of Central Asia is established.

The Ingush Autonomous Oblast, the Committee of the North, the North Ossetian Autonomous Oblast, the Tajikistan Autonomous Soviet Socialist Republic, the Volga German Autonomous Soviet Socialist Republic and the Kara-Kirgiz Autonomous Oblast are established.

The Basmachi Revolt is crushed in Turkestan.

The caliphate in Turkey is dissolved.

1925   The Chuvash Autonomous Soviet Socialist Republic is formed out of the Chuvash Autonomous Oblast.

The Karakalpak Autonomous Oblast and the Mountainous Badakhshan Autonomous Oblast are established.

The Kazakh Autonomous Oblast becomes the Kazakh Autonomous Soviet Socialist Republic.

The Kyrgyz Autonomous Soviet Socialist Republic is established after southern Kazakhstan is taken from the jurisdiction of the Turkestan Autonomous Soviet Socialist Republic.

1926   Stalin wins the power struggle and takes control of the country.

The Karachai Autonomous Oblast and the Circassian National Okrug are created.

The Soviet Union establishes a neutrality agreement with Afghanistan.

1927   The Soviet Union establishes a neutrality agreement with Iran.

1928   The Circassian Autonomous Oblast is established.

1929   Stalin begins forced collectivization of Soviet agriculture.
        Tajikistan splits off from Uzbekistan to form a separate republic.
        The Komi-Permyak National Okrug, the Nenets National Okrug, and the Shor-
        ian National Okrug are established.
        Soviet authorities crush the Union for the Liberation of Ukraine.

1930   The Koryak National Okrug, the Chuchki National Okrug, the Evenki National
        Okrug, the Mordva Autonomous Soviet Socialist Republic, and the Khanty-
        Manti National Okrug are established.

1932   The Karakalpak Autonomous Soviet Socialist Republic is established.
        Forced famine begins in Ukraine and the northern Caucasus.
        The Votyak Autonomous Oblast is renamed Udmurt Autonomous Oblast.

1933   The Kalmyk Autonomous Soviet Socialist Republic is established.

1934   The Chechen-Ingush Autonomous Oblast, the Jewish Autonomous Oblast, and
        the Udmurt Autonomous Soviet Socialist Republic are formed.

1936   The Kabardino-Balkar Autonomous Soviet Socialist Republic is established.
        Kazakhstan and Kyrgyzia become Soviet republics.
        The Transcaucasian Soviet Federated Republic is dissolved into the Armenian,
        Azerbaijan, and Georgian republics.
        The Chechen-Ingush Autonomous Soviet Socialist Republic, the Komi Auton-
        omous Soviet Socialist Republic, and the North Ossetian Autonomous Soviet
        Socialist Republic are established.
        The Karakalpak Autonomous Soviet Socialist Republic is transferred from the
        authority of the Russian Soviet Federated Socialist Republics to the Uzbek
        Soviet Socialist Republic.

1938   The Russian language is required in all schools in the Soviet Union.

1939   The Soviet Union and Germany sign the Molotov-Ribbentrop (Non-Aggression)
        Pact.
        Soviet troops re-occupy Poland, Latvia, Lithuania, and Estonia.
        The Russo-Finnish War begins.
        Remaining portions of Ukraine and Belarus are annexed into the Soviet Union.
        The Shorian National Okrug is dissolved.
        Transcarpathia is given to Hungary.

1940   The Soviet Union seizes Northern Bukovina and Bessarabia from Romania,
        incorporating them into Ukraine and the newly established Moldavian Soviet
        Socialist Republic.
        The Soviet Union annexes Estonia, Latvia, and Lithuania.
        The Karelian ASSR becomes the Karelo-Finnish Union Republic.
        Most Baltic Germans are repatriated to Germany.

1941   The Russo-Finnish War ends in a Soviet victory.
        Germany invades the Soviet Union.
        All Russian Germans not living in Nazi-occupied regions are deported to western
        Siberia.
        Soviet and British troops invade Iran.

The Volga German ASSR is dissolved.

Germany returns Northern Bukovina to Romania.

1943   Stalin allows the Russian Orthodox Church to appoint its own patriarch.

The Karachai Autonomous Oblast is dissolved.

1944   Anti-Soviet rebellions erupt in Ukraine, Belarusia, Latvia, Estonia, and Lithuania.

Northern Bukovina is restored to the Soviet Union.

Soviet troops reconquer the Crimean Peninsula. Because of their alleged collaboration with the Germans, mass deportations of Crimean Tatars, Balkars, Chechens, Ingushes, Karachais, and Kalmyks begin; their republics and autonomous oblasts are dissolved.

The Tuva People's Republic is brought into the Soviet Union.

1945   World War II ends. Soviet troops remain in Eastern Europe and begin establishing puppet regimes in Poland, Hungary, East Germany, Bulgaria, and Romania.

Soviet forces move into Manchuria and northern Korea.

Czechoslovakia formally cedes to Russia what becomes the Transcarpathian Oblast.

1946   Stalin abolishes the Ukrainian Catholic Church.

1948   In Czechoslovakia, the Communists gain full control of the government, and a new constitution is adopted.

1953   Stalin dies, and a struggle for power begins among Lavrenty Beria, Nikolai Bulganin, Nikita Khrushchev, Georgii Malenkov, and Viacheslav Molotov.

1954   Russia cedes the Crimean Peninsula to Ukraine.

1955   The Soviet government issues a decree providing for the deportation of Gypsies if they refused to engage in "productive work."

1956   Soviet forces crush the Hungarian rebellion.

The Karelo-Finnish Union Republic is dissolved, and the Karelian Autonomous Soviet Socialist Republic is re-established.

The de-Stalinization campaign begins.

1957   Khrushchev wins the power struggle following Stalin's death and takes control.

The rehabilitation of the ethnic groups that had been deported in 1943–1944 begins.

1958   The Buryat Autonomous Soviet Socialist Republic and the Kalmyk Autonomous Soviet Socialist Republic are established.

1962   The Cuban Missile Crisis almost brings the Soviet Union and the United States to war.

1963   The United States and the Soviet Union sign the Nuclear Test Ban Treaty.

1964   Khrushchev falls from power and is replaced by Leonid Brezhnev and Aleksei Kosygin.

1965   The Soviet government rehabilitates the Volga Germans.

1967   The Crimean Tatars are rehabilitated but not allowed to return from exile.

1968   Prague Spring is suppressed by the Soviets.

1970   Jewish emigration from the Soviet Union increases dramatically.

1975   Brezhnev consolidates political power in his own hands as General Secretary.

1979   The Soviet Union invades Afghanistan.

1982   Brezhnev dies, and Yuri Andropov comes to power.

1984   Andropov dies, and Konstantin U. Chernenko comes to power.

1985   Chernenko dies, and Mikhail Gorbachev comes to power.
The collapse of world oil prices robs the Soviet Union of its primary source of hard currency, and the economy begins to disintegrate.

1986   Gorbachev announces the beginning of his policies of *glasnost* (openness) and *perestroika* (restructuring).
The Chernobyl nuclear disaster occurs.
Ethnic riots erupt in Alma-Ata.

1988   The millennium of Russian Christianity is celebrated in Moscow.
Gorbachev formally recognizes the ethnic terrorism of the Stalin era in the Soviet Union.

1989   Gorbachev withdraws the last Soviet troops from Afghanistan and agrees to withdraw Soviet troops from Eastern Europe; the Communist governments of Poland, Hungary, Czechoslovakia, and East Germany collapse.
The Berlin Wall crumbles, and the re-unification of West Germany and East Germany begins.
The independence movements in the Baltic republics gain momentum.

1990   The Karelian Republic declares its autonomy within the Soviet Union.

1991   A right-wing coup against Gorbachev fails, and Boris Yeltsin gains new prominence.
Centralized authority in the Soviet Union collapses.
The presidents of Russia, Ukraine, Belarus, and Kazakhstan establish the Commonwealth of Independent States. Other republics soon join. On December 25, 1991, the Soviet Union ceases to exist.

Appendix E
Major Political Subdivisions of the
Soviet Union in 1990

1. ARMENIAN SOVIET SOCIALIST REPUBLIC

   The Armenian SSR had no autonomous political subdivisions.

2. AZERBAIDZHAN (AZERBAIJAN) SOVIET SOCIALIST REPUBLIC

   Nakhichevan Autonomous Soviet Socialist Republic

   Nagorno-Karabakh (Karabagh) Autonomous Oblast

3. BELORUSSIAN (BELARUSIAN) SOVIET SOCIALIST REPUBLIC

   The Belorussian SSR had no autonomous political subdivisions.

4. ESTONIAN SOVIET SOCIALIST REPUBLIC

   The Estonian SSR had no autonomous political subdivisions.

5. GEORGIAN SOVIET SOCIALIST REPUBLIC

   Abkhazian Autonomous Soviet Socialist Republic

   Adzhar (Adjar) Autonomous Soviet Socialist Republic

   South Ossetian Autnomous Oblast

6. KAZAKH SOVIET SOCIALIST REPUBLIC

   The Kazakh SSR had no autonomous political subdivisions.

7. KIRGHIZ (KYRGYZ) SOVIET SOCIALIST REPUBLIC

   The Kirghiz (Kyrgyz) SSR had no autonomous political subdivisions.

8. LATVIAN SOVIET SOCIALIST REPUBLIC

   The Latvian SSR had no autonomous political subdivisions.

9. LITHUANIAN SOVIET SOCIALIST REPUBLIC

The Lithuanian SSR had no autonomous political subdivisions.

10. MOLDAVIAN (Moldovan) SOVIET SOCIALIST REPUBLIC

The Moldavian (Moldovan) SSR had no autonomous political subdivisions.

11. RUSSIAN SOVIET FEDERATED SOCIALIST REPUBLIC

Bashkir Autonomous Soviet Socialist Republic

Buryat Autonomous Soviet Socialist Republic

Chechen-Ingush Autonomous Soviet Socialist Republic

Chuvash Autonomous Soviet Socialist Republic

Kabardino-Balkar Autonomous Soviet Socialist Republic

Kalmyk Autonomous Soviet Socialist Republic

Karelian Autonomous Soviet Socialist Republic

Komi Autonomous Soviet Socialist Republic

Mari Autonomous Soviet Socialist Republic

Mordvinian Autonomous Soviet Socialist Republic

North Ossetian Autonomous Soviet Socialist Republic

Tatar Autonomous Soviet Socialist Republic

Tuva Autonomous Soviet Socialist Republic

Udmurt Autonomous Soviet Socialist Republic

Yakut Autonomous Soviet Socialist Republic

Adygei (Adyghe) Autonomous Oblast

Gorno-Altai Autonomous Oblast

Jewish (Yevreyskaya) Autonomous Oblast

Karachai-Circassian Autonomous Oblast

Khakass Autonomous Oblast

Aginsk-Buryat Autonomous Okrug

Chukot Autonomous Okrug

Evenk Autonomous Okrug

Khanty-Mansi Autonomous Okrug

Komi-Permyak Autonomous Okrug

Koryak Autonomous Okrug

Nenet Autonomous Okrug

Taymyr Autonomous Okrug

Ust-Ordyn Buryat-Mongol Autonomous Okrug

Yamalo-Nenet Autonomous Okrug

12. TADZHIK (TAJIK) SOVIET SOCIALIST REPUBLIC

Gorno-Badakhshan Autonomous Oblast

13. TURKMEN SOVIET SOCIALIST REPUBLIC

The Turkmen SSR had no autonomous political subdivisions.

14. UKRAINIAN SOVIET SOCIALIST REPUBLIC

The Ukrainian SSR had no autonomous political subdivisions.

15. UZBEK SOVIET SOCIALIST REPUBLIC

Karakalpak Autonomous Soviet Socialist Republic

Source: Richard Sakwa, Soviet Politics: An Introduction (London: Routledge, 1989), 289.

Appendix F
Nationality, Language Loyalty, and Religion in the Soviet Union, 1989

Nationality Group	Percent Who Speak the National Language as Native Language	Percent Who Are Fluent in Russian	Dominant Religion
Abaza	93.4	78.1	Muslim
Abkhaz	93.3	78.2	Muslim, Orthodox
Adyghe	94.7	81.7	Muslim
Afghan	65.4	35.7	Muslim
Agul	94.4	65.8	Muslim
Albanian	52.0	49.2	Orthodox, Muslim
*Aleut	---	---	Animist, Orthodox
Altai	84.4	65.2	Orthodox
American	61.3	39.5	Protestant, Catholic
Arab	72.4	63.5	Muslim
Armenian	91.6	47.1	Orthodox
Assyrian	59.7	43.6	Nestorian
Austrian	45.7	30.2	Catholic
Avar	96.9	60.6	Muslim
Azerbaijan	97.6	34.4	Muslim
Balkar	92.9	77.2	Muslim
Bashkir	72.3	71.8	Muslim
Belarusian	70.9	54.7	Orthodox, Catholic
Beluchi	95.7	5.0	Muslim
British	70.0	50.2	Protestant
Bulgarian	67.9	60.3	Orthodox
Buryat	86.3	72.0	Orthodox, Animist, Buddhist

Nationality Group	Percent Who Speak the National Language as Native Language	Percent Who Are Fluent in Russian	Dominant Religion
Chechen	98.0	74.0	Muslim
Chinese	33.0	30.6	Taoist, Buddhist
*Chukchi	---	---	Animist, Orthodox
Chuvash	76.5	65.1	Orthodox, Muslim
Circassian	90.4	76.3	Muslim
Crimean Tatar	92.5	76.0	Muslim
Croat	59.3	47.7	Catholic
Cuban	73.3	73.1	Catholic
Czech	36.0	37.3	Catholic
Dargin	97.5	68.0	Muslim
*Dolgan	---	---	Animist, Orthodox
Dungan	94.7	70.5	Muslim
Dutch	35.1	32.7	Protestant
*Ent	---	---	Animist, Orthodox
*Eskimo	---	---	Animist, Orthodox
Estonian	95.5	33.8	Lutheran
*Even	---	---	Animist, Orthodox
*Evenk	---	---	Animist, Orthodox
Finn	35.7	34.4	Lutheran
French	50.3	44.4	Catholic
Gagauz	87.4	71.7	Orthodox
Georgian	98.2	33.1	Orthodox
German	48.7	45.0	Lutheran, Catholic
Greek	44.5	35.5	Orthodox
Gypsy	77.4	63.3	Orthodox, Muslim

Nationality Group	Percent Who Speak the National Language as Native Language	Percent Who Are Fluent in Russian	Dominant Religion
Indian	77.1	40.7	Hindu
Ingush	96.9	80.0	Muslim
Iranian (Persian)	33.4	45.9	Muslim
Italian	40.4	28.4	Catholic
*Itelmen	---	---	Animist, Orthodox
Izhora	36.9	38.0	Orthodox
Japanese	45.9	38.6	Shinto, Buddhist
Jews	11.1	10.1	Jewish
Kabard	96.9	77.1	Muslim
Kalmyk	89.9	85.1	Buddhist
Karachai	96.7	79.1	Muslim
Karakalpak	94.1	20.7	Muslim
*Karapapakh	---	---	Muslim
Karelian	47.9	45.5	Orthodox
Kazakh	97.0	60.4	Muslim
*Ket	---	---	Animist, Orthodox
Khakass	76.1	66.6	Muslim
*Khant	---	---	Animist, Orthodox
Komi	70.4	62.1	Orthodox
Komi-Permyak	70.1	61.2	Orthodox
Korean	49.4	43.3	Animist, Confucian
*Koryak	---	---	Animist, Orthodox
Kumyk	97.4	74.5	Muslim
Kurd	80.5	28.5	Muslim
Kyrgyz	97.8	37.2	Muslim

Nationality Group	Percent Who Speak the National Language as Native Language	Percent Who Are Fluent in Russian	Dominant Religion
Lak	93.5	76.4	Muslim
*Lapp	---	---	Animist, Lutheran
Latvian	94.8	64.4	Lutheran
Lezgin	91.5	53.4	Muslim
Lithuanian	97.7	27.7	Catholic
Magyar	93.7	43.3	Catholic
*Manchu	---	---	Buddhist
*Mansi	---	---	Animist, Orthodox
Mari	80.8	68.8	Orthodox
*Meskhetian	---	---	Muslim
Moldovan	91.6	53.8	Orthodox
Mordvinian	67.0	62.5	Orthodox
*Nanai	---	---	Animist, Orthodox
*Negidal	---	---	Animist
*Nenet	---	---	Animist, Orthodox
*Nganasan	---	---	Animist
*Nivkhi	---	---	Animist, Orthodox
Nogai	89.9	79.3	Muslim
*Orochi	---	---	Animist, Orthodox
Ossetian	87.0	68.9	Muslim
*Pakistani	---	---	Muslim
Pole	30.4	43.9	Catholic
Romanian	60.9	50.9	Orthodox
Russian	99.8	100.0	Orthodox
Rutul	94.5	63.0	Muslim
*Selkup	---	---	Animist
Serb	40.6	50.2	Orthodox, Muslim
Shor	57.7	52.8	Orthodox

Nationality Group	Percent Who Speak the National Language as Native Language	Percent Who Are Fluent in Russian	Dominant Religion
Slovak	42.7	51.8	Catholic
Spaniard	48.7	43.5	Catholic
Tabasaran	92.9	77.2	Muslim
Tajik	97.7	27.7	Muslim
Talysh	90.1	6.1	Muslim
Tat	71.8	64.0	Muslim, Jewish, Christian
Tatar	83.2	70.8	Muslim
*Tofalar	---	---	Orthodox
Tsakhur	95.1	23.6	Muslim
Turk	91.0	40.2	Muslim
Turkmen	98.5	27.8	Muslim
Tuvinian	98.5	59.1	Lamaist
*Udegei	---	---	Animist
Udi	85.3	49.4	Orthodox
Udmurt	69.6	61.3	Orthodox
Uigur	86.5	58.3	Muslim
Ukrainian	81.1	56.2	Orthodox, Uniate
*Ulchi	---	---	Animist
Uzbek	98.3	23.8	Muslim
Vep	52.6	49.2	Orthodox
Vietnamese	98.5	25.0	Buddhist
Yakut	93.8	54.9	Orthodox
*Yukagir	---	---	Animist

*Percentages unknown.

Source: Ronald Wixman, The Peoples of the USSR (Armonk, NY: M. E. Sharpe, 1984); Michael Mandelbaum, ed. The Rise of Nations in the Soviet Union (New York: Council on Foreign Relations, 1991); Raymond Zickel, ed., Soviet Union. A Country Study (Washington, D.C.: Department of the Army, 1991).

Appendix G
Soviet Residence Patterns by Major
Nationality Group, 1989

Nationality	Republic of Residence	Population	Percentage
RUSSIAN	Russian	119,807,165	82.6
	Ukrainian	11,340,250	7.8
	Kazakh	6,226,400	4.3
	Uzbek	1,652,179	1.1
	Belarusian	1,341,055	0.9
	Kyrgyz	916,543	0.6
	Latvian	905,515	0.6
	Moldovan	560,423	0.4
	Estonian	474,815	0.3
	Azerbaijan	392,303	0.3
	Tajik	386,630	0.3
	Lithuanian	343,957	0.2
	Georgian	338,645	0.2
	Turkmen	334,477	0.2
	Armenian	51,553	0.04
	Total Russian	145,071,550	
UKRAINIAN	Ukrainian	37,370,368	84.7
	Russian	4,363,992	9.9
	Kazakh	895,964	2.0
	Moldovan	599,777	1.4
	Belarusian	290,368	0.7
	Uzbek	154,155	0.3
	Kyrgyz	108,027	0.2
	Latvian	92,101	0.2
	Georgian	51,472	0.1
	Estonian	48,273	0.1
	Lithuanian	44,397	0.1
	Tajik	40,646	0.09
	Turkmen	35,814	0.08
	Azerbaijan	32,344	0.07
	Armenian	8,341	0.02
	Total Ukrainian	44,135,989	
UZBEK	Uzbek	14,123,626	84.6
	Tajik	1,197,091	7.2
	Kyrgyz	550,095	3.3
	Kazakh	332,016	2.0
	Turkmen	317,252	1.9
	Russian	127,169	0.8
	Ukrainian	27,753	0.2
	Belarusian	3,550	0.02
	Moldovan	2,018	0.01

Nationality	Republic of Residence	Population	Percentage
	Lithuanian	1,452	0.01
	Azerbaijan	1,379	0.01
	Georgian	1,073	0.01
	Latvian	925	0.01
	Estonian	595	0.00
	Armenian	246	0.00
	Total Uzbek	16,686,240	
BELARUSIAN	Belarusian	7,897,781	78.7
	Russian	1,205,887	12.0
	Ukrainian	439,858	4.4
	Kazakh	182,514	1.8
	Latvian	119,702	1.2
	Lithuanian	63.076	0.6
	Uzbek	31,737	0.3
	Estonian	27,711	0.3
	Moldovan	19,431	0.2
	Turkmen	9,285	0.1
	Kyrgyz	9,187	0.1
	Georgian	8,338	0.09
	Azerbaijan	7,833	0.08
	Tajik	7,042	0.07
	Armenian	1,059	0.01
	Total Belarusian	10,030,444	
KAZAKH	Kazakh	6,531,921	80.3
	Uzbek	808,090	9.9
	Russian	686,083	7.8
	Turkmen	87,595	1.1
	Kyrgyz	37,318	0.5
	Ukrainian	12,120	0.1
	Tajik	11,371	0.1
	Belarusian	4,530	0.06
	Georgian	2,545	0.03
	Moldovan	1,933	0.02
	Azerbaijan	1,638	0.02
	Latvian	1,044	0.01
	Lithuanian	658	0.01
	Armenian	608	0.01
	Estonian	424	0.01
	Total Kazakh	8,137,878	
AZERBAIJAN	Azerbaijan	5,800,994	85.4
	Russian	336,908	5.0
	Georgian	307,908	4.5
	Kazakh	90,082	1.3
	Armenian	84,860	1.2

Nationality	Republic of Residence	Population	Percentage
	Ukrainian	59,149	0.9
	Uzbek	44,393	0.7
	Turkmen	33,334	0.5
	Kyrgyz	15,775	0.2
	Belarusian	6,634	0.1
	Tajik	3,689	0.05
	Latvian	2,765	0.04
	Moldovan	2,554	0.04
	Lithuanian	1,307	0.02
	Estonian	1,238	0.02
Total Azerbaijan		6,791,106	
TATAR	Russian	5,519,605	83.1
	Uzbek	467,676	7.0
	Kazakh	327,871	4.9
	Ukrainian	86,789	1.3
	Tajik	72,168	1.1
	Kyrgyz	70,068	1.1
	Turkmen	39,243	0.6
	Azerbaijan	28,019	0.4
	Belarusian	12,352	0.2
	Lithuanian	5,107	0.1
	Latvian	4,828	0.1
	Estonian	4,058	0.1
	Georgian	3,999	0.1
	Moldovan	3,335	0.05
	Armenian	470	0.01
Total Tatar		6,645,588	
ARMENIAN	Armenian	3,081,920	66.6
	Russian	532,675	11.5
	Georgian	436,615	9.4
	Azerbaijan	390,495	8.4
	Ukrainian	60,047	1.3
	Uzbek	50,516	1.1
	Turkmen	31,838	0.7
	Kazakh	19,105	0.4
	Tajik	5,630	0.1
	Belarusian	5,251	0.1
	Kyrgyz	3,975	0.1
	Latvian	3,069	0.07
	Moldovan	2,774	0.06
	Estonian	1,669	0.04
	Lithuanian	1,648	0.04
Total Armenian		4,627,227	

Nationality	Republic of Residence	Population	Percentage
TAJIK	Tajik	3,168,193	75.1
	Uzbek	931,547	22.1
	Russian	38,327	0.9
	Kyrgyz	33,842	0.8
	Kazakh	25,514	0.6
	Ukrainian	10,476	0.3
	Turkmen	3,418	0.08
	Belarusian	1,417	0.03
	Georgian	1,133	0.03
	Moldovan	720	0.02
	Azerbaijan	702	0.02
	Lithuanian	516	0.01
	Armenian	432	0.01
	Latvian	343	0.01
	Estonian	113	0.00
	Total Tajik	4,216,693	
GEORGIAN	Georgian	3,379,385	95.1
	Russian	130,719	3.3
	Ukrainian	23,689	0.6
	Azerbaijan	13,986	0.4
	Kazakh	9,496	0.2
	Uzbek	4,726	0.1
	Belarusian	2,968	0.07
	Latvian	1,378	0.03
	Armenian	1,364	0.03
	Kyrgyz	1,143	0.03
	Moldovan	1,077	0.03
	Tajik	971	0.02
	Turkmen	960	0.02
	Lithuanian	647	0.02
	Estonian	606	0.02
	Total Georgian	3,983,115	
MOLDOVAN	Moldovan	2,709,769	83.2
	Ukrainian	324,480	9.7
	Russian	172,784	5.1
	Kazakh	33,096	1.0
	Uzbek	11,424	0.3
	Belarusian	5,348	0.2
	Latvian	3,223	0.1
	Georgian	2,814	0.1
	Turkmen	2,678	0.08
	Azerbaijan	1,915	0.06
	Kyrgyz	1,875	0.06
	Tajik	1,646	0.05
	Lithuanian	1,448	0.04
	Estonian	1,215	0.04
	Armenian	525	0.02
	Total Moldovan	3,355,240	

Nationality	Republic of Residence	Population	Percentage
LITHUANIAN	Lithuania	2,924,048	95.3
	Russian	70,386	2.3
	Latvian	34,630	1.1
	Ukrainian	11,385	0.4
	Kazakh	10,938	0.4
	Belarusian	7,589	0.3
	Estonian	2,568	0.1
	Uzbek	2,234	0.07
	Moldovan	1,438	0.05
	Georgian	921	0.03
	Azerbaijan	533	0.02
	Tajik	530	0.02
	Kyrgyz	493	0.02
	Turkmen	372	0.01
	Armenian	231	0.01
Total Lithuanian		3,068,296	
TURKMEN	Turkmen	2,524,138	92.9
	Uzbek	122,566	4.5
	Russian	39,738	1.5
	Tajik	20,527	0.8
	Kazakh	4,046	0.1
	Ukrainian	3,990	0.1
	Kyrgyz	899	0.03
	Belarusian	755	0.03
	Moldovan	399	0.01
	Azerbaijan	340	0.01
	Georgian	305	0.01
	Latvian	228	0.01
	Lithuanian	193	0.01
	Estonian	106	0.00
	Armenian	67	0.00
Total Turkmen		2,718,297	
KYRGYZ	Kyrgyz	2,228,482	88.0
	Uzbek	174,899	6.9
	Tajik	63,831	2.5
	Russian	43,083	1.7
	Kazakh	14,271	0.6
	Ukrainian	3,881	0.2
	Turkmen	727	0.03
	Belarusian	555	0.02
	Armenian	271	0.01
	Azerbaijan	224	0.01
	Moldovan	216	0.01
	Latvian	189	0.01

Nationality	Republic of Residence	Population	Percentage
	Georgian	170	0.01
	Lithuanian	118	0.01
	Estonian	81	0.00
Total Kyrgyz		2,530,998	
GERMAN	Kazakh	956,235	47.0
	Russian	840,980	41.3
	Kyrgyz	101,198	5.0
	Tajik	32,493	1.6
	Other	104,191	5.1
Total German		2,035,807	
CHUVASH	Russian	1,771,047	93.8
	Other	68,181	6.2
Total Chuvash		1,839,228	
LATVIAN	Latvian	1,387,646	93.8
	Russian	46,818	3.2
	Ukrainian	7,169	0.5
	Lithuanian	4,228	0.3
	Kazakh	3,370	0.2
	Estonian	3,135	0.2
	Belarusian	2,655	0.2
	Uzbek	1,130	0.1
	Turkmen	859	0.06
	Georgian	524	0.04
	Moldovan	461	0.03
	Kyrgyz	392	0.03
	Azerbaijan	324	0.02
	Tajik	300	0.02
	Armenian	145	0.01
Total Latvian		1,459,462	
BASHKIR	Russian	1,345,231	92.8
	Other	104,231	7.2
Total Bashkir		1,449,462	
JEW	Russian	536,422	39.0
	Ukrainian	485,975	35.3
	Belarusian	111,789	8.1

795

Nationality	Republic of Residence	Population	Percentage
	Moldovan	65,668	4.8
	Uzbek	65,369	4.7
	Azerbaijan	25,190	1.8
	Latvian	22,897	1.7
	Kazakh	18,379	1.3
	Lithuanian	12,312	0.9
	Georgian	10,302	0.7
	Tajik	9,576	0.7
	Other	13,031	1.0
Total Jew		1,376,910	
MORDVINIAN	Russian	1,072,517	93.0
	Other	80,999	7.0
Total Mordvinian		1,153,516	
POLE	Belarusian	417,648	37.1
	Lithuanian	257,988	22.9
	Ukrainian	218,891	19.4
	Latvian	60,338	5.4
	Other	171,222	15.2
Total Pole		1,126,137	
ESTONIAN	Estonian	963,269	93.8
	Russian	46,358	4.5
	Ukrainian	4,208	0.4
	Kazakh	3,397	0.3
	Latvian	3,312	0.3
	Uzbek	948	0.1
	Belarusian	797	0.1
	Lithuanian	598	0.06
	Turkmen	560	0.05
	Kyrgyz	430	0.04
	Azerbaijan	324	0.03
	Armenian	295	0.03
	Moldovan	276	0.03
	Tajik	171	0.02
Total Estonian		1,027,255	
OTHER		12,173,338	
TOTAL		285,639,467	

REFERENCE: Raymond E. Zickel, ed., Soviet Union: A Country Study
(Washington, DC: Department of the Army, 1991).

Appendix H
Ethnic Composition of the Autonomous Units
of the Soviet Union in 1991

Autonomous Republic	Group	Percent Native Group	Percent Russian
Bashkir ASSR	Bashkir	21.9	39.3
Buryat ASSR	Buryat	24.0	70.0
Chechen-Ingush ASSR	Chechen	57.9	23.1
	Ingush	12.9	
Chuvash ASSR	Chuvash	67.8	26.7
Daghestan ASSR	Avar	27.5	9.2
	Agul	0.8	
	Dargin	15.6	
	Kumyk	12.9	
	Lak	5.1	
	Lezgin	11.3	
	Nogai	1.6	
	Rutul	0.8	
	Tabasaran	4.3	
	Tsakhur	0.3	
Kabardino-Balkar ASSR	Kabard	48.2	32.0
	Balkar	9.4	
Kalmyk ASSR	Kalmyk	45.4	37.7
Karelian ASSR	Karelian	10.0	73.6
Komi ASSR	Komi	23.3	57.7
Mari ASSR	Mari	43.3	47.5
Mordvinian ASSR	Mordvinian	32.5	60.8
North Ossetian ASSR	Ossetian	53.0	29.9
Tatar ASSR	Tatar	48.5	43.3
Tuva ASSR	Tuvinian	64.3	32.0
Udmurt ASSR	Udmurt	30.9	58.9

Autonomous Republic	Group	Percent Native Group	Percent Russian
Yakut ASSR	Yakut	33.4	50.3

Autonomous Province	Group	Percentage of Total Population	
		Group	Russian
Adyghe AP	Adyghe	22.1	68.0
Gorno-Altai AP	Altai	31.0	60.4
Jewish AP	Jew	4.2	83.2
Karachai-Cherkess AP	Karachai	31.2	42.4
	Cherkess	9.7	
Khakass AP	Khakass	11.1	79.5

Autonomous Region	Group	Percentage of Total Population	
		Group	Russian
Aginsk-Buryat AR	Buryat	54.9	40.8
Chukchi AR	Chukchi	7.3	66.1
Evenki AR	Evenk	14.0	67.5
Khanty-Mansi AR	Khant	0.9	66.3
	Mansi	0.5	
Komi-Permyak AR	Komi-Permyak	60.2	36.1
Koryak AR	Koryak	16.5	62.0
Nenets AR	Nenet	11.9	65.8
Taymyr (Dolgan-Nenets) AR	Dolgan	8.9	67.1
	Nenet	4.8	
Ust-Orda Buryat AR	Buryat	36.3	56.5
Yamalo-Nenets AR	Nenet	4.2	59.2

....

Source: "Ethnic Data for Russia's Autonomous Units," The Current Digest of the
         Soviet Press, 43 (June 26, 1991), 8.

Selected Bibliography of Titles in English

Abramzon, S. M. "Reflections of the Process of the Coming Together of Nations in the Family Life and Daily Habits of the Peoples of Central Asia and Kazakhstan." *Soviet Sociology* 1 (1962).

Adamovich, Anthony. *Opposition to Sovietization in Belorussian Literature, 1917–1957.* 1958.

Agarwal, N. N. *Soviet Nationalities Policy.* 1969.

Aitmatov, Chingis. *The Day Lasts More Than a Hundred Years.* 1983.

Akiner, Shirin. *Islamic Peoples of the Soviet Union.* 1983.

Alexandrov, Victor. *The End of the Romanovs.* 1966.

Alexeyeva, Ludmilla. *Soviet Dissent: Contemporary Movements for National, Religious, and Human Rights.* 1985.

———. "Unrest in the Soviet Union." *The Washington Quarterly* 13 (Winter 1990).

Alexiev, Alexander R. *Dissent and Nationalism in the Soviet Baltic.* 1983.

Alexiev, Alexander R., and S. Enders Wimbush. *The Ethnic Factor in the Soviet Armed Forces.* 1983.

Allen, William Edward David. *A History of the Georgian People: From the Beginning Down to the Russian Conquest in the Nineteenth Century.* 1932.

Allen, William Edward David, and Paul Muratoff. *Caucasian Battlefields.* 1953.

Allworth, Edward. *Uzbek Literary Politics.* 1964.

———. *Central Asian Publishing and the Rise of Nationalism.* 1965.

———. *Central Asia: A Century of Russian Rule.* 1967.

———. *Ethnic Russia Today: The Dilemma of Dominance.* 1980.

———. *Tatars of the Crimea: Their Struggle for Survival.* 1988.

———, ed. *Soviet Nationality Problems.* 1971.

———, ed. *The Nationality Question in Soviet Central Asia.* 1973.

———, ed. *Nationality Group Survival in Multi-Ethnic States: Shifting Support Patterns in the Soviet Baltic Region.* 1977.

Almedingen, Edith Martha. *So Dark a Stream: A Study of Emperor Paul I of Russia, 1754–1801.* 1959.

———. *The Emperor Alexander II: A Study.* 1962.

———. *The Emperor Alexander I.* 1964.

Altay, A. T. "Kirgizia During the Great Purge." *Central Asian Review* 12 (1964).

Alstadt, Audrey L. "Nagorno-Karabakh: 'Apple of Discord' in the Azerbaydzhan SSR." *Central Asian Survey* [Oxford] 7 (1988): 63–78.

Altshuler, Mordechai. *Soviet Jewry since the Second World War: Population and Social Structure*. 1987.

Anderson, John. *Religion and the Soviet State: A Report on Religious Repression in the USSR on the Occasion of the Christian Millennium*. 1988.

Anderson, M. S. "The Great Powers and the Russian Annexation of the Crimea, 1783–1784." *Slavonic and East European Review* 37 (1958).

———. *Peter the Great*. 1978.

Andersons, Edgars. *Cross Road Country, Latvia*. 1953.

Armstrong, John A. *The Politics of Totalitarianism: The Communist Party of the Soviet Union from 1934 to the Present*. 1961.

———. *Ideology, Politics, and Government in the Soviet Union*. 1962.

Arnovitz, Benton. "Zion in Siberia." *Survey* 29 (Autumn 1985): 129–52.

Aron, Leon. "Gorbachev's Mounting Nationalities Crisis." *Heritage Foundation Backgrounder* No. 695 (March 1989): 1–12.

Aslanyan, A. A. *Soviet Armenia*. 1971.

Aspaturian, Vernon V. *The Union Republics in Soviet Diplomacy: A Study of Soviet Federalism in the Service of Soviet Foreign Policy*. 1960.

———. *The Soviet Union in the World Communist System*. 1966.

Austin, Paul M. "Soviet Karelian." *Slavic Review* 51 (Spring 1992).

Avalishvili, Zourab. *The Independence of Georgia in International Politics, 1918–1921*. 1940.

Avrich, Paul. *Russian Rebels, 1600–1800*. 1972.

Azrael, Jeremy R., ed. *Soviet Nationality Policies and Practices*. 1978.

Babakhanov, Mufti Ziyauddin Khan. *Islam and the Muslims in the Land of the Soviets*. 1980.

Bacon, Elizabeth. *Central Asians Under Russian Rule: A Study in Culture Change*. 1966.

Baddeley, John F. *The Russian Conquest of the Caucasus*. 1908.

———. *The Rugged Flanks of Caucasia*. 2 vols. 1942.

Bagramov, Eduard. *One Hundred Nationalities: One People*. 1982.

Bahry, Donna, and Carol Nechemias. "Half Full or Half Empty?" *Slavic Review* 40 (Fall 1981).

Balic, Smail. "Eastern Europe: The Islamic Dimension." *Journal of the Institute of Minority Affairs* 1 (1979): 29–37.

Balzer, Marjorie M. "Ethnicity Without Power: The Siberian Khanty in Soviet Society." *Slavic Review* 42 (Winter 1983): 633–48.

Barghoorn, Frederick C. *Soviet Russian Nationalism*. 1956.

Baron, Salo. *The Russian Jew under Tsars and Soviets*. 1964.

Bartol'd, V. V. *Four Studies on the History of Central Asia*. 4 volumes. 1956–1963.

———. *Turkestan Down to the Mongol Invasion*. 1958.

Baskakov, N. A. *The Turkic Languages of Central Asia: Problems of Planned Culture Contact*. 1960.

———. *The Turkic Peoples of USSR: The Development of Their Languages and Writing*. 1960.

Baytugan, B. S. "The North Caucasus." *Studies on the Soviet Union* 11 (1971): 1–34.

Bazhan, M. P., ed. *Soviet Ukraine*. 1969.

Beloff, Nora. *Inside the Soviet Empire: The Myth and the Reality*. 1979.

Bennigsen, Alexandre. *The Evolution of the Muslim Nationalities of the USSR and Their Linguistic Problems*. 1961.

———. "The Problem of Bilingualism and Assimilation in the North Caucasus." *Central Asian Survey*, 15 (1967): 205–11.

———. "Muslim Religious Conservatism and Dissent in the USSR." *Religion in Communist Lands* 6 (1978): 153–61.

———. " 'Official' Islam in the Soviet Union." *Religion in Communist Lands* 7 (1979): 148–59.

———. "Marxism or Pan-Islamism: Russian Bolsheviks and Tatar National Communists at the Beginning of the Civil War, July, 1918." *Central Asian Survey* [Oxford] 6 (1987): 55–66.

———. "Unrest in the World of Soviet Islamism." *Third World Quarterly* 10 (April 1988): 770–86.

Bennigsen, Alexandre, and Marie Broxup. *The Islamic Threat to the Soviet State*. 1983.

Bennigsen, Alexandre, and Chantal Lemercier-Quelquejay. *The Evolution of the Muslim Nationalities of the USSR and Their Linguistic Problems*. 1960.

———. *Islam in the Soviet Union*. 1967.

Bennigsen, Alexandre, and S. Enders Wimbush. *Muslim National Communism in the Soviet Union: A Revolutionary Strategy for the Colonial World*. 1979.

———. *Mystics and Commissars: Sufism in the Soviet Union*. 1983.

———. *Muslims of the Soviet Empire: A Guide*. 1986.

Bescançon, Alain. "The Nationalities Issue in the USSR." *Survey* 30 (June 1989).

Bethell, Nicholas. *The Last Secret: Forcible Repatriation to Russia, 1944–1947*. 1974.

Bialar, Seweryn. *Stalin's Successors*. 1981.

———, ed. *Politics, Society, and Nationality: Inside Gorbachev's Russia*. 1988.

Bilinsky, Yaroslav. *The Second Soviet Republic: The Ukraine after World War II*. 1964.

———. "Education of the Non-Russian Peoples of the USSR, 1917–1967: An Essay." *Slavic Review* 27 (1968).

———. "Nationality Policy in Gorbachev's First Year." *Orbis* 30 (Summer 1986): 331–42.

Billington, James. *The Icon and the Axe: An Interpretive History of Russian Culture*. 1970.

Bilmanis, Alfred. *A History of Latvia*. 1951.

Bilocerkowycz, Jaroslav. *Soviet Ukrainian Dissent: A Study of Political Alienation*. 1988.

Birch, J. T. "Border Disputes and Disputed Borders in the Soviet Federal System." *Nationalities Papers* 15 (Spring 1987).

———. "The 1986 Party Program and the National Minorities in the USSR." *Nationalities Papers* 15 (Fall 1987).

———. *The Ukrainian Nationalist Movement in the USSR Since 1956*. 1971.

Blanch, Lesley. *The Sabres of Paradise*. 1960.

Blank, Stephen. "The Origins of Soviet Language Policy 1917–1921." *Russian History* 15 (1988).

———. *The Sorcerer as Apprentice: Stalin and the Soviet Commissariat of Nationalities, 1917–1924*. 1989.

Blum, Jerome. *Lord and Peasant in Russia from the Ninth to the Nineteenth Centuries*. 1961.

Bociurkiw, Bohdan. "The Uniate Church in the Soviet Ukraine: A Case Study in Soviet Church Policy." *Canadian Slavonic Papers* 7 (1965).

————. "The Orthodox Church and the Soviet Regime in the Ukraine, 1953–1971." *Canadian Slavonic Papers* 14 (Summer 1972).

————. *Ukrainian Churches under Soviet Rule: Two Case Studies.* 1984.

Bociurkiw, B. R., and J. W. Strong. *Religion and Atheism in the USSR and Eastern Europe.* 1975.

Bohr, Annette. "A Belated Step in the Repatriation of the Chechen and Ingush." *Radio Liberty Research Bulletin* (April 19, 1985).

————. "Breaking the Silence: The Mass Deportation of Koreans under Stalin." *Radio Liberty Research Bulletin* (September 1, 1988).

Bourdeaux, Michael. *Religious Ferment in Russia.* 1968.

Bremmer, Ian, and Norman Naimark, eds. *Soviet Nationality Problems.* 1972.

Brown, Archie, John Fennell, Michael Kaser, and W. T. Willets, eds. *The Cambridge Encyclopedia of Russia and the Soviet Union.* 1982.

Brown, Archie, and Michael Kaser, eds. *The Soviet Union since the Fall of Khrushchev.* 1975.

Browne, Michael, ed. *Ferment in the Ukraine.* 1971.

Bruchis, Michael. "The Language Policy of the CPSU and the Linguistic Situation in Soviet Moldavia." *Soviet Studies* 36 (January 1984).

————. "The Language Policy of the Soviet Communist Party: Comments and Observations." *East European Quarterly* 21 (June 1987).

Brumberg, Abraham, ed. *In Quest of Justice.* 1970.

Bryan, Robert J. "Cultural Versus Structural Explanation of Ethnic Intermarriage in the USSR: A Statistical Re-Analysis." *Russian History* 15 (1988).

Budreckis, Algirdas M. *The Lithuanian National Revolt of 1941.* 1968.

Bungs, Dzintra. "The Deportation of Balts to the USSR: Still a Touchy Subject." *Radio Free Europe Research* [Munich] 13 (June 10, 1988).

Burg, Steven L. "Soviet Policy and the Central Asian Problem." *Survey* 24 (1979).

————. "The Soviet Union's Nationalities Question." *Current History* 88 (October 1989).

Brzezinski, Zbigniew. "Post-Communist Nationalism." *Foreign Affairs* (Winter, 1989/ 1990).

Cang, Joel. *The Silent Millions: A History of the Jews in the Soviet Union.* 1969.

Caroe, Sir Olaf K. *Soviet Empire: The Turks of Central Asia and Stalinism.* 1967.

Carr, Edward Hallett. *History of Soviet Russia.* 14 vols. 1952–1978.

Carrère d'Encasse, Hélène C. *Decline of an Empire: The Soviet Socialist Republics in Revolt.* 1979.

Charques, Richard D. *The Twilight of Imperial Russia: The Reign of Tsar Nicholas II.* 1958.

Chew, Allen F. *An Atlas of Russian History.* 1967.

Churchward, L. G. *Contemporary Soviet Government.* 1968.

Clark, Charles Upsham. *Bessarabia.* 1927.

Clarkson, J. A. *A History of Russia.* 1961.

Clem, Ralph S. "The Changing Geography of Soviet Nationalities and Its Socioeconomic Correlates: 1926–1970." Ph.D. diss., Columbia University, 1975.

————, ed. *The Soviet West: Interplay between Nationality and Social Organization.* 1975.

Clemens, Walter C., Jr. *Baltic Independence and Russian Empire.* 1991.

Coates, W. P., and Zelda K. Coates. *Soviets in Central Asia.* 1969.

Cohen, Stephen F., Alexander Rabinowitch, and Robert Sharlet. *The Soviet Union Since Stalin*. 1980.

Cole, J. P., and F. C. German. *A Geography of the U.S.S.R.* 1970.

Connor, Walker. "Nation-Building or Nation-Destroying?" *World Politics* 24 (April 1972).

Connors, Walter. *The National Question in Marxist-Leninist Theory and Strategy*, 1984.

Conquest, Robert. *Soviet Russian Nationalism*. 1956.

———. *Power and Policy in the USSR: The Study of Soviet Dynamics*. 1961.

———. *The Great Terror: Stalin's Purges of the Thirties*. 1968.

———. *The Nation Killers: Soviet Deportation of Nationalities*. 1970.

———. *The Harvest of Sorrow: Soviet Collectivization and the Terror-Famine*. 1986.

———, ed. *Back to Life*. 1958.

———, ed. *Soviet Nationality Policy in Practice*. 1967.

———, ed. *The Last Empire: Nationality and the Soviet Future*. 1986.

Cottam, Richard W. *Nationalism in Iran*. 1964.

Crankshaw, Edward. *Khrushchev's Russia*. 1959.

———. *In the Shadow of the Winter Palace: The Drift to Revolution, 1825–1917*. 1976.

Curtiss, John S. *The Russian Church and the Soviet State, 1917–1950*. 1953.

Czaplicka, M. M. *The Turks of Central Asia*. 1918.

Dallin, Alexander. *German Rule in Russia, 1941–1945: A Study of Occupation Policies*. 1957.

Dallin, David J. *The New Soviet Empire*. 1951.

———. *From Purge to Coexistence: Essays on Stalin's and Khrushchev's Russia*. 1964.

Davies, R. W., and J. B. Denis, eds. *The Soviet Union*. 1978.

Davitaya, F. F. *Soviet Georgia*. 1972.

de Lageard, Helene A. "The Revolt of the Basmachi According to Red Army Journals (1920–1922)." *Central Asian Survey* [Oxford] 6 (1987).

DeGeorge, Richard T., and James Scanlan, eds. *Marxism and Religion in Eastern Europe*. 1974.

Demko, George J. *The Russian Colonization of Kazakhstan, 1896–1916*. 1960.

D'Encansse, Hélène Carrère. *Islam and the Russian Empire: Reform and Revolution in Central Asia*. 1966.

Der Nersessian, Sirarpie. *The Armenians*. 1970.

Deutschev, Isaac. *The Unfinished Revolution: Russia 1917–1967*. 1967.

Dienes, Leslie. "Pastoralism in Turkestan: Its Decline and Its Persistence." *Soviet Studies* 27 (July 1975).

Dodge, N. T., ed. *Soviets in Asia*. 1972.

Dostal, Petr, and Hans Knippenberg. "The Russification of Ethnic Minorities in the U.S.S.R." *Soviet Geography* 20 (1979).

Douglas, William O. *Strange Lands and Friendly Peoples*. 1951.

Dreifelds, Juris. "Demographic Trends in Latvia." *Nationalities Papers* 12 (No. 1, 1984).

———. "Latvian National Rebirth." *Problems of Communism* (July-August 1989).

Dubnow, S. M. *History of the Jews in Russia and Poland*. 1920.

Dukes, Paul. *Catherine the Great and the Russian Nobility: A Study Based on the Materials of the Legislative Commission of 1767*. 1967.

Duncan, Peter J. "The Fate of Russian Nationalism: The Samizdat Journal *Veche* Revisited." *Religion in Communist Lands* 16 (Spring 1988).

Dunlop, John B. *The Faces of Contemporary Russian Nationalism*. 1983.

————. "The Contemporary Russian Nationalist Spectrum." *Radio Liberty Research Bulletin* (December 19, 1988).

Dunn, Dennis J. *The Catholic Church and The Soviet Government, 1939–1949.* 1977.

Dunn, Stephen P., and Ethel Dunn. "Soviet Regime and Native Culture in Central Asia and Kazakhstan: The Major Peoples." *Current Anthropology* 8 (1967): 147–208.

Dvornik, Francis. *The Slavs in European History and Civilization.* 1962.

Dyer, S. Rimsky-Korsakoff. *Soviet Dungan Kolkhozes in the Kirghiz SSR and the Kazakh SSR.* 1979.

Dzyuba, Ivan. *Internationalism or Russification? A Study in the Soviet Nationalities Problems.* 1970.

Ekmanis, Rolfs. "Soviet Attitudes Toward Pre-Soviet Latvian Writers." *Journal of Baltic Studies* 3 (Spring 1972).

————. *Latvian Literature Under the Soviet Union 1940–1975.* 1978.

Eliav, Arie L. *Between Hammer and Sickle.* 1969.

Elliott, Mark R. *Pawns of Yalta: Soviet Refugees and America's Role in Their Repatriation.* 1982.

Ellis, C. H. *The Transcaspian Episode, 1918–1919.* 1963.

Ellis, Jane. *The Russian Orthodox Church: A Contemporary History.* 1986.

————. "The Events in Kazakhstan: An Eyewitness Report." *Central Asian Survey* [Oxford] 6 (1987).

Emerson, Rupert. *From Empire to Nation: The Rise to Self-Assertion of Asian and African Peoples.* 1960.

Fainsod, Merle. *Smolensk under Soviet Rule.* 1958.

Fedoseyev, P. N. *Lenin and the National Question.* 1977.

Fedotov, Georgii P. *The Russian Religious Mind.* 2 vols. 1946–1966.

Feizuillin, G. R. "The Persecution of National-Religious Traditions of the Moslems of the USSR." *Caucasian Review* 3 (1956).

Fennell, John L. I. *Ivan the Great of Moscow.* 1961.

————. *The Emergence of Moscow, 1304–1359.* 1968.

Fireside, Harvey. "Valentyn Moroz: Individualist in Jeopardy." *Survey* 22 (Winter 1976).

Fischer-Galati, Stephen. *The New Rumania: From People's Democracy to Socialist Republic.* 1967.

Fisher, Alan W. *The Russian Annexation of the Crimea 1772–1783.* 1970.

————. *The Crimean Tatars.* 1987.

Fisher, Wesley A. "Ethnic Consciousness and Intermarriage: Correlates of Endogamy Among the Major Soviet Nationalities." *Soviet Studies* 29 (July 1977).

Fitzpatrick, Sheila. *The Russian Revolution.* 1983.

Florinsky, Michael T. *The End of the Russian Empire.* 1931.

————. *McGraw-Hill Encyclopedia of Russia and the Soviet Union.* 1961.

Forsyth, James. *A History of the Peoples of Siberia.* 1992.

Frankland, Noble. *Crown of Tragedy: Nicholas II.* 1960.

Fraser, Glenda. "Basmachi—I." *Central Asian Survey* [Oxford] 6 (No. 1, 1987).

————. "Basmachi—II." *Central Asian Survey* [Oxford] 6 (No. 2, 1987).

Fuller, Elizabeth. "Georgian Nuclear Reactor to Close in Wake of Public Protest." *Radio Liberty Research Bulletin* (April 20, 1990).

————. "Georgia Edges toward Secession." *Radio Liberty Research Bulletin* (June 1, 1990).

————. "Georgian Alternative Election Results Announced." *Radio Liberty Research Bulletin* (October 26, 1990).

————. "Georgia on the Eve of the Supreme Soviet Elections." *Radio Liberty Research Bulletin* (November 9, 1990).

————. "Georgian Parliament Votes to Abolish Ossetian Autonomy." *Radio Liberty Research Bulletin* (December 21, 1990).

Gardanov, V. K., B. O. Dolgikh, and T. A. Zhdanko. "Major Trends in Ethnic Processes Among the Peoples of the USSR." *Soviet Anthropology and Archaeology* 1 (1962).

Geiger, Bernhard, et al. *Peoples and Languages of the Caucasus.* 1959.

Gellner, Ernest. *Muslim Societies.* 1981.

Germroth, David S. "The Soviet Republics and Nationalism." *Global Affairs* 4 (Spring 1989).

Gibb. H.A.R. *The Arab Conquests in Central Asia.* 1923.

Gibson, Michael. *Russia Under Stalin.* 1972.

Gidney, James B. *A Mandate for Armenia.* 1967.

Gilboa, Yehoshua A. *The Black Years of Soviet Jewry: 1939–1945.* 1971.

Girnius, Kestutis K. "The Collectivization of Lithuanian Agriculture, 1944–1950." *Soviet Studies* 40 (July 1988).

Gobel, Paul. "Ethnic Politics in the USSR." *Problems of Communism* (July-August 1989).

Goldberg, B. Z. *The Jewish Problem in the Soviet Union: Analysis and Solutions.* 1961.

Goldhagen, Erich, ed. *Ethnic Minorities in the Soviet Union.* 1968.

Goldman, Guido. *Zionism Under Soviet Rule, 1917–1928.* 1960.

Goldman, Marshall. "The USSR's New Class Struggle." *World Monitor* 2 (February 1989).

Gorer, Geoffrey, and John Rickman. *The People of Great Russia: A Psychological Study.* 1962.

Grabski, Stanislaw. *The Polish-Soviet Frontier.* 1943.

Graham, Stephen. *A Life of Alexander II, Tsar of Russia.* 1935.

Greenberg, Louis. *The Jews in Russia: The Struggle for Emancipation.* 1976.

Grey, Ian. *Ivan III and the Unification of Russia.* 1964.

————. *Ivan the Terrible.* 1964.

————. *Boris Godunov, the Tragic Tsar.* 1973.

Gross, Jan T. *Revolution from Abroad: The Soviet Conquest of Poland's Western Ukraine and Western Belorussia.* 1988.

Grunwald, Constantin de. *Tsar Nicholas I.* 1954.

Guthier, Steven L. "The Belorussians: National Identification and Assimilation, 1897–1970. Part I, 1897–1939." *Soviet Studies* 29 (January 1977).

————. "The Belorussians: National Identification and Assimilation, 1897–1970. Part II, 1939–1970." *Soviet Studies* 29 (April 1977).

Hackel, Sergei A. *The Orthodox Church.* 1971.

Hajda, Lubomyr. "The Nationalities Problem in the Soviet Union." *Current History* 87 (October 1988).

Hajda, Lubomyr, and Mark Beissinger, eds. *The Nationalities Factor in Soviet Politics and Society.* 1990.

Hájdu, Péter. *The Samoyedic Peoples of the Soviet Union.* 1962.

Hambly, G. R., et al. *Central Asia.* 1969.

Hamm, Henry. *Albania.* 1963.

Harding, Neil, ed. *The State in Socialist Society*. 1984.

Hayward, Max, and William C. Fletcher, eds. *Religion and the Soviet State: A Dilemma of Power*. 1969.

Heer, Nancy. *Politics and History in the Soviet Union*. 1971.

Heller, Mikhail. *Cogs in the Wheel: The Formation of Soviet Man*. 1988.

Henze, Paul. "The Last Empire." *Journal of Democracy* (Spring 1990).

Hodnett, Grey. "The Debate Over Soviet Federalism." *Soviet Studies* 18 (1966–1967).

Hodnett, Gary. "What's in a Nation?" *Problems of Communism* 16 (1967).

Hooson, D. R. *The Soviet Union: Peoples and Regions*. 1966.

Horak, Stephen M., ed. *Guide to the Study of the Soviet Nationalities*. 1982.

Hosking, Geoffrey A., ed. *Church, Nation, and State in Russia and Ukraine*. 1991.

Hostler, Charles W. *Turkism and the Soviets: The Turks of the World and Their Political Objectives*. 1957.

Hovannisian, Richard. *Armenia on the Road to Independence*. 1967.

———, ed. *The Armenian Genocide*. 1992.

Hrushevsky, M. T. *A History of the Ukraine*. 1941.

Hvat, Ivan. "The Ukrainian Catholic Church, the Vatican, and the Soviet Union During the Pontificate of Pope John Paul II." *Religion in Communist Lands* 11 (Winter 1983).

Isayev, M. I. *National Languages in the USSR: Problems and Solutions*. 1977.

Janos, Andrew. "Ethnicity, Communism and Political Change in Eastern Europe." *World Politics* 23 (1971).

Jones, Ellen, and Fred W. Grupp. "Measuring Nationality Trends in the Soviet Union." *Slavic Review* 41 (1982).

———. "Modernization and Traditionality in a Multiethnic Society: The Soviet Case." *American Political Science Review* 79 (June 1985).

Jones, Stephen. "The Establishment of Soviet Power in Transcaucasia: The Case of Georgia, 1921–1928." *Soviet Studies* 40 (October 1988).

Jukes, Geoffrey. *The Soviet Union in Asia*. 1973.

Junger, H. I., ed. *The Literatures of the Soviet Peoples: A Historical and Biographical Survey*. 1970.

Jurgela, Constantine R. *History of the Lithuanian Nation*. 1948.

Kamenetsky, Ihor. *Nationalism and Human Rights: Processes of Modernization in the USSR*. 1977.

Kandelaki, Constantin. *The Georgian Question Before the Free World*. 1953.

Kandelaki, Constantin. "Soviet Nationality Policy in the Caucasus." *Caucasian Review* 2 (1956).

Karakashley, K. T. "A Contribution to the History of the Social Structure of the Population of the Lesser Caucasus." *Soviet Anthropology and Archaeology* 8 (1970).

Karklins, Rasma. "A Note on 'Nationality' and 'Native Tongue' as Census Categories in 1979." *Soviet Studies* 32 (July 1980).

———. "Nationality Power in Soviet Republics: Attitudes and Perceptions." *Studies in Comparative Communism: An International Interdisciplinary Journal* 21 (1981).

———. *Ethnic Relations in the USSR: The Perspective from Below*. 1986.

———. "Nationality Policy and Ethnic Relations in the USSR." In James R. Miller, ed. *Politics, Work and Daily Life in the USSR: A Survey of Former Soviet Citizens*, 1987.

Kaser, Michael. "A Source on the Soviet Far East." *Soviet Studies* 27 (October 1975).

Kassof, Allan, ed. *Prospects for Soviet Society*. 1968.

Kats, Zev, Rosemarie Rogers, and Frederic Harned, eds. *Handbook of Major Soviet Nationalities*. 1975.

Kaushik, D. R. *Central Asia in Modern Times*. 1970.

Kazemzadeh, Firuz. *The Struggle for Transcaucasia, 1917–1921*. 1951.

Kendrick, D. T. *The Destiny of Europe's Gypsies*. 1972.

Khodarkovsky, Michael. "The Arrival of the Kalmyks on the Muscovite Southern Frontier, 1600–1670." *Russian History* 15 (1988).

Kim, Maxim. *The Soviet Peoples: A New Historical Community*. 1974.

King, Gundar Julian. *Economic Policies in Occupied Latvia*. 1965.

King, Robert. *Minorities Under Communism*. 1973.

Klier, John Doyle. *Russia Gathers Her Jews: The Origins of the Jewish Question in Russia, 1772–1825*. 1986.

Kochan, Lionel. *The Russian Revolution*. 1971.

———, ed. *The Jews in Soviet Russia Since 1917*. 1970.

Kochan, Miriam. *The Last Days of Imperial Russia*. 1976.

Kolarz, Walter. *Russia and Her Colonies*. 1952.

———. "The Nationalities Under Khrushchev: Gains and Losses." *Soviet Survey* 24 (April-June 1958).

———. *Religion in the Soviet Union*. 1961.

———. *Communism and Colonialism*. 1964.

———. *The Peoples of the Soviet Far East*. 1969.

Komarnicki, Titus. *Rebirth of the Polish Republic: A Study in the Diplomacy of Europe, 1914–1920*. 1957.

Korey, William. *The Soviet Cage: Anti-Semitism in Russia*. 1973.

———. "Soviet Decision-Making and the Problem of Jewish Emigration Policy." *Survey* 22 (Winter 1976).

Koropeckyj, Iwan S. *The Ukraine Within the USSR*. 1982.

———. *Vsevolod Holubnychy: Selected Works*. 1982.

Koslów, Jules. *Ivan the Terrible*. 1961.

Krader, Lawrence. *Peoples of Central Asia*. 1963.

Krawchenko, Bohdan. *Social Change and National Consciousness in Twentieth-Century Ukraine*. 1985.

———, ed. *Ukraine After Shelest*. 1983.

Kreindler, Isabelle. *The Mordvinians: A Doomed Soviet Nationality?* 1984.

———. "The Soviet Deported Nationalities: A Summary and Update." *Soviet Studies* 38 (July 1986).

———, ed. *Sociolinguistic Perspectives on Soviet National Languages: Their Past, Present, and Future*. 1985.

Krushinsky, S. Y. *Byelorussian Communism and Nationalism*. 1953.

Kuzio, Taras. "Nationalist Ferment in Western Ukraine." *Soviet Analyst* 17 (August 3, 1988).

———. "Nationalist Riots in Kazakhstan." *Central Asian Survey* [Oxford] 7 (No. 4, 1988).

Lane, C. R. *Christian Religion in the Soviet Union: A Sociological Study*. 1978.

Lane, D. T. *Politics and Society in the USSR*. 1978.

Lang, David Marshall. *A Modern History of Soviet Georgia*. 1962.

———. *The Georgians*. 1966.

————. *Armenia: Cradle of Civilization.* 1978.

————. *The Armenians: A People in Exile.* 1988.

Lapidus, Gail. "Gorbachev's Nationality Problem." *Foreign Affairs* 68 (Fall 1989).

Lawrence, Gunther. *Three Million More.* 1970.

Lazzerini, Edward. "Ismail Bey Gasprinskii and Muslim Modernism in Russia." Ph.D. diss., University of Washington, 1973.

Lemercier-Quelquejay, Chantal. "The Crimean Tatars: A Retrospective Summary." *Central Asian Review* 16 (1968).

Lenin, V. I. *National Liberation and Socialism.* 1927.

Lentin, A. T. *Russia in the Eighteenth Century: From Peter the Great to Catherine the Great, 1696–1796.* 1973.

Levin, M. G., and L. P. Potapov. *Peoples of Siberia.* 1964.

Levin, Nora. *The Jews in the Soviet Union Since 1917: Paradox of Survival.* 1975.

Lewis, E. Glyn. *Multilingualism in the Soviet Union: Aspects of Language Policy and Its Implementation.* 1972.

Lewis, Robert A., Richard H. Rowland, and Ralph S. Clem. *Nationality and Population Change in Russia and the USSR: An Evaluation of Census Data, 1897–1970.* 1977.

Lewytzkyj, Borys. *Politics and Society in Soviet Ukraine: 1953–1980.* 1984.

Liely, Helmut. "Shepherds and Reindeer Nomads in the Soviet Union." *Soviet Studies* 31 (July 1979).

Lieven, Dominic. *Gorbachev and the Nationalities.* 1988.

Lipsett, H. L. "The Status of National Minority Languages in Soviet Education." *Soviet Studies* 19 (1967–68).

Livezeanu, Irina. "Urbanization in a Low Key and Linguistic Change in Soviet Moldavia, Part I." *Soviet Studies* 33 (July 1981).

————. "Urbanization in a Low Key and Linguistic Change in Soviet Moldavia, Part II." *Soviet Studies* 33 (October 1981).

Loewenthal, R. S. "The Extinction of the Krimchaks in World War II." *Slavic Review* 10 (1951).

Lorimar, Frank. *The Population of the Soviet Union: History and Prospects.* 1946.

Low, A. D. *Lenin on the National Question.* 1958.

Lubachko, Ivan S. *Belorussia under Soviet Rule: 1917–1957.* 1972.

Lubin, Nancy. *Labour and Nationality in Soviet Central Asia: An Uneasy Compromise.* 1972.

————. "Women in Soviet Central Asia: Progress and Contradictions." *Soviet Studies* 33 (April 1981).

Luckyj, George S. N. "Polarity in Ukrainian Intellectual Dissent." *Canadian Slavonic Papers* 14 (1972).

————, ed. *Discordant Voices: The Non-Russian Soviet Literatures.* 1975.

Luzbetak, Louis J. *Marriage and Family in Caucasia.* 1966.

Mace, James E. *Communism and the Dilemmas of National Liberation: National Communism in Soviet Ukraine 1918–1933.* 1983.

Maclean, Fitzroy. *To Caucasus, End of all the Earth.* 1976.

Mamullaku, Ramadan. *Albania and the Albanians.* 1975.

Mandel, William M. *Soviet But Not Russian: The "Other" Peoples of the Soviet Union.* 1984.

Mandelbaum, Michael, ed., *The Rise of Nations in the Soviet Union.* 1991.

Manning, Clarence. *Twentieth-Century Ukraine*. 1951.

Manz, Beatrice Forbes. "Central Asian Uprisings in the Nineteenth Century: Ferghana Under the Russians." *Russian Review* 46 (1987).

Marin, Yuri. "Central Asia Through Soviet Eyes." *Studies on the Soviet Union* 8 (1968).

Marples, David R. *Chernobyl and Nuclear Power in the USSR*. 1986.

———. *Ukraine Under Perestroika: Ecology, Economics and the Workers' Revolt*. 1991.

Marshall, Richard H., ed. *Aspects of Religion in the Soviet Union, 1917–1967*. 1971.

Massell, Gregory. *The Surrogate Proletariat: Moslem Women and Revolutionary Strategies in Soviet Central Asia, 1919–1929*. 1974.

Matossian, Mary Kilbourne. *The Impact of Soviet Policies in Armenia*. 1962.

———. "The Armenians." *Problems of Communism* 16 (September-October 1967).

Mazour, Anatole Grigorevich. *The First Russian Revolution 1825: The Decembrist Movement, Its Origins, Development and Significance*. 1961.

McCagg, W. A., Jr., and Brian D. Silver, eds. *Soviet Asian Ethnic Frontiers*. 1979.

McCauley, Martin, ed. *The Soviet Union Under Gorbachev*. 1987.

Medlin, W. K., F. S. Carpenter, and W. M. Cave. *Education and Development in Central Asia: A Case Study on Social Change in Uzbekistan*. 1971.

Medvedev, Roy. *Let History Judge: The Origins and Consequences of Stalinism*. 1972.

Mellor, Roy E. H. *The Soviet Union and its Geographical Problems*. 1982.

Menges, Karl. *The Turkic Peoples and Languages: An Introduction to Turkic Studies*. 1968.

Mihalisko, Kathleen. "A Profile of Informal Patriotic Youth Groups in Belorussia." *Radio Liberty Research Bulletin* (July 27, 1988).

———. "Belorussian Activists Charged with Violating Law of Assembly." *Radio Liberty Research Bulletin* (September 28, 1988).

———. "Historian Outlines Revisionist View of Belorussia's Past." *Radio Liberty Research Bulletin* (September 28, 1988).

Miller, Jack. *Jews in Soviet Culture*. 1984.

Miller, James, ed. *Politics, Work, and Daily Life in the USSR*. 1987.

Miller, Marshall L. "Between Moscow and Mecca: Ethnic Minorities in the Soviet Union." *Armed Forces Journal International* 124 (March 1987).

Misiunas, Romuald J., and Rein Taagepera. *The Baltic States: Years of Dependence 1940–1980*. 1983.

Mosse, W. E. *Perestroika Under the Tsars*. 1992.

———. *Alexander II and the Modernization of Russia*. 1992.

Motyl, Alexander J. *Will the Non-Russians Rebel? State, Ethnicity, and Stability in the USSR*. 1987.

Mowat, Farley. *The Siberians*. 1971.

Muiznieks, Nils. "The Daugavpils Hydro Station and 'Glasnost' in Latvia." *Journal of Baltic Studies* 18 (Spring 1987).

Muraka, Dev. *The Soviet Union*. 1971.

Nahaylo, Bohdan. "Four Decades of Resistance: An Interview with Danylo Shumuk." *Radio Liberty Research Bulletin* (August 25, 1987).

———. "Political Demonstration in Minsk Attests to Belorussian National Assertiveness." *Radio Liberty Research Bulletin* (November 26, 1987).

———. "National Ferment in Moldavia." *Radio Liberty Research Bulletin* (January 24, 1988).

―――. "Concern Voiced About Six Million Ukrainians Condemned to 'Denationalization.' " *Radio Liberty Research Bulletin* (February 27, 1988): 1–7.
―――. "Representatives of Non-Russian National Movements Establish Coordinating Committee." *Radio Liberty Research Bulletin* (June 22, 1988).
―――. "Ukrainian Writers' Plenum Reveals Growing Frustration and Radicalization." *Radio Liberty Research Bulletin* (August 10, 1988).
―――. "Independent Groups in the Ukraine Under Attack." *Radio Liberty Research Bulletin* (September 28, 1988).
Nahaylo, Bohdan, and C. J. Peters. *The Ukrainians and Georgians.* 1981.
Nahaylo, Bohdan, and Victor Swoboda. *Soviet Disunion: A History of the Nationalities Problem in the USSR.* 1990.
Nekrich, Alexsandr M. *The Punished Peoples: The Deportation and Tragic Fate of Soviet Minorities at the End of the Second World War.* 1978.
Newman, Sally. "Soviet Scholars Advocate Fostering Cultures of National Minorities." *Radio Liberty Research Bulletin* (June 29, 1988).
Nichols, Mary F. *Problems and Prospects of Soviet Nationalities.* 1982.
Nicolson, Harold. *Curzon: The Last Phase, 1919–1925.* 1934.
Nove, Alec, and J. A. Newth. *The Soviet Middle East: A Communist Model for Development.* 1966.
Olcott, Martha Brill. "Yuri Andropov and the 'National Question.' " *Soviet Studies* 37 (January 1985).
―――. *The Kazakhs.* 1987.
―――. "Gorbachev's National Dilemma." *Journal of International Affairs* 42 (Spring 1989).
Ostrowski, Wiktor. *Spotlight on Byelorussia and Her Neighbours.* 1959.
Pajanjis-Javis, J. S. *Soviet Genocide in Lithuania.* 1980.
Palmer, Alan W. *Alexander I, Tsar of War and Peace.* 1974.
Pano, Nicholas C. *The People's Republic of Albania.* 1968.
Pares, Bernard. *A History of Russia.* 1926.
―――. *The Fall of the Russian Monarchy: A Study of the Evidence.* 1939.
Park, Alexander G. *Bolshevism in Turkestan, 1917–1927.* 1957.
Parker, W. H. *An Historical Geography of Russia.* 1969.
Parming, Tonu. "Population Changes in Estonia, 1935–1970." *Population Studies* 26 (January 1972).
―――. "Population Processes and Nationality Issues in the Soviet Baltic." *Soviet Studies* 32 (July 1980).
Parming, T. S., and E. J. Jarvesoo, eds. *A Case Study of a Soviet Republic: The Estonian SSR.* 1978.
Parsons, J.W.R. "National Integration in Soviet Georgia." *Soviet Studies* 34 (October 1982).
Pelenski, Jaroslaw. *Russia and Kazan: Conquest and Imperial Ideology.* 1974.
Pennar, Jaan, et al. *Modernization and Diversity in Soviet Education, With Special Reference to Nationality Groups.* 1971.
Perfecky, George A. "The Status of the Ukrainian Language in the Ukrainian SSR." *East European Quarterly* 21 (June 1987).
Pierce, R. T. *Russian Central Asia, 1867–1917: A Study in Colonial Rule.* 1960.
Pinkus, Benjamin. *The Jews of the Soviet Union: The History of a National Minority.* 1988.

Pipes, Richard. "The First Experiment in Soviet National Policy: The Bashkir Republic, 1917–1920." *Russian Review* (October 1950).

———. "Demographic and Ethnographic Changes in Transcaucasia." *Middle East Journal* 13 (1959).

———. "The Forces of Nationalism." *Problems of Communism* (January-February 1964).

———. *The Formation of the Soviet Union: Communism and Nationalism 1917–1923.* 1964.

———. " 'Solving' the Nationality Problem." *Problems of Communism* (September-October 1967).

———. *Russia Under the Old Regime.* 1974.

Pirzada, Shaziae. "Federalism in the USSR: The Central Asian Context." *Strategic Studies* 10 (Winter 1987).

Pokshishevsky, V. V. "Urbanization and Ethnographic Processes." *Soviet Geography: Review and Translation* 13 (February 1972).

Polansky, Antony, and Norman Davies. *Jews in Eastern Poland and the USSR, 1939–1946.* 1991.

Popp, Gary E., and Syed T. Anwar. "From Perestroika to Ethnic Nationalism." *International Perspectives* 18 (March-April 1989).

Potichnyj, Peter J., ed. *Ukraine in the Seventies.* 1975.

Pozner, Vladimir. *Parting with Illusions.* 1990.

Pyle, Emily. "Calls for Legalization of the Ukrainian Catholic Church." *Report on the USSR* 1 (July 21, 1988).

Ra'anan, Uri, and Charles M. Perry. *The USSR Today and Tomorrow.* 1987.

Rakowska-Harmstone, Teresa. *Russia and Nationalism in Central Asia: The Case of Tadzhikistan.* 1970.

———. "The Dialectics of Nationalism in the USSR." *Problems of Communism* 23 (May-June 1974).

Ramet, Pedro. *Religion and Nationalism in Soviet and East European Politics.* 1984.

Ramet, Pedro, ed. *Eastern Christianity and Politics in the Twentieth Century.* 1988.

Rauch, Georg von. *A History of Soviet Russia.* 1957.

———. *The Baltic States: The Years of Independence 1917–1940.* 1974.

Raun, Toivo U. *Estonia and the Estonians.* 1987.

Reddaway, Peter. *Uncensored Russia: The Human Rights Movement in the Soviet Union.* 1972.

Reddel, Carl W. "S. M. Solov'ev and Multi-National History." *Russian History* 13 (Winter 1986).

Rei, August. *The Drama of the Baltic Peoples.* 1970.

Remeikis, Thomas. *Opposition to Soviet Rule in Lithuania, 1945–1980.* 1980.

Riasanovsky, Nicholas V. *A History of Russia.* 1977.

Rigby, T. H. *Communist Party Membership in the USSR, 1917–1967.* 1968.

Rigby, T. H., Archie Brown, and Peter Reddaway, eds. *Authority, Power and Policy in the USSR.* 1980.

Ritter, William S. "The Final Phase in the Liquidation of Anti-Soviet Resistance in Tadzhikstan: Ibrahim Bek and the Basmachi, 1924–1931." *Soviet Studies* 37 (October 1985).

Roberts, Henry L. *Rumania: Political Problems of an Agrarian State.* 1951.

Roberts, Ian W. *Nicholas I and the Russian Intervention in Hungary.* 1991.

Rogov, Vladimir. *Languages and Peoples of the USSR.* 1966.

Ro'i, Yaacov. "The Task of Creating the New Soviet Man: 'Atheistic' Propaganda in the Soviet Muslim Areas." *Soviet Studies* 26 (January 1984).

Rorlich, Azade-Ayse. "Islam Under Communism: Volga-Ural Muslims." *Central Asian Survey* 1 (1982).

———. *The Volga Tatars: A Profile in National Resilience.* 1986.

Rothberg, Abraham. *The Heirs of Stalin: Dissidence and the Soviet Regime, 1953–1970.* 1972.

Rothenberg, Joshua. *The Jewish Religion in the Soviet Union.* 1971.

Rozitis, Ojars. "The Rise of Latvian Nationalism." *Swiss Review of World Affairs* 38 (February 1989).

Ruble, Blair A. "Ethnicity and Soviet Cities." *Soviet Studies* 41 (July 1989).

Rudnytsky, Ivan L. "The Role of the Ukraine in Modern History." *Slavic Review* 22 (June 1963).

———. "The Soviet Ukraine in Historical Perspective." *Canadian Slavonic Papers* 14 (Summer 1972).

Rudolph, Richard L., and David Good. *Nationalism and Empire: The Hapsburg Monarchy and the Soviet Union.* 1991.

Rutkis, J. S., ed. *Latvia: Country and People.* 1967.

Rywkin, Michael. *Russia in Central Asia.* 1963.

———. *Moscow's Muslim Challenge: Soviet Central Asia.* 1981.

———. "Islam and the New Soviet Man: 70 Years of Evolution." *Central Asian Survey* [Oxford] 6 (No. 4, 1987).

———, ed. *Russian Colonial Expansion to 1917.* 1988.

Sabaliunas, Leonas. *Lithuania in Crisis: Nationalism to Communism, 1939–1940.* 1972.

Sallnow, John. "Belorussia: The Demographic Transition and the Settlement Network in the 1980s." *Soviet Geography* 28 (January 1987).

Saunders, George, ed. *Samizdat: Voices of the Soviet Opposition.* 1974.

Sawchuk, Konstantyn. "Opposition in the Ukraine: Seven Versus the Regime." *Survey* 20 (Winter 1974).

Schlesinger, Rudolf, ed. *The Nationalities Problem and Soviet Administration: Selected Readings on the Development of Soviet Nationalities Policy.* 1956.

Schopflin, George, ed. *The Soviet Union and Eastern Europe: A Handbook.* 1969.

Schroeter, Leonard. *The Last Exodus.* 1974.

Schulman, Elias. *A History of Jewish Education in the Soviet Union.* 1971.

Schwartz, Solomon W. *The Jews in the Soviet Union.* 1951.

Semyonov, Yuri. *Siberia: Its Conquest and Development.* 1963.

Seton-Watson, Hugh. *The Decline of Imperial Russia, 1855–1914.* 1952.

———. *The Russian Empire, 1801–1817.* 1967.

Shabad, Theodore. *Geography of the USSR: A Regional Study.* 1951.

Sheehy, Ann. "The Andizhan Uprising of 1898 and Soviet Historiography." *Central Asian Review* 14 (1966).

———. *The Crimean Tatars and Volga Germans: Soviet Treatment of Two National Minorities.* 1971.

———. "Moldavians Gain Some Language Concessions." *Radio Liberty Research Bulletin* (August 27, 1987).

———. "Migration to RSFSR and Baltic Republics Continues." *Radio Liberty Research Bulletin* (November 30, 1987).

————. "Interethnic Relations in the Soviet Armed Forces." *Radio Liberty Research Bulletin* (June 29, 1988).

————. "Kazakh Minister Defends Territorial Integrity of Kazakhstan." *Radio Liberty Research Bulletin* (June 29, 1988).

Sheehy, Ann, and Bohdan Nahaylo. *The Crimean Tatars, Volga Germans and Meskhetians: Soviet Treatment of Some National Minorities*. 1980.

Shimoniak, Wasyl. "A Study of Soviet Policies in Uzbekistan and their Implementation." Ph.D. diss., University of Michigan, 1963.

Shragin, Boris. *The Challenge of the Spirit*. 1978.

Shtromas, Alexander. "Soviet Occupation of the Baltic States and Their Incorporation into the USSR: Political and Legal Aspects." *East European Quarterly* 19 (September 1985).

Shtromas, Alexander, and Morton A. Kaplan, eds. *The Soviet Union and the Challenge of the Future*. Vol. 3. *Ideology, Culture, and Nationality*. 1972.

Shuiskii, S. A. "Muslims in the Soviet State: Islam a Privileged Religion?" *Oriente Moderno* 7–12 (1980).

Shukman, Harry. *Encyclopedia of the Russian Revolution*. 1988.

Silde, Adolfs. *Resistance Movements in Latvia*. 1972.

Silver, Brian. "Ethnic Identity Change Among Soviet Nationalities: A Statistical Analysis." Ph.D. diss., University of Wisconsin, 1972.

————. "The Status of Minority Languages in Soviet Education: An Assessment of Recent Changes." *Soviet Studies* 26 (January 1974): 28–40.

————. "The Impact of Urbanization and Geographical Dispersion on the Linguistic Russification of Soviet Nationalities." *Demography* 2 (February 1974).

————. "Social Mobilization and Russification of Soviet Nationalities." *American Political Science Review* 68 (March 1974).

————. "Methods of Deriving Data on Bilingualism from the 1970 Soviet Census." *Soviet Studies* 27 (October 1975).

Simmonds, George W., ed. *Nationalism in the USSR & Eastern Europe in the Era of Brezhnev & Kosygin*. 1977.

Simons, Thomas W., Jr. *Eastern Europe in the Postwar World*. 1991.

Sinyasky, Andrei. "Russian Nationalism." *Radio Liberty Research Bulletin* (December 19, 1988).

Skendi, Stavro. *The Albanian National Awakening, 1878–1912*. 1967.

Skilling, H. Gordon. *Czechoslovakia, 1918–1988*. 1991.

Slider, Darrell. "A Note on the Class Structure of Soviet Nationalities." *Soviet Studies* 37 (October 1985).

Smirnov, N. A. *Islam and Russia*. 1956.

Smith, Hedrick. *The Russians*. 1976.

————. *The New Russians*. 1991.

Sokol, E. D. *The Revolt of 1916 in Russian Central Asia*. 1954.

Solchanyk, Roman. "Russian Language and Soviet Politics." *Soviet Studies* 34 (January 1982).

————. "Belorussian Ministry of Education Accused of Sabotaging the Native Language." *Radio Liberty Research Bulletin* (November 10, 1986).

————. "Shcherbitsky on Nationalism and Religion." *Radio Liberty Research Bulletin* (April 6, 1987).

————. "Catastrophic Language Situation in Major Ukrainian Cities." *Radio Liberty Research Bulletin* (July 15, 1987).

————. "Ukrainians and Belorussians Focus on Language and Ecology." *Radio Liberty Research Bulletin* (April 6, 1988).

————. "Belorussian Informal Groups Criticized for Nationalism." *Radio Liberty Research Bulletin* (November 16, 1988).

————. "A Strong Center and Strong Republics: The CPSU's Draft 'Platform' on Nationalities Policy." *Report on the USSR*, No. 35 (September 1, 1989).

————. "Letters to Belorussian Weekly Evidence Strong Support for Native Language." *Radio Liberty Research Bulletin* (November 9, 1989).

————. *Ukraine: From Chernobyl to Sovereignty.* 1992.

Soper, John. " 'Unofficial' Islam: A Muslim Minority in the USSR." *Religion in Communist Lands* 7 (1979).

————. "Kirgiz Intelligentsia Seeking to Lessen Russian Influence on Native Language." *Radio Liberty Research Bulletin* (September 24, 1987).

————. "Nationality Issues Under Review in Kirgizia." *Radio Liberty Research Bulletin* (January 29, 1988).

————. "Classical Central Asian Language to be Taught in Uzbek Schools?" *Radio Liberty Research Bulletin* (June 29, 1988).

Stackelberg, George von. "The Tenacity of Islam in Soviet Central Asia." *Studies on The Soviet Union* 5 (1966).

Strakhovsky, Leonid Ivan. *Alexander I of Russia: The Man Who Defeated Napoleon.* 1947.

Strobe, Talbot. *Khrushchev Remembers.* 1971.

Strong, J. W., ed. *The Soviet Union Under Brezhnev and Kosygin: The Transition Years.* 1971.

Stukas, Jack J. *Awakening in Lithuania.* 1966.

Subtelny, Orest. *The Ukraine: A History.* 1988.

Sumner, Benedict H. *Peter the Great and the Emergence of Russia.* 1951.

Suny, Ronald Grigor. *The Baku Commune, 1917–1918.* 1972.

————. *Sakartvelo: The Making of the Georgia Nation.* 1987.

————. *The Making of the Georgian Nation.* 1988.

————. "Russian Nationalism in the Era of Glasnost and Perestroika." *Radio Liberty Research Bulletin* (December 19, 1988).

————. "Nationalist and Ethnic Unrest in the Soviet Union." *World Policy Journal* 6 (Summer 1989).

Swoboda, Victor, and Ann Sheehy. *Ethnic Pressures in the Soviet Union.* 1972.

Sword, Keith. *The Soviet Takeover of the Polish Eastern Provinces, 1939–1941.* 1991.

Symmons-Symonolewicz, Konstantin. *The Non-Slavic Peoples of the Soviet Union.* 1972.

Sysyn, Frank E. *The Ukrainian Orthodox Question in the USSR.* 1987.

Szporluk, Roman. "West Ukraine and West Belorussia: Historical Tradition, Social Communication, and Linguistic Assimilation." *Soviet Studies* 31 (January 1979).

————. "History and Russian Nationalism." *Survey* 24 (Summer 1979).

————. "Dilemmas of Russian Nationalism." *Problems of Communism* (July/August 1989).

————, ed. "The Nations of the USSR in 1970." *Survey* 17 (Summer 1971).

————, ed. *The Influence of East Europe and the Soviet West on the USSR.* 1975.

Taagepera, Rein. "National Differences Within Soviet Demographic Trends." *Soviet Studies* 20 (1968).

———. "Soviet Collectivization of Estonian Agriculture: The Deportation Phase." *Soviet Studies* 32 (July 1980).

———. "Estonia in September 1988: Stalinists, Centrists and Restorationists." *Journal of Baltic Studies* 20 (Summer 1989).

———. "Estonia's Road to Independence." *Problems of Communism* (November-December 1989).

Talbot-Rice, Tamara. *Elizabeth, Empress of Russia.* 1970.

Tarulis, Albert N. *Soviet Policy Toward the Baltic States 1918–1940.* 1959.

Terauda, Vita. *The Rise of Grass Roots Environmental Groups under Gorbachev: A Case Study of Latvia.* 1988.

Tillet, Lowell. *The Great Friendship: Soviet Historians on the Non-Russian Nationalities.* 1969.

Tolstoi, Nikolai. *Victims of Yalta.* 1978.

Tomingas, William. *The Soviet Colonization of Estonia.* 1973.

Treadgold, Donald W. *Twentieth-Century Russia.* 1964.

Turkay, Osman. "The Tragedy of the Crimean Tatars." *Index on Censorship* 3 (1974).

Tuzmuhamedov, R. T. *How the National Question was Solved in Soviet Central Asia.* 1973.

Ulam, Adam B. *Bolsheviks.* 1968.

Utechin, S. V. *Everyman's Concise Encyclopedia of Russia.* 1961.

Uustalu, E. S. *History of the Estonian People.* 1952.

Vaidyanath, R. I. *The Formation of the Soviet Central Asian Republics: A Study in Soviet Nationalities Policy, 1917–1936.* 1967.

Vakar, Nicholas P. "The Name 'White Russia.' " *American Slavic and East European Review* 8 (October 1949).

———. *Belorussia: The Making of a Nation.* 1956.

Vakhabov, A. S. *Muslims in the USSR.* 1980.

Vali, Ferenc A. *Bridge Across the Bosporus.* 1971.

Vardys, V. Stanley. "Soviet Colonialism in the Baltic States: A Note on the Nature of Modern Colonialism." *Lituanus* 10 (Summer 1964).

———. *Lithuania Under the Soviets.* 1965.

———. "Lithuania's Catholic Movement Reappraised." *Survey* 25 (Summer 1980).

———. "Lithuanian National Politics." *Problems of Communism* (July-August 1989).

———, ed. *The Catholic Church, Dissent and Nationality in Soviet Lithuania.* 1978.

Vernadsky, George. *A History of Russia.* 1961.

Vernadsky, George, and Michael Karpovich. *A History of Russia.* 5 vols. 1943–1969.

Vucinich, Wayne, ed. *Russia and Asia: Essays on the Influence of Russia on the Asian Peoples.* 1972.

Wandycz, Piotr S. *Soviet-Polish Relations, 1917–1921.* 1969.

Werth, Alexander. *Russia: Hopes and Fears.* 1969.

Wheeler, Geoffrey. *The Modern History of Soviet Central Asia.* 1964.

———. *The Peoples of Soviet Central Asia.* 1966.

Wheeler, Lowell. *Racial Problems in Soviet Muslim Asia.* 1960.

Widmer, Michael Jean. "Nationalism and Communism in Latvia: The Latvian Communist Party Under Soviet Rule." Ph.D. diss., Harvard University, 1969.

Wieczynski, Joseph L. *Modern Encyclopedia of Russian and Soviet History.* 1976.

Williams, Robert C. "The Nationalization of Early Soviet Culture." *Russian History* 9 (1982).

Wimbush, S. Enders. *Iran's Ethnic Factions Threaten to Split the State.* 1980.

———, ed. *Soviet Nationalities in Strategic Perspective.* 1985.

Wimbush, S. Enders, and Alexander Alexiev, eds. *Ethnic Minorities in the Red Army.* 1988.

Wimbush, S. Enders, and Ronald Wixman. "The Meskhetian Turks: A New Voice in Soviet Central Asia." *Canadian Slavonic Papers* 17 (1975).

Winnifrith, Tom. *Perspectives on Albania.* 1992.

Wishnevsky, Julia. "A Tribute to the Crimean Tatar Movement." *Radio Liberty Research Bulletin* (July 29, 1987).

———. "The Origins of Pamyat." *Survey* 30 (October 1988).

Wixman, Ronald. *Language Aspects of Ethnic Patterns and Processes in the North Caucasus.* 1980.

———. "Territorial Russification and Linguistic Russianization in Some Soviet Republics." *Soviet Geography* 22 (1981).

———. "Ethnic Nationalism in the Caucasus." *Nationalities Papers* 10 (1982).

———. *The Peoples of the USSR: An Ethnographic Handbook.* 1984.

Wurm, Stefan. *Turkic Peoples of the USSR.* 1954.

Yanov, Alexander. *The Russian New Right.* 1978.

———. *The Russian Challenge and the Year 2000.* 1987.

———. "Russian Nationalism as the Ideology of Counterreform." *Radio Liberty Research Bulletin* (December 19, 1988).

Zajaczkowski, A. A. *Karaims in Poland: History, Language, Folklore, Science.* 1961.

Zaslovsky, Viktor, and Robert Brym. *Soviet-Jewish Emigration and Soviet Nationality Policy.* 1983.

Zenkovsky, Serge A. *Pan-Turkism and Islam in Russia.* 1960.

Zwick, Peter. "Ethnoregional Economic Fragmentation and Soviet Budgetary Policy." *Soviet Studies* 31 (July 1979).

Index

Note: Page numbers in **bold** indicate main entries in the dictionary.

About the Editors and Contributors

JAMES S. OLSON is professor of history at Sam Houston State University in Huntsville, Texas.

LEE BRIGANCE PAPPAS is a Ph.D. candidate at the University of California at Los Angeles and a historian at Sam Houston State University in Huntsville, Texas.

NICHOLAS C. J. PAPPAS teaches history at Sam Houston State University in Huntsville, Texas.

ANTHONY J. AMATO is a graduate student in the department of history at Indiana University.

GEORGE BOURNOUTIAN is a faculty member with the department of history at Iona College in New Rochelle, New York.

JOHN A. FINK lives and writes in Brooklyn, New York.

SAMUEL FREEMAN is a political scientist at the University of Texas-Pan American in Edinburgh, Texas.

REUEL HANKS teaches political science at Kennesaw State College in Marietta, Georgia.

NEIL M. HEYMAN teaches history at San Diego State University in San Diego, California.

GARY R. HOBIN is a career military officer specializing in Middle Eastern affairs.

ROSS MARLAY is a political scientist at Arkansas State University in State University, Arkansas.

SAMUEL A. OPPENHEIM is a historian at California State University, Stanislaus, in Turlock, California.

ALEXANDER SYDORENKO is a member of the history department at Arkansas State University in State University, Arkansas.